Windows® 98 Programming Bible

Windows® 98 Programming Bible

Richard C. Leinecker
Tom Archer

with contributions by
Clayton Walnum
Kevin Smith

IDG BOOKS WORLDWIDE

IDG Books Worldwide, Inc.
An International Data Group Company

Foster City, CA ✦ Chicago, IL ✦ Indianapolis, IN ✦ New York, NY

Windows® 98 Programming Bible

Published by
IDG Books Worldwide, Inc.
An International Data Group Company
919 E. Hillsdale Blvd., Suite 400
Foster City, CA 94404
www.idgbooks.com (IDG Books Worldwide Web site)

Library of Congress Catalog Card No.: 98-70258

ISBN: 0-7645-3185-9

Printed in the United States of America

10 9 8 7 6 5 4 3 2 1

1B/RW/QW/ZY/FC

Distributed in the United States by IDG Books Worldwide, Inc.

Distributed by Macmillan Canada for Canada; by Transworld Publishers Limited in the United Kingdom; by IDG Norge Books for Norway; by IDG Sweden Books for Sweden; by Woodslane Pty. Ltd. for Australia; by Woodslane (NZ) Ltd. for New Zealand; by Addison Wesley Longman Singapore Pte Ltd. for Singapore, Malaysia, Thailand, Indonesia, and Korea; by Norma Comunicaciones S.A. for Colombia; by Intersoft for South Africa; by International Thomson Publishing for Germany, Austria, and Switzerland; by Toppan Company Ltd. for Japan; by Distribuidora Cuspide for Argentina; by Livraria Cultura for Brazil; by Ediciencia S.A. for Ecuador; by Ediciones ZETA S.C.R. Ltda. for Peru; by WS Computer Publishing Corporation, Inc., for the Philippines; by Unalis Corporation for Taiwan; by Contemporanea de Ediciones for Venezuela; by Computer Book & Magazine Store for Puerto Rico; by Express Computer Distributors for the Caribbean and West Indies. Authorized Sales Agent: Anthony Rudkin Associates for the Middle East and North Africa.

For general information on IDG Books Worldwide's books in the U.S., please call our Consumer Customer Service department at 800-762-2974. For reseller information, including discounts and premium sales, please call our Reseller Customer Service department at 800-434-3422.

For information on where to purchase IDG Books Worldwide's books outside the U.S., please contact our International Sales department at 650-655-3200 or fax 650-655-3297.

For information on foreign language translations, please contact our Foreign & Subsidiary Rights department at 650-655-3021 or fax 650-655-3281.

For sales inquiries and special prices for bulk quantities, please contact our Sales department at 650-655-3200 or write to the address above.

For information on using IDG Books Worldwide's books in the classroom or for ordering examination copies, please contact our Educational Sales department at 800-434-2086.

For press review copies, author interviews, or other publicity information, please contact our Public Relations department at 650-655-3000 or fax 650-655-3299.

For authorization to photocopy items for corporate, personal, or educational use, please contact Copyright Clearance Center, 222 Rosewood Drive, Danvers, MA 01923, or fax 978-750-4470.

ABOUT IDG BOOKS WORLDWIDE

Welcome to the world of IDG Books Worldwide.

IDG Books Worldwide, Inc., is a subsidiary of International Data Group, the world's largest publisher of computer-related information and the leading global provider of information services on information technology. IDG was founded more than 25 years ago and now employs more than 8,500 people worldwide. IDG publishes more than 275 computer publications in over 75 countries (see listing below). More than 60 million people read one or more IDG publications each month.

Launched in 1990, IDG Books Worldwide is today the #1 publisher of best-selling computer books in the United States. We are proud to have received eight awards from the Computer Press Association in recognition of editorial excellence and three from *Computer Currents'* First Annual Readers' Choice Awards. Our best-selling *...For Dummies®* series has more than 30 million copies in print with translations in 30 languages. IDG Books Worldwide, through a joint venture with IDG's Hi-Tech Beijing, became the first U.S. publisher to publish a computer book in the People's Republic of China. In record time, IDG Books Worldwide has become the first choice for millions of readers around the world who want to learn how to better manage their businesses.

Our mission is simple: Every one of our books is designed to bring extra value and skill-building instructions to the reader. Our books are written by experts who understand and care about our readers. The knowledge base of our editorial staff comes from years of experience in publishing, education, and journalism — experience we use to produce books for the '90s. In short, we care about books, so we attract the best people. We devote special attention to details such as audience, interior design, use of icons, and illustrations. And because we use an efficient process of authoring, editing, and desktop publishing our books electronically, we can spend more time ensuring superior content and spend less time on the technicalities of making books.

You can count on our commitment to deliver high-quality books at competitive prices on topics you want to read about. At IDG Books Worldwide, we continue in the IDG tradition of delivering quality for more than 25 years. You'll find no better book on a subject than one from IDG Books Worldwide.

IDG BOOKS WORLDWIDE

John Kilcullen
CEO
IDG Books Worldwide, Inc.

Steven Berkowitz
President and Publisher
IDG Books Worldwide, Inc.

VIII WINNER
Eighth Annual Computer Press Awards 1992

IX WINNER
Ninth Annual Computer Press Awards 1993

1995 COMPUTER CURRENTS READERS' CHOICE 1995

X WINNER
Tenth Annual Computer Press Awards 1994

XI WINNER
Eleventh Annual Computer Press Awards 1995

IDG Books Worldwide, Inc., is a subsidiary of International Data Group, the world's largest publisher of computer-related information and the leading global provider of information services on information technology. International Data Group publishes over 275 computer publications in over 75 countries. Sixty million people read one or more International Data Group publications each month. International Data Group's publications include: **ARGENTINA:** Buyer's Guide, Computerworld Argentina, PC World Argentina; **AUSTRALIA:** Australian Macworld, Australian PC World, Australian Reseller News, Computerworld, IT Casebook, Network World, Publish, Webmaster; **AUSTRIA:** Computerwelt Osterreich, Networks Austria, PC Tip Austria; **BANGLADESH:** PC World Bangladesh; **BELARUS:** PC World Belarus; **BELGIUM:** Data News; **BRAZIL:** Annuário de Informática, Computerworld, Connections, Macworld, PC Player, PC World, Publish, Reseller News, Supergamepower; **BULGARIA:** Computerworld Bulgaria, Network World Bulgaria, PC & MacWorld Bulgaria; **CANADA:** CIO Canada, Client/Server World, ComputerWorld Canada, InfoWorld Canada, NetworkWorld Canada, WebWorld; **CHILE:** Computerworld Chile, PC World Chile; **COLOMBIA:** Computerworld Colombia, PC World Colombia; **COSTA RICA:** PC World Centro America; **THE CZECH AND SLOVAK REPUBLICS:** Computerworld Czechoslovakia, Macworld Czech Republic, PC World Czechoslovakia; **DENMARK:** Communications World Danmark, Computerworld Danmark, Macworld Danmark, PC World Danmark, Techworld Denmark; **DOMINICAN REPUBLIC:** PC World Republica Dominicana; **ECUADOR:** PC World Ecuador; **EGYPT:** Computerworld Middle East, PC World Middle East; **EL SALVADOR:** PC World Centro America; **FINLAND:** MikroPC, Tietoverkko, Tietoviikko; **FRANCE:** Distributique, Hebdo, Info PC, Le Monde Informatique, Macworld, Reseaux & Telecoms, WebMaster France; **GERMANY:** Computer Partner, Computerwoche, Computerwoche Extra, Computerwoche FOCUS, Global Online, Macwelt, PC Welt; **GREECE:** Amiga Computing, GamePro Greece, Multimedia World; **GUATEMALA:** PC World Centro America; **HONDURAS:** PC World Centro America; **HONG KONG:** Computerworld Hong Kong, PC World Hong Kong, Publish in Asia; **HUNGARY:** ABCD CD-ROM, Computerworld Szamitastechnika, Internetto online Magazine, PC World Hungary, PC-X Magazin Hungary; **ICELAND:** Tolvuheimur PC World Island; **INDIA:** Information Communications World, Information Systems Computerworld, PC World India, Publish in Asia; **INDONESIA:** InfoKomputer PC World, Komputek Computerworld, Publish in Asia; **IRELAND:** ComputerScope, PC Live!; **ISRAEL:** Macworld Israel, People & Computers/Computerworld; **ITALY:** Computerworld Italia, Macworld Italia, Networking Italia, PC World Italia; **JAPAN:** DTP World, Macworld Japan, Nikkei Personal Computing, OS/2 World Japan, SunWorld Japan, Windows NT World, Windows World Japan; **KENYA:** PC World East African; **KOREA:** Hi-Tech Information, Macworld Korea, PC World Korea; **MACEDONIA:** PC World Macedonia; **MALAYSIA:** Computerworld Malaysia, PC World Malaysia, Publish in Asia; **MALTA:** PC World Malta; **MEXICO:** Computerworld Mexico, PC World Mexico; **MYANMAR:** PC World Myanmar; **NETHERLANDS:** Computer! Totaal, LAN Internetworking Magazine, LAN World Buyers Guide, Macworld Netherlands, Net, WebWereld; **NEW ZEALAND:** Absolute Beginners Guide and Plain & Simple Series, Computer Buyer, Computer Industry Directory, Computerworld New Zealand, MTB, Network World, PC World New Zealand; **NICARAGUA:** PC World Centro America; **NORWAY:** Computerworld Norge, CW Rapport, Datamagasinet, Financial Rapport, Kursguide Norge, Macworld Norge, Multimediaworld Norge, PC World Ekspress Norge, PC World Nettverk, PC World Norge, PC World ProduktGuide Norge; **PAKISTAN:** Computerworld Pakistan; **PANAMA:** PC World Panama; **PEOPLE'S REPUBLIC OF CHINA:** China Computer Users, China Computerworld, China InfoWorld, China Telecom World Weekly, Computer & Communication, Electronic Design China, Electronics Today, Electronics Weekly, Game Software, PC World China, Popular Computer Week, Software Weekly, Software World, Telecom World; **PERU:** Computerworld Peru, PC World Profesional Peru, PC World SoHo Peru; **PHILIPPINES:** Click!, Computerworld Philippines, PC World Philippines, Publish in Asia; **POLAND:** Computerworld Poland, Computerworld Special Report Poland, Cyber, Macworld Poland, Networld Poland, PC World Komputer; **PORTUGAL:** Cerebro/PC World, Computerworld/Correio Informático, Dealer World Portugal, Mac*In/PC*In Portugal, Multimedia World; **PUERTO RICO:** PC World Puerto Rico; **ROMANIA:** Computerworld Romania, PC World Romania, Telecom Romania; **RUSSIA:** Computerworld Russia, Mir PK, Publish, Seti; **SINGAPORE:** Computerworld Singapore, PC World Singapore, Publish in Asia; **SLOVENIA:** Monitor; **SOUTH AFRICA:** Computing SA, Network World SA, Software World SA; **SPAIN:** Communicaciones World España, Computerworld España, Dealer World España, Macworld España, PC World España; **SRI LANKA:** Infolink PC World; **SWEDEN:** CAP&Design, Computer Sweden, Corporate Computing Sweden, Internetworld Sweden, it.branschen, Macworld Sweden, MaxiData Sweden, MikroDatorn, Nätverk & Kommunikation, PC World Sweden, PCaktiv, Windows World Sweden; **SWITZERLAND:** Computerworld Schweiz, Macworld Schweiz, PCtip; **TAIWAN:** Computerworld Taiwan, Macworld Taiwan, NEW ViSiON/Publish, PC World Taiwan, Windows World Taiwan; **THAILAND:** Publish in Asia, Thai Computerworld; **TURKEY:** Computerworld Turkiye, Macworld Turkiye, Network World Turkiye, PC World Turkiye; **UKRAINE:** Computerworld Kiev, Multimedia World Ukraine, PC World Ukraine; **UNITED KINGDOM:** Acorn User UK, Amiga Action UK, Amiga Computing UK, Apple Talk UK, Computing, Macworld, Parents and Computers UK, PC Advisor, PC Home, PSX Pro, The WEB; **UNITED STATES:** Cable in the Classroom, CIO Magazine, Computerworld, DOS World, Federal Computer Week, GamePro Magazine, InfoWorld, I-Way, Macworld, Network World, PC Games, PC World, Publish, Video Event, THE WEB Magazine, and WebMaster; online webzines: JavaWorld, NetscapeWorld, and SunWorld Online; **URUGUAY:** InfoWorld Uruguay; **VENEZUELA:** Computerworld Venezuela, PC World Venezuela; and **VIETNAM:** PC World Vietnam.

3/24/97

Credits

Acquisitions Editor
John Osborn

Development Editors
Laura Brown
Kathi Duggan
Matt Lusher

Technical Editors
Bob Turner
Allen Wyatt

Copy Editors
Marcia Baker
Tim Borek
Tracy Brown
Barry Childs-Helton
Eric Hahn
Ami Knox

Project Coordinator
Susan Parini

Cover Design
Murder By Design

Graphics and Production Specialists
Jude Levinson
Chris Pimentel

Quality Control Specialists
Mick Arellano
Mark Schumann

Illustrator
Donna Reynolds

Proofreader
David Wise

Indexer
Donald Glassman

About the Authors

Richard C. Leinecker is a professional software developer. He holds the position of Software Engineer with Landmark Community Interests, where he writes imaging software. His previous positions include Senior Programmer at MCI's Digital Imaging division, Director of Technology at IntraCorp, Inc., and Manager of Programming and Online Services at COMPUTE publications.

He has had many of his software titles published, including Championship Chess, BridgeMaster, and Miami Vice.

Rick also wrote a regular column and dozens of feature articles and reviews for *COMPUTE Magazine*. Many of *COMPUTE*'s software disk offerings (such as *COMPUTE*'s PC Utility Disk) were the result of his programming labors. He also brought *COMPUTE* and *OMNI* magazines online, creating two of the first online magazines. He is the author of *Visual J++ Bible* (IDG Books Worldwide, Inc.), *Visual C++ 5 Bible* (IDG Books Worldwide, Inc.), *Visual C++ 5 Power Toolkit*, and *Visual C++ Programmer's Reference*.

When Rick isn't writing books or software, he's playing with his three girls or roller-blading with his wife. He enjoys the position of musical director for the Rockingham County Theater Guild, and singing in a contemporary Christian group named Gentle Healer.

Tom Archer is a senior-level software developer with over 13 years of experience designing and coding everything from small-business accounting applications to full-blown distribution systems for companies such as IBM (World Book Encyclopedia) and Peachtree Software (Peachtree Accounting for Windows). He has also written advanced 32-bit Windows vertical-market software systems for AT&T, Data General, and Equifax.

Tom is co-author of *Visual C++ Bible* (IDG Books Worldwide, Inc.), *Windows 98 Programming Bible* (IDG Books Worldwide, Inc.) and *Visual J++ Bible* (IDG Books Worldwide, Inc.). When Tom isn't programming or writing books, he can usually be found helping other developers on various programming newsgroups.

Clayton Walnum started programming computers in 1982, when he traded in an IBM Selectric typewriter to buy an Atari 400 computer (16K of RAM!). Clay soon learned to combine his interest in writing with his newly acquired programming skills and started selling programs and articles to computer magazines. In 1985, *ANALOG Computing*, a nationally distributed computer magazine, hired him as a technical editor, and, before leaving the magazine business in 1989 to become a freelance writer, Clay had worked his way up to Executive Editor. He has since acquired a degree in Computer Science, and written more than 30 books (translated into many languages) covering everything from computer gaming to 3D graphics programming. He has also written hundreds of magazine articles and software reviews, as well as countless programs. His recent books include *Windows 98 Programming Secrets* (IDG Books Worldwide, Inc.), among others. Clay's biggest disappointment in life is that he wasn't one of the Beatles. To compensate, he writes and records rock music in his home studio.

Kevin Smith has been involved in software development for over five years. His past projects include network automation, problem-management systems, and developing Internet-enabled applications. His current projects include finding new ways to extend Microsoft's Internet Information Server and designing database-connectivity middleware for Java. Kevin currently resides in Greensboro, North Carolina, with his wife and two ferrets. When he isn't being a geek, Kevin enjoys cycling and racquetball.

To a wonderful family: Tammy, Jane, Judy, and Beth.—*Richard C. Leinecker*

To my incredible parents for all their years of sacrifice and love.
You're the best!—*Tom Archer*

To Lynn.—*Clayton Walnum*

To my wife Dawn, whose patience let me fulfill a dream.—*Kevin Smith*

Preface

It's a privilege to be able to write a book on such an awesome subject as applications development for Windows 98. Windows 98 is a continuation of the fantastic work that Microsoft started with Windows 95. Consumer PCs can now perform preemptive multitasking; this feature has probably contributed the most to the quality and robustness of current Windows software.

The second biggie is that Windows 98 is a 32-bit operating system. Software developers don't have to worry about segmented memory architecture and all the headaches that go with it. Things just work better and faster as 32-bit applications.

What's in This Book

This book will teach you how to write killer Windows 98 applications. It takes you from such basics as menus and mouse input to such advanced topics as Internet programming and database connectivity. Each chapter teaches a subject, shows you how to use the techniques described, and then follows up with at least one demonstration program.

There's also a CD-ROM included with the book that you'll find to be worth its weight in gold. You won't have to type anything to try the techniques presented in the book. Just open the files on the CD-ROM, look at the code, and make any changes you want. There are many third-party demo programs and libraries included, too. You'll have the chance to try out some of the best add-ons available for Windows 98 program development.

Who This Book Is For

This book is for anyone who needs to learn about Windows 98 programming. If you're new to Visual C++, or even new to Windows programming, you can learn the basics and master Windows programming fundamentals in no time.

Some programmers, even seasoned veterans, want to have a comprehensive manual on Windows 98 programming that covers all bases. You won't find many programming books that cover the range of topics that are covered here. We've made an effort to cover valuable topics such as Internet programming and database connectivity—subjects that other books shy away from, or deal with on a superficial level.

Others will find a specific section with which they need help. For instance, you might have the responsibility at work for writing a program that sends and receives files to and from an FTP server. If you don't know how to do this, just turn to Chapter 29 and learn all about it. You won't have to spend days poring over manuals, plowing through the online help, and scouring the Internet for help on the subject. We teach you how to FTP files in such a way that you'll learn in less than an hour.

In short, almost everyone can benefit from this book. It's a comprehensive guide to writing Windows 98 applications that you won't want to miss.

How Things Are Organized

This book is divided into eight main parts. The first is entitled "Fundamentals" and covers the basics of Windows 98 programming. The second part is called "Architecture" and talks about subjects such as document/view architecture and printing. The third part, "Advanced Topics in MFC Programming," teaches techniques for advanced programming such as effective use of toolbars and extending MFC controls. Next, the fourth part("Database Programming") covers the all-important topic of database connectivity. Our fifth part is "Extending Applications," and it addresses topics such as writing and using DLLs. Next in the list is Part VI, "ActiveX Programming," which covers the relatively new subject of ActiveX controls. Part VII, "Internet Programming," comes next; there you learn how to write applications that communicate over the Internet. The eighth and final part is entitled "Using Visual Studio Tools."

Almost every chapter follows the same basic format. We present a topic along with some short code examples. Besides the explanation of the subject, we give expert tips. These expert tips are the result of countless hours of struggle—which we're hoping to save you. Summaries of many techniques are given for your convenience in what we call the "Nutshell" features.

Most of the chapters have at least one demonstration program. The demo programs take the concepts that were presented in the chapter and ties them together so you can see how to use them in a real program. The entire program's source code is never included—this would be a waste of paper. Instead, we just pull out portions of the program that best illustrate what's going on. You find all the source code on the accompanying CD-ROM.

Icons Used in This Book

Several icons are used throughout the book. They're intended to make it easier for you to identify key sections within the text. Familiarity with these icons can greatly enhance your ability to quickly find the information you need.

This is simply a useful piece of information for future reference.

This icon identifies a short section in which a topic is summarized "in a nutshell." Typically, these sections enumerate a procedure in a step-by-step manner.

This icon identifies a section in which it's recommended that you learn by creating a project similar to the one that's being described.

This icon identifies an insight that can't be found by reading normal documentation. The expert tips are the result of the authors' experience in uncovering and solving difficult problems. You'll benefit immeasurably from them.

This icon identifies a demonstration program. These programs can be found throughout the book, and they illustrate the salient points of the current topic by showing you a complete program using the principles presented.

This icon identifies a Web resource that relates to the current topic. You can use resources such as FTP and Web sites to find additional information with which you can further your knowledge and understanding.

This icon identifies an element that was added with the ClassWizard. Below the icon, you are shown the name of the message (or virtual function), followed by the function that's created, and in which source code module it's placed.

Contacting the Authors

All the authors welcome your comments and feedback. We're all carrying a heavy load with full-time jobs and writing in the evenings, so sometimes it takes us a few days to respond, but we're eager to hear from you.

You can contact Richard C. Leinecker at `ivt-rcl@interpath`. His Web page addresses are `http://www.interpath.com/~phaedrus` and `http://www.infinitevision.net`. Tom Archer can be e-mailed at `tarcher@mindspring.com`. His Web page is `http://www.mindspring.com/~tarcher`. Clayton Walnum's Web page is `http://www.connix.com/~cwalnum`. You can contact Kevin Smith at `smithka@earthlink.com`.

Acknowledgments

Richard C. Leinecker would like to thank Matt Lusher for his perseverance and dedication to the project. It's nice to be working with such a fantastic development editor who actually cares about the authors. John Osborn is an acquisitions editor extraordinaire — without John, this and other projects just wouldn't have been possible. The group of coauthors who made it possible for the book to meet its deadline deserve a round of applause. And to Matt Wagner of Waterside Productions, keep those projects coming!

Tom Archer wishes to express gratitude and thanks to his unbelievably caring, loving and supportive girlfriend, Krista. In addition, this book simply would not have been the same had it not been for the added loving support of my two children, Peter and Christopher, and their mother, Maria — one of my closest and dearest friends. Thanks to you guys also, Christopher Duncan, Jerry Galloway, and Doyle Vann, for showing me what true friends are made of while I pushed myself to do the best I could for this book. My name may be on the cover, but this book belongs as much to every one of you! Thanks for being there!

Clayton Walnum would like to thank the many people who had a hand in getting this book from the authors' heads to the bookshelf. Special thanks go to Greg Croy for recommending me for this project, and to Rick Leinecker for accepting that recommendation, to John Osborn for his support and flexibility, and to Matt Lusher for ensuring that the text made sense. As always, thanks goes to my family: Lynn, Christopher, Justin, Stephen, and Caitlynn.

Contents at a Glance

Preface xi
Acknowledgments xiv

Part I: Fundamentals 1

Chapter 1: Getting Started 3
Chapter 2: Menus....................25
Chapter 3: Mouse and Keyboard....................63
Chapter 4: Graphics....................97
Chapter 5: Bitmaps, Palettes, DIBs, and Double Buffering 155
Chapter 6: MFC Exception Handling....................195
Chapter 7: Dialogs and Controls 225
Chapter 8: Property Sheets and Property Pages....................267
Chapter 9: Data I/O 289
Chapter 10: Sound 323
Chapter 11: Timers and Idle Processing....................349

Part II: Application Architecture....................367

Chapter 12: Documents, Views, and SDI....................369
Chapter 13: Splitter Windows 389
Chapter 14: MDI 411
Chapter 15: Printing and Print Preview 425

Part III: Advanced Topics in MFC Programming....................453

Chapter 16: Extending MFC Classes 455
Chapter 17: Toolbars and Status Bar 479
Chapter 18: Threads 501

Part IV: Database Programming 523

Chapter 19: ODBC 525
Chapter 20: MFC Database Classes....................563
Chapter 21: DAO Database Programming 607

Part V: Extending Applications 643

Chapter 22: Working with DLLs 645
Chapter 23: Extending Applications with Third-Party Libraries....................675
Chapter 24: Data Encryption 713

Part VI: Common Object Model Programming 735

Chapter 25: Introduction to ActiveX....................737

Chapter 26: Containers and Servers 749
Chapter 27: Automation and ActiveX Controls 781
Chapter 28: Active Template Library 813

Part VII: Distributed Computing 829

Chapter 29: Internet Programming 831
Chapter 30: CHtmlView 867

Part VIII: Using Visual Studio Tools 885

Chapter 31: Using J++ with C++ 887
Chapter 32: Using C++ and Visual Basic Together 913
Chapter 33: Writing a Custom AppWizard 931

Appendix: What's on the CD-ROM? 955
Index 981
End-User License Agreement 1022
CD-ROM Installation Instructions 1026

Contents

Preface xi

Acknowledgments xiv

Part I: Fundamentals 1

Chapter 1: Getting Started 3

What's New in Windows 98 3
What Does This Mean for Users? 4
What Does This Mean for Developers? 4
What's New in Visual Studio 6 5
The Visual C++ HelloWorld1 Program 6
The Visual C++ Win32 Console Application 10
The HelloWorld3 ATL Control 11
The HelloWorld4 Java Applet 14
The HelloWorld5 Java Application 18
The HelloWorld6 Visual Basic Application 23
Summary 24

Chapter 2: Menus 25

Changing Default Menus 25
    Editing a menu resource 26
    Creating Menus 29
    Creating menu handlers 29
Menu Messages in MFC 31
Menu Command Ranges 33
Handling Menu Input 34
Keyboard Accelerators 40
    About keyboard input 40
    Defining accelerator keys 41
    Selecting appropriate keyboard accelerators 43
    Multiple accelerator tables 46
Changing Menus Dynamically During Program Execution 48
    Getting the current CMenu object 48
    Changing an existing pop-up menu 49
    MFC's permanent and temporary handle maps 52
Context Menus 54
Creating Context Menus to Change Windows 56
Summary 61

Chapter 3: Mouse and Keyboard 63

Input Basics and System State 64
Mouse Input 64
Creating Mouse Message Handlers 65
Converting Between Screen and Window Coordinates 67
Creating an MFC Program that Handles Mouse Events 68
Nonclient Mouse Events 74
Changing the Mouse Cursor 75
Creating an MFC Demo Program that Changes Mouse Cursors 76
Capturing the Mouse 79
Limiting Mouse Movement 81
Keyboard Input 81
- Translation of keyboard input 82
- Echoing keyboard focus 86

Keyboard Demo Program 93
Summary 95

Chapter 4: Graphics 97

Introduction to the Graphics Device Interface 97
Types of Graphics 98
- Text as graphics 99
- Raster graphics 99
- Vector graphics 100

GDI Devices 101
- Physical devices 101
- Pseudodevices 102

The Device Context 103
- DC drawing attributes 103
- A simple OnDraw() function 107

The WM_PAINT Message 108
- Drawing coordinates 109
- Requesting a PAINT message 110
- Drawing outside PAINT messages 111

Controlling the Appearance of Text 112
- Basic text attributes 113
- All about fonts 118

Pens and Brushes 124
- The CPen class 124
- The CBrush class 127
- The PenBrushDemo Program 129

Mapping Modes 133
Raster Operations 135
Drawing to a Window 136
- The GraphicsDemo1 Program 136
- Text drawing functions 142
- Text coordinate calculations 144

Clipping Regions 149
Summary 153

Chapter 5: Bitmaps, Palettes, DIBs, and Double Buffering 155

Creating CBitmap Objects 157
Loading and Setting Bitmap Content 159
Drawing CBitmaps to the Screen 161
Raster Operations 164
The BlitDemo Program 167
Palettes and Color 173
    Logical palettes 174
    Palette events 179
    The SetSystemPaletteUse() function 180
Device-Independent Bitmaps 180
    The anatomy of a DIB file 181
    The CDib class 183
    The ShowDIB demo program 189
Double Buffering 192
Summary 194

Chapter 6: MFC Exception Handling 195

C++ Exception Handling Versus SEH 195
Exception-Handling Syntax 196
    Throwing the exception 196
    Catching the exception 197
Exception Handling Versus Return Codes 198
    Dealing with error conditions 198
    Handling errors in the correct context 199
    Improving code readability 201
    Throwing exceptions from constructors 203
The CException Class 203
    Creating and deleting CException objects 204
    Retrieving error information from a CException object 205
    Catching multiple exception types 206
Defining CException-Derived Classes 207
    Discovering the CFileException class 208
    Defining your own CException-derived classes 212
Advanced Exception-Handling Techniques 215
    Deciding what function should catch an exception 216
    Deciding what code to put in a try block 217
    Deciding what code to put in a catch block 218
    Throwing exceptions from virtual functions 219
Summary 223

Chapter 7: Dialogs and Controls 225

Dialogs and Controls — A Brief Description 226
Using the Resource Editor 226
    Creating a dialog-based application 227
    Using the resource editor 228
Programming with CDialog and MFC Control Classes 235
    The CDialog class — a brief description 235

MFC control classes....235
Dialog Data Exchange (DDX)....236
Message handling....239
Putting it all together....240
Serializing Dialog Data....249
Adding serialization to the CProject class....249
Updating the dialog to serialize the CProject objects....250
Working with Modal Dialogs....253
Creating the AddKeyword dialog template and its class....253
Invoking the Dialog....255
Modeless Dialogs — A Find Dialog Box....258
Creating the modeless dialog box....259
Invoking a modeless dialog box....260
Communication between modal and modeless dialog boxes....261
Summary....266

Chapter 8: Property Sheets and Property Pages....267

Understanding CPropertySheet and CPropertyPage....268
Using the resource editor to create property pages....269
Creating a CPropertyPage....269
Creating and displaying a modal CPropertySheet....269
Creating and displaying a modeless CPropertySheet....270
Creating and displaying a property sheet within an existing dialog....271
Modal Property Sheet Demo....272
Creating the demo application....272
Removing standard buttons....276
Repositioning standard buttons....277
Changing the standard button's caption....278
Disabling tabs....279
Re-enabling tabs....281
Dynamically setting CPropertyPage tab captions....283
Changing a tab's font....286
Using mnemonics with CPropertyPage tabs....286
Summary....288

Chapter 9: Data I/O....289

The CString Class....289
File I/O and the CFile Class....302
Opening a file with the Open() member function....303
The FileDemo program....305
The CMemFile Class....313
The CStdioFile Class....313
The CSerial Class for Serial Communications....314
Serial communications overview....314
The CSerial class....315
The Registry....317
Registry values....317
Predefined Registry keys....317

Commonly used Registry keys 318
Subtrees in HKEY_CLASSES_ROOT 319
Subtrees in HKEY_USERS 319
Subtrees in HKEY_CURRENT_USER 319
The CRegistry class 319
Summary 321

Chapter 10: Sound 323

Playing Recorded Sounds 323
The CWave class in brief 324
Playing .WAV files using the Windows API 324
The CWave Class Functions 326
The WaveDemo Program 329
Playing MIDI Files 332
What is MIDI? 333
The CMidi class in brief 333
The MIDIDemo Program 334
CD Audio 338
The CCDAudio class library in brief 339
The CDPlayer Program 342
Summary 348

Chapter 11: Timers and Idle Processing 349

Timers 350
Setting a timer using WM_TIMER 350
Setting a timer with a callback procedure 352
The Clock Program 354
CWinApp's OnIdle Capability 361
The OnIdleDemo Program 363
Summary 366

Part II: Application Architecture 367

Chapter 12: Documents, Views, and SDI 369

Implementing Document/View Architecture 369
Step 1: Create a skeleton application 372
Step 2: Declare the document's data objects 373
Step 3: Complete the OnNewDocument() function 374
Step 4: Override the DeleteContents() function 375
Step 5: Complete the Serialize() function 377
Step 6: Complete the OnDraw() function 378
Step 7: Add editing code 379
Persistent Objects 381
Saving Persistent and Nonpersistent Objects 387
Summary 388

Chapter 13: Splitter Windows 389

Introducing Splitter Windows 389
MFC's CSplitterWnd Class 391
The DynSplitter Application 393
    Exploring dynamic splitter windows 395
    Dynamic splitters and AppWizard 395
The StatSplitter Application 399
    Exploring static splitter windows 400
    Static splitters and AppWizard 401
Splitter Windows and MDI 402
The MDISplitter Application 403
    Exploring the MDI dynamic splitter window 404
    MDI dynamic splitters and AppWizard 404
Splitter Windows and Differing Views 405
The MultViewSplitter Application 405
    Exploring the multiple-view splitter window 406
    Multiple view splitters and AppWizard 407
Summary 409

Chapter 14: MDI 411

Introducing MDI Applications 411
The MDIDemo Application 414
The Child Frame Window 417
Creating an MDI Application 420
Exploring an MDI Application 421
Summary 423

Chapter 15: Printing and Print Preview 425

An Overview of Printing in Windows 425
Printing Text in an MFC Application 428
    The TextPrint sample application 430
    MFC member functions for printing 432
Printing Graphics in an MFC Application 446
    The RectPrint sample application 446
    Scaling between the screen and printer 447
    The OnCreate() function 450
    The OnDraw() function 451
    The OnPreparePrinting() function 452
Summary 452

Part III: Advanced Topics in MFC Programming 453

Chapter 16: Extending MFC Classes 455

UI Controls 455
    CAutoCompleteComboBox 456
    CGreyEdit 458

CUnderlineEdit 464
Views and Dialogs 469
CFormBackground....469
CListBoxView 474
Summary 477

Chapter 17: Toolbars and Status Bars 479

Understanding Toolbars 479
Examining MFC control bars 480
Creating a toolbar 481
Showing and hiding toolbars....483
Understanding Status Bars 484
Creating a status bar....484
Displaying toolbar help 485
Expanding status bars 486
Status bar demo program 492
Summary 499

Chapter 18: Threads....501

Distinguishing Threads 502
Creating a worker thread 503
The thread function 504
Creating a user interface thread 505
Suspending and Resuming Threads 507
Putting Threads to Sleep 507
Terminating a Thread....508
Terminating a Thread from Another Thread 508
Exploring Thread Scheduling 512
Examining Process Priority Classes 513
Sharing MFC Objects Among Threads 514
Using C Runtime Functions in Multithreaded Applications....517
Summary 522

Part IV: Database Programming 523

Chapter 19: ODBC....525

Key Concepts....525
DBMS (database management system)....525
SQL (Structured Query Language) 526
Data source 526
ODBC—the Need for a Standard 526
The ODBC Standard....527
ODBC conformance levels (driver functionality) 529
ODBC conformance levels (SQL grammar) 530
ODBC—Implementation....530
Configuring ODBC 530
Connecting to a data source....532

Querying the data and the data source 534
Preparing and executing SQL requests 534
Retrieving data 535
Disconnecting from a data source 536
A Simple ODBC Application to Fetch Data 537
Adding ODBC support to a Visual C++ project 538
Modifying the ODBCDemo dialog 538
Adding the initialization and database code 539
Encapsulating Advanced ODBC Functionality 545
CODBCInfo class “multi-header” file 546
Creating the header file for the CODBCInfo class 547
Defining the CODBCInfo class 549
Building the CODBCInfo DLL 560
Testing the CODBCInfo class 560
Summary 562

Chapter 20: MFC Database Classes 563

The MFC Database Classes 563
CDatabase 564
CRecordset 568
An MFC Database Classes Demo 578
Creating the Visual C++ 6.0 Project 579
Adding support for the MFC database classes 579
Adding a dialog to the application 579
Adding a utility class to encapsulate the user's data 581
Creating a CRecordset class for the UserMaster table 581
Modifying the dialog's header file 582
Modifying the dialog's implementation file 582
Building the User Maintenance application 591
Parameterized Recordsets and Queries 592
Creating and using parameterized recordsets 593
Building the Application 599
Creating parameterized queries 600
Summary 605

Chapter 21: DAO Database Programming 607

DAO Overview 608
The history of DAO 608
The DAO hierarchy 610
The many (inter)faces of DAO 614
Using the MFC DAO Classes 615
CDaoDatabase 616
CDaoWorkspace 619
CDaoRecordset 620
Creating a maintenance application using MFC Database classes 630
Summary 641

Part V: Extending Applications 643

Chapter 22: Working with DLLs 645

Regular DLLs....................645
Understanding the regular DLL internals....................646
Dynamically loading DLLs....................648
Examples of when to dynamically load a DLL....................649
Demo to dynamically load a DLL....................650
Writing Windows hooks....................658
MFC Extension DLLs....................666
Understanding the MFC Extension DLL internals....................666
Exporting classes via MFC Extension DLLs....................667
More on the AFX_EXT_CLASS....................667
Using nested MFC Extension DLLs....................668
Exporting resources....................669
Writing a demo that encapsulates documents and views in a DLL....................669
Summary....................674

Chapter 23: Extending Applications with Third-Party Libraries 675

Using a Third-Party Library....................676
The ImageObject Library in Brief....................678
Supported Image File Formats....................680
The BMP file format....................682
The GIF file format....................682
The JPEG file format....................683
The PCX file format....................684
The TGA file format....................684
The TIFF file format....................684
Working with the ImageObject Library....................685
Loading images with the ImageObject library....................685
Saving images with the ImageObject library....................689
Drawing images with the ImageObject library....................692
The Display Program....................697
Cropping and Stretching Images....................699
The CropStretch Program....................700
Changing Color Depth of an Image....................703
Image Processing....................704
The ProcessImage Program....................707
Summary....................711

Chapter 24: Data Encryption 713

Basic Cryptographic Terms....................713
Different Types of Cryptography....................714
Symmetric algorithms....................714
The Substitution Algorithm demo program....................715
Public-key cryptography....................720
Hash Functions....................721

The HFDemo Program 722
Using Microsoft's CryptoAPI 726
The CryptDemo Program 728
Summary 733

Part VI: Common Object Model Programming 735

Chapter 25: Introduction to ActiveX 737

OLE 1.0 737
OLE 2.0 740
COM 742
ActiveX Applications and Components 742
- ActiveX container applications 743
- ActiveX server applications 744
- ActiveX automation applications 746
- ActiveX controls 747
- ActiveX documents 747

Summary 748

Chapter 26: Containers and Servers 749

Container Applications 749
- Creating a skeleton container application 749
- Managing an embedded object's size and position 755
- Using the mouse to select items 756
- Deleting embedded items 763

Server Applications 764
- Creating a skeleton server application 764
- Customizing the application's resources 768
- Completing the application's document class 772
- Completing the server item's class 773
- Completing the view class 774
- Running the server application 776

Summary 780

Chapter 27: Automation and ActiveX Controls 781

Automation Servers 781
- The Automation Server Application 782
- Creating a skeleton automation server 782
- Customizing the automation server's resources 784
- Completing the automation server's document class 785
- Completing the automation server's view class 785
- Defining the server's properties and methods 788

The Automation Client Application 790
- Creating the automation client skeleton 791
- Customizing the client application's resources 792
- Completing the client application's view class 793

Initializing ActiveX in the client application 795
Controlling the Server from the Client 796
ActiveX Controls 797
Creating a skeleton ActiveX control 798
Creating the ActiveX control's user interface 800
Creating properties and methods 803
Responding to the control's button 806
Testing the ActiveX control 808
Persistent properties 808
Placing an ActiveX control on a Web page 809
Summary 812

Chapter 28: Active Template Library 813

Creating an ATL Control 814
Adding a COM Object to the Project 816
Adding the Draw Code 818
Implementing the Interface Functions 820
Using the Control from C++ 822
Data Types 824
Converting to and from BSTRs 824
Comparing BSTRs 825
Viewing the contents of a BSTR in the debugger 826
Embedding an ActiveX Control in a Web Page 826
Summary 827

Part VII: Distributed Computing 829

Chapter 29: Internet Programming 831

Getting Started with CInternetSession 831
Creating a Simple Web Browser 834
Connecting to an FTP Server 836
Retrieving a File from an FTP Server 838
The FtpDemo Program 840
Web Robots 847
Agents 847
The trouble with robots 848
The Crawler Program 849
Guidelines for Robot Writers 863
Be accountable 863
Test locally 864
Don't hog resources 864
Stay with it 866
Summary 866

Chapter 30: CHtmlView 867

Creating a CHtmlView Project 868
Converting Projects to Use CHtmlView 869

Navigating CHtmlViews 870
CHtmlDemo1 872
HTML Document Information Retrieval 875
Blocking and Logging URLs for a CHtmlView Application 876
CHtmlViewDemo2 879
Summary 884

Part VIII: Using Visual Studio Tools 885

Chapter 31: Using J++ with C++ 887

Creating a J++ Project 887
 Making a threaded applet 889
 Removing unnecessary code 891
 Adding code that draws to the applet window 891
 Applet parameters 892
Java Images 893
 Loading images 893
 Drawing images 895
Making Java Live on the Web 897
 Uploading applets 897
 Editing the HTML file 900
The Banner Applet 900
The MakeBanner Program 907
Summary 912

Chapter 32: Using C++ and Visual Basic Together 913

The RegistryControl ATL Control 914
The Register Visual Basic Program 919
The OhmsCalculator Basic ActiveX Control 921
The UseOhmsCalculator C++ Program 924
Visual Basic Graphics Coordinates 928
An Imaging Control for Visual Basic 928
Summary 930

Chapter 33: Writing a Custom AppWizard 931

The Internal Workings of the AppWizard 932
Creating a Custom AppWizard 934
Changing a Project's Default Settings 936
 Creating the SDIAutomationWiz demo project 936
 Changing AppWizard macros 936
 Defining the CCustomAppWiz class 936
 Working with macro dictionaries 938
Including Personal Information on Every About Box 939

Creating the AboutWiz demo project 939
Adding a custom dialog 939
Creating your own templates 941
Changing the newproj.inf file 943
Changing the AppWizard templates 945
Changing the CONFIRM.INF file 949
Using the Registry for persistent macros 950
Summary 953

Appendix: What's on the CD-ROM? 955

Index 981

End-User License Agreement 1022

CD-ROM Installation Instructions 1026

P A R T

I

Fundamentals

The first eleven chapters teach you the basics of Windows 98 programming. After working through the fundamentals section, you'll probably be able to write Windows programs easily.

The topics covered in this first section range from menus and mouse-and-keyboard input to using GDI and bitmaps to draw to the screen. You learn how to create and use dialog boxes, as well as how to handle errors by catching exceptions.

These first eleven chapters provide a solid foundation for the more advanced topics introduced in the remainder of the book.

✦ ✦ ✦ ✦

In This Part

Chapter 1
Getting Started

Chapter 2
Menus

Chapter 3
Mouse and Keyboard

Chapter 4
Graphics

Chapter 5
Bitmaps, Palettes, DIBs, and Double Buffering

Chapter 6
MFC Exception Handling

Chapter 7
Dialogs and Controls

Chapter 8
Property Sheets and Property Pages

Chapter 9
Data I/O

Chapter 10
Sound

Chapter 11
Timers and Idle Processing

✦ ✦ ✦ ✦

CHAPTER 1

Getting Started

✦ ✦ ✦ ✦

In This Chapter

Discovering what's new in Windows 98

Examining what's new in Visual Studio 6

Exploring Visual C++ programs

Checking out Visual J++ programs

Investigating Visual Basic programs

✦ ✦ ✦ ✦

Many motivational speakers have said, "What the mind can conceive and believe, it can achieve." When it comes to Windows 98 programming, it might be easier than you think to achieve your dreams. That's because Windows 98 is a fantastic operating system that gives the developer power and provides the user with great features and robustness.

Add Microsoft's Visual Studio 6 to Windows 98, and you have a one-two punch that's going to blow your socks off. The possibilities are endless. I get excited just thinking about them.

What's New in Windows 98

Windows 98 isn't just a 32-bit operating system that sits on top of DOS, as is Windows 95. It's a fully integrated 32-bit protected-mode operating system. The need for a separate copy of MS-DOS is eliminated.

New as of Windows 95, and even better in Windows 98, is the ability for programs to spawn multiple threads. Windows 98 manages these threads with its ability to perform preemptive multitasking. These capabilities enable system responsiveness and smooth background processing.

Windows is no longer shackled by the old DOS FAT file system. Those 12- and 16-bit FAT indexes are no more. Now 32-bit indexes rule! No longer do you have to worry about disk cluster size or a batch file committing from 8K to 32K of disk space. Besides the savings in disk space where small files are concerned, the enhanced file system makes long filenames easy to manage. After living for years with filenames limited by the 8.3 convention, this is a real benefit.

Device drivers can now be written in native 32-bit code. These drivers deliver high performances and intelligent memory use, as long as the code is written to take advantage of the native 32-bit programming model.

In addition, unlike Windows 95, the Windows 98 kernel is completely 32-bit. This means memory management, process scheduling, and process management are far more efficient.

The system is more stable and far more robust. I recall many conversations with friends during which, after telling them how much more I liked Windows 95 than Windows 3.1, they proceeded to tell me they wanted Windows 3.1 back because Windows 95 crashes so often (the preemptive multitasking in Windows 95 has caused many Windows 95 problems).

The system is far better at detecting hardware and managing system resources. This is useful when you're installing new hardware.

Probably the most controversial feature of Windows 98 is its ability to integrate with Internet Explorer. This makes the Internet an extension of your computer, not an abstract set of computers out there in cyberspace.

What Does This Mean for Users?

For users, some of this might not mean anything. That's not to say they won't reap the benefits of the beefed-up operating system. For the most part, they won't notice that it doesn't crash like Windows 95. Who notices when things go smoothly? It's only when things don't go smoothly that anyone notices.

The enhanced ability to detect and manage resources is a big benefit to users. But here again, they may not notice that Windows 98 just works as it's supposed to, whereas Windows 95 was more "plug and pray" than "plug and play."

The only thing users might really notice is the integration of Windows 98 and Internet Explorer. The Department of Justice has certainly noticed this and has given Microsoft a big headache over the issue. In spite of the legal problems, I think most users will move toward the integrated operating system because it has many advantages.

What Does This Mean for Developers?

Windows 98 is a gift to developers, as was Windows 95, mainly because Windows 98 gives developers the chance to take advantage of preemptive multitasking. Instead of performing processor-intensive functions as part of a timer scheme, you can just spawn a thread and let it do its work. The operating system worries about how to divide the time between processes so that no one process brings the system to its knees.

The integration of Internet Explorer and Windows 98 is another good thing for developers. Those of us who used the Internet Browser control in our applications had to always make sure Internet Explorer was installed in the client machine. If it wasn't, we had to install it because the required DLLs weren't in the System directory, which resulted in the Browser control failing miserably. (By the way, Microsoft doesn't allow redistribution of the DLLs, only of the full Internet Explorer package.)

The Internet Explorer control has even been wrapped by some of the Microsoft Foundation Classes (MFC). It's now easier than ever to use the Web Browser control. Check out Chapter 31 for more details on the new `CHtmlView` class.

What's New in Visual Studio 6

Visual Studio 6 is in some ways light years ahead of the last rendition, and in other ways it's about the same. Visual C++ resides in the same integrated development environment (IDE) that it always did. Actually, after spending a lot of time really learning the Visual C++ IDE, I'm relieved it stayed the same. Visual C++'s MFC libraries don't have much new, either. The `CHtmlView` class is nice, and there are some new controls. Of course, if I really wanted to, I guess I could make a long list of new features, but most of them are minor.

Visual Basic, like Visual C++, is still in a similar IDE as the last version. Visual Basic has a few new features and is more robust, but unless you get excited about things such as DHTML or IDE extensibility, there's not much new.

Visual J++, on the other hand, is radically different. I had to spend a large amount of time to learn this new environment. Microsoft is making an effort to have all the Visual Studio tools reside in the same IDE. The one in which Visual J++ resides now is where they're all headed, but there wasn't enough time before the Visual Studio version 6 release to shoehorn in Visual C++ and Visual Basic. The Visual C++ development team is hoping that by the next release (code-named "Ranier") all of the Visual Studio tools can share the same IDE. Dream on!

Visual InterDev is also in the same IDE where Visual J++ resides. This is a tool I use only when the DBA (database administrator) at work frowns and sternly tells me, "You can do that yourself from Visual InterDev." I then reluctantly enter the realm of Visual InterDev. From what I've seen, though, the new version makes this task much easier.

For the remainder of this chapter, I'm going to give you a tour of Visual Studio 6 by creating some applications, a control, and an applet. During each project I talk about the tools used and show you the highlights of the tool. This overview will prepare you for the rest of the book, which gets into the nitty-gritty of Visual Studio 6 programming for Windows 98.

The Visual C++ HelloWorld1 Program

The first program created for this chapter is a variation of the traditional "Hello World" program that all C and C++ programmers start with. The program was created with the MFC AppWizard. The only default setting that was changed throughout the AppWizard process was the one that makes the application a single-document interface program. Most of the same project types that came with version 5, such as AppWizard, ATL Wizard, and MFC DLL, are included in Visual C++ 6. Figure 1-1 shows the available selections.

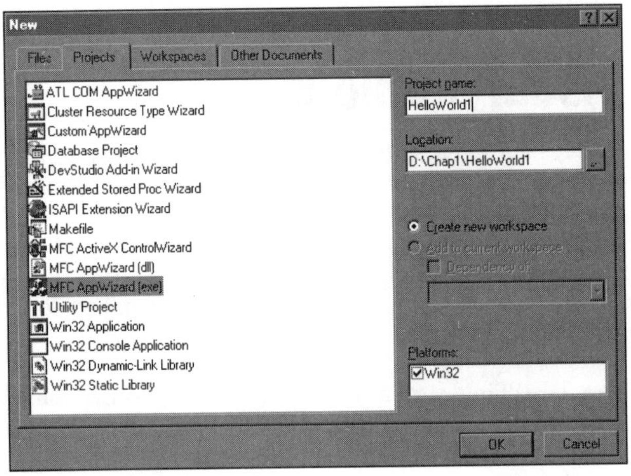

Figure 1-1: The project types in Visual C++ version 6 are almost identical to those in Visual C++ version 5.

The project types are about the same for Visual C++ 6 as they were for Visual C++ 5. One important thing to note is you can now create programs with AppWizard that don't have document/view architecture support. For me this is a tremendously valuable option. I can't tell you how many times I've created document/view programs that simply display graphics or images and totally ignore all the document features. Every time this happened, I'd look at the files in the project and long to delete the document source code files. (Good thing I never did, otherwise the project wouldn't have compiled.)

The first time I used Visual C++ 6, when I went to add the code to the view class' `OnDraw()` function, I was surprised by the *IntelliSense* feature, which took over and tried to make my job easier. IntelliSense is a system in which the editor gives you a list of functions and function arguments based on the context of what you're typing. For instance, if I type **TextO**, a list containing `TextOut` will be displayed. If I press Enter (or Tab), the function name is completed, and I have less to type. IntelliSense also gives you a list of arguments for the function. This greatly reduces the number of trips to online help you'll have to make. Figure 1-2 shows the IntelliSense feature as it appeared when I created the HelloWorld1 program.

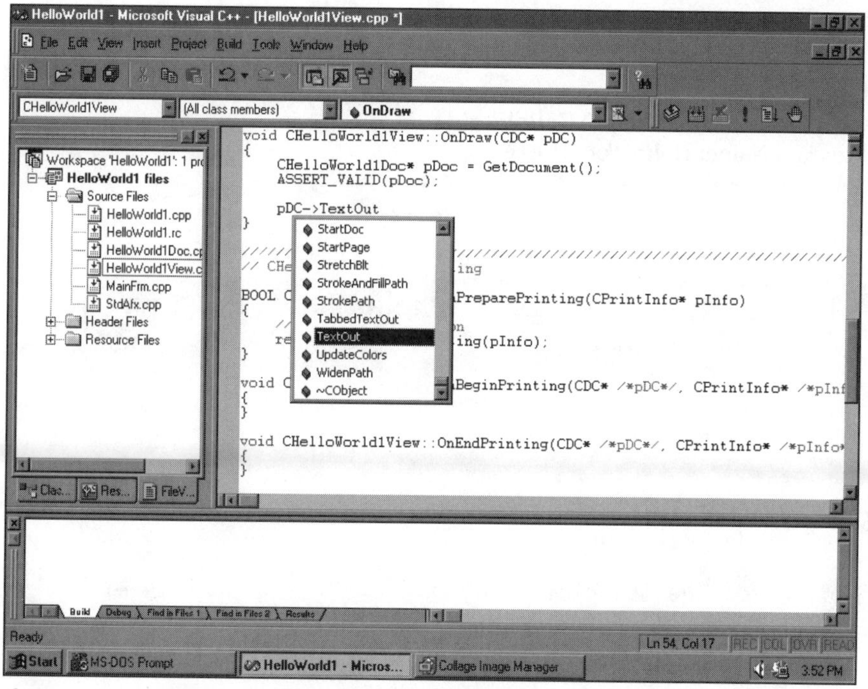

Figure 1-2: IntelliSense and statement completion make editing simple, but more importantly they help you remember class-member functions.

Another new feature of the AppWizard is the ability to create Explorer-style programs that have a tree-view control to display objects. Figure 1-3 shows a program that uses an Explorer-style look.

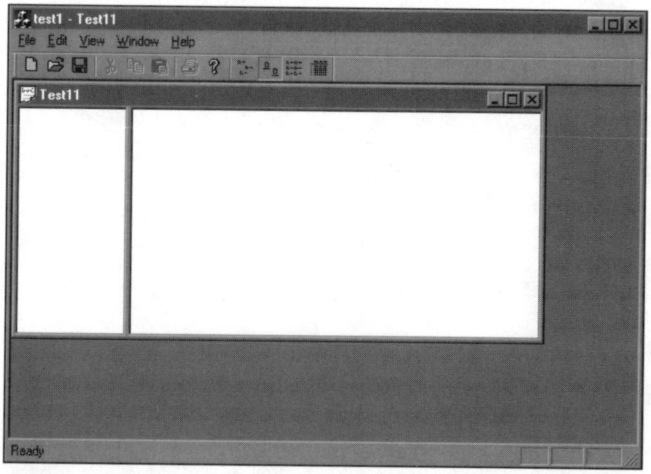

Figure 1-3: You can easily create Explorer-style applications.

Listing 1-1 shows highlights of the HelloWorld1 program's view class.

Demo Program

HelloWorld1
CD-ROM Location: **Chap1\HelloWorld1**
Program Name: **HelloWorld1.exe**
Source Code Modules in Text: **HelloWorld1View.cpp**

◆ ◆ ◆ ◆ ◆

Listing 1-1: Highlights of the HelloWorld1 Program's View Class

```
// HelloWorld1View.cpp : implementation of the
// CHelloWorld1View class
//

#include "stdafx.h"
#include "HelloWorld1.h"

#include "HelloWorld1Doc.h"
#include "HelloWorld1View.h"

/////////////////////////////////////////////////////////////
// CHelloWorld1View

IMPLEMENT_DYNCREATE(CHelloWorld1View, CView)

BEGIN_MESSAGE_MAP(CHelloWorld1View, CView)
  //{{AFX_MSG_MAP(CHelloWorld1View)
  //}}AFX_MSG_MAP
  // Standard printing commands
  ON_COMMAND(ID_FILE_PRINT, CView::OnFilePrint)
  ON_COMMAND(ID_FILE_PRINT_DIRECT, CView::OnFilePrint)
  ON_COMMAND(ID_FILE_PRINT_PREVIEW, CView::OnFilePrintPreview)
END_MESSAGE_MAP()

/////////////////////////////////////////////////////////////
// CHelloWorld1View construction/destruction

CHelloWorld1View::CHelloWorld1View()
{
}

CHelloWorld1View::~CHelloWorld1View()
{
}

BOOL CHelloWorld1View::PreCreateWindow(CREATESTRUCT& cs)
{
  return CView::PreCreateWindow(cs);
}
```

```
/////////////////////////////////////////////////////////////////
// CHelloWorld1View drawing

void CHelloWorld1View::OnDraw(CDC* pDC)
{
  CHelloWorld1Doc* pDoc = GetDocument();
  ASSERT_VALID(pDoc);

  pDC->TextOut( 20,20, "Hello Visual C++ World!" );

}

/////////////////////////////////////////////////////////////////
// CHelloWorld1View printing

BOOL CHelloWorld1View::OnPreparePrinting(
  CPrintInfo* pInfo)
{
  // default preparation
  return DoPreparePrinting(pInfo);
}

void CHelloWorld1View::OnBeginPrinting(CDC* /*pDC*/,
  CPrintInfo* /*pInfo*/)
{
}

void CHelloWorld1View::OnEndPrinting(CDC* /*pDC*/,
  CPrintInfo* /*pInfo*/)
{
}
```

When the HelloWorld1 program runs, you should see the familiar SDI application. In the view window, the text string "Hello Visual C++ World!" appears, as you can see in Figure 1-4.

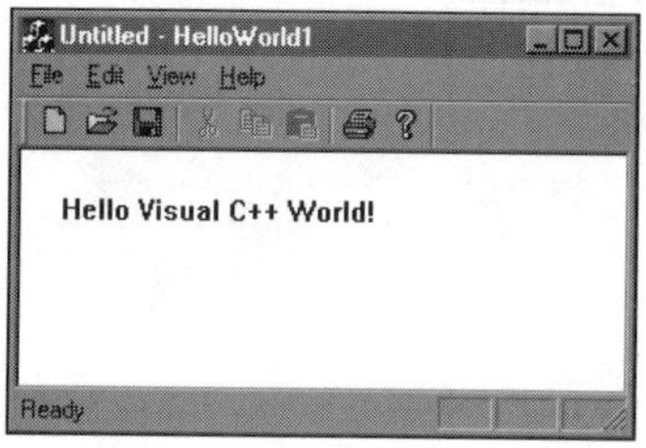

Figure 1-4: The AppWizard still creates the familiar SDI application.

The Visual C++ Win32 Console Application

I never thought there was a place for Win32 console applications until two things happened. First, I started teaching C++ at Rockingham Community College. I began my instruction by creating AppWizard-based Windows applications. It only took me about 15 minutes to realize how lost everyone was. I then quickly learned about Win32 console applications. With these gems I was able to teach C++ concepts without students getting lost in myriad project and MFC classes. Second, using Win32 console applications, I discovered I could quickly and easily get a program running that performs utility functions.

Once I made this startling revelation, I began to realize that the Win32 console applications are really handy for utilities that don't need a user interface. With almost no effort, I can create programs that do useful tasks such as move and rename files, convert binary files to source code, and other things software developers such as myself need. I don't yearn for the old days when I could whip up a DOS application in five minutes to automate some programming tasks. And I don't even have to worry about segmented pointers or running out of memory (usually).

This second demonstration program is a Win32 console application that displays the message "Hello Visual C++ Console World!". When you create a Win32 console application, one of the choices, believe it or not, is a "Hello World" application (see Listing 1-2).

Demo Program

HelloWorld2

CD-ROM Location: **Chap1\HelloWorld2**
Program Name: **HelloWorld2.exe**
Source Code Modules in Text: **HelloWorld2.cpp**

◆ ◆ ◆ ◆ ◆

Listing 1-2: The Entire Source Code for the HelloWorld2 Program

```
// HelloWorld2.cpp : Defines the entry point
// for the console application.
//

#include "stdafx.h"

int main(int argc, char* argv[])
{
  printf("Hello Visual C++ Console World!\n");
  return 0;
}
```

When the program runs, you should see a console window. In this console window, the message "Hello Visual C++ Console Application World!" appears, as shown in Figure 1-5.

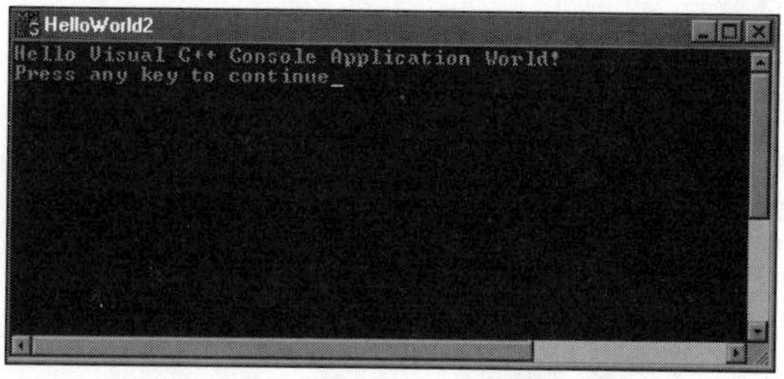

Figure 1-5: You may find yourself in need of a Win32 console application.

The HelloWorld3 ATL Control

If you haven't tackled ActiveX controls or used the Active Template Library (ATL), it won't be long, especially with the direction in which Microsoft is pushing, before you'll need to create ActiveX controls. For most situations, the best way to do this is with the Active Template Library Wizard. It creates the startup code for an ATL project and saves you the time and drudgery of doing it yourself (see Listing 1-3).

In spite of the ease with which you can create an ATL control, the footprint turns out to be relatively small. A full control with minimal code that's added, such as the HelloWorld3 control, ends up at about 37K. ATL controls have a lot of options, one being the ability to use MFC. If you want to use MFC, be prepared for another 80K to 100K to be added to the footprint.

Demo Program

HelloWorld3

CD-ROM Location: **Chap1\HelloWorld3**
Program Name: **HelloWorld3.dll**
Source Code Modules in Text: **Full.h**

◆ ◆ ◆ ◆ ◆

Listing 1-3: The Source Code for the ATL Wizard-created CFull Class In Which the Text Is Displayed

```
// Full.h : Declaration of the CFull

#ifndef __FULL_H_
#define __FULL_H_

#include "resource.h"       // main symbols
#include <atlctl.h>
```

(continued)

Listing 1-3 *(continued)*

```
/////////////////////////////////////////////////////////////////////////////
// CFull
class ATL_NO_VTABLE CFull :
  public CComObjectRootEx<CComSingleThreadModel>,
  public IDispatchImpl<IFull, &IID_IFull,
    &LIBID_HELLOWORLD3Lib>,
  public CComControl<CFull>,
  public IPersistStreamInitImpl<CFull>,
  public IOleControlImpl<CFull>,
  public IOleObjectImpl<CFull>,
  public IOleInPlaceActiveObjectImpl<CFull>,
  public IViewObjectExImpl<CFull>,
  public IOleInPlaceObjectWindowlessImpl<CFull>,
  public IPersistStorageImpl<CFull>,
  public ISpecifyPropertyPagesImpl<CFull>,
  public IQuickActivateImpl<CFull>,
  public IDataObjectImpl<CFull>,
  public IProvideClassInfo2Impl<&CLSID_Full, NULL,
    &LIBID_HELLOWORLD3Lib>,
  public CComCoClass<CFull, &CLSID_Full>
{
public:
  CFull()
  {
  }

DECLARE_REGISTRY_RESOURCEID(IDR_FULL)

BEGIN_COM_MAP(CFull)
  COM_INTERFACE_ENTRY(IFull)
  COM_INTERFACE_ENTRY(IDispatch)
  COM_INTERFACE_ENTRY(IViewObjectEx)
  COM_INTERFACE_ENTRY(IViewObject2)
  COM_INTERFACE_ENTRY(IViewObject)
  COM_INTERFACE_ENTRY(IOleInPlaceObjectWindowless)
  COM_INTERFACE_ENTRY(IOleInPlaceObject)
  COM_INTERFACE_ENTRY2(IOleWindow,
    IOleInPlaceObjectWindowless)
  COM_INTERFACE_ENTRY(IOleInPlaceActiveObject)
  COM_INTERFACE_ENTRY(IOleControl)
  COM_INTERFACE_ENTRY(IOleObject)
  COM_INTERFACE_ENTRY(IPersistStreamInit)
  COM_INTERFACE_ENTRY2(IPersist, IPersistStreamInit)
  COM_INTERFACE_ENTRY(ISpecifyPropertyPages)
  COM_INTERFACE_ENTRY(IQuickActivate)
  COM_INTERFACE_ENTRY(IPersistStorage)
  COM_INTERFACE_ENTRY(IDataObject)
  COM_INTERFACE_ENTRY(IProvideClassInfo)
  COM_INTERFACE_ENTRY(IProvideClassInfo2)
END_COM_MAP()
```

```
BEGIN_PROP_MAP(CFull)
  PROP_DATA_ENTRY("_cx", m_sizeExtent.cx, VT_UI4)
  PROP_DATA_ENTRY("_cy", m_sizeExtent.cy, VT_UI4)
  // Example entries
  // PROP_ENTRY("Property Description", dispid, clsid)
  // PROP_PAGE(CLSID_StockColorPage)
END_PROP_MAP()

BEGIN_MSG_MAP(CFull)
  CHAIN_MSG_MAP(CComControl<CFull>)
  DEFAULT_REFLECTION_HANDLER()
END_MSG_MAP()
// Handler prototypes:
//  LRESULT MessageHandler(UINT uMsg, WPARAM wParam,
//    LPARAM lParam, BOOL& bHandled);
//  LRESULT CommandHandler(WORD wNotifyCode, WORD wID,
//    HWND hWndCtl, BOOL& bHandled);
//  LRESULT NotifyHandler(int idCtrl, LPNMHDR pnmh,
//    BOOL& bHandled);

// IViewObjectEx
  DECLARE_VIEW_STATUS(VIEWSTATUS_SOLIDBKGND |
VIEWSTATUS_OPAQUE)

// IFull
public:

  HRESULT OnDraw(ATL_DRAWINFO& di)
  {
    RECT& rc = *(RECT*)di.prcBounds;
    Rectangle(di.hdcDraw, rc.left, rc.top,
      rc.right, rc.bottom);

    SetTextAlign(di.hdcDraw, TA_CENTER|TA_BASELINE);
    LPCTSTR pszText = _T("Hello Visual C++ ATL World!");
    TextOut(di.hdcDraw,
      (rc.left + rc.right) / 2,
      (rc.top + rc.bottom) / 2,
      pszText,
      lstrlen(pszText));

    return S_OK;
  }
};

#endif //__FULL_H_
```

The first thing you have to realize about this project is you can't just execute it. You need some sort of container into which to load it. A container in this case is some program that loads and executes the control. And even before you load the control into a container, you have to register it. To register the control so that applications can use it, run Regsvr32 (in the Windows\System directory) with a parameter of the control you want to register—for example, `C:\Windows\System\Regsvr32 HelloWorld3.dll`.

If you compile the project, Visual C++ registers the control for you. This makes it easy to test controls when you develop them. Once a control is registered, though, it's always expected to be in the directory in which it was registered. If you change it to a different directory, you must reregister it.

Visual C++ gives you a container program into which you can load controls. This saves you from having to write your own container just to test a control out. To run the test container program, just select ActiveX Control Test Container from the Tools menu. Figure 1-6 shows the HelloWorld3 control loaded into the test container.

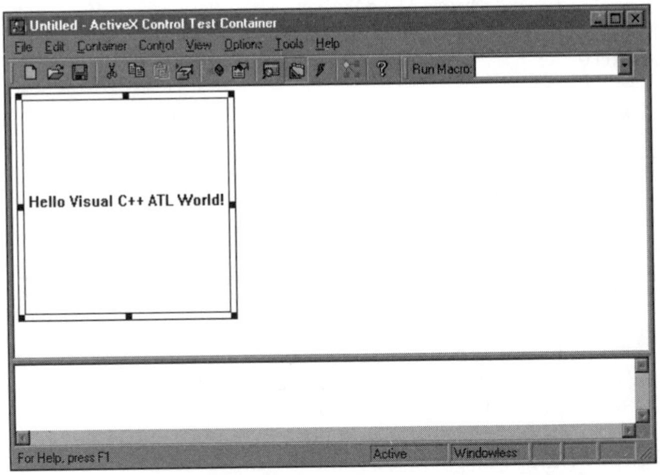

Figure 1-6: The HelloWorld3 control must be loaded into a control container. Here it's loaded into the ActiveX Control Test Container tool that comes with Visual C++.

The HelloWorld4 Java Applet

Somewhere along the way, everyone creates several Java applets and/or applications. Some go on to master the language and extensively use J++ as a development tool. I initially got into Java because it's so easy to use images, and I liked spicing up my Web site. Eventually, I learned all of the other aspects of Java, and lo and behold, I inherited several e-commerce applets that I maintain at work. (This was an unwanted side benefit of my Java development.)

All kidding aside, you're going to need to know some Java in order to keep up with today's development requirements. And Visual Studio gives you J++, a powerful, easy-to-use tool for Java development.

The HelloWorld4 applet, shown in Listing 1-4, was written in about two minutes. Java is fairly easy to learn, and J++ creates enough startup code so you don't have to fool with it yourself.

Demo Program

HelloWorld4
CD-ROM Location: **Chap1\HelloWorld4**
Program Name: **HelloWorld4.class**
Source Code Modules in Text: **HelloWorld4.java**

◆ ◆ ◆ ◆ ◆

Listing 1-4: **The Source Code for the HelloWorld4 Applet**

```
// HelloWorld4.java

import java.awt.*;
import java.applet.*;

/**
 * This class reads PARAM tags from its HTML host page
 * and sets the color and label properties of the applet.
 * Program execution begins with the init() method.
 */
public class HelloWorld4 extends Applet
{
  /**
   * The entry point for the applet.
   */
  public void init()
  {
    initForm();

    usePageParams();

}

  private  final String labelParam = "label";
  private  final String backgroundParam = "background";
  private  final String foregroundParam = "foreground";

  /**
   * Reads parameters from the applet's HTML host and
   * sets applet properties.
   */
  private void usePageParams()
  {
    final String defaultLabel = "Default label";
    final String defaultBackground = "C0C0C0";
    final String defaultForeground = "000000";
    String labelValue;
```

(continued)

Listing 1-4 *(continued)*

```
    String backgroundValue;
    String foregroundValue;

    /**
     * Read the <PARAM NAME="label" VALUE="some string">,
     * <PARAM NAME="background" VALUE="rrggbb">,
     * and <PARAM NAME="foreground" VALUE="rrggbb"> tags
     * from the applet's HTML host.
     */
    labelValue = getParameter(labelParam);
    backgroundValue = getParameter(backgroundParam);
    foregroundValue = getParameter(foregroundParam);

    if ((labelValue == null) || (backgroundValue == null)
     ||(foregroundValue == null))
    {
      /**
       * There was something wrong with the HTML host
       * tags. Generate default values.
       */
      labelValue = defaultLabel;
      backgroundValue = defaultBackground;
      foregroundValue = defaultForeground;
    }

    /**
     * Set the applet's string label, background color,
     * and foreground colors.
     */
    label1.setText(labelValue);
    label1.setBackground(stringToColor(backgroundValue));
    label1.setForeground(stringToColor(foregroundValue));
    this.setBackground(stringToColor(backgroundValue));
    this.setForeground(stringToColor(foregroundValue));
  }

  /**
   * Converts a string formatted as "rrggbb" to an
   * awt.Color object
   */
  private Color stringToColor(String paramValue)
  {
    int red;
    int green;
    int blue;

    red = (Integer.decode("0x" +
      paramValue.substring(0,2))).intValue();
```

```
    green = (Integer.decode("0x" +
      paramValue.substring(2,4))).intValue();
    blue = (Integer.decode("0x" +
      paramValue.substring(4,6))).intValue();

    return new Color(red,green,blue);
  }

  /**
   * External interface used by design tools to show
   * properties of an applet.
   */
  public String[][] getParameterInfo()
  {
    String[][] info =
    {
      { labelParam, "String",
        "Label string to be displayed" },
      { backgroundParam, "String",
        "Background color, format \"rrggbb\"" },
      { foregroundParam, "String",
        "Foreground color, format \"rrggbb\"" },
    };
    return info;
  }

  Label label1 = new Label();

  /**
   * Intializes values for the applet and its components
   */
  void initForm()
  {
    this.setBackground(Color.lightGray);
    this.setForeground(Color.black);
    label1.setText("label1");
    this.setLayout(new BorderLayout());
    this.add("North",label1);
  }
}
```

When the HelloWorld4 Java applet runs, it first invokes Internet Explorer (IE). IE then loads the HelloWorld4.htm file. The .htm file then loads the applet and gives it parameters such as background color and the text that's displayed in the applet window. In this case, the text that's displayed is "Hello Visual J++ World from the HTML host," as you can see in Figure 1-7.

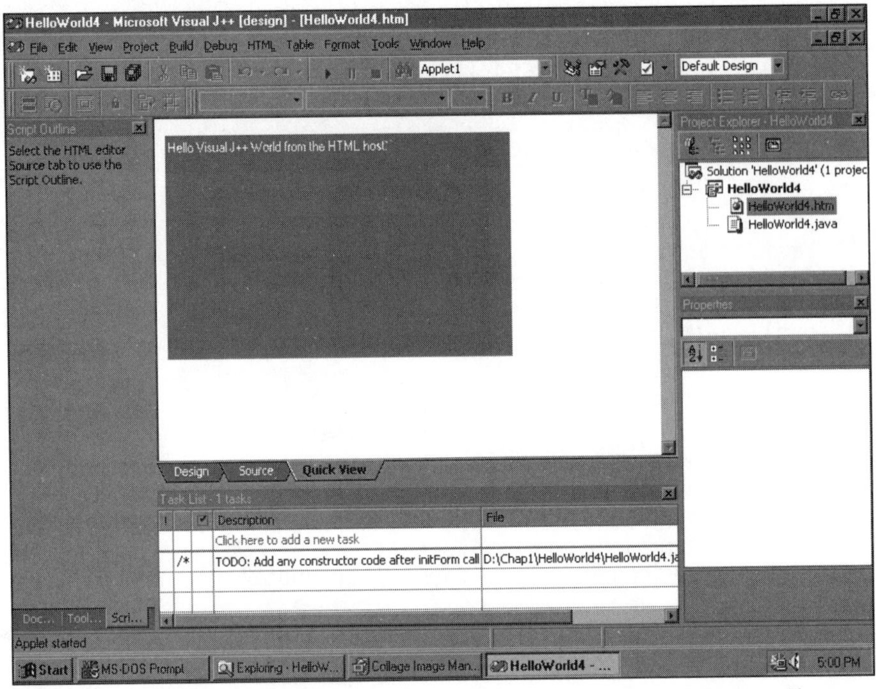

Figure 1-7: The HelloWorld4 Java applet loads a text string from the HTML file as a parameter and displays it.

The HelloWorld5 Java Application

Someone out there is probably now saying, "Java is a real language? What about applications?" Serious Java devotees might even be mixing it up with some expletives. Yes, Java is a real language that can be used to write very good applications. As a matter of fact, Id Software, developers of Doom and Quake, are now using Java to develop some of their utility programs. If it's good enough for them, it's good enough for us.

In fact, Java is a great language. It's really object oriented, not like the hybrid variety of OOP that C++ implements. You can write a serious application with Java, no question about it. My only concern is that the Virtual Machine (VM) is not all that fast. I haven't written any large applications with Java yet — I think I'll wait until the VM gets faster. But for small applications, it's a good choice.

The HelloWorld5 program is a Java application that displays a text string in the application's window caption bar (see Listing 1-5).

HelloWorld5
CD-ROM Location: **Chap1\HelloWorld5**
Program Name: **HelloWorld5.class**
Source Code Modules in Text: **HelloWorld5.java**

◆ ◆ ◆ ◆ ◆

Listing 1-5: The Source Code for the HelloWorld5 Application

```
//JPad.java
import wfc.app.*;
import wfc.core.*;
import wfc.ui.*;

public class JPad extends Form
{

  private void JPad_click(Object sender, Event e)
  {
  }

  public void newMenu_click(Object sender, Event e)
  {
  }

  private void saveAsMenu_click(Object sender, Event e)
  {
  }

  private void saveMenu_click(Object sender, Event e)
  {
  }

  private void openMenu_click(Object sender, Event e)
  {
  }

  public void wordWrapMenu_click(Object sender, Event e)
  {
  }

  public void dateTimeMenu_click(Object sender, Event e)
  {
  }

  public void pasteMenu_click(Object sender, Event e)
  {
    try
    {
    }
```

(continued)

Listing 1-5 *(continued)*

```
    catch (Exception ecx)
    {
    }
  }

  public void copyMenu_click(Object sender, Event e)
  {
  }

  public void cutMenu_click(Object sender, Event e)
  {
  }

  public void exitMenu_click(Object sender, Event e)
  {
      Application.exit();
  }

  public JPad()
  {
    //Required for Visual J++ Form Designer support
    initForm();

}

  public static void main(String args[])
  {
    Application.run(new JPad());
  }

  /*
   * NOTE: The following code is required by the Visual
   * J++ form designer.  It can be modified using the
   * form editor.  Do not modify it using the code
   * editor.
   */

  Container components = new Container();
  MainMenu mainMenu1 = new MainMenu();
  MenuItem fileMenu = new MenuItem();
  MenuItem newMenu = new MenuItem();
  MenuItem openMenu = new MenuItem();
  MenuItem saveMenu = new MenuItem();
  MenuItem seperator3Menu = new MenuItem();
  MenuItem exitMenu = new MenuItem();
  MenuItem editMenu = new MenuItem();
  MenuItem cutMenu = new MenuItem();
  MenuItem copyMenu = new MenuItem();
```

```
MenuItem pasteMenu = new MenuItem();
MenuItem separator1Menu = new MenuItem();
MenuItem dateTimeMenu = new MenuItem();
MenuItem separator2Menu = new MenuItem();
MenuItem wordWrapMenu = new MenuItem();
MenuItem helpMenu = new MenuItem();
MenuItem aboutMenu = new MenuItem();
MenuItem saveAsMenu = new MenuItem();

private void initForm()
{

  newMenu.setText("&New");
  newMenu.addOnClick(
    new EventHandler(this.newMenu_click));
  openMenu.setText("&Open...");
  openMenu.addOnClick(
    new EventHandler(this.openMenu_click));
  saveMenu.setText("&Save");
  saveMenu.addOnClick(
    new EventHandler(this.saveMenu_click));
  seperator3Menu.setText("-");
  exitMenu.setText("E&xit");
  exitMenu.addOnClick(
    new EventHandler(this.exitMenu_click));
  cutMenu.setText("Cu&t");
  cutMenu.addOnClick(
    new EventHandler(this.cutMenu_click));
  copyMenu.setText("&Copy");
  copyMenu.addOnClick(
    new EventHandler(this.copyMenu_click));
  pasteMenu.setText("&Paste");
  pasteMenu.addOnClick(
    new EventHandler(this.pasteMenu_click));
  separator1Menu.setText("-");
  dateTimeMenu.setText("&Date/Time");
  dateTimeMenu.addOnClick(
    new EventHandler(this.dateTimeMenu_click));
  separator2Menu.setText("-");
  wordWrapMenu.setText("&Word Wrap");
  wordWrapMenu.addOnClick(
    new EventHandler(this.wordWrapMenu_click));
  editMenu.setMenuItems(new MenuItem[] {
    cutMenu,
    copyMenu,
    pasteMenu,
    separator1Menu,
    dateTimeMenu,
    separator2Menu,
    wordWrapMenu});
```

(continued)

Listing 1-5 *(continued)*

```
    editMenu.setText("&Edit");
    aboutMenu.setText("&About");
    helpMenu.setMenuItems(new MenuItem[] {
      aboutMenu});
    helpMenu.setText("&Help");
    saveAsMenu.setText("Save &As...");
    saveAsMenu.addOnClick(
      new EventHandler(this.saveAsMenu_click));
    fileMenu.setMenuItems(new MenuItem[] {
      newMenu,
      openMenu,
      saveMenu,
      saveAsMenu,
      seperator3Menu,
      exitMenu});
    fileMenu.setText("&File");
    mainMenu1.setMenuItems(new MenuItem[] {
      fileMenu,
      editMenu,
      helpMenu});
    /* @designTimeOnly mainMenu1.setLocation(
      new Point(100, 60)); */
    this.setBackColor(Color.CONTROL);
    this.setLocation(new Point(298, 88));
    this.setSize(new Point(300, 240));
    this.setTabIndex(-1);
    this.setTabStop(true);
    this.setText("HelloWorld5");
    this.setAutoScaleBaseSize(13);
    this.setClientSize(new Point(292, 193));
    this.setMenu(mainMenu1);
  }
  //NOTE: End of form designer support code.

  public static class ClassInfo extends Form.ClassInfo
  {
    //TODO: Add your property and event infos here
  }
}
```

When the application runs, you should see a window appear with the text "HelloWorld5" in the caption bar, as shown in Figure 1-8.

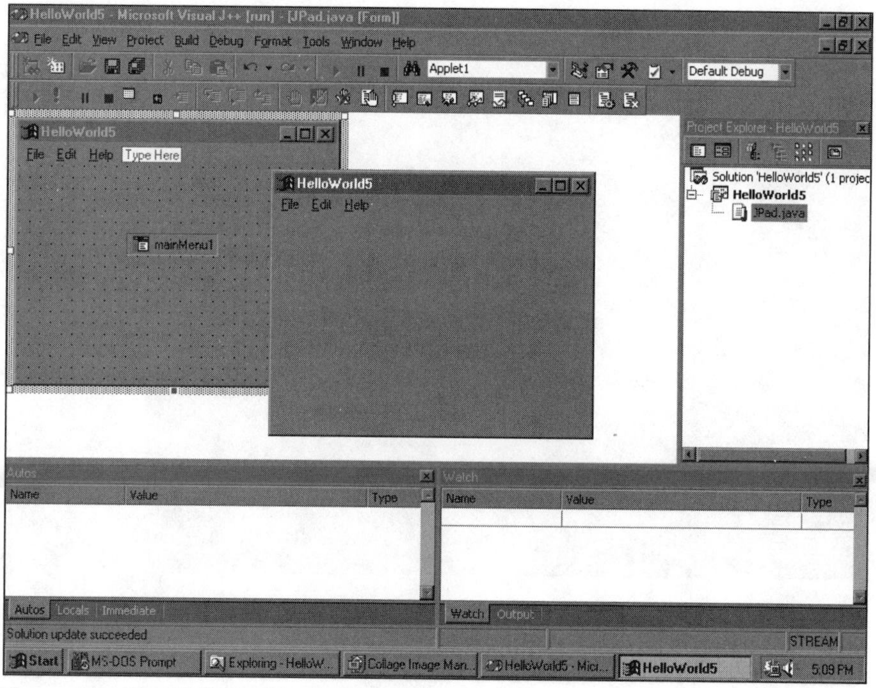

Figure 1-8: The HelloWorld5 Java application is a good example of how easy it is to create a Java application, and of how many features J++ builds into the code.

The HelloWorld6 Visual Basic Application

Visual Basic is another power tool in the Visual Studio 6 arsenal. With Visual Basic, you can create useful applications in several minutes. And it's not just form-based applications that are easy. Writing NT services is a snap. Creating ActiveX components is a piece of cake. If you don't currently use Visual Basic, you need to take another look at it. It's a sophisticated tool that, in many cases, can save you time and money.

The HelloWorld6 application took about a minute and a half to write, which was less time than it took to run the program, capture the screen, and save the image shown in Figure 1-9. And there's absolutely no source code for the program. What you see is all automatic, based on some form properties and a single object placed on the form.

Demo Program

HelloWorld6

CD-ROM Location: **Chap1\HelloWorld6**

Program Name: **HelloWorld6.exe**

Source Code Modules in Text: **None**

✦ ✦ ✦ ✦ ✦

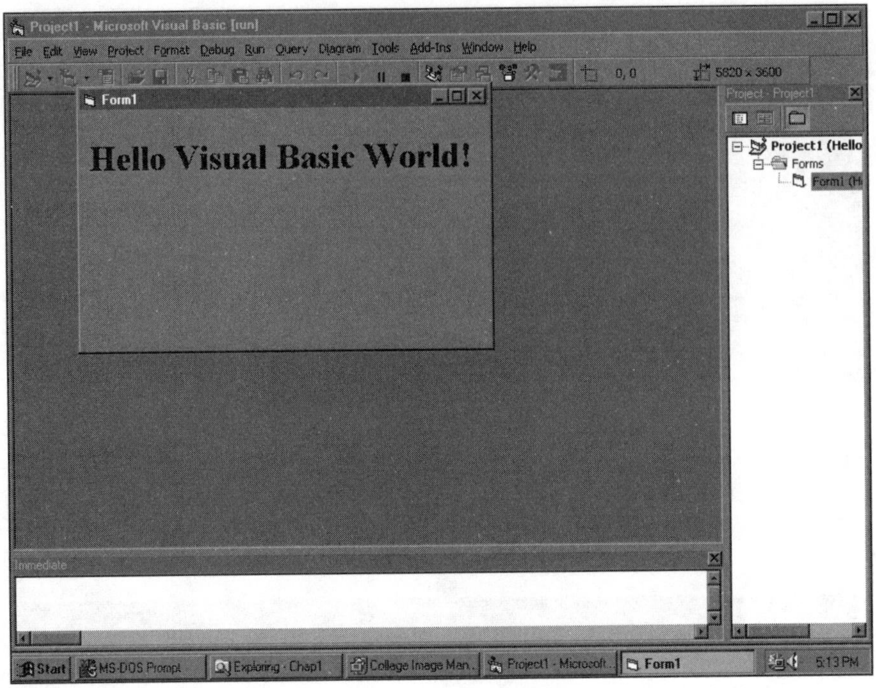

Figure 1-9: This Visual Basic program was easy to write – it only took about 1 1/2 minutes.

Summary

As a software developer, you have some of the most unbelievable opportunities in front of you. I remember the days of 256K machines with CGA graphics. Programmers had to squeeze to get anything to work well, and getting something to look good was a challenge.

Windows 98 brings a solid, stable, and feature-filled platform to the equation. It's an operating system that makes development a pleasure. My vote for what's been the greatest single contribution to software is preemptive multitasking. It's a blessing.

Visual Studio complements Windows 98 in ways I'm discovering every day. It's a well-rounded, robust, and flexible tool that will allow you to achieve your wildest software dreams.

✦ ✦ ✦

CHAPTER 2

Menus

✦ ✦ ✦ ✦

In This Chapter

Editing menu resources

Creating menu command and update handlers

Learning about menu messages in MFC programs

Studying a demo program and learning more about menus

Examining keyboard accelerators

Creating context menus

Viewing context menus in a demo program

✦ ✦ ✦ ✦

Next to windows, the most important user-interface objects probably are menus. After all, every user relies on menus to figure out the available commands. The number of menu-support functions in the Windows 98 API reflects the importance of menus.

This chapter covers available MFC support for two user-interface objects used to receive command input: *menus* and *accelerator tables* (commonly known as *shortcut keys*). After all, the first thing a user does when an application's window appears is to tell the application what to do—which involves using one of these two command input mechanisms. We'll show you how to get these user-interface objects ready to do your users' bidding.

Even casual users of Microsoft Windows 98 know that a menu bar appears at the top of an application's main window. Since the introduction of Windows 95 (and now in Windows 98), Microsoft has promoted the use of per-object context menus that appear when the user clicks the right mouse button. One of the sample programs shown in this chapter shows you how easy it is to create and respond to these menus.

An *accelerator* is a keystroke that a program interprets as a command. From your program's perspective, the result of a menu selection or an accelerator keystroke is identical because Windows 98 generates identical messages for both. You can connect the two in the mind of a user by displaying the accelerator name in the menu, to the right of the equivalent menu command. For example, you'll often see Ctrl+V next to the Paste command in an Edit menu. Although both types of commands are connected in the user's mind, from a programming perspective the two are defined separately. Specifically, menus are defined using menu resources, and accelerators are defined with accelerator resources.

Changing Default Menus

When AppWizard creates a Doc/View application for you, it provides a default menu (or a pair of default menus when building a multiple-document application). In this section, you'll work through some of the steps you might take to change that menu to one more suitable for your application.

Similar to an operating system's file system, menus are defined as hierarchies. In both cases, the hierarchies consist of two basic types of entities. A file system has subdirectories and files, and menus have pop-up menus (sometimes called submenus) and menu items (called commands). Subdirectories are used by the file system to organize files and other subdirectories. Pop-up menus organize menu item groups and other pop-up menus.

Editing a menu resource

A menu resource lives in a resource script (.RC) file, along with an application's other resources. To access the resource file, click on the resource tab in the InfoViewer window. This displays a summary of available resource types and available resources.

The resource summary list shows all the types of resources available in your application—for example, bitmaps, dialogs, icons, menus, a string table, and a version resource. When you double-click Menu, a list of menu resources is displayed. To open a particular menu resource in the menu editor, double-click its name in this list. (If you're using an AppWizard-generated resource list, the name of your main menu will be `IDR_MAINFRAME`.) The selected menu resource is displayed in the menu editor.

From the menu editor, you can open the Menu Item Properties dialog box. This dialog box lists all the details of individual menu items. It also allows you to change any detail of a menu. To see this important user-interface object, double-click any menu item displayed in the menu editor.

When the Menu Item Properties dialog box is displayed, the first thing you'll probably want to do is make sure it doesn't disappear unexpectedly. To make it remain in place, click the Thumbtack icon in the dialog's top-left corner.

When you're defining a menu item, three fields play the most important roles: ID, Caption, and Prompt. To make sure you're getting what you want, you need to check all three carefully when creating a menu item. This is true even for the ID field, which is automatically provided for you by the menu editor. Let's examine each of these three fields, starting with the ID.

When you are creating a new menu item, you start with one of two fields in the Menu Item Properties dialog box: the ID or the Caption. You start with the ID when creating a menu item using one of MFC's predefined identifier values. You use a predefined value for commands that the MFC framework may handle for you. For example, the ID for New in the File menu is `ID_FILE_NEW`, the ID for Cut in the Edit menu is `ID_EDIT_CUT`, and the ID for New in the Window menu is `ID_WINDOW_NEW`. For a complete list of these predefined identifier values, see `AFXRES.H`, the MFC include file in which all of its default resource IDs are defined.

To create a menu item for which MFC has no built-in support, you start by selecting the blank menu item and entering a menu item name in the Caption field. As you type the caption, the menu editor instantly modifies the menu to show you the results of your changes. If you enter the caption first, the menu editor defines an ID value for you (to see the symbolic name, click another menu item, and then click back on the item you're creating). If you don't like the name of the ID that the menu editor supplies, you can always define your own name by typing over the supplied name.

Try This

Creating an Application and Editing the Menus

This exercise will get you familiar with the basics of editing menus in your programs.

1. Create a single-document application with AppWizard.
2. Click the resource tab in the InfoViewer window.
3. Double click the menu folder.
4. Double click the `IDR_MAINFRAME` menu resource.
5. In the File menu, delete all entries except the Exit entry.
6. Click the Help menu.
7. Press the Insert key —this will create a new menu.
8. Edit the new menu so it says "Test."
9. Add three menu entries to the Test menu as shown in Figure 2-1.

✦ ✦ ✦ ✦ ✦

As you may notice, the menu editor follows the convention of using the `ID_` prefix at the beginning of command ID names. If you don't like the name (or the convention), it's a simple matter to type in a new symbolic name.

Expert Tip

Naming Conventions

You're better off if you accept the default IDs generated at this point because it'll be easier to remember what the IDs refer to. Their names are based on the menu text and the menu entry text.

✦ ✦ ✦ ✦ ✦

When filling in the Caption field, you will want to give some thought to a menu item's *keyboard mnemonic.* A keyboard mnemonic defines the keyboard interface to a menu item (or a pop-up menu). The mnemonic comes into play when the user activates a menu by holding the Alt key while pressing the underlined letter, or *mnemonic*, for that menu. For example, because of keyboard mnemonics, Open from the File menu can be selected with the Alt+F+O key combination—that is, by holding down the Alt key and pressing F and O. To a user, keyboard mnemonics are similar to accelerator keystrokes. From a programming perspective, however, they differ: Mnemonic support comes from the menu system. Accelerators, as you'll see in this chapter, are defined in an accelerator table. To define a mnemonic, insert an ampersand (&) before the letter you want underlined. To insert an ampersand in your menu text, insert two ampersands (&&) in the Caption field.

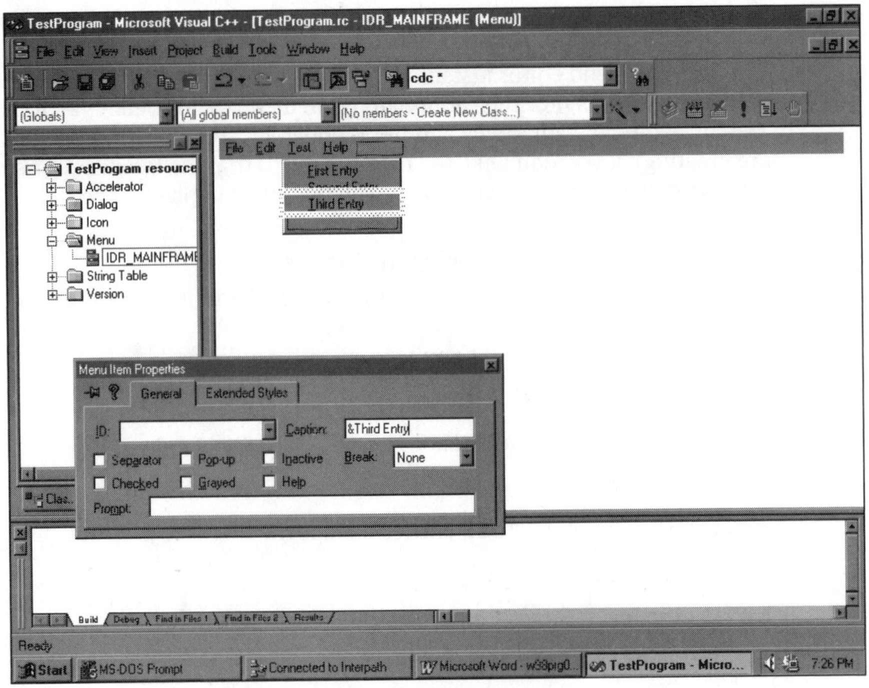

Figure 2-1: This exercise will get you familiar with editing menus.

✦ ✦ ✦ ✦ ✦

The third field you should always define for a menu item is the Prompt field. You use this field to enter a character string that you want displayed in the status bar when the user browses over (without selecting) a menu item. Even though you fill in this field in the menu editor, the string itself isn't stored as part of the menu resource. Instead, an entry is made in the string table resource, with the string ID set to the same value as the menu item command ID.

The Prompt field has two parts: the status bar string and the ToolTip string. You already know about the status bar string. The ToolTip string isn't used with a menu item, but rather applies to another command input device: toolbar buttons. A ToolTip string is displayed when the mouse cursor pauses over a toolbar button. As shown in the following example (which shows the prompt value that MFC creates for the Exit command), you separate the two parts with a newline (`\n`) character:

```
Quits the application; prompts to save documents\nExit
```

Try This

Adding Prompts to Your Menu

With the application you created in the previous TryThis exercise, add prompts including ToolTip strings.

✦ ✦ ✦ ✦ ✦

Creating Menus

There are several ways to create a menu. The most common way is to define the menu at program build time using a menu resource. As will be discussed in the next chapter, when a frame window is initialized, MFC's frame window class creates several user-interface objects from resource data. Included among these objects are accelerator tables and menus. Both are identified by a resource ID passed as the first parameter to `CFrameWnd::LoadFrame()`. Visual Studio provides a set of resource editing tools, including a graphical menu editor for editing a menu's contents.

Each menu item has two essential elements: a string name (such as "Copy") and an integer command ID (3, for example). In a menu resource, each menu item needs a unique command ID. By generating unique IDs for your menu items, the Visual Studio resource editor ensures this requirement is met. It also creates a symbolic constant by combining the pop-up menu name with the menu item name.

After you've created a menu resource, you need to run the ClassWizard to create code for each menu item. As you'll see, ClassWizard treats each menu item as a separate user-interface object (listed in the Object ID list box). For each menu item, you have to decide which class should handle that item. Then, you have to decide whether you want code for the `COMMAND` menu message, the `UPDATE_COMMAND_UI` menu message, or both. To help you make these choices, the following section details the meaning of these two messages.

Creating menu handlers

The menu resource is nothing more than a data structure that defines how the system should construct a menu. MFC automatically connects a menu to a frame window when the menu resource ID is provided. But MFC cannot automatically decide how a program should respond to menu item selections (aside from default handling provided in AppWizard-generated code). That's your job, accomplished by the handling of menu messages.

For menu items, ClassWizard lets you choose between two messages: `COMMAND` and `UPDATE_COMMAND_UI`. Within the MFC source files, these messages have slightly different names: `WM_COMMAND` and `CN_UPDATE_COMMAND_UI`.

Expert Tip

Default Names for Update Functions

The default function names that the ClassWizard creates for command functions are normally OK. But the ones it creates for update functions are longer because ClassWizard adds "Update" to the function names. Under some circumstances, this extends the function name to a cumbersome length. Make sure update functions aren't too long. Consider renaming them.

◆ ◆ ◆ ◆ ◆

A WM_COMMAND message means a user has selected a menu item (or an accelerator key or a toolbar button). This message is a request from the user for action, and some response is expected. As such, you must provide a WM_COMMAND message handler for each menu item in your menus. If MFC cannot find a WM_COMMAND handler for a given menu item, that menu item is grayed (disabled) and made unavailable to the user. Here's an example of an empty WM_COMMAND handler function created by ClassWizard:

```
{
    // TODO: Add your command handler code here
}
```

On the other hand, handling of the CN_UPDATE_COMMAND_UI message is entirely optional. This message is a request from MFC to update the appearance of individual menu items. For example, you might place a check mark next to a menu item, gray out a menu item, or enable a menu item. Here's an example of a CN_UPDATE_COMMAND_UI message handler that does it all:

```
{
    // Set check mark if d_bMenuChecked is TRUE,
    // Otherwise clear check mark.
    pCmdUI->SetCheck(d_bMenuChecked);

    // Enable if d_bMenuEnable is TRUE,
    // Otherwise gray out.
    pCmdUI->Enable(d_bMenuEnable);
}
```

As shown in this code fragment, you are passed a pointer to a CCmdUI object. You control the menu item state by calling CCmdUI member functions.

Try This

Adding Command Handlers to Your Program

With the application you've used in the last two TryThis exercises, add command functions for the menu entries under the Test menu.

◆ ◆ ◆ ◆ ◆

A single message, WM_COMMAND, lets you know the user wants some work done. You just need to make sure a message-handler function is ready to do the work. If you've already built Windows programs in C, be forewarned: This is the only similarity between MFC and Windows 98 API menu-message handling.

MFC allows other objects besides window objects to handle messages. This is an improvement over SDK-style programming, in which windows are the only objects that receive messages of any kind. To take advantage of this feature, you need to know which other objects can receive messages. You also need to know in what order MFC queries objects for command message handlers. In other words, you need to know how MFC routes command messages. That's our next topic for discussion.

Nutshell

Editing and Using Menus

Here are the steps to edit and respond to menu items.

1. Click the resource tab in the InfoViewer window.
2. Double click the menu folder.
3. Double click the `IDR_MAINFRAME` menu resource.
4. Add and delete menus and menu entries until your menu structure meets your needs.
5. Using the ClassWizard, add command functions for each of your newly added menu entries.
6. Add update functions for menu entries that must maintain a check, enabled state, or any other update property.

◆ ◆ ◆ ◆ ◆

Menu Messages in MFC

Most of the messages you handle in an MFC program are directed at one object type: a window. This follows the model used by the Windows 98 API, and—given the types of messages—it seems to make sense. After all, windowing messages such as `WM_CREATE`, `WM_MOVE`, and `WM_SIZE` notify us that a window has been created, moved, or sized. In the Windows 98 API and in MFC, only a window object is interested in such events. In addition, non-windowing messages—for example, mouse and keyboard messages—direct data to a particular window, and therefore cannot be rerouted without creating confusion.

MFC departs from the Windows 98 API in its handling of the two menuing messages. When an application creates a menu command, the frame window holding a menu doesn't have to process every menu message (although it usually handles some). Instead, the work can be delegated to message handlers within objects that own the resources to which the command applies. Among the candidates for handling menu messages are `CCmdTarget`-derived classes, which include windows (such as view windows), and application (`CWinApp`-derived) objects. In a Doc/View application, document objects and view objects (which are windows) are also candidates for handling menu messages.

Although any `CCmdTarget`-derived class *can* receive menu messages, in fact, menu messages take a specific path when they are routed. Table 2-1 lists the order that MFC uses to check the message maps when delivering command messages for non-Doc/View applications, single-document Doc/View applications, and multiple-document Doc/View applications.

If MFC's command message routing isn't to your liking, you can define your own priorities and send command messages to any object. However, you will have to override the `OnCmdMsg()` command message routing functions in several classes. Before doing this, you'll want to spend some time reviewing the MFC source files to make sure your changes are in sync with the base classes. In particular, look for the default `OnCmdMsg()` handlers in the following classes: `CView`, `CDocument`, `CFrameWnd`, and `CMDIFrameWnd`. (You could also override `PreTranslateMessage()` to get the same result.)

Although it isn't likely you'll modify the routing of menu messages, you will probably need to modify menus dynamically at one time or another. In the next section, we'll cover some of the possibilities for runtime changes to menus. We won't provide in-depth coverage of every capability; we'll just introduce the basics and give you an idea of what is possible.

Table 2-1
Routing of Command Messages for Different Application Types

Application Type	***Base Class***	***Comments***
Non-Doc/View	`CFrameWnd`	Frame window gets first crack at messages.
	`CWinApp`	The application object is handled second.
Single-Document	`CView`	The active view is checked first for menu interface (SDI) handlers.
Doc/View	`CDocument`	The document of the active view comes next.
	`CSingleDocTemplate`	The document template of the active view is third.
	`CFrameWnd`	The frame window comes next.
	`CWinApp`	The application object comes last.
Multiple-document	`CView`	The currently active view is checked first for menu interface (MDI) handlers.
Doc/View	`CDocument`	The document of the active view comes next.
	`CMultiDocTemplate`	The document template for the active view comes third.
	`CMDIChildFrame`	The child frame comes next, although this class relies on the `CFrameWnd` (its base class) implementation.
	`CMDIFrameWnd`	The parent frame window is next.
	`CWinApp`	The application object is last.

Menu Command Ranges

If you dynamically create menu items, you need to provide command handlers. Although you could use ClassWizard to "dummy up" a set, you don't always know how many command handlers you need to create. For such situations, MFC lets you handle a range of command IDs with a single command handler. Because ClassWizard can't deal with a range of command IDs, you must write the code by hand that ClassWizard would otherwise create for you.

Your first concern is picking a range of command IDs that doesn't interfere with existing command IDs. Table 2-2 summarizes how the available command ranges are used by ClassWizard in particular and the MFC framework in general. As shown in this table, what's left for your use is a range of IDs from 0x9000 (36864) to 0xDFFF (57343).

Table 2-2
How the MFC and ClassWizard Use Command Ranges

Range	*Description*
0x8000-0x8FFF	ClassWizard uses this range for application-defined menus.
0x9000-0xDFFF	This range of command IDs is available for your use.
0xE000-0xFFFF	MFC uses this range for its own purposes.

Next, you need to add a function to the class declaration. ClassWizard creates three pieces of code for every message: an include file declaration, a message map definition, and a function definition. Here's an example of a function declaration for a message-handling function that can handle a range of command IDs:

```
{    ...
   void OnCommandRange (UINT id);
   ...
};
```

The next piece is the message map entry, which MFC's message-handling mechanism must have to be able to find your function. To create this message map entry, you need to add an `ON_COMMAND_RANGE()` message map macro between the boundaries of a `BEGIN_MESSAGE_MAP()` and `END_MESSAGE_MAP()` pair. This message map macro takes three parameters: start of range, end of range, and function:

```
ON_COMMAND_RANGE(ID_MIN, ID_MAX, OnCommandRange);
```

The final piece is the function definition itself. It takes a single parameter, which is the command ID for a selected menu item. Here's an example:

```
{
   switch (id)
   {
       case ID_DYNA_COMMAND_1: ...
       case ID_DYNA_COMMAND_2: ...
       ...
   }
}
```

When you understand the basics, dynamic changes to existing menus are fairly straightforward. In most cases, however, you'll rely on static menus — that is, menus built from menu resources — to inform your users about their command options.

Handling Menu Input

In order to illustrate the basic techniques of handling menu input, we've created a demo program named `MenuDemo1`. It performs simple menu command and update functions in response to menu input.

Demo Program

MenuDemo1
CD-ROM Location: **Chap02\MenuDemo1**
Program Name: **MenuDemo1.EXE**
Source Code Modules in Text: **MenuDemo1View.cpp**

✦ ✦ ✦ ✦ ✦

Listing 2-1: MenuDemo1

```
// MenuDemo1View.cpp : implementation of
// the CMenuDemo1View class
//

/////////////////////////////////////////////////////////////////////
// CMenuDemo1View construction/destruction

CMenuDemo1View::CMenuDemo1View()
{

  // Set the initial color
  // to black.
  m_nColor = COLOR_BLACK;

}

CMenuDemo1View::~CMenuDemo1View()
{
}

/////////////////////////////////////////////////////////////////////
// CMenuDemo1View drawing
```

```
void CMenuDemo1View::OnDraw(CDC* pDC)
{
  CMenuDemo1Doc* pDoc = GetDocument();
  ASSERT_VALID(pDoc);

  // Define the four colors that
  // we'll use.
  static COLORREF Color[] = {
    RGB( 0, 0, 0 ), RGB( 255, 255, 255 ),
    RGB( 255, 0, 0 ), RGB( 0, 255, 0 ),
    RGB( 0, 0, 255 ) };

  // Create a brush.
  CBrush Brush( Color[m_nColor] );

  // Get the client RECT so we know
  // the size of the RECT to draw.
  RECT Rect;
  GetClientRect( &Rect );

  // Draw the rect.
  pDC->FillRect( &Rect, &Brush );

}

/////////////////////////////////////////////////////////////////////////////
// CMenuDemo1View message handlers

void CMenuDemo1View::OnInformationScreenwidthandheight()
{

  CString strInfo;

  // Format a CString object with
  // information about the screen's
  // width and height.
  strInfo.Format(
    "Screen Width:%d, Screen Height:%d",
    GetSystemMetrics( SM_CXFULLSCREEN ),
    GetSystemMetrics( SM_CYFULLSCREEN ) );

  // Display the information.
  AfxMessageBox( strInfo );

}

void CMenuDemo1View::OnInformationScreencolordepth()
{

  // Get a DC to the window.
  CClientDC ClientDC( this );
```

(continued)

Listing 2-1 *(continued)*

```
  CString strInfo;

  // Format a CString object with
  // information about the DC's
  // color depth.
  strInfo.Format(
    "Screen Bits:%d, Planes:%d",
    ClientDC.GetDeviceCaps( BITSPIXEL ),
    ClientDC.GetDeviceCaps( PLANES ) );

  AfxMessageBox( strInfo );

}

void CMenuDemo1View::OnColorsBlack()
{

  // Set the redraw color
  // to black.
  m_nColor = COLOR_BLACK;

  // Cause a screen redraw.
  InvalidateRect( NULL, TRUE );
  UpdateWindow();

}

void CMenuDemo1View::OnColorsBlue()
{

  // Set the redraw color
  // to blue.
  m_nColor = COLOR_BLUE;

  // Cause a screen redraw.
  InvalidateRect( NULL, TRUE );
  UpdateWindow();

}

void CMenuDemo1View::OnColorsGreen()
{

  // Set the redraw color
  // to green.
  m_nColor = COLOR_GREEN;

  // Cause a screen redraw.
  InvalidateRect( NULL, TRUE );
  UpdateWindow();
```

```
}

void CMenuDemo1View::OnColorsRed()
{

  // Set the redraw color
  // to red.
  m_nColor = COLOR_RED;

  // Cause a screen redraw.
  InvalidateRect( NULL, TRUE );
  UpdateWindow();

}

void CMenuDemo1View::OnColorsWhite()
{

  // Set the redraw color
  // to white.
  m_nColor = COLOR_WHITE;

  // Cause a screen redraw.
  InvalidateRect( NULL, TRUE );
  UpdateWindow();

}

void CMenuDemo1View::OnOptionsMaximizewindow()
{

  // Get a pointer to the frame window
  // and maximize it.
  CMainFrame *pFrame = (CMainFrame *) AfxGetMainWnd();
  pFrame->ShowWindow( SW_SHOWMAXIMIZED );

}

void CMenuDemo1View::OnOptionsMinimizewindow()
{

  // Get a pointer to the frame window
  // and minimize it.
  CMainFrame *pFrame = (CMainFrame *) AfxGetMainWnd();
  pFrame->ShowWindow( SW_SHOWMINIMIZED );

}

void CMenuDemo1View::OnOptionsShownormalwindow()
{

  // Get a pointer to the frame window
  // and have it show normal.
```

(continued)

Listing 2-1 *(continued)*

```
  CMainFrame *pFrame = (CMainFrame *) AfxGetMainWnd();
  pFrame->ShowWindow( SW_SHOWNORMAL );

}

void CMenuDemo1View::OnUpdateColorsBlack(CCmdUI* pCmdUI)
{

  // Set the menu check if the color
  // is set to black.
  pCmdUI->SetCheck( m_nColor == COLOR_BLACK );

}

void CMenuDemo1View::OnUpdateColorsBlue(CCmdUI* pCmdUI)
{

  // Set the menu check if the color
  // is set to blue.
  pCmdUI->SetCheck( m_nColor == COLOR_BLUE );

}

void CMenuDemo1View::OnUpdateColorsGreen(CCmdUI* pCmdUI)
{

  // Set the menu check if the color
  // is set to green.
  pCmdUI->SetCheck( m_nColor == COLOR_GREEN );

}

void CMenuDemo1View::OnUpdateColorsRed(CCmdUI* pCmdUI)
{

  // Set the menu check if the color
  // is set to red.
  pCmdUI->SetCheck( m_nColor == COLOR_RED );

}

void CMenuDemo1View::OnUpdateColorsWhite(CCmdUI* pCmdUI)
{

  // Set the menu check if the color
  // is set to white.
  pCmdUI->SetCheck( m_nColor == COLOR_WHITE );

}
```

```
void
CMenuDemo1View::OnUpdateOptionsMaximizewindow(
  CCmdUI* pCmdUI)
{

  // Get a pointer to the frame window and
  // pull out WINDOWPLACEMENT information.
  WINDOWPLACEMENT WindowPlacement;
  CMainFrame *pFrame = (CMainFrame *) AfxGetMainWnd();
  pFrame->GetWindowPlacement( &WindowPlacement );

  // Enable if we're not maximized.
  pCmdUI->Enable( WindowPlacement.showCmd !=
    SW_SHOWMAXIMIZED );

}

void
CMenuDemo1View::OnUpdateOptionsMinimizewindow(
  CCmdUI* pCmdUI)
{

  // Get a pointer to the frame window and
  // pull out WINDOWPLACEMENT information.
  WINDOWPLACEMENT WindowPlacement;
  CMainFrame *pFrame = (CMainFrame *) AfxGetMainWnd();
  pFrame->GetWindowPlacement( &WindowPlacement );

  // Enable if we're not minimized.
  pCmdUI->Enable( WindowPlacement.showCmd
    != SW_SHOWMINIMIZED );

}

void
CMenuDemo1View::OnUpdateOptionsShownormalwindow(
  CCmdUI* pCmdUI)
{

  // Get a pointer to the frame window and
  // pull out WINDOWPLACEMENT information.
  WINDOWPLACEMENT WindowPlacement;
  CMainFrame *pFrame = (CMainFrame *) AfxGetMainWnd();
  pFrame->GetWindowPlacement( &WindowPlacement );

  // Enable if we're not already shown normally.
  pCmdUI->Enable( WindowPlacement.showCmd
    != SW_SHOWNORMAL );

}
```

Keyboard Accelerators

An accelerator, sometimes known as a keyboard shortcut, lets a user issue a command using keyboard input. The Windows 98 API provides the accelerator table resource for holding sets of accelerator key definitions. AppWizard provides an accelerator table when it generates a single- or multiple-document application. If a frame (`CFrameWnd`) window is initialized by calling `CFrameWnd::LoadFrame()`, the accelerator table is automatically connected to the frame window.

Microsoft recommends against creating keyboard commands "as the only way to access a particular operation." In fact, they refer to accelerators as "shortcuts," a reminder that they provide an alternative — not a substitute — for other command input mechanisms such as menus and toolbars.

History underscores the supporting role that accelerators are supposed to play. When Microsoft started to build Windows back in 1983, accelerator keys were not part of the system's original design. Reflecting the influence of other GUI systems such as the Xerox Star and the Apple Macintosh, early Windows had a mouse- and menu-centered design. Microsoft added support for accelerators only after getting feedback from software companies that keyboard commands were important to users. Microsoft complied because they realized its success was dependent on Windows software developed by third parties.

Our exploration of keyboard accelerators starts with a general discussion of keyboard input. Next, we'll cover the creation of keyboard accelerators using the accelerator table editor. To help you figure out which keys to use and which ones to avoid, we'll provide some guidelines for appropriate accelerator key assignment. Then, we'll examine the Windows 98 API mechanisms behind accelerators, and show you how to dynamically install an accelerator table.

About keyboard input

There are clear categories of keyboard input: text keys, access keys, mode keys, and shortcut keys. The term *shortcut keys* refers to accelerator keys. Let's examine each of these four types of keyboard input, paying special attention to the relationship between accelerator keys and one other category of keys.

The term *text keys* refers to printable characters — that is, upper- and lowercase letters, numbers, punctuation marks, and other symbols. Nothing in MFC or the Windows 98 API prevents you from using text keys for command keys. If you've spent much time in a character-based, mainframe world, you have probably encountered this type of command key. Coming from that background, simple text commands seem natural. But this practice is inconsistent with the user-interface style that has evolved for Windows 98. Put simply, users expect letter and number keys to generate printable letters and numbers.

The design guide's second category of keyboard input is access keys. An access key (sometimes called a *mnemonic*) is an alphanumeric key which, when pressed in combination with the Alt key, accesses a pop-up menu, a menu item, or a dialog-box control. Adding an access key to a menu or a dialog box control isn't difficult; a simple ampersand (&) identifies the access key to the system, and Windows just makes them work. You need to make sure your accelerator keys don't conflict with access keys. The simplest solution is to avoid defining accelerator keys that take the form of the Alt key plus a letter or number key.

Mode keys, the third type of keyboard input, have a significant effect on possible accelerator key combinations. Mode keys "change the actions of other keys (or other input devices)." There are two subcategories of mode keys: toggle keys and modifier keys. Toggle keys are somewhat of an artifact from the IBM PC family of computers. A standard Windows-compatible keyboard has three toggle keys: Caps Lock, Num Lock, and Scroll Lock.

The second type of mode keys — modifier keys — is even more important. Although there are a few single-key accelerators (function keys, for example), the presence of modifier keys multiplies the number of key combinations available for defining accelerator keys. The standard 101-key keyboard defines three modifier keys: Shift, Ctrl, and Alt. Microsoft has defined a specification for a new, 104-key keyboard in which the basic 101-key layout is enhanced with three new keys: two Windows keys (sporting the Windows logo) and an Applications key. The Windows key is an additional modifier key. Its use is reserved for the operating system.

The final category is the shortcut keys, or accelerators. Any keys that are not included in the other categories are available for use as single-key accelerators. This group includes the function keys (F1, F2, and so on) and the cursor (insertion point) movement keys (Home, the up-arrow key, and so on). With these keys and the modifier-plus key combinations, you have a wide range of choices for creating accelerator keys. Let's look at the mechanics of defining an accelerator key assignment.

Defining accelerator keys

Defining an accelerator key involves two basic steps. First, you need to create an accelerator table resource. The accelerator table resource defines the key codes and the command ID that will result when a user presses the accelerator key. Then, you need to advertise the availability of the key combination to the user. For key combinations that match menu item selections, you do this by modifying the menu item text. Let's look at what's involved in each of these steps.

Creating an accelerator-table resource

Visual Studio has a built-in accelerator-table editor. Just like the menu editor, the accelerator-table editor provides access to a properties dialog box which lets you edit individual items. To open the Accel Properties dialog box, which is shown in Figure 2-2, double-click any accelerator. To make this dialog box stick around, click the Thumbtack icon.

By clicking the Help button in the Accel Properties dialog box, you can obtain details about each control. The accelerator table itself has three columns: ID, key, and type. These correspond roughly to the four sets of fields in the Accel Properties dialog box. You'll probably need only a little experimentation to feel comfortable with creating and editing accelerator entries. To fill in some of the gaps, let's look at each set of accelerator properties, starting with the command ID.

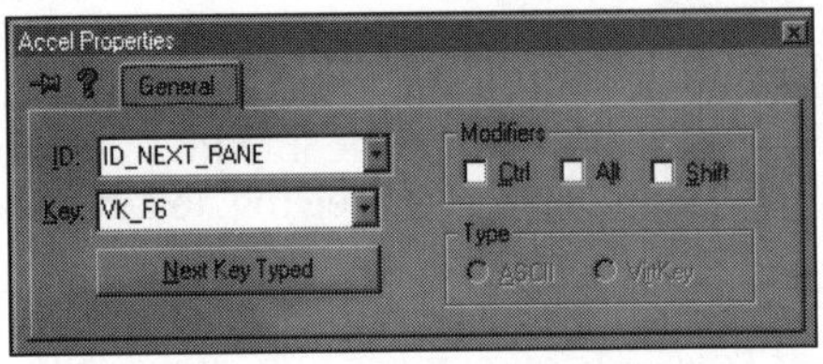

Figure 2-2: Use the Accel Properties dialog box to modify accelerator properties.

The command ID identifies the command code passed—via a `WM_COMMAND` message—when a user presses an accelerator key. The command list is filled with values from your program's RESOURCE.H file, along with a set of MFC's predefined values from AFXRES.H. When you define an accelerator, be sure that its command ID matches the command ID for the corresponding menu item. By doing so, you only have to provide a single command handler function that works for both menu input and accelerator input.

The Key field identifies the keyboard key for the accelerator. For alphanumeric characters, you simply type the number or letter. For nonprintable characters, you use virtual key codes. As you scroll through the combo box that's connected to this field, you'll see that it contains 72 virtual key codes, each with a `VK_` prefix. For example, `VK_F1` is the virtual key code for the F1 function key, and `VK_DOWN` is the virtual key code for the down-arrow key.

If you're not sure which virtual key code to use, the simplest solution is to click the Next Key Typed button. You can then press a modifier-key combination that you want to use for your accelerator, and the accelerator editor will automatically fill in the correct entries for the Key, Modifiers, and Type fields in the Accel Properties dialog box.

You choose the modifier key for your accelerator by clicking one of the check boxes in the Modifiers field. The design guide recommends that you use the Ctrl key as a modifier before the others. In addition, you should avoid using the Alt key with an alphanumeric accelerator because it might conflict with a menu access key. Even if you find Alt+alphanumeric-key combinations that don't conflict with your menu access keys, the access keys in internationalized versions often differ.

The Type field gives you a choice between ASCII and VirtKey. Almost every accelerator key should be a virtual key, because these transcend the different types of keyboards used around the world. However, you'll occasionally have to define an

ASCII accelerator, most notably for using punctuation marks (for example, <, >, or /) as commands. Selecting the ASCII option in the Type field lets you define character commands instead of keyboard key commands. The ASCII Type lets you differentiate between upper- and lowercase letters. However, even though it's possible, for example, to have an "A" command that differs from an "a" command, you should avoid this practice. After all, users expect case-insensitive commands.

Creating accelerator menu hints

To let users know about your accelerator keys, you'll want to advertise them. The best place for doing this is next to the corresponding menu item. Following the menu item name within a menu resource, you simply insert a tab character (`\t`) and the accelerator key name. For example, the standard accelerator for the Paste menu item is Ctrl+V. The following menu resource entry shows how the hint for this accelerator is included in the Paste menu item:

```
&Paste\tCtrl+V
```

In some cases, your accelerator keys don't correspond to menu item selections. To make sure that your users can take advantage of these accelerator keys, you should add a help database entry.

You know how to create accelerator keys and how to add hints within menus, but you still need to figure out which keys to use for keyboard commands. We cover this subject in the following section.

Selecting appropriate keyboard accelerators

When you define keyboard accelerators, be sure to use standard accelerator key combinations that are consistent with other Windows applications. Table 2-3 summarizes the standard Windows keyboard commands. Two of the five categories in this table are implemented for you by the operating system (system commands) or by an MFC class (`CMDIFrameWnd` implements the MDI accelerator keys). The rest are up to you to implement in your own accelerator table. You'll want to be aware of all of them, however, to avoid defining an accelerator that conflicts with standard Windows keyboard commands. You can check Table 2-1 for standard Windows keyboard commands.

The following suggestions should help you pick a reasonable set of accelerator keys:

- Assign single keys where possible because these keystrokes are the easiest for the user to perform.
- Make modifier-letter-key combinations case-insensitive.
- Use Shift+key combinations for actions that extend or complement the actions of the key or key combination used without the Shift key. For example, Alt+Tab switches windows in a top-to-bottom order. Shift+Alt+Tab switches windows in reverse order. However, avoid Shift+text keys, because the effect of the Shift key may differ for some international keyboards.

✦ Use Ctrl+key combinations for actions that represent a larger-scale effect. For example, in text editing contexts, Home moves to the beginning of a line, Ctrl+Home moves to the beginning of the text. Use Ctrl+key combinations for access to commands where a letter key is used — for example, Ctrl+B for bold. Remember that such assignments might only be meaningful for English-speaking users.

✦ Avoid Alt+key combinations, because they may conflict with the standard keyboard access for menus and controls. The Alt+key combinations — Alt+Tab, Alt+Esc, and Alt+spacebar — are reserved for system use. Alt+numeric-key combinations enter special characters.

✦ Avoid assigning shortcut keys defined in the design guide to other operations in your software. For example, if Ctrl+C is the shortcut for the Copy command and your application supports the standard copy operation, don't assign Ctrl+C to another operation.

✦ Provide support for allowing the user to change the shortcut key assignments in your software, when possible.

✦ Use the Esc key to terminate a function in process or to cancel a direct manipulation operation. It is also usually interpreted as the shortcut key for a Cancel button.

Table 2-3
Standard Keyboard Commands in Microsoft Windows

Category	*Keystroke(s)*	*Description*
System Commands	Ctrl+Alt+Del	Local reboot in Windows 3.1. Logon/logoff in Windows 95, 98, and Windows NT.
	Alt+Tab	Select the next active application.
	Alt+Esc	Select the next active application.
	Ctrl+Esc	Display the Start menu on Windows 95 and 98.
		(Display the Task List on Windows 3.1).
	Alt+Spacebar	Open the windows' system menu.
	PrtScr	Make a snapshot of the display screen and place it on the clipboard.
	Alt+PrtScr	Make a snapshot of the currently active window and place it on the clipboard.
	Alt	Activate or deactivate the application menu bar.
	Alt+Enter	Toggle DOS windows into and out of full screen text mode.

Category	*Keystroke(s)*	*Description*
Application Modes	Esc	Cancel the current mode or operation.
	Enter	In dialog boxes, the same action as a mouse click on the default pushbutton.
	Tab	In a dialog box, select the next control.
	Alt+F4	Close the currently active top-level window.
	Applications key	Display a context menu (on Windows 98-compatible, 104-key keyboards).
	Shift+F10	Display a context menu.
	F1	Summon application help.
	Shift+F1	Summon context help.
File Commands	Ctrl+N	New.
	Ctrl+O	Open. . .
	Ctrl+P	Print. . .
	Ctrl+S	Save.
Clipboard Commands	Ctrl+Z	Undo.
	Alt+ Backspace	Undo (for backward compatibility with Windows 3.*x*).
	Ctrl+X	Cut.
	Shift+Del	Cut (for backward compatibility with Windows 3.*x*).
	Ctrl+C	Copy.
	Ctrl+Ins	Copy (for backward compatibility with Windows 3.*x*).
	Ctrl+V	Paste.
	Shift+Ins	Paste (for backward compatibility with Windows 3.*x*).
Multiple-Document Interface (MDI) Commands	Ctrl+F4	Close the document window that is currently active (CMDIFrameWnd handles this).
	Ctrl+F6	Activate the next document window (CMDIFrameWnd handles this).
	Shift+Ctrl+F6	Activate the previous document window (CMDIFrameWnd handles this).

When you've selected the accelerator keys for your application, you have to decide whether to put them all in a single accelerator table or spread them out between multiple accelerator tables. For small- to medium-sized applications, a single accelerator table is sufficient. For larger, more complex applications working with several different types of data, you might find that you need several accelerator tables. The following section explores the issues involved in using multiple accelerator tables in an MFC application.

Multiple accelerator tables

The use of multiple accelerator tables allows you to divide the work that's to be done, and gives you greater flexibility in enabling different keyboard-command sets. MFC's Doc/View classes take advantage of this capability to support multiple accelerator tables. But we're avoiding Doc/View for now, so we'll show you how to use multiple accelerator tables in a non-Doc/View application. (Incidentally, we are avoiding Doc/View so that we can focus on MFC fundamentals, not because there's anything wrong with it. When you grasp MFC fundamentals, Doc/View is simpler to understand and use.) To help you understand what's required, we'll start with a review of how the native Windows 98 API provides accelerator support.

Native Windows 98 API accelerator support

For all that accelerators do for you, the Win32 API has only six accelerator functions. (The scarcity of native API functions is one reason why you *don't* find a `CAccelerators` class in MFC.) The most important features are provided by two of these accelerator functions: `LoadAccelerators()` and `TranslateAccelerator()`. `LoadAccelerators()` creates a RAM-resident accelerator table from an accelerator resource. The second function, `TranslateAccelerator()`, tests whether a particular keyboard message corresponds to an accelerator table command entry.

In a Windows program written in C, you would call the load function to create the accelerator table and then call the translate function from your program's message loop. MFC provides the message loop that every MFC-based program uses. The message loop in the thread class's `CWinThread::Run()` function calls `CWinThread::PumpMessage()`, which does the following:

```
 if (!PreTranslateMessage(&m_msgCur))
{
    ::TranslateMessage(&m_msgCur);
    ::DispatchMessage(&m_msgCur);
}
```

In this code fragment, the three functions with the global scope operators (: :) are native Windows 98 API functions. The fourth function, `PreTranslateMessage()`, is the name of an overloaded function that appears in several MFC classes. These functions exist for one primary reason: to check for accelerator keys. To experienced Windows 98 API programmers, this is a familiar message loop, with the exception that `Translate-Accelerator()` is usually called instead of `PreTranslateMessage()`.

By the way, the function's name comes from the fact that it is called before `::TranslateMessage()`. This latter function takes raw keyboard (virtual key) messages and turns them into cooked ASCII character input. For accelerator keys to be handled properly, they must be raw. Also, if a particular message is associated with an accelerator, the caller returns TRUE, and no further processing is required. Otherwise, the normal message loop functions are called.

Although many MFC classes have `PreTranslateMessage()` functions, not all can support an accelerator table. In some cases—such as with `CWinApp` and `CWinThread`—the base member function simply calls the corresponding member in the windowing classes. This implies that accelerator tables can be used only by window classes. However, this limitation is not a design feature of MFC; it is a trait that MFC inherits from the native Windows 98 API.

The basic flow of messages is from the innermost data window to the outermost container window. The command is handled by whichever window first claims it. In a single-document Doc/View application, the view window gets the first chance to handle an accelerator, followed by the frame window. In a multiple-document Doc/View application, the sequence progresses from the view window to the child frame, and then to the parent frame. In our Doc/View-free world, a program has only one window—a frame window—which alone among the MFC objects can receive accelerator-key commands.

Let's take a closer look at the mechanics of providing accelerator tables to MFC's windowing classes.

Connecting a new accelerator table to a windowing class

To connect an accelerator table to a window class, you start by loading the accelerator table into memory. You'll do this sometime during the initialization of your window—`PreCreateWindow()` is a good choice. Incidentally, this function gets its name from the fact that it is called before `::CreateWindow()`, the native Win32 function that creates a Windows system window.

You load an accelerator table into memory by calling `::LoadAccelerators()`, which is defined as follows:

```
    HINSTANCE  hinst,       // EXE file instance handle
   LPCTSTR  lpTableName);  // Accelerator table name
```

The first parameter, the instance handle, identifies who you are in this system. This is passed to your program's `WinMain()` entry point. The second parameter is the accelerator table name, which you specified in the resource file.

The following code fragment loads an accelerator table named `IDR_VIEW_COMMMANDS`:

```
  LPCTSTR lpID = MAKEINTRESOURCE(IDR_VIEW_COMMMANDS);
 HACCEL d_hAccel = LoadAccelerators (hInst, lpID);
```

The AfxGetResourceHandle() function helps make sure that we get the correct instance handle — for code in an application as well as in a dynamic link library. The MAKEINTRESOURCE() macro converts the accelerator table's integer ID into a character string, which is the type required by the function. The return value, d_hAccel, is a Windows system handle that gives our program access to the accelerator table in memory.

When an accelerator table is loaded into memory, the next step is to make sure it is called at the right time. This is a simple matter of overloading the PreTranslateMessage() function in a CWnd-derived class. Here's a sample implementation that does just that:

```
{
   if (d_hAccel == NULL)
      return FALSE;  // we didn't process

   return ::TranslateAccelerator(m_hWnd, d_hAccel, pMsg);
}
```

Changing Menus Dynamically During Program Execution

In general, any change you can make to a menu in the menu editor can also be made dynamically at runtime. For example, you can create menus from scratch, add menu items, or remove menu items. Certain menu features — for example, owner-draw menu items and custom bitmap check marks — are accessible *only* at run-time. (An owner-draw menu item contains a graphic image — such as a bitmap, or geometric figure drawn using calls to GDI — instead of a text string.)

Although MFC provides a menu class (CMenu), AppWizard's code doesn't use this class to create a menu. Instead, the Windows 98 API supports the simultaneous creation of a window with a menu. When creating a Windows window, MFC's CFrameWnd class requests the creation of a menu. In the process, it also creates a bit of an object-oriented design paradox. Although a CFrameWnd *logically* contains a CMenu, it *physically* contains no CMenu data type.

Getting the current CMenu object

Although you won't use CMenu to create the menu attached to your program's frame window, you'll use it extensively for dynamic menu operations. To get a CMenu pointer to the menu that is connected to a window, you call CWnd::GetMenu():

```
CMenu * pmenu = GetMenu();
```

You might notice another twist to the paradox we mentioned. This line of code fetches a pointer to an object that we never created. What's happening? The short answer, on which we'll soon elaborate, is that MFC creates a CMenu for us while adding it to a temporary object storage list.

For now, we're going to examine some of the issues involved in making dynamic modifications to menus. We'll start with the most common task you'll probably need: modifying the contents of an existing pop-up menu.

Changing an existing pop-up menu

Using a CMenu pointer from CWnd::GetMenu(), you can do such things as inserting a new pop-up menu between the File menu and the Help menu. That's a subject we'll explore a bit later in this chapter.

For now, we're interested in a more common operation: adding menu items to and removing menu items from an existing pop-up menu. For this, you need another CMenu * pointer—in this case, to one of our submenus. As shown in the following lines of code, you use CMenu::GetSubMenu() to get a submenu pointer:

```
CMenu * pmSub = pmenu->GetSubMenu(1);
```

CMenu::GetSubMenu() is defined as follows:

```
CMenu* GetSubMenu( int nPos)
```

The sole parameter, nPos, is a zero-based index to the submenu that you want to access.

Table 2-4 summarizes some common CMenu functions for modifying (or simply querying) the contents of a menu.

Table 2-4
A Basic Set of CMenu Class Functions for Modifying and Querying a Menu

Function	*Description*
AppendMenu()	Adds a new menu item to the end of an existing menu or to a new pop-up menu.
CheckMenuItem()	(Rarely called.) Sets or clears the menu check mark. In place of this function, you should provide an UPDATE_COMMAND_UI handler.
GetMenuItemID()	Queries a menu item's command ID.
GetMenuString()	Queries a menu item's text label.

(continued)

Table 2-4 (continued)	
Function	***Description***
`EnableMenuItem()`	Enables and disables menu items (only works if `CFrameWnd::m_b-AutoMenuEnable` is set to `FALSE`). In place of this function, you should provide an `UPDATE_COMMAND_UI` handler.
`InsertMenu()`	Inserts a new menu item at a specified offset within an existing menu.
`RemoveMenu()`	Deletes a specific menu item.

For example, using the `pmSub` submenu pointer from the previous example, you can append a new menu item to an existing submenu like this:

```
ID_MENU_ADDMENUITEM, // Command id.
"Add Menu &Item");   // Menu string.
```

Although the MFC help database describes the parameters for you, let's take a closer look at the declaration for `CMenu::AppendMenu()`:

```
UINT nIDNewItem = 0,
LPCTSTR lpszNewItem = NULL);
```

The first parameter, nFlags, is a flag field for specifying the state of the menu item you create. Many menu modification functions use these flags, so we've summarized them for you in Table 2-5. When appending a menu item, you'll always choose one of the five flags from the group labeled "Type of Menu Item" at the beginning of the table. Common settings include `MF_STRING`, which creates a menu item identified by a string; `MF_SEPARATOR`, which adds a menu item separator bar; and `MF_POPUP`, which creates a new pop-up menu.

The meaning of the second parameter, `nIDNewItem`, depends on whether you're inserting a new menu item or a new pop-up menu (indicated by `MF_POPUP` in nFlags). If you're inserting a menu item, this parameter holds an integer command ID for the menu item. If you're inserting a new pop-up menu, this field is the menu handle of the menu to be inserted. (As you'll see, you use the value of `CMenu::m_hMenu` for this field.)

The meaning of the last parameter, `lpszNewItem`, depends on what type of item you're inserting. It's either a pointer to a character string for an `MF_STRING` item, or a unique item identifier for an `MF_OWNERDRAW` item.

You should note that when you dynamically create menu items, MFC doesn't know how to display help strings in the status window. (Recall that MFC does this automatically for static menu resources, using strings that you enter in the menu editor's Prompt field.) To enable this feature for dynamically created menu items, override `CFrameWnd::GetMessageString()` with your own version of `GetMessageString()`. For dynamically created menu items, you supply the required strings. For statically created menu items, call the default handler which reads in the correct string from the string table.

Although the menu modification techniques that we've been describing certainly work as advertised, we've glossed over an important issue. We started out by saying that an MFC program doesn't create a `CMenu` object for its menu, but we clearly are using a `CMenu` object to change the menu. Where did this object come from? And who will delete the object when we're done with it? The answer to these questions is addressed in a later section, "MFC's Permanent and Temporary Handle Maps."

By adding menu items on the fly, your programs can be responsive to changes in the user's environment. Dynamic menu items are commonly used to update the lists of most recently used files, which often appear in File menus. Sometimes, you only know at runtime how many dynamic menu items you're going to create. To simplify the receipt of command notifications for such items, MFC lets you create command handlers for a range of command IDs. Unfortunately, ClassWizard doesn't (yet) support this feature. The following section shows you how it's done manually.

Table 2-5
Menu Flags Used as Parameters to Many CMenu Class Functions

Category	*Menu Flag*	*Description*
Menu Item	`MF_BITMAP`	Contains a bitmap image instead of a string.
	`MF_OWNERDRAW`	Relies on the application to draw its contents. This is more flexible than `MF_BITMAP` for embedding graphic images in a menu.
	`MF_POPUP`	A pop-up menu.
	`MF_SEPARATOR`	A half-height space with a line for visually dividing groups of menu items.
	`MF_STRING`	A menu item or a pop-up menu (`MF_POPUP`) with a string.
Check State	`MF_CHECKED`	A check mark is displayed.
	`MF_UNCHECKED`	No check mark is displayed.
Enabled State	`MF_DISABLED`	The menu is not available to the user.
	`MF_ENABLED`	The menu is available to the user.
	`MF_GRAYED`	The menu is not available to the user *and* it appears grayed out. This makes more sense than `MF_DISABLED`, which doesn't give the user a visual cue about its state.

(continued)

Table 2-5 *(continued)*

Category	***Menu Flag***	***Description***
Menu Break	MF_MENUBREAK	At a menu item with this flag, the menu changes direction. For example, a menu bar menu—which normally travels in a horizontal direction— wraps to a new line; a pop-up menu—which normally travels in a vertical direction—wraps to start a new column.
	MF_MENUBARBREAK	The same as MF_MENUBREAK, except that in pop-up menus a line is drawn to separate columns.
Identifying	MF_BYCOMMAND	Pick menu items with the command ID. Menu Items
	MF_BYPOSITION	Pick items with a zero-based offset in the current menu.

MFC's permanent and temporary handle maps

To bridge the gap between MFC objects and Windows 98 API objects, MFC maintains a set of look-up tables, called *handle maps.* CObject-derived classes use *pointer semantics* instead of *value semantics*. So, to access an object created from a CObject-derived class, you need a pointer to the object.

In simplest terms, Windows uses handles to identify objects, and MFC uses pointers. The origin of pointer semantics was primarily for maintaining a one-to-one ratio between Windows system objects (windows and menus, for example) and C++/MFC objects (such as CWnd and CMenu objects). And while we identify a C++ object with a pointer, a Windows system object is always identified by a *handle*. Remember, a handle is a number that uniquely identifies a particular object. The meaning of the number is known only to the part of the system that issued the handle. Internal to the operating system, a handle might be a pointer or an index, but to the outside world it's just a number.

MFC uses handle maps to identify the C++ object that corresponds to a given Windows object handle. After all, when MFC calls Windows 98 API functions, it cannot use the C++ object; MFC must use a handle. And when the Windows system libraries communicate back to MFC, they also use handles. Although MFC can easily figure out the handle from a C++ object (after all, it's usually one of the first data members), a little extra work is required for MFC to convert a system handle to a C++ pointer. To assist in this task, MFC creates handle maps.

MFC creates handle maps for two user-interface objects (windows and menus) and for seven graphic output objects (bitmaps, brushes, device contexts, fonts, palettes, pens, and regions). The creation of handle maps and handle map entries is handled transparently most of the time by individual MFC objects as needed.

In a few cases, such as when merging existing Windows 98 API code into an MFC application, you'll find that you have to convert system handles to MFC object pointers. Each of the MFC classes that wrap Windows 98 API objects has member functions that can help with this task. For example, `CWnd::Attach()` connects a `CWnd` object to an existing system window and creates the proper handle map entry. `CWnd::Detach()` deletes a window handle entry from the MFC handle maps.

MFC creates two types of handle maps: permanent and temporary. A *permanent handle map* exists for Windows 98 API objects that are created via an MFC class. For example, when you initialize a `CFrameWnd` object by calling `CFrameWnd::Create()` or `CFrameWnd::LoadFrame()`, an entry is made in the permanent handle table. When you delete an MFC object that has a permanent handle table entry, the object knows that it can also destroy the corresponding Windows 98 API object.

Programmers who are experienced with SDK-style programming might wonder why an alternative mechanism wasn't chosen. In particular, why does MFC use handle tables for windows instead of window extra bytes? (Window extra bytes are a fixed number of extra bytes allocated by Windows on a per-window basis.) The reason is that predefined window types—such as dialog box controls—already use window extra bytes. Microsoft designed MFC to be able to wrap around pre-existing classes. If MFC tried using window extra bytes with a window that already used window extra bytes, there would be a conflict.

MFC's automatic destruction of Windows system objects can cause you untold grief if you don't understand some of the subtler implications. In particular, you should avoid creating `CObject`-derived objects as local variables. At the end of the function—when the local objects go out of scope—the destructor will be called, which will destroy the Windows 98 API object. The following code fragment taught this lesson to one of the authors:

```
// DON'T DO THIS!!! - When local variable goes out
// of scope, Windows 98 API object is destroyed.
CMenu cm;
cm.LoadMenu(IDR_POPUP_MENU);

// The append operation will be short-lived...
CMenu * pmenu = GetMenu();
pmenu->AppendMenu(MF_POPUP, (UINT)cm.m_hMenu, "Popup");
```

With one important change, this code fragment could work properly. The only reason the object is destroyed is because `CMenu::~CMenu()` finds the object in the permanent handle map. By calling `CMenu::Detach()`, you disconnect the handle map entry and avoid this particular headache.

On the other hand, for objects that are not created via an MFC class, MFC has a *temporary handle map*. MFC creates an entry in the temporary handle map for objects that it must create on the fly to wrap Windows system objects. Such objects are very short-lived, though, because all entries to the temporary handle map are deleted during idle time processing. For this reason, you'll always reference temporary objects using pointers that are created as local variables. This way, you avoid the problem of having a pointer to an object that has been automatically deleted.

Every MFC function that wraps Windows 98 API objects has the two functions we've described: `Attach()` and `Detach()`. There's also a third function, `FromHandle()`, which is a universal "get pointer from handle" function. This function first searches a permanent handle map, and then the temporary handle map. If no entry is found in either map, an object is created and an entry is made in the temporary handle map.

Here's an example that clarifies when an entry is made in the temporary handle map. The menu function we've been discussing, `CWnd::GetMenu()`, calls `CMenu::FromHandle()`. When you call this function in an AppWizard-generated program—which loads a menu from a resource—MFC automatically creates a `CMenu` for you. To ensure that you have complete access to this object, MFC adds an entry to the temporary handle map. Your access to the object will last at least until your program fetches its next message, because cleanup is handled at idle time.

So, how does MFC determine when things are idle? Idle time occurs only when you're not in the middle of handling a message. Idle time is a Windows 98 API artifact that was first created long ago to provide printer spooling support (for Windows 1.01, which perhaps should now be renamed Windows 85). Idle time occurs whenever the user pauses a moment and allows all message queues to empty. Even the busiest worker on the slowest machine must pause sometime, whether it's to answer a phone, talk to a friend, or just think. A blink is all it takes for an idle moment to occur, at which time MFC frees the C++ objects (but *not* the Windows 98 API objects) that are referenced in temporary handle maps.

To summarize: When you allocate and initialize an object yourself, MFC creates a permanent handle map entry. When you fetch a pointer to an object that you have never allocated, MFC creates an object and a temporary handle map entry.

Context Menus

Since the introduction of Windows 95, Microsoft has promoted the creation of *context menus*. A context menu—sometimes called a *pop-up menu*—is not connected to the menu bar. Instead, it is displayed when the user selects an object and then clicks with the secondary (usually the right) mouse button. (It's also possible to simultaneously select an object and summon a context menu with just a single click of the secondary mouse button.) Visual Studio already makes extensive use of this type of menu, as do many other commercially available applications. Starting with Windows 95, the operating system itself uses context menus for handling numerous routine operations. To fit into this environment, you should consider adding them to your applications as well.

Besides clicking the right mouse button, a user can summon a context menu using a keystroke. The Applications key appears on newer 104-key keyboards, such as the Microsoft Natural keyboard. On keyboards that are so equipped, users can open a context menu by pressing the Applications key. To accommodate users whose keyboards are not equipped with this key, applications should define the Shift+F10 accelerator for summoning context menus.

Like most other MFC objects that wrap Windows 98 API objects, two steps are required for creating a fully functioning object. First, you allocate a C++ object, and then you initialize the object. These lines of code show one way to create and initialize a `CMenu` object:

```
// Allocate CMenu for context menu.
d_pmenuContext = new CMenu();
if (!d_pmenuContext) return -1;

// Initialize CMenu (connect menu to MFC menu object).
BOOL bSuccess = d_pmenuContext->LoadMenu(IDR_CONTEXT);
if (!bSuccess) return -1;
```

This code fragment is from a function that expects a return value of –1 on failure (the handler function for the `WM_CREATE` message). Allocation involves the new operator. Initialization involves a call to `CMenu::LoadMenu()`, which takes as its only parameter a menu resource identifier.

After it's created and initialized, the context menu is ready to appear whenever you want to see it. From the user's perspective, you want to see this menu when the user clicks the right mouse button. The following `WM_RBUTTONDOWN` message handler displays the context menu:

```
void CMainFrame::OnRButtonDown(UINT nFlags, CPoint point)
{
  // Convert client coordinate to screen coordinates.
  ClientToScreen(&point);

  // Display context menu at mouse location.
  CMenu * psubmenu = d_pmenuContext->GetSubMenu(0);
  psubmenu->TrackPopupMenu(
    TPM_LEFTALIGN | TPM_RIGHTBUTTON,
    point.x, point.y, this );

  CFrameWnd::OnRButtonDown(nFlags, point);
}
```

The second of the two parameters to OnRButtonDown(), point, gives the location of the mouse in client-area coordinates. But TrackPopupMenu() expects screen coordinates, so you call CWnd::ClientToScreen(). This function converts from client-area coordinates (the origin in the top-left corner of client area) to screen coordinates (the origin in the top-left corner of the screen).

Most of the parameters to CMenu::TrackPopupMenu() are reasonably straightforward. However, the last parameter is worth discussing. When the context menu appears, a stream of messages is generated that must be sent to some window or another. The pointer *this*, in the context of a CFrameWnd-derived class, identifies the window that should receive the menu messages.

The final step that you'll need to consider is how to clean up a context menu when you're done using it. Our example simply deletes the CMenu object when you're finished using it. Like all other entries in the permanent handle map table, when the object is destroyed, the system object is destroyed and the handle map entry is erased. Although you might delete the menu object in any of several different places, you could do it in the destructor for the window frame object:

```
  {
   if( m_pMenuContext != NULL )
     m_pMenuContext->DestroyMenu();
  }
```

As part of the Windows user-interface standard, Microsoft recommends using the right mouse button for context menus. Users will expect this feature, and you put yourself at a disadvantage if you don't make use of it.

Menus are the most obvious command input device, but they aren't the only one. Keyboard accelerators provide another mechanism by which users can issue commands to your program. In particular, experienced users prefer working with keyboard accelerators for more commonly used commands, simply because they are quicker than choosing commands from menus.

Creating Context Menus to Change Windows

The following program, called MenuDemo2, shows you how to create context menus and use them to affect changes in a window. The program divides the view window into four quadrants. One is red, one green, one blue, and one white. If you click the right mouse button in the view window, the program calculates which quadrant you're in. It then displays a context menu and allows you to set the brightness of the quadrant's color as shown in Figure 2-3.

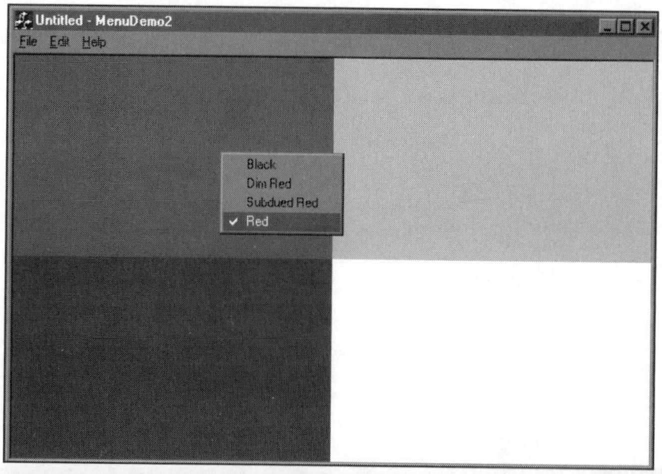

Figure 2-3: This demo program shows you how to use context menus.

Demo Program

MenuDemo2

CD-ROM Location: **Chap02\MenuDemo2**
Program Name: **MenuDemo2.EXE**
Source Code Modules in Text: **MenuDemo2View.cpp**

◆ ◆ ◆ ◆ ◆

Listing 2-2: **MenuDemo2**

```
// MenuDemo2View.cpp : implementation of
// the CMenuDemo2View class
//

/////////////////////////////////////////////////////////
// CMenuDemo2View construction/destruction

CMenuDemo2View::CMenuDemo2View()
{

  // Remember that the current menu

  m_nCurrentMenu = 0;

  // Keep a static list of the color
  // hues we'll be using.
  static CString strColors[] = { "Red",
    "Green", "Blue", "White" };

  CString strInfo;
```

(continued)

Listing 2-2 *(continued)*

```
  // Loop through and create four
  // popup menus.
  for( int i=0; i<4; i++ ){

    // Set the current level to 3.
    m_nColorLevel[i] = 3;

    // Allocate and create the
    // new menu.
    m_pPopup[i] = new CMenu;
    m_pPopup[i]->CreatePopupMenu();

    // At level 0, the color is always black.
    m_pPopup[i]->AppendMenu( MF_ENABLED | MF_STRING,
      IDC_COLORMENU0, "Black" );

    // Create and add the menu entry for the
    // dim version of the hue.
    strInfo = "Dim " + strColors[i];
    m_pPopup[i]->AppendMenu( MF_ENABLED | MF_STRING,
      IDC_COLORMENU1, strInfo );

    // Create and add the menu entry for the
    // subdued version of the hue.
    strInfo = "Subdued " + strColors[i];
    m_pPopup[i]->AppendMenu( MF_ENABLED | MF_STRING,
      IDC_COLORMENU2, strInfo );

    // Create and add the menu entry for the
    // full-color version of the hue.
    strInfo = strColors[i];
    m_pPopup[i]->AppendMenu( MF_ENABLED | MF_STRING,
      IDC_COLORMENU3, strInfo );
    }

}

CMenuDemo2View::~CMenuDemo2View()
{
}

/////////////////////////////////////////////////////////////////////////////
// CMenuDemo2View drawing

void CMenuDemo2View::OnDraw(CDC* pDC)
{
  CMenuDemo2Doc* pDoc = GetDocument();
  ASSERT_VALID(pDoc);

  // Keep a list of multipliers
  // for each of the three color channels.
```

```
   // These multiplers are multipied
   // by the current level for the color.
   static int nFactors[] = { 85, 0, 0,
     0, 85, 0, 0, 0, 85, 85, 85, 85 };

   // Loop through and draw the four
   // color rectangles.
   for( int i=0; i<4; i++ ){

     // Get the client rectangle so that
     // we can dynamically size the RECT
     // that we'll draw.
     RECT Rect;
     GetClientRect( &Rect );

     // Even numbers are on the left side
     // of the window.
     if( !( i & 1 ) ) Rect.right /= 2;
     else Rect.left = Rect.right / 2;

     // Numbers less than two are on
     // the top half of the window.
     if( i < 2 ) Rect.bottom /= 2;
     else Rect.top = Rect.bottom / 2;

     // Create the brush based on the color
     // for this rectangle and the current
     // color level.
     CBrush Brush( RGB( nFactors[i*3] * m_nColorLevel[i],
       nFactors[i*3+1] * m_nColorLevel[i],
       nFactors[i*3+2] * m_nColorLevel[i] ) );

     // Draw the filled rectangle.
     pDC->FillRect( &Rect, &Brush );
     }

}

/////////////////////////////////////////////////////////////////
// CMenuDemo2View message handlers

void CMenuDemo2View::OnRButtonDown(UINT nFlags,
CPoint point)
{

  // Get the client rectangle so that
  // we'll know how to divide the window
  // into quadrants. This is essential
  // in order to calculate the current
  // quadrant in which the mouse was
  // clicked.
  RECT Rect;
  GetClientRect( &Rect );
```

(continued)

Listing 2-2 *(continued)*

```
  // Divide x by two to get a
  // left/right value.
  if( point.x < Rect.right / 2 )
    m_nCurrentMenu = 0;
  else
    m_nCurrentMenu = 1;

  // Divide y by two to get the
  // vertical component of the
  // quadrant number.
  if( point.y > Rect.bottom / 2 )
    m_nCurrentMenu += 2;

  // Loop through and set the appropriate
  // check value for each menu item.
  for( int i=0; i<4; i++ )
    m_pPopup[m_nCurrentMenu]->CheckMenuItem(
      IDC_COLORMENU0 + i,
      MF_BYCOMMAND |
      ( ( i == m_nColorLevel[m_nCurrentMenu] ) ?
      MF_CHECKED : MF_UNCHECKED ) );

  // Cause the menu to appear by calling
  // TrackPopupMenu.
  m_pPopup[m_nCurrentMenu]->TrackPopupMenu(
    TPM_LEFTALIGN | TPM_LEFTBUTTON,
    point.x, point.y, this, &Rect );

  CView::OnRButtonDown(nFlags, point);
}

BOOL CMenuDemo2View::OnCommand(WPARAM wParam,
  LPARAM lParam)
{

  // Remember the old color level.
  int nOldLevel = m_nColorLevel[m_nCurrentMenu];

  // Set to the new color level.
  switch( wParam ){
    case IDC_COLORMENU0:
      m_nColorLevel[m_nCurrentMenu] = 0;
      break;
    case IDC_COLORMENU1:
      m_nColorLevel[m_nCurrentMenu] = 1;
      break;
    case IDC_COLORMENU2:
      m_nColorLevel[m_nCurrentMenu] = 2;
      break;
    case IDC_COLORMENU3:
```

```
      m_nColorLevel[m_nCurrentMenu] = 3;
      break;
    }

  // If this color level is different than the one
  // previously set, cause a window redraw.
  if( nOldLevel != m_nColorLevel[m_nCurrentMenu] ){
    InvalidateRect( NULL, FALSE );
    UpdateWindow();
    }

  return CView::OnCommand(wParam, lParam);
}
```

Summary

In this chapter, we've described two Windows 98 mechanisms for getting command input from the user: menus and accelerator tables. Both send the same message—WM_COMMAND—to notify your program of a command. Both also send a CN_UPDATE_COMMAND_UI message to ask whether a particular command is enabled or whether menu and toolbar items should be checked. As you've seen, most of the work in using these command input mechanisms is in setting them up.

In the next chapter, we're going to explore mouse and keyboard input. These are two important ways to interact with users. Without them, Windows would not be a friendly place.

✦ ✦ ✦

CHAPTER 3

Mouse and Keyboard

✦ ✦ ✦ ✦

In This Chapter

Learning about mouse input

Creating mouse message handlers

Examining keyboard input and mouse events by studying a demo program

Learning about nonclient mouse messages

Changing mouse cursors

Understanding keyboard input

✦ ✦ ✦ ✦

Microsoft's image slogan is "Where do you want to go today?" Although this might initially seem more appropriate for a bus company than a software company, it starts to make sense if you think about it a bit. After all, transportation isn't a bad metaphor for the way a personal computer takes you where you haven't been before. New information, like a new place, can have elements that are disorienting, useful, and exciting all at the same time.

If a PC is your mode of transportation, the mouse is the steering wheel, moving your program's operation in new directions. And the keyboard is the engine, driven by piston-like fingers that transport the data from your mind to its destination. Whether a user is entering numbers into a spreadsheet or cranking out a C++ program, everything screeches to a halt when the fingers stop.

In this chapter, we show you how to handle mouse and keyboard input. For background, we discuss the various pieces of state information the system stores. Windows 98 (and Windows 95 before it) uses the idea of local input state—a concept that Microsoft first introduced with Windows NT—to support both a multitasking scheduler and a view of input state that is compatible with previous versions of Windows.

Next, we look at mouse input. You can avoid dealing with low-level mouse input by using higher-level user-interface objects. At a minimum, though, you want to manage state information that's related to mouse input. Here, we consider such issues as the shape of the mouse pointer (cursor), the capture of mouse input, and the clipping of the mouse pointer to a specific clipping rectangle.

From there, we look at the various ways that a program can use keyboard input. If desired, you can avoid dealing with low-level keyboard input by using user-interface objects such as edit controls. With this in mind, we're going to pay particular attention to the less obvious but nevertheless important ways an application must manage its keyboard state. As part of this discussion, we consider the keyboard focus, the keyboard cursor (insertion point), the selection state, and other user-interface constructs related to keyboard input.

Input Basics and System State

The challenge to properly handling mouse and keyboard input in Windows 98 is understanding and managing the context in which input occurs. The input itself is rather simple; you get several types of messages for both mouse and keyboard events. When you write code for keyboard input, you decide between two keyboard messages. The most critical mouse input is communicated by two or three mouse messages.

Once you've written the basic message-handling code, an even more important step awaits you. You need to write supporting code to make your application behave in a predictable and consistent manner. To accomplish this, you must understand the context of input messages — the not-so-obvious yet critical ways that input interacts with application state, as viewed by both a user and Windows 98 itself. Let's start by looking at the input state of first the mouse and then the keyboard.

Mouse Input

Most C programmers are used to getting input — particularly keyboard input — by polling the system via function calls. For example, the C run-time library contains the `getc()` function, which reads the "next character" from standard input:

```
char ch = getc();
```

Windows 98 doesn't use the notion of standard input for mouse and keyboard input; instead, it sends input to a program's windows as messages, which get stored in a hardware input queue. Table 3-1 lists the main Windows 98 mouse messages to which you'll respond when handling user input.

Table 3-1
The Windows Mouse-Input Messages

Message	*Description*
WM_MOUSEMOVE	The pointer has moved over a window's client area.
WM_LBUTTONDOWN	The left (primary) button has been pushed while the pointer is over the client area.
WM_LBUTTONUP	The left (primary) button has been released.

Message	Description
WM_RBUTTONDOWN	The right (secondary) button has been pushed while the pointer is over the client area.
WM_RBUTTONUP	The right (secondary) button has been released.
WM_MBUTTONDOWN	The middle button has been pushed while the pointer is over the client area.
WM_MBUTTONUP	The middle button has been released.

Creating Mouse Message Handlers

It's easy to create handler functions for the mouse messages in Table 3-1. Start by bringing up the ClassWizard. In the Class Name combo box, select the class in which you want to add the event handlers—this is usually either the `MainFrame` or `View` class. In the Object IDs list box, make sure the top entry, the class name, is highlighted.

If you scroll down through the messages list box, you should see `WM_LBUTTONDOWN`, `WM_MOUSEMOVE`, and other mouse messages, as shown in Figure 3-1.

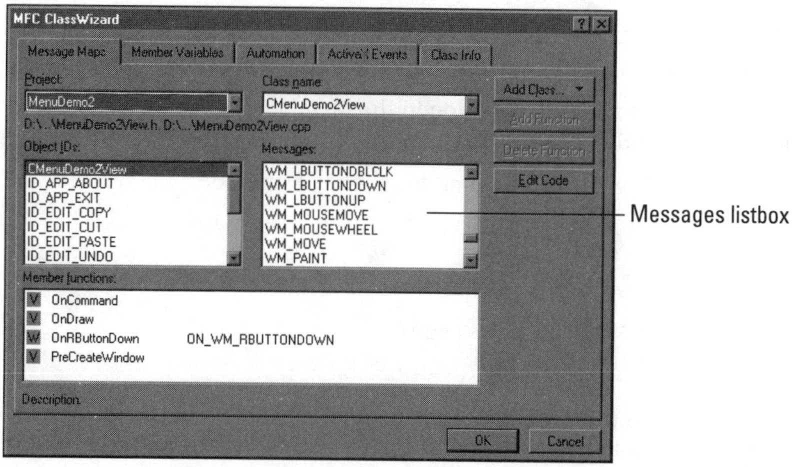

Figure 3-1: The Messages list box contains the mouse messages.

To create a message handler for the mouse, double-click the message for which you want to create a handler function. A function is created and automatically added to the Member Functions list box. The message appears in bold text in the messages list box, indicating there's a message handler function for the message in the selected class.

Nutshell

How to Add a Mouse Event Handler

Here's how you add a mouse event handler to your program.

1. Bring up the ClassWizard.
2. Select the class in which you want to add the handler function. This will usually be the MainFrame or View class.
3. Make sure the class is selected in the Object IDs list box.
4. Find the message for which you want to creating a handler in the messages list box and double-click it. The handler is added to the Member Functions list box.

◆ ◆ ◆ ◆ ◆

Try This

Adding Your Own Mouse Handler

Now that you've learned how to create handler functions for mouse messages, you should take a minute and create one. This ensures you understand everything that's been discussed to this point.

1. Create a single-document interface application named CreateHandler.
2. Invoke the ClassWizard.
3. Select `CreateHandlerView` in the Class Name combo box.
4. Select `CreateHandlerView` in the Object IDs combo box.
5. Find the `WM_MOUSEMOVE` message in the Messages list box and double-click it.
6. Click the `OnMouseMove()` function in the Member Functions list box and then click the Edit Code button.
7. Add the following code to the `OnMouseMove()` function:

```
CClientDC ClientDC( this );
CString strInfo;
strInfo.Format( "X:%d Y:%d      ",
  point.x, point.y );
ClientDC.TextOut(10,10, strInfo,
 strInfo.GetLength() );
```

8. Compile and run the program. As you move the mouse in the client window, you'll see the mouse position coordinates as they're drawn in the window (see Figure 3-2).

◆ ◆ ◆ ◆ ◆

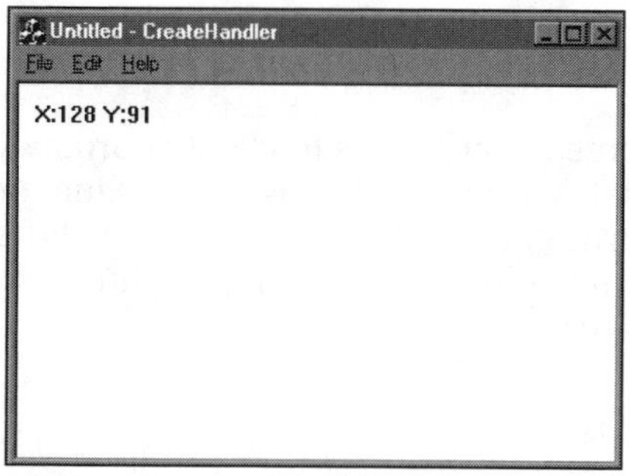

Figure 3-2: This program shows you the mouse coodinates.

Converting Between Screen and Window Coordinates

The coordinates sent to the `OnMouseMove()` function are relative to the view window's client area. The lowest value you can get for both *x* and *y* is zero. The greatest value for the *x* and *y* values is equal to the width and height of the view window, respectively.

There may be occasions when you want to know what the mouse coordinates are in terms of the entire screen. MFC includes a convenient conversion member function named `ClientToScreen()`. It takes as an argument a `CPoint` class and converts the values in the class from client window values to screen values.

For instance, a window might be placed on the screen at 50, 75, in which case the mouse coordinates returned to `OnMouseMove()` will be with reference to the coordinate pair of 50, 75. If the user is pointing to a location inside of the window that's 15 pixels to the right of the window's top-left corner and 25 pixels down from the window's top-left corner, the coordinates sent to `OnMouseMove()` will be 15, 25. By using the `ClientToScreen()` function, those values will be converted to literal screen values by adding the offset into the window to the screen position of the window. In this case, the screen coordinates will be 65, 100. A small code fragment follows that illustrates the use of this function.

```
void CMyClassView::OnMouseMove(UINT nFlags, CPoint point)
{
  CPoint pt;
  pt = point;
  ClientToScreen( pt );
  CString strInfo;
  strInfo( "Scrn X:%d ScrnY:%d    ",
    pt.x, pt.y );
  CClientDC ClientDC( this );
  ClientDC.TextOut(10,10, strInfo, strInfo.GetLength() );
```

```
    CScrollView::OnMouseMove(nFlags, point);
  }
```

Another option is to convert from screen coordinates to client coordinates. This is helpful when you get mouse coordinates from the Windows 98 API function `GetCursorPos()`. This function returns coordinate values in terms of the entire screen. Following is an example in which the mouse position is obtained and then converted to client window coordinates:

```
void CMyClassView::TestFunction()
{
  POINT point;
  ::GetCursorPos( &point );
  CPoint pt( point );
  ScreenToClient( pt );
  CString strInfo;
  strInfo( "Scrn X:%d ScrnY:%d ClntX:%d ClntY:%d",
    point.x, point.y, pt.x, pt.y );
  AfxMessageBox( strInfo );
  CScrollView::OnMouseMove(nFlags, point);
}
```

Creating an MFC Program that Handles Mouse Events

We've created a simple demo program, highlights of which are given in Listing 3-1, that shows you how to respond to the main mouse events. It handles mouse movement events, mouse-button down events, and mouse-button up events. It does not handle middle mouse-button events.

MouseDemo1
CD-ROM Location: **Chap03\MouseDemo1**
Program Name: **MouseDemo1.EXE**
Source Code Modules in Text: **MouseDemo1View.cpp**

✦ ✦ ✦ ✦ ✦

Listing 3-1: MouseDemo1View.cpp Source Code File Highlights

```
// MouseDemo1View.cpp : implementation of the
// CMouseDemo1View class
//

////////////////////////////////////////////////////////////
// CMouseDemo1View construction/destruction

CMouseDemo1View::CMouseDemo1View()
{
```

```
  // Start in the mode that shows mouse
  // info, not the grid of rectangles.
  m_nInfoMode = MOUSE_SHOWINFO;

  // Clear the two dimensional grid array.
  for( int y=0; y<10; y++ )
    for( int x=0; x<10; x++ )
      m_nGrid[x][y] = 0;

}

CMouseDemo1View::~CMouseDemo1View()
{
}

/////////////////////////////////////////////////////////
// CMouseDemo1View drawing

void CMouseDemo1View::OnDraw(CDC* pDC)
{
  CMouseDemo1Doc* pDoc = GetDocument();
  ASSERT_VALID(pDoc);

  // We only perform a redraw when we're
  // set to MOUSE_SHOWGRID mode.
  if( m_nInfoMode == MOUSE_SHOWGRID ){

    // Use the client rectangle
    // in order to draw the grid
    // rectangles in a size proportional
    // to the client rectangle.
    RECT Rect;
    GetClientRect( &Rect );

    // Create red, white and blue brushs.
    CBrush RedBrush( RGB( 255, 0, 0 ) );
    CBrush BlueBrush( RGB( 0, 0, 255 ) );
    CBrush WhiteBrush( RGB( 255, 255, 255 ) );
    CBrush *pUseBrush;

    // The grid has ten horizontal and ten
    // vertical components.
    for( int y=0; y<10; y++ ){
      for( int x=0; x<10; x++ ){

        // Assign DrawRect by calculating
        // one tenth of the client
        // rectangle.
        RECT DrawRect;
        DrawRect.left =
          ( x * Rect.right ) / 10;
        DrawRect.top =
          ( y * Rect.bottom ) / 10;
```

(continued)

Listing 3-1 *(continued)*

```
        DrawRect.right =
          DrawRect.left + ( Rect.right / 10 ) + 1;
        DrawRect.bottom =
          DrawRect.top + ( Rect.bottom / 10 );

        // Select the brush for drawing
        // based on whether the grid
        // is empty, set to left, or
        // set to right.
        pUseBrush = &WhiteBrush;
        if( m_nGrid[x][y] == 1 )
          pUseBrush = &BlueBrush;
        else if( m_nGrid[x][y] == 2 )
          pUseBrush = &RedBrush;

        // Draw the filled rectangle.
        pDC->FillRect( &DrawRect, pUseBrush );
        }
      }
    }

}

/////////////////////////////////////////////////////////////////////////////
// CMouseDemo1View message handlers

void CMouseDemo1View::OnLButtonDown(UINT nFlags,
  CPoint point)
{

  // Call the function that displays the mouse
  // information.
  ShowMouseInfo( "LButtonDown", point, 1 );

  // Call the default OnLButtonDown() function.
  CView::OnLButtonDown(nFlags, point);
}

void CMouseDemo1View::OnLButtonUp(UINT nFlags,
  CPoint point)
{

  // Call the function that displays the mouse
  // information.
  ShowMouseInfo( "LButtonUp", point );

  // Call the default OnLButtonUp() function.
  CView::OnLButtonUp(nFlags, point);
}

void CMouseDemo1View::OnLButtonDblClk(UINT nFlags,
```

```
  CPoint point)
{

  // Call the function that displays the mouse
  // information.
  ShowMouseInfo( "LButtonDblClk", point );

  // Call the default OnLButtonDblClk() function.
  CView::OnLButtonDblClk(nFlags, point);
}

void CMouseDemo1View::OnRButtonDown(UINT nFlags,
  CPoint point)
{

  // Call the function that displays the mouse
  // information.
  ShowMouseInfo( "RButtonDown", point, 2 );

  // Call the default OnRButtonDown() function.
  CView::OnRButtonDown(nFlags, point);
}

void CMouseDemo1View::OnRButtonUp(UINT nFlags,
  CPoint point)
{

  // Call the function that displays the mouse
  // information.
  ShowMouseInfo( "RButtonUp", point );

  // Call the default OnRButtonUp() function.
  CView::OnRButtonUp(nFlags, point);
}

void CMouseDemo1View::OnRButtonDblClk(UINT nFlags,
  CPoint point)
{

  // Call the function that displays the mouse
  // information.
  ShowMouseInfo( "RButtonDblClk", point );

  // Call the default OnRButtonDblClk() function.
  CView::OnRButtonDblClk(nFlags, point);
}

void CMouseDemo1View::OnMouseMove(UINT nFlags,
  CPoint point)
{

  // Only show the mouse position if
  // we're set to MOUSE_SHOWINFO
```

(continued)

Listing 3-1 *(continued)*

```
  if( m_nInfoMode == MOUSE_SHOWINFO ){
    CClientDC ClientDC( this );

    CString strInfo;

    // Copy the CPoint class so
    // that we can convert it to
    // screen coordinates.
    CPoint pt = point;

    // Convert to screen coordinates.
    ClientToScreen( &pt );

    // Format the information.
    strInfo.Format(
      "X:%d Y:%d ScnX:%d ScnY:%d             ",
      point.x, point.y,
      pt.x, pt.y );

    // Draw the information string to
    // the window.
    ClientDC.TextOut( 0, 0,
      strInfo, strInfo.GetLength() );
    }

  // Call the default OnMouseMove() function.
  CView::OnMouseMove(nFlags, point);
}

void CMouseDemo1View::ShowMouseInfo(
  const char *lpszText, CPoint point, int nFlag )
{

  // Perform the following code if
  // we're set to MOUSE_SHOWGRID.
  if( m_nInfoMode == MOUSE_SHOWGRID ){
    if( nFlag != -1 ){

      // Get the client rectangle
      // so that we can calculate which
      // x and y index the current
      // click position.
      RECT Rect;
      GetClientRect( &Rect );

      // Use the client rectangle
      // and divide by ten to calculate
      // the x and y grid indexes.
      int x = ( point.x * 10 ) / Rect.right;
      int y = ( point.y * 10 ) / Rect.bottom;
```

```
      // Either set the grid to left or right
      // button states, or clear them so that
      // the grid array is empty.
      if( m_nGrid[x][y] == nFlag )
        m_nGrid[x][y] = 0;
      else
        m_nGrid[x][y] = nFlag;

      // Cause the window to redraw.
      InvalidateRect( NULL, FALSE );
      UpdateWindow();
      }
    return;
    }

  // Get a DC to the client window.
  CClientDC ClientDC( this );

  CString strInfo;

  // Format the output string.
  strInfo.Format(
    "X:%d Y:%d %s         ",
    point.x, point.y, lpszText );

  // Draw the output string to the
  // window.
  ClientDC.TextOut( point.x, point.y,
    strInfo, strInfo.GetLength() );

}

void CMouseDemo1View::OnFileMouseGriddisplay()
{

  // Set to MOUSE_SHOWGRID mode.
  if( m_nInfoMode != MOUSE_SHOWGRID ){
    m_nInfoMode = MOUSE_SHOWGRID;
    InvalidateRect( NULL, TRUE );
    UpdateWindow();
    }

}

void CMouseDemo1View::OnUpdateFileMouseGriddisplay(
  CCmdUI* pCmdUI)
{

  // Set the menu check if we're
  // in MOUSE_SHOWGRID mode.
  pCmdUI->SetCheck( m_nInfoMode == MOUSE_SHOWGRID );

}
```

(continued)

Listing 3-1 *(continued)*

```
void CMouseDemo1View::OnFileMousePositioninformation()
{

  // Set to MOUSE_SHOWINFO mode.
  if( m_nInfoMode != MOUSE_SHOWINFO ){
    m_nInfoMode = MOUSE_SHOWINFO;
    InvalidateRect( NULL, TRUE );
    UpdateWindow();
    }

}

void CMouseDemo1View::OnUpdateFileMousePositioninformation(
  CCmdUI* pCmdUI)
{

  // Set the menu check if we're
  // in MOUSE_SHOWINFO mode.
  pCmdUI->SetCheck( m_nInfoMode == MOUSE_SHOWINFO );

}
```

Nonclient Mouse Events

Windows 98 uses about half of the defined input messages for nonclient-area objects. The mouse messages with names containing the letters *NC* are messages that Windows 98 handles for the nonclient-area components of a window. For example, Windows receives a WM_NCLBUTTONDOWN message when a user selects a menu command, resizes a window frame, or minimizes a window. The differences between these actions depend on the mouse location when the mouse button is clicked.

The nonsystem mouse messages are for application use—that is, they are for your use. With the help of ClassWizard, creating and responding to the basic set of messages is fairly straightforward. Table 3-2 shows the nonclient mouse messages Windows 98 manages.

Table 3-2
Nonclient Mouse Messages

Message	*Description*
WM_NCMOUSEMOVE	The mouse has moved over a nonclient area of a window.
WM_NCLBUTTONDOWN	The left (primary) button has been pushed while the pointer is over the nonclient area.

Message	Description
WM_NCLBUTTONUP	The left (primary) button has been released.
WM_NCRBUTTONDOWN	The right (secondary) button has been pushed while the pointer is over the nonclient area.
WM_NCRBUTTONUP	The right (secondary) button has been released.
WM_NCMBUTTONDOWN	The middle button has been pushed while the pointer is over the nonclient area.
WM_NCMBUTTONUP	The middle button has been released.
WM_NCHITTEST	This query message asks, "Where in the window is the mouse pointer?" The NC in this query message doesn't mean that it's only for the nonclient area, although that is the system's primary interest. Instead, this message returns a hit-test code that identifies the pointer position in the window—for example, over a border, over a menu, or over the client area.

Changing the Mouse Cursor

One of the most obvious ways to give the user feedback is with the shape of the mouse pointer. Of the stock pointers, the hourglass pointer is the easiest to display because MFC provides two helper functions. One function, `BeginWaitCursor()`, displays the hourglass cursor. The other function, `EndWaitCursor()`, returns the pointer to its normal shape. Both functions should be called during the long time it takes to perform such tasks as a large disk I/O access.

We should point out that this is not the only way to display an hourglass pointer. You could also do this by handling the `WM_SETCURSOR` message. If a program needs to interact with the user—that is, retrieve any type of message—while still displaying the hourglass pointer, you *must* respond to the `WM_SETCURSOR` solution. Windows 98 sends a constant stream of these messages to each window, causing a continual updating of each window's pointer. (To see this for yourself, run SPY++.)

The function call for displaying pointers is a Windows 98 API function, `SetCursor()`. For example, here is the line of code that displays the right-arrow pointer:

```
::SetCursor( ::LoadCursor( AfxGetInstanceHandle(), IDC_ARROW )
);
```

Creating an MFC Demo Program that Changes Mouse Cursors

To demonstrate how to change mouse cursors within an application, we've written a special program named MouseDemo2; highlights of this program are shown in Listing 3-2. The program loads 16 cursors and sets the cursor depending on the mouse position.

The application looks at where the mouse currently is inside of the view window. Dividing the view window into 16 rectangular regions enables the program to decide which of 16 mouse cursors to use. When you run the program and move the mouse around inside of the view window, you'll see the mouse cursor change. The name of the mouse cursor is also displayed, as shown in Figure 3-3.

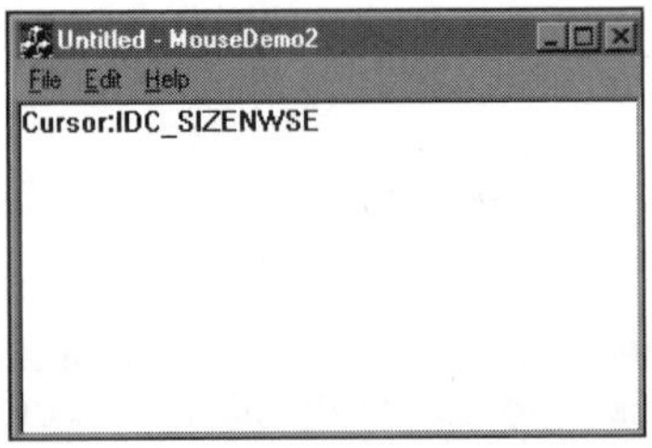

Figure 3-3: This program changes mouse cursors and displays the cursor name in the view window.

Demo Program

MouseDemo2
CD-ROM Location: **Chap03\MouseDemo2**
Program Name: **MouseDemo2.EXE**
Source Code Modules in Text: **MouseDemo2View.cpp**

Listing 3-2: MouseDemo2View.cpp Source Code File Highlights

```
// MouseDemo2View.cpp : implementation of
// the CMouseDemo2View class
//

//////////////////////////////////////////////////////////////
// CMouseDemo2View construction/destruction

CMouseDemo2View::CMouseDemo2View()
{

  // Keep a list of the cursor IDs that
  // we'll load in.
  static char *szCursor[] = {
    IDC_ARROW, IDC_IBEAM, IDC_WAIT,
```

```
    IDC_CROSS, IDC_UPARROW, IDC_SIZENWSE,
    IDC_SIZENESW, IDC_SIZEWE, IDC_SIZENS,
    IDC_SIZEALL, IDC_NO, IDC_APPSTARTING,
    IDC_HELP, IDC_ARROW, IDC_ARROW, IDC_ARROW };

  // Load the cursors.
  for( int i=0; i<16; i++ )
    m_hCursor[i] =
      ::LoadCursor( NULL, szCursor[i] );

}

CMouseDemo2View::~CMouseDemo2View()
{
}

/////////////////////////////////////////////////////////////
// CMouseDemo2View message handlers

BOOL CMouseDemo2View::OnSetCursor(CWnd* pWnd, UINT nHitTest,
  UINT message)
{

  // See if this is a HTCLIENT
  // hit test.
  if( nHitTest == HTCLIENT ){

    // Get the mouse position. This
    // will be in terms of the
    // entire screen.
    POINT pt;
    GetCursorPos( &pt );

    // Convert the coordinates to
    // client rectangle coordinates.
    ScreenToClient( &pt );

    // Call the function that we created
    // which gets the cursor region.
    int nCursor = GetCursorRegion( &pt );

    // Set the window cursor.
    ::SetCursor( m_hCursor[nCursor] );

    // Return indicating that we responded
    // to this message.
    return( TRUE );
    }

  // Call the default OnSetCursor() function.
  return CView::OnSetCursor(pWnd, nHitTest, message);
}
```

(continued)

Listing 3-2 *(continued)*

```
int CMouseDemo2View::GetCursorRegion( POINT *lpPt )
{

  // We'll need the client
  // rectangle so that we can
  // calculate the cursor region.
  // It'll be an x value from 0-3
  // and a y value from 0-3.
  RECT Rect;
  GetClientRect( &Rect );

  // Divide the client rectangle width
  // by four to obtain the x region
  // index.
  int x =
    ( lpPt->x * 4 ) / Rect.right;
  if( x > 3 ) x = 3;


  // Divide the client rectangle height
  // by four to obtain the y region
  // index.
  int y =
    ( lpPt->y * 4 ) / Rect.bottom;
  if( y > 3 ) y = 3;

  // Return the index. It'll be a value
  // from 0-15.
  return( y * 4 + x );

}

void CMouseDemo2View::OnMouseMove(UINT nFlags, CPoint point)
{

  // Keep a list of the cursor names
  // so that we can display them
  // in the client window.
  static CString strCursor[] = {
    "IDC_ARROW", "IDC_IBEAM", "IDC_WAIT",
    "IDC_CROSS", "IDC_UPARROW", "IDC_SIZENWSE",
    "IDC_SIZENESW", "IDC_SIZEWE", "IDC_SIZENS",
    "IDC_SIZEALL", "IDC_NO", "IDC_APPSTARTING",
    "IDC_HELP", "IDC_ARROW", "IDC_ARROW",
    "IDC_ARROW" };

  // Get the cursor region. This
  // will be a value from 0-15 and
  // will correspond to the 16
  // cursors we loaded.
  int nCursor =
```

```
    GetCursorRegion( &point );

  // Get a DC to the client window
  // so that we can draw.
  CClientDC ClientDC( this );

  CString strInfo;

  // Format a string.
  strInfo = "Cursor:" +
    strCursor[nCursor] +
    "              ";

  // Draw the string to the client window.
  ClientDC.TextOut( 0, 0,
    strInfo, strInfo.GetLength() );

  // Call the default OnMouseMove() function.
  CView::OnMouseMove(nFlags, point);
}
```

Capturing the Mouse

From time to time, you have to ask the mouse to give its full attention to a single window. You do this by *capturing the mouse*. Although you might think that mouse capture somehow limits the movement of the pointer, it doesn't. (That happens when you *clip the pointer*, a subject that we address shortly.) Instead, capturing the mouse forces all mouse messages to be sent to a single window. Here's the real kicker: The window that has captured the mouse continues to get mouse input *even when the pointer is not over the window.*

So, when does a window want to grab the mouse's full attention? This is necessary when one mouse message—typically the left-button down message (WM_LBUTTONDOWN)—starts a multiple-mouse-message action. Examples include drag and drop, dragging to select multiple items (such as multiple lines in a word processor), and dragging to draw.

If the mouse flew off without letting you know about the button up message, it could leave your application in an indeterminate state. After all, when a multiple-mouse-message action starts, you'll probably set some flags to indicate the action is taking place. You want to avoid having such actions terminated in midstride. In other words, capturing the mouse is necessary to force the mouse to stay in touch until it finishes what it has started.

To understand mouse capture, it helps to see it in action. Run almost any application and open the File Open dialog box. The mouse can be captured by two dialog box controls: list boxes and edit controls. Mouse capture takes place when you click to select an item in a list box or text in the edit control. After clicking such controls, when you drag the mouse outside the border, you see the control scrolling its contents. The scrolling is caused by mouse capture.

Another place you can see mouse capture work is within most text editing windows (including the Visual C++ editor). These windows scroll when you click a window filled with text and drag beyond the window border. These windows are only able to continue receiving mouse input — in the form of `WM_MOUSEMOVE` messages — because the mouse has been captured.

Now that you've seen it at work, you probably want to know how you can capture the mouse yourself. It's easy; you just call `CWnd::SetCapture()`. As we mentioned, you typically do this in response to a mouse-down message. To *release* the mouse capture — something you must be sure to do — call `CWnd::ReleaseCapture()`. A good time to release the mouse capture is in response to the button-up message (`WM_LBUTTONUP`).

Here's some ClassWizard-generated code that shows a typical scenario for mouse capture and release. The mouse is captured when the left mouse button is clicked (in reply to the `WM_LBUTTONDOWN` message), and it is released when the left mouse button comes up (in reply to the `WM_LBUTTONUP` message):

```
void CMainFrame::OnLButtonDown(UINT nFlags,
  CPoint point)
{
  // Grab the mouse.
  SetCapture();

  CFrameWnd::OnLButtonDown(nFlags, point);
}

void CMainFrame::OnLButtonUp(UINT nFlags, CPoint point)
{
  // Release the mouse.
  ReleaseCapture();

  CFrameWnd::OnLButtonUp(nFlags, point);
}
```

Incidentally, when you capture the mouse, Windows 98 doesn't send you any hit-test (`WM_NCHITTEST`) or pointer-setting (`WM_SETCURSOR`) messages. The assumption is you already have complete control of the mouse, and you will change the pointer when you need to. If you want to change the pointer during mouse capture, you would probably do so in response to `WM_MOUSEMOVE`, the only mouse message you get when the mouse is captured.

Limiting Mouse Movement

Another facility Windows 98 enables you to control is *mouse-pointer clipping*. It's not something you'll do very often, but to complete our discussion of mouse state, we need to at least mention it. Mouse-pointer clipping — like the clipping GDI does for graphic drawings — involves the definition of a rectangle boundary. The mouse pointer can move only within its defined pointer clipping rectangle.

One example of pointer clipping is obvious when using Windows 98. Windows 98 itself clips the pointer to the display screen. If it didn't, a user might accidentally send the pointer over the edge of the screen and into oblivion. We've seen some display drivers that have an option to enable the pointer to wrap around the left edge of the screen onto the right and over the top of the screen onto the bottom. Although it's not our taste in mouse pointer, some users undoubtedly appreciate being able to do this.

So, why should a program clip the pointer? Obviously, it's necessary to prevent the user from moving the pointer outside a given area. For example, a security program might let the user move the pointer only within the password dialog box. It's tough to come up with good examples of when to use pointer clipping, because the few places where it's done, it's disconcerting. For example, the Paintbrush program in Windows 3.1 clips the pointer when you're drawing shapes such as Bézier curves. (We find this more annoying than useful.)

Microsoft's MFC developers apparently agree with our assessment that this isn't a general-purpose function. They don't include the Windows 98 API function that controls pointer clipping, `::ClipCursor()`, in any MFC class. What's interesting, though, is that although MFC doesn't wrap this function in any of its own classes, it *does* clip the pointer in one specific circumstance. When resizing an OLE toolbar, the pointer is clipped to the parent window's client area. This is one use that makes sense, because the size of a child window should be limited by the size of the parent window.

Keyboard Input

The handling of individual keyboard messages is fairly straightforward. Once you know which message(s) to look for, it's a simple matter to set up the message handling that springs into action when a particular key is pressed. You'll probably package keyboard commands as accelerators, which we discussed in Chapter 2. As command input, accelerators generate `WM_COMMAND` messages.

For keyboard input not handled by an accelerator table, you'll choose either the `WM_KEYDOWN` message or the `WM_CHAR` message to detect keyboard input. In this section, we describe the differences between these two messages as well as when you should choose one over the other.

We're also going to cover some of the less obvious aspects of keyboard input. We start with a look at how the keyboard hardware's scan codes are translated into visible character codes. Next, we discuss general user-interface issues that relate to keyboard input — namely, what to do when a window gets the keyboard focus.

Translation of keyboard input

Keyboard data undergoes two translations. The first is performed by the keyboard device driver when it converts scan codes into virtual key (`WM_KEYDOWN`) messages. Next, applications call a Windows 98 API function, `::TranslateMessage()`, which filters virtual key messages for printable characters. When printable characters are found, Windows 98 generates an entirely new message, `WM_CHAR`, and adds it to the message stream.

How much of this translation process do you really need to understand? That depends on your needs. If you spent a lot of time as an MS-DOS programmer, you probably want to know how Windows 98 enhances the basic keyboard scan codes created by MS-DOS interrupts. If you plan to support international versions of your Windows 98 software, you'll certainly want to know how Windows 98 handles the different keyboards used around the world. Even if these two issues aren't important for your purposes, you should at least know when to use each of the two types of keyboard messages. Keyboard data starts with the keyboard, so that's where we begin.

The physical keyboard

Keyboards haven't changed much since the first IBM PCs were shipped back in the summer of 1981. Those first machines shipped with an 83-key keyboard. In 1984, IBM introduced the 84-key keyboard with the IBM-AT computer (the SysReq key was added). IBM subsequently introduced the 101/102-key keyboard, which mostly duplicated existing keys. That keyboard has become the standard for IBM-compatible computers.

At COMDEX in the fall of 1994, Microsoft introduced the Microsoft Natural Keyboard. In addition to sporting a curvy, ergonomic design, this keyboard adds two keys to the standard set. As mentioned in our discussion of keyboard accelerators in Chapter 2, the two new keys are the Applications key and the Windows key.

The Applications key is intended for application use; it summons context menus. And in Windows 98, Windows 98 itself responds to the Windows key by displaying the Task Manager. Both represent relatively minor but useful additions to keyboard operation, although it's too early to say whether other keyboard manufacturers will adopt these new keys.

Getting keyboard input to an MS-DOS program often involves an intimate knowledge of how a low-level keyboard code, known as a *scan code*, is generated. Although C run-time functions translate keyboard input for you, MS-DOS programmers who opt for high performance will grab keyboard scan codes directly. Scan codes are not related to any character set; instead, they are a set of 8-bit codes that indicate which key has been pressed. For example, the key that generates a *Y* on a U.S.-English keyboard has a scan code of 15 hex. It doesn't take too much imagination—or code—to build a table for converting scan code data to ASCII characters. That's what many MS-DOS programmers must do.

Intimate knowledge of the keyboard is required because MS-DOS programmers have to ignore about half of the scan codes generated. Each key on the keyboard actually has *two* scan codes. One indicates a key has been pressed, and the other indicates the key has been released. The difference between the two scan codes is 80 hex. For example, the *Y* key we discussed a moment ago sends a scan code of 15 hex when pressed and 95 hex when released. Of these two, the down transition is more interesting. When reading scan codes, the up transition—which has the sign bit set—is usually ignored.

One problem with scan codes is they are a very hardware-dependent, low-level type of input. To properly perform scan code conversion, you must take into account the keyboard currently installed on the system. Most types of keyboards are distinguished on the basis of language or, in some cases, country.

One example, the Swiss-German keyboard, takes into account both language and country. On that keyboard, the *Z* key and the *Y* key are reversed from what they are on the U.S.-English keyboard. As a result, an MS-DOS program that relies on scan code conversions according to the U.S.-English keyboard layout won't work correctly in Switzerland without some modification.

When we say that keyboard scan codes are hardware dependent, we really mean they are dependent on the different way keys are laid out to follow various cultural conventions. For a scan code-dependent program that could work worldwide, approximately two dozen different translation tables are required. And that's only taking into account the keyboards that use the Roman alphabet. For other keyboards, such as Cyrillic, Arabic, and the various Asian keyboards, a whole new set of problems arise.

In addition to being hardware dependent, scan codes are so low level that they don't take into account keyboard state, such as the Shift key or the Caps Lock key. As a result, considerable effort is required to simply detect the difference between an upper- and a lowercase letter. For example, a scan code–dependent program can't tell the difference between *Y* and *y* without a lot of extra work. Scan codes aren't case sensitive because keyboards aren't case sensitive.

Windows 98 has different solutions for each of these two problems. To avoid relying on country-specific keyboard layouts, Windows 98 keyboard drivers convert scan codes into a standard set of *virtual key codes*. This set of keys make up what is sometimes called the *Windows logical keyboard*. To solve the problem of keyboard state, Windows 98 provides a helper function to convert virtual key codes into printable characters. This latter conversion creates the distinction between upper- and lowercase that we rely on when reading text.

The Windows 98 logical keyboard

The logical keyboard is an abstraction that serves to hide differences between keyboards in countries that use Roman characters. You won't see a keyboard layout for the logical keyboard anywhere in the Windows 98 documentation. What you will see, however, are the definitions for virtual key (`VK_`) codes. It's the job of the keyboard device driver to convert hardware-specific scan codes into virtual key codes.

In particular, Windows 98 calls the keyboard driver to convert raw hardware scan codes into virtual key codes. These virtual key codes are sent to applications as messages. Because each keyboard key has two scan codes—that is, a key pressed code and a key released code—each key also has two messages. The `WM_KEYDOWN` message indicates a keyboard key has been pressed, and the `WM_KEYUP` message indicates a key has been released.

With virtual key messages, you don't have to worry about different keyboards. The device driver does whatever translation is necessary to produce a uniform set of key codes. However, although virtual key messages solve this first problem with scan codes, they don't solve the second problem.

The problem that still exists is virtual key codes are fairly low level. In particular, you have to do a lot of work to decide whether letters are upper- or lowercase. And virtual key codes aren't influenced by changes to shift key states, which include the Shift, Ctrl, and Alt keys. Virtual key codes also ignore the state of the Caps Lock, Num Lock, and Scroll Lock keys.

Although they don't provide enough information to get character input, virtual key codes are suitable for use as accelerator key codes. Two types of accelerators are available: VIRTKEY and ASCII. We recommend that you always use VIRTKEY, which, as the name suggests, corresponds to virtual keys. The other type of accelerator, ASCII, is created from the other type of keyboard message, which we discuss next.

Printable character messages

The Windows 98 API contains a function for converting between virtual key code messages and `WM_CHAR` messages. We call these the *printable character messages*, because most are uppercase letters, lowercase letters, numbers, or punctuation marks. That is, they correspond to characters you can see on the display screen and send to the printer.

The `::TranslateMessage()` function is the Windows 98 API function that converts virtual key messages into `WM_CHAR` messages. Unless you've written Windows SDK programs, you've probably never seen this function. And because MFC calls this function for you in its message loop, you don't ever have to worry about it.

What's important is this function adds `WM_CHAR` messages to your application's message queue. Every `WM_CHAR` message you receive will be preceded by a `WM_KEYDOWN` message and followed by a `WM_KEYUP` message. You get printable character input from the WM_CHAR message, and you can safely ignore the associated virtual key messages.

If you ignore WM_KEYDOWN messages, why does Windows bother sending them to you? This message is for all the keys that *don't* have a corresponding printable character. We should mention that such keystrokes seem more like commands than data, and the easiest way to handle keyboard commands is with an accelerator table. You can't always use an accelerator table, however. In particular, it's something of a convention that only one accelerator table is active at any point in time. That accelerator table would be the one for an application's frame window. All other windows must process low-level keyboard input directly, without the benefits accelerator tables provide.

Table 3-3 lists the virtual key codes for keys that don't create printable characters. When you can't create accelerator table entries, you'll rely on the WM_KEYDOWN message to detect when these keys have been pressed.

To summarize, keyboard input starts as scan codes. A Windows 98 keyboard driver converts these codes to a hardware-independent form: virtual key codes. Typically, Windows 98 applications then send the virtual key code messages to a Windows 98 API function that generates WM_CHAR character messages when printable characters are typed. For nonprintable characters — such as function keys and navigation keys — you must rely on the WM_KEYDOWN virtual key message.

Table 3-3
Virtual Key Codes for Keys That Don't Produce Printable Characters

Key	*Virtual Key Code*
Alt	VK_MENU
Application	VK_APPS
Ctrl	VK_CONTROL
Del	VK_DELETE
Down arrow	VK_DOWN
End	VK_END
F1	VK_F1
F2	VK_F2
F3	VK_F3
F4	VK_F4
F5	VK_F5
F6	VK_F6

Table 3-3 *(continued)*

Key	***Virtual Key Code***
F7	`VK_F7`
F8	`VK_F8`
F9	`VK_F9`
F10	`VK_F10`
F11	`VK_F11`
F12	`VK_F12`
Home	`VK_HOME`
Ins	`VK_INSERT`
Left arrow	`VK_LEFT`
Pause	`VK_PAUSE`
PgDn	`VK_NEXT`
PgUp	`VK_PRIOR`
PrtScr	`VK_SNAPSHOT`
Right arrow	`VK_RIGHT`
Shift	`VK_SHIFT`
Up arrow	`VK_UP`

Now that you understand the types of keyboard input messages Windows 98 can send you, it's time to address input issues related to application state. Toward that end, the following section describes how an application lets the user know a window has the keyboard focus. This can be done using several techniques, which we call *echoing the keyboard focus.*

Echoing keyboard focus

When you build support for keyboard input into a window, you must provide a visual cue that lets the user know when that support is enabled. Because a window gets keyboard input when it has the focus, the proper time for displaying those visual cues is when the window has the focus. It follows, then, that you should disable the visible signs of the focus when the window loses the focus.

To help you build windows that display the proper visual cues, the following sections describe three ways a window can advertise its ownership of the focus. We start with a look at creating insertion points, which are Windows' keyboard pointers. Next, we talk about focus rectangles, something often seen in dialog-box controls but which can also be displayed in other types of windows. Finally, we talk about the relationship between a window's selection state and the keyboard focus.

Creating and maintaining keyboard cursors

A keyboard cursor or insertion point is a blinking bitmap that lets the user know where keyboard input will have an effect.

Table 3-4 lists the eight `CWnd` member functions that create and manage keyboard cursors. This group of functions is fairly small and easy to understand. The challenge with keyboard cursors revolves around timing issues, such as when to create, show, hide, and destroy the cursors.

Table 3-4
CWnd Member Functions for Creating and Managing Keyboard Cursors

Function	***Description***
`CreateCaret()`	Creates a keyboard cursor using a bitmap you provide.
`CreateGrayCaret()`	Creates a solid gray cursor using the size you specify.
`CreateSolidCaret()`	Creates a solid black cursor using the size you specify.
`GetCaretPos()`	Returns the location of the cursor. Because of local input state in Windows 95, 98, and Windows NT, you can only find the location of a cursor if it's contained within a window that's created by the calling thread.
`DestroyCaret()`	Destroys a cursor. To avoid putting your application in an unknown state, destroy the cursor when you lose the keyboard focus (and create a cursor when you gain the keyboard focus).
`HideCaret()`	Makes a cursor invisible.
`SetCaretPos()`	Moves a cursor to a position in a window. When a window containing a cursor is scrolled, the cursor gets scrolled with the window data.
`ShowCaret()`	Makes a cursor visible.

You create a keyboard cursor when a window gets the keyboard focus. Although you might be tempted to create it earlier, you should resist the temptation. After all, you only need a cursor to echo the results of keyboard input. And without the focus, you don't have any keyboard input. In addition to creating the cursor, you need to position it within your window and make it visible. Here's a fragment of code that does the right thing in response to a `WM_SETFOCUS` message:

```
void CMainFrame::OnSetFocus(CWnd* pOldWnd)
{
  // First call default handler.
  CFrameWnd::OnSetFocus(pOldWnd);

  // Create, position, and make caret appear.
  CreateSolidCaret(0, d_cyLineHeight );
  SetCaretPos( d_ptCaretLocation );
  ShowCaret();
}
```

Just as you create a keyboard cursor when you get the focus, the logical time to destroy the cursor is when you lose the focus. In response to the `WM_KILLFOCUS` message, you first hide the cursor and then destroy it. Here's a code fragment that shows how this is done:

```
void CMainFrame::OnKillFocus(CWnd* pNewWnd)
{
  CFrameWnd::OnKillFocus(pNewWnd);

  // Query and save current caret position.
  d_ptCaretLocation = GetCaretPos();

  // Eliminate caret.
  HideCaret();
  DestroyCaret();
}
```

The only other keyboard cursor issue involves drawing outside of the normal `WM_PAINT` drawing. If a cursor is in a window, you must hide the cursor before any non-`WM_PAINT` drawing. Otherwise, you might overwrite the cursor. When the non-`WM_PAINT` drawing is done, you can restore the cursor. Here's a code fragment that shows what we mean:

```
void CMainFrame::OnChar(UINT nChar, UINT nRepCnt,
  UINT nFlags)
{
  CSize sizeTextBox;

  // Fetch caret position.
  CPoint pt = GetCaretPos();

  // Hide caret before fetching DC.
  HideCaret();

  // Drawing in non-WM_PAINT message.
  // Bracket required to force DC to disappear.
  {
    CClientDC ClientDC( this );
    ClientDC.TextOut(pt.x, pt.y, (LPCTSTR)&nChar, 1);
    sizeTextBox =
```

```
        ClientDC.GetTextExtent( (LPCTSTR)&nChar, 1 );
    }

    // Advance caret position.
    pt.x += sizeTextBox.cx;
    SetCaretPos( pt );

    // Display caret.
    ShowCaret();
}
```

This code fragment actually does more than just hide the keyboard cursor. It shows how you respond to the WM_CHAR message to both draw the character that's typed and advance the cursor. Such drawn objects won't be a permanent part of a window's contents unless they are also drawn in response to the WM_PAINT message. Because our code makes no provision for saving the text anywhere, this isn't done. (When you understand why this code fragment is "broken," you truly understand the meaning of the WM_PAINT message.)

To test your cursor-creation code, be sure to force the focus to switch away from your program. Do this by activating the Task Manager (Ctrl-Esc) or any other application that's currently running. When you switch away, the cursor should disappear without a trace. When you switch back, the cursor should be in the same place it was before you switched focus.

The keyboard cursor is called the insertion point because it shows users the exact point in a window at which keyboard input will have an effect. Users expect to be able to navigate insertion points around a window through the use of the arrow keys. Another way to echo the keyboard focus is with a focus rectangle, which we discuss next.

Focus rectangles

A focus rectangle provides an alternative to a cursor for signaling the keyboard focus location. Unlike cursors, focus rectangles don't blink. Instead, they provide subtle highlighting that draws a user's eye to a particular part of a window. Whether you use a focus rectangle or a cursor depends on what you are trying to highlight. The most common examples of focus rectangles occur in dialog boxes. For all non-edit controls, focus rectangles are drawn as the user moves the focus—via the Tab key or the mouse—to the different controls in the dialog.

Focus rectangles aren't solely for dialog box controls, although this is the most obvious and most common use. You can use them anywhere a cursor doesn't seem appropriate. One difference between focus rectangles and cursors is cursors are always solid rectangles. Focus rectangles, on the other hand, are hollow, and they wrap around other objects. If you need to echo the focus in a way that is solid or blinking, you want a cursor. For a subtler, hollow pointer, try a focus rectangle instead.

Drawing a focus rectangle is extremely easy. You simply call MFC's `CDC::DrawFocusRect()` function. The following example shows how to draw a focus rectangle around a block of text:

```
void CMainFrame::OnLButtonDown(UINT nFlags, CPoint point)
{
  CClientDC ClientDC( this );

  // Draw a line of text at mouse cursor location.
  CString str;
  str.Format("Focus rectangle around this text");
  ClientDC.TextOut(point.x, point.y, str);

  // Calculate width and height of text.
  CSize sizeText =
    ClientDC.GetTextExtent( str, str.GetLength() );

  // Calculate a margin around the focus rectangle.
  int cxMargin = GetSystemMetrics( SM_CXBORDER ) * 4;
  int cyMargin = GetSystemMetrics( SM_CYBORDER ) * 1;

  // Calculate size of focus rectangle.
  CRect rTextBox;
  rTextBox.left = point.x - cxMargin;
  rTextBox.top = point.y - cyMargin;
  rTextBox.right = point.x + sizeText.cx + cxMargin;
  rTextBox.bottom = point.y + sizeText.cy + cyMargin;

  // Draw a focus rectangle around a block of text.
  ClientDC.DrawFocusRect( &rTextBox );

  CFrameWnd::OnLButtonDown(nFlags, point);
}
```

This code fragment draws a focus rectangle in response to a `WM_LBUTTONDOWN` message. We show this simply as an example of *how* to call `CDC::DrawFocusRect()`. The truth of the matter is that button messages aren't the events that typically trigger the drawing of focus rectangles.

You're more likely to draw the focus rectangle when a window gets the focus. The reason should be obvious: That's when you are certain your window has the focus. As you may recall from our earlier discussion, this means you draw a focus rectangle in response to a `WM_SETFOCUS` message. Here's a fragment of code taken from an MFC program that shows how to do this:

```
void CMainFrame::OnSetFocus(CWnd* pOldWnd)
{
  CFrameWnd::OnSetFocus(pOldWnd);

  CClientDC ClientDC( this );

  // Draw focus rectangle when we get the focus.
  CRect rFocus;
```

```
    rFocus.left = d_ptFocusRect.x;
    rFocus.top = d_ptFocusRect.y;
    rFocus.right = d_ptFocusRect.x + d_cxIcon;
    rFocus.bottom = d_ptFocusRect.y + d_cyIcon;
    ClientDC.DrawFocusRect( &rFocus );
}
```

If you draw a focus rectangle, you must be sure to erase it. Because a focus rectangle exists just to show focus ownership, the logical time to erase a focus rectangle is when the window loses the focus. Interestingly enough, a focus rectangle is erased by calling the same function that drew it in the first place: `CDC::DrawFocusRect()`. The following code fragment erases the focus rectangle we drew a moment ago. This is done in response to—what else?—the `WM_KILLFOCUS` message:

```
void CMainFrame::OnKillFocus(CWnd* pNewWnd)
{
  CFrameWnd::OnKillFocus(pNewWnd);

  CClientDC ClientDC( this );

  // Hide focus rectangle when we lose the focus.
  CRect rFocus;
  rFocus.left = d_ptFocusRect.x;
  rFocus.top = d_ptFocusRect.y;
  rFocus.right = d_ptFocusRect.x + d_cxIcon;
  rFocus.bottom = d_ptFocusRect.y + d_cyIcon;
  ClientDC.DrawFocusRect(&rFocus);
}
```

You might find it a bit puzzling that the same code can erase *and* draw a focus rectangle. To explain how this is possible, we need to describe how `CDC::DrawFocusRect()` works. This function uses Boolean arithmetic to invert a set of pixels. To draw a focus rectangle, pixels are inverted. To erase the same focus rectangle, the same pixels are inverted again, which completely and effectively erases the focus rectangle. This is often referred to as a Boolean operation, and it makes use of GDI's Boolean *raster operations* (or *ROP codes*).

So far, we've described how you make a focus rectangle appear when you get a `WM_SETFOCUS` message, and how you make it disappear in response to a `WM_KILLFOCUS` message. But there's one more message that can affect the health and well-being of a focus rectangle. To provide complete support for a focus rectangle, you must redraw the focus rectangle in response to the `WM_PAINT` message.

You need to draw a focus rectangle when handling a `WM_PAINT` message for the same reason that you draw any other object in a window's client area. You can't determine ahead of time when some outside event will damage the contents of a window's client area. Such an event might be as simple as a screen saver that automatically starts after ten minutes of idle time. Whatever the reason, you draw a focus rectangle with the same function we described earlier, `CDC::DrawFocusRect()`. With `WM_PAINT`, however, you must first determine whether the window has the focus. If it doesn't, you don't draw the focus rectangle. Only if it has the focus do you draw the focus rectangle. Here's a `WM_PAINT` handler that first checks for the presence of the focus before drawing a focus rectangle:

```
void CMainFrame::OnPaint()
{
  CPaintDC PaintDC( this ); // DC for painting

  // Only draw focus rectangle if our window has focus.
  if( GetFocus() == this ){
    // Calculate coordinate
    CRect rFocus;
    rFocus.left = d_ptFocusRect.x;
    rFocus.top = d_ptFocusRect.y;
    rFocus.right = d_ptFocusRect.x + d_cxIcon;
    rFocus.bottom = d_ptFocusRect.y + d_cyIcon;

    // Draw actual focus rectangle.
    PaintDC.DrawFocusRect(&rFocus);
    }
}
```

Both types of focus-echoing mechanisms — keyboard cursors and focus rectangles — are relatively easy to create and use. But a third issue — the selection state — is closely related to the keyboard focus. By *selection state*, we mean the display of objects selected by a user in a window. To support the Windows standards for user-interface activity, the selection state must be visible only when a window has focus. At all other times, the selection state of objects must be hidden.

Selection state and keyboard focus

With Windows 98 applications, a common mode of operation involves *noun-verb* operations. This means the user first selects an object and then chooses the action to take on that object. For example, to change the formatting of a word in a word processing program, the user first selects the word and then chooses the format command. Although this mode of operation is obvious to experienced Windows users, the opposite — that is, *verb-noun* operation — is quite common in character-based environments.

Objects can be selected using either the mouse or the keyboard. Regardless of how it's done, Windows 98 programs change the color of selected objects to help users distinguish them from other objects. We talk about selecting text colors in Chapter 5. But for now, suffice it to say that you fetch the colors to use by calling `::GetSysColor()` with the appropriate color indices. You then perform a bitwise exclusive OR to determine the color of selected text. This is summarized in the following lines of code:

```
COLORREF d_crForeground = GetSysColor(COLOR_WINDOWTEXT);
COLORREF d_crBackground = GetSysColor( COLOR_WINDOW );
COLORREF d_crSelectFore = d_crForeground ^ 0x00ffffff;
COLORREF d_crSelectBack = d_crBackground ^ 0x00ffffff;
```

In general, when a window loses the keyboard focus, it should hide its selection. When focus is restored, the window should again show the selection. We say "in general" because a few situations exist in which a window will still show its selection state even though it has lost the focus. In particular, two windows might need to simultaneously display the selected state. For a more detailed discussion on this topic, see *The Windows Interface Guidelines for Software Design: An Application Design Guide* (Microsoft Press).

To get a sense for when to show the selection state and when to hide it, run some of the popular Windows applications (either Windows 95, 98, or NT). If you watch closely, you should see that numerous small visual cues indicate changes in activation and focus. Some of these — for example, the change in title bar color — are handled by Windows 98. Other state changes — such as the three we've discussed here — must be handled by your application. But rather than dictate hard-and-fast rules, we should point out that the most important criterion is what works for your users.

Keyboard Demo Program

Now that you've learned about keyboard input, it's time to show you a program that demonstrates the principles, highlights of which are given in Listing 3-3. We've built and included a simple program named KeyboardDemo. It displays `WM_KEYDOWN`, `WM_KEYUP`, and `WM_CHAR` messages sent to the View window.

Demo Program

KeyboardDemo
CD-ROM Location: **Chap03\KeyboardDemo**
Program Name: **KeyboardDemo.EXE**
Source Code Modules in Text: **KeyboardDemoDlg.cpp**

◆ ◆ ◆ ◆ ◆

Listing 3-3: KeyboardDemoDlg.cpp Source Code File Highlights

```
// KeyboardDemoDlg.cpp : implementation file
//

/////////////////////////////////////////////////////////////////
// CKeyboardEventList message handlers

void CKeyboardEventList::OnChar(UINT nChar, UINT nRepCnt,
  UINT nFlags)
{

  // Call the function that adds the event
  // to the list.
  AddEvnt( "WM_CHAR", nChar, nRepCnt, nFlags );
```

(continued)

Listing 3-3 *(continued)*

```
  // Call the default handler.
  CListBox::OnChar(nChar, nRepCnt, nFlags);
}

void CKeyboardEventList::OnKeyDown(UINT nChar, UINT nRepCnt,
  UINT nFlags)
{

  // Call the function that adds the event
  // to the list.
  AddEvnt( "WM_KEYDOWN", nChar, nRepCnt, nFlags );

  // Call the default handler.
  CListBox::OnKeyDown(nChar, nRepCnt, nFlags);
}

void CKeyboardEventList::OnKeyUp(UINT nChar, UINT nRepCnt,
  UINT nFlags)
{

  // Call the function that adds the event
  // to the list.
  AddEvnt( "WM_KEYUP", nChar, nRepCnt, nFlags );

  // Call the default handler.
  CListBox::OnKeyUp(nChar, nRepCnt, nFlags);
}

void CKeyboardEventList::AddEvnt( const char *lpszEvent,
  UINT nChar, UINT nRepCnt, UINT nFlags )
{
  CString strEvent;

  // Format the string. It'll have
  // message name, char, repeat count,
  // flags, extended key flag, context code,
  // previous key state, and transition
  // state value.
  strEvent.Format(
    "%-10s  %3d  %2d  %3d   %d   %d   %d   %d",
    lpszEvent,
    nChar, nRepCnt, nFlags & 0xff,
    ( nFlags > 8 ) & 1,
    ( nFlags > 13 ) & 1,
    ( nFlags > 14 ) & 1,
    ( nFlags > 15 ) & 1 );

  // Add the string to the event list.
  AddString( strEvent );

  // We'll limit the entries in the list
```

```
    // to 30 so it doesn't get too long.
    if( GetCount() >= 30 )
      DeleteString( 0 );

  }
```

Summary

In contrast to its support for graphic output and user-interface objects, Windows 98 support for mouse and keyboard input is fairly low level. You are notified of individual keyboard keystrokes — that is, down and up transitions — as well as individual mouse movement and mouse button transitions. This gives you a great deal of flexibility for shaping your software's user interface, but it requires a lot of work on your part if it is to be handled robustly.

The next chapter shows you how to draw to a window using the Windows Graphics Device Interface (GDI). You should then be ready to create useful applications by combining what you know about mouse and keyboard input with the graphics capabilities of Windows 98.

✦ ✦ ✦

CHAPTER 4

Graphics

In This Chapter

Examining the Graphics Device Interface

Understanding different types of graphics

Learning about the device context

Demonstrating pens and brushes

Evaluating coordinates and mapping modes

Drawing to a window

Programs have come a long way since 1985, when text-based menus using function keys for user input were common. If you pressed the wrong function key, the computer beeped in the most annoying way. During this time, Atari and Amiga computers enjoyed advanced graphical user interfaces. Pull-down menus and dialog boxes were common on these two machines. It's a testament to Microsoft and IBM that IBM-compatible computers survived while the more capable and attractive competition died.

Today, everything in Windows 98 is graphical. Programmers don't have to worry about drawing menus and dialog boxes; such objects are built into the operating system. But they do have to worry about graphical representations of data and other information in applications. Many programs draw such items as graphs, charts, and diagrams.

Fortunately, Windows 98 provides all of the services necessary for application developers to create graphical programs. This chapter shows you how to take advantage of Windows' native graphics functionality to make your programs come alive.

Introduction to the Graphics Device Interface

GDI, the Graphics Device Interface, is one of three dynamic link libraries that form the core of Microsoft Windows 98. GDI manages all the graphical output from a Windows 98 program. When a drawing package creates a circle, when a word-processing program sends a page of text to a printer, when a screen saver flashes fancy graphics — all of these operations use GDI services to create their output.

Windows 98 itself uses GDI to draw the various parts of the user interface. When you see a window, a menu, or a dialog box, each of these has been drawn with calls to GDI. GDI is even responsible for the mouse cursor (pointer), which seems to float above the other objects on the display screen.

GDI's presence in the system provides you with high-level drawing functions that allow you to produce interesting graphical effects with little effort. For example, it's easy to draw text in a multitude of sizes and colors. You can move and manipulate bitmaps with just a few calls. You can produce sophisticated vector drawings without having to fuss over the math they might otherwise require. All of this comes with a minimum of code because GDI defines the programming interface and — through a large set of device drivers — provides uniform results across a large number of devices.

Types of Graphics

GDI functions let a program create three types of graphical output: text, raster graphics, and vector graphics. Figure 4-1 shows examples of each type. Although these categories might seem arbitrary, they aren't. At the device-driver level, each type has its own set of entry points and ways of operating. At the programming interface, a program controls the appearance of each type using slightly different sets of drawing attributes. By understanding the distinctions between these three types, you can often avoid the confusion that is sometimes caused by inconsistencies in the handling of each type.

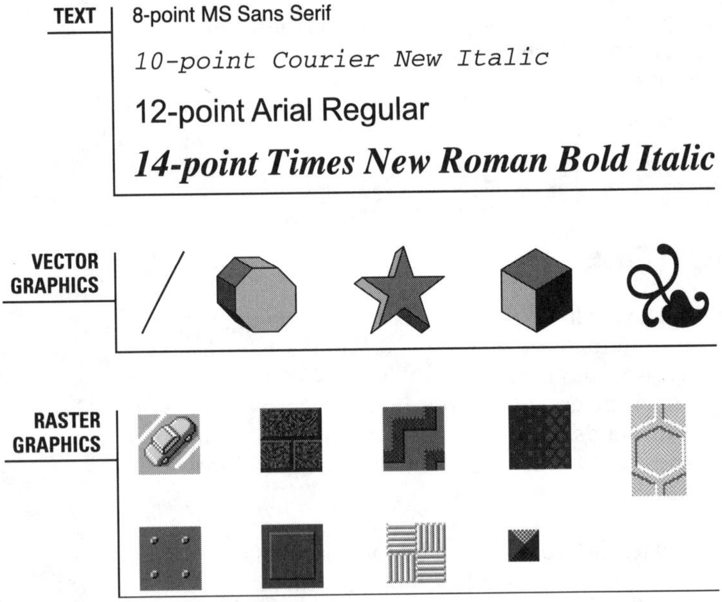

Figure 4-1: GDI functions enable a program to create text, raster graphics, and vector graphics.

Text as graphics

An irony of Windows programming is that although GDI simplifies the creation of raster and vector graphics, it's harder to create text output in a Windows program than in a character-based program. By harder, we mean that quite a few more lines of code are required to get similar results. It's harder to create text because text is treated as graphics.

Why is handling text as graphics a difficult procedure? Perhaps an example will help explain why. Calling the C-runtime function `printf()` for text output is simple. You don't have to worry about the color of the text, the font, or even (in most cases) where the text appears — it simply shows up on the next available line or character position.

Text requires more work in Windows because you can control more aspects than you were ever able to control in the character-based world. Do you want red text? No problem. Need 18-point, bold letters? No problem; you can choose from a large set of such letters. Are you planning to create shadowed effects by drawing the same text overlapping itself by just a pixel or two? You certainly can't do any of that in a character-based environment, but you can do all of it in Windows.

As an example of text as graphics, consider the fact that Windows 98 itself uses text to draw the ornaments of a window (this started with Windows 95). The Minimize box, the Maximize box, and the Close box are all characters from the Marlett font. Because previous versions of Windows used bitmaps for these ornaments, the switch to a TrueType font — which is scalable — gives Windows 98 the flexibility of allowing users to change the title bar size. For the extra work that fonts require, the added benefit is greater flexibility in controlling the resulting output.

Raster graphics

GDI's second type of graphical output is raster graphics. A raster graphics function operates on data stored in arrays called bitmaps. (Chapter 5 covers bitmaps in greater detail.) The most obvious example of a bitmap is projected onto the display screen of a computer when the power is on. A standard VGA monitor's 640x480 image is little more than a bitmap that the display adapter hardware makes visible on the display screen. Part of Windows' support for raster graphics is the capability to create offscreen bitmap images. Like the image on your display screen, such bitmaps can hold all kinds of graphic data.

Other examples of raster graphics are icons and cursors (mouse pointers), which you add to a program by editing the resource file. Window movement on the display screen is yet another example of raster graphics. When the user picks up a window and moves it to another location on the display screen, a raster graphics function picks up the rectangle of pixels at the source and moves it to the destination rectangle.

Windows' user interface also makes use of raster graphics in other ways. For example, most of the pixels in a typical Windows 98 application are drawn by making raster graphics function calls. In particular, all of the white (or background color) space that's not text in a window is drawn by calling the `PatBlt()` function. The thin lines that make up window borders are also drawn using this pattern fill function, with the destination rectangle set to draw a very thin pattern.

Because the data on the display screen is stored in arrays of raster data, bitmaps are useful for caching complex graphical objects for fast-display screen drawing. You can build complex drawings ahead of time—either on the fly or at program build time—so the bitmap image is ready and waiting. Whether the image is a cartoon character, a logo, or some other complex symbol, it can be quickly copied from the bitmap cache to your display screen, as needed. The only problem with bitmaps is the space that they consume, both in RAM and on disk. For example, a screen-size, 640x480, 8-bit-per-pixel, 256-color bitmap occupies approximately 300K. To ensure that your bitmaps are worth the space they consume, you'll want to cache only your most commonly drawn graphical objects.

One very practical use of raster data involves capturing screen shots for documentation purposes. This capability is useful for creating everything from an application's design document to end-user documentation. The PrtScr key copies the entire screen to the clipboard. A slight variation, Alt+PrtScr, copies only the top-level window. From the clipboard, these bitmap images can then be pasted to a word-processing document. For example, that's how we created all the screen shots that you see in this book.

Vector graphics

In the context of GDI, the term vector graphics refers to the drawing functions that create lines and filled figures. GDI has a whole set of functions for drawing straight lines, curves, polygons, pie wedges, and rectangles. You can call these functions with any raster or text function to mix text and graphics in any way that suits you.

When most people think of graphics, they think of geometric shapes. It's ironic, then, that very few vector graphic functions are called by Windows 98 when it draws the user interface. Instead, menus, dialog boxes, and all parts of windows are drawn using only text and raster graphic calls. Even though a window border looks like a straight line and therefore might seem to involve vector graphic calls, in fact, window borders are drawn with raster graphic calls.

Aside from drawing packages, most applications don't make much use of GDI's vector graphics. There's nothing wrong with these functions; it's just that most business uses are text-based. And for complex images, most programs use bitmaps (or icons).

GDI's three types of graphic output—text, raster, and vector—combine to provide numerous choices for creating a wide range of visual effects. To make the most of each type requires a bit of imagination. For example, most programmers don't typically think of text as graphics. But the window ornaments in Windows 98 show one way that this can be done.

GDI Devices

Built-in support for text, raster graphics, and vector graphics isn't required for a graphics device to be a GDI device. Some devices can do it all — most notably printers that use Adobe's Postscript language and printers that use the Microsoft At Work print technology. But the vast majority of graphics devices — that is, display adapters and printers — don't have anywhere near this sophistication.

The only requirement for being a GDI device is the capability to turn on a pixel. Beyond that, GDI can do most of the work of decomposing drawing requests into a simpler form. It's up to each device driver to tell GDI exactly what that specific device can and cannot do. The driver passes GDI a set of device capability bits that GDI uses to modify its drawing requests.

On devices with limited capabilities, GDI does most of the drawing work. Using its built-in drawing simulations, GDI can convert all text and vector calls into raster data. Although raster data occupies more space than higher-level drawing functions, this is offset by the benefit of being able to render highly complex GDI drawings on even the least capable device.

For more capable devices, GDI does less of the work. After all, if a device can handle a drawing request — perhaps using special hardware — GDI puts less demand on the system's CPU. Also, higher-level drawing requests take much less memory and disk space, providing even greater improvement in overall system throughput.

The capability to work on a wide range of devices is one reason why Microsoft calls GDI a device-independent graphics package. If a drawing capability doesn't exist on the device itself, GDI steps in with a software simulation to create a reasonable result. If a device does have a built-in capability, GDI gets out of the way and lets the user enjoy the speed advantage of hardware-based graphics.

The types of devices supported by GDI can be divided into two categories: physical devices and pseudodevices. It's a useful distinction because it helps clarify GDI's device-independent nature. The distinction also points to another aspect of GDI: A single set of drawing calls can be used to draw on both physical and logical drawing surfaces.

Physical devices

From an application's point of view, there are two basic physical devices: display screens and printers. When drawing on a display screen, an application is always drawing inside a window. The window manager makes sure that the drawing from one application doesn't accidentally spill over into the windows that belong to other applications.

GDI enforces window boundaries using a feature known as clipping. Clipping is the definition of drawing boundaries. The most obvious drawing boundaries are the borders of windows, which the system manages for you. In addition, you can create your own drawing boundaries by creating your own clipping regions. For example, you might use this capability to create a brick wall between the drawings done by two different parts of an application without creating additional windows.

In the same way that clipping serves to enforce boundaries between drawings on the display screen, GDI uses another technique — spooling — to enforce the boundaries between drawings done to the printer. Although the Windows implementation of spooling might differ from that of other operating systems, the principle is the same. Print jobs are stored until the printer is ready to receive them.

When sending output to a printer, you must make some special considerations, such as the paper size, the orientation, and the available fonts. But you'll use the same set of GDI functions whether you're drawing on the display screen or on a printer. In practical terms, this means that you can write a single piece of drawing code for both types of devices.

Pseudodevices

Pseudodevices provide a way to store pictures. GDI has two types of pseudodevices: bitmaps and metafiles. When using the term *pseudodevice*, we refer to the fact that the API gives both of these storage devices the same respect that it gives a physical device. But bitmaps and metafiles obviously aren't devices in the traditional sense. Aside from the RAM or the disk space in which they are stored, they have no physical hardware. They are, in effect, software simulations of a logical device.

A bitmap is an array of picture elements. In the same way that you can call GDI functions to draw on the display screen or on the printer, you can call GDI functions to draw on a bitmap. Although a bitmap simulates a raster drawing surface, you aren't limited to using only raster graphics calls. Instead, you can make any text, raster graphic, or vector graphic drawing calls to draw on a bitmap.

GDI's second type of pseudodevice is the metafile. While a bitmap is an array of pixels, metafiles are lists of drawing calls. Like bitmaps, metafiles store pictures. Bitmaps hold the pixels that are drawn after a function call. Metafiles capture GDI function calls before any pixels are illuminated. A metafile is basically a recording of a set of drawing calls, including parameters, that can be played back to create a picture on any other GDI device.

To give you a better idea of what's in a metafile, we should point out that there is nothing intrinsically graphical about capturing function call parameters. You could, for example, create a similar mechanism to log calls made to the C-runtime string routines. After a program runs, you might have a list containing several thousand references to `strcpy()`, `strcat()`, and other functions, along with the parameters used. We're not sure what good this would do, because you wouldn't know the meaning of all those parameters without some additional data. However, when you record GDI drawing calls in a metafile, you have a very good chance of re-creating your original picture when you replay the metafile.

The record-and-playback nature of metafiles provides a great deal of flexibility for storing pictures. However, that flexibility comes at a cost. For complicated pictures, drawing is slower with a metafile than with a comparable bitmap. The drawback to bitmaps, though, is that they tend to consume quite a bit of memory. To decide which pseudodevice you should use, you must study both and decide when the tradeoffs make one more useful to you than the other.

The Device Context

Whenever you draw to any GDI device—whether it is a physical device or a pseudodevice—you always need access to a data structure called a device context (DC). In fact, a handle to a device context is always the first parameter to a GDI drawing call in the native API.

MFC wraps GDI's DC into a set of C++ classes. This includes CDC and the CDC-derived classes. Many of the members of these classes are simple inline wrapper functions around native GDI drawing calls.

To draw on the display screen, a Windows 98 program must have a DC for the display. And to create output on a printer, yet another DC is required—this one created specifically for the printer. If the same program also wants to create output in a metafile and a bitmap, a third and a fourth DC are required. The role of a DC, then, is to provide a connection between a program and either a physical device or a pseudodevice.

In addition to providing a device connection, a DC holds a collection of drawing attribute settings. For example, one drawing attribute in the DC is the text color. When a text drawing function is called, the function refers to the text color attribute to determine the correct color for the text.

You can change any drawing attribute at any time by calling specific GDI functions. For example, the `SetTextColor()` function sets the text color. For every attribute-setting function, there is a comparable attribute query function. For example, to find out the current text color settings, you call `GetTextColor()`.

DC drawing attributes

Table 4-1 summarizes the 25 attributes that GDI stores in a DC. The Description column provides details about default settings and how to change each attribute; check marks indicate which drawing attributes affect each of the three types of graphic objects (text, raster graphic, vector graphic). The functions mentioned in Table 4-1 are member functions of CDC, the MFC class that wraps the GDI device context.

Table 4-1
Drawing Attributes That GDI Stores in a Device Context

Attribute	*Description*	*Text*	*Raster*	*Vector*
Arc direction	Default=Counterclockwise. Determines whether arcs are drawn in a clockwise (`AD_CLOCKWISE`) or counterclockwise (`AD_COUNTERCLOCKWISE`) direction. Set by calling `SetArcDirection()`.			✓
Background color	Default=`RGB`(255,255,255) – that is, white. Used for the background of normal text, in color-to-monochrome bitmap conversions, and for the background of styled (nonsolid) pens and hatched brushes. Set by calling `SetBkColor()`.	✓	✓	✓
Background mode	Default=`OPAQUE`. Turns use of background color ON (`OPAQUE`) or OFF (`TRANSPARENT`). Set by calling `SetBkMode()`.	✓	✓	✓
Bounds rectangle	Default=Disabled. When enabled, tells GDI to keep track of the area into which it has drawn. Control with `SetBoundsRect()`.	✓	✓	✓
Brush	Default=White brush. Defines the interior color of closed figures. In MFC, create a `CBrush` object, and then select it into the DC by calling `SelectObject()`.		✓	✓
Brush origin	Default=(0,0). Sets the point in device space to align a brush. Necessary only for hatched and dithered brushes, because only these types can have misalignments. Set by calling `SetBrushOrg()`.			✓
Clipping region	Default=Entire drawing surface. Defines drawing boundaries. Set by creating a clipping region (`CRgn`) and selecting it into a DC (`SelectClipRgn()`).	✓	✓	✓
Color adjustment	Default=No adjustment. Defines the changes to bitmaps stretched with calls to `StretchBlt()` and `StretchDIBits()`. Set by calling `SetColorAdjustment()`.	✓		

Attribute	*Description*	*Text*	*Raster*	*Vector*
Current position	Default=(0,0). An (x,y) pair originally created to assist in line drawing. Enable for text by calling `SetText.` `Align()` with the `TA_UPDATECP` flag. Set attribute by calling `SetCurrentPosition()`.	✓		✓
Drawing mode	Default=`R2_COPYPEN`. Determines how Boolean operators are used when vector graphics are drawn. Set by calling `SetROP2()`.			✓
Font	Default=System font. Determines which set of graphic figures are used for drawing text. In MFC, set by creating a `CFont` object and connecting it to a DC by calling `SelectObject()`.	✓		
Graphics mode	Default=`GM_COMPATIBLE`. Determines whether GDI ignores world transform and other Win32 enhancements (Windows 3.1-compatible) or whether these are used (`GM_ADVANCED`). Set by calling `SetGraphicsMode()`.	✓	✓	✓
Mapping mode	Default=`MM_TEXT`. Controls much of coordinate mapping. In the default mode, one logical unit equals one device unit. Set by calling `SetMapMode()`.	✓	✓	✓
Miter limit	Default=10.0. Determines how much miter (pointiness) to allow in a join of a geometric line before capping off the corner. (Note: This setting only affects lines drawn with pens that have the `PS_JOIN_MITER` style.) Set by calling `SetMiterLimit()`.			✓
Palette	Default=System palette. Supported only by certain devices, it gives applications control over how the physical color table, or palette, is set. To use this attribute, create a `CPalette` object and connect to a device by calling `SelectPalette()`.	✓	✓	✓
Pen	Default=Black pen. Used by vector graphics functions to draw the borders of geometric figures such as rectangles and pie wedges, as well as for drawing straight and curved lines. Set by creating a `CPen` object and connecting to a device by calling `SelectObject()`.			✓

(continued)

Table 4-1 *(continued)*

Attribute	*Description*	*Text*	*Raster*	*Vector*
Polygon filling mode	Default=ALTERNATE. Determines how the interior spaces of complex, overlapping polygons are to be filled. With a five-pointed star, for example, should the center be filled or not? The default, ALTERNATE, means *No*. The other choice, WINDING, means *Yes*. Change by calling SetPolyFillMode().			✓
StretchBlt mode	Default=BLACKONWHITE. Determines how pixels are removed when a bitmap is shrunk using the StretchBlt() API. Set by calling SetStretchBltMode().		✓	
Text alignment	Default=TA_LEFT | TA_TOP. Determines the alignment between text drawing coordinates and the resulting text box. Default is upper-left, but eight other alignments are possible. Set by calling SetTextAlign().	✓		
Text color	Default=RGB(0,0,0) – that is, black. Determines the foreground color of pixels. (See also the background color attribute). Set by calling SetTextColor().	✓		
Text extra spacing	Default=0. Determines how many pixels are to be padded into each character cell in a string. Used to expand a string to fill a margin. Set by calling SetTextCharacterExtra().	✓		
Text justification	Default=(0,0). Determines how many pixels to pad into *break characters* (that is, spaces) to help a line of text fill out a margin. Set by calling SetTextJustification().		✓	
Viewport extent	Default=(1,1). Used with a mapping mode of MM_ISOTROPIC or MM_ANISOTROPIC. Helps scale a drawing by modifying the device coordinate side of the scaling ratio. Set by calling SetViewportExt().	✓	✓	✓
Viewport origin	Default=(0,0) – that is, the upper-left corner of device space. Moves the origin around the device space. Set by calling SetViewportOrg().	✓	✓	✓

Attribute	Description	Text	Raster	Vector
Window extent	Default=(1,1). Used with a mapping mode of MM_ISOTROPIC or MM_ANISOTROPIC. Scales a drawing by modifying the world coordinate side of the scaling ratio. Set by calling SetWorldExt().	✓	✓	✓
Window origin	Default=(0,0). Moves the origin around the world coordinate space. Set by calling SetWindowOrg().	✓	✓	✓

A simple OnDraw() function

When you create a single- or multiple-document AppWizard program, you'll find a function in the view class named OnDraw(). This function is automatically created by the AppWizard. It receives a message every time your view window gets a WM_PAINT message (more about this message in the next section). A CDC class pointer is passed to the OnDraw() function. The CDC pointer can be used to draw to the view window. A simple OnDraw() function follows that draws a rectangle to the view window:

```
void CMyView::OnDraw(CDC* pDC)
{
  CMyDoc* pDoc = GetDocument();
  ASSERT_VALID(pDoc);

  // Here is where the code we add
  // to draw a rectangle begins.
  RECT Rect;
  Rect.left = Rect.top = 10;
  Rect.right = Rect.bottom = 100;

  // Create a red brush.
  // The RGB macro lets you specify
  // the R, G, and B color components
  // respectively. Their values range
  // from 0 to 255.
  CBrush Brush( RGB( 255, 0, 0 ) );

  // Draw to the window using the GDI
  // FillRect() function.
  pDC->FillRect( &Rect, &Brush );

}
```

The default DC settings provide a good starting place for drawing. The best way to learn about GDI drawing is by writing small programs that draw a few simple objects. As you begin to experiment with new drawing functions, you won't have to make many changes to DC attributes to get reasonable results. Once you have a clearer understanding of how various drawing functions work, you can begin to explore the role of individual drawing attributes.

Try This

Getting Started with GDI Functions

This exercise is intended to get your feet wet by creating a simple program with which you can experiment.

1. With the AppWizard, create a single-document program named Graphics.
2. Open the GraphicsView.cpp file and find the `OnDraw()` function.
3. Add your code below the `ASSERT_VALID()` macro.

   Start by drawing a line that goes from 10, 10 to 100, 100 as follows:

   ```
   pDC->MoveTo( 10, 10 );
   pDC->LineTo( 100, 100 );
   ```
4. Compile the program and run it.
5. Change the line drawing code so that your program draws a rectangle as follows:

   ```
   pDC->Rectangle( 10, 10, 100, 100 );
   ```
6. Compile and run the program.

◆ ◆ ◆ ◆ ◆

The WM_PAINT Message

For drawing in a window, the most important message is `WM_PAINT`. In simplest terms, this message asks a window to redraw its contents. There are many reasons why you might get this message. For example, another window might open on top of your window and overwrite its contents. Or, a user might decide to unminimize a previously minimized window. Or, it might simply be that your program is just starting up.

Whatever the reason for a window getting a `WM_PAINT` message, the system can't re-create the contents of a window's client area. The original Windows development team considered various ways that the system might be able to store window data. One possibility was to take a snapshot of a window before it was covered by other windows. The sheer amount of memory required for this approach made it an unworkable solution.

In the character-based world, a screen full of data can be stored in a tiny, 2K buffer. In the graphics world of Windows 98, however, a 256-color, 640x480 window needs 300K. With several applications running, a megabyte or more would be quickly eaten up. This was too high a price to pay for the first version of Windows, when system memory totaled only one megabyte! With Windows 98 targeted to run in 16 megabytes, a megabyte of window snapshots is still too much memory for too little benefit.

Even if memory wasn't a problem, however, another problem remains. If the system stores window snapshots and any part of a window's data changed, the cache would be worthless. In such a situation, the application would have to redraw the contents of the window anyway. As a result, all of the memory and all of the processor time spent saving the snapshot would be wasted.

The WM_PAINT message is the solution to the problem of keeping the state of a window up to date. Windows makes every application entirely responsible for maintaining the contents of its windows. The WM_PAINT message provides the mechanism by which the system tells you that it's time to refresh a window. All you have to do is make sure that your program retains whatever state information it needs for accomplishing this task.

Drawing coordinates

When a DC is first created, its default coordinates are pixel—or device—units. As needed, you can modify the entire coordinate system to use inches, centimeters, or printer point units. You can also arbitrarily scale your drawings using *rubber sheet graphics,* where you change the mapping mode and the origin. But the default units, which we're going to use, are device units. In DC attribute terms, this is known as the MM_TEXT mapping mode.

The default origin—that is, coordinate (0,0)—is located in the upper-left corner of the drawing surface. On the display screen, this means the upper-left corner of the window's client area. On the printed page, it means the upper-left corner of whatever would be the top of the page. Just as you can change the coordinate system, you can also change the location of the origin. For our purposes, though, we're going to stick with the default origin.

The default direction of movement along the *x* and *y* axes is a little different from the Cartesian coordinate system you may have studied in school. Figure 4-2 shows the default orientation of both axes, along with the location of the origin in the window.

In a window, the default coordinate system is called client-area coordinates. Because the same coordinates are used for mouse input, client-area coordinates make it easy to match mouse clicks to objects you've drawn in your window.

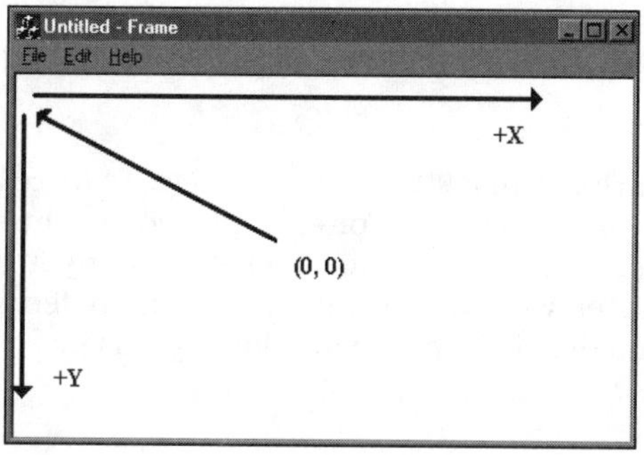

Figure 4-2: Client-area coordinates use device units, have the origin in the upper-left corner, and orient positive x toward the right and positive y toward the bottom.

Requesting a PAINT message

When we introduced the WM_PAINT message, we described it as the most important drawing message. We also noted that you can never know the cause of the message; your window might have changed size, or it might have been previously covered by another window. However, you don't really need to worry about the cause. You simply need to redraw whatever is in your window.

In some cases, however, the cause of a paint message isn't an external factor such as the user changing a window size. Instead, it's an internal factor that only you can recognize. For example, the user might have entered some additional text in a text input window. Or, the user might have added or removed a column of data from a spreadsheet window. Whatever the internal cause, when the data represented in the window changes, you need to generate a paint message.

To generate a paint message, you declare that the contents of the window are invalid. You can do this by calling a few different CWnd member functions. Of these, Invalidate() is the simplest because it takes only a single parameter, a Boolean value that specifies whether to erase the background before drawing. This function declares the entire client area to be invalid:

```
// Force redraw of entire window—first erase contents.
Invalidate( TRUE );
```

Another function that generates paint messages is InvalidateRect(). This function lets you identify the specific rectangle to be redrawn. On slower hardware, this helps minimize screen flicker. On any hardware, you'll want to be conservative when you request a redraw, because too much screen flicker can annoy users. From an ergonomic point of view, such flicker causes fatigue—which not only annoys users but forces them to take more frequent breaks than might otherwise be necessary when using your software. Here's how to request a paint message for a rectangle that's bounded by the coordinates 10, 10, and 100, 100:

```
// Define invalid rectangle and request paint message.
CRect Rect( 10, 10, 100, 100 );
InvalidateRect( &Rect, TRUE );
```

Compared to other messages—for example, those that are associated with mouse or keyboard input—paint messages have a very low priority. After all, if more data comes in, additional paint messages might be necessary. When you declare a window to be invalid, the window might receive other messages before getting the WM_PAINT message.

In some cases, you need to raise the priority of a WM_PAINT message. To force an immediate paint message, you call UpdateWindow(). For example, you might need to do this if you've already called Invalidate() to request a redraw but you also want to immediately draw on the updated window. It's not uncommon to declare part of a window invalid and then immediately force a paint message, as in:

```
InvalidateRect( &Rect, TRUE );
UpdateWindow();
```

But you should save this for cases in which you really need to have your window redrawn. Otherwise, you create too much screen flicker on slower display devices. More about screen flicker in the latter part of chapter 5 in the section labeled Double Buffering.

To summarize, when you want the image in a window to be changed, you invalidate the area in which the change will be seen. This area will be drawn during a subsequent WM_PAINT message. The UpdateWindow() call does not declare part of a window to be invalid. It simply accelerates repainting for invalidated areas. If no area is invalid, calls to UpdateWindow() have no effect on the contents of a window. Windows' conservative paint policy limits the drawing—via clip rectangles—to only the part of a window that is invalid.

We mentioned that calling UpdateWindow() forces an immediate repaint so that you can draw over a valid window. However, this makes sense only if you're drawing in response to some other message besides WM_PAINT. Let's talk about how you'd do this, and explore some of the issues you must address.

Drawing outside PAINT messages

In some cases, you need to draw in response to messages other than WM_PAINT. We should mention that one school of thought suggests that you draw only when you get a paint message. This centralizes your drawing code, which helps to make it more robust. This is a good goal to work toward.

However, to enhance a program's performance or its interactivity for the user, you might need to draw in response to other messages. For example, consider a text editing window. If such a program generated a paint message for every character typed, it would run very slowly (particularly noticeable on slower systems). The overhead associated with continually creating paint messages would use too much processing time.

Or, consider a drawing program that lets a user pick up a graphic object and move it around a window. As the object is moved, it must be redrawn to show the user its new, tentative location. Once again, creating a paint message for each new location would create too much overhead. For both of these cases, you'll want to draw in response to other messages besides the paint message.

However, a word of caution is needed here. If you draw and erase a temporary object—for example, a stretchable rubber rectangle—there's no problem. But if you draw more permanent objects, your painting code will have to know about those objects. After all, you don't know when a user will force a redraw of a window. All the user needs to do to make this happen is to minimize and then maximize your window. The same result occurs when another application's window is maximized over your window. When your application becomes the active application, you'll have to handle a paint message for your entire window. Any lack of synchronization between your paint and nonpaint drawing code will become painfully obvious to your users.

Setting aside these caveats and concerns, it's relatively easy to draw in response to other messages. Instead of using the CDC class, you use a `CClientDC` object. The clipping for a `CClientDC` is set to the entire client area of a window. For example, here is how to say "Hello Windows 98," which is centered under the cursor, when the user clicks the left mouse button:

```
void CMyView::OnLButtonDown(UINT nFlags, CPoint point)
{
  // Create a CClientDC class.
  CClientDC ClientDC( this );

  // Create a CString object with the text.
  CString strText = "Hello Windows 98";

  // Get the size of this text string in terms of
  // this DC.
  CSize size = ClientDC.GetTextExtent( strText,
   strText.GetLength() );

  // Calculate the coordinates to which we need to draw
  // in order to center the text about the mouse point.
  int xCentered = point.x - ( size.cx / 2 );
  int yCentered = point.y - ( size.cy / 2 );

  // Draw the text to the window.
  ClientDC.TextOut( xCentered, yCentered, strText );
}
```

So far, the sample code in this chapter has shown you how to fetch a DC and draw a line of text using the default DC attributes. The default settings are useful, but you'll eventually want to control some or all of the attributes that affect the appearance of text. We'll delve into those topics next.

Controlling the Appearance of Text

To change the appearance of text, you change one of the DC attributes that affect text. As summarized in Table 4-2, eight attributes affect the appearance or the positioning of text. The most effective way to understand the changes that a DC attribute controls is to see the text change in a real program. If your computer is handy, you might consider generating a tiny AppWizard program so that you can experiment with each attribute, as it is discussed. In a Doc/View application, don't forget that you'll want to paint in a view window.

Table 4-2
DC Attributes That Affect the Appearance of Text

Attribute	*Description*
Background color	Default=RGB(255,255,255), or white. Used for the background of normal text, in color-to-monochrome bitmap conversions, and for the background of styled (nonsolid) pens and hatched brushes. Set by calling SetBkColor().
Background mode	Default=`OPAQUE`. Turns use of background color ON (`OPAQUE`) or OFF (`TRANSPARENT`). Set by calling SetBkMode().
Current position	Default=`(0,0)`. An (x,y) pair originally created to assist in line drawing. Enable for text by calling `SetTextAlign()` with the `TA_UPDATECP` flag. Set attribute by calling `SetCurrentPosition()`.
Font	Default=System font. Determines which set of graphic figures are used for drawing text. In MFC, set by creating a CFont object and connecting to a DC by calling `SelectObject()`.
Text alignment	Default=`TA_LEFT | TA_TOP`. Determines the alignment between text drawing coordinates and the resulting text box. Default is upper-left, but eight other alignments are possible. Set by calling `SetTextAlign()`.
Text color	Default=`RGB(0,0,0)`, or black. Determines the foreground color of pixels. (See also Background color). Set by calling `SetTextColor()`.
Text extra spacing	Default=0. Determines how many pixels are to be padded into each character cell in a string. Used to expand a string to fill a margin. Set by calling `SetTextCharacterExtra()`.
Text justification	Default=(0,0). Determines how many pixels to pad into break characters (that is, spaces) to help a line of text fill out a margin. Set by calling `SetTextJustification()`.

Basic text attributes

Aside from the font, which we'll cover later, the two basic categories of text attributes are used to control the color and the positioning of text.

GDI color support

Before you can change the color of text, you need to understand how to specify color in GDI. The basic Windows 98 data type for holding color values is `COLORREF`. The easiest way to define colors is by using the `RGB()` macro, which takes three parameters that define the red, green, and blue color components. For each color component, you specify a value in the range 0-255. For example, here are three color values — one each for red, green, and blue:

```
COLORREF crRed   = RGB( 255, 0, 0 );
COLORREF crGreen = RGB( 0,255, 0 );
COLORREF crBlue  = RGB( 0, 0,255 );
```

Although this might seem fairly straightforward, a number of factors make this more complex than it first seems. In GDI, these types of color references are called logical colors. Here, logical doesn't mean Boolean. Instead, this term is used to differentiate between logical colors and physical colors, which are the colors that a physical hardware device can actually display. A high-resolution, 16-million color device shouldn't have a problem displaying various combinations of red, green, and blue. But it's a different story for a black-and-white printer. How are these differences handled?

You should think about logical colors in terms of requests. If you request red, and the device can produce red, you get what you asked for. If you request red, and the device can't give you what you want, the device provides the closest possible match. That might mean black! To solve the problem of the black-and-white printer, you start by not asking for colors that aren't available. To find out the number of available colors, you call `CDC::GetDeviceCaps()`, as in:

```
int nColors = pDC->GetDeviceCaps( NUMCOLORS );
```

On color display screens, the system creates a default palette with 20 colors. For devices that support only 16 colors, only the first 16 of these 20 colors are used (the rest turn into white or gray). On devices that support more than 16 colors, these 20 form the default set that are available to applications. Listing 4-1 lists the standard RGB values for fetching these colors.

Listing 4-1: The 20 Standard RGB Values in the Default System Palette

```
// 16-color device support
const COLORREF g_crBlack     = RGB(  0,  0,  0);
const COLORREF g_crYellow    = RGB(255,255,  0);
const COLORREF g_crDkYellow  = RGB(128,128,  0);
const COLORREF g_crRed       = RGB(255,  0,  0);
const COLORREF g_crDkRed     = RGB(128,  0,  0);
const COLORREF g_crMagenta   = RGB(255,  0,255);
const COLORREF g_crDkMagenta = RGB(128,  0,128);
const COLORREF g_crBlue      = RGB(  0,  0,255);
const COLORREF g_crDkBlue    = RGB(  0,  0,128);
const COLORREF g_crCyan      = RGB(  0,255,255);
const COLORREF g_crDkCyan    = RGB(  0,128,128);
const COLORREF g_crGreen     = RGB(  0,255,  0);
const COLORREF g_crDkGreen   = RGB(  0,128,  0);
const COLORREF g_crGray      = RGB(192,192,192);
const COLORREF g_crDkGray    = RGB(128,128,128);
const COLORREF g_crWhite     = RGB(255,255,255);
```

```
// Additional four colors for displays with more than 16
colors.
const COLORREF g_crLtYellow  = RGB(255,251,240);
const COLORREF g_crLtGreen   = RGB(192,220,192);
const COLORREF g_crLtBlue    = RGB(166,202,240);
const COLORREF g_crMedGray   = RGB(160,160,164);
```

On displays that support more than 16 colors, you can always define your own custom palette. When selected into a DC, this gives you access to a much wider range of colors. However, the use of palettes is beyond the scope of this book. The default palette serves nicely for all but the most demanding applications.

Text color

Now that you know how to use the RGB() macros to pick colors, let's look at the three DC attributes that affect text color. These attributes are: text color, background color, and background mode. When you first get a DC, it contains the following default settings for these three values as shown in Table 4-3.

Table 4-3
Default Color Values

Text Color Attributes	*Default Setting*
Text color	Black text: RGB(0,0,0)
Background color	White background: RGB(255,255,255)
Background mode	Use the background color: OPAQUE

To set the color to be used for drawing the foreground pixels of text, you call CDC::SetTextColor(). This function is defined as follows:

```
COLORREF SetTextColor( COLORREF crColor );
```

This function takes a color value as input, and returns the previous text color setting. For example, here's how to get red text:

```
pDC->SetTextColor(RGB( 255,  0,  0 ) );
pDC->TextOut ( x, y, "This is red text" );
```

To set the color for background text pixels, call CDC::SetBkColor(). This function is defined as follows:

```
COLORREF SetBkColor( COLORREF crColor )
```

As you may have surmised, the background pixels are those that are inside the text box but not part of letter strokes. Here's how you set the background color to black:

```
pDC->SetBkColor(RGB(  0,  0,  0));
pDC->TextOut (x, y, "This text has a black background", 32);
```

The final DC attribute that affects the color of text is the background mode. It's basically an on/off toggle for the background mode. The default setting, `OPAQUE`, tells GDI to use the background color. The alternate setting, `TRANSPARENT`, tells GDI not to use the background color in drawing text. You set the background mode by calling `CDC::SetBkMode()`, which is defined as follows:

```
int SetBkMode( int nBkMode );
```

If you're interested in letting your users set the foreground or background colors, you'll probably want to use the Color Selector dialog. This is one of the common dialog boxes that is included as part of Windows 98. With just a few lines of code, you get a fully functioning dialog as follows:

```
CColorDialog ColorDialog;
if( ColorDialog.DoModal() == IDOK ){

  COLORREF Color = ColorDialog.GetColor();

  CString strText;
  strText.Format( "The selected color was RGB( %d, %d, %d )",
    GetRValue( Color ), GetGValue( Color ), GetBValue( Color )
);

  AfxMessageBox( strText );
  }
```

Text alignment

Text alignment describes the relationship between the (*x*,*y*) text coordinate and the text box. The default setting aligns the text below and to the right of the text coordinate.

To set the text alignment, you call `CDC::SetTextAlign()`. This function takes a single parameter, a combination of the flags listed in Table 4-2. The flags in each column are mutually exclusive—that is, you take one flag from each column. The first row of Table 4-4 lists the default settings, which are also marked with an asterisk (*).

Table 4-4
Text Alignment Flags for CDC::SetTextAlign()

x-axis alignment	*y-axis alignment*	*Update current position*
TA_LEFT (*)	TA_TOP (*)	TA_NOUPDATECP (*)
TA_CENTER	TA_BASELINE	TA_UPDATECP
TA_RIGHT	TA_BOTTOM	

You might want to change the default settings if you're going to mix text of different sizes (or even the same size and different fonts) on the same line. The *y*-axis default alignment, TA_TOP, would yield strange results if you didn't adjust the *y*-axis values yourself. Here's how you set the text alignment to accommodate multifont drawing:

```
pDC->SetTextAlign( TA_LEFT | TA_BASELINE );
```

It's also convenient to change the text alignment when you are trying to align the right side of text with another graphic object. Although you could tinker with the *x*-axis value, it's easier to set the alignment as follows:

```
pDC->SetTextAlign( TA_RIGHT | TA_TOP );
```

Another situation in which you might want to change the text alignment is when you want to use the DC's current position value for text. The current position is an (*x*,*y*) coordinate pair that's typically used for vector graphics. However, you can use it for text when you set the TA_UPDATECP flag:

```
pDC->SetTextAlign( TA_UPDATECP );
```

With this setting, the only coordinate used for text drawing is the current position. As each line of text is drawn, the position is updated so it's ready for the next text. You set the current position by calling CDC::MoveTo(). Because it uses the TA_UPDATECP flag, the following code draws its text at (12, 92) instead of at the coordinates specified in the TextOut() call:

```
// Request that text drawing use current position.
pDC->SetTextAlign( TA_UPDATECP );

// Set current value of current position.
pDC->MoveTo( 12, 92 );

// Even though coordinates are specified here, they are ignored.
   pDC->TextOut( 100,200,"This text is not drawn at 100,200",33);
```

Text justification and extra spacing

There are two final text attributes in our basic set: text justification and text extra spacing. Each of these helps you pad out lines of text. You'll pad out text lines to produce WYSIWYG (what-you-see-is-what-you-get) output. For the most part, this means that you tweak the display screen output to mimic the printed output.

To adjust the settings of these two attributes, you call `CDC::SetTextJustification()` and `CDC::SetTextCharacterExtra()`, respectively. `SetTextJustification()` lets you specify the number of pixels to add to each space character. This setting represents additional room beyond what the font would normally use for spaces. If even more padding is needed, you call `SetTextCharacterExtra()` instead of `SetTextJustification()`. `SetTextCharacterExtra()` adds extra pixels to every character (not just the space characters).

We should mention that these two drawing attributes date back to the very first version of Windows, and that other techniques for accomplishing the same results have since been added to Windows. For example, the `ExtTextOut()` function gives you complete control over the width of individual character cells. If you can take the time for the extra work it requires, it's well worth the results. The addition of TrueType fonts to Windows has also cut down on the differences between display screen fonts and printer fonts. An application that exclusively uses TrueType fonts can get reasonably close to WYSIWYG output with little or no character cell padding.

We've covered all the basic text attributes first because they are the simplest. In the following section, we direct our attention to the text attribute that has the greatest effect on the appearance of text, the font.

All about fonts

In this section, we'll cover the basics for creating and using fonts. The easiest approach for working with fonts is to use GDI's stock fonts. But to access a broader range of fonts that are installed in a typical Windows 98 system, you'll need to create a `CFont` object.

A font is a collection of complex graphical images, of a single size and design, that are used to represent character data. Fonts are commonly identified by point size and by name, such as Arial or Times Roman, and perhaps also by style. In common parlance, we refer to specific fonts using such terms as *18-point Times Roman* or *8-point bold Arial*.

If you've never been exposed to the world of fonts, it can be quite a shock to learn that literally thousands of different fonts are available. Windows 98 ships with a basic set of fonts, but numerous font packs are sold to add to this set. And it's not at all uncommon for Windows applications to include even more fonts. For example, Corel Corporation's CorelDRAW application ships with more than 800 fonts.

By default, Windows 98 ships with a few dozen basic fonts. Windows 98 includes a font preview utility—the character map program, CHARMAP—which lets you quickly see the fonts that are loaded in the system. In Figure 4-3, CHARMAP is displaying a basic set of characters from the Times New Roman font.

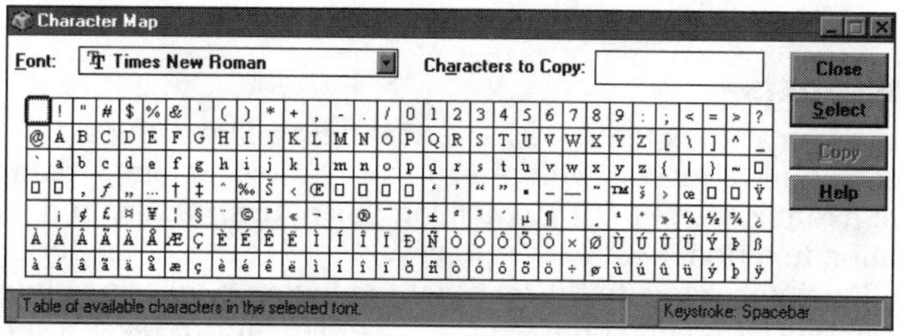

Figure 4-3: The CHARMAP character map program, showing the set of characters in the Times New Roman font.

Selecting a stock font

To select a font, you start by getting your hands on one. In an MFC program, this means having a properly initialized `CFont` object. The simplest way to get a font is to use one of the predefined stock fonts that Windows 98 provides. The following example shows how to get one of the stock fonts:

```
CFont fontStock;
fontStock.CreateStockObject( ANSI_FIXED_FONT );
```

Like every other drawing attribute, a font must be connected to a DC before it affects the appearance of any output. To connect a font to a DC, you call `CDC::SelectObject()`. For example, this code fragment connects the font that we just created to a DC:

```
pDC->SelectObject( &fontStock );
```

Until we select a different font into the DC, all text that we draw will appear using this font.

Fonts differ from other drawing attributes in an important way. Most attributes are simply numbers that are stored in the DC. Within the system, however, a font is its own object, and it has its own life separate from the DC. For every font object that you create, you need to make sure that you destroy the object when you're done using it. Otherwise, there is space wasted somewhere.

In practical terms, this means simply making sure that you destroy every `CFont` object that you create. The destructor to this class helps you make sure that no system memory is wasted. But how do you catch those `CFont` objects that you forget to delete? Fortunately, the Visual C++ tools can help you catch them. Just run the Debug build of your program in the debugger that's built into the Visual C++

development environment. When the program shuts down, you'll see a laundry list of objects that haven't been properly cleaned up.

We should mention that stock fonts aren't actually cleaned up even when you delete their CFont wrapper. The reason is that the system created those fonts for everyone to use.

Selecting nonstock fonts

To select a font other than a stock font, you have to submit a font request to GDI. One way to represent a font request is with the `LOGFONT`—logical font—data structure. To submit a font request to GDI, you fill in this data structure and pass it to a `CFont` initialization function, `CFont::CreateFontIndirect()`. The term indirect in this function name refers to the fact that the function takes a pointer parameter. Another initialization function, `CFont::CreateFont()`, takes a series of parameters that, when taken together, match `LOGFONT`.

A logical font is a lot like the logical color we described earlier in this chapter when we discussed setting text color. A logical font represents a logical request that GDI and the device driver use to figure out which specific physical font to use. In the same way that you can ask for red and get black, you might ask for 24-point Times New Roman and get 12-point Courier.

The problem of mismatched fonts has many solutions, including PANOSE font IDs, font enumeration, and applying your own font mapping algorithms. We won't go into them here, because they are not of general interest. But we have a few suggestions.

The simplest solution would be to always use the device default. A font that you can create using a stock font always provides the device default. It is generally a 10- or 12-point device font. Or, limit your choices to the dozen or so fonts that are built into Windows 98. This is the same general solution that we applied to the red-black color mismatch: Don't ask for something that the system doesn't have.

The following example shows you how to create and use a font in a program's `OnDraw()` function:

Listing 4-2: **Using OnDraw to Create a Font**

```
void CFrameView::OnDraw(CDC* pDC)
{
  CFrameDoc* pDoc = GetDocument();
  ASSERT_VALID(pDoc);

  // Create a CFont object, then create the
  // font with the CreateFont() function.
  CFont NewFont;
  NewFont.CreateFont( 45, 45,
    0, 0, FW_DONTCARE,
```

```
        FALSE, FALSE, FALSE,
        DEFAULT_CHARSET,
        OUT_CHARACTER_PRECIS, CLIP_CHARACTER_PRECIS,
        DEFAULT_QUALITY, DEFAULT_PITCH | FF_DONTCARE,
        "Times New Roman" );

    // Select the newly created font into the
    // DC and remember the old font so that
    // we can restore it later.
    CFont *pOldFont;
    pOldFont = pDC->SelectObject( &NewFont );

    // Draw the text.
    pDC->TextOut( 10, 10, "Hello Fonts!" );

    // Select the old font back into the DC.
    pDC->SelectObject( pOldFont );

}
```

CreateFont() function parameters

The `CreateFont()` function expects a lot of parameters. Here's an explanation of the 14 `CreateFont()` parameters.

The first parameter is the height. It specifies the desired height (in logical units) of the font. The font height can be specified as a value greater than 0, in which case the height is transformed into device units and matched against the cell height of the available fonts. It can be equal to 0, in which case a reasonable default size is used. Otherwise, it can be less than 0, in which case the height is transformed into device units and the absolute value is matched against the character height of the available fonts. The absolute value of `nHeight` must not exceed 16,384 device units after it is converted. For all height comparisons, the font mapper looks for the largest font that does not exceed the requested size or the smallest font if all the fonts exceed the requested size.

The second parameter is the width. It specifies the average width (in logical units) of characters in the font. If the width is 0, the aspect ratio of the device will be matched against the digitization aspect ratio of the available fonts to find the closest match, which is determined by the absolute value of the difference.

The third parameter is the font's *escapement*. It specifies the angle (in 0.1-degree units) between the escapement vector and the x-axis of the display surface. The escapement vector is the line through the origins of the first and last characters on a line. The angle is measured counterclockwise from the *x* axis.

The fourth parameter is the font's orientation. It specifies the angle (in 0.1-degree units) between the baseline of a character and the *x* axis. The angle is measured counterclockwise from the *x* axis for coordinate systems in which the *y* direction is down, and clockwise from the *x* axis for coordinate systems in which the *y* direction is up.

The fifth parameter is the font's weight. It specifies the font weight (in inked pixels per 1,000). Although `nWeight` can be any integer value from 0 to 1,000, the common constants can be `FW_DONTCARE`, `FW_THIN`, `FW_EXTRALIGHT`, `FW_ULTRALIGHT`, `FW_LIGHT`, `FW_NORMAL`, `FW_REGULAR`, `FW_MEDIUM`, `FW_SEMIBOLD`, `FW_DEMIBOLD`, `FW_BOLD`, `FW_EXTRABOLD`, `FW_ULTRABOLD`, `FW_BLACK`, or `FW_HEAVY`. These values are approximate; the actual appearance depends on the typeface. Some fonts have only `FW_NORMAL`, `FW_REGULAR`, and `FW_BOLD` weights. If `FW_DONTCARE` is specified, a default weight is used.

The sixth parameter is a Boolean value that specifies whether the font is italic.

The seventh parameter is a Boolean value that specifies whether the font is underlined.

The eighth parameter is a Boolean value that specifies whether characters in the font are struck out.

The ninth parameter specifies the font's character set. The predefined constants that can be used are `ANSI_CHARSET`, `DEFAULT_CHARSET`, `SYMBOL_CHARSET`, `SHIFTJIS_CHARSET`, and `OEM_CHARSET`. The OEM character set is system-dependent. Fonts with other character sets may exist in the system. An application that uses a font with an unknown character set must not attempt to translate or interpret strings that are to be rendered with that font. Instead, the strings should be passed directly to the output device driver. The font mapper does not use the `DEFAULT_CHARSET` value. An application can use this value to allow the name and size of a font to fully describe the logical font. If a font with the specified name does not exist, a font from any character set can be substituted for the specified font. To avoid unexpected results, applications should use the `DEFAULT_CHARSET` value sparingly.

The tenth parameter specifies the desired output precision. The output precision defines how closely the output must match the requested font's height, width, character orientation, escapement, and pitch. The values it can be are `OUT_CHARACTER_PRECIS`, `OUT_STRING_PRECIS`, `OUT_DEFAULT_PRECIS`, `OUT_STROKE_PRECIS`, `OUT_DEVICE_PRECIS`, `OUT_TT_PRECIS`, and `OUT_RASTER_PRECIS`. Applications can use the `OUT_DEVICE_PRECIS`, `OUT_RASTER_PRECIS`, and `OUT_TT_PRECIS` values to control how the font mapper chooses a font when the system contains more than one font with a given name. For example, if a system contains a font named Symbol in raster and TrueType form, specifying `OUT_TT_PRECIS` forces the font mapper to choose the TrueType version. (Specifying `OUT_TT_PRECIS` forces the font mapper to choose a TrueType font whenever the specified font name matches a device or raster font, even when there is no TrueType font of the same name.)

The eleventh parameter specifies the desired clipping precision. The clipping precision defines how to clip characters that are partially outside the clipping region. The values it can be are CLIP_CHARACTER_PRECIS, CLIP_MASK, CLIP_DEFAULT_PRECIS, CLIP_STROKE_PRECIS, CLIP_ENCAPSULATE, CLIP_TT_ALWAYS, and CLIP_LH_ANGLES. To use an embedded read-only font, an application must specify CLIP_ENCAPSULATE. To achieve consistent rotation of device, TrueType, and vector fonts, an application can use the OR operator to combine the CLIP_LH_ANGLES value with any of the other clip precision values. If the CLIP_LH_ANGLES bit is set, the rotation for all fonts depends on whether the orientation of the coordinate system is left-handed or right-handed. For more information about the orientation of coordinate systems, see the description of the orientation parameter. If CLIP_LH_ANGLES is not set, device fonts always rotate counterclockwise, but the rotation of other fonts is dependent on the orientation of the coordinate system.

The twelfth parameter specifies the font's output quality, which defines how carefully the GDI must attempt to match the logical-font attributes to those of an actual physical font. The values it can be are DEFAULT_QUALITY, DRAFT_QUALITY, and PROOF_QUALITY.

The thirteenth parameter specifies the pitch and family of the font. The two low-order bits specify the pitch of the font and can be a combination of either DEFAULT_PITCH, VARIABLE_PITCH, or FIXED_PITCH; and FF_DECORATIVE, FF_DONTCARE, FF_MODERN, FF_ROMAN, FF_SCRIPT, or FF_SWISS. An application can specify a value for the pitch and family by using the boolean OR operator to join a pitch constant with a family constant. Font families describe the look of a font in a general way. They are intended for specifying fonts when the exact typeface desired is not available.

The fourteenth and final parameter is a pointer to a null-terminated string that specifies the typeface name of the font. The length of this string must not exceed 30 characters. The Windows EnumFontFamilies() function can be used to enumerate all currently available fonts. If this parameter is NULL, the GDI uses a device-independent typeface.

Expert Tip

Selecting Devices into DCs

Any time you select a non-stock object in a DC, it's a good idea to remember what object was previously selected into the DC. You always get a pointer to the object when you use the SelectObject() function. For instance, if you use the SelectObject() function to select a newly-created font into the DC, a pointer to a CFont object will be returned. You can record the font that was selected into the DC before you selected your non-stock font in the following way.

```
CFont *pOldFont;
pOldFont = pDC->SelectObject( &NewFont );
```

After you're done using the non-stock font (or any other GDI object for that matter), you must select the old object back into the DC. If your newly-created GDI object is still selected into the DC when you try to delete it (or the object's destructor tries to delete it), the deletion will fail and the memory that the GDI object occupies will be locked until your application quits. Following is the final line that you should add once you're done drawing with the non-stock GDI object:

```
pDC->SelectObject( pOldFont );
```

◆ ◆ ◆ ◆ ◆

Pens and Brushes

GDI provides a number of API functions that an application can call to create custom pens and brushes, including `CreatePen()`, `CreateSolidBrush()`, `CreateHatchBrush()`, and `CreatePatternBrush()`. MFC wraps these functions into the `CPen` and `CBrush` classes so pens and brushes can be dealt with as objects rather than through the raw handles that GDI provides.

The CPen class

The simplest way to create a GDI pen is to construct a `CPen` object and pass it the parameters define the pen as follows:

```
CPen Pen( PS_SOLID, 1, RGB( 255, 0, 0 ) );
```

A second way to create a GDI pen is to construct an uninitialized `CPen` object. This is used most often when the pen declaration and the pen creation come in different places. For instance, the same pen instance might be used, but the color changed at various times. Each time the pen is re-created, you call the `CreatePen()` function. This technique of `CPen` create follows:

```
CPen Pen;
Pen.CreatePen( PS_SOLID, 1, RGB( 255, 0, 0 ) );
```

A third method is to construct an uninitialized `CPen` object, fill in a `LOGPEN` structure describing the pen, and then call `CPen::CreatePenIndirect()` to create the pen. This method probably seems like a lot of trouble. It is. I rarely use it. But it does have a place if you store pen definitions in arrays or in data files. The technique is as follows:

```
CPen Pen;
LOGPEN LogPen;
LogPen.lopnStype = PS_SOLID;
LogPen.lopnWidth = 1;
LogPen.lpenColor = RGB( 255, 0, 0 );
Pen.CreatePenIndirect( &LogPen );
```

`CreatePen()` and `CreatePenIndirect()` return `TRUE` if a pen is successfully created, `FALSE` if it is not. If you allow the object's constructor to create the pen, an exception of type CResourceException is thrown if the pen can't be created. This should happen only if the system is critically low on memory.

A pen has three defining characteristics: style, width, and color. All three of the pen examples in this chapter create a pen whose style is PS_SOLID, whose width is 1 logical unit, and whose color is bright red.

Pen style

The first of the three parameters passed to the CPen constructor, CreatePen(), or CreatePenIndirect() specifies the pen style, which defines the type of line the pen will draw. PS_SOLID creates a pen that draws solid, unbroken lines. The other pen styles are listed in Table 4-5.

Table 4-5
GDI Line Styles

Style	*Description*
PS_SOLID	Creates a solid pen.
PS_DASH	Creates a dashed pen. Valid only when the pen width is 1 or less, in device units.
PS_DOT	Creates a dotted pen. Valid only when the pen width is 1 or less, in device units.
PS_DASHDOT	Creates a pen with alternating dashes and dots. Valid only when the pen width is 1 or less, in device units.
PS_DASHDOTDOT	Creates a pen with alternating dashes and double dots. Valid only when the pen width is 1 or less, in device units.
PS_NULL	Creates a NULL pen.
PSINSIDEFRAME	Creates a pen that draws a line inside the frame of closed shapes produced by the Windows GDI output functions that specify a bounding rectangle (for example, the Ellipse(), Rectangle(), RoundRect(), Pie(), and Chord() member functions). When this style is used with Windows GDI output functions that do not specify a bounding rectangle (for example, the LineTo member function), the drawing area of the pen is not limited by a frame.

The NULL pen draws nothing. Why would you ever want to create a NULL pen? Believe it or not, there are times when a NULL pen comes in handy. Suppose, for example, that you want to draw a solid red circle with no border. If you draw the circle with MFC's CDC::Ellipse() function, Windows will automatically border the circle with the pen currently selected into the device context. You can't tell the Ellipse() function you don't want a border, but you can select a NULL pen into the device context so that the circle will have no visible border. NULL brushes are used in a simpler way. If you want the circle to have a border but want the interior of the circle to be transparent, you select a NULL brush into the device context before doing your drawing.

Pen width

The second parameter passed into CPen's pen-create functions specifies the pen width—the width of the lines the pen will draw. Pen widths are specified in logical units whose physical meanings depend on the mapping mode. You can create PS_SOLID, PS_NULL, and PS_INSIDEFRAME pens of any logical width. But the other pen styles must be one logical unit in width. Specifying a pen width of zero in any style creates a pen that is one pixel width, no matter what the mapping mode.

Pen color

The third and final parameter specified when a pen is created is the pen's color. This is a 24-bit RGB color in which each possible color is defined by red, green, and blue color values ranging from 0 to 255.

Windows predefines three special solid, 1-pixel-wide pens you can use without explicitly creating a pen object. Called stock pens, these pens belong to a group of GDI objects known as stock objects and are created with the CreateStockObject(). The stock pens that are available are defined at WHITE_PEN, BLACK_PEN, and NULL_PEN. The following code creates a stock white pen:

```
CPen Pen;
Pen.CreateStockObject( WHITE_PEN );
```

The following code creates an identical white pen that's not a stock object:

```
CPen Pen;
Pen.CreatePen( PS_SOLID, 1, RGB( 255, 255, 255 ) );
```

In case none of the basic pen styles fits your needs, the CPen class provides a separate constructor for cosmetic and geometric pens that support a wide variety of styling options. You can create a geometric pen, for example, that draws a pattern described by a bitmap image, and you can exercise precise control over endpoints and joins by specifying the end cap style (flat, round, or square) and join style (beveled, mitered, or rounded). The following code creates a geometric pen 16 units wide and draws green solid lines with flat ends. Where two lines meet, the adjoining ends are rounded to form a smooth intersection:

```
LOGBRUSH LogBrush;
LogBrush.lbStyle = BS_SOLID;
LogBrush.lbColor = RGB( 0, 255, 0 );
CPen Pen( PS_GEOMETRIC | PS_SOLID | PS_ENDCAP_FLAT |
PS_JOIN_ROUND,
  16, &LogBrush );
```

Windows 98 places several restrictions on the use of cosmetic and geometric pens, not the least of which is that for the endpoint and join styles to work, figures must first be drawn to paths and then rendered with the `CDC::StrokePath()` function. You define a path by enclosing drawing commands between calls to `CDC::BeginPath()` and `CDC:EndPath()` functions as follows:

```
pDC->BeginPath();
pDC->MoveTo( 0, 0 );
pDC->LineTo( 200, 0 );
pDC->LineTo( 200, 200 );
pDC->LineTo( 0, 200 );
pDC->CloseFigure();
pDC->EndPath();
pDC->StrokePath();
```

The CBrush class

MFC's `CBrush` class encapsulates GDI brushes. Brushes come in three basic varieties: solid brushes, hatch brushes, and pattern brushes. The `CBrush` class provides a constructor for each different brush style.

Solid brushes

Solid brushes paint with solid colors. If your display hardware won't allow a particular solid brush color to be displayed directly, Windows simulates the color by dithering colors that can be displayed.

You can create a solid brush in one step by passing a `COLORRREF` value to the `CBrush` constructor as follows:

```
CBrush Brush( RGB( 255, 0, 0 ) );
```

Or you can create a solid brush in two steps by creating an uninitialized `CBrush` object and calling `CBrush::CreateSolidBrush()` as follows:

```
CBrush Brush;
Brush.CreateSolidBrush( RGB( 255, 0, 0 ) );
```

Both examples create a solid brush that paints bright red. You can also create a brush by initializing a `LOGBRUSH` structure and calling `CBrush::CreateBrushIndirect()`. As with `CPen` constructors, all `CBrush` constructors that create a brush for you throw a resource exception if GDI is critically low on memory and a brush can't be created.

Windows makes seven stock brushes available: `BLACK_BRUSH`, `DKGRAY_BRUSH`, `GRAY_BRUSH`, `LTGRAY_BRUSH`, `HOLLOW_BRUSH`, `NULL_BRUSH`, and `WHITE_BRUSH`. All are solid brushes, and in each case, the identifier is an accurate indicator of the brush's color. `HOLLOW_BRUSH` and `NULL_BRUSH` are two different ways of referring to the same thing: a brush that paints nothing.

Hatch brushes

A *hatch brush* paints with one of six predefined hatch styles modeled after hatching patterns used in engineering and architectural drawings. Hatch brushes are created by passing CBrush's constructor both a hatch index and a COLORREF value, or by calling CBrush::CreateHatchBrushIndirect(). Following is an example that creates a hatch brush with perpendicular crosshatch lines that are oriented at 45-degree angles:

```
CBrush Brush( HS_DIAGCROSS, RGB( 255, 0, 0 ) );
```

The next example creates the same hatch brush in two steps:

```
CBrush Brush;
Brush.CreateHatchBrush( HS_DIAGCROSS, RGB( 255, 0, 0 ) );
```

HS_DIAGCROSS is one of six hatch styles you can choose from. Table 4-6 shows all six hatch styles that are available.

Table 4-6
The Six Hatch Styles

Hatch Style	*Description*
HS_BDIAGONAL	Downward hatch (left to right) at 45 degrees
HS_CROSS	Horizontal and vertical crosshatch
HS_DIAGCROSS	Crosshatch at 45 degrees
HS_FDIAGONAL	Upward hatch (left to right) at 45 degrees
HS_HORIZONTAL	Horizontal hatch
HS_VERTICAL	Vertical hatch

When painting with a hatch brush, Windows fills the space between hatch lines with the default background color unless you change the device context's current background color with CDC::SetBkColor(), or turn off background fills by changing the background mode from OPAQUE to TRANSPARENT with CDC::SetBkMode(). The following example draws a rectangle 100 units square and fills it with white crosshatch lines drawn against a light gray background:

```
CBrush Brush( HS_DIAGCROSS, RGB( 255, 255, 255 ) );
CBrush *pOldBrush;
pOldBrush = pDC->SelectObject( &Brush );
pDC->SetBkColor( RGB( 192, 192, 192 ) );
pDC->Rectangle( 0, 0, 100, 100 );
pDC->SelectObject( pOldBrush );
```

The next example draws a black crosshatched rectangle against the existing background. The background color mode also determines how Windows fills the gaps in lines drawn with stylized pens and fills between the characters in text strings.

```
CBrush Brush( HS_DIAGCROSS, RGB( 0, 0, 0 ) );
CBrush *pOldBrush
pOldBrush = pDC->SelectObject( &Brush );
pDC->SetBkMode( TRANSPARENT );
pDC->Rectangle( 0, 0, 100, 100 );
pDC->SelectObject( pOldBrush );
```

The PenBrushDemo Program

The first demo program in this chapter shows you how to use `CPen` and `CBrush` objects. Because these MFC classes encapsulate GDI pens and brushes, they make it easier for programmers to draw with pens and brushes.

With a menu selection, you can alternate between drawing lines and rectangles to the window. Another menu selection lets you set the line width with which the lines and rectangle border will be drawn.

When lines are drawn to the window, you'll see the defined line patterns such as `PS_DASH` and `PS_DOT` as shown in Figure 4-4. When rectangles are drawn to the window, you'll see the defined fill patterns such as `HS_BDIAGONAL` and `HS_CROSS`.

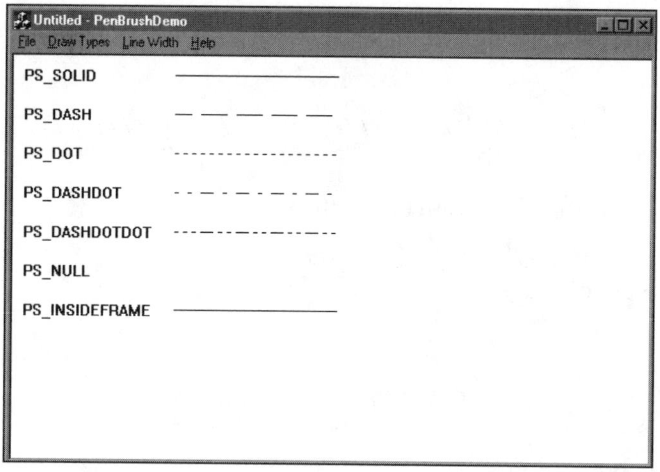

Figure 4-4: This program is showing the different pen styles.

Demo Program

PenBrushDemo
CD-ROM Location: **Chap04\PenBrushDemo**
Program Name: **PenBrushDemo.EXE**
Source Code Modules in Text: **PenBrushDemoView.cpp**

◆ ◆ ◆ ◆ ◆

Listing 4-1: **PenBrush Demo**

```
// PenBrushDemoView.cpp : implementation of
// the CPenBrushDemoView class
//

//////////////////////////////////////////////////////////
// CPenBrushDemoView construction/destruction

CPenBrushDemoView::CPenBrushDemoView()
{

  // Set the initial operation type to line.
  m_nOperationType = 0;

  // Lines will have a width of 1 initially.
  m_nLineWidth = 0;

}

CPenBrushDemoView::~CPenBrushDemoView()
{
}

//////////////////////////////////////////////////////////
// CPenBrushDemoView drawing

void CPenBrushDemoView::OnDraw(CDC* pDC)
{
  CPenBrushDemoDoc* pDoc = GetDocument();
  ASSERT_VALID(pDoc);

  int i;

  // Keep the text strings describing
  // the line styles in a static array.
  static char *szLineStyles[] = {
    "PS_SOLID", "PS_DASH", "PS_DOT", "PS_DASHDOT",
    "PS_DASHDOTDOT", "PS_NULL", "PS_INSIDEFRAME" };

  // Keep the line style definitions in a
  // static array.
  static int nLineStyles[] = {
    PS_SOLID, PS_DASH, PS_DOT, PS_DASHDOT,
    PS_DASHDOTDOT, PS_NULL, PS_INSIDEFRAME };
```

```
// Keep the text strings describing
// the brush styles in a static array.
static char *szBrushStyles[] = {
  "HS_BDIAGONAL", "HS_CROSS", "HS_DIAGCROSS",
  "HS_FDIAGONAL", "HS_HORIZONTAL", "HS_VERTICAL" };

// Keep the brush style definitions in a
// static array.
static int nBrushStyles[] = {
  HS_BDIAGONAL, HS_CROSS, HS_DIAGCROSS,
  HS_FDIAGONAL, HS_HORIZONTAL, HS_VERTICAL };

switch( m_nOperationType ){
  case 0:
    for( i=0; i<7; i++ ){

      // Display the text string describing
      // the line style.
      pDC->TextOut( 10, 10 + i * 35,
        szLineStyles[i] );

      // Create the pen based on the
      // style and width
      CPen Pen( nLineStyles[i],
        1 << m_nLineWidth,
        RGB( 0, 0, 0 ) );

      // Select the CPen object into the DC
      // and remember the CPen object that's
      // selected out.
      CPen *pOldPen = pDC->SelectObject( &Pen );

      // Draw the line.
      pDC->MoveTo( 150, 17 + i * 35 );
      pDC->LineTo( 300, 17 + i * 35 );

      // Select the old CPen object back into
      // the DC.
      pDC->SelectObject( pOldPen );
      }
    break;

  case 1:
    // Create a CPen object based on the line width
    // that the user selected.
    CPen Pen( PS_INSIDEFRAME, 1 << m_nLineWidth,
      RGB( 0, 0, 0 ) );

    // Select the newly-created CPen object into
    // the DC and remember the old CPen object
    // that's selected out.
    CPen *pOldPen = pDC->SelectObject( &Pen );
```

(continued)

Listing 4-1 *(continued)*

```
      for( i=0; i<6; i++ ){

        // Display the text string describing
        // the brush style.
        pDC->TextOut( 10, 23 + i * 55,
          szBrushStyles[i] );
        // Create a CBrush object based on the selected
        // brush style.
        CBrush Brush( nBrushStyles[i], RGB( 0, 0, 0 ) );

        // Select the newly-created CBrush object into
        // the DC and remember the CBrush object that's
        // selected out.
        CBrush *pOldBrush = pDC->SelectObject( &Brush );

        // Create a CRect object with the coordinates
        // of the destination rectangle.
        CRect Rect( 150, 10 + i * 55, 300, 60 + i * 55 );

        // Draw the rectangle.
        pDC->Rectangle( Rect );

        // Select the old CBrush object into the DC.
        pDC->SelectObject( pOldBrush );
        }

      // Select the old CPen object into the DC.
      pDC->SelectObject( pOldPen );
      break;
    }

}

/////////////////////////////////////////////////////////////////////////////
// CPenBrushDemoView message handlers

void CPenBrushDemoView::OnOperationtype()
{

  m_nOperationType =
    LOWORD( GetCurrentMessage()->wParam -
      ID_OPERATIONTYPE_LINES );

  InvalidateRect( NULL, TRUE );
  UpdateWindow();

}

void CPenBrushDemoView::OnUpdateOperationtype(
  CCmdUI* pCmdUI)
{
```

```
    pCmdUI->SetCheck( (int) pCmdUI->m_nIndex ==
      m_nOperationType );

}

void CPenBrushDemoView::OnLinewidth()
{

    m_nLineWidth =
      LOWORD( GetCurrentMessage()->wParam -
        ID_LINEWIDTH_ONE );

    InvalidateRect( NULL, TRUE );
    UpdateWindow();

}

void CPenBrushDemoView::OnUpdateLinewidth(CCmdUI* pCmdUI)
{

    pCmdUI->SetCheck( (int) pCmdUI->m_nIndex ==
      m_nLineWidth );

}
```

Mapping Modes

When an application draws a line from point A to point B, the coordinates passed to `MoveTo()` and `LineTo()` don't specify physical locations on the screen. Instead, they specify coordinates within a logical coordinate system whose properties are defined by the device context. GDI translates logical coordinates into physical coordinates on the screen, or device coordinates, using equations that factor in the current mapping mode as well as other attributes of the device context. In the device coordinate system, the point (0, 0) corresponds to the upper left corner of the device context's display surface, values of *x* and *y* increase as you move to the right and down, and one device unit equals one pixel. In a logical coordinate system, the point (0, 0) defaults to the upper left corner of the display surface but can be moved, and the orientation of the *x* and *y* axes and the physical distance that corresponds to one unit in the *x* or *y* direction are governed by the mapping mode. You can change the mapping mode with the `CDC::SetMapMode()` function, and you can move the origin of a logical coordinate system with the `CDC:SetViewportOrg()` and `CDC::SetWindowOrg()` functions.

Windows 98 supports eight different mapping modes, summarized in Table 4-7.

Table 4-7
Windows Mapping Modes

Mapping Mode	***Description***
MM_ANISOTROPIC	Logical units are converted to arbitrary units with arbitrarily scaled axes. Setting the mapping mode to MM_ANISOTROPIC does not change the current window or viewport settings. To change the units, orientation, and scaling, call the SetWindowExt() and SetViewportExt() member functions.
MM_HIENGLISH	Each logical unit is converted to 0.001 inch. Positive *x* is to the right; positive *y* is up.
MM_HIMETRIC	Each logical unit is converted to 0.01 millimeter. Positive *x* is to the right; positive *y* is up.
MM_ISOTROPIC	Logical units are converted to arbitrary units with equally scaled axes; that is, 1 unit along the *x* axis is equal to 1 unit along the *y* axis. Use the SetWindowExt() and SetViewportExt() member functions to specify the desired units and the orientation of the axes. GDI makes adjustments as necessary to ensure that the *x* and *y* units remain the same size.
MM_LOENGLISH	Each logical unit is converted to 0.01 inch. Positive *x* is to the right; positive *y* is up.
MM_LOMETRIC	Each logical unit is converted to 0.1 millimeter. Positive *x* is to the right; positive *y* is up.
MM_TEXT	Each logical unit is converted to 1 device pixel. Positive *x* is to the right; positive *y* is down.
MM_TWIPS	Each logical unit is converted to 1/20 of a point. (Because a point is 1/72 inch, a twip is 1/1440 inch.) Positive *x* is to the right; positive *y* is up.

The default MM_TEXT mapping mode is the easiest of all the mapping modes to understand because in that mode, logical coordinates translate directly to device coordinates: One logical unit in the *x* or *y* direction equals one pixel on the screen, and values of *x* and *y* increase as you move right and down. In MM_TEXT, as in all of the other mapping modes, the origin of the logical coordinate system coincides with the origin of the device coordinate system unless it is moved with CDC::SetWindowOrg() or CDC::SetViewportOrg(). For a client-area device context, this means that the pixel in the upper left corner of the window's client area initially has the logical coordinates (0, 0).

If you'd prefer that the origin of the coordinate system be in the center of the display surface rather than in the upper left corner, you can move it with CDC:SetWindowOrg() or CDC::SetViewportOrg(). This option applies to all mapping modes, not just MM_TEXT. If you use CWnd::GetClientRect() to initialize a CRect object named Rect with the device coordinates of a window's client area and the DC represents a client-area device context, the following example moves the origin of the coordinate system to the center of the client area:

```
CRect Rect;
GetClientRect( Rect );
pDC->SetViewportOrg( Rect.Width() / 2, Rect.Height() / 2 );
```

Raster Operations

One thing you can do is to change how the color with which you're drawing combines with the destination color. Most of the time, though, drawing to the screen to have it appear exactly how you'd expect is what you'll want. For instance, if you draw a red circle, 99 percent of the time you'll want a red circle to be drawn. Other times, a simple draw operation won't do.

An example in which you might want to use another raster operation is in some animations. A common technique for moving figures around on the screen is to XOR them before moving them to a new location. That is, you set the drawing mode (ROP code) to an exclusive OR operation, then draw the figure where it currently is. XORing one figure over itself completely removes it. Here's why. When you first draw the figure to the screen using an XOR raster operation, the image source combines with the destination. Anywhere the source has a bit that's set, it toggles the corresponding bit in the destination to its opposite value. For instance, if the source bit is set (a one) and the destination bit is not set (a zero), the result will be a one. If the animation must be moved, XORing the same figure in the same location toggles those same bits, once again restoring them to their original state. The bitmap can then be drawn in a new location using an XOR raster operation. Table 4-8 defines the raster operation codes.

Table 4-8
Raster Operations for GDI Drawing

Raster Operation	*Description*
R2_BLACK	Pixel is always black.
R2_WHITE	Pixel is always white.
R2_NOP	Pixel remains unchanged.
R2_NOT	Pixel is the inverse of the screen color.
R2_COPYPEN	Pixel is the pen color.
R2_NOTCOPYPEN	Pixel is the inverse of the pen color.

(continued)

Table 4-8 *(continued)*

Raster Operation	***Description***
R2_MERGEPENNOT	Pixel is a combination of the pen color and the inverse of the screen color (final pixel = (NOT screen pixel) OR pen).
R2_MASKPENNOT	Pixel is a combination of the colors common to both the pen and the inverse of the screen (final pixel = (NOT screen pixel) AND pen).
R2_MERGENOTPEN	Pixel is a combination of the screen color and the inverse of the pen color (final pixel = (NOT pen) OR screen pixel).
R2_MASKNOTPEN	Pixel is a combination of the colors common to both the screen and the inverse of the pen (final pixel = (NOT pen) AND screen pixel).
R2_MERGEPEN	Pixel is a combination of the pen color and the screen color (final pixel = pen OR screen pixel).
R2_NOTMERGEPEN	Pixel is the inverse of the R2_MERGEPEN color (final pixel = NOT(pen OR screen pixel)).
R2_MASKPEN	Pixel is a combination of the colors common to both the pen and the screen (final pixel = pen AND screen pixel).
R2_NOTMASKPEN	Pixel is the inverse of the R2_MASKPEN color (final pixel = NOT(pen AND screen pixel)).
R2_XORPEN	Pixel is a combination of the colors that are in the pen or in the screen, but not in both (final pixel = pen XOR screen pixel).
R2_NOTXORPEN	Pixel is the inverse of the R2_XORPEN color (final pixel = NOT(pen XOR screen pixel)).

Drawing to a Window

This section shows you how to use GDI to draw to a window. The demo program gives you the basics of this procedure.

The GraphicsDemo1 Program

The GraphicsDemo1 program illustrates the basic techniques of drawing to a window. When the program runs, you can draw lines, rectangles, and ellipses. You can select the color with which the program will draw with the color selector common dialog. Additionally, you can set the ROP code so that draw operations are performed with different results.

To draw in the window, just click the left mouse in the window as shown in Figure 4-5. To change the draw operation, draw color, and ROP code use the menu selections.

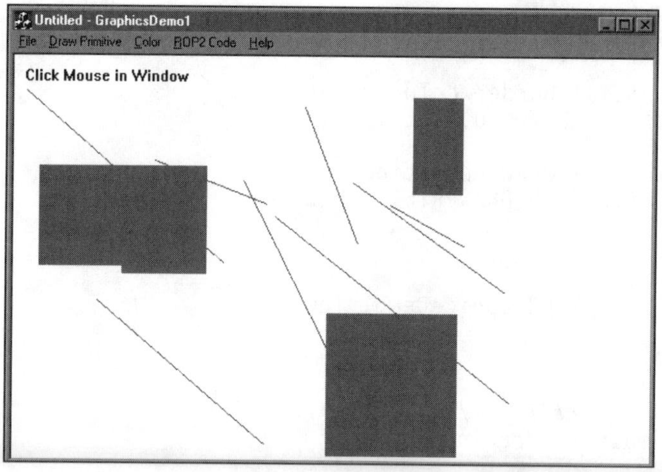

Figure 4-5: This program shows you how to draw into a window in many different ways.

Demo Program

GraphicsDemo1
CD-ROM Location: **Chap04\GraphicsDemo1**
Program Name: **GraphicsDemo1.EXE**
Source Code Modules in Text: **GraphicsDemo1View.cpp**

✦ ✦ ✦ ✦ ✦

Listing 4-2: **GraphicsDemo1**

```
// GraphicsDemo1View.cpp : implementation of
// the CGraphicsDemo1View class
//

///////////////////////////////////////////////////////////
// CGraphicsDemo1View construction/destruction

CGraphicsDemo1View::CGraphicsDemo1View()
{

  // Set the initial raster operation
  // to R2_COPYPEN.
  m_nROP2Code = R2_COPYPEN;

  // Set the initial fill color to red.
  m_FillColor = RGB( 255, 0, 0 );
```

(continued)

Listing 4-2 (continued)

```
  // Set the initial border color to blue.
  m_BorderColor = RGB( 0, 0, 255 );

  // Set the initial draw operation to line.
  m_nDrawPrimitive = ID_DRAWPRIMITIVE_LINE;

}

CGraphicsDemo1View::~CGraphicsDemo1View()
{
}

/////////////////////////////////////////////////////////////
// CGraphicsDemo1View drawing

void CGraphicsDemo1View::OnDraw(CDC* pDC)
{
  CGraphicsDemo1Doc* pDoc = GetDocument();
  ASSERT_VALID(pDoc);

  // OnDraw() doesn't do much. Just display the
  // instructions "Click Mouse in Window".
  pDC->TextOut( 10, 10, "Click Mouse in Window", 21 );
}

/////////////////////////////////////////////////////////////
// CGraphicsDemo1View message handlers

// Store the actual GDI ROP codes in an
// array so that we can easily set the
// ROP code depending on the value of
// m_nROP2Code.
static int nROP2Code[] = {
   R2_BLACK, R2_WHITE, R2_NOP, R2_NOT,
   R2_COPYPEN, R2_NOTCOPYPEN, R2_MERGEPENNOT,
   R2_MASKPENNOT, R2_MERGENOTPEN, R2_MASKNOTPEN,
   R2_MERGEPEN, R2_NOTMERGEPEN, R2_MASKPEN,
   R2_NOTMASKPEN, R2_XORPEN, R2_NOTXORPEN };

// This array contains the IDs for the
// menu items so that we can easily
// scan the list and obtain a zero-based
// index into this list. That way, we'll
// have a value from 0-whatever that lets
// us know which menu item the user selected.
static int nMenuID[] = {
   ID_ROP2CODE_R2BLACKPEN, ID_ROP2CODE_R2WHITE,
   ID_ROP2CODE_R2NOP, ID_ROP2CODE_R2NOT,
   ID_ROP2CODE_R2COPYPEN, ID_ROP2CODE_R2NOTCOPYPEN,
   ID_ROP2CODE_R2MERGEPENNOT, ID_ROP2CODE_R2MASKPENNOT,
   ID_ROP2CODE_R2MERGENOTPEN, ID_ROP2CODE_R2MASKNOTPEN,
```

```
    ID_ROP2CODE_R2MERGEPEN, ID_ROP2CODE_R2NOTMERGEPEN,
    ID_ROP2CODE_R2MASKPEN, ID_ROP2CODE_R2NOTMASKPEN,
    ID_ROP2CODE_R2XORPEN, ID_ROP2CODE_R2NOTXORPEN };

void CGraphicsDemo1View::OnRop2code()
{

  // Obtain the menu ID that was selected.
  int nID = (UINT) LOWORD( GetCurrentMessage()->wParam );

  // Loop through and match the menu ID with the
  // menu ID in the static list. Use this match
  // to get a zero-based value for the menu selection.
  for( int i=0; i<sizeof(nMenuID)/sizeof(int); i++ ){
    if( nID == nMenuID[i] ){
      m_nROP2Code = nROP2Code[i];
      break;
      }
    }

}

void CGraphicsDemo1View::OnUpdateRop2code(CCmdUI* pCmdUI)
{

  // Loop through and match the ID of this menu
  // item with the ID of the menu item in the static
  // list. Then, see if m_nROP2Code matches the loop
  // value. If so, set the check; if not, don't set
  // the check.
  for( int i=0; i<sizeof(nMenuID)/sizeof(int); i++ ){
    if( (int) pCmdUI->m_nID == nMenuID[i] ){
      pCmdUI->SetCheck( m_nROP2Code == nROP2Code[i] );
      break;
      }
    }

}

void CGraphicsDemo1View::OnColorSelectcolor()
{

  // Get the ID of the menu selection.
  int nID = (UINT) LOWORD( GetCurrentMessage()->wParam );

  CColorDialog ColorDialog;

  // Invoke the common color selector
  // dialog box.
  if( ColorDialog.DoModal() == IDOK ){
    // We've set either the fill color or the
    // border color.
    if( nID == ID_COLOR_SELECTFILLCOLOR )
```

(continued)

Listing 4-2 *(continued)*

```
      m_FillColor = ColorDialog.GetColor();
    else m_BorderColor = ColorDialog.GetColor();
    }

}

void CGraphicsDemo1View::OnDrawprimitive()
{

  // Get the ID for the selected menu
  // item and store it in m_nDrawPrimitive.
  m_nDrawPrimitive =
    (UINT) LOWORD( GetCurrentMessage()->wParam );

}

void CGraphicsDemo1View::OnUpdateDrawprimitive(
  CCmdUI* pCmdUI)
{

  // If this ID matches the ID in m_nDrawPrimitive,
  // set the menu item check.
  pCmdUI->SetCheck( m_nDrawPrimitive ==
    (int) pCmdUI->m_nID );

}

void CGraphicsDemo1View::OnLButtonDown(UINT nFlags,
  CPoint point)
{

  // Create a DC for the drawing operations.
  CClientDC ClientDC( this );

  // Generate four random points based on
  // the mouse position.
  int x1 = point.x - ( rand() & 0x7f );
  int y1 = point.y - ( rand() & 0x7f );
  int x2 = point.x + ( rand() & 0x7f );
  int y2 = point.y + ( rand() & 0x7f );

  // Create a CRect object with which we'll
  // perform some of our draw operations.
  CRect Rect( x1, y1, x2, y2 );

  // Create a CBrush object based on the fill color.
  CBrush Brush( m_FillColor );

  // Create a CPen object based on the border color.
  CPen Pen( PS_SOLID, 1, m_BorderColor );
```

```
// Select the newly-created CBrush object into the
// DC and remember the CBrush object that got
// selected out.
CBrush *pOldBrush =
  (CBrush *) ClientDC.SelectObject( &Brush );

// Select the newly-created CPen object into the
// DC and remember the CPen object that got
// selected out.
CPen *pOldPen = (CPen *) ClientDC.SelectObject( &Pen );

// Set the ROP code.
ClientDC.SetROP2( m_nROP2Code );

// For the filled rectangle and ellipse,
// we create a pen based on the fill color.
// This causes the rectangle to draw with
// the same color in the border and fill
// interior.
CPen MatchPen( PS_SOLID, 1, m_FillColor );

switch( m_nDrawPrimitive ){

  case ID_DRAWPRIMITIVE_LINE:
    // For a simple line we use
    // the four integer coordinates
    // instead of the CRect object.
    ClientDC.MoveTo( x1, y1 );
    ClientDC.LineTo( x2, y2 );
    break;

  case ID_DRAWPRIMITIVE_FILLEDRECTANGLE:
    // For the filled rectangle, we create
    // a pen based on the fill color. This
    // causes the rectangle to draw with
    // the same color in the border and fill
    // interior.
    ClientDC.SelectObject( &MatchPen );

  case ID_DRAWPRIMITIVE_BORDEREDRECTANGLE:
    // For both the bordered rectangle and
    // the filled rectangle, we make the same
    // call to the Rectangle() function. The
    // only difference is that for the filled
    // rectangle we made sure we set to a
    // pen of a color that matches the fill color.
    ClientDC.Rectangle( &Rect );
    break;

  case ID_DRAWPRIMITIVE_FILLEDELLIPSE:
    // For the filled ellipse, we create
    // a pen based on the fill color. This
    // causes the rectangle to draw with
```

(continued)

Listing 4-2 *(continued)*

```
        // the same color in the border and fill
        // interior.
        ClientDC.SelectObject( &MatchPen );

      case ID_DRAWPRIMITIVE_BORDEREDELLIPSE:
        // For both the bordered ellipse and
        // the filled ellipse, we make the same
        // call to the Rectangle() function. The
        // only difference is that for the filled
        // rectangle we made sure we set to a
        // pen of a color that matches the fill color.
        ClientDC.Ellipse( &Rect );
        break;

      }

    // Select the old CPen and CBrush objects
    // back into the DC.
    ClientDC.SelectObject( pOldPen );
    ClientDC.SelectObject( pOldPen );

    CView::OnLButtonDown(nFlags, point);
  }
```

Text drawing functions

GDI provides five text drawing functions. You'll find yourself using them over and over again when you draw text to a window. They are summarized in Table 4-9.

Table 4-9
GDI Text Drawing Functions

Function	*Description*
`DrawText()`	Provides some text formatting while text is drawn. Among the 14 flags that set draw options, some control text alignment (for example, left, right, center, top). Another flag requests that tab characters be expanded to tab stops, and the `DT_WORDBREAK` flag requests enabling of word wrapping to produce multiple lines of text output.

Function	Description
`ExtTextOut()`	Draws a single line of text with three added features. First, you can specify a clipping rectangle to limit text to an arbitrary rectangle. Second, you can specify an opaque rectangle, which involves filling in a rectangle with the background text color. And third, you can control the spacing of characters by providing an array of character cell width values.
`GrayString()`	Creates mottled text, like that used in menus to show a disabled menu item.
`TabbedTextOut()`	Draws a line of text, just like `TextOut()`. The only difference is that you can define an array of tab stop positions for the support of tab characters.
`TextOut()`	Draws a single line of text.

To draw a single line of text, the easiest function to call is `CDC::TextOut()`. This function is defined in two different ways, the first of which looks like this:

```
BOOL TextOut( int x, int y, LPCTSTR lpszString, int nCount);
```

The alternative looks like this:

```
BOOL TextOut( int x, int y, const CString& strText );
```

For the `TextOut()` function, *x* and *y* are coordinates for positioning the text string. By default, text hangs below and to the right of this point. The `lpszString` parameter is a pointer to a character string. The fourth paramenter, `nCount`, is the count of characters in the string. `strText` is a `CString`, which therefore contains both character string and string length information about the text that is to be drawn.

Here's an example of a `WM_PAINT` handling function that calls `TextOut()` to display the text "Hello Windows 98" at location (100,100):

```
void CMyView::OnFunction ()
{
  CClientDC ClientCD( this );
  LPCTSTR lpszText = "Hello Windows 98";
  ClientDC.TextOut( 100, 100, lpszText, strlen( lpszText ) );
}
```

Here's the same function, rewritten for the second form of `TextOut()`:

```
void CMyView::OnFunction()
{
  CClientDC ClientDC( this );
  CString strText = "Hello Windows 98";
  ClientDC.TextOut( 100, 100, strText );
}
```

When specifying drawing coordinates in GDI drawing functions such as `TextOut()`, remember that Windows 98 recognizes only 16 bits of significance. Even though you might pass a 32-bit integer value, GDI under Windows 98 operates in only 16 bits (just like GDI did under Windows 3.*x*). Under Windows NT, however, all 32 bits of precision are recognized and supported. Unless you want your programs to run only on Windows NT, limit the range of your drawing coordinates to those that fit in 16-bit integers.

`CDC::TextOut()` draws a single line of text. In many cases, however, you want to draw multiple lines of text, which requires several calls to `TextOut()` with different coordinates for each call. Unlike text drawing in a character-oriented environment, drawing coordinates in GDI are something other than character cells (for now, pixels). To properly space the text that's drawn by different calls, you need to do some text coordinate calculation. We'll explore this subject in the following section.

Text coordinate calculations

GDI provides several functions that are useful in the calculation of text coordinates. You need to use this set of functions because the spacing of text strings depends not only on the font specified by the user, but on the resolution of the target device. Before drawing any text, you need to ask GDI for the required text coordinate values.

Table 4-10 lists some of GDI's more useful text measurement functions. To help you understand these functions, we'll take a look at some of their more common uses. We'll start by discussing how to calculate point size, a common concern when working with text. We'll then describe how to get to the next string—whether it's on the same line as the current string, or the next line. Our last text coordinate topic is centering a line of text around a point.

Font point size

Even a casual user of word-processing programs knows that text is measured in *points*. One point is approximately 1/72.54 inches, which makes a point small, but not too small to be seen by the unaided eye. Windows uses a value of 1/72 inch for a point—a reasonable approximation for most uses. Common sizes for regular text range between 8 points and 12 points. Headlines can be anywhere from 14 points up to 24 or 36 points, or even larger. Text is usually measured by its height and not by its width, although in Windows you can request a font using either or both attributes.

As we mentioned earlier, our focus is on device units, which are the simplest to deal with. The basic formula for converting between device units and point size is as follows:

```
PointSize = ( 72 * DeviceUnits ) / LogicalInch
```

Going the other way, here's the formula for converting points to device units:

```
DeviceUnits = ( PointSize * LogicalInch ) / 72
```

Incidentally, you'll probably want to use the Windows `MulDiv()` helper function rather than let the compiler do the math. This function eliminates rounding and overflow errors that sometimes occur with plain-integer arithmetic. Here's the previous formula, written to use this function:

```
DeviceUnits = ::MulDiv( PointSize, LogicalInch, 72 );
```

Table 4-10
Common GDI Text Coordinate Calculation Functions

Function	*Description*
`GetCharWidth()`	Gets a copy of the default character width values for a range of letters in the font currently selected in a DC.
`GetDeviceCaps()`	Gets various bits of device-specific data. In the context of text, LOGPIXELSY provides the number of pixels in a logical vertical inch. This is useful for calculating font point size.
`GetTabbedTextExtent()`	Like `GetTextExtent()`, this function gets the width and height that a character string would occupy when drawn with the font selected in a DC. This also takes into account tab settings.
`GetTextExtent()`	Gets the width and height that a given string would occupy when drawn with the font currently selected in a DC.
`GetTextMetrics()`	Gets a copy of the TEXTMETRIC data for the font currently selected in a DC. This data structure contains basic font measurement information.

We need to explain a few things about these formulas. First, the term logical inch refers to the number of pixels in an inch. It's called logical because of the way this measurement is defined for display screens. On display screens, a logical inch is usually larger than a physical inch. This helps ensure that 8-point fonts — which are typically the smallest size used — are readable. On printers, logical inches and physical inches are the same.

To obtain the logical inch for a particular device, you call `CDC::GetDeviceCaps()`, the device capabilities function. `GetDeviceCaps()` takes a single parameter, an index of the capability to query. Two indices return logical inch values: `LOGPIXELSX` for movement in the *x* direction, and `LOGPIXELSY` for movement in the *y* direction. Because point size refers to the height of text — that is, its size along the *y* axis — you use `LOGPIXELSY` to find out the logical inches for a given device:

```
LogicalInch = dc.GetDeviceCaps( LOGPIXELSY );
```

Another point worth mentioning is that our formulas use a ratio of 1:72 instead of the more accurate 1:72.54 ratio of points to inches. This rounding down is done because GDI in particular — and Windows in general — doesn't use any floating-point arithmetic. The reason is performance. Intel x86 processors prior to the 80486 lacked hardware support for floating-point arithmetic. Because floating-point arithmetic in software can be very slow, Windows uses integer arithmetic, which allows for faster operation and a reasonable degree of accuracy. Although this may change in future versions, for now Windows relies solely on integer arithmetic.

Next string, same line

You must sometimes split a single line of text between multiple text drawing calls [that is, multiple calls to `TextOut()`]. This can happen for any number of reasons. It might simply be more convenient, given the way your data is stored. Or, you might want to display a line of text in which parts of the text use different drawing attributes. For example, displaying red text next to blue text requires two calls to `TextOut()`. Using two fonts in the same line of text also requires two text drawing calls.

To calculate the position for the next string, you call `CDC::GetTextExtent()`. This function tells you both the width and height of a character string for the currently selected font. This function is defined as follows:

```
CSize GetTextExtent( LPCTSTR lpszString, int nCount ) const;
```

where the following conditions apply:

✦ `lpszString` is a pointer to the character string.

✦ `nCount` is the number of characters to include.

The return value, `CSize`, is a structure with two members: `cx` is the width of the character string, and `cy` is the height. For example, here's how you write "Hello Windows 98" on the same line using two calls to `TextOut()`:

```
int x, y;
x = 100;
y = 100;
LPCTSTR lpszHello = "Hello ";
LPCTSTR lpszWin95 = "Windows 98";

// Draw the first string.
ClientDC.TextOut( x, y, lpszHello, strlen( lpszHello ) );

// Calculate size of first string.
CSize sizeString = ClientDC.GetTextExtent( lpszHello, strlen(
   lpszHello ) );

// Adjust x-coordinate.
x += sizeString.cx;

// Draw second string.
ClientDC.TextOut( x, y, lpszWin95, strlen( lpszWin95 ) );
```

To preserve the space between the strings, the first string—"Hello"—ends with a space.

Next string, next line

Another common text calculation involves determining how much space to put between two lines of text. As a shortcut, we could use the return value from the function we looked at a moment ago, `GetTextExtent()`. After all, this function provides both the width and the height of a character string. Here's how to use this function to calculate the spacing between two lines of text:

```
// Draw first string.
ClientDC.TextOut( x, y, lpszHello, strlen( lpszHello ) );

// Calculate size of first string.
CSize sizeString = ClientDC.GetTextExtent( lpszHello, strlen(
    lpszHello ) );

// Adjust y-coordinate.
y += sizeString.cy;

// Draw second string.
ClientDC.TextOut( x, y, lpszWin95, strlen( lpszWin95 ) );
```

Although this is workable for many situations, it's not the most accurate calculation. It takes into account the character cell height, but the font designer might have decided that more space is needed between lines of text. And if the font designer went to the trouble of defining additional pixels for interline spacing, it's worthwhile for you to use that spacing.

The term that font designers use for the space between lines of text is *external leading*. With its origins in the days when type was set by hand as tiny pieces of metal, the term leading refers to flat bars of metal that were placed between lines of text. It is considered external leading because it's not included—that is, it's outside of—the character cell height. Another term, internal leading, refers to intercharacter spacing that's been built into each character cell.

Both the internal and external leading values are stored in a `TEXTMETRIC` data structure. To get a copy of this data structure for a given font, you call `CDC::GetTextMetrics()`. This function provides text metric data for the font that's currently selected in the DC. Here's an example of calling this function:

```
TEXTMETRIC TmSys;
ClientDC.GetTextMetrics( &TmSys );
```

(As an aside, note that the data structure—`TEXTMETRIC`—is singular, while the function call—`GetTextMetrics()`—is plural. This annoying inconsistency has bubbled up from the native Windows 98 API.)

To calculate the space between lines of text, you need to use two TEXTMETRIC members: character cell height and external leading size. For the text metric structure we just filled, here's how you calculate the value that must be added to the *y* coordinate before drawing the next line:

```
int cyLineHeight = TmSys.tmHeight + TmSys.tmExternalLeading;
```

In our earlier example, we'd add this to the *y* coordinate before drawing the second line of text:

```
// Adjust y-coordinate.
y += cyLineHeight;

// Draw second string.
ClientDC.TextOut( x, y, lpszWin95, strlen( lpszWin95 ) );
```

We've shown two ways to get the height of a character cell, and you might be wondering how this value relates to a font's point size. Watch out, they are probably not the same. We say probably because it's possible that they are the same. But to be absolutely sure, you must check another text metric value, the internal leading.

As we've discussed, leading is a typesetting word for interline spacing. External leading is the space not included in the character cell height. Internal leading, on the other hand, is the space that is included in the character cell height. Dennis Adler, a font guru at Microsoft, pointed this out to one of the authors. To calculate the point size of a font, you subtract the value of the internal leading from the font height. In code terms, that means:

```
int DeviceUnits = TmSys.tmHeight - TmSys.tmInternalLeading;
```

The result of this calculation is the height of the character cells in device units. To convert this value to points, we need to take into account the device's logical inch. Using the size from the previous formula, here's how you get the font size in points:

```
int LogicalInch = ClientDC.GetDeviceCaps( LOGPIXELSY );
int PointSize = ::MulDiv( 72, DeviceUnits, LogicalInch );
```

Centering text

It's often useful to center a string of text over a particular point. For example, you might want to center a text label over a column of text. Or, you might want to center a label within another graphic object. Whatever the reason, when you need to solve problems like this, it's helpful to think of text as a graphic object. Like a birthday present, text comes in a box—which we sometimes call a text box.

By default, a character string hangs below and to the right of the text coordinate. As a result, the centering of text requires figuring out how to shift the control point up and to the left. The size of the shift is equal to one-half the size of the text box—that is, we shift the text up by one-half of the text box height, and to the left by one-half of the text box width. To show you what we mean, here's a code fragment that centers a text string over a given (*x,y*) point:

```
// The string.
CString strText = "Centered Line of Text";

// Calculate the shift up and to the left.
CSize size = ClientDC.GetTextExtent( strText,
strText.GetLength() );
int xCentered = x - ( size.cx / 2 );
int yCentered = y - ( size.cy / 2 );

// Draw line of centered text
ClientDC.TextOut( xCentered, yCentered, strText );
```

Clipping Regions

There will be many occasions when you must limit your draw operations to a specific region and prevent anything from being drawn outside of this region. The `SelectClipRgn()` function takes care of this by limiting draw operations in a particular device context.

The `SelectClipRgn()` function selects the given region as the current clipping region for the device context. Only a copy of the selected region is used. The region itself can be selected for any number of other device contexts, or it can be deleted. The function assumes that the coordinates for the given region are specified in device units.

The `CRgn` class encapsulates a Windows GDI region. A region is an elliptical or polygonal area within a window. To use regions, you use the member functions of class `CRgn` with the clipping functions defined as members of class CDC. The following example shows how to create a simple rectangular region bounded by the coordinates (10, 10) and (100, 100):

```
CRgn Rgn;
Rgn.CreateRectRgn( 10, 10, 100, 100 );
```

With a region created, you can then limit the device context's drawing to only the region that's been created as follows:

```
pDC->SelectClipRgn( &Rgn );
```

A more advanced version of `SelectClipRgn()` allows you to choose between five different modes. These modes affect the way the clipping region is combined with regions that are already selected into the device context, and how the region is to be used. The five modes are shown in Table 4-11.

Table 4-11
The Modes Available for SelectClipRgn

Mode	*Description*
RGN_AND	The new clipping region combines the overlapping areas of the current clipping region and the region identified by pRgn.
RGN_COPY	The new clipping region is a copy of the region identified by pRgn. This functionality is identical to the first version of SelectClipRgn. If the region identified by pRgn is NULL, the new clipping region becomes the default clipping region (a null region).
RGN_DIFF	The new clipping region combines the areas of the current clipping region with those areas excluded from the region identified by pRgn.
RGN_OR	The new clipping region combines the current clipping region and the region identified by pRgn.
RGN_XOR	The new clipping region combines the current clipping region and the region identified by pRgn but excludes any overlapping areas.

The GraphicsDemo2 program shows you how to create a clipping rectangle and use it to limit the window area in which draw operations occur. The program lets you move the clipping rectangle around on the screen so that you can experiment. To change the clipping rectangle to a different location, click the left mouse button in the window.

To draw the star-shaped figure, just move the mouse around in the window. It'll draw in the window, centered around the mouse coordinates. You will, however, only see part of the figure since there's a rectangular clipping region that's selected, as shown in Figure 4-6.

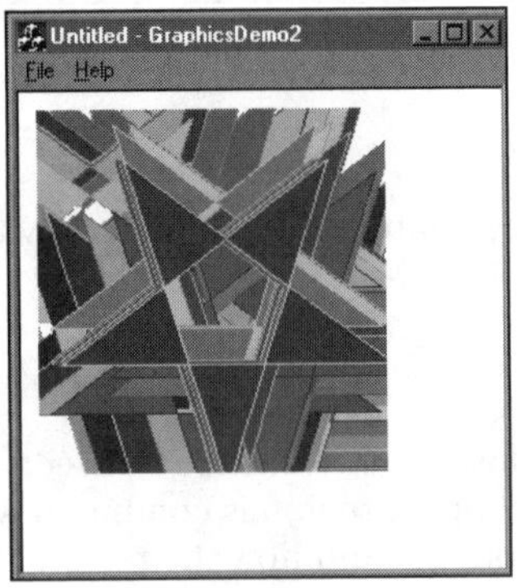

Figure 4-6: This program draws a star, but it's clipped to a rectangle so you won't always see the entire figure.

Demo Program

GraphicsDemo2
CD-ROM Location: **Chap04\GraphicsDemo2**
Program Name: **GraphicsDemo2.EXE**
Source Code Modules in Text: **GraphicsDemo2View.cpp**

◆ ◆ ◆ ◆ ◆

Listing 4-3: The GraphicsDemo2View.cpp Source Code Module

```
// GraphicsDemo2View.cpp : implementation of
// the CGraphicsDemo2View class
//

/////////////////////////////////////////////////////////
// CGraphicsDemo2View construction/destruction

CGraphicsDemo2View::CGraphicsDemo2View()
{

  // The clipping regions upper
  // left corner will be at 10, 10.
  m_nRgnX = m_nRgnY = 10;

}

CGraphicsDemo2View::~CGraphicsDemo2View()
{
}

/////////////////////////////////////////////////////////
// CGraphicsDemo2View message handlers

void CGraphicsDemo2View::OnMouseMove(UINT nFlags,
  CPoint point)
{

  // Form an array of the star definition.
  // We don't make it static since it's
  // altered by addition each time OnMouseMove()
  // is called.
  POINT Point[] = {
    -59, -81, 0, 100, 59, -81,
    -95, 31, 95, 31 };

  // Loop through and add the mouse
  // coordinates to the star definition
  // vertices.
  for( int i=0; i<5; i++ ){
```

(continued)

Listing 4-3 *(continued)*

```
    Point[i].x += point.x;
    Point[i].y += point.y;
    }

  // Create a CBrush object with random red, green,
  // and blue hues.
  CBrush Brush( RGB( ( rand() & 0xff ),
    ( rand() & 0xff ), ( rand() & 0xff ) ) );

  // Create a CPen object with random red, greeen,
  // and blue hues.
  CPen Pen( PS_SOLID, 1, RGB( ( rand() & 0xff ),
    ( rand() & 0xff ), ( rand() & 0xff ) ) );

  // Create a DC for drawing into the window.
  CClientDC ClientDC( this );

  // Select the newly-created CBrush object into the DC
  // and remember the old CBrush object that was selected
  // out.
  CBrush *pOldBrush =
    (CBrush *) ClientDC.SelectObject( &Brush );

  // Select the newly-created CPen object into the DC
  // and remember the old CPen object that was selected
  // out.
  CPen *pOldPen = (CPen *) ClientDC.SelectObject( &Pen );

  // Create a rectangular region with which to
  // clip all draw operations.
  CRgn Rgn;
  Rgn.CreateRectRgn( m_nRgnX, m_nRgnY,
    m_nRgnX + 200, m_nRgnY + 200 );

  // Select the newly-created region into the DC.
  ClientDC.SelectClipRgn( &Rgn );

  // Use the GDI Polygon() function to draw the
  // polygon into the DC.
  ClientDC.Polygon( Point,
    sizeof( Point ) / sizeof( POINT ) );

  // Set the clipping region to none.
  ClientDC.SelectClipRgn( NULL );

  // Restore the old CBrush and CPen objects
  // back into the DC.
  ClientDC.SelectObject( pOldPen );
  ClientDC.SelectObject( pOldBrush );
```

```
  CView::OnMouseMove(nFlags, point);
}

void CGraphicsDemo2View::OnLButtonDown(UINT nFlags,
  CPoint point)
{

  // Move the clipping region. Do this by taking
  // the mouse coodinates at which the left
  // button was clicked. Subtract 100 to arrive at
  // the upper left corner of the clipping region.
  m_nRgnX = point.x - 100;
  if( m_nRgnX < 0 ) m_nRgnX = 0;
  m_nRgnY = point.y - 100;
  if( m_nRgnY < 0 ) m_nRgnY = 0;

  CView::OnLButtonDown(nFlags, point);
}
```

Summary

In this chapter, you've learned how to draw vector and text graphics to a window. Because Windows 98 applications rely so heavily on text and graphics, these techniques are very important when you write your programs.

✦ ✦ ✦

CHAPTER 5

Bitmaps, Palettes, DIBs, and Double Buffering

✦ ✦ ✦ ✦

In This Chapter

Creating CBitmap objects

Loading bitmap data from the resource file

Drawing with CBitmap objects

Comparing different raster operations for drawing CBitmap objects

Learning about palettes

Creating a new class for loading, displaying, and saving DIBs

Reducing screen flicker by double buffering

✦ ✦ ✦ ✦

At the heart of your computer's video system is memory. This memory contains data that represent the patterns which appear on the monitor. Every time the mouse moves, a small amount of data in memory changes. You then see the mouse move across the screen. Each and every graphics operation affects video memory as GDI makes its calculations, and alters video memory in an appropriate way.

Bitmaps represent rectangular regions of RAM similar to video memory. At their core is a handle for a chunk of RAM. In terms of Windows API, this handle is known as an `HBITMAP`. In this memory resides data that, if moved into video memory, would cause a pattern to appear on the monitor. A good example of this is a desktop icon. Icons are loaded from disk into memory. This memory is then moved into video memory at the appropriate addresses so when video memory is rendered on the screen by the video hardware, the icon becomes visible.

Bitmaps add graphical objects to the screen in a different way than drawn objects such as lines and ellipses. Lines and ellipses are mathematically calculated, then the pixels in video memory are set in such a way that the object appears. Bitmap data isn't calculated. The pattern already exists in bitmap memory. It's simply a matter of copying a block of memory from the bitmap to video memory. Because of this, using bitmaps is preferable to using a series of draw operations when the end result is a complex graphics image. Imagine how many separate operations it would take to draw your photograph on the screen — it may take thousands. By using a bitmap, the complex photographic image can reside in bitmap memory. Then, with a single operation, the bitmap memory can be quickly copied to a region of video memory.

This chapter will talk about two types of bitmap objects. One is wrapped in the MFC `CBitmap` class. Bitmaps of this type are called device-dependent bitmaps. They can only be drawn successfully on a video system that matches their own configuration. For instance, a device-dependent bitmap that has a color depth of 24 bits per pixel will only draw to a video system that's 24 bits per pixel. The only exception to this rule are monochrome bitmaps of one bit plane with a color depth of one bit per pixel. These are able to be drawn to video memory of any configuration.

Before we get started, a few words on terminology are in order. In this chapter, the Windows GDI object known as an `HBITMAP` is called a *bitmap*. The MFC class that wraps a bitmap is called a *`CBitmap` object*. A logical palette is a Windows GDI object, and we'll call them *palettes* in this chapter. The MFC class that wraps a palette is known as a *`CPalette` object*. A *device-independent bitmap* such as the kind that makes up BMP files will be called a *DIB*. DIBs can't be found in the Windows API or MFC anywhere as separate items. Instead, this chapter's code loads them into `HGLOBAL` memory objects. They're still called DIBs, though, so you know what's in the memory. A special class (built later on in the chapter) that wraps a DIB is called a *`CDib` object*.

No discussion of bitmaps would be complete without talking about palettes. We'll use MFC's `CPalette` object to perform all of our palette operations. For video adapters with pixel depths of 8 bits or less, effective use of palettes is essential for optimizing the appearance of bitmaps.

The second type of bitmap covered in this chapter, a device-independent bitmap (DIB), is not wrapped in an MFC class of any kind. Toward the end of this chapter, however, we'll create a class similar to `CBitmap` that will make it easier for you to work with DIBs. The advantage that DIBs have over device-dependent bitmaps is that the DIB's configuration doesn't have to match the video configuration for a draw operation to be successful. The bitmap is drawn to the screen, taking the configurations of the bitmap and the video into account. For instance, a 24-bit DIB will draw successfully to a video system of 8, 16, 24, and 32 bits per pixel. When there's a color-depth mismatch, a color-matching algorithm is used to achieve the best possible match. For instance, a 24-bit DIB that's drawn to an 8-bit video system has to reduce to the 256 colors available in the video system. When the DIB is drawn to the screen, the color downsizing is done during the draw operation. This doesn't affect the DIB data that's in memory. The drawback to this is that performance is greatly reduced. For this reason, if performance is an issue, DIBs should not be used. Instead, device-dependent bitmaps are recommended.

The last thing you'll learn in this chapter is how to use `CBitmap` objects to reduce or eliminate screen flicker during screen redraws.

Bit Planes, Bits-Per-Pixel, and Color Depth

Back when CGA video was the standard, there were four colors to choose from: black, cyan, magenta, and white. (Another, seldom-used variation produced black, yellow, green, and red.) CGA video memory stored data for each pixel in two contiguous bits. Each byte of video memory contained enough data for four screen pixels. Oddly enough, the data was stored in two banks of memory. The first bank contained data for the odd scanlines; the second contained data for the even scanlines.

With the advent of EGA and VGA monitors, the number of possible colors expanded. EGA and VGA presented four variables to contend with: the red, blue, and green color bits, and the high/low intensity bit. Combining these four bits created 16 colors (high-intensity green, low-intensity green, high-intensity green and red, and so on). The four variables became known as *bit planes*; each resided in a different bank of memory. For instance, all the red memory for an EGA setting of 320x200 pixels resided in a memory bank of 8,000 bytes.

MCGA systems introduced 8 bits of information for each pixel. Since the concept of a color plane doesn't describe the capabilities of this type of system, the 8 bits of information for each color have become known as the *bits-per-pixel value*. MCGA video memory contains a single byte for each screen pixel. To get the RGB value with which the video system renders the pixel, a *lookup* into a palette is used. MCGA palettes have only 256 entries, so MCGA video can only display 256 simultaneous colors.

All video cards support older modes such as CGA and EGA. But most of them support newer modes in which the actual RGB values are stored in video memory. The most common of these new modes is 24-bit *truecolor* video, in which each screen pixel is represented by three consecutive bytes. Each byte has an RGB value for red, green, and blue. There are two other common modes in which literal RGB values reside in video memory. They use 16 or 32 bits of data to represent the RGB color.

To determine the actual *bit depth* of a given video system, you must check two other values: the bits-per-pixel value and the number of bit planes. You can call the `GetDeviceCaps()` API function with the BITSPIXEL constant to determine the bits-per-pixel value. To determine the number of color planes, you can call the same API function with the PLANES constant.

A simple way to calculate the true bit-depth value is to retrieve both of these values and multiply them. This calculation is valid because an EGA/VGA system returns 1 for the bits-per-pixel value, and a *truecolor/highcolor* system returns 1 as the color-planes value.

Creating CBitmap Objects

`CBitmap` objects are empty when they're first instantiated. The bitmap that the class wraps must eventually be created for the object to be useful. There are several ways to create bitmaps within a `CBitmap` class. The first uses the `CreateBitmap()` function and has the following syntax:

```
CBitmap::CreateBitmap( int nWidth, int nHeight,
  int nPlanes, int nBits, const *void lpBits );
```

The `nWidth` and `nHeight` parameters specify the size of the bitmap in pixels. The `nPlanes` argument specifies the number of bit planes that the bitmap will be—this will almost always be 1. The `nBits` argument specifies the number of bits for each pixel. The last argument, `lpBits`, enables you to initialize the bitmap with a bit pattern. The bit pattern is copied into the bitmap memory, but it's still the caller's responsibility to maintain and dispose of the original bit pattern memory. Normally a bit pattern isn't specified when creating a bitmap, and in this case, the `lpBits` parameter will be `NULL`. Without initializing the bitmap pattern, it will contain meaningless data and look like a jumbled up mess. The following example creates a bitmap with a width of 50, a height of 60, one bit plane, 24 bits per pixel, and no initial bit pattern:

```
CBitmap Bitmap;
Bitmap.CreateBitmap( 50, 60, 1, 24, NULL );
```

Often it's important to find out the configuration of a bitmap that's already created. To do this, you must use the `GetObject()` function to have a `BITMAP` structure filled in with information about the bitmap. When you retrieve information about the CBitmap object, the `bmBits` member will be NULL because you can't get a direct pointer to bitmap memory. However, if you use CBitmap's `CreateBitmapIndirect()` function, `bmBits` will be used to initialize the bitmap data if the structure member is not `NULL`. The `bmType` member will always be zero. The `BITMAP` structure definition shown here is followed by an example of filling in a `BITMAP` structure:

```
typedef struct tagBITMAP{
  int bmType;
  int bmWidth;
  int bmHeight;
  int bmWidthBytes;
  BYTE bmPlanes;
  BYTE bmBitsPixel;
  void *bmBits;
} BITMAP;
```

The two fields that need explaining are the `bmType` and `bmWidthBytes` members. The `bmType` member will always contain the value '`BM`'. That's why .BMP files always start with the character pair '`BM`'. The `bmWidthBytes` member contains the number of bytes for each scanline of the bitmap. It's not simply the number of bytes per pixel multiplied by the width. The value must be divisible by four.

```
// Bitmap is a CBitmap object. It may or may not
// contain valid data, but the BITMAP structure will
// be faithfully filled in with information about
// the bitmap.
BITMAP bm;
Bitmap.GetObject( sizeof( BITMAP ), &bm );
```

Another way to create a bitmap is with the `CreateBitmapIndirect()` function. To do this, a `BITMAP` structure must first be filled in with the values for the bitmap that's to be created. A call to `CreateBitmapIndirect()` then uses the members of the structure to create the bitmap. An example which uses the `CreateBitmapIndirect()` function to create a bitmap with a width of 100, a height of 200, one bit plane, and 16 bits of color depth follows:

```
BITMAP bm;
bm.bmType = 0;
bm.bmWidth = 100;
bm.bmHeight = 200;
bm.bmWidthBytes = 200;
bm.bmPlanes = 1;
bm.bmBitsPixel = 16;
bm.bmBits = NULL;

CBitmap Bitmap;
Bitmap.CreateBitmapIndirect( &bm );
```

Expert Tip

RGB Really Means BGR in Video Memory

Even though the term RGB is commonly used, the order of the RGB triplets in video memory is B-G-R, the reverse of what the term says. If each pixel is represented by three bytes in video memory, the first byte is for blue, the second for green, and the third for red.

◆ ◆ ◆ ◆ ◆

Often you simply want to create a bitmap that's compatible with the video system. You can do this without having to specify the bit planes or bits per pixel by using the `CreateCompatibleBitmap()` function. This function takes a pointer to a device context, and uses the device context to figure out how many bit planes and how many bits per pixel the bitmap must be. Following is an example of using this from the `OnDraw()` function:

```
void CBitmapView::OnDraw(CDC* pDC)
{
 CBitmapDoc* pDoc = GetDocument();
 ASSERT_VALID(pDoc);

 CBitmap Bitmap;
 Bitmap.CreateCompatibleBitmap( pDC );
}
```

Loading and Setting Bitmap Content

Before using a bitmap, you'll want to set its contents with meaningful data. When bitmaps are first created, their memory contains unpredictable data. If you display a bitmap on the screen before setting the data, what you'll see will resemble a television that's not set to a station and is just producing random patterns. We'll talk about two different ways to set the contents of a bitmap. The first uses the SetBitmapBits() function, and the second uses the LoadBitmap() function.

The SetBitmapBits() function copies the contents of a memory buffer into the bitmap memory. The source memory must be created and subsequently managed and deleted by the calling code. There are two reasons you'd want to set bitmap contents from a memory buffer. The first is because you want to create a pattern algorithmically in memory and move it into the bitmap. The second reason is that you want to load bitmap data from disk and then move it into bitmap memory. The example below creates a 24-bit bitmap, creates a memory buffer that'll produce a red rectangle when copied to memory, and then sets the contents of the bitmap to the red pattern.

```
// Instantiate CBitmap and create the bitmap.
// This example is explicitly for 24-bit images.
CBitmap Bitmap;
Bitmap.CreateBitmap( 50, 50, 1, 24, NULL );

// Get the bitmap dimensions and allocation a buffer
// large enough for its contents.
BITMAP bm;
Bitmap.GetObject( sizeof( BITMAP ), &bm );
unsigned char pData =
    new unsigned char [bm.bmHeight*bm.bmWidthBytes];
// Loop through and set the buffer values so
// that the pattern will be solid red.
for( int y=0; y<bm.bmHeight; y++ ){
 for( int x=0; x<bm.bmWidth; x++ ){
  pData[x*3+y*bm.bmWidthBytes] = 0;
  pData[x*3+1+y*bm.bmWidthBytes] = 0;
  pData[x*3+2+y*bm.bmWidthBytes] = 255;
  }
 }

// Set the bitmap with the red data.
Bitmap.SetBitmapBits( bm.bmHeight * bm.bmWidthBytes,
 pData );

// Delete the data buffer.
delete [] pData;
```

For bitmaps of 16 colors (four bits per pixel) or less, there's another alternative. You can put the bitmap into your program as a resource, and then use the LoadBitmap() function to transfer the data into a bitmap. A bonus of using LoadBitmap() is that you don't have to use CreateBitmap() or any of the other bitmap creation functions; it's done for you by LoadBitmap(). Another nice thing is that LoadBitmap() will create a bitmap that's compatible with the current video system, regardless of the format of the resource bitmap. Following is an example of loading a bitmap with a resource id of IDB_BITMAP1 into a CBitmap object:

```
CBitmap Bitmap;
Bitmap.LoadBitmap( IDB_BITMAP1 );
```

One other function that you might find useful is `LoadMappedBitmap()`. It takes the same argument that `LoadBitmap()` takes, but converts various colors in the bitmap according to how the user's system colors are set. For instance, it converts black pixels to the color of button text, and converts dark gray to the color of button shadows.

Drawing CBitmaps to the Screen

When you have a `CBitmap` object which contains a valid bitmap, you're ready to draw it to the screen. Most of the time, you'll rely on the `BitBlt()` function. This function is fast. The `BitBlt()` function is hard to beat when it comes to data transfer between memory and video. It's evident that Microsoft placed a high priority on fast algorithms for blitting operations — and with the importance of these in such a graphically intensive environment, it's a wise priority.

The first thing you must understand is that `BitBlt()` technically copies data from one device context to another. That means a device context must be created for a bitmap before operations to and from it are carried out. Additionally, the bitmap must be selected into the device context before performing operations.

The `BitBlt()` function is a member of the CDC class and has the following syntax:

```
CDC:BitBlt( int x, int y, int nWidth, int nHeight,
    CDC *pSrcDC, int xSrc, int ySrc, DWORD dwROP );
```

The `x` and `y` parameters are the destination coordinates to which the bitmap will be drawn. The `nWidth` and `nHeight` parameters are the width and height of the destination rectangle and must match the source bitmap. The `pSrcDC` parameter is a pointer to the source device context — the source bitmap must have previously been selected into this device context for the operation to work correctly. The `xSrc` and `ySrc` parameters are the upper left corner of the source bitmap that's to be copied. By changing the `xSrc` and `ySrc`, and the `nWidth` and `nHeight` parameters, you can draw partial bitmaps to the screen. The `dwROP` parameter specifies the raster operation that's to be performed. It's a DWORD variable and thus can contain 32 bits describing the operation. With a total of 32 bits for the raster operation descriptor, it's unlikely that Windows will exceed its capacity by introducing more raster operations than the DWORD can hold. A more detailed discussion of raster codes appears later in the chapter; see Raster Operations.

The example that follows loads a bitmap with the `LoadBitmap()` function in an application's view class constructor. The example then shows how to draw the bitmap to the screen using the `OnDraw()` function. One very important item to note: When you select the bitmap into the newly-created device context, you obtain a pointer to the old bitmap. This allows you to select the old bitmap back into the device context after the bitmap is drawn.

```
CmyView::CmyView()
{

 m_Bitmap.LoadBitmap( IDC_BITMAP1 );

}
CmyView::OnDraw(CDC *pDC)
{
 CBitmapDoc* pDoc = GetDocument();
 ASSERT_VALID(pDoc);

 CDC MemDC;
 MemDC.CreateCompatibleDC( pDC );
 CBitmap *pOldBitmap = MemDC.SelectObject( &m_Bitmap );
 BITMAP bm;
 m_Bitmap.GetObject( sizeof( BITMAP ), &bm );
 pDC->BitBlt( 10, 10, bm.bmWidth, bm.bmHeight, &MemDC,
  0, 0, SRCCOPY );
 MemDC.SelectObject( pOldBitmap );

}
```

Nutshell

Drawing Bitmaps

The following steps sum up the process necessary to display a CBitmap object.

1. Create a device context for the bitmap that's compatible with the video device context.
2. Select the CBitmap object into the newly-created device context and save a pointer to the old bitmap.
3. Fill in a BITMAP structure using `GetObject()` so you know what the bitmap's dimensions are. (Skip this step if you already know the dimensions.)
4. Perform the `BitBlt()` function.
5. Select the old bitmap back into the newly-created device context.

✦ ✦ ✦ ✦ ✦

Expert Tip

Taking Everything Into Account

So far, the examples you've seen don't take into account mapping mode and the difference between device and logical coordinates. Most applications you write won't change the mapping mode, and most applications have device and logical coordinates that are the same. If you're not sure, though, of the situation in which you'll find yourself, you must add some extra code (and additional overhead). A `DrawBitmap()` function follows in which these additional factors are accounted for:

```
void DrawBitmap( int x, int y, CDC *pDC, CBitmap *pBitmap )
{
 BITMAP bm;
 pBitmap->GetObject( sizeof( BITMAP ), &bm );
```

```
CPoint size( bm.bmWidth, bm.bmHeight );
pDC->DPtoLP( &size );

CPoint org( 0, 0 );
pDC->DPtoLP( &org );

CDC MemDC;
MemDC.CreateCompatibleDC( pDC );
CBitmap *pOldBitmap = MemDC.SelectObject( pBitmap );
MemDC.SetMapMode( pDC->GetMapMode() );
pDC->BitBlt( x, y, size.x, size.y, &MemDC,
 org.x, org.y, SRCCOPY );
MemDC.SelectObject( pOldBitmap );
 }
```

◆ ◆ ◆ ◆ ◆

Try This

Creating and Displaying Bitmaps

By creating this application, you'll learn how to create and display bitmaps. Only three of the seven bitmaps will successfully draw to the screen. The other four won't draw because they don't match your video's configuration. The monochrome (1-bit) bitmap will display in all video configurations.

Create a single-document application.

Declare an array of seven `CBitmap` objects in the view class.

Import a bitmap as a resource object and give it an id of `IDB_BITMAP1`.

Initialize the seven bitmaps in the view class constructor as follows:

```
static int nBits[] = { 1, 4, 8, 16, 24, 32 };
 for( int i=0; i<6; i++ )
 m_Bitmap[i].CreateBitmap( 40, 40, 1, nBits[i], NULL );
 m_Bitmap[6].LoadBitmap( IDB_BITMAP1 );
```

Draw the bitmaps in the `OnDraw()` function as follows:

```
for( int i=0; i<7; i++ ){
 CDC MemDC;
 CBitmap *pOldBitmap;
 MemDC.CreateCompatibleDC( pDC );
 pOldBitmap = MemDC.SelectObject( &m_Bitmap[i] );
 pDC->BitBlt( 20 + i * 50, 30, 40, 40, &MemDC,
  0, 0, SRCCOPY );
 MemDC.SelectObject( pOldBitmap );
 }
```

◆ ◆ ◆ ◆ ◆

There are times when it's necessary to copy video memory into a bitmap. Since `BitBlt()` doesn't care what the source and destination are as long as it gets two valid device contexts, it couldn't be easier. All you have to do in order to copy from the screen to a bitmap is reverse the roles of the two device contexts.

For instance, the previous examples all used the pDC device context pointer as the destination, and the function call was structured as pDC->BitBlt(). In order to specify the second device context, the address of MemDC was passed in as a function argument to BitBlt(). The destination will be MemDC and the function call will be structured MemDC.BitBlt(). The pDC pointer will be passed in as an argument to BitBlt() so it knows what the second device context from which the source will be obtained is. A function named GetImage() follows which copies from the screen into a bitmap:

```
void GetImage( int x, int y, CDC *pDC, CBitmap *pBitmap )
{

 BITMAP bm;
 pBitmap->GetObject( sizeof( BITMAP ), &bm );

 CDC MemDC;
 MemDC.CreateCompatibleDC( pDC );

 CBitmap *pOldBitmap = MemDC.SelectObject( pBitmap );
 MemDC.BitBlt( 0, 0, bm.bmWidth, bm.bmHeight, pDC,
  x, y, SRCCOPY );
 MemDC.SelectObject( pOldBitmap );

}
```

Raster Operations

The last argument in the BitBlt() function determines how the source will combine with the destination. Most of the time, though, copying a bitmap to the screen to have it appear exactly as it does in the bitmap data is what you want. At other times, a simple data copy won't do. One example of this is when you want to draw a bitmap to the screen allowing a transparent color to be masked out. The transparent color, when it appeared in the source bitmap would be rejected. Whatever color was in the destination at any pixel location in which the source contained the transparent color would remain unchanged.

This masking technique must be carried out with two separate BitBlt() calls. The first part of the process creates a mask based on the source bitmap. It finds the transparent pixels and is created based on them. It then masks the destination in such a way as to eliminate all destination pixels into which the non-transparent source pixels will be drawn. The same mask is then used to mask the source and remove the unwanted transparent-color pixels. The source is then ORed (or XORed) into the destination. The original bitmap must then be restored to its original state, otherwise the transparent color will no longer exist and the pair of transparent operations won't work correctly.

A faster way to accomplish this double masking process is to create a mask ahead of time. That way it doesn't have to be created every time you want to go through the process. If execution time is important, seriously consider this option. The BlitDemo program uses such preformed masks when it draws the fly images. Taking a good look at this demo program will give you a good idea of how it's done.

Another example in which you might want to use another raster operation is in some animations. A common technique for moving bitmaps around on the screen is to XOR them before moving them to a new location. XORing one image over itself completely removes it. Here's why. When you first draw the image to the screen using an XOR raster operation, the image source combines with the destination. Anywhere the source has a bit that's set, XOR toggles the corresponding bit in the destination to its opposite value. For instance, if the source bit is set (a 1) and the destination bit is not set (a zero), the result will be a 1. If the animation must be moved, XORing the same bitmap in the same location toggles those same bits, once again restoring them to their original state. The bitmap can then be drawn in a new location using an XOR raster operation. Following is a chart of the raster operation codes defined in Table 5-1.

Table 5-1
Raster Operations

Operation	*Description*
BLACKNESS	Turns all output black.
DSTINVERT	Inverts the destination bitmap.
MERGECOPY	Combines the pattern and the source bitmap using the Boolean AND operator.
MERGEPAINT	Combines the inverted source bitmap with the destination bitmap using the Boolean OR operator.
NOTSRCCOPY	Copies the inverted source bitmap to the destination.
NOTSRCERASE	Inverts the result of combining the destination and source bitmaps using the Boolean OR operator.
PATCOPY	Copies the pattern to the destination bitmap.
PATINVERT	Combines the destination bitmap with the pattern using the Boolean XOR operator.
PATPAINT	Combines the inverted source bitmap with the pattern using the Boolean OR operator. Combines the result of this operation with the destination bitmap using the Boolean OR operator.
SRCAND	Combines pixels of the destination and source bitmaps using the Boolean AND operator.
SRCCOPY	Copies the source bitmap to the destination bitmap.
SRCERASE	Inverts the destination bitmap and combines the result with the source bitmap using the Boolean AND operator.
SRCINVERT	Combines pixels of the destination and source bitmaps using the Boolean XOR operator.
SRCPAINT	Combines pixels of the destination and source bitmaps using the Boolean OR operator.
WHITENESS	Turns all output white.

If you need a function that draws a bitmap to the screen and masks a single transparent color, the following `DrawTransparent()` function will come in handy. You can add it to your program, or better yet, derive a class from `CBitmap` that you can always use. Source code for the `DrawTransparent()` function can be found in **Transparent.c** in the **Chap5** directory of the CD-ROM accompanying this book.

Listing 5-1: The DrawTransparent() Function

```
void DrawTransparent( int x, int y, CDC *pDC,
 CBitmap *pBitmap, COLORREF Color )
{
 BITMAP bm;
 pBitmap->GetObject( sizeof( BITMAP ), &bm );

 CDC ImageDC;
 ImageDC.CreateCompatibleDC( pDC );
 CBitmap *pOldImageBitmap =
   ImageDC.SelectObject( pBitmap );

 CDC MaskDC;
 MaskDC.CreateCompatibleDC( pDC );

 CBitmap MaskBitmap;
 MaskBitmap.CreateBitmap( bm.bmWidth, bm.bmHeight,
   1, 1, NULL );
 CBitmap *pOldMaskBitmap =
   MaskDC.SelectObject( &MaskBitmap );

 ImageDC.SetBkColor( Color );
 MaskDC.BitBlt( 0, 0, bm.bmWidth, bm.bmHeight,
   &ImageDC, 0, 0, SRCCOPY );

 CDC OrDC;
 OrDC.CreateCompatibleDC( pDC );

 CBitmap OrBitmap;
 OrBitmap.CreateCompatibleBitmap( &ImageDC,
   bm.bmWidth, bm.bmHeight );
 CBitmap *pOldOrBitmap = OrDC.SelectObject( &OrBitmap );

 OrDC.BitBlt( 0, 0, bm.bmWidth, bm.bmHeight,
   &ImageDC, 0, 0, SRCCOPY );
 OrDC.BitBlt( 0, 0, bm.bmWidth, bm.bmHeight,
   &MaskDC, 0, 0, 0x220326 );

 CDC TempDC;
 TempDC.CreateCompatibleDC( pDC );

 CBitmap TempBitmap;
 TempBitmap.CreateCompatibleBitmap( &ImageDC,
   bm.bmWidth, bm.bmHeight );
 CBitmap *pOldTempBitmap =
```

```
    TempDC.SelectObject( &TempBitmap );

  TempDC.BitBlt( 0, 0, bm.bmWidth, bm.bmHeight,
    pDC, x, y, SRCCOPY );
  TempDC.BitBlt( 0, 0, bm.bmWidth, bm.bmHeight,
    &MaskDC, 0, 0, SRCAND );
  TempDC.BitBlt( 0, 0, bm.bmWidth, bm.bmHeight,
    &OrDC, 0, 0, SRCPAINT );

  pDC->BitBlt( x, y, bm.bmWidth, bm.bmHeight,
    &TempDC, 0, 0, SRCCOPY );

  TempDC.SelectObject( pOldTempBitmap );
  OrDC.SelectObject( pOldOrBitmap );
  MaskDC.SelectObject( pOldMaskBitmap );
  ImageDC.SelectObject( pOldImageBitmap );}@sr
}
```

The BlitDemo Program

The BlitDemo program that's included on the CD-ROM shows you how to perform common operations using `CBitmap` objects. The actual bitmaps are contained as resource objects and are loaded using the `LoadBitmap()` member function.

The program begins by displaying one of three rising bubble images as shown in Figure 5-1. Clicking the left mouse button in the client window displays the next image in the sequence. After the third image has been displayed, the initial image is drawn.

You can use the Operations menu to select one of four different image sequences. The second is a set of four images that show a man on an old-fashioned railroad trolley. The third and fourth use a set of flies. When you click the left mouse button, the fly moves vertically on the screen as if it's flying.

Figure 5-1: The BlitDemo program begins by showing the first of three in a sequence of rising bubbles.

The flies are drawn in two different ways according to your menu selection. The third menu selection causes the flies to be drawn with a combination of an AND operation and an OR operation. There's a mask image for each fly that's loaded in at the start of the program. These are used for the AND operation.

The fourth menu selection causes the flies to move across the screen with an XOR operation. You'll notice that the resultant color of the fly depends on the color of the client window.

CD-ROM Location: **Chap5\BlitDemo**
Program Name: **BlitDemo.EXE**
Source Code Modules in Text: **BlitDemoView.cpp**

✦ ✦ ✦ ✦ ✦

Listing 5-2: **BlitDemoView.cpp Source Code File Highlights**

```
// BlitDemoView.cpp:implementation of CBlitDemoView class
//
//////////////////////////////////////////////////////////////////
// CBlitDemoView construction/destruction

CBlitDemoView::CBlitDemoView()
{

 // Start the program showing bubbles.
 m_nOperation = OPERATION_BUBBLES;

 // Initialize our indexes to the fly,
 // bubble, and trolley.
 m_nCurrentFly = 2;
 m_nCurrentBubble = 0;
 m_nCurrentTrolley = 0;

 // Set the fly's position.
 m_nFlyX = 20;
 m_nFlyY = 10;

 static int nBubble[] = {
 IDB_BUBBLE1, IDB_BUBBLE2, IDB_BUBBLE3 };

 static int nFly[] = {
 IDB_FLY1, IDB_FLY2, IDB_FLY3, IDB_FLY4 };

 static int nFlyMask[] = {
 IDB_FLYMASK1, IDB_FLYMASK2,
 IDB_FLYMASK3, IDB_FLYMASK4 };

 static int nTrolley[] = {
 IDB_TROLLEY1, IDB_TROLLEY2,
 IDB_TROLLEY3, IDB_TROLLEY4 };
```

```
 // Load in the bitmaps using LoadBitmap().
 for( int i=0; i<4; i++ ){
  if( i < 3 )
   m_Bubble[i].LoadBitmap( nBubble[i] );
  m_Fly[i].LoadBitmap( nFly[i] );
  m_FlyMask[i].LoadBitmap( nFlyMask[i] );
  m_Trolley[i].LoadBitmap( nTrolley[i] );
  }

}

CBlitDemoView::~CBlitDemoView()
{
}

///////////////////////////////////////////////////////////
// CBlitDemoView drawing

void CBlitDemoView::OnDraw(CDC* pDC)
{
 CBlitDemoDoc* pDoc = GetDocument();
 ASSERT_VALID(pDoc);

 // When a redraw message comes, just
 // call DrawBitmaps()
 DrawBitmaps( pDC );

}

void CBlitDemoView::DrawBitmaps( CDC *pDC )
{

 // Create a DC into which the bitmap
 // will be selected.
 CDC MemDC;
 MemDC.CreateCompatibleDC( pDC );
 CBitmap *pOldBitmap;

 BITMAP bm;

 switch( m_nOperation ){
  case OPERATION_BUBBLES:
   // Select the appropriate bitmap into
   // the DC.
   pOldBitmap =
    (CBitmap *) MemDC.SelectObject(
     &m_Bubble[m_nCurrentBubble] );
   // We need the width and height of the
   // bitmap for the BitBlt() function.
   m_Bubble[m_nCurrentBubble].GetObject(
    sizeof( BITMAP ), &bm );
   // Perform the BitBlt() function to the destination
```

(continued)

Listing 5-2 *(continued)*

```
        // coordinates 0, 0.
        pDC->BitBlt( 0, 0, bm.bmWidth, bm.bmHeight, &MemDC,
          0, 0, SRCCOPY );
        break;
      case OPERATION_TROLLEY:
        // Select the appropriate bitmap into
        // the DC.
        pOldBitmap =
          (CBitmap *) MemDC.SelectObject(
            &m_Trolley[m_nCurrentTrolley] );
        // We need the width and height of the
        // bitmap for the BitBlt() function.
        m_Trolley[m_nCurrentTrolley].GetObject(
          sizeof( BITMAP ), &bm );
        // Perform the BitBlt() function to the destination
        // coordinates 0, 0.
        pDC->BitBlt( 0, 0, bm.bmWidth, bm.bmHeight, &MemDC,
          0, 0, SRCCOPY );
        break;
      case OPERATION_XORFLY:
        // Select the appropriate bitmap into
        // the DC.
        pOldBitmap =
          (CBitmap *) MemDC.SelectObject(
            &m_Fly[m_nCurrentFly] );
        // We need the width and height of the
        // bitmap for the BitBlt() function.
        m_Fly[m_nCurrentFly].GetObject(
          sizeof( BITMAP ), &bm );
        // Perform the BitBlt() function to the destination
        // coordinates calculated by using m_nFlyX and m_nFlyY
        // as the center of the object. The width and height
        // of the bitmap are then used to draw the object
        // centered on m_nFlyX and m_nFlyY.
        pDC->BitBlt( m_nFlyX - ( bm.bmWidth / 2 ), m_nFlyY,
          bm.bmWidth, bm.bmHeight, &MemDC,
          0, 0, SRCINVERT );
        break;
      case OPERATION_MASKFLY:
        // Select the appropriate bitmap into
        // the DC.
        pOldBitmap =
          (CBitmap *) MemDC.SelectObject(
            &m_FlyMask[m_nCurrentFly] );
        // We need the width and height of the
        // bitmap for the BitBlt() function.
        m_FlyMask[m_nCurrentFly].GetObject(
          sizeof( BITMAP ), &bm );
        pDC->BitBlt( m_nFlyX - ( bm.bmWidth / 2 ), m_nFlyY,
          bm.bmWidth, bm.bmHeight, &MemDC,
          0, 0, SRCAND );
```

```
    MemDC.SelectObject( &m_Fly[m_nCurrentFly] );
    // Perform the BitBlt() function to the destination
    // coordinates calculated by using m_nFlyX and m_nFlyY
    // as the center of the object. The width and height
    // of the bitmap are then used to draw the object
    // centered on m_nFlyX and m_nFlyY.
    pDC->BitBlt( m_nFlyX - ( bm.bmWidth / 2 ), m_nFlyY,
     bm.bmWidth, bm.bmHeight, &MemDC,
     0, 0, SRCINVERT );
    break;
   }

 // Select the old bitmap back
 // into the DC.
 MemDC.SelectObject( pOldBitmap );

}

/////////////////////////////////////////////////////////////
// CBlitDemoView message handlers

void CBlitDemoView::OnLButtonDown(UINT nFlags,
 CPoint point)
{

 CClientDC ClientDC( this );

 switch( m_nOperation ){
  case OPERATION_BUBBLES:
   // Increment to next bubble.
   m_nCurrentBubble++;
   // Make sure the bubble value in in range.
   if( m_nCurrentBubble >= 3 )
    m_nCurrentBubble = 0;
   break;
  case OPERATION_TROLLEY:
   // Increment to next trolley.
   m_nCurrentTrolley++;
   // Make sure the trolley value is in range.
   if( m_nCurrentTrolley >= 4 )
    m_nCurrentTrolley = 0;
   break;
  case OPERATION_XORFLY:
   // XORFLY uses the same movement calculations
   // as MASKFLY. The only difference is that
   // to erase the previous image, XORFLY
   // calls DrawBitmaps() and MASKFLY draws
   // a rectangle.
   DrawBitmaps( &ClientDC );
  case OPERATION_MASKFLY:
   if( m_nOperation == OPERATION_MASKFLY ){
    // Get the bitmap size so that we
```

(continued)

Listing 5-2 *(continued)*

```
    // can calculate the rectangle which
    // we must draw to erase the fly.
    BITMAP bm;
    m_FlyMask[m_nCurrentFly].GetObject(
     sizeof( BITMAP ), &bm );
    RECT Rect;
    Rect.left = m_nFlyX - ( bm.bmWidth / 2 );
    Rect.top = m_nFlyY;
    Rect.right = Rect.left + bm.bmWidth;
    Rect.bottom = Rect.top + bm.bmHeight;
    // Create a brush that's the same as the
    // window color and then draw a rectangle.
    CBrush Brush( GetSysColor( COLOR_WINDOW ) );
    ClientDC.FillRect( &Rect, &Brush );
    }
   // We're toggling between 2 and 3 going down
   // and 0 and 1 going up. We can use ^ 1 to
   // accomplish this. If the fly moves past a
   // threshold point, we reverse the direction.
   m_nCurrentFly ^= 1;
   if( m_nCurrentFly >= 2 ){
    m_nFlyY += 10;
    if( m_nFlyY > 300 )
     m_nCurrentFly -= 2;
    }
   else{
    m_nFlyY -= 10;
    if( m_nFlyY <= 10 )
     m_nCurrentFly += 2;
    }
   break;
  }

 DrawBitmaps( &ClientDC );

 CView::OnLButtonDown(nFlags, point);
}

void CBlitDemoView::OnOperationsMaskfly()
{

 // Set the operation to OPERATION_MASKFLY.
 m_nOperation = OPERATION_MASKFLY;
 // Invalidate the client window and force
 // an immediate redraw.
 InvalidateRect( NULL, TRUE );
 UpdateWindow();

}
```

```
void CBlitDemoView::OnOperationsShowbubbles()
{

 // Set the operation to OPERATION_BUBBLES.
 m_nOperation = OPERATION_BUBBLES;
 // Invalidate the client window and force
 // an immediate redraw.
 InvalidateRect( NULL, TRUE );
 UpdateWindow();

}

void CBlitDemoView::OnOperationsShowtrolley()
{

 // Set the operation to OPERATION_TROLLEY.
 m_nOperation = OPERATION_TROLLEY;
 // Invalidate the client window and force
 // an immediate redraw.
 InvalidateRect( NULL, TRUE );
 UpdateWindow();

}

void CBlitDemoView::OnOperationsXorfly()
{

 // Set the operation to OPERATION_XORFLY.
 m_nOperation = OPERATION_XORFLY;
 // Invalidate the client window and force
 // an immediate redraw.
 InvalidateRect( NULL, TRUE );
 UpdateWindow();

}
```

Palettes and Color

The representation of color on IBM-compatible video systems is done using RGB triplets. Each of the RGB triplets contains a value for the red, green, and blue components of a color. The combination of the three component values determines the color that's seen on the screen.

RGB is a common color space (or color definition). The colors red, green, and blue are considered fundamental and undecomposable. Color systems can be separated into two categories: additive color systems and subtractive color systems. Colors in additive systems, such as the RGB system, are created by adding colors to black to create new colors. The more color that's added, the more the resulting color tends toward white. The presence of all the primary colors in sufficient amounts creates pure white; the absence of all the primary colors creates pure black.

We'll use the common RGB macro in this section to describe RGB triplets. The RGB macro converts three byte values ranging from 0 to 255 into a COLORREF value. The macro's first argument is the red value, the second green, and the third blue. Values range from 0 to 255. For instance, an RGB value with a red component of 244, a green component of 142, and a blue component of 34 can be notated as `RGB( 244, 142, 34 )`. Table 5-2 lists some common colors found in the default Window palette.

Table 5-2
RGB Colors in the Default Windows Palette

RGB Value	***Color***
RGB(0, 0, 0)	Black
RGB(255, 255, 255)	White
RGB(255, 0, 0)	Red
RGB(0, 255, 0)	Green
RGB(0, 0, 255)	Blue
RGB(255, 255,)	Yellow
RGB(255, 0, 255)	Magenta
RGB(0, 255, 255)	Cyan
RGB(128, 128, 128)	Dark Gray
RGB(192, 192, 192)	Light Gray

Logical palettes

In video systems set for 16-, 24-, and 32-bit display, individual pixels appear on the screen as the result of storing RGB values in video memory. Video systems set for 8-bit display (and lower values) operate in a more indirect way, and often are called *palletized* devices. Thus images that have a data depth of 8 bits or less are called palletized images.

Palletized video memory doesn't contain the actual RGB data with which a pixel is rendered. Instead, it contains an index into a table of 256 RGB values. This table resides in a section of video memory known as the Digital Adapter Color (DAC). You can't directly set the DAC table yourself from Windows; it's a shared resource. Instead, you must use GDI to set the hardware palette store in the DAC.

The GDI palette manager performs many roles as arbitrator of the hardware palette. One important thing it does is maintain 20 colors (know as static colors) with which Windows draws common items such as dialog objects and icons. You can force GDI to override the 20 static colors, but it's not a good idea. There will be more about this later.

The palette manager prevents duplicate entries from getting into the hardware palette. Duplicate palette entries would diminish the effectiveness of your application to display images in an optimal way. This feature is very valuable for palettized display systems. As with the palette manager's enforcement of the 20 static colors, the rule against duplicate colors can be overridden. We'll mention how this can be done shortly.

A logical palette is created with a `LOGPALETTE` structure. Within the `LOGPALETTE` structure is a list of `PALETTEENTRY` structures. The `PALETTEENTRY` list contains the RGB values with which Windows will set the hardware palette. The number of `PALETTEENTRY` structures that can be in the list ranges from 1 to 256. If your video system supports more than 256 palette entries, your logical palette can be more. The real limit to the size of palette entries is the size of your hardware's palette. Most of the time this will be 256. The `LOGPALETTE` structure definition follows:

```
typedef struct tagLOGPALETTE{
 WORD palVersion;
 WORD palNumEntries;
 PALETTEENTRY palPalEntry[1];
} LOGPALETTE;
```

The `palVersion` member specifies the `LOGPALETTE` version. In all current releases of Windows, this value should be 0x300. The `palNumEntries` member contains the number of palette entries that can be found in the `PALETTEENTRY` list. The `PALETTEENTRY` structure definition is as follows:

```
Typedef struct tagPALETTEENTRY{
 BYTE peRed;
 BYTE peGreen;
 BYTE peBlue;
 BYTE peFlags;
} PALETTEENTRY;
```

The `peRed`, `peGreen`, and `peBlue` members contain the RGB values. The `peFlags` member contains a value of one or more flags describing the type of palette entry. Table 5-3 shows these flags.

Table 5-3
Palette Entry Flags

Flag	*Description*
`PC_EXPLICIT`	Creates a palette entry that specifies an index into the system palette rather than an RGB color. Used by programs that display the contents of a system palette.
`PC_NOCOLLAPSE`	Creates a palette entry that's mapped to an unused entry in the system palette even if there is already an entry for that color. Used to ensure the uniqueness of palette colors when two entries map to the same color.

(continued)

Table 5-3 (continued)

Flag	*Description*
`PC_RESERVED`	Creates a palette entry that's private to this application. When a `PC_RESERVED` entry is added to the system palette, it isn't mapped to colors in other logical palettes even if the colors match. Used by programs that perform palette animation.

Two Other Color Spaces That You May Encounter

RGB is the most common color space used in graphics programming, but there are several others; of these, you're most likely to encounter CMY and HSV. Here's a quick rundown.

CMY Color Space

CMY (cyan, magenta, and yellow) is a subtractive color system used by printers and photographers for the rendering of colors with ink of emulsion, normally on a white surface. It is used by most hard-copy devices that deposit color pigments on white paper, such as laser and ink-jet printers. When illuminated, each of the three colors absorbs its complementary light color. Cyan absorbs red; magenta absorbs green; and yellow absorbs blue. By increasing the amount of yellow ink, for instance, the amount of blue in the image is decreased.

As in all subtractive systems, we say that the CMY system colors are subtracted from white light by pigments to create new colors. The new colors are the wavelengths of light reflected, rather than absorbed, by the CMY pigments. For example, when cyan and magenta are absorbed, the resulting color is yellow. The yellow pigment is said to subtract the cyan and magenta components from the reflected light. When all of the CMY compoments are subtracted, or absorbed, the resulting color is black. It is, however, difficult to achieve a good black color in CMY space. A variant of CMY, known as CMYK, has been spawned. CMYK color has a separate component for the color black.

You can calculate a CMY value from an RGB value. To calculate cyan, subtract the RGB red value from 255; for magenta, subtract the RGB green value from 255; and for yellow, subtract the RGB blue from 255. For instance, RGB(240, 12, 135) have equivalent CMY values of 15, 243, and 120.

HSV

HSV is one of many color systems that vary the degree of properties of colors to create new colors, rather than using a mixture of the colors themselves. Hue specifies color in the common use of the term, such as red, orange, blue, and so on. Saturation (also called chroma) refers to the amount of white in a hue: a fully saturated hue contains no white and appears pure. By extensions, a partly saturated hue appears lighter in color due to the mixture of white. Red hue with 50 percent saturation appears pink, for instance. Value (also called brightness) is the degree of self-luminescence of a color-that is, how much light it emits. A hue with high intensity is very bright, while a hue with low intensity is dark.

HSV most closely resembles the color system used by painters and other artists, who create colors by adding white, black, and gray to pure pigments to create tints, shades, and tones.

A tint is a pure, fully saturated color combined with white, and a shade is a fully saturated color combined with black. A tone is a fully saturated color with both black and white added to it. If we related HSV to this color mixing, saturation is the amount of white, value is the amount of black, and hue is the color that the black and white are added to.

You can convert a color from RGB space to HSV space with the following function, which can be found in a file named **HSV.c** in the Chap05 directory on the CD-ROM:

```
#define mid( a, b, c ) \
  ( a >= b && a <= c ? \
   a : ( b >= a && b <= c ? b : c ) )

void RGB2HSV( int nRed, int nGreen, int nBlue,
  int *nH, int *nS, int *nV )
{
  int nLow, nMid, nHigh;

  if( nRed == nGreen &&
    nGreen == nBlue ){
    *nH = 0;
    *nS = 0;
    *nV = nRed;
    return;
  }

  nLow = min( nRed, min( nGreen, nBlue ) );
  nHigh = max( nRed, max( nGreen, nBlue ) );
  nMid = mid( nRed, nGreen, nBlue );

  *nV = ( nLow + nHigh ) / 2;
  *nS = nHigh - nLow;

  int nCommon = (int)
    ( 60.0 * (double) ( nMid - nLow ) /
    (double) ( nHigh - nLow ) );

  if( nRed == nLow && nBlue == nHigh )
    *nH = 240 - nCommon;
  else if( nRed == nLow && nGreen == nHigh )
    *nH = 120 + nCommon;
  else if( nGreen == nLow && nRed == nHigh )
    *nH = 360 - nCommon;
  else if( nGreen == nLow && nBlue == nHigh )
    *nH = 240 - nCommon;
  else if( nBlue == nLow && nGreen == nHigh )
    *nH = 120 - nCommon;
  else if( nBlue == nLow && nRed == nHigh )
    *nH = nCommon;
}
```

Here's how you'd create a logical palette with 16 colors in which the RGB colors are calculated based on the loop counter:

```
LOGPALETTE *pLogPal;
pLogPal = (LOGPALETTE *)
 new char [sizeof(LOGPALETTE)+16*sizeof(PALETTEENTRY)];

pLogPal->palVersion = 0x300;
pLogPal->palNumEntries = 16;

for( int i=0; i<16; i++ ){
 pLogPal->palPalEntry[i].peRed =
  (unsigned char) ( i * 16 );
 pLogPal->palPalEntry[i].peGreen =
  (unsigned char) ( i * 12 );
 pLogPal->palPalEntry[i].peBlue =
  (unsigned char) ( i * 8 );
 pLogPal->palPalEntry[i].peFlags = 0;
}
```

You can use a `LOGPALETTE` in conjunction with Windows API functions to set the palette. It's better, though, to use the MFC `CPalette` class. This class makes it more convenient to perform palette operations; the `CDC` class that wraps the GDI API expects a `CPalette` object. If you don't use a `CPalette` class, the CDC class won't be of any use when you set the palette.

When you have a `LOGPALETTE`, creating a `CPalette` object couldn't be easier. The following code takes the `LOGPALETTE` created in the last code fragment (named `pLogPal`) and creates a `CPalette` object with it. Once the `CPalette` object is created, the `LOGPALETTE` memory can be deleted as follows:

```
CPalette Palette;
Palette.CreatePalette( pLogPal );
delete [] pLogPal;
```

When you've created a `CPalette` object, you must select the palette into the device context, then realize it. As with most GDI objects, the old object must be selected back into the device context after you're done. Following is code in an `OnDraw()` function which takes the `CPalette` object created in the last code fragment and uses it to set the Windows palette:

```
CPalette *pOldPalette;
pOldPalette = pDC->SelectPalette( &Palette, FALSE );
pDC->RealizePalette();
pDC->SelectPalette( pOldPalette, FALSE );
```

You can create a `CPalette` object which contains a generic and fairly uniform distribution of colors. These palettes are known as halftone palettes, and can be created with the `CreateHalftonePalette()` function. Following is an example of creating such a `CPalette` object:

```
CPalette Palette;
Palette.CreateHalftonePalette( pDC );
```

If you pass an argument of `NULL` to the `CreateHalftonePalette()` function, you create a 256-color halftone palette that's independent of the output device.

Palette events

When you write an application that sets the palette, you'll need to be aware that other applications may receive the focus and set the palette differently. If this happens, your graphics may not look like what you expect when your application gets the focus back. For this reason, you'll have to add some event handlers so you can restore the palette when it's appropriate.

The `WM_QUERYNEWPALETTE` message is sent to an application's top-level window (usually a `CMainFrame` object for AppWizard-created applications) when a palette realization causes a change in the system palette. Palette realization causes Windows to send the palette data that resides in the selected palette to the video hardware that is to effect a change. The `WM_PALETTECHANGED` message is sent to the top-level window when it receives the focus. For multiple-document interface applications which maintain different palettes, each child window should look for a `WM_GETFOCUS` message so the child window can set its own palette.

The following example assumes that a `CPalette` object named `m_Palette` has already been created. It shows how a `WM_QUERYNEWPALETTE` message should be handled:

Class Wizard

Handling a WM_QUERYNEWPALETTE message

Message: **WM_QUERYNEWPALETTE**
Function Created: `OnQueryNewPalette()`
Source Code Module: **MainFrm.cpp**

```
BOOL CMainFrame::OnQueryNewPalette()
{

 CClientDC ClientDC( this );
 CPalette *pOldPalette =
  ClientDC.SelectPalette( &m_Palette, FALSE );

 if( ClientDC.RealizePalette() > 0 )
  Invalidate();

 ClientDC.SelectPalette( pOldPalette, FALSE );

}
```

✦ ✦ ✦ ✦ ✦

Class Wizard

Handling a WM_PALETTECHANGED message
Message: WM_PALETTECHANGED
Function Created: `OnPaletteChanged()`
Source Code Module: **MainFrm.cpp**

```
BOOL CMainFrame::OnPaletteChanged(CWnd *pFocusWnd)
{

 if( pFocusWnd != this ){

  CClientDC ClientDC( this );
  CPalette *pOldPalette =
   ClientDC.SelectPalette( &m_Palette, FALSE );

  if( ClientDC.RealizePalette() > 0 )
   Invalidate();

  ClientDC.SelectPalette( pOldPalette, FALSE );
 }

}
```

◆ ◆ ◆ ◆ ◆

The SetSystemPaletteUse() function

There are times when you may want to have access to the entire system palette, including the 20 static colors. If you find yourself in this situation, you can use the `SetSystemPaletteUse()` function to change the number of static colors Windows reserves for itself. The following code reduces the number of static colors down to two — one for white and one for black:

```
CClientDC ClientDC( this );
SetSystemPalette( ClientDC.m_hDC, SYSPAL_NOSTATIC );
```

Device-Independent Bitmaps

One of the biggest drawbacks to device-dependent bitmaps is the inability to draw to device contexts with different pixel depths. This problem can be overcome by using a DIB. Unfortunately, DIBs aren't wrapped by any MFC classes. This creates extra work for developers; they must write load, save, draw, manipulation, and support code into their application.

To overcome the lack of a DIB class, this section creates a class named `CDib` that conveniently wraps a DIB. A demo program that uses the class comes next, and shows how easy it is to load and display DIBs in programs using the `CDib` class.

The anatomy of a DIB file

Files containing DIBs always start with a BITMAPFILEHEADER data structure. There isn't much useful information in this structure except the size of the file and the offset of the actual DIB data within the file. The offset refers to the number of bytes from the beginning of the file at which the actual image data (as opposed to header information) begins. The first two bytes contain a signature of 'BM' which can be useful for an initial validity check. (The 'BM' signature must be called 'MB' because of the way intel processors swap bytes.) The BITMAPFILEHEADER structure follows:

```
typedef struct tagBITMAPFILEHEADER {
 WORD bfType;
 DWORD bfSize;
 WORD bfReserved1;
 WORD bfReserved2;
 DWORD bfOffBits;
} BITMAPFILEHEADER;
```

The bfType member is always set to BM to indicate that it's a bitmap file. The bfSize member contains a value equal to the file size. The reserved members aren't used and should be zero. The bfOffBits member contains the offset from the beginning of the file to the actual image date.

The next thing that comes in a DIB file is a BITMAPINFOHEADER data structure. In this structure resides information about the DIB that's essential. It contains such things as width, height, and color depth. The BITMAPINFOHEADER structure follows:

```
typedef struct tagBITMAPINFOHEADER{
 DWORD biSize;
 LONG biWidth;
 LONG biHeight;
 WORD biPlanes;
 WORD biBitCount
 DWORD biCompression;
 DWORD biSizeImage;
 LONG biXPelsPerMeter;
 LONG biYPelsPerMeter;
 DWORD biClrUsed;
 DWORD biClrImportant;
} BITMAPINFOHEADER;
```

The biSize field is simply the size of the BITMAPINFOHEADER structure. The biWidth and biHeight members refer to the image width and height. The biPlanes and biBitCount members describe the image color depth. The biCompression member is almost always zero, but in rare cases may be a value that represents some sort of compression. The biSizeImage member contains the size in bytes of the image. The next two members, biXPelsPerMeter and biYPelsPerMeter, refer to the image resolution and are rarely used. The biClrUsed member is usually zero — the only exception is when the number of colors used is actually less than the maximum number of colors for the specified color depth. The biClrImportant member indicates how many of the colors are important — zero, which is usually used, means they're all important.

The last information in the file before the actual DIB data is the palette information. For DIBs with bit depths greater than 8, there will be no palette data. For DIBs of 8 bits or less, the number of palette entries can be calculated by the following formula:

```
int nNumPaletteEntries = 1 << BitmapInfoHeader.biBitCount;
```

It's allowable for DIBs to contain fewer palette entries than the maximum allowable. For instance, an 8-bit DIB has a maximum of 256 colors allowed. Applications that save DIBs may choose to save fewer than 256 palette entries in the disk file.

The BITMAPINFOHEADER member biClrUsed can be used to determine if a DIB has been saved with an explicit number of palette entries. If biClrUsed is zero, the DIB file contains the maximum number of palette entries for the DIB's color depth. If it's non-zero, the DIB file contains exactly the number of palette entries in biClrUsed.

Palette entries are stored in an RGBQUAD structure. The format of the RGBQUAD structure follows:

```
typedef struct tagRGBQUAD {
 BYTE rgbBlue;
 BYTE rgbGreen;
 BYTE rgbRed;
 BYTE rgbReserved;
} RGBQUAD;
```

Finally, after the BITMAPFILEHEADER, the BITMAPINFOHEADER, and any palette entries, comes the DIB data. For 8-bit DIBs, each byte represents a pixel; for 16-bit DIBs, every two bytes represents a pixel; for 24-bit DIBs, every three bytes represents a pixel; for 32-bit DIBs, every four bytes represents a pixel.

Expert Tip

Simple Math Isn't Enough for DIB Widths

If you find yourself needing to calculate an offset into DIB data, heed this warning. To find the number of bytes of each line of a DIB, most programs would take the pixel width and multiply it by the number of bytes per pixel. This may not give you accurate results since the number of bytes for each DIB line must be an even multiple of four. The following code calculates the byte width of a DIB.

```
int nWidthBytes = BitmapInfoHeader.biWidth;
if( BitmapInfoHeader.biBitCount == 16 )
 nWidthBytes *= 2;
else if( BitmapInfoHeader.biBitCount == 24 )
 nWidthBytes *= 3;
else if( BitmapInfoHeader.biBitCount == 32 )
 nWidthBytes *= 4;
while( ( nWidthBytes & 3 ) != 0 )
 nWidthBytes++;
```

✦ ✦ ✦ ✦ ✦

The CDib class

The CDib can save you time, and help you keep your program tidy. In this section, the class is described one function at a time.

CDib::Load()

The Load() function takes a single argument of a char pointer, which points to a NULL-terminated ASCII string of the file name. If the function is successful, it returns TRUE. If for some reason it fails, it returns FALSE.

If a DIB has already been loaded, the Load() function will delete the old DIB if the new one is successfully loaded. Source code for the Load() function follows in Listing 5-3.

Listing 5-3: Source code for the CDib::Load() function

```
BOOL CDib::Load( const char *pszFilename )
{

  CFile cf;

  // Attempt to open the DIB file for reading.
  if( !cf.Open( pszFilename, CFile::modeRead ) )
    return( FALSE );

  // Get the size of the file and store
  // in a local variable. Subtract the
  // size of the BITMAPFILEHEADER structure
  // since we won't keep that in memory.
  DWORD dwDibSize;
  dwDibSize =
    cf.GetLength() - sizeof( BITMAPFILEHEADER );

  // Attempt to allocate the DIB memory.
  unsigned char *pDib;
  pDib = new unsigned char [dwDibSize];
  if( pDib == NULL )
    return( FALSE );

  BITMAPFILEHEADER BFH;

  // Read in the DIB header and data.
  try{

    // Did we read in the entire BITMAPFILEHEADER?
    if( cf.Read( &BFH, sizeof( BITMAPFILEHEADER ) )
      != sizeof( BITMAPFILEHEADER ) ||
```

(continued)

Listing 5-3 *(continued)*

```
      // Is the type 'MB'?
      BFH.bfType != 'MB' ||

      // Did we read in the remaining data?
      cf.Read( pDib, dwDibSize ) != dwDibSize ){

      // Delete the memory if we had any
      // errors and return FALSE.
      delete [] pDib;
      return( FALSE );
      }
    }

  // If we catch an exception, delete the
  // exception, the temporary DIB memory,
  // and return FALSE.
  catch( CFileException *e ){
    e->Delete();
    delete [] pDib;
    return( FALSE );
    }

  // If we got to this point, the DIB has been
  // loaded. If a DIB was already loaded into
  // this class, we must now delete it.
  if( m_pDib != NULL )
    delete m_pDib;

  // Store the local DIB data pointer and
  // DIB size variables in the class member
  // variables.
  m_pDib = pDib;
  m_dwDibSize = dwDibSize;

  // Pointer our BITMAPINFOHEADER and RGBQUAD
  // variables to the correct place in the DIB data.
  m_pBIH = (BITMAPINFOHEADER *) m_pDib;
  m_pPalette =
   (RGBQUAD *) &m_pDib[sizeof(BITMAPINFOHEADER)];

  // Calculate the number of palette entries.
  m_nPaletteEntries = 1 << m_pBIH->biBitCount;
  if( m_pBIH->biBitCount > 8 )
    m_nPaletteEntries = 0;
  else if( m_pBIH->biClrUsed != 0 )
    m_nPaletteEntries = m_pBIH->biClrUsed;

  // Point m_pDibBits to the actual DIB bits data.
  m_pDibBits =
    &m_pDib[sizeof(BITMAPINFOHEADER)+
      m_nPaletteEntries*sizeof(RGBQUAD)];
```

```
    // If we have a valid palette, delete it.
    if( m_Palette.GetSafeHandle() != NULL )
      m_Palette.DeleteObject();

    // If there are palette entries, we'll need
    // to create a LOGPALETTE then create the
    // CPalette palette.
    if( m_nPaletteEntries != 0 ){

      // Allocate the LOGPALETTE structure.
      LOGPALETTE *pLogPal = (LOGPALETTE *) new char
          [sizeof(LOGPALETTE)+
          m_nPaletteEntries*sizeof(PALETTEENTRY)];

      if( pLogPal != NULL ){

        // Set the LOGPALETTE to version 0x300
        // and store the number of palette
        // entries.
        pLogPal->palVersion = 0x300;
        pLogPal->palNumEntries = m_nPaletteEntries;

        // Store the RGB values into each
        // PALETTEENTRY element.
        for( int i=0; i<m_nPaletteEntries; i++ ){
          pLogPal->palPalEntry[i].peRed =
            m_pPalette[i].rgbRed;
          pLogPal->palPalEntry[i].peGreen =
            m_pPalette[i].rgbGreen;
          pLogPal->palPalEntry[i].peBlue =
            m_pPalette[i].rgbBlue;
          }

        // Create the CPalette object and
        // delete the LOGPALETTE memory.
        m_Palette.CreatePalette( pLogPal );
        delete [] pLogPal;
        }
      }

    return( TRUE );

  }
```

To use the `Load()` function, just call it with a valid filename. If the function successfully loads a valid .bmp file, the function returns `TRUE`. If for some reason the function fails, it'll return `FALSE`. An example of using the `Load()` function follows:

```
CDib Dib;
BOOL bRet;
```

```
bRet = Dib.Load( "C:\\Windows\\Clouds.bmp" );
if( bRet )
 AfxMessageBox( "The Load() function succeeded." );
else
 AfxMessageBox( "The Load() function failed." );
```

CDib::Save

You may find it necessary to save a DIB. This situation will arise if you modify the DIB data and want to save it back to disk. The `Save()` function takes the DIB data that's in the `CDib` memory and saves it to disk. The only argument it takes is a pointer to a filename. It returns `TRUE` if the save operation was successful, `FALSE` if it wasn't. The source code for the `CDib::Save()` function follows in Listing 5-4:

Listing 5-4: Source code for the CDib::Save() function

```
BOOL CDib::Save( const char *pszFilename )
{

 // If we have no data, we can't save.
 if( m_pDib == NULL )
  return( FALSE );

 CFile cf;

 // Attempt to create the file.
 if( !cf.Open( pszFilename,
  CFile::modeCreate | CFile::modeWrite ) )
  return( FALSE );

 // Write the data.
 try{

  // First, create a BITMAPFILEHEADER
  // with the correct data.
  BITMAPFILEHEADER BFH;
  memset( &BFH, 0, sizeof( BITMAPFILEHEADER ) );
  BFH.bfType = 'MB';
  BFH.bfSize = sizeof( BITMAPFILEHEADER ) + m_dwDibSize;
  BFH.bfOffBits = sizeof( BITMAPFILEHEADER ) +
   sizeof( BITMAPINFOHEADER ) +
   m_nPaletteEntries * sizeof( RGBQUAD );

  // Write the BITMAPFILEHEADER and the
  // DIB data.
  cf.Write( &BFH, sizeof( BITMAPFILEHEADER ) );
  cf.Write( m_pDib, m_dwDibSize );
  }

 // If we get an exception, delete the exception and
 // return FALSE.
```

```
  catch( CFileException *e ){
   e->Delete();
   return( FALSE );
   }

  return( TRUE );

}
```

To use the Save() function, just call it with a valid file name. A word of caution is in order. If a file exists with the same name as the one that's specified as an argument, that file will be overwritten by the newly-created file. It might be a good idea to check for the existence of the file before saving. If the function successfully saves the .bmp file, the function returns TRUE. If for some reason the function fails, it'll return FALSE. An example of using the Save() function follows:

```
CDib Dib;
BOOL bRet;
bRet = Dib.Save( "C:\\Windows\\NewClouds.bmp" );
if( bRet )
 AfxMessageBox( "The Save() function succeeded." );
else
 AfxMessageBox( "The Save() function failed." );
```

CDib::Draw()

Of course, a CDib class isn't much good if you can't draw the DIB to the screen. An essential function for the class is one that draws the DIB to a device context. The Draw() function does just this. It has one required parameter, a CDC pointer. The next two arguments, the *x* and *y* coordinates, are optional. If you don't specify the *x* and *y* coordinates the DIB will be drawn to 0, 0. The fourth and fifth arguments, width and height, are also optional. If you don't specify either of them, they'll default to the width and/or height of the DIB itself. Otherwise, the function will take the DIB data and stretch (or shrink or both) the data so it exactly fits the width and height that are specified. Source code for the CDib::Draw() function follows in Listing 5-5.

Listing 5-5: Source code for the CDib::Draw() function

```
BOOL CDib::Draw( CDC *pDC, int nX, int nY, int nWidth,
 int nHeight )
{

 // If we have not data we can't draw.
 if( m_pDib == NULL )
  return( FALSE );
```

(continued)

Listing 5-5 *(continued)*

```
// Check for the default values of -1
// in the width and height arguments. If
// we find -1 in either, we'll set them
// to the value that's in the BITMAPINFOHEADER.
if( nWidth == -1 )
 nWidth = m_pBIH->biWidth;
if( nHeight == -1 )
 nHeight = m_pBIH->biHeight;

// Use StretchDIBits to draw the DIB.
StretchDIBits( pDC->m_hDC, nX, nY,
 nWidth, nHeight,
 0, 0,
 m_pBIH->biWidth, m_pBIH->biHeight,
 m_pDibBits,
 (BITMAPINFO *) m_pBIH,
 BI_RGB, SRCCOPY );

return( TRUE );

}
```

To use the `Draw()` function in its simplest form, just pass in a CDC pointer. The function returns `TRUE` if it was successful and `FALSE` if it was not:

```
CDib Dib;
Dib.Load( C:\\Windows\\Clouds.bmp" );
```

Following are three examples of using the `CDib::Draw()` function. The first just passes a CDC pointer. The second passes a CDC pointer and *x* and *y* coordinates. The third passes a CDC pointer, *x* and *y* coordinates, and width and height values.

✦ Using a CDC Only:

```
Dib.Draw( pDC );
```

✦ Using a CDC and Screen Coordinates:

```
Dib.Draw( pDC, 10, 25 );
```

✦ Using a CDC, Screen Coordinates, and Width and Height:

```
Dib.Draw( pDC, 10, 25, 100, 150 );
```

CDib::SetPalette

The last function you'll need to correctly draw the DIBs to the screen is one that sets the palette. For DIBs with pixel depths greater than 8, this function does nothing. For DIBs with pixel depths of 8 bits or less, the palette that was obtained from the DIB data became part of the `CDib` class' `Cpalette` member. Source code for the `SetPalette()` function follows in Listing 5-6.

Listing 5-6: Source Code for the SetPalette() Function

```
BOOL CDib::SetPalette( CDC *pDC )
{

  // If we have not data we
  // won't want to set the palette.
  if( m_pDib == NULL )
    return( FALSE );

  // Check to see if we have a palette
  // handle. For DIBs greater than 8 bits,
  // this will be NULL.
  if( m_Palette.GetSafeHandle() == NULL )
    return( TRUE );

  // Select the palette, realize the palette,
  // then finally restore the old palette.
  CPalette *pOldPalette;
  pOldPalette = pDC->SelectPalette( &m_Palette, FALSE );
  pDC->RealizePalette();
  pDC->SelectPalette( pOldPalette, FALSE );

  return( TRUE );

}
```

The ShowDIB demo program

A demo program that shows you how to use the `CDib` class is included on the book's CD-ROM. It's called `ShowDIB` and it loads, displays, and saves DIBs. Since the `CDib` class does most of the work, the source code for the program is limited to the `ShowDIBView.cpp` source-code file and is minimal. Figure 5-2 shows the program running with a DIB loaded. The source code for the ShowDIB program can be found in Listing 5-7.

Figure 5-2: The ShowDIB program allows you to load DIBs in from a disk file and display them in the view window.

Demo Program

ShowDib
CD-ROM Location: **Chap05\ShowDIB**
Program Name: **ShowDIB.EXE**
Source Code Modules in Text: **ShowDIBView.cpp**

◆ ◆ ◆ ◆ ◆

```
// ShowDIBView.cpp:implementation of CShowDIBView class
//

#include "stdafx.h"
#include "ShowDIB.h"

#include "ShowDIBDoc.h"
#include "ShowDIBView.h"

#ifdef _DEBUG
#define new DEBUG_NEW
#undef THIS_FILE
static char THIS_FILE[] = __FILE__;
#endif

///////////////////////////////////////////////////////////
// CShowDIBView

IMPLEMENT_DYNCREATE(CShowDIBView, CView)

BEGIN_MESSAGE_MAP(CShowDIBView, CView)
 //{{AFX_MSG_MAP(CShowDIBView)
 ON_COMMAND(ID_FILE_OPEN, OnFileOpen)
 //}}AFX_MSG_MAP
END_MESSAGE_MAP()
```

```
/////////////////////////////////////////////////////////////
// CShowDIBView construction/destruction

CShowDIBView::CShowDIBView()
{
}

CShowDIBView::~CShowDIBView()
{
}

BOOL CShowDIBView::PreCreateWindow(CREATESTRUCT& cs)
{
 return CView::PreCreateWindow(cs);
}

/////////////////////////////////////////////////////////////
// CShowDIBView drawing

void CShowDIBView::OnDraw(CDC* pDC)
{
 CShowDIBDoc* pDoc = GetDocument();
 ASSERT_VALID(pDoc);

 RECT Rect;
 GetClientRect( &Rect );
 m_Dib.SetPalette( pDC );
 m_Dib.Draw( pDC, 0, 0,
  Rect.right, Rect.bottom );

}

/////////////////////////////////////////////////////////////
// CShowDIBView diagnostics

#ifdef _DEBUG
void CShowDIBView::AssertValid() const
{
 CView::AssertValid();
}

void CShowDIBView::Dump(CDumpContext& dc) const
{
 CView::Dump(dc);
}

CShowDIBDoc* CShowDIBView::GetDocument()
 // non-debug version is inline
{
 ASSERT(
  m_pDocument->IsKindOf(RUNTIME_CLASS(CShowDIBDoc)));
 return (CShowDIBDoc*)m_pDocument;
}
#endif //_DEBUG
```

```
/////////////////////////////////////////////////////////////////////////////
// CShowDIBView message handlers

void CShowDIBView::OnFileOpen()
{
 static char szFilter[] = "BMP Files(*.BMP)|*.BMP||";

 CFileDialog FileDlg( TRUE, NULL, NULL,
  OFN_HIDEREADONLY, szFilter );

 if( FileDlg.DoModal() == IDOK &&
  m_Dib.Load( FileDlg.GetPathName() ) ){
  InvalidateRect( NULL, TRUE );
  UpdateWindow();
  }

}
```

Double Buffering

There are times when your applications draw to the window with a large number of GDI calls. Often this causes noticeable flicker as the window clears and is then drawn. There's an easy way to eliminate this flicker using the `CBitmap` class. You simply create a `CBitmap` object and a device context, select the bitmap into the device context, draw to the newly-created device context, then draw the bitmap to the window. It's a way to draw to memory with GDI, then move the entire memory object to the visible window with one single, fast `BitBlt()` function call. In almost every case, this will eliminate the redraw flicker that's so annoying.

Try This

Create an Application with Flicker

By creating this application, you'll see a great example of screen flicker. This program will be modified later to eliminate the screen flicker by using a `CBitmap`. It's best if you create this project from scratch—you'll learn more. If you would rather not, however, a complete project for this program can be found on the CD-ROM in the `Chap05\Flicker` directory.

1. Create a single-document application.
2. Set a timer to go off every second.
3. In the timer use the `InvalidateRect( NULL, TRUE )` and `UpdateWindow()` functions to cause the view window to redraw.
4. Add the following code to the `OnDraw()` function.

```
RECT Rect;
GetClientRect( &Rect );

static BOOL bColor = FALSE;
```

```
if( bColor )
 pDC->SelectStockObject( WHITE_PEN );
else
 pDC->SelectStockObject( BLACK_PEN );
bColor = !bColor;

for( int i=0; i<Rect.right; i++ ){
 pDC->MoveTo( i, 0 );
 pDC->LineTo( i, Rect.bottom );
 }
```

5. Run the program and maximize it.

◆ ◆ ◆ ◆ ◆

When the program is running, you'll see the window flicker every second. That's because there's a delay between the time that the line drawing begins and the time it ends. Since the lines are drawn in alternating colors (white and black), you can easily see the delay and the resulting flicker.

Here's how we can get rid of the screen flicker in the Flicker program that you just created. In the `OnDraw()` function before the lines are drawn, use `CreateCompatibleDC()` and `CreateCompatibleBitmap()` to create in-memory device context and bitmap objects to which you'll do your drawing. Perform all draw operations. Finally, use `BitBlt()` to move the entire memory bitmap to the visible window. A replacement `OnDraw()` function follows.

```
RECT Rect;
GetClientRect( &Rect );

static BOOL bColor = FALSE;

CDC MemDC;
MemDC.CreateCompatibleDC( pDC );

CBitmap MemBitmap;
MemBitmap.CreateCompatibleBitmap( pDC,
 Rect.right, Rect.bottom );

CBitmap *pOldBitmap = MemDC.SelectObject( &MemBitmap );

if( bColor )
 MemDC.SelectStockObject( WHITE_PEN );
else
 MemDC.SelectStockObject( BLACK_PEN );
bColor = !bColor;

for( int i=0; i<Rect.right; i++ ){
 MemDC.MoveTo( i, 0 );
 MemDC.LineTo( i, Rect.bottom );
 }

pDC->BitBlt( 0, 0, Rect.right, Rect.bottom,
```

```
    &MemDC, 0, 0, SRCCOPY );

  MemDC.SelectObject( pOldBitmap );
```

Nutshell

Double Buffering

These steps sum up the process for double-buffering a series of draw operations:

1. Create a compatible device context using a `CDC` object.
2. Create a compatible bitmap using a `CBitmap` object.
3. Select the `CBitmap` object into the `CDC` object and store the old bitmap so it can be restored when you're done.
4. Perform all draw operations to the newly-created `CDC` object.
5. Use the `BitBlt()` function to quickly move the newly-created `CBitmap` object to the window's device context.
6. Restore the old bitmap in the newly-created `CDC` object.

The `CDC` and `CBitmap` objects will be cleaned up by their destructors.

◆ ◆ ◆ ◆ ◆

Summary

In this chapter, you've learned how to create and use device-dependent bitmaps with the `CBitmap` class. Now that you've read this chapter, it's a good time to roll up your sleeves and do your own experimentation. First, however, you may want to review some high points:

- Palettes and the `CPalette` class are especially important for images of 8-bit pixel depth.
- You can make DIB manipulation easier by creating a `CDib` class.
- Double buffering is a way to optimize performance.
- Bitmaps and DIBs are powerful and flexible tools in your arsenal. In an age of visual applications, it would be difficult to overstate their importance.

✦ ✦ ✦

CHAPTER 6

MFC Exception Handling

In This Chapter

- Understanding the benefits of exception handling
- Discovering the CException class
- Examining how MFC defines CException-derived classes
- Discovering the CSimpleException and CUserException classes
- Learning advanced exception-handling techniques

Aside from templates, perhaps the single most overlooked and least utilized feature of the C++ language is exception handling. Exceptions are events that are unexpected and whose effects make completion of a particular code path impossible. An example of this can be seen in the `CFile` class. Let's say that you're attempting to open a file using the `CFile` class. One of its constructors takes as its first argument the name of the file to be opened. Even so, if the file can not be opened for some reason, an exception of type `CFileException` is thrown. Therefore, exception handling is the process of handling these unexpected conditions in an orderly and controlled manner.

One important thing to note here is that exception handling should not be used to handle "normal" or "expected" errors that the application should be able to recover from quite easily. Because functions exist to test for the existence of a file before attempting to open it, the programmer in the example would naturally have expected to be able to open the specified file. The fact that the file could not be opened represents an unexpected or abnormal condition; in all likelihood the function that attempted to open the file in the first place would not be able to continue with its task. Therefore, exception handling should be used in this case.

C++ Exception Handling Versus SEH

Because there are a couple of ways to implement exception handling in a Win32 application, it's important to clear up some terminology at this point. Windows 98, Windows 95 and Windows NT support a form of exception handling at the operating-system level called *SEH (structured exception handling)*. SEH works for almost any programming language, even when the language itself does not provide direct SEH support. Microsoft recognizes this capability, but specifies C++ exception handling in the MSDN documentation.

Note

Microsoft states: "Although structured exception handling can also be used with C++, the new C++ exception-handling method should be used for C++ programs."

◆ ◆ ◆ ◆ ◆

The Microsoft Visual C++ compiler implements the C++ exception-handling model on the basis of the ISO WG21/ANSI X3J16; therefore, when this chapter uses the general term "exception handling," it refers specifically to C++ exception handling.

Exception-Handling Syntax

Exception-handling syntax is extremely simple and straightforward, consisting of only three keywords: `try`, `catch` and `throw`. Exception handling uses only two participants: the function that is "raising" or *throwing* the exception and the function that is "handling" or *catching* the exception.

Throwing the exception

When a function needs to relay the fact that an exception has occurred, it *throws* an exception by using the following syntax:

```
throw assignment-expression
```

The manner in which the `throw` statement is called is similar to the C/C++ `return` statement. In C++, the `assignment-expression` shown in the syntax can be any type. For example, a function can even throw a `char` pointer, as shown in the following code:

```
void GetBuffer(char** ppBuffer, unsigned int uiSize)
{
 *ppBuffer = NULL;
 *ppBuffer = new char(uiSize);
 if (NULL == *ppBuffer)
 {
  throw "Memory Error: Could not allocate memory";
 }
}
```

MFC provides a base class called `CException`, however, and this chapter will concentrate on the throwing and catching exceptions of type `CException` as well as classes that are derived from `CException`. Using the `CException` class and developing your own `CException`-derived classes will be covered shortly.

Throwing objects instead of simple types enables you to use classes (like CException) that also implement functions that can be called to discover why the exception occurred in the first place.

Catching the exception

Because a called function can throw an exception, the calling function needs to be able to respond to this event. This is done via the catch statement. All you have to do to catch an exception is bracket your code in a try block and specify which types of exceptions your function is capable of handling in a catch block. All the statements in the try block will be processed in the same order as usual; if an exception is caught, control is passed to the first line of the appropriate catch block. Using the example just given, the calling function might appear like this:

```
#include <iostream.h>

int main()
{
 char* pBuffer;
 try
 {
  GetBuffer(&pBuffer, 512);
  cout << pBuffer;
 }
 catch(char* szException)
 {
  cout << szException;
 }

 return 0;
}
```

As you probably know, if your function attempted to call the cout function with an invalid char pointer, your application would probably receive some type of Access Validation error. Note, however, that if the string buffer in the example just given could not be allocated by the GetBuffer() function, an exception would have been thrown by GetBuffer() and caught in the main's catch block. Therefore, in the event that the memory could not be allocated, the cout function would not be executed.

So what would happen if you call a function that throws an exception and you don't catch it? This depends on the design of your application. When an exception is caught, control is passed down the call stack until a function is located that catches an exception of the type that was thrown. If a function with the appropriate catch statement is not located, the application aborts. Therefore, if you write a function that calls another function that can throw an exception—and your function doesn't catch that exception—you must make sure that some function in the call stack *does* handle the exception.

Another handy technique to know is how to catch multiple types of exceptions: Simply add a `catch` block for every exception type to be caught. Another way to catch multiple types of exceptions in C++ is to define a catch block for the base class of all the exceptions in your system; then you can use C++ *RTTI* (runtime type information) to figure out which exception was thrown within a single catch block. Because the MFC exception classes offer special support for checking class types at runtime, we'll cover this topic in more detail in the section entitled "The `CException` Class."

That's it! Now that you know how easy it is to implement exception handling, let's look at why you would want to use it as an alternative to the more familiar approach of returning an error code to signal an error condition.

Exception Handling Versus Return Codes

The standard approach to error handling has always been to return an error code to the calling function and let the caller figure out what to do on the basis of the returned value. The return value can be as simple as a basic C/C++ type or a pointer to a C++ class. In more elaborate systems that return a value to signify that an error occurred in the called function, a global function retrieves information about the error. Even so, the concept is still the same: The calling function in some way calls a function and needs to inspect a returned value to verify the success or failure of the function that was called.

This approach is severely flawed in a number of important ways. What follows are a few of the areas where exception handling provides tremendous benefits over using return codes.

Dealing with error conditions

When using return codes, the called function returns an error code and the error condition is handled by the calling function. Because the error handling occurs outside the scope of the called function, there is no guarantee the caller will check the returned error code. As an example, let's say you write a class called `CCommaDelimitedFile` that wraps the functionality of reading and writing comma-delimited files. Among other things, your class would need to expose functions to open the file and read data from the file. Using the older "return code" method of reporting errors, these functions would return some variable type that would need to be checked by the caller to verify the success of the function call. Undesired results could emerge if the user of your class called the `CCommaDelimitedFile::Open()` function, for example, and then attempted to call the `CCommaDelimitedFile::Read()` function without checking whether the file actually opened. If the class's open function threw an exception instead, the caller would be forced to deal with the fact that the file did not open; any time a function throws an exception, control is passed back up the call stack until it is caught. Here's an example of what that code may look like:

```
try
{
 CCommaDelimitedFile file;
 file.Open("c:\\test.csv");

 CString strFirstLine;
 file.Read(strFirstLine);
}
catch(CException* pe)
{
 AfxMessageBox("Exception caught");
}
```

As you can see, if the `CCommaDelimitedFile::Open()` throws an exception, the calling function is forced to catch it. This is because if this function does not catch the exception and no other function in the current code path attempts to catch an exception of this type, the application will abort. Also pay particular attention to this: Because both the `Open()` and `Read()` functions were placed in the same `try` block and an exception was caught, an invalid read will not be attempted. This is because programmatic control is passed from the open call in the `try` block to the first line of the `catch` block. Therefore, exception handling ensures you that a failure in your function cannot go ignored.

Handling errors in the correct context

The calling function often does not have enough information to handle the error. This is the area where exception handling shines brightest. If your function calls another function that you know carries out a simple task, it is easy to deal with an error code. Even so, what if the function you're calling is more complex than that? In other words, what if the function you're calling needs to perform many tasks to fulfill its requirements? The function you call may have to call a function. How can your function deal with the fact an error occurred several function layers down? Using our `CAccessDb` described, let's look at an example that illustrates the problem. Let's add a static function to our `CAccessDb` class called `GenerateDb()`. This function will be used to create new access databases. The `GenerateDb()` function needs to perform several tasks to create the database. For example, it needs to create the physical database and the specified tables and columns, and to define any necessary indexes. The `GenerateDb()` function may even need to create some default users and permissions. Figure 6-1 illustrates the number of function levels traversed in this example.

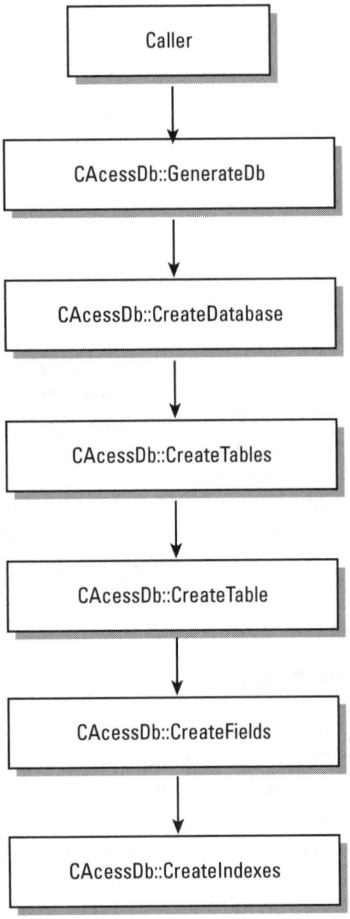

Figure 6-1: An example of calling a function that leads to a long code path. Code paths like this make it difficult for the calling function to handle returned errors.

An example of the programmatic design problem: If an error were to occur in the `CreateIndex()` function, which function would handle it and how? At some point, the function that originally called the `GenerateDb()` function would need to handle the error, but how could it? It would have no idea how to handle an error that occurred several function calls deep in the code path. The calling function would not be in the correct "context" to handle the error. In other words, the only function that could logically create any meaningful error information about the error is the function that failed. Having said that, if return codes were used here, each function in the code path would have to check for every single error code that every single function following it could return. One obvious problem with this is the calling function would need to handle a ridiculously large number of error codes. In addition, maintenance would be extremely difficult because every time an error condition is added to any of the functions in the code path, every other function would need to be updated. In addition, remember we are only talking about one code path here! Now try to imagine if CAccessDb::GenerateDb() is called by other functions and if some of the functions within this code path are called directly by other functions.

Exception handling resolves all these issues by allowing the calling function to trap for a given class of exception. In this example, if a class named CAccessDb was derived from CException, it could be used for any types of errors that occur within the CAccessDb functions. Therefore, if the CAccessDb::CreateIndexes() function failed, it would throw an CAccessDb function. The calling function would catch that exception and be able to call one of its member functions to find out exactly what went wrong. Therefore, instead of handling every possible type of return code that CAccessDb::GenerateDb() and any of its called functions could return, the calling function would be assured that if *any* of the functions in that code path failed, the proper error information would be returned. An additional bonus is, because the error information is contained with a class, new error conditions can be added and the calling function would remain unchanged.

Improving code readability

With exception handling, code readability is greatly improved; code maintenance is easier and less costly. The reason for this is the way in which return codes are handled versus the exception-handling syntax.

Using the CAccessDb::GenerateDb() function mentioned, similar code would be needed to handle return codes.

```
void CCallingClass::CallingFunction()
{
 if (CAccessDb::GenerateDb())
 {
  ...
 }
}

RETURN_CODE CAccessDb::GenerateDb()
{
 if (CreatePhysicalDb())
 {
  if (CreateTables())
  {
   if (CreateIndexes())
   {
    return SUCCESS;
   }
   else
   {
    // handle error
   }
  }
```

```
    else
    {
     // handle error
    }
   }
   else
   {
    // handle error
   }
  }
```

Add a couple of pointer validations to the code and you have a tremendous amount of error-validation code mixed in with the rest of the code. If you have your editor set to display tabs instead of spaces and the tab value is set to 4 (the DevStudio default), there are times when the first character of a line of code will start around column 20! Although none of this is disastrous for your code, it does make the code more difficult to maintain. Code that is difficult to maintain is code that invites bugs. Let's look at how this same example would look if exception handling were used.

```
void CCallingClass::CallingFunction()
{
 try
 {
  CAccessDb::GenerateDb();
  ...
 }
 catch(CAccessDbException* pe)
 {
  TCHAR   szErrorMessage[CHAR_MAX];

  if (pe->GetErrorMessage(szErrorMessage,
   _countof(szErrorMessage)))
  {
   AfxMessageBox(szErrorMessage);
  }

  pe->Delete();
 }
}

void CAccessDb::GenerateDb()
{
 // all these functions throw exceptions
 // therefore, any function calling this function
 // should catch the CAccessDbException
 CreatePhysicalDb();
 CreateTables();
 CreateIndexes();
}
```

Notice how much cleaner and more elegant the second solution is. This is because error detection and recovery code is no longer mixed with the logic of the calling code itself. As you can see, because exception handling has made this code much more straightforward, the capability to maintain this code has been greatly increased.

Throwing exceptions from constructors

Because constructors cannot return values, exceptions are a great way of signaling an error has occurred during the construction of an object. Therefore, if you know that the class you're attempting to instantiate throws an exception, you'll need to bracket its construction in a `try` block. This includes scenarios where you're constructing the object on the stack frame. Here are two examples of catching exceptions thrown during object construction. The first example shows an attempt to construct an object on the heap (or free store) and the second example shows an attempt to construct an object on the stack frame.

```
// example of handling exception when constructing
// an object on the heap
try
{
 CTest pTest = new CTest();
}
catch(someexceptiontype)
{
 // handle exception
}

// example of handling exception when constructing
// an object on the stack frame
try
{
 CTest Test();
}
catch(someexceptiontype)
{
 // handle exception
}
```

The CException Class

As mentioned earlier, C++ exception handling enables you to catch exceptions of almost any type. Even so, using C++ classes gives you the benefit of catching an object that includes the information necessary to describe the error condition, as well as functions to retrieve that information. MFC provides a set of classes for just this purpose. The base class for all MFC exception classes is called `CException`.

As you may imagine, the base `CException` class is not at all complex. In fact, aside from the constructor, the class includes just three functions: `GetErrorMessage()`, `ReportError()` and `Delete()`.

Creating and deleting CException objects

Although the `CException` class does define functions for retrieving information about a specific exception, it does **not** contain any member variables for defining that information. This is because you should never instantiate a `CException` object directly. Instead, you should use one of the MFC CException-derived classes or derive your own exception classes from `CException` and implement the `GetErrorMessage()` and `ReportError()` virtual functions.

The `CException` constructor takes as its only argument a Boolean value (`m_bAutoDelete`) that represents whether the exception object should automatically be deleted. Setting this value to `TRUE` specifies that the exception object was created on the heap. This causes the exception object to be deleted when the `Delete()` member function is called. The only time you should set `m_bAutoDelete` to `FALSE` is when the exception object was created on the stack frame or when the exception object is a global object. In all but a few cases, you set this value to `TRUE`.

The `CException` class provides a member function called `Delete()` for deleting an exception object. Calling this function is straightforward; however, there are a few guidelines to follow when deleting an exception object:

- ✦ Never delete an exception object directly using the C++ `delete` operator. Instead use the `CException::Delete()` function.
- ✦ If an exception is caught and will be thrown or somehow still used outside the scope of the current catch block, do not delete it.
- ✦ If an exception is caught and will not be used outside the current catch block, you must delete it. This includes scenarios where you catch an exception of one type and want to throw an exception of another type. You must still delete the first exception object when you finish referencing it.

Expert Tip

Why Delete Exceptions?

If you're new to the C++ `try-catch` mechanism and are, instead, familiar with the MFC `TRY/CATCH` macros, you're probably wondering why you have to delete the exceptions your function catches. Actually, you have always had to delete any caught exceptions that were not re-thrown. Even so, the MFC macros deleted the exception for you "under the hood." Therefore, if you're going to use the C++ `try-catch` mechanism, you're now responsible for this clean-up.

✦ ✦ ✦ ✦ ✦

Retrieving error information from a CException object

The `CException` class has two functions for retrieving information as to the cause of the exception: `ReportError()` and `GetErrorMessage()`.

The `ReportError()` function displays a message box to the user indicating the cause of the exception. Because you're usually going to want to format any messages displayed to the user, this function is normally only used when debugging your application. Here's an example of the `ReportError()` function in use.

```
CStdioFile file;
CFileException fe;

try
{
 file.Open("IKnowThisFileDoesNotExist.txt",
  CFile::typeText | CFile::modeReadWrite,
  &fe);
 file.Close();
}
catch(CFileException* pe)
{
 pe->ReportError();
}
```

As you can see in the example, the `CFileException` class was used. The `CFileException` class is used for exceptions when dealing with the `CFile` class and any of its derived classes. We'll look at this class in more detail shortly. Also notice the exception was not deleted. This is because the exception object was constructed on the stack. Therefore, the exception object will be destructed when it goes out of scope.

Although the `ReportError()` function displays the exception's description to the user without giving you an opportunity to format what will be displayed, the `GetErrorMessage()` function returns a textual description of the error that occurred. When calling this function, supply an `LPTSTR` for the description's buffer and a maximum length for the description. When the function returns, you can then use the description to do such things as formatting an error message for display and logging the error condition to a file. Using the example given, here's how you might format a `CFileException` description and display the result to the user.

```
CStdioFile file;
CFileException fe;

try
{
 file.Open("IKnowThisFileDoesNotExist.txt",
  CFile::typeText | CFile::modeReadWrite,
  &fe);
 file.Close();
}
```

```
catch(CFileException* pe)
{
 TCHAR szErrorMessage [CHAR_MAX];
 if (pe->GetErrorMessage(szErrorMessage,
  _countof(szErrorMessage)))
 {
  CString strErrorMessage;
  strErrorMessage.Format("File error encountered: %s",
   szErrorMessage);
  AfxMessageBox(strErrorMessage);
 }
}
```

Catching multiple exception types

Times occur when the functions in a `try` block need to catch exceptions that are different from one another. For example, say you create a class called `CValidatePtr` that validates pointers. If this class throws an exception, you need to catch it. Even so, what if in the same `try` block, another function is being called that could throw an exception that is not a `CValidatePtrException`? This scenario can be handled in two ways.

The first way is to declare multiple `catch` blocks. Each `catch` block exists for the exception type that it is prepared to handle. Here's an example of a function that saves the current dialog's data.

```
CTestDlg::OnOk()
{
 try
 {
  CValidatePtrException::ValidatePtr(m_pTestPtr,
   RUNTIME_CLASS(CTestPtr));

  m_pTestPtr->DoSomeThing();
 }
 catch(CValidatePtrException* pe)
 {
  // do something with this type of ptr
  pe->Delete();
 }
 catch(CTestPtrException* pe)
 {
  // do something else with this ptr
  pe->Delete();
 }
```

The second way to catch multiple exception types from the same `try` block is to use the `IsKindOf()` function. Because the `CException` class specifies the `DECLARE_DYNAMIC` and `IMPLEMENT_DYNAMIC` macros, you can use the `CObject::IsKindOf()` function to find out what type of exception was thrown even if you only have an "upcasted" pointer. Here is an example of how the `IsKindOf()` function would be implemented using the example.

```
CTestDlg::OnOk()
{
 try
 {
  CValidatePtrException::ValidatePtr(m_pTestPtr,
   RUNTIME_CLASS(CTestPtr));

  m_pTestPtr->DoSomeThing();
 }
 catch(CException* pe)
 {
  if (pe->IsKindOf(RUNTIME_CLASS(CValidatePtrException)))
  {
   // do something with this type of ptr
   pe->Delete();
     }
     else if (pe->IsKindOf(CTestPtrException))
     {
   // do something else with this ptr
   pe->Delete();
     }
 }
}
```

Defining CException-Derived Classes

As explained earlier, because the `CException` class does not have any member variables for holding the information that would explain the cause of an exception, you must derive a class from `CException`. The following list shows the MFC-provided exception classes derived from `CException`.

```
CSimpleException
CArchiveException
CFileException
CDaoException
CDBException
COleException
COleDispatchException
CInternetException
```

Although defining your own `CException` is by no means difficult, one of the greatest benefits of using MFC is you have the MFC source code readily available. In addition, who better to take tips from insofar as deriving a class from an MFC base class than an MFC-derived class? Therefore, before we look how to derive your own class from `CException`, let's see how MFC did the same thing with the `CFileException` class.

Discovering the CFileException class

The CFileException class is used when dealing with the errors in association with the CFile class or any of its derived classes. A CFileException can be thrown for quite a few reasons. Among those reasons are things such as the specified file not being found, an invalid directory path, and a sharing violation.

The CFileException class needs to associate a string value for each exception for use in the CFileException::Dump() and AfxThrowFileException() functions. Even so, the designers of the CFileException class wanted to allow the function instantiating the CFileException to be able to specify a numeric value that would represent the cause of the exception. These numeric values are defined in an enum within the CFileException class itself. Because each enum automatically has a number associated with it, a static string array is defined for the CFileException class. That way the textual description of any given CFileException can be found by using the enum value as an index into this static string array. Because this is a good technique for using in your own CException-derived classes, the enum structure and the static string array are found in the following code list:

```
enum {
 none,
 generic,
 fileNotFound,
 badPath,
 tooManyOpenFiles,
 accessDenied,
 invalidFile,
 removeCurrentDir,
 directoryFull,
 badSeek,
 hardIO,
 sharingViolation,
 lockViolation,
 diskFull,
 endOfFile
};

static const LPCSTR rgszCFileExceptionCause[] =
{
 "none",
 "generic",
 "fileNotFound",
 "badPath",
 "tooManyOpenFiles",
 "accessDenied",
 "invalidFile",
 "removeCurrentDir",
 "directoryFull",
 "badSeek",
```

```
    "hardIO",
    "sharingViolation",
    "lockViolation",
    "diskFull",
    "endOfFile",
  };
```

As you can see, each `enum` value matches a specific textual description in the `rgszCFileExceptionCause` static string array. Therefore, when a `CFileException` object is constructed and thrown, it can be done in the following manner.

```
throw new CFileException(CFileException::fileNotFound);
```

This is a good example of how to implement specific error types with your exception classes. Actually, an even better way exists to deal with situations where you associate a text value with an exception. One thing you did not see in the definition of the static string array was that it is only defined for debug builds. In other words, the `rgszCFileExceptionCause` array is only defined within an `#ifdef _DEBUG/#endif` block. So how does the `CFileException` class get its error descriptions and how are they associated with the `int` value passed to its constructor? The answer is the resource file. Due to having to localize all messages the user sees, the `CFileException` class stores its error descriptions in the resource file. If you peek at how the `CFileException::GetErrorMessage()` is defined, you see the following:

```
BOOL CFileException::GetErrorMessage(LPTSTR lpszError, UINT
nMaxError,
 PUINT pnHelpContext)
{
 ASSERT(lpszError != NULL && AfxIsValidString(lpszError,
nMaxError));

 if (pnHelpContext != NULL)
  *pnHelpContext = m_cause + AFX_IDP_FILE_NONE;

 CString strMessage;
 CString strFileName = m_strFileName;
 if (strFileName.IsEmpty())
  strFileName.LoadString(AFX_IDS_UNNAMED_FILE);
 AfxFormatString1(strMessage,
  m_cause + AFX_IDP_FILE_NONE, strFileName);
 lstrcpyn(lpszError, strMessage, nMaxError);

 return TRUE;
}
```

The first few lines validate the `LPTSTR` address and set the help context. Next, the filename specified when the `CFileException` was constructed is retrieved. If a filename was not passed to the constructor, a string value of "unnamed file" is loaded from the resource file.

Notice the line that calls `AfxFormatString1`. This function formats a `CString` using a string resource identified by the resource id in the second argument. As you can see, a value identified as `AFX_IDP_FILE_NONE` is used. Actually what is happening here in a release build is much like what happens in a debug build. The only difference is, when you build a debug version of your application, the `enum` value is used as an index into a static string array. In the release build of your application, however, the `enum` value is added to the `AFX_IDP_FILE_NONE` value and used as a string resource ID. This way, all the `CFileException` error descriptions are kept in the MFC DLL for release builds that use the MFC in a shared DLL. For release builds that statically link MFC into their applications, the same resources are compiled into the application.

Expert Tip

Viewing DLL and EXE Resources

If you want to view the resources of a DLL or EXE, you can do so in DevStudio. For example, if you want to view the string resources specified in the MFC42.DLL files, simply click the File Open toolbar icon, locate the files in your Windows system32 directory, and remember to select the "Resources" entry in the "Open As" combo box on the File Open dialog.

✦ ✦ ✦ ✦ ✦

Demo Program

FileExceptionTest

CD-ROM Location: **Chap06\FileExceptionTest**
Program Name: **FileExceptionTest.EXE**
Source Code Modules in Text: **FileExceptionTest.cpp**

✦ ✦ ✦ ✦ ✦

What follows is a demo application that shows the `CFileException` class in action. Because you now have seen how the `CFileException` class is defined, the purpose of this demo is to illustrate how easy it is to throw and catch exceptions of this type. Figure 6-2 shows the results of selecting a `CFileException` error type. As you can see, an exception was thrown and caught. Upon catching the exception, the `CFileException::GetErrorMessage()` function was called and the resulting string was used in the message box. All this is pretty obvious, but what you should pay attention to here is how the design and implementation of the `CFileException` class with `enum` values and string resources make the use of this class flexible. You are going to use a similar technique in the next section to create your own `CException`-derived classes. Note that because only the dialog's `OnOK()` and `GetException()` functions are pertinent to this topic, they are the only functions listed.

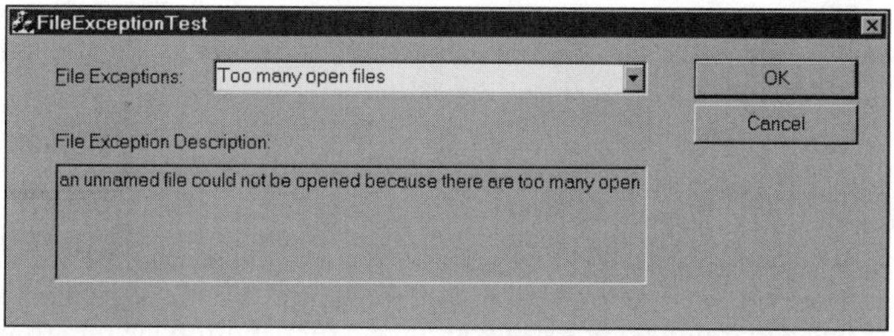

Figure 6-2: Looking at the code for the FileExceptionTest dialog illustrates how easy it is to implement exceptions using the CFileException class as a template.

Listing 6-1: FileExceptionTest

```
void CFileExceptionTestDlg::OnOk()
{
 try
 {
  if (UpdateData(TRUE))
  {
   GetException();
   CFileExceptionTestDlg::OnOK();
  }
 }
 catch(CFileException* pe)
 {
  TCHAR szErrorMessage[CHAR_MAX];
  if (pe->GetErrorMessage(szErrorMessage,
   _countof(szErrorMessage)))
  {
   AfxMessageBox(szErrorMessage);
  }

  pe->Delete();
 }
}

void CFileExceptionTestDlg::GetException()
{
 throw new CFileException(m_iFileExceptionEnum,
  -1, m_strFileName);
}
```

As you can see in the listing, the only thing the `GetException()` function does is create a `CFileException` with the value specified on the dialog. Also note, the

CFileExceptionTestDlg::OnOK() function will never be called. This is because, as you learned earlier in the chapter, when a function is called in a try block that throws an exception, control is passed to the first line of the catch block.

Defining your own CException-derived classes

Now that you know how CFileException is designed, it's time to derive your own exception classes from CException. We begin by imagining a real-life scenario where you would use exceptions. Let's say you have a distribution system that has a few maintenance dialogs, one in particular for entities such as customers and suppliers. In keeping with good object-oriented design, the customer maintenance dialog and supplier maintenance dialog won't actually maintain the respective customers and suppliers. Instead, each dialog contains a pointer to its respective customer or supplier object that is being created or edited on the dialog. When the user chooses to save the entity in question, the dialog will call UpdateData(TRUE) and then call the entity's save function. Because there is a CFile class and a CFileException class for exceptions that occur with CFile objects, we'll create an exception class for each class that needs one. Therefore, the save code for the customer maintenance dialog may look something like this:

```
CCustomerMaintenanceDlg::OnOK()
{
 try
 {
  if (UpdateData(TRUE))
  {
   m_pCustomer->Save();
   CDialog::OnOK();
  }
}
 catch(CCustomerException* pe)
 {
  TCHAR szErrorMessage[CHAR_MAX];
  if (pe->GetErrorMessage(szErrorMessage,
   _countof(szErrorMessage)))
  {
   AfxMessageBox(strErrorMessage);
  }

  pe->Delete();
 }
}
```

Here's an example of how the CCustomerException class's exception might be defined.

```
const int CUSTOMER_EXCEPTION_STRING_RESOURCE = 1000;

class CCustomerException : public CException
{
DECLARE_DYNAMIC(CCustomerException)
```

```
public:
 CCustomerException(int iCause);
protected:
 int m_iCause;

public:
 enum
 {
  causeDuplicateCustomer = 0,
  causeInvalidTermsCode,
  causeInvalidSupplierCode
 }
public:
 virtual BOOL GetErrorMessage(LPTSTR lpszError,
   UINT nMaxError, PUINT pnHelpContext = NULL);
};
```

Notice the `const int CUSTOMER_EXCEPTION_STRING_RESOURCE` defined. This would be used just like the `AFX_IDP_FILE_NONE` value was used in the `CFileException::GetErrorMessage()` function. In other words, the `m_iCause` member variable would be added to this value and the result would use the string resource id to retrieve the exception description at runtime.

But now we start to see a few problems with this approach. First, you need to create a new exception class for every class in the system that would need to signal an exception. In a large system, this could be a ridiculously large number of classes and files to maintain. The second problem is, if a different class were created for every exception with the only difference in their class declarations being the values of an `enum` structure, this would definitely not be following good object-oriented design techniques. In other words, you should only declare a new class type when a class does not exist that exhibits the same behavior that is needed. Therefore, a better way must exist of defining exceptions for the entire system without having an exception class for each one. Actually, there is a simple way to do this.

We can start by examining a class derived from `CException`: the `CSimpleException` class. This class is said to be a "resource critical" exception. In other words, the `CException` class does not declare any variables that contain the cause of a specific exception; the `CSimpleException` does. Actually, there is yet another level of abstraction to traverse. Although the `CSimpleException` class does declare a member variable to hold a string resource ID, it does not declare a function to set that resource id. You must use the `CUserException` for that purpose. The `CUserException` class has a constructor that takes as one of its arguments a string resource ID. This way, when you call its `GetErrorMessage()` function, it loads the string resource and returns it as the cause of the exception. Here is how the `CSimpleException::GetErrorMessage()` function is defined:

```
BOOL CSimpleException::GetErrorMessage(LPTSTR lpszError,
 UINT nMaxError, PUINT pnHelpContext)
{
 ASSERT(lpszError != NULL
 && AfxIsValidString(lpszError, nMaxError));
```

```
 if (pnHelpContext != NULL)
  *pnHelpContext = 0;

 // if we didn't load our string (eg, we're a
 // console app) return a null string and FALSE

 if (!m_bInitialized)
  InitString();

 if (m_bLoaded)
  lstrcpyn(lpszError, m_szMessage, nMaxError);
 else
  lpszError[0] = '\0';

 return m_bLoaded;
}

void CSimpleException::InitString()
{
 m_bInitialized = TRUE;
 m_bLoaded = (AfxLoadString(m_nResourceID,
 m_szMessage, _countof(m_szMessage)) != 0);
}
```

Instead of creating a new exception class for every class that needs to throw an exception, you can instantiate a `CSimpleException` object. Even so, one problem is still left. When a `CCustomer` exception occurs (which results in a `CSimpleException` being thrown), should a string resource id be used to construct the `CSimpleException`? It can be. Even so, it is much more elegant and clear in your code to follow the design of the `CFileException` and use an `enum` structure in your `CCustomer` class to define all the values that will be used in the `CSimpleException`'s constructor and in the `CSimpleException::InitString()` function to retrieve the string resource.

To see just how easy this is to implement, let's look at some code that illustrates two example classes that can throw exceptions: `CCustomer` and `CSupplier`. Because the `CSimpleException` does most of the work for you, all you have to do is define the exception causes in the `CCustomer` and `CSupplier` class declarations. The code would look like this:

```
class CCustomer : public CObject
{
...
public:
 enum
 {
  causeDuplicateCustomer = 1000,
  causeInvalidTermsCode,
  causeInvalidSupplierCode
 ...
 };
```

```
class CSupplier : public CObject
{
enum
 {
  causeDuplicateSupplier = 2000,
  causeInvalidDiscountRate
};
```

Notice how `enum` values are set. It is always a good idea to "space," or distribute, the starting numbers for your exception resource ids far enough apart to allow for future exception descriptions.

Using this approach, you would only have one exception class for all the exception types in your application. The only thing you have to do at this point is to create the string resources with the ids that you specify in the different class's `enum` structures.

The `CCustomerMaintenanceDlg::OnOK()` function would now look like this:

```
CCustomerMaintenanceDlg::OnOK()
{
 try
 {
  if (UpdateData(TRUE))
  {
   m_pCustomer->Save();
   CDialog::OnOK();
  }
}
 catch(CSimpleException* pe)
 {
  TCHAR szErrorMessage[CHAR_MAX];
  if (pe->GetErrorMessage(szErrorMessage,
   _countof(szErrorMessage)))
  {
   AfxMessageBox(szErrorMessage);
  }

  pe->Delete();
 }
}
```

A demo implementing this class can be found on the CD-ROM in the Chap06\SimpleExceptionDemo folder.

Advanced Exception-Handling Techniques

So far we've covered the basic concepts of using exception handling, the semantics related to throwing and catching exceptions, and a few of the MFC classes that make doing all this very easy. Even so, now that the basics are understood, some important questions still remain.

Let's say `FunctionA()` calls `FunctionB()`, which, in turn, calls `FunctionC()`. If `FunctionC()` can advertises that it can throw a particular kind of exception, does `FunctionB()` need to catch it even though it won't, or can't, do anything with it? How should code be split regarding the `try to catch` blocks? Are there any special considerations for throwing exceptions from virtual functions? Now that we've covered the basics of implementing MFC exception handling, let's look at these issues as we delve a little more deeply into how to make exception handling work for you to deliver on its promise of making your code tighter.

Deciding what function should catch an exception

Now you know how to catch an exception that a called function may throw, and you know that control will pass up the call stack until an appropriate `catch` block is found. The question is: Should a `try` block catch every possible exception a function within it may throw? The answer to this is no. As mentioned earlier, two of the biggest benefits to using exception handling in your application are reduced coding and lower maintenance cost. Here's an example to illustrate the point:

```
#include <iostream.h>

int main()
{
 try
 {
  PerformWork()
  cout << "Program terminated without any problems";
 }
 catch(char* szException)
 {
  cout << szException;
 }

 return 0;
}

void PerformWork()
{
 try
 {
  char* pBuffer;
  GetBuffer(&pBuffer, 512);
  cout << pBuffer;
 }
 catch(char* szException)
 {
  throw szException;
 }
}
```

```
void GetBuffer(char** ppBuffer, unsigned int uiSize)
{
 *ppBuffer = NULL;
 *ppBuffer = new char(uiSize);
 if (NULL == *ppBuffer)
 {
  throw "Memory Error: Could not allocate memory";
 }
}
```

As you can see in the example, the `PerformWork()` function catches the exception `GetBuffer()` may throw, even though it doesn't do anything with the exception except re-throw it. The `main()` function then catches the re-thrown exception and truly handles it by doing something (in this case, displaying an error message). Here are a few reasons why functions that simply re-throw an exception shouldn't catch the exception to start.

Because the function doesn't do anything with the exception, you would be left with a `catch` block in its function that is, at best, superfluous. It's never a good idea to have code in a function simply for the sake of its existence.

If the exception type being thrown by the `GetBuffer()` function changed, you would have to go back and change both the `main()` function and the `PerformWork()` functions. This results in an increased maintenance cost for the system.

Doing this enough times in a large application can degrade your system performance. This is because while an exception is being handled, every function in the stack would be returned to — and would simply re-throw the exception back up the call stack.

Because C++ will automatically continue up the call stack until a function catches the exception, intermediate functions can ignore the exceptions it cannot process.

Deciding what code to put in a try block

Determining what code to put in a try block is often a stylistic issue. Normally you would only put code in a `try` block whose operation could result in an exception being thrown. Even so, many programmers tend to put almost the entire function in a `try` block for reasons of readability. Therefore, you routinely see code like the following:

```
void SomeClass::SomeFunction(CWnd* pWnd)
{
 try
 {
  CString strWindowText;
  pWnd->GetWindowText(strWindowText);
```

```
    m_pRecord->Save(strWindowText);

    ...
   }
   catch(CException* pe)
   {
    pe->ReportError();
    pe->Delete();
   }
  }
```

As you can see in the SomeClass::SomeFunction() function, the first two lines of code to define a CString object and to retrieve text from a window have nothing to do with the possibility of the Save() function throwing an exception. Therefore, these two lines of code could have been placed before the try block like this:

```
void SomeClass::SomeFunction(CWnd* pWnd)
{
 CString strWindowText;
 pWnd->GetWindowText(strWindowText);

 try
 {
  m_pRecord->Save(strWindowText);

  ...
 }
 catch(CException* pe)
 {
  pe->ReportError();
  pe->Delete();
 }
}
```

As mentioned earlier, this comes down to a stylistic choice. Personally, I think placing all the code in the try block makes it more readable. Even so, both techniques are perfectly valid.

Deciding what code to put in a catch block

The only code that should ever appear in a catch block is code that will at least partially process the exception. For example, there will be times when a function will catch an exception, do what it can to process the exception, and then re-throw the exception, so further exception handling can be done. Let's look at a scenario that illustrates this.

```
CMyDialog::OnOk()
{
 try
 {
  m_pDoc->SaveInvoice(*m_pInvoice);
```

```
    CDialog::OnOK();
  }
  catch(CException* pe)
  {
    pe->ReportError();
    pe->Delete();
  }
}

CMyDoc::Save(CInvoice const& rInvoice)
{
  try
  {
    m_pDB->Commit();

    m_pDB->SaveInvoiceHdr(rInvoice->GetHeader());
    m_pDB->SaveInvoiceDtl(rInvoice->GetDetail());

    m_pDB->Commit();

    SetModifiedFlag(TRUE);
  }
  catch(CDBException* pe)
  {
    m_pDB->Rollback();

    throw pe;
  }
}
```

In this example, a dialog called `CMyDialog` is used to enter invoices. Upon handling the `OnOk()` function, the `CMyDialog::OnOk()` function uses its embedded document member variable (`m_pDoc`) to attempt to save the invoice. If the `SaveInvoice()` function throws an invoice, `CMyDialog::OnOk()` catches it and displays the error message. Otherwise, the dialog is dismissed (as the invoice has been saved). You've already seen this type of "call and catch" done several times in this chapter. Even so, look at the `CMyDoc::Save()` function. As you can see, this function calls the `Commit()` function, saves the data, and then calls the `Commit()` function again before exiting. Now look at the `catch` block. Before this function re-throws the exception, it calls the `Rollback()` function to undo any uncompleted changes from the database. Times occur when a function may need to catch an exception to do some internal clean-up before the previous function in the call stack does its processing of the exception.

Throwing exceptions from virtual functions

Throwing exceptions from virtual functions can definitely be a tricky issue. As is always the case with overriding a virtual function, you should never do anything that previously written code cannot handle. In other words, say you have the following class declaration:

```
class CTest
{
 ...

public:
 // Upon failure, DoSomething() throws
 // CTestException
 virtual void DoSomething();

 ...
};

class CTestException : public CException
{
 ...

public:
 void LogException ();

 ...
};


CSomeClass::SomeFunction(CTest* pTest)
{
 try
 {
  pTest->DoSomething();
 }
 catch(CTestException* pe)
 {
  pe->LogException();
  pe->Delete();
 }
}
```

In the example, an exception has been derived from the `CException` base class. This class adds the functionality of logging an exception to a file when the `LogException()` function is called. Therefore, the `CSomeClass:SomeFunction()` function places the `CTest::DoSomething()` function in a `try` block to catch the `CTestException` exception if it's thrown.

Even so, what happens now if another programmer derives a new class from `CTest`, overrides the `CTest::DoSomething()` virtual function, and wants to throw a different type of exception? The answer is simple. If the exception is derived from a class that the `CTest::SomeFunction()` function is documented as throwing, there is no problem. In other words, all previous code continues to work as before. Even so, if the new class's implementation of the `DoSomething()` function throws an exception that was not documented when code was developed using the `CTest::DoSomething()` function, you need to go back and modify all the existing code that calls the `CTest::DoSomething()` function. Otherwise, the functions that receive an upcasted pointer to the new class will not catch the new exception. Here's an example of how that would fail:

```
class CNewTest : public CTest
{
 ...

public:
 // Upon failure, DoSomething() throws
 // CNewTestException
 virtual void DoSomething();

 ...
};

CSomeClass::SomeFunction(CTest* pTest)
{
 try
 {
  pTest->DoSomething();
 }
 catch(CTestException* pe)
 {
  pe->LogException();
  pe->Delete();
 }
}
```

Now if the `CSomeClass::SomeFunction()` function is called with a pointer to a `CNewTest` object and the `DoSomething()` function throws an exception, it will not be caught. One of the biggest selling points of C++ is the capability to add new code to a system without having to rewrite existing code. In this case, however, existing code has been broken. The reason is the `CTest::DoSomething()` function was documented as throwing an exception of one type and then an overridden version of this function threw an exception of another type. Luckily, two ways exist to solve this problem.

If you override a function documented as throwing a specific type of exception and throw a different type of exception, throw an exception derived from the originally documented exception type. In the example, that means because the `CTest::DoSomething()` function was originally documented as throwing an exception of type `CTestException`, the `CNewTest::DoSomething()` should only throw exceptions of that type or any class that is derived from that type.

Another way to solve this problem is for the calling function generically to catch an exception type that represents the base class to all the exception types in the system. Then the system can use the `IsKindOf()` function to check for specific exception types. This type of approach should definitely be used when you're designing a class that has functions you know will be overridden. Here is a better way of handling the example shown.

```
class CTest
{
 ...

 // Upon failure, DoSomething() throws
 // CTestException (derived from CException)
 virtual void DoSomething();

 ...
};

class CTestException : public CException
{
 ...

public:
 void LogException ();

 ...
};

class CNewTest : public CTest
{
 ...

 // Upon failure, DoSomething() throws
 // CNewTestException (NOT derived from CException)
 virtual void DoSomething();

 ...
}

CSomeClass::SomeFunction(CTest* pTest)
{
 try
 {
  pTest->DoSomething();
 }
 catch(CTestException* pe)
 {
  pe->LogException();
  pe->Delete();
 }
 catch(CException* pe)
 {
  TCHAR szErroMessage[512];
  if (pe->GetErrorMessage(szErrorMessage,
   _countof(szErrorMessage)))
  {
   // call global logging function
   // passing szErrorMessage so that
   // all exceptions get logged
  }
```

```
      pe->Delete();
    }
  }
```

When processing exceptions, C++ will pass control back up the call stack to the *first* `catch` block that handles this specific type of exception. Therefore, control will be passed to the first `catch` block when a `CTestException` is thrown. Because the `CNewTestException` was derived from `CException` and not `CTestException`, control will be passed to the second `catch` block when an exception of this type is thrown.

Summary

As you've seen throughout this chapter, exception-handling syntax is simple, the MFC exception classes are straightforward, and implementing exception handling in your application is as easy as designing your functions ahead of time. What makes exception handling so powerful is not an obtuse syntax or complex lattice of C++ classes. It is the overall technique of using exceptions in your application and the benefits derived therein that make exception handling an incredibly important tool to developing dependable applications with robust and complete error checking.

✦ ✦ ✦

CHAPTER 7

Dialogs and Controls

✦ ✦ ✦ ✦

In This Chapter

Creating a dialog-based application

Learning how to use the resource editor

Working with the CDialog class

Discovering MFC control classes

Understanding DDX and how to use it

Implementing message handlers for control notification messages

Discovering how to use serialization from a dialog-based application

Learning how to work with modal dialogs

Learning about modeless dialogs and how to invoke them

Communicating between a modal and modeless dialog

✦ ✦ ✦ ✦

Instead of covering the subject of dialogs and controls by presenting the usual "hello, world" example, this chapter does something a little different: You'll learn the subject by coding a realistic application from start to finish, adding in different bits of functionality as you proceed.

There are two main benefits derived from this approach. First, for the beginner-level MFC programmer, this chapter allows you to work through an entire real-world application in a tutorial manner. And second, for the more advanced reader who is simply trying to look up something specific about dialogs and controls, this chapter serves as a reference where you can jump to your specific area of need.

In keeping with a logical, step-by-step approach to teaching the ins and outs of dialogs and controls, this chapter is broken into several sections. The first section is simply a brief description, or definition, of what a dialog is and what controls are used for. The next section introduces you to the sample application that you'll be building throughout the remainder of the chapter. In that section, you'll learn how to use the resource editor to edit your dialog and to create and edit your dialog's controls. The following sections are then devoted to adding different features to the sample application. Each of these features teaches you a whole new set of techniques to use when dealing with dialogs and controls in your Windows applications.

Dialogs and Controls – A Brief Description

One of the most important user-interface elements in a Windows application is the *dialog*. Dialogs (sometimes referred to as "dialog boxes") are used to display information as well as receive input from the user. For the beginning Windows programmers, it is important to understand that dialogs, like any other window on your screen, are simply another type of window. From a programmatic standpoint, that means that anything you can do with a window (size, move, minimize, maximize, and so on), you can do with a dialog. We get into exactly how to control the creation and operation of dialogs shortly.

Controls are the user interface elements such as edit boxes, list boxes, and buttons that interact with the user. Almost without exception, a dialog box contains at least a few controls. Controls, like dialogs, are also windows. Therefore, dialogs are windows that contain other windows (controls) for the purpose of interacting with the user.

In addition to controls like the edit fields, push buttons, combo boxes, and list boxes, new controls were introduced with Windows 95. These controls are called the *Window Common Controls* and include tree controls, list controls, and sliders, among others. This chapter focuses on the basic controls; the Windows Common Controls are covered in Chapter 8.

Using the Resource Editor

As mentioned earlier, a real-life example can teach the most important and relevant facts about the dialogs in Windows applications. That way, instead of seeing an endless list of techniques for controlling the dialog programmatically—with no real emphasis on when to *use* those techniques— you'll see first-hand the issues that surround programming a dialog for a practical application.When you've finished this chapter, you'll not only know the techniques for dealing with dialogs and controls, you'll also know when and how to use those techniques to make your application robust and user-friendly.

Having said that, the sample application for this chapter is a dialog-based application called "CodeFinder." The CodeFinder application was designed to solve a very common problem experienced by many a programmer. After a few applications have been written and a certain amount of source code has been amassed, most programmers run into one very frustrating problem—locating that code when it's needed. I've been programming for 13 years now, and I can't tell you how many times I've needed to find a routine I wrote a couple of years ago. I usually spend about 30 minutes just trying to remember where I was working when I wrote the application that contains the code. After I remember that, I then have to remember where the code for that application is now located. Is it on my FTP server? No, maybe that's the code that's on the Jaz disc I lent Jerry. No, that's not it. . . . As you can see, it is extremely frustrating to know that you've written a nice piece of code in the past and not be able to find it. The purpose of the CodeFinder application is to help in eliminating that frustration. Figure 7-1 shows the completed version of the CodeFinder application.

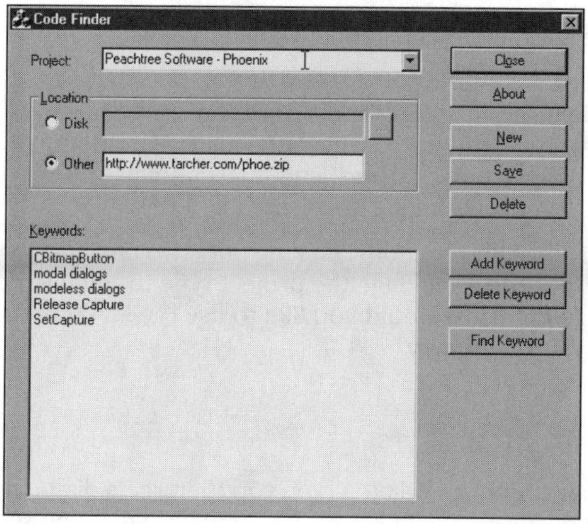

Figure 7-1: Preview of the finished CodeFinder application that teaches how to use dialogs and controls

The finished application enables you to specify a project and define a list of keywords for that project. For example, let's say you've written systems for Borland and Microsoft. You would enter Borland as a project. You would then add the different API calls you used in that system in the Keyword list box. You would do the same thing for Microsoft. You would also define the current location for the source code for each system. For example, maybe the Borland system's source code is on your local hard disk and the Microsoft system's source code is on your FTP server. Now, let's say you start a new job at another company and you need to work with bitmap buttons. Instead of racking your brain trying to recall where you last used bitmap buttons and where that source code is located, you can use the Find Keyword button and bring up a list of all the projects you were a part of that used bitmap buttons. In addition, you would see the location of that source code.

Creating a dialog-based application

As you read previously, CodeFinder is a dialog-based application. What that means is that unlike many Windows applications, CodeFinder will not have the same look and feel as, say, Microsoft Word for Windows or DevStudio. These products have an enormous number of features; and therefore, they require many windows (or views), different toolbars, a menu, and more to perform their specific functions. However, just as many applications don't have a need for all those extra UI elements. For those applications, where everything required to interface to the user can be contained on a single window, the dialog-based application is a good approach.

As is always the case in this book, if you just want to read along and look at the source code later, this demo can be located on the accompanying CD in the \Demos\CodeFinder folder. If, however, you do want to code the application as you read through the explanations of the code that makes it up, then start by creating a dialog-based application, as follows:

1. Press Ctrl+N to create a new file.
2. From the New dialog, select the Projects tab and select the "MFC AppWizard (exe)" entry.

   Please note that I actually used the "MFC AppWizard (exe) – About Box" entry created with a custom AppWizard. Writing this particular custom AppWizard is covered in Chapter 33; the actual DLL for it and instructions for installing it are on the CD-ROM in the Demos\AboutWiz folder.
3. Follow the AppWizard dialogs' instructions, making only two changes to the default settings. On the first dialog, change the project type to "dialog-based." On second dialog, change the "How would you like to use the MFC library" option to "As a statically linked library."

Using the resource editor

After you have finished the last AppWizard dialog box, you then see a dialog box inside DevStudio. This dialog box is shown in Figure 7-2. Actually, what you see is something called a *dialog template resource* and you are in the *resource editor* part of DevStudio. The dialog box you see is what AppWizard created for you as the main dialog for your dialog-based application.

The MFC AppWizard has not only created the dialog box for you, it has also created the entire framework needed to make the application display the dialog box, handle the OK and Cancel buttons, and close the dialog box. In fact, without adding a line of code, you already have the functionality I just mentioned. Selecting and executing Build CodeFinder.exe from the Build menu will illustrate how much has been done for you. In theory, it's nice to think AppWizard magically created this code and you don't have to understand any of it to get your application. However, to do anything productive with your new dialog (like writing CodeFinder), you need to do a lot more to it.

The resource editor is used to create and edit the resources your application uses, such as menus, icons, or bitmaps. In addition to these resource types, dialogs are also considered resources, as are the controls placed on dialog boxes. Such dialog resources are often called dialog *templates*. There is no better way to explain how to use something than to jump right in and start using it. So, let's start using the resource editor, and I'll explain as we go along.

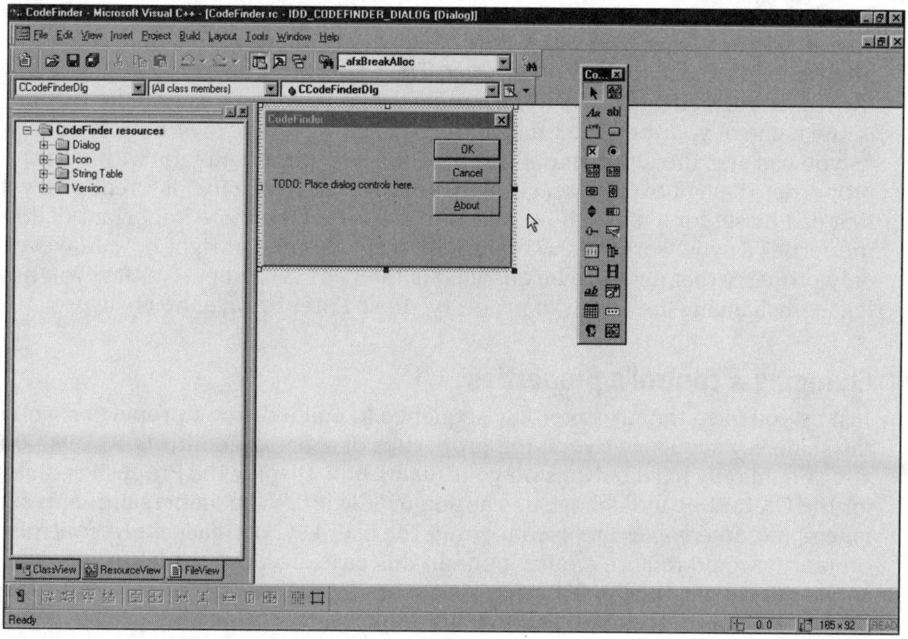

Figure 7-2: A default dialog box created by AppWizard

Changing a dialog box's properties

Figure 7-2 showed you the default dialog template created by AppWizard. The dialog box already contains three controls: a static text control, an OK button, and a Cancel button. If you used the custom AppWizard from Chapter 33, you will also see a fourth control (an About box button). Alongside the dialog box you should see a floating vertical toolbar. This toolbar contains all the controls you can place on a dialog box, including the ones already on it now.

Let's start your Resource Editor training by changing some dialog properties. To display the dialog's properties, click the mouse anywhere on the dialog's background that does not contain a control, and then press Alt+Enter. This method can be used to view or edit any resource's properties. After the dialog properties have been displayed, you will see two important pieces of information: the dialog's resource ID and its `Caption` property. Figure 7-3 shows the dialog's properties.

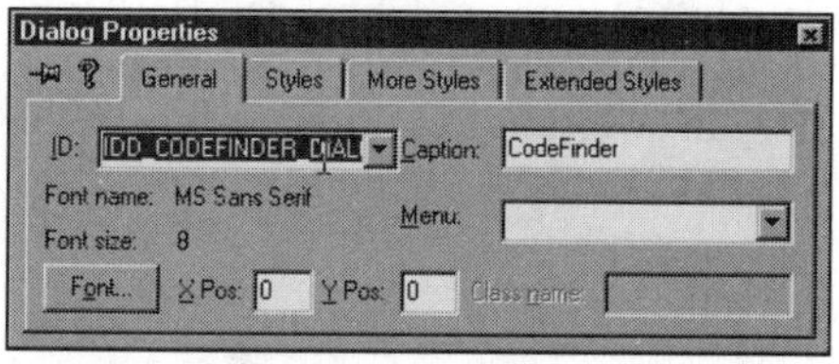

Figure 7-3: Editing a dialog template resource's properties

The dialog's resource ID is extremely important because it is how you refer to your dialog box when you write your application. You can think of it as the programmatic name of your dialog box. The `Caption` property is what you see at the top of the dialog box when the application is run. AppWizard defaults this value to the name of your project. Change this, by simply typing over it, to "Code Finder." As you can see, the different dialog properties are placed on tabs within the properties dialog box. Click each of these tabs now to see the different properties that can be set for a dialog box. We get into a few of the more important dialog properties as you work your way through this chapter. For right now, however, the only property that needs to be changed is the `Caption` property. After you have finished changing the `Caption` property, press Enter to save the changes.

Changing a control's properties

Just as you used the Alt+Enter key sequence to edit a dialog's properties, you use the same key sequence to edit the properties of a dialog's controls. At this point, you should only have buttons on your dialog box. Display the Properties dialog box for the OK button and change its caption to "Cl&ose." The ampersand represents a mnemonic. *Mnemonics* are used to grant the user keyboard access to controls that ordinarily would require mouse input. In this case, because the letter *o* was chosen as the mnemonic, the Close button is activated if the user presses the Alt+O key sequence. As with the dialog's `Caption` property, this is the only property we'll change for now, but you will learn quite a few more properties before the chapter is through.

Expert Tip

Using Mnemonics

You saw how to use mnemonics to enable a user to activate a button quickly using the keyboard instead of the mouse. You can also use mnemonics to enable the user to jump quickly to other controls. For example, let's say you have a static control on your dialog labeled "Project" and an edit control for the project's value. To allow the user to jump to the Project edit control by pressing Alt+C, simply define the static control's caption as "&Project" and make sure the edit control follows the static control in the tab order.

◆ ◆ ◆ ◆ ◆

When a user presses an Alt key sequence for a read-only control (such as a static control), Windows passes control, or *focus*, to the next control in the tab order.

Removing a control from a dialog box

The next thing you must do is to remove the static text control AppWizard placed on the dialog box. Simply select the static control whose text reads "TODO: Place dialog controls here." by clicking it once with your mouse, and then press the Delete key to remove it from the dialog box. In addition to removing the TODO static control, also remove the Cancel button in the same fashion.

Resizing a control

Before you can add the controls we need to write the CodeFinder application, you need to resize the controls so all the controls fit. Resizing a dialog box is accomplished using the same technique as resizing any control. First, select the dialog box by clicking anywhere on its background. You will know the dialog box is selected when you see a sizing rectangle around it. At different points on this rectangle, you should see light- and dark-colored blocks. The dark-colored blocks are used to size the dialog box. The light-colored blocks mean the dialog box cannot been resized in that direction.

Moving your mouse pointer over one of these blocks changes your mouse pointer to a two-headed arrow. This standard Windows mouse pointer is used when an application (in this case, DevStudio) is enabling you to resize something. In the lower-right corner of DevStudio's status bar, you should see two numbers separated by a comma. These values represent the current size of the dialog box in dialog units. To resize the dialog box, hold the mouse button down over one of the dark resizing blocks and move the mouse until the dialog box is large enough to hold all the controls that will be placed on it.

Adding controls to a dialog box

The Controls toolbar is used to create new controls for a dialog box. Figure 7-4 shows this toolbar with a brief description of each of the different controls at your disposal. If your Controls toolbar is not visible, right-mouse click the DevStudio menu (to the right of any actual menu items). A menu will display that will enable you to toggle the visible state of any menus and toolbars that are available. If the option for the Control menu is not checked, clicking it will display the menu.

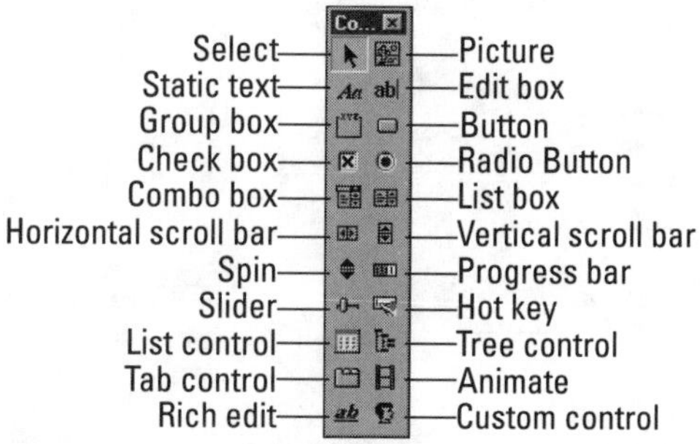

Figure 7-4: The Controls toolbar

Adding controls to your dialog box couldn't be easier. Simply click the desired control in the Controls toolbar and drag that item onto the dialog box. Now that you know how to create controls and change their properties, do so for the following controls:

```
Project static: Caption="&Project:"
Project combo box: ID=IDC_CBO_Project, Type=Dropdown
Location group box: Caption="&Location"
Disk radio button: ID=IDC_RBTN_DISK, Caption="Disk"
Disk edit: ID=IDC_EDT_DISK
Disk button: ID=IDC_BTN_DISK, Caption="..."
Other radio button: ID=IDC_RBTN_OTHER, Caption="Other"
Other edit: ID=IDC_EDT_OTHER
Keywords static: Caption="Keywords"
Keywords list box: ID=IDC_LBX_KEYWORDS
New button: ID=IDC_BTN_NEW, Caption="&New"
Save button: ID=IDC_BTN_SAVE, Caption="Sa&ve"
Delete button: ID=IDC_BTN_DELETE, Caption="De&lete"
Add Keyword button: ID=IDC_BTN_ADD_KEYWORD, Caption="Add
Keyword"
Delete Keyword button: ID= IDC_BTN_DELETE_KEYWORD,
   Caption="Delete Keyword"
Find Keyword button: ID=IDC_BTN_FIND_KEYWORD,
   Caption="Find Keyword"
```

Figure 7-5 shows the finished dialog box. (Don't worry about positioning and sizing the controls right now; simply create the controls and set their properties.)

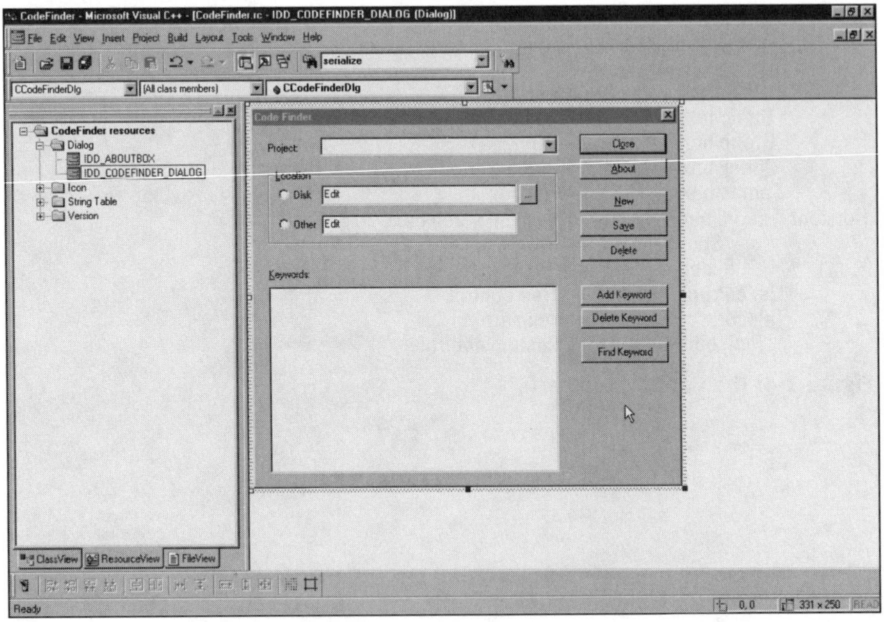

Figure 7-5: The CodeFinder dialog box after controls have been added.

Expert Tip

Resizing a Combo Box

To resize the drop-down part of a combo box, click the combo box's arrow (to the right of the edit portion of the combo box). A resizing rectangle should appear that shows how large the drop-down list will be. Simply *grab* one of the dark -colored blocks and drag to resize the combo box's drop-down area.

◆ ◆ ◆ ◆ ◆

Wow! That's seven different controls on your first dialog box. Although you simply dragged them to the dialog box and set a few basic properties thus far, you will definitely become more intimate with these controls once you start coding your new application in the next section of this chapter.

After all the controls have been created and their properties set, you need to size and align them. The toolbar that appears at the bottom of the resource editor when editing a dialog is useful when adding a large number of controls. This is called the Dialog toolbar and it contains a number of buttons that make the alignment and sizing of controls on a dialog box much easier. Viewing the actions of each button can be accomplished by moving your mouse pointer over each button in the Dialog toolbar and looking at the status bar for a description of that button's action.

An example of using one of these buttons is when you want to align a given set of controls. Say you want to align several controls along the left side. Simply select each control you want to align by first clicking one control and then holding down the Shift key for each additional control you want to select. You will see each control you click is selected. If you make a mistake and select a control you do not want to align, simply hold down the Shift key and click the control again. It will then be deselected; the other controls remain selected. After you have selected all the controls you want to align, you need to select the "dominant" control. In other words, you need to tell the resource editor which control to align with the rest of the controls. You do this by holding down the Ctrl key and clicking a given control. After you finish selecting this control, click the "Align left" button on the Dialog toolbar, and all the controls will have their left edge aligned with the left edge of the "dominant control." As you can see, this dramatically increases your speed in aligning and sizing controls.

Remember earlier in the chapter when I explained a control's property ID is used to refer to that control in your C++ source code? You may wonder why I set the ID property of only some of the controls. The reason is I wanted to use a meaningful ID for those controls that will be referenced in code. Because CodeFinder will not attempt to do anything with the static controls, there was no need to alter their default IDs.

Setting a dialog's tab order

The last thing you need in this section is to set the dialog's tab order. When the user presses the Tab key, the control that receives focus is determined by the tab order. To define the tab order, start by pressing Ctrl+D. The first control you click with your mouse will be the first item in the tab order. The second control you click will result in that control being the second control in the tab order, and so on. Set the tab order as you see it in Figure 7-6.

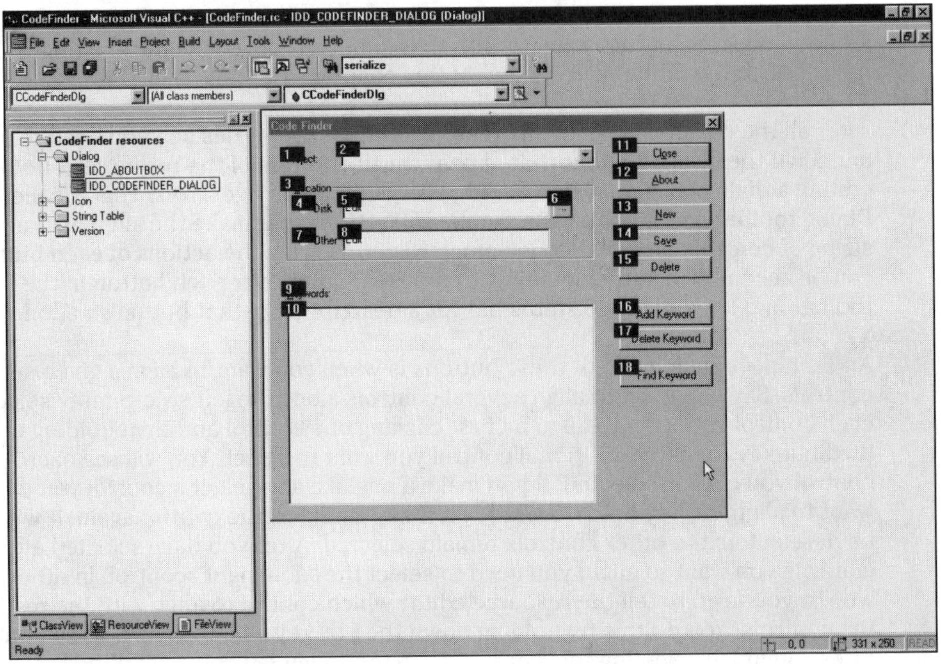

Figure 7-6: How to set a dialog's controls tab order in DevStudio.

But what happens if you make a mistake and click the wrong control? Or, what if you add a control and you want to make it the ninth control in the tab order? Do you have to start over and re-tab the entire dialog box? Luckily, there is a neat trick to avoid this. Remember the idea of a "dominant" control when doing multiple control selections? Well, the same concept applies here.

Here's an example. As you just read, the first control you click becomes the first control in the tab order. However, say you clicked three controls and you made a mistake on the fourth control. Let's say the fourth control you clicked was supposed to be the fifth control in the tab order. All you have to do is hold down the Ctrl key and click the third control again. After doing that, the third control becomes your starting point. Now any control you click after setting that "starting point" control will be the fourth control in the tab order. This saves you from having to re-tab the controls correctly selected before you made the mistake.

I know by now you must be itching to get to the code! Well, you're almost there. Now that you have a good idea of how to use the resource editor, let's first look at the MFC control classes and then we'll start coding.

Programming with CDialog and MFC Control Classes

It's finally time to start diving into learning how to program the dialog portion of your application. In this section, you discover the MFC `CDialog` class that makes programming dialog boxes a breeze. After this, you learn how to manipulate the controls you placed on the dialog box programmatically, using the various MFC controls classes. In addition to learning about these classes, you learn the three most important aspects of coding any dialog: DDX, message routing, and initialization.

The CDialog class – a brief description

You have now seen the main dialog of the sample application in two forms. First, you saw the dialog template resource when you added controls to the dialog box. After that, you ran the application and saw the finished product. In other words, you saw the dialog box as the user of your application sees it. However, what bridged the gap between a resource in your application's source code and the finished product you saw when you ran the application? The answer is the `CDialog` class.

Earlier in this chapter, you learned a dialog box is simply another window. MFC provides a class called `CWnd` that encapsulates much of the functionality of a window. For example, using a `CWnd` object, you can move the window, resize it, handle its input from users, and so on. Because `CDialog` is itself a window, the `CDialog` class is derived from the `CWnd` class and inherits its basic functionality. The `CDialog` class then extends that base functionality by implementing the features specific to dialogs. These features include functions for creating and displaying the dialog box, iterating through the dialog's controls, setting and retrieving the default button, and dismissing the dialog box. (We get into some of the more important aspects of this class shortly.)

MFC control classes

Developers place controls on dialogs to display and accept information from the user. To make Windows programming easier and more flexible, MFC provides a set of classes that encapsulate the functionality of the common user-interface controls, such as edit controls, list boxes, and checkboxes. You sometimes hear these controls referred to as *child controls* or *child window controls* because they always appear on another window (such as a dialog box) and are seen as *children* of that window. In this chapter, these controls are referred to simply as *controls* or *dialog controls*.

Two main advantages exist to using the MFC control classes. First, they enable you to interact with the controls on your dialog in an object-oriented manner. Because there is an MFC class for each basic control type, each class has member functions specific to the type of Windows control whose functionality they encapsulate. This makes using the controls much easier and more intuitive. Take, for example, the case of an edit control. Say you have an edit control on your dialog box and you want to limit the number of characters that can be typed into this control. Without using the `CEdit` class, you would have to do something similar to the following:

```
HWND hwndEdit = ::GetDlgItem(hwndDlg, IDC_MYEDITCONTROL);
if (hwndEdit)
{
 ::SendMessage(hwndEdit, EM_LIMITTEXT, 10, 0);
}
```

If you had a `CEdit` member variable, however, your code would look more like this:

```
m_edtMyEdit.LimitText(10);
```

The second advantage to using the MFC control classes is, like any other C++ class, they can be extended to meet your own unique requirements. If you are familiar with Microsoft's Internet Explorer or Netscape Navigator, you have no doubt noticed that when you type an entry into the URL Address combo box, the combo box attempts to find the closest match to what you are typing as you type it. Unfortunately, a `CComboBox` class does exist, but it does not implement this functionality. Therefore, if your application has a need for a control of this type, you would have to program that functionality yourself. This scenario—needing to extend an existing control—is where the true power of the MFC control classes can be seen. Because you would want to keep the basic functionality of the `CComboBox` itself and include the additional functionality that the Explorer and Navigator combo boxes exhibit, all you must do is derive a class from `CComboBox` and implement the desired new behavior. Now, instead of associating the combo box control on your dialog box with the standard MFC `CComboBox` class, you would use your new combo box class. Although the topic of extending MFC controls is covered thoroughly in Chapter 16, you get a chance to implement the type of combo box described here in this chapter's second demo.

Dialog Data Exchange (DDX)

Right now, you are probably overflowing with questions. Some of the pieces should start to fall into place at this point. For example, you now know that to create a dialog for use in your application you create it in the resource editor. You have learned how to use the resource editor to create, position, and size the controls you wish to place on a dialog box. In addition, you have learned of the existence of a set of classes used to control the dialog (`CDialog`) and any controls on your dialog box (MFC controls classes). However, how do you actually use or reference a given control in your source code? In other words, you learned of the existence of a class called CComboBox used to control a combo box, but how do you make the connection between an object of that type and a combo box on your dialog?

The answer lies in a mechanism called *Dialog Data Exchange* (DDX), which provides a means for you to map a given control to a member variable in your dialog's class. Instead of rambling on in the abstract, let's look at how to do this by creating a CComboBox object for the Project combo box.

The first thing you need to do is open the dialog for editing. After you are in the resource editor, locate the Project combo box, and while holding down the Ctrl key, double-click the left mouse button on this control. What you should see next is the Add Member Variable dialog. This dialog (shown in Figure 7-7) contains three fields needed for adding a member variable to your dialog's class. The first field is the name of the member variable. The second field is the Category of the member variable you are attempting to create. The only options are Value and Control. The third field is the Variable type. With the Category set to Value, click the Variable type combo box arrow to see its list. You'll see that the only Value type of member variable you can create for a combo box is a CString object. This is because combo boxes only hold strings. If you want a combo box full of integers, let's say, you would have to enter them into the combo box as strings and extract them from the combo box as strings. You would then have to do the formatting yourself to convert them to integers. However, we are interested in mapping a dialog control to an MFC control class. Therefore, change the Category to Control and click the Variable type combo box to reveal the options for this type of member variable. Upon doing this, you see your only option is the CComboBox. This is because DevStudio knows the control's type as you defined it and only lists the applicable MFC control classes that would be valid. Use the value shown in Figure 7-7 and, when finished, click the OK button to create the CComboBox member variable.

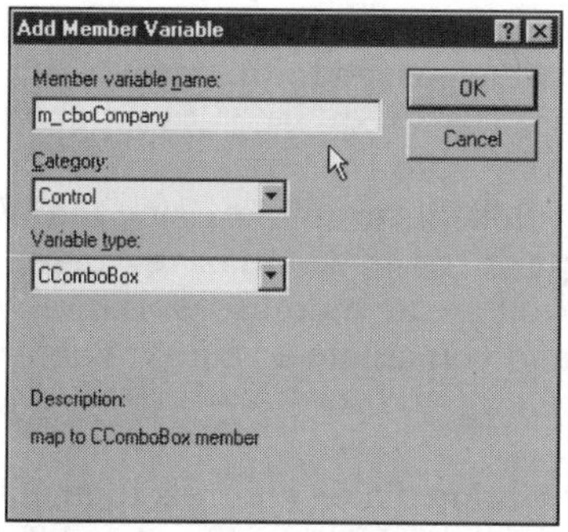

Figure 7-7: The Add Member Variable dialog box

Now that you've mapped the dialog's control to a member variable of type CComboBox (m_cboProject), let's look at exactly what happened.

Open the CodeFinderDlg.cpp file and locate the `CCodeFinderDlg::DoDataExchange` function. It should look like the following:

```
void CCodeFinderDlg::DoDataExchange(CDataExchange* pDX)
{
 CDialog::DoDataExchange(pDX);
 //{{AFX_DATA_MAP(CCodeFinderDlg)
 DDX_Control(pDX, IDC_CBO_PROJECT, m_cboProject);
 //}}AFX_DATA_MAP
}
```

Notice the line that contains a call to the `DDX_Control` function. A control's ID property is used via the `DDX_Control` function to associate a given control on a dialog box with a member variable of the dialog's class. If you open the CodeFinderDlg.h file, you'll see `m_cboProject` has been defined as a variable of type `CComboBox`. This means that once the `DoDataExchange` function is called, the `m_cboProject` variable is mapped to the control represented by the resource ID `IDC_CBO_PROJECT`. Therefore, any function calls involving the `m_cboProject` object will affect the Project combo box you originally placed on your dialog.

Let's test this by calling one of the `m_cboProject` member functions. Locate the `CCodeFinder::OnInitDialog` function. This function is called when a dialog box is first initialized and is, therefore, the function in which you place the majority of your dialog's initialization code. Look for the comment that reads "TODO: Add extra initialization here" and add the following lines of code:

```
m_cboProject.AddString("A");
m_cboProject.AddString("B");
m_cboProject.AddString("C");
    m_cboProject.SetCurSel(1);
```

Building and running the application results in what you may expect. The three strings (A, B, and C) are added to the Project combo box. In addition, the second item in the combo box is selected because the value passed to the `CComboBox::SetCurSel` function is relative to zero.

We created a member variable of type `CCombBox` for this example. Using the "Value" Category and creating a member variable of type `CString` would have worked in almost exactly the same way. The difference is you create a Control variable when you want to do something to the control itself and you create a Value variable when you simply want to set or get the control's value.

In summary, DDX gives you an easy way of associating dialog controls to member variables in the definition of the dialog's class. You'll be using DDX quite a bit with the sample application—to manipulate controls and exchange data with the control on your dialog box.

Message handling

The next major bit of functionality you need to know about concerning the `CDialog` class is message handling. You have your controls on the dialog box and you know how to create member variables of the correct type so you can work with them. However, how do you know when a user has done anything to them? For example, how do you get notified when the user clicks a button or chooses another item in the combo box?

The answer lies in the fact that a dialog control is simply a window and, as such, it receives messages from the Windows operating system when a user-precipitated event takes place and the control has focus. What happens next depends on the type of control. When a button control is clicked, for example, that control sends a notification message to its owner. In this case, the owner of the button control is the dialog. Therefore, the dialog receives a notification message stating the button was clicked. There are many different notification messages for each control. For example, the button control only has two notification messages: one for when the button is clicked and another for when the button is double-clicked. A combo box, on the other hand, has over ten different notification messages that it can send to its owner window. These messages include such things as notification that the drop-down list has been displayed and the control has lost focus.

But, the question still remains. How do you, as an MFC developer, handle these messages in your code? The answer is something akin to what you did in creating a member variable for use with DDX. Just as DDX enables you to create an association between a control's resource ID and a member variable, the *message handler* provides you with a means of associating a window's message with a function.

Look at a quick example to illustrate exactly how you would go about creating a message handler for a given control's notification message. Continuing with the previous example in which you added the lines of code to the `OnInitDialog()` function to initialize the Project combo box, let's add a message handler to show a message every time the combo box's selection has been changed. This dialog will, along with many other things, enable you to add message handlers for the different classes in your application.

To add the message handler we want, first select the correct class from the Class Name combo box. After that, locate the `IDC_CBO_PROJECT` resource ID in the Object IDs list box. The fact that you have to locate the controls by resource ID is why it is important to use names that in some way relate to the control. For example, if when you added the controls to the dialog box, you had not changed the resource IDs of the controls you expect to use in this application, you would see controls with names like `IDC_EDIT1`, `IDC_EDIT2`, `IDC_EDIT3`, and so on. Such names make it much more difficult to locate specific controls.

After you have selected the IDC_CBO_PROJECT resource ID, the different notification messages that can be handled are listed in the Message list box. Notice the CBN_ prefix. This prefix stands for *combo box notification.* This same naming standard is used for all the controls. Therefore, when you see a reference to a message that begins with BN_, you know it is a "button notification" message; LBN_ means "list box notification" and so on. Select the CBN_SELCHANGE entry. Notice the Add Function button has been enabled. Click that button now to indicate you want to create a new function for the CBN_SELCHANGE message. The ClassWizard presents you with a dialog box that has a default function name. Although you have the ability to change the name, just accept the default for this demo, and click the OK button. Now click the Edit Code button to see your new function and add the following line of code to it so we know this function is being called when a new Project is selected:

```
AfxMessageBox("new selection");
```

Before you build and test the application, look at the new message map:

```
BEGIN_MESSAGE_MAP(CCodeFinderDlg, CDialog)
//{{AFX_MSG_MAP(CCodeFinderDlg)
 ON_WM_SYSCOMMAND()
 ON_BN_CLICKED(ID_APP_ABOUT, OnAbout)
 ON_WM_PAINT()
 ON_WM_QUERYDRAGICON()
 ON_CBN_SELCHANGE(IDC_CBO_PROJECT, OnSelchangeCboProject)
  //}}AFX_MSG_MAP
END_MESSAGE_MAP()
```

This is what is used to map a control resource ID and a notification message to a specific function. As you can see, when the control with a resource ID of IDC_CBO_PROJECT sends a notification message of IDC_CBN_SELCHANGE, a function named OnSelchangeCboProject will be called. Thanks to ClassWizard, it's that easy to create message handlers in your code.

Putting it all together

Now that you know how to implement DDX and message handlers, let's put that to work and make this application actually do something. Before we get started, you need to delete the test lines of code you placed in the OnInitDialog() function. After that, invoke ClassWizard and delete the OnSelchangeCboProject function by selecting it in the "Member functions" list box and clicking the Delete button.

Now it's time to start putting in the "real" code.

Creating the CProject class

Ultimately, this application will be used to create companies and keywords with a many-to-many relationship between the two. However, this section concentrates on getting the project data first. (Adding and removing keywords is covered when we get to the section on programming modal dialogs.)

At this point, you need to create the `CProject` class. Normally, you would put this class declaration into another header file. However, to keep this sample as simple as possible, we place the class in the dialog's header file. Therefore, open the CodeFinderDlg.h file and add the following class declaration:

```
class CProject
{
public:
 CProject(CString const& rstrProjectName,
  int iLocationType, CString const& rstrLocation);

protected:
 CString m_strProjectName;
 int m_iLocationType;
 CString m_strLocation;

public:
void SetLocationType(int iLocationType)
 { m_iLocationType = iLocationType; }
void SetLocation(CString const& rstrLocation)
 { m_strLocation = rstrLocation; }

public:
 typedef enum
 {
 loctypeDisk,
 loctypeOther
 };

public:
 CString GetProjectName() { return m_strProjectName; }
 int GetLocationType() { return m_iLocationType; }
 CString GetLocation() { return m_strLocation; }
};
```

After adding the class declaration to the dialog's header file, add the following constructor at the top of the CodeFinderDlg.cpp file:

```
CProject::CProject(CString const& rstrProjectName,
 int iLocationType, CString const& rstrLocation)
{
 m_strProjectName = rstrProjectName;
 m_iLocationType = iLocationType;
 m_strLocation = rstrLocation;
}
```

Dialog initialization and the New button

To create a new project, we simply blank out the fields on the dialog box. We want to create a new record whenever the dialog box is first displayed and when the user clicks the New button.

In the section on DDX, you learned how to create member variables associated with the different controls on your dialog box. Using what you learned in that section, create the following member variables:

✦ **Project combo box:** `Variable Name: m_strProject, Type=CString`

✦ **Location Disk edit control:** `Variable Name: m_strDiskLocation, Type=CString`

✦ **Location Other edit control:** `Variable Name: m_strDiskOther, Type=CString`

After you create these "Value" DDX member variables, you need to create two "Control" DDX member variables for the two radio buttons. Unfortunately, one of the limitations of ClassWizard is that it does not create member variables for radio buttons. Therefore, you have to create them manually. To do this, add the following member variable declarations to your dialog's header file:

```
CButton m_rbtnLocationDisk;
CButton m_rbtnLocationOther;
```

After you have declared the two button member variables, add the following lines to the dialog's `DoDataExchange()` function:

```
DDX_Control(pDX, IDC_RBTN_DISK, m_rbtnLocationDisk);
DDX_Control(pDX, IDC_RBTN_OTHER, m_rbtnLocationOther);
```

Now that you have the radio button member variables, you can use the `CButton::SetCheck()` function to set which button you want checked upon initialization or when the user creates a new project. Because dialog initialization is usually done in the `OnInitDialog()` function, place the following code at the end of that function (before the return statement):

```
InitDialogControls();
```

And implement the `InitDialogControls()` function as follows:

```
void CCodeFinderDlg::InitDialogControls()
{
 m_strProject = _T("");
 m_strLocationDisk = _T("");
 m_strLocationOther = _T("");

 m_rbtnLocationDisk.SetCheck(1);
 m_rbtnLocationOther.SetCheck(0);
```

```
 UpdateData(FALSE);
}
```

After you have added the `InitDialogControls` function, you need to add a handler for the New button. To do this, simply add a line to it that calls the `InitDialogControls()` function and sets the focus to the Project combo box, like this:

```
void CCodeFinderDlg::OnBtnNew()
{
 InitDialogControls();
 m_cboProject.SetFocus();
}
```

Enabling and Disabling controls

You may have noticed the CodeFinder application has an edit control alongside two different radio buttons used to determine where the source of the project currently resides. However, if users click the Disk radio button, they should not be allowed to enter a value into the Other edit control. Conversely, if users click the Other radio button, they should not be able to enter data into the Disk edit control.

Enabling and disabling controls can be accomplished using the `EnableWindow()` function. Because this function is implemented in the `CWnd` class, all MFC control classes have this inherited function. Therefore, to enable or disable a control, simply call this function and pass a Boolean value that indicates whether you are enabling or disabling the control. For example, if you want to disable an edit control for which you have a `CEdit` member variable defined, you would enter the following:

```
m_edtMyEditControl.EnableWindow(FALSE);
```

At this point, use ClassWizard to create the following control member variables:

```
IDC_BTN_DISK: Variable Name: m_btnDisk, Type: CButton
IDC_EDT_DISK: Variable Name: m_edtLocationDisk,
 Type: CEdit
IDC_EDT_OTHER: Variable Name: m_edtLocationOther,
 Type: CEdit
```

After you create the necessary member variables, bring ClassWizard up so you can create the message handlers for the radio buttons. Locate the `IDC_RBTN_DISK` control in the Object IDs list box and add a function for the `BN_CLICKED` message. Now, do the same thing for the `IDC_RBTN_OTHER` control.

After these functions have been created by ClassWizard, edit them to look like the following:

```
void CCodeFinderDlg::OnRbtnDisk()
{
```

```
  m_edtLocationDisk.EnableWindow(TRUE);
  m_strLocationDisk = _T("");
  m_btnDisk.EnableWindow(TRUE);

  m_edtLocationOther.EnableWindow(FALSE);
  m_strLocationOther = _T("");
 }

void CCodeFinderDlg::OnRbtnOther()
{
  m_edtLocationDisk.EnableWindow(FALSE);
  m_strLocationDisk = _T("");
  m_btnDisk.EnableWindow(TRUE);

  m_edtLocationOther.EnableWindow(TRUE);
  m_strLocationOther = _T("");
}
```

Also edit the `InitDialogControls` and add a call to the `OnRbtnDisk` function at the end.

Saving the dialog data

Now, let's add the code necessary to save the information on the dialog box so, when the user clicks the "Save" button, the necessary `CProject` objects are added to the combo box. This way, when the user clicks an existing project, you can display the already saved information for that project. By the way, at this point the data is not persistent. In other words, every project saved only exists in the combo box until the user ends the application. The act of making this data persistent is covered in the section entitled "Serializing Dialog Data."

Because we know we will serialize this data at some point, we will add a map to keep track of the projects that have been entered. In the dialog's header file, add the following declarations:

```
CMapStringToOb m_mapProjectNameToProject;
```

Now, add a message handler for the `IDC_BTN_SAVE` button. The `Save()` function should look like this:

```
void CCodeFinderDlg::OnBtnSave()
{
 UpdateData(TRUE);

 CProject* pProject;
 if (NULL != (pProject = SaveProject(m_strProject)))
 {
  UpdateProjectCombo box(pProject);
  InitDialogControls();
 }
}
```

As you can see, the first thing this function does is to call UpdateData(TRUE) — which, as you already learned, is done to update your dialog's member variables from the values on the dialog box. After that, a function is called to create the project, and then another function is called to add the project to the combo box.

Next, implement the following SaveProject() function, which simply looks in the Project map you created earlier to see if the project already exists. If it does, this function returns that project pointer to the calling function. If the project doesn't exist in the dialog project's map, this function creates the project object and adds it to that map. Notice the call to the radio button's GetCheck() function to see which button is clicked.

```
CProject* CCodeFinderDlg::SaveProject(CString const&
rstrProject)
{
 CProject* pProject = NULL;

 if (!m_mapProjectNameToProject.Lookup(rstrProject,
 (CObject*&)pProject))
 {
  int iLocationType;
  CString strLocation;
  if (1 == m_rbtnLocationDisk.GetCheck())
  {
   iLocationType = CProject::loctypeDisk;
   strLocation = m_strLocationDisk;
  }
  else
  {
   iLocationType = CProject::loctypeOther;
   strLocation = m_strLocationOther;
  }
  pProject = new CProject(rstrProject, iLocationType,
   strLocation);

  if (pProject)
  {
   m_mapProjectNameToProject.SetAt(m_strProject,
   (CObject*)pProject);
  }
 }
 else
 {
  if (1 == m_rbtnLocationDisk.GetCheck())
  {
   pProject->SetLocationType(CProject::loctypeDisk);
   pProject->SetLocation(m_strLocationDisk);
  }
  else
  {
   pProject->SetLocationType(CProject::loctypeOther);
   pProject->SetLocation(m_strLocationOther);
```

```
        }
    }

    return pProject;
}
```

Now that a project object has been created or retrieved via the `SaveProject()` function, it needs to be added to the combo box. Implement the `UpdateProjectCombBox` to do just that. Pay special attention to the different `CComboBox` functions being used:

- The `FindString()` function is done to search the combo box for a given string. The -1 value passed to it simply means to search all the elements in the combo box.
- The `AddString()` function does exactly what its name implies. However, I mention it here to bring a few facts to light. If (in the resource editor) you specified the `Sort` property for the combo box, the `AddString()` function will insert the string into the correct position in the combo box. If, however, you did not specify the `Sort` property for the combo box, the string being added will be the last string in the combo box.
- The `InsertString()` function is an alternative means of adding items to combo boxes (or list boxes, for that matter, seeing as how they work almost identically). In addition to taking as an argument the string to be added, the `InsertString()` enables you to specify exactly where in the combo box (or list box) you want the string to appear. For example, if you want to add a string and make it the third entry in the list, simply specify the following:

  ```
  m_cboMyCombobox.InsertString(2, "my new entry");
  ```

  Note that the index value is relative to zero; therefore, the third entry would be specified as 2.

The last new function being introduced in this code has to with *item data*. Item data is a powerful tool, used when you want to associate the entries in a combo box or list box with other data. For example, say you want to present a list of invoice numbers to the user and when the user makes a selection, you want to display that invoice. You could read all the invoices you want to show the user, create an invoice object for each invoice, and call the `AddString()` or `InsertString()` function to add the invoice number to the combo box or list box. You would then set the combo box entry's item data to a pointer to the invoice object. Now, when the user clicks an invoice number, you query the combo box as to which entry is being selected and retrieve its item data. The item data will contain the invoice's object's pointer so you can display the rest of the invoice information. This is exactly what is happening in the following code—once the project object has been retrieved and the Project Name has been added to the combo box, its item data is set to the project object's pointer for later retrieval.

```
void CCodeFinderDlg::UpdateProjectCombo box(CProject* pProject)
{
 if (CB_ERR == m_cboProject.FindString(-1,
  pProject->GetProjectName()))
 {
  int iIndex = m_cboProject.AddString(
   pProject->GetProjectName());
  if (CB_ERR != iIndex)
  {
   m_cboProject.SetItemData(iIndex, (DWORD)pProject);
  }
 }
}
```

Because we are creating objects and adding them to a map, we must make sure any object we created is cleaned up when the application ends. To do this, create a destructor for the dialog, as follows:

```
CCodeFinderDlg::~CCodeFinderDlg()
{
 POSITION posProject;
 CString strProjectName;
 CProject* pProject;

 for (posProject =
  m_mapProjectNameToProject.GetStartPosition();
  NULL != posProject;)
 {
  m_mapProjectNameToProject.GetNextAssoc(posProject,
   strProjectName, (CObject*&)pProject);
  if (pProject)
  {
   m_mapProjectNameToProject.RemoveKey(strProjectName);
   delete pProject;
  }
 }

 ASSERT(0 == m_mapProjectNameToProject.GetCount());
}
```

After the user selects a project from the combo box, we want to redisplay the information for that project. As you learned earlier in the chapter, a combo box sends a notification message to its parent window when an item is selected from the combo box entries. Add a `(CBN_SELCHANGE)` message handler for this message ID via ClassWizard and define it as follows:

```
void CCodeFinderDlg::OnSelchangeCboProject()
{
 InitDialogControls();
 m_rbtnLocationDisk.SetCheck(0);
```

```
int iIndex = m_cboProject.GetCurSel();
if (CB_ERR != iIndex)
{
 CProject* pProject =
 (CProject*)m_cboProject.GetItemData(iIndex);
 if (pProject)
 {
  m_strProject = pProject->GetProjectName();

  if (CProject::loctypeDisk ==
   pProject->GetLocationType())
  {
   m_rbtnLocationDisk.SetCheck(1);
   OnRbtnDisk();
   m_strLocationDisk = pProject->GetLocation();
  }
  else
  {
   m_rbtnLocationOther.SetCheck(1);
   OnRbtnOther();
   m_strLocationOther = pProject->GetLocation();
  }
 }
 UpdateData(FALSE);
}
}
```

This function does nothing more than initialize the dialog controls, retrieve the project object from the combo box's item data, and update the dialog box with that project's information.

We introduced a lot in this section, but we have one more item to cover: deleting a project. For this, create a `BN_CLICKED` message handler for the `IDC_BTNDELETE` button control and code it as follows:

```
void CCodeFinderDlg::OnBtnDelete()
{
 UpdateData(TRUE);

 CProject* pProject = NULL;

 if (m_mapProjectNameToProject.Lookup(m_strProject,
  (CObject*&)pProject))
 {
  int iIndex;
  if (CB_ERR != (iIndex =
   m_cboProject.FindString(-1, m_strProject)))
  {
   m_cboProject.DeleteString(iIndex);
  }

  delete pProject;
  m_mapProjectNameToProject.RemoveKey(m_strProject);
```

```
    }

    InitDialogControls();
  }
```

So now you know about the `CDialog` class and the MFC controls classes, implementing DDX, and handling notification messages from controls via the definition of message handlers in the message map. However, if you build and run the application right now, you'll have one glaring problem with it: When you click the Save button, the data is stored in a map and the project name is added to the combo box, but the data is not persistent. In other words, when you quit the application and restart it, the data is no longer there. The next section takes care of this.

Serializing Dialog Data

The quickest and easiest way to save data from an MFC application is through serialization. *Serialization* is the storing and retrieving of objects to disk. Before proceeding, it is important to understand what this section will and won't illustrate.

Normally the act of serializing data is done in conjunction with the application having document support. However, because sometimes you'll have a dialog-based application (such as CodeFinder) that needs to save its data, this chapter shows what calls you need to make to implement serialization without going into the details of what these MFC functions are doing. The more full and comprehensive explanation of how serialization works is described in Chapter 12.

Adding serialization to the CProject class

The first thing you must do is to set up the `CProject` class so it can be serialized. To take advantage of serialization, it must meet some basic requirements. First, change the base class of `CProject Cobject`, as follows:

```
class CProject : public CObject
{
 ...
```

Next, you need to add the following `DECLARE_SERIAL` macro within the `CProject` declaration. Without going into a lot of detail (covered in Chapter 12), this macro basically gives the `CProject` class the capability to be serialized.

```
DECLARE_SERIAL(CProject)
```

After the `DECLARE_SERIAL` macro, add a default constructor that has no body. The only reason we must do this is because serialization needs to have a way to create the object. (The `Serialize()` function, which is coming up shortly, explains how the object gets its values.)

```
CProject() {};
```

Add the following function declaration to `CProject`. This is the function that will be called to serialize the data to and from disk.

```
protected:
        void Serialize(CArchive& ar);
```

In the CodeFinderDlg.cpp file, add the following macro:

```
IMPLEMENT_SERIAL(CProject, CObject, 1)
```

Now it's time to implement the following `CProject::Serialize()` function. As you can see, it is incredibly simple. All you have to do is find out whether you are storing or loading the values and use the appropriate insertion or extraction operators.

```
void CProject::Serialize(CArchive& ar)
{
 CObject::Serialize(ar);

 if (ar.IsLoading())
 {
  ar > m_strProjectName;
  ar > m_iLocationType;
  ar > m_strLocation;
 }
 else
 {
  ar << m_strProjectName;
  ar << m_iLocationType;
  ar << m_strLocation;
 }
}
```

Updating the dialog to serialize the CProject objects

Now that the `CProject` object can be serialized, it's time to make the dialog box do its job. Add the following `#include` to the top of the CodeFinderDlg.cpp file. Because we need to check for the existence of the data file in the `OnInitDialog()` function, we will use the C "_access" function declared in this header file.

```
#include "io.h"
```

Add a `#define` to store the name of the data file that will be used to hold the project data, as follows:

```
#define DATA_FILENAME "CodeFinder.dat"
```

After the data file's name has been defined, add the following `Serialize()` function. Notice the call to serialize the project map. When you call the `Serialize()` function of a map (in this case, `CMapStringToOb`), MFC automatically calls each map element's `Serialize()` function. Therefore, if you add three projects to the map and call the map's `Serialize()` function, each of these objects will have their `Serialize()` function called.

```
void CCodeFinderDlg::Serialize(CArchive& ar)
{
 try
 {
  CDialog::Serialize(ar);

   m_mapProjectNameToProject.Serialize(ar);

   if (ar.IsStoring())
   {  // storing code
   }
   else
   {  // loading code
   }
  }
  catch (CArchiveException* pe)
  {
  if (CArchiveException::endOfFile == pe->m_cause)
  {
   pe->Delete();
  }
  else
  {
   throw pe;
  }
 }
}
```

The next thing you must do is to update the `OnInitDialog()` function to create the data file and read any data present. Add the following code just before the Return statement at the end of the `OnInitDialog()` function. The call to the `_access` function is to see if the file is present. That knowledge is used to determine the flags that will be used in opening the file. If the file doesn't exist, we need to specify to the `CFile` constructor to create the file. Otherwise, we simply want to open it in read/write mode. After the file has been serialized in, the Project map will be filled with any previously saved projects. A call is then made to `FillProjectComboBox()` to fill the combo box with these projects.

```
// Serialize articles in
int flags;
if (!_access(DATA_FILENAME, 6))
{
```

```
  flags = CFile::modeReadWrite;
 }
 else
 {
  flags = CFile::modeCreate;
 }
 CFile file(DATA_FILENAME, flags);

 CArchive ar(&file, CArchive::load);
 Serialize(ar);

 FillProjectCombo box();
```

The CCodeFinderDlg::Serialize() function has restored the project map; now define the FillProjectCombo() function:

```
void CCodeFinderDlg::FillProjectComboBox()
{
 POSITION posProject;
 CString strProjectName;
 CProject* pProject;
 int iIndex;

 for (posProject =
  m_mapProjectNameToProject.GetStartPosition();
  NULL != posProject;)
 {
  m_mapProjectNameToProject.GetNextAssoc(posProject,
   strProjectName, (CObject*&)pProject);
  if (pProject)
  {
   iIndex = m_cboProject.AddString(strProjectName);
   m_cboProject.SetItemData(iIndex, (DWORD)pProject);
  }
 }
}
```

The OnInitDialog() pretty much takes care of loading the data. But where do you store the data? We do it when the dialog box is destroyed. Use ClassWizard to add the following message handler for the WM_DESTROY message and have it do the following. The first thing it does is to create a CFile() object on the stack using the filename defined at the top of the file. Notice that unlike the OnInitDialog() function, it does not check to see if the file exists. This is because it was already created in that OnInitDialog() function. After the CFile() object is created, a CArchive() object is created. Take note of the second parameter. The CArchive::store() enum value basically stipulates that this CArchive() object is being used to save data. After a valid CArchive() object is created, the dialog's Serialize() function is called to save the data and the OnDestroy() function of the dialog's base class.

```
void CCodeFinderDlg::OnDestroy()
{
 CFile file(DATA_FILENAME, CFile::modeReadWrite);
 CArchive ar(&file, CArchive::store);
 Serialize(ar);

 CDialog::OnDestroy();
}
```

Now when you build and run the application, it should be able not only to save the data, but also to read the data back in upon initialization.

Working with Modal Dialogs

The next function to add to the sample application is a modal dialog used to add keywords to the project. (After all, the whole reason for this application is to associate keywords, or API calls with a given project!) As you'll quickly see, you already know how to do almost everything required to create and display a modal dialog box.

Creating the AddKeyword dialog template and its class

Let's begin by using the resource editor to create the dialog box. Because you already learned how to use the resource editor when you created this application's main dialog box, I won't go into the details a second time. Simply look at Figure 7-8 and create your new dialog box accordingly.

After you have created the dialog and its controls, set the dialog resource ID to `IDD_ADDKEYWORD` and the edit control's resource ID to `IDC_EDT_KEYWORD`.

After the resource IDs have been set, you'll need to create a member variable for the edit control. However, if you hold down the Ctrl key and double-click the control, you'll find you can't create the member variable just yet — because you don't have a class associated with the new dialog. Why were you able to do this with the main dialog? Because when you create an AppWizard-generated application that is also dialog-based, AppWizard not only creates the dialog template resource automatically for the main dialog, it also creates the necessary dialog classes for you to begin programming. To create the new dialog class, simply choose the "Create a new class" option (the default) and press the Enter key.

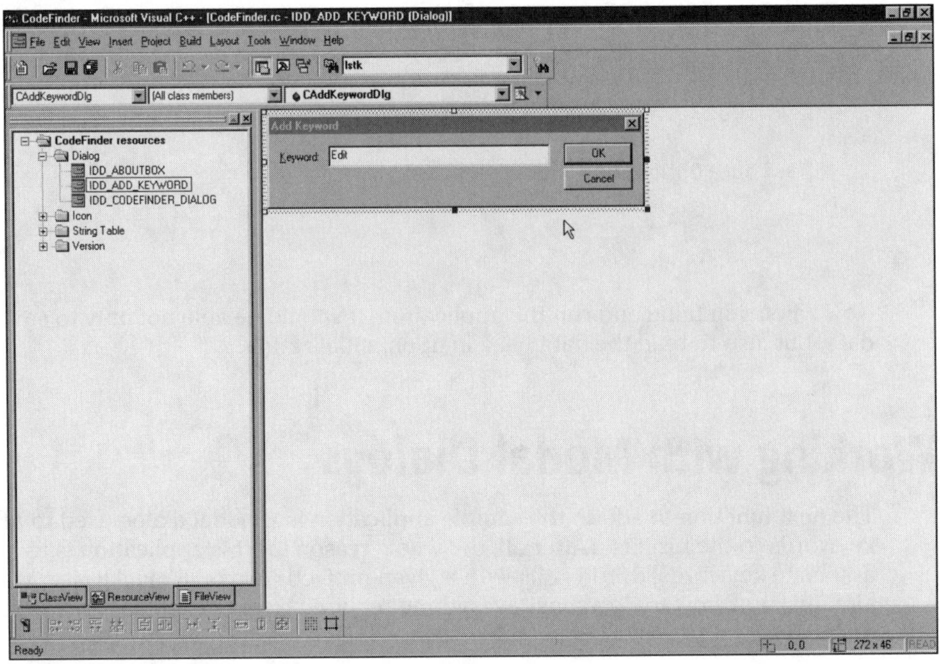

Figure 7-8: This Add Keyword dialog box illustrates how to use a modal dialog.

The New Class dialog box is the next one you see. The dialog box already has the name of the resource ID and the class type specified. Simply choose a class name of `CAddKeywordDlg` and press the Enter key. This creates the new class for you and invokes ClassWizard.

At this point, you have two ways to create the member variable for the `IDC_EDT_KEYWORD` edit control. You can dismiss the ClassWizard dialog box and return to the resource editor to create the member variable, or you can create the member variable by using the Member Variables tab in ClassWizard. If you want to use the ClassWizard, simply click the MemberVariables tab to view the available controls and their IDs, and double-click the `IDC_EDT_KEYWORD` ID to invoke the Add Member Variable dialog box. Create a `CString` variable named `m_strKeyword`.

Because you do not want the user to be able to enter blank keywords, add a message handler to the IDOK control of `CAddKeywordDlg`. To verify the keyword is not blank, make sure your `OnOk` handler looks like the following:

```
void CAddKeywordDlg::OnOK()
{
 UpdateData(TRUE);

 m_strKeyword.TrimRight();
 m_strKeyword.TrimLeft();
```

```
 if (m_strKeyword.IsEmpty())
 {
  AfxMessageBox("Sorry, the Keyword cannot be blank.");
 }
 else
 {
  CDialog::OnOK();
 }
}
```

Now that the CAddKeywordDlg is done, you need to update the CCodeFinderDlg to invoke it and retrieve the newly entered keyword.

Invoking the Dialog

After the dialog template resource has been created and you have used ClassWizard to create a class for it, it's time to start using it.

1. Create a member variable of type CListbox for the main dialog's "Keyword" list box. Name the variable m_lbxKeywords.
2. At the top of the "CodeFinderDlg.cpp" file, add the following #include:

   ```
   #include ""AddKeywordDlg.h""
   ```

A call to the CDialog::DoModal() function is what invokes a modal dialog box. The DoModal function will return a numeric value that can be used to determine how the dialog was ended. Because the IDD_ADD_KEYWORD dialog box has only OK and Cancel buttons, the only return values you need to be concerned with are IDOK and IDCANCEL. With this in mind, use ClassWizard to create a message handler for the main dialog's IDC_BTN_ADDKEYWORD button and code it as follows. This is all you need to invoke a dialog, handle its return value, and retrieve any needed values from the dialog box. After you have the new keyword, simply add it to the Keyword list box. Notice the CListbox::AddString() function works exactly like that of the CComboBox.

```
void CCodeFinderDlg::OnBtnAddKeyword()
{
 CAddKeywordDlg dlg;
 if (IDOK == dlg.DoModal())
 {
  CString strKeyword = dlg.m_strKeyword;
  m_lbxKeywords.AddString(strKeyword);
 }
}
```

Technically, this is all you need to do to invoke and work with a modal dialog. However, to complete the changes so the sample application can work properly, there a few steps should be followed.

First, create a new class called CKeyword. Here's the declaration. By now a few things should be obvious—for example, that the DECLARE_SERIAL macro is used so the CKeyword objects can be serialized.

```
class CKeyword : public CObject
{
DECLARE_SERIAL(CKeyword)

public:
 CKeyword() {};
 CKeyword(CString const& rstrKeyword);

protected:
 CString m_strKeyword;
public:
 CString GetKeyword() { return m_strKeyword; }

protected:
  void Serialize(CArchive& ar);
};
```

Because we know we are going to have to associate the different keywords with a given project, you need to create the mechanism for that association. A CStringList will work nicely here. Modify the CProject definition to declare the following member variables and member functions that will be used to maintain each CProject object's keyword list:

```
public:
 CStringArray m_arrKeywords;
public:
 void DeleteAllKeywords() { m_arrKeywords.RemoveAll(); }
 void AddKeyword(CString const& rstrKeyword)
  { m_arrKeywords.Add(rstrKeyword); }
```

After you have finished modifying the CProject declaration, you need to add another map to the CCodeFinderDlg class so the application can track all keywords, in addition to keeping track of all projects:

```
protected:
 CMapStringToOb m_mapKeywords;
```

Now, it's time to update the Save code, so when the user chooses to save a project, the associated keywords are also saved. First, update the CCodeFinderDlg::OnBtnSave() function to look like the following. Because this code needs to run, regardless of whether a new project is being created or an existing project is being updated, add this code just before the return statement.

```
pProject->DeleteAllKeywords();
CString strKeyword;
```

```
for (int i = 0; i < m_lbxKeywords.GetCount(); i++)
{
m_lbxKeywords.GetText(i, strKeyword);
pProject->AddKeyword(strKeyword);

CKeyword* pKeyword = new CKeyword(strKeyword);
if (pKeyword)
{
 m_mapKeywords.SetAt(strKeyword, (CObject*)pKeyword);
}
```

Now that the project's keywords are being saved in its internal keyword map, we need to make sure these keywords are saved to disk when the project is saved. Because MFC map and list objects automatically call their elements' `Serialize()` function, simply add the following function to the top of the `CProject::Serialize()` function *after* the call to the base class' `Serialize` function. Because the `m_arrKeywords()` is a `CStringArray()`, this code serializes the string that represents the keywords (not the keyword objects).

```
m_arrKeywords.Serialize(ar);
```

We now need to make sure the dialog's map of all keywords gets serialized as well. This is where the keyword objects are being stored. Update the `CCodeFinderDlg::Serialize()` as follows (the function in bold is the only change):

```
m_mapProjectNameToProject.Serialize
m_mapKeywords.Serialize(ar);
```

Because the application is creating objects, once again you have to write the code to free these objects when the application is terminated. Add the following code to the end of the `CCodeFinderDlg` destructor:

```
POSITION posKeyword;
CString strKeyword;
CKeyword* pKeyword;

 for (posKeyword = m_mapKeywords.GetStartPosition(); NULL !=
 posKeyword;)
 {
 m_mapKeywords.GetNextAssoc(posKeyword, strKeyword,
 (CObject*&)pKeyword);
 if (pKeyword)
 {
  m_mapKeywords.RemoveKey(strKeyword);
  delete pKeyword;
 }
}

ASSERT(0 == m_mapKeywords.GetCount());
```

Next, update the `CCodeFinderDlg::InitDialogControls()` so the Keyword list box is initialized with the rest of the controls on the dialog box. Simply add the following function before the call to the `UpdateData` function:

```
m_lbxKeywords.ResetContent();
```

Now that you have done this, you are almost finished. You are saving the keywords with their respective project. However, when you select a project, its keywords are not appearing. Why? Remember the function you added to handle the Project combo box's `CBN_SELCHANGE` notification message? You now need to add the code to that function to display the newly selected project's keywords in the Keyword list box. Simply add the following code to the `CCodeFinderDlg::OnSelchangeCboProject()` function right before the call to the `UpdateData()` function:

```
for (int i = 0;
 i < pProject->m_arrKeywords.GetSize(); i++)
{
 m_lbxKeywords.AddString(pProject->m_arrKeywords[i]);
}
```

Building and running the application will show you that you now have an application that enables you to keep track of the different API calls you have worked with on your different projects. Each time you select a project from the Project combo box, a list of its keywords is shown in the Keyword list box. But, what if you want to search across all projects for a given keyword or API call? Because most applications that provide search, or find, functionality implement it via a modeless dialog, adding this functionality is the subject of the next section.

Modeless Dialogs — A Find Dialog Box

As you know, when a dialog box is created, an owner window is specified. When a modal dialog is displayed, the user cannot interact with its owner until the dialog box has been dismissed. An example of a modal dialog is the About box. Most Windows applications implement this feature to display application information, such as the application name, copyright, and version information. After the user invokes this About box, the user is not allowed to interact with the rest of the application until the dialog box has been dismissed. In addition, when the user of this sample application invokes a dialog to add a new keyword, the user cannot interact with the main dialog until the Add Keyword dialog box has been dismissed.

As you have seen, the `CDialog` class is so powerful that creating a modal dialog box and displaying it can be accomplished simply by creating a dialog template resource, using ClassWizard to create your own `CDialog`-derived class and then calling the `DoModal()` function. This is precisely what you did in the last section.

A *modeless* dialog box, on the other hand, enables the user to continue interacting with its owner even while the dialog is still active. In other words, the dialog box can "float" in the background while the user interacts with the owner window. The user is then free to switch back and forth between working with the dialog box and its owner. An example of a modeless dialog box can be found in most applications that support a Search or Find feature.

One common design factor used in deciding whether to make a dialog modal or modeless is the issue of usability. Most UI designers feel that in the case of the About box, the user has no need to have the dialog box present while continuing to work with the rest of the application. The case of the Find dialog box, however, is normally an exception. Let's take the sample `CDialog` application you created in the last section. If a user wanted to search for a keyword across all projects, it would be natural to invoke a dialog that enables him or her to enter a keyword and then present a list of projects that contain that keyword in a list box. If the user then selects a project in the list box, that project's data should be shown on the main dialog box. But, what if that particular project is on another PC? Keeping the Find dialog modeless enables the user to go and look at this project, and then return to it without having to issue the search all over again.

As you'll see in this section, managing modeless dialogs is only marginally more difficult than working with modal dialogs.

Creating the modeless dialog box

To get started, take a look at the dialog box in Figure 7-9. Using the resource editor, create this dialog box and its controls.

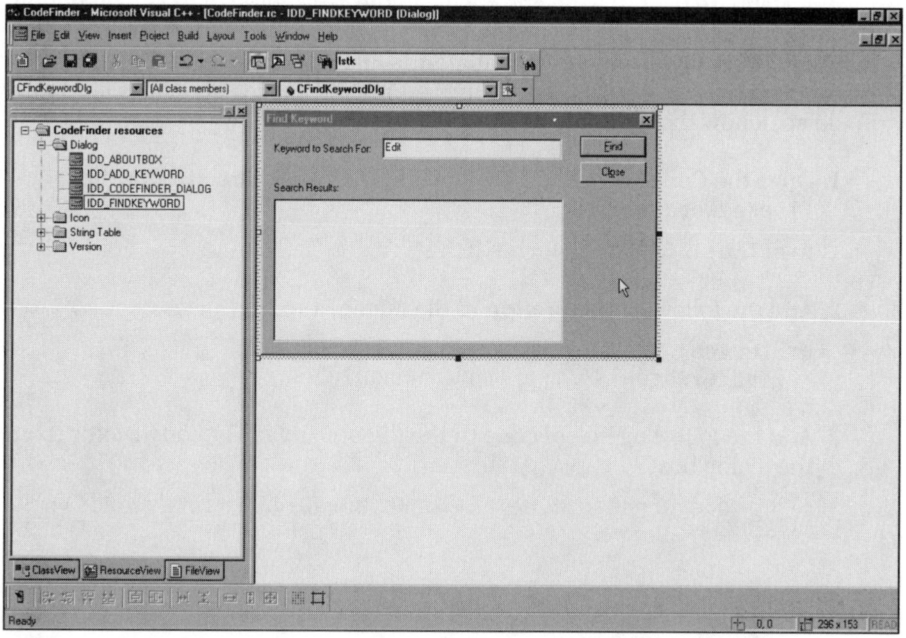

Figure 7-9: This Find dialog box illustrates how to use a modeless dialog.

After you have created the dialog template resource, make the following changes:

- ✦ The dialog's resource ID should be IDD_FIND_KEYWORD.
- ✦ The Keyword edit resource ID should be IDD_EDT_KEYWORD.
- ✦ The Search Results list box resource ID should be IDD_LBX_SEARCHRESULTS.
- ✦ Create a new class based on this dialog template, and call it CFindKeywordDlg.
- ✦ Create a member variable of type CString for the IDC_EDT_KEYWORD, and call it m_strKeyword.
- ✦ Create a member variable of type CListbox for the IDC_LBX_SEARCHRESULTS.

Invoking a modeless dialog box

Although there is generally only one step necessary to invoke a modal dialog box — the DoModal() function call invoking a modeless dialog box involves setting a dialog property and using two functions.

Begin by editing the dialog's properties in the resource editor and setting its Visible property to "on." For a modal dialog box, you don't have to do this — but in the case of a modeless dialog, forgetting to set this property results in your having an invisible dialog box on-screen.

Next, instantiate the CDialog and then call the CDialog::Create() function. Because the user will be able to invoke the Find Keyword dialog box an infinite number of times, you should instantiate the dialog in the CCodeFinderDlg constructor and call its Create() function whenever the user clicks Find Keyword. To do so, follow these steps:

1. Open the CodeFinderDlg.h file and add #include directive for the FindKeywordDlg.h:

```
#include ""FindKeywordDlg.h""
```

2. Add the following declaration to the CCodeFinderDlg class:

```
protected:
 CFindKeywordDlg* m_pFindKeywordDlg;
```

3. Add the following line of code to the CCodeFinderDlg constructor to create the dialog box:

```
m_pFindKeywordDlg = new CFindKeywordDlg(m_mapKeywords);
```

4. Because the Find Keyword dialog box will be created on the heap, be sure to delete it in the `CCodeFinderDlg` destructor, as follows:

```
if (m_pFindKeywordDlg)
{
 delete m_pFindKeywordDlg;
}
```

5. Add a message handler for the `IDC_BTN_FINDKEYWORD` button on the `CCodeFinderDlg`. The function should look like the following code snippet:

```
void CCodeFinderDlg::OnBtnFindKeyword()
{
 if (!m_pFindKeywordDlg->GetSafeHwnd())
 {
  // displays the modeless dialog
  m_pFindKeywordDlg->Create(IDD_FINDKEYWORD);
 }
}
```

As the comment indicates, the `Create()` function call displays the modeless dialog, which users can now invoke. The major reason for using a sample application like CodeFinder in this example is to see a realistic application of the different dialog functions. The next task, therefore, is to make sure these two dialog boxes can communicate when they are both visible.

Communication between modal and modeless dialog boxes

After the modeless `CFindKeywordDlg` dialog box is displayed, it needs to communicate with the modal `CCodeFinderDlg` dialog box. This communication needs to take place at two different times.

- ✦ First is when a user enters a keyword to search for. The `CFindKeywordDlg` dialog needs to search the main dialog's keyword map for all the projects that have this keyword defined. To do this, we simply pass a pointer to the keyword map to the `CFindKeywordDlg` constructor.
- ✦ Second is after the user has performed the search and selected a project. The `CFindKeywordDlg` should communicate that fact to the `CCodeFinderDlg`, and the `CCodeFinderDlg` should in turn display that particular project.

Getting information to the modeless dialog

Of the two communication problems just mentioned, the second is easier to deal with. Because the `CFindKeywordDlg` needs access to the `CCodeFinderDlg` keyword map, we simply pass it through the constructor.

To change the CFindKeywordDlg, replace its constructor with the following lines of code. As you can see, the constructor has been changed to accept a reference to the CCodeFinderDlg keyword map. A keyword map pointer is then declared to hold the value passed to the constructor.

```
public:
 CFindKeywordDlg(CMapStringToOb const& rmapKeywords,
  CWnd* pParent = NULL);   // standard constructor

protected:
 CMapStringToOb* m_pmapKeywords;
```

Next, change the CFindKeywordDlg constructor to read like the following:

```
CFindKeywordDlg::CFindKeywordDlg(
 CMapStringToOb const& rmapKeywords,
 CWnd* pParent /*=NULL*/)
: CDialog(CFindKeywordDlg::IDD, pParent)
{
 //{{AFX_DATA_INIT(CFindKeywordDlg)
 m_strKeyword = _T("");
 //}}AFX_DATA_INIT

 m_pmapKeywords = (CMapStringToOb*)&rmapKeywords;
}
```

After you have modified both the declaration and definition of the CFindKeywordDlg constructor, add a message handler for its OK button and code it like this. This function simply verifies that the keyword entered by the user is not blank, searches the keyword map for it, and if the keyword is found, loads the "Search Results" list box with all the projects that have it defined.

```
void CFindKeywordDlg::OnOk()
{
 m_lbxSearchResults.ResetContent();

 UpdateData(TRUE);
 m_strKeyword.TrimLeft();
 m_strKeyword.TrimRight();
 if (m_strKeyword.IsEmpty())
 {
   AfxMessageBox("Sorry, the Keyword can not be blank");
 }
 else
 {
  CKeyword* pKeyword = NULL;
  if (!m_pmapKeywords->Lookup(
   m_strKeyword, (CObject*&)pKeyword))
  {
   AfxMessageBox("The Keyword you entered is not "
    "being used on any Projects");
  }
```

```
    else
    {
     if (!pKeyword)
     {
      AfxMessageBox("The Keyword you entered is not "
       "being used on any Projects");
     }
     else
     {
      for (int i = 0;
       i < pKeyword->m_arrProjects.GetSize();
       i++)
      {
       m_lbxSearchResults.AddString(
        pKeyword->m_arrProjects[i]);
      }
     }
    }
   }
  }
```

You may have noticed the reference to the CKeyword project array. There's only one problem with that. It doesn't exist yet. Therefore, the next thing we'll do in this section is to remedy this problem.

Add the following declaration to the CKeyword class. Much like the CProject class, which has a member variable that represents an array of associated keywords, the CKeyword class will now have an array of associated projects. This enables us to efficiently perform the searches that are necessary in this application.

```
public:
 CStringArray m_arrProjects;
```

Because another member variable has been added to the CKeyword class, it also must be serialized. Add the following line of code to the CKeyword::Serialize() function (after the call to the Serialize() function of the base class):

```
m_arrProjects.Serialize(ar);
```

Now that each CKeyWord object has an array of associated projects, the SaveProject() function of the CCodeFinderDlg must be modified to update this map as well. Therefore, locate SaveProject() and delete the following lines of code:

```
CKeyword* pKeyword = new CKeyword(strKeyword);
if (pKeyword)
{
 m_mapKeywords.SetAt(strKeyword, (CObject*)pKeyword);
}
```

Insert the following lines of code to replace the ones you just deleted. Note, this code should be inserted after the `pProject->AddKeyword` function call. This code attempts to locate the keyword in the dialog's keyword map. If the keyword cannot be found, a new `CKeyword` object is created and added to the keyword map. After this, either the found or newly created `CKeyword` object's project map is updated with the value of the project currently being saved.

```
// Update keyword to project map
CKeyword* pKeyword = NULL;
if (!m_mapKeywords.Lookup(strKeyword,
 (CObject*&)pKeyword))
{
 pKeyword = new CKeyword(strKeyword);
 m_mapKeywords.SetAt(strKeyword, (CObject*)pKeyword);
}

pKeyword->m_arrProjects.Add(m_strProject);
```

Communicating back to the modal dialog

After the user has selected a project by double-clicking it, you somehow need to inform the dialog of that fact. Actually, this is not difficult. So far in this chapter, you have worked with messages that were created and then sent to a class you wrote. Now you need to create a user-defined message—that is, one created uniquely for your purposes. When the user double-clicks a project, this message will be sent from the `CFindKeywordDlg` to the `CCodeFinderDlg`. The message will include the project's name. That project name will then be located in the Project combo box, and the dialog will be updated.

To get the ball rolling, add a message handler for the `LBN_DBLCLICK` notification message for the `IDC_LBX_SEARCHRESULT` control ID of the `CFindKeywordDlg`. Modify it to look like the following. As you can see, after the user's requested project name has been retrieved from the "Search Results" list box, a pointer to the `CCodeFinderDlg` is acquired. Because this is a modeless dialog that was created, a child window of the `CCodeFinderDlg`, the `CDialog::GetParent()` function can be used to accomplish this. After a pointer to the `CCodeFinderDlg` object has been acquired, a message is sent to it (`WM_SHOWPROJECT`) with the first parameter containing the selected project name.

```
void CFindKeywordDlg::OnDblclkLbxSearchresults()
{
 int iIndex;
 if (CB_ERR != (iIndex = m_lbxSearchResults.GetCurSel()))
 {
  CWnd* pWnd = GetParent();
  if (pWnd)
  {
   CString strProject;
   m_lbxSearchResults.GetText(iIndex, strProject);
```

```
    pWnd->SendMessage(WM_SHOWPROJECT,
    (WPARAM)(&strProject));
   }
  }
 }
```

You'll need to add support manually for the capability of receiving the new `WM_SHOWPROJECT` message. Start by defining this message ID in the CodeFinderDlg.h file:

```
#define WM_SHOWPROJECT (WM_USER + 1)
```

Next, locate the declarations for the `CCodeFinderDlg` message map functions and add the following declaration:

```
afx_msg void OnShowProject(WPARAM wParam, LPARAM lParam);
```

The last thing you need to do is handle the message. This is done in two steps. First, update the message map in the CodeFinderDlg.cpp file, as follows:

```
ON_MESSAGE(WM_SHOWPROJECT, OnShowProject)
```

Next, add the following `CCodeFinderDlg::OnShowProject()` function. This function simply casts the `WPARAM` variable back into a `CString` pointer and uses it to search the Project combo box. When located, that specific project is selected as if the user had selected it from the combo box.

```
void CCodeFinderDlg::OnShowProject(WPARAM wParam,
 LPARAM lParam)
{
 CString* pstrProject = (CString*)wParam;
 if (pstrProject)
 {
  int iIndex;
  if (CB_ERR == (iIndex = m_cboProject.FindString(-1,
   *pstrProject)))
  {
   AfxMessageBox("Error - Project not found in "
    "combo box");
  }
  else
  {
   m_cboProject.SetCurSel(iIndex);
   OnSelchangeCboProject();
  }
 }
}
```

Summary

In this chapter, you learned a great deal about the power and flexibility of the `CDialog` class. In addition, you worked with seven different basic controls, learned about DDX, implemented message handlers for control notification messages, implemented user-defined messages, and coded both modal and modeless dialog boxes. As you've seen, knowing about each of these things individually is helpful, but fully understanding how to incorporate all of them into an application is what will make you a more productive programmer.

✦ ✦ ✦

CHAPTER 8

Property Sheets and Property Pages

In This Chapter

Understanding the CPropertySheet and CPropertyPage classes

Working with modal and modeless property sheets

Writing a modal CPropertySheet demo

Removing the standard CPropertySheet buttons

Repositioning the standard CPropertySheet buttons

Enabling and disabling CPropertyPage tabs

Changing a tab's caption and font

Using mnemonics with CPropertyPage tabs

Tabbed dialogs are certainly no stranger to anyone who has used 32-bit Windows operating systems. In fact, it is difficult to use Windows without running into these dialogs. Tabbed dialogs are found not only within operating system applications, but also within popular applications such as Word for Windows, Excel, and even DevStudio. Tabbed dialogs benefit developers by providing a means of defining a single interface point (for example, a menu option) to access a given task while still enabling the developer to separate the subtasks into different tabs. This functionality enables the developer to use the tabs that define each level of granularity. Figure 8-1 shows an example of tabbed dialogs in Word for Windows.

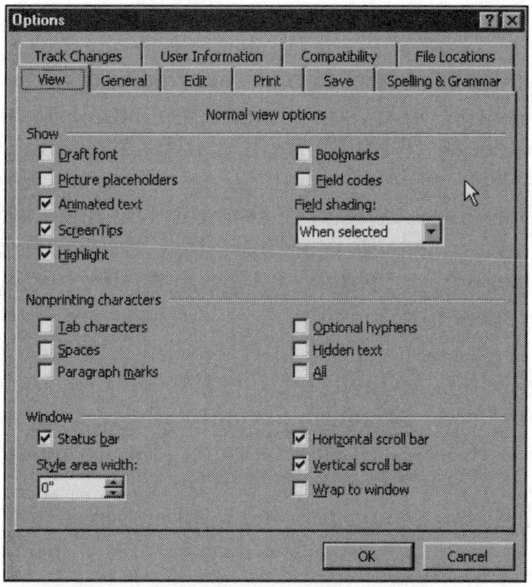

Figure 8-1: Example of tabbed dialog (Word for Windows Option dialog)

After taking a look at the 10 tabs in this dialog, imagine what it would be like to go to a different menu option for each of these options. This sample dialog is a great example of why tabbed dialogs were invented. Instead of having to search through several different dialogs to view and set different options, the user views only one dialog for all the application's options. Each tab is then defined to contain a given set of logically related options.

When MFC 3.0 (Visual C++ 2.0) shipped, tabbed dialogs were among the most notable new classes. Even so, the name was changed from tabbed dialogs to property sheets and property pages in MFC parlance. These entities are supported by the `CPropertySheet` and `CPropertyPage` MFC classes. In Figure 8-1, the property sheet is defined as the entire dialog and the property pages are the 10 different tabs that exist therein.

In this chapter, you'll examine these two MFC classes and learn how to implement them in both a modal and modeless environment. After you have learned the different options and ways in which to implement these classes, a demo with several variations will be presented. While working your way through the demo, you'll learn how to complete frequently requested tasks with regard to property sheets and property pages. These tasks include property sheet level functions such as removing, renaming, and repositioning the standard property sheet buttons. Also included are property page level functions such as changing the tabs' caption and font as well as implementing mnemonics on tabs.

Understanding CPropertySheet and CPropertyPage

Describing either the `CPropertySheet` class or the `CPropertyPage` class in a linear manner produces a chicken-and-egg problem. In other words, because each class was meant to work intimately with the other, it is almost impossible to talk exclusively about one class without referring to the other. If you examine the MFC source code for these classes, you'll see that the `CPropertyPage` class is a friend class of the `CPropertySheet` class. Therefore, instead of separately explaining each class, I will explain both classes together with their interdependence spelled out as I go along. That way, the two classes will be described and illustrated as they are designed to be used: as a single programmatic entity.

Refer back to the tabbed dialog in Figure 8-1. As mentioned earlier, tabbed dialogs are implemented in MFC via the `CPropertySheet` and `CPropertyPage` classes. If MFC was used to implement this dialog, the entire tabbed dialog (the frame, titlebar text, "OK" button, and "Cancel" button) would be represented by a `CPropertySheet` object. The individual tabs would then be implemented via `CPropertyPage` objects.

As a result, you might assume that the CPropertySheet is derived from CDialog. Actually, the CPropertySheet class is derived directly from CWnd. As you learned in Chapter 7, the CDialog class encapsulates a Windows dialog functionality and Windows dialogs are based on dialog template resources. Using this little nugget of trivia is important when implementing your own CPropertySheet-derived class. Because the separate CPropertyPage objects are used to represent each tab, the CPropertyPage class is derived from CDialog.

Using the resource editor to create property pages

Creating property pages is almost the same as creating dialogs. In both cases, the resource editor lays out the controls on a dialog template resource. Even so, some of the dialog properties change with property pages, as follows:

- The Caption property appears on the tab instead of on the dialog's titlebar
- Set the Style property to *Child*
- Set the dialog's Border style to *Thin*
- Check the dialog's Disabled property

Luckily, you don't need to remember these different styles because the "Insert Resource" dialog has three different options for creating property pages. All of the created property pages have the correct styles set. The only difference between the different default property pages created with the "Insert Resource" dialog is the initial size of the dialog.

Creating a CPropertyPage

After you design the property pages, you create a CPropertyPage-derived class to associate with each of the dialog template resources. You can create this CPropertyPage-derived class in a similar fashion to creating a CDialog-derived class. Simply invoke ClassWizard — but instead of selecting CDialog as the base class, select CPropertyPage. Be careful about the last part. If you invoke the ClassWizard to create a new class of a dialog template resource, ClassWizard always defaults the base class to CDialog. Unfortunately, ClassWizard doesn't look at the styles to determine that a CPropertyPage is probably the correct method in some cases.

Creating and displaying a modal CPropertySheet

Although the CPropertySheet is not derived from CDialog, it is implemented in a similar manner to the CDialog class. For example, to create modal property sheets, you normally declare a CPropertySheet object on the stack and call its DoModal() function, just as you'd call a CDialog object. With a property page, however, you must add the relevant property pages before calling the `DoModal()` function or risk having a boring property sheet. The following example adds `CPropertyPage` objects to a `CPropertySheet` object via the `CPropertySheet::AddPage()` function:

```
void ShowModalPropertySheet()
{
 CPropertySheet sheet;
 CMyPropertyPage1 pageMyPage1;
 CMyPropertyPage2 pageMyPage2;

 sheet.AddPage(&pageMyPage1);
 sheet.AddPage(&pageMyPage2);
 sheet.DoModal();
}
```

Creating and displaying a modeless CPropertySheet

Displaying a modeless property sheet is almost identical to displaying a modal property sheet. Instead of using the `DoModal()` function to display the property sheet, however, the `CPropertySheet::Create()` function is used. In addition, you should remember the following points when dealing with modeless property sheets and property pages. First, the `CPropertySheet` and `CPropertyPage` objects must be allocated on the heap. By definition, you create a modeless property sheet in an asynchronous manner. In other words, the function that created and displayed the property sheet will normally end while the property sheet remains on the screen. Therefore, if you create the `CPropertySheet` and `CPropertyPage` objects on the stack, they go out of scope with the property sheet still active on the screen. Also, because the function that allocates the `CPropertyPage` objects usually ends before the user dismisses the property sheet, the memory needs to be de-allocated by another function. This process is normally accomplished by deriving a class from the `CPropertySheet` class and implementing the `PostNcDestroy()` member function. Because the `CPropertySheet` object has an array of its `CPropertyPages`, the act of de-allocating the `CPropertyPages` can be done in this function, which is called when the property sheet is dismissed. The following example is a simple example of how to create and display a modeless property sheet. This code snippet assumes that the `CMyPropertySheet`, `CMyPropertyPage1`, and `CMyPropertyPage2` classes have already been created. If you have further questions, this process will also be covered later in this chapter in the demo for creating modeless property sheets.

```
void ShowModelessPropertySheet()
{
 CMyPropertySheet* psheet = new CMyPropertySheet();
 CMyPropertyPage1* ppageMyPage1 = new CMyPropertyPage1();
 CMyPropertyPage2* ppageMyPage2 = new CMyPropertyPage2();

 psheet->AddPage(ppageMyPage1);
 psheet->AddPage(ppageMyPage2);
 psheet->Create();
}
```

As you can see, the `GetPageCount()` function returns the total number of pages added to the `CPropertySheet` object. Because `CPropertyPage` objects are stored in an array in the `CPropertySheet` object, the `GetPage()` function returns a pointer to a `CPropertyPage` object using the passed integer value as an index into that array:

```
for (int i = 0; i < GetPageCount(); i++)
{
 CPropertyPage* pPage = GetPage(i);
 if (pPage)
 {
  delete pPage;
 }
}
```

Unlike a modal property sheet, modeless property sheets are not automatically created with an "OK" and "Cancel" button; you have to create them manually. You'll learn this skill in the next section as we further delve into the `CPropertySheet()`.

Creating and displaying a property sheet within an existing dialog

So far, you've seen how to create and display both a modal and modeless property sheet. Even so, you may need to display a property sheet within an already existing dialog, such as in the Windows "Find in Files" application. When you start the Find application, you only see what appears to be a `CPropertySheet` with the buttons aligned along the right-hand side of the dialog, instead of along the bottom of the dialog. Even so, the existing menu and the visible list control upon clicking the "Find" file confirms that this is no ordinary `CPropertySheet`. Actually, it is a dialog (with a menu) that has an embedded `CPropertySheet`.

If you need this advanced user-interface functionality, use the following simple steps:

First, declare the `CPropertySheet` and `CPropertyPage` objects as member variables:

```
class CYourDialog : public CDialog
{
 ...
protected:
 CPropertySheet m_sheet;
 CMyPropertyPage1 m_pageMyPage1;
 CMyPropertyPage2 m_pageMyPage2;
 ...
```

Next, in the dialog's `OnInitDialog()` function, call the `CPropertySheet::AddPage()` function to add the `CPropertyPage` objects. Then, create the property sheet (specifying that the property sheet is a child of the dialog with the `WS_CHILD` flag). After the `CPropertySheet` object has been created, modify a couple of styles that deal with tabbing. Finally, position the property sheet on the dialog via a call to the `SetWindowPos()` function. Here's how your `OnInitDialog()` may look:

```
void CYourDialog::OnInitDialog()
{
 ...
 m_sheet.Create(this, WS_CHILD | WS_VISIBLE, 0);
 m_sheet.ModifyStyleEx (0, WS_EX_CONTROLPARENT);
 m_sheet.ModifyStyle( 0, WS_TABSTOP );
 CRect rect;
 GetDlgItem(IDC_PROPSHEET)->GetWindowRect(&rect);
 ScreenToClient(&rect);
 m_sheet.SetWindowPos(NULL, rect.left-7, rect.top-7,
  0, 0, SWP_NOZORDER | SWP_NOSIZE | SWP_NOACTIVATE);
 ...
```

Modal Property Sheet Demo

The first demo in this chapter teaches you many aspects of using modal property sheets by writing a "Find" dialog. The "Find" dialog is similar to other application dialogs with one exception: Once a search has been completed, the results are displayed on a second tab. This capability handles scenarios where a search results in more than one "hit."

Programming this type of demo enables you to deal with many realistic scenarios concerning programming property sheets. For example, in a "Find" dialog you wouldn't want to enable the "Results" tab unless matches are found. Therefore, after you get the basic property sheet up and running, you'll learn to enable and disable tabs. In addition, it's a nice touch for the user to see the number of matches on the "Result" tab. To accomplish that task, you need to change a tab caption dynamically.

Creating the demo application

Because the main objective of this demo is to teach the different aspects of the `CPropertySheet` and `CPropertyPage` classes, we will dummy up (or fake) the main application's role with regards to the "Find" dialog. In other words, the main application will only instantiate and display the `CPropertySheet` and `CPropertyPage` objects. In addition, the main application displays a message indicating any data sent back from the `CPropertySheet` object. Here's how to create the application:

1. Create a new MFC SDI application named "ModalPropertySheetDemo."
2. Start the resource editor and create two property sheets.
3. From the DevStudio's "Insert" menu option, select the "Resource" entry.
4. After you see the "Insert Resource" dialog, a tree control of resource types appears. Expanding the "Dialog" option will expose several "types" of dialogs. Actually, all these types are represented by a dialog template resource. Even so, each type has a different style set to function properly with their associated MFC classes.
5. Create a small property page by double-clicking the `IDD_PROPPAGE_SMALL` entry.
6. After you create the dialog resource, rename its resource ID to `IDP_FINDBOOK_FIND` and add the necessary control to make it look like the dialog in Figure 8-2. You may need to resize the dialog to have your controls look the way you want.
7. Make sure to disable the "Author" and "Publisher" Edit controls. As mentioned earlier, you want to focus on the task of dealing with property sheets. Therefore, many aspects of this demo will be faked so that the demo doesn't address issues irrelevant to property sheets.

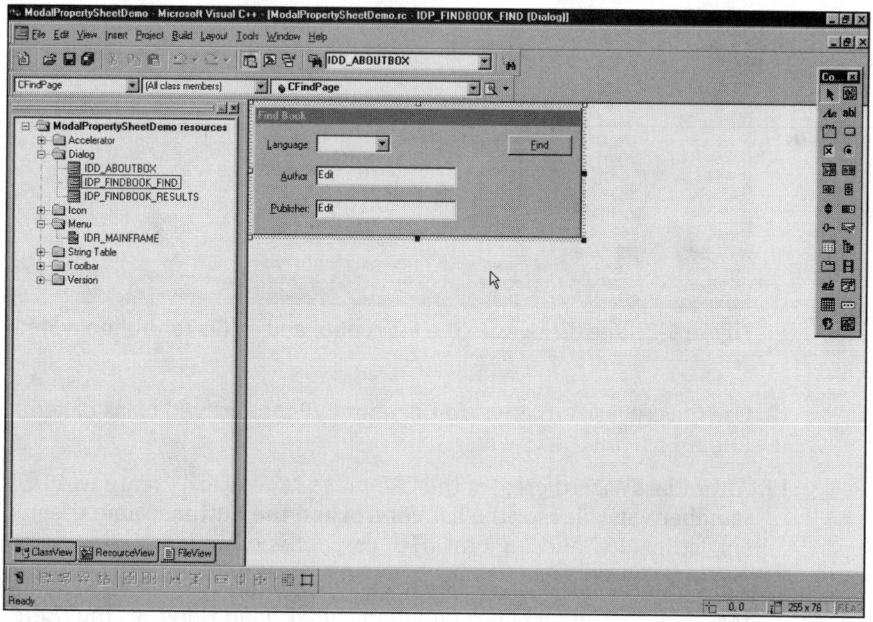

Figure 8-2: PropertySheetDemo1 — Find Property Page after controls are added

8. After the control is placed on the IDP_FINDBOOK_FIND dialog, use the ClassWizard to create a CPropertyPage class called CFindPage.

9. Next, create DDX control member variables for the "Language" combo box and the "Find" button. Name them "m_cboLanguages" and "m_btnFind" respectively.

10. After the "Find" property page is complete, create a second property page called IDP_FINDBOOK_RESULTS.

11. Add a list control and a "Go To" button to the dialog so that it looks like the dialog in Figure 8-3.

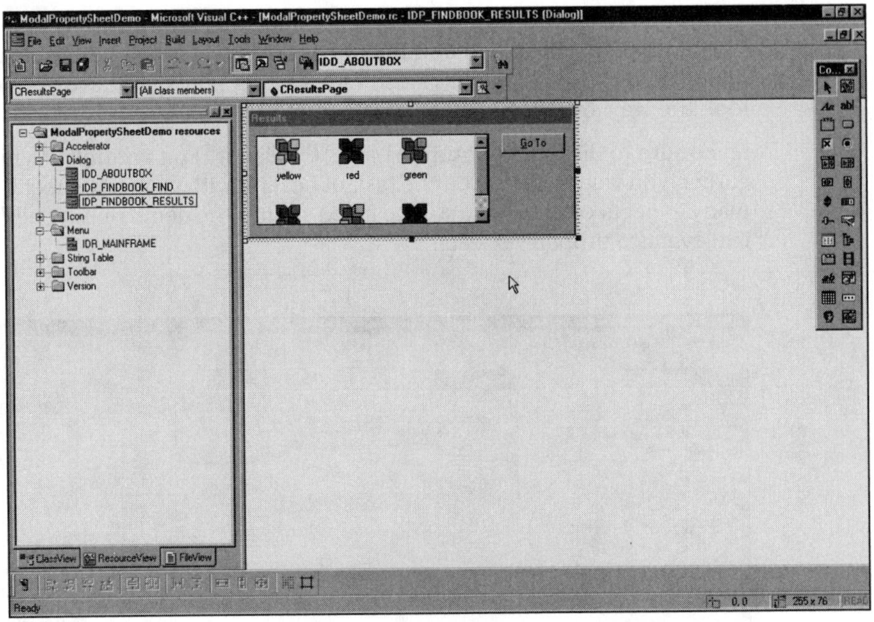

Figure 8-3: The dialog with the list control and a "Go To" button added

12. Use ClassWizard to create a CPropertyPage-derived class called CResultsPage.

13. After ClassWizard creates the CResultsPage class, create two DDX control member variables for the list control and the button. Name them "m_lstResults" and "m_btnGoTo" respectively.

14. After you create the property pages, locate the IDR_MAINFRAME menu resource and add a new menu item called "Find Book" to the "Edit" menu.

15. Create a menu handler via ClassWizard for your new menu entry in the `CMainFrame` class. The code should look like the following when you're done:

```
void CMainFrame::OnEditFindbook()
{
 CPropertySheet sheet(_T("Find Book"));
 CFindPage pageFind;
 CResultsPage pageResults;

 sheet.AddPage(&pageFind);
 sheet.AddPage(&pageResults);
 sheet.DoModal();
}
```

In the code, a `CPropertySheet` is created on the stack using the constructor that takes a string displayed in the title bar as its only argument. Next, two `CPropertyPage` objects are instantiated. After the pages are created, they are both added to the `CPropertySheet` via the `CPropertySheet::AddPage()` function and the `CPropertySheet::DoModal()` function is called to display the property sheet.

Finally, before compiling the demo, add the following two `#include` directives to the beginning of the `mainfrm.cpp` file for the two `CPropertyPage`-derived classes:

```
#include "FindPage.h"
#include "ResultsPage.h"
```

At this point, you can build and run the application. After you select the "Find" option from the "Edit" menu, your modal property sheet should look like Figure 8-4.

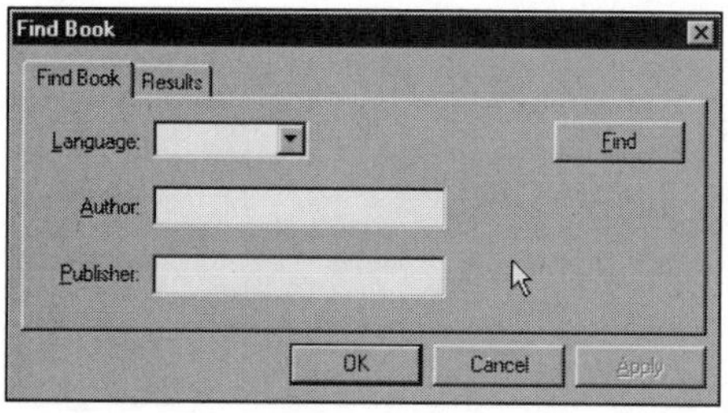

Figure 8-4: Example of the modal property sheet

Pretty easy, huh? Unfortunately, most books leave off at this point. Even so, you aren't reading this chapter to learn something that can be covered in just a few pages. Roll up your sleeves and let's start doing some real work with this dialog.

Removing standard buttons

When a CPropertySheet is displayed, several buttons are automatically created and displayed for you. Even so, there may be situations where your application doesn't have a need for all these standard buttons. If the buttons are displayed automatically, how does the programmer specify that they are not needed? Actually, as you're about to see, removing any or all of the standard buttons from a CPropertySheet is not difficult.

First, remove the "Cancel" and "Apply" buttons. The "Cancel" button is used when the property sheet makes changes to data or preferences. That way, the user can back out (or cancel) at any time before committing the changes. The "Apply" button gives the user the ability to apply the changes while remaining on the property sheet. In other words, when using a dialog, it is customary to expect that changes will only be made once the dialog has been dismissed. Even so, with property sheets you can use the "Apply" button to enable the user to view her changes while the property sheet remains active. This capability enables users to continue making changes and, depending on the application, see the effects as they work their way through the property sheet's pages.

This demo is about a "Find" property sheet, however, and because data will not be changed, neither of these buttons is applicable to this application. The question now becomes how to remove these buttons when you don't have the dialog template resource for the property sheet. With a CPropertySheet, you get these buttons (and the "OK" button) for free.

Because MFC is creating these buttons automatically for you, they are all created with static, nonchanging resource IDs. Therefore, their IDs are documented as follows:

Button	***Resource ID***
OK	IDOK
Cancel	IDCANCEL
Help	IDHELP
Apply	ID_APPLY_NOW

To move the standard buttons, you only need to do the following for each control (where IDXX is one of the IDs listed):

```
CWnd* pWnd = GetDlgItem(IDXX);
if (pWnd)
{
 pWnd->ShowWindow(FALSE);
}
```

To implement this change to the FindBook demo, make the following modifications:

1. Derive a class from CPropertySheet called CFindSheet.
2. Include the FileSheet.h file at the beginning of the Mainfrm.cpp file.
3. Modify the CMainFrame:: OnEditFindbook() function to instantiate this new CFindSheet class (instead of the standard CPropertySheet).
4. Using ClassWizard, override the CFindSheet::OnInitInstance() function to hide the unwanted buttons (IDCANCEL and ID_APPLY_NOW).

Your OnInitDialog should now look like the following:

```
void CFindSheet::OnInitDialog()
{
 BOOL bResult = CPropertySheet::OnInitDialog();

 int ids[] = {ID_APPLY_NOW, IDCANCEL};
 for (int i = 0; i < sizeof ids / sizeof ids[0]; i++)
 {
  CWnd* pWnd = GetDlgItem(ids[i]);
  ASSERT(pWnd);
  if (pWnd) pWnd->ShowWindow(FALSE);
 }
}
```

If you run the application, you still have one problem concerning the standard buttons. The only remaining button (IDOK) appears as if it has been marooned in the middle of the dialog. The next section shows an example of how to move the standard buttons.

Repositioning standard buttons

The dialog looks a little strange now with only one button positioned almost in the middle of the dialog. In addition, both property pages have buttons aligned along the right-hand side of the property page. The dialog would certainly look better if the "OK" button was also aligned along the right-hand side of the property sheet. Unfortunately, there is no single member function along the lines of AlignButtons(). Therefore, you will have to do this the old-fashioned way: the MoveWindow() function. The following code should be added to the OnInitDialog() function (or a function that is called from OnInitDialog()).

Here's a brief explanation of the code in Listing 8-1. First, use the technique described in "Removing the Standard Buttons" to get a button to calculate the button size. In this example, you are only going to move the "OK" button (since it's the only one left!). Even so, this code could easily be modified to move any buttons. From there, simply shorten the property page (via the MoveWindow() function call) by the height of a button and widen the property sheet the width of a button. After the property sheet is properly sized, use the screen position of the first property page to properly align the "OK" button with the property page.

Listing 8-1: Code Snippet to Move Buttons in a Property Sheet

```
CWnd* pbtnOk = GetDlgItem(IDOK);
ASSERT(pbtnOk);

CRect rectSheet;
GetWindowRect(rectSheet);

// get size of ok button
CRect rectOkBtn;
pbtnOk->GetWindowRect(rectOkBtn);

// get border space between btn bottom and sheet bottom
int iBorder = rectSheet.bottom - rectOkBtn.bottom;

// resize sheet
rectSheet.right += rectOkBtn.Width() + iBorder;
rectSheet.bottom = rectOkBtn.top;
MoveWindow(rectSheet);

// find first page
CPropertyPage* pPage = GetPage(0);
ASSERT(pPage);
CRect rectPage;
pPage->GetWindowRect(rectPage);

// save width and height
int cxOk = rectOkBtn.Width();
int cyOk = rectOkBtn.Height();

// move ok button
rectOkBtn.top = rectPage.top;
rectOkBtn.bottom = rectOkBtn.top + cyOk;
rectOkBtn.left = rectSheet.right - (cxOk + iBorder);
rectOkBtn.right = rectOkBtn.left + cxOk;
ScreenToClient(rectOkBtn);
pbtnOk->MoveWindow(rectOkBtn);
```

Changing the standard button's caption

Next, change the "OK" button's caption. A button's caption should reflect what will happen if the button is clicked. If someone is using this "Find" dialog and sees an "OK" button, they would naturally be confused as to what will happen once that button is clicked. In other words, does the pressing of an "OK" button on a "Find" dialog close the dialog or perform the search? Therefore, the next task changes the "OK" button's caption.

Because the `CPropertySheet` and its standard buttons are created dynamically, you have to change a standard button's caption in your code. The following code changes the "OK" button's caption (including setting a mnemonic). Any of the property sheet's standard button IDs could be used (as listed), as well as any IDs for controls added to the property sheet.

```
CWnd* pWnd = GetDlgItem(IDOK);
pWnd->SetWindowText(_T("Cl&ose"));
```

Disabling tabs

At the time of this writing, there is no elegant means of disabling a tab. The only means of disabling tabs are as follows:

1. Create a member variable to store the current tab index.
2. Create an array member variable to hold all the index values for the currently disabled tabs.
3. Handle the `TCN_SELCHANGING` notification message to set the current tab index.
4. Handle the `TCN_SELCHANGED` notification message to decide if you want to allow the tab to be activated. If you don't, post a `PSM_SETCURSEL` message. In this message, the last active tab index is specified.

In addition to all this work to disable a tab, you cannot change the font for a given tab. In other words, you cannot "gray out" the text of the tab so the user can intuitively see that the tab is not accessible. Therefore, Microsoft recommends that you simply append the text "- Disabled" to the tab's caption. Bogus? Absolutely. Unfortunately, this is the only available strategy at this point.

Create a member variable to store the current tab index

Add a member variable to the `CFindSheet` class to hold the current tab index. When a user attempts to access a disabled tab, this index value represents the tab that will be activated. Actually, it happens so fast that the user only perceives his inability to switch to the disabled tab.

```
protected:
 int m_iLastActivePage;
```

Create a member variable to hold currently disabled tabs

Add a member variable of type `CUIntArray` to the `CFindSheet` class. This array will hold all the indexes to the currently disabled tabs on the property sheet.

```
CUIntArray m_arrDisabledPages;
```

Add member functions to disable specified tabs

Next, add the following function declaration to the `CFindSheet` class to allow the disabling of tabs. The tabs that need to be disabled are specified in a variable argument list that is terminated with the standard value of -1. This function adds the specified tab indexes to the "m_arrDisabledPages" array. After that, the `SetDisabledText()` function is called to append the " - Disabled" text to the tab's caption.

```
void CFindSheet::DisablePage(int iFirstPage, ...)
{
 int iPage = iFirstPage;

 va_list marker;
 va_start (marker, iFirstPage);
 int nArgs = 0;

 while (iPage != -1)
 {
  // add page to disabled page index array
  m_arrDisabledPages.Add(iPage);

  SetDisabledText(iPage);

  // Get next page index
  iPage = va_arg(marker, UINT);

  // the list MUST end with a -1!!!
  ASSERT(nArgs++ < 100);
 }
}
```

Add member functions to set captions of disabled tabs

After you have added the `DisablePage()` function, add the following `#define` function. This function will append the `DISABLED_TEXT` value to the tab's caption so that the user knows that the tab cannot be activated.

```
#define DISABLED_TEXT " - Disabled"

void CFindSheet::SetDisabledText(int iPage)
{
 CTabCtrl* pTab = GetTabControl();
 ASSERT(pTab);
 TC_ITEM ti;
 char szText[100];
 ti.mask = TCIF_TEXT;
 ti.pszText = szText;
 ti.cchTextMax = 100;
 VERIFY(pTab->GetItem(iPage, &ti));
 strcat(szText, DISABLED_TEXT);
 VERIFY(pTab->SetItem(iPage, &ti));
}
```

Handle tab notification messages for disabled tabs

Now that you have everything in place to know whether a tab should be disabled, add the function that will disallow user activation of a disabled tab. Use the ClassWizard to implement the `OnNotify()` virtual function and edit it to look like the following. Whenever the user attempts to activate a tab, this function checks to see if the desired tab is disabled. If so, this function will reset the current tab to the last active tab by posting a `PSM_SETCURSEL` message to itself.

```
BOOL CFindSheet::OnNotify(WPARAM wParam,
 LPARAM lParam, LRESULT* pResult)
{
 NMHDR* pnmh = (NMHDR*)lParam;
 ASSERT(pnmh);
 if (TCN_SELCHANGING == pnmh->code)
 {
  m_iLastActivePage = GetActiveIndex();
 }
 else if (TCN_SELCHANGE == pnmh->code)
 {
  int iCurrPage = GetActiveIndex();
  if (PageIsDisabled(iCurrPage))
  {
   PostMessage(PSM_SETCURSEL, m_iLastActivePage);
  }
 }

 return CPropertySheet::OnNotify(wParam,
  lParam, pResult);
}
```

Test the capability to disable tabs

Because the "Find" dialog has a tab for the search criteria and one for the search results, it would be logical to assume that the "Results" tab be disabled until the user has initiated the search. Therefore, add the following line at the end of the `CFindSheet::OnInitDialog()` function. When you call any function that takes a variable argument list, you must send a value that is recognized as the terminating value to the list. In this case, I have used the standard value of –1. Testing and running the application at this point should produce a property sheet where the "Results" property page is not accessible. Because you want to re-enable this tab once the user initiates a search, the next section will show how to re-enable tabs.

```
DisablePage(1, -1);
```

Re-enabling tabs

Now that you have disabled the tab(s), you need to be able to re-enable them. To accomplish this, simply add the following functions to both enable a given tab and to remove the " - Disabled" text from the tab's caption.

Understanding the EnablePage function

This function simply searches the "m_arrDisabledPages" array for a specified page. If the page is found, it is removed from the array and the SetEnabledText() function is called.

```
void CFindSheet::EnablePage(int iPage)
{
 BOOL bFoundEntry = FALSE;
 int iSize = m_arrDisabledPages.GetSize();

 int i = 0;
 while (i < iSize && !bFoundEntry)
 {
  if (m_arrDisabledPages.GetAt(i) == (UINT)iPage)
  {
   bFoundEntry = TRUE;
  }
  else
  {
   i++;
  }
 }

 if (bFoundEntry)
 {
  m_arrDisabledPages.RemoveAt(i);
  SetEnabledText(iPage);
 }
}
```

Examining the SetEnabledText function

After a tab has re-enabled, this function is called by the EnableTab() function to strip the " - Disabled" string from the end of the tab's caption.

```
void CFindSheet::SetEnabledText(int iPage)
{
 CTabCtrl* pTab = GetTabControl();
 ASSERT(pTab);
 TC_ITEM ti;
 char szText[100];
 ti.mask = TCIF_TEXT;
 ti.pszText = szText;
 ti.cchTextMax = 100;
 VERIFY(pTab->GetItem(iPage, &ti));
 char* pFound = strstr(szText, DISABLED_TEXT);
 if (pFound)
 {
  *pFound = '\0';
  VERIFY(pTab->SetItem(iPage, &ti));
 }
}
```

Testing the EnableTab function

To test the capability to re-enable a tab, use the ClassWizard to add a message handler for the "Find" button on the `CFindPage` property page. Get a pointer to the property page's parent window (the property sheet). This will be a pointer to the `CFindSheet` object. After completing these steps, you can call the `CFindSheet::EnablePage()` function.

```
void CFindPage::OnBtnFind()
{
 CFindSheet* pParentSheet = (CFindSheet*)GetParent();

 ASSERT(pParentSheet-IsKindOf(
  RUNTIME_CLASS(CFindSheet)));

 pParentSheet->EnablePage(1);
}
```

Now, if you build and run the application, you'll see that the "Results" tab is disabled until you click the "Find" button on the "Find Book" tab.

Dynamically setting CPropertyPage tab captions

When you created the dialog template resources for the two property pages, you specified a caption property. Even so, what happens when you want to change a tab's label or caption at run-time? The demo provides a great example of this situation. Because the "Results" tab contains a list control of the found items, the tab should also indicate the number of items found.

Using the SetItem function to set a tab's caption

To set a tab's caption, simply get a pointer to the tab control (`CTabCtrl`) object, retrieve the current text (`CTabCtrl::GetItem()`), and then set the text with the `CTabCtrl::SetItem()` function call. At its simplest, this sequence can be performed as follows:

```
CTabCtrl* pTab = GetTabControl();
ASSERT(pTab);
TC_ITEM ti;
char szText[100];
ti.mask = TCIF_TEXT;
ti.pszText = szText;
ti.cchTextMax = 100;
VERIFY(pTab->GetItem(iIndexOfDesiredTab, &ti));

strcpy(szText, "Your new tab Caption");
VERIFY(pTab->SetItem(iIndexOfDesiredTab, &ti));
```

Testing the SetItem function to set a tab's caption

The preceding example is very simple. But what if you want to format the caption? For example, what if you needed to show the caption as "Results: 5 books found?" Here's how to add this functionality:

Add the following #defines to the top of the "FindSheet.cpp" file:

```
#define RESULTS_TAB_INDEX 1
#define RESULTS_TAB_CAPTION "Results: %ld books found"
```

After the #defines are done, add the following functions to the CFindSheet class. As you can see, the SetResults() function simply calls a function to alter the "Results" tab's caption and then enables or disables the tab based on the value of "nHits." Because the CFindPage will be calling the SetResults() function, declare it as a public function.

```
void CFindSheet::SetResults(int nHits)
{
 SetResultsTabCaption(nHits);
 if (0 == nHits)
 {
  DisablePage(1, -1);
 }
 else
 {
  EnablePage(1);
 }
}
```

After retrieving the tab's caption via the CTabCtrl::GetItem() function call, the RESULTS_TAB_CAPTION is used to format the new caption.

```
void CFindSheet::SetResultsTabCaption(int nHits)
{
 CTabCtrl* pTab = GetTabControl();
 ASSERT(pTab);
 TC_ITEM ti;
 char szText[100];
 ti.mask = TCIF_TEXT;
 ti.pszText = szText;
 ti.cchTextMax = 100;
 VERIFY(pTab->GetItem(RESULTS_TAB_INDEX, &ti));

 sprintf(szText, RESULTS_TAB_CAPTION, nHits);
 VERIFY(pTab->SetItem(RESULTS_TAB_INDEX, &ti));
}
```

After the functions are defined, you just need to call them. Update the CFileSheet::OnInitDialog by removing the call to DisablePage() and replacing it with a call to the SetResults() function. You no longer have to disable the tab — the SetResults() function automatically disables the tab if a value of 0 (indicating no hits) is passed to it.

```
SetResults(0);
```

To test this example for both finding and not finding books via the CFindPage's "Find" button, we will hardcode a couple of entries in its "Languages" combo box. Use ClassWizard to add the OnInitDialog() function to the CFindPage class and update the function as follows:

```
BOOL CFindPage::OnInitDialog()
{
 CPropertyPage::OnInitDialog();

 m_cboLanguages.AddString(_T("Visual C++"));
 m_cboLanguages.AddString(_T("Visual J++"));
 m_cboLanguages.SetCurSel(0);

 return TRUE;
}
```

Finally, update the CFindPage::OnBtnFind() function to "find" 2 books if the "Visual C++" combo box entry is selected and to "find" 0 books if the "Visual J++" combo box entry is chosen. For the purposes of this example, these numbers are hard-coded so that you can concentrate on simply testing the code that dynamically changes a tab's caption. When you build and test the application at this point, you'll see that if you select the "Visual C++" entry to click the "Find" button, the "Results" tab's caption changes and also becomes enabled so you can activate it. Conversely, if you select the "Visual J++" entry to click the "Find" button, the "Results" tab's caption will indicate that no books could be located and the "Results" tab will be disabled.

```
void CFindPage::OnBtnFind()
{
 CFindSheet* pParentSheet = (CFindSheet*)GetParent();
 ASSERT(pParentSheet- >IsKindOf(
  RUNTIME_CLASS(CFindSheet)));

 int iIndex;
 if (0 == (iIndex = m_cboLanguages.GetCurSel()))
 {
  pParentSheet->SetResults(2);
 }
 else
 {
  pParentSheet->SetResults(0);
 }
}
```

Changing a tab's font

If you take a close look at the different tabs you added to the demo application, you may notice that the tab captions don't stand out. In other words, the captions fade into the background. Although many people don't worry about this characteristic, you can use the following steps to change the tab caption's font:

1. Create the desired font.
2. Acquire a pointer to the `CTabCtrl` object.
3. Call the `CTabCtrl::SetFont()` function.

Unfortunately, you cannot change the font for the "active" tab. All the tab's captions are displayed with the same font, which is changed with the `CTabCtrl::SetFont()` function. To change the font in the demo application, declare a member variable of type `CFont` in the `CFindSheet` class called "m_fontTab." Then, add the following lines of code to the end of the `CFindSheet::OnInitDialog()` function:

```
m_fontTab.CreateFont(-8, 0, 0, 0, FW_BOLD, 0, 0, 0,
 1, 0, 0, 0, 0, _T("MS Sans Serif"));
CTabCtrl* pTab = GetTabControl();
ASSERT(pTab);
pTab->SetFont(&m_fontTab);
```

Using mnemonics with CPropertyPage tabs

In regards to other operating systems, the Windows interface has superior user-interface consistency. For example, whenever you see static text on the screen with one of the letters underlined, the underlined letter is known as a *mnemonic*. When you hold down the Alt key and press the mnemonic, the field usually gains focus. Actually, as you learned in Chapter 7, if the control is read-only, the next control in the tab order receives focus. In the case of a push button, pressing a mnemonic produces the same effect as clicking the push button with the mouse.

Just when you get comfortable with the concept of putting mnemonics in all your dialogs, along comes the `CPropertyPage` class, which completely ignores mnemonics. For example, if you set a `CPropertyPage`'s caption to "&Result" and press the <Alt><R> key, nothing will happen. To get around this glaring shortcoming of the `CPropertyPage` class, you'll have to override the `CPropertySheet`'s `PreTranslateMessage`. Every single keystroke will be filtered through this function for every property page owned by the property sheet.

At this point, use ClassWizard to create the `PreTranslateMessage()` function. The demo's implementation is listed in Listing 8-2. As you can see, the listing only cares about `WM_SYSKEYDOWN` messages. These messages are sent when a key is pressed while the Alt key is held down. The `pMsg->wParam` value is then evaluated to make sure that the pressed key was a number or a letter. After that evaluation, the function simply iterates through the property sheet's property pages and compares the typed mnemonic to the mnemonic (if any) for each property page. If a matching property page is found, the `SetActivePage()` is called only if the page is not disabled. Figure 8-5 shows the demo after implementing the changes outlined in this section.

Listing 8-2: The Completed PreTranslateMessage() Function

```
BOOL CFindSheet::PreTranslateMessage(MSG* pMsg)
{
 BOOL bHandledMsg = FALSE;

 switch(pMsg->message)
 {
  case WM_SYSKEYDOWN:
  {
   // we only want 0-9 and letters
   if ((0x2f < pMsg->wParam)
   && (0x5b > pMsg->wParam))
   {
    CTabCtrl *pTab = GetTabControl();
    ASSERT(pTab);

    TC_ITEM ti;
    char szText[100];
    ti.mask = TCIF_TEXT;
    ti.pszText = szText;

    char szMnemonic[3];
    sprintf(szMnemonic, "&%c", pMsg->wParam);

    BOOL bFoundMatchingPage = FALSE;
    int iCurrPage = 0;
    while ((iCurrPage < pTab->GetItemCount())
    && (!bFoundMatchingPage))
    {
     ti.cchTextMax = 99;
     pTab->GetItem(iCurrPage, &ti);

     CString strText = szText;
     strText.MakeUpper();
     if (-1 != strText.Find(szMnemonic))
     {
      bFoundMatchingPage = TRUE;
      if (!PageIsDisabled(iCurrPage))
      {
       SetActivePage(iCurrPage);
       bHandledMsg = TRUE;
      }
     }
```

(continued)

Listing 8-2 *(continued)*

```
        else
        {
        iCurrPage++;
        }
      }
    }
  }
  break;

  default: break;
 }

 return (TRUE == bHandledMsg ?
  TRUE : CPropertySheet::PreTranslateMessage(pMsg));
}
```

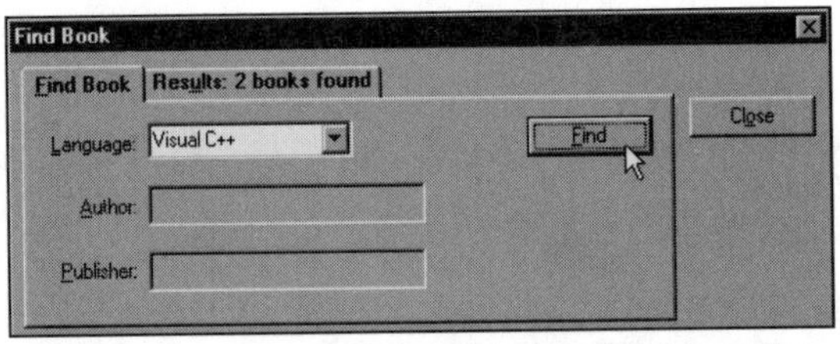

Figure 8-5: Here is the modal Property Sheet after removing some standard buttons, repositioning the others, and changing the tab's caption, mnemonic, and font.

Summary

In this chapter, you learned about the `CPropertySheet` and `CPropertyPage` classes and how to use them in both a modal and modeless environment. You also learned that while these classes encapsulate their intended functionality, they do not always meet the expected standard of providing functions to enable and disable tabs, support tab navigation through keyboard mnemonics, and set a particular tab's font and caption. The code in this chapter should make these and other related tasks easier to complete.

✦ ✦ ✦

CHAPTER 9

Data I/O

✦ ✦ ✦ ✦

In This Chapter

Discovering the CString class and viewing its demo program

Examining the CFile class and seeing its demo program

Identifying MFC classes derived from CFile

Investigating a special class—Cserial

Learning about the Registry

Using the CRegistry class

✦ ✦ ✦ ✦

Most programs use, create, and transfer data while doing their jobs. Word processors maintain the document as data and perform operations such as loading, saving, and spell-checking to this data. Spreadsheets not only load and save data, they make calculations to it. Even a computer card game such as Solitaire keeps track of the cards and treats this information as a *dataset*.

MFC gives you plenty of tools to deal with the input and output of data. In this chapter, we cover the `CString`, `CFile`, `CMemFile`, and the `CWnd` classes. We also introduce some non-MFC classes that make it easier to deal with other types of data. One class is intended to give you easy access to the serial port. With our `CSerial` class you can communicate with other computers through your modem. Another thing that MFC left out was easy access to the Registry. The accepted way of storing configuration information for applications is to use the Registry, and as an application developer you'll go to the Registry often.

The CString Class

The `CString` class provides support for manipulating strings. It's intended to replace and extend the functionality normally provided by the C runtime library string package. The `CString` class supplies member functions and operators for simplified string handling similar to those found in Basic. The class also provides constructors and operators for constructing, assigning, and comparing `CString`s and standard C++ string data types.

`CString` is enabled for both Unicode and multibyte character sets (MBCS). This support makes it easier for you to write portable applications that you can build for either Unicode or ANSI characters.

A `CString` object can store up to 2,147,483,647 characters. Unlike character arrays, the `CString` class has a built-in memory-allocation capability. This enables `CString` objects to automatically grow as needed (that is, you don't have to worry about expanding a `CString` object to fit longer strings).

A `CString` object can also act like a literal C-style string (an `LPCTSTR`, which is the same as `const char*`). The `LPCTSTR` conversion operator enables `CString` objects to be freely substituted for character pointers in function calls.

Use the `GetBuffer()` and `ReleaseBuffer()` member functions when you need to directly access a `CString` as a nonconstant character pointer (`LPTSTR` instead of a `const` character pointer, `LPCTSTR`).

Where possible, allocate `CString` objects on the frame rather than on the heap. This saves memory and simplifies parameter passing.

When `CString` objects are copied, MFC increments a reference count rather than copying the data. This makes passing parameters by value and returning `CString` objects by value more efficient. These operations cause the copy constructor to be called, sometimes more than once. Incrementing a reference count reduces that overhead for these common operations and makes using `CString` a more attractive option. As each copy is destroyed, the reference count in the original object is decremented. The original `CString` object is not destroyed until its reference count is reduced to zero. You can use the `CString` member functions `LockBuffer()` and `UnlockBuffer()` to disable or enable reference counting.

The `CString` class provides member functions and overloaded operators that duplicate and, in some cases, surpass the string services of the C run-time libraries (for example, `strcat`).

You can assign C-style literal strings to a `CString` just as you can assign one `CString` object to another as follows:

```
CString strText = "This is a test";
```

You can also assign the value of one `CString` object to another:

```
CString strText = "This is a test";
CString strCopy = strText;
```

In the latter of these two cases, the contents of a `CString` object are copied when one `CString` object is assigned to another. Thus, the two strings do not share a reference to the actual characters that make up the string.

Expert Tip

Unicode Strings

To write your application so it can be compiled for Unicode or for ANSI, code literal strings using the `_T` macro as follows:

```
CString strText = _T( "This is a test" );
```

You can access individual characters within a CString object with the GetAt() and SetAt() member functions. You can also use the *array* (or *subscript*) operator [] instead of GetAt() to get individual characters (this is similar to accessing array elements by index, as in standard C-style strings). Index values for CString characters are zero based.

To concatenate two CString objects, use the concatenation operators (+ or +=) as follows:

```
CString strOne = "This ";
strOne += "is a ";
CString strTwo = "test";
CString strMessage = strOne + "big " + strTwo;
// strMessage contains "This is a big test".
```

At least one of the arguments to the concatenation operators must be a CString object, but you can use a constant character string (such as "big") or a char (such as *x*) for the other argument.

The CString class overrides the relational operators (<, <=, >=, >, ==, and !=). You can compare two CStrings using these operators, as follows:

```
CString strOne( "Tom" );
CString strTwo( "Jerry" );
if( strOne < strTwo )
  AfxMessageBox( "Tom < Jerry" );
else
  AfxMessageBox( "Tom >= "Jerry" );
```

Even though CString objects are dynamically growable objects, they act like built-in primitive types and simple classes. Each CString object represents a unique value. CString objects should be thought of as the actual strings rather than as pointers to strings.

The most obvious consequence of using CString objects as values is that the string contents are copied when you assign one CString to another. Thus, even though two CString objects may represent the same sequence of characters, they do not share those characters. Each CString has its own copy of the character data. When you modify one CString object, the copied CString object is not modified, as shown by the following example:

```
CString strOne, strTwo;
strOne = strTwo = "Hi there";

if( strOne == strTwo )
  AfxMessageBox( "The strings are equal" );
else
  AfxMessageBox( "The strings are not equal" );

strOne.MakeUpper(); // Does not modify strTwo
if( strTwo[0] == 'h' )
```

```
AfxMessageBox("TRUE since strTwo is still 'hi there'");
```

Notice in the example the two CString objects are considered "equal" because they represent the same character string. The CString class overloads the equality operator (==) to compare two CString objects based on their value (contents) rather than their identity (address).

In the simplest case, you can cast a CString object to be an LPCTSTR. The LPCTSTR type conversion operator returns a pointer to a read-only, C-style, null-terminated string from a CString object. The pointer returned by LPCTSTR points into the data area used by the CString. If the CString goes out of scope and is automatically deleted or something else changes the contents of the CString, the LPCTSTR pointer will no longer be valid. Treat the string to which the pointer points as temporary.

You can use CString functions, such as SetAt(), to modify individual characters in the string object. However, if you need a copy of a CString object's characters that you can modify directly, use strcpy to copy the CString object into a separate buffer where the characters can be safely modified, as shown by the following example:

```
CString theString( "This is a test" );
LPTSTR lpszString = new char[theString.GetLength()+1];
strcpy( lpszString, theString );
//... modify lpszString as much as you want
```

The second argument to strcpy is a const char* (ANSI). The preceding example passes a CString for this argument. The C++ compiler automatically applies the conversion function defined for the CString class that converts a CString to an LPCTSTR. The ability to define casting operations from one type to another is one of the most useful features of C++.

In most situations, you should be able to find CString member functions to perform any string operation for which you might consider using the standard C runtime library string functions, such as strcmp().

If you need to use the C run-time string functions, you can convert to an equivalent C-style string buffer, perform your operations on the buffer, and then assign the resulting C-style string back to a CString object.

In most situations, you should use CString member functions to modify the contents of a CString object or to convert the CString to a C-style character string. However, certain situations, such as working with operating-system functions, require a character buffer, where it is advantageous to directly modify the CString contents.

Nutshell

Gaining Access to CString's Internal Character Buffer

The `GetBuffer()` and `ReleaseBuffer()` member functions enable you to gain access to the internal character buffer of a `CString` object and modify it directly. The following steps show how to use these functions for this purpose:

1. Call `GetBuffer()` for a `CString` object, specifying the length of the buffer you require.
2. Use the pointer returned by `GetBuffer()` to write characters directly into the `CString` object.
3. Call `ReleaseBuffer()` for the `CString` object to update all the internal `CString` state information (such as the length of the string). After modifying a `CString` object's contents directly, you must call `ReleaseBuffer()` before calling any other `CString` member functions.

◆ ◆ ◆ ◆ ◆

Some C functions take a variable number of arguments. A notable example is `printf()`. Because of the way this kind of function is declared, the compiler cannot be sure of the type of the arguments and cannot determine which conversion operation to perform on each argument. Therefore, it is essential you use an explicit type cast when passing a `CString` object to a function that takes a variable number of arguments. To use a `CString` object in a variable argument function, explicitly cast the `CString` to an `LPCTSTR` string.

For most functions that need a string argument, it's best to specify the formal parameter in the function prototype as a `const` pointer to a character (`LPCTSTR`) instead of a `CString`. When a formal parameter is specified as a `const` pointer to a character, you can pass a literal string such as "hi there" or a `CString` object. The `CString` object is automatically converted to an `LPCTSTR`. Any place you can use an `LPCTSTR`, you can also use a `CString` object.

You can also specify a formal parameter as a constant string reference (that is, `const CString&`) if the argument will not be modified. Drop the `const` modifier if the string will be modified by the function. If a default null value is desired, initialize it to the null string "" as follows:

```
void AddCustomer( const CString& name,
  const CString& address, const CString& comment = "" );
```

For most function results, you can simply return a `CString` object by value.

When you define a class interface, you must determine the argument-passing convention for your member functions. There are some standard rules for passing and returning `CString` objects.

If a string is an input to a function, in most cases it is best to declare the string function parameter as `LPCTSTR`. Convert to a `CString` object as necessary within the function using constructors and assignment operators. If the string contents are to be changed by a function, declare the parameter as a nonconstant `CString` reference (`CString&`).

Normally you can return `CString` objects from functions because `CString` objects follow value semantics like primitive types. To return a read-only string, use a constant `CString` reference (`const CString&`). The following example illustrates the use of `CString` parameters and return types:

```
class CName : public CObject
{
private:
  CString m_firstName;
  char m_middleInit;
  CString m_lastName;
public:
  CName() {}
  void SetData( LPCTSTR fn, const char mi, LPCTSTR ln )
  {
    m_firstName = fn;
    m_middleInit = mi;
    m_lastName = ln;
  }
  void GetData( CString& cfn, char mi, CString& cln )
  {
    cfn = m_firstName;
    mi = m_middleInit;
    cln = m_lastName;
  }
  CString GetLastName()
  {
   return m_lastName;
  }
};

CName name;
CString last, first;
char middle;
name.SetData( "John", 'Q', "Public" );
ASSERT( name.GetLastName() == "Public" );
name.GetData( first, middle, last );
ASSERT( ( first == "John" ) && ( last == "Public" ) );
```

The entire class library is conditionally enabled for Unicode characters and strings. In particular, class `CString` is Unicode-enabled.

Installing Unicode Support

The Unicode versions of the MFC libraries are not copied to your hard drive unless you select them during a custom installation. If you attempt to build or run an MFC Unicode application without the MFC Unicode files, you may get errors.

To copy the files to your hard drive, rerun Setup, choose Custom installation, clear the check boxes for all other components except "Microsoft Foundation Class Libraries," click the Details button, and select both "Static Library for Unicode" and "Shared Library for Unicode."

`CString` is based on the `TCHAR` data type. If the symbol _UNICODE is defined for a build of your program, `TCHAR` is defined as type `wchar_t`, a 16-bit character encoding type; otherwise, it is defined as `char`, the normal 8-bit character encoding. Under Unicode, then, `CString`s are composed of 16-bit characters. Without Unicode, they are composed of characters of type `char`.

To complete Unicode programming of your application, you must also use the `_T` macro to conditionally code literal strings to be portable to Unicode.

When you pass strings, pay attention to whether function arguments require a length in characters or a length in bytes. The difference is important if you're using Unicode strings.

Use portable versions of the C runtime string-handling functions.

Use the following data types for characters and character pointers:

- `TCHAR`—where you would use `char`
- `LPTSTR`—where you would use `char*`
- `LPCTSTR`—where you would use `const char*`

`CString` provides the operator `LPCTSTR` to convert between `CString` and `LPCTSTR`. `CString` also supplies Unicode-aware constructors, assignment operators, and comparison operators.

The class library is also enabled for multibyte character sets—specifically for double-byte character sets (DBCS).

Under this scheme, a character can be either one or two bytes wide. If it is two bytes wide, its first byte is a special *lead byte*, chosen from a particular range depending on which code page is in use. Taken together, the lead and *trail bytes* specify a unique character encoding.

If the symbol `_MBCS` is defined for a build of your program, type `TCHAR`, on which `CString` is based, maps to char. It's up to you to determine which bytes in a `CString` are lead bytes and which are trail bytes. The C runtime library supplies functions to help you determine this.

Under `DBCS`, a given string can contain all single-byte ANSI characters, all double-byte characters, or a combination of the two. These possibilities require special care in parsing strings, including `CString` objects.

To show you how to use the basic `CString` functions, we've created a demo program named StringDemo (see Listing 9-1). The application loads a file named AESOP.txt when it first runs. This text file contains many fables from Aesop's Fables.

You can search the text for any string, as shown in Figure 9-1. You can choose to do a case-sensitive search or a non-case-sensitive search. You can also perform a search-and-replace operation on the file. Once the search-and-replace operation is done, you should be able to see the altered text inside of WordPad. (When you see it in WordPad, though, make sure WordPad's set for text wrapping.)

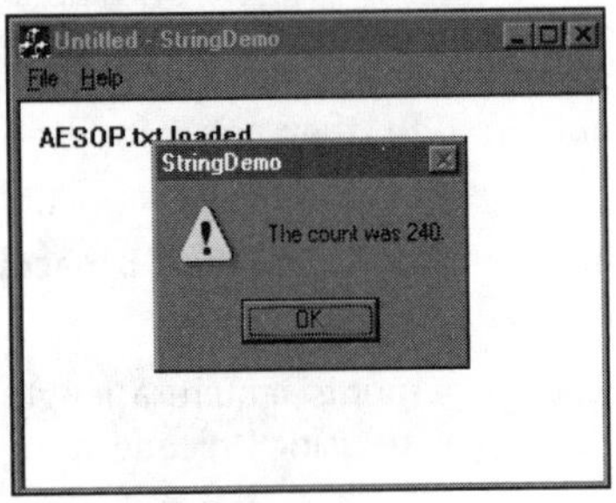

Figure 9-1: You can search through the Aesop.txt file for any word or phrase.

Demo Program

StringDemo
CD-ROM Location: **Chap09\StringDemo**
Program Name: **StringDemo.EXE**
Source Code Modules in Text: **StringDemoView.cpp**

◆ ◆ ◆ ◆ ◆

Listing 9-1: **StringDemo**

```
// StringDemoView.cpp : implementation of
// the CStringDemoView class
//

/////////////////////////////////////////////////////////////
// CStringDemoView construction/destruction

CStringDemoView::CStringDemoView()
{

  // Attempt to open the data file.
  CFile cf;
  if( cf.Open( "AESOP.txt", CFile::modeRead ) ){

    // Get the file length.
    int nFileLength = cf.GetLength();

    // Allocate a temporary buffer.
```

```
        char *lpBuffer = new char [nFileLength+1];

        try{
          // Read the data.
          cf.Read( lpBuffer, nFileLength );
          }

        // Catch a Read exception if it's
        // thrown.
        catch( CFileException *e ){
          e->Delete();
          delete [] lpBuffer;
          return;
          }

        // NULL terminate the string.
        lpBuffer[nFileLength] = 0;

        // Set the m_strOriginalText and
        // m_strAlteredText CString objects.
        m_strOriginalText = lpBuffer;
        m_strAlteredText = m_strOriginalText;

        // Free the temporary buffer.
        delete [] lpBuffer;
        }

}

CStringDemoView::~CStringDemoView()
{
}

/////////////////////////////////////////////////////////////////////////////
// CStringDemoView drawing

void CStringDemoView::OnDraw(CDC* pDC)
{
  CStringDemoDoc* pDoc = GetDocument();
  ASSERT_VALID(pDoc);

  // Let users know if the file was
  // loaded or not.
  if( m_strOriginalText.GetLength() > 0 )
    pDC->TextOut( 10, 10, "AESOP.txt loaded." );
  else
    pDC->TextOut( 10, 10, "AESOP.txt not loaded." );

}

/////////////////////////////////////////////////////////////////////////////
// CStringDemoView message handlers
```

(continued)

Listing 9-1 *(continued)*

```
void CStringDemoView::OnFilePerformwordcount()
{
  CGetWord GetWord;

  // Get the word in a dialog box.
  if( GetWord.DoModal() == IDOK ){

    // Set the count to 0.
    int nCount = 0;
    int nIndex;
    CString strTempString;

    // Set a temporary CString object
    // to contain the altered text.
    strTempString = m_strAlteredText;

    // Set a temporary string to
    // contain the word for which
    // we're searching.
    CString strTempWord =
      GetWord.m_strWordToCount;

    // If we're not making a case sensitive
    // search, make both strings upper case.
    if( !GetWord.m_bCaseSensitive ){
      strTempWord.MakeUpper();
      strTempString.MakeUpper();
      }

    do{
      // Attempt to find the word.
      nIndex =
        strTempString.Find( strTempWord );

      // If nIndex != -1, we found the word.
      if( nIndex != -1 ){

        // Make sure the character before the
        // word is not an alphanumeric character.
        // If it is, the word we found is
        // embedded in something else.
        if( nIndex == 0 ||
          !isalnum( strTempString.GetAt( nIndex - 1 ) )){

          // Make sure the character after the
          // word is not an alphanumeric character.
          // If it is, the word we found is
          // embedded in something else.
          if( !isalnum( strTempString.GetAt(
            nIndex + strTempWord.GetLength() ) ) )
```

```
                // Increment the count.
                nCount++;
              }

            // Shorten the string containing the
            // body of data.
            strTempString =
              strTempString.Right(
                strTempString.GetLength() -
                strTempWord.GetLength() -
                nIndex );
            }
          } while( nIndex != -1 );

        // Format a string and tell users
        // how many matches were found.
        CString strInfo;
        strInfo.Format( "The count was %d.", nCount );
        AfxMessageBox( strInfo );

        }

}

void CStringDemoView::OnFileRestoreoriginalfiledata()
{

  // Restore the working text string
  // with the original text string.
  m_strAlteredText = m_strOriginalText;

}

void CStringDemoView::OnFileSearchandreplace()
{
  CSearchReplace SearchReplace;

  // Get the search and replace word.
  if( SearchReplace.DoModal() == IDOK ){

    // See if both strings are identical.
    if( SearchReplace.m_strWordToFind ==
      SearchReplace.m_strWordToReplace ){
      AfxMessageBox( "Those two strings are identical!");
      return;
      }

    // Set the count to 0.
    int nCount = 0;
    int nIndex;
    CString strTempString;
```

(continued)

Listing 9-1 *(continued)*

```
// Set a temporary CString object
// to contain the altered text.
strTempString = m_strAlteredText;

// Set a temporary string to
// contain the word for which
// we're searching.
CString strTempWord =
  SearchReplace.m_strWordToFind ;

// If we're not making a case sensitive
// search, make both strings upper case.
if( !SearchReplace.m_bCaseSensitive ){
  strTempWord.MakeUpper();
  strTempString.MakeUpper();
  }

do{
  BOOL bReplaced = FALSE;

  // Attempt to find the word.
  nIndex =
    strTempString.Find( strTempWord );

  // If nIndex != -1, we found the word.
  if( nIndex != -1 ){

    // Make sure the character before the
    // word is not an alphanumeric character.
    // If it is, the word we found is
    // embedded in something else.
    if( nIndex == 0 ||
      !isalnum( strTempString.GetAt( nIndex - 1 ) )){

      // Make sure the character after the
      // word is not an alphanumeric character.
      // If it is, the word we found is
      // embedded in something else.
      if( !isalnum( strTempString.GetAt(
        nIndex + strTempWord.GetLength() ) ) ){

        // Increment the count.
        nCount++;

        // Calculate the number of
        // characters to the right
        // of the word that was found.
        int nRightLength =
          strTempString.GetLength() -
          nIndex -
          strTempWord.GetLength();
```

```
                // Calculate the number of
                // characters to the left
                // of the word that was found.
                int nLeftLength =
                  m_strAlteredText.GetLength() -
                  nRightLength -
                  strTempWord.GetLength();

                // Form a left and right string.
                CString strLeft, strRight;
                strLeft =
                  m_strAlteredText.Left( nLeftLength );
                strRight =
                  m_strAlteredText.Right( nRightLength );

                // Put the altered text string
                // together.
                m_strAlteredText = strLeft +
                  SearchReplace.m_strWordToReplace +
                  strRight;

              }
            }

          // Shorten the temporary string.
          strTempString =
            strTempString.Right(
              strTempString.GetLength() -
              strTempWord.GetLength() -
              nIndex );

          }

        } while( nIndex != -1 );

      // Format a string and tell users
      // how many replacements were made.
      CString strInfo;
      strInfo.Format( "%d replacements made.", nCount );
      AfxMessageBox( strInfo );

      }

}

void CStringDemoView::OnFileViewalterationsinnotepad()
{
  CFile Out;

  // Attempt to create a temporary file
  // which will be loaded into wordpad.
  if( Out.Open( "StringDemoTempFile.txt",
    CFile::modeCreate | CFile::modeWrite ) ){
```

(continued)

Listing 9-1 *(continued)*

```
        try{
          // Write the data.
          Out.Write( m_strAlteredText,
            m_strAlteredText.GetLength() );
          }

        // Catch a write exception if it's thrown.
        catch( CFileException *e ){
          e->Delete();
          return;
          }

        // Close the file so wordpad
        // won't get a sharing violation.
        Out.Close();

        // Use WinExec() to bring up wordpad.
        WinExec( "WRITE.EXE StringDemoTempFile.txt",
          SW_NORMAL );
        }

}
```

File I/O and the CFile Class

`CFile` is the base class for Microsoft Foundation file classes. It directly provides unbuffered, binary disk-input/output services, and it indirectly supports text files and memory files through its derived classes. `CFile` works in conjunction with the `CArchive` class to support serialization of MFC objects.

The hierarchical relationship between this class and its derived classes enables your program to operate on all file objects through the polymorphic `CFile` interface. A memory file, for example, behaves like a disk file.

Normally a disk file is opened automatically on `CFile` construction and closed on destruction. Static member functions permit you to interrogate a file's status without opening the file.

The `CFile` class provides an interface for general-purpose binary file operations. The `CStdioFile` and `CMemFile` classes derived from `CFile` and the `CSharedFile` class derived from `CMemFile` supply more specialized file services.

Opening a file with the Open() member function

File objects are usually created on the stack frame by declaring a `CFile` variable. If you use the `CFile()` constructor (which takes no arguments), you must then call the `Open()` member function for the file object, supplying a path and permission flags.

The return value for `Open()` is nonzero if the file was opened successfully or 0 if the specified file could not be opened. The `Open()` member function is prototyped as follows:

```
virtual BOOL Open( LPCTSTR lpszFileName, UINT nOpenFlags,
  CFileException* pError = NULL );
```

The open flags specify which permissions, such as read-only, you want for the file. The possible flag values are defined as enumerated constants within the `CFile` class, so they are qualified with `CFile::`, as in `CFile::modeRead`. The flag definitions can be seen in Table 9-1. Use the `CFile::modeCreate` flag if you want to create the file.

Table 9-1
CFile Open Modes

Mode	*Description*
`CFile::modeCreate`	Directs the constructor to create a new file. If the file exists already, it is truncated to 0 length.
`CFile::modeNoTruncate`	You can combine this value with `modeCreate`. If the file being created already exists, it is not truncated to 0 length. Thus the file is guaranteed to open, either as a newly created file or as an existing file. This might be useful, for example, when opening a settings file that may or may not exist already. This option applies to `CStdioFile` as well.
`CFile::modeRead`	Opens the file for reading only.
`CFile::modeReadWrite`	Opens the file for reading and writing.
`CFile::modeWrite`	Opens the file for writing only.
`CFile::modeNoInherit`	Prevents the file from being inherited by child processes.
`CFile::shareDenyNone`	Opens the file without denying other processes read or write access to the file. The `Create` function fails if the file has been opened in compatibility mode by any other process.
`CFile::shareDenyRead`	Opens the file and denies other processes read access to the file. Create fails if the file has been opened in compatibility mode or for read access by any other process.

(continued)

Table 9-1 *(continued)*

Mode	*Description*
`CFile::shareDenyWrite`	Opens the file and denies other processes write access to the file. Create fails if the file has been opened in compatibility mode or for write access by any other process.
`CFile::shareExclusive`	Opens the file with exclusive mode, denying other processes both read and write access to the file. Construction fails if the file has been opened in any other mode for read or write access, even by the current process.
`CFile::shareCompat`	Maps to `CFile::shareExclusive` when used in `CFile::Open()`. This flag is not available in 32-bit MFC.
`CFile::typeText`	Sets text mode with special processing for carriage return–linefeed pairs (used in derived classes only).
`CFile::typeBinary`	Sets binary mode (used in derived classes only).

The following example shows how to create a new file with read/write permission (replacing any previous file with the same path):

```
char * lpszFileName = "c:\\test\\myfile.dat";
CFile myFile;
CFileException fileException;

if( !myFile.Open( lpszFileName, CFile::modeCreate |
  CFile::modeReadWrite ), &fileException ){
    TRACE( "Can't open file %s, error = %u\n",
      lpszFileName, fileException.m_cause );
  }
```

This example creates and opens a file. If there are problems, the `Open()` call can return a `CFileException` object in its last parameter, as shown here. The `TRACE` macro prints both the filename and a code indicating the reason for failure. You can call the `AfxThrowFileException()` function if you require more detailed error reporting.

Use the `Read()` and `Write()` member functions to read and write data in the file. The `Seek()` member function is also available for moving to a specific offset within the file.

`Read()` takes a pointer to a buffer and the number of bytes to read and returns the actual number of bytes that were read. If the required number of bytes could not be read because end-of-file is reached, the actual number of bytes read is returned. If any read error occurs, an exception is thrown. `Write()` is similar to `Read()`, but the number of bytes written is not returned. If a write error occurs, including not writing all the bytes specified, an exception is thrown. If you have a valid `CFile` object, you can read from it or write to it as shown in the following example:

```
char cbBuffer[256];
UINT nActual = 0;
CFile myFile;

myFile.Write( cbBuffer, sizeof( cbBuffer ) );
myFile.Seek( 0, CFile::begin );
nActual = myFile.Read( cbBuffer, sizeof( cbBuffer ) );
```

You should normally carry out input/output operations within a try/catch exception handling block.

Use the `Close()` member function. This function closes the file-system file and flushes buffers if necessary. If you allocated the `CFile` object on the frame (as in the examples shown earlier), the object will automatically be closed and then destroyed when it goes out of scope. Deleting the `CFile` object does not delete the physical file in the file system.

`CFile` also supports getting file status, including whether the file exists, creation and modification dates and times, logical size, and path. Use the `CFile` class to get and set information about a file. One useful application is to use the `CFile` static member function `GetStatus()` to determine if a file exists. `GetStatus()` returns 0 if the specified file does not exist.

Thus, you could use the result of `GetStatus()` to determine whether to use the `CFile::modeCreate` flag when opening a file, as shown by the following example:

```
CFile theFile;
char *szFileName = "c:\\test\\myfile.dat";
BOOL bOpenOK;

CFileStatus status;
if( CFile::GetStatus( szFileName, status ) ){
  // Open the file without the Create flag
  bOpenOK = theFile.Open( szFileName,
    CFile::modeWrite );
  }
else{
  // Open the file with the Create flag
  bOpenOK = theFile.Open( szFileName,
    CFile::modeCreate | CFile::modeWrite );
  }
```

The FileDemo program

You'll use the `CFile` class to load and save buffers of data often. For that reason, a program named FileDemo, shown in Listing 9-2, was written that does just that. It lets you create a list of files, and then saves all the files to one large file.

You can also copy a single file from one source to a destination. To do this, just select Copy ➪ First File. The program then copies the first file in the list to a destination file you select.

One very handy function that you may want to remove and place in your own program is the `CopyFile()` function. It's useful for a wide variety of applications that need to copy files from one place to another.

Demo Program

FileDemo

CD-ROM Location: **Chap09\FileDemo**
Program Name: **FileDemo.EXE**
Source Code Modules in Text: **FileDemoView.cpp**

◆ ◆ ◆ ◆ ◆

Listing 9-2: **FileDemo**

```
// FileDemoView.cpp : implementation of
// the CFileDemoView class
//

/////////////////////////////////////////////////////////////
// CFileDemoView drawing

void CFileDemoView::OnDraw(CDC* pDC)
{
  CFileDemoDoc* pDoc = GetDocument();
  ASSERT_VALID(pDoc);

  // Draw the list of files in the list.
  int y = 0;
  for( int i=0; i<m_Filename.GetSize(); i++ ){
    // Get the string at this index.
    CString strText = m_Filename.GetAt( i );
    // Draw it to the DC.
    pDC->TextOut( 0, y, strText );
    // Get the size so we can increment
    // the y coordinate.
    CSize size =
      pDC->GetTextExtent( strText, 1 );
    // Increment the y coordinate by
    // the text height.
    y += size.cy;
    }

}

/////////////////////////////////////////////////////////////
// CFileDemoView message handlers

char szFilter[] = "All Files(*.*)|*.*||";

void CFileDemoView::OnFileAddtolist()
{
```

```
  // Common dialog box.
  CFileDialog FileDlg( TRUE, NULL, NULL,
    OFN_HIDEREADONLY, szFilter );

  if( FileDlg.DoModal() == IDOK ){
    // Add the full path and filename
    // to the m_Pathname list.
    m_Pathname.Add( FileDlg.GetPathName() );
    // Add the filename to the m_Filename
    // list.
    m_Filename.Add( FileDlg.GetFileName() );

    // Cause a window redraw.
    InvalidateRect( NULL, TRUE );
    UpdateWindow();
    }

}

void CFileDemoView::OnFileSavefilesinlist()
{

  // Check to make sure we have some
  // files in the list.
  if( m_Pathname.GetSize() == 0 ){
    AfxMessageBox( "There are no files in the list." );
    return;
    }

  // Common dialog box.
  CFileDialog FileDlg( FALSE, NULL, NULL,
    OFN_HIDEREADONLY, szFilter );

  if( FileDlg.DoModal() == IDOK ){

    // Attempt to open the output file.
    CFile Out;
    if( Out.Open( FileDlg.GetPathName(),
      CFile::modeWrite | CFile::modeCreate ) ){

      // Loop through each file.
      for( int i=0; i<m_Pathname.GetSize(); i++ ){

        // Attempt to create the input
        // file.
        CFile In;
        if( In.Open( m_Pathname.GetAt( i ),
          CFile::modeRead ) ){
          // Temporary buffer.
          char cbBuffer[4000];
```

(continued)

Listing 9-2 *(continued)*

```
// Get the input file size so we
// know when we're done writing.
int nFilesize = In.GetLength();

while( nFilesize > 0 ){

  // Start off by assuming
  // we'll read in enough bytes
  // to fill the buffer.
  int nSize = sizeof( cbBuffer );

  // If the number of bytes remaining
  // isn't enough to fill the
  // buffer, adjust the size.
  if( nSize > nFilesize )
    nSize = nFilesize;

  // Read in the bytes and make
  // sure we catch any exceptions
  // that are thrown.
  try{
    In.Read( cbBuffer, nSize );
    }
  catch( CFileException *e ){

    // Format a message from
    // the system.
    char *lpMsgBuf;
    if( FormatMessage(
      FORMAT_MESSAGE_ALLOCATE_BUFFER |
      FORMAT_MESSAGE_FROM_SYSTEM,
      NULL, e->m_lOsError,
      MAKELANGID( LANG_NEUTRAL,
        SUBLANG_DEFAULT ),
      (LPSTR) &lpMsgBuf, 0, NULL ) > 0 ){
      AfxMessageBox( lpMsgBuf );
      LocalFree( lpMsgBuf );
      }

    // Free the exception and
    // return.
    e->Delete();
    return;
    }

  // Write out the bytes and make
  // sure we catch any exceptions
  // that are thrown.
  try{
    Out.Write( cbBuffer, nSize );
    }
```

```
            catch( CFileException *e ){

              // Format a message from
              // the system.
              char *lpMsgBuf;
              if( FormatMessage(
                FORMAT_MESSAGE_ALLOCATE_BUFFER |
                FORMAT_MESSAGE_FROM_SYSTEM,
                NULL, e->m_lOsError,
                MAKELANGID( LANG_NEUTRAL,
                  SUBLANG_DEFAULT ),
                (LPSTR) &lpMsgBuf, 0, NULL ) > 0 ){
                AfxMessageBox( lpMsgBuf );
                LocalFree( lpMsgBuf );
                }

              // Free the exception and
              // return.
              e->Delete();
              return;
              }
            nFilesize -= nSize;
            }
          }

        // Alert user to problem.
        else
          AfxMessageBox( "Could not open "
            + m_Pathname.GetAt( i ) );
        }
      }

    // Alert user to problem.
    else
     AfxMessageBox( "Could not create the output file.");
    }

}

void CFileDemoView::EmptyStringArrays( void )
{

  // Empty the arrays which contain
  // the full path and filename,
  // and just the filename.
  m_Pathname.RemoveAll();
  m_Filename.RemoveAll();

}

void CFileDemoView::OnFileEmptylist()
{
```

(continued)

Listing 9-2 *(continued)*

```
  // Empty everything and then
  // cause a screen redraw.
  EmptyStringArrays();
  InvalidateRect( NULL, TRUE );
  UpdateWindow();

}

BOOL CFileDemoView::CopyFile( const char *lpSrcFilename,
  const char *lpDestFilename, int nBuffersize )
{
  CFile Out, In;
  int nFilesize;
  char *lpBuffer;

  // Attempt to open the input file.
  if( !In.Open( lpSrcFilename, CFile::modeRead ) ){
    AfxMessageBox( "Could not open the input file." );
    return( FALSE );
    }

  // Attempt to create the output file.
  if( !Out.Open( lpDestFilename,
    CFile::modeWrite | CFile::modeCreate ) ){
    AfxMessageBox( "Could not open the output file." );
    return( FALSE );
    }

  // Create the copy buffer.
  lpBuffer = new char [nBuffersize];
  if( lpBuffer == NULL ){
   AfxMessageBox( "Could not allocate the copy buffer.");
    return( FALSE );
    }

  // Get the input file status so that
  // we can set the output file's status
  // to the same. This will preserve
  // things such as time and date.
  CFileStatus rStatus;
  In.GetStatus( lpSrcFilename, rStatus );

  // Get file file size so we know
  // when we're done copying.
  nFilesize = In.GetLength();

  while( nFilesize > 0 ){

    // Start off by assuming
    // we'll read in enough bytes
    // to fill the buffer.
```

```
int nSize = nBuffersize;

// If the number of bytes remaining
// isn't enough to fill the
// buffer, adjust the size.
if( nSize > nFilesize )
  nSize = nFilesize;

// Read in the bytes and make
// sure we catch any exceptions
// that are thrown.
try{
  In.Read( lpBuffer, nSize );
  }
catch( CFileException *e ){

  // Format a message from
  // the system.
  char *lpMsgBuf;
  if( FormatMessage(
    FORMAT_MESSAGE_ALLOCATE_BUFFER |
    FORMAT_MESSAGE_FROM_SYSTEM,
    NULL, e->m_lOsError,
    MAKELANGID( LANG_NEUTRAL,
      SUBLANG_DEFAULT ),
    (LPSTR) &lpMsgBuf, 0, NULL ) > 0 ){
    AfxMessageBox( lpMsgBuf );
    LocalFree( lpMsgBuf );
    }

  // Free the exception and
  // return.
  e->Delete();
  return( FALSE );
  }

// Write out the bytes and make
// sure we catch any exceptions
// that are thrown.
try{
  Out.Write( lpBuffer, nSize );
  }

catch( CFileException *e ){

  // Format a message from
  // the system.
  char *lpMsgBuf;
  if( FormatMessage(
    FORMAT_MESSAGE_ALLOCATE_BUFFER |
    FORMAT_MESSAGE_FROM_SYSTEM,
    NULL, e->m_lOsError,
```

(continued)

Listing 9-2 *(continued)*

```
          MAKELANGID( LANG_NEUTRAL,
            SUBLANG_DEFAULT ),
          (LPSTR) &lpMsgBuf, 0, NULL ) > 0 ){
          AfxMessageBox( lpMsgBuf );
          LocalFree( lpMsgBuf );
          }

        // Free the exception and
        // return.
        e->Delete();
        return( FALSE );
        }

      nFilesize -= nSize;

      }

    // Close the output file so the
    // SetStatus() function won't fail.
    Out.Close();
    CFile::SetStatus( lpDestFilename, rStatus );

    // Delete the buffer.
    delete [] lpBuffer;

    return( TRUE );

}


void CFileDemoView::OnFileCopyfirstfile()
{


  // Check to make sure we have some
  // files in the list.
  if( m_Pathname.GetSize() == 0 ){
    AfxMessageBox( "There are no files in the list." );
    return;
    }

  // Common dialog box.
  CFileDialog FileDlg( FALSE, NULL, NULL,
    OFN_HIDEREADONLY, szFilter );

  // If the selected OK, do the copy.
  if( FileDlg.DoModal() == IDOK )
    CopyFile( m_Pathname.GetAt( 0 ),
      FileDlg.GetPathName() );

}
```

The CMemFile Class

CMemFile is the CFile-derived class that supports memory files. These memory files behave like disk files except that the file is stored in RAM rather than on disk. A memory file is useful for fast, temporary storage or for transferring raw bytes or serialized objects between independent processes.

CMemFile objects can automatically allocate their own memory, or you can attach your own memory block to the CMemFile object by calling Attach(). In either case, memory for expanding the memory file automatically is allocated in nGrowBytes-sized increments if nGrowBytes is not zero. nGrowBytes is an optional parameter that's passed to the CMemFile constructor.

The memory block is automatically deleted on destruction of the CMemFile object if the memory was originally allocated by the CMemFile object; otherwise, you are responsible for deallocating the memory you attached to the object.

You can access the memory block through the pointer supplied when you detach it from the CMemFile object by calling Detach().

The most common use of CMemFile is to create a CMemFile object and use it by calling CFile member functions. Creating a CMemFile automatically opens it; you do not call CFile::Open(), which is only used for disk files. Because CMemFile doesn't use a disk file, the data member CFile::m_hFile is not used and has no meaning.

The CFile member functions Duplicate(), LockRange(), and UnlockRange() are not implemented for CMemFile. If you call these functions on a CMemFile object, you get a CNotSupportedException.

CMemFile uses the run-time library functions malloc(), realloc(), and free() to allocate, reallocate, and deallocate memory—and the intrinsic memcpy() to block-copy memory when reading and writing. If you'd like to change this behavior or the behavior when CMemFile grows a file, derive your own class from CMemFile and override the appropriate functions.

The CStdioFile Class

A CStdioFile object represents a C runtime stream file as opened by the runtime function fopen(). Stream files are buffered and can be opened in either text mode (the default) or binary mode.

Text mode provides special processing for carriage return–linefeed pairs. When you write a newline character (0x0A) to a text-mode CStdioFile object, the byte pair (0x0D, 0x0A) is sent to the file. When you read a newline character, the byte pair (0x0D, 0x0A) is translated to a single 0x0A byte.

The `CFile` functions `Duplicate()`, `LockRange()`, and `UnlockRange()` are not supported for `CStdioFile`. If you call these functions on a `CStdioFile`, you get a `CNotSupportedException`.

The CSerial Class for Serial Communications

This section describes the `CSerial` class, a class for performing serial communications through the PC COM ports. This class can empower your programs with all of the computer-accessible information in the world.

A common use of remote communications is a business application that links different sites in order to keep tabs on inventories and transactions. For example, I once wrote a large drug-dispensing program in which many clinic sites automatically received new orders and updated pharmacy information each evening from a central host location. The central host received inventory levels and transaction information from each site during evening hours. A large part of my time was spent constructing telecommunications routines that sent and received information packets. If I had had the class library that's included on the CD-ROM that comes with this book, my development time would have been reduced significantly.

Serial communications overview

The PC communications port uses asynchronous communication, or asynch for short. Each byte of data is potentially a separate unit. The PC sending data can pause between any two bytes of a message. The receiver, however, may have to catch the data as quickly as it arrives.

To accomplish this trick, asynch data requires an extra bit's worth of time to announce the beginning of a new byte (the "start" bit) and one extra bit's worth of time at the end (the "stop" bit). A 9600 baud modem can transfer only 9600 bytes of data per second, because each byte requires a minimum of 10 bits to be transferred.

Modern high-speed modems do not actually transmit the start and stop bits. They are squeezed out as parts of the general data compression. However, the start and stop bits are generated on the wire that connects a COM port to an external modem (the RS-232 interface). Because of this and the general availability of data compression, the modern COM port is usually configured to use a higher speed (between the COM port and the modem) than the actual data transmission will support (between the two modems over the phone line). As an example, modems may operate at 14,400 bits per second, but the COM port is configured for 38,400 bits per second.

This is just an example of older conventions adapted to new requirements. The standards for asynchronous communications go back to the days before computers. The first modems were used by Teletype machines to send cablegrams.

When the first computers were developed, the existing population of Teletype machines provided convenient terminals.

The standards made sense up to the point where it became possible to put computer chips inside the modems. "Smart" modems can dial the phone, send a fax, compress data, and correct transmission errors. None of these functions were even imagined when standards such as RS-232 were originally developed. Although the rules have been adapted to accommodate modern technology, some of the old junk still pops up.

The CSerial class

This section describes the member functions for the `CSerial` class. Most function descriptions have examples showing how to use them.

CSerial

This is the `CSerial` class constructor, and it takes no arguments. It initializes all the class member variables.

CSerial::Open

This member function opens the communication port. It takes two integer arguments. The first argument is an integer—number of the port through which you want to communicate—and its valid values normally range from 1 to 4. The second argument is the baud rate, with valid values of 300, 1200, 2400, 4800, 9600, 19200, 38400, and 76800. The function returns a Boolean value indicating success or failure. You get a `TRUE` if everything worked as expected, a `FALSE` if the port didn't open. Following is an example of opening communication port 2 at 9600 baud:

```
CSerial Serial;
if( Serial.Open( 2, 9600 ) )
  AfxMessageBox( "The port opened OK." );
else
  AfxMessageBox( "The port didn't open." );
```

CSerial::Close

This function closes the communication port. The `CSerial` destructor calls this function, so you don't have to call this explicitly unless you have a reason to close the port before you destroy the class. The following two example functions, `FunctionOne()` and `FunctionTwo()`, create a `CSerial` class. The first example explicitly closes the port:

```
void FunctionOne( void )
{
  CSerial Serial;
  if( Serial.Open( 2, 9600 ) )
    Serial.Close();  // Explicit closing of port.
}
```

The second example enables the class destructor to close the port:

```
void FunctionTwo( void )
{
  CSerial Serial;
  Serial.Open( 2, 9600 );
  // Implicit closing of port, the CSerial
  // destructor takes care of it.
}
```

CSerial::SendData

This function writes data from a buffer to the serial port. The first argument it takes is to a `const char *` buffer that contains the data to be sent. The second argument is the number of bytes to be sent. The function returns the actual number of bytes that have been written to the port. Following is an example in which the communication port is opened and a text string is sent to the port:

```
void Function( void )
{
  CSerial Serial;
  if( Serial.Open( 2, 9600 ) ){
    static char *szMessage[] = "This is a test message";
    int nBytesSent;
    nBytesSent = Serial.SendData( szMessage,
      strlen( szMessage ) );
  }
}
```

CSerial::ReadDataWaiting

This function returns the number of incoming bytes that are waiting in the communication port's buffer. It takes no arguments.

CSerial::ReadData

This function reads data from the port's incoming buffer. The first argument it takes is a `void *` to a buffer into which the data is to be placed. The second argument is an integer value that gives the size of the buffer. For instance, if the buffer passed in is allocated at 500 bytes, this value is 500. This prevents buffers from becoming overrun. The `ReadData()` function returns an integer value for the actual number of bytes that were read. Following is an example in which a serial port is opened and waiting serial data is read into an allocated buffer:

```
void Function( void )
{
  CSerial Serial;
  if( Serial.Open( 2, 9600 ) ){
    char *lpBuffer = new [500];
    int nBytesRead;
    nBytesRead = Serial.ReadData( lpBuffer, 500 );
   delete [] lpBuffer;
```

```
    }
}
```

You can find the .cpp and the .h files for the `CSerial` class in the **Chap09\Serial** directory. To use them, copy the files into your project's directory and add them to the project.

The Registry

This mysterious object appeared with the introduction of OLE under Windows 3.1. No matter how hard programmers try to ignore it, it's here to stay; in fact, while we were looking the other way, it quietly took over the role of initialization, or INI files, among other things.

The Registry is a hierarchically organized store of information. Each entry in this tree-like structure is called a *key*. A key may contain any number of *subkeys*; it can also contain data entries called *values*. In this form, the Registry stores information about the system: its configuration, hardware devices, and software applications. It also assumes the role of the ubiquitous INI files by providing a place where application-specific settings can be stored. A Registry key is identified by its name. Keynames consist of printable ASCII characters except the backslash (\), space, and wildcard (* or ?) characters. The use of keynames that begin with a period (.) is reserved. Keynames are not case sensitive.

Registry values

A value in the Registry is identified by its name. Value names consist of the same characters as keynames. The value itself can be a string, binary data, or a 32-bit unsigned value.

Generally, storing items larger than a kilobyte or two in the Registry is not recommended. For larger items, use a separate file, and use the Registry for storing the filename. Under Windows 98/95, Registry values are limited to 64KB. Another consideration when using the Registry is that storing a key generally requires substantially more storage space than storing a value. Whenever possible, organize values under a common key rather than using several keys for the same purpose.

Predefined Registry keys

The Registry contains several predefined keys.

The HKEY_LOCAL_MACHINE key contains entries that describe the computer and its configuration. This includes information about the processor, system board, memory, and installed hardware and software.

The HKEY_CLASSES_ROOT key is the rear key for information relating to document types and OLE/COM. This key is a subordinate key to HKEY_LOCAL_MACHINE. (It is equivalent to HKEY_LOCAL_MACHINE\SOFTWARE\Classes.) Information that is stored here is used by shell applications, such as the Program Manager, File Manager, or the Explorer, and by OLE/ActiveX applications.

The HKEY_USERS key serves as the key for the default user preference settings as well as individual user preferences.

The HKEY_CLASSES_USER key is the root key for information relating to the preferences of the current (logged in) user. Under Windows 95 and Windows 98, there are two additional predefined keys.

The HKEY_CURRENT_CONFIG key contains information about the current system configuration settings. This key is equivalent to the system key of HKEY_LOCAL_MACHINE\Config.

The HKEY_DYN_DATA key provides access to dynamic status information, such as information about plug-and-play devices.

Commonly used Registry keys

Information about Registry keys is often difficult to find. This section lists information on some frequently used Registry keys that are of interest to programmers.

A number of subtrees appear in HKEY_LOCAL_MACHINE. Keys in HKEY_LOCAL_MACHINE contain information about the computer's software and hardware configuration. Of these, the Config and Enum subkeys are specific to Windows 98/95 and its plug-and-play capabilities. The Config subkey is where Windows stores various hardware configurations; the Enum subkey contains Windows 98/95 bus enumerators that build the tree of hardware devices.

Windows maintains the System subkey under HKEY_LOCAL_MACHINE. The System\CurrentControlSet subkey contains configuration information for services and device drivers.

Other subkeys in HKEY_LOCAL_MACHINE include Software and Classes.

The Software subkey is where information about installed software packages can be found. HKEY_CLASSES_ROOT points to the classes subkey. The Software subtree is of particular interest to application programmers. This is where you should store configuration and installation information specific to your application. Microsoft recommends that you build a series of subtrees under HKEY_LOCAL_MACHINE\Software. These subkeys should represent your company name, the name of your product, and the product's version.

What you store under such a key is entirely application dependent. You should not store anything here that is user specific; user-specific information pertinent to your application should be organized under a subkey of HKEY_CURRENT_USER.

Of particular interest is the key HKEY_LOCAL_MACHINE\Software\Microsoft\Windows \Currrent Version, which describes the current Windows configuration.

Subtrees in HKEY_CLASSES_ROOT

The HKEY_CLASSES_ROOT key contains two types of subkeys: subkeys that correspond to filename extensions and class definition subways. A filename extension subkey has a name that corresponds to the filename extension (such as .doc). The key typically contains one unnamed value, which holds the name of the class definition subkey. A class definition subkey describes the behavior of a document class. The information stored here includes data on shell- and OLE-related properties. A subkey under HKEY_CLASSES_ROOT is CLSID. This is the place where COM class identifiers are stored. When you create an MFC application using the Visual C++ AppWizard, a series of subkeys to be installed under HKEY_CLASSES_ROOT are also created. These identify the document type and filename extension of your new application and also its OLE properties (such as the OLE class identifier).

Subtrees in HKEY_USERS

The key HKEY_USERS contains a subkey named Default. Default, and possibly other keys (but not necessarily), correspond to users on the system. The .Default subkey corresponds to the default user profile. Other entries correspond to profiles of existing users.

Subtrees in HKEY_CURRENT_USER

The HKEY_CURRENT_USER key corresponds to the profile of the currently logged-in user. Application configuration information specific to the current user should be stored under the subkey software. Information should be organized by keys corresponding to company name, product name, and product version number.

The CRegistry class

Class Library

To make it easier for you to access the Registry, a special class named `CRegistry` is included on the CD-ROM in the **Chap09\Registry** directory. To use it, just copy the two files (`Registry.cpp` and `Registry.h`) into your project's directory and add them to your project. Descriptions of the class functions — along with specific examples — follow.

CRegistry::CRegistry

Two forms exist for the `CRegistry` constructor. One creates a `CRegistry` object and takes no arguments, and the other creates a `CRegistry` object and tries to open the Registry key passed in as a pair of arguments. Two examples follow:

```
CRegistry Registry;
// Create a CRegistry object that''s not opened.
```

or

```
CRegistry Registry( HKEY_LOCAL_MACHINE,
  ""SOFTWARE\\GreatSoftware"" );
// Create a CRegistry object that
// attempts to open SOFTWARE\GreatSoftware.
```

CRegistry::Open

This function opens a Registry key. It takes two arguments: a subtree keyname and a keyname of the subtree that you wish to open. The function returns `TRUE` if the Registry key opened successfully and `FALSE` if it did not. Following is an example:

```
CRegistry Registry;
  if( Registry.Open( HKEY_LOCAL_MACHINE,
   "SOFTWARE\\GreatSoftware" ) )
    AfxMessageBox( "The registry key opened OK." );
else
  AfxMessageBox( "The registry key didn't open." );
```

CRegistry::Close

This function closes the Registry key that was opened. You don't need to explicitly call this because the `CRegistry` destructor closes the key.

CRegistry::IsOpen

This function returns `TRUE` if the Registry key is currently open, `FALSE` if it is not.

CRegistry::ReadDWORD

This function reads a `DWORD` value from an open Registry key. The first argument the function takes is the value name. The second argument is a pointer to a `DWORD` that accepts the value that's read in. A third optional argument is a pointer to a `DWORD` that accepts an error code if this third argument is given. The function returns `TRUE` if successful, `FALSE` if not. An example that opens a Registry key and reads a `DWORD` value follows:

```
CRegistry Registry;
DWORD dwValue;
if( Registry.Open( HKEY_LOCAL_MACHINE,
  "SOFTWARE\\GreatSoftware" ) )
  Registry.ReadDWORD( "WindowColor", &dwValue );
```

CRegistry::ReadString

This function reads a character string from an open Registry key. The first argument the function takes is the value name. The second argument is a pointer to a character buffer that accepts the string that's read in. The third argument is the size of the buffer to which the data is to be copied. A fourth optional argument is a pointer to a DWORD that accepts an error code if this fourth argument is given. The function returns TRUE if successful, FALSE if not. An example that opens a Registry key and reads a string follows:

```
CRegistry Registry;
char cbBuffer[250];
if( Registry.Open( HKEY_LOCAL_MACHINE,
  "SOFTWARE\\GreatSoftware" ) )
  Registry.ReadString( "UserName", cbBuffer, 250 );
```

CRegistry::WriteDWORD

This function writes a DWORD value to an open Registry key. The first argument the function takes is the value name. The second argument is a DWORD value that's to be written. A third optional argument is a pointer to a DWORD that accepts an error code if this third argument is given. The function returns TRUE if successful, FALSE if not. An example that opens a Registry key and writes a DWORD value follows:

```
CRegistry Registry;
if( Registry.Open( HKEY_LOCAL_MACHINE,
  "SOFTWARE\\GreatSoftware" ) )
  Registry.WriteDWORD( "WindowColor", 50 );
```

CRegistry::WriteString

This function writes a character string to an open Registry key. The first argument the function takes is the value name. The second argument is a pointer to a character buffer that contains the string data that's to be written. A third optional argument is a pointer to a DWORD that accepts an error code if this third argument is given. An example that opens a Registry key and writes a string follows:

```
CRegistry Registry;
if( Registry.Open( HKEY_LOCAL_MACHINE,
  "SOFTWARE\\GreatSoftware" ) )
  Registry.WriteString( "UserName", "John Doe" );
```

Summary

This chapter gives the basics of data I/O. Your programs will certainly use the techniques described. Mastery of working with data is an essential first step to creating useful applications.

✦ ✦ ✦

CHAPTER 10

Sound

✦ ✦ ✦ ✦

In This Chapter

Understanding the importance of sound for applications

Learning to use the CWave class

Exploring a CWave class demo

Examining the CMidi class

Investigating a CMidi class demo

Understanding the CCDAudio class

Looking over a CCDAudio class demo

One of your five senses is hearing. According to many psychologists, this sense accounts for 30 to 45 percent of a person's perception. Such an important sense should be used by application developers. Windows 98 makes it easy to play music and sounds, so there's no excuse for neglecting what could be the sensory stimulus that transforms your program from boring and mundane to pleasant, communicative, and interesting. Built into the Windows 98 architecture is a sophisticated multimedia kernel. Many applications use these functions to enhance the way they present themselves, and now people expect this capability in programs.

This chapter shows you how to play music from a MIDI file, replay recorded sounds from .WAV files, and play CD audio from CD tracks. Three different class libraries: `CWave`, `CMidi`, and `CCDAudio`, have been created to encapsulate the Windows 98 API functions and make your programming job easier.

Playing Recorded Sounds

Comedian Steven Wright once said, "My friend has a baby. I'm recording all the noises he makes so later I can ask him what he meant." If Steven Wright were using the `CWave` class from this chapter, he could write his own Visual C++ application to record the sounds, save them to disk, and play them back many years later. That's just a small example of what you can do with the routines from this chapter. We will cover the basics of playing waveform audio (also known as .WAV or *wave* files) in addition to recording, saving, and playing multiple sounds at the same time. We will also examine the workings of the functions behind the class library, although you can easily use the classes to add sound to your programs without learning this functionality.

Adding sound effects, digital audio, and music to your application can truly enhance the user's experience. By appealing to several of your users' senses, you involve them on a deeper level and bring them closer to the world you are trying to create for them. Sound is also a great way to give feedback to users and let them know that they are really interacting with your application. If you use your imagination, the possibilities for sound in Visual C++ programs are endless.

Visual C++ does include support for playing waveform audio. In this chapter, we will expand on that support and provide you with a class library that makes it much easier to add sound to your Windows 98 applications. The Wave class library that comes with this book, along with the Windows multimedia library `winmm.lib` (provided with Visual C++), can provide a quick and easy way to add sound effects to Windows 95, Windows 98, or Windows NT. We have also created a class library that takes advantage of the DirectSound technology built in to Visual C++ to play multiple wave files at the same time.

The CWave class in brief

The `CWave` class can be added to any Visual C++ project (you must also link `winmm.lib`). Now, you are ready to add sound to your own applications. You don't necessarily have to know what's happening within the class; it will do all the work for you.

The class offers more than just the capability to play wave files. The class has a big advantage over the Windows sound routines, in that it loads the sound data into memory and can repeatedly play the sounds without a delay for loading the sound. The library also provides the capability to record and save your own wave files. If you want to examine the class library in detail or make changes to the member functions, the source code is part of the WaveDemo program in the Sound library source code.

You can open a wave file by two different methods with the `CWave` class. You can load a file from disk or from the resource file. To open a wave from an application's resource file, the application must be compiled with the wave files in the resource segment.

Playing .WAV files using the Windows API

The Microsoft API provides three different ways for applications to work with wave files:

- ✦ The `PlaySound()` function is a powerful function that allows playback of waveform audio with one line of code. We will use this as the basis for the `CWave` class, but enhance it by pre-loading the sound data into memory.
- ✦ The Media Control Interface (MCI). This is similar to the method we use to play MIDI files. The `CWave` class uses this method for the recording and saving of wave files.
- ✦ Low-level waveform audio services. Applications that require complete control over the waveform data can use these services.

The PlaySound() Function

The Windows API includes a function called PlaySound() that plays waveform audio. The function has two minor limitations: the entire sound must fit into available physical memory and the sound must be in a data format supported by one of the installed audio drivers. A good rule of thumb is to use PlaySound() for files under 100K and MCI for files larger than that. The PlaySound() function offers the programmer a lot of flexibility for digitized sound playback. It will play disk-based wave files, wave resources, or specific system-event sounds. It can loop sounds, play them asynchronously, and play them from memory. The CWave class uses this function extensively; a major advantage of the class library is that it loads the waveform data into memory then uses the PlaySound() function to play the sound. The application need load the sound only once, which eliminates delay at the start of sound playback. Let's examine the Windows API PlaySound() function:

```
BOOL PlaySound( LPCSTR pszSound, HMODULE hmod, DWORD fdwSound );
```

The first parameter, pszSound, specifies the filename, resource identifier, or system event. If this parameter is NULL, playback is stopped. The second parameter, hmod, is the handle of the resource. The third parameter, fdwSound, specifies flags for the command; Table 10-1 lists these flags.

Table 10-1
PlaySound() Flags

Flag	*Description*
SND_SYNC	Plays the sound synchronously (default).
SND_ASYNC	Plays the sound asynchronously.
SND_NODEFAULT	Blocks the use of the default sound.
SND_MEMORY	The first parameter points to a memory file.
SND_LOOP	Loops the sound until next PlaySound.
SND_NOSTOP	Keeps any currently playing sound from stopping.

The Media Control Interface

The Media Control Interface (MCI) allows for control of the Windows waveform audio devices. The CWave class uses the MCI to record and save wave files.

The MCI can be implemented with one of two functions: mciSendCommand() or mciSendString(). Although they both serve the same purpose and both produce the same result, they have different syntax. One uses a command-based interface and the other uses a string-based interface. We will only use mciSendCommand because the command-based interface usually seems more logical to programmers accustomed to the Windows command-based API.

The `mciSendCommand()` function communicates with the MCI device by sending command messages such as `MCI_OPEN` and `MCI_PLAY`. The MCI command-based messaging interface allows for a lot of flexibility through the use of MCI parameter blocks. The *parameter blocks* are structures defined in MMSYSTEM.H that allow large amounts of information to be passed to and returned from the `mciSendCommand()` function. Let's examine the Windows API `mciSendCommand()` function:

```
DWORD mciSendCommand( UINT wDeviceID, UINT wMessage,  dwParam1,
DWORD dwParam2 );
```

The first parameter, `wDeviceID`, is the device that receives the message. The second parameter, `wMessage`, is the MCI command message. The third parameter, `dwParam1`, specifies flags for the command. The last parameter, `dwParam2`, specifies a pointer to the parameter block to be used.

The MCI device ID identifies which device has been opened. This value is returned in the parameter block when you send the `MCI_OPEN` command and should be saved for later use. The ID identifies this device when you send subsequent commands. Table 10-2 is a brief overview of the MCI commands that are relevant to waveform audio.

Table 10-2
MCI Commands for Playing Waveform Audio

Command	*Description*
`MCI_OPEN`	Opens the device.
`MCI_CLOSE`	Closes the device.
`MCI_PLAY`	Starts the file playback.
`MCI_STOP`	Stops the file playback.
`MCI_SEEK`	Seeks a specific position within the file.
`MCI_RECORD`	Begins recording of waveform audio.
`MCI_SAVE`	Saves recorded audio to disk.

The CWave Class Functions

This section is provided as a reference to the public function calls of the `CWave` class. The calls should be easy to use and easy to implement in your own programs.

CWave Class Functions

The CWave Class can easily be used in your own program. Just add the source code to your project. It'll greatly simplify your task of programming sounds.

CWave::CWave

This example is the CWave class constructor. It simply creates a CWave object and initializes its internal variables.

CWave::GetDevices

Most of the time, you'll want to make sure the computer on which your program is running is capable of playing wave files. This function, GetDevices(), returns an integer value to indicate how many devices installed on the system support wave audio output. This function takes no parameters.

CWave::LoadFromDisk

You'll want to use this function, LoadFromDisk(), if you're trying to load a .WAV sound directly from a .WAV file. Don't use it when you want to load a sound from the resource file. This function opens the file and reads the waveform data into memory. The sound remains in memory until another sound is loaded into the CWave class, or until the CWave class is destroyed. The function takes a CString object as a parameter. It returns TRUE for success, FALSE for failure. An example follows:

```
CWave Wave;
CString strFilename;
strFilename = "Sound.wav";
BOOL bSuccess = Wave.LoadFromDisk( strFilename );
```

CWave::LoadFromRes

You'll want to use this function, LoadFromRes(), if you're trying to load a .WAV sound as a resource—but not when you want to load directly from a disk file. This function loads waveform data into memory. The sound remains in memory until another sound is loaded into the CWave class, or until the CWave class is destroyed. The function takes a CString object and an HINSTANCE handle as parameters. It returns TRUE for success, FALSE for failure. An example follows:

```
CWave Wave;
CString strResname;
strResname = "IDR_SOUND1";
BOOL bSuccess = Wave.LoadFromRes( strResname,
AfxGetInstanceHandle() );
```

CWave::Close

This function stops the file from playing and releases the memory that is storing the waveform data. You should not need to call this function; the destructor calls it automatically. You can call it yourself if you want to free up memory sooner. The `Close()` function takes no arguments and returns `TRUE` for success, `FALSE` for failure.

CWave::Play

This function plays the sound that's in memory. It first checks to see whether a sound has been loaded. If no sound is loaded, it returns `FALSE`. Then, any sound that's currently playing will be stopped. Finally, the sound that's currently loaded is begun. This function takes one Boolean parameter that allows you to specify whether the sound will loop repeatedly. It returns `TRUE` for success, `FALSE` for failure.

CWave::Stop

This function stops the current sound from playing if it's currently playing. This function takes no arguments and returns nothing.

CWave::Record

When you want to enable a user to record a sound, this function will provide the capability, provided a microphone is plugged into the back of the user's sound card. This function records new waveform data. Recording will continue until the `Stop()` function is called. The `Record()` function takes no parameters. It returns `TRUE` for success, `FALSE` for failure.

CWave::Save

Most of the time you'll be loading sounds for playback. But if you've recorded a sound, you might want to save it to disk. This function allows you to save the sound that's in the class's memory to disk. It takes a single argument, a `CString` object which contains the filename to which the data will be saved.

CWave::PlayFromDisk

This static function, plays a sound synchronously from disk. It takes a single argument, a `CString` object that contains the filename from which the sound data will be played. It returns `TRUE` for success, `FALSE` for failure.

CWave::PlayFromRes

This static function also plays a sound synchronously from disk. The function takes two arguments — a `CString` object (which contains the resource name from which the sound data will be played) and an `HINSTANCE` handle for the application. It returns `TRUE` for success, `FALSE` for failure.

✦ ✦ ✦ ✦ ✦

The WaveDemo Program

The first demo program in this chapter plays six different pre-recorded sounds. Three of the sounds are saved to disk as .WAV files. The other three are part of the program's resource file. Users can select any of the six sounds and have them play. The sounds can either be played directly from disk or the resource file, or they can be loaded and then played at a later time. You can see what the program looks like in Figure 10-1.

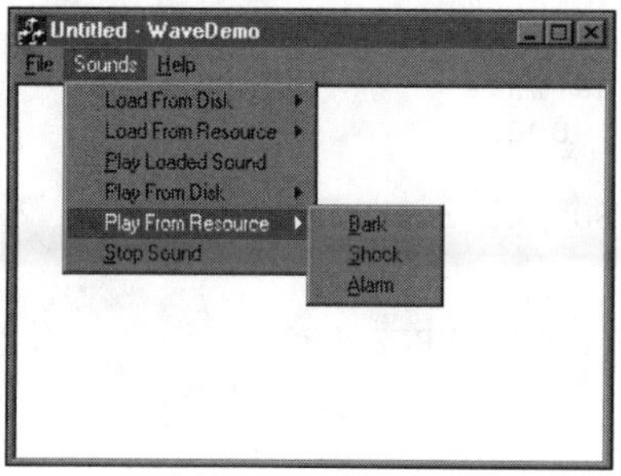

Figure 10-1: The WaveDemo program shows you how to use the CWave class.

CD-ROM Location: **Chap10\WaveDemo**
Program Name: **WaveDemo.EXE**
Source Code Modules in Text: **WaveDemoView.cpp**

◆ ◆ ◆ ◆ ◆

Listing 10-1: **WaveDemo**

```
// WaveDemoView.cpp : implementation of
// the CWaveDemoView class
//

////////////////////////////////////////////////////////////
// CWaveDemoView message handlers

void CWaveDemoView::OnSoundsLoadfromdisk()
{
  // Get the menu ID for this message.
  WORD wID = GetCurrentMessage()->wParam;

  // Have the CWave object load the .wav
  // file from disk for the sound that's
  // been selected.
  if( wID == ID_SOUNDS_LOADFROMDISK_CARDS )
    m_Wave.Load( "Sample1.wav" );
  else if( wID == ID_SOUNDS_LOADFROMDISK_BOING )
    m_Wave.Load( "Sample2.wav" );
```

(continued)

Listing 10-1 *(continued)*

```
  else
    m_Wave.Load( "Sample3.wav" );

}

void CWaveDemoView::OnSoundsLoadfromresource()
{
  // Get the menu ID for this message.
  WORD wID = GetCurrentMessage()->wParam;

  // Have the CWave object load the wave
  // resource for the sound that's been
  // selected.
  if( wID == ID_SOUNDS_LOADFROMRESOURCE_BARK )
    m_Wave.Load( IDR_WAVE3,
      AfxGetInstanceHandle() );
  else if( wID == ID_SOUNDS_LOADFROMRESOURCE_SHOCK )
    m_Wave.Load( IDR_WAVE2,
      AfxGetInstanceHandle() );
  else
    m_Wave.Load( IDR_WAVE1,
      AfxGetInstanceHandle() );

}

void CWaveDemoView::OnSoundsPlayfromdisk()
{
  // Get the menu ID for this message.
  WORD wID = GetCurrentMessage()->wParam;

  // Let them know when we start
  // by changing the mouse cursor
  // to the hourglass.
  BeginWaitCursor();

  // Have the CWave object play the .wav
  // file from disk for the sound that's
  // been selected.
  if( wID == ID_SOUNDS_PLAYFROMDISK_CARDS )
    m_Wave.PlayFromDisk( "Sample1.wav" );
  else if( wID == ID_SOUNDS_PLAYFROMDISK_BOING )
    m_Wave.PlayFromDisk( "Sample2.wav" );
  else
    m_Wave.PlayFromDisk( "Sample3.wav" );

  // Change the mouse cursor back to
  // it's original state before
  // the call to BeginWaitCursor().
  EndWaitCursor();

}
```

```
void CWaveDemoView::OnSoundsPlayfromresource()
{
  // Get the menu ID for this message.
  WORD wID = GetCurrentMessage()->wParam;

  // Let them know when we start
  // by changing the mouse cursor
  // to the hourglass.
  BeginWaitCursor();

  // Have the CWave object play the wave
  // resource for the sound that's been
  // selected.
  if( wID == ID_SOUNDS_PLAYFROMRESOURCE_BARK )
    m_Wave.PlayFromRes( IDR_WAVE3,
      AfxGetInstanceHandle() );
  else if( wID == ID_SOUNDS_PLAYFROMRESOURCE_SHOCK )
    m_Wave.PlayFromRes( IDR_WAVE2,
      AfxGetInstanceHandle() );
  else
    m_Wave.PlayFromRes( IDR_WAVE1,
      AfxGetInstanceHandle() );

  // Change the mouse cursor back to
  // it's original state before
  // the call to BeginWaitCursor().
  EndWaitCursor();

}

void CWaveDemoView::OnSoundsPlayloadedsound()
{

  // Let them know when we start
  // by changing the mouse cursor
  // to the hourglass.
  BeginWaitCursor();

  // Play the loaded sound.
  m_Wave.Play();

  // Change the mouse cursor back to
  // it's original state before
  // the call to BeginWaitCursor().
  EndWaitCursor();

}

void CWaveDemoView::OnUpdateSoundsPlayloadedsound(
  CCmdUI* pCmdUI)
{
```

(continued)

Listing 10-1 *(continued)*

```
    // Enable the menu item if a sound has
    // been loaded.
    pCmdUI->Enable( m_Wave.IsLoaded() );

}

void CWaveDemoView::OnSoundsStopsound()
{

    // Stop the sound that's playing.
    m_Wave.Stop();

}
```

Playing MIDI Files

Believe it or not, you don't need to know anything about music or MIDI to add music to your Visual C++ applications. Although we cover the basics of MIDI and the Windows MIDI interface in this chapter, you could easily use the classes presented here to add music to your programs without such a background.

Music is one of the easiest ways to enhance your multimedia applications. Nearly every popular game or multimedia title features some sort of background music, either MIDI or CD audio. Music is very effective for putting the user in a specific mood or evoking certain feelings. The right music at the right time can work wonders for you and your Visual C++ programs.

You may wonder why you would want to use MIDI when you could skip to the `CCDAudio` class and add CD audio to your applications. Although CD audio is the current trend and is of a much higher quality, MIDI music does still have its advantages. Of course, your applications may not be CD-based or you're not requiring your user to have a CD-ROM drive. MIDI is cheaper to produce than CD audio; a huge library of MIDI music is available on the Internet, as well as through freeware and shareware. Finally, if you are producing a high-end CD-ROM product, consider that you would need to pause CD audio every time your program accessed the disc; you can continue to play MIDI music uninterruptedly.

Although Microsoft provides support for playing MIDI files, nothing built into Visual C++ or MFC helps you implement this support. The CMidi class described in this chapter along with the Windows multimedia library (`winmm.lib`) provided with Visual C++ provide a quick and easy method for adding MIDI music to any Windows 98 (or Windows 95/NT) application. Good luck making your programs come alive with MIDI music!

What is MIDI?

The *Musical Instrument Digital Interface* (MIDI) is a protocol originally developed within the music industry by several large companies involved in production of electronic music synthesizers. MIDI has since been adopted by the computer industry as the standard format for multimedia music files. A MIDI file is a set of commands for storing and transmitting information about music. MIDI devices on your computer (such as a sound card) interpret this information and use it to create music. In simpler terms, a MIDI file is the electronic equivalent of sheet music.

Windows supports the General MIDI Specification, the industry standard for how MIDI is developed and used. This standard defines the particular sounds and instruments that are supported, as well as the commands that control them. Microsoft and most MIDI sound-card manufacturers support this standard.

The CMidi class in brief

The `CMidi` class can be linked with any Visual C++ project (you must also link winmm.lib). Before you know it, you will be playing MIDI files in your own applications. You don't need to know what's going on behind the scene, the class will do all the work for you.

The library offers much more than just the capability to play MIDI files. You can pause the playback, skip around to different positions within the file, and even change the tempo of the playback. Of course, if you want to examine the class library in detail or make changes to the member functions, the source code is part of the MIDI demo program and is also included in the Sound library project.

Class Library

CMidi Class Functions

This reference lists the functions found in the `CMidi` class. Use it when you study the MIDIDemo program and create your own programs that use the `CMidi` class.

CMidi::CMidi

This example is the `CMidi` class constructor. It simply creates a `CMidi` object and initializes its internal variables.

CMidi::DeviceCount

This function returns the number of MCI devices capable of playing MIDI tracks. It takes no arguments and returns an integer value containing the number of MIDI-capable devices.

CMidi::Open

The `Open()` function opens the MCI for playing MIDI files. It issues the necessary `mciSendCommand()` functions to set everything up. The `CMidi` class retains a handle to the open MCI device for its own internal use. The function takes one argument: a character pointer to a string containing the file name of the MIDI file that's to be loaded. It returns `TRUE` if successful, `FALSE` if it fails.

CMidi::Close

This function stops a MIDI track if it's currently playing, and then closes the MCI device. It sets all internal flags to indicate that everything is closed down properly. This function is called any time a `CMidi` class is destroyed so that things are cleaned up. The `Close()` function takes no arguments and returns `TRUE` if successful, `FALSE` if it fails.

CMidi::Play

The `Play()` function begins the playback of the MIDI file that's been loaded into memory. If the `CMidi` class hasn't been opened, this function returns `FALSE`. The `Play()` function takes no arguments and returns `TRUE` if successful, `FALSE` if it fails.

CMidi::Stop

The `Stop()` function, causes the MIDI track that's currently playing to stop. The `Stop()` function takes no arguments and returns `TRUE` if successful, `FALSE` if it fails.

CMidi::IsPlaying

This function returns a Boolean value indicating whether the MIDI track is currently playing. It returns `TRUE` if the MIDI track is playing, `FALSE` if it isn't. `IsPlaying()` takes no parameters.

CMidi::Pause

This function in the library pauses the playback of the MIDI track that's currently being played. The `Pause()` function takes no arguments and returns `TRUE` if successful, `FALSE` if it fails.

◆ ◆ ◆ ◆ ◆

The MIDIDemo Program

The MIDIDemo program shows you how to play and manage MIDI files. Four MIDI files are in the MIDIDemo directory, and any one of them can be loaded and played. The program uses the `CMidi` class for performing MIDI operations. It will make playing MIDI files very easy. The MIDIDemo program can be seen in Figure 10-2.

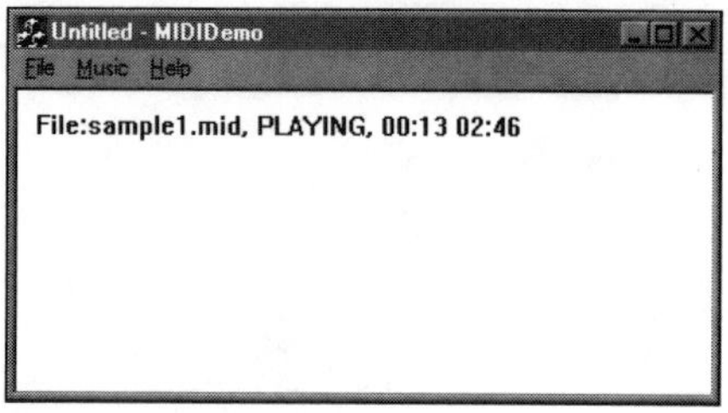

Figure 10-2: Studying the MIDIDemo program teaches you to use the `CMidi` class.

MIDIDemo
CD-ROM Location: **Chap10\MIDIDemo**
Program Name: **MIDIDemo.EXE**
Source Code Modules in Text: **MIDIaveDemoView.cpp**

◆ ◆ ◆ ◆ ◆

Listing 10-2: **MIDIDemo Program**

```
// MIDIDemoView.cpp : implementation of
// the CMIDIDemoView class
//

/////////////////////////////////////////////////////////
// CMIDIDemoView construction/destruction

static char *szFilename[] = {
  "sample1.mid", "sample2.mid",
  "sample3.mid", "sample4.mid" };

CMIDIDemoView::CMIDIDemoView()
{

  // Set the initial song to 0
  // and the initial file to sample1.mid.
  m_nSong = 0;
  m_Midi.Open( szFilename[0] );

}

CMIDIDemoView::~CMIDIDemoView()
{
}

/////////////////////////////////////////////////////////
// CMIDIDemoView message handlers

void CMIDIDemoView::OnMusicSelectsong()
{
  // Remember if the file is playing.
```

(continued)

Listing 10-2 *(continued)*

```
  BOOL bIsPlaying = m_Midi.IsPlaying();

  // Close the midi file.
  m_Midi.Close();

  // Get the menu message ID.
  WORD wID = GetCurrentMessage()->wParam;

  // Set the song number to 0, 1, 2, or 3
  // depending on the menu ID.
  if( wID == ID_MUSIC_SELECTSONG_JUNGLE )
    m_nSong = 0;
  else if( wID == ID_MUSIC_SELECTSONG_WINTER )
    m_nSong = 1;
  else if( wID == ID_MUSIC_SELECTSONG_CANDYLAND )
    m_nSong = 2;
  else
    m_nSong = 3;

  // Open the CMidi object with the selected
  // song's filename.
  m_Midi.Open( szFilename[m_nSong] );

  // If we were playing when we came into
  // this function, start the audio.
  if( bIsPlaying )
    m_Midi.Play();

}

void CMIDIDemoView::OnUpdateMusicSelectsong(
CCmdUI* pCmdUI)
{

  // Set the check for the currently
  // selected song.
  pCmdUI->SetCheck( m_nSong ==
    (int) pCmdUI->m_nIndex );

}

void CMIDIDemoView::OnMusicStop()
{

  // Stop the playing.
  m_Midi.Stop();

}

void CMIDIDemoView::OnUpdateMusicStop(CCmdUI* pCmdUI)
{
```

```
  // Enable the 'stop' menu selection
  // if the file is currently playing.
  pCmdUI->Enable( m_Midi.IsPlaying() );

}

void CMIDIDemoView::OnMusicPlay()
{

  // Play the midi file.
  m_Midi.Play();

}

void CMIDIDemoView::OnUpdateMusicPlay(CCmdUI* pCmdUI)
{

  // Enable the 'play' menu selection
  // if the file is not currently playing.
  pCmdUI->Enable( !m_Midi.IsPlaying() );

}

int CMIDIDemoView::OnCreate(
  LPCREATESTRUCT lpCreateStruct)
{
  if (CView::OnCreate(lpCreateStruct) == -1)
    return -1;

  // Kick off the timer.
  SetTimer( 1, 500, NULL );

  return 0;
}

void CMIDIDemoView::OnTimer(UINT nIDEvent)
{

  // Get a DC to the window.
  CClientDC ClientDC( this );

  // We'll need a CString object
  // to form the information text.
  CString strInfo;

  // Use the GetMinutes() and GetSeconds()
  // functions to obtain the current minutes
  // and seconds. We'll get negative values
  // if the midi file isn't opened, so check
  // for this.
  int nMinutes = m_Midi.GetMinutes();
  if( nMinutes < 0 )
    nMinutes = 0;
```

(continued)

Listing 10-2 (continued)

```
    int nSeconds = m_Midi.GetSeconds();
    if( nSeconds < 0 )
      nSeconds = 0;

    // Use the GetLength() function to obtain
    // the total midi file length. We'll get
    // negative values if the midi file isn't
    // opened, so check for this.
    int nTotalMinutes, nTotalSeconds;
    m_Midi.GetLength( &nTotalMinutes, &nTotalSeconds );
    if( nTotalMinutes < 0 )
      nTotalMinutes = 0;
    if( nTotalSeconds < 0 )
      nTotalSeconds = 0;

    // Format the information string so that we can display
    // it to the window.
    strInfo.Format( "File:%s, %s, %02d:%02d %02d:%02d     ",
      szFilename[m_nSong],
      m_Midi.IsPlaying() ? "PLAYING" : "!PLAYING",
      nMinutes, nSeconds,
      nTotalMinutes, nTotalSeconds );

    // Write the information string to the
    // window.
    ClientDC.TextOut( 10, 10, strInfo );

    CView::OnTimer(nIDEvent);
  }
```

CD Audio

CD audio. Sounds cool, doesn't it? Just having sound and music in your application is not enough anymore. Publishers want high-quality CD audio to compete with the top-of-the-line multimedia productions.

What makes CD audio so great? First, and probably most important, is sound quality. CD audio has the unique advantage of sounding exactly the way the composer designed it and the musicians produced it. While a MIDI file playing on one person's computer could sound completely different than on another, CD audio will always sound exactly the same. Along with this improved sound quality comes the capability to completely immerse the user in the musical experience. You might be surprised at the effects high-quality audio can have on a computer user.

Another advantage of using CD audio is that it's easy to skip to different tracks on a CD or to different positions within a track; CDs are organized in a format that most people are already familiar with.

Are there disadvantages to CD audio? Well, yes; CD audio, like everything else, is not perfect. The main disadvantage involves disc access. You can't play CD audio while you are accessing the disc for other purposes. So when your application accesses the CD to read data, you must pause the CD audio until the process is complete. Also, unless you happen to run your own music studio, CD quality audio may be expensive and hard to produce.

When you make the decision to use CD audio in your applications, you must take all these factors into account. But if you have the resources and the know-how to use CD audio, no other one feature can add more to the user experience. The `CCDAudio` class that comes on the book's CD-ROM, along with the Windows multimedia library (winmm.lib) provided with Visual C++, can provide a quick and easy method for adding CD audio to any application written for Windows 95, Windows 98, or Windows NT. You can now make your programs sound like the ones the pros offer.

The CCDAudio class library in brief

We've built a class that encapsulates all of the MCI commands necessary to play CD audio. The `CCDAudio` class is linked into the CDAudio program as a .cpp file. For your convenience, a .lib file named Sound.lib and a .h file named Sound.h are provided which contain the `CWave`, `CMidi`, and `CCDAudio` classes. These two files, along with the entire project, can be found in the Chap10\Library directory on the CD-ROM.

If you link in the `CCDAudio` class, with just a few additions to your application you can have all the features of a CD player in your own program. You don't have to learn the programming required to play CD audio. The class library will do all the work for you.

In addition to playing audio from the CD, you're provided with a set of functions that allow you to do much more: skip around on the CD, get information on different tracks, and even open and close the CD drive. All of this is handled in a way that's transparent to the program. Of course, if you want to examine the class library in detail or make changes to the member functions, you can.

The Media Control Interface

The brains behind the `CCDAudio` class is the Media Control Interface. This is how Microsoft Windows talks to such devices as VCRs, video-disc players, and of course CD audio.

The MCI can be implemented with one of two functions: `mciSendCommand()` or `mciSendString()`. Although they both serve the same purpose and both produce the same result, they have different syntax. One uses a command-based interface and the other uses a string-base interface. We only use the `mciSendCommand()` function because the command-based interface usually seems more logical to programmers accustomed to the Windows command-based API.

The mciSendCommand() function communicates with the MCI device, either sending command messages (MCI_OPEN and MCI_PLAY) or querying for information (MCI_STATUS) on the device. The MCI command-based messaging interface (see Table 10-3) allows for a lot of flexibility through the use of MCI parameter blocks. The MCI parameter blocks (also known as *flags* — see Table 10-4) are structures defined in MMSYSTEM.H that allow larger amounts of information to be passed to a return from the mciSendCommand() function.

Table 10-3
MCI Commands for Playing CD Audio

Command	*Description*
MCI_OPEN	Opens the device.
MCI_CLOSE	Closes the device.
MCI_PLAY	Starts the audio playing.
MCI_STOP	Stops the audio playing.
MCI_PAUSE	Pauses the audio playing.
MCI_SEEK	Seeks to a specific position in the CD.
MCI_SET	Used in conjunction with the MCI flags.
MCI_STATUS	Used in conjunction with the MCI flags.

Table 10-4
MCI Flags for CCDAudio Class

Set Flags	*Description*
MCI_SET_TIME_FORMAT	Changes the time format.
MCI_SET_DOOR_OPEN	Opens the CD drive.
MCI_SET_DOOR_CLOSED	Closes the CD drive.
Status Flags	***Description***
MCI_STATUS_CURRENT_TRACK	Gets the current track.
MCI_STATUS_LENGTH	Gets the length of the CD or a specific track.
MCI_STATUS_MODE	Gets the current status of the drive.
MCI_STATUS_NUMBER_OF_TRACKS	Gets the number of tracks on the CD.
MCI_STATUS_POSITION	Gets the current position in the current time format.

Status Flags	*Description*
`MCI_STATUS_READY`	Checks to see whether the device is ready.
`MCI_STATUS_TIME_FORMAT`	Gets the current time format.
`MCI_CDA_STATUS_TYPE_TRACK`	Checks to make sure the track is an audio track.
`MCI_STATUS_MEDIA_PRESENT`	Checks to make sure a CD is in the drive.

Class Library

CCDAudio Class Functions

This section will serve as a reference for the functions found in the `CCDAudio` class. Use it when you study the CDPlayer program and create your own programs that use the `CCDAudio` class.

CCDAudio::CCDAudio

This example is the `CCDAudio` class constructor. It simply creates a `CCDAudio` object and initializes its internal variables.

CCDAudio::Open

The `Open()` function, opens the MCI for playing CD audio tracks. It issues the necessary `mciSendCommand()` functions to set everything up. The `CCDAudio` class retains a handle to the open MCI device for its own internal use. The `Open()` function takes no arguments. It returns `TRUE` if successful, `FALSE` if it fails.

CCDAudio::Close

This example is a function that stops a CD audio track if it's currently playing, and closes the MCI device. It sets all internal flags to indicate that everything is closed down properly. This function is called any time a `CCDAudio` class is destroyed so that things are cleaned up. The `Close()` function takes no arguments and returns nothing.

CCDAudio::Play

The `Play()` function causes the currently selected track to begin playing. If the audio device isn't opened, this function returns `FALSE`. The `Play()` function takes no arguments. It returns `TRUE` if successful, `FALSE` if it fails.

CCDAudio::Stop

This example is a function that stops the playback of the current track. If the track isn't playing or the CD device isn't opened, this function returns `FALSE`. The `Stop()` function takes no arguments. It returns `TRUE` if successful, `FALSE` if it fails.

CCDAudio::Pause

This example is a function that pauses the playback of the current track. If the track isn't playing or the CD device isn't opened, this function returns `FALSE`. The `Pause()` function takes no arguments. It returns `TRUE` if successful, `FALSE` if it fails.

◆ ◆ ◆ ◆ ◆

The CDPlayer Program

Very few programs play CD audio music. Most programs load and play MIDI files. This program plays the high-quality sound data that's found on audio CDs. It does so with the `CCDAudio` class.

Because the CD-ROM that comes with the book has no CD audio tracks, you'll have to put an audio CD of your own in the CD-ROM drive. After you've done so, the program enables you to play any track on your audio CD. You can pause playback and move around inside each track. You can see the CDPlayer application pictured in Figure 10-3.

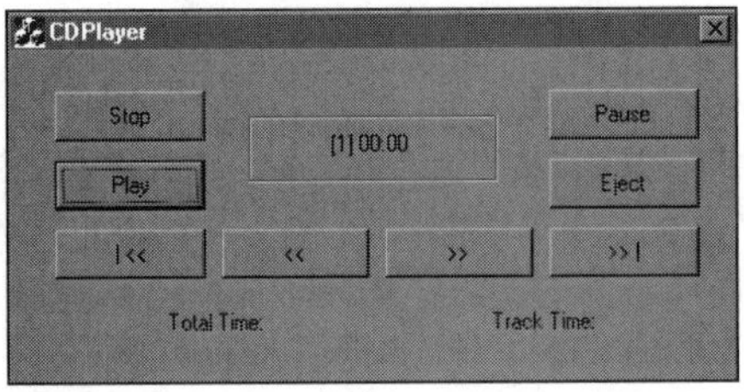

Figure 10-3: The CDPlayer application is dialog-based.

Demo Program

CDPlayer

CD-ROM Location: **Chap10\CDPlayer**

Program Name: **CDPlayer.EXE**

Source Code Modules in Text: **CDPlayerDlg.cpp**

◆ ◆ ◆ ◆ ◆

Listing 10-3: **CDPlayer Program**

```
// CDPlayerDlg.cpp : implementation file
//


/////////////////////////////////////////////////////////////////
// CCDPlayerDlg dialog
```

```
CCDPlayerDlg::CCDPlayerDlg(CWnd* pParent /*=NULL*/)
  : CDialog(CCDPlayerDlg::IDD, pParent)
{
  //{{AFX_DATA_INIT(CCDPlayerDlg)
    // NOTE: the ClassWizard will add member
// initialization here
  //}}AFX_DATA_INIT
  m_hIcon = AfxGetApp()->LoadIcon(IDR_MAINFRAME);

  // Open the CD device.
  m_CDAudio.Open();

}

/////////////////////////////////////////////////////////////
// CCDPlayerDlg message handlers

int CCDPlayerDlg::OnCreate(LPCREATESTRUCT lpCreateStruct)
{
  if (CDialog::OnCreate(lpCreateStruct) == -1)
    return -1;

  // Kick off the timer.
  SetTimer( 1, 1000, NULL );

  return 0;
}

void CCDPlayerDlg::OnTimer(UINT nIDEvent)
{

  BOOL bDriveReady = TRUE;

  // Format an information string. We'll use
  // it to display the track and current time
  // within the track.
  CString strStatus;
  strStatus.Format( "[%d] %02d:%02d",
    m_CDAudio.GetCurrentTrack(),
    m_CDAudio.GetMinutes(),
    m_CDAudio.GetSeconds() );

  // If the current track is -1, that means
  // we have no audio CD. Update the information
  // string to reflect this condition.
  if( m_CDAudio.GetCurrentTrack() == -1 ){
    strStatus = "No CD Audio";
    bDriveReady = FALSE;
    }
  SetDlgItemText( IDC_TRACKINFO, strStatus );
```

(continued)

Listing 10-3 *(continued)*

```
  // The next information string will contain the total
// time for this CD. We'll use the GetTotalLength()
// function to obtain the minutes and seconds.
  CString strLength;
  int nMinutes, nSeconds;
  m_CDAudio.GetTotalLength( &nMinutes, &nSeconds );
  strLength.Format( "Total Time: %02d:%02d",
nMinutes, nSeconds );
  if( nMinutes == -1 )
    strLength = "Total Time: 00:00";
  SetDlgItemText( IDC_TOTALTIME, strLength );

  // The next information string will contain the total
// time for this track. We'll use the GetTrackLength()
// function to obtain the minutes and seconds.
  m_CDAudio.GetTrackLength(
    m_CDAudio.GetCurrentTrack(),
    &nMinutes, &nSeconds );
  strLength.Format( "Track Length: %02d:%02d",
nMinutes, nSeconds );
  if( nMinutes == -1 )
    strLength = "Total Time: 00:00";
  SetDlgItemText( IDC_TRACKTIME, strLength );

  // We'll use the boolean flags we've already
  // gotten in this function to update the
  // dialog buttons.
  CWnd *pWnd;
  pWnd = GetDlgItem( IDC_BACK );
  pWnd->EnableWindow( bDriveReady );
  pWnd = GetDlgItem( IDC_FORWARD );
  pWnd->EnableWindow( bDriveReady );
  pWnd = GetDlgItem( IDC_SKIPBACK );
  pWnd->EnableWindow( bDriveReady );
  pWnd = GetDlgItem( IDC_SKIPFORWARD );
  pWnd->EnableWindow( bDriveReady );

  // Update the approriate buttons
  // that depend on whether the CD is playing.
  BOOL bPaused;
  if( m_CDAudio.IsPlaying( &bPaused ) ){
    pWnd = GetDlgItem( IDC_PLAY );
    pWnd->EnableWindow( bPaused );
    pWnd = GetDlgItem( IDC_STOP );
    pWnd->EnableWindow( bDriveReady );
    pWnd = GetDlgItem( IDC_PAUSE );
    pWnd->EnableWindow( bDriveReady && !bPaused );
    }
  else{
    pWnd = GetDlgItem( IDC_PLAY );
    pWnd->EnableWindow( bDriveReady );
```

```
      pWnd = GetDlgItem( IDC_STOP );
      pWnd->EnableWindow( FALSE );
      pWnd = GetDlgItem( IDC_PAUSE );
      pWnd->EnableWindow( FALSE );
      }

  CDialog::OnTimer(nIDEvent);
}

void CCDPlayerDlg::OnPlay()
{

  // If the drive is ready, begin the
  // audio playback.
  if( m_CDAudio.IsDriveReady() )
    m_CDAudio.Play();

}

void CCDPlayerDlg::OnStop()
{

  // Stop the playback.
  m_CDAudio.Stop();

}

void CCDPlayerDlg::OnPause()
{

  // Pause the playback.
  m_CDAudio.Pause();

}

void CCDPlayerDlg::OnEject()
{

  // If the drive is read, close it.
  // Otherwise, attempt to open the drive.
  if( !m_CDAudio.IsDriveReady() )
    m_CDAudio.CloseDrive();
  else m_CDAudio.OpenDrive();

}

void CCDPlayerDlg::OnForward()
{

  // Get the current minutes, seconds
  // and track.  int nMinutes = m_CDAudio.GetMinutes();
  int nSeconds = m_CDAudio.GetSeconds();
```

(continued)

Listing 10-3 *(continued)*

```
  int nTrack = m_CDAudio.GetCurrentTrack();

  // If minutes == -1, then the
  // CD device didn't open or there's
  // some other problem.
  if( nMinutes == -1 )
    return;

  // Go forward five seconds. Make
  // sure that the seconds haven't gone
  // out of range.
  nSeconds += 5;
  if( nSeconds > 59 ){
    nMinutes++;
    nSeconds -= 60;
    }

  // Get the length of this track so
  // that we can check to make sure
  // we haven't gone past the end
  // of the track.
  int nTrackMinutes, nTrackSeconds;
  m_CDAudio.GetTrackLength( nTrack,
    &nTrackMinutes, &nTrackSeconds );

  // Check that the new values will be
  // in range, not past the end of the
  // track.
  if( nMinutes * 60 + nSeconds >
    nTrackMinutes * 60 + nTrackSeconds ){
    nMinutes = nTrackMinutes;
    nSeconds = nTrackSeconds;
    }

  // Seek to the new location in this track.
  m_CDAudio.SeekTo( nTrack,
    nMinutes, nSeconds, 0 );

}

void CCDPlayerDlg::OnBack()
{

  // Get the current minutes, seconds
  // and track.
  int nMinutes = m_CDAudio.GetMinutes();
  int nSeconds = m_CDAudio.GetSeconds();
  int nTrack = m_CDAudio.GetCurrentTrack();

  // If minutes == -1, then the
  // CD device didn't open or there's
```

```
  // some other problem.
  if( nMinutes == -1 )
    return;

  // Back up five seconds. Make sure
  // we haven't gone out of range.
  nSeconds -= 5;
  if( nSeconds < 0 ){
    nMinutes—;
    nSeconds += 60;
    if( nMinutes < 0 )
      nMinutes = 0;
    }

  // Seek to the new location in this track.
  m_CDAudio.SeekTo( nTrack,
    nMinutes, nSeconds, 0 );

}

void CCDPlayerDlg::OnSkipback()
{

  // Get the current track and deccrement.
  int nTrack = m_CDAudio.GetCurrentTrack() - 1;

  // If we're below the lowest allowable
  //track, go up to the highest track.
  if( nTrack < 1 )
    nTrack = m_CDAudio.GetTotalTracks();

  // Seek to the beginninig of the
  // previous track.
  m_CDAudio.SeekTo( nTrack, 0, 0, 0 );

}

void CCDPlayerDlg::OnSkipforward()
{

  // Get the current track and increment.
  int nTrack = m_CDAudio.GetCurrentTrack() + 1;

  // Get the total number of tracks and
  // make sure nTrack hasn't exceeded it.
  if( nTrack > m_CDAudio.GetTotalTracks() )
    nTrack = 1;

  // Seek to the beginning of the next track.
  m_CDAudio.SeekTo( nTrack, 0, 0, 0 );

}
```

Summary

This chapter has shown you three useful classes that take nearly all the work out of Windows sound.

- ✦ Use these classes to add sound and music to your applications: `CWave` class, `CMidi` class, and `CCDAudio` class.
- ✦ Three demonstration programs showed you exactly how to take advantage of the functionality each class offers; now you can use these classes to add sound and music to your applications.
- ✦ For convenience, use the Sound.lib and Sound.h files found in the Chap10\Library directory of the CD-ROM. You won't have to link in any source code, which will make sound easier to add to your applications.

✦ ✦ ✦

CHAPTER 11

Timers and Idle Processing

In This Chapter

Implementing timer processing

Setting a timer using WM_TIMER

Setting a timer with a callback procedure

Creating a clock application

Using CWinApp's OnIdle capability

Overriding and using the OnIdle() function

Not all processing is performed in response to user input in Windows 98. Some processing is inherently time-based — the actions performed by an autosave routine that saves open documents at 5- or 10-minute intervals, for instance. Windows helps out by providing timers that can be programmed to notify an application at regular intervals. Another useful form of time-based processing is idle processing — work performed during idle periods, when there are no messages waiting to be processed. MFC provides a framework for idle-time processing by calling an application's virtual `OnIdle()` function each time the message pump in `CWinThread` finds the message queue empty.

In the first half of this chapter, we look at timers, which can be programmed for intervals as low as 55 milliseconds. Here are just a few of the ways in which timers can be put to use:

- In applications that simulate a wall clock or display the current time in a status bar. Most such applications set a timer to fire at intervals ranging from a half second to as many as 60 seconds. When a timer notification arrives, the display is updated to reflect the current time.
- In unattended backup programs, disk defragmenters, and other applications that sit dormant until a specified time and then spring into action.
- In resource monitors, free-memory gauges, and other applications that monitor the state of the system.

In the second half of the chapter, we leave timers behind and move on to idle processing. A few of the many uses for the framework's `OnIdle` mechanism include background print spooling and garbage collection. Some chores that were ideal candidates for idle processing in 16-bit Windows are better done in background threads in Windows 98, but `OnIdle` still has its uses. We look at one example of how idle calls can be put to work in a 32-bit application in the second of this chapter's two sample programs.

Timers

There are only two functions you need to know to use timers. `CWnd::SetTimer()` programs a timer to fire at specified intervals, and `CWnd::KillTimer()` stops a running timer. Depending on the parameters passed to `SetTimer()`, a timer notifies an application that a timer interval has elapsed in two ways: by sending a `WM_TIMER` message, and by calling an application-defined callback function.

The `WM_TIMER` method is the simpler of the two, but the callback method is sometimes preferable when multiple timers are used. Both types of timer notifications receive low priority when they are sent to an application. They're processed only when the message queue is devoid of other messages.

Timer notifications are never allowed to stack up in the message queue. If you've set a timer to fire every 100 milliseconds and a full second goes by while your application is busy processing other messages, it won't suddenly receive ten rapid-fire timer notifications when the message queue empties. Instead, it will receive just one. You don't need to worry about taking so much time to process a timer notification that another will arrive before you're finished with the first one, starting a race condition. Still, a Windows 98 application should never spend an excessive amount of time processing a message unless processing has been delegated to a secondary thread because responsiveness will suffer if the primary thread goes too long without checking the message queue.

Setting a timer using WM_TIMER

The easiest way to set a timer is to call `SetTimer()` with nothing more than a timer ID and a time-out value and then map `WM_TIMER` messages to an `OnTimer()` function in your application's window class. A timer ID is a nonzero value that identifies the timer. When `OnTimer()` is activated in response to a `WM_TIMER` message, the timer ID is passed as an argument. If you use only one timer, the ID value probably won't interest you because all `WM_TIMER` messages will come from the same timer. An application that uses two or more timers can use the timer ID to determine which timer a message has come from.

The time-out value passed to `SetTimer()` specifies the interval between `WM_TIMER` messages in thousandths of a second. Values range from 1 through the highest number a 32-bit integer will hold: $^{2}/_{32}$ -1 milliseconds, which equals slightly more than 49$^{1}/_{2}$ days. The following code allocates a timer, assigns it the ID of 1m, and programs it to send the window whose `SetTimer()` function called a `WM_TIMER` message every 500 milliseconds. The `NULL` third parameter configures the timer to send `WM_TIMER` messages rather than use a callback function.

```
SetTimer( 1, 500, NULL );
```

Although the programmed interval is 500 milliseconds, the window will actually receive a `WM_TIMER` message about once every 550 milliseconds because the hardware timer upon which timers are based ticks once every 54.9 milliseconds. In effect, Windows rounds the value you pass to `SetTimer()` up to the next multiple of 55 milliseconds. Thus, the following two lines of code both program a timer to send a `WM_TIMER` message roughly every 55 milliseconds:

```
SetTimer( 1, 1, NULL );
SetTimer( 1, 50, NULL );
```

If you change the timer to an interval of 60 as in the following line, `WM_TIMER` messages will arrive every 110 milliseconds:

```
SetTimer( 1, 60, NULL );
```

Timers can't be relied upon for stopwatch-like accuracy. If you write a clock application that programs a timer for 1,000-millisecond intervals and updates the display each time a `WM_TIMER` message arrives, you shouldn't assume that 60 `WM_TIMER` messages means one minute has passed. Instead, you should check the current time whenever a message arrives and update the clock accordingly. Then, if the flow of timer messages is interrupted, the clock's accuracy will be maintained.

If you write an application that demands precision timing, you can use Windows multimedia timers in lieu of conventional timers and program them for intervals of 1 millisecond or less. Multimedia timers offer superior precision and are ideal for specialized applications such as MIDI sequencers, but they also incur more overhead and can adversely impact other programs running on the system.

The value returned by `SetTimer()` is the timer ID if the function succeeded, or 0 if it failed. In versions of Windows before Windows 95, timers were a shared global resource of which a limited number were available. Beginning with Windows 95, the number of timers the system can dole out is limited only by available memory. Failures should be rare, but it's still prudent to check the return value just in case the system is critically low on resources. The timer ID returned by `SetTimer()` will equal the timer ID you specified in the function's first parameter unless you specify 0, in which case `SetTimer()` will return a timer ID of 1. `SetTimer()` won't fail if you assign two or more timers the same ID. Rather, it will assign duplicate IDs as requested.

`SetTimer()` can also be used to change a previously assigned time-out value. If timer 1 already exists, the following statement will reprogram it for intervals of 1,000 millliseconds:

```
SetTimer( 1, 1000, NULL );
```

Reprogramming a timer also resets its internal clock so the next notification won't arrive until the specified time period has elapsed.

Nutshell

Creating and Using a Timer

This section will describe how to create and use a timer. It uses the ClassWizard to create `OnCreate()` and `OnTimer()` functions for a single-document view window.

To create and use a timer, follow these steps:

1. With the AppWizard, create a single-document application named UseTimer.
2. Run the ClassWizard and select the `CUseTimerView` class in the Class Name combo box.
3. In the Messages listbox, find the `WM_CREATE` and `WM_TIMER` messages and add handlers for them.
4. In the `OnCreate()` function, add the following:

```
SetTimer( 1, 1000, NULL );
```

5. In the `OnTimer()` function add the following:

```
static int nCounter = 0;
CString strText;
strText.Format( "Counter=%d    ", nCounter );
nCounter++;
CClientDC ClientDC( this );
ClientDC.TextOut( 10, 10, strText );
```

6. Compile and run the program. You see the counter increment at approximately every second.

✦ ✦ ✦ ✦ ✦

An important point to take home is that `WM_TIMER` messages are not processed asynchronously with respect to other messages. That is, one `WM_TIMER` message will never interrupt another `WM_TIMER` message in the same thread; it will not interrupt a nontimer message, for that matter. `WM_TIMER` messages wait their turn in the message queue just as other messages do and are not processed until they are retrieved and dispatched by the message loop. If a regular message handling function and `OnTimer()` modify the same member variable, then you can safely assume that access to that variable will be serialized so `OnTimer()` won't modify the variable's value while another message is being processed. (Of course, this rule doesn't hold true if the two timers were created by separate threads.)

Setting a timer with a callback procedure

Timers don't have to generate `WM_TIMER` messages. If you prefer, you can configure a timer to call a callback function inside your application rather than post a `WM_TIMER` message to the message queue. This method is often used in applications using multiple timers so each timer can be handled independently.

A common misconception among Windows programmers is that timer callbacks are processed more expediently than timer messages because callbacks are sent directly to the application's window procedure whereas `WM_TIMER` message are posted to the message queue. In reality, callbacks and messages are handled identically up to the point at which `DispatchMessage()` is called. When a timer fires, Windows sets a flag in the message queue to indicate that a timer message or callback is awaiting processing. If GetMessage() finds that the message queue is empty and no windows need repainting, it checks the timer flag. If the flag is set, GetMessage() builds a WM_TIMER message subsequently dispatched by DispatchMessage(). If the timer that generated the message is of the WM_TIMER variety, the message is dispatched to the window procedure. But if a callback function is registered instead, DispatchMessage() calls the callback function. Therefore, callback timers enjoy virtually no performance advantage over message timers. Slightly less overhead is involved when a timer callback is invoked because no sorting of message IDs has to be done in the message map or the window procedure, but the difference is all but immeasurable. In practice, you find that WM_TIMER-type timers and callback timers work with the same regularity.

To set a timer that uses a callback function, specify the name of the callback function in the third parameter as follows:

```
SetTimer( 1, 100, TimerProc );
```

The callback procedure, which is named TimerProc, is prototyped as follows:

```
void CALLBACK TimerProc( HWND hWNd, UINT nMsg,
  UINT nTimerId, DWORD dwTime );
```

The hWnd parameter to TimerProc() contains the window handle, nMsg contains the message ID WM_TIMER, nTimerID holds the timer ID, and dwTime specifies the number of milliseconds that have elapsed since Windows 98 was started. The callback function should be declared as a static member function of the window class, or other measures should be taken to prevent this pointer from being passed on the stack.

One obstacle you run into when you're using a static member function as a timer callback is that the timer procedure doesn't receive a user-defined lParam value as some Windows callback functions do. In a timer procedure, you have to manufacture that window pointer yourself if you want to access nonstatic function and data members. Fortunately, you can get a pointer to your application's main window with MFC's AfxGetMainWnd() function as follows:

```
CmainWindow *pMainWd = (CmainWindow *) AfxGetMainWnd();
```

Casting the return value to a CMainWindow pointer is necessary if you want to access CMainWindow function and data members because the pointer returned by AfxGetMainWnd() is a generic CWnd pointer. After pMainWnd is initialized in this way, a TimerProc() function that is also a member of CMainWindow can access nonstatic CMainWindow functions and data members as if it, too, were a nonstatic member function.

The counterpart of CWnd::SetTimer() is CWnd::KillTimer(), which stops a timer and stops the flow of WM_TIMER messages or callbacks. The following statement releases the timer whose ID is 1:

```
KillTimer( 1 );
```

A good place to kill a timer create in `OnCreate()` is in the window's `OnClose()` or `OnDestroy()` handler. If an application fails to free a timer before it terminates, Windows 98 will clean up after it when the process ends.

The Clock Program

The first demo program in this chapter shows you how to create a clock application using a timer. The `SetTimer()` function passes a `NULL` as its third parameter, therefore causing a `WM_TIMER` message to be posted to the window.

This program allows you to view either an analog clock or a digital clock. To change the display, simply change the setting in the Type menu. The program is shown in Figure 11-1.

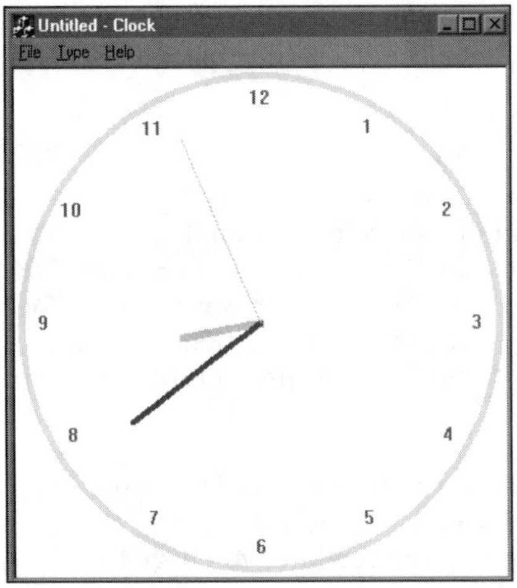

Figure 11-1: The Clock program lets you see the time with an analog or a digital display.

Demo Program

Clock
CD-ROM Location: **Chap11\Clock**
Program Name: **Clock.EXE**
Source Code Modules in Text: **ClockView.cpp**

◆ ◆ ◆ ◆ ◆

Listing 11-1: The Clock Program

```
// ClockView.cpp : implementation of
// the CClockView class
//
```

```
/////////////////////////////////////////////////////////////////////
// CClockView construction/destruction

CClockView::CClockView()
{

  // Set the initial clock type
  // to analog.
  m_nClockType = CLOCK_ANALOG;

}

CClockView::~CClockView()
{
}

/////////////////////////////////////////////////////////////////////
// CClockView drawing

void CClockView::OnDraw(CDC* pDC)
{
  CClockDoc* pDoc = GetDocument();
  ASSERT_VALID(pDoc);

  // Get the client rectangle so that we
  // can dynamically fit the clock to
  // the window.
  RECT Rect;
  GetClientRect( &Rect );

  // For easier calculations, get the
  // x and y coordinates of the
  // window center.
  int nCenterX = Rect.right / 2;
  int nCenterY = Rect.bottom / 2;

  // Get the current time.
  CTime Time = CTime::GetCurrentTime();

  CString strDigits;
  int i, x, y;
  CSize size;

  switch( m_nClockType ){
    case CLOCK_ANALOG:
      {
      // Create a yellow pen with which we'll
      // draw the ellipse.
      CPen Pen( PS_SOLID, 5, RGB( 255, 255, 0 ) );

      // Select the new pen into the DC and
      // remember the pen that was selected out.
```

(continued)

Listing 11-1 *(continued)*

```
CPen *pOldPen = pDC->SelectObject( &Pen );
// Draw the clock face border with
// the Ellipse function.
pDC->Ellipse( 5, 5, Rect.right - 5,
  Rect.bottom - 5 );

double Radians;

// Out text color will be red.
pDC->SetTextColor( RGB( 255, 0, 0 ) );

for( i=1; i<=12; i++ ){

  // Format the digit CString object
  // for the current clock number.
  strDigits.Format( "%d", i );

  // Get the text extent of the
  // text so that we can center
  // it about a point.
  size =
    pDC->GetTextExtent( strDigits,
    strDigits.GetLength() );

  // Calculate the number of radians
  // for the current clock number.
  Radians = (double) i * 6.28 / 12.0;

  // Calculate the x coordinate. We
  // use the text extent to center
  // the text about a point.
  x = nCenterX -
    ( size.cx / 2 ) +
    (int) ( (double) ( nCenterX - 20 ) *
           sin( Radians ) );

  // Calculate the y coordinate. We
  // use the text extent to center
  // the text about a point.
  y = nCenterY -
    ( size.cy / 2 ) -
    (int) ( (double) ( nCenterY - 20 ) *
          cos( Radians ) );

  // Draw the text.
  pDC->TextOut( x, y, strDigits );

  }

// Calculate the radians for the hour hand.
Radians = (double) Time.GetHour() +
```

```
  (double) Time.GetMinute() / 60.0 +
  (double) Time.GetSecond() / 3600.0;
Radians *= 6.28 / 12.0;

// Create a pen for the hour hand that's five
// pixels wide with a green color.
CPen HourPen( PS_SOLID, 5, RGB( 0, 255, 0 ) );

// Select the newly-created CPen object
// into the DC.
pDC->SelectObject( &HourPen );

// Move to the center of the clock, then
// draw the hour hand line.
pDC->MoveTo( nCenterX, nCenterY );
pDC->LineTo(
  nCenterX + (int) ( (double) ( nCenterX / 3 ) *
      sin( Radians ) ),
  nCenterY - (int) ( (double) ( nCenterY / 3 ) *
      cos( Radians ) ) );

// Calculate the radians for the minute hand.
Radians = (double) Time.GetMinute() +
  (double) Time.GetSecond() / 60.0;
Radians *= 6.28 / 60.0;

// Create a pen for the minute hand that's three
// pixels wide with a blue color.
CPen MinutePen( PS_SOLID, 3, RGB( 0, 0, 255 ) );

// Select the newly-created CPen object
// into the DC.
pDC->SelectObject( &MinutePen );

// Move the to center of the clock, then
// draw the minute hand line.
pDC->MoveTo( nCenterX, nCenterY );
pDC->LineTo(
  nCenterX + (int) ( (double) (
      ( nCenterX * 2 ) / 3 ) * sin( Radians ) ),
  nCenterY - (int) ( (double) (
      ( nCenterY * 2 ) / 3 ) * cos( Radians ) ) );

// Calculate the radians for the second hand.
Radians = (double) Time.GetSecond();
Radians *= 6.28 / 60.0;

// Create a pen for the second hand that's one
// pixels wide with a cyan color.
CPen SecondPen( PS_SOLID, 1, RGB( 0, 255, 255 ) );

// Select the newly-created CPen object
```

(continued)

Listing 11-1 *(continued)*

```
      // into the DC.
      pDC->SelectObject( &SecondPen );
      // Move the to center of the clock, then
      // draw the second hand line.
      pDC->MoveTo( nCenterX, nCenterY );
      pDC->LineTo(
        nCenterX + (int) ( (double) (
            ( nCenterX * 4 ) / 5 ) * sin( Radians ) ),
        nCenterY - (int) ( (double) (
            ( nCenterY * 4 ) / 5 ) * cos( Radians ) ) );

      // Select the old CPen object back into
      // the DC.
      pDC->SelectObject( pOldPen );
      }
      break;
    case CLOCK_DIGITAL:
      {

      // Begin by creating the text string
      // that represents the digital time.
      strDigits.Format( "%d:%02d:%02d",
        Time.GetHour(),
        Time.GetMinute(),
        Time.GetSecond() );

      CFont Font, *pOldFont;
      int nWidth = 100;
      int nHeight = 140;

      do{

        // We may have already created
        // a font in the CFont object. Here
        // we make sure it's deleted.
        if( Font.GetSafeHandle() != NULL )
          Font.DeleteObject();

        // Create the font with mostly default
        // values. Use a Times New Roman font.
        Font.CreateFont( nHeight, nWidth, 0, 0,
          FW_DONTCARE, 0, 0, 0, ANSI_CHARSET,
          OUT_CHARACTER_PRECIS, CLIP_CHARACTER_PRECIS,
          DEFAULT_QUALITY, DEFAULT_PITCH | FF_DONTCARE,
          "Times New Roman" );

        // Select the newly-created CFont object into
        // the DC and remember the CFont object that
        // was selected out.
        pOldFont = pDC->SelectObject( &Font );
```

```
        // Get the text extent so we can decide if
        // this font is too large.
        size =
          pDC->GetTextExtent( strDigits,
            strDigits.GetLength() );

        // Select the old font back into the DC.
        pDC->SelectObject( pOldFont );

        // If the text extent is too wide,
        // reduce the font width.
        if( size.cx > Rect.right )
          nWidth -= 5;

        // If the text extent is too high,
        // reduce the font height.
        if( size.cy > Rect.bottom )
          nHeight -= 5;

        } while( size.cx > Rect.right ||
          size.cy > Rect.bottom );

      // Select the final font into the
      // DC and remember the CFont object
      // that's selected out.
      pOldFont = pDC->SelectObject( &Font );

      // Draw the text.
      pDC->TextOut( nCenterX - ( size.cx / 2 ),
        nCenterY - ( size.cy / 2 ),
        strDigits );

      // Select the old font back into the DC.
      pDC->SelectObject( pOldFont );

      }
      break;
    }

}

int CClockView::OnCreate(LPCREATESTRUCT lpCreateStruct)
{
  if (CView::OnCreate(lpCreateStruct) == -1)
    return -1;

  // Kick off the timer.
  SetTimer( 1, 1000, NULL );

  return 0;
}
```

(continued)

Listing 11-1 *(continued)*

```
void CClockView::OnTimer(UINT nIDEvent)
{
  // The timer just causes a redraw to occur.
  // In the OnDraw() function the current
  // time is obtained.
  InvalidateRect( NULL, TRUE );
  UpdateWindow();

  CView::OnTimer(nIDEvent);
}

void CClockView::OnTypeAnalog()
{

  // Set to an analog clock and
  // cause a window redraw.
  m_nClockType = CLOCK_ANALOG;
  InvalidateRect( NULL, TRUE );
  UpdateWindow();

}

void CClockView::OnUpdateTypeAnalog(CCmdUI* pCmdUI)
{

  // Set the check if we have an analog clock.
  pCmdUI->SetCheck( m_nClockType == CLOCK_ANALOG );

}

void CClockView::OnTypeDigital()
{

  // Set to an digital clock and
  // cause a window redraw.
  m_nClockType = CLOCK_DIGITAL;
  InvalidateRect( NULL, TRUE );
  UpdateWindow();

}

void CClockView::OnUpdateTypeDigital(CCmdUI* pCmdUI)
{

  // Set the check if we have an digital clock.
  pCmdUI->SetCheck( m_nClockType == CLOCK_DIGITAL );

}
```

CWinApp's OnIdle Capability

As mentioned earlier, an application can perform idle processing of its own by overriding the application object's virtual OnIdle() function. OnIdle() is prototyped as follows:

```
virtual BOOL OnIdle( LONG lCount );
```

The lCount parameter is a 32-bit value that specifies the number of times OnIdle() has been called since the last message was processed. The count continually increases until the message loop in CWinThread::Run calls PumpMessage() to retrieve and dispatch another message. The count is then reset to 0 and starts again. Mouse messages, WM_PAINT messages, and WM_SYSTIMER messages don't cause lCount to be reset. lCount can be used as a rough measure of the time elapsed since the last message, or of the length of time the application has been idle. If you have two background tasks you'd like to perform during idle time — one high-priority and one low-priority — you can use lCount to determine when to execute each task. For example, the high-priority task might be executed when lCount reaches 10, and the low-priority task might be deferred until lCount is 100 or even 1,000.

If you could log the calls to an application's OnIdle() function without slowing it down, you'd find that 1,000 is not all that high a number, Typically, OnIdle() is called 100 or more times per second when the message queue is empty, so a low-priority background task that kicks off when lCount reaches 1,000 would be executed when the user stopped typing or moving the mouse for a few seconds. A high-priority task that begins when lCount reaches 10 would be executed much more often because the count frequently reaches or exceeds 10 even when the message loop is relatively busy. Idle processing should be carried out as quickly as possible because message traffic is blocked until the OnIdle() function returns.

The value returned by OnIdle() determines whether OnIdle() will be called again. If OnIdle() returns a nonzero value, it is called again if the message queue is still empty. If OnIdle() returns 0, however, further calls to OnIdle() are suspended until another message finds its way into the message queue, and the idle state is reentered after the message is dispatched. The mechanism that makes this work is the bIdle flag in CWinThread::Run, which is initially set to TRUE but is set to FALSE if OnIdle() returns FALSE. The while loop that calls OnIdle() tests the value of bIdle at the beginning of each iteration and fails if bIdle is FALSE. bIdle is set to TRUE again when a message shows up in the message queue and PumpMessage() is called to retrieve and dispatch it. From a practical standpoint, you can save a few CPU cycles by returning FALSE from your OnIdle() override if background processing is complete for the moment and you don't want OnIdle() to be called again until the flow of messages resumes. Be careful, however, not to return FALSE before the framework has finished its most recent spate of idle processing chores and thus deprives it of the idle time it needs. There's an easy way to avoid this trap that we'll see in just a moment.

This cardinal rule in using OnIdle() is to call the base class version of OnIdle() from the overridden version. The following OnIdle() override demonstrates the proper technique. The base class's OnIdle() function is called first, and after the call returns, the application performs its own idle processing.

```
BOOL CMyApp::OnIdle( LONG lCount )
{
  CwinApp::OnIdle( lCount );
  DoIdleWork(); // Do idle processing
  return( TRUE );
}
```

An even better approach is to accord higher priority to the framework's OnIdle() handler by delaying the start of your own idle processing until lCount reaches a value of 2 or higher, as follows:

```
BOOL CMyApp::OnIdle( LONG lCount )
{
  CwinApp::OnIdle( lCount );
  if( lCount > 2 )
    DoIdleWork(); // Do idle processing
  return( TRUE );
}
```

The framework does its processing when lCount is 0 and 1. You can find out exactly what's done and when by looking at the source code for CWinThread::OnIdle() in Thrdcore.cpp and CWinApp::OnIdle in Appcore.cpp.

Because the version of OnIdle() shown in the preceding example always returns TRUE, an application will continue receiving OnIdle() calls even if both it and the framework are finished doing idle chores for the time being. The following OnIdle() override minimizes wasted clock cycles by returning FALSE when the application's own idle processing is complete:

```
BOOL CMyApp::OnIdle( LONG lCount )
{
  CwinApp::OnIdle( lCount );
  BOOL bContinue = TRUE;
  if( lCount > 2 ){
    DoIdleWork(); // Do idle processing
    BContinue = FALSE;
    }
  return( bContinue );
}
```

Because application-specific idle processing isn't started until lCount equals 2, the framework won't be deprived of the idle time it needs if the application's OnIdle() function returns FALSE.

It's important to do idle processing as quickly as possible to avoid reducing the application's responsiveness. If necessary, break up large OnIdle() tasks into smaller, more manageable pieces and process one piece at a time in successive calls to `OnIdle()`. The following `OnIdle()` function begins its work when `lCount` reaches 2 and continues responding to `OnIdle()` calls until `DoIdleWork()` returns `FALSE`, indicating that no further idle time is required:

```
BOOL CMyApp::OnIdle( LONG lCount )
{
  CwinApp::OnIdle( lCount );
  BOOL bContinue = TRUE;
  if( lCount > 2 )
    bContinue = DoIdleWork(); // Do idle processing
  return( bContinue );
}
```

The OnIdleDemo Program

The OnIdleDemo program shows you how to override and use the `OnIdle()` function. It shows numeric values for the `OnIdle lCount` value, and the elapsed time since `lCount` was reset. The OnIdleDemo program is shown in Figure 11-2.

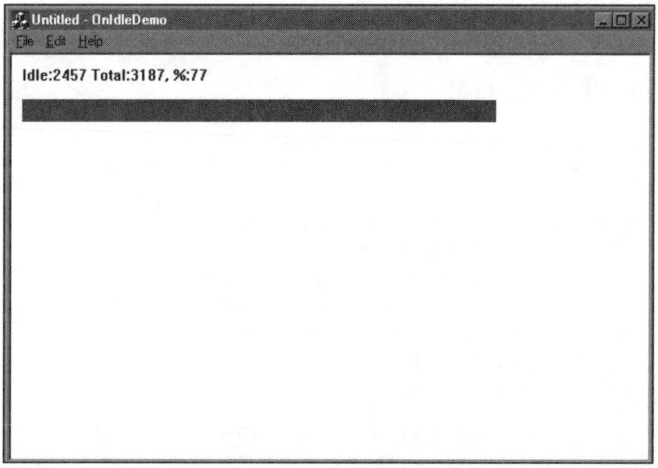

Figure 11-2: The OnIdleDemo program shows you a bargraph with the relative amount of time given to the program's OnIdle() function.

The program also draws a bar graph to give a graphical indication of the relative amount of idle processing that the application has made available to the `OnIdle()` function. If you move the mouse around or perform window operations such as resizing, the graph will decrease. That's because all the messages that Windows 98 services reduce the amount of processing time available to the `OnIdle()` function.

Demo Program

OnIdleDemo
CD-ROM Location: **Chap11\OnIdleDemo**
Program Name: **OnIdleDemo.EXE**
Source Code Modules in Text: **OnIdleDemo.cpp**

◆ ◆ ◆ ◆ ◆

Listing 11-2: **The OnIdleDemo Program**

```
// OnIdleDemo.cpp : Defines the class behaviors
// for the application.
//

///////////////////////////////////////////////////////////
// COnIdleDemoApp commands

DWORD dwTotal = 0, dwIdle = 0, dwFirst, dwLast;

BOOL COnIdleDemoApp::OnIdle(LONG lCount)
{
  CWinApp::OnIdle(lCount);

  // If dwTotal == 0, this is the first time through
  // and we need to record dwFirst.
  if( dwTotal == 0 )
    dwFirst = GetTickCount();

  // Get the current clock tick.
  DWORD dwTemp = GetTickCount();

  // Calculate dwTotal—this is the total tick count
  // since the first time into OnIdle(). We add one
  // because the very first time through, dwTotal
  // will be 0 and cause a divide by zero error. This
  // extra '1' won't affect the percentage significantly
  // since the values get so large.
  dwTotal = dwTemp - dwFirst + 1;

  // If lCount != 0, then we haven't had a skip in the
  // OnIdle processing. That means we need to add to
  // dwIdle the elapsed time since we came through last
  // time. If lCount == 0 that means the application
  // processed some messages and didn't come through
  // OnIdle(). For this reason, we don't add the elapsed
  // time in this case since it was chewed up while
  // processing messages.
  if( lCount != 0 )
    dwIdle += ( dwTemp - dwLast );
```

```
// Record the current time in dwLast since all of
// our calculations have been made.
dwLast = dwTemp;

// We need a DC so we'll get the CMainFrame class and
// then the COnIdleDemoView class. From this, we
// create a CClientDC object for painting.
CMainFrame *pFrame =
  (CMainFrame *) AfxGetMainWnd();
COnIdleDemoView *pView =
  (COnIdleDemoView *) pFrame->GetActiveView();
CClientDC ClientDC( pView );

// Calculate the percentage and store in a local
// variable since we need the value twice.
int nPercent = dwIdle * 100 / dwTotal;

// Format a CString object, and draw it to the window.
CString strInfo;
strInfo.Format( "Idle:%ld Total:%ld, %%:%d       ",
  dwIdle, dwTotal, nPercent );
ClientDC.TextOut( 10, 10, strInfo );

// Get the client RECT for the view window DC.
// We'll scale the bar graph to fit nicely in the
// window, regardless of its size.
RECT Rect;
pView->GetClientRect( &Rect );

// Indent the bar graph from the left, top, bottom
// so it doesn't go to the edge of the window and
// it's below the text we just drew. Calculate the
// length of the bar based on the percentage of
// OnIdle time we've gotten.
Rect.left += 10;
Rect.top += 40;
int nRight = Rect.right - 10;
Rect.bottom = Rect.top + 20;
int nWidth = nRight - Rect.left;
nWidth = nWidth * nPercent / 100;
Rect.right = Rect.left + nWidth;

// Draw the blue rectangle to indicate
// the relative amount of OnIdle time
// we've gotten.
CBrush BlueBrush( RGB( 0, 0, 255 ) );
ClientDC.FillRect( &Rect, &BlueBrush );

// Draw a white rectangle to the right
// of the blue bar so that any blue
// from an old value will be erased.
```

(continued)

Listing 11-2 *(continued)*

```
    Rect.left = Rect.right;
    Rect.right = nRight;
    CBrush WhiteBrush( RGB( 255, 255, 255 ) );
    ClientDC.FillRect( &Rect, &WhiteBrush );

    return( TRUE );
}
```

Summary

This chapter shows you how to use two very powerful techniques — timer setting and idle processing. Both allow applications to perform tasks without requiring a user action. I end up implementing at least one of these techniques in almost every program I write.

✦ ✦ ✦

PART

II

Application Architecture

The Microsoft Foundation Classes promote an application architecture commonly referred to as *document/view* architecture. It provides a practical way to organize applications.

Documents and data are separated into a document class that is engineered to make storage and retrieval easy. The many support functions built into MFC assist in this process.

The visual representation of data within applications is handled by a View class, engineered to make display easy. A special window update function is provided as standard startup code so developers can easily draw to the screen.

This section on application architecture shows you how to take advantage of Microsoft's application architecture scheme.

✦ ✦ ✦ ✦

In This Part

Chapter 12
Documents, Views, and SDI

Chapter 13
Splitter Windows

Chapter 14
MDI

Chapter 15
Printing and Print Preview

✦ ✦ ✦ ✦

CHAPTER 12

Documents, Views, and SDI

✦ ✦ ✦ ✦

In This Chapter

Understanding document and view classes

Creating a document/view application with AppWizard

Writing custom document and view classes

Loading and saving document data

Editing and displaying document data

Writing classes for persistent objects

✦ ✦ ✦ ✦

Documents are the focus of an operating system like Windows 98. That is, the user is encouraged to think about the document (s)he wants to create or edit, rather than the application needed to edit the document. Of course, most full-featured Windows 98 applications enable you to create and edit some sort of document. This document might be a letter, a spreadsheet, a drawing, or any number of other types of data. A couple of things all these document-oriented applications have in common is a way to store and load a document and a way to view and edit a document. When Microsoft created MFC, they took these ideas of documents and views and created classes that encapsulate the functionality needed to handle documents and views of those documents more easily. In this chapter, you see how MFC's document/view architecture works.

Implementing Document/View Architecture

MFC provides a way — through the document/view architecture — for an application to separate the way data is stored from how it's viewed. Specifically, the application's *document class* serves two purposes: holding the data for the currently open document and *serializing* (saving and loading) the data to and from a disk file. The *view class* has two purposes of its own: displaying the data and enabling the user to edit the data in whatever way is appropriate for the application.

Note

A single instance of a view class can display and enable editing for only a single document. A document object, however, can be associated with any number of views. For example, suppose a document object holds the contents of an area of memory. This document object could be associated with several views that display the memory area in different ways. One view might display the memory area as binary values, another as hexadecimal values, and still another as string data. Each of these different view objects would enable the user to edit the memory area in ways appropriate to the type of display.

◆ ◆ ◆ ◆ ◆

MFC features the `CDocument` and `CView` classes, from which you can create your own customized document and view classes. Although `CDocument` is not related to MFC's extensive set of window classes, `CView` derives directly from `CWnd` and so inherits all the capabilities of an MFC window. MFC also defines a set of special-purpose view classes, including `CEditView`, `CListView`, `CRichEditView`, `CTreeView`, and `CScrollView`, that add special capabilities to the generic `CView` class. The important thing to remember, however, is that your application's view object is a window, albeit a window without a frame, title bar, toolbar, status bar, or other visual component.

The easiest way to implement document/view architecture in an application is to create the application with AppWizard. The source code that AppWizard generates contains all the nuts and bolts required to implement functional document and view classes. You only need to add the source code to handle the specific type of data for your application.

Nutshell

Implementing the Document/View Architecture

To implement the document/view architecture, you must complete the following steps:

1. Use AppWizard to create a skeleton application.
2. In the document class, declare the data objects needed to hold the document's data.
3. Complete the document class's `OnNewDocument()` function to initialize a new document.
4. Override the `DeleteContents()` function in the document class to delete data from the previous document.
5. Complete the document class's `Serialize()` function to save and load document data.
6. Complete the view class's `OnDraw()` function to display the contents of the current document.
7. In the view class, add the code needed to enable the user to edit the document's data.

◆ ◆ ◆ ◆ ◆

Demo Program

RectApp
CD-ROM Location: **Chap12\RectApp**
Program Name: **RectApp.EXE**
Source Code Modules in Text: **None**

◆ ◆ ◆ ◆ ◆

In the **Chap12\RectApp** directory of this book's CD-ROM, you will find the source code and executable file for the RectApp application, a program that uses the document/view architecture to enable the user to save, load, and edit an array of rectangle objects. When you run the application, you see the window shown in Figure 12-1. As you can see, at startup, a RectApp document already contains a single object: a default rectangle.

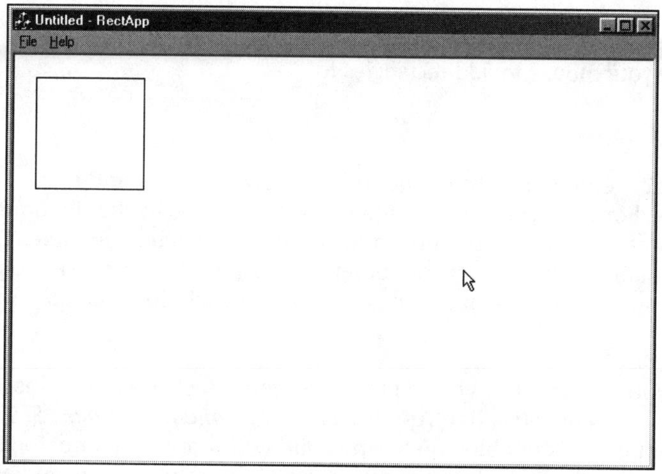

Figure 12-1: The RectApp application when first run

To edit a RectApp document, click in the window with your mouse. A rectangle appears at each point you click, as shown in Figure 12-2. You can add as many rectangles as you like. The program adds each rectangle to the document's internal storage. The view class can access this storage to display the document or to add new rectangles to the document.

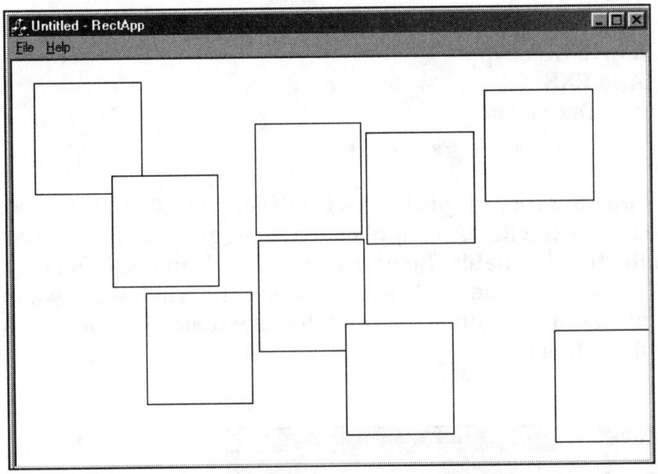

Figure 12-2: You use your mouse to add rectangles to RectApp's document.

The File menu contains commands that enable you to create, save, and load RectApp documents. For example, after adding a few rectangles to the document, select the Save command and save the file under whatever filename you like. Then, select the New command to start a new document. Finally, select Open to reload your saved document. The document should display in the window just as it was when you saved it.

Note

Notice that before you can use it to view a new document, RectApp must close the current document. This is because RectApp is a *single-document interface (SDI)* application. Applications that enable you to open and edit more than one document simultaneously are called *multiple-document interface (MDI)* applications and are covered in Chapter 14.

◆ ◆ ◆ ◆ ◆

The previous seven steps were used to create the RectApp application. Examining each step in detail shows how RectApp was built.

Step 1: Create a skeleton application

Earlier in this book, you learned how to create an application with AppWizard (if you need a refresher course, please refer to that chapter). To create the RectApp application, start a new project workspace called **RectApp**. Then use the following settings in AppWizard's six wizard pages to finish the skeleton application:

Step 1 page Select the single document interface, and be sure that Document/View Architecture Support is selected.

Step 2 page Accept all default settings.

Step 3 page Accept all default settings.

Step 4 page Shut off all features except 3D controls.

Step 5 page Select the statically linked library.

Step 6 page Accept all default settings.

When you click the Finish button on the Step 6 wizard page, the New Project Information dialog box appears, as shown in Figure 12-3.

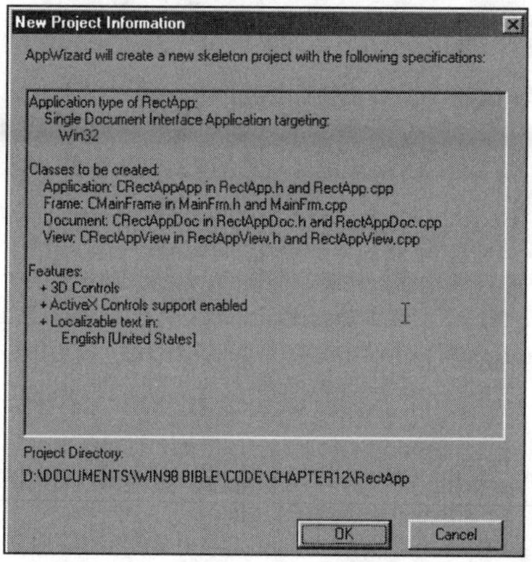

Figure 12-3: After you choose settings in the six wizard pages for the RectApp application, AppWizard displays the New Project Information dialog box.

Step 2: Declare the document's data objects

Now that you have the basic project created, the next step is to declare member variables for the application's data. Because the RectApp application's data consists of an array of rectangle coordinates — each coordinate stored in a `CPoint` object — the MFC `CPtrArray` class is the perfect data type for this purpose. Add a data member called `m_rectArray` to the `CRectAppDoc` document class, as follows:

1. Right-click the `CRectAppDoc` class in the project workspace window. Select the Add Member Variable command from the menu that appears, as shown in Figure 12-4.

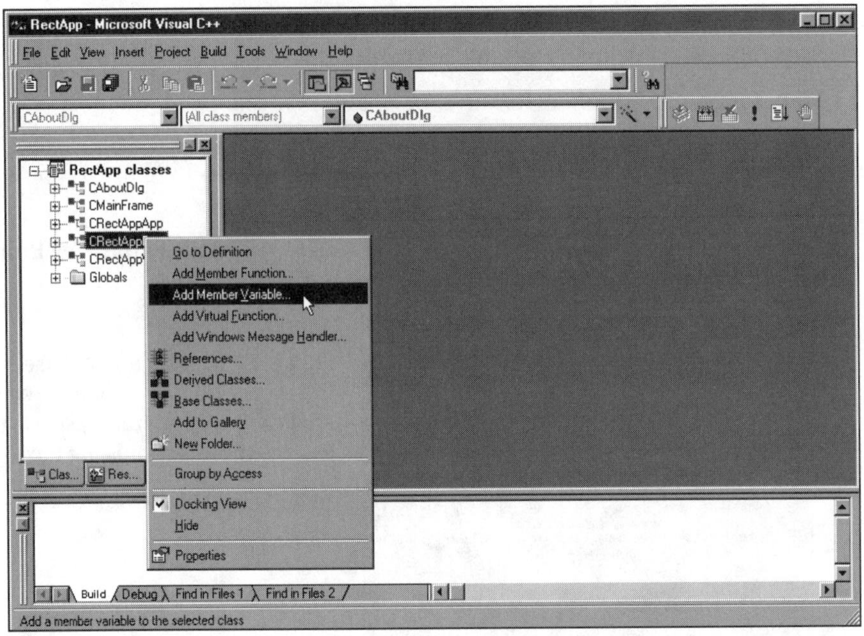

Figure 12-4: You can add member variables from this pop-up menu.

2. In the Add Member Variable dialog box, type **CPtrArray** into the Variable Type box, type **m_rectArray** into the Variable Name box, and select the Public access option (see Figure 12-5).

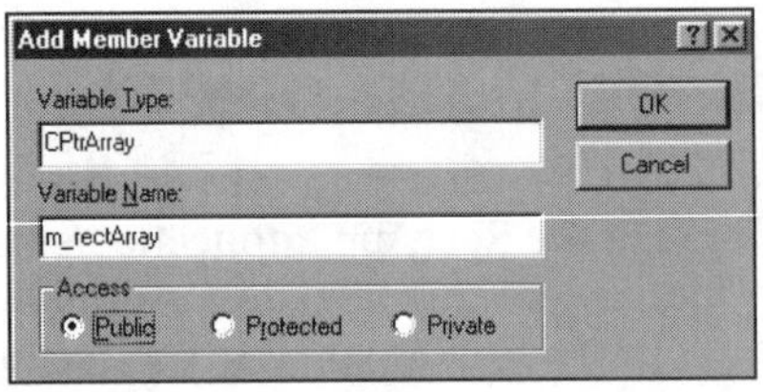

Figure 12-5: The document class's new data member.

3. Click OK to add the new member variable to the document class.

Step 3: Complete the OnNewDocument() function

All document-oriented applications need a way to generate a new document. Whenever the user creates a new document in an MFC application using the document/view architecture, MFC calls the document class's `OnNewDocument()` function, which gives the application a chance to initialize the new document. In the case of the RectApp application, OnNewDocument() adds a single default rectangle to the rectangle array. Every RectApp document has this default rectangle, which the application displays at the top left of the window.

You can see RectApp's completed OnNewDocument() function in Listing 12-1. If you're building the application, you need to add the two lines that appear right before the return statement in the listing; the rest of the lines were created by AppWizard. The first of the two new lines creates a CPoint object to hold the coordinate of the default rectangle; the second adds the CPoint object to the rectangle array.

Listing 12-1: The OnNewDocument() function

```
BOOL CRectAppDoc::OnNewDocument()
{
  if (!CDocument::OnNewDocument())
    return FALSE;

  // TODO: add reinitialization code here
  // (SDI documents will reuse this document)

  CPoint* point = new CPoint(20, 20);
  m_rectArray.Add(point);

  return TRUE;
}
```

Step 4: Override the DeleteContents() function

Just as a document-oriented application needs a way to create new documents, it also needs a way to close an existing document, deleting the existing document's data from memory as it closes. In an MFC application with documents and views, when the user creates a new application document (either explicitly or just by starting the application), MFC calls DeleteContents() so the application can delete any data objects that remain from the previous document. This gives the new document a fresh start. Because MFC calls DeleteContents() when the application first runs, you must be sure to check for empty documents to avoid crashing the program when there is no previous document. (You don't, after all, want to try to access objects before they're created.)

You can override DeleteContents() using ClassWizard, as shown in Figure 12-6. Listing 12-2 shows RectApp's completed DeleteContents() function. If you're building the RectApp application, you need to add all the lines between the comments and the call to CDocument's DeleteContents().

In this version of `DeleteContents()`, the program first checks the size of the rectangle array. If `GetSize()` returns 0, the program skips over the entire `if` statement and so doesn't try to delete data objects that don't yet exist. If the array's size is greater than 0, the `for` loop steps through the array, deleting each `CPoint` object whose pointers are stored in the array. Finally, the call to the array class's `RemoveAll()` function removes all pointers from the array, leaving its size at 0.

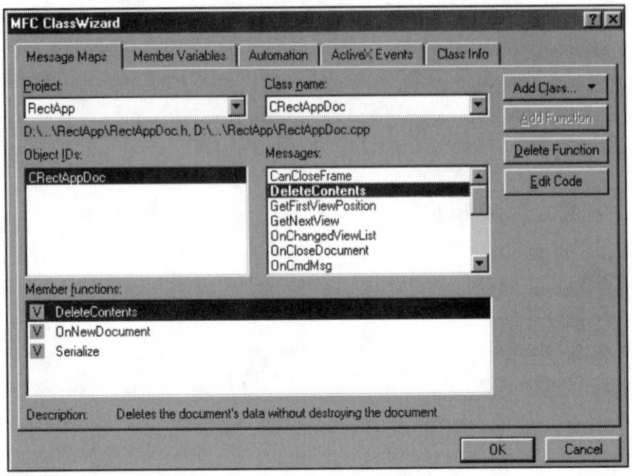

Figure 12-6: You can override DeleteContents() with ClassWizard.

Class Wizard

Overriding a Document Class's DeleteContents() Function

Message: None
Function Created: `DeleteContents()`
Source Code Module: **RectAppDoc.cpp**

◆ ◆ ◆ ◆ ◆

Listing 12-2: **The DeleteContents() function**

```
void CRectAppDoc::DeleteContents()
{
  // TODO: Add your specialized code here
  //   and/or call the base class

  int size = m_rectArray.GetSize();

  if (size > 0)
  {
    for (int x=0; x<size; ++x)
    {
      CPoint* point =
```

```
            (CPoint*)m_rectArray.GetAt(x);
          delete point;
        }
        m_rectArray.RemoveAll();
      }

      CDocument::DeleteContents();
    }
```

Step 5: Complete the Serialize() function

When the user creates a new document or edits an existing one, (s)he needs a way to save the changes to disk. This is where the document class's `Serialize()` function comes into play. `Serialize()`'s single parameter is a `CArchive` object that can serialize (save and load) many types of data. To serialize data to the archive, use the << operator. To serialize data from the archive, use the > operator. MFC defines both of these operators in the `CArchive` class so you can easily save and load many types of data.

Unfortunately, a `CPtrArray` object is not one of the data types supported by the `CArchive` class. (Anyway, saving a bunch of pointers wouldn't help the program much; if you tried to reload pointers, they'd all be invalid.) So, to save or load the rectangles contained in the `m_rectArray` data member, the program extracts the coordinate points from the array before serializing them. Listing 12-3 shows the completed `Serialize()` function.

Note

In the `Serialize()` function, notice the call to `UpdateAllViews()` after loading a document. This call ensures that the document's view is updated to display the newly loaded data.

✦ ✦ ✦ ✦ ✦

Listing 12-3: The Serialize() function

```
void CRectAppDoc::Serialize(CArchive& ar)
{
  int size;

  if (ar.IsStoring())
  {
    // TODO: add storing code here

    size = m_rectArray.GetSize();
    ar << size;
    for (int x=0; x<size; ++x)
    {
      CPoint* point =
```

(continued)

Listing 12-3 *(continued)*

```
            (CPoint*)m_rectArray.GetAt(x);
          ar << point->x;
          ar << point->y;
        }
    }
    else
    {
      // TODO: add loading code here

      int x, y;

      ar > size;
      for (int z=0; z<size; ++z)
      {
        ar > x;
        ar > y;
        CPoint* point = new CPoint(x, y);
        m_rectArray.Add(point);
      }

      UpdateAllViews(NULL);
    }
}
```

Step 6: Complete the OnDraw() function

A document wouldn't be much use if an application had no way to display the document on the screen. In an MFC application's view class, the `OnDraw()` function is charged with displaying the current document in the application's window. How you display this data in your own applications is, of course, completely dependent upon the data and how you think it's best displayed. Listing 12-4 shows the `CRectAppView` class's completed `OnDraw()` function. You can see that `OnDraw()` simply iterates through the points stored in the `m_rectArray` array, drawing a rectangle at each stored coordinate.

Listing 12-4: The OnDraw() function

```
void CRectAppView::OnDraw(CDC* pDC)
{
  CRectAppDoc* pDoc = GetDocument();
  ASSERT_VALID(pDoc);
```

```
    // TODO: add draw code for native data here

    int size = pDoc->m_rectArray.GetSize();
    for (int z=0; z<size; ++z)
    {
      CPoint* point =
        (CPoint*)pDoc->m_rectArray.GetAt(z);
      pDC->Rectangle(point->x, point->y,
        point->x + 100, point->y + 100);
    }
}
```

Step 7: Add editing code

Getting a document displayed in the application's window is only half the battle. Now you need to provide editing functions so the user can modify the document as she sees fit. In the RectApp application, the user can edit the document by clicking in the window to add rectangles to the display, as well as add the rectangles to the document class's internal rectangle array. In an MFC application, you enable the program to respond to mouse clicks by adding the `OnLButtonDown()` function to the program, which you can do with ClassWizard, as shown in Figure 12-7.

Listing 12-5 shows the application's completed `OnLButtonDown()` function, where the program creates a new `CPoint` object from the user's mouse click and adds the new point to the rectangle array. The call to `GetDocument()` obtains a pointer to the document that's associated with the view. The call to the document class's `SetModifiedFlag()` function tells the document that its data needs to be saved. If the user should try to exit the application without saving the data, the program will warn the user of his oversight. The call to `Invalidate()` forces the program to redraw its display, so the newly added rectangle appears in the window.

Class Wizard

Responding to Mouse Button Clicks

Message: `WM_LBUTTONDOWN`
Function Created: `OnLButtonDown()`
Source Code Module: **RectAppView.cpp**

✦ ✦ ✦ ✦ ✦

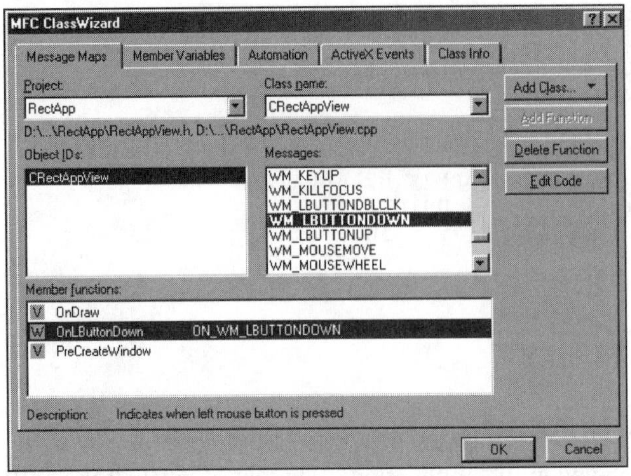

Figure 12-7: You can use ClassWizard to add the OnLButtonDown() function to the application's view class.

Listing 12-5: **The editing function**

```
void CRectAppView::OnLButtonDown(UINT nFlags,
  CPoint point)
{
  // TODO: Add your message handler code here
  //   and/or call default

  CPoint* rectPoint = new CPoint(point.x, point.y);
  GetDocument()->m_rectArray.Add(rectPoint);
  GetDocument()->SetModifiedFlag();
  Invalidate();

  CView::OnLButtonDown(nFlags, point);
}
```

Now you've had a close look at the steps needed to implement MFC's document/view architecture in your own applications. However, often there are more elegant solutions to a problem than the brute-force methods described in a basic program like RectApp. For example, a more elegant way to serialize data in a document class is to create serializable classes for the data objects. Such data objects are called *persistent objects*, and are covered in the following section.

Documents, Views, and OOP

Traditionally, MFC document classes expose their data as `public` member variables. Storing data in `public` member variables makes it easy for the view class to gain access to the data. All the view class needs is a pointer to the document object, and it can do whatever it likes with the document data. For some people, though, this type of access to a class's data members is tantamount to sacrilege. Why? Because strict OOP programming rules dictate that a class's data members never be `public`. They should always be declared at least `protected`.

If making your document class's storage `public` runs a shiver of dread up your spine, you can follow OOP programming rules and still use MFC's document/view architecture. Just as with any class, you need only supply your document class with public functions that return or modify the class's `protected` data members. Another solution might be to declare your application's view class as a `friend` of the document class. Then, the view class will have direct access to the document class's `protected` data members, but other classes will be kept out.

If you're not a stickler for rules, however, you'll probably want to go with `public` data members in your document classes. Most programmers, including Microsoft's, work this way. In fact, I can't remember the last time I saw a document class written with anything but `public` data members. Keep in mind, though, that this rule-breaking applies only to the document data members that store the document's data. Any data members that the document class uses only internally should still be declared `protected` or `private`.

Persistent Objects

The term *persistent object* may sound high-tech, but it's really a simple concept: an object that can *serialize* (save or load) its state and contents. To save or load the object's contents to and from a file, you need only call the object's `Serialize()` function with a reference to a `CArchive` object. Many MFC classes are already persistent. For example, the collection classes like `CByteArray`, `CWordArray`, and `CStringArray` all implement MFC's serialization abilities. MFC classes, however, aren't the only classes that can be serialized. Any class that you create can be made persistent.

Making a Class Persistent

You can make any class persistent simply by following a few easy steps:

1. Derive your new class from MFC's `CObject` class.
2. Include the `DECLARE_SERIAL` macro in the class's declaration.
3. Provide a default constructor for the class.
4. Provide a `Serialize()` function in the class.
5. Include the `IMPLEMENT_SERIAL` macro in the class's definition.

◆ ◆ ◆ ◆ ◆

Demo Program

RectApp2
CD-ROM Location: **Chap12\RectApp2**
Program Name: **RectApp2.EXE**
Source Code Modules in Text: **Rectangles.h and Rectangles.cpp**

◆ ◆ ◆ ◆ ◆

In the **Chap12\RectApp2** directory of this book's CD-ROM is a new version of RectApp, which you developed earlier in this chapter. The new version uses a persistent class to store the document's rectangles. From the user's point of view, this new version of RectApp works just like the old one; the differences are all internal.

Listing 12-6 shows the header file for the class that the program uses to store its document data.

Listing 12-6: **The header file for the CRectangles class**

```
///////////////////////////////////////////////////
// Rectangles.h
///////////////////////////////////////////////////

class CRectangles : public CObject
{
  DECLARE_SERIAL(CRectangles)
  CRectangles();

protected:
  CPtrArray m_rectArray;

public:
  void Add(CPoint point);
  int GetCount();
  void Get(int rectNum, CPoint* point);
  void DeleteAll();
  void Serialize(CArchive& ar);
};
```

The header listing shows that the `CRectangles` class has the MFC `CObject` as its immediate base class. That is, `CRectangles` is derived from `CObject`. The class declaration also includes the `DECLARE_SERIAL` macro. (The macro's single argument is the name of the class you're declaring as serializable.) The new class also provides a default constructor. The constructor is defined in the class's implementation file.

The `CRectangles` class has a single data member, which is an object of the `CPtrArray` class. You used the `CPtrArray` class in the original version of the CircleApp application to store the rectangles that make up a RectApp document.

The CRectangles class uses the CPtrArray object, m_rectArray, in exactly the same way. Now, however, the details of handling m_rectArray are hidden from the main program, which accesses the array only through the public member functions provided by CRectangles. The public member functions, along with their descriptions, are listed in Table 12-1.

Table 12-1
Public Member Functions

Function	*Description*
Add()	Adds a rectangle to the circle array
DeleteAll()	Deletes all rectangles from the circle array
Get()	Gets the data for a given circle
GetCount()	Returns the current number of rectangles in the circle array
Serialize()	Performs object serialization for the class

The header file declares the class's Serialize() function. The class also has to define the Serialize() function, which it does in its implementation file, shown in Listing 12-7. The first thing to notice here is the IMPLEMENT_SERIAL macro. The macro's three arguments are the name of the class you're declaring as serializable, the name of the immediate base class, and a schema, or version number.

Listing 12-7: The implementation file for the CRectangles class

```
///////////////////////////////////////////////////
// Rectangles.cpp
///////////////////////////////////////////////////

#include "stdafx.h"
#include "CRectangles.h"

IMPLEMENT_SERIAL(CRectangles, CObject, 1)
CRectangles::CRectangles()
{
}

void CRectangles::Add(CPoint point)
{
  CPoint* rectPoint = new CPoint(point.x, point.y);
  m_rectArray.Add(rectPoint);
}
```

(continued)

Listing 12-7 *(continued)*

```
int CRectangles::GetCount()
{
  return m_rectArray.GetSize();
}

void CRectangles::Get(int circleNum, CPoint* point)
{
  CPoint* rectPoint =
    (CPoint*)m_rectArray.GetAt(circleNum);
  point->x = rectPoint->x;
  point->y = rectPoint->y;
}

void CRectangles::DeleteAll()
{
  int size = GetCount();
  for (int x=0; x<size; ++x)
  {
    CPoint* point =
      (CPoint*)m_rectArray.GetAt(x);
    delete point;
  }
  m_rectArray.RemoveAll();
}

void CRectangles::Serialize(CArchive& ar)
{
  CObject::Serialize(ar);

  if (ar.IsStoring())
  {
    CPoint point;
    int size = GetCount();
    ar << size;

    for (int x=0; x<size; ++x)
    {
      Get(x, &point);
      ar << point.x;
      ar << point.y;
    }
  }
  else
  {
    int size;
    ar > size;

    for (int x=0; x<size; ++x)
    {
      CPoint point;
      ar > point.x;
```

```
        ar > point.y;
        Add(point);
      }

    }
  }
```

When it comes to file handling, the `Serialize()` function is the heart of the class, the function that makes `CRectangles` persistent. The `Serialize()` function, which transfers the object's data (or state) to and from a file, looks quite a bit like the `Serialize()` function you wrote for the document class in the original version of RectApp. Listing 12-8 shows the original document class's `Serialize()` function. Compare it with the `Serialize()` function in Listing 12-7. The main difference is that `CRectangles`'s `Serialize()` function calls the class's own member functions where appropriate, rather than always calling `CPtrArray` member functions.

Listing 12-8: The original document class's Serialize() function

```
void CRectAppDoc::Serialize(CArchive& ar)
{
  int size;

  if (ar.IsStoring())
  {
    // TODO: add storing code here

    size = m_rectArray.GetSize();
    ar << size;
    for (int x=0; x<size; ++x)
    {
      CPoint* point = (CPoint*)m_rectArray.GetAt(x);
      ar << point->x;
      ar << point->y;
    }
  }
  else
  {
    // TODO: add loading code here

    int x, y;

    ar > size;
    for (int z=0; z<size; ++z)
    {
      ar > x;
```

(continued)

Listing 12-8 *(continued)*

```
            ar > y;
            CPoint* point = new CPoint(x, y);
            m_rectArray.Add(point);
        }

        UpdateAllViews(NULL);
    }
}
```

You may now wonder how making `CRectangles` a persistent class changes the way that the document class serializes a RectApp document. Listing 12-9 shows the document class's new `Serialize()` function. As you can see, all the function does is call `m_rects.Serialize()` (`m_rects` is a `CRectangles` object). The `m_rects` object then handles the serialization, whether the application is loading or saving the object. In the case of loading a document, `CRectAppDoc::Serialize()` must also call `UpdateAllViews()` to ensure that the view window gets updated with the newly loaded document.

Listing 12-9: The document class's new Serialize() function

```
void CRectAppDoc::Serialize(CArchive& ar)
{
  m_rects.Serialize(ar);

  if (ar.IsStoring())
  {
    // TODO: add storing code here

  }
  else
  {
    // TODO: add loading code here

    UpdateAllViews(NULL);
  }
}
```

Several other changes were made to the original RectApp application to create RectApp2. For example, Listing 12-10 shows how the new view class's `OnLButtonDown()` adds a rectangle to the document by calling a `CRectangles` member function rather than a `CPtrArray` member function. Ditto for `OnDraw()`, which displays the rectangles in the view window.

Listing 12-10: The new OnLButtonDown() function

```
void CRectAppView::OnLButtonDown(UINT nFlags, CPoint point)
{
  // TODO: Add your message handler code here
  //   and/or call default

  CPoint rectPoint(point.x, point.y);
  GetDocument()->m_rects.Add(rectPoint);
  Invalidate();

  CView::OnLButtonDown(nFlags, point);
}
```

Listing 12-11 shows the new `OnDraw()` function. There are a few other modifications to RectApp's document and view classes to accommodate the change from the `CPtrArray` data storage to the persistent `CRectangles` object. If you want to examine those changes, you can find the complete source code in the **Chap12\RectApp2** directory of this book's CD-ROM.

Listing 12-11: The new OnDraw() function

```
void CRectAppView::OnDraw(CDC* pDC)
{
  CRectAppDoc* pDoc = GetDocument();
  ASSERT_VALID(pDoc);

  // TODO: add draw code for native data here

  int size = pDoc->m_rects.GetCount();
  for (int z=0; z<size; ++z)
  {
    CPoint point;
    pDoc->m_rects.Get(z, point);
    pDC->Rectangle(point.x, point.y,
      point.x + 100, point.y + 100);
  }
}
```

Saving Persistent and Nonpersistent Objects

The best way to demonstrate a concept in a programming book is to use simple examples. Unfortunately, sometimes simple examples don't represent solutions to real-world programming problems. For example, a real paint application would have much more complex data to serialize than the rectangle sample program in this chapter. Some of this data may be stored in persistent classes, whereas other document data may be stored in nonpersistent data objects.

The good news is that a document's `Serialize()` function doesn't force you into an either/or situation. If you need to save both persistent objects and nonpersistent objects, write a `Serialize()` function like that shown in Listing 12-12. In this listing, the function first serializes persistent objects and then, in the `if` statement, saves or loads nonpersistent objects.

Note

If you try this combined approach to serialization, be sure that you save the data objects in the same order that you load them. This is true, of course, for any type of file handling. There's nothing magical about serialization.

◆ ◆ ◆ ◆ ◆

Listing 12-12: A Serialize() function that serializes both persistent and nonpersistent data objects

```
void CRectAppDoc::Serialize(CArchive& ar)
{
  m_rects.Serialize(ar);

  if (ar.IsStoring())
  {
    // TODO: add storing code here

    ar << msg;
  }
  else
  {
    // TODO: add loading code here

    ar > msg;
    UpdateAllViews(NULL);
  }
}
```

Summary

In this chapter, you learn to manage document and view classes in your MFC programs. Along the way, you discover that an application's document class stores, loads, and saves document data, whereas the view class displays the data and enables the user to edit the data. Finally, you see how to write classes that implement their own `Serialize()` functions and how to use these classes to create persistent objects.

✦ ✦ ✦

CHAPTER 13

Splitter Windows

✦ ✦ ✦ ✦

In This Chapter

Discovering the difference between dynamic and static splitter windows

Adding splitter windows to existing programs

Creating splitter-window applications with AppWizard

Programing MDI splitter-window applications

Displaying multiple views in splitter panes

Writing custom splitter-window classes

✦ ✦ ✦ ✦

These days many applications enable the user to display different views of a document in separate panes of the main window. For example, a word processor may enable the user to display the beginning of the document in one pane while the user scrolls through the document in another pane. Another example might be an application that enables the user to view one document in different formats. A disk editor, for example, might display ASCII data in one pane and hexadecimal data in another. This type of functionality can be added to an MFC application through the use of splitter windows. In this chapter, you learn how these handy types of windows work and how to add them to new or existing MFC applications.

Introducing Splitter Windows

Splitter windows enable an application to divide its main window into multiple views, each with its own scroll bars. The view in each pane of a splitter window can show different areas of the same document, display the same document in different ways, or show completely different documents. It's all up to you, although showing different areas of the same document is the easiest type of splitter view to implement and is almost automatically handled by AppWizard-generated programs, provided you select the correct AppWizard options when you generate the program.

There are actually two types of splitter windows: dynamic and static. *Dynamic splitter windows*, which are the type directly supported by AppWizard, enable the user to decide how to split the window. By dragging a small handle down from the top of the window or from the left of the window, the user can divide the window horizontally, vertically, or both. Figure 13-1 shows a splitter window divided horizontally, Figure 13-2 shows the same window divided vertically, and Figure 13-3 shows the window divided both ways.

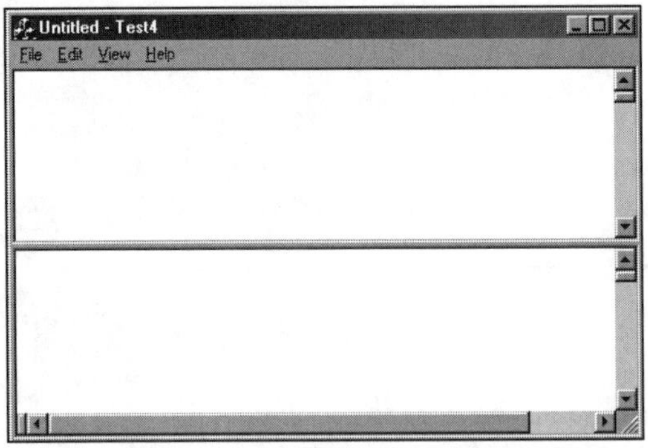

Figure 13-1: Here's a splitter window divided horizontally.

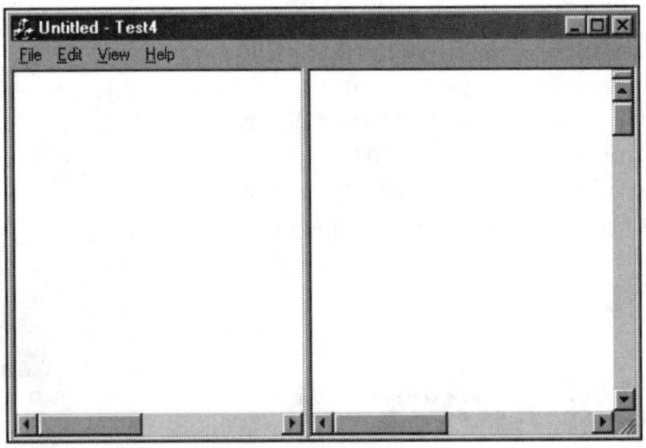

Figure 13-2: This splitter window is divided vertically.

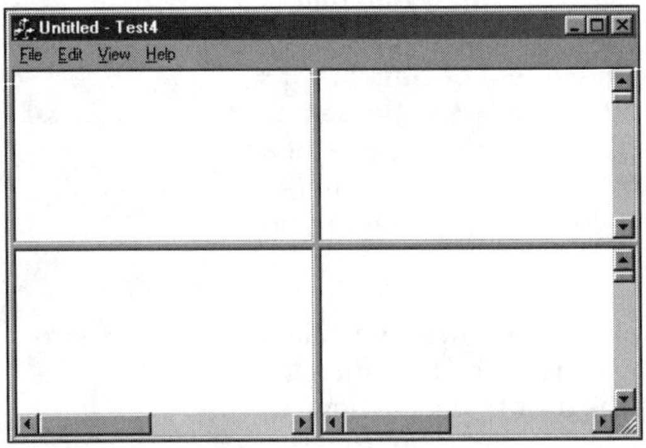

Figure 13-3: This splitter window is divided both horizontally and vertically.

Although a dynamic splitter window gives the user a powerful tool for configuring an application's display, such a window comes with a limitation. A dynamic splitter can contain no more than four panes, arranged as shown in Figure 13-3. In most cases, however, four panes are plenty.

If you want to display more than four panes, or you want to create the panes from within the application, you should use a static splitter window. Static splitter windows can display as many as 256 panes in a 16 x 16 grid. However, the panes must be created from within the application; the user cannot create panes as he can with a dynamic splitter window. The user can still change the size of the panes, though, by dragging the splitter bars with his mouse. Figure 13-4 shows a static splitter window containing 16 panes.

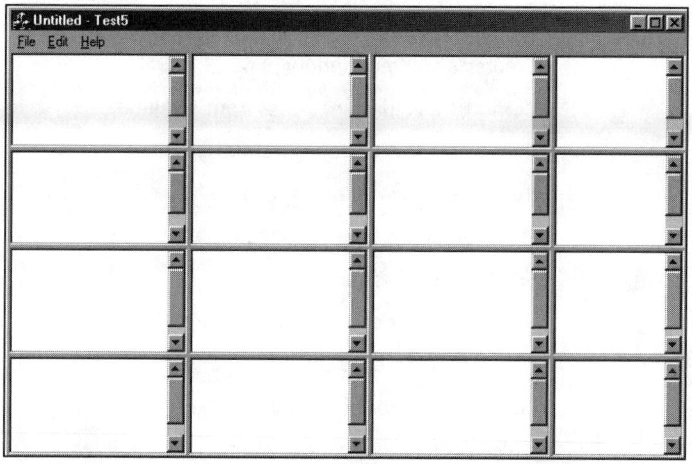

Figure 13-4: A static splitter window allows more than four panes.

You may wonder how a splitter window fits in with the architecture of your application. Normally in an MFC program the application's main window (represented by the `CMainFrame` class in an AppWizard-generated program) displays the view class's window in its client area. When you add a splitter window to the mix, however, the main frame window holds the splitter window, and the splitter window then holds the view window. This is mostly transparent to you, the programmer, because once you have the splitter window installed you can go about programming your view class just as you would without the splitter window.

MFC's CSplitterWnd Class

In MFC, splitter windows — both dynamic and static — are represented by the `CSplitterWnd` class. MFC derives `CSplitterWnd` from `CWnd`, so a splitter window doesn't inherit any of the added power that frame windows or view windows enjoy. Still, with the might of the `CWnd` class behind it, `CSplitterWnd` offers a lot of versatility. Besides the functions `CSplitterWnd` inherits from `CWnd`, the class also defines a set of its own, all of which are listed in Table 13-1.

Table 13-1
Member Functions of the CSplitterWnd Class

Function	*Description*
`ActivateNext()`	Handles the Next Pane and Previous Pane commands
`CanActivateNext()`	Determines whether the Next Pane and Previous Pane commands can be executed
`Create()`	Creates a dynamic splitter window
`CreateScrollBarCtrl()`	Creates a scroll bar
`CreateStatic()`	Creates a static splitter window
`CreateView()`	Creates a splitter-window pane
`DeleteColumn()`	Removes a column of panes from a splitter
`DeleteRow()`	Removes a row of panes from a splitter
`DeleteView()`	Removes a view from a splitter window
`DoKeyboardSplit()`	Handles the keyboard split command
`DoScroll()`	Scrolls split windows
`DoScrollBy()`	Scrolls split windows a specified amount
`GetActivePane()`	Returns a pointer to the active pane
`GetColumnCount()`	Gets the number of columns in the splitter
`GetColumnInfo()`	Gets information about a column in the splitter
`GetPane()`	Gets a pointer to a pane in a splitter
`GetRowCount()`	Gets the number of rows in the splitter
`GetRowInfo()`	Gets information about a row in a splitter
`GetScrollStyle()`	Gets the splitter's scroll bar style
`IdFromRowCol()`	Returns the child window ID of the pane at the specified row and column
`IsChildPane()`	Returns `TRUE` if the window is a splitter child pane
`OnDrawSplitter()`	Draws the splitter window
`OnInvertTracker()`	Draws a splitter with the same size and shape as the frame window
`RecalcLayout()`	Redraws the splitter window after resizing
`SetActivePane()`	Activates a pane
`SetColumnInfo()`	Sets information about a column in the splitter
`SetRowInfo()`	Sets information about a row in the splitter

Function	Description
`SetScrollStyle()`	Sets the splitter's scroll bar style
`SplitColumn()`	Creates a vertical split at the given location
`SplitRow()`	Creates a horizontal split at the given location

The DynSplitter Application

In the Chap13\DynSplitter folder of this book's CD-ROM, you can find the DynSplitter application, which demonstrates how to program dynamic splitter windows. When you run the application, you see the window shown in Figure 13-5. The application's document displays 100 lines of text, numbered 0 through 99. You can, of course, use the scroll bar to see the lines not currently visible in the window.

Demo Program

DynSplitter
CD-ROM Location: **Chap13\DynSplitter**
Program Name: **DynSplitter.exe**
Source Code Modules in Text: **None**

◆ ◆ ◆ ◆ ◆

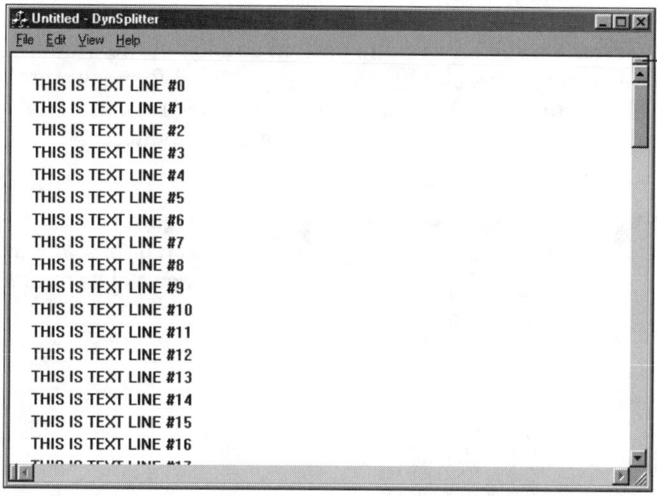

Figure 13-5: Here's the DynSplitter application when you first run it.

If you look just above the up-arrow button on the vertical scroll bar, you'll see a small bar. If you use your mouse to drag this bar downward, you'll create a horizontal splitter bar that divides the main window into two views of the document. You can scroll the contents of the panes separately, and so see different parts of the document in each pane, as shown in Figure 13-6.

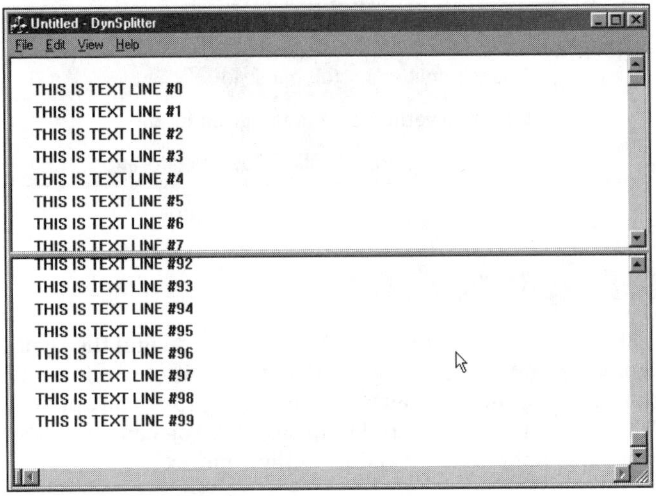

Figure 13-6: Here's DynSplitter after you create horizontal panes and scroll the lower document view.

Now look just to the left of the left-arrow button on the horizontal scroll bar. You should see a small vertical bar. If you drag this bar to the right, you can divide the window vertically, giving you four panes, all showing a view of the current document. You might think that you can now scroll each of these panes separately in order to see four different parts of the document. However, as shown in Figure 13-7, dynamic splitters only create scroll bars on the bottom and left of the window. This means two panes share each vertical and horizontal scroll bar. When you scroll the upper vertical scroll bar down, both of the panes in the top row respond. Similarly, if you scroll a horizontal scroll bar, both of the panes above it respond.

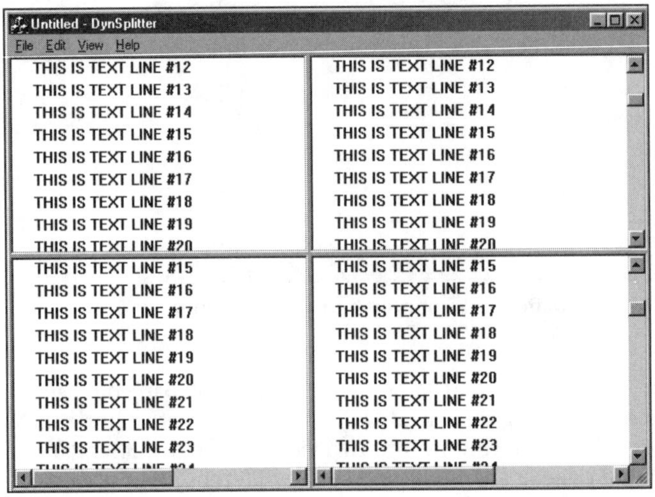

Figure 13-7: DynSplitter can display four different views of its document.

Exploring dynamic splitter windows

Now that you've had a chance to experiment with a dynamic splitter window from the user's point of view, you'll probably want to take a look under the application's hood. Dynamic splitters are so easy to create that you can easily add them to most any MFC application. All you have to do is create a `CSplitterWnd` object as a data member of the main window class and then override the main window's `OnCreateClient()` function, creating your splitter window there, as shown in Listing 13-1.

Listing 13-1: The OnCreateClient() Function

```
BOOL CMainFrame::OnCreateClient(LPCREATESTRUCT lpcs,
    CCreateContext* pContext)
{
  // TODO: Add your specialized code here and/or
  //      call the base class

  //return CFrameWnd::OnCreateClient(lpcs, pContext);

  return m_splitterWnd.Create(this, 2, 2,
    CSize(10, 10), pContext);
}
```

In Listing 13-1, the commented-out `return` line is the line originally generated by ClassWizard for `OnCreateClient()`. To add a splitter window, you call the `CSplitterWnd` object's `Create()` function, instead of calling the base class's `OnCreateClient()`. The function's five arguments are a pointer to the frame window, the maximum number of horizontal panes, the maximum number of vertical panes, the minimum size of a pane, and the `pContext` pointer (which points to information about the view) that was passed as a parameter to `OnCreateClient()`.

If you want to prohibit splitting the window horizontally or vertically, simply provide a 1 instead of a 2 for the appropriate argument in the call to `Create()`. For example, the following line creates a splitter window that doesn't allow vertical splits because it specifies a maximum of one vertical pane:

```
m_splitterWnd.Create(this, 2, 1, CSize(10, 10), pContext);
```

Dynamic splitters and AppWizard

If you know in advance that you want to use a dynamic splitter window in your application, you can build it in when you generate the skeleton application with AppWizard. You can also build in automatic scrolling functionality by inheriting your view window class from `CScrollView` rather than from `CView`. To create an AppWizard application with a splitter window and working scroll bars, follow these steps:

Nutshell

Creating a Dynamic Splitter Window

Follow these steps to create an AppWizard application with a splitter window and working scroll bars.

1. Start your AppWizard project as you normally would.
2. When you get to the MFC AppWizard - Step 4 of 6 dialog box, click the Advanced button, shown in Figure 13-8. The Advanced Options dialog box appears.

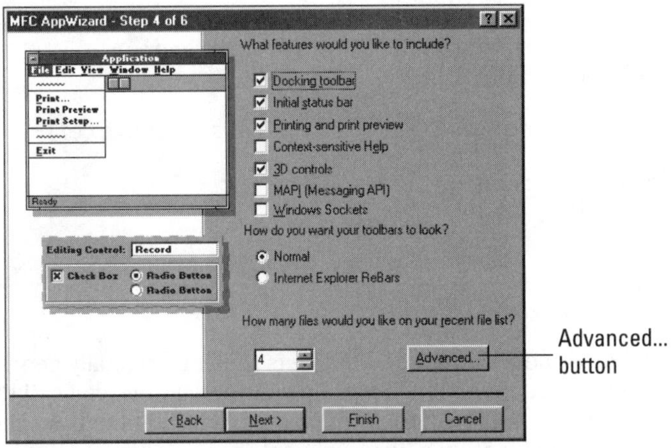

Figure 13-8: The Advanced button brings up advanced application options.

3. Click the Window Styles tab, and select the Use split window option, as shown in Figure 13-9.
4. In the MFC AppWizard - Step 6 of 6 dialog box, select the application's view class in the upper pane, and then select CScrollView in the Base Class box (Figure 13-10).
5. Click the Finish button to generate the skeleton application.

✦ ✦ ✦ ✦ ✦

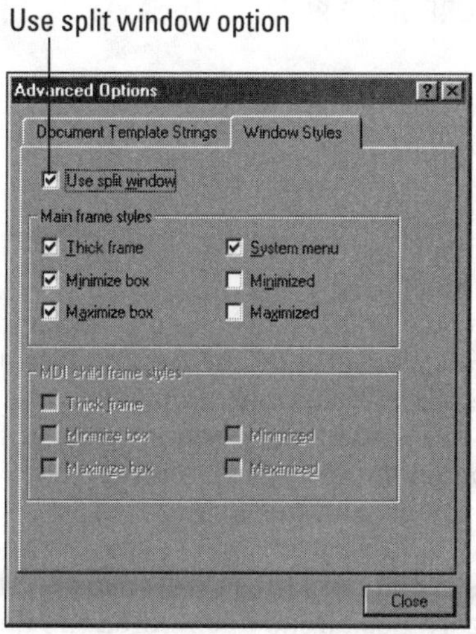

Figure 13-9: Selecting the Use Split Window option gives your application a dynamic splitter window.

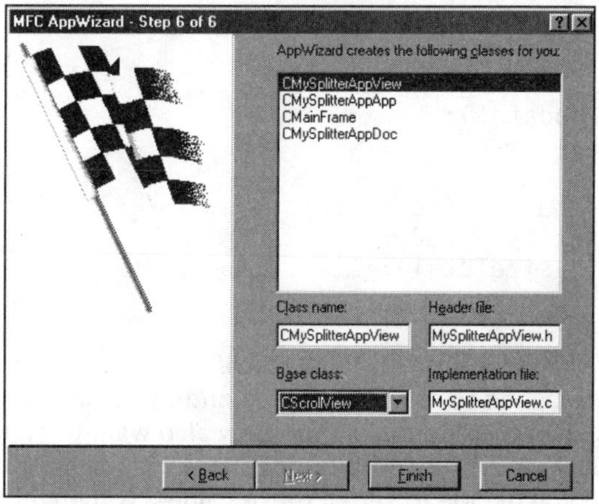

Figure 13-10: Here's the Step 6 dialog box after you select the CScrollView class.

At this point, you can compile and run your new application, which will appear with a complete splitter window. If you want to disable horizontal or vertical splits, you need to modify the frame window's `OnCreateClient()` function, which was generated by AppWizard. You can also modify the minimum pane size. The following code fragment shows the `OnCreateClient()` function that AppWizard generates. Note the `TODO` comments that indicate where to customize the function:

```
BOOL CMainFrame::OnCreateClient(LPCREATESTRUCT /*lpcs*/,
  CCreateContext* pContext)
{
  return m_wndSplitter.Create(this,
    2, 2, // TODO: adjust the number of rows, columns
    CSize(10, 10), // TODO: adjust the minimum pane size
    pContext);
}
```

When you have `OnCreateClient()` the way you want it, you can go ahead and complete your application's document and view classes, just as you would in any other MFC program. You need to know the details of the application's document before you can add the final pieces that'll get the scroll bars working, though. In this case, you need to know the size of the document, because it's up to your program to properly set the scroll bar's range, page, and line size.

The place to go to fine tune your application's scroll bars is the view class's `OnInitialUpdate()` function, where AppWizard has already generated the default source code needed to initialize the scroll bars. The following code fragment shows AppWizard's version of the `OnInitialUpdate()` function:

```
void CMySplitterAppView::OnInitialUpdate()
{
  CScrollView::OnInitialUpdate();

  CSize sizeTotal;
  // TODO: calculate the total size of this view
  sizeTotal.cx = sizeTotal.cy = 100;
  SetScrollSizes(MM_TEXT, sizeTotal);
}
```

To get your scroll bars working as appropriate for your specific application, you at least need to change the values assigned to `sizeTotal`'s `cx` and `cy` elements, which are the horizontal and vertical size of the document. You may also want to supply additional arguments to the `SetScrollSizes()` function. These arguments can specify the page and line sizes. If you decide to set all these values, you might as well comment out AppWizard's default code and supply a completely new `SetScrollSizes()` function call that looks something like this:

```
SetScrollSizes(MM_TEXT, CSize(500,2050),
  CSize(100,510), CSize(20,20));
```

Here, `SetScrollSizes()`'s arguments are the view's mapping mode, a `CSize` object representing the document's width and height, a `CSize` object representing the document's horizontal and vertical page size, and a `CSize` object representing the document's horizontal and vertical line size.

There's no one way to determine the size of a document. For example, a 640 x 480 picture would have a document width of 640 and a document height of 480.

However, what if your application's document is made up of text? In this case, you need to determine the width of a line of text. You also need to determine the height of the text by multiplying the number of lines times the character height.

The document's horizontal and vertical page sizes are the amounts the display should scroll when the user clicks in the horizontal or vertical scroll bar's track. The document's horizontal and vertical line sizes, on the other hand, are the amounts the display should scroll when the user clicks the horizontal or vertical scroll bar's arrow buttons.

The StatSplitter Application

In the `Chap13\StatSplitter` folder of this book's CD-ROM, you can find the StatSplitter application, which demonstrates how to program static splitter windows. When you run the application, you see the window shown in Figure 13-11. Just as with the DynSplitter application, the StatSplitter application's document displays 100 lines of text, numbered 0 through 99. You can't create additional columns in the window, nor can you remove existing columns. You can, however, adjust the size of any column or row.

Demo Program

StatSplitter
CD-ROM Location: **Chap13\StatSplitter**
Program Name: **StatSplitter.exe**
Source Code Modules in Text: **None**

◆ ◆ ◆ ◆ ◆

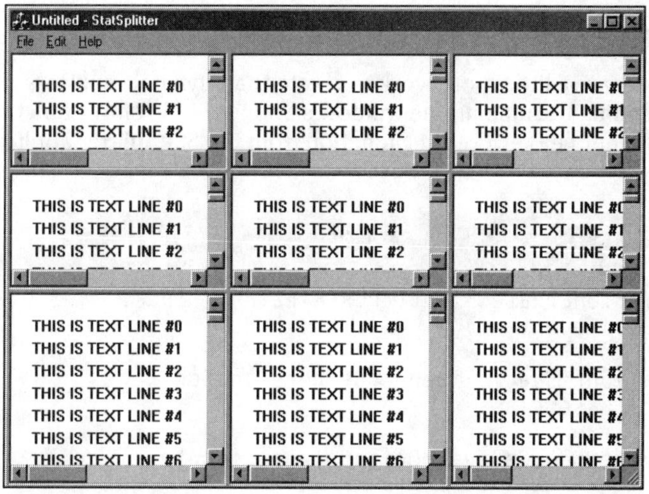

Figure 13-11: Here's the StatSplitter application when you first run it.

Try scrolling several of the panes. You'll soon discover that, unlike dynamic splitter windows, a static splitter window enables you to scroll each pane independently of the other panes. That is, a static splitter window has no shared scroll bars. Because StatSplitter's window has nine panes, you can get nine different views of the current document, as shown in Figure 13-12. In the figure, notice how each view of the document starts with a different text line.

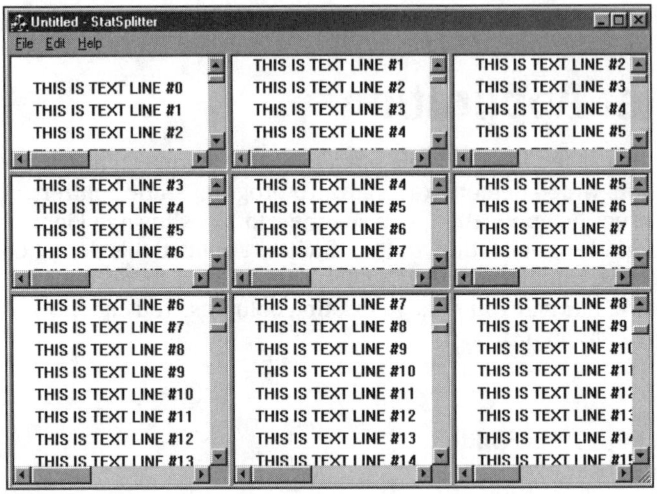

Figure 13-12: StatSplitter can display nine different document views.

Exploring static splitter windows

Static splitter windows are a little more work to create than dynamic splitters. Still, you start off by overriding the main frame window's `OnCreateClient()` function. Listing 13-2 shows the `OnCreateClient()` function from the StatSplitter application.

Listing 13-2: StatSplitter's OnCreateClient() Function

```
BOOL CMainFrame::OnCreateClient(LPCREATESTRUCT lpcs,
  CCreateContext* pContext)
{
  // TODO: Add your specialized code here and/or
  //   call the base class

  //return CFrameWnd::OnCreateClient(lpcs, pContext);

  m_splitterWnd.CreateStatic(this, 3, 3);

  for (int x=0; x<3; ++x)
    for (int y=0; y<3; ++y)
```

```
        m_splitterWnd.CreateView(x, y,
            RUNTIME_CLASS(CStatSplitterView),
            CSize(200, 100), pContext);

    return TRUE;
}
```

As you can see, the first thing you do in `OnCreateClient()` is call the splitter-window object's `CreateStatic()` function rather than the `Create()` function. This function call takes three arguments: a pointer to the main window, the number of rows, and the number of columns. With a dynamic splitter window, after calling `Create()`, you'd be all done, because the user is the one who creates the panes. With static splitters, however, your application must create the panes. It does this by calling the `CreateView()` function for each pane in the window. `CreateView()` takes five arguments, which are the pane's row, the pane's column, the run-time class of the view, the pane's size, and the `pContext` pointer passed to `OnCreateClient()`.

Note

Because the `RUNTIME_CLASS` macro requires the name of your application's view class, you need to include the header files for the document and view classes in the main window class. In the case of the StatSplitter application, you must add the lines `#include "StatSplitterDoc.h"` and `#include "StatSplitterView.h"` at the top of the MainFrm.cpp file.

✦ ✦ ✦ ✦ ✦

Static splitters and AppWizard

Unfortunately, AppWizard directly supports only dynamic splitter windows. If your application requires a static splitter window, you should create your AppWizard-generated project using the option settings you'd use for the application without the splitter window, except you'll still want to change your view's base class from `CView` to `CScrollView` to take advantage of MFC's powerful scroll bar class. After generating the skeleton source code, use ClassWizard to override the `OnCreateClient()` function and modify the function so it creates your static splitter window, as described in the previous section.

An alternative approach would be to generate your AppWizard project such that it includes the dynamic splitter window. (Select the Use Split Window option in the Step 6 of 6 dialog box's advanced options.) After AppWizard generates the source code, modify the `OnCreateClient()` function as needed to create your static splitter window. This method saves you from having to override `OnCreateClient()` and create a `CSplitterWnd` data member on your own.

Listing 13-3 shows the `OnCreateClient()` function you might end up with if you took the approach described in the previous paragraph. Notice first that the programmer has commented out the original function body generated by

AppWizard. (You could, of course, just remove the lines completely.) The programmer then added his own code to create the static splitter window. The `m_wndSplitter` data member (which is an object of the `CSplitterWnd` class) was generated by AppWizard to create the original dynamic splitter window, but by calling the object's `CreateStatic()` instead of the `Create()` function, the same object can create the static splitter window.

Listing 13-3: A Customized AppWizard-Generated OnCreateClient() Function

```
BOOL CMainFrame::OnCreateClient(LPCREATESTRUCT /*lpcs*/,
  CCreateContext* pContext)
{
  /*return m_wndSplitter.Create(this,
    2, 2,  // TODO: adjust the number of rows, columns
    CSize(10, 10),  // TODO: adjust the minimum pane size
    pContext);*/

  m_wndSplitter.CreateStatic(this, 3, 3);

  for (int x=0; x<3; ++x)
    for (int y=0; y<3; ++y)
      m_wndSplitter.CreateView(x, y,
        RUNTIME_CLASS(CTestView),
        CSize(200, 100), pContext);

  return TRUE;
}
```

Splitter Windows and MDI

You can also use splitter windows in your multiple-document interface (MDI) applications. Because MDI applications can display several child document windows simultaneously, however, the application's architecture varies from that of a single-document interface (SDI) application. As you now know, in an SDI application with a splitter window, the frame window holds the splitter window and the splitter window panes hold the document's current view. An MDI application adds a layer to this window organization. In an MDI application, the main frame window holds one or more child document windows, each of which holds a view of its current document. When you add the splitter window, each child window then holds the splitter window, whose panes hold the view of the document.

The MDISplitter Application

In the Chap13\MDISplitter folder of this book's CD-ROM, you can find the MDISplitter application, which demonstrates how to program dynamic splitter windows in an MDI application. When you run the application, you see the window shown in Figure 13-13. As with previous versions of the splitter-window sample application, the application's document displays 100 lines of text, numbered 0 through 99.

Demo Program

MDISplitter

CD-ROM Location: **Chap13\MDISplitter**

Program Name: **MDISplitter.exe**

Source Code Modules in Text: **None**

✦ ✦ ✦ ✦ ✦

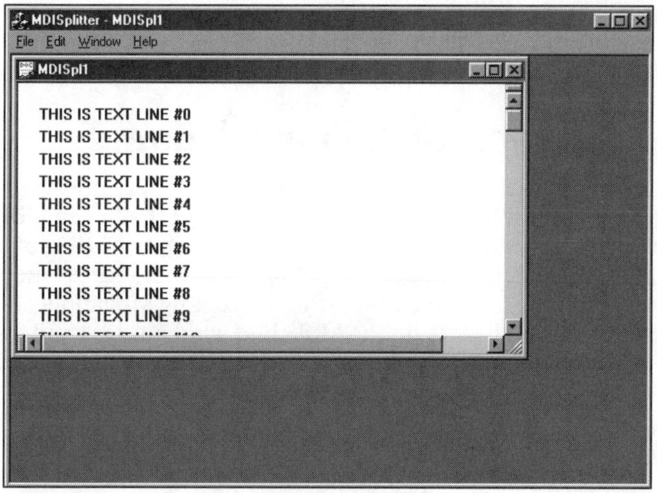

Figure 13-13: Here's the MDISplitter application when you first run it.

By selecting the File menu's New command, you can create additional child document windows, each of which contains a splitter window displaying the current document. You can split each of the document windows differently. For example, one window can have a vertical split, whereas another can have a horizontal split. Figure 13-14 shows the MDISplitter application with three child document windows, each of which is split in a different way.

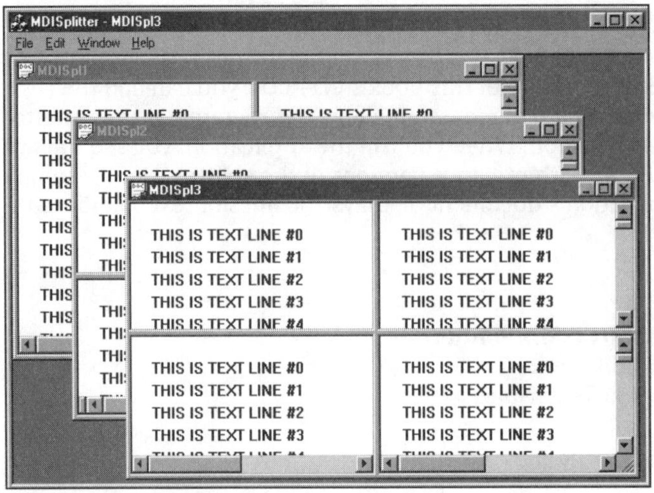

Figure 13-14: MDISplitter can display multiple child windows, each with its own splitter.

Exploring the MDI dynamic splitter window

Creating splitter windows in an MDI application is not all that different from creating them in an SDI application. You just have to remember that, in an MDI application, the child window (derived from `CMDIChildWnd`) contains the splitter, so it is the child-window class's `OnCreateClient()` function that creates the splitter window. If you're adding a splitter window to an existing MDI application, you should override `OnCreateClient()` in the MDI child window class and then add the code needed to create the splitter window. The following code segment shows the `OnCreateClient()` function from the MDISplitter application.

```
BOOL CChildFrame::OnCreateClient(LPCREATESTRUCT /*lpcs*/,
  CCreateContext* pContext)
{
  return m_wndSplitter.Create( this,
    2, 2,    // TODO: adjust the number of rows, columns
    CSize( 10, 10 ),// TODO: adjust the minimum pane size
    pContext );
}
```

You can see by the `TODO` comments that AppWizard generated this `OnCreateClient()` function, which brings you to the next topic.

MDI dynamic splitters and AppWizard

Using AppWizard to create an MDI application with splitter windows is almost as easy as creating the equivalent SDI application. Just perform the following general steps.

Nutshell: Creating an MDI Dynamic Splitter Window

Follow these steps to create an AppWizard multiple-document interface application that supports splitter windows:

1. Start your AppWizard project as you normally would.
2. In the MFC AppWizard – Step 1 of 6 dialog box, select the Multiple Documents option.
3. When you get to the MFC AppWizard – Step 4 of 6 dialog box, click the Advanced button. The Advanced Options dialog box appears.
4. Click the Window Styles tab, and select the Use split window option.
5. In the MFC AppWizard – Step 6 of 6 dialog box, select the application's view class in the upper pane, and then select CScrollView in the Base Class box.
6. Click the finish button to generate the skeleton application.

◆ ◆ ◆ ◆ ◆

Notice these steps are very similar to the steps you used to create an SDI application with a splitter window. The main difference is the selection of multiple documents in Step 2.

Splitter Windows and Differing Views

There's nothing to say that each view in a splitter window's panes has to be exactly the same document in exactly the same data format. You could display the same document in two different ways or even display two completely different documents. It all depends on how you put together the application. One of the most common uses for splitter windows is to provide two views of the same document displayed in different formats. A drawing program, for example, could display graphical objects in one pane and a list of the objects' coordinates in another. In the following section, you see how to add this sort of functionality to your MFC programs.

The MultViewSplitter Application

In the Chap13\MultViewSplitter folder of this book's CD-ROM, you can find the MultViewSplitter application, which demonstrates how to display two different views in a dynamic splitter window. When you run the application, you see the application's main window, which features a horizontal dynamic splitter. If you split the window, you see the two different views, as shown in Figure 13-15.

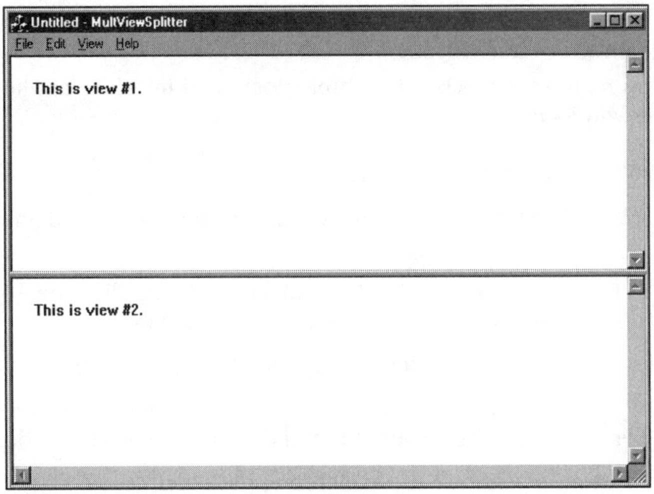

Figure 13-15: Here's the MultViewSplitter application when you first run it.

Exploring the multiple-view splitter window

Accomplishing the multiple-view stunt is only slightly tricky. First, you create the main application just as you would any application with a splitter window. However, you create two view classes, one for each view you want to appear in the splitter panes. Also, you must derive your own custom splitter-window class from `CSplitterWnd`, overriding the class's `CreateView()` function. It is in `CreateView()` that the splitter window determines the view to display.

Listing 13-4 shows how you might program `CreateView()`. As you can see, the function receives five parameters: the new view's row, the new view's column, the new view's runtime class pointer, the size of the view, and a pointer to the view's context information. By examining the `row` and `col` parameters, you can tell if the requested view is the original view or the alternate view. That is, if `col` and `row` are 0, the view should be the normal view because it is being positioned in the first pane (which may even be the only pane at this time). Otherwise, the view is being positioned in the second pane and so should be the alternate view.

Listing 13-4: The Custom CreateView() Function

```
BOOL CCustomSplitterWnd::CreateView(int row,
  int col, CRuntimeClass* pViewClass,
  SIZE sizeInit, CCreateContext* pContext)
{
  if ((row == 0) && (col == 0))
    return CSplitterWnd::CreateView(row, col,
      pViewClass, sizeInit, pContext);
```

```
    return CSplitterWnd::CreateView(row, col,
      RUNTIME_CLASS(CAltView), sizeInit, pContext);
}
```

In Listing 13-4, notice that the alternate view (represented by the `CAltView` class) must be capable of generating runtime-class information with the `RUNTIME_CLASS` macro. This means the class must support dynamic creation, which is a whole ball of wax we won't get into here. The easiest way to provide the proper type of view class for your alternate view is to create the basic application with AppWizard and then use ClassWizard to generate the second view class. In the following section, you discover the missing pieces to that part of the multiple-view puzzle.

Multiple view splitters and AppWizard

As is typical with a lot of MFC programs, AppWizard offers the fastest route to creating an application like MultViewSplitter. Not only does AppWizard generate a lot of source code for you, it enables you to use ClassWizard to add classes to the project, also generating the basic code for these new classes. In this particular case, ClassWizard is especially useful because it can generate a view class that supports MFC dynamic creation through the `DECLARE_DYNCREATE` and `IMPLEMENT_DYNCREATE` macros. You don't have to know anything about dynamic object creation to take advantage of the class's extra capabilities. To use AppWizard and ClassWizard to create an application like MultViewSplitter, follow these steps.

Creating a Splitter Window with Differing Views

Follow these steps to create an application with a custom splitter-window class that enables the application to display different views of a document:

1. Create a normal splitter AppWizard project.
2. Bring up ClassWizard, click the Add Class button, and select New from the menu. The New Class dialog box appears.
3. Type the new view class's name into the Name box, and select the CScrollView class in the Base Class box, as shown in Figure 13-16.
4. Write your custom splitter-window class, deriving the class from `CSplitterWnd` and overriding `CreateView()`. (For some reason, ClassWizard won't let you create a new class based on `CSplitterWnd`. You have to write it by hand.)
5. In the frame window class's header file, change `m_wndSplitter` from a `CSplitterWnd` object to an object of your custom splitter-window class. You also need to `#include` the custom class's header file in the frame window's header file.

✦ ✦ ✦ ✦ ✦

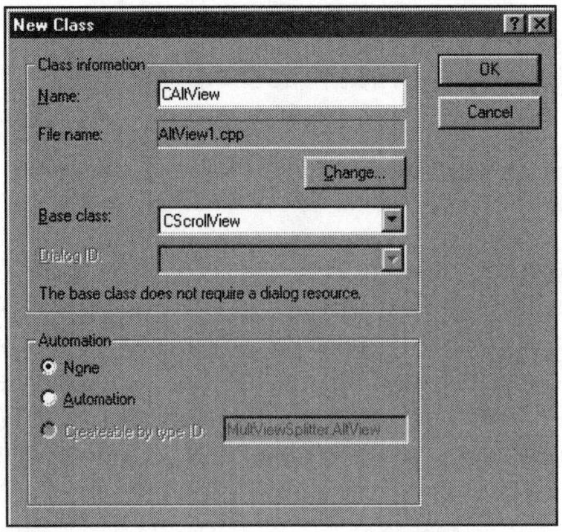

Figure 13-16: You create your alternate view class in the New Class dialog.

And that's all there is to it! Well, almost. You still need to complete your document and view classes, not to mention the entire application.

If you're a little fuzzy on how to derive your custom splitter-window class from `CSplitterWnd`, take a look at Listings 13-5 and 13-6. The former is the header file for the MultViewSplitter application's splitter class, and the latter is the implementation file. To get the class into your project, just select the Project menu's Add To Project command, choosing Files from the submenu that appears. Next, select the class's implementation (.cpp) file.

Demo Program

MultViewSplitter
CD-ROM Location: **Chap13\MultViewSplitter**
Program Name: **MultViewSplitter.exe**
Source Code Modules in Text: **CCustomSplitterWnd.h and CCustomSplitterWnd.cpp**

◆ ◆ ◆ ◆ ◆

Listing 13-5: The CCustomSplitterWnd Class's Header File

```
///////////////////////////////////////////
// CCustomSplitterWnd.h
///////////////////////////////////////////

class CCustomSplitterWnd : public CSplitterWnd
{
public:
  CCustomSplitterWnd();
  ~CCustomSplitterWnd();
```

```
  BOOL CreateView(int row, int col,
    CRuntimeClass* pViewClass, SIZE sizeInit,
    CCreateContext* pContext);
};
```

Listing 13-6: The CCustomSplitterWnd Class's Implementation File

```
///////////////////////////////////////////////
// CCustomSplitterWnd.cpp
///////////////////////////////////////////////

#include "stdafx.h"
#include "AltView.h"
#include "CustomSplitterWnd.h"

CCustomSplitterWnd::CCustomSplitterWnd()
{
}

CCustomSplitterWnd::~CCustomSplitterWnd()
{
}

BOOL CCustomSplitterWnd::CreateView(int row,
  int col, CRuntimeClass* pViewClass,
  SIZE sizeInit, CCreateContext* pContext)
{
  if ((row == 0) && (col == 0))
    return CSplitterWnd::CreateView(row, col,
      pViewClass, sizeInit, pContext);

  return CSplitterWnd::CreateView(row, col,
    RUNTIME_CLASS(CAltView), sizeInit, pContext);
}
```

Summary

Using splitter windows, you can provide your application's users with various views of a document or even views of different documents. Dynamic splitter windows enable the user to create split views but are limited to only four panes. Static splitter windows can hold up to 256 individual panes, but the panes must be created from within the application.

The key to adding splitter windows to an application is to override the frame-window class's `OnCreateClient()` function to create a splitter window instead of the normal view window. The view window will then be displayed in the splitter window. If you want easy control over the splitter window's scroll bars, you should derive your view classes from `CScrollView` rather than from `CView`.

Splitter windows often provide different view positions within a single document. However, you can display a document in different formats in a splitter's panes or even display totally different documents, depending on your application's needs. If you want to control the view that's displayed in a splitter window's panes, you must derive a custom splitter-window class from `CSplitterWnd` and write your own `CreateView()` function.

✦ ✦ ✦

CHAPTER 14

MDI

In This Chapter

Understanding how MDI applications help the user to manage documents

Exploring a working MDI application

Creating your own MDI applications

Examining the classes AppWizard generates for an MDI application

Noting some differences between MDI and SDI applications

In the previous chapter, you learned one method for displaying different views and documents in a single application. Specifically, you discovered splitter windows, which give your application's user the power to divide a window into multiple panes. Splitter windows are often used to show different views of a single document. If you want an application that can display and edit multiple documents concurrently, you may find that an MDI application fits the bill better than an application with a splitter window. In this chapter, you discover what MDI applications are, as well as how to build them.

Introducing MDI Applications

You've been working mostly with single-document interface (SDI) applications up to now, which can display only a single document at a time. That's sufficient for most applications. To display more than one document at a time, you use *multiple-document interface (MDI)* applications.

An MDI frame window is a lot like a mini-desktop. On it, the user can arrange several document windows (called MDI child windows). Document windows in an MDI application can even be reduced to icons inside the frame window, just as applications can be reduced to icons on the Windows taskbar.

You can create MDI applications easily with AppWizard. In fact, MDI applications are the default type in the AppWizard Step 1 dialog box. Figure 14-1 shows the Step 1 dialog box. You can select three options — Single document, Multiple documents, and Dialog based — at the top of the dialog box. To create an MDI application, you select the Multiple documents option.

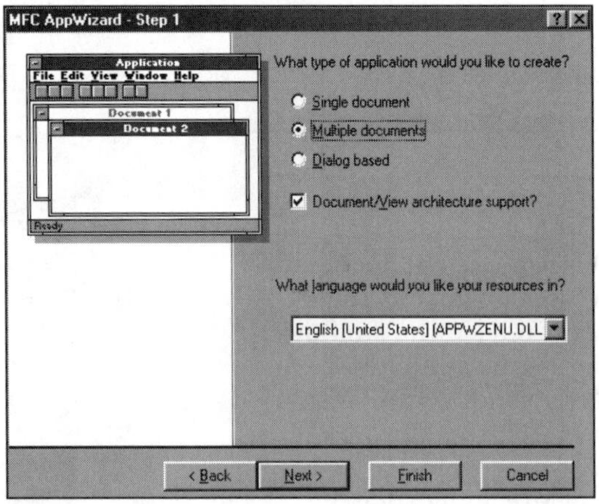

Figure 14-1: AppWizard when creating an MDI application

The other options in the remaining AppWizard dialog boxes are unaffected by the Multiple documents selection. If you leave those options set to their default values, you get the application shown in Figure 14-2. As you can see, when the application runs, it displays two windows: the frame window and a child window. It's the child window that represents a document in the application. As such, the child window's client area contains the view window for the document.

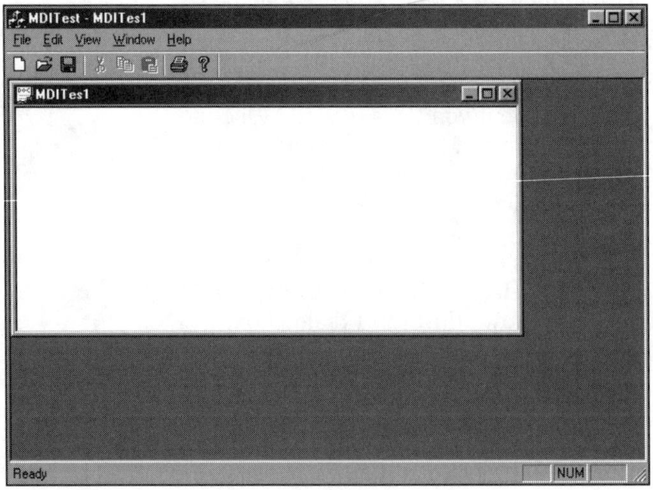

Figure 14-2: A basic MDI application

One major way an MFC MDI application differs from an SDI application is in the base classes from which MFC derives its window classes. Specifically, an MDI frame window derives from the CMDIFrameWnd class, which itself derives from CFrameWnd. This derivation should tell you that a CMDIFrameWnd window is just a frame window with some extra features. Those features include the ability to manage multiple documents.

Similarly, in an AppWizard-generated application, an MDI child window's class is CChildFrame, which MFC derives from CMDIChildWnd. The child window is a frame window that appears inside an MDI frame window. An MDI child window doesn't have a menu bar; instead, it places menu commands in the MDI frame window's menu bar. MDI child windows can never leave the MDI frame window's client area.

As you know, an MDI application can display several documents concurrently. For example, the MDI application shown in Figure 14-3 has several open document windows. Notice how the MDITes3 child window is positioned such that it doesn't fit entirely inside the MDI frame window. Rather than extend onto the Windows desktop, though, the portion of the child window that doesn't fit is not visible at all. This is similar to what happens on the Windows 98 desktop if you try to move an application window beyond the limits of the screen.

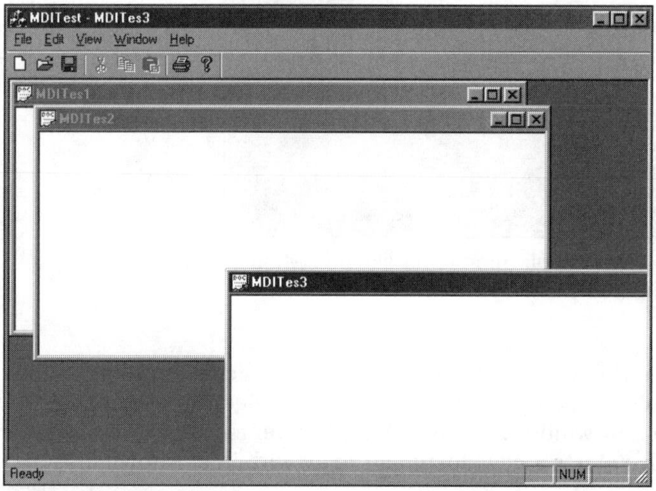

Figure 14-3: The MDI application with multiple document windows open

Because SDI applications rarely display child windows, AppWizard never creates a child-window class for an SDI application. Child document windows are, in fact, the main difference between SDI and MDI applications. In the following section, you get a chance to experiment with this chapter's MDI sample program.

The MDIDemo Application

In the Chap14\MDIDemo folder of this book's CD-ROM, you can find the MDIDemo application, which demonstrates how to program MDI applications. When you run the application, you see the window shown in Figure 14-4. MDIDemo is an MDI version of the RectApp2 application from Chapter 12. You may remember that a RectApp2 document consists of a set of rectangles, with a new document starting off with one default rectangle. With RectApp2, the default starting document appears in the application's main window. As you can see, with MDIDemo the default starting document appears in a child window.

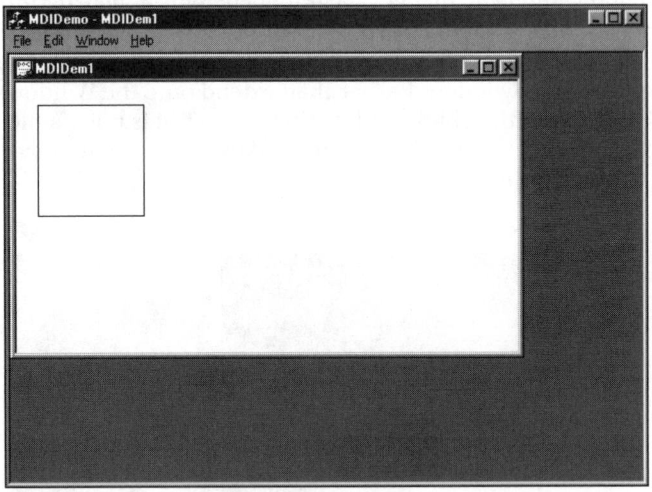

Figure 14-4: The MDIDemo application looks like this when you first run it.

Go ahead and click in the document window. Each click adds a new rectangle to the document. After you've added a bunch of rectangles, select the File menu's New command to open a new window. When you do, MDIDemo not only opens a new child window, but also starts a new document to go with it, as shown in Figure 14-5.

Add rectangles to this new document, and then try to exit the application. MDIDemo asks whether you want to save your work. Go ahead and save both documents. When you rerun MDIDemo, you can reload the documents from the File menu's document list, as shown in Figure 14-6.

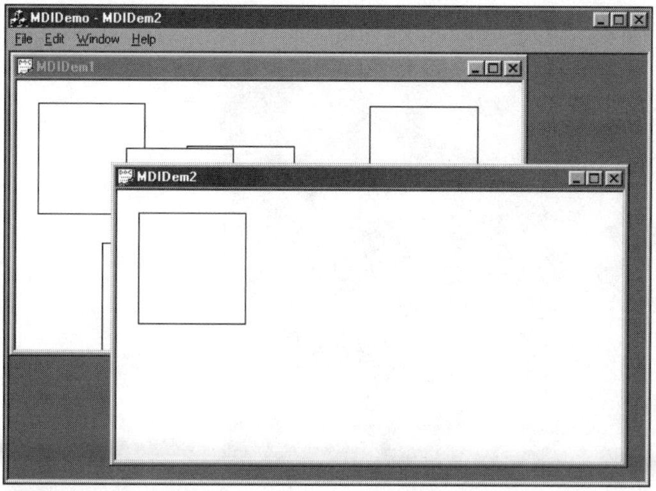

Figure 14-5: The New command creates a new default document.

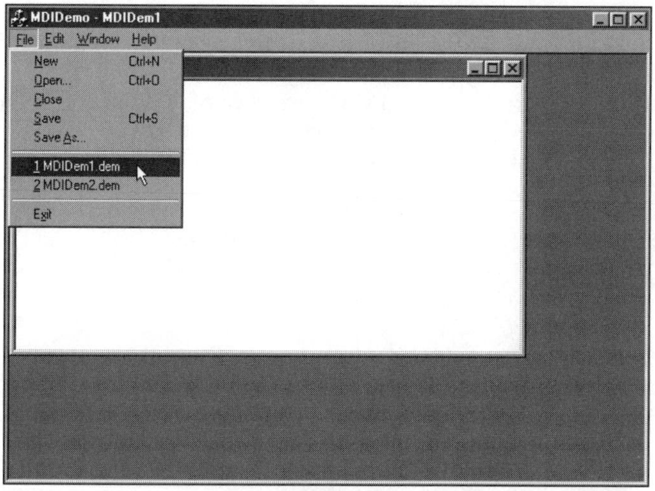

Figure 14-6: The File menu lists recently opened documents.

Another thing to notice about the MDI application is it actually uses two menu bars: one for when child windows are present and one for when no child windows are present. Currently, you can see MDIDemo has four menus in its menu bar: File, Edit, Window, and Help. (Using the commands on the Window menu, you can manipulate child windows in various ways.) Close all the child windows, and the Edit and Window menus disappear (Figure 14-7). Those menus contain commands that are appropriate only when a child window is active.

Figure 14-7: MDIDemo's menu bar changes when no child windows are present.

Because MDIDemo's main window acts as a kind of desktop, you can minimize document windows, after which they appear as icons at the bottom of the window. Figure 14-8 shows MDIDemo with three child windows, two of which have been minimized. To restore a minimized child window, you can click its restore or maximize button, or you can just double-click the icon.

Figure 14-8: Minimized child windows appear as icons at the bottom of the window.

Finally, if you maximize a document window, it takes over the full client area of the frame window, merging its window control buttons with the frame window's menu bar. Figure 14-9 shows MDIDemo with a maximized child window. In this state, the application looks much like a normal SDI application. The big difference is the other open documents are still available. You can switch to one of them by selecting it from the Window menu, or you can return the maximized document to its previous size and select the next document by clicking its window.

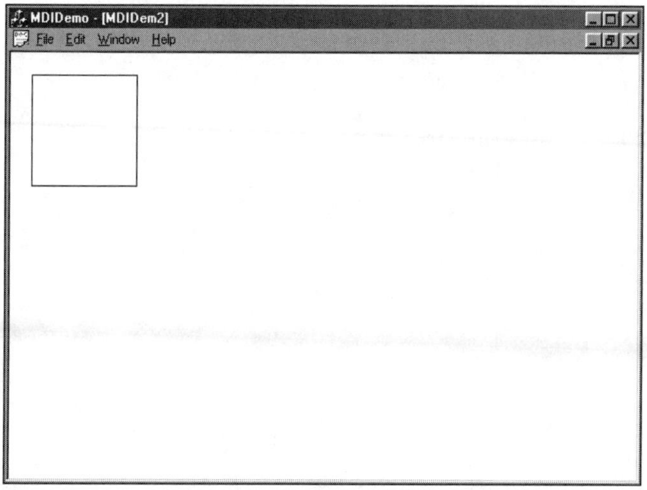

Figure 14-9: Maximized child windows fill the frame window's client area.

The Child Frame Window

As you now know, a big difference between the AppWizard-generated files for an SDI application and those for an MDI application is that the MDI application has a child-window class, called `CChildFrame`, that represents the application's document windows. Each time the user opens a new document, the application creates a new instance of `CChildFrame` in which to display the document within the main frame window. Listing 14-1 shows the child-window class's header file, whereas Listing 14-2 shows the class's implementation file. (The files were slightly modified to fit the page and to remove some extraneous AppWizard-generated lines.) Of special note is the `PreCreateWindow()` function, in which you can modify the child window's size, location, and style by changing the values in the `cs` structure.

Demo Program

MDIDemo

CD-ROM Location: **Chap14\MDIDemo**
Program Name: **MDIDemo.exe**
Source Code Modules in Text: **CChildFrame.h** and **CChildFrame.cpp**

◆ ◆ ◆ ◆ ◆

Listing 14-1: The Header File for the CChildFrame Class

```
// ChildFrm.h : interface of the CChildFrame class
//
/////////////////////////////////////////////////////////////

class CChildFrame : public CMDIChildWnd
{
  DECLARE_DYNCREATE(CChildFrame)
public:
  CChildFrame();

// Attributes
public:

// Operations
public:

// Overrides
  // ClassWizard generated virtual function overrides
  //{{AFX_VIRTUAL(CChildFrame)
  virtual BOOL PreCreateWindow(CREATESTRUCT& cs);
  //}}AFX_VIRTUAL

// Implementation
public:
  virtual ~CChildFrame();
#ifdef _DEBUG
  virtual void AssertValid() const;
  virtual void Dump(CDumpContext& dc) const;
#endif

// Generated message map functions
protected:
  //{{AFX_MSG(CChildFrame)
    // NOTE - the ClassWizard will add and remove
    //   member functions here.
    //    DO NOT EDIT what you see in these blocks
    //    of generated code!
  //}}AFX_MSG
  DECLARE_MESSAGE_MAP()
};
```

Listing 14-2: The Implementation File for the CChildFrame Class

```
// ChildFrm.cpp : implementation of the CChildFrame class
//

#include "stdafx.h"
#include "MDIDemo.h"

#include "ChildFrm.h"

#ifdef _DEBUG
#define new DEBUG_NEW
#undef THIS_FILE
static char THIS_FILE[] = __FILE__;
#endif

/////////////////////////////////////////////////////////////
// CChildFrame

IMPLEMENT_DYNCREATE(CChildFrame, CMDIChildWnd)

BEGIN_MESSAGE_MAP(CChildFrame, CMDIChildWnd)
  //{{AFX_MSG_MAP(CChildFrame)
    // NOTE - the ClassWizard will add and remove
    //   mapping macros here.
    // DO NOT EDIT what you see in these blocks
    //   of generated code !
  //}}AFX_MSG_MAP
END_MESSAGE_MAP()

/////////////////////////////////////////////////////////////
// CChildFrame construction/destruction

CChildFrame::CChildFrame()
{
  // TODO: add member initialization code here

}

CChildFrame::~CChildFrame()
{
}

BOOL CChildFrame::PreCreateWindow(CREATESTRUCT& cs)
{
  // TODO: Modify the Window class or styles here
  //  by modifying
  //  the CREATESTRUCT cs
```

(continued)

Listing 14-2 *(continued)*

```
  if( !CMDIChildWnd::PreCreateWindow(cs) )
    return FALSE;

  return TRUE;
}

/////////////////////////////////////////////////////////////////////////////
// CChildFrame diagnostics

#ifdef _DEBUG
void CChildFrame::AssertValid() const
{
  CMDIChildWnd::AssertValid();
}

void CChildFrame::Dump(CDumpContext& dc) const
{
  CMDIChildWnd::Dump(dc);
}

#endif //_DEBUG
```

Creating an MDI Application

Creating a basic MDI application with AppWizard is a snap. Just create the application as you normally would, except be sure to select the Multiple documents option in the MFC AppWizard - Step 1 of 1 dialog box. That's all there is to it. Once you've created the skeleton application, you complete the document and view classes as you normally would, except you don't need to implement the document class's `DeleteContents()` function. This is because MDI applications don't reuse document objects.

The MFC framework takes care of all the other details, including starting a new document when the user creates a new child window, tracking changes in each document to warn the user when a document needs to be saved, and managing the commands in the Window menu. You'll have to implement whatever editing commands your application needs, of course. You can implement the commands on the default Edit menu or add your own commands. As always, editing functions are completely dependent on the type of your application.

Nutshell

Creating an MDI Application

Follow these steps to create an AppWizard MDI application:

1. Start your AppWizard project as you normally would.

2. In the MFC AppWizard - Step 1 of 1 dialog box, be sure the Multiple documents option is selected.
3. After generating the skeleton source code, complete the application's document and view classes.

◆ ◆ ◆ ◆ ◆

Exploring an MDI Application

Although you don't need to dig too deeply into the innards of an MDI application (thanks to AppWizard), you might be interested to know some of the things AppWizard does differently when generating an MDI application. The biggest difference you'll notice right off is the addition of a child-window class to your project. This child-window class, called `CChildFrame` by default, is derived from MFC's `CMDIChildWnd` class and represents the application's document windows. The following list shows and describes the classes that AppWizard generates for the MDIDemo application:

- `CAboutDlg` — Derived from `CDialog`, this class represents the application's About dialog box. Declared and defined in MDIDemo.cpp.
- `CChildFrame` — Derived from `CMDIChildWnd`, this class represents the application's child (document) windows. Declared in ChildFrm.h and defined in ChildFrm.cpp.
- `CMainFrame` — Derived from `CMDIFrameWnd`, this class represents the application's main window. Declared in MainFrm.h and defined in MainFrm.cpp.
- `CMDIDemoApp` — Derived from `CWinApp`, this class represents the application object. Declared in MDIDemo.h and defined in MDIDemo.cpp.
- `CMDIDemoDoc` — Derived from `CDocument`, this class represents the application's document. Declared in MDIDemoDoc.h and defined in MDIDemoDoc.cpp.
- `CMDIDemoView` — Derived from `CView`, this class represents the application's document view. Declared in MDIDemoView.h and defined in MDIDemoView.cpp.

The project still has a `CMainFrame` class, but now it's derived from `CMDIFrameWnd` rather than from `CFrameWnd`. This MDI frame window has a lot of extra work to do, what with managing child document windows. In its client area, the frame window actually contains a special MDI client window. Rather than being directly associated with the frame window, the child windows, then, are children of the MDI client window.

Each child window acts as a miniframe, holding the view window for its document in the child window's client area. In this way, the child window resembles an SDI application's main frame window, except a child window never has a menu bar; instead, it merges its menus with the MDI frame window's menu bar.

If you want to dig into the source code, you can find some notable differences between an SDI and an MDI application. The first place to look is in the application's `InitInstance()` function, where the application creates the document template from `CMultiDocTemplate` rather than from `CSingleDocTemplate`. So you can see the difference, here's the appropriate code segment from the SDI application, RectApp2:

```
CSingleDocTemplate* pDocTemplate;
pDocTemplate = new CSingleDocTemplate(
  IDR_MAINFRAME,
  RUNTIME_CLASS(CRectAppDoc),
  RUNTIME_CLASS(CMainFrame),       // main SDI frame window
  RUNTIME_CLASS(CRectAppView));
AddDocTemplate(pDocTemplate);
```

Now, here's the same code segment from MDIDemo:

```
CMultiDocTemplate* pDocTemplate;
pDocTemplate = new CMultiDocTemplate(
  IDR_MDIDEMTYPE,
  RUNTIME_CLASS(CMDIDemoDoc),
  RUNTIME_CLASS(CChildFrame), // custom MDI child frame
  RUNTIME_CLASS(CMDIDemoView));
AddDocTemplate(pDocTemplate);
```

You'll find another difference in your application's resources, where an MDI application defines two menus. In the case of MDIDemo, these two menus have the IDs `IDR_MAINFRAME` and `IDR_MDIDEMTYPE`. Figure 14-10 shows the two menus displayed in the ResourceView pane, with the `IDR_MAINFRAME` menu loaded into the menu editor.

The `IDR_MAINFRAME` menu is the menu you see when no child windows are open. If you have menu commands that aren't associated with child windows, you should place them in this menu bar. Usually, you'll also want to duplicate such menus in the child-window menu. The `IDR_MDIDEMTYPE` menu is the menu bar that MDIDemo displays when a child window is open. All menus associated with child windows belong here. Most main application commands (those defined in the `IDR_MAINFRAME` menus) should also appear here, so those commands are still available when a child window is open. The name that AppWizard assigns to the child-window menu depends on the application's name.

MFC handles most of the other MDI details internally. Unless you want to start browsing through MFC's source code (that'll keep you busy!), you have to take it on faith that MFC knows what it's doing when it comes to managing an MDI application. If you want to build an MDI application from scratch, without using AppWizard, you have a lot of studying in front of you. Frankly, I don't know why anyone would bother trying to write an MDI application by hand. One thing's for sure: It would be an educational experience!

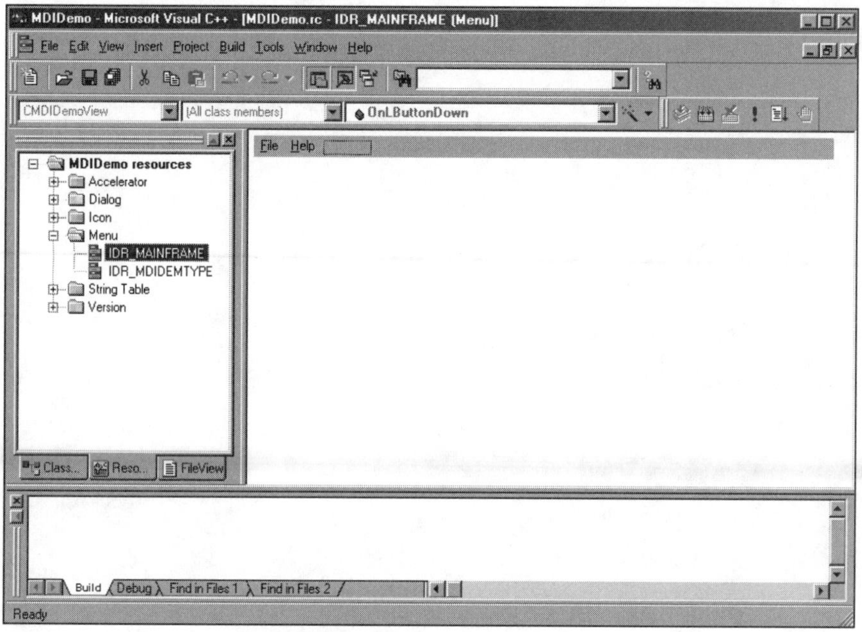

Figure 14-10: MDI applications define two menu bars.

Summary

MDI applications enable the user to open and edit multiple documents simultaneously. Each open document gets its own MDI child window, which acts much like an SDI frame window, except that it can't display a menu bar. Instead, MDI child windows merge their menus into the main frame window's menu bar. Creating an MDI application with AppWizard is as easy as selecting the Multiple documents option in the MFC AppWizard – Step 1 of 1 dialog box. From the programmer's point of view, MDI and SDI applications have very similar document and view classes, although the MFC framework handles a lot of the details in the background.

✦ ✦ ✦

CHAPTER 15

Printing and Print Preview

✦ ✦ ✦ ✦

In This Chapter

Printing from a traditional Windows application

Discovering how to print text in an MFC application

Printing graphics in an MFC application

✦ ✦ ✦ ✦

If you've ever tried to program document printing in a traditional (non-MFC) Windows program, you know that it can be a meticulous task. This is especially true for earlier versions of Windows, which required the programmer to learn a lot of archaic codes. In fact, handling printers under Windows was once a task that made even experienced programmers want to run for cover. These days, giving a Windows application printing capabilities is much easier, thanks to printing functions added to Windows, but traditional Windows printing still requires that you handle many details. MFC makes printing even easier, though there's still much to learn. In this chapter, you discover the techniques you need to know to successfully print text and graphics from an MFC Windows application.

An Overview of Printing in Windows

Although this chapter is dedicated to printing documents from MFC programs, in order to understand what's going on behind the scenes in MFC, it helps to learn to print data from a traditional C Windows program. You tackle that topic in this section.

Nutshell

Printing Under Windows

Under Windows, the basic printing process involves six steps:

1. Call the `CreateDC()` function to acquire a printer device context (DC).
2. Call the `StartDoc()` function to begin the document.
3. Call the `StartPage()` function to begin a page.
4. Render the document onto the printer DC.

5. Call the `EndPage()` function to end a page. (Repeat Steps 3 through 5 for each page in the document.)
6. Call the `EndDoc()` function to end the print job.

✦ ✦ ✦ ✦ ✦

Your first task is to call `CreateDC()` to create a printer device context. Just as you need a device context to draw data in an application's window, so, too, do you need a DC to send data to a printer. There are two ways to determine the type of printer connected to the system. Using the first method, the application examines the user's WIN.INI file. Using the second method, the application calls the Windows API `EnumPrinters()` function. Calling `EnumPrinters()` is the easiest method. The `EnumPrinters()` function's signature looks like this:

```
BOOL EnumPrinters(
  DWORD Flags,
  LPTSTR Name,
  DWORD Level,
  LPBYTE pPrinterEnum,
  DWORD cbBuf,
  LPDWORD pcbNeeded,
  LPDWORD pcReturned,
);
```

The function's arguments are described as follows:

`Flags`	A flag indicating the type of printer needed
`Name`	The name of the printer object
`Level`	The type of printer info structure
`pPrinterEnum`	A pointer to the printer info structures
`cbBuf`	The size of the printer info array
`pcbNeeded`	A pointer to the variable that holds the number of bytes copied to the printer info array
`pcReturned`	A pointer to the variable that holds the number of print info structures copied to the array

Depending on how you want Windows to describe the printers available on the system, some of `EnumPrinters()`'s arguments have many different possible values. Most of the time, however, you need only get the default printer. (If you're interested in all the other hairy details, look up `EnumPrinters()` in your Visual C++ online documentation.) To program your application to ask Windows for the default printer, use the following code:

```
PRINTER_INFO_5 printerInfo5[3];
DWORD needed, returned;

EnumPrinters(PRINTER_ENUM_DEFAULT, NULL, 5,
```

```
(LPBYTE)printerInfo5, sizeof(printerInfo5),
&needed, &returned);
```

After the previous lines execute, the name of the default printer appears in the first printer info structure's `pPrinterName` member, which you can access like this:

```
printerInfo5[0].pPrinterName
```

The printer name is exactly what you need in order to create a DC for the printer. To get the DC, call `CreateDC()`:

```
HDC printDC;

printDC = CreateDC(NULL,
  printerInfo5[0].pPrinterName, NULL, NULL);
```

In this call to `CreateDC()`, the second argument is the printer's system name. The remaining arguments should be `NULL`.

When you have created the printer DC, you can start printing the document. To do this, you first call the Windows API function `StartDoc()`, which sets up Windows to begin spooling your document to the system print spooler. If `StartDoc()` succeeds, it returns an ID for the print job; otherwise, it returns a value less than or equal to zero.

`StartDoc()` passes a pointer to a `DOCINFO` structure as one of its arguments. Your program must initialize this structure's members before calling `StartDoc()`. In most cases, you just place the size of the structure in the `cbSize` member and a pointer to the document's name in the `lpszDocName` member. The remaining members can be `NULL` or zero. The entire process looks something like Listing 15-1.

Listing 15-1: **Calling the StartDoc() Function**

```
char docName[] = "RectangleDoc";
DOCINFO docInfo;
docInfo.cbSize = sizeof(docInfo);
docInfo.lpszDocName = docName;
docInfo.lpszOutput = NULL;
docInfo.lpszDatatype = NULL;
docInfo.fwType = 0;

result = StartDoc(printDC, &docInfo);

if (result <= 0)
{
  MessageBox(0, "StartDoc() failed",
    "Basic Print App", MB_OK | MB_ICONERROR );
  return;
}
```

If the call to `StartDoc()` succeeds, you're ready to start printing your first page, which you do by calling the `StartPage()` function. `StartPage()` requires a single argument, the printer DC. The function returns a value greater than zero if it succeeds; otherwise, it returns a value less than or equal to zero. The code to start a page will be similar to the following snippet:

```
result = StartPage(printDC);
if (result <= 0)
{
  MessageBox(0, "StartPage() failed",
    "Basic Print App", MB_OK | MB_ICONERROR );
  return;
}
```

With the page started, your application can send data to the printer in much the same way the application displays data in its window. The application just directs the output to the printer DC, rather than to a window DC. Of course, a printer isn't as versatile as a video display. For example, your printer probably can't display a bitmap the same way a window does. Also, the dots on the screen are a different size than the dots on most printers, so you often need to scale data destined for the printer.

When a page has finished printing, the application calls the `EndPage()` function. `EndPage()`, like `StartPage()`, requires the printer DC as its single argument. Also like `StartPage()`, `EndPage()` returns a value greater than zero if it succeeds and zero or less if it doesn't succeed. The code to end a page will be similar to the following snippet:

```
result = EndPage(printDC);
if (result <= 0)
{
  MessageBox(0, "EndPage() failed",
    "Basic Print App", MB_OK | MB_ICONERROR );
  return;
}
```

At this point, the application can call `StartPage()` again to begin another page. If the document has been completely printed, the application should call `EndDoc()` to end the print job:

```
EndDoc(printDC);
```

Printing Text in an MFC Application

There's a big advantage to using AppWizard to generate the skeleton code for your new application, which is that AppWizard automatically generates basic printing and print preview functions. To get this functionality, just be sure you select the Printing and Print Preview option in AppWizard's Step 4 of 6 dialog box, as shown in Figure 15-1. Such an AppWizard application handles all the details of getting the printer's name and acquiring the printer DC. You only need to refine the generated source code to produce the kind of printout that's appropriate for the application.

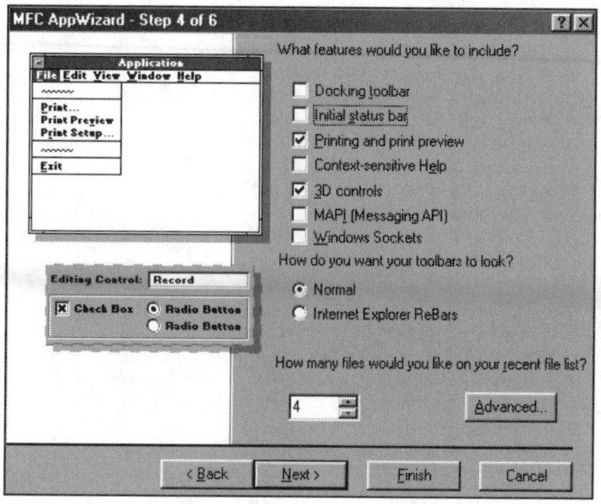

Figure 15-1: The AppWizard Printing and Print Preview option generates printing functions in your application.

The AppWizard-generated code uses the `OnDraw()` function to display the application's document both on the screen and on the printer. However, when displaying data on the screen, the DC object sent to `OnDraw()` is for the client window, whereas the DC is for the current printer when displaying data on the printer. This clever bit of DC switching enables one function to render output for both the screen and the printer, making it easier to produce WYSIWYG (What You See Is What You Get) output. The complication sets in when the coordinates used for screen display don't match those needed for printing. This is where scaling printer output comes in.

Depending on the type of document the application needs to print, you may also need to deal with creating fonts, managing pagination, and generating headers and footers. Luckily, MFC takes much of the busywork out of printing documents by not only creating the printer context, but also providing member functions in the view class that enable view windows to access the printing process at various stages. In the next section, you get a look at those functions and how they work. Along the way, you'll learn printing skills such as pagination and scaling.

The TextPrint sample application

In the Chapter15\TextPrint directory of this book's CD-ROM, you can find the TextPrint application. Run the application, and then select a text file to view. To do this, select the File menu's Open menu, and then select any ASCII file. When you do, the file appears in the window. Figure 15-2 shows the application after loading the TextPrint source-code file TextPrintView.cpp.

Demo Program

TextPrint

CD-ROM Location: **Chap15\TextPrint**
Program Name: **TextPrint.exe**
Source Code Modules in Text: **None**

◆ ◆ ◆ ◆ ◆

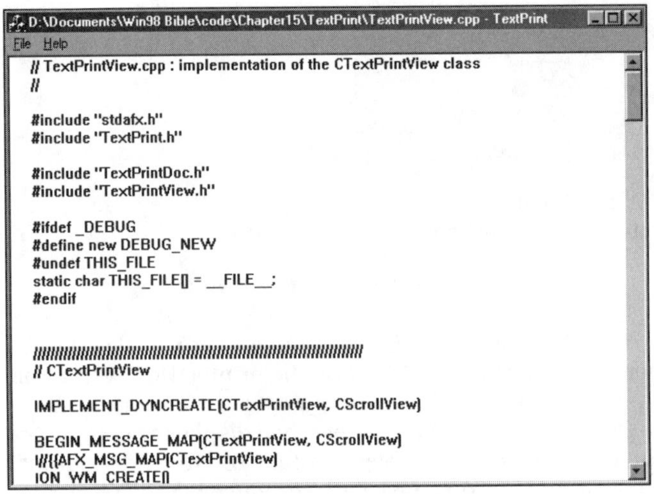

Figure 15-2: TextPrint after loading a source code file

As with most text-oriented Windows applications, you can use the scroll bars to view the parts of the document not currently displayed in the window. More importantly, you can use the File menu's Print, Print Preview, and Print Setup commands. For example, if you choose the Print Preview command, you see the window shown in Figure 15-3. If you like, you can click the Two Page button in order to see two pages of the document. Figure 15-4 shows the two-page print preview window.

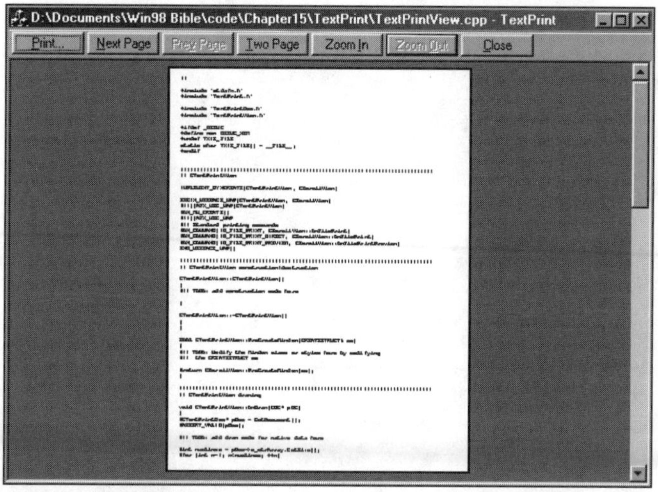

Figure 15-3: TextPrint's print preview window

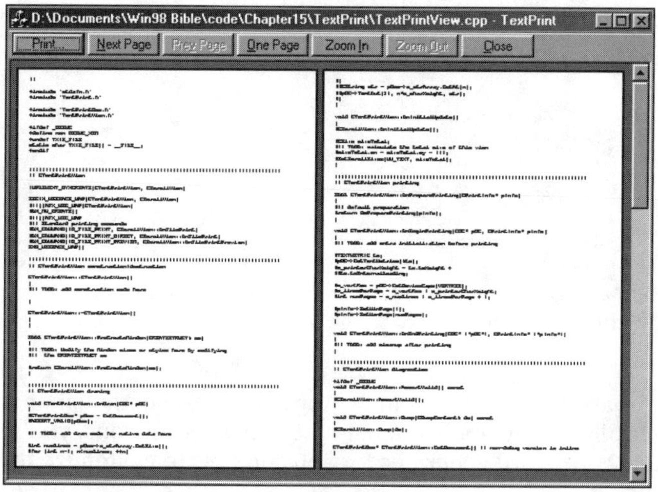

Figure 15-4: TextPrint's print preview window showing two pages

When you click the Print button or select the File menu's Print command, the Print dialog box appears (Figure 15-5). In the Print dialog box, you can select a printer, the number of pages to print, and other print-related options. If you leave the options set as displayed, TextPrint prints all of the displayed document to the default printer. If you choose the File menu's Print Setup command, the Print Setup dialog box for your default printer appears (Figure 15-6).

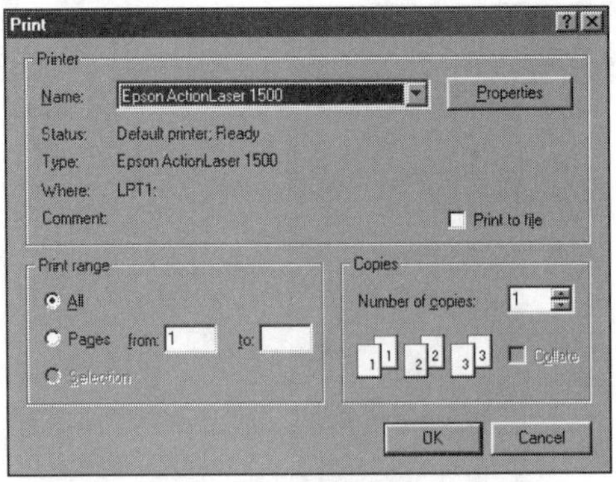

Figure 15-5: You can choose print options from the Print dialog box.

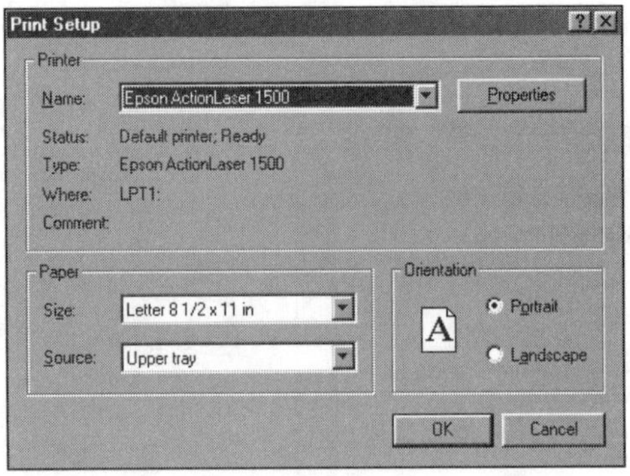

Figure 15-6: You can choose general print options from the Print Setup dialog box.

Many of TextPrint's capabilities were built in by AppWizard. Some, though, had to be programmed especially for the application. In the following sections, you see the printing functions that AppWizard generates for you and how to customize them for your own applications.

MFC member functions for printing

An MFC AppWizard-generated program with printing features already knows how to get the current printer's name and how to create the printer DC. The application can also display the Print dialog box. The application can even send its document to the printer. MFC handles all these details for you. Often, though, you need to refine the default MFC printing features for a specific application. The `CView` class, from which you derive your application's view window, defines five functions that enable you to take control of different phases of the printing process:

- `OnPreparePrinting()`
- `OnBeginPrinting()`
- `OnPrepareDC()`
- `OnPrint()`
- `OnEndPrinting()`

In the following sections, you have a chance to examine these five functions in detail to see how you can use them to customize MFC's printing capabilities.

The OnPreparePrinting() function

When a printing or print preview job begins, `OnPreparePrinting()` is the first of the five special functions that MFC calls. This function displays the Print dialog box and creates the printer DC. In `OnPreparePrinting()` you can also change some of the values displayed in the Print dialog box to set the minimum and maximum page count—if you can calculate the page count without the printer DC. When MFC calls `OnPreparePrinting()`, the printer DC has not yet been created.

As mentioned previously, AppWizard provides many printing functions for you. All you have to do is select the Printing and Print Preview option in the AppWizard dialog box. When you do, AppWizard automatically overrides the `OnPreparePrinting()` function (and many other functions) for you, as shown here:

```
BOOL CTextPrintView::OnPreparePrinting(CPrintInfo* pInfo)
{
  // default preparation
  return DoPreparePrinting(pInfo);
}
```

In its default form, `OnPreparePrinting()` calls `DoPreparePrinting()`, which displays the Print dialog box. You can control the options displayed in the dialog box by initializing members of the `CPrintInfo` object that's passed to the function as its single parameter. For example, if you know that the document will be three pages, you can add calls to the `CPrintInfo` object's `SetMinPage()` and `SetMaxPage()` member functions, as follows:

```
BOOL CTextPrintView::OnPreparePrinting(CPrintInfo* pInfo)
{
  // default preparation

  pInfo->SetMinPage(1);
  pInfo->SetMaxPage(3);

  return DoPreparePrinting(pInfo);
}
```

Besides telling MFC how many pages to print, the `SetMinPage()` and `SetMaxPage()` functions also determine the values shown in the Print dialog box's From and To boxes. If you don't call `SetMinPage()` and `SetMaxPage()`, the From box defaults to 1 and the To box remains empty (although MFC will assume only one page is to be printed).

The CPrintInfo Object

In order to successfully manage a print or print preview job, an application must have access to information about the print job. In an MFC program, the framework stores information about a print job in an object of the `CPrintInfo` class. The `CPrintInfo` class contains a number of data members that hold the print job information, as well as member functions that enable an application to manipulate the object. When a user begins a print job, MFC creates the `CPrintInfo` object and maintains it, passing it to functions that need print information, until the print job has completed. In this way, the `CPrintInfo` object is the connection between MFC's internal printing functions and your application's view class.

Information stored in the `CPrintInfo` object includes whether the document is being printed or previewed, the number of the page currently being printed, the number of pages displayed in the print preview window, whether the printing should continue, and whether the document should be printed without displaying the Print dialog box. The `CPrintInfo` object also maintains a pointer to the `CPrintDialog` object that represents the Print dialog box.

When you want to pass print job information from your application's view class to MFC, you call one of the `CPrintInfo` object's member functions. For example, to set the number of the first and last pages in the document, the application can call the `CPrintInfo` object's `SetMinPage()` and `SetMaxPage()`, respectively. The application can call `GetMinPage()` or `GetMaxPage()` to retrieve this information.

To get the number of the first and last page to be printed (the values the user entered into the Print dialog box's From and To boxes), the application can call the `CPrintInfo` object's `GetFromPage()` and `GetToPage()` member functions.

Another way an application can manipulate the `CPrintInfo` object is to set its data members directly. For example, to stop the print job, an application can set the `m_bContinuePrinting` data member to `FALSE`. Another example would be changing the print job's page number format by setting the `CPrintInfo` object's `m_strPageDesc` data member to a custom format string, which you can do in your view class' `OnPreparePrinting()` function. For more information on these topics, check your Visual C++ online documentation.

If your document is a fixed size, as in the preceding example, you know in advance how many pages will be printed. This enables you to set the minimum and maximum pages in `OnPreparePrinting()`. The problem with `OnPreparePrinting()` is that the application does not yet have access to the printer DC, which limits how much information you can determine about the current document and printer. In many cases, you need the printer DC in order to determine how much of the document will fit on a page. If this is the case, you can modify the `OnBeginPrinting()` function.

The OnBeginPrinting() function

After calling `OnPreparePrinting()`, MFC calls the `OnBeginPrinting()` function, where you can create GDI resources (pens, brushes, and fonts) needed by the print job. Also, because `OnBeginPrinting()` is the first place the view window has access to both the printer DC and the `CPrintInfo` structure, you can set page counts and other values here when those values may depend upon the settings of the printer DC.

When you create your application with MFC AppWizard and select the option labelled "Printing and print preview" for the application, AppWizard automatically overrides the `OnBeginPrinting()` function for you, as shown here:

```
void CTextPrintView::OnBeginPrinting(CDC* /*pDC*/,
  CPrintInfo* /*pInfo*/)
{
  // TODO: add extra initialization before printing
}
```

Notice that AppWizard comments out the names of the printer DC and `CPrintInfo` objects in its version of `OnBeginPrinting()`. Obviously, if you're going to access these parameters, you must remove the comments.

Your application will often need to calculate different character sizes for the screen and printer. As far as dots per inch (DPI) goes, screen and printer fonts are rarely the same size. For example, a 10-point font might be 20 pixels high on the screen, but 50 dots high on the printer. If you try to use the same character height for the screen and the printer, the printer output will almost certainly overlap. Figure 15-7 shows a print preview window using the screen character height to print text.

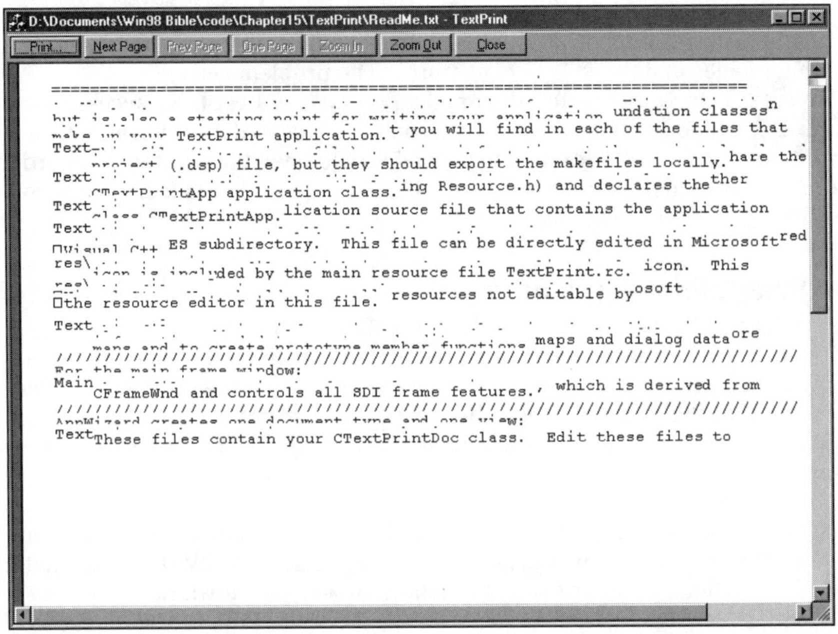

Figure 15-7: If an application uses the screen character size for printing, the text will probably overlap.

When you need to scale text output or calculate page sizes based on printer attributes, you override OnBeginPrinting(), which is the first place you have access to the printer DC. By calling printer DC member functions such as GetTextMetrics(), you can determine the correct character height for the printer, as well as calculate the number of lines per page and the number of pages needed to display the entire document. Listing 15-2 shows an example of the OnBeginPrinting() function calculating character sizes and page counts.

Listing 15-2: The OnBeginPrinting() Function

```
void CTextPrintView::OnBeginPrinting(CDC* pDC,
  CPrintInfo* pInfo)
{
  // TODO: add extra initialization before printing

  TEXTMETRIC textMetric;
  pDC->GetTextMetrics(&textMetric);
  m_printerCharHeight = textMetric.tmHeight +
    textMetric.tmExternalLeading;

  m_vertRes = pDC->GetDeviceCaps(VERTRES);
  m_linesPerPage = m_vertRes / m_printerCharHeight;
  int numPages = m_numLines / m_linesPerPage + 1;
```

```
    pInfo->SetMinPage(1);
    pInfo->SetMaxPage(numPages);
}
```

Understanding the GetTextMetrics() Function

`GetTextMetrics()` enables you to obtain information about the currently selected font. Although `GetTextMetrics()` is a Windows API function, MFC encapsulates the function in its `CDC` class (and classes derived from `CDC`) so you can more easily get information about the font currently associated with the DC. The MFC version of `GetTextMetrics()` requires a single argument, which is the address of a `TEXTMETRIC` structure.

Windows defines a `TEXTMETRIC` structure as shown in the code below. The table following describes each of the structure's members. Unless you know a bit about typography, some of the terms used in the table will be new to you. In most cases, however, you won't need to deal with the more esoteric members of the `TEXTMETRIC` structure. Many of `TEXTMETRIC`'s members are easily understood from their names. For example, `tmHeight` is the height of the font, whereas `tmItalic` determines whether the font is italic.

```
typedef struct tagTEXTMETRIC {  /* tm */
  int  tmHeight;
  int  tmAscent;
  int  tmDescent;
  int  tmInternalLeadinga;
  int  tmExternalLeading;
  int  tmAveCharWidth;
  int  tmMaxCharWidth;
  int  tmWeight;
  BYTE tmItalic;
  BYTE tmUnderlined;
  BYTE tmStruckOut;
  BYTE tmFirstChar;
  BYTE tmLastChar;
  BYTE tmDefaultChar;
  BYTE tmBreakChar;
  BYTE tmPitchAndFamily;
  BYTE tmCharSet;
  int  tmOverhang;
  int  tmDigitizedAspectX;
  int  tmDigitizedAspectY;
} TEXTMETRIC;
```

(continued)

(continued)

Members of the TEXTMETRIC structure

Member	*Description*
`tmAscent`	Character ascent, which is the height above the baseline
`tmAveCharWidth`	Average character width
`tmBreakChar`	Break character for text justification
`tmCharSet`	Font's character set
`tmDefaultChar`	Character to be substituted for those not included in the font
`tmDescent`	Character descent, which is the height below the baseline
`tmDigitizedAspectX`	Horizontal element of the aspect ratio
`tmDigitizedAspectY`	Vertical element of the aspect ratio
`tmExternalLeading`	External leading, which is extra space between lines of text
`tmFirstChar`	Value of the font's first character
`tmHeight`	Character height
`tmInternalLeading`	Internal leading, which is space used for adding marks such as accents
`tmItalic`	Value indicating italic (zero=no italic; nonzero=italic)
`tmLastChar`	Value of the font's last character
`tmMaxCharWidth`	Width of the widest character
`tmOverhang`	Extra width that may be added in order to add attributes such as bold or italic to characters
`tmPitchAndFamily`	Pitch, technology, and family of a physical font
`tmStruckOut`	Value indicating strikeout (zero=no strikeout; nonzero=strikeout)
`tmUnderlined`	Value indicating underlined (zero=no underline; nonzero=underlined)
`tmWeight`	Font weight

In Listing 15-2, after setting the value of `m_printerCharHeight` (which you add as a member variable to the view class), you can use `m_printerCharHeight` to properly space the text. First, though, you need to determine whether `OnDraw()` is being called to display data on the screen or on the printer. The `CDC` object passed to `OnDraw()` defines a member function, called `IsPrinting()`, that returns `TRUE` if MFC is calling the function to render data for the printer. Listing 15-3 shows one way to write the `OnDraw()` function so it displays text correctly on both the screen and the printer. Figure 15-8 shows the print preview window when the application uses the `OnDraw()` function from Listing 15-3.

Listing 15-3: An OnDraw() Function That Uses Different Character Sizes for the Screen and Printer

```
void CTextPrintView::OnDraw(CDC* pDC)
{
  CTextPrintDoc* pDoc = GetDocument();
  ASSERT_VALID(pDoc);

  // TODO: add draw code for native data here

  int charHeight;
  int numLines = pDoc->m_strArray.GetSize();

  if (pDC->IsPrinting())
    charHeight = m_printerCharHeight;
  else
    charHeight = m_charHeight;

  for (int x=0; x<numLines; ++x)
  {
    CString str = pDoc->m_strArray.GetAt(x);
    pDC->TextOut(20, x*charHeight, str);
  }
}
```

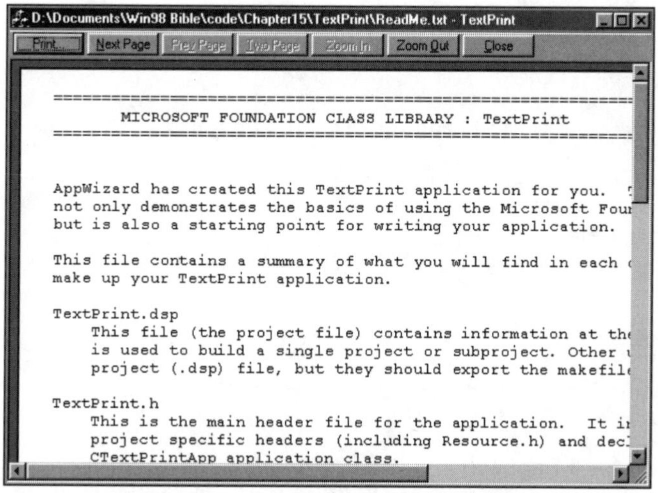

Figure 15-8: The print preview window now shows that the text spacing is correct for the printer.

In Listing 15-3, `OnDraw()` determines whether the output is going to the screen or to the printer by calling `IsPrinting()`. If `IsPrinting()` returns `TRUE`, the data is about to be rendered on the printer, so `OnDraw()` sets `charHeight` to `m_printerCharHeight`, which got its value in `OnBeginPrinting()`. If `IsPrinting()` returns `FALSE`, the data is about to be rendered on the screen, so `OnDraw()` sets `charHeight` to `m_charHeight`, which holds the character height for the screen.

You may now wonder where `m_charHeight` came from. It's a member variable of the view class that you need to add on your own. You can initialize `m_charHeight` in the class' `OnCreate()` function, which you override in the view class. `OnCreate()` responds to the Windows `WM_CREATE` message, so MFC calls `OnCreate()` after the application's window has been created, but right before it displays the window on the screen. To initialize `m_charHeight` to the screen character size, you create a DC for the client window and call its `GetTextMetrics()` member function. Listing 15-4 shows the entire process.

Class Wizard

Handling a WM_CREATE message

Message: `WM_CREATE`
Function Created: `OnCreate()`
Source Code Module: **TextPrintView.cpp**

◆ ◆ ◆ ◆ ◆

Listing 15-4: An OnCreate() Function That Determines the Screen Character Height

```
int CTextPrintView::OnCreate
  (LPCREATESTRUCT lpCreateStruct)
{
  if (CScrollView::OnCreate(lpCreateStruct) == -1)
    return -1;

  // TODO: Add your specialized creation code here

  TEXTMETRIC tm;
  CClientDC clientDC(this);
  clientDC.GetTextMetrics(&tm);
  m_charHeight = tm.tmHeight + tm.tmExternalLeading;

  return 0;
}
```

Expert Tip

Selecting GDI Objects for a Print Job

If you use `OnBeginPrinting()` to create GDI objects for a print job, don't select the new GDI objects into the printer DC right away. Instead, select them in the

OnPrint() member function that gets called for each page. This rule applies because the DC is reinitialized for each page of the document. MFC calls OnBeginPrinting() only once for the entire document but calls OnPrint() for each page. That is, you can access information about the printer in OnBeginPrinting(), but you shouldn't modify the DC until OnPrint().

◆ ◆ ◆ ◆ ◆

The OnPrepareDC() function

Now, you're ready to examine the third MFC printing function, OnPrepareDC(). MFC calls OnPrepareDC() for each page in the document. Moreover, MFC calls OnPrepareDC() right before the page gets printed. This means when you're using OnDraw() to render data for both the screen and the printer, you can use OnPrepareDC() to control exactly what portion of the document MFC is sent to the printer. You might override OnPrepareDC() when the application must print multiple-page documents. You can also use OnPrepareDC() to set mapping modes and other attributes of the printer device context for each page of the document.

For example, you previously discovered how you can determine the printer character size. Using the printer character size when sending data to the printer yields properly spaced text. However, if the document length exceeds one page, it still doesn't print correctly. You get all the pages, but each page starts with the first text line and runs off the bottom of the page. This phenomenon occurs because for each page of the document, OnDraw() draws the entire document. To paginate properly, you need some way to tell OnDraw() to start printing further into the document, as appropriate for each page. You do this by calling the printer DC's SetViewportOrg() function, as shown in Listing 15-5.

Listing 15-5: An OnPrepareDC() Function That Sets the Viewport Origin

```
void CTextPrintView::OnPrepareDC(CDC* pDC,
  CPrintInfo* pInfo)
{
  // TODO: Add your specialized code here
  // and/or call the base class

  if (pDC->IsPrinting())
  {
    int start = (pInfo->m_nCurPage - 1) * m_vertRes;
    pDC->SetViewportOrg(0, -start);
  }

  CView::OnPrepareDC(pDC, pInfo);
}
```

You can use the SetViewportOrg() to tell Windows that the document starts at a different point, later in the document rather than right at the beginning. SetViewportOrg() takes two arguments: the *x* and *y* coordinates of the new origin (where the document starts).

As you now know, MFC calls OnPrepareDC() once for each page in the document. When MFC calls OnPrepareDC() for the first page, the function sets the document's origin to 0,0, which is the real beginning of the document. The program sends the entire document to the page, starting at coordinates 0,0. The part of the document that doesn't fit on the page runs off the bottom of the page and doesn't appear.

When MFC calls OnPrepareDC() for the second page, the function sets the origin to the start of the second page. Again, the program sends the entire document to the page, but now the program thinks the document starts at the second page, determined by the new origin. If the document is still too long for the second page, the remaining data runs off the bottom of the second page and doesn't appear.

This process continues for each page in the document, with OnPrepareDC() moving the document's origin forward a page at a time.

Note

Notice that OnPrepareDC() calls the DC's IsPrinting() member function before doing anything. This function call is important because MFC calls OnPrepareDC() when displaying data on the screen, as well as on the printer. When displaying data on the screen, you may not want to fiddle with the origin.

✦ ✦ ✦ ✦ ✦

At this point, your application is close to having fully functional printing capabilities. However, there's still a problem. For many printers, the number of lines that fit on the printed page will not be a whole number. For example, a printer with a vertical page resolution of 3,175 (the number of dots that fit vertically on the page) and a character height of 50 (the size of the DC's current font) can display 63.5 lines per page. (To get the lines per page, you divide the printer's vertical page resolution by the character height.) And when you print the document, 63.5 lines is exactly what you get. For example, Figure 15-9 shows the print preview for the bottom of a document's first page. As you can see, the printer has split a line between the current page and the next.

At this point, it's no longer prudent to use OnDraw() to render the document for both the screen and the printer. Now you need to move the printing tasks to the OnPrint() function, which you do in the next section.

Note

When you create your application with AppWizard, AppWizard doesn't automatically override OnPrepareDC() in your view window's class. You must override OnPrepareDC() using ClassWizard (or add it by hand).

✦ ✦ ✦ ✦ ✦

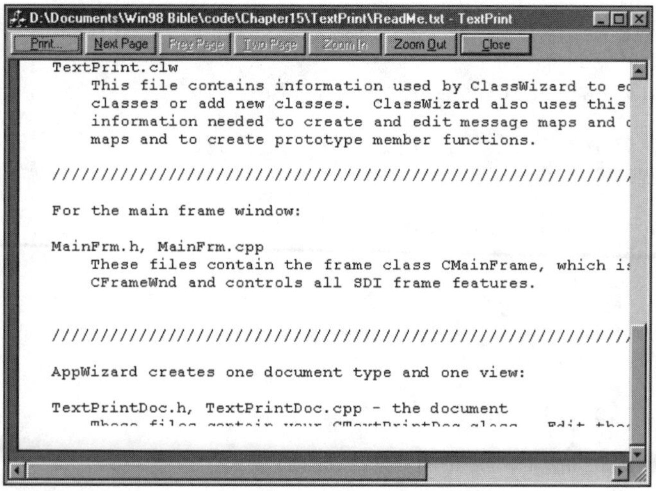

Figure 15-9: The print preview shows the bottom line running off the document's first page.

The OnPrint() function

`OnPrint()` is where you can add the code you need for a specific printing task, without having to contend with `OnDraw()`'s generic printer handling. MFC calls `OnPrint()` for each page, right after calling `OnPrepareDC()`. If you like, you can even set the viewport origin (which, you should remember, controls what portion of the document is output for the page) in `OnPrint()` rather than in `OnPrepareDC()`. Usually, though, you'll override `OnPrint()` when you want to output the document's data differently for the printer than for the screen. You can also use `OnPrint()` to output headers and footers before the document itself is rendered by the `OnDraw()` function.

Note

When you create your application with AppWizard, AppWizard doesn't automatically override `OnPrint()` in your view window's class. You must override `OnPrint()` using ClassWizard. When you do, make sure you comment out the call to `CView::OnPrint()` (or `CScrollView::OnPrint()`, as is the case with the TextPrint application) because that's where MFC calls the `OnDraw()` function, which your application should not do when it's doing all its printing in `OnPrint()`.

◆ ◆ ◆ ◆ ◆

Previously, the application's printer text output for each page had its last line cut in half. To get pagination to work properly in this case, you can separate the screen-display code from the code that draws to the printer. The program can then handle the entire printing task in one place, rather than having to keep calling `IsPrinting()` and performing different tasks based on the result. Listing 15-6 shows how `OnPrint()` might look for this section's text example. The listing also shows the functions that need to be changed to accommodate the `OnPrint()` function. For example, `OnPrepareDC()` no longer sets the viewport origin for each page. `OnDraw()`, on the other hand, contains only the code needed to draw the document in the application's window.

Listing 15-6: The OnPrint() and OnPrepareDC() Functions

```
void CTextPrintView::OnPrint(CDC* pDC, CPrintInfo* pInfo)
{
  // TODO: Add your specialized code here and/or
  //   call the base class

  int startLine = (pInfo->m_nCurPage - 1) *
    m_linesPerPage + 1;
  int endLine = startLine + m_linesPerPage - 1;
  if (endLine > m_numLines)
    endLine = m_numLines;

  int curLine = 0;
  CTextPrintDoc* pDoc = GetDocument();

  for(int x=startLine; x<=endLine; ++x)
  {
    if (x < m_numLines)
    {
      CString str = pDoc->m_strArray.GetAt(x);
      pDC->TextOut(20, curLine*m_printerCharHeight, str);
      ++ curLine;
    }
  }

  //CScrollView::OnPrint(pDC, pInfo);
}

void CTextPrintView::OnPrepareDC(CDC* pDC,
    CPrintInfo* pInfo)
{
  // TODO: Add your specialized code here and/or
  //   call the base class

  CScrollView::OnPrepareDC(pDC, pInfo);
}

void CTextPrintView::OnDraw(CDC* pDC)
{
  CTextPrintDoc* pDoc = GetDocument();
  ASSERT_VALID(pDoc);

  // TODO: add draw code for native data here

  int numLines = pDoc->m_strArray.GetSize();
  for (int x=0; x<numLines; ++x)
  {
    CString str = pDoc->m_strArray.GetAt(x);
    pDC->TextOut(20, x*m_charHeight, str);
  }
}
```

The version of OnPrint() in Listing 15-6 determines exactly which lines of the document should be drawn on the current page. OnPrint() then draws only those lines, without leaving a partial line at the bottom of the page. MFC passes the current page to OnPrint() in the CPrintInfo object member m_nCurPage. Here's a quick rundown on what the OnPrint() function does in Listing 15-6:

- ✦ Calculates the number of the first line to print
- ✦ Calculates the number of the last line to print
- ✦ Uses the first and last line numbers as the control values in a for loop
- ✦ Prints a line of text in each iteration of the loop

Figure 15-10 shows the application's working pagination. In the figure, you can see the program no longer prints partial lines at the bottom of the first page.

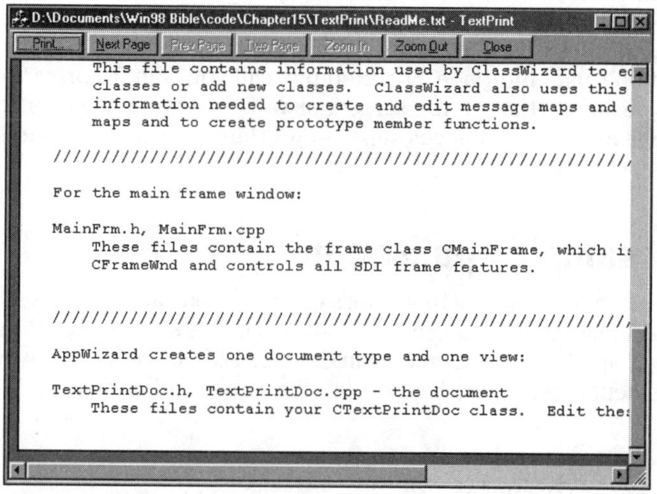

Figure 15-10: Print preview now shows the first page ending with a complete line.

The OnEndPrinting() function

MFC defines one last function that you need to examine in order to give your application complete printing capabilities. That function is OnEndPrinting(), which is the counterpart for the OnBeginPrinting() function. MFC calls OnEndPrinting() when the print job has been completed, giving your application a chance to release resources allocated in OnBeginPrinting(). AppWizard overrides OnEndPrinting() in your application as shown here:

```
void CTextPrintView::OnEndPrinting(CDC* /*pDC*/,
  CPrintInfo* /*pInfo*/)
{
  // TODO: add cleanup after printing
}
```

Notice that the `CDC` and `CPrintInfo` objects passed to the function are commented out. You need to remove the comments if you want to access these objects in the body of the function.

You now know how to add text printing capabilities to your MFC applications. It's time to move on to graphics printing. In most cases, graphical screens don't need to deal with text sizes and line spacing. Instead, scaling is accomplished using a physical measurement, such as inches or millimeters. In the following sections, you learn how this scaling works.

Printing Graphics in an MFC Application

When you print a text document, you need to be aware of text sizes to space the lines of the document correctly. When you print a document that contains graphics, you need to scale all the elements that compose the document so the output looks reasonably similar to that on the screen. How you want to perform this scaling depends on the application's needs, and this is a choice you need to make as you design your application's user interface. For example, will you want to print the output so it's the same size as that on the screen, or will you enable the user to scale the screen image and printer images separately? Here, you can examine one approach to printing scaled images.

The RectPrint sample application

In the Chapter15\RectPrint directory of this book's CD-ROM, you can find the RectPrint application, which demonstrate the concepts you learned in this section. RectPrint is based on the RectApp2 application you created in Chapter 12. This version, however, prints rectangle documents scaled properly on both the screen and printer.

Demo Program

RectPrint
CD-ROM Location: **Chap15\RectPrint**
Program Name: **RectPrint.exe**
Source Code Modules in Text: **None**

◆ ◆ ◆ ◆ ◆

When you run the application, you can draw rectangles in the window just as you did with the Chapter 12 version, by clicking in the window. This version, however, features a ruler at the top of the screen, which indicates the size of the screen's logical inches, as shown in Figure 15-11. Figure 15-12 shows how the rectangle document appears in print preview. As you can see, the printer output is properly scaled.

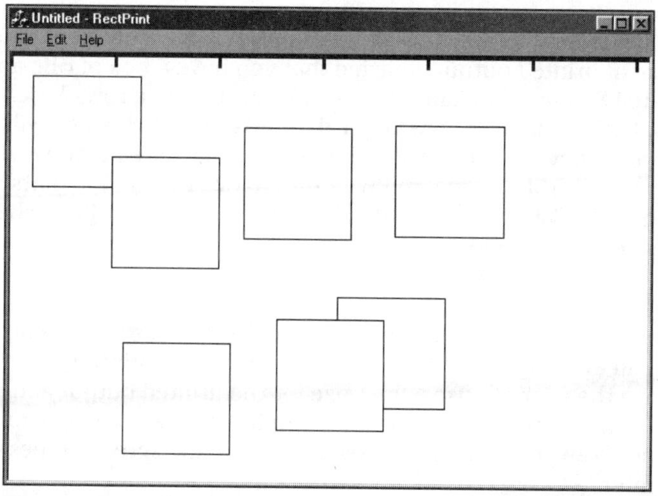

Figure 15-11: The RectPrint screen displaying a set of rectangles

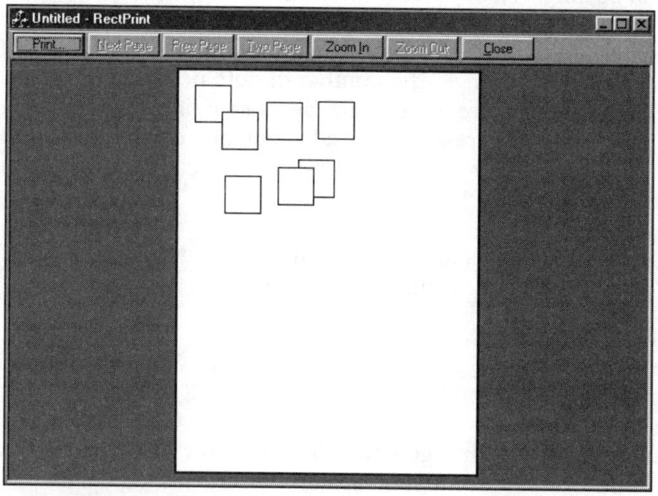

Figure 15-12: RectPrint's print preview showing the document just created

Scaling between the screen and printer

As you learned in the section on printing text, the screen and the printer usually have different resolutions. For example, the horizontal and vertical dots per inch on the screen may be 96, whereas the printer's horizontal and vertical dots per inch may be 300 or more. (The horizontal and vertical values aren't necessarily the same.) Because the screen has larger dots, when you print an image on both the screen and the printer, the printer's image looks small.

Note

If you have a hard time understanding how the dots-per-inch measurement of a device affects the size of printed output, imagine that you have a box of BBs and a box of marbles. Lay 100 BBs in a row, and then lay 100 marbles in a row. Which line is longer? Obviously, because marbles are larger than BBs, the marble line will be longer than the BB line. A device's dots-per-inch measurements are no more mysterious than BBs and marbles. If you tell Windows to draw a line 100 units long on a 96 DPI device and on a 300 DPI device, the 300 DPI device's line will be shorter, because the device's dots are smaller.

You can solve this resolution problem in several ways. You can use a different mapping mode (instead of the default `MM_TEXT`) for drawing and printing your graphics. You can have the user choose a final size for the printed output and scale the output based on that choice. Or, if it suits your application, you can use one of the simplest solutions: Draw the images so a logical inch on the screen comes out as an inch on the printer.

The Windows API function `GetDeviceCaps()` will give you the information you need to do this type of scaling. When you call `GetDeviceCaps()` with the constant `LOGPIXELSX` as its single argument, the function returns the number of dots per logical horizontal inch on the screen. Similarly, when you call `GetDeviceCaps()` with the argument `LOGPIXELSY`, you get the number of dots per logical, vertical inch on the screen. The keyword here is "logical." Because monitors come in different sizes but display the same resolutions, a logical inch on one screen may truly be an inch, whereas on a larger or smaller screen, a logical inch will be larger or smaller than an inch.

So, the first step in printer output scaling is to get the logical dots per inch for the screen. Following is an example of how this could be done:

```
CClientDC clientDC(this);
screenHDotsPerInch = clientDC.GetDeviceCaps(LOGPIXELSX);
screenVDotsPerInch = clientDC.GetDeviceCaps(LOGPIXELSY);
```

In these sample lines, the program first gets the client window's DC and then calls the DC's `GetDeviceCaps()` member function to get the screen's logical inch. You can place the previous lines anywhere in the program after the system has created the application's window. In an MFC program, a good place is in the `OnCreate()` function, which responds to the Windows `WM_CREATE` message.

After getting the screen's logical inch, you need to get the printer's logical inch. To do that, you would use code similar to the following snippet:

```
int printerHDotsPerInch = pDC->GetDeviceCaps(LOGPIXELSX);
int printerVDotsPerInch = pDC->GetDeviceCaps(LOGPIXELSY);
```

Notice that you call `GetDeviceCaps()` through a pointer named `pDC`. The `pDC` pointer is the address of a printer DC, so in order to call `GetDeviceCaps()` for the printer, you must already have a printer DC. If you're using `OnDraw()` to send data to the printer, you can place the previous lines there, checking the DC's `IsPrinting()` flag to be sure the DC is a printer DC and not the screen DC, as shown in Listing 15-7.

Listing 15-7: Checking for a Printer DC and Calculating the Scaling Values for the Printer

```
float hScale = 1.0;
float vScale = 1.0;

if (pDC->IsPrinting())
{
  int printerHDotsPerInch =
    pDC->GetDeviceCaps(LOGPIXELSX);
  int printerVDotsPerInch =
    pDC->GetDeviceCaps(LOGPIXELSY);
  hScale = (float)printerHDotsPerInch /
    (float)screenHDotsPerInch;
  vScale = (float)printerVDotsPerInch /
    (float)screenVDotsPerInch;
}
```

Here, the program creates horizontal and vertical scaling values by dividing the printer's logical inch by the screen's logical inch. You can then use these scaling factors with output coordinates to create a display that's appropriate for both the screen and the printer. For example, suppose the variables `x1`, `y1`, `x2`, and `y2` contain the screen coordinates for a shape. You might scale the coordinates as follows:

```
x1 = (int)(x1 * hScale);
y1 = (int)(y1 * vScale);
x2 = (int)(x2 * hScale);
y2 = (int)(y2 * vScale);
```

Referring back to Listing 15-7, if the DC passed to `OnDraw()` is a screen DC, `hScale` and `vScale` end up set to 1.0. The coordinates, when multiplied by `hScale` and `vScale`, stay the same, with the scaling values replaced by the actual values:

```
x1 = (int)(x1 * 1.0);
y1 = (int)(y1 * 1.0);
x2 = (int)(x2 * 1.0);
y2 = (int)(y2 * 1.0);
```

If the DC is a printer DC, however, `hScale` and `vScale` are set to the result of dividing printer logical inches by screen logical inches. Suppose, for example, that the screen logical inch is 96 pixels, both horizontally and vertically, and the printer's logical inch is 300, both horizontally and vertically. Substituting actual values for the `printerHDotsPerInch` and `screenHDotsPerInch` variables, you get the following calculation:

```
hScale = 300 / 96;
vScale = 300 / 96;
```

This calculation yields the following results:

```
hScale = 3.125;
vScale = 3.125;
```

You can see from these scaling values that the screen's logical inch contains a little over three times as many dots as the printer's logical inch, both horizontally and vertically. When printing, all screen coordinates must be multiplied by the scaling values so a logical inch on the screen equals an inch on the printer:

```
x1 = (int)(x1 * 3.125);
y1 = (int)(y1 * 3.125);
x2 = (int)(x2 * 3.125);
y2 = (int)(y2 * 3.125);
```

The OnCreate() function

To perform the scaling, the program needs to calculate the screen's logical inch, which it can do in the `OnCreate()` function. Listing 15-8 shows the program's `OnCreate()` function, which was added to the program using ClassWizard.

Listing 15-8: Calculating Scaling Values for the Printer

```
int CRectPrintView::OnCreate
  (LPCREATESTRUCT lpCreateStruct)
{
  if (CView::OnCreate(lpCreateStruct) == -1)
    return -1;

  // TODO: Add your specialized creation code here

  CClientDC clientDC(this);
  m_winHDotsPerInch =
    clientDC.GetDeviceCaps(LOGPIXELSX);
  m_winVDotsPerInch =
    clientDC.GetDeviceCaps(LOGPIXELSY);

  return 0;
}
```

The OnDraw() function

Unlike TextPrint, which had to separate screen data display from printing, RectPrint uses `OnDraw()` for drawing on both the screen and the printer. Listing 15-9 shows the `OnDraw()` function, which performs the following tasks:

✦ Initializes the horizontal and vertical scaling variables to 1.0

✦ If the DC is for the printer, gets the printer's logical inch and divides it by the window's logical inch, resetting the horizontal and vertical scaling variables

✦ Processes the application's rectangle document, scaling the output as appropriate

✦ If the DC is not for the printer, draws a ruler on the screen

Listing 15-9: **RectPrint's OnDraw() Function**

```
void CRectPrintView::OnDraw(CDC* pDC)
{
  CRectPrintDoc* pDoc = GetDocument();
  ASSERT_VALID(pDoc);

  // TODO: add draw code for native data here

  float hScale = 1.0;
  float vScale = 1.0;

  if (pDC->IsPrinting())
  {
    int printHDotsPerInch =
      pDC->GetDeviceCaps(LOGPIXELSX);
    int printVDotsPerInch =
      pDC->GetDeviceCaps(LOGPIXELSY);
    hScale = (float)printHDotsPerInch /
      (float)m_winHDotsPerInch;
    vScale = (float)printVDotsPerInch /
      (float)m_winVDotsPerInch;
  }

  int size = pDoc->m_rects.GetCount();
  for (int z=0; z<size; ++z)
  {
    CPoint point;
    pDoc->m_rects.Get(z, &point);
    int x1 = (int)(point.x * hScale);
    int y1 = (int)(point.y * vScale);
    int x2 = (int)((point.x+100) * hScale);
    int y2 = (int)((point.y+100) * vScale);
    pDC->Rectangle(x1, y1, x2, y2);
  }
```

(continued)

Listing 15-9 (continued)

```
    if (!pDC->IsPrinting())
    {
      CPen newPen(PS_SOLID, 3, RGB(0,0,0));
      CPen* pOldPen = pDC->SelectObject(&newPen);
      pDC->MoveTo(0, 1);
      pDC->LineTo(800, 1);

      for (int i=0; i<10; ++i)
      {
        pDC->MoveTo(i*m_winHDotsPerInch, 1);
        pDC->LineTo(i*m_winHDotsPerInch, 10);
      }
      pDC->SelectObject(pOldPen);
    }
}
```

The OnPreparePrinting() function

Unlike the text printing application you learned about earlier in this chapter, RectPrint doesn't take advantage of the `OnPreparePrinting()`, `OnBeginPrinting()`, and `OnEndPrinting()` functions, except to set the maximum page count to 1, as shown here:

```
BOOL CRectPrintView::OnPreparePrinting(CPrintInfo* pInfo)
{
  // default preparation

  pInfo->SetMaxPage(1);

  return DoPreparePrinting(pInfo);
}
```

Summary

Many of the applications you write for Windows 98 will require the capability to print documents. Although printing under Windows can become a complex task, MFC takes over some of the burden by not only providing a printer context for the print job, but also handling the Print dialog box and providing functions that enable you to access the printing process at various points. The printing functions you study in this chapter are `OnPreparePrinting()`, `OnBeginPrinting()`, `OnPrepareDC()`, `OnPrint()`, and `OnEndPrinting()`. You also learn how functions like `OnDraw()` and `OnCreate()` can fit into the printing process.

✦ ✦ ✦

PART III

Advanced Topics in MFC Programming

This section on advanced MFC programming separates the professionals from the rookies. You learn how to take full advantage of the MFC classes to produce professional user interfaces on par with world-class applications such as Word and Excel.

Besides showing you how to take full advantage of MFC, this part offers tricks and tips that can help you advance your programs to an even higher level. Instructions on extending MFC classes enable you build on them to create your own proprietary classes.

In This Part

Chapter 16
Extending MFC Classes

Chapter 17
Toolbars and Status Bar

Chapter 18
Threads

CHAPTER 16

Extending MFC Classes

In This Chapter

Seeing how easy it is to build on the MFC classes

Writing an auto-completion Combo box

Writing a "grey edit" control

Writing an underline edit" control

Writing a "page view" control

Writing a "list-box view" control

As you've worked through this book, you've seen that MFC does a great job of not only encapsulating basic Windows functionality, but also extending it via C++ classes. Other chapters, particularly in this section of the book, have illustrated how to work with these MFC classes; we also presented some classes that extend basic MFC functionality. For example, Chapter 19 shows how to use the MFC database classes to access ODBC data sources. In addition, this chapter presents a class that goes beyond the basic MFC database classes and provides a way to dynamically query any data source, even when the database schema is not known.

Efficiency forbids illustrating every feature of MFC *and* presenting extensions to all MFC classes to implement those features. Nevertheless, this chapter is devoted to extending the MFC classes by implementing additional functionality not found in the base MFC classes. All code for these classes can be found in the `\Chap16\MFCExtensions` folder on the book's accompanying CD-ROM.

UI Controls

This first section looks at extending some MFC control classes. Although MFC certainly does a great job of giving us a tremendous amount of flexibility and power there are always going to be times when a particular application calls for something a little different in terms of user interface. The first extension in this section — an "auto-complete" combo box like the one you may know from your favorite Web browser — illustrates just what I mean. As you type the entry into the Edit portion of the combo box, the combo box finds the nearest match in its list of entries and displays it. After you see just how easy it is to implement this cool little control, two `CEdit`-derived classes are presented: `CGreyEdit` and `CUnderlineEdit`. These classes need not offer functionality beyond what they inherit from their `CEdit` parent class —

they help tremendously when you need to present a dialog whose appearance more closely resembles a real-world document such as an invoice or purchase order.

CAutoCompleteComboBox

One of the nice things about the Microsoft Explorer is that the Address combo box not only contains the last several addresses typed in, but it also supports a handy capability called *auto complete*: As you type text into the combo box's edit control, the combo box is busy finding the nearest match in its list of entries. For example, let's say the combo box has the following entries:

```
c:\mycode\docviewtest
c:\mycode\editcontroltest
```

Let's say you want to search for the `c:\mycode\editcontroltest`. When you type the letter **c**, the first entry that matches what you typed, `c:\mycode\docviewtest`, is selected into the combo box. Actually, what you see is the letter you typed plus the rest of the entry; the selected text color helps you distinguish what you've typed from the rest of the text. As you continue typing, the entry doesn't change until you type the letter **e** of `editcontroltest` (because both entries contain the `\mycode\` text). At this point, the combo box automatically selects the second entry in the combo box. For a combo box with just a couple of entries, that may not seem like such a big deal. If you have hundreds of entries, however, you'll be much more popular with your users if they *don't* have to scroll through the entire list manually to find a specific entry.

Curiously enough, the regular Windows combo box does provide partial support for this auto-complete function; the biggest limitation is that the Windows combo box control offers no way to distinguish between what you've typed and what the combo box filled in. Using the previous example again, as you type the string **c:\mycode**, there is no change in what you see in the combo box. The combo box only changes when it finds another match. According to the usability testing done at some of the companies I've worked for, the user has no idea that the combo box is searching for a match, quickly abandons the idea of typing an entry, and resorts to searching manually for the desired entry in the drop-down list.

CAutoCompleteComboBox source code

Implementing this functionality is straightforward: You create a `CComboBox`-derived class, implement a handler for the `CBN_EDITUPDATE` notification message, and override the `PreTranslateMessage()` function. Figure 16-1 shows an auto-complete CcomboBox control in action.

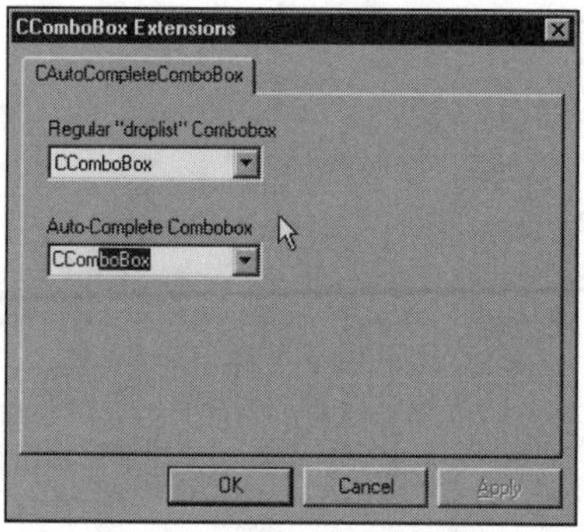

Figure 16-1: Example of an auto-complete combo box

The first thing the `OnEditUpdate()` function does is to check a member variable called `m_bFindNearestMatch` to see whether we want to keep searching for matches (I'll explain this flag in a moment). The text typed in the combo box's edit control is used as an argument to the `CComboBox::FindString()` member function. This is basically a function that allows you to perform a case-independent search of a combo box for a string. If the search is successful, the index of the corresponding entry is returned. If an index is returned, it sets the current selection of the combo box (via a call to `CComboBox::SetCurSel()`). The length of the original string that the user typed is then used to determine the starting position for the `CComboBox::SetEditSel()` function. Using this value, we can be sure that the only characters that appear as selected text are the characters that have not been typed in, but are a result of the `FindString()` function.

```
void CAutoCompleteComboBox::OnEditUpdate()
{
 if (m_bFindNearestMatch)
 {
  char szEntry[CHAR_MAX];
  int nLen = GetWindowText(szEntry,
   CHAR_MAX);

  int iIndex;
  if (CB_ERR != (iIndex = FindString(-1,
   szEntry)))
  {
   SetCurSel(iIndex);
   SetEditSel(nLen, -1);
  }
 }
}
```

All that's left to do is to implement an override of the `PreTranslateMessage()` function, so that pressing the Del or the Backspace key stops the search for a match to the text typed in so far. If the user presses one of those keys, a member variable called (`m_bFindNearestMatch`) is set. This variable is used by `OnEditUpdate()` to decide whether it should continue searching the combo box while the user types.

```
BOOL CAutoCompleteComboBox::PreTranslateMessage(MSG* pMsg)
{
 if (WM_KEYDOWN == pMsg->message)
 {
  if ((VK_BACK == pMsg->wParam)
  || (VK_DELETE == pMsg->wParam))
  {
   m_bFindNearestMatch = FALSE;
  }
  else
  {
   m_bFindNearestMatch = TRUE;
  }
 }

 return CComboBox::PreTranslateMessage(pMsg);
}
```

Using the CAutoCompleteComboBox

As you would with any other class, you can simply use DDX to subclass a dialog's combo box with this class. After you've done that, you're finished! No other code is required to make this class work.

CGreyEdit

If you've ever used Intuit's Quicken or Peachtree Accounting for Windows, you may have noticed something called a "grey edit control" on some of the dialogs. As you can see in Figure 16-2, a grey edit control is one in which the text is grey and italicized until the control has focus or until data has been entered into the control. Where this little control becomes very useful is in situations where there is no room on the dialog box for a static control that properly describes what the edit control is for. For example, let's say you have a group of edit controls that make up an address (name, street one, street two, and so on). Because the controls are nestled so closely, you don't have any room for any static controls. Another example that we faced at Peachtree was on the registry screens. Again, the controls (date, check number, payee, and so on) are closely coupled, leaving no room to tell users what they need to enter into each edit control. Using the `CGreyEdit` control, a user can see the description of an edit control in the edit control itself; the grey, italicized font signals that this description is not the actual value for the field. After the control receives focus, the grey text disappears so the user is not distracted. When the control loses focus, whether or not the grey text returns depends on whether the user typed any information into the control.

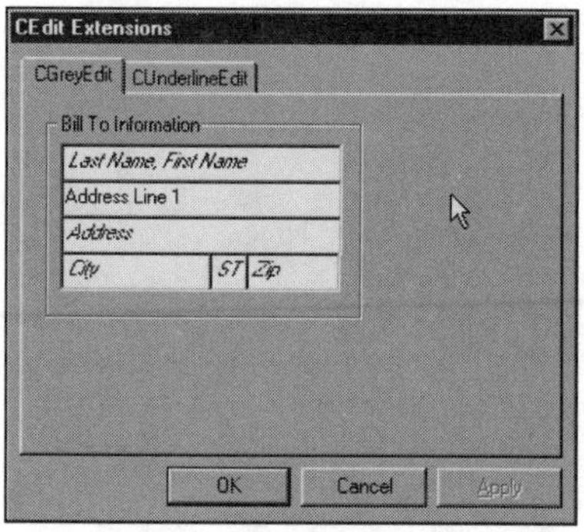

Figure 16-2: Example of the "CGreyEdit" class at work.

CGreyEdit source code

Consistently throughout this book, rather than print out entire source files for both headers and implementation files, I've placed only the salient code here, along with descriptions of what each function does.

To use the `CGreyEdit` class, all you need to do is instantiate it and call its `Init()` member function. The first argument is the resource ID of the edit control you want subclassed. The second and third arguments are the parent window of the edit control and the default text you want displayed in the control. The last two arguments both have defaults. The `clrBackgroundColor` argument defaults to the Window's `COLOR_WINDOWTEXT`, and the `uiAlignment` argument defaults to left-alignment. After that, the `Init` function creates two fonts and stores them as member variables: one for the italicized text and another "regular" font. After that's done, some basic initialization is performed for the control:

```
BOOL CGreyEdit::Init(UINT uiControlId,
 CWnd *pParent, const char *lpszDefaultText,
 COLORREF lBackgroundColor,
 UINT uiAlignment)
{
 BOOL bStat =
  SubclassDlgItem(uiControlId,pParent);
 if (bStat)
 {
  CClientDC dcClient(CWnd::GetDesktopWindow());
  LOGFONT lf;

  memset(&lf, 0, sizeof LOGFONT);
  lf.lfHeight = PointSizeToHeight(8, &dcClient);
  lf.lfWeight = FW_NORMAL;
  strcpy(lf.lfFaceName, "MS Sans Serif");
  lf.lfWeight = FW_NORMAL;

  VERIFY(m_DialogFont.CreateFontIndirect(&lf));

  lf.lfItalic = TRUE;
```

```
VERIFY(m_DialogItalicFont.CreateFontIndirect(&lf));

  m_sDefaultText = lpszDefaultText;
  m_uiAlignment = uiAlignment;

  // don't trust it to be blank before we start
  SetWindowText(m_sDefaultText);
  SetBlankFieldToDefaultText();
  m_lBackgroundColor = lBackgroundColor;
  CreateBackgroundBrush();

  m_bInitialized = TRUE;
 }

 return(bStat);
}
```

The following is a very simple function used to convert a font's point size to a pixel value for the height:

```
int CGreyEdit::PointSizeToHeight(int iPointSize, CDC *pDC)
{
 return (-( MulDiv (iPointSize,
  pDC->GetDeviceCaps(LOGPIXELSY),72)));
}
```

When the edit control is destroyed, the following function is internally called to "unsubclass" the control:

```
BOOL CGreyEdit::UnSubclass()
{
 WNDPROC     OldWndProc;
 WNDPROC*    lplpfn = GetSuperWndProcAddr();

 // return if null
 if ( !*lplpfn ) return FALSE;

 // Set the original window procedure
 OldWndProc = (WNDPROC)::SetWindowLong(
  m_hWnd, GWL_WNDPROC, (LONG) *lplpfn );

 if ( OldWndProc != AfxWndProc ) return FALSE;

 Detach();

 return TRUE;
}

void CGreyEdit::OnDestroy()
{
 UnSubclass();
 CEdit::OnDestroy();
}
```

Here are a couple of "helper" functions that simply set the edit control's font and text color:

```
void CGreyEdit::SetToGreyItalic()
{
 SetFont(&m_DialogItalicFont);
 m_clrTextColor = RGB(192,192,192);
}

void CGreyEdit::SetToNormal()
{
 SetFont(&m_DialogFont);
 m_clrTextColor = ::GetSysColor(COLOR_WINDOWTEXT);
}

void CGreyEdit::SetText(CString &strText)
{
 SetWindowText(strText);
 SetBlankFieldToDefaultText();
}

CString CGreyEdit::GetText()
{
 CString strText;
 GetWindowText(strText);
 strText.TrimLeft();
 strText.TrimRight();
 if (strText == m_sDefaultText)
 {
  strText = "";
 }

 return(strText);
}
```

As its name implies, the following function resets an edit control's text to the defined default text if it is blank:

```
void CGreyEdit::SetBlankFieldToDefaultText()
{
 CString sText;

 // set to default if it's blank
 GetWindowText(sText);
 sText.TrimRight();
 sText.TrimLeft();
 if (!sText.GetLength())
 {
  SetWindowText(m_sDefaultText);
```

```
 }

 // if it's default, set to grey italic
 GetWindowText(sText);
 if(sText == m_sDefaultText)
 {
  SetToGreyItalic();
 }
 else
 {
  SetToNormal();
 }

 Invalidate(FALSE);
}

void CGreyEdit::OnSetFocus(CWnd* pOldWnd)
{
 SetToNormal();

 CString sText;
 GetWindowText(sText);
 if(sText == m_sDefaultText)
 {
  sText = "";
  SetWindowText(sText);
 }

 CEdit::OnSetFocus(pOldWnd);
}

void CGreyEdit::OnKillFocus(CWnd* pNewWnd)
{
 SetBlankFieldToDefaultText();

 CEdit::OnKillFocus(pNewWnd);
}
```

Here we need to do a little `OnCtlColor` work to ensure that the correct brush is being used when Windows paints the edit control and its text:

```
HBRUSH CGreyEdit::OnCtlColor(CDC* pDC, CWnd* pWnd, UINT
nCtlColor)
{
 HBRUSH hbrReturnBrush;
 CPoint ptBrushOrigin(0,0);

 // make sure we have the most recent color for the background
 m_brBackground.DeleteObject();
 CreateBackgroundBrush();

 switch (nCtlColor)
 {
```

```
    case CTLCOLOR_EDIT:
     pDC->SetTextColor(GetTextColor());
     pDC->SetBkMode(TRANSPARENT);
     ClientToScreen(&ptBrushOrigin);
     m_brBackground.UnrealizeObject();
     pDC->SetBrushOrg(ptBrushOrigin.x, ptBrushOrigin.y);
     hbrReturnBrush = (HBRUSH)m_brBackground.m_hObject;
    break;

    case CTLCOLOR_MSGBOX:
     ClientToScreen(&ptBrushOrigin);
     m_brBackground.UnrealizeObject();
     pDC->SetBrushOrg(ptBrushOrigin.x, ptBrushOrigin.y);
     hbrReturnBrush = (HBRUSH)m_brBackground.m_hObject;
    break;

    default:
     // return a brush provided by the default window procedure
    hbrReturnBrush = (HBRUSH)Default();
   }

  return(hbrReturnBrush);
 }
```

The following function returns the background brush to `OnCtlColor` so that the background of the edit control is painted correctly:

```
void CGreyEdit::CreateBackgroundBrush()
{
 ASSERT(m_lBackgroundColor > -1);
 COLORREF clrBackground;

 // an RGB value up to RGB(255,255,255)
 if (m_lBackgroundColor < MAXRGB)
 {
  clrBackground = (COLORREF)m_lBackgroundColor;
 }
 else
 {
  clrBackground = ::GetSysColor(m_lBackgroundColor - MAXRGB);
 }

 m_brBackground.CreateSolidBrush(clrBackground);
}

BOOL CGreyEdit::IsDirty()
{
 CString strCurrentText;
 GetWindowText(strCurrentText);

 return(strCurrentText != m_strInitialText && strCurrentText !=
 m_sDefaultText);
}
```

Using the CGreyEdit control

To use this control, simply create a member variable of type CGreyEdit in your dialog or view class, and call the object's Init function, just as in the code from the MFCExtensions sample on the CD-ROM:

```
BOOL CGreyEditPage::OnInitDialog()
{
 CPropertyPage::OnInitDialog();

 m_edtName.Init(IDC_EDT_NAME, this,
  _T("Last Name, First Name"), RGB(255,0,0));
 m_edtAddr1.Init(IDC_EDT_ADDR1, this, _T("Address"));
 m_edtAddr2.Init(IDC_EDT_ADDR2, this, _T("Address"));
 m_edtCity.Init(IDC_EDT_CITY, this, _T("City"));
 m_edtState.Init(IDC_EDT_STATE, this, _T("ST"));
 m_edtZipCode.Init(IDC_EDT_ZIPCODE, this, _T("Zip"));
 ...
```

To see this sample, simply run the MFCExtensions application and select the MFC Extensions menu option. From there, select the CEdit menu. When the property sheet appears, select the CGreyEdit property page to play around with the sample.

CUnderlineEdit

User-interface designers use a multitude of techniques such as coloring schemes, fonts, and different controls when designing an application meant for mass consumption. The obvious attempt here is to emulate what the user is familiar with so that he or she feels more at home. For example, if the dialog is emulating what the user would normally see on a physical piece of paper, then the UI designer wants the dialog to look as much like the original document as possible. Unfortunately, with the MFC control classes, you basically get the dialog controls that only an experienced computer-user would expect to see. I don't know about you, but I've never seen an invoice or a purchase order with an OK and Cancel button drawn on it.

This is where the next class comes in. The CUnderlineEdit class is used where the user would expect to see a simple underline where data is to be entered (see Figure 16-3). This is as opposed to the normal rectangular box that represents an edit control. An example of where this control can be used is in a dialog box used to enter purchase orders. There would probably be an edit control at the bottom of the dialog box where the user types his or her name. Because the physical purchase order that was used when designing the dialog box probably has an underline instead of a box for the issuer's name, the CUnderlineEdit control would be perfect for this dialog box.

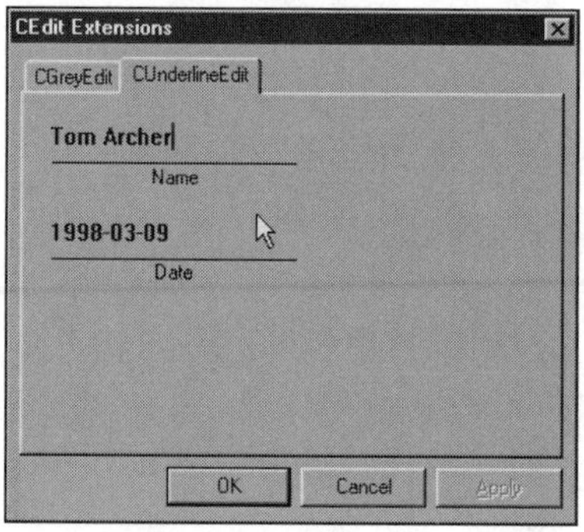

Figure 16-3: Example of an underline edit control

CUnderlineEdit source code

The first function that you'll look at is the `CreateBackgroundBrush` function. This function creates the brush that will be used for painting the background of the edit control. Actually, it will be used in the `OnCtlColor` override. Anytime you create a GDI object (as is the case with this brush) you need to delete it. The `m_brBackground` brush is deleted in this class destructor. The function uses the Win32 SDK `GetSysColor()` function to set the edit control's background color according to the user's defined system colors.

```
void CUnderlineEdit::CreateBackgroundBrush()
{
 ASSERT(m_lBackgroundColor > -1);
 COLORREF clrBackground;

 // an RGB value up to RGB(255,255,255)
 if (m_lBackgroundColor < PHOENIX_MAXRGB)
 {
  clrBackground =
  (COLORREF)m_lBackgroundColor;
 }
 else
 {
  clrBackground =
   ::GetSysColor(m_lBackgroundColor
   - PHOENIX_MAXRGB);
 }

 m_brBackground.CreateSolidBrush(
  clrBackground);
}
```

The following special DDX functions are used to subclass the control (notice the removal of the control's `WS_BORDER` style):

```
void AFXAPI DDX_UnderlineEditControl(CDataExchange* pDX, int
nIDC, CUnderlineEdit& rUnderlineEdit)
{
```

```
 // not subclassed or created
 if (rUnderlineEdit.m_hWnd == NULL)
 {
  CWnd *pwndOld = CWnd::FromHandle(
   pDX->PrepareEditCtrl(nIDC));
  CRect rect;
  pwndOld->GetWindowRect(rect);
  pDX->m_pDlgWnd->ScreenToClient(rect);
  DWORD dwStyle = ::GetWindowLong(
   pwndOld->m_hWnd,GWL_STYLE);

  // turn off the border
  dwStyle &= ~WS_BORDER;
  pwndOld->DestroyWindow();

  BOOL bStat = rUnderlineEdit.Create(dwStyle, rect,
   pDX->m_pDlgWnd, nIDC);
 }
}

void AFXAPI DDX_UnderlineEditText(CDataExchange* pDX,
CUnderlineEdit& rUnderlineEdit, CString &strText)
{
 if (rUnderlineEdit.m_hWnd != NULL)
 {
  if (pDX->m_bSaveAndValidate)
  rUnderlineEdit.GetWindowText(strText);
  else
  rUnderlineEdit.SetWindowText(strText);
 }
}
```

The `CWnd::OnCtlColor()` function creates and returns a handle to the brush used to paint the control's background:

```
HBRUSH CUnderlineEdit::OnCtlColor(CDC* pDC, CWnd* pWnd, UINT
nCtlColor)
{
 ASSERT(m_bInitialized);


 HBRUSH hbrReturnBrush;
 CPoint ptBrushOrigin(0,0);

 // make sure we have the most recent color for the background
 m_brBackground.DeleteObject();
 CreateBackgroundBrush();

 switch (nCtlColor)
 {
  case CTLCOLOR_EDIT:
   pDC->SetBkMode(TRANSPARENT);
   ClientToScreen(&ptBrushOrigin);
```

```
      m_brBackground.UnrealizeObject();
      pDC->SetBrushOrg(ptBrushOrigin.x, ptBrushOrigin.y);

      hbrReturnBrush = (HBRUSH)m_brBackground.m_hObject;
     break;

     case CTLCOLOR_MSGBOX:
      ClientToScreen(&ptBrushOrigin);
      m_brBackground.UnrealizeObject();
      pDC->SetBrushOrg(ptBrushOrigin.x, ptBrushOrigin.y);

      hbrReturnBrush = (HBRUSH)m_brBackground.m_hObject;
     break;

     default:
      hbrReturnBrush = (HBRUSH)Default();
     break;
    }

    return(hbrReturnBrush);
   }
```

As you probably guessed, here is the real meat of the class. It is in the `Paint()` function that the underline is drawn. However, since we are taking over control of drawing the line, we also need to draw the text "manually" as well. This operation includes dealing with whether all or part of the text is highlighted, as shown in the following function:

```
void CUnderlineEdit::OnPaint()
{
 CPaintDC dc(this);
 CRect rect;
 CFont *pOldFont;
 int iStart,
 iEnd;
 UINT uiAlignFlags = 0;
 int iUnderlinePos;

 // draw the underline
 GetClientRect(rect);
 iUnderlinePos = rect.Height();

 dc.MoveTo(rect.TopLeft().x + 1,iUnderlinePos);
 dc.LineTo(rect.BottomRight().x - 1,iUnderlinePos);

 pOldFont = dc.SelectObject(GetFont());
 CString strText;
 GetWindowText(strText);
 GetSel(iStart,iEnd);

 dc.SetTextAlign(uiAlignFlags);

 // nothing selected, just do it
```

```
if (iStart == iEnd)
{
 dc.TextOut(0,0,strText);
}
else
{
 CString strTmp;
 COLORREF clrBackColor = dc.GetBkColor();
 COLORREF clrTextColor = dc.GetTextColor();

 // there's unhilited characters before the start
 // of the selection
 if (iStart)
 {
  strTmp = strText.Left(iStart);
  dc.TextOut(0,0,strTmp);
  uiAlignFlags |= TA_UPDATECP;
  dc.SetTextAlign(uiAlignFlags);
 }

 dc.SetBkColor(::GetSysColor(COLOR_HIGHLIGHT));
 dc.SetTextColor(::GetSysColor(COLOR_HIGHLIGHTTEXT));
 strTmp = strText.Mid(iStart,iEnd - iStart);
 dc.TextOut(0,0,strTmp);
 if (!iStart)
 {
  uiAlignFlags |= TA_UPDATECP;
  dc.SetTextAlign(uiAlignFlags);
 }

 int iLen = strText.GetLength();
 if (iLen > iEnd)
 {
  strTmp = strText.Right(iLen - iEnd);
  dc.SetBkColor(clrBackColor);
  dc.SetTextColor(clrTextColor);
  dc.TextOut(0,0,strTmp);
 }
}

dc.SelectObject(pOldFont);
}
```

Using the CUnderlineEdit control

Through the magic of DDX, all you need to do to use this class is simply subclass the control with the provided `DDX_UnderlineEditControl()` function. A DDX value function (`DDX_UnderlineEditText()`) is also provided to easily retrieve and set the control's value.

Views and Dialogs

Now that we've looked at three examples of extended UI controls, let's take a look at a couple of extended controls that work in view and dialogs.

CFormBackground

Because (so far) a couple of the controls have been directed at helping a dialog resemble a real-life document, I thought that I would add another class that completes this look and feel. No matter how cool the controls look, if they are sitting on a dull grey or white background, they still look like controls on a dialog. Therefore, this very simple class illustrates how easy it is to create a view base class whose background has a 3D piece of paper drawn on it. Figure 16-4 shows an example of a dialog that uses the `CFormBackground` class.

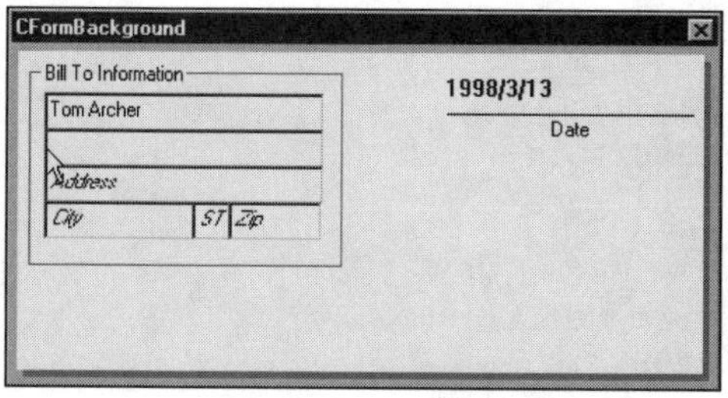

Figure 16-4: Example of the CFormBackground class being used to draw a 3D piece of paper on the background of a dialog

CFormBackground source code

In the `CFormBackground` class constructor, the necessary background, border, and shadow colors are set. As you can see, all of these have defaults to make the class even easier to use. However, the class is still flexible enough to allow the user to dictate all these colors. In addition, a constructor can be used to specify the margin (the space between the page and the view frame) and whether a border is drawn.

```
CFormBackground::CFormBackground(CWnd* pParent,
 BOOL bUseBorder /* = FALSE */,
 COLORREF clrBackground /* = RGB(255,255,255) */,
 COLORREF clrClient /* = RGB(128,128,128) */,
 COLORREF clrShadow /* = RGB(64,64,64) */,
 int iMargin /* = 4 */,
 int iBorderInset /* = 4 */)
{
 // Save passed parms that will be
 // needed in member functions that
 // are called later
 m_clrBorder = RGB(0,0,0);
 m_clrBackground = clrBackground;
 m_clrClient = clrClient;
 m_clrShadow = clrShadow;
```

```
 m_bUseBorder = bUseBorder;
 m_iBorderInset = iBorderInset;
 m_iMargin = iMargin;
 m_pwndParent = pParent;
}
```

The main function of this class is the `OnDraw()` function. If you look closely, you'll see a few tricks introduced in the graphics chapters of this book. Specifically, look at the comments concerning the handling of the memory device context. The `OnDraw` function calls a helper function, `DrawFormBackground()`, to draw on the memory device context. After the `DrawFormBackground()` function returns, the results are then "blitted" onto the real device context. (For a more comprehensive look at topics like bit-blitting, please refer to the chapters on graphics programming, especially Chapters 4 and 5.)

```
void CFormBackground::OnDraw(CDC* pDC)
{
 CDC dcMem;
 CBitmap bmpMem,
 *pbmpOld;

 // memory dc compatible with display
 dcMem.CreateCompatibleDC(NULL);

 // set new size
 m_pwndParent->GetClientRect(&m_rectClient);
 CClientDC dcClient(m_pwndParent);

 if (!m_rectClient.IsRectEmpty())
 {
  // create a bitmap large enought
  // for the entire client area
  if (bmpMem.CreateCompatibleBitmap(
   &dcClient,m_rectClient.Width(),
   m_rectClient.Height()))
  {
   // Select the new bitmap into
   // the memory dc
   pbmpOld = dcMem.SelectObject(&bmpMem);
   if (pbmpOld)
   {
    dcMem.SetBkMode(OPAQUE);
    dcMem.SetBkColor(m_clrBackground);

    // redraw the form onto the memory dc.
    DrawFormBackground(dcMem);

    // Blit the changes to the screen dc
    pDC->BitBlt(0,
     0,
     m_rectClient.Width(),
     m_rectClient.Height(),
     &dcMem,
```

```
        0,
        0,
        SRCCOPY);

      dcMem.SelectObject(pbmpOld);
      bmpMem.DeleteObject();
    }
  }
  else
  {
   AfxThrowMemoryException();
  }
 }
}
```

The following function draws the actual page on the parent window's background. After the page is drawn, two additional functions are called to draw the page's border and shadow. As you can see, a few of the arguments that were passed to this class constructor are used in the drawing process.

```
void CFormBackground::DrawFormBackground(CDC &rDC)
{
 CBrush brClient, brBackground;

 BOOL bStat = brClient.CreateSolidBrush(
  m_clrClient);
 if (bStat)
 {
  bStat = brBackground.CreateSolidBrush(
   m_clrBackground);

  if (bStat)
  {
   // paint outside of form
   // and erase background
   // fill rect does not include the
   // right or bottom borders
   CRect rectClientFill = m_rectClient;
   rectClientFill.BottomRight().x++;
   rectClientFill.BottomRight().y++;
   rDC.FillRect(rectClientFill,&brClient);

   CRect rectFormRect;

   rectFormRect.TopLeft().x = m_iMargin;

   rectFormRect.BottomRight().x =
    m_rectClient.Width() - (m_iMargin
    + ciShadowDepth);

   rectFormRect.TopLeft().y = m_iMargin;

   rectFormRect.BottomRight().y =
```

```
      m_rectClient.Height() - (m_iMargin
      + ciShadowDepth);

     CRect rectFormFill = rectFormRect;

     // fill rect does not include the
     // right or bottom borders
     // but the math above handles it in
     // this case

     // paint inside of form
     rDC.FillRect(rectFormFill,&brBackground);

     // paint optional border
     if (m_bUseBorder)
     {
      DrawBorder(rDC);
     }

     // paint the shadow
     DrawShadow(rDC,rectFormRect);

     brBackground.DeleteObject();
    }

   brClient.DeleteObject();
  }
}
```

If the border argument for the class constructor is set to `TRUE`, the following function will be called from the `DrawFormBackground()` function. Once again, you can see many of the things in the graphics chapters being put to use here. For example, take a look at how the pens and brushes are being utilized.

```
void CFormBackground::DrawBorder(CDC &rDC)
{
 const int ciTotalInset = m_iBorderInset
  + m_iMargin;

 CPen penBorder;

 BOOL bStat = penBorder.CreatePen(
  PS_SOLID, 0, m_clrBorder);

 if (bStat)
 {
  // select the border pen
  CPen* ppenOld = rDC.SelectObject(
   &penBorder);
  if (ppenOld)
  {
   // Start at upper left corner
   rDC.MoveTo(ciTotalInset,ciTotalInset);
```

```
      // draw top
      rDC.LineTo(m_rectClient.Width()
       - ciTotalInset,ciTotalInset);

      // draw right side
      rDC.LineTo(m_rectClient.Width() -
       ciTotalInset,m_rectClient.Height() -
       ciTotalInset);

      // draw bottom
       rDC.LineTo(ciTotalInset,
       m_rectClient.Height() - ciTotalInset);

      // draw left side
      rDC.LineTo(ciTotalInset,ciTotalInset);

      // finished with border - select old pen
      rDC.SelectObject(ppenOld);
     }
    }
   }
```

The last `CFormBackground` function is `DrawShadow()`. Without this function, our page would look like no more than a shaded rectangle:

```
void CFormBackground::DrawShadow(CDC &rDC, CRect &rectForm)
{
 CPen penShadow;
 BOOL bStat = penShadow.CreatePen(
  PS_SOLID,0,m_clrShadow);

 if (bStat)
 {
  CPen* ppenOld = rDC.SelectObject(
   &penShadow);

  if (ppenOld)
  {
   int iDepth = ciShadowDepth - 1;
   for (int i = 0; i < ciShadowDepth; i++)
   {
    // Start at upper right corner
    rDC.MoveTo(rectForm.BottomRight().x
    + i,rectForm.TopLeft().y
    + ciShadowDepth);

    // draw right side
    rDC.LineTo(rectForm.BottomRight().x
     + i,rectForm.BottomRight().y + i);

    // draw bottom
    rDC.LineTo(rectForm.TopLeft().x
     + iDepth,rectForm.BottomRight().y + i);
```

```
    }

    // finished with shadow - select old pen
    rDC.SelectObject(ppenOld);
  }
 }
}
```

Using the CFormbackground source code

This class can be used for either a view or a dialog. All you have to do is declare a class member variable of type `CFormBack`, construct the `CFormBack` object in the view's constructor, call the `CFormBack::OnDraw()` function in your view's `OnDraw()` function, and delete the object when the view is destroyed.

CListBoxView

One pretty cool little class that Microsoft introduced in version 4 of MFC was the `CCtrlView` class. This class allows you to define almost any control as a view. In fact, this is how the `CTreeView` and `CListView` classes work. For example, if you look at the MFC source code for the `CTreeView` class, you'll see that it does almost nothing above and beyond its parent `CCtrlView` class. However, it does do one important thing in its constructor that makes it work. As the following code excerpt from the `AFXCVIEW.H` file shows, the `CTreeView` constructor calls the `CCtrlView` constructor and passes it a value of `WC_TREEVIEW`.

```
_AFXCVIEW_INLINE CTreeView::CTreeView():
  CCtrlView(WC_TREEVIEW,     AFX_WS_DEFAULT_VIEW)
  { }
```

A little more digging turns up the following in the COMMCTRLS.H file:

```
#define WC_TREEVIEW              "SysTreeView"
```

Now, when you trace into the `CCtrlView` constructor, you see the following:

```
CCtrlView::CCtrlView(LPCTSTR lpszClass,
 DWORD dwStyle)
{
 m_strClass = lpszClass;
 m_dwDefaultStyle = dwStyle;
}

BOOL CCtrlView::PreCreateWindow(CREATESTRUCT& cs)
{
 ASSERT(cs.lpszClass == NULL);
 cs.lpszClass = m_strClass;

 // initialize common controls
 VERIFY(AfxDeferRegisterClass(
  AFX_WNDCOMMCTLS_REG));
```

```
  // map default CView style to default style
  // WS_BORDER is insignificant
  if ((cs.style | WS_BORDER) == AFX_WS_DEFAULT_VIEW)
   cs.style = m_dwDefaultStyle
   & (cs.style | ~WS_BORDER);

  return CView::PreCreateWindow(cs);
}
```

Thus the `CCtrlView` class creates a window using the class name that is passed to its constructor. Because this class is derived from `CView`, the window in question will have a frame placed around it automatically when the view is created as a part of an SDI or MDI document template.

By the way, this is one reason a `CTreeView` class and a `CTreeCtrl` class are essentially the same. Both are C++ classes that encapsulate windows created with the `SysTreeView` class name. It just happens that in the case of `CTreeView`, you have to dig a little to see the window creation taking place.

So now that you know this bit of internal MFC trivia, how does it help you? Well, it helps if you ever need to create a view whose entire client area is covered by one control. You already know that Microsoft has given this treatment to a few controls (such as `CEditView`, `CTreeView`, and `CListView`), but let's see how easy it is to do for another control: `CListBox`. In the following section, we'll create a class called `CListboxView`. Figure 16-5 shows the `CListboxView` class in action.

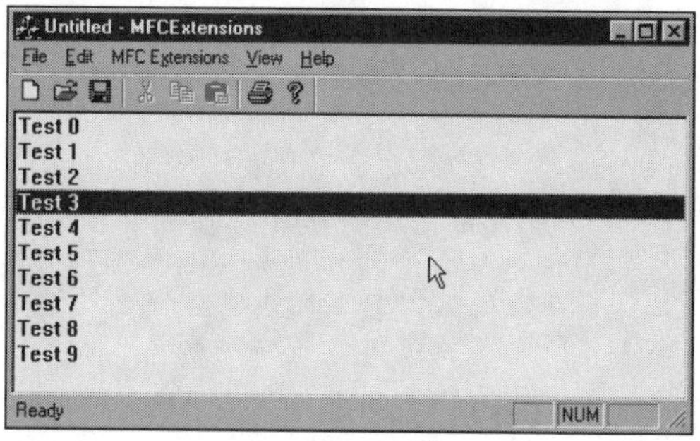

Figure 16-5: Example of extending the `CCtrlView` class with the `CListBoxView`.

CListBoxView source code

To create this class, simply declare the `CListBoxView` class, as follows:

```
#pragma once

class CListBoxView : public CCtrlView
{
 DECLARE_DYNCREATE(CListBoxView)

// Construction
```

```
public:
 CListBoxView();

// Attributes
public:
 CListBox& GetListBox() const;

 //{{AFX_MSG(CListBoxView)
 //}}AFX_MSG
DECLARE_MESSAGE_MAP()
};
```

Next, implement the source code as follows. Take note of the constructor's initializer list and the fact that it passes the class name of the list-box control (`LISTBOX`) to the `CCtrlView` constructor. By doing so, this class we call a `CCtrlView` reveals that it's a list-box control at heart.

The only function of any interest is the `GetListBox()` function. How can you return a view pointer to a function that requested a list-box object? Remember that almost all MFC control classes are thin wrappers for their associated Windows controls. As an example, when you call the `CListbox::AddString()` function, the `CListbox` object simply sends a Windows message to its associated window to add the specified string. Therefore, if a user of `CListBoxView` requests the `CListBox` control in order to call a `CListBox` member function, the resulting Windows message will be sent to the window associated with the `CListBoxView`, as follows:

```
#include "stdafx.h"
#include "listboxview.h"

IMPLEMENT_DYNCREATE(CListBoxView, CCtrlView)

CListBoxView::CListBoxView() :
 CCtrlView(_T("LISTBOX"),    AFX_WS_DEFAULT_VIEW)
 { };

CListBox& CListBoxView::GetListBox() const
 {  return *(CListBox*)this; }

BEGIN_MESSAGE_MAP(CListBoxView, CCtrlView)
 //{{AFX_MSG_MAP(CListBoxView)
 ON_WM_NCDESTROY()
 //}}AFX_MSG_MAP
END_MESSAGE_MAP()
```

Using the CListBoxView control

Testing this class is as easy as writing it. Simply use the AppWizard to create an SDI application called `LbxViewTest`. When you're finished, simply open the LbxViewTestView.cpp and lbxViewTextView.h files and replace all occurrences of `CView` with `CListBoxView`. That's it. Now when you run this test application, you'll see a view whose entire client is covered by a list box.

As a matter of fact, that is exactly how the MFCExtensions demo on the CD-ROM was done. After the search and replace was finished, all I had to do was implement the `OnInitialUpdate` function, like this:

```
void CMFCExtensionsView::OnInitialUpdate()
{
 CListBoxView::OnInitialUpdate();

 CListBox* pLbx = (CListBox*)this;
 if (pLbx)
 {
  CString str;
  for (int i = 0; i < 10; i++)
  {
   str.Format("Test %ld", i);
   pLbx->AddString(str);
  }
 }
}
```

Summary

Although it would be less than feasible to pick four or five classes that all readers of this book would need in their applications, this chapter showed you how to write several classes that illustrate extending the basic MFC classes.

- Three cool UI controls were included: an auto-complete combo box, a grey edit control, and an underline edit control.
- In addition, you wrote a form-background class and a `CCtrlView`-derived class.
- This chapter illustrated just how easily you can extend the MFC class architecture once you've defined exactly what special classes your application needs.
- MFC's flexible design makes it perfect for those times when you need to extend its capabilities and make it do something a little different.
- MFC excels in giving you a broad range of powerful classes upon which to build your applications.
- No one except *you* can know the exact functionality of the classes you need for your applications.

✦ ✦ ✦

CHAPTER 17

Toolbars and Status Bars

✦ ✦ ✦ ✦

In This Chapter

Creating and controlling toolbars

Showing and hiding toolbars

Creating and using status bars

Using a demo program to illustrate customizing status-bar appearance at runtime

✦ ✦ ✦ ✦

This chapter covers available MFC support for two user-interface objects: toolbars and status bars. *Toolbars* are windows with buttons that allow users to issue commands with a single mouse click. This makes toolbar commands somewhat more accessible to users, because menus require at least two mouse clicks (or a mouse click-and-drag). Because they occupy screen space, however, toolbars should be used for only the most commonly requested commands. For the same reason, most users want to be able to hide unwanted toolbars. AppWizard automatically provides this capability in the toolbars it creates for you. We'll show you how to create additional toolbars as well as how to show them and hide them as desired.

MFC provides another user-interface object often associated with command input: status bars. A *status bar* is typically a window at the bottom of an application's main window. A status bar displays text messages so users know the current status of an application. As part of its support for command input, MFC automatically displays helpful tips in the status window when the user browses menu items or toolbar buttons.

Understanding Toolbars

For a user, toolbars provide instant access to program commands. Rather than digging into a menu or remembering a keystroke, toolbars are right there to see. Because they occupy precious screen space, you'll want to make sure your toolbars include only the most frequently used commands. Large programs tend to have multiple toolbars for different user tasks. Even if your program has only a single toolbar, make sure you give the user the option of hiding it when it gets in the way.

From a programming perspective, a toolbar is a child window that displays a series of bitmap buttons. After you create a toolbar and make it visible, you can all but ignore it because it generates the same message — `WM_COMMAND` — that menus and accelerators generate. However, you will want to synchronize toolbar command IDs with the command IDs in menus and accelerators.

The following sections cover several topics that can help you work with toolbars. We start with a quick look at the place of toolbars in the MFC hierarchy. Then we cover some of the details involved in dynamically creating and modifying toolbars. We'll conclude by introducing CTRLBARS, a sample program that shows some toolbar programming techniques.

Examining MFC control bars

MFC's toolbar class, `CToolBar`, is one of several classes that create windows for receiving some kind of command input and displaying status information to the user. The base class for this group, known collectively as control bars, is `CControlBar`. This class is derived from `CWnd`.

This inheritance relationship has some useful implications. For example, because all control bars are derived from `CWnd`, all control bars are connected to a Windows API window. As a result, all of the functional capabilities of `CWnd` — creating, moving, showing, and hiding windows — are available when you're working with control bars.

`CToolBar` has several sibling classes, including `CStatusBar`, `CDialogBar`, and `COleResizeBar`. When asked, AppWizard gladly creates a status bar by spinning code that creates a `CStatusBar` object. As mentioned in our discussion of menus, status bars sit at the bottom of a frame window and can display helpful information about menu choices. A status bar will also display helpful details about different toolbar buttons as the user moves the mouse cursor over the buttons.

The `CDialogBar` class creates dialog bars, which are a cross between a toolbar and a dialog box. A dialog bar can hold controls like a dialog box, but it stays visible in a frame window like a toolbar.

The final MFC control bar is `COleResizeBar`, which supports resizing of in-place OLE objects, a subject that is beyond the scope of this book.

MFC toolbars (and dialog bars) are dockable. When this feature is enabled, a user can pick up a toolbar and move it to a different edge of a frame window. It is up to the frame window, however, to indicate which edges are acceptable docking sites. As an alternative, toolbars can also be moved away from any frame edge and left in a free-floating palette.

MFC toolbars also support *ToolTips*. ToolTips are intended to help users understand the purpose of individual toolbar buttons. Users summon ToolTip support — when it's enabled — by moving the mouse cursor over a toolbar button (without clicking the button). After a short wait, the Tooltip—a brief word or phrase—appears in a tiny text window that hovers over the toolbar buttons.

To put toolbars to work in your MFC program, you must coordinate several items, including a bitmap resource, the toolbar itself, and the frame window. To help with this effort, the following section shows how to create a toolbar of your own.

Creating a toolbar

AppWizard automatically generates a toolbar for you, but some of its features—for example, showing and hiding the toolbar—are buried in existing MFC classes. To give you a more complete picture of toolbars, we're going to create a second toolbar. Then the sample program CTRLBARS will show you how two toolbars can coexist in the same program, demonstrating how easy it is to create additional toolbars.

Toolbar creation is a five-step process. First, you create a bitmap that holds the button images. Second, you build an array that maps your buttons to your program's command codes. Third, you write the code to create the toolbar and initialize it appropriately. After the toolbar window is created, steps four and five involve connecting button images and command IDs to the toolbar. When you have accomplished these minimum steps, you can fine-tune the behavior of your toolbar.

The first step, then, is to create a bitmap that holds all of the button images. You'll store the bitmap as a bitmap resource, which means you'll first open your project's resource (.RC) file. You create your bitmap button images in a row, using the bitmap editor. The default size of each image is 16 pixels wide by 15 pixels high. Although you can use different sizes, a change from the default requires you to tell your toolbar object by calling `CToolBar::SetSizes()`.

The next step is to define an array of command codes that map button images to command IDs. As shown in the following example, this is an array of unsigned `int`s (`UINT`):

```
// toolbar buttons - IDs are command buttons
static UINT BASED_CODE buttons[] =
{
    // same order as in the bitmap 'bitmap1.bmp'
    ID_TOOLBAR_CREATE,
        ID_SEPARATOR,
    ID_TOOLBAR_SHOW
};
```

The two command codes are `ID_TOOLBAR_CREATE` and `ID_TOOLBAR_SHOW`. The other item, `ID_SEPARATOR`, adds a bit of spacing between these two buttons.

The third step is to create and initialize the toolbar object. As with other windows, you create a toolbar by first instantiating the object, and then calling an initialization function. Here's an example:

```
// Create C++ object and WinAPI window.
d_pToolbar2 = new CToolBar();
d_pToolbar2->Create(this, WS_CHILD | CBRS_TOP, 0x9100);
```

The initialization function, `CToolBar::Create()`, overrides the base function `CWnd::Create()`. As with other types of window objects, the style field—that is, the middle field—controls quite a few object attributes. This example has two style flags: `WS_CHILD` and `CBRS_TOP`. The first style, `WS_CHILD`, is a standard windowing style that makes this a child window. The second style, `CBRS_TOP`, is a control-bar-specific style that puts the toolbar at the top of the frame window. Table 17-1 lists some other style flags that might be useful.

Table 17-1
Useful Style Flags

Flag	***Description***
WS_VISIBLE	Makes the toolbar window visible initially.
WS_CHILD	Makes the toolbar a child of the parent frame window
CBRS_TOP	Places the control bar at the top of the frame
CBRS_BOTTOM	Places the control bar at the bottom of the frame.
CBRS_FLYBY	Causes command descriptions to be displayed in the status window when the mouse cursor pauses over buttons.
CBRS_NOALIGN	Prevents repositioning of the control bar when its parent window is resized.
CBRS_TOOLTIPS	Displays tooltips when the mouse cursor pauses over the toolbar's buttons.
CBRS_TOP	Places the control bar at the top of the frame.

After the toolbar window is created, a few more initialization steps must be performed. For one thing, you need to connect the button images to your toolbar. They are stored in the bitmap resource. You accomplish this by calling `CToolBar::LoadBitmap()`, as in:

```
d_pToolbar2->LoadBitmap(IDR_TOOLS);
```

You also need to associate command IDs with buttons. As shown in the following example, you do this by calling `CToolBar::SetButtons()`, with a pointer to the array created in step two:

```
d_pToolbar2->SetButtons(buttons,
  sizeof(buttons)/sizeof(UINT));
```

At this point, the toolbar is complete. However, you might still want to fine-tune the toolbar's operation.

By default, a `CToolBar` toolbar can be moved only by program control. However, you can allow users to move the toolbar to other parts of the frame. To do so, you notify both the toolbar and the frame window. As shown in the following example, you do this by calling `CToolBar::EnableDocking()` and `CFrameWnd::EnableDocking()`:

```
d_pToolbar2->EnableDocking(CBRS_ALIGN_ANY);
EnableDocking(CBRS_ALIGN_ANY);
```

Users can then dock and undock the toolbar. One other option: Under program control, you can dock the toolbar by calling `CFrameWnd::DockControlBar()`, and you can undock the toolbar by calling `CFrameWnd::FloatControlBar()`.

After you create a toolbar, it remains attached to your frame window and works on its own. There aren't many things you'll need to do, except perhaps hide it or show it on demand. Doing so involves a process all its own.

Showing and hiding toolbars

The key point when showing or hiding a toolbar is that a toolbar is a window. In practice, this means you'll rely more on `CWnd` member functions than on `CToolBar` functions.

Before you can show or hide a toolbar, it helps to know the current visibility state of the toolbar window. The `WS_VISIBLE` windowing style is the key to toolbar visibility. To query all of the style bits for a window, you call `CWnd::GetStyle()`. This code fragment sets a flag based on the visibility of a toolbar window:

```
// Query current visibility.
BOOL bVisible = (d_pToolbar2->GetStyle() &
  WS_VISIBLE);
```

A call to `CWnd::SetStyle()` lets you change certain window styles; unfortunately, `WS_VISIBLE` is not one of them. Instead, you call `CWnd::ShowWindow()` and pass `SW_HIDE` to make the toolbar invisible and `SW_SHOWNORMAL` to make it reappear. The following code fragment toggles the visibility flag queried in the previous example:

```
// Show or hide.
int nShow = (bVisible) ? SW_HIDE : SW_SHOWNORMAL;
d_pToolbar2->ShowWindow(nShow);
```

Whenever you programmatically change a toolbar, you must inform the frame window about the change. You do this by simply asking it to recalculate the positioning of control bars. You make this request by calling `CFrameWnd::RecalcLayout()`, which takes no parameters:

```
// Reconfigure remaining toolbar items.
RecalcLayout();
```

Understanding Status Bars

A status bar is the multifield bar that appears at the bottom of a frame window. It has become almost customary for all Windows applications to include a status bar and to use the bar to display such user interface information as toolbar-button help and application-specific information (such as) the state of the Caps Lock key in a word processor. Because users will expect to see status bars in the applications you create, it's reassuring to know that creating and using status bars is generally straightforward.

Creating a status bar

A status bar object is represented in the MFC framework by the CStatusBar class. Typically, a status bar is declared as a CStatusBar object that is a member of the frame window class:

```
protected:
CStatusBar  m_wndStatusBar;
CToolBar    m_wndToolBar;
```

The status bar is created and initialized in the frame window's OnCreate() function:

```
UINT nSeparator = ID_SEPARATOR;
m_wndStatusBar.Create(this);
m_wndStatusBar.SetIndicators(&nSeparator,1);
```

ID_SEPARATOR is a universal resource ID which tells MFC there is no string resource associated with this status bar field. The example just given creates a status bar with a blank field you can use to dynamically display information. If you wanted to display several string resources in the status bar, the code would look like this:

```
UINT nIndicators[]={IDS_BARTEXT1, IDS_BARTEXT2,
  IDS_BARTEXT3};
m_wndStatusBar.Create(this);
m_wndStatusBar.SetIndicators(nIndicators,3);
```

IDS_BARTEXT1, IDS_BARTEXT2, and IDS_BARTEXT3 are resource ID values for string resources which reside in the application's string table.

Now, this technique is great if all you want to do is display static text within the status-bar fields. However, this isn't how most status bars are used. Typically, status bars convey dynamic information about the application to the user. As indicated before, they can include such things as displaying the state of the Caps Lock or Num Lock keys, as well as displaying toolbar help.

Fortunately, MFC provides some pre-defined constants which do some of the work for us. These constants are summarized in Table 17-2.

Table 17-2
MFC Status Bar Constants

Status Bar Constant	*Status Bar Information*
ID_INDICATOR_CAPS	Displays the current state of the Caps Lock key.
ID_INDICATOR_NUM	Displays the current state of the Num Lock key.
ID_INDICATOR_SCRL	Displays the current state of the Scroll Lock key.

The following code snippet will create and display a status bar that displays the current states of the Caps Lock and Num Lock keys:

```
UINT nIndicators[]={ID_SEPARATOR, ID_INDICATOR_CAPS,
  ID_INDICATOR_NUM};
m_wndStatusBar.Create(this);
m_wndStatusBar.SetIndicators(nIndicators,3);
```

Pretty simple, huh?

Displaying toolbar help

MFC provides a simple and technically elegant solution for displaying toolbar and menu-selection help on a status bar. Basically, MFC takes the resource ID for a toolbar button or a menu selection and checks to see whether the application has a string resource defined in its string table with the same ID. This may sound confusing at first, but remember: Resource IDs must be unique only within their section of the .RC file.

This means you can create a useful capability: If the application has a toolbar button with the ID `ID_DATABASE_CONNECT` and also has a string resource defined with the same ID, then MFC automatically displays that string whenever the user "hovers" the mouse cursor over that button. The following code snippets illustrate this technique:

From the application resource file's menu section:

```
POPUP "&Database"
BEGIN
  MENUITEM "&Connect", ID_DATABASE_CONNECT
END
```

And in the resource file's string table section:

```
BEGIN
  ID_DATABASE_CONNECT "Connect to remote database"
END
```

The constant `ID_DATABASE_CONNECT` represents the same numerical value. MFC uses the shared value to associate the two resources. This association will cause the application to display the string `"Connect to remote database"` as toolbar help in a status bar pane.

And if this wasn't already easy enough, MFC and the App Wizard already provide many of the most common help strings. An example is displayed in Figure 17-1. This is only a small sampling of the help strings that the AppWizard and MFC automatically provide.

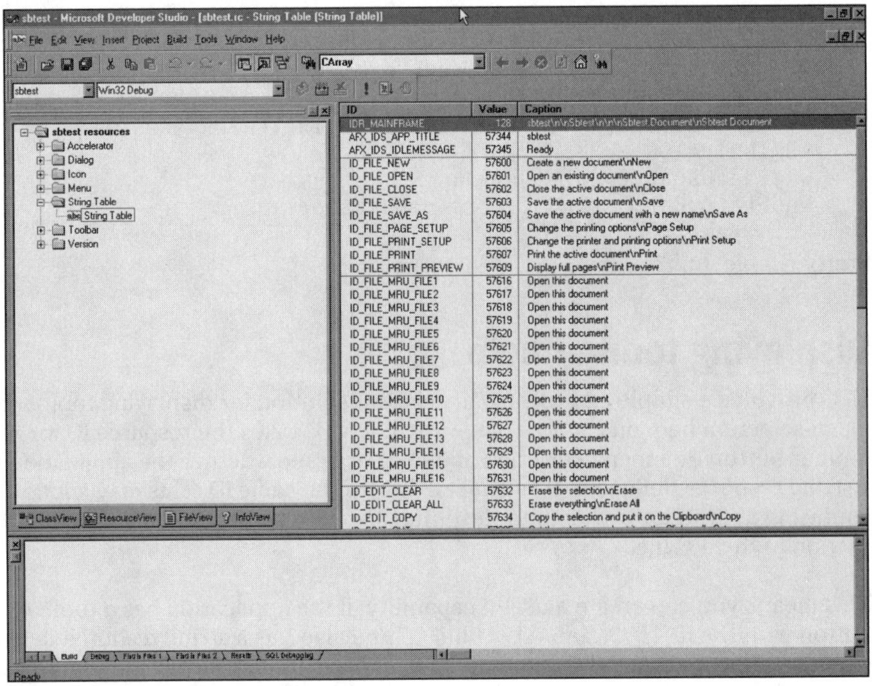

Figure 17-1: Basic status bar display

Expanding status bars

As you've seen in other parts of MFC, status bars can be customized and extended in several different ways. This section discusses creating custom status bars and how to take complete control of the status bar.

Creating custom status bars

Normally, a status bar is created in the main frame window's OnCreate() member function like this:

```
m_wndStatusBar.Create(this);
```

Calling CStatusBar::Create() and passing only the window handle of the frame window creates a status bar which is bound to the default status bar object ID AFX_IDW_STATUS_BAR. Status bars created in this manner also have the default attributes of a bottom-aligned, visible, child window linked to the main frame window. The full prototype of CStatusBar::Create() is shown next. Default values are indicated in italics.

```
BOOL Create( CWnd* pParentWnd,
  DWORD dwStyle = WS_CHILD | WS_VISIBLE | CBRS_BOTTOM,
  UINT nID = AFX_IDW_STATUS_BAR );
```

As you can see, Create() accepts several style flags which control the appearance and behavior of the status bar. In addition to many of the style flags accepted by all CWnd derived classes, such as WS_CHILD, Create() also accepts six style flags which are specific to CStatusBar. These style flags are summarized next in Table 17-3:

Table 17-3
Create() Style Flags Specific to CStatusBar

Style Flag	*Description*
CBRS_TOP	Status bar is at top of frame window.
CBRS_BOTTOM	Status bar is at bottom of frame window.
CBRS_NOALIGN	Status bar is not repositioned when the parent is resized.

The following function call creates a status bar top-aligned with the main frame window (Figure 17-2):

```
m_wndStatusBar.Create( this,
  WS_CHILD | WS_VISIBLE | CBRS_TOP);
```

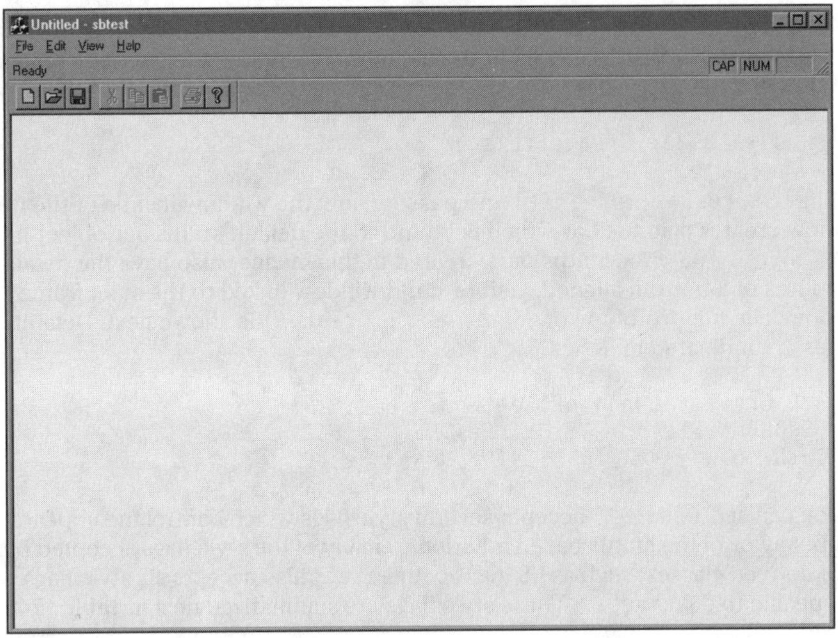

Figure 17-2: The status bar is created at the top of the window, directly under the toolbar.

You can also customize the appearances of each of the individual panes of a status bar with a different set of style flags. The member function `CStatusBar::SetPaneStyle()` is used to change the style, or appearance, of the individual status bar panes. The function prototype looks like this:

```
void SetPaneStyle( int nIndex, UINT nStyle )
```

The parameter, nIndex, is used as an index into the array of status bar indicator resources. This value is used during the status bar creation process to select which indicators are displayed in the different status bar panes. It is also used any time you may want to change the indicator displayed by the status bar.

Remember, since the indicator array is zero-based, if you want to change the style of the third pane in a status bar, then `nIndex = 2`. `nStyle` is used to set the style of the pane. `SetPaneStyle()` accepts the style flags listed in Table 17-4.

Using the flags listed previously, the code to disable a status bar pane looks like this:

```
m_wndStatusBar.SetPaneStyle(2,SBS_DISABLED);
```

Table 17-4
SetPaneStyle() Style Flags

Style Flag	*Description*
SBPS_NOBORDERS	Creates a pane flush with the status bar.
SBPS_POPOUT	Creates a pane that protrudes from the status bar.
SBPS_NORMAL	Creates a pane recessed on the status bar.
SBPS_DISABLED	Disables the pane. A disabled pane displays no text.
SBPS_STRETCH	Stretches the pane to take up any "slack" space on the status bar. Only one pane per status bar can have this style.
SBPS_OWNERDRAW	Creates an owner-drawn pane.

Taking control of the status bar

When you use the App Wizard to create an MFC-based application, the App Wizard creates a default status bar with the child window ID AFX_IDW_STATUS_BAR. In some cases you may choose not to use the default behavior of the wizard-created status bar. To disable the behavior, you'll need to take control of the status bar and handle its updates with your own code.

First, add custom strings to the application's string table. For our example we'll add ID_CONNECT_STATUS.

The next thing you must do is change the child window ID to your own ID. Using your own window ID "disconnects" the status bar from the functionality that the App Wizard generates automatically. This ID should be defined in the application's resources. You can view these resources by selecting View ➪ Resource Symbols. Our examples use the constant ID_CUSTOM_STATUS_BAR. The status bar's window ID is assigned in the frame window's OnCreate member function. The App Wizard-generated function looks like this:

```
int CMainFrame::OnCreate(LPCREATESTRUCT lpCreateStruct)
{
. . .

  if (!m_wndStatusBar.Create(this) ||
    !m_wndStatusBar.SetIndicators(indicators,
      sizeof(indicators)/sizeof(UINT)))
  {
    TRACE0("Failed to create status bar\n");
    return -1;      // fail to create
. . .
  }

  return 0;
}
```

The line `m_wndStatusBar.Create(this)` creates the status bar with the default child window ID and binds it to the frame window. The customized version of `OnCreate()` that uses the custom window ID looks like this (changes in bold):

```
int CMainFrame::OnCreate(LPCREATESTRUCT lpCreateStruct)
{
. . .

  if (!m_wndStatusBar.Create(WS_CHILD | WS_VISIBLE |
       CBRS_BOTTOM, ID_CUSTOM_STATUS_BAR) ||
       !m_wndStatusBar.SetIndicators(indicators,
       sizeof(indicators)/sizeof(UINT)))
  {
    TRACE0("Failed to create status bar\n");
    return -1;      // fail to create
. . .
  }

  return 0;
}
```

The next step is to replace the default status bar indicators with your own. The indicators are stored in a static array of `UINT`s called `indicators`. The array is located in the frame window's .cpp file. The AppWizard-generated code looks like this:

```
static UINT indicators[] =
{
  ID_SEPARATOR,           // status line indicator
  ID_INDICATOR_CAPS,
  ID_INDICATOR_NUM,
  ID_INDICATOR_SCRL,
};
```

These indicator constants create a status bar which contains a "stretchy" pane for help and message text and three additional panes which display the status of the caps, num, and Scroll Lock keys. You'll need to replace these with resource IDs of your own:

```
static UINT indicators[] =
{
  ID_SEPARATOR,           // status line indicator
  ID_CONNECT_STATUS,
  ID_POSITION
};
```

Replacing our example indicators with resources of your own is straightforward. As you've done before, create your own string resources using the resource editor and use these new resource IDs in place of our example resources.

Our example creates a status bar that contains the same help and message pane but also includes two customized panes for displaying the application's connect status to (for example) a database or remote server, as well as the current cursor position.

Next, you'll need to add your own message handlers for the status bar. You need to do this because the Class and App Wizards only understand the default values they generate. Since the status bar's window ID and the indicator's resource IDs differ from the defaults normally generated by the wizards, you'll need to handle the message processing manually for the status bar. It's generally easiest to use the Class Wizard to add the message handlers. You should add handlers for both `COMMAND` and `UPDATE_COMMAND_UI` messages. Continuing with our example, the following handlers should be added:

Object ID	***Message***	***Handler Function***
ID_CUSTOM_STATUS_BAR	COMMAND	OnViewStatusBar
ID_CUSTOM_STATUS_BAR	UPDATE_COMMAND_UI	OnUpdateViewStatusBar

Now that you have the message handlers added to the class, you need to add the message-handler prototypes to the main frame window. You have to do this manually because the ClassWizard won't recognize the customized message IDs. The code to do this looks like this (customized code in bold):

```
protected:
  //{{AFX_MSG(CMainFrame)
  afx_msg int OnCreate(LPCREATESTRUCT lpCreateStruct);
  afx_msg void OnViewStatusBar();
  afx_msg void OnUpdateViewStatusBar(CCmdUI* pCmdUI);
  afx_msg void OnUpdateConnect(CCmdUI* pCmdUI);
  //}}AFX_MSG
```

In order for the message-handler functions to work, you need to map them to some messages; add some code to the application's message map (customized code in bold):

```
BEGIN_MESSAGE_MAP(CMainFrame, CFrameWnd)
  //{{AFX_MSG_MAP(CMainFrame)
  ON_WM_CREATE()
  ON_UPDATE_COMMAND_UI(ID_CONNECT_STATUS,
    OnUpdateConnect)
  //}}AFX_MSG_MAP
END_MESSAGE_MAP()
```

With the addition of the message-handler functions and the message map entries, our custom function `OnUpdateConnect` will be called to update the status bar. The prototype for the function looks like this:

```
void CMainFrame::OnUpdateConnect(CCmdUI* pCmdUI)
```

The code contained in this function will test the state of the database connection and update the status bar appropriately.

Nutshell

Customizing the Status Bar

These are the steps required to customize the behavior of the status bar:

1. Add a string resource for each of the custom status bar panes.
2. Add a new child window ID and use this ID during status bar creation.
3. Replace the stock indicators with customized ones.
4. Add message handlers for the custom status bar.
5. Create message-map entries to connect the messages to the custom status-bar-handler functions.
6. Add code to each of the message-handler functions to update the status bar.

◆ ◆ ◆ ◆ ◆

Status bar demo program

The demo program in this section illustrates how to customize the appearance of a status bar at runtime. Many of the techniques discussed in this chapter are used in this application. These techniques include custom status-bar indicators, controlling the status bar, and dynamically changing the status-bar panes.

The process for creating a status bar resides in MainFrm.cpp, specifically in the member function `CMainFrame::OnCreate()`. In here you can find the modifications made to the indicators array as well as the initial call to `CStatusBar::Create()`.

Most of the actual modifications to the status bar are located in `Sbdemoview.cpp`. The dynamic modification of the status bar occurs in the mouse-command message handlers `OnLButtonDown`, `OnRButtonDown`, and `OnMouseMove`. In the button-handler functions, each of the status-bar panes are toggled between a "popped-out" and recessed appearance. The code contained in the `OnMouseMove` handler updates two of the status bar panes with the current x and y coordinates of the mouse cursor.

Demo Program

SBDemo

CD-ROM Location: **Chap17\SBDemo**
Program Name: **SBDemo.EXE**
Source Code Modules in Text: **MainFrm.h, MainFrm.cpp, CDemoView.h, CDemoView.cpp**

◆ ◆ ◆ ◆ ◆

Listing 17-1: SB Demo program

MainFrm.h

```
class CMainFrame : public CFrameWnd
{
protected: // create from serialization only
  CMainFrame();
  DECLARE_DYNCREATE(CMainFrame)

// Attributes
public:

// Operations
public:

// Overrides
  // ClassWizard generated virtual function overrides
  //{{AFX_VIRTUAL(CMainFrame)
  virtual BOOL PreCreateWindow(CREATESTRUCT& cs);
  //}}AFX_VIRTUAL

// Implementation
public:
  virtual ~CMainFrame();
#ifdef _DEBUG
  virtual void AssertValid() const;
  virtual void Dump(CDumpContext& dc) const;
#endif

protected:  // control bar embedded members


// Generated message map functions
protected:
  //{{AFX_MSG(CMainFrame)
  afx_msg int OnCreate(LPCREATESTRUCT lpCreateStruct);
  //}}AFX_MSG
  DECLARE_MESSAGE_MAP()

public:
    CStatusBar  m_wndStatusBar;

};
```

MainFrm.cpp

```
// MainFrm.cpp : implementation of the CMainFrame class
//

#include "stdafx.h"
#include "sbdemo.h"
```

(continued)

Listing 17-1 *(continued)*

```
#include "MainFrm.h"

/////////////////////////////////////////////////////////////
// CMainFrame

IMPLEMENT_DYNCREATE(CMainFrame, CFrameWnd)

BEGIN_MESSAGE_MAP(CMainFrame, CFrameWnd)
  //{{AFX_MSG_MAP(CMainFrame)
  ON_WM_CREATE()
  //}}AFX_MSG_MAP
END_MESSAGE_MAP()

static UINT indicators[] =
{
  ID_SEPARATOR,  // status line indicator
  ID_SEPARATOR,
  ID_SEPARATOR,
  ID_INDICATOR_CAPS
};

/////////////////////////////////////////////////////////////
// CMainFrame construction/destruction

CMainFrame::CMainFrame()
{

}

CMainFrame::~CMainFrame()
{
}

int CMainFrame::OnCreate(LPCREATESTRUCT lpCreateStruct)
{
  if (CFrameWnd::OnCreate(lpCreateStruct) == -1)
    return -1;

  if (!m_wndStatusBar.Create(this) ||
    !m_wndStatusBar.SetIndicators(indicators,
      sizeof(indicators)/sizeof(UINT)))
  {
    TRACE0("Failed to create status bar\n");
    return -1;      // fail to create
  }

  return 0;
}

BOOL CMainFrame::PreCreateWindow(CREATESTRUCT& cs)
{
```

```
    return CFrameWnd::PreCreateWindow(cs);
}
```

Sbdemoview.h

```
class CSbdemoView : public CView
{
protected: // create from serialization only
  CSbdemoView();
  DECLARE_DYNCREATE(CSbdemoView)

// Attributes
public:
  CSbdemoDoc* GetDocument();

// Operations
public:

// Overrides
  // ClassWizard generated virtual function overrides
  //{{AFX_VIRTUAL(CSbdemoView)
  public:
  virtual void OnDraw(CDC* pDC);
  virtual BOOL PreCreateWindow(CREATESTRUCT& cs);
  protected:
  //}}AFX_VIRTUAL

// Implementation
public:
  virtual ~CSbdemoView();
#ifdef _DEBUG
  virtual void AssertValid() const;
  virtual void Dump(CDumpContext& dc) const;
#endif

protected:

// Generated message map functions
protected:
  //{{AFX_MSG(CSbdemoView)
  afx_msg void OnMouseMove(UINT nFlags, CPoint point);
  afx_msg void OnLButtonDown(UINT nFlags, CPoint point);
  afx_msg void OnRButtonDown(UINT nFlags, CPoint point);
  //}}AFX_MSG
  DECLARE_MESSAGE_MAP()
};

#ifndef _DEBUG  // debug version in sbdemoView.cpp
inline CSbdemoDoc* CSbdemoView::GetDocument()
   { return (CSbdemoDoc*)m_pDocument; }
#endif

/////////////////////////////////////////////////////////////////
```

(continued)

Listing 17-1 *(continued)*

```
//{{AFX_INSERT_LOCATION}}
// Microsoft Developer Studio will insert additional
declarations immediately before the previous line.
```

Sbdemoview.cpp

```
// sbdemoView.cpp : implementation of the CSbdemoView class
//

#include "stdafx.h"
#include "sbdemo.h"

#include "sbdemoDoc.h"
#include "sbdemoView.h"
#include "MainFrm.h"

/////////////////////////////////////////////////////////////
// CSbdemoView

IMPLEMENT_DYNCREATE(CSbdemoView, CView)

BEGIN_MESSAGE_MAP(CSbdemoView, CView)
  //{{AFX_MSG_MAP(CSbdemoView)
  ON_WM_MOUSEMOVE()
  ON_WM_LBUTTONDOWN()
  ON_WM_RBUTTONDOWN()
  //}}AFX_MSG_MAP
END_MESSAGE_MAP()

/////////////////////////////////////////////////////////////
// CSbdemoView construction/destruction

CSbdemoView::CSbdemoView()
{

}

CSbdemoView::~CSbdemoView()
{
}

BOOL CSbdemoView::PreCreateWindow(CREATESTRUCT& cs)
{
  return CView::PreCreateWindow(cs);
}

void CSbdemoView::OnDraw(CDC* pDC)
{
  CSbdemoDoc* pDoc = GetDocument();
  ASSERT_VALID(pDoc);
```

```
  pDC->TextOut(0,0,"Use the mouse and watch the status
   bar behavior");
}

void CSbdemoView::OnMouseMove(UINT nFlags, CPoint point)
{
  CString strTemp;
  UINT nPaneID;
  UINT nPaneStyle;
  int nPaneWidth;

  CMainFrame* pFrame = (CMainFrame*)
   AfxGetApp()->m_pMainWnd;

CStatusBar* pBar = &pFrame->m_wndStatusBar;
  if (pBar)
  {
    strTemp.Format("x=%d",point.x);
    pBar-> GetPaneInfo(1,
                         nPaneID,
                         nPaneStyle,
                         nPaneWidth);

    pBar->SetPaneText(1,strTemp);

    pBar->SetPaneInfo(1,nPaneID,nPaneStyle,
                     7 * strTemp.GetLength());

    strTemp.Format("y=%d",point.y);
    pBar-> GetPaneInfo(2,
                      nPaneID,
                      nPaneStyle,
                      nPaneWidth);

    pBar->SetPaneText(2,strTemp);
    pBar->SetPaneInfo(2,nPaneID,nPaneStyle,
                     7 * strTemp.GetLength());
    pFrame->RecalcLayout();
  }
  CView::OnMouseMove(nFlags, point);
}

void CSbdemoView::OnLButtonDown(UINT nFlags, CPoint
  point)
{
  UINT nPaneID;
  UINT nPaneStyle;
  int nPaneWidth;

  CMainFrame* pFrame = (CMainFrame*)
   AfxGetApp()->m_pMainWnd;

  CStatusBar* pBar = &pFrame->m_wndStatusBar;
```

(continued)

Listing 17-1 *(continued)*

```
  pBar->GetPaneInfo(1,nPaneID,nPaneStyle,nPaneWidth);

if (nPaneStyle==SBPS_NORMAL)
    pBar-> SetPaneInfo(1,
                          nPaneID,
                          SBPS_POPOUT,
                          nPaneWidth);
  else
    pBar-> SetPaneInfo(1,
                          nPaneID,
                          SBPS_NORMAL,
                          nPaneWidth);

  pBar->GetPaneInfo(2,nPaneID,nPaneStyle,nPaneWidth);
  pBar->SetPaneInfo(2,nPaneID,SBPS_NORMAL,nPaneWidth);
  CView::OnLButtonDown(nFlags, point);
}

void CSbdemoView::OnRButtonDown(UINT nFlags, CPoint
  point)
{
  UINT nPaneID;
  UINT nPaneStyle;
  int nPaneWidth;

  CMainFrame* pFrame = (CMainFrame*)
   AfxGetApp()->m_pMainWnd;

  CStatusBar* pBar = &pFrame->m_wndStatusBar;

  pBar->GetPaneInfo(1,nPaneID,nPaneStyle,nPaneWidth);
  pBar->SetPaneInfo(1,nPaneID,SBPS_NORMAL,nPaneWidth);
  pBar->GetPaneInfo(2,nPaneID,nPaneStyle,nPaneWidth);

if (nPaneStyle==SBPS_NORMAL)
    pBar-> SetPaneInfo(2,
                          nPaneID,
                          SBPS_POPOUT,
                          nPaneWidth);
  else
    pBar-> SetPaneInfo(2,
                          nPaneID,
                          SBPS_NORMAL,
                          nPaneWidth);

  CView::OnRButtonDown(nFlags, point);
}
```

Summary

This chapter explores two basic user-interface objects: toolbars and status bars.

- ✦ Creating toolbars involves a five-step process; when you have created a toolbar, you can customize it to your own specific needs.
- ✦ Incorporating status bars into an application begins with the defaults used by MFC during status bar creation. Becoming familiar with this process results in the capability to create and control your own status bars.
- ✦ The member functions of `CStatusBar` give you the means to customize the appearance of your status bars at runtime.

✦ ✦ ✦

CHAPTER 18

Threads

In This Chapter

Learning what a thread is

Understanding the difficulties of programming with threads

Exploring ways to start and stop threads

Examining MFC classes from threads

Viewing a demo program that uses threads

Within Windows 98 and in the Win32 environment, each running application constitutes a *process* and each process consists of one or more *threads* — paths of execution through the code of a process. The way a program uses threads can make a crucial difference. One fundamental difference between 16- and 32-bit Windows, for example, is that 32-bit Windows doesn't limit its applications to one thread each. A process in a 32-bit Windows application begins its life as a single thread, but that thread can spawn additional threads. A preemptive scheduler inside the operating system divides CPU time among active threads so they appear to run simultaneously. Secondary threads are ideal for performing background tasks such as paginating documents and performing garbage collection. They can also play more visible roles by creating windows and processing messages to those windows, just as the primary thread processes messages sent to an application's main window.

Multithreading is not for everyone. Multithreaded applications are difficult to write and debug because the parallelism of the concurrently running threads adds an extra layer of complexity to the code. But used properly, multiple threads can dramatically improve an application's responsiveness. A word processor that does its spell checking in a dedicated thread, for example, can continue to process input in the primary thread so that the user doesn't have to wait for the spell checker to finish. What makes writing a threaded spell checker difficult is that the spell-checking thread will invariably have to synchronize its actions with other threads in the application. Most programmers have been conditioned to think about their code in synchronous terms — function A calls function B, function B initializes variable C and returns to A, and so on. But threads are asynchronous by nature in a multithreaded application; you have to think about what happens if, say, two threads call function B at the same time or one thread reads a variable while another writes it. If function A launches function B in a separate thread, you also must anticipate what problems could occur if function A continues to run while function B executes. For example, it's common to pass the address of a variable created on the stack in function A to function B for processing. But if function B is in another thread, the variable may no longer exist when function B gets around to accessing it. Even the most innocent looking code can be fatally flawed when it involves the use of multiple threads.

MFC encapsulates threads of execution in the `CWinThread` class. It also includes synchronization classes encapsulating events, mutexes (the process of restricting thread code to execution by a single simultaneous process), and other thread synchronization objects found in the Windows kernel. Does MFC make multithreading easier? Not exactly. Developers who have written multithreaded Windows applications in C are often surprised to learn that MFC adds complexities all its own. The key to writing multithreaded programs in MFC is to have a keen understanding of what you're doing and to know where the trouble spots are. This chapter is designed to help you do both.

Distinguishing Threads

As far as Windows is concerned, all threads are alike. MFC, however, distinguishes between two types: *user interface* (UI) *threads* and *worker threads*. UI threads have message loops, and worker threads do not. UI threads can create windows and process messages sent to those windows. Worker threads perform background tasks that receive no direct input from the user and therefore don't need windows and message loops. When you open a folder in the Windows shell, the shell launches a UI thread that creates a window showing the folder's contents. If you drag-copy a group of files to the newly opened folder, that folder's thread performs the file transfers. (Sometimes the UI thread creates yet another thread — this time a worker thread — to copy the files). The benefit of this multithreaded architecture is that after the copy operation begins, you can switch to windows already opened onto other folders — and continue working there while files are copied in the background. Launching a UI thread that creates a window is conceptually similar to launching an application within an application. The most common use for UI threads is to create multiple windows serviced by separate threads of execution.

Worker threads are ideal for performing isolated tasks that can be broken off from the rest of the application and performed in the background while other processing takes place in the foreground. A classic example of a worker thread is the thread an animation control uses to play AVI clips. Basically all the thread does is draw a frame, put itself to sleep for a fraction of a second, and wake up and start again. It adds little to the processor's workload because it spends most of its life suspended between frames, and yet it also provides a valuable service. This is a great example of multithreaded design because the background thread is given a specific task to do and then allowed to perform that task over and over until the primary thread signals it's time to end.

Creating a worker thread

There are two ways to create a worker thread in an MFC application. You can construct a CWinThread object and call that object's CreateThread() function to create the thread, or you can use AfxBeginThread() to construct a CWinThread object and create a thread in one step. MFC defines two different versions of AfxBeginThread(): one for UI threads and another for worker threads. Don't use the Win32 ::CreateThread() function to create a thread in an MFC program unless the thread doesn't use MFC.

AfxBeginThread() and CWinThread::CreateThread() aren't merely wrappers around ::CreateThread(); in addition to launching threads of execution, they also initialize internal variables used by the framework, perform sanity checks at various points during the thread creation process, and take steps to ensure that functions in the C runtime library are accessed in a thread-safe way.

AfxBeginThread() makes it simple—almost trivial, in fact—to create a worker thread. The following statement starts a worker thread and passes it the address of an application-defined data structure named ThreadInfo that contains input to the thread:

```
CWinThread *pThread = AfxBeginThread( ThreadFunc,
  &ThreadInfo );
```

ThreadFunc is the thread function—the function executed when the thread itself begins to execute.

A simple thread function that spins in a loop, eating CPU cycles, and then terminates looks like this:

```
UINT ThreadFunc( LPVOID pParam )
{
  UINT nIterations = (UINT) pParam;
  for( UINT i=0; i<nIterations; i++ )
    return( 0 );
}
```

We'll look at thread functions in more detail in the next section. The worker thread form of AfxBeginThread() accepts as many as four additional parameters that specify the thread's priority, stack size, creation flags, and security attributes. The complete function prototype follows:

```
CWinThread *AfxBeginThread( AFX_THREADPROC pfnThreadPro,
  LPVOID pParam, int nPriority = THREAD_PRIORITY_NORMAL,
  UINT nStackSize = 0, DWORD dwCreateFlags = 0,
  LPSECUTIRY_ATTRIBUTES lpSecutiryAttrs = NULL );
```

The nPriority parameter specifies the thread's execution priority. High-priority threads are always scheduled for CPU time before low-priority threads, but in practice even threads with extremely low priorities usually get all the processor time they need. nPriority doesn't specify an absolute priority level. It specifies a priority level relative to the priority level of the process to which the thread belongs. The default is THREAD_PRORITY_NORMAL, which assigns the thread the same priority as the process that owns it. A thread's priority level can be changed at any time with CWinThread::SetThreadPriority().

The nStackSize parameter passed to AfxBeginThread() specifies the thread's maximum stack size. In the Win32 environment, each thread receives its own stack. The 0 default nStackSize value allows the stack to grow as large as 1 MB. This doesn't mean that every thread receives a minimum of 1 MB of memory; it means that each thread is assigned 1 MB of address space in the larger 4-GB address space in which 32-bit Windows applications execute. Memory isn't committed (assigned) to the stack's address space until it's needed, so most thread stacks never use more than a few kilobytes of physical memory. Placing a limit on the stack size allows the operating system to trap runaway functions that recurse endlessly and eventually consume the stack. The default limit of 1 MB is fine for almost all applications.

The dwCreateFlags parameter can be one of two values. The default value 0 tells the system to start executing the thread immediately. If CREATE_SUSPENDED is specified instead, the thread starts out in a suspended state and doesn't begin running until another thread (usually the thread that created it) calls CWinThread::ResumeThread() on the suspended thread, as demonstrated here:

```
CWinThread *pThread = AfxBeginThread( ThreadFunc,
  &ThreadInfo, THREAD_PRIORITY_NORMAL, 0,
  CREATE_SUSPENDED );
```

Sometimes it's useful to create a thread but defer its execution until later. As you'll see later, it's also possible to create a thread that suspends itself until a specified event occurs.

The final parameter in the AfxBeginThread() argument list, lpSecurityAttrs, is a pointer to a SECURITY_ATTRIBUTES structure that specifies the new thread's security attributes and also tells the system whether child processes should inherit the thread handle. The NULL default value assigns the new thread the same properties the thread that created it has.

The thread function

A worker thread's thread function can be a static class member function or a function declared outside a class. It is prototyped this way:

```
UINT ThreadFunc ( LPVOID pParam );
```

The pParam argument is a 32-bit value whose value equals the pParam passed to AfxBeginThread(). Often pParam is the address of an application-defined data structure containing information passed to the worker thread by the thread that created it. It can also be a scalar value, a handle, or even a pointer to an MFC object. It's perfectly legal to use the same thread function for two or more threads, but you should be sensitive to re-entrancy problems caused by global and static variables. As long as the variables (and objects) a thread uses are created on the stack, there are no re-entrancy problems since each thread gets its own stack.

Creating a user interface thread

Creating a UI thread is an altogether different process than creating a worker thread. A worker thread is defined by its thread function, but a UI thread's behavior is governed by a dynamically creatable class derived from CWinThread that much resembles an application class derived from CWinApp. The UI thread class shown below in Listing 18-1 creates a top-level frame window that closes itself when clicked with the left mouse button. Closing the window terminates the thread, too, because CWnd::OnNcDestroy() posts a WM_QUIT message to the thread's message queue. Posting a WM_QUIT message to a secondary thread ends the thread. Posting a WM_QUIT message to a primary thread ends the thread and ends the application, too.

Listing 18-1: A User Interface Thread That Stops When the Window Is Closed

```
// The CUIThread class
class CUIThread : public CWinThread
{

  DECLARE_DYNCREATE( CUIThread )

public:
  virtual BOOL InitInstance();

};

IMPLEMENT_DYNCREATE( CUIThread, CWinThread );

BOOL CUIThread::InitInstance()
{
  m_pMainWnd = new CMainWindow();
  m_pMainWnd->ShowWindow( SW_SHOW );
  m_pMainWnd->UpdateWindow();

  return( TRUE );

}
```

(continued)

Listing 18-1 *(continued)*

```
// The CmainWindow class
class CMainWindow : public CFrameWnd
{

public:
  CMainWindow();

protected:
  afx_msg void OnLButtonDown( UINT, CPoint );
  DECLARE_MESSAGE_MAP()

};

BEGIN_MESSAGE_MAP( CMainWindow, CFrameWnd )
  ON_WM_LBUTTONDOWN()
END_MESSAGE_MAP()

CMainWindow::CMainWindow()
{
  Create( NULL, "UI Thread Window" );
}

void CMainWindow::OnLButtonDown( UINT nFlags,
  CPoint Point )
{

  PostMessage( WM_CLOSE, 0, 0 );

}
```

Note the `SW SHOW` parameter passed to `ShowWindow()` in place of the normal `m_nCmdShow` parameter. `m_nCmdShow` is a `CWinApp` data member, so when you create a top-level window from a UI thread, it's up to you to specify the window's initial show state.

A `CUIThread` is launched by calling the form of `AfxBeginThread()` that accepts a `CRuntimeClass` pointer to the thread class as follows:

```
CWinThread *pThread =
  AfxBeginThread( RUNTIME_CLASS ( CUIThread ) );
```

The UI-thread version of `AfxBeginThread()` accepts the same four optional parameters as the worker-thread version, but it doesn't accept a `pParam` value. Once started, a UI thread runs asynchronously with respect to the thread that created it, almost as if it belonged to another application.

Suspending and Resuming Threads

A running thread can be suspended with `CWinThread::SuspendThread()` and started again with `CWinThread::ResumeThread()`. A thread can call `SuspendThread()` on itself, or another thread can call `SuspendThread()` for it. However, a suspended thread can't call `ResumeThread()` to wake itself up; someone else must call `ResumeThread()` on its behalf. A suspended thread consumes next to no processor time and imposes essentially zero overhead on the system.

For each thread, Windows maintains a suspend count that's incremented by `SuspendThread()` and decremented by `ResumeThread()`. A thread is scheduled for processor time only when its suspend count is 0. If `SuspendThread()` is called twice in succession, `ResumeThread()` must be called twice also. A thread created without a `CREATE_SUSPENDED` flag is assigned an initial suspend count of 0. A thread created with a `CREATE_SUSPENDED` flag begins with a suspend count of 1. Both `SuspendThread()` and `ResumeThread()` return the thread's previous suspend count, so you can make sure a thread gets resumed no matter how high its suspend count is by calling `ResumeThread()` repeatedly until it returns 1. `ResumeThread()` returns 0 if the thread it's called on is not currently suspended.

Putting Threads to Sleep

A thread can put itself to sleep by calling the API function `::Sleep()`. A sleeping thread uses no processor time and is automatically awakened after a specified number of milliseconds The following statement suspends the current thread for ten seconds:

```
::Sleep( 10000 );
```

One use for `::Sleep()` is for implementing threads whose actions are inherently time-based, such as the background thread in an animation control or a thread that moves the hands of a clock. Another use for `::Sleep()` is for relinquishing the remainder of a thread's timeslice to other threads waiting to execute. The following statement suspends the current thread and allows the scheduler to run other threads of equal priority:

```
::Sleep( 0 );
```

If there are no other equal-priority threads awaiting execution time, the function call returns immediately and the scheduler resumes executing the current thread. If you write an application that uses multiple threads to draw to a display surface, a few strategically placed `::Sleep( 0 )` statements can do wonders for the quality of the output.

Terminating a Thread

Once a thread begins, it can terminate in two ways. A worker thread ends when the thread function executes a return statement or calls `AfxEndThread()`. A UI thread terminates when a `WM_QUIT` message is posted to its message queue or a function within the thread calls `AfxEndThread()`. A thread can post a `WM_QUIT` message to itself with the API function `::PostQuitMessage()`. `AfxEndThread()`, `::PostQuitMessage()`, and return all except a 32-bit exit code that can be retrieved with `::GetExitCodeThread()` after the thread has terminated. The statement that follows copies the exit code of the thread referenced by `pThread` to the `DWORD` variable `dwExitCode`:

```
DWORD dwExitCode;
::GetExitCodeThread( pThread->m_hThread, &dwExitCode );
```

If called for a thread that's still executing, `::GetExitCodeThread()` sets `dwExitCode` equal to `STILL_ACTIVE` (0x103).

One complication in calling `::GetExitCode()` in an MFC application is that by default a `CWinThread` object automatically deletes itself when the corresponding thread terminates. Therefore, a `::GetExitCodeThread()` statement like the one above will probably generate an access violation if the thread has terminated because `pThread` will no longer be valid. You can avoid such problems by setting the thread object's `m_bAutoDelete` data member to `FALSE` so that the `CWinThread` object won't be deleted automatically upon thread termination. (Don't forget to delete the `CWinThread` object yourself to avoid memory leaks.) An alternative approach is to save the thread handle stored in the `CWinThread` object's `m_hThread` data member and pass it to `::GetExitCodeThread()` directly. Thread handles passed to `::GetExitCodeThread()` can identify existing threads or threads that once existed but have since terminated.

Terminating a Thread from Another Thread

Generally speaking, threads can terminate only themselves. If you want thread A to terminate thread B, you need to set up a signaling mechanism that allows thread A to tell thread B to terminate itself. In most cases, a simple variable can serve as a flag that signals a thread to terminate, as demonstrated here in Listing 18-2:

Listing 18-2: Terminating a Thread from Another Thread

```
// Thread A
static BOOL bContinue = TRUE;

CWinThread *pThread =
  AfxBeginThread( ThreadFunc, bContinue );

// Do some work
```

```
// Tell thread B to terminate
bContinue = FALSE;

// Thread B
UINT ThreadFunc( LPVOID pParam )
{
  BOOL *pContinue = (BOOL*) pParam;

  while( *pContinue ){
    // Do some work
    }

  return( 0 );

}
```

Conventional wisdom says that this is a poor way for threads to communicate, but in fact it's just as effective as using a thread synchronization object. Of course, to prevent access violations, you need to ensure that `bContinue` doesn't go out of scope while thread B is running. That's why `bContinue` is declared static in the example. Even if the function that sets `bContinue` to `FALSE` in thread A returns before thread B terminates, the variable will still be valid because it's located in the application's data segment, not on the stack.

Now suppose that you'd like to modify this example so that, once it sets `bContinue` to `FALSE`, thread A stops what it's doing until thread B is no longer running. Listing 18-3 shows the proper way to do it:

Listing 18-3: **Waiting for a Thread to End**

```
// Thread A
static BOOL bContinue = TRUE;
CWinThread *pThread =
  AfxBeginThread( ThreadFunc, &bContinue );

// Do some work

// Save the thread handle
HANDLE hThread = pThread->m_hThread;

// Tell thread B to terminate
bContinue = FALSE;

::WaitForSingleObject( hThread, INFINITE );
```

(continued)

Listing 18-3 (continued)

```
// Thread B
UINT ThreadFunc( LPVOID pParam )
{
  BOOL *pContinue = (BOOL *) pParam;
  while( *pContinue ){
    // Do some work
    }
  return( 0 );
}
```

`::WaitForSingleObject()` waits until the specified object—in this case, another thread—enters a signaled state. A thread object goes from nonsignaled to signaled when the thread terminates. The first parameter passed to `::WaitForSingleObject()` is the handle of the object you want to wait on. (It can also be a process handle, the handle of a synchronization object, or a file-change notification handle, among other things.) The handle is retrieved from the `CWinThread` object before `bContinue` is set to `FALSE` because the `CWinThread` object may no longer exist when the call to `::WaitForSingleObject()` is executed. The second parameter is the length of time the thread that calls `::WaitForSingleObject()` is willing to wait. `INFINITE` means wait as long as it takes. When you specify `INFINITE`, you take the chance that the calling thread could lock up if the object it's waiting on never becomes signaled. If you specify a number of milliseconds instead, as in `::WaitForSingleObject( hThread, 5000 )`, then `WaitForSingleObject()` will return after the specified time—in this case, 5 seconds—elapses, even if the object still hasn't become signaled. You can check the return value to determine why the function returned. `WAIT_OBJECT_0` means that the object became signaled, and `WAIT_TIMEOUT` means that it did not.

Given a thread handle or a `CWinThread` object wrapping a thread handle, you can quickly determine whether the thread is still running by calling `::WaitForSingleObject()` and specifying 0 for the time-out period, as shown here:

```
if( ::WaitForSingleObject( hThread, 0 ) ==WAIT_OBJECT_0 )
  // The thread no longer exists
else
  // The thread still exists
```

Called this way, `::WaitForSingleObject()` doesn't wait; it returns immediately. A return value equal to `WAIT_OBJECT_0` means that the thread is signaled (no longer exists), and a return value equal to `WAIT_TIMEOUT` means that the thread is nonsignaled (still exists). Remember: Because a `CWinThread` object is automatically deleted when a thread terminates, it doesn't make sense to call `::WaitForSingleObject()` to find out whether a `CWinThread` is signaled or nonsignaled unless the CWinThread object's m_bAutoDelete data member is set to FALSE.

Don't make the mistake of waiting for a thread to terminate by writing code like this:

```
// Thread A (don't do this!)

static BOOL bContinue = TRUE;

CWinThread *pThread =
  AfxBeginThread( ThreadFunc, bContinue );
// Do some work
HANDLE hThread = pThread->m_hThread;

// Save the thread handle
bContinue = FALSE;

// Tell thread B to terminate
DWORD dwExitCode;
do{
  ::GetExitCodeThread( hThread, &dwExitCode );
   } while( dwExitCode == STILL_ACTIVE );

// Thread B
UINT ThreadFunc( LPVOID pParam )
{
  BOOL *pContinue = (BOOL*) pParam;

  while( *pContinue ){
    // Do some work
    }

  return( 0 );

}
```

In addition to spending CPU time needlessly by forcing the primary thread to spin in a do-while loop, this code will probably cause the application to lock up. When a thread calls ::WaitForSingleObject(), it waits efficiently because it is effectively suspended until the function call returns. The thread is said "to be blocked" or "to block" until ::WaitForSingleObject() returns.

There is one way a thread can kill another directly, but you should use it only as a last resort. The statement ::TerminateThread(pThread->m_hThread, 0); terminates pThread and assigns it an exit code of 0. The Win32 API reference documents some of the many problems ::TerminateThread() can cause, which range from orphaned thread synchronization objects to DLLs that don't get a chance to execute normal thread-shutdown code.

Exploring Thread Scheduling

The *scheduler* is the component of the operating system that decides which threads run when and for how long. Thread scheduling is a complex task whose goal is to divide CPU time among multiple threads of execution as efficiently as possible to create the illusion that all of them are running at once. On machines with multiple CPUs, Windows NT really does run two or more threads at the same time by assigning different threads to different processors. This feature is known as *symmetric multiprocessing*, or *SMP*. Windows 98 is not an SMP system, so it schedules all of its threads on the same CPU even if several CPUs are present.

The Windows 98 scheduler uses a variety of techniques to improve multitasking performance and to try to ensure that each thread in the system gets an ample amount of CPU time, but ultimately the decision about which thread should execute next boils down to the thread with the highest priority. At any given moment, each thread is assigned a priority level from 0 through 31, with higher numbers indicating higher priorities. If a priority-16 thread is waiting to execute and all of the other threads vying for CPU time have priority levels of 15 or less, the priority-16 thread gets scheduled next. If two priority-16 threads are waiting to execute, the scheduler executes the one that has executed the least recently. When that thread's time slice is up, the other priority-16 thread gets executed if all of the other threads still have lower priorities. As a rule, the scheduler always gives the next time slice to the thread waiting to execute that has the highest priority.

Does this mean that lower-priority threads will never get executed? Not at all. First, remember that Windows 98 is a message-based operating system. If a thread's message queue is empty when the thread calls `::GetMessage()` to retrieve a message, the thread blocks until a message becomes available. This gives lower-priority threads a chance to execute because blocked threads receive no time slices. Most UI threads spend the major part of their time blocked on the message queue waiting for input, so as long as a high-priority worker thread doesn't monopolize the CPU, even low-priority threads typically get all the CPU time they need. (A worker thread never blocks on the message queue because it doesn't process messages.)

The scheduler also plays a lot of tricks with threads' priority levels to enhance the overall responsiveness of the system and reduce the chance that any thread will be starved for CPU time. A thread may have a priority level of 7, but if that thread goes for too long without receiving a time slice, the scheduler may temporarily boost the thread's priority level to 8 or 9 (or even higher) to give it a chance to execute. Windows boosts the priorities of all threads that belong to the foreground process to improve the responsiveness of the application in which the user is working, and it boosts a thread's priority even more when the thread has an input message to process. The system also uses a technique called *priority inheritance* to prevent high-priority threads from blocking for too long on synchronization objects owned by low-priority threads. For example, if a priority-16 thread tries to access a critical section owned by a priority-10 thread, the scheduler will treat the priority-10 thread as if it had priority 16 until the thread releases the critical section. This way, the critical section will come free faster and the priority-16 thread won't get stuck waiting on a lower-priority thread.

How do thread priorities get assigned in the first place? When you call `AfxBeginThread()` or `CWinThread::SetThreadPriority()`, you specify the relative thread-priority value. (An aside: The `::CreateThread()` API function that starts a thread doesn't accept a relative thread-priority value. When `AfxBeginThread()` starts a thread for you, it calls `SetThreadPriority()` after it creates the thread to set the thread's relative priority.) The operating system combines the relative priority level with the priority class of the process that owns the thread to compute a base priority level for the thread. The thread's actual priority level—a number from 0 through 31—varies from moment to moment depending on whether the process that owns it is running in the foreground or the background. The actual priority level is also subject to change from the system's dynamic boosting, but most of the time it stays within 2 or 3 digits of the base priority level. You can't control boosting (and you wouldn't want to even if you could), but you can control the base priority level by setting the priority class for the process and the relative priority level for the thread.

Examining Process Priority Classes

Most processes begin life with the priority class `NORMAL_PRIORITY_CLASS`. Once started, however, a process can change its priority class by calling `::SetPriorityClass()`, which accepts a process handle (obtainable with `::GetCurrentProcess()`) and one of the specifiers shown in Table 18-1.

Most applications don't need to change their priority classes. `HIGH_PRIORITY_CLASS` and `REALTIME_PRIORITY_CLASS` processes can severely inhibit the responsiveness of the system and even delay critical system activities such as flushing of the disk cache. One legitimate use for `HIGH_PRIORITY_CLASS` is for system applications that remain hidden most of the time but pop up a window when a certain input event occurs. These applications impose little overhead on the system while they're blocked and waiting for input, but when the input appears, they receive priority over normal applications. `REALTIME_PRIORITY_CLASS` is provided primarily for the benefit of real-time data-acquisition programs that must have the lion's share of the CPU time to work properly.

`IDLE_PRIORITY_CLASS` is ideal for screen savers, system monitors, and other low-priority applications that operate unobtrusively in the background.

Table 18-1
Relative Thread Priorities

Priority Class	*Description*
IDLE_PRIORITY CLASS	The process runs only when the system is idle – for example, when other threads are blocked on the message queue waiting for input.
NORMAL_PRIORITY_CLASS	The default process priority class. The process has no special scheduling needs.
HIGH_PRIORITY_CLASS	The process should receive priority over IDLE_PRIORITY CLASS and NORMAL_PRIORITY_CLASS processes.
REALTIME_PRIORITY_CLASS	The process must have the highest possible priority, and its threads should preempt even threads belonging to H1GH_PRIORITY_CLASS processes.

Sharing MFC Objects Among Threads

Now for the bad news about writing multithreaded MFC applications. As long as threads are written so that they don't call member functions belonging to objects created by other threads, there are few restrictions on what they can do. However, if thread A passes a CWnd pointer to thread B and thread B calls a member function of that CWnd object, MFC is likely to halt a debug build of the application with an assertion error. A release build might work fine—but then again, it might not. There's also a possibility in this situation that a debug build not only won't assert but that it won't work properly, either. It all depends on what goes on inside the framework when that particular CWnd member function is called. You can avoid a potential minefield of problems by compartmentalizing your threads and having each thread create the objects it uses rather than rely on objects created by other threads. But for cases in which that's simply not practical, here are a few rules to go by.

First, there are many MFC member functions that can be safely called on objects in other threads. Most of the inline functions defined in the .inl files in MFC's include directory can be called through object pointers passed in from other threads because they are little more than wrappers around API functions. But calling a non-inline member function is asking for trouble. For example, the following code in Listing 18-4, which passes a CWnd pointer named pWnd from thread A to thread B and has B call CWnd::GetParent() through the pointer, works without problems:

Listing 18-4: ThreadDemo1View

```
CwinThread *pThread =
  AfxBeginThread( ThreadFunc, (LPVOID) pWnd );

UINT ThreadFunc( LPVOID pParam )
{
  CWnd *pWnd = (CWnd *) pParam;
  CWnd *pParent = pWnd->GetParent();

  return( 0 );

}
```

Simply changing `GetParent()` to `GetParentFrame()`, however, causes an assertion error the moment thread B is started. Look what that does to this code:

```
CwinThread *pThread =
  AfxBeginThread( ThreadFunc, pWnd);

UINT ThreadFunc( LPVOID pParam )
{
  CWnd *pWnd = (CWnd *) pParam;
  // Get ready for an assertion error!
  CWnd *pParent = pWnd->GetParentFrame();

  return( ) );
}
```

Why does `GetParent()` work when `GetParentFrame()` doesn't? Because `GetParent()` calls through almost directly to the `::GetParent()` function in the API. No problem there; `m_hWnd` is valid because it's part of the `CWnd` object that `pWnd` points to, and `FromHandle()` converts the `HWND` returned by `GetParent()` into a `CWnd` pointer.

But now consider what happens when you call `GetParentFrame()`. The line that causes the assertion error is `ASSERT_VALID(this)`. `ASSERT_VALID` calls `CWnd::AssertValid()`, which performs a sanity check—making sure that the associated `HWND` appears in the permanent or temporary handle map that the framework uses to convert `HWND`s into `CWnd`s. Going from a `CWnd` to an `HWND` is easy because the `HWND` is a data member of the class, but going from an `HWND` to a `CWnd` can be done only through the handle maps. And here's the problem: Handle maps are local to each thread and are not visible to other threads. If the `CWnd` whose address is passed to `ASSERT_VALID` was created by another thread, the corresponding `HWND` won't appear in the current thread's permanent or temporary handle map and MFC will assert. Many of MFC's non-inline member functions call ASSERT_VALID, but inline functions do not—at least not in current releases.

Frequently MFC's assertions protect you from calling functions that wouldn't work anyway. In a release build, GetParentFrame() returns NULL when called from a thread other than the one in which the parent frame was created. But in cases in which assertion errors are spurious—that is, when the function would work okay despite the per-thread handle tables—you can avoid assertions by passing real handles instead of object pointers. For example, it's safe to call CWnd::GetTopLevelParent() in a secondary thread if FromHandle() is called first to create an entry in the thread's temporary handle map, as shown here:

```
CwinThread *pThread =
  AfxEeginThread( ThreadFunc, (LPVOID) pWnd->m_hWnd );

UINT ThreadFunc( LPVOID pParam )
{
  CWnd *pWnd = CWnd::FromHandle( (HWND) pParam );
  CWnd *pParent = pWnd->GetTopLevelParent();

  return( ) );

}
```

That's why the MFC documentation warns that windows, GDI objects, and other objects should be passed between threads by means of handles instead of by means of pointers to MFC objects. In general, you'll have fewer problems if you pass handles instead of object pointers and then use FromHandle() to "re-create" objects in the temporary handle map of the current thread. But don't take that to mean that just any function will work. It won't.

What about calling member functions belonging to objects created from "pure" MFC classes such as CDocument and CRect—classes that don't wrap HWNDs, HDCs, or other handle types and therefore don't rely on handle maps? Just what you wanted to hear: *Some work and some don't.* There's no problem with this code:

```
CWinThread *pThread =
  AfxBeginThread( ThreadFunc, pRect );

UINT ThreadFunc( LPVOID pParam )
{
  CRect *pRect = (CRect *) pParam;
  int nArea = pRect->Width() * pRect->Height();

  return( 0 );

}
```

But the following code will assert on you:

```
CWinThread *pThread =
  AfxBeginThread( ThreadFunc, pDoc );

UINT ThreadFunc( LPVOID pParam )
{
  CMyDocument *pDoc = (CMyDocument *) pParam;
  PDoc->UpdateAllViews( NULL );

  return( 0 );

}
```

Even seemingly innocuous functions frequently don't work when they're called from secondary threads. The bottom line is that before you go calling member functions of MFC objects created in other threads, you must understand the implications. And the only way to understand the implications is to study the MFC source code to see how a particular member function behaves. Also keep in mind that MFC isn't thread-safe, a subject we'll explore later in this chapter. So even if a member function appears to be safe, ask yourself what might happen if an object created by thread A were accessed by thread B and thread A preempted thread B in the middle of the access. This is incredibly difficult stuff to sort out and only adds to the complexity of writing multithreaded applications. Avoid crossing thread boundaries with calls to MFC member functions; you'll avoid a lot of problems.

Using C Runtime Functions in Multithreaded Applications

Certain functions in the standard C runtime library pose problems for multithreaded applications. `strtok()`, `time()`, and many other C runtime functions use global variables to store intermediate data. If thread A calls one of these functions and thread B preempts thread A and calls the same function, global data stored by thread A could be overwritten by global data stored by thread B. Most modern C and C++ compilers come with two versions of the C runtime library: one that's thread-safe (multiple concurrent threads can call into it) and one that isn't. The thread-safe versions of the runtime library typically won't rely on thread-synchronization objects. Instead, they store intermediate values in per-thread data structures. Visual C++ 6 comes with six versions of the C runtime library, described in Table 18-2. Which one you should choose depends on whether you're compiling a debug build or a release build, whether you want to link with the C runtime library statically or dynamically, and, of course, whether your application is single-threaded or multithreaded.

Table 18-2
C Runtime Libraries

Library	*Use*
Libc.lib	Single-threaded release builds
Libcd.lib	Single-threaded debug builds
Libcmt.lib	Multithreaded release builds
Libcmtd.lib	Multithreaded debug builds
Msvcrt.lib	Single- or multithreaded, dynamic-linking, release builds
Msvcrtd.lib	Single- or multithreaded, dynamic-linking, debug builds

The `ThreadDemo1` program implements a multiple-document framework. Each separate window is drawn by a separately instantiated thread. So if you create four child windows, there are four threads at work drawing each window.

The thread functions draw a spirograph pattern in the windows. There are three values that determine the shape and pattern of the spirograph pattern: the integers `nFixedRadius`, `nMovingRadius`, and `nMovingOffset`. Each time the window is drawn, these values are incremented. This makes the pattern change over time for a continuous variety of effects.

Demo Program

ThreadDemo1
CD-ROM Location: **Chap18\ThreadDemo1View**
Program Name: **ThreadDemo1View.EXE**
Source Code Modules in Text: **ThreadDemo1View.cpp**

✦ ✦ ✦ ✦ ✦

Listing 18-5: ThreadDemo1View

```
// ThreadDemo1View.cpp : implementation of
// the CThreadDemo1View class
//

UINT ThreadProc( LPVOID lpParam )
{
  // Get a THREAD_INFO pointer from the
  // parameter that was passed in.
  THREAD_INFO *lpThreadInfo =
    (THREAD_INFO *) lpParam;

  // The next six variables represent
  // values used to draw the spirograph;
  unsigned char Red, Green, Blue;
```

```
int nFixedRadius = 80;
int nMovingRadius = 10;
int nMovingOffset = 70;

// Begin colors based on the system time. This
// makes the color somewhat random.
Red = (unsigned char)
  ( GetTickCount() & 0x000000ff );
Green = (unsigned char)
  ( ( GetTickCount() & 0x00000ff0 ) > 4 );
Blue = (unsigned char)
  ( ( GetTickCount() & 0x0000ff00 ) > 8 );

while( *lpThreadInfo->lpKillThread == FALSE ){

  // Get a DC for the window.
  HDC hdc = ::GetDC( lpThreadInfo->hWnd );

  // Get the client rect so we can
  // calculate the center point.
  RECT Rect;
  ::GetClientRect( lpThreadInfo->hWnd, &Rect );
  int nMidx = Rect.right / 2;
  int nMidy = Rect.bottom / 2;

  // Clear the window.
  ::InvalidateRect( lpThreadInfo->hWnd, NULL, TRUE );
  ::UpdateWindow( lpThreadInfo->hWnd );

  // Create a pen based on the color. Select it
  // into the DC and remember the old pen so
  // we can select it back in later.
  HPEN hPen, hOldPen;
  hPen =
    ::CreatePen( PS_SOLID, 1, RGB( Red, Green, Blue ));
  hOldPen = (HPEN) ::SelectObject( hdc, hPen );

  // Iterate through a bunch of times and
  // draw the spirograph.
  int prevx, prevy, x, y;
  for( int i=0; i<=500; i++ ){

    // Remember x and y.
    prevx = x;
    prevy = y;

    // Calculate the new x and y.
    x = (int) ( ( nFixedRadius + nMovingRadius ) *
      cos( (double) i ) -
      ( nMovingRadius + nMovingOffset ) *
      cos((double)(( ( nFixedRadius + nMovingRadius ) /
      nMovingRadius ) * i ) ) );
```

(continued)

Listing 18-5 *(continued)*

```
      y = (int) ( ( nFixedRadius + nMovingRadius ) *
        sin( (double) i ) -
        ( nMovingRadius + nMovingOffset ) *
        sin((double)(( ( nFixedRadius + nMovingRadius ) /
        nMovingRadius ) * i ) ) );

      // Draw the line (or move to the first
      // point if this is the first time through).
      if( i > 0 )
        ::LineTo( hdc, x + nMidx, y + nMidy );
      else
        ::MoveToEx( hdc, x + nMidx, y + nMidy, NULL );

      }

    // Increment the color variables so
    // that the colors move around.
    Red += 6;
    Green += 5;
    Blue += 4;

    // Increase the fixed radius and
    // limit it to a max of 150.
    nFixedRadius++;
    if( nFixedRadius > 170 )
      nFixedRadius = 90;
    // Increase the moving radius and
    // limit it to a max of 120.
    nMovingRadius++;
    if( nMovingRadius > 40 )
      nMovingRadius = 10;

    // Increase the moving offset and
    // limit it to a max of 90.
    nMovingOffset++;
    if( nMovingOffset > 100 )
      nMovingOffset = 70;

    // Select the old pen into the DC,
    // delete the pen we created, and
    // release the DC we got.
    ::SelectObject( hdc, hOldPen );
    ::DeleteObject( hPen );
    ::ReleaseDC( lpThreadInfo->hWnd, hdc );

    // Sleep so we don't chew up too
    // much CPU time.
    Sleep( 200 );
    }

  return( 0 );
```

```
}

///////////////////////////////////////////////////////////////
// CThreadDemo1View construction/destruction

CThreadDemo1View::CThreadDemo1View()
{

  // This is the flag that tells the thread to quit.
  m_bKillThread = FALSE;

  // NULL the pointer to the thread so we know
  // it hasn't been created.
  m_pThread = NULL;

}

CThreadDemo1View::~CThreadDemo1View()
{
  // Get the thread handle into local space since
  // the thread will delete itself.
  HANDLE hThread = m_pThread->m_hThread;

  // Set the flag to kill the thread to TRUE;
  m_bKillThread = TRUE;

  // Wait for the thread to end.
  ::WaitForSingleObject( m_hThread, 5000 );

}

///////////////////////////////////////////////////////////////
// CThreadDemo1View drawing

void CThreadDemo1View::OnDraw(CDC* pDC)
{
  CThreadDemo1Doc* pDoc = GetDocument();
  ASSERT_VALID(pDoc);

  // If the m_pThread is NULL, we need to kick
  // off the thread.
  if( m_pThread == NULL ){

    // Store the window handle and the Kill flag.
    m_ThreadInfo.hWnd = m_hWnd;
    m_ThreadInfo.lpKillThread = &m_bKillThread;

    // Start the thread.
    m_pThread =
      AfxBeginThread(ThreadProc, (LPVOID) &m_ThreadInfo);
    }
}
```

Notice that the drawing was all done with straight Windows API graphics functions. This avoids the problems that can occur in threads. The best way to understand the program would be to recompile it and make your own changes.

Summary

The `ThreadDemo1` program in this chapter teaches you there's no such thing as a free lunch. When several threads are running, the designs are drawn much more slowly.

✦ Any thread that performs a task will consume CPU cycles.

✦ The more threads running, the more processor time required.

✦ With clever planning, you can avoid unnecessary system conflicts and delays.

✦ Using `::sleep()` to yield to other threads is a polite and efficient way of making sure a thread doesn't hog CPU time.

✦ Use `::WaitForSingleObject()` to wait for threads to end.

✦ Threads seem daunting at first—but once under control, they make your applications smoother and more efficient.

✦ ✦ ✦

P A R T

IV

Database Programming

You can't do much in this day and age without retrieving data from — or storing data to — a database. Database types run the gamut from Access to SQL Server to Oracle; this section covers them all.

You learn how to use the MFC database classes to access databases through ODBC drivers. This connectivity standard enables your programs to meet almost every database need.

Continuing from ODBC database access, you'll learn about DAO and other more specialized classes and functions. These advanced concepts and techniques will have your programs outperforming most others — and if you take advantage of the clear presentation found in these chapters, it won't be hard.

✦ ✦ ✦ ✦

In This Part

Chapter 19
ODBC

Chapter 20
MFC Database Classes

Chapter 21
DAO Database Programming

✦ ✦ ✦ ✦

CHAPTER 19

ODBC

✦ ✦ ✦ ✦

In This Chapter

Discovering ODBC

Learning the different conformance levels of ODBC

Learning the different ODBC functions

Writing a simple ODBC application to fetch data

Writing a C++ class to encapsulate advanced ODBC functionality

✦ ✦ ✦ ✦

Most database connectivity you're likely to encounter in Visual C++ is based on one of three distinct technologies: ODBC (Open Database Connectivity), DAO/RDO, and OLE (for example, OLE DB and ADO). In this chapter, you'll explore the first of these, learning how to develop database applications using the ODBC 3.0 SDK. MFC also provides a set of object-oriented database classes for the ODBC functionality covered in the Chapter 20. DAO and its interfaces are presented in Chapter 21.

This chapter begins with the basic concepts and principles around which the ODBC SDK came to be; once these are introduced, you'll write two demos. In the first demo, you learn how to use basic ODBC function calls to connect to, fetch data from, and disconnect from a data source. After you understand these basic ODBC functions, you'll write a C++ class (`CODBCInfo`) that encapsulates the `SQLGetTypeInfo()` function. This class will illustrate how to use advanced ODBC functions to retrieve data from a data source when the data types of the columns are not known until runtime.

Key Concepts

Before you go any further, you'll need a few definitions of terms used throughout this chapter. In some cases, these are standard entities with recognized definitions (for example, DBMS and SQL). In other cases, I define an otherwise-ambiguous term and explain how it's used in the chapter.

DBMS (database management system)

A DBMS, or *database management system*, is software that provides access to and manipulation of structured data. Examples of popular DBMSs are Microsoft Access, Microsoft SQL Server, Oracle Server, and Sybase SQL Server. Most DBMSs (including all the aforementioned databases) provide an SQL interface.

SQL (Structured Query Language)

As the language used to access and manipulate data in a DBMS, SQL statements divide into two categories: *DDL (data definition language)* statements — used to create tables, indexes, and so on — and *DML (data manipulation language)* statements that retrieve data, update data, and perform other such operations.

Data source

This chapter uses the term *data source* to represent a specific instance of a DBMS that (let's say) you're using. For example, if you're using Microsoft Access and create a database called Test, then assume that *DBMS* refers to Microsoft Access and its functionality; *data source* would refer to the Test database.

ODBC – The Need for a Standard

In the early days of the PC, database applications were developed to run on only one (standalone) workstation and supported only one data source. The DBMS that the application supported typically provided a proprietary API (application programming interface) that the application used to interface with the database. Very little PC development was being done (most applications were still written on — and for — larger computers); DBMSs were rarely, if ever, changed, and this arrangement worked very well for many years. When more companies began accepting the PC as a viable platform on which to develop their software, problems arose that ODBC was created to solve:

- **Scalability** — With PCs becoming more common on every employee's desk, there usually came a time when the application had to become "network" capable. In other words, the application needed to run on each desktop and interface to a DBMS running on a server. If the application had been written as a stand-alone application, that usually meant switching to another DBMS (one that supported multiple concurrent users). This meant incurring the cost of rewriting the application.
- **Interoperability** — If a company developed software to sell it typically needed to target a specific DBMS. If it wanted to target more than one DBMS, the company needed to develop a special version of the software for each one it wished to support. This was an extremely costly proposition. What was needed was a way to write the software so it could interface with any DBMS without having to rewrite custom versions of the application for everyone.
- **Software-development costs** — Because the APIs used to interface to the different DBMSs were almost always proprietary, if a company wanted to develop software to use a particular DBMS, the company needed to hire developers who were proficient with that specific DBMS and its idiosyncrasies. Then, if the company wanted to add support for additional DBMS systems, it needed to hire additional experts for those systems as well.

What was needed was a standard database API. In other words, an API that would enable programmers to interface generically to a data source without regard to the specific DBMS implementation.

The ODBC Standard

ODBC provides a means of communicating with a DBMS using a standard application programming interface and SQL syntax. There is a very important distinction to make here. Although ODBC enables you to access a DBMS with an SQL-like interface, it would *not* be correct to understand that to mean ODBC is a means of accessing SQL databases. Although it's true that most DBMSs do indeed support SQL, ODBC does not place this restriction on any DBMS. You can interact with any DBMS if an ODBC driver exists for it. (ODBC drivers will be covered shortly.) Just keep in mind that if the DBMS you want to interface to has an ODBC driver, then you can use ODBC in your application. This gives you, the developer, tremendous power and flexibility in developing your applications. You need only write your application *once*, swapping out the DBMS and ODBC driver when and if you ever want to change the DBMS. ODBC offers you this flexibility by providing the following features:

- The capability to use SQL syntax on the basis of the X/Open and SQL Access Group (SAG) SQL CAE specification
- A standard set of error codes that can be returned from an ODBC function call
- A standard way of configuring and maintaining the definition of your databases
- A standard way of connecting to your DBMS
- A standard way of interacting with your DBMS in terms of saving and retrieving data
- A standard way of interfacing with your DBMS in terms of configuring your database
- A standard way of disconnecting from your DBMS

As you can see by now, the name of the game here is "standard." The entire concept behind using ODBC is that you have one way of interfacing to your DBMS, regardless of the actual DBMS implementation on the back end. ODBC provides this level of abstraction a *function seam*—a layer between your application and the DBMS you want to connect to. This seam relieves the programmer of the burden of dealing with the idiosyncrasies of the underlying DBMS; you need only interact with the components of ODBC.

To provide this layer of programmatic abstraction, the original designers of ODBC had to provide two advantages:

- Give the application developer a means of generically interfacing to any database that adhered to the ODBC standards
- Provide the capability to interact with the local DBMS

The concept took the form of an ODBC Driver Manager and ODBC Driver. When an application makes an ODBC function call, it's actually calling an exported function of the ODBC Driver Manager. The ODBC Driver Manager then calls an exported function of the ODBC Driver. It's the responsibility of the developer of the ODBC Driver to respond to the ODBC Driver Manager. Therefore, the only layer that has any knowledge of the inner workings of the DBMS is the ODBC Driver. You can see these components at work in Figure 19-1.

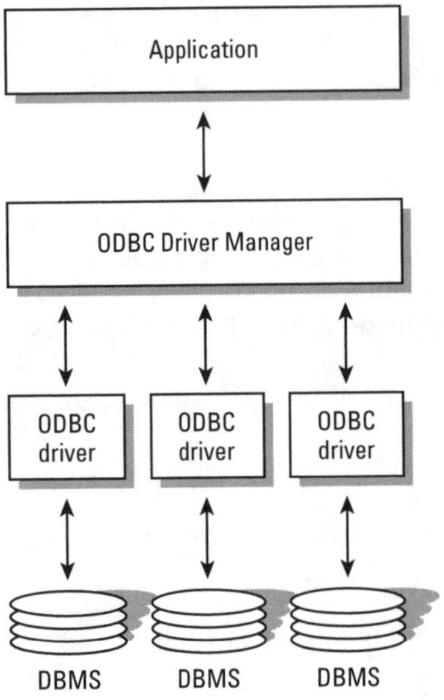

Figure 19-1: ODBC Components at work – notice that your application never talks directly to the DBMS.

Application

This is your application. Although you can use any HLL (high-level language) that supports DLLs (dynamic link libraries), this section represents your Visual C++ application.

ODBC Driver Manager

The ODBC Driver Manager, a DLL (dynamic link library) provided by Microsoft, is the gateway through which you, the application's developer, interface to the DBMS. The ODBC APIs that you call are all exported from this DLL.

ODBC Driver

As just mentioned, the ODBC Driver is the component that actually interfaces to the DBMS once the ODBC Driver Manager makes a request to it on your behalf. Any information or response is also passed back through the Driver Manager to you. For you to be able to use a particular DBMS with ODBC, you must acquire an ODBC Driver for it.

Note

This chapter assumes that you're an application developer and are not developing an ODBC Driver.[1]

End FootnoteData Source

For ODBC to be able to work with your database, it must be *registered*— known to the ODBC Driver Manager. You register ODBC by defining a *DSN*, or *data source name*; Microsoft provides a utility called the ODBC Data Source Administrator for this purpose. Figure 19-2 shows what the ODBC Driver Manager looks like.

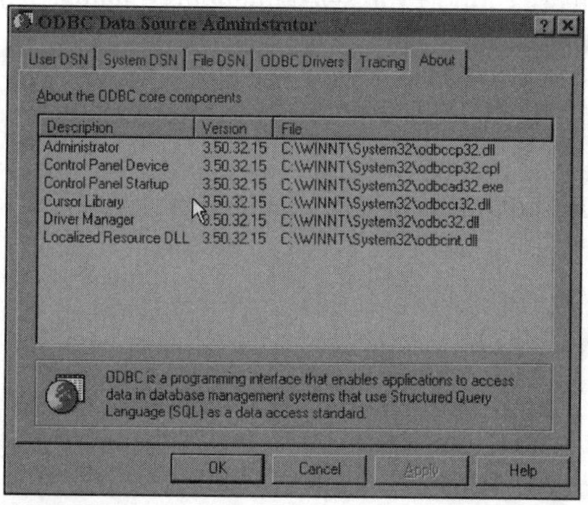

Figure 19-2: The ODBC Data Source Administrator

ODBC conformance levels (driver functionality)

To provide an API that would work with all DBMSs, the designers of ODBC had to define certain minimum characteristics that each and every ODBC-compliant driver has to have (Core level). Even while defining this minimum conformance level, the designers wanted to enable more robust DBMSs to make their services available as well. Therefore, ODBC drivers are defined, or categorized, by their level of conformance. The Core level is defined by the X/Open SQL Access Group (SAG) Call Level Interface (CLI) specification. It's important to understand that for a driver's manufacturer to claim that it corresponds to any given conformance level, it must implement all the functionality defined within that level (whether or not the underlying data source does). Therefore an application developer who wishes to make an ODBC call *without* defining it as a Core-level call must ensure that the driver supports the function. There are two ways to fulfill this responsibility. The simplest, and least flexible, way is to contact the driver's manufacturer and find out

[1]For developing ODBC Drivers, *Microsoft ODBC Programmer's Reference and SDK Guide* is a good reference book.

whether the driver supports the function(s) in question. If the application is being written to work heterogeneously, on multiple platforms, this approach is too limiting. Therefore, ODBC offers a second approach: defining a function (`SQLGetFunctions()`) that can be called at runtime to query the driver's capabilities.

ODBC conformance levels (SQL grammar)

In addition to the different ODBC Driver conformance levels, there are also conformance levels for SQL, as defined by SQL-92. The Microsoft ODBC 3.0 Programmer's Reference defines a subset of SQL-92 called the SQL Minimum Grammar. All ODBC-compliant drivers support the SQL Minimum Grammar. If a driver purports to conform to a given SQL-92 level then it must support all syntax included in that level. Even so, if a driver supports a given SQL-92 level, it can also support higher-level functionality. For example, let's say that a driver will only support the minimum grammar, but the developers of this driver also want to support some higher-level functionality. They can do this as long as they advertise the driver as simply being compliant with the Minimum Grammar.

ODBC – Implementation

The best way to proceed from this point would be to split the different ODBC functions into logical groups that correspond to the order in which you're most likely to use them in your application. Therefore, the groupings are as follows:

- Configuring ODBC
- Connecting to a data source
- Querying the data and the data source
- Preparing and executing SQL requests
- Retrieving data
- Disconnecting from a data source

Configuring ODBC

As mentioned earlier, ODBC provides a program (the ODBC Data Source Administrator) for configuring ODBC on your system. This program, located in the Control Panel, enables you to configure both the ODBC drivers and the DSNs (data source name) on your system. Figure 19-3 shows an example list of configured drivers.

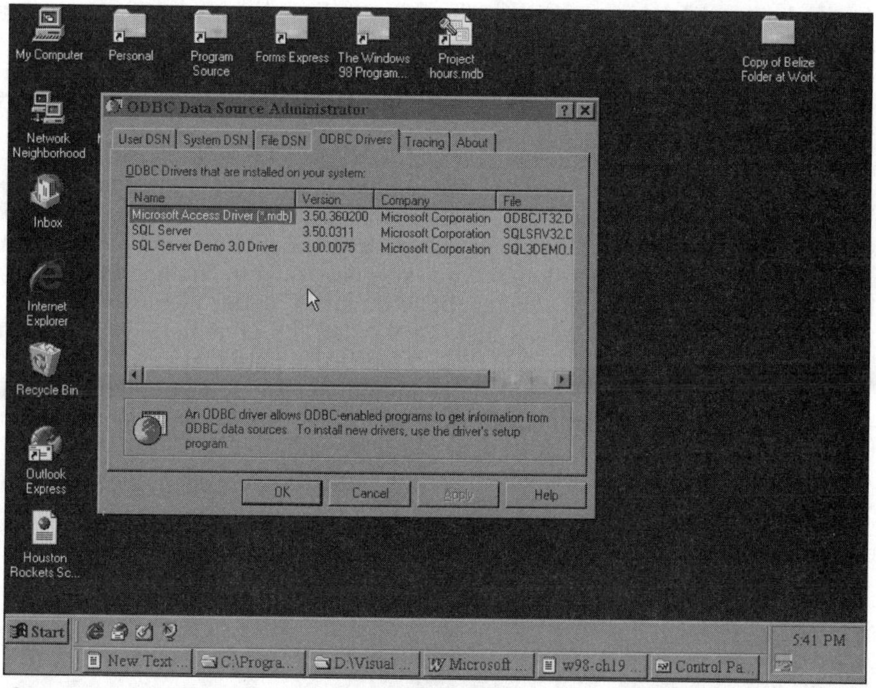

Figure 19-3: Example of installed ODBC drivers

The drivers in this particular group are known as the Desktop Drivers because they support the more popular desktop DBMS software. You'll sometimes hear these drivers incorrectly referred to as the "Access Drivers," probably because most developers use them with the Microsoft Access product. Even so, as you can see, the Desktop Drivers support several DBMSs. After you've installed the driver for your DBMS and have created a database using that DBMS, you can "register" your database with ODBC by defining a DSN. You can define a data source as one of the following three types:

✦ **User data source**—A data source created as a user data source is local to a computer and can only be used by the user that creates the data source.

✦ **System data source**—Data sources created as system data sources belong to a computer, or a system, rather than a specific user. A user would have to have privileges to use a system data source.

✦ **File data source**—A data source defined as a file data source is specific to a file. In other words, the data source can be used by any user that has the appropriate driver installed.

A DSN defines a database to ODBC. The driver defines the information you need to specify to create a DSN. When you specify (a) that you want to add a data source and (b) the driver you're using, the ODBC Data Source Administrator instructs the driver to display its configuration dialog so you can configure that specific type of database.

At minimum, most drivers need to know such data as filename, system (local or remote), directory, and so on. If it's a Microsoft Access file, the driver needs to know other data, such as the system database file, user name, and password. You'll need to read the documentation for your specific driver to configure the data source. Figure 19-4 shows the System DSNs on my PC under Windows 98. As you can see, I have already added a System DSN called "Programming W98—Chapter 19," used for some of the demos in this chapter. Also note that you have the flexibility (in terms of name length and embedding spaces, dashes, and such) to give your DSN a very readable name.

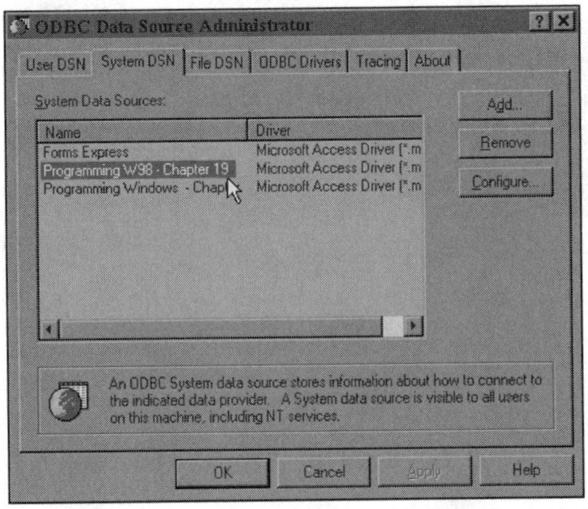

Figure 19-4: Example of installed ODBC system data source names (DSNs)

Connecting to a data source

After you've configured your data source via the ODBC Data Source Administrator program, you're ready to program your application. The first programmatic step to using ODBC is to connect to your data source. This is done via a series of function calls. The general flow of connecting to a data source is as follows:

1. Initialize ODBC and acquire a unique environment handle, or `henv`, that uniquely represents this thread's use of ODBC. This is achieved via a call to `SQLAllocHandle()`. The application first declares a variable of type `SQLHENV`.

It then calls SQLAllocHandle specifying that an henv is desired and passes the address of the henv variable. Here is an example of how to allocate an henv:

```
SQLHENV henv;
SQLRETURN rc = SQLAllocHandle(SQL_HANDLE_ENV,
  SQL_NULL_HANDLE, &henv);
```

2. Set the version of ODBC to which the application conforms. This is done via a call to SQLSetEnvAttr(). The application calls this function and passes the SQL_ATTR_ODBC_VERSION constant to indicate the supported ODBC version. In the example below, the fact that the constant SQL_OV_ODBC3 is being passed indicates that ODBC 3.0 is the version supported by this application.

```
SQLSetEnvAttr(henv, SQL_ATTR_ODBC_VERSION, (SQLPOINTER)
SQL_OV_ODBC3,
  SQL_IS_INTEGER)
```

3. Before an application can connect to a database it must acquire a database connection handle, hdbc, from ODBC. This is accomplished by calling the SQLAllocHandle() function using the SQL_HANDLE_HDBC constant as its first argument. The second argument must be a valid henv that was acquired using step 1 above. The third and last argument must be a pointer to a variable of type SQLHDBC. An example of how to acquire an hdbc can be seen below:

```
SQLHDBC hdbc;
SQLRETURN  rc = SQLAllocHandle(SQL_HANDLE_ENV, henv, &hdbc);
```

4. After you have an hdbc you can connect to the database. Connecting to a database can be accomplished using any of three different ODBC function calls: SQLConnect(), SQLDriverConnect(), and SQLBrowseConnect(). SQLConnect is a very straightforward and simple way of connecting to a data source. Using this function, you simply pass the DSN, user id, and password to ODBC to connect to the data source. SQLDriverConnect() is an alternative for ODBC drivers that require more information than can be passed using SQLConnect. SQLBrowseConnect() is an even more advanced means of connecting to a data source. Using one or more calls to SQLBrowseConnect(), you can iteratively request the information needed to connect to a data source. The way this works is that the function returns the value SQL_NEEDS_DATA until the application has provided all the information needed to connect to the data source, at which time the function returns SQL_SUCCESS. So that the more important topics of ODBC functionality can be concentrated on, the basic SQLConnect function will be used in the upcoming demos. Here is an example of using the SQLConnect() function to connect to a data source named "Programming W98— Chapter 19":

```
SQLRETURN rc = SQLConnect(hdbc,
(SQLCHAR*)"Programming W98 - Chapter 19", SQL_NTS,
  (SQLCHAR*)"", SQL_NTS, (SQLCHAR*)"", SQL_NTS);
```

The SQL_NTS constants simply tell ODBC that the previous argument passed was a null-terminated string.

Querying the data and the data source

In order for ODBC to provide a way for your application to interface to multiple DBMSs that have different and distinct capabilities, functions were needed that would enable an application to dynamically query an ODBC driver. These functions include `SQLGetFunctions()`, `SQLGetInfo`, and `SQLGetTypeInfo()`.

`SQLGetFunctions()` queries an ODBC driver about the different functions, or groups of functions, the driver supports. To use this function, the application simply calls this function and passes it a valid `hdbc`, along with a numeric value (defined in the SQLEXT.H file that ships with the ODBC SDK) that represents either a specific ODBC function or group of ODBC functions. The application must also pass a pointer to a variable that ODBC will set to indicate whether support is available for the function or group of functions.

`SQLGetInfo()` returns information about the ODBC driver and its capabilities. Examples of using this function include ascertaining an ODBC driver's version and name as well as its level of ODBC conformance.

An application calls `SQLGetTypeInfo()` when seeking information regarding what types are supported by the data source. The tricky part about this function is that the function does not directly return a value. Instead, the driver returns the information in the form of a result set. In this way, it works in much the same way a retrieval of data from a data source would. Therefore, once the function returns, the application must retrieve the results accordingly. You'll see how to retrieve data in the next section, as well as in the demos and hands-on exercise later in the chapter.

Preparing and executing SQL requests

After you've connected to a data source, the last thing your application will need to do before executing SQL requests against the data source is to acquire a statement handle, or `hstmt`. To allocate the `hstmt`, simply declare a variable of type `SQLHSTMT` and call the `SQLAllocHandle()` function specifying that an `hstmt` is desired (using the `SQL_HANDLE_STMT` constant) and passing the address of the `hstmt` variable. An example of this two-step process can be seen following:

```
SQLSTMT hstmt;
SQLRETURN  rc = SQLAllocHandle(SQL_HANDLE_STMT, hdbc, &hstmt);
```

After you've acquired an `hstmt`, you're ready to issue SQL statements against the data source. There are two different ways of executing an SQL query against a data source. One way is to call the `SQLExecDirect()` function while specifying the SQL statement in the function's second argument. Here's an example of doing just that.

```
SQLRETURN rc = ::SQLExecDirect(hstmt, (unsigned char*)"INSERT
INTO UserMaster
  VALUES('UserID', 'User Name', 0)", SQL_NTS))
```

If the statement is to be executed multiple times, a more efficient means of issuing the SQL statement is to call the `SQLPrepare()` function first followed by a call to the `SQLExecute()` function. This can be seen in this example:

```
SQLRETURN rc;
LPCSTR szSQL = "INSERT INTO UserMaster values('UserID2', 'Just
Another User', 0)";

if (SQL_SUCCESS == (rc = ::SQLPrepare(hstmt, (unsigned
char*)szSQL, SQL_NTS)))
{
  if (SQL_SUCCESS == (rc = ::SQLExecute(hstmt)))
  ...
```

Retrieving data

In the previous section you saw how to execute an SQL statement that carries out a request on your behalf (inserted data), but does not return any data. But, what do you do if the SQL statement returns data and how do you map that data to your application's variables? That's where the next group of ODBC functions come into play. When an ODBC function is said to have returned a result set, "bind" your variables to the different columns of data that will be returned. As you might imagine, ODBC provides a great deal of flexibility in retrieving the data, depending on the type of application you're developing.

If you're developing an application whose principal goal is flexibility, using the `SQLNumResultCols()`, the `SQLDescribeCol()` and `SQLGetData()` functions can be a tremendous benefit. These functions enable you to develop your application without knowing how many columns are going to be returned or the data types involved. An example of how these functions could be put to good use is if you were developing an ad-hoc query tool designed to enable end-users to define their own queries. Due to the dynamic nature of an application of this type (the query is being defined by the end-user at run time), you could not know the number of columns and their respective data types when you develop the application. Therefore, after building and running the user-defined SQL statement, you would need to call `SQLNumResultCols()` to find out how many columns had been returned in the result set and then call `SQLDescribeCol()` iteratively to determine the data type for each column. After you know the data type for a given column you would call the `SQLGetData()` function to retrieve the value for that column. You'll see how to use these functions in more detail in the second ODBC demo.

Not everyone needs the level of flexibility just described. The majority of developers will be issuing SQL statements that they code in their applications and therefore, do not need to query ODBC as to the type of data being returned in the result set. In these situations, the `SQLBindCol()` and `SQLFetch()` functions can be used to retrieve the data from an ODBC result set into your application's variables. The `SQLBindCol()` function enables you to specify the column number in the result set that you're binding, the type of data at that column position and the address of a variable to hold the data once SQLFetch() is called to retrieve the data. You do not have to bind every column. You need only bind the columns whose data you wish to map into your variables. After you've called SQLBindCol() for each desired column, you can call SQLFetch() as often as necessary, or until you've read the entire result set. Here is an example of how to use these two functions to retrieve your data from a result set. This code segment assumes that an SQL statement has already been run to retrieve the data into a result set:

```
#define LEN_USERID 16

SDWORD cb;
char szUserID[LEN_USERID];

if (SQL_SUCCESS == (rc = SQLBindCol(hstmt, 1, SQL_C_CHAR,
szUserID, LEN_USERID, &cb)))
{
  if (SQL_SUCESS == (rc = SQLFetch(hstmt)))
  {
    // szUserID now contains the value from the first row of
    // the returned result set
    ...
```

Disconnecting from a data source

After you've finished using a connection to a data source, you must disconnect from the data source (via the SQLDisconnect() function) and release any handles that have been allocated. Here is an example of what your "clean-up" code might look like:

```
if (henv)
{
  if (hdbc)
  {
    if (bIsConnected)
    {
      if (hstmt)
      {
       ::SQLFreeHandle(SQL_HANDLE_STMT, hstmt);
      }
      ::SQLDisconnect(hdbc);
      bIsConnected = FALSE;
    }
    ::SQLFreeHandle(SQL_HANDLE_DBC, hdbc);
    hdbc = NULL;
  }
  ::SQLFreeHandle(SQL_HANDLE_ENV, henv);
  henv = NULL;
}
```

A Simple ODBC Application to Fetch Data

This demo is a very simple ODBC application that will utilize many of the functions that you've read about up to now. This demo illustrates the basic ODBC functions of allocating the different ODBC handles, connecting to a data source, fetching data, de-allocating the ODBC handles, and disconnecting from the data source. Although this is a very simple application, you can use these same functions in your own application regardless of its scope or complexity.

Demo Program

ODBCDemo

CD-ROM Location: **Chap19\odbcDemo**
Program Name: **ODBCDemo.cpp**
Source Code Modules in Text: **none**

◆ ◆ ◆ ◆ ◆

If you want to type the application in as you read through the explanation, simply create a Visual C++ dialog-based application and then follow the steps given here. To run the demo, you'll need to create the ODBC DSN—and point it to the database provided on the companion CD-ROM—before your application will run correctly.

Note

As mentioned earlier, this chapter assumes you've installed the ODBC 3.0 SDK, as well as Microsoft Access and the Microsoft ODBC Desktop Drivers 3.5. The database used in this demo is located in the same directory as the source code. The steps required to create the DSN are listed under "Creating an ODBC DSN."

◆ ◆ ◆ ◆ ◆

Nutshell

Creating an ODBC DSN

To create an ODBC System DSN, simply do the following:

1. Open the ODBC Data Source Administrator (via the Control Panel), and select the System DSN tab.
2. Click the Add button on the right side of the dialog box.
3. Select the appropriate ODBC Driver. For this demo select the entry with the name "Microsoft Access Driver (*.mdb)," and click the Finish button in the lower-right corner of the dialog box.
4. In the Data Source Name text box, type the name of the DSN. For this demo use "Programming W98 - Chapter 19." After you've typed in the DSN, click the Select button on the left side of the dialog box.
5. Using the File dialog box, select the database you want to represent the data source for the new DSN. For purposes of this demo, the database to use is located on the CD-ROM in the `\Chap19\ODBCDemo` folder. After you've selected the database and have returned to the Setup dialog box, click the OK button in the upper-right corner of the dialog box.
6. Click the OK button in the lower-left corner of the dialog box to signify that you've finished.

◆ ◆ ◆ ◆ ◆

Adding ODBC support to a Visual C++ project

To start using the ODBC SDK in an application, include the appropriate header files in one of the project's files. If different modules within the project contain calls to the ODBC SDK it's easier to simply include the ODBC header files in the project's stdafx.h file. The most common header files that an ODBC application would need are the following:

```
sql.h
sqlext.h
sqltypes.h
```

In addition to including the appropriate header file, you'll also need to link with the odbc32.lib library shipped with the ODBC SDK.

Modifying the ODBCDemo dialog

Because this is a dialog-based application, you already have a dialog to use for the display of the customer data. At this point, locate the `IDD_ODBCDEMO_DIALOG` dialog template resource and make the following modifications.

1. Remove the "TODO" static text control and insert the controls as they appear in Figure 19-5. Note that the control under the "Term Codes" static text is a list box.

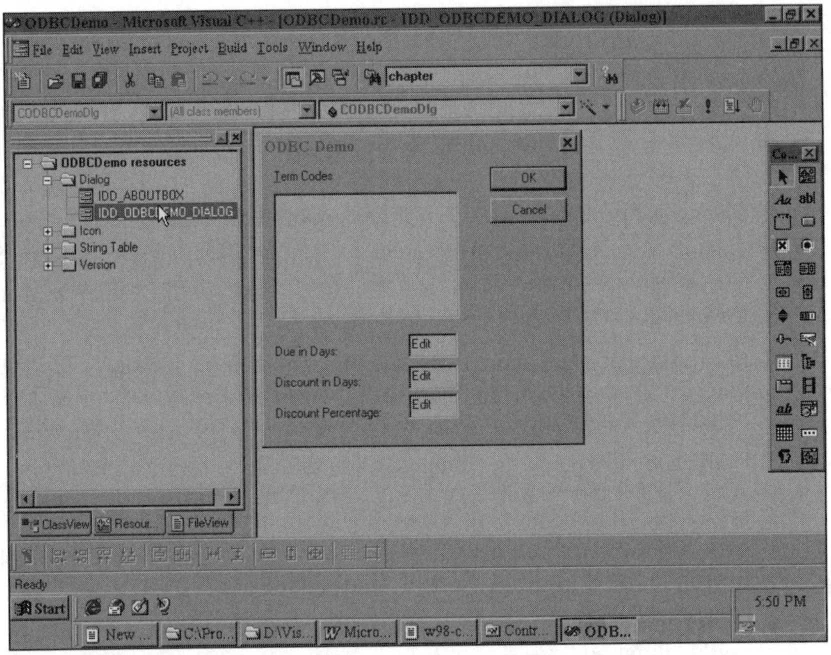

Figure 19-5: The ODBCDemo dialog box after adding the new controls

2. You should now have four input controls (a list box for the Term Code list and three Edit fields for the "Due In Days," "Discount In Days," and "Discount Percentage"). Click the list box control. Hold down the Alt key and press the Enter key. Give this control an ID of `IDC_LBX_TERM_CODES`. Using the same key sequence, rename the remaining controls as follows:

   "Due in Days" edit control = `IDC_EDT_DUE_IN_DAYS`

   "Discount in Days" edit control = `IDC_EDT_DUE_IN_DAYS`

   "Discount Percentage" edit control = `IDC_EDT_DISCOUNT_PCTG`

3. Create the member variables that will be used with DDX (dynamic data exchange) for the different controls by holding down the Ctrl button and double-clicking the control. You'll see an Add Member Variable dialog box that enables you to specify Member variable name, Category, and Variable Type. Do so for the following controls, filling in the appropriate information:

Control Name	*Member Variable(s) to Add*
"Term Code" list box control	`m_lbxTermCodes, Control, CListbox`
"Due in Days" edit control	`m_lDueInDays, Value, long`
"Discount in Days" edit control	`m_lDiscountInDays, Value, long`
"Discount Percentage" edit control	`m_dDiscountPctg, Value, double`

Adding the initialization and database code

1. Open the ODBCDemoDlg.h file and find the following line:

```
// Implementation
protected:
```

   Add the following function declaration. This function will be called to fill the list box with all the Term Codes in the database:

```
void FillTermCodesListbox();
```

2. Open the ODBCDemoDlg.cpp file and find the following line:

```
#include "ODBCDemoDlg.h"
```

   Now insert the following `#include` directive:

```
#include "TermCode.h"
```

3. Find the following line in ODBCDemoDlg.cpp:

```
// CAboutDlg dialog used for App About
```

Now add the following `#define` that will be used when retrieving the data from the data source:

```
#define LEN_TERM_CODE 20
```

4. Find the `OnInitDialog()` function in the `ODBCDemoDlg.cpp` file. After the "TODO" comment, add the following function call. This call will load the list box upon initialization of the dialog box.

```
FillTermCodesListbox ();
```

5. Add the following function at the end of the `ODBCDemoDlg.cpp` file:

```
void CODBCDemoDlg:: FillTermCodesListbox ()
{
```

6. Declare and initialize the following variables to be used in this function:

```
BOOL bSuccess = FALSE;

CString strFunction;

SQLHENV henv = NULL;
SQLHDBC hdbc = NULL;
BOOL bIsConnected = FALSE;
SQLHSTMT hstmt = NULL;

SQLRETURN rc;

SWORD    sMsgNum = 0;
char     szState[7]="";
SDWORD   pfNative=0;
```

The ODBC handles are set to `NULL` so that upon exiting the function, it's easier to tell which handles were successfully allocated (the ones that are not `NULL`).

7. Next, the following function calls (`::SQLAllocHandle()`, `::SQLSetEnvAttr()` and `::SQLAllocHandle()`) will initialize ODBC and return handles to use in subsequent ODBC function calls.

```
if (SQL_SUCCESS == (rc = ::SQLAllocHandle(SQL_HANDLE_ENV,
  SQL_NULL_HANDLE, &henv)))
{
 if (SQL_SUCCESS == (rc = ::SQLSetEnvAttr(henv,
  SQL_ATTR_ODBC_VERSION, (SQLPOINTER) SQL_OV_ODBC3,
  SQL_IS_INTEGER)))
 {
  if (SQL_SUCCESS == (rc = ::SQLAllocHandle(SQL_HANDLE_DBC,
  henv, &hdbc)))
  {
```

8. The call to `::SQLConnect()` connects this application to the DSN that was created in the section "Creating the Demo ODBC DSN," as follows:

```
rc = ::SQLConnect(hdbc,
 (SQLCHAR*)"Programming W98 - Chapter 19 ",
 SQL_NTS,
 (SQLCHAR*)"", SQL_NTS, (SQLCHAR*)"", SQL_NTS);
if ((SQL_SUCCESS == rc)
|| (SQL_SUCCESS_WITH_INFO == rc))
{
 bIsConnected = TRUE;
```

9. After you've connected to the DSN, allocate a statement handle to use when you submit your SQL to the data source:

```
if (SQL_SUCCESS == (rc =
     ::SQLAllocHandle(SQL_HANDLE_STMT, hdbc, &hstmt)))
     {
```

10. The following code builds an SQL `SELECT` string, prepares it (via `::SQLPrepare()`) and executes it (via `::SQLExecute()`):

```
LPCSTR szSQL = "SELECT * FROM TermCodeMaster";
if (SQL_SUCCESS == (rc = ::SQLPrepare(hstmt,
(unsigned char*)szSQL, SQL_NTS)))
{
 if (SQL_SUCCESS == (rc = ::SQLExecute(hstmt)))
 {
```

11. After the SQL statement executes, bind the local variables to their corresponding columns by calling `::SQLBindCol()` for each desired column. Then call `::SQLFetch()` to retrieve the data into the bound variables. The needed coding looks like this:

```
SDWORD cb;
char szTermCode[LEN_TERM_CODE];
long lDueInDays;
long lDiscountInDays;
double dDiscountPctg;

SQLBindCol(hstmt, 1, SQL_C_CHAR, szTermCode,
 LEN_TERM_CODE, &cb);
SQLBindCol(hstmt, 2, SQL_C_LONG, &lDueInDays, 0,
 &cb);
SQLBindCol(hstmt, 3, SQL_C_LONG,
 &lDiscountInDays, 0, &cb);
SQLBindCol(hstmt, 4, SQL_C_DOUBLE,
 &dDiscountPctg, 0, &cb);

int iIndex;

rc = SQLFetch(hstmt);
while (SQL_SUCCESS == rc)
{
```

12. Create an object (CTermCode) that will contain all information for each Term Code read from the database; this prevents the database from getting "hit" every time a Term Code is selected from the list box to retrieve that Term Code's information.

```
            CTermCode* pTermCode = new CTermCode();
            pTermCode->m_strTermCode = szTermCode;
            pTermCode->m_lDueInDays = lDueInDays;
            pTermCode->m_lDiscountInDays = lDiscountInDays;
            pTermCode->m_dDiscountPctg = dDiscountPctg;

            iIndex = m_lbxTermCodes.AddString(szTermCode);
            m_lbxTermCodes.SetItemData(iIndex,
            (DWORD)pTermCode);

            rc = SQLFetch(hstmt);
           }
          }
         }
        }
       }
      }
     }
    }
```

The Term Code will be added to the list box and its Item Data will be set to the CTermCode object pointer, making retrieval of the Term Code's information much more efficient.

13. After all records have been read from the data source, clean up and deinitialize ODBC by disconnecting from the data source and releasing the ODBC handles:

```
if (henv)
{
 if (hdbc)
 {
  if (bIsConnected)
  {
   if (hstmt)
   {
    ::SQLFreeHandle(SQL_HANDLE_STMT, hstmt);
   }
   ::SQLDisconnect(hdbc);
   bIsConnected = FALSE;
  }
  ::SQLFreeHandle(SQL_HANDLE_DBC, hdbc);
  hdbc = NULL;
 }
 ::SQLFreeHandle(SQL_HANDLE_ENV, henv);
 henv = NULL;
 }
}
```

14. You now need to add a function so that when a Term Code is selected from the list box the proper information is displayed in the dialog box. Begin by bringing up the Class Wizard by pressing Ctrl+W. Make sure the selected class name is CODBCDemoDlg.

15. In the Object IDs list box, select the Listbox ID (IDC_LBX_TERM_CODES). Double-click the LBN_SELCHANGE entry in the Messages list box on the right.

16. When the Add Member Function dialog box appears, press Enter to accept the default function name.

17. Click the Edit button on the right side of the MFC Class Wizard dialog box to edit your new function. Make sure the function looks like the following code list:

```
void CODBCDemoDlg:: OnSelChangeTermCodes ()
{
 int iIndex = m_lbxTermCodes.GetCurSel();
 if (LB_ERR != iIndex)
 {
  CTermCode* pTermCode =
(CTermCode*)m_lbxTermCodes.GetItemData(iIndex);

  if (pTermCode)
  {
   m_lDueInDays = pTermCode->m_lDueInDays;
   m_lDiscountInDays = pTermCode->m_lDiscountInDays;
   m_dDiscountPctg = pTermCode->m_dDiscountPctg;

   UpdateData(FALSE);
  }
 }
}
```

The code just given does the following: When an item (a Term Code) in the list box is selected, this function is called. The first necessary task is to get the index of the Term Code that was selected (via the CListbox::GetCurSel() function). If no error occurred while getting this index, the Item Data is retrieved. This is the same Item Data that was set in the FillTermCodesListbox() function earlier. This Item Data, therefore, is a pointer to the information about this specific Term Code that was read from the data source when the dialog was initialized.

18. When the process in the previous step is complete, the member variables that correspond to the different dialog controls are changed to reflect the current Term Code's information. The UpdateData function is then called to move the data from these member variables to the controls on the dialog box.

19. You now need to add a function so that when the dialog box is closed, the CTermCode objects that were created will be deleted and their memory freed. To begin this process, bring up the Class Wizard by pressing Ctrl+W. Make sure the selected class name is CODBCDemoDlg.

20. In the Object IDs list box, select the CODBCDemoDlg Object ID from the list on the left side. Double-click the DestroyWindow entry in the Messages list box on the right.

21. Click the Edit button on the right side of the MFC Class Wizard dialog box to edit your new function. Make sure the function looks like the following code list:

```
BOOL CODBCDemoDlg::DestroyWindow()
{
 CTermCode* pTermCode;
 int nTermCodes = m_lbxTermCodes.GetCount();
 for (int i = 0; i < nTermCodes; i++)
 {
  pTermCode = (CTermCode*)m_lbxTermCodes.GetItemData(i);
  if (pTermCode)
  {
   delete pTermCode;
  }
 }

 return CDialog::DestroyWindow();
}
```

The code just listed will walk through every Term Code in the Listbox and then, after retrieving its Item Data, call the C++ delete operator to free the associated memory.

22. Create a file named TermCode.h and type in the following lines of code:

```
#pragma once

class CTermCode
{
public:
  CString m_strTermCode;
  long m_lDueInDays;
  long m_lDiscountInDays;
  double m_dDiscountPctg;
};
```

The resulting object serves to hold information about each Term Code read from the data source.

23. Add the ODBC library to the project; begin by clicking the Project menu option. From there, click the Add To Project menu. You'll be presented with yet another menu.

24. On this latest menu, select the Files menu and locate where you've installed the ODBC 3.0 SDK. Under that directory, you should find a subdirectory named LIB32. Change the Files of Type option to list files of type **Library Files (*.lib)**. Then double-click the Odbc32.lib file.

25. Press the F7 button to build the application, and then run it by pressing Ctrl+F5. After you build and run the application, the results should be similar to what you see in Figure 19-6.

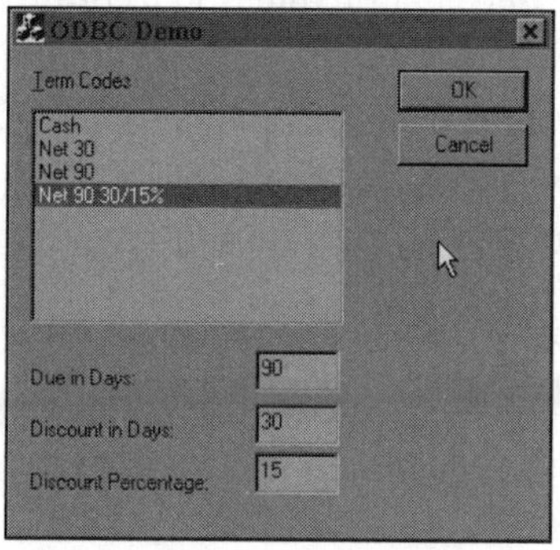

Figure 19-6: The ODBCDemo application that demonstrates basic ODBC functionality

Encapsulating Advanced ODBC Functionality

One of the most powerful features of ODBC is its set of APIs that enable a developer to query the ODBC Driver and the underlying DBMS as to its capabilities. As you read earlier, this is what gives ODBC its flexibility. As you'll see in the next section of this chapter, the MFC Database Classes encapsulate many of the ODBC functions that connect to a data source, retrieve data, and disconnect from a data source. Even so, one of the glaring weaknesses of the MFC Database Classes is that they provide no encapsulation of the `SQLGetFunctions()`, `SQLGetInfo()`, and `SQLGetTypeInfo()` ODBC SDK functions.

In the following exercise (a copy of which can be found on the companion CD-ROM in the \Chap19\ODBCInfoDll and \Chap19\ODBCInfoClient directories), you'll write a C++ program to encapsulate the functionality of the `SQLGetTypeInfo()` function. The `SQLGetTypeInfo()` function returns information about the different data types supported by a data source. When I first got the idea for this program, I envisioned a class that would retrieve all this data upon instantiation. Using this method, the user of this class would have to call a different member function for each data type and data type attribute. I quickly realized that although this class would have been useful, it would have had several severe drawbacks:

- ✦ The class's programmer would have needed to write a member function for every data type and data type attribute.
- ✦ The user would have needed to know not only what identifier ODBC used for the data type attribute in question, but also the class's corresponding member-function name used to retrieve this information.
- ✦ As with any standard, ODBC continues to be enhanced; this class would probably be out-of-date with the next release of ODBC. Therefore, the class would have needed continual maintenance to function correctly.

To resolve these issues, you'll encapsulate the functionality of `SQLGetTypeInfo()` and use some advanced ODBC SDK functions that are used when you don't know the type of data being retrieved until runtime. When you finish, you'll have attained some distinct advantages:

- Your new class needs to expose only one generic function to return the needed data.
- Your new class will work with all versions of ODBC, past and future.
- In addition—just as valuably—you'll have learned how to dynamically retrieve data whose attributes are not known until runtime.

As with the first ODBC demo in the section "Writing a Simple ODBC Application to Fetch Data," you'll need to copy the demo database from the companion CD-ROM and create an ODBC DSN. If you've not already done so, please follow the instructions under "Creating the Demo ODBC DSN."

Nutshell

Creating the Visual C++ 6.0 DLL

Let's begin by creating a project for the DLL that will contain the `CODBCInfo` class.

1. From the File menu, select the New command.
2. In the New dialog box, select the Projects tab, and select MFC App Wizard (dll) from the list box.
3. Type the project name (**ODBCInfoDll**) and select the location, or directory under which you want to create this demo. Make sure the "Create new workspace" option button is selected, then click the OK button or press Enter.
4. Because you're exporting an MFC class from a DLL, under the heading "What type of DLL would you like to create?", click the option button that corresponds to the MFC Extension DLL. Click the Finish button, and click the OK button or press Enter in the New Project Information dialog box.

◆ ◆ ◆ ◆ ◆

CODBCInfo class "multi-header" file

The "multi-header" file is (as you might have guessed) a header file that includes other header files. The benefit of this file is that it enables the user of your class to include one file that will in turn include all the files that your class needs. That way the user doesn't have to dig through the source trying to figure out which include files are needed and in what order they need to be included.

1. To create a new include file via the Microsoft Developer Studio, from the File menu, select the New command.
2. In the New dialog box, select the Files tab, and then select C/C++ Header File from the list box.

3. Type the filename (in this case, **ODBCInfo.hpp**) and click the OK button or press Enter.

4. Make sure your `ODBCInfo.hpp` file looks like the following short code list. *All users of the CODBCInfo class must include this principal header file.* Do not include the `odbcinfo.h` file; the header file will include it for you.

```
#ifndef _ODBCINFO_HPP_
#define _ODBCINFO_HPP_

#include "afxdb.h"
#include "sql.h"
#include "sqlext.h"
#include "sqltypes.h"
#include "odbcinfo.h"

#endif
```

Creating the header file for the CODBCInfo class

The next step is to create a header file for the `CODBCInfo` class declaration.

1. Following the same instructions outlined earlier, create the include file that will house the `CODBCInfo` class's declaration. Name the file **ODBCInfo.h**.

2. Add the standard `#ifndef/#define` block to ensure that the file is not included more than once.

```
#ifndef _ODBCINFO_H_
#define _ODBCINFO_H_
```

3. Add the class declaration. The `AFX_EXT_CLASS` macro specifies that the class is to be exported. This eliminates the need for a DEF file where you would have to specify the decorated, or "mangled," C++ names to export.

```
class AFX_EXT_CLASS CODBCInfo
{
```

4. Add the constructor, destructor and initialization variables. The only constructor provided by this class will take as its argument a string that represents an ODBC DSN.

```
public:
 CODBCInfo(LPCSTR lpszDSN);

 ~CODBCInfo();

protected:
 BOOL m_bIsInitialized;
```

5. Declare the ODBC handles and other variables below that represent the connection to the ODBC data source.

```
protected:
 SQLHENV m_henv;
 SQLHDBC m_hdbc;
 BOOL m_bIsConnected;
```

6. Declare a function called `GetTypeInfo()`. This public function is the only function the user of this class will need. The user simply specifies the data type and the name of the column desired. The values to be used for the first two parameters are already documented in the ODBC documentation for `SQLGetTypeInfo()`. The `#define`s for the data types are found in the "sqlext.h" file distributed with the ODBC SDK.

```
public:
 BOOL GetTypeInfo(UINT iDataType, LPCSTR lpszColName,
CDBVariant** ppvarValue);
```

7. Declare the map that will be used to store the data types and data type attributes looked up when the user calls the `GetTypeInfo()` function. Each data type has its own set of data attributes. Therefore, this map (`mapDataTypeToDataAttrMap`) is a "map of maps." In other words, there is one element in this map for each supported data type. Each element maps a data type to another map. This second map associates a data type attribute (the column name) to its value. For example, let's say that only one data type is supported (`STRING`) and it has only one data type attribute (`DELIMITER`). The first map would have an element for the `STRING` data type that would contain a pointer to its data attribute map. The data attribute map would contain a single element that would map the column name "DELIMITER" to its value (for example, a single quotation mark):

```
protected:
 CMapWordToOb m_mapDataTypeToDataAttrMap;
```

These maps are internal to the class and the user will never see them. These *internals* of the class are responsible for maintaining these maps and retrieving the correct data when the user calls the `GetTypeInfo()` function.

8. Declare the following internal "helper" functions (explained later):

```
protected:
  BOOL InternalGetTypeInfo();
  short GetFieldTypeFromSQLType(short nSQLType);

  void* GetDataBuffer(CDBVariant* pvarValue,
    short nFieldType, int* pnLen,
    short nSQLType, UDWORD nPrecision);
```

```
    long GetData(SQLHSTMT hstmt, short nFieldIndex,
      short nFieldType, LPVOID pvData,
      int nLen, short nSQLType);
};

#endif
```

Defining the CODBCInfo class

Now that the header file is completed, it's time to define the class's member functions.

1. Create a new file and name it **ODBCInfo.cpp**. This file will contain the `CODBCInfo` class's member function definitions.
2. Add the include-file directives. As with any user of the class, the only file that needs to be included is odbcinfo.hpp. The odbcinfo.hpp file will include all files needed to support the class.

```
#include "stdafx.h"
#include "odbcinfo.hpp"
```

3. The `MAX_COLNAME` `#define` will be used later on, when you call `SQLDescribeCol()`to specify the maximum length of a column name:

```
#define MAX_COLNAME 50
```

4. As the only constructor for the class, the next function is responsible for initializing the class. It takes as its argument the name of an ODBC DSN, connects to the specified ODBC DSN, and retrieves information about the data source (in this case, the SQL data type) from the ODBC driver:

```
CODBCInfo::CODBCInfo(LPCSTR lpszDSN)
{
 SQLRETURN rc;

 m_henv = NULL;
 m_hdbc = NULL;
 m_bIsConnected = FALSE;
 m_bIsInitialized = FALSE;

  if (SQL_SUCCESS == (rc =
  ::SQLAllocHandle(SQL_HANDLE_ENV, SQL_NULL_HANDLE,
  &m_henv)))
  {
    if (SQL_SUCCESS == (rc = ::SQLSetEnvAttr(m_henv,
      SQL_ATTR_ODBC_VERSION, (SQLPOINTER), SQL_OV_ODBC3,
      SQL_IS_INTEGER)))
    {
      if (SQL_SUCCESS == (rc =
```

```
        ::SQLAllocHandle(SQL_HANDLE_DBC, m_henv, &m_hdbc)))
      {
        rc = ::SQLConnect(m_hdbc, (unsigned char*)lpszDSN,
          SQL_NTS,(unsigned char*)"", SQL_NTS,
          (unsigned char*)"", SQL_NTS);
        if ((SQL_SUCCESS == rc)
          || (SQL_SUCCESS_WITH_INFO == rc))
        {
          m_bIsConnected = TRUE;
```

5. If a successful connection to the ODBC DSN is made, call the function that will retrieve the SQL data type info. A member variable (`m_bIsInitialized`) is set, based on the return value of `InternalGetTypeInfo()`.

```
          m_bIsInitialized = InternalGetTypeInfo();
        }
      }
    }
  }
}
```

This boolean member variable is checked later when the user calls `GetTypeInfo()` to ensure that the data type information was successfully obtained during the object's construction.

6. As you create the destructor, you'll want it to disconnect from the data source and free any allocated handles. The handles were set to `NULL` in the constructor so that the destructor would know exactly what had been successfully accomplished. Therefore, only handles that were successfully returned from ODBC are freed. It looks like this:

```
CODBCInfo::~CODBCInfo()
{
if (m_bIsInitialized)
  {
    if (m_henv)
    {
      if (m_hdbc)
      {
        if (m_bIsConnected)
        {
          ::SQLDisconnect(m_hdbc);
          m_bIsConnected = FALSE;
        }
        ::SQLFreeHandle(SQL_HANDLE_DBC, m_hdbc);
        m_hdbc = NULL;
      }
      ::SQLFreeHandle(SQL_HANDLE_ENV, m_henv);
      m_henv = NULL;
    }
    m_bIsInitialized = FALSE;
  }
```

7. Now we need some basic code to "clean up" the maps and objects allocated during the `InternalGetTypeInfo()` function. It's given here:

```
  POSITION pos1;
  WORD wKey;
  CMapStringToOb* pmapColNameToDataAttr;

  POSITION pos2;
  CString strKey;
  CDBVariant* pvarValue;

  for (pos1 =
    m_mapDataTypeToDataAttrMap.GetStartPosition();
    pos1 != NULL;)
  {
    m_mapDataTypeToDataAttrMap.GetNextAssoc(pos1, wKey,
    (CObject*&)pmapColNameToDataAttr);
    for (pos2 =
      pmapColNameToDataAttr->GetStartPosition(); pos2
      != NULL;)
    {
      pmapColNameToDataAttr->GetNextAssoc(pos2, strKey,
      (CObject*&)pvarValue);
      delete pvarValue;
    }
    delete pmapColNameToDataAttr;
  }
}
```

Because the `m_mapDataTypeToDataAttrMap` is a map that associates a *word* to an object pointer, this map must be iterated to clean up the associated maps. Each object pointer that is retrieved points to another map. The second map is then iterated one element at a time. Each element in this map also contains an object pointer (to the data attribute value). This object is then deleted. After a data type's map is deleted, the data type's entry in the `m_mapDatatypeToDataAttrMap` is deleted. This continues until all dynamically allocated objects are deleted.

8. The next function, `GetFieldTypeFromSQLType()`, is a simple "helper" function; it takes a *short* that identifies an SQL type (defined in sqlext.h) and maps it to a corresponding C type. These values are also defined by ODBC and listed in the sqlext.h `include` file distributed with the ODBC SDK. The code looks like this:

```
short CODBCInfo::GetFieldTypeFromSQLType(short nSQLType)
{
  short nFieldType;

  switch (nSQLType)
  {
    case SQL_BIT:
      nFieldType = SQL_C_BIT;
    break;
```

```
    case SQL_TINYINT:
      nFieldType = SQL_C_UTINYINT;
    break;

    case SQL_SMALLINT:
      nFieldType = SQL_C_SSHORT;
    break;

    case SQL_INTEGER:
      nFieldType = SQL_C_SLONG;
    break;

    case SQL_REAL:
      nFieldType = SQL_C_FLOAT;
    break;

    case SQL_FLOAT:
    case SQL_DOUBLE:
      nFieldType = SQL_C_DOUBLE;
    break;

    case SQL_DATE:
    case SQL_TIME:
    case SQL_TIMESTAMP:
      nFieldType = SQL_C_TIMESTAMP;
    break;

    case SQL_NUMERIC:
    case SQL_DECIMAL:
    case SQL_BIGINT:
    case SQL_CHAR:
    case SQL_VARCHAR:
    case SQL_LONGVARCHAR:
      nFieldType = SQL_C_CHAR;
    break;

    case SQL_BINARY:
    case SQL_VARBINARY:
    case SQL_LONGVARBINARY:
      nFieldType = SQL_C_BINARY;
    break;

    default:
    ASSERT(FALSE);
  }

  return nFieldType;
}
```

9. You'll want to make this class capable of handling any type of data from the data source. The GetDataBuffer() function retrieves the data and maps it into a CDBVariant variable:

```
void* CODBCInfo::GetDataBuffer(CDBVariant* pvarValue,
  short nFieldType, int* pnLen, short nSQLType,
  UDWORD nPrecision)
{
  void* pvData = NULL;
```

Note

The MFC documentation claims that a CDBVariant class lets you encapsulate data without worrying about data type. The bad news is: You still have to worry about data type—because you have to specify which member variable is to hold the data. The good news is: The user of your class has only to check a specific member variable (m_dwType) to know which member variable contains the data. You'll see how this works when you actually instantiate the class and attempt to retrieve data from it.

10. Next, the CDBVariant::m_dwType member variable is set on the basis of the field type. When this CDBVariant object is returned, the member variable is queried so the user will know what type of data was returned. In addition, a void pointer—which will be passed to SQLGetData() to retrieve the data—is set to the address of the corresponding CDBVariant member variable. That way SQLGetData() writes the requested data directly into the correct member variable of the CDBVariant object.

```
  switch (nFieldType)
  {
    case SQL_C_BIT:
      pvData = &pvarValue->m_boolVal;
      pvarValue->m_dwType = DBVT_BOOL;
      *pnLen = sizeof(pvarValue->m_boolVal);
    break;

    case SQL_C_UTINYINT:
      pvData = &pvarValue->m_chVal;
      pvarValue->m_dwType = DBVT_UCHAR;
      *pnLen = sizeof(pvarValue->m_chVal);
    break;

    case SQL_C_SSHORT:
      pvData = &pvarValue->m_iVal;
      pvarValue->m_dwType = DBVT_SHORT;
      *pnLen = sizeof(pvarValue->m_iVal);
    break;

    case SQL_C_SLONG:
      pvData = &pvarValue->m_lVal;
      pvarValue->m_dwType = DBVT_LONG;
      *pnLen = sizeof(pvarValue->m_lVal);
    break;
```

```
case SQL_C_FLOAT:
  pvData = &pvarValue->m_fltVal;
  pvarValue->m_dwType = DBVT_SINGLE;
  *pnLen = sizeof(pvarValue->m_fltVal);
break;

case SQL_C_DOUBLE:
  pvData = &pvarValue->m_dblVal;
  pvarValue->m_dwType = DBVT_DOUBLE;
  *pnLen = sizeof(pvarValue->m_dblVal);
break;

case SQL_C_TIMESTAMP:
  pvData = pvarValue->m_pdate = new TIMESTAMP_STRUCT;
  pvarValue->m_dwType = DBVT_DATE;
  *pnLen = sizeof(*pvarValue->m_pdate);
break;

case SQL_C_CHAR:
{
  pvarValue->m_pstring = new CString;
  pvarValue->m_dwType = DBVT_STRING;

  // Need to have at least a length of 1 for
  // the NULL terminator
  *pnLen = 1;

  if ((nSQLType != SQL_LONGVARCHAR)
  && (nSQLType != SQL_LONGVARBINARY))
  {
    *pnLen = nPrecision + 1;

    // If type is Numeric or Decimal add 2
    // bytes for decimal point and sign
    if ((nSQLType == SQL_NUMERIC)
    || (nSQLType == SQL_DECIMAL))
    {
      *pnLen += 2;
    }
  }
  pvData =
    pvarValue->m_pstring->GetBufferSetLength(*pnLen);
}
break;

case SQL_C_BINARY:
  pvarValue->m_pbinary = new CLongBinary;
  pvarValue->m_dwType = DBVT_BINARY;

  if (nSQLType == SQL_LONGVARBINARY)
  {
    *pnLen = 1;
  }
```

```
        else
        {
          *pnLen = nPrecision;
        }

        pvarValue->m_pbinary->m_hData =
          ::GlobalAlloc(GMEM_MOVEABLE, *pnLen);
        pvarValue->m_pbinary->m_dwDataLength = *pnLen;

        pvData =
          ::GlobalLock(pvarValue->m_pbinary->m_hData);
      break;

      default: ASSERT(FALSE);
    }

  return pvData;
}
```

11. The GetData() function is another “helper” function that simply calls SQLGetData(), using the void pointer that was set up in the GetDataBuffer() function:

```
long CODBCInfo::GetData(SQLHSTMT hstmt, short nFieldIndex,
  short nFieldType, LPVOID pvData, int nLen, short nSQLType)
{
  UNUSED(nSQLType);

  long nActualSize = -1;

  SQLRETURN rc;
  if (SQL_SUCCESS != (rc = ::SQLGetData(hstmt, nFieldIndex,
    nFieldType, pvData, nLen, &nActualSize)))
  {
    UCHAR lpszMsg[SQL_MAX_MESSAGE_LENGTH];
    UCHAR lpszState[SQL_SQLSTATE_SIZE];
    CString strMsg;
    CString strState;
    SDWORD lNative;
    SWORD nOutlen;

    ::SQLError(m_henv, m_hdbc, hstmt, lpszState, &lNative,
      lpszMsg, SQL_MAX_MESSAGE_LENGTH-1, &nOutlen);
    TRACE1("SQLGetData failed: %s\n", lpszMsg);
  }

  return nActualSize;
}
```

If this function fails, SQLError() is called to find out why it failed.

12. The `InternalGetTypeInfo()` function is really the heart and soul of this class. This function retrieves the data from the data source and inserts the corresponding elements into the maps described earlier. When you code it, the function looks like this:

```
BOOL CODBCInfo::InternalGetTypeInfo()
{
  BOOL bSuccess = FALSE;
  SQLRETURN rc;
  SQLHSTMT hstmt = NULL;
```

13. What comes next is the definition of all supported SQL types:

```
  int aiDataTypes[] = {
    SQL_CHAR,
    SQL_NUMERIC,
    SQL_DECIMAL,
    SQL_INTEGER,
    SQL_SMALLINT,
    SQL_FLOAT,
    SQL_REAL,
    SQL_DOUBLE,
#if (ODBCVER >= 0x0300)
    SQL_DATETIME,
#endif
    SQL_VARCHAR
  };

  int nDataTypes = (sizeof(aiDataTypes) /
    sizeof(aiDataTypes[0]));
```

14. Next, a `for` loop is executed that will iterate through the array of valid SQL data types just listed:

```
  for (int iCurrDataType = 0; iCurrDataType < nDataTypes;
    iCurrDataType++)
  {
```

15. For each SQL data type, create a map to hold its data-type attributes:

```
    CMapStringToOb* pmapColNameToDataAttr =
      new CMapStringToOb();

    m_mapDataTypeToDataAttrMap.SetAt(
      aiDataTypes[iCurrDataType],
      (CObject*)pmapColNameToDataAttr);
```

16. To call `SQLGetTypeInfo()`, a `hstmt` must be allocated as follows:

```
    if (SQL_SUCCESS == (rc =
      ::SQLAllocHandle(SQL_HANDLE_STMT, m_hdbc, &hstmt)))
    {
```

Notice that the `hdbc` that was allocated in the constructor is used.

17. `SQLGetTypeInfo()` is then called for the current data type:

```
if (SQL_SUCCESS == (rc = ::SQLGetTypeInfo(hstmt,
  aiDataTypes[iCurrDataType])))
{
```

18. After `SQLGetTypeInfo()` is called, `SQLFetch()` must be called to actually retrieve the data from the result set:

```
if (SQL_SUCCESS == (rc = ::SQLFetch(hstmt)))
{
  SWORD FAR iNumResultCols = 0;
```

The `SQLGetData()` function, used later, will retrieve the data into the local variables.

19. Now that you've retrieved the data type attributes for the current data type via the `SQLGetTypeInfo()` and `SQLFetch()` functions (see Steps 17 and 18), you must find out how many columns of data were returned. The documentation specifies 15 columns, but you'll want this class to be more dynamic in case this number changes in future releases of ODBC. Therefore, use a call to `SQLNumResult Cols()` to return the number of columns that were retrieved into a result set:

```
if (SQL_SUCCESS == (rc =
  ::SQLNumResultCols(hstmt, &iNumResultCols)))
{
```

20. Once the exact number of columns is known, you can start a `for` loop to loop through all of them:

```
for (int iCurrDataTypeAttr = 1;
iCurrDataTypeAttr <= iNumResultCols;
iCurrDataTypeAttr++)
{
  char lpszColName[MAX_COLNAME + 1];
  SWORD nLen;
  SWORD nSQLType;
  UDWORD nPrecision;
  SWORD nScale;
  SWORD nNullability;
```

21. Next, to retrieve the data-type attribute, you need to know its type, length, precision, scale, and so on. For each column (that is, for each datatype attribute), call `SQLDescribeCol()` to dynamically retrieve information about the column:

```
          if (SQL_SUCCESS == (rc = ::SQLDescribeCol(
            hstmt, iCurrDataTypeAttr,
(UCHAR*)lpszColName,
            MAX_COLNAME, &nLen, &nSQLType, &nPrecision,
            &nScale, &nNullability)))
          {
```

This information will be used later — when allocating memory to hold the value, and when calling `SQLGetData()` to retrieve the data into that memory.

22. As the comment states in the following short list, a call to `GetFieldTypeFromSQLType()` retrieves the C data type that corresponds to the SQL data type returned from the `SQLDescribeCol()` function call:

```
// Determine the default field type and
// get the data buffer
short nFieldType =
  GetFieldTypeFromSQLType(nSQLType);
```

23. Create a new `CDBVariant()` object that will hold the data-type attribute and call its `Clear()` member function to initialize it:

```
CDBVariant* pvarValue = new CDBVariant();
pvarValue->Clear();
```

24. Next, a call to `GetDataBuffer()` allocates the memory needed to retrieve the data-type attribute. `GetDataBuffer()` also sets this pointer to the address of one of the `CDBVariant` object's member variables that will hold the data once `SQLGetData()` is called:

```
int nGetDataBufferLen = 0;
void* pvData = GetDataBuffer(pvarValue,
  nFieldType,  &nGetDataBufferLen,
  nSQLType, nPrecision);
```

25. Now that you have the correct amount of memory allocated (via `GetDataBuffer()`) and the `CDBVariant` object set up, call `GetData()` to finally retrieve the data into your variable. After this call, the `CDBVariant`'s member variable that corresponds to the data type attribute's data type should contain the data type attribute's value.

```
long nActualSize = GetData(hstmt,
  iCurrDataTypeAttr, nFieldType, pvData,
  nGetDataBufferLen, nSQLType);
```

26. If the field type was a character string, the `CDBVariant::m_pstring` member variable (which is a `CString` pointer) needs to be released via a call to `ReleaseBuffer()`:

```
if (nFieldType == SQL_C_CHAR)
{
  // Release the string buffer
  CString strValue = (*pvarValue->m_pstring);
  strValue.ReleaseBuffer(nActualSize < nLen
  ? nActualSize : nLen);
}
```

27. Now that you have the data type attribute, add an element into the map that associates the data-type attribute name with its value:

```
pmapColNameToDataAttr->SetAt(lpszColName,
```

```
                    (CObject*)pvarValue);
                }
              }
            }
          }
        }
```

28. Now that this data type has been processed, free the statement handle. The handle will be reallocated for the next data type at the top of the `for` loop.

```
      ::SQLFreeHandle(SQL_HANDLE_STMT, &hstmt);
      }
    }
```

If at least one data type was processed, the function returns `true`.

```
    bSuccess = (0 < m_mapDataTypeToDataAttrMap.GetCount());
    return bSuccess;
  }
```

29. As mentioned in the header file, the `GetTypeInfo()` function is the only function the user of this class has to call. The first argument is a `uint` that represents a data type. The valid values are defined in the `GetTypeInfo()` ODBC documentation and can be found in the sqlext.h include file. The second argument is a string that represents the column name, or data-attribute name, also documented in the ODBC documentation for the `SQLGetTypeInfo()` function. The third argument is a pointer to a `CDBVariant()` pointer.

```
BOOL CODBCInfo::GetTypeInfo(UINT iDataType, LPCSTR
lpszColName,
  CDBVariant** ppvarValue)
{
  BOOL bSuccess = FALSE;

If the InternalGetTypeInfo() function ran successfully, the
m_bIsInitialized boolean variable is set to true. Check this
variable to make sure that the class was constructed
correctly.
  if (m_bIsInitialized)
  {

The Lookup() function is called for the
m_mapDataTypeToDataAttrMap to find the data type attribute
map for the requested data type.
    CMapStringToOb* pmapColNameToDataAttr;
    if (m_mapDataTypeToDataAttrMap.Lookup(iDataType,
    (CObject*&)pmapColNameToDataAttr))
    {
```

30. Once the correct map is found, call its Lookup function to get the data-type attribute in the form of a `CDBVariant` object:

```
      if (pmapColNameToDataAttr->Lookup(lpszColName,
```

```
        (CObject*&)*ppvarValue))
        {

If the data type attribute was found, return true to indicate
success.
          bSuccess = TRUE;
        }
      }
    }

    return bSuccess;
}
```

In the code just given, the user's `CDBVariant` pointer to pointer is used to display the data-type attribute's value—just where the user would expect to find it.

Building the CODBCInfo DLL

Now that the code has been entered for the class, simply build the DLL and move it to a directory where it can be used by the test application. Good news—it's a two-step process:

1. Press the F7 button to build the DLL.
2. Copy the resulting DLL to a folder in your *path*; for example, I copied the file to my `c:\winnt\system32` folder.

Testing the CODBCInfo class

After you've copied the DLL, it's time to use the class in a test application. You can build a new application via App Wizard or simply use the following steps with an existing application:

1. Add the ODBCInfoDll.lib import library to the test application's project.
2. At the top of the file that will instantiate the class, include the following line:

   ```
   #include "ODBCInfo.hpp"
   ```

   Adding this line includes all files needed to use the CODBCInfo class.
3. The only remaining task is to instantiate and use your new class! The following code shows you just how easy it is to use the `CODBCInfo` class:

   ```
   static struct
     {
       LPSTR lpszColName;
   ```

```
}
columns[] =
{
  "TYPE_NAME",
  "LITERAL_PREFIX",
  "LITERAL_SUFFIX"
};

CODBCInfo odbcInfo("Programming W98 - Chapter 19");
CDBVariant* pvarValue;
CString str;

for (int i = 0; i < (sizeof columns / sizeof columns[0]);
  i++)
{
  if (odbcInfo.GetTypeInfo(SQL_CHAR,
columns[i].lpszColName,
    &pvarValue))
  {
    str += CString(columns[i].lpszColName) + _T("=");
    CString strValue = CString(*pvarValue->m_pstring);
    str += strValue.GetBuffer(strValue.GetLength());
    str += _T("\n");
  }
}

AfxMessageBox(str);
```

In this example, the `type name`, `literal prefix` and `literal suffix` values are requested from the data source for the `char` type. You can use this one function, `CODBCInfo::GetTypeInfo()`, for every data type — and every data-type attribute combination — that the ODBC SDK's `SQLGetTypeInfo()` function supports.

Figure 19-7 shows the results of running the `ODBCInfoClient.exe` program found on the CD-ROM in the `\Chap19\ODBCInfoClient` directory.

Figure 19-7: The CODBCInfo class at work. This class dynamically encapsulates the ODBC SQLGetTypeInfo functionality.

To retrieve the data source's literal prefix for character field types, the application uses the exact code just shown.

Summary

This chapter introduced you to ODBC and how it provides a single API that can be used to interface to almost any DBMS from a single code base. You also encountered some challenges that go along with using the ODBC SDK to write database applications.

- ✦ You learned how to use the ODBC SDK to connect to, fetch data from, and disconnect from a data source.
- ✦ You wrote a C++ class to encapsulate some advanced ODBC SDK functions that enable you to access a data source without knowing the database's schema until runtime.
- ✦ Having the power and flexibility of a robust API like the ODBC SDK does involve a tradeoff: The programming is more difficult, both in terms of what you as a programmer are responsible for and the number of lines of code necessary to carry out a given task.
- ✦ As you saw in the ODBCDemo application, the simple task of writing a loop to read and display all the records in a single table required about a dozen different ODBC function calls and almost 100 lines of code!

Luckily, Microsoft recognized this difficulty and released a set of MFC classes, collectively known as the *MFC database classes*. These classes, covered in the next chapter, give the database developer a much simpler object-oriented interface to the ODBC functionality that you've learned about throughout this chapter.

✦ ✦ ✦

CHAPTER 20

MFC Database Classes

In This Chapter

Discovering the MFC database classes

Writing an application using the MFC database classes

Accessing a parameterized recordset

Calling a parameterized MS Access query that returns data

As you read in Chapter 19, ODBC was created to provide a single API to generically interface to multiple DBMS systems from a single codebase. Although programming to the ODBC SDK certainly has its advantages, it's not without its drawbacks. If you use ODBC SDK functions in your MFC applications, the first and most obvious problem is mixing the object-oriented MFC code of your application with the straight C functions exported by ODBC. Additionally, the ODBC SDK does give you a tremendous amount of flexibility in terms of querying different data sources as to levels of compliance, functionality, and so on; there are times when all that power simply isn't needed.

For these cases, MFC includes a set of classes that encapsulate the ODBC functionality. These classes, referred to as the "database classes," are presented in this chapter. After learning about the base MFC database classes (`CDatabase` and `CRecordset`), you'll solidify your new-found knowledge with two demos. The first demo is a maintenance application that shows basic CRUD (Create/Read/Update/Delete) functionality. In the chapter's last demo you'll learn how to use parameterized recordsets and how to call MS Access parameterized queries that return data using CRecordset-derived classes. One thing to note before attempting any of the demos is that you'll need to create the ODBC DSN presented in Chapter 19 before they run correctly. Please refer to that chapter for instructions on how to do that.

The MFC Database Classes

The Microsoft MFC Development team has made the life of the Windows programmer easier by encapsulating functionality from the Windows SDK in the form of a C++ framework of classes. Although Microsoft has usually stuck to encapsulating only elements found in the Windows SDK, one exception is the MFC Database Classes. The entire purpose of the database classes is to make programming with ODBC much easier. Although the ODBC SDK certainly provides for a tremendous amount of flexibility and power, it also has numerous drawbacks that make it inappropriate for some application development. Let's say you want to write a simple maintenance application that enables you to maintain employee records. If this application is only going to offer CRUD (create/read/update/delete) capabilities, ODBC might very well be overkill. As you'll see in the rest of this chapter, you can perform quite a few functions with the MFC Database classes that you can do with the ODBC SDK while writing 1/10th of the code.

Three main classes make up the MFC Database Classes: `CDatabase`, `CRecordset`, and `CRecordView`. The `CDatabase` and `CRecordset` classes will be explored in this chapter. The `CRecordView` class is not included in this chapter because it's a simple class, adequately covered in the online help and MFC tutorials. The `CRecordView` class is really nothing more than a `CFormView` class with an embedded `CRecordset` object. Therefore, instead of basically rehashing what is already in the online help, I'll cover issues such as parameterized recordsets and parameterized queries; they are not adequately explained in other books and technical notes on MFC database programming.

CDatabase

This class represents a connection to a data source. After constructing the `CDatabase` object, the data source is specified when the `Open()` or `OpenEx()` member function is called. The `CDatabase` class can be used in conjunction with one or more `CRecordsets` (which I'll explain shortly) or it can be used by itself. An example of when you would want to use the `CDatabase` class by itself is when you need to issue an SQL statement against a data source that does not return any data. The `CDatabase::ExecuteSQL()` function exists for just this purpose. Following is an example of how easy it is to insert a record into a table using the `CDatabase` class:

```
TRY
{
  CDatabase db;
  if (db.Open("Programming W98 - Chapter 19"))
  {
    db.ExecuteSQL("INSERT INTO UserMaster
      VALUES('TestID', 'Test User Name', 0)");

    db.Close();
  }
}
CATCH(CDBException, p)
{
  AfxMessageBox(p->m_strError);
}
END_CATCH
```

Compare this code segment to the 50-plus lines of ODBC SDK code you would have to write to accomplish the same thing! The database classes, though not as powerful as directly using the ODBC SDK, are much easier and faster to use in cases where the power of the ODBC SDK is not needed.

Let's take a minute and take a more detailed look at the code just given. The first thing you see in the code snippet is a TRY/CATCH block:

```
TRY
{
  ...
}
CATCH(CDBException, p)
{
  AfxMessageBox(p->m_strError);
}
END_CATCH
```

Most database-class member functions throw an exception of type CDBException if an abnormal condition occurs. The CDBException class doesn't really need much functionality. In fact, it has no member functions at all (except those inherited from its base class: CException). The three data members it does contain — *member variables* — serve to tell the application what went wrong at the time the exception was thrown. Here are the three member variables and what they mean in terms of determining the cause of the exception.

Member Variable	***Description***
m_nRetCode	This variable contains the ODBC return code (of type SQLRETURN).
m_strError	This variable is a string that describes the error.
m_strStateNativeOrigin	Like m_strError, this variable is a string that describes the error that occurred. However, it does so in terms of the error codes returned by ODBC.

Because member functions of the database class can throw exceptions of type CDBException, it's wise to "wrap" all your database code in TRY/CATCH blocks even if you don't expect the function to fail.

The next line in the example constructs the CDatabase object and opens it:

```
CDatabase db;
if (db.Open("Programming W98 - Chapter 19"))
...
```

The CDatabase's constructor doesn't do anything special. You must call the CDatabase::Open() or CDatabase::OpenEx() member function to actually connect to a data source:

```
virtual BOOL Open( LPCTSTR lpszDSN, BOOL bExclusive = FALSE,
BOOL bReadOnly = FALSE, LPCTSTR lpszConnect = "ODBC;", BOOL
bUseCursorLib = TRUE );
throw( CDBException, CMemoryException );
```

As you can see in the prototype, there are several options you can set in opening a database connection using the CDatabase::Open() function. Even so, only the first parameter is explicitly required. In the example just given, only this parameter was passed and represented the DSN for our data source. Other options could have been used as well.

The bExclusive flag specifies whether to allow other connections to a data source. Even so, this flag actually has no use because it's not supported. Therefore, if you specify TRUE with this option, the function will assert.

The bReadOnly flag enables you to specify whether updates to the data source will be allowed. The default value is FALSE. Any recordsets created and attached to this CRecordset will inherit this flag.

The lpszConnect argument enables you to specify the ODBC connect string. If you use this argument, specify NULL as the lpszDSN. The benefit of using this argument is in terms of flexibility. For example, if you need to specify a userID and password, you can do so within the lpszConnect. The format of the argument is dictated by the ODBC driver you're using.

Finally, the bUseCursorLib flag specifies whether the ODBC cursor library is to be used. If you set this value to TRUE (which is the default), you'll only be able to use cursors of type static snapshot or forward-only. To use dynasets, you must set this value to FALSE.

After opening the recordset, the next line executes the SQL statement and closes the database:

```
db.ExecuteSQL("INSERT INTO UserMaster VALUES('TestID', 'Test
User Name', 0)");
db.Close();
```

As you can see, the CDatabase::ExecuteSQL() has a straightforward syntax. You simply pass it the string that represents the SQL statement you wish to execute. Note that this function is only used when you're not expecting data to be returned.

An alternative method of opening a database connection using the database classes is via the CDatabase::OpenEx() function. Actually, according to the MFC documentation, this is now the preferred way of opening a database connection.

```
virtual BOOL OpenEx( LPCTSTR lpszConnectString,
  DWORD dwOptions = 0 );
throw( CDBException, CMemoryException );
```

The `CDatabase::Openex()` function takes only two parameters: the connect string and a `DWORD` that represents options for the connection. The `lpszConnectString` passes the ODBC connect string to the function; the `dwOptions` argument sets up how the connection is to be made. The following values can be used together using the logical "or" operator.

```
CDatabase::openExclusive
CDatabase::openReadOnly
CDatabase::useCursorLib
CDatabase::noODBCDialog
CDatabase::forceODBCDialog
```

These values work exactly as they did in the `CDatabase::Open()` function. The only difference is in the `CDatabase::noODBCDialog` and the `CDatabase::forceODBCDialog` flags, which indicate whether the application wishes for the ODBC Driver Manager to present the user with the ODBC connection dialog box when the connection is attempted.

The `CDatabase` class supports a useful set of member functions that support transactions. Transactions give the application the capability to bracket a set of functions in a logical group so that if any one of those functions fail, no changes are made. For those of you not familiar with transactions, an example might be in order here. Let's say that you're writing an accounting application and you wish to move an amount from one account to another. What would happen if after removing the amount from one account, the attempt to update the second account's balance failed? You would end up with incorrect data. That is where transactions come in. Now you can specify that either both of these functions must complete successfully or neither of them should.

Here's the way it works: You set a "transaction boundary" by calling `CDatabase::BeginTrans()`. Anything done after this point is subject to being "rolled back," or undone. Once you call `CDatabase::CommitTrans()`, you're committing (making permanent) all the changes you've made to the database since the last transaction boundary. If for some reason you wish to back out of the changes since the last transaction boundary, simply call the `CDatabase::Rollback()` function.

Note Before you attempt to use transactions, it would be wise to call the `CDatabase::CanTransact()` function to see whether the driver supports them.

✦ ✦ ✦ ✦ ✦

CRecordset

A `CDatabase` object represents a connection to a data source; a `CRecordset` object represents a set of records from a data source. There are basically two types of recordsets: dynasets and snapshots. A *dynaset* is a dynamic set of data that stays synchronized with the updates made by other users of the data source. A *snapshot*, on the other hand, is a static picture of the data taken at the time the recordset was filled. This set of data is not affected by changes made by other users.

The simplest way to get started using recordsets is to create one using the Class Wizard. Here we will walk you through creating a `CRecordset`-derived class using the Class Wizard. The record set will use the UserMaster table you've seen throughout this chapter. Figure 20–1 shows the UserMaster table in Microsoft Access 97 that the recordset will be based on.

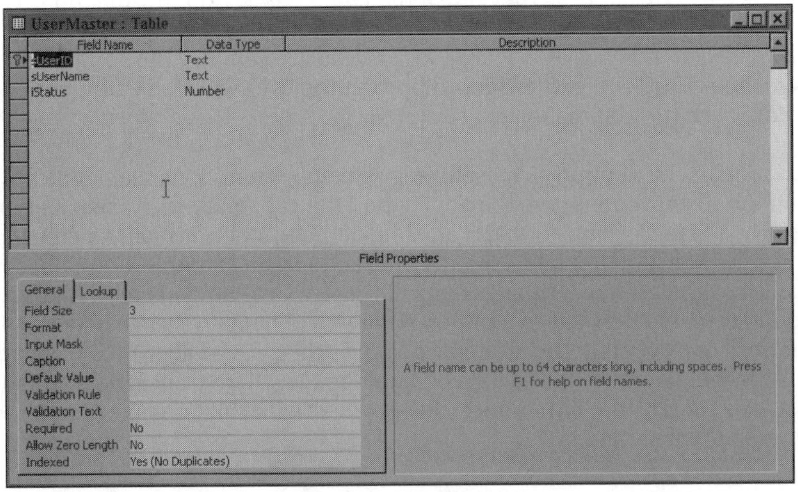

Figure 20-1: The UserMaster table definition in Microsoft Access 97

Begin by bringing up the Class Wizard from the Microsoft Visual Studio. From the Class Wizard, click the Add Class button. From the menu that appears, then select the New option. Figure 20-2 shows the resulting New Class dialog box.

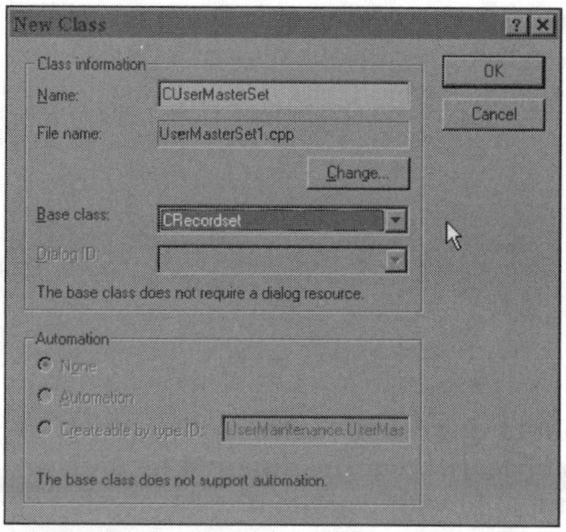

Figure 20-2: The New Class dialog box initiated from Class Wizard

When you specify that you want to create a `CRecordset`-derived class, Class Wizard prompts you to specify the type of database access used with your recordset class. Figure 20-3 shows this dialog.

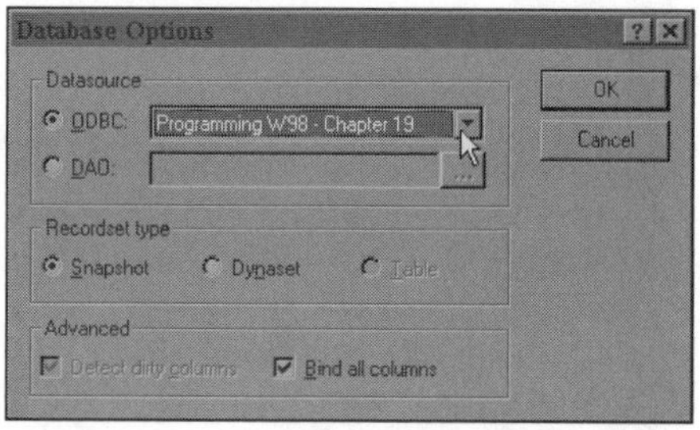

Figure 20-3: Database options dialog box for a new CRecordset-derived class

After selecting the DSN, simply select the desired table (as shown in Figure 20-4) and click OK. That's how easy it is to create a `CRecordset`-derived class!

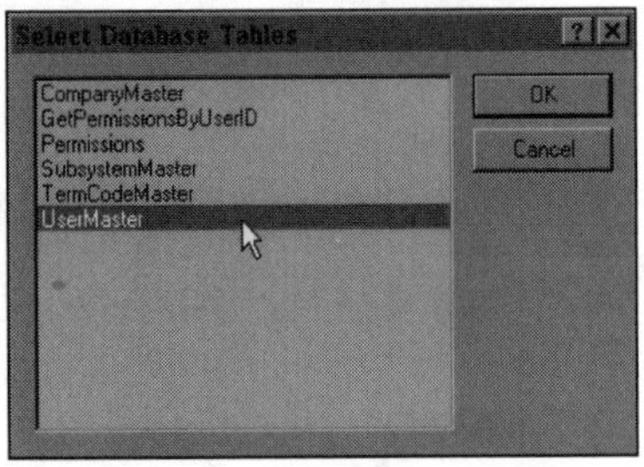

Figure 20-4: Use the Select Database Tables dialog box to complete the creation of a CRecordset-derived class from Class Wizard.

Listings 20-1 and 20-2 show you the amount of work the Class Wizard does for you. Throughout this part of the chapter you'll learn what the different member variables and member functions are for and how to use them.

Listing 20-1: **UserMasterSet.h**

```
#pragma once

#if _MSC_VER >= 1000
#pragma once
#endif // _MSC_VER >= 1000
// UserMasterSet.h : header file
//

/////////////////////////////////////////////////////////////////
// CUserMasterSet recordset

class CUserMasterSet : public CRecordset
{
public:
  CUserMasterSet(CDatabase* pDatabase = NULL);
  DECLARE_DYNAMIC(CUserMasterSet)

  // Field/Param Data
  //{{AFX_FIELD(CUserMasterSet, CRecordset)
  Cstring   m_sUserID;
  Cstring   m_sUserName;
  int       m_iStatus;
  //}}AFX_FIELD


  // Overrides
  // ClassWizard generated virtual function overrides
  //{{AFX_VIRTUAL(CUserMasterSet)
  public:
  virtual CString GetDefaultConnect();    // Default connection
                                          // string
  virtual CString GetDefaultSQL();    // Default SQL for
                                      //Recordset
```

```
   virtual void DoFieldExchange(CFieldExchange* pFX); // RFX
                                                      // support
   //}}AFX_VIRTUAL

   // Implementation
   #ifdef _DEBUG
   virtual void AssertValid() const;
   virtual void Dump(CDumpContext& dc) const;
   #endif
};

//{{AFX_INSERT_LOCATION}}
// Microsoft Developer Studio will insert additional
// declarations immediately before the previous line.
```

Listing 20-2: UserMasterSet.cpp

```
// UserMasterSet.cpp : implementation file
//

#include "stdafx.h"
#include "dbtest.h"
#include "UserMasterSet.h"

#ifdef _DEBUG
#define new DEBUG_NEW
#undef THIS_FILE
static char THIS_FILE[] = __FILE__;
#endif

/////////////////////////////////////////////////////////////////////
// CUserMasterSet

IMPLEMENT_DYNAMIC(CUserMasterSet, CRecordset)

CUserMasterSet::CUserMasterSet(CDatabase* pdb)
: CRecordset(pdb)
{
  //{{AFX_FIELD_INIT(CUserMasterSet)
  m_sUserID = _T("");
  m_sUserName = _T("");
  m_iStatus = 0;
  m_nFields = 3;
  //}}AFX_FIELD_INIT
  m_nDefaultType = snapshot;
}

CString CUserMasterSet::GetDefaultConnect()
{
```

(continued)

Listing 20-2 (continued)

```
  return _T("ODBC;DSN=Programming W98 - Chapter 19");
}

CString CUserMasterSet::GetDefaultSQL()
{
  return _T("[UserMaster]");
}

void CUserMasterSet::DoFieldExchange(CFieldExchange* pFX)
{
  //{{AFX_FIELD_MAP(CUserMasterSet)
  pFX->SetFieldType(CFieldExchange::outputColumn);
  RFX_Text(pFX, _T("[sUserID]"), m_sUserID);
  RFX_Text(pFX, _T("[sUserName]"), m_sUserName);
  RFX_Int(pFX, _T("[iStatus]"), m_iStatus);
  //}}AFX_FIELD_MAP
}

/////////////////////////////////////////////////////////////////
// CUserMasterSet diagnostics

#ifdef _DEBUG
void CUserMasterSet::AssertValid() const
{
  CRecordset::AssertValid();
}

void CUserMasterSet::Dump(CDumpContext& dc) const
{
  CRecordset::Dump(dc);
}
#endif //_DEBUG
```

After you have a recordset to work with, you can do any of the following:

- Construct a recordset
- Open a recordset
- Read and write data using RFX (record field exchange)
- Filter records
- Sort the records returned with a recordset
- Move through the result set
- Save records
- Delete records

Constructing a recordset

The CRecordset constructor takes only one argument: a pointer to a CDatabase object. This argument has a default value of NULL. If you choose not to specify a CDatabase object when calling this constructor, MFC automatically creates a temporary one for you, using the information specified when you used the Class Wizard to create the recordset; specifically, that information can be found in the CRecordset::GetDefaultConnect() function. If you're planning to use multiple recordsets, however, it's much more efficient to create one CDatabase object to use for your recordsets. One way of doing this is to create your CDatabase object when the application initializes and store the pointer in the application object. That way, whenever you need to construct a recordset, you can acquire it from the application object and pass its pointer to the recordset's constructor.

Opening a recordset

After the recordset has been constructed, you can then open it using the CRecordset::Open() function. The syntax for this function is as follows:

```
virtual BOOL Open( UINT nOpenType = AFX_DB_USE_DEFAULT_TYPE,
  LPCTSTR lpszSQL = NULL, DWORD dwOptions = none );
throw( CDBException, CMemoryException );
```

The nOpenType argument specifies the type of recordset you want: dynaset or snapshot. The default is CRecordset::snapshot.

The lpszSQL argument enables you to specify the SQL statement you want to execute against the data source when the recordset is opened. If you allow this argument to default to NULL, the code in the CRecordset::GetDefaultSQL will be used. In most cases, you'll see only the name of a table or query in this function; in this situation, however, MFC will retrieve all columns from this table or query without filtering or sorting the data in any way. If you need to filter or sort your data, these issues will be covered shortly.

Reading and writing data using RFX

As you read in the section "Opening a recordset," to retrieve all the records from a table without regard to order, you simply need to create a CRecordset-derived class (as shown) and call its CRecordset::Open() member function. Even so, at this point you may be wondering how does the data get from the data source into your application's variables. The answer is *RFX* (record field exchange). When a CRecordset-derived class is created using the Class Wizard, it enumerates all the columns in the selected table or query and declares variables of the appropriate type in the class' header file. It also generates a function called DoFieldExchange() that serves to tie the member variables to their corresponding columns in the data source. This function is called when MFC needs to move data from the data source to your member variables or vice versa. The underlying MFC code actually does all the nitty-gritty ODBC SDK functions (for example, binding the columns, fetching the data, and so on) that you learned how to do in the first part of this chapter. Even so, now it all happens automatically for you! When you open a recordset, the CRecordset::Open() function moves to the first record so that you can immediately start using your data. You can then start navigating through the resulting data using the CRecordset::MoveFirst(), CRecordset::MovePrev(), CRecordset::MoveNext(), and CRecordset::MoveLast() member functions. These functions will be explained shortly.

Filtering records

Now that you know how to open and retrieve data from a data source, you need to learn how to filter that data to get just the records you desire. Actually, there are several ways to accomplish this. As you saw in the section entitled "Opening a recordset," you can specify the SQL in the lpszSQL argument. Here is an example of filtering the records when the recordset is opened. This code reads only the records that represent users whose status code equals 0:

```
TRY
{
  CDatabase db;
  if (db.Open("Programming W98 - Chapter 19"))
  {
    CUserMasterSet* pUserMasterSet =
      new CUserMasterSet();
    pUserMasterSet->Open(CRecordset::snapshot,
      "SELECT * from usermaster where iStatus = 0");

    // use the data that was returned

    pUserMasterSet->Close();
    db.Close();
  }
}
CATCH(CDBException, p)
{
  AfxMessageBox(p->m_strError);
}
END_CATCH
```

A second way of filtering the data returned in a recordset is to use a parameterized recordset. Using the CUserMasterSet (see Listings 20–1 and 20-2) created earlier in the chapter, you'll change this recordset so that upon opening the recordset, only records that represent users with iStatus equal to 0 will be retrieved.

1. The first step is to declare a variable that will hold the parameter data in the UserMasterSet.h file. First, declare the following block of variables:

```
// Field/Param Data
  //{{AFX_FIELD(CUserMasterSet, CRecordset)
  Cstring    m_sUserID;
  Cstring    m_sUserName;
  int        m_iStatus;
  //}}AFX_FIELD
```

Then add the following variable declaration:

```
Int         m_iStatusParam;
```

2. The next step is to initialize the variable in the recordset's constructor and set the `m_nParams` value to the number of parameters that will be used (in this case it's 1). This is extremely important. If you attempt to use a parameterized recordset and do not set this value, the recordset's `Open()` will fail during the call to `DoFieldExchange()`:

```
//{{AFX_FIELD_INIT(CUserMasterSet)
  m_sUserID = _T("");
  m_sUserName = _T("");
  m_iStatus = 0;
  m_nFields = 3;
  //}}AFX_FIELD_INIT
```

becomes

```
//{{AFX_FIELD_INIT(CUserMasterSet)
  m_sUserID = _T("");
  m_sUserName = _T("");
  m_iStatus = 0;
  m_nFields = 3;
  m_iStatusParam = 0;
  m_nParams = 1;
  //}}AFX_FIELD_INIT
```

3. The next step is to update the `DoFieldExchange()` function. After finished, it will look like the following:

```
//{{AFX_FIELD_MAP(CUserMasterSet)
  pFX->SetFieldType(CFieldExchange::outputColumn);
  RFX_Text(pFX, _T("[sUserID]"), m_sUserID);
  RFX_Text(pFX, _T("[sUserName]"), m_sUserName);
  RFX_Int(pFX, _T("[iStatus]"), m_iStatus);
  pFX->SetFieldType(CFieldExchange::param);
  RFX_Int(pFX, _T("[iStatus]"), m_iStatusParam);
  //}}AFX_FIELD_MAP
```

Note

Please note: The `CfieldExchange::SetFieldType()` must be called with the `CfieldExchange::param` argument, and the second argument of the `RFX_Text()` function points to the column used to filter the data (`iStatus`).

◆ ◆ ◆ ◆ ◆

4. After the appropriate calls are made, one requirement remains before you open the recordset: Set the parameter's value. Here is an example of how to do this:

```
TRY
{
  CDatabase db;
  if (db.Open("Programming W98 - Chapter 19"))
  {
```

```
      CUserMasterSet* pUserMasterSet = new CUserMasterSet();
      pUserMasterSet->m_strFilter = "iStatus = ?";
      pUserMasterSet->m_iStatusParam = 0;
      pUserMasterSet->Open();

      // use the data that was returned

      pUserMasterSet->Close();
      db.Close();
    }
  }
  CATCH(CDBException, p)
  {
    AfxMessageBox(p->m_strError);
  }
  END_CATCH
```

As you can see, using parameterized recordsets is not very complex, but if you forget to do any of the steps involved you can end up losing a lot of time tracking down why your `Open()` isn't working.

Sorting records returned with a recordset

As you just saw in the section entitled "Filtering Records," MFC provides you with a member variable (`m_strFilter`) to filter the records that your recordset represent. MFC also provides you with a member variable to specify the order in which the records are returned. This member variable is `m_strSort`. To use this member variable, simply set it to the name of the column that you want to sort by. For example, if you wanted to sort the sample code just shown by user name, your code would look like the following:

```
TRY
{
  CDatabase db;
  if (db.Open("Programming W98 - Chapter 19"))
  {
    CUserMasterSet* pUserMasterSet = new CUserMasterSet();
    pUserMasterSet->m_strFilter = "iStatus = ?";
    pUserMasterSet->m_iStatusParam = 0;

    pUserMasterSet->m_strSort = "sUserID";
    pUserMasterSet->Open();

    // use the data that was returned

    pUserMasterSet->Close();
    db.Close();
  }
}
CATCH(CDBException, p)
{
```

```
    AfxMessageBox(p->m_strError);
}
END_CATCH
```

If you need to sort by more than one column, just separate the columns by giving each one a name followed by a comma.

Moving through the result set

After you've opened the recordset and you have only the data you wish (via filtering) in the sequence you desire (via the m_strSort member variable), you'll need to know how to move through the resulting records. MFC makes this process easy—you can use the MoveFirst(), MovePrev(), MoveNext(), and MoveLast() functions. Although you can see what each function does from its name, you should know about several aspects of the functions before you attempt to navigate through a recordset:

- ✦ The MoveXXX function throws an exception if the recordset did not return any records. Therefore, you should always call the CRecordset::IsBOF() or CRecordset::IsEOF() before you call one of the move functions.
- ✦ The MoveFirst() and MovePrev() functions are not supported for recordsets defined as forward-only.
- ✦ If you're moving through a recordset and a record in that recordset has been deleted by another user, you should call the CRecordset::IsDeleted() function to know whether the record is still valid.
- ✦ If you move to the last record in the recordset and call MoveNext(), a CDBException will be thrown. Therefore, when using MoveNext() to move sequentially through a recordset, always call IsEOF() before you call MoveNext() again.

Here is a simple example of moving through a recordset with a while loop. As you can see, CRecordset::IsEOF() is called after every move so an invalid call to CRecordset::MoveNext() is not made once all the records have been read.

```
pUserMasterSet->Open();
while (!pUserMasterSet->IsEOF())
{
  AfxMessageBox(pUserMasterSet->m_sUserID);
  pUserMasterSet->MoveNext();
}
```

Saving records

It's very easy to save data using a recordset. There are basically two different ways of saving data: adding new records and updating existing records.

To add a new record, you simply do the following:

1. Call the `CRecordset::AddNew()` function. This will prepare a new, blank record for you.
2. Move your application's data into the recordset's member variables.
3. Call the `CRecordset::Update()` function to update the data source.

To update an existing record, follow these steps:

1. Call the `CRecordset::Edit()` function. This will prepare a new, blank record for you.
2. Move your application's data into the recordset's member variables.
3. Call the `CRecordset::Update()` function to update the data source.

Note

Take special care to establish the order in which you call these functions. You must move the data into the member variables *after* calling the `Edit()` function. Otherwise, MFC will not update your data. The reason is that when the database classes cache (buffer) the data, they do a memory-compare process when you call the `Update()` function. *If no changes have been made to the member variables since you called the* `Edit()` *function, the data will not be saved*—even though you explicitly called the `Update()` function.

◆ ◆ ◆ ◆ ◆

Deleting Records

To delete a record from a recordset, you must first be positioned on a record. Then, to delete the record, you simply call the `CRecordset::Delete()` function. After deleting the record, you must call one of the `MoveXXX` functions to move to another record since the current record is no longer valid.

An MFC Database Classes Demo

In the following program (which can be found on the companion CD-ROM in the \Chap20\UserMaintenance directory), you'll develop a fully functional maintenance application using the MFC database classes. This application will have all the capabilities of a traditional maintenance application (creating, reading, updating, deleting) for maintaining Users. As with the ODBC program presented earlier in the chapter, you can read along or you can enter the exercise. Once again, however—*before* you type in the following exercise—you must create the ODBC DSN and point it to the database provided on the companion CD-ROM. Otherwise your application will not run correctly. The steps required to create the appropriate DSN are listed earlier in this chapter, in the section entitled "Creating the Demo ODBC DSN."

Creating the Visual C++ 6.0 Project

Begin by creating a new project, using the Microsoft Developer Studio as follows:

1. From the File menu, select the New command.
2. In the New dialog box, select the Projects tab, and select MFC App Wizard (exe) from the list box.
3. Type the project name (**UserMaintenance**) and then select the location (such as a folder) where you want to create the program. Make sure the *Create new workspace* option button is selected before you click OK or press Enter.
4. On the first dialog box of the MFC App Wizard, specify that you want a Dialog-based application. Then click the Finish button and click OK (or press Enter in the New Project Information dialog box).

Adding support for the MFC database classes

With MFC, you only need to include the `afxdb.h` header file to incorporate MFC database class support into your application.

1. Open the stdafx.h source-code file and find the following line:

```
// Microsoft Developer Studio will insert additional
declarations immediately before the previous line.
```

2. Add the following `#include` directive, which is needed for database-class declarations:

```
#include "afxdb.h"
```

Adding a dialog to the application

1. On the left side of the Developer Studio you should see the Project window. Double-click the Resource tab at the bottom and double-click the User Maintenance resources entry. A list of resource entries will then be displayed in outline format below Parameterized Resources. Double-click the Dialog entry.
2. At this point, you'll see two dialog boxes created for you by App Wizard. When you locate the `IDD_USERMAINTENANCE_DIALOG` entry, select it by double-clicking it. This will cause the dialog box to be opened in edit mode so that you can make the necessary changes for this program.
3. Double-click the dialog box with the resource ID `IDD_USERMAINTENANCE_DIALOG`. The Developer Studio will open this dialog box for you to view and edit.
4. Change the dialog box by removing the "TODO" static text control and insert the controls shown in Figure 20-5. Most of the Visual Studio toolbars have

been hidden so more of the dialog box can be seen. Note that the control under the Users static text is a list box.

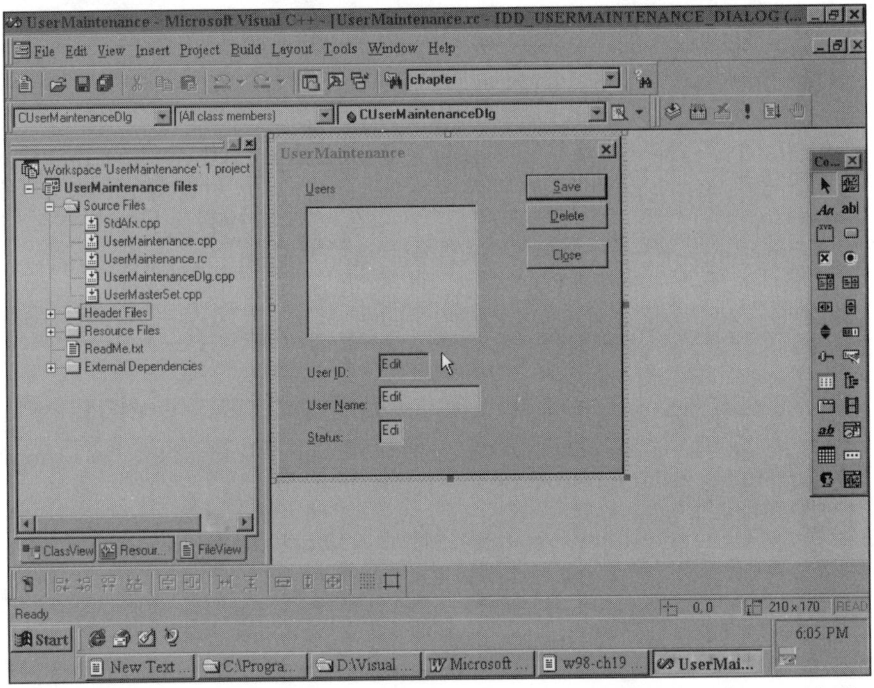

Figure 20-5: The dialog for the program (after the new controls have been added)

3. You should now have four input controls (a list box for the User list and three Edit fields for the User ID, User Name, and Status). Click the Listbox control. Hold down the Alt key and press the Enter key. Give this control an ID of `IDC_LBXUSERS`.

4. Using the same key sequence, rename the remaining controls as follows:

   User ID Edit field = `IDC_EDTUSERID`

   User Name Edit field = `IDC_EDTUSERNAME`

   Status Edit field = `IDC_EDTSTATUS`

   Also be sure to click the Read-Only attribute for the User ID field.

5. Using the same key sequence, rename the button controls as follows:

   Save Button = `IDC_BTNSAVE`

   Delete Button = `IDC_BTNDELETE`

   Close Button = `IDC_BTNCLOSE`

6. Create the member variables that will be used with DDX (dynamic data exchange) for the different controls. This is done by holding down the Ctrl button and double-clicking the control. You'll see the Add Member Variable dialog that enables you to specify Member variable name, Category, and Variable Type. Do this for the following controls, filling in the appropriate information:

Control	*Variable Name*
User Listbox	`m_lbxUsers, Control, CListbox`
User ID Edit	`m_strUserID, Value, CString`
User Name Edit	`m_strUserName, Value, CString`
Status Edit	`m_iStatus, Value, int`
Save Button	`m_btnSave, Control, Cbutton`
Delete Button	`m_btnDelete, Control, Cbutton`
Close Button	`m_btnClose, Control, CButton`

Adding a utility class to encapsulate the user's data

A utility class is needed to encapsulate each record's data. As you'll see later, once a record is read, a `CUser` class is created. An entry is then made into the list box that represents that record. This list box entry, in turn, points back to the class that contains the record's data.

1. Create a file named **User.h**.
2. The `User.h` file should look like the following:

```
#ifndef _USER_H_
#define _USER_H_

class CUser
{
public:
  CString m_strUserID;
  CString m_strUserName;
  int m_iStatus;
};

#endif
```

Creating a CRecordset class for the UserMaster table

You now need a recordset class to access the data in the UserMaster table. Call this class `CUserMasterSet`.

Tip

If you don't remember how to create a CRecordset-derived class, follow the directions in the section entitled "CRecordset" (presented earlier in the chapter).

Modifying the dialog's header file

You'll need to make a couple of minor changes to the dialog's header file for this program.

1. Open the UserMaintenanceDlg.h file and add the following #include right before the declaration of the CUserMaintenanceDlg class:

```
#include "User.h"
```

2. Find the following comment:

```
// Implementation
```

3. Add the following member-function declarations:

```
void FillListboxWithUsers();
BOOL GetSelectedUser(int* piIndex, CUser** ppUser);
void InitControls();
BOOL SaveUser(CUser* pUser);
BOOL DeleteUser(CUser* pUser);
```

Modifying the dialog's implementation file

The last thing to do for this program is to modify the dialog's code to perform the database I/O.

1. Open the UserMaintenanceDlg.cpp file and find the OnInitialUpdate() function. At the top of the file, locate the following #include directives:

```
#include "stdafx.h"
#include "UserMaintenance.h"
#include "UserMaintenanceDlg.h"
```

   Add this #include directive after them:

```
#include "UserMasterSet.h"
```

2. Find the OnInitialUpdate() function, and then find in the OnInitDialog() function — after which add this comment:

```
// TODO: Add extra initialization here
```

   Then add the following function calls: The FillListboxWithUsers() function fills the list box with all users found in the database; the InitControls() function performs operations such as initializing the state of the Buttons. (For example, disabling the Save and Delete Buttons when a user is not selected, or enabling the Save and Delete Buttons when a user is selected.)

```
FillListboxWithUsers();
InitControls();
```

3. At the end of the `UserMaintenanceDlg.cpp` file, add the following function:

```
void CUserMaintenanceDlg::FillListboxWithUsers()
{
  int iIndex;
  CDatabase db;
  CUserMasterSet* pUserMasterSet = NULL;
```

4. Because most database classes throw an exception upon encountering unexpected conditions, it's wise to "wrap" all your database class with a `TRY/CATCH` block.

```
  TRY
  {
```

5. Open the database, using the DSN created in the earlier section entitled "Creating the Demo ODBC DSN," as follows:

```
  if (db.Open("Programming W98 - Chapter 19"))
  {
```

6. Create a new recordset object and open it.

```
    pUserMasterSet = new CUserMasterSet();
    pUserMasterSet->Open();

    while (!pUserMasterSet->IsEOF())
    {
```

Note that because you're not using the filtering techniques discussed in the "Filtering Records" section, you'll be retrieving all the users from the data source.

7. To guard the database against being "hit" for user information every time a user is selected from the list box, create an object (`CUser`) that will contain all the information for every user read from the database:

```
      CUser* pUser = new CUser();
      pUser->m_strUserID = pUserMasterSet->m_sUserID;
      pUser->m_strUserName = pUserMasterSet->m_sUserName;
      pUser->m_iStatus = pUserMasterSet->m_iStatus;

      iIndex = m_lbxUsers.AddString(
        pUserMasterSet->m_sUserName);
      m_lbxUsers.SetItemData(iIndex, (DWORD)pUser);
```

Each user will then be added to the list box and its Item Data will be set to the `CUser` object pointer; doing so makes retrieving user information much more efficient. Note that simply by calling the recordset's `Open()` and `MoveNext()` function, you set its member variables to the current record's information without any further work on your part. Compare this to all the work required to code the ODBC SDK level "manually."

8. Call the recordset's `MoveNext()` function to retrieve the next record in the recordset:

```
      pUserMasterSet->MoveNext();
    }

    pUserMasterSet->Close();
    delete pUserMasterSet;
    db.Close();
  }
}
CATCH(CDBException, p)
{
```

9. If a `CDBException` is thrown during one of the database function calls, display the error message—and then clean up by closing the database and/or recordset (if open) and deleting the appropriate recordset pointer (if created). The process looks like this:

```
    AfxMessageBox(p->m_strError);

    if (pUserMasterSet)
    {
      if (pUserMasterSet->IsOpen())
      {
        pUserMasterSet->Close();
      }
      delete pUserMasterSet;
    }

    if (db.IsOpen())
    {
      db.Close();
    }
  }
  END_CATCH

}
```

10. Add the following initialization function to the end of the `UserMaintenanceDlg.cpp` file:

```
void CUserMaintenanceDlg::InitControls()
{
```

11. Initialize the controls by setting all Edit fields to blanks and disabling the Save and Delete buttons (which are enabled when a User is selected from the list box), like this:

```
m_lbxUsers.SetCurSel(-1);
```

```
    m_strUserID = "";
    m_strUserName = "";
    m_iStatus = -1;

    m_btnSave.EnableWindow(FALSE);
    m_btnDelete.EnableWindow(FALSE);
    m_btnClose.EnableWindow(TRUE);

    m_lbxUsers.SetFocus();

    UpdateData(FALSE);
  }
```

12. You now need to add a function so that when a user is selected from the list box, the proper information appears in the dialog box. Begin by bringing up the Class Wizard, making sure the selected class name is the `CODBCDemoDlg`, and pressing Ctrl+W.

13. In the Object IDs list box that appears, select the Listbox ID (`IDC_LBXUSERS`). Double-click the `LBN_SELCHANGE` entry in the Messages list box on the right. You'll be prompted with the Add Member Function dialog box.

14. Press Enter to accept the default function name, and then click the Edit button on the right side of the MFC Class Wizard dialog box to edit your new function. Make sure the function looks like the following:

```
void CUserMaintenanceDlg::OnSelchangeLbxusers()
{
  int iIndex;
  CUser* pUser;

  if (GetSelectedUser(&iIndex, &pUser))
  {
```

15. Update the member variables with the currently selected User's information:

```
  m_strUserID = pUser->m_strUserID;
  m_strUserName = pUser->m_strUserName;
  m_iStatus = pUser->m_iStatus;
```

16. Because a User is now selected, enable both the Save and Delete Buttons as follows:

```
  m_btnSave.EnableWindow(TRUE);
  m_btnDelete.EnableWindow(TRUE);
```

Calling `UpdateData()` with an argument of `FALSE` will cause DDX (dynamic data exchange) to update the dialog box's controls from the member variables. It looks like this:

```
    UpdateData(FALSE);
  }
}
```

17. You'll need to get the selected user at different times (such as when the Update Button or the Delete Button is clicked); add the following function at the end of the UserMaintenanceDlg.cpp file to perform this task:

```
BOOL CUserMaintenanceDlg::GetSelectedUser(int* piIndex,
  CUser** ppUser)
{
  BOOL bSuccess = FALSE;

  int iIndex;
  if (LB_ERR != (iIndex = m_lbxUsers.GetCurSel()))
  {
    *piIndex = iIndex;
    *ppUser = (CUser*)m_lbxUsers.GetItemData(iIndex);
    bSuccess = TRUE;
  }

  return bSuccess;
}
```

18. Add a handler for the Close button. Begin by bringing up the Class Wizard and selecting the IDC_BTNCLOSE entry from the ID list box.

19. Double-click the BN_CLICKED entry in the Messages list box and accept the default function name.

20. After clicking the Edit button to exit the Class Wizard and bringing up the function, make sure it looks like the following:

```
void CUserMaintenanceDlg::OnBtnclose()
{
  CDialog::OnCancel();
}
```

At this point, you can now read all the users from the data source and display their respective information when they are selected from the list box. Now you're ready to add Update capability to the application.

21. Add a handler for the Save button. Begin by bringing up the Class Wizard and selecting the IDC_BTNSAVE entry from the ID list box.

22. Double-click the BN_CLICKED entry in the Messages list box and accept the default function name.

23. After clicking the Edit button to exit the Class Wizard and then bringing up the function, make sure it looks like the following:

```
void CUserMaintenanceDlg::OnBtnsave()
{
  int iCurrIndex;

  CUser* pUser = NULL;
```

```
if (GetSelectedUser(&iCurrIndex, &pUser))
{
  ASSERT(pUser);
  if (pUser)
  {
    UpdateData();
```

24. Save the data the user has typed in. That way, if the `SaveUser()` function call fails, the data is not lost and the Save can be attempted again without having to retype the information. The code looks like this:

```
    CString strPrevUserID;
    strPrevUserID = m_strUserID;
    CString strPrevUserName;
    strPrevUserName = m_strUserName;
    int iPrevStatus = m_iStatus;

    pUser->m_strUserID = m_strUserID;
    pUser->m_strUserName = m_strUserName;
    pUser->m_iStatus = m_iStatus;
```

25. Next, call the `SaveUser()` function to save the current User:

```
    if (SaveUser(pUser))
    {
```

26. Because the User Name is being used in the list box and it could have changed, delete it from the list box and add the User back. Although the User Name could be checked to verify it had been changed, this “quick and dirty” way of doing it costs nothing in terms of performance.

```
      if (LB_ERR == m_lbxUsers.DeleteString(iCurrIndex))
      {
        AfxMessageBox("The User ID was Saved, but the
          previous User ID could not be "
         removed from the listbox.");
      }
      else
      {
        int iNewIndex = m_lbxUsers.AddString(
          pUser->m_strUserName);
        if ((LB_ERR == iNewIndex) || (LB_ERRSPACE ==
          iNewIndex))
        {
          AfxMessageBox("The User ID was Saved, but
            the new User ID could not
            be added to the listbox.");
        }
        if (LB_ERR == m_lbxUsers.SetItemData(iNewIndex,
          (DWORD)pUser))
        {
```

```
                    AfxMessageBox("SetItemData returned LB_ERR.
                      This will probably cause
                      serious problems if you attempt to update
                      or delete this item from the listbox");
                  }
                }

                InitControls();

                UpdateData(FALSE);
              }
              else
              {
```

If the SaveUser() function failed, set the dialog box's values back to what had been typed in.

```
                pUser->m_strUserID = strPrevUserID;
                pUser->m_strUserName = strPrevUserName;
                pUser->m_iStatus = iPrevStatus;
                AfxMessageBox("SaveUser failed");
              }
            }
          }
          else
          {
            // should never get here because of
            // enabling/disabling button on lbx selection
            AfxMessageBox("You must first select a
              User ID to Save");
          }
        }
```

27. Add the following helper function at the end of UserMaintenanceDlg.cpp to save the record:

```
BOOL CUserMaintenanceDlg::SaveUser(CUser* pUser)
{
  BOOL bSuccess = FALSE;
  CDatabase db;

  TRY
  {
    if (db.Open("Programming W98 - Chapter 19"))
    {
```

28. Add a handler for the Delete button. Begin by bringing up the Class Wizard and selecting the `IDC_BTNDELETE` entry from the ID list box.

29. Double-click the `BN_CLICKED` entry in the Messages list box and accept the default function name.

30. After clicking the Edit button to exit the Class Wizard and bringing up the function, make sure it looks like the following:

```
void CUserMaintenanceDlg::OnBtndelete()
{
  int iIndex;
  CUser* pUser = NULL;
  if (GetSelectedUser(&iIndex, &pUser))
  {
    ASSERT(pUser);
    if (pUser)
    {
      UpdateData();
      CString strMsg;

      strMsg = "Are you sure that you want to delete
        the User ";
      strMsg += "'";
      strMsg += pUser->m_strUserName;
      strMsg += "'?";
      if (IDYES == AfxMessageBox(strMsg, MB_YESNOCANCEL))
      {
        if (DeleteUser(pUser))
        {
          if (LB_ERR == m_lbxUsers.DeleteString(iIndex))
          {
            AfxMessageBox("The User was successfully
              Deleted, but there was an error in
              removing it from the listbox.");
          }

          InitControls();

          UpdateData(FALSE);
        }
        else
        {
          AfxMessageBox("DeleteUser failed");
        }
      }
    }
  }
else
{
  // should never get here because of
  // enabling/disabling button on lbx selection
  AfxMessageBox("You must first select a User
    ID to Delete");
}
```

31. Add the following helper function at the end of `UserMaintenanceDlg.cpp` to delete the record:

```
BOOL CUserMaintenanceDlg::DeleteUser(CUser* pUser)
{
  BOOL bSuccess = FALSE;
  CDatabase db;

TRY
{
  if (db.Open("Programming W98 - Chapter 19"))
  {
```

This process is another example of using a `CDatabase` object by itself; it's more efficient to use the `CDatabase::ExecuteSQL()` function to get the current User (instead of filtering the recordset) and then call the `CRecordset::Delete()` function to remove the record. Compare this process with the code that follows:

```
    CString strSQL = CString("DELETE FROM UserMaster
      WHERE ");
    strSQL += CString("sUserID = '") +
      pUser->m_strUserID + CString("'");

    db.ExecuteSQL(strSQL);

    bSuccess = TRUE;
  }
}
CATCH(CDBException, p)
{
  AfxMessageBox(p->m_strError);

  if (db.IsOpen())
  {
    db.Close();
  }
}
END_CATCH

return bSuccess;
}
```

Building the User Maintenance application

To see your new application at work, simply press the F7 button to build the application and then run it by pressing Ctrl+F5. After you build and run the application, the results should be similar to what you see in Figure 20-6.

Using a CDatabase Object by Itself

Here is an example of using a CDatabase object by itself (instead of using a CRecordset object). In cases like this, where you know you're going to issue an SQL statement (such as the following SQL UPDATE) against a data source and you don't already have a current record, it's more efficient to use the CDatabase::ExecuteSQL() function. The SQL statement is built and passed to the ExecuteSQL() function for processing.

```
        CString strSQL = CString("UPDATE UserMaster SET ");
        strSQL += CString("sUserName = '") +
          pUser->m_strUserName + CString("', ");

        strSQL += CString("iStatus = ");
        char szStatus[10];
        itoa(pUser->m_iStatus, szStatus, 10);
        strSQL += szStatus;

        strSQL += CString(" WHERE sUserID = ");
        strSQL += CString("'") + pUser->m_strUserID +
          CString("'");

        db.ExecuteSQL(strSQL);

        bSuccess = TRUE;
      }
    }
    CATCH(CDBException, p)
    {
      AfxMessageBox(p->m_strError);

      if (db.IsOpen())
      {
        db.Close();
      }
    }
    END_CATCH

    return bSuccess;
  }
```

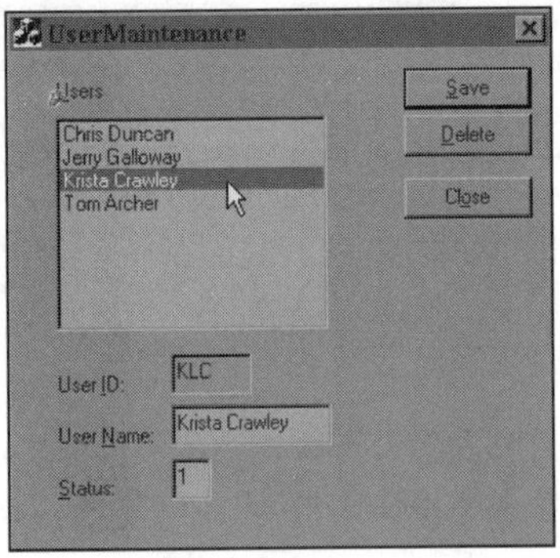

Figure 20-6: The User Maintenance application that demonstrates the MFC databases at work

Parameterized Recordsets and Queries

The following application is split into two sections ("Creating and Using Parameterized Recordsets" and "Creating Parameterized Queries"). This will give you the opportunity to learn two very important ways in which to use the `CRecordset` class. Like the first MFC Database Classes demo, this one displays a dialog to retrieve information about Users from the User Master table — with two important differences:

✦ In the first demo, all Users were read from the database and inserted into a list box from which a user could select one. This time, however, the application will enable the user to search for a specific User by typing the User name into a provided Edit control on the dialog. When the user clicks the "Find" button, a *parameterized recordset* queries the table to see whether the User exists.

✦ If the specified User is successfully found in the database, a *parameterized query* reads data from a join of multiple tables.

Is this the way I would normally program this in a "real-world" application? Probably not — but this example serves to illustrate the use of parameterized recordsets and parameterized queries.

If you simply want to copy this demo from the companion CD-ROM and follow along, it can be found in the \Chap20\Parameterized directory. As with the other demos in this chapter that use ODBC, you must create an ODBC DSN based on the database provided with the CD-ROM. If you have not already created the DSN, please follow the instructions in the section entitled "Creating the Demo ODBC DSN" (which can be found in the ODBC SDK demo called "Writing a Simple ODBC Application to Fetch Data").

Creating and using parameterized recordsets

Now you'll learn how to create and use a parameterized recordset. This application will enable the user to retrieve information about specific users. The difference between this demo and the User Maintenance demo is that this time you'll only retrieve the requested User, without having to retrieve all Users and present them in a list box. To retrieve a specific User, you'll use a parameterized recordset to "filter" which Users are read from the User Master table. To summarize this process, creating parameterized recordsets is as easy as doing the following. When you actually type the code in, or follow along in the book, you'll see each of these steps described in more detail:

- Create a `CRecordset`-derived class using Class Wizard
- Declare a parameter variable(s) in the recordset's header file
- Initialize the parameter variable(s) in the recordset's constructor
- Set the recordset's `m_nParams` member variable to the number of parameters you're going to use
- Update the recordset's `DoFieldExchange`
- Set the recordset's `m_strFilter` variable before calling its `Open()` function
- Assign a value to the recordset's parameter variable(s)
- Call the recordset's `Open()` function

Creating the Visual C++ 6.0 project

Begin by creating a new project using the Microsoft Developer Studio, as follows:

1. From the File menu, select the New command.
2. In the New dialog box, select the Projects tab and select MFC App Wizard (exe) from the list box.
3. Type the project name (**Parameterized**) and select the location, or folder, where you want to create the demo. Make sure the "Create new workspace" option button is selected; when it is, click the OK button or press Enter to start the process of creating your new project.
4. In the first dialog box of the MFC App Wizard, specify that you want a Dialog-based application and then click the Finish button (or press Enter) to continue.
5. Click the OK button or press Enter in the New Project Information dialog box.

Adding database support to the application

1. Open the `stdafx.h` source code file and find the following line:

```
// Microsoft Developer Studio will insert additional
   declarations immediately before the previous line.
```

2. Add the following `#include` directive, which is needed for the database-class declarations:

```
#include "afxdb.h"
```

Adding controls to the dialog

For this application, you'll need to add a number of controls to the dialog to display the data requested by the user.

1. On the left side of the Developer Studio, you should see the Project window. Double-click the Resource tab at the bottom and double-click the "Parameterized resources" entry. A list of resource entries appears, in outline format, just below Parameterized Resources. Double-click the Dialog entry.
2. At this point, you'll see two dialog boxes created for you by App Wizard. When you've located the `IDD_PARAMETERIZED_DIALOG` entry, select it by double-clicking it. The dialog box opens in edit mode so you can make the necessary changes for this demo.
3. Begin the changes by removing the "TODO" static text control, and then insert the controls shown in Figure 20-7. Most Developer Studio toolbars have been hidden so more of the dialog box can be seen. Note that the control under the Permissions static text is a "tree control."

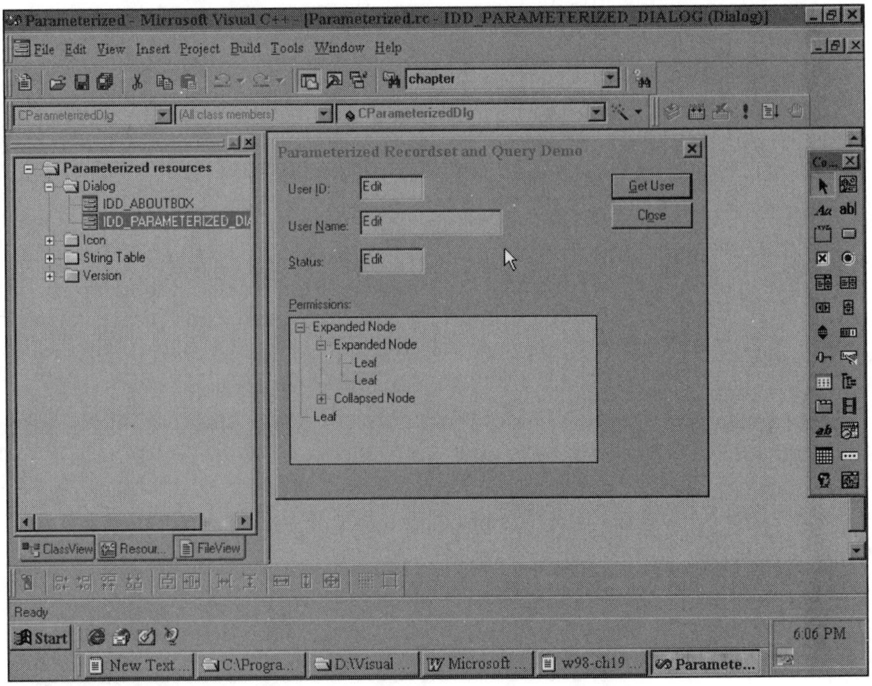

Figure 20-7: The dialog box for a Parameterized CRecordset and Query demo (after the new controls have been added)

4. You should now have four input controls (three Edit fields for the User ID, User Name, and Status, and a Tree Control for the permissions). Click the Tree Control, hold down the Alt key, and press Enter. On the General tab, give this control an ID of `IDC_PERMISSIONS`. On the Styles tab, specify the "Has buttons," "Has lines," and "Lines at Root" options.

5. Using the same key sequence, rename the remaining controls as follows:

   User ID Edit field = `IDC_USERID`

   User Name Edit field = `IDC_USERNAME`

   Status Edit field = `IDC_STATUS`

6. Make the `UserName` and `Status` fields read-only by selecting that option from the Style tab.

7. Create the member variables to be used with DDX (dynamic data exchange) for the different controls. Do so by holding down Ctrl and double-clicking each on-screen control button.

8. When you see the Add Member Variable dialog box, use it to specify Member-variable name, Category, and Variable Type. Do so for the following controls, filling in the appropriate information:

Control	***Variable(s) to Fill In***
User ID Edit	`m_strUserID, Value, CString`
User Name Edit	`m_strUserName, Value, CString`
Status Edit	`m_iStatus, Value, int`
Permissions Tree Control	`m_treePermissions, Control, CTreeControl`

Creating a CRecordset class for the UserMaster table

You now need a recordset class to access the data in the UserMaster table. Call this class `CUserMasterSet`. If you don't remember how to create a `CRecordset`-derived class, follow the directions in the section entitled "CRecordset" (presented earlier in the chapter).

Modifying the CRecordset class to accept parameters

After you've created the `CRecordset`-derived class, you'll need to modify it so that it can accept parameters.

1. Open the UserMasterSet.h file and find the following comment:

```
//}}AFX_FIELD comment.
```

2. Now add the following variable declaration:

```
CString m_sUserIDParam;
```

This variable serves as the "parameter" to the recordset, holding the value used to search the UserMaster table and return corresponding records into the CUserMasterSet recordset.

3. When you create parameter variables for a recordset, it's standard practice to simply copy the member variable that corresponds to the column in the table you plan to use, using that copied variable as the key to the table. Then you append "Param" to the end of the variable name, as follows:

4. Open the UserMasterSet.cpp file and locate the `CUserMasterSet::CUserMasterSet` constructor. At the end of the function, you should see a line similar to the following:

```
//}}AFX_FIELD_INIT
```

5. Add the following initialization lines. The first line initializes your parameter variable. This specifies how many parameters you have in this recordset.

```
m_sUserIDParam = _T("");
m_nParams = 1;
```

Caution

Don't leave out the `m_nParams = 1;` *line.* If you do, you'll receive an Assert when you call the `CRecordset::Open()` function. I've seen many a programmer code everything else perfectly and forget this one very important line.

6. Now locate the `CUserMasterSet::DoFieldExchange()` function and add the following lines immediately before the end of the function:

```
pFX->SetFieldType(CFieldExchange::param);
RFX_Text(pFX, _T("[sUserID]"), m_sUserIDParam);
```

These two lines associate the parameter variable with the correct column in the `UserMaster` table. Take special note that the column name is the `sUserID` column. In the case of a parameterized recordset, you'll generally have two variables pointing to the same column for each parameter defined for that recordset. One of these variables (`m_sUserID` in this demo) sends and receives data to and from the column in your table; the other (`m_sUserIDParam` in this demo) serves as the key to search on.

Adding search capability to the application

Now it's time to add the functionality that enables the user to search the UserMaster table for specific users.

1. Open the `ParameterizedDlg.cpp` file.

2. At the top of the file you'll see the following `#include` directives:

```
#include "ParameterizedDlg.h"
#include "UserMasterSet.h"
```

3. Add a function so that when a user presses the Enter key or clicks the button labeled "Get User," the proper information is displayed in the dialog box. Begin by pressing Ctrl+W to bring up the Class Wizard. Make sure the selected class name is `CParameterizedDlg`.

4. In the Object IDs list box, select the Get Users button ID (`IDOK`). Double-click the `BN_CLICKED` entry in the Messages list box on the right.

5. When you're prompted with the Add Member Function dialog box, press Enter to accept the default function name.

6. Click the Edit button on the right side of the MFC Class Wizard dialog box to edit your new function. Make sure the function looks like the following:

```
void CParameterizedDlg::OnOK()
{
```

7. Declare and initialize the recordset pointer:

```
CUserMasterSet* pUserMasterSet = NULL;

TRY
{
  pUserMasterSet = new CUserMasterSet();
}
  CATCH(CMemoryException, pe)
{
  TRACE("CParameterizedDlg::OnOk - Memory
    Exception creating recordset\n");
  pUserMasterSet = NULL;
}
END_CATCH

if (pUserMasterSet)
{
  UpdateData(TRUE);

  TRY
  {
```

8. Set the `CRecordset::m_strFilter` member variable to the value that you want to search for. Set this variable the same way you would specify an SQL `WHERE` clause, using a "placeholder" for the data. MFC substitutes your variable's value for the question mark before it makes the call to ODBC to fetch the data into the recordset.

9. Because you've called `UpdateData()`, the dialog's member variables now contain the values that were typed into the dialog box. Set the recordset's parameter variable to the User ID that was entered.

10. After you've set the filter and parameter value(s), call the `CRecordSet::Open()` function to retrieve the data and move to the first row. The code looks like this:

```
pUserMasterSet->m_strFilter = "sUserID = ?";
pUserMasterSet->m_sUserIDParam = m_strUserID;
if (pUserMasterSet->Open())
{
```

11. Check to see whether you've reached end-of-file. If not, you know that ODBC returned at least one row of data. Don't forget that since `CRecordset::Open()` automatically "moves" you to the first record, you don't have to call `CRecordset::MoveFirst()`. Here's all it takes:

```
  if (!pUserMasterSet->IsEOF())
  {
```

12. Copy the recordset's data to the member variables that are mapped to the controls of the dialog box, and then call `UpdateData(FALSE)` to update the dialog box:

```
    m_strUserName = pUserMasterSet->m_sUserName;
    m_iStatus = pUserMasterSet->m_iStatus;

    UpdateData(FALSE);
  }
  else
  {
```

13. If the requested User ID does not exist, tell the user about it so he/she can enter another User ID and retry:

```
    CString str = m_strUserID + CString(" was not
      found");
    AfxMessageBox(str);
  }
```

14. Close the recordset:

```
  pUserMasterSet->Close();
}
```

15. Delete the recordset pointer:

```
  delete pUserMasterSet;
}
```

16. The final important item to include is the `CATCH` block in case any database operation throws an exception:

```
CATCH(CDBException, pe)
{
  if (pUserMasterSet->IsOpen())
```

```
            {
              pUserMasterSet->Close();
            }
            delete pUserMasterSet;
            TRACE("CParameterizedDlg::OnOk - Database Exception
              - %s\n", pe->m_strError);
          }
          END_CATCH
        }
      }
```

If you got all the way through the code for this project, close the recordset and delete the recordset's pointer.

Building the Application

Now that the code has been entered to search the database for a specific record, simply build the application and run it. Doing so at this point should give you results similar to what you see in Figure 20-8.

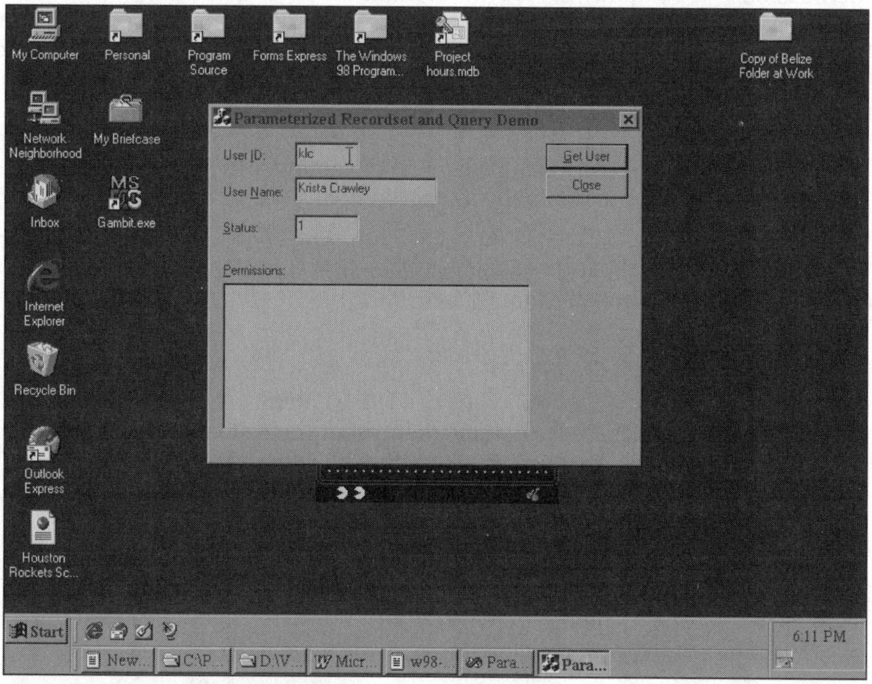

Figure 20-8: The Parameterized CRecordset and Query demo (after the Parameterized CRecordset code has been entered)

Notice that this User ID was entered in lowercase, yet the User ID in the table is shown in uppercase. Not to worry. Remember the `CODBCInfo` class presented in an earlier demo? A call to the `CODBCInfo::GetTypeInfo()` function specifying `SQL_CHAR` as the data type and "CASE_SENSITIVE" and the Column Name (data type attribute) will tell you that Microsoft Access character types are not case-sensitive.

Creating parameterized queries

In the second part of building this application, you'll create and use a `CRecordset`-derived class that uses a Microsoft Access parameterized query. You'll use the `UserMaster` table (seen throughout this chapter) as well as some new tables. In this example, pretend you're writing a large system that includes multiple subsystems. (An example would be a distribution system that supports subsystems such as Order Entry, Invoicing, Receiving, Purchasing, and so on.)

Your system might also need to support multiple companies; many large corporations are broken into smaller companies or divisions. Because every employee would probably not have access to every subsystem for every company, your system would need to support some type of security. User "Bob" might have access to Order Entry and Invoicing in Company A, but he might not have any "permissions" in Company B. A Permissions table could be used to limit access to different parts of the system. In this example, "Bob" would have two records in the Permissions table (one for each company/subsystem pair to which he has access). This scenario is the basis for the final application in this chapter; it requires three new tables (already in the demo database):

✦ **Company Master**—This table lists all the companies for the system. The only columns are for the Company ID and Company Name.

✦ **Subsystem Master**—This table lists all the subsystems for the system (for example, Order Etnry, Receiving, and so on). The only columns are for the Subsystem ID and Subsystem Name.

✦ **Permissions**—Because a User can have permissions for any number of companies/subsystems, an "intersection" table is needed to handle this *many-to-many* scenario. This table only has three columns: User ID, Company ID, and Subsystem ID. These columns represent the primary keys for their respective tables. A record exists in this table for every User/Company/Subsystem for which the User has permissions.

The demo database also includes a query (`GetPermissionsByUserID`) that is actually a join that connects all four tables. The query takes a User ID as a parameter and retrieves the Company Name and Subsystem Name for all the companies and subsystems for which this User has permissions.

Creating a CRecordset class based on a parameterized query

Basing a CRecordset-derived class on a parameterized query in Visual C++ is much easier now than it was with previous versions. The steps to follow are similar to those you would use to create any recordset, with just a couple of differences (indicated in boldface type). As with the first part of this demo, you'll see each technique in more detail when you follow these numbered steps:

1. **Create a CRecordset-derived class using Class Wizard.**
2. **Change the recordset's GetDefaultSQL member function to use the CALL syntax. Following is an example of this syntax.**

   ```
   {CALL GetPermissionsByUserID(?)}
   ```

3. **Declare a parameter variable(s) in the recordset's header file.**
4. **Initialize the parameter variable(s) in the recordset's constructor.**
5. **Set the recordset's m_nParams member variable to the number of parameters you're going to use.**
6. **Update the recordset's DoFieldExchange.**

When you use a parameterized query, you do not need to set the m_strFilter variable. Instead, assign a value to the recordset's parameter variable(s) and call the recordset's Open function in read-only mode, as in the following steps:

1. **Create a CRecordset-derived class called CPermissionsQry. (Follow the directions in the earlier section entitled "CRecordset.") Be sure to select the GetPermissionsByUserID query on the Select Database Tables dialog box.**
2. **Open the PermissionsQry.cpp file and change the GetDefaultSQL() member function to look like the following code list:**

   ```
   CString CPermissionsQry::GetDefaultSQL()
   {
     return _T("{CALL GetPermissionsByUserID(?)}");
   }
   ```

   When you use the Microsoft Desktop Drivers to access a parameterized query, you must use the CALL syntax. When you call the CRecordset::Open() function, MFC checks to see whether the string returned by the CRecordset::GetDefaultSQL() starts with {CALL. If it does not, MFC attempts to build an SQL SELECT statement. The question mark represents the parameter that will be passed. For multiple parameters, simply add a question mark for each desired parameter, adding a comma to separate it from the other parameters.

3. **Add the following two lines of code at the end of the CPermissionsQry's constructor:**

   ```
   m_sUserIDParam = _T("");
   m_nParams = 1;
   ```

4. Add the following two lines of code at the end of the `CPermissionsQry::DoFieldExchange()` function:

```
pFX->SetFieldType(CFieldExchange::param);
RFX_Text(pFX, _T("[sUserID]"), m_sUserIDParam);
```

5. Open the `PermissionsQry.h` file and declare the following member variable:

```
CString m_sUserIDParam;
```

6. Declare the following member variable in the `ParameterizedDlg.h` file:

```
protected:
 void ShowPermissions();
```

This function will be called to read all the permissions for the User. These permissions will then be displayed in the `CTreeCtrl` control.

7. Open the ParameterizedDlg.cpp file and add the following `#include` directive after the `#include` directive for the "UserMasterSet.h" file:

```
#include "PermissionsQry.h"
```

8. Open the ParameterizedDlg.cpp file and find the following line:

```
UpdateData(FALSE);
```

Add a line to show the permissions before the UpdateData function call:

```
ShowPermissions();
```

9. Add the following function at the end of the ParameterizedDlg.cpp file:

```
void CParameterizedDlg::ShowPermissions()
{
```

10. Clear out the previous permissions:

```
m_treePermissions.DeleteAllItems();

CPermissionsQry* pPermissionsQry = NULL;

TRY
{
  pPermissionsQry = new CPermissionsQry();
}
CATCH(CMemoryException, pe)
{
  TRACE("CParameterizedDlg::OnOk - Memory Exception
    creating recordset\n");
  pPermissionsQry = NULL;
}
END_CATCH

if (pPermissionsQry)
{
```

```
TRY
{
  pPermissionsQry->m_sUserIDParam = m_strUserID;
  if (pPermissionsQry->Open())
  {
    if (!pPermissionsQry->IsEOF())
    {
      TV_INSERTSTRUCT tvinsert;
      HTREEITEM hCompany = NULL;

      CString strPrevCompanyID;
```

11. Here is typical "control break" logic: The query is ordered by Company ID and Subsystem ID. For each Company it reads, the demo adds that Company Name to the `CTreeCtrl` control; then it goes into a `while` loop until the Company ID changes. As it runs in that `while` loop, the demo adds each Subsystem to the `CTreeCtrl` control below the current Company Name. This whole process continues until all the Permissions records have been read for the User. The code that makes it happen looks like this:

```
      while (!pPermissionsQry->IsEOF())
      {
        tvinsert.hParent = NULL;
        tvinsert.hInsertAfter = TVI_LAST;
        tvinsert.item.mask = TVIF_TEXT;
        tvinsert.item.hItem = NULL;
        tvinsert.item.state = 0;
        tvinsert.item.stateMask = 0;
        tvinsert.item.cchTextMax =
          pPermissionsQry->m_sCompanyName.GetLength() + 1;
        tvinsert.item.iSelectedImage = 0;
        tvinsert.item.cChildren = 0;
        tvinsert.item.lParam = 0;
        tvinsert.item.pszText =
          pPermissionsQry->m_sCompanyName.GetBuffer(
          tvinsert.item.cchTextMax);
        hCompany = m_treePermissions.InsertItem(&tvinsert);

        strPrevCompanyID = pPermissionsQry->m_sCompanyID;
        while ((!pPermissionsQry->IsEOF())
          && (strPrevCompanyID ==
          pPermissionsQry->m_sCompanyID))
        {
          if (hCompany)
          {
            tvinsert.hParent = hCompany;
            tvinsert.item.cchTextMax =
              pPermissionsQry->m_sSubsystemName.GetLength()
              + 1;
            tvinsert.item.pszText =
              pPermissionsQry->m_sSubsystemName.GetBuffer(
              tvinsert.item.cchTextMax);
            m_treePermissions.InsertItem(&tvinsert);
```

```
                    }

                    pPermissionsQry->MoveNext();
                  }
                }
              }
              else
              {
                CString str = m_strUserID + CString(" was
                  not found");
                AfxMessageBox(str);
              }

              pPermissionsQry->Close();
            }
            delete pPermissionsQry;
          }
          CATCH(CDBException, pe)
          {
           if (pPermissionsQry->IsOpen())
            {
              pPermissionsQry->Close();
            }
            delete pPermissionsQry;
            TRACE("CParameterizedDlg::OnOk - Database Exception
              - %s\n", pe->m_strError);
          }
          END_CATCH
        }
      }
```

12. Build the application and run it. Running it should give you results similar to what you see in Figure 20-9.

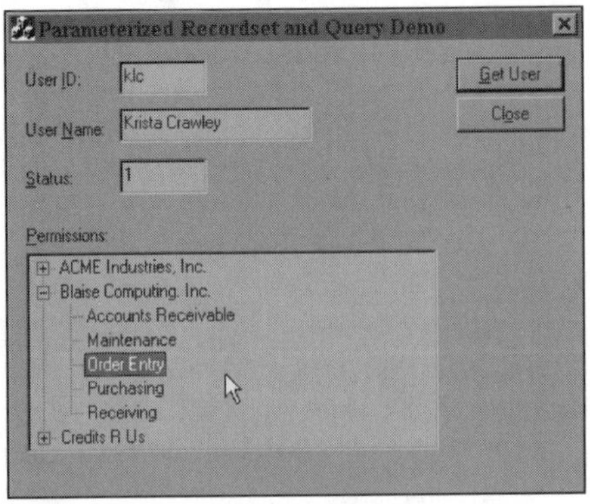

Figure 20-9: Running the final Parameterized CRecordset and Query demo

Summary

In light of what you've learned about the ODBC SDK and the MFC Database Classes — including their respective strengths and weaknesses — one important question remains: *Should MFC database classes use ODBC or the MFC Database Classes?* The following considerations, in addition to summing up what the chapter has presented, may help you answer that question:

- As you've seen, having both the ODBC SDK and the MFC Database Classes gives you, the applications developer, the best of both worlds in terms of power and flexibility versus ease of use.
- The ODBC SDK is a good choice when you're developing robust systems that need to be scalable and have to operate with different DBMS programs.
- The MFC Database Classes make your job much easier by providing a simpler, easier-to-use programmatic interface.
- Choosing either ODBC or MFC often reflects the priorities for the current project you're working on — hence it's a personal choice that only *you* can make at that point.

✦ ✦ ✦

CHAPTER 21

DAO Database Programming

✦ ✦ ✦ ✦

In This Chapter

Learning about the current version of DAO

Learning about the DAO object model

Discovering the different ways to interface to DAO

Discovering the MFC DAO classes

Creating a parameterized DAO recordset

Filtering and sorting records with the CDaoRecordset class

Writing a simple maintenance application using MFC DAO classes

✦ ✦ ✦ ✦

DAO (data access objects) is the programmatic interface to the Microsoft Access database, which is also known as the *Jet* engine. Because of this, you will often hear the terms DAO and Jet used interchangeably. This chapter covers DAO version 3.5 and how to interface to it from a Visual C++ application.

DAO was originally designed for Microsoft Access and (later Visual Basic) and Visual Basic for Applications. Accordingly, for several years, programmers who needed to use an Access database from any other language only had one option: ODBC. Although ODBC is a great tool for certain jobs, it is inappropriate for applications that only need to work with an Access database. As you learned in Chapter 19, the greatest benefit of ODBC is its ability to allow a single code base to interface to many different databases. By definition, this results in "least-common-denominator" code. If you are writing a single code base to work with multiple databases, then you will not be able to take advantage of any specific database's capabilities without writing special case code for each database. In addition, some of the functionality of the Access database simply is not supported through the Access ODBC Driver (Microsoft Desktop Drivers). However, in DAO 3.0, Microsoft addressed this issue by exposing the full functionality of the Jet engine through *Automation* (formerly called *OLE Automation*).

In version 3.0, DAO was released in the form of an Automation in-process server (DLL) that contains an embedded type library. As with any Automation type library, a client application can query the Automation server for descriptions of exposed objects via the OLE `IDispatch` interface. This ability opened up an entirely new paradigm to application development involving an Access database. Now, any language that supported Automation could have access to almost every facet of the Jet's functionality through the DAO Automation interfaces.

In this chapter, you will learn about the different objects that constitute the DAO object hierarchy. In addition, you will be exposed to the different DAO APIs that enable you to programmatically manipulate the different DAO objects from your applications. Once these APIs have been covered, the MFC DAO classes will be covered in detail.

DAO Overview

Before we jump into the different ways to program to the DAO interface, it is important to understand a little background on DAO as well as the DAO object hierarchy.

The history of DAO

DAO was introduced in Visual Basic 2.0. At that time it didn't have an official name, though many VB programmers referred to it as the "database objects." From that point, DAO has continued to evolve to its current incarnation as an Automation in-process server. Here is a brief sketch of this evolution.

Jet 1.0

This was the initial release of Jet. It was one of the first desktop databases to include features such as updatable views, query capabilities, and seamless access to heterogeneous data.

Jet 1.1

Improvements included in this release included much better connectivity between the Jet and Open Database Connectivity (ODBC) databases, and an increased database size from 128MB to approximately 1.1GB. This upgrade of DAO also added Data Definition Language (DDL) capabilities.

These benefits were available in Visual Basic 3.0, but not in Microsoft Access 1.1.

Jet 2.0

This version was introduced with Microsoft Access 2.0. It offered major enhancements over previous versions. The major areas of improvement included the following:

- ✦ Enforced referential integrity and data validation at the engine level
- ✦ Optimized query performance using Rushmore technology gained in the merger with FoxPro
- ✦ Increased conformance to ANSI-standard SQL syntax rules

- Support for `UNION`, sub-`SELECT`, and data-definition queries
- A full programming interface to Jet using DAO 2.0
- Cascading update and delete support
- Capability to send transactions (via remote transaction management) to servers that support them
- SQL pass-through queries
- New MSysConf settings controlling how often and how many data fetches are made against ODBC data sources
- Support for remote index joins
- New initialization settings for debugging and tuning data operations

As you can see, Jet 2.0 introduced so many new features that it was almost considered to be a totally new relational database.

Jet 2.5

Jet 2.5 was really delivered as an interim build between 2.0 and 3.0 to handle problems related to databases being incorrectly marked as corrupt. However, along with this major fix, version 2.5 also introduced support for the new ODBC Desktop Drivers shipped for the first time as a 32-bit product. And modifications were finally made to support Visual Basic for Applications (VBA) for use with the Desktop Database Drivers (VBA[32].DLL).

Jet 3.0

This was the version where DAO DLL moved to an Automation server containing an embedded type library.

Jet 3.0 also introduced new features and improved performance. The most important and eagerly anticipated aspect of this upgrade was its full 32-bit implementation for use in environments such as Microsoft Windows 95 and Microsoft Windows NT.

Numerous changes were made to the database format and the way the engine handles data, with the goal of making most operations substantially faster. Among these changes was the implementation of multithreading. To deal with the fact that Jet was now being used in workplace applications, Jet 3.0 introduced replication capabilities, which allow developers to create replicable databases that can be used in different locations. Microsoft Jet can synchronize these replicas and keep data current.

Jet 3.5

One major change made in Jet 3.5 is the fact that it allows users to replicate only specified portions of database tables, whereas previous versions of Jet allowed full replication of these tables.

Jet 3.5 also introduced a new Type argument for the `OpenRecorder()` method: `dbOpenForwardOnly`. This new recordset type behaves in the same way as a DAO 3.0 snapshot-type `CdbRecordset` opened with the `dbForwardOnly` option.

In addition, a new `SetOption()` method allows you to override Microsoft Jet Registry settings at runtime. This lets you fine-tune Microsoft Jet query performance, timeout delays, and so on.

The DAO hierarchy

Conceptually, DAO is the programmatic interface to the Jet engine. More specifically stated, the interface is a hierarchy of objects and collections of objects packaged in a DLL. At the top of this hierarchy is the `DBEngine` object. Every other object is, in turn, a sub-object of the `DBEngine` object. Before we take a look at some of the more important objects in more detail, take a look at Figure 21-1. This layout illustrates the DAO object hierarchy.

The DBEngine object

DAO is the top-level object in the DAO object hierarchy. Therefore, the `DBEngine` object contains and controls all the other objects in the DAO object model. Although many of the other DAO objects have an associated collection object, the `DBEngine` does not. That means there is one and only one `DBEngine` object, and it is not an element of any collection.

The `DBEngine` object contains numerous methods and properties as well as two collections: the Workspaces collection and the Errors collection. The `DBEngine` object is used to do such high-level tasks as create Workspace objects and carry out database maintenance tasks such as "compact" and "repair."

The Workspaces collection object

The Workspaces collection object is a non-ordered collection of all active Workspace objects. One way to think of a Workspace is as a session between your application and the Jet engine. The Workspaces object is used to start new sessions or manage existing sessions.

As with any DAO collection object, you can retrieve any of the contained objects either by name or ordinal number. Like C/C++ arrays, DAO collection indexes are relative to zero. This means that to retrieve the first Workspace object from the Workspaces collection by ordinal number, you would need to specify a value of 0.

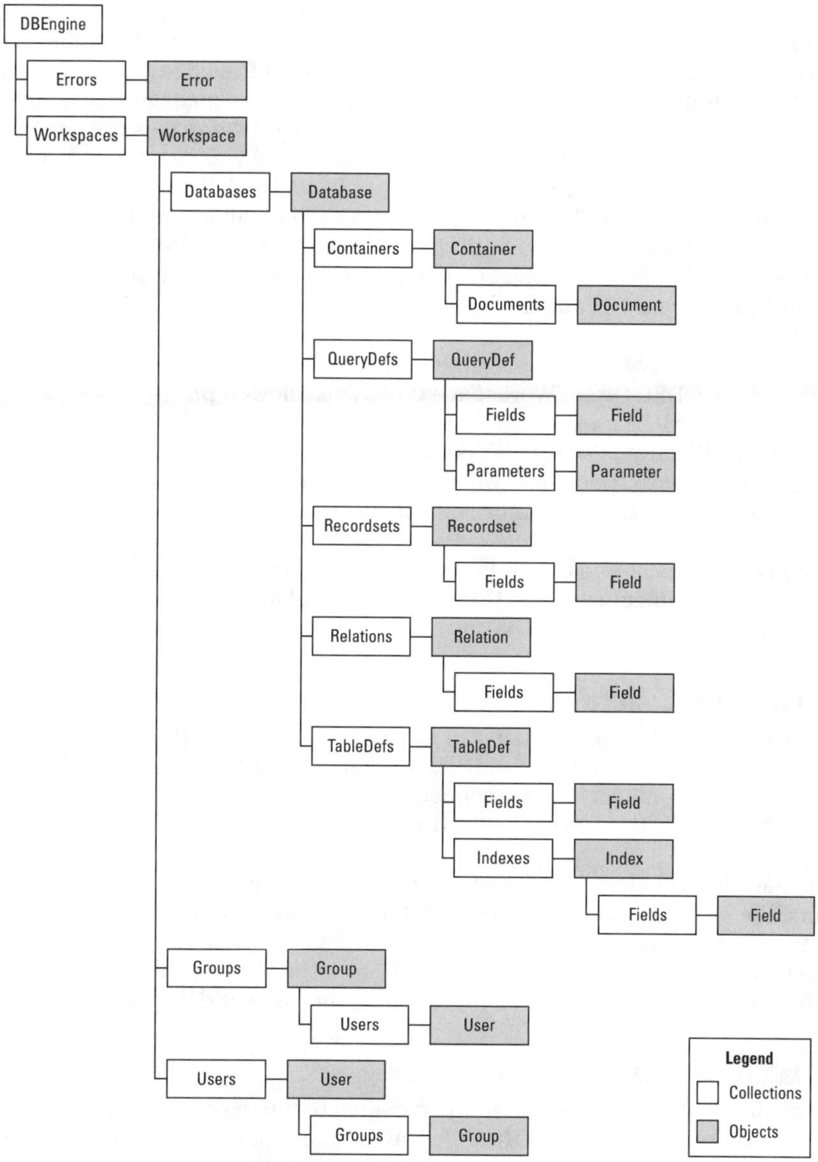

Figure 21-1: The DAO object hierarchy (Jet Workspace)

The Workspace object

A Workspace object specifies an active, named session with the Jet engine. You can use the Workspace object for managing transactions, creating and opening databases, and performing security-level functions like creating users and groups.

In general, you will not need to create this object because a default Workspace object is created for you. However, if you do need to create a unique, named Workspace object, the `CreateWorkspace()` method of the `DBEngine` object can be used. For example, when using the Workspace methods to manage transactions (`BeginTrans()`, `CommitTrans()`, and `Rollback()`), *all* databases open within the specified `Workspace` are affected. For instance, let's say you've opened two databases using the `Workspace OpenDatabase()` method. If you call the `BeginTrans()` method followed by changes to each database, and then call the Rollback method, all changes to both databases will be lost. You would need to create additional `Workspace` objects if you want to manage transactions independently across `Database` objects.

There are two types of `Workspace` objects: Jet and ODBCDirect. In Jet 3.5, Microsoft introduced the ODBC Direct Workspace type. This allowed programmers using DAO to also access ODBC data sources without going through the Jet engine. Figure 21-1, shown earlier, illustrates the Jet Workspace. Because this chapter concentrates solely on the Jet Workspace, you will need to refer to the *Microsoft Jet Database Engine Programmer's Guide* for more information on using ODBCDirect.

Although each `Workspace` object is contained within the `Workspaces` collection, each `Workspace` object contains three collections of its own: `Databases`, `Users`, and `Groups`.

The Databases collection

The `Databases` collection contains all the open `Database` objects created or opened in its parent `Workspace` object. When a database is created or changed via `theWorkspace` object, the associated `Database` object is appended to that `Workspace` object's `Databases` collection.

Other than simply being a container for all of a `Workspace` object's open `Database` objects, the `Databases` collection doesn't provide much in terms of functionality. About the only `Database Collection` properties and methods you might find yourself needing are the `Count()` method to retrieve the total number of open `Databases` and the `Refresh` method to reflect the current database schema.

The Database object

The `Database` object references an open connection to a database. A physical database can only be managed through DAO via an associated `Database` object. Once you have created the `Database` object, you can then manipulate the database through the various `Database` object's properties and methods.

The `Database` object contains several collections that directly correlate to the database schema of the associated database file. For example, the `QueryDefs`, `TableDefs`, `Relations`, and `Containers` collections are all defined within the `Database` object.

It's important to realize that creating a `Database` object doesn't automatically establish a link with associated database's tables or queries. To do this, you must use the `TableDefs` collection or the `Recordsets` collection.

A database's schema can be changed through the Database object via its CreateQueryDef, `CreateTableDef()`, `CreateRelation()`, and `CreateProperty()` methods. In addition, the `MakeReplica()`, `Synchronize()`, and `PopulatePartial()` methods can be used to create and synchronize full or partial replicas of the database file associated with the Database objects.

The Recordsets collection

The `Recordsets` collection contains all the open `Recordset` objects for a given `Database` object. The `Recordset` object is most often how you will deal with data using DAO. Much like the `Databases` collection, the `Recordsets` collection doesn't provide much functionality beyond the `Count` property and `Refresh()` method provided by all DAO collection objects.

The Recordset object

The `Recordset` object represents the data returned from executing a query. The major difference between the `Recordset` object and most of the other DAO objects is that it is not persistent. Although other DAO objects such as the `Database`, `TableDef`, and `QueryDef` objects relate to a part of a physical database, the `Recordset` object represents only the set of records produced by running a query against one or more tables or queries.

There are five types of supported DAO `Recordsets`, as follows:

- **Table**—Represents an Access table that you can manipulate by adding, changing, and deleting records.
- **Dynaset**—A dynamic set of records that can also be manipulated by adding, changing, and deleting records.
- **Snapshot**—A static set of records. This type of recordset is not updateable.
- **Forward-Only**— Identical to the `Snapshot` recordset type except you can only proceed forward through the recordset. This newly defined recordset is ideal for a situation where you only need to traverse a recordset once.
- **Dynamic**—Similar to a Dynaset recordset, with one very important difference. After you run the query that results in a recordset of this type, if another user adds or deletes records that would have been included in this recordset, the changes will be reflected in this recordset automatically.

The `Recordset` type is specified when the `OpenRecordset` method is called. The default `Recordset` type is a table-type recordset.

Because the `Recordset` object represents a set of records produced as a result of a query, the `Recordset` object also exposes methods to navigate this set of records. These methods include `MoveFirst()`, `MoveNext()`, `MovePrevious()`, and `MoveLast()`. Creating and updating records is done via the `AddNew()`, `Edit()`, and `Update()` methods. The `Move()` and `Seek()` methods provide additional means of traversing the records.

The many (inter)faces of DAO

Although the ability to communicate with the Jet engine through an industry standard mechanism like Automation was a much-heralded breakthrough, programming with DAO through Automation is generally thought to be a somewhat tedious task. In answer to these complaints, Microsoft released a DAO SDK that included header files to make using the DAO Automation interface easier, as well as two additional mechanisms for interfacing to the Jet engine: the dbDAO C++ classes (also included in the DAO SDK) and the MFC DAO classes.

DAO Automation interfaces

Because DAO provides a standard vtable-based implementation of Automation, the DAO SDK was released to provide C++ header files that define the DAO vtable interfaces. This, in turn, eliminated the need to use the `IDispatch` interface. With the DAO SDK, once an application creates an instance of the `DBEngine` object, instances of objects can be created through their parent objects using the DAO hierarchy previously shown in Figure 21-1. Otherwise, these objects are standard COM objects and as such, need to be explicitly released when the application has finished using them. If you are familiar with COM or Automation programming, this interface may be perfect for your application. However, if you are programming in C++ and would rather use a more C++ friendly method of interfacing to the Jet engine, there are two other methods that may be more appealing to you.

Note

If you still want to try your hand at using the Automation programming method, refer to the *OLE Automation Programmer's Reference* published by Microsoft Press.

✦ ✦ ✦ ✦ ✦

dbDAO C++ classes

The dbDAO C++ classes (included as a part of the DAO SDK) were the first alternatives to directly using the DAO Automation interface. These classes not only provided C++ programmers with the convenience of encapsulating the DAO in C++ classes, but they also provided a Visual Basic-like syntax to database programming. The decision to make the dbDAO functions have a Visual Basic-like syntax was made for two reasons. First, most programmers familiar with Access databases had at least started using the Access database with Visual Basic. And second, because the ratio of Visual Basic programmers to Visual C++ programmers at the time was estimated at about five to one, it only made sense to cater to the majority. Therefore, with dbDAO, Microsoft killed two birds with one stone.

Another major advantage of dbDAO over the native DAO Automation interface is that with dbDAO, only a limited amount of COM and Automation knowledge is necessary to effectively use the classes. This is because the dbDAO classes abstract the developer from many of the underlying details of dealing directly with the DAO Automation interface. For example, dbDAO automatically handles reference counting (using the AddRef and Release methods), dynamic allocation and de-allocation of objects, and many lower-level Automation details that the programmer would normally have to deal with.

In short, the dbDAO classes afford the database developer the same benefits as the DAO Automation interface, with the lowest possible overhead short of programming directly to the DAO Automation interfaces.

Note

Because this chapter concentrates on the MFC DAO classes, you might want to check out the *Microsoft Jet Database Engine Programmer's Guide*, published by Microsoft Press, if you want to learn how to use the dbDAO classes from a Visual C++ application.

◆ ◆ ◆ ◆ ◆

MFC DAO classes

Not to be outdone, the developers of MFC released their own DAO interface with Visual C++ 4.0. The MFC DAO classes are based on the MFC Database classes you learned about in Chapter 20. The advantage to MFC database programmers is that they could easily leverage existing knowledge and experience. In addition, the MFC DAO classes are fully integrated with the MFC wizards and the MFC class hierarchy.

Note

Even though the syntax of the MFC DAO classes is very distinct from the dbDAO classes, both class hierarchies simply wrap the DAO Automation interface. Hence, if something can't be done using the DAO Automation interface, it's a good bet it can't be done at all with either dbDAO or MFC.

◆ ◆ ◆ ◆ ◆

Using the MFC DAO Classes

Eight classes make up the MFC DAO classes: `CDaoDatabase`, `CDaoWorkspace`, `CDaoRecordset`, `CDaoTableDef`, `CDaoQueryDef`, `CDaoException`, `CDaoRecordView`, and `CDaoFieldExchange`. With the exception of the MFC Doc/View-specific `CDaoRecordView` and `CDaoFieldExchange` classes, each of these classes relates to a DAO object.

In addition, the MFC DAO classes are designed from a user standpoint in a very similar manner to the MFC Database classes. Besides the fact that the MFC Database classes use the ODBC SDK internally to carry out their work (as opposed to DAO Automation), the major difference between the two sets of classes is that the MFC DAO classes are much more robust in terms of functionality. For example, the MFC DAO classes can access ODBC data sources via their own database. In addition, Data Definition Language (DDL) operations are directly supported by the MFC DAO classes.

As noted, the MFC DAO classes only number eight, compared to almost 30 objects defined in the DAO object model (Jet Workspace). This disparity in the number of classes is due to several factors:

- The MFC DAO classes are a "flattened out" representation of the DAO object model. In the DAO object model, if an object can contain a collection of another type of object, separate objects represent both the collection and the contained object type. For example, because a Database object can contain multiple `TableDef` objects, a `TableDefs` collection object and a TableDef object are defined in the DAO object model. However, in the case of the `Database/TableDef` example, the MFC DAO classes define a member variable of type `CMapPtrToPtr` within the `CDaoDatabase` class to hold all the `CDaoTableDef` objects, thereby eliminating the need to have a separate class for each collection object.
- The MFC DAO classes do not support all the functionality available via DAO Automation. For example, the MFC DAO classes do not support any of the Jet security operations. To manage security for an Access database using DAO from a Visual C++ application, you will need to use either the dbDAO classes or the DAO Automation interfaces. This means the DAO Users and Groups objects have no corollary classes in MFC.

In this chapter, we will concentrate on the `CDaoDatabase`, `CDaoWorkspace`, `CDaoRecordset`, and `CDaoException` classes. The `CDaoRecordView` class is not included in this chapter because it is a very simple class, adequately covered in the online help and MFC tutorials.

CDaoDatabase

This class represents a connection to a database. After constructing the `CDaoDatabase` object, the database is specified as the first argument to the `CDaoDatabase::Open()` member function. The `CDaoDatabase` class can be used in conjunction with one or more `CDaoRecordset` objects (which I'll explain shortly) or it can be used by itself. An example of when you would want to use the `CDaoDatabase` class by itself is if you need to issue an SQL statement against a database that does not return any data. The `CDaoDatabase::Execute` function exists for just this purpose. Below is an example of how easy it is to insert a record into a table using the `CDaoDatabase` class. The table used here is a very simple test Access database that can be found on the accompanying CD in the \Chap21\DaoUserMaintenance folder.

```
try
 {
  CDaoDatabase db;
  db.Open("DaoDemo.mdb");

  db.Execute("INSERT INTO UserMaster "
    "VALUES('TST', 'Test User Name', 0)");

  db.Close();
 }
 catch(CDaoException* pe)
 {
  AfxMessageBox(pe->m_pErrorInfo->m_strDescription,
   MB_ICONEXCLAMATION );
  pe->Delete();
 }
```

Expert Tip

When you use the AppWizard to create an application, one of the options you are given is whether or not you will want DAO support. If you elect to use this support, the appropriate header files are included in your project. However, if you need to add DAO support to an existing project, you simply include the DAO header file (afxdao.h) to the appropriate files in your project.

✦ ✦ ✦ ✦ ✦

Let's take a minute and look at the previous code in more detail. The first thing you see in the code snippet is a C++ try/catch block:

```
try
{
  ...
}
CATCH(CDaoException* pe)
{
 AfxMessageBox(pe->m_pErrorInfo->m_strDescription,
  MB_ICONEXCLAMATION );
 pe->Delete();
}
```

When using the MFC DAO classes, all DAO errors are expressed as exceptions of type `CDaoException`. Because the DAO object model supports the existence of an Errors collection, the `CDaoException` class defines member functions to retrieve any information from any DAO error objects stored in the database engine's `Errors` collection. When a DAO error occurs, one or more `Error` objects are added to the database engine's Errors collection. However, if a DAO operation results in one or more of the `Error` objects being created and added to the `Errors` collection, the previous `Error` objects are discarded first. If a DAO operation does not produce an error of any kind, then the Errors collection retains its previous content. Here are a couple of the more important member functions and variables you use when dealing with the `CDaoException` class:

✦ m_nAfxDaoError—This member variable is set when a DAO component error has occurred, such as the Jet engine not being able to be initialized.

✦ m_pErrorInfo—This is a pointer to a CDaoErrorInfo structure that includes, among other things, a member variable containing the textual representation of the error.

✦ GetErrorCount—This member function returns the number of Error objects in the database engine's Errors collection.

Because all the MFC DAO class's member functions can throw exceptions of type CDaoException, it is wise to wrap all your DAO database code in try/catch blocks, even if you don't expect the function to fail.

The first thing the previous example is attempting to do in the try block is construct a CDaoDatabase object and open it. Obviously, I've hard-coded the name and location of the database file to save space:

```
CDaoDatabase db;
db.Open("DaoDemo.mdb"))
...
```

The CDaoDatabase constructor doesn't do anything special. You must call the CDaoDatabase::Open member function to actually connect to a database, as follows:

```
virtual void Open(LPCTSTR lpszName,
 BOOL bExclusive = FALSE, BOOL bReadOnly = FALSE,
 LPCTSTR lpszConnect = _T("") );
  throw( CDaoException, CMemoryException );
```

As you can see in this prototype, there are several options you can set when opening a database using the CDaoDatabase::Open() function. However, only the first parameter is explicitly required for this function, and it was the only one passed in the example. It simply represents the fully qualified name of the database being opened.

The remaining parameters serve the following purposes:

✦ The bExclusive flag is used to specify if you want to open the database for exclusive access. If the specified file is already opened and this flag is set to TRUE, an exception of type CDaoException will be thrown by the Open() function.

✦ The bReadOnly flag allows you to specify whether or not updates to the data source will be allowed. The default value is FALSE. Any recordsets created and attached to this CDaoDatabase object will inherit this flag.

✦ The lpszConnect argument allows you to specify the ODBC connect string. However, if you are using an Access database (the subject of this chapter), this argument must be an empty string.

After opening the CDaoDatabase object, the next lines execute the SQL statement and close the database:

```
db.Execute("INSERT INTO UserMaster "
 "VALUES('TST', 'Test User Name', 0)");

db.Close();
```

As you can see, CDaoDatabase::Execute() has a very straightforward syntax. You simply pass it the string that represents the SQL statement you wish to execute or the name of an action query you want to run. Note that this function is only used when you are not expecting data to be returned. In fact, calling an action query that returns a value will result in an exception being thrown by the Execute() function.

A second argument can also be specified in the Execute() function call that specifies options relating to the integrity of the query. For example, you can use this argument to stipulate things such as the database performing a rollback on any updates if an error occurs.

CDaoWorkspace

The CDaoWorkspace class is used to manage a named database session. As mentioned previously in the section describing the DAO objects, you will not normally need multiple Workspaces. In fact, you will very rarely need to create explicit Workspace objects. This is because when you open a database and its associated Recordset objects, the DAO default Workspace is used. The ability, however, does exist to create additional Workspaces for performing such tasks as logically grouping transactions. Remember that the transaction operations (such as BeginTrans(), Commit(), and the like) are performed on the Workspace-level. This means that to manage transactions independently across CDaoDatabase objects, you need to explicitly create additional CDaoWorkspace objects.

The CDaoWorkspace object therefore provides access to the default Workspace created when the database engine is initialized. In addition, when a Workspace is opened or created (or one of its static member functions is called), the DAO database engine is initialized, which then creates the default workspace for that instance of the database engine.

As noted, another useful set of member functions that the CDaoWorkspace class supports are the functions for supporting transactions. Transactions give the application the ability to bracket a set of functions in a logical group so if any one of those functions fail, no changes are made. For those of you not familiar with transactions, an example might be in order here. Let's say you're writing an accounting application and you wish to move an amount from one account to another. What would happen if after removing the amount from one account, the attempt to update the second account's balance failed? You would end up with incorrect data. That is where transactions come in. Now you can specify that either or both of these functions must complete successfully — or neither of them should.

Here's the way it works. You set a "transaction boundary" by calling `CDaoWorkspace::BeginTrans()`. Anything done after this point is subject to being rolled back, or undone. Once you call `CDaoWorkspace::CommitTrans()`, you are committing (making permanent) all the changes you've made to the database since the last transaction boundary. If for some reason, you wish to back out of the changes since the last transaction boundary, simply call the `CDaoWorkspace::Rollback()` function. Please note that before attempting to call the `CommitTrans()` function, you must first call the `BeginTrans()` function.

In addition to the functions that support transactions, the `CDaoWorkspace` class also defines functions such as `CompactDatabase()` and `RepairDatabase()` to manage the maintenance of an Access database.

CDaoRecordset

Although a `CDaoDatabase` object represents a connection to a database, a `CDaoRecordset` object represents a set of records from one of those connections. As you may recall from earlier in the chapter, the DAO `Recordset` object supports five different types of recordsets. The `CDaoRecordset`, however, only supports three of those: table-type, dynaset, and snapshot. A table-type object represents a single base table whose data you can change. A dynaset object is the outcome of a query whose results you can update. And a snapshot object is a static picture of the data taken at the time the recordset was filled. This data can not be updated.

The simplest way to get started using recordsets is to create one using ClassWizard. The recordset we create will use the UserMaster table of the DaoDemo.mdb file introduced earlier in the chapter. If you are following along, this file can be located on the accompanying CD in the \Chap21\DaoUserMaintenance folder. Actually, this file is a replica of the file used in Chapter 19's example code. Therefore, the following examples and demos will, for the most part, be identical to those in Chapter 19. This is done so that if you are reading both the ODBC and the DAO chapters, you will be able to decide for yourself which of these two technologies is best suited for your application. Figure 21-2 shows the UserMaster table in Microsoft Access 97 on which the recordset will be based.

To use ClassWizard, you will need to have an active project open in DevStudio. Therefore, create a "dummy" project at this point. You can name this project anything you like. Once you have created the project, invoke Class Wizard and click the Add Class button. From the menu that appears, select the New submenu option. Figure 21-3 shows the resulting New Class dialog box and the values you should enter.

When you specify that you want to create a `CDaoRecordset`-derived class, Class Wizard prompts you to specify the type of database access used with your recordset class. Figure 21-4 shows this dialog with the demo database selected.

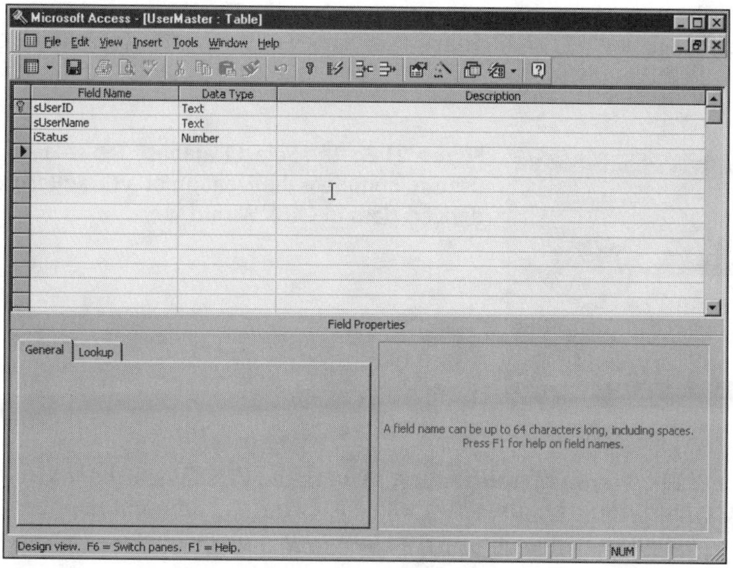

Figure 21-2: The UserMaster table definition in Microsoft Access 97

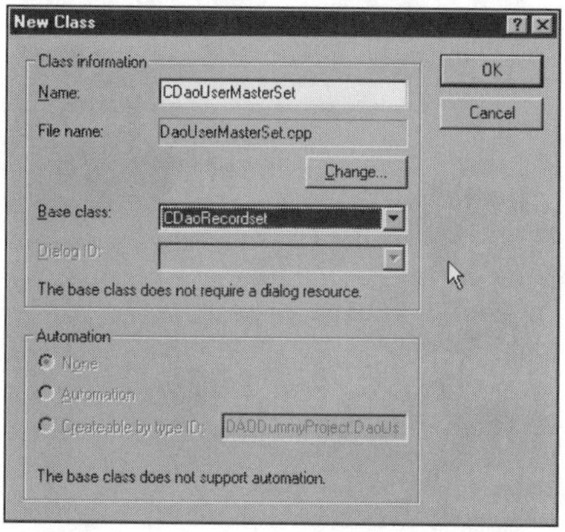

Figure 21-3: The New Class dialog box initiated from Class Wizard for the CUserMasterSet class

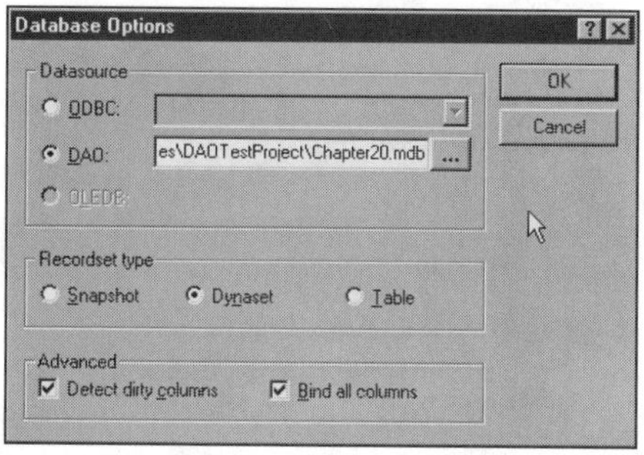

Figure 21-4: The Database Options dialog box for a new CDaoRecordset-derived class

After selecting the Access database file, simply select the UserMaster table (as shown in Figure 21-5) and click OK. That's how easy it is to create a CDaoRecordset-derived class!

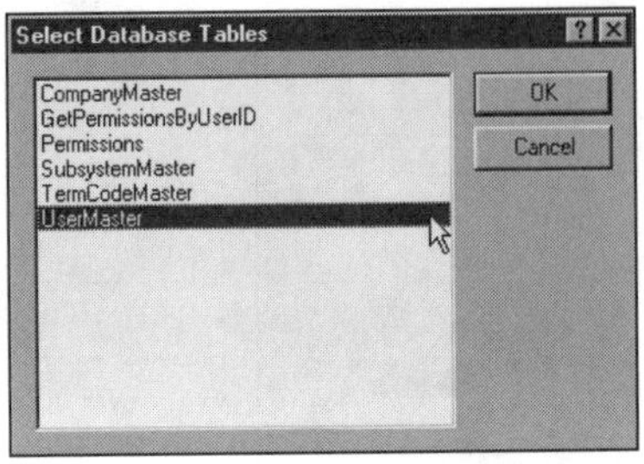

Figure 21-5: The Select Database Tables dialog box used to complete the creation of a CDaoRecordset-derived class in Class Wizard

Listings 21-1 and 21-2 show you the amount of work the Class Wizard does for you. Throughout this part of the chapter, you will learn what the different member variables and member functions are for and how to use them.

Listing 21-1: DaoUserMasterSet.h

```
#if !defined _DAO_USER_MASTER_SET_H_
#define _DAO_USER_MASTER_SET_H_


#if _MSC_VER > 1000
#pragma once
#endif // _MSC_VER > 1000
// DaoUserMasterSet.h : header file
//

/////////////////////////////////////////////////////////////////////////////
// CDaoUserMasterSet DAO recordset

class CDaoUserMasterSet : public CDaoRecordset
{
public:
 CDaoUserMasterSet(CDaoDatabase* pDatabase = NULL);
 DECLARE_DYNAMIC(CDaoUserMasterSet)

 // Field/Param Data
 //{{AFX_FIELD(CDaoUserMasterSet, CDaoRecordset)
 CString  m_sUserID;
 CString  m_sUserName;
 short m_iStatus;
 //}}AFX_FIELD

 // Overrides
 // ClassWizard generated virtual function overrides
```

```
 //{{AFX_VIRTUAL(CDaoUserMasterSet)
 public:
 virtual CString GetDefaultDBName();
 virtual CString GetDefaultSQL();
 virtual void DoFieldExchange(CDaoFieldExchange* pFX);  // RFX
support
 //}}AFX_VIRTUAL

 // Implementation
 #ifdef _DEBUG
 virtual void AssertValid() const;
 virtual void Dump(CDumpContext& dc) const;
 #endif
};

//{{AFX_INSERT_LOCATION}}
// Microsoft Visual C++ will insert additional
// declarations immediately before the previous line.

#endif // _DAO_USER_MASTER_SET_H_
```

Listing 21-2: **DaoUserMasterSet.cpp**

```
// DaoUserMasterSet.cpp : implementation file
//

#include "stdafx.h"
#include "DAOTestProject.h"
#include "DaoUserMasterSet.h"

#ifdef _DEBUG
#define new DEBUG_NEW
#undef THIS_FILE
static char THIS_FILE[] = __FILE__;
#endif

/////////////////////////////////////////////////////////////
// CDaoUserMasterSet

IMPLEMENT_DYNAMIC(CDaoUserMasterSet, CDaoRecordset)

CDaoUserMasterSet::CDaoUserMasterSet(CDaoDatabase* pdb)
: CDaoRecordset(pdb)
{
 //{{AFX_FIELD_INIT(CDaoUserMasterSet)
 m_sUserID = _T("");
 m_sUserName = _T("");
```

(continued)

Listing 21-2 (continued)

```
 m_iStatus = 0;
 m_nFields = 3;
 //}}AFX_FIELD_INIT
 m_nDefaultType = dbOpenDynaset;
}


CString CDaoUserMasterSet::GetDefaultDBName()
{
 return
_T("C:\\WINNT\\Profiles\\Administrator\\Personal\\Books\\Window
s 98 Programming Bible\\Chapter 20 - DAO Database
Programming\\DAOTestProject\\Chapter20.mdb");
}

CString CDaoUserMasterSet::GetDefaultSQL()
{
 return _T("[UserMaster]");
}

void CDaoUserMasterSet::DoFieldExchange(CDaoFieldExchange* pFX)
{
 //{{AFX_FIELD_MAP(CDaoUserMasterSet)
 pFX->SetFieldType(CDaoFieldExchange::outputColumn);
 DFX_Text(pFX, _T("[sUserID]"), m_sUserID);
 DFX_Text(pFX, _T("[sUserName]"), m_sUserName);
 DFX_Short(pFX, _T("[iStatus]"), m_iStatus);
 //}}AFX_FIELD_MAP
}

/////////////////////////////////////////////////////////////
// CDaoUserMasterSet diagnostics

#ifdef _DEBUG
void CDaoUserMasterSet::AssertValid() const
{
 CDaoRecordset::AssertValid();
}

void CDaoUserMasterSet::Dump(CDumpContext& dc) const
{
 CDaoRecordset::Dump(dc);
}
#endif //_DEBUG
```

Once you have a recordset to work with, you can do just about anything you want to the returned records. This includes the following:

- Construct a recordset.
- Open a recordset.
- Read and write data using DFX (DAO field exchange).
- Filter records.
- Sort records returned with a recordset.
- Move through the recordset.
- Save records.
- Delete records.

Constructing a CDaoRecordset object

The `CDaoRecordset` constructor takes only one argument: a pointer to a `CDaoDatabase` object. This argument has a default value of `NULL`. If you choose not to specify a `CDaoDatabase` object when calling this constructor, MFC will automatically create a temporary one for you, using the information specified when the recordset was created with the Class Wizard. You can find that information in the `CDaoRecordset::GetDefaultDBName()` function.

However, if you are planning on using multiple recordsets, it is much more efficient to create one `CDaoDatabase` object and use that object for all your recordsets. One way of doing this is to create a `CDaoDatabase` object when the application initializes and store the pointer in the application or document object. Then, whenever you need to construct a recordset, you can use this global database object.

Opening a recordset

Once the `CDaoRecordset` object has been constructed, you can open it using the `CDaoRecordset::Open()` function. One of the arguments for this function is the recordset type. This argument is used to specify whether the recordset you are opening will be a dynaset, table, or snapshot recordset type. These types are represented by the `dbOpenDynaset`, `dbOpenTable`, and `dbOpenSnapshot` constants, respectively. If you do not specify a recordset type, the type of recordset opened will be dictated by the value entered when the class was created. This value is stored in the `m_nDefaultType` member variable and is initialized in the class constructor.

Using the various overloaded `CDaoRecordset::Open()` functions, you can specify an SQL string to run against a table, or specify a `TableDef` or `QueryDef` to open. If you do not specify an SQL statement, the `GetDefaultSQL()` function is used to determine which records will end up in the recordset after the `Open()` function returns.

Reading and writing data using DFX

To retrieve all the records from a table without regard to order, you simply need to create a CDaoRecordset-derived class (as shown previously) and call its CDaoRecordset::Open() member function. However, at this point you may be wondering how the data gets from the data source into your application's variables. The answer is DFX (DAO field exchange).

When a CDaoRecordset-derived class is created using Class Wizard, it enumerates all the columns in the selected table or query and declares variables of the appropriate type in the class header file. It also generates code for a function called DoFieldExchange() that serves to tie the member variables to their corresponding columns in the database. The DoFieldExchange() function is called when MFC needs to move data from the database to your member variables or vice versa. The underlying MFC code actually does all the low-level DAO work, like binding the columns and fetching the data, that you would have to do manually if it weren't for this "helper" function.

When you open a CDaoRecordset via its Open() member function, it moves to the first record so the application can immediately start using the data. The application can then start navigating through the resulting data using the CDaoRecordset::MoveFirst(), CDaoRecordset::MovePrev(), CDaoRecordset::MoveNext(), and CDaoRecordset::MoveLast() member functions. (These functions will be explained shortly.)

Filtering records

Now that you know how to open and retrieve data from a data source, you need to learn how to filter that data to get just the records you desire. Actually, there are several ways to accomplish this. As you saw in the section entitled "Opening a recordset," one way is to specify the SQL in the CDaoRecordset::Open() function. The following code is an example of using that function to filter the desired records from the UserMaster table. This code reads only the records that represent users whose status code is equal to 0.

```
CDaoDatabase db;
CDaoUserMasterSet rs;
try
{
 rs.Open(AFX_DAO_USE_DEFAULT_TYPE,
 "SELECT * from UserMaster where iStatus = 0");

 while (!rs.IsEOF())
 {
 AfxMessageBox(rs.m_sUserName);
 rs.MoveNext();
 }
}
catch(CDaoException* pe)
{
 AfxMessageBox(pe->m_pErrorInfo->m_strDescription,
```

```
   MB_ICONEXCLAMATION);
  pe->Delete();
 }
```

A second way of filtering the data returned in a recordset is to use a parameterized recordset. Using the CDaoUserMasterSet created earlier in the chapter (see Listings 21-1 and 21-2), you will change this recordset so only records whose iStatus has a value of zero will be retrieved. To accomplish this, follow these steps:

1. Locate the following block of variables:

   ```
   // Field/Param Data
    //{{AFX_FIELD(CDaoUserMasterSet, CDaoRecordset)
    CString   m_sUserID;
    CString   m_sUserName;
    short m_iStatus;
    //}}AFX_FIELD
   ```

2. Add the following variable declaration after the variable block you located in step 1:

   ```
   short m_iStatusParam;
   ```

   This variable will hold the parameter data in the DaoUserMasterSet.h file.

3. Initialize the variable in the recordset's constructor and set the m_nParams value to the number of parameters you want to use, as follows (the boldface lines represent the new lines of code you need to add):

   ```
   //{{AFX_FIELD_INIT(CDaoUserMasterSet)
   m_sUserID = _T("");
   m_sUserName = _T("");
   m_iStatus = 0;
   m_nFields = 3;
   m_iStatusParam = 0;
   m_nParams = 1;
   //}}AFX_FIELD_INIT
   m_nDefaultType = dbOpenDynaset;
   ```

   This is extremely important. If you attempt to use a parameterized recordset and do not set this value, the recordset's Open() will fail and you will receive an ASSERT during the call to DoFieldExchange().

4. Update the DoFieldExchange() function to look like the following:

   ```
   void CDaoUserMasterSet::DoFieldExchange(
    CDaoFieldExchange* pFX)
   {
     //{{AFX_FIELD_MAP(CDaoUserMasterSet)
     pFX->SetFieldType(CDaoFieldExchange::outputColumn);
     DFX_Text(pFX, _T("[sUserID]"), m_sUserID);
     DFX_Text(pFX, _T("[sUserName]"), m_sUserName);
     DFX_Short(pFX, _T("[iStatus]"), m_iStatus);
     //}}AFX_FIELD_MAP
   }
   ```

Please note that the `CDaoFieldExchange::SetFieldType()` must be called with the `CDaoFieldExchange::param` argument, and the second argument of the `DFX_Short()` function points to the column used to filter the data (iStatus).

5. Set the parameter's value. Here is an example of how to do this:

```
CDaoDatabase db;
CDaoUserMasterSet rs;
try
{
 rs.m_strFilter = "iStatus = ?";
 rs.m_iStatusParam = 0;
 rs.Open();

 while (!rs.IsEOF())
 {
  AfxMessageBox(rs.m_sUserName);
  rs.MoveNext();
 }
}
catch(CDaoException* pe)
{
 AfxMessageBox(pe->m_pErrorInfo->m_strDescription,
  MB_ICONEXCLAMATION );
 pe->Delete();
}
```

As you can see, using parameterized recordsets is not very complex, but if you forget to do any of the steps involved, you can end up losing a lot of time tracking down why your `Open` function call is not working.

Sorting records returned with a recordset

As you just saw in the section entitled "Filtering Records," MFC provides you with a member variable (`m_strFilter`) to filter the records your recordset represents. MFC also provides you with a member variable to specify the order in which the records are returned. This member variable is `m_strSort`. To use this member variable, simply set it to the name of the column you want to sort by. For example, in the sample code previously used, if you wanted to sort by the iStatus column in the UserMaster table, your code would look like the following:

```
CDaoDatabase db;
CDaoUserMasterSet rs;
try
{
 rs.m_strSort = _T("iStatus");
 rs.Open();

 while (!rs.IsEOF())
 {
 AfxMessageBox(rs.m_sUserName);
 rs.MoveNext();
```

```
  }
 }
 catch(CDaoException* pe)
 {
  AfxMessageBox(pe->m_pErrorInfo->m_strDescription,
   MB_ICONEXCLAMATION);
  pe->Delete();
 }
```

If you need to sort by more than one column, just separate each column name with a comma.

Moving through the result set

Once you have opened the recordset and you have only the data you want (via filtering) in the sequence you desire (via the `m_strSort` member variable), you will need to know how to move through the resulting records. MFC makes this extremely easy with the `MoveFirst()`, `MovePrev()`, `MoveNext()`, and `MoveLast()` functions. It's not hard to figure out from the function names what each function does. However, there are some things you should know when attempting to navigate through a recordset:

- `MoveXXX` will throw an exception if the recordset did not return any records. Therefore, you should always call `CDaoRecordset::IsBOF` or `CDaoRecordset::IsEOF` before attempting to call one of the move functions.
- The `MoveFirst` and `MovePrev` functions are not supported for recordsets defined as forward-only. This point is only applicable for Workspaces that use ODBCDirect.
- If you are moving through a recordset, and a record in that recordset has been deleted by another user, you should call the `CDaoRecordset::IsDeleted` function to verify the record is still valid.
- If you move to the last record in the recordset and call `MoveNext`, a `CDaoException` will be thrown. Therefore, when using `MoveNext` to move sequentially through a recordset, you should always call `IsEOF` before calling `MoveNext` again.

Saving records

It is very easy to save data using a recordset. There are basically two different ways to save data: by adding new records and by updating existing records.

To add a new record, you simply do the following:

1. Call the `CDaoRecordset::AddNew()` function. This will prepare a new, blank record for you.
2. Move your application's data into the recordset's member variables.
3. Call the `CDaoRecordset::Update()` function.

To update an existing record, you simply do the following:

1. Call the `CDaoRecordset::Edit()` function.
2. Move your application's data into the recordset's member variables.
3. Call the `CDaoRecordset::Update()` function.

There is something very important to note here about the order in which you call these functions. You must move the data into the member variables after calling the `Edit()` function. Otherwise, MFC will not update your data. The reason for this is that the database classes cache, or buffer, the data and do a memory compare when you call the `Update()` function. If no changes have been made to the member variables since you called the `Edit()` function, the data will not be saved even though you explicitly called the `Update()` function.

Deleting records

To delete a record from a recordset, the current record must be the record your application needs to delete. Then, simply call the `CRecordset::Delete()` function. After deleting the record, you must call one of the `MoveXXX` functions to move to another record because the current record is no longer valid.

Creating a maintenance application using MFC Database classes

In the following program (which can be found on the companion CD in the \Demos\DaoUserMaintenance folder), you will develop a fully functional maintenance application using the MFC DAO classes. This application will have all the create, update, and delete capabilities of a traditional maintenance application for maintaining users. As with all the demos in this book, you can read along or you can perform the exercise.

Creating the Visual C++ 6.0 project

Begin by creating a new project with the following criteria:

- ✦ The name of the project should be "DaoUserMaintenance."
- ✦ Check the Dialog-based option.

Adding support for the MFC DAO classes

As mentioned earlier, with MFC you only need to include the afxdao.h header file to incorporate MFC DAO support into your application. To do this, simply add the following `#include` directive to the stdafx.h file:

```
#include <afxdao.h>
```

Editing the dialog for the demo application

After adding the header file for the DAO classes, you will need to edit the application's main dialog. Open the `IDD_USER_MAINTENANCE_DIALOG` dialog template resource and make the necessary edits so the resulting dialog looks like Figure 21-6. (Actually, if you use the following tip, you can save yourself some time.)

Expert Tip

Duplicating Dialog Functions with the Clipboard

When duplicating the work of one dialog that exists in one resource file to another resource file, you can use the clipboard functions. For example, because the dialog in Figure 21-6 is almost exactly like the dialog used for the `UserMaintenance` project in Chapter 20, you can use the clipboard so you don't have to duplicate work you've already done.

Simply open the UserMaintenance.rc file on the CD. Notice that it appears in a view instead of in the project workspace dialog bar. This is because only the current project's resources are displayed in the dialog bar. Once you have located the dialog from which you wish to copy the controls, select the desired controls and copy them to the clipboard. Make sure to note the size of the dialog. Now, return to the `IDD_USER_MAINTENANCE_DIALOG` and after resizing the dialog, paste the controls into the dialog. Not only does this save you the work of creating the controls, but even the control IDs have been set correctly.

◆ ◆ ◆ ◆ ◆

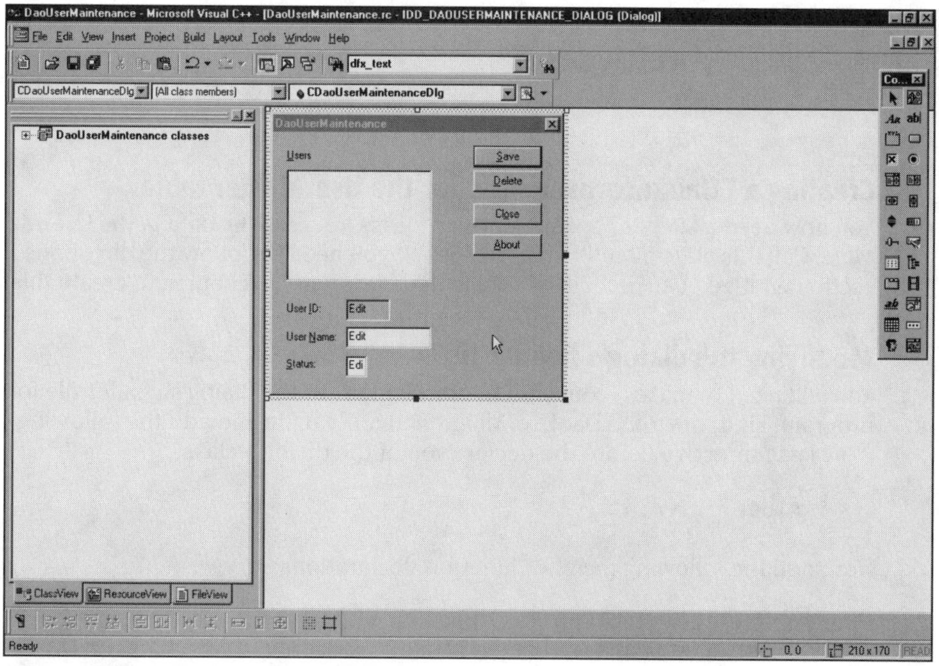

Figure 21-6: The DaoUserMaintenance dialog after the new controls have been added

Once you have copied the controls onto the dialog, create the member variables that will be used with DDX (dynamic data exchange) for the different controls, as follows:

User Listbox — `m_lbxUsers, Control, CListbox`

User ID Edit — `m_strUserID, Value, CString`

User Name Edit — `m_strUserName, Value, CString`

Status Edit — `m_iStatus, Value, int`

Save Button — `m_btnSave, Control, CButton`

Delete Button — `m_btnDelete, Control, CButton`

Adding a utility class to encapsulate the user's data

A utility class is needed to encapsulate each record's data. As you will see later, once a record is read, a `CUser` class is created. An entry is then made into the list box that represents that record. This list-box entry, in turn, points back to the class that contains the record's data. At this point, create a file named User.h and edit it to look like the following:

```
#pragma once

class CUser
{
public:
 CString m_strUserID;
 CString m_strUserName;
 int m_iStatus;
};
```

Creating a CDaoRecordset class for the UserMaster table

You now need a `CDaoRecordset`-derived class to access the data in the UserMaster table. Call this class `CDaoUserMasterSet`. If you need to, follow the directions in the section entitled `CDaoRecordset`, presented earlier in the chapter, to create this class.

Modifying the dialog's header file

You will need to make a couple of minor changes to the dialog's header file for this program. First, open the DaoUserMaintenanceDlg.h file and add the following `#include` directive before the declaration of the dialog's class:

```
#include "User.h"
```

Now, add the following member function declarations:

```
void FillListboxWithUsers();
BOOL GetSelectedUser(int* piIndex, CUser** ppUser);
```

```
void InitControls();
BOOL SaveUser(CUser* pUser);
BOOL DeleteUser(CUser* pUser);
```

Modifying the dialog's implementation file

The last thing you need to do for this program is to modify the dialog's code to perform the database I/O. First, open the DaoUserMaintenanceDlg.cpp file, and at the top of the file, add the following `#include` directive (it should be listed last):

```
#include "DaoUserMasterSet.h"
```

Now locate the `OnInitDialog` function and add the following function calls:

```
FillListboxWithUsers();
InitControls();
```

The `FillListboxWithUsers()` function will fill the list box with all the users found in the database. The `InitControls()` function will do things like initialize the state of the buttons (disabling the Save and Delete buttons when a user is not selected, enabling the Save and Delete buttons when a user is selected, and so on).

At the end of the DaoUserMaintenanceDlg.cpp file, add the following function definition:

```
void CUserMaintenanceDlg::FillListboxWithUsers()
{
 int iIndex;
 CDaoDatabase db;
 CDaoUserMasterSet rs;
```

Because the MFC DAO classes throw exceptions upon encountering unexpected conditions, we need to "wrap" the database code with a `try/catch` block:

```
 try
 {
```

Open the recordset and start a `while` loop based on reaching the end-of-file:

```
  rs.Open();

  while (!rs.IsEOF())
  {
```

Note that because this code is not using any of the filtering techniques discussed in the "Filtering Records" section, all the users from the database will be retrieved.

To keep the database from being "hit" again every time a user is selected from the list box to retrieve that user's information, add the following:

```
    CUser* pUser = new CUser();
    pUser->m_strUserID = rs.m_sUserID;
    pUser->m_strUserName = rs.m_sUserName;
    pUser->m_iStatus = rs.m_iStatus;

    iIndex = m_lbxUsers.AddString(rs.m_sUserName);
    m_lbxUsers.SetItemData(iIndex, (DWORD)pUser);
```

This code creates a CUser object to contain all the information that is read from the database for each user. The user will then be added to the list box and its item data will be set to the CUser object pointer, making retrieval of user information much more efficient. Note that by simply calling the recordset's Open() and MoveNext() functions, its member variables are set to the current record's information without any further work on your part.

Now call the recordset's MoveNext() function to retrieve the next record in the recordset, as follows:

```
    rs.MoveNext();
   }
  }
  catch(CDaoException* pe)
  {
   AfxMessageBox(pe->m_pErrorInfo->m_strDescription,
    MB_ICONEXCLAMATION );
  }
 }
```

Add the following initialization function to the end of the DaoUserMaintenanceDlg.cpp file:

```
void CDaoUserMaintenanceDlg::InitControls()
{
```

Initialize the controls by setting all the Edit fields to blanks and disabling the Save and Delete buttons. These buttons will be enabled when a User is selected from the Listbox.

```
  m_lbxUsers.SetCurSel(-1);

  m_strUserID = "";
  m_strUserName = "";
  m_iStatus = -1;

  m_btnSave.EnableWindow(FALSE);
  m_btnDelete.EnableWindow(FALSE);

  m_lbxUsers.SetFocus();

  UpdateData(FALSE);
}
```

You now need to add a function so when a user is selected from the list box the proper information is displayed in the dialog box. To do this, use Class Wizard to implement a message handler for the LBN_SELCHANGE notification message, as follows:

```
void CDaoUserMaintenanceDlg::OnSelchangeLbxusers()
{
 int iIndex;
 CUser* pUser;

 if (GetSelectedUser(&iIndex, &pUser))
 {
```

Update the member variables with the currently selected user's information:

```
  m_strUserID = pUser->m_strUserID;
  m_strUserName = pUser->m_strUserName;
  m_iStatus = pUser->m_iStatus;
```

Because a user is now selected, enable both the Save and Delete buttons:

```
  m_btnSave.EnableWindow(TRUE);
  m_btnDelete.EnableWindow(TRUE);
```

Calling UpdateData() with an argument of FALSE will cause DDX (dynamic data exchange) to update the dialog box controls from the member variables.

```
  UpdateData(FALSE);
 }
}
```

Because you are going to require information about the selected user at different times (when the Update button is clicked, when the Delete button is clicked, and so on), go ahead and write a "helper" function to perform this task:

```
BOOL CDaoUserMaintenanceDlg::GetSelectedUser(
 int* piIndex, CUser** ppUser)
{
 BOOL bSuccess = FALSE;

 int iIndex;
 if (LB_ERR != (iIndex = m_lbxUsers.GetCurSel()))
 {
  *piIndex = iIndex;
  *ppUser = (CUser*)m_lbxUsers.GetItemData(iIndex);
  bSuccess = TRUE;
 }

 return bSuccess;
}
```

At this point, you can read all the users from the data source and display their respective information when they are selected from the list box. Now, the ability to add records will be implemented in the application.

Add a `BN_CLICKED` handler for the Save button and edit it so you have the following results when finished:

```
void CDaoUserMaintenanceDlg::OnBtnsave()
{
 int iCurrIndex;

 CUser* pUser = NULL;
 if (GetSelectedUser(&iCurrIndex, &pUser))
 {
  ASSERT(pUser);
  if (pUser)
  {
   UpdateData();
```

Add the following code to save the data the user has typed in. That way, if the `SaveUser()` function call fails, the data is not lost and the `Save` can be attempted again without the user having to retype the information.

```
   CString strPrevUserID;
   strPrevUserID = m_strUserID;
   CString strPrevUserName;
   strPrevUserName = m_strUserName;
   int iPrevStatus = m_iStatus;

   pUser->m_strUserID = m_strUserID;
   pUser->m_strUserName = m_strUserName;
   pUser->m_iStatus = m_iStatus;
```

Now, call the `SaveUser` function to save the current User:

```
   if (SaveUser(pUser))
   {
```

Because the User Name information is being used in the list box, and it could have changed, delete it from the list box and add the User back:

```
    if (LB_ERR == m_lbxUsers.DeleteString(iCurrIndex))
    {
     AfxMessageBox("The User ID was Saved, "
      "but the previous User ID could not be "
      "removed from the listbox.");
    }
    else
    {
     int iNewIndex = m_lbxUsers.AddString(
      pUser->m_strUserName);
     if ((LB_ERR == iNewIndex) || (LB_ERRSPACE ==
```

```
        iNewIndex))
       {
        AfxMessageBox("The User ID was Saved, but "
         "the new User ID could not "
         "be added to the listbox.");
       }
       if (LB_ERR == m_lbxUsers.SetItemData(iNewIndex,
       (DWORD)pUser))
       {
        AfxMessageBox("SetItemData returned LB_ERR. "
         "This will probably cause "
         "serious problems if you attempt to update "
         "or delete this item from the listbox");
       }
      }

      InitControls();

      UpdateData(FALSE);
     }
     else
     {
```

Obviously, the User Name could have been checked to verify if it had been changed, but this is the "quick and dirty" way of doing it and costs nothing in terms of performance.

Next, enter the following code to ensure that if the `SaveUser()` function fails, the dialog box values are set back to what was typed in:

```
      pUser->m_strUserID = strPrevUserID;
      pUser->m_strUserName = strPrevUserName;
      pUser->m_iStatus = iPrevStatus;
      AfxMessageBox("SaveUser failed");
     }
    }
   }
   else
   {
    // should never get here because of
    // enabling/disabling button on lbx selection
    AfxMessageBox("You must first select a "
    "User ID to Save");
   }
  }
```

Now you add the function that will actually do the work necessary to save a given record:

```
BOOL CDaoUserMaintenanceDlg::SaveUser(CUser* pUser)
{
 BOOL bSuccess = FALSE;
```

```
CDaoDatabase db;

try
{
db.Open(_T("Chapter20.mdb"));
```

You can also use a `CDaoDatabase` object by itself (instead of with a `CDaoRecordset` object). In cases where you know you are going to issue an SQL statement (like the following SQL `UPDATE`) against a database, and you do not already have a current record, it is more efficient to use the `CDaoDatabase::Execute()` function. Here the SQL statement is built and passed to the `Execute()` function for processing:

```
 CString strSQL = CString("UPDATE UserMaster SET ");
 strSQL += CString("sUserName = '") +
  pUser->m_strUserName + CString("', ");

 strSQL += CString("iStatus = ");
 char szStatus[10];
 itoa(pUser->m_iStatus, szStatus, 10);
 strSQL += szStatus;

 strSQL += CString(" WHERE sUserID = ");
 strSQL += CString("'") + pUser->m_strUserID +
  CString("'");

 db.Execute(strSQL);

 bSuccess = TRUE;
}
catch(CDaoException* pe)
{
 AfxMessageBox(pe->m_pErrorInfo->m_strDescription,
  MB_ICONEXCLAMATION );

 pe->Delete();
}

return bSuccess;
}
```

Finally, it's time to see how to delete a record using DAO. To do this, add a handler for the Delete button, as follows:

```
void CDaoUserMaintenanceDlg::OnBtndelete()
{
 int iIndex;
 CUser* pUser = NULL;
 if (GetSelectedUser(&iIndex, &pUser))
 {
  ASSERT(pUser);
```

```
 if (pUser)
 {
  UpdateData();
  CString strMsg;

  strMsg = "Are you sure that you want to delete "
   "the User ";
  strMsg += "'";
  strMsg += pUser->m_strUserName;
  strMsg += "'?";
  if (IDYES == AfxMessageBox(strMsg, MB_YESNOCANCEL))
  {
   if (DeleteUser(pUser))
   {
    if (LB_ERR == m_lbxUsers.DeleteString(iIndex))
    {
     AfxMessageBox("The User was successfully "
      "Deleted, but there was an error in "
      "removing it from the listbox.");
    }

             InitControls();

    UpdateData(FALSE);
   }
   else
   {
    AfxMessageBox("DeleteUser failed");
   }
  }
 }
}
else
{
 // should never get here because of
 // enabling/disabling button on lbx selection
 AfxMessageBox("You must first select a User "
  "ID to Delete");
}
}
```

Add the following helper function at the end of the DaoUserMaintenanceDlg.cpp file to do the actual work of deleting a record:

```
BOOL CDaoUserMaintenanceDlg::DeleteUser(CUser* pUser)
{
 BOOL bSuccess = FALSE;
 CDaoDatabase db;

 try
 {
```

Once again, we are hard-coding the database name in the following code. Obviously, in a real application, a pointer to a database object with dialog-level scope would have been created for efficiency, or at the very least a constant would be used for the database name.

```
    db.Open(_T("Chapter20.mdb"));

    CString strSQL;
    strSQL.Format("DELETE FROM UserMaster WHERE "
     "sUserID = '%s'", pUser->m_strUserID);

    db.Execute(strSQL);

    bSuccess = TRUE;
   }
   catch(CDaoException* pe)
   {
    AfxMessageBox(pe->m_pErrorInfo->m_strDescription,
     MB_ICONEXCLAMATION );

    pe->Delete();
   }

   return bSuccess;
  }
```

Once you have added the support to delete records, add one last function to free up the memory allocated when the `CUser` objects were created. This can be done by adding a handler for the dialog's `WM_DESTROY` message and adding the following code:

```
void CDaoUserMaintenanceDlg::OnDestroy()
{
 CDialog::OnDestroy();

 CUser* pUser;

 for (int i = 0; i < m_lbxUsers.GetCount(); i++)
 {
  pUser = (CUser*)m_lbxUsers.GetItemData(i);
  if (pUser)
  {
   delete pUser;
  }
 }
}
```

Testing the UserMaintenance application

Once you build and test the application, the results should be similar to what you see in Figure 21-7.

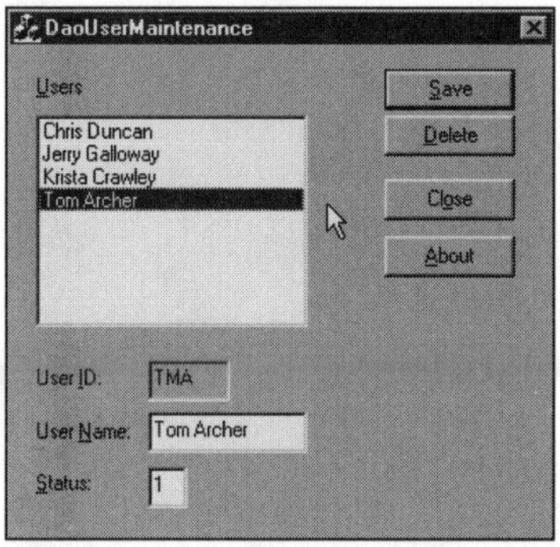

Figure 21-7: The DaoUserMaintenance application, which demonstrates the MFC DAO classes at work

Summary

In this chapter, you have learned about the basics of DAO, the different objects that constitute the DAO object hierarchy, and the different DAO APIs that enable you to programmatically manipulate the Microsoft Jet engine from your application. In addition, you learned how to use the MFC DAO classes to write a simple maintenance application. Although no one can argue with the fact that you don't have the programmatic level of control using DAO as you do with the ODBC SDK, there are times when a nice simple, clean database API like DAO is all you need.

✦ ✦ ✦

P A R T

V

Extending Applications

Single developers — even teams of developers — can't do it all. There comes a time when you need to rely on third-party libraries to provide the functionality that your program needs. Some add-on libraries can cost just several hundred dollars, yet still save the development team hundreds or thousands of hours of time. This section shows you how to extend your applications with such third-party libraries.

In This Part

Chapter 22
Working with DLLs

Chapter 23
Extending Applications with Third-Party Libraries

Chapter 24
Data Encryption

CHAPTER 22

Working with DLLs

✦ ✦ ✦ ✦

In This Chapter

Creating a DLL

Implementing your own DllMain() to handle multiple thread attachments

Learning about AFX_MANAGE_STATE

Creating resource-only DLLs for multilingual support

Loading and calling DLLs dynamically

Writing a system-wide keyboard hook

Learning about MFC Extension DLLs

Exporting entire classes and parts of classes from a DLL

Seeing how to properly define nested Extension DLLs

Encapsulating documents and views in a DLL

✦ ✦ ✦ ✦

Dynamic Link Libraries (or DLLs) have been around as long as the Windows operating system has. In fact, the Windows APIs are all located in DLLs. Therefore, this chapter assumes you are already familiar with the concept of DLLs and concentrates on how to create and use DLLs with Visual C++ 6.0.

DLLs basically come in two types with regards to Visual C++: regular DLLs and MFC Extension DLLs. In the first section, you learn the advantages of using regular DLLs and how to create them with ClassWizard. You also learn how to manage the current "module state" so the DLL can make calls to the shared version of the MFC DLLs. In addition, I show you how to write two demos: a system-level keyboard hook and an application that dynamically loads and uses DLLs with the `LoadLibrary()` and `GetProcAddress()` functions.

In the second section, you learn about MFC Extension DLLs that enable you to export whole classes or specific member functions of a class. The two demos in this section teach you how to use nested MFC Extension DLLs and how to place documents and views in a DLL separate from the main application.

Regular DLLs

Unlike MFC Extension DLLs, which are covered later in this chapter, regular DLLs are used when the function interfaces being exported are C functions or C++ classes. Note here the expression *C++ classes* is used rather than *MFC classes*. If you need to export an MFC class, you have to look into writing and managing MFC Extension DLLs. Because MFC Extension DLLs can do everything a regular DLL can do and more, you may be wondering why you would ever need to use a regular DLL. Actually, there are a couple of important advantages to using a regular DLL when programming with Visual C++:

✦ The application or DLL using the DLL does not need to be an MFC application. It simply needs to be able to call C-like functions. This could be anything from an MFC application to a Delphi or Visual Basic application.

✦ A regular DLL can use C++ classes internally and then export only the C function wrappers. That way, any changes to these C++ classes would not affect the calling application or DLL.

Regular DLLs can be created from Visual C++ with the aid of the AppWizard. After invoking the AppWizard, simply choose the MFC AppWizard (dll) project type. The first dialog box enables you to specify whether you want to use the MFC library and how you want the MFC libraries linked to your DLL: statically or dynamically.

Just as using regular DLLs over MFC Extension DLLs has its advantages, so, too, are there advantages and disadvantages regarding how you choose to link MFC support to your DLL:

✦ If a regular DLL dynamically links to the MFC libraries, its file size will be much smaller than a regular DLL that uses static linking. However, the disadvantage here is the MFC DLLs must now be shipped with the product. Obviously, this is only a problem if you are distributing your application. If the application you are developing will run on only one PC or in an environment that you control, this is not a liability.

✦ If you are distributing your DLL for use by another MFC application, and the other application dynamically links to the MFC libraries, there will always be a concern over which version of MFC each DLL is using. However, if your DLL is statically linking to the MFC libraries for the MFC support it needs, there is never a question about which version your DLL is using.

As you can see, before you start working with DLLs, you need to make some decisions. These decisions, by and large, are predicated on factors such as whether or not you control the environment where the DLL will be used, what language the calling application will be written in, and whether or not you want to worry about distributing the MFC DLLs with your code. In all likelihood, this will be a decision process that you have to go through with each application and DLL that you write.

Understanding the regular DLL internals

If you take a look at the AppWizard-generated source code for a regular DLL, you will find a `CWinApp`-derived class that represents your DLL. If you are already familiar with creating DLLs, you may be wondering where the `DllMain()` function went. As you know, every Win32 DLL must have a `DllMain()` entry point. The answer is that much like the `WinMain` function for Win32 applications, Visual C++ automatically creates a `DllMain()` function for you.

The advantage here is you can program your main DLL modules as you would any other `CWinApp`-derived class. For example, because initialization for `CWinApp` classes usually takes place in the `InitInstance()` function, you can also override the `CWinApp::InitInstance()` function for the DLL and provide global initialization there. In addition, deinitialization should be placed in the `ExistInstance` function derived from your DLL's `CWinApp`-derived class.

Expert Tip

Implementing Your Own DllMain() Function

Whereas MFC provides a default `DllMain()` implementation, and the MFC documentation generally advises you to do your initialization in the `InitInstance()` function of your DLL's `CWinApp`-derived class, there may be times when you will need to implement your own `DllMain()` function. One potential problem with using the MFC-provided `DllMain()` function in conjunction with an `InitInstance()` function override is the `InitInstance()` function is only called when a process attaches to the DLL or detaches from the DLL. This is fine in most cases, but there may be times that your DLL will need to perform initialization and deinitialization when a thread attaches or detaches. In order to handle this scenario, it may be necessary to implement your own `DllMain()`.

You have a `DllMain()` function automatically compiled into your DLL because the MFC source code links code to your DLL from the Dllmodul.cpp file. In fact, if you navigate to the folder on your hard disk that contains the MFC source code, you will not only find this file, but inside it you will find the definition of the `DllMain()` function. In addition to the `DllMain()` function, the Dllmodul.cpp file contains most of the code used to support a regular DLL. The recommended way to override or altar this function is to copy this file into the DLL's source code folder and include it in the DLL's project. Now you can make the changes you deem necessary, and the local, modified copy of the Dllmodul.cpp file will be compiled and linked to your DLL.

◆ ◆ ◆ ◆ ◆

Another important point about regular DLLs is an issue that only arises if a regular DLL needs to call into the MFC. As you probably already know, MFC keeps some internal global state information pertaining to the application or DLL. Therefore, if an exported function in the DLL attempts to call a function that depends on this information, the wrong data will be used. The following is a simple example to illustrate my point.

Use AppWizard to create a new MFC DLL project called DisplayAppName. Don't forget to define this DLL as being a regular DLL (it's the default AppWizard setting). Declare the following function in the DisplayAppName.h file:

```
void DisplayAppName();
```

In the DisplayAppName.cpp file, define the `DisplayAppName` function as follows:

```
void DisplayAppName()
{
 CString str = AfxGetAppName();
 AfxMessageBox(str);
}
```

Now add the function to the DisplayAppName.def file in the `EXPORTS` section. The `EXPORTS` section should now look like the following:

```
EXPORTS
 DisplayAppName
```

Build the DLL and copy it to a folder in your path. Create an MFC application project called RegDllTest. After including the DisplayAppName.h file somewhere in your code and adding the DisplayAppName.lib file to the project, place a call to the `DisplayAppName()` function.

When you build and run this test, you will see that the name displayed is the application name of your EXE, not the DLL. This is because MFC has placed global data on the stack that represents the current module—in this case, the application. To specify that you want to use the global data associated with the DLL, you need to use the `AFX_MANAGE_STATE` macro in your code. This macro is used to push or pop the global data associated with the module. Therefore, at the beginning of every exported function, you need to set the current module state to that of the DLL. Don't worry about resetting the module state, because the `AFX_MANAGE_STATE` macro actually resolves to a class whose destructor will reset the previous state when the object goes out of scope. Here's how you would change the example code so the message box reflects the name of the DLL instead of the application:

```
void DisplayAppName()
{
 AFX_MANAGE_STATE(AfxGetStaticModuleState());
 CString str = AfxGetAppName();
 AfxMessageBox(str);
}
```

Dynamically loading DLLs

As mentioned earlier, when an application is loaded, the Windows operating system loads the necessary DLLs required to run the application. However, many developers need to dynamically load a DLL instead of having Windows do it automatically. To load a DLL at runtime, you simply call the `LoadLibrary()` function. As you can see in the prototype shown here, it only takes one argument: the name of the file.

```
HINSTANCE LoadLibrary(LPCTSTR lpLibFileName);
```

The returned `HINSTANCE` is a global handle that represents that DLL. It can be used in other functions referencing the DLL. For example, if you want to call a function exported by the DLL, you can call the `GetProcAddress()` function (passing the `HINSTANCE`) to retrieve the function's address. That address is then stored in a function pointer and can be called like any other function.

Examples of when to dynamically load a DLL

Now that you know the semantics of loading a DLL, here are some examples of when and how you would want to dynamically load a DLL, instead of using the more common method of linking to an import library at build time and letting Windows resolve the function addresses at runtime.

Programming function seams

A *function seam* is a layer of abstraction between a function and its caller. Its purpose is to insulate the caller from the internals of the function to be called. Let's say you have an application that supports multiple communications protocols. The application might support APPC, NetBios, and Named Pipes, to name a few. How would you have your application support all of these completely different communications APIs without changing your main module's source code for each one?

Each communications API would be placed in a separate DLL. Each DLL would then export the exact same set of functions. For example, each DLL would export a generic Read function with a universally agreed on function definition. Using this technique, the calling function could load the appropriate DLL and call its Read function, and not have to be informed about what the DLL is doing internally to satisfy the read request.

An example of using function seams is ODBC (covered in Chapter 19). After you make a request of the ODBC Driver Manager, it must be able to pass that request to the specified ODBC Driver. Microsoft accomplishes this by mandating that all ODBC Drivers export a specific set of functions per the published specification on writing ODBC Drivers. That way, the ODBC Driver Manager never has to have any understanding of how the request is being carried out, and therefore doesn't require any special coding for different ODBC Drivers.

Writing multilingual applications

Programming multilingual applications is another instance when you need to dynamically load a DLL. A couple of different ways exist to support more than one language, but by far the most popular technique is to use resource-only DLLs. This is done by creating a DLL for each language that needs to be supported. Once the DLL has been created, the necessary resources (string tables, menus, and so on) are added to each DLL. The only important thing here is that the resources ids are consistent across the different DLL's resource files. For example, if the resource id for the main menu is 100 in the English DLL, it must be 100 in the Spanish DLL.

Once you have done this, the calling program only needs to do two things to finish the process of providing multilingual capabilities: it must load the library and provide the `HINSTANCE` returned to the `AfxSetResourceHandle` function call. Now when the application refers to resource ids, the resources in the desired resource-only DLL will be used.

When the header file or import library is not available

At times your application may need to call into a DLL whose header file or import library is not available to you. You can place the calls to the exported functions in your application, but without the header file you probably won't be able to compile your application, and without the import library you won't be able to link your application.

If you can dump a list of the functions the DLL exports, however, you can have your application dynamically load the library and get the address of the functions you need to call. At that point, you can call the desired functions.

Retrieving resources from a binary file

Another popular reason for dynamically loading a library is to retrieve its resources. Because the resource compiler binds the resources to the application or DLL at "make" time, the resources are located in the binary file itself. An example of this would be the standard mouse cursors in Windows. These cursors can be retrieved from the User32.DLL by dynamically loading the DLL and calling the `LoadCursor()` function that is passing the resource id of the desired cursor.

Expert Tip

Viewing Binary Resources

You can view the resources of a binary file from DevStudio. Simply invoke the File Open dialog and locate the binary file that contains the resources you want to view. After you have specified the desired binary file, change the Open As combo box to Resources. When the file is opened, you will see all of its resources just as if you were opening up any resource file.

✦ ✦ ✦ ✦ ✦

Demo to dynamically load a DLL

If you've ever used the Control Panel, you know it displays all the Control Panel applets in the system. These applets are generally system-level maintenance applications. Because the Control Panel must communicate with each applet, the way you write a Control Panel applet is to export a few very specific, documented functions for the Control Panel to load and call. For example, applets must export functions used to retrieve the applet's description and the icon to be displayed in the Control Panel. The demo used here is very similar in nature to how the Control Panel communicates with its applets.

This demo is built on the idea of a product that enables its end-users to configure different communications APIs. Because each communications API resides in a DLL, the application will need to use the `LoadLibrary()` function to load appropriate DLLs (using a mask for the filename). The application will then attempt to use `GetProcAddress()` for a function that will return the description of the communications API being used in the DLL. Obviously, if this function fails, you can assume the DLL was not the correct type for this application. Each communications API DLL will then have its description inserted into a list box on the application's main dialog box. Once all of the communications DLLs have been loaded and their descriptions inserted into the main application's list box, the end-user can then select one of these DLLs to have a communications-API-specific dialog displayed.

Because all the source code for this demo can be found on the accompanying CD in the `Chap22\CommClientApp`, `Chap22\CommSvrAppc`, and `Chap22\CommSvrTcpIp` folders, I didn't copy and paste all the code here. Instead, I only explain the salient points pertaining to the topic of this section.

Creating the regular DLLs

The first thing to do is create the demo DLLs. The first DLL you will create is the APPC DLL. Create a project named `CommSvrAppc` with the following settings:

- ✦ "MFC AppWizard (dll)" in the New dialog box
- ✦ "Regular DLL with MFC statically linked" as the DLL type

When the project has been created, add a simple "dummy" dialog box, as follows:

- ✦ Set the dialog box caption to read "Edit APPC Properties" to identify the dialog when the demo is run.
- ✦ Create a class for this dialog named `CEditAppcPropertiesDlg`.

Next, open the CommSvrAppc.h file and add the following function prototypes to the beginning of the file (before the class declaration). These functions will be used to query the DLL for its description and invoke its dialog.

```
void GetDescription(LPSTR lpszDesc);
void DisplayEditPropertiesDlg();
```

Open the CommSvrAppc.cpp file and add the following `#include` directive to the top of the file:

```
#include "EditAppcPropertiesDlg.h"
```

Implement the `GetDescription` and `DisplayEditPropertiesDlg` functions, as follows:

```
void GetDescription(LPSTR lpszDesc)
{
strcpy(lpszDesc, _T("Advanced Program to "
 "Program Communications"));
}

void DisplayEditPropertiesDlg()
{
 CEditAppcPropertiesDlg().DoModal();
}
```

Export the functions through the CommSvrAppc.def file so that the `EXPORTS` section looks like the following when finished:

```
EXPORTS
   GetDescription @1
   DisplayEditPropertiesDlg @2
```

Now, you need to create the second demo DLL: the TCP/IP DLL. Create a project named "CommSvrTcpip" with the following settings:

✦ "MFC AppWizard (dll)" in the New dialog box

✦ "Regular DLL with MFC statically linked" as the DLL type

When the project has been created, add a simple "dummy" dialog, as follows:

✦ Set the dialog box caption to read "Edit TCP/IP Properties" to identify the dialog.

  Note that on the CD, the demo dialog box has a couple of extra controls that were added to simply make the screen shot look a little more realistic. All you really need is something that distinguishes this DLL's dialog box from the APPC DLL's dialog box.

✦ Create a class for this dialog box named `CEditTcpipPropertiesDlg`.

Next, open the CommSvrTcpip.h file and add the following function prototypes to the beginning of the file (before the class declaration). These functions will be used to query the DLL for its description and invoke its dialog.

```
void GetDescription(LPSTR lpszDesc);
void DisplayEditPropertiesDlg();
```

Open the CommSvrTcpip.cpp file and add the following `#include` directive to the top of the file:

```
#include "EditTcpipPropertiesDlg.h"
```

Implement the `GetDescription()` and `DisplayEditPropertiesDlg()` functions as follows:

```
void GetDescription(LPSTR lpszDesc)
{
strcpy(lpszDesc, _T("TCP/IP Support"));
}

void DisplayEditPropertiesDlg()
{
 CEditTcpipPropertiesDlg().DoModal();
}
```

Export the functions through the CommSvrTcpip.def file so that the `EXPORTS` section looks like this when finished:

```
EXPORTS
    GetDescription @1
    DisplayEditPropertiesDlg @2
```

Creating the demo application and dialog

Once the demo DLLs have been built, it's time to create the main application to test the loading of these DLLs and the calling of their exported functions. To do this:

1. Using AppWizard, create a dialog-based application named "CommClientApp."
2. Create a dialog box to be used in displaying the DLL descriptions. Model the dialog box after the one illustrated in Figure 22-1.

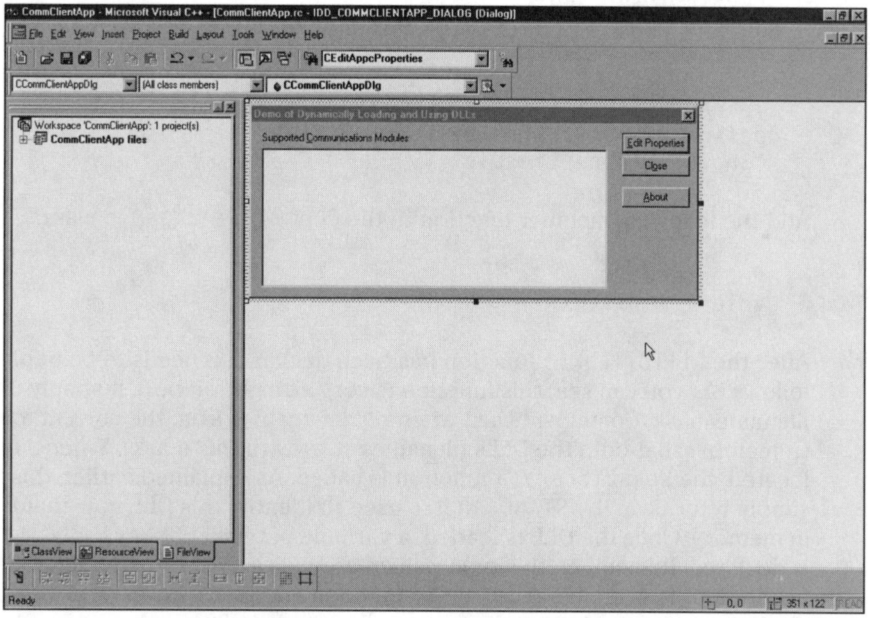

Figure 22-1: Dynamic DLL load demo dialog box

3. Once you have created the dialog box, create a member variable of type `CListbox` for the list box and call it `m_lbxDlls`.

Using the LoadLibrary and GetProcAddress functions

So far, everything has been pretty cut and dried. A couple of DLLs were created (CommSvrAppc and CommSvrTcpip). Each of these DLLs defined two functions (GetDescription and DisplayEditPropertiesDlg). Finally, each DLL used its .DEF file to export its respective functions. Now, it's time to define these functions in such a way that the calling application, or client, can use them.

As mentioned earlier, dynamically loaded DLLs have their functions called through function pointers. Therefore, you need to declare variables of that function type. To do that, you must first create a typedef of the function so you have a valid type to use when declaring the function pointer. If you've never done this before, it is actually much easier to do than it sounds. Here's what you need to enter at the top of the CommClientAppDlg.h file (before the dialog class declaration) to declare the types necessary to call the two functions being exported from the DLLs:

```
typedef void (* COMM_API_DLL_INFORMATION)
 (LPSTR lpszDesc);
#define COMM_API_DLL_INFORMATION_FUNCTION \
 "GetDescription"

typedef void (* COMM_API_DLL_EDITPROPS)();
#define COMM_API_DLL_EDITPROPS_FUNCTION \
 "ShowEditPropertiesDlg"
```

Add the following member function to the CCommClientAppDlg class:

```
protected:
 void FillDllLbx();
```

After the FillDllLbx() function has been declared, it needs to be implemented as follows. As you can see, this function is very straightforward. It simply uses a filename mask, CommSvr*.DLL, when retrieving files from the current folder (remember that both the DLLs filenames start with this mask). When a file is located, the LoadLibrary() function is called. As explained earlier, this function simply returns an HINSTANCE that is used to identify this DLL now that it is loaded in memory. Once the DLL is loaded, a variable of type COMM_API_DLL_INFORMATION is declared. Remember, this type was created via a typedef statement in the header file. The GetProcAddress() function is then called to retrieve a pointer to the function referred to by the COMM_API_DLL_INFORMATION_FUNCTION #define (GetDescription()). If the GetProcAddres() function call is successful, this function pointer will have a non-NULL value. This function is then called simply by placing parentheses behind it. The whole process is performed for each file corresponding to the CommSvr*.DLL filename mask found in the current working folder. When this function has completed, all the appropriate DLL descriptions will have been loaded in the dialog's list box, and its Item Data will have been set to the DLL's HINSTANCE returned by the LoadLibrary() function call.

```
void CCommClientAppDlg::FillDllLbx()
{
 WIN32_FIND_DATA findData;
```

```
  HANDLE hFile;
  CString strFileMask = "CommSvr*.DLL";

  char szCurrentDirectory[CHAR_MAX];
  GetCurrentDirectory(sizeof(szCurrentDirectory),
   szCurrentDirectory);

  ZeroMemory(&findData, sizeof(findData));
  hFile = FindFirstFile(strFileMask, &findData);
  if (INVALID_HANDLE_VALUE != hFile)
  {
   do
   {
    if ((findData.dwFileAttributes
    & FILE_ATTRIBUTE_NORMAL) ||
    (findData.dwFileAttributes & FILE_ATTRIBUTE_ARCHIVE))
    {
     TRACE1("*** Found '%s'\n", findData.cFileName);

     HINSTANCE hInst = NULL;
     hInst = LoadLibrary(findData.cFileName);

     TRACE2("*** LoadLibrary on '%s' %s\n",
      findData.cFileName, (NULL != hInst ? _T("succeeded")
      : _T("failed")));

     if (hInst)
     {
      COMM_API_DLL_INFORMATION pfnCommApiDllInfo
      = (COMM_API_DLL_INFORMATION)GetProcAddress(hInst,
      COMM_API_DLL_INFORMATION_FUNCTION);

      TRACE2("*** GetProcAddress for '%s' %s\n",
      COMM_API_DLL_INFORMATION_FUNCTION,
      (NULL != pfnCommApiDllInfo ? _T("succeeded")
      : _T("failed")));

      if (pfnCommApiDllInfo)
      {
       char szDesc[255];
       pfnCommApiDllInfo(szDesc);

       int iIndex = m_lbxDlls.AddString(szDesc);
       m_lbxDlls.SetItemData(iIndex, (DWORD)hInst);
      }
     }
    }
   } while (FindNextFile(hFile, &findData));
  }
 FindClose(hFile);
}
```

Now that all the DLLs have been loaded and their descriptions inserted into the list box, it is time to code the Edit Properties command button so the end-user can display the appropriate dialog box for each DLL. To do this, use ClassWizard to add an `OnOK()` handler to the dialog box. The Edit Properties command button should have an ID of IDOK for this to work. This function simply checks to see if an item is currently selected in the list box. If an item is selected, its Item Data is retrieved and cast to an `HINSTANCE`. This `HINSTANCE` is then used to call `GetProcAddress()` for the DLL's `ShowEditPropertiesDlg()` function, which is used to invoke that DLL's dialog box.

```
void CCommClientAppDlg::OnOK()
{
 int iIndex = m_lbxDlls.GetCurSel();
 if (CB_ERR == iIndex)
 {
  AfxMessageBox("You must first select an "
   "communications API DLL");
 }
 else
 {
  HINSTANCE hInst =
  (HINSTANCE)m_lbxDlls.GetItemData(iIndex);
  if (NULL == hInst)
  {
   AfxMessageBox("Invalid HINSTANCE");
  }
  else
  {
   COMM_API_DLL_EDITPROPS pfnEditProps =
   (COMM_API_DLL_EDITPROPS)GetProcAddress(hInst,
   COMM_API_DLL_EDITPROPS_FUNCTION);

   TRACE2("*** GetProcAddress for '%s' %s\n",
    COMM_API_DLL_EDITPROPS_FUNCTION, (NULL != pfnEditProps
    ? _T("succeeded") : _T("failed")));

   if (pfnEditProps)
   {
    pfnEditProps();
   }
  }
 }
}
```

The next thing that needs to be done to the code is some cleanup work. Every time you use the `LoadLibrary()` function to dynamically load a library, you must call the `ReleaseLibrary()` function to release the resources Windows has associated with it. Therefore, because the `LoadDllsLbx()` function placed an entry into the list box for every valid DLL found and set its Item Data to the loaded DLL's `HINSTANCE`, a function is needed to cycle through that list box, retrieve the `HINSTANCE` for each DLL that was loaded, and call `ReleaseLibrary()` for each one. Because this is the last thing that should be done before this application exits, a good place to put it would be in the `OnDestroy()` virtual function. At this pointer, use ClassWizard to implement a message handler for the `WM_DESTROY` message and modify it so it looks like the following:

```
void CDynLibLoadTestDlg::OnDestroy()
{
 CDialog::OnDestroy();

 HINSTANCE hInst;
 CString strCommApiDll;
 BOOL bSuccess;

 for (int i = 0; i < m_lbxCommAPIs.GetCount(); i++)
 {
  m_lbxCommAPIs.GetText(i, strCommApiDll);
  TRACE1("*** Attempting to locate hinst for '%s' "
   "from listbox's ItemData\n", strCommApiDll);

  hInst = (HINSTANCE)m_lbxCommAPIs.GetItemData(i);
  if (hInst)
  {
   bSuccess = ::FreeLibrary(hInst);

   TRACE2("*** FreeLibrary on '%s' %s\n", strCommApiDll,
    (NULL != hInst ? _T("succeeded") : _T("failed")));
  }
 }
}
```

Testing the demo

To test the demo, you need to copy the DLLs to the folder that the application will run from. This is because the `FillDllLbx()` function will only look in the current folder to find the communications API DLLs.

When the DLLs have been copied, run the application. The results should be similar to what you see in Figure 22-2.

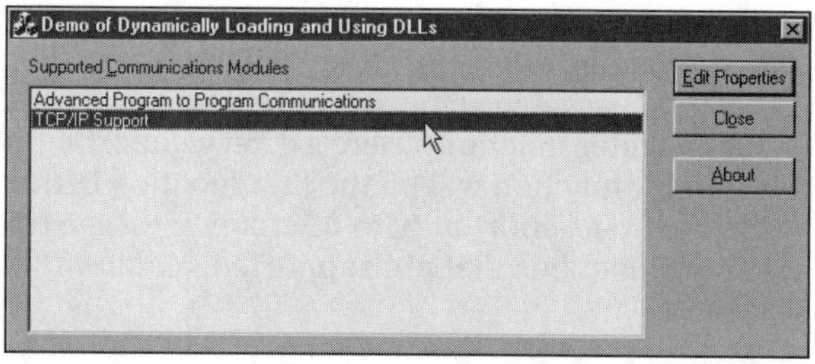

Figure 22-2: Dynamic DLL load demo after `LoadLibrary` and `GetProcAddress` have been executed on DLLs

Selecting the TCP/IP entry should then result in a similar outcome to what you see in Figure 22-3.

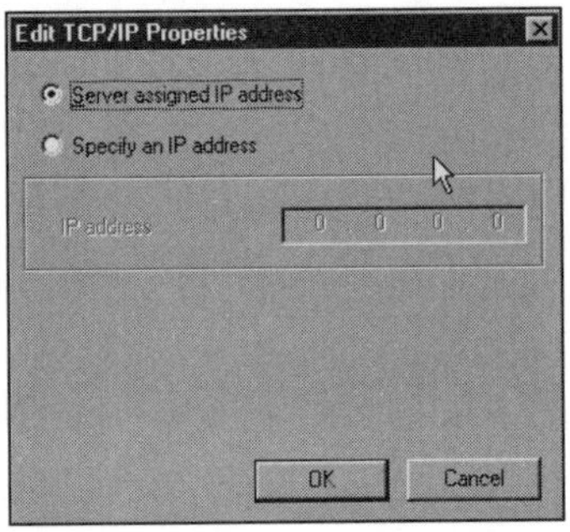

Figure 22-3: Dynamic DLL load demo after a DLL entry has been selected and the DLL displays a dialog specific to its functionality.

Writing Windows hooks

During my stint at Microsoft's MFC newsgroup (`microsoft.public.vc.mfc`), I have seen many a post directed at finding out how to write hooks of one type or another. (By the way, let me interject that if you are not already using this newsgroup, you should probably look into it — it's a tremendous source of free support, tips, knowledge, links to source code, and the like.) In addition to seeing other programmers request hook instructions in the various newsgroups, I have also been asked personally to explain this process quite a few times. Therefore, because hooks are implemented via DLLs, a system-level keyboard hook constitutes the subject of this section.

Definitions and terminology for Windows hooks

Before we go any further, let's take a look at some terminology. *Hooks* are points in the Windows messaging path where subroutines are injected or attached to filter certain types of messages before they reach their target destination. Once these messages are caught, they can be modified, logged, or simply discarded. The subroutines themselves are called *filters*. These filters are classified according to the types of events they are filtering. For example, the hook that you write in this section is known as a *keyboard hook*. When a filter function is attached to a hook, this is known as *setting a hook*. As you might imagine, there will be times when more than one hook of the same type has been set. In order to deal with this, Windows keeps track of the chain of filter functions. Here's a very important point to note: the most recently added filter function will be the first function in that chain and, therefore, it will have the first opportunity to filter any message traffic. The following table shows the hook functions that are supported, along with a brief description of each.

Table 22-1
Windows Hook Functions

Function	***Description***
WH_CALLWNDPROC	Used to monitor all Windows messages before the message is sent to its destination window procedure (see WH_CALLWNDPROCRET).
WH_CALLWNDPROCRET	Used to monitor messages after they have been processed by the destination window procedure.
WH_CBT	Monitors messages used by Computer-Based-Training applications.
WH_DEBUG	Used to aid in debugging other hook functions.
WH_GETMESSAGE	Monitors Windows messages posted to a message queue.
WH_JOURNALPLAYBACK	Used to post messages previously recorded by a WH_JOURNALRECORD hook procedure.
WH_JOURNALRECORD	Used to record input messages posted to the system message queue.
WH_KEYBOARD	Used to monitor keyboard activity.
WH_KEYBOARD_LL	Used to monitor low-level keyboard input events (Windows NT only).
WH_MOUSE	Used to monitor mouse messages.
WH_MOUSE_LL	Used to monitor low-level mouse input events (Windows NT only).
WH_MSGFILTER	Used to monitor messages generated as a result of an input event in a dialog box, message box, menu, or scroll bar.
WH_SHELL	Used to receive notification of events meaningful to shell applications.
WH_SYSMSGFILTER	Used to monitor messages generated as a result of an input event in a dialog box, message box, menu, or scroll bar, similar to the WH_MSGFILTER. However, WH_SYSMSGFILTER monitors these messages for all active applications.

SetWindowsHookEx

To set a hook, the SetWindowsHookEx() function must be called. Its prototype looks like this:

```
SetWindowsHookEx(int idHook, HOOKPROC lpfn,
 HINSTANCE hMod, DWORD dwThreadId)
```

The first argument, `idHook`, represents a constant that identifies what type of hook is being set. About 15 types of hooks can be set for Windows. The value that will be used in the demo application is the `WH_KEYBOARD` constant, which indicates to the `SetWindowsHookEx()` function that a keyboard hook is being set. (Refer to the online help or MSDN for information on the other types of hooks that can be used.)

The second argument, `lpfn`, is simply a pointer to a function of type `HOOKPROC`. For a keyboard hook, the function passed to the `SetWindowsHookEx()` must have the following prototype:

```
LRESULT CALLBACK KeyboardProc(int code, WPARAM, LPARAM);
```

An example of this function and an explanation of its arguments are covered in the source code explanation.

The third argument, `hMod`, is the `HINSTANCE` of the DLL that contains the filter function.

The fourth and last argument to the `SetWindowsHookEx()` function enables you to specify the thread for which the hook is being set. For example, you can set a hook for one single thread or for all threads that are currently active. For the latter, simply specify a value of NULL for this argument.

When the `SetWindowsHookEx()` function returns, it returns a value of type `HHOOK` (handle to a hook). If the hook was not successfully set, this returned value is `NULL`, and you then need to call the `GetLastError()` function to determine the cause of its failure.

UnhookWindowsHookEx

To remove a hook from the hook chain, you must call the `UnhookWindowsHookEx()` function. This function (shown as follows) simply takes the `HHOOK` value returned by the successful setting of a hook via the `SetWindowsHookEx()` function. The `UnhookWindowsHookEx()` function returns a Boolean value, which can be used to test for the success or failure of this function.

```
BOOL UnhookWindowsHookEx(HHOOK hHook);
```

CallNextHook

The only other function that is of major importance when programming filter functions is `CallNextHook()`. As explained earlier, when a filter function is set for a given hook type, the filter function is placed at the head of a chain of filter functions for that hook type. Once a filter function completes its task, it can call the `CallNextHook()` function for the next filter function to perform its work. However, occasionally you won't want processing to continue. For example, if you write a keyboard hook and want to discard the keystroke, you would not call this function. If you are simply logging an event and you want the message to continue along its intended messaging path, you would need to call the `CallNextHook()` function. If there are no other filter functions for this type of hook, Windows delivers the message to the appropriate message queue.

Writing the keyboard hook DLL

The first thing you need to do is create the DLL that will contain the filter function for the keyboard hook. Create a project named KeybdHook with the following settings:

- ✦ "MFC AppWizard (dll)" in the New dialog box
- ✦ "Regular DLL with MFC statically linked" as the DLL type

Open the KeybdHook.h file and add the following lines before the CKeybdHookApp's class declaration. The first `#define` simply provides an easy way of exporting functions that have the `__stdcall` calling mechanism. The second function is the actual filter function. It is the function that will be called for every single keystroke Windows processes. Its arguments are explained shortly.

```
#define EXPORTED_DLL_FUNCTION \
 __declspec(dllexport) __stdcall

LRESULT EXPORTED_DLL_FUNCTION KbdHookProc (int nCode,
 WPARAM  wParam, LPARAM lParam);
```

Now, open the KeybdHook.cpp file and add the following lines to the top of the file. What this does is create a shared data segment across all uses of this DLL. That way, the values defined within it are global to all uses of this DLL. Always remember: when using this technique to create variables like this, you are required to initialize those variables.

```
#pragma data_seg(".SHARDAT")
static HWND      hWndMain  = 0;
static HHOOK     hKeyHook = NULL;
#pragma data_seg()

HINSTANCE hInstance = 0;
HOOKPROC  lpfnHookProc = 0;
```

After declaring the global variables that will be used in this DLL, you define the filter function (`KbdHookProc`) that will be called every time Windows processes a keystroke. Add the following filter function that you declared earlier. As you can see, I am simply catching the F10 keystroke here to show how you would catch specific keystrokes in your own keyboard filter function. Obviously, once your specific filter function catches the keystrokes it is filtering, you are then free to run whatever application-specific logic you need. Notice that if the keystroke is handled, and you do not want Windows to continue processing the keystroke, simply return a value of `TRUE` from this function instead of calling the next filter function for this hook type.

```
LRESULT EXPORTED_DLL_FUNCTION KbdHookProc (int nCode, WPARAM
wParam, LPARAM lParam)
{
 BOOL bHandledKeystroke = FALSE;
```

```
if (((DWORD)lParam & 0x40000000)
&& (HC_ACTION == nCode))
{
 switch (wParam)
 {
  case VK_F10:
   AfxMessageBox("Caught the F10 key!");
   bHandledKeystroke = TRUE;
  break;

  default :
  break ;
 }
}

return (bHandledKeystroke ?
 TRUE :
 ::CallNextHookEx (ghKeyHook, nCode, wParam, lParam));
}
```

Let's do a quick run-through of the different arguments passed to a keyboard hook function like the one just used.

One of the values that the first argument, `nCode`, might contain is the `HC_ACTION` constant. Actually, this variable will only contain one of two values: `HC_ACTION` and `HC_NOREMOVE`. In both cases, the `WPARAM` and `LPARAM` variables will contain information about the keystroke. However, when `nCode` has a value of `HC_NOREMOVE`, the destination application for this keystroke has used the `PeekMessage` function, specifying the `PM_NOREMOVE` flag. In addition, if the value of `nCode` is less than zero, the filter function should not attempt to process the keystroke; it should call the `CallNextHookEx()` function instead.

The `WPARAM` value contains the virtual key code of the generated keystroke. As you can see in the `KbdHookProc()` function just shown, this value can be used to verify which key was pressed.

Finally, the `LPARAM` value is used to find out more information about the keystroke, such as the repeat count and whether the key was down or up before the message was sent. In the previous example, the `LPARAM` is used to determine the latter case.

Once you have defined the keyboard filter function, you need to export a couple of functions to set and release the keyboard hook. First, open the KeybdHook.h file and declare the following function, which will be used to install or set the keyboard hook:

```
BOOL EXPORTED_DLL_FUNCTION InstallKeyboardHook
 HWND hWnd);
```

Once you have declared the function, define it as follows in the KeybdHook.cpp file. If this function works successfully and the keyboard hook is set, the ghKeyHook variable will have the HHOOK returned from the SetWindowsHookEx() function. Therefore, the first thing InstallKeyboardHook() does is check this variable to see if it has a value. If it does, the hook has already been set, and this function simply returns. If the ghKeyHook variable does not have a value, this function attempts to set the keyboard hook. You already defined the glpfnHookProc in the preceding global data segment, but what about the ghInstance variable being set? This variable will be set in the InitInstance() function for this DLL. (I'll get to this shortly.) This function then returns success or failure based on whether or not the SetWindowsHookEx() successfully set the hook.

```
BOOL EXPORTED_DLL_FUNCTION InstallKeyboardHook
 (HWND hWnd)
{
 BOOL bSuccess = FALSE;

 if (!ghKeyHook)
 {
  ghWndMain     = hWnd ;
  glpfnHookProc = (HOOKPROC) KbdHookProc ;

  bSuccess = (NULL != (ghKeyHook =
   ::SetWindowsHookEx (WH_KEYBOARD, glpfnHookProc,
   ghInstance, NULL)));
 }

 return bSuccess;
}
```

Now that you have exported a function to set the keyboard hook, you also need to export a function to release the keyboard hook. Declare the following function above the InstallKeyboardHook() function declaration in the KeybdHook.h file:

```
BOOL EXPORTED_DLL_FUNCTION DeInstallKeyboardHook();
```

After declaring the function to remove the keyboard hook, place the following function definition in the KeybdHook.cpp file. Note that the ghKeyHook variable is reset to NULL if the UnHookWindowsHookEx() function works successfully. This is so the user of this DLL can call InstallKeyboardHook() again to reset the hook if needed.

```
BOOL EXPORTED_DLL_FUNCTION DeInstallKeyboardHook()
{
 if (ghKeyHook)
 {
  if (TRUE == (0 != ::UnhookWindowsHookEx(ghKeyHook)))
  {
```

```
      ghKeyHook = NULL;
    }
  }

  return (NULL == ghKeyHook);
}
```

Now that all the code for setting and removing a keyboard hook is in place, use ClassWizard to add both an `InitInstance()` function and an `ExitInstance()` function to the `CKbdHookApp` object. They should be defined as follows:

```
BOOL CKbdHookApp::InitInstance()
{
  AFX_MANAGE_STATE(AfxGetStaticModuleState());
  ghInstance = AfxGetInstanceHandle();
  return TRUE;
}

int CKbdHookApp::ExitInstance()
{
  DeInstallKeyboardHook();
  return CWinApp::ExitInstance();
}
```

Building a test for the keyboard hook DLL

Now that you have written the hook function, it is time to do the easy part: testing it. To test your new keyboard hook, simply use AppWizard to create a dialog-based application named KeybdHookClient.

After the project has been created, use ClassWizard to create a function for the IDOK button being clicked. In the handler, simply call the DLL's exported `InstallKeyboardHook()` function. Your `OnOK` function should look like this:

```
void CKeybdHookClientDlg::OnOK()
{
 InstallKeyboardHook(GetSafeHwnd());
}
```

Next, use ClassWizard to override the dialog's `OnCancel()` function. This function will simply make sure the keyboard hook is removed before the application terminates. When finished, the `OnCancel()` function should look like the following:

```
void CKeybdHookClientDlg::OnCancel()
{
 DeInstallKeyboardHook();
 CDialog::OnCancel();
}
```

As with any DLL, now all you have to do is include the header file that contains the declarations for the functions you want to call. Add the following `#include` at the top of the KeybdHookClientDlg.cpp file. Obviously, you have to either fully qualify this name or place the folder where this file resides in your include folder path.

```
#include "KeybdHook.h"
```

The only thing left to do before building and running the test application is to include the keyboard hook DLL's import library, KeybdHook.lib.

Testing the keyboard hook DLL

As a test of the keyboard hook, simply find a product that uses the F10 key to do something. Because the F10 key is defined by Common User Access (CUA) to provide keyboard access to the menu, plenty of applications implement this keystroke. I used the Notepad application. To test the keyboard hook DLL in Notepad, simply do the following:

1. Start the Notepad application.

   Your cursor is placed in the body of the document (actually a multiline edit control).

2. Press the F10 key.

   This places you on the File menu.

3. Press the Esc key to return from the menu to the document.

4. Run the KeybdHookClient application and press the Enter key.

   This sets the keyboard hook.

5. Return to the Notepad application and press the F10 key.

   Instead of being placed on Notepad's File menu, you see a message box that states the F10 key was successfully filtered. Because the keyboard hook filter function did not call the `CallNextHook()` function, this key was not sent to the Notepad application, and you are not able to get to the Notepad menu via this keystroke. In other words, this keystroke has been filtered and essentially discarded.

6. Close the KeybdHookClient application.

   This releases the keyboard hook.

7. Return to the Notepad application and press the F10 key.

   The F10 key now works as it originally did because the keyboard hook has been released.

Figure 22-4 shows an example of this procedure. Notice that although the Notepad application was the current application when the F10 key was pressed, the filter function caught it and displayed its own message instead of allowing the Notepad application to process it.

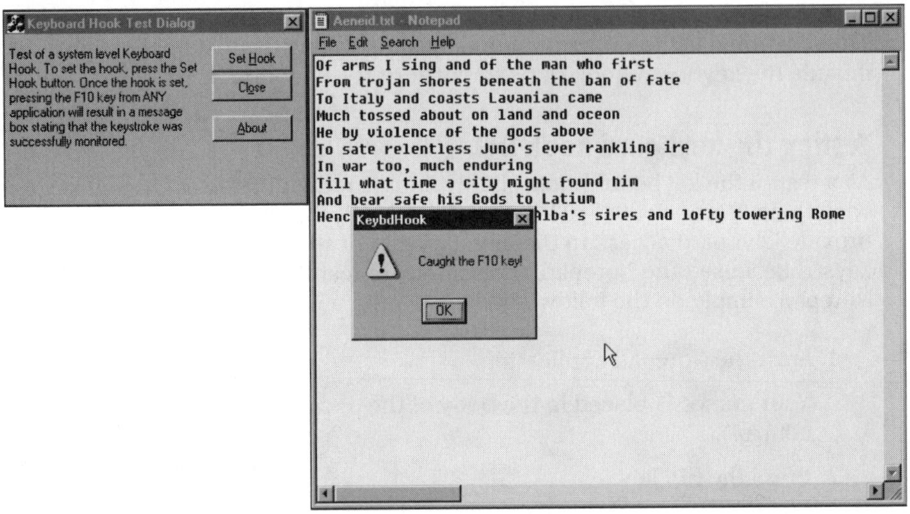

Figure 22-4: Example of the keyboard hook in progress. This example filters and discards the F10 key so that the Notepad application never has an opportunity to process it.

MFC Extension DLLs

Whereas regular DLLs are typically used to export C functions for non-MFC clients, MFC Extension DLLs are used to export functions and classes that enhance MFC. For example, let's say you have created a new toolbar derived from the MFC `CToolbar` class. To export this class, you need to place it in an MFC Extension DLL. Another example of when to use an MFC Extension DLL is if you want to encapsulate each view or logical group of views in a separate DLL in an MDI application.

Understanding the MFC Extension DLL internals

Whereas both MFC Extension DLLs and regular DLLs can be created via the AppWizard and therefore can be built in a similar fashion, there are a number of fundamental differences between the two DLL types:

- ✦ An MFC Extension DLL client *must* be an MFC application.
- ✦ Unlike a regular DLL, an MFC Extension DLL does not have a `CWinApp`-derived object.

✦ Whereas regular DLLs typically do their initialization through the InitInstance() and ExitInstance() functions, an MFC Extension DLL must provide its own DllMain() for this purpose.

✦ MFC Extension DLLs introduce a new class, CDynLinkLibrary, to enable the export of CRuntimeClasses or resources.

Exporting classes via MFC Extension DLLs

MFC Extension DLLs are usually implemented when a need arises to export classes that are based on MFC. Classes and their functions are exported in one of two ways, depending on how much of a class the DLL wants to export. In other words, the developer of an MFC Extension DLL can choose to export either entire classes or a limited subset of the functionality of a particular class.

In the section covering regular DLLs, you saw that the .DEF file is normally used to export functions from a regular DLL. This causes some inconvenience with C++ classes (such as the MFC classes), in that if you want to use the .DEF file to export them, you must specify the compiler-dependent mangled or decorated name. Luckily, MFC has a couple of macros that make this job much easier. When exporting entire classes from a DLL, the AFX_EXT_CLASS macro is used in the class declaration like this:

```
class AFX_EXT_CLASS CMyFancyToolbar : public CToolbar
...
```

Exporting parts of a class is just as easy. Instead of using the AFX_EXT_CLASS macro when declaring the class, simply place the macro in front of the function being defined that you wish to export, as follows:

```
class CMyFancyDialog : public CDialog
{
public:
 AFX_EXT_CLASS CMyFancyDialog();
 AFX_EXT_CLASS int DoModal();
public:
  BOOL Create(LPCTSTR lpszTemplateName,
   CWnd* pParentWnd = NULL);
  BOOL Create(UINT nIDTemplate, CWnd* pParentWnd = NULL);
...
```

Note that in the CMyFancyDialog class, the class constructor and DoModal() functions will be exported and the two overloaded Create() functions will not.

More on the AFX_EXT_CLASS

As you just saw, the AFX_EXT_CLASS macro can be used to export either entire classes or parts of classes. When a client application includes the header file that contains the declaration of the classes the DLL is exporting, however, a problem arises: Both modules are stating to the linker that they are responsible for exporting the class. This potential problem is resolved by the AFX_EXT_CLASS macro definition being dependent on the following preprocessor definitions for the project:

✦ If _AFXDLL and _AFXEXT are defined for the project, the AFX_EXT_CLASS macro resolves to the following:

```
__declspec(dllexport)
```

✦ If _AFXEXT is *not* defined, the AFX_EXT_CLASS macro resolves to the following for import purposes:

```
__declspec(dllimport)
```

Therefore, when AppWizard is used to create an MFC Extension DLL, both _AFXDLL and the _AFXEXT are defined. Any time the DLL's source code refers to the AFX_EXT_CLASS, the class is being exported.

Using nested MFC Extension DLLs

As mentioned previously, the AFX_EXT_CLASS macro is used to export an entire class or parts of a class from a DLL. Problems may arise, however, if you nest MFC Extension DLLs. As an example, let's say you have an MFC Extension DLL of common routines and classes that you use on all projects. Let's call this DLL the Common DLL. You may then have another MFC Extension DLL that contains common routines and classes for a specific project, which is called the Project DLL. The Project DLL would almost certainly use the Common DLL. This is what is meant by the phrase "nested MFC Extension DLLs"—one MFC Extension DLL uses another.

When you attempt to link the Project DLL, you may receive linker errors. This is because both the Common and Project DLLs are using the same macro and declaring the same classes, when in fact the Project DLL needs to import the classes it needs from Common DLL.

The workaround to this problem is very simple. Instead of using the AFX_EXT_CLASS macro, you need to use a macro that takes into consideration the project using it. For example, you could create a common macro called COMMON_IMPORT_EXPORT and define it as follows. The header file used to declare the classes and functions that the Common DLL exports will use the COMMON_IMPORT_EXPORT macro instead of the AFX_EXT_CLASS macro. The advantage is that only the Common DLL will be exporting its classes. Any other modules will be importing them. One way to define the _COMMON_DLL for the Common DLL would be to define it in the Project Setting dialog for that DLL.

```
#ifdef _COMMON_DLL
 #define COMMON_IMPORT_EXPORT  _declspec(dllexport)
#else
 #define COMMON_IMPORT_EXPORT  _declspec(dllimport)
#endif
```

Exporting resources

Each MFC application contains a linked list of CDynLinkLibrary objects. If your code in an MFC application requests that MFC load a resource on its behalf, MFC first attempts to load the requested resource from the current module. MFC locates this module's resources by calling the AfxGetResourceHandle function. If the requested resource cannot be located, MFC "walks" the application's linked list of CDynLinkLibrary objects in an attempt to locate the resource. To set the default module that MFC uses to first locate requested resources, you need to use the AfxSetResourceHandle function to specify the HINSTANCE of the module.

Writing a demo that encapsulates documents and views in a DLL

As this is the day and age of component-based reusable software, the MFC Extension DLL demo will illustrate how to place document and view support into a DLL. Let's say you have written a document and view to support the reading of .JPG files. Maybe you had to write an application that, among many other things, needed to display these files. You would normally create the document and view classes to support these files within the scope of the main application. However, what happens if tomorrow you need to provide the same JPG viewing functionality for another application? It would obviously be a much better practice to place application-independent logic (like the viewing of JPG files) into a DLL that any application could use.

Creating the ImageViewer DLL

The first thing you will need to do is to create the MFC Extension DLL named ImageViewer. Once you have created the project, use ClassWizard to create a CScrollView-derived class called CImageViewerView. After ClassWizard has created the files for this new class, open the ImageViewerView.cpp file and delete the following line.

```
#include "   \ add additional includes here"
```

Since this demo will use the ImageObject library to display the images, open the "ImageViewerView.h" file and add the following #include directive. A demo of this imaging library can be found on the accompanying CD.

```
#include "imageobject.h"
```

After inserting the #include directive, add the following member variable to the CImageViewer class. This object is all you will need to display graphics files.

```
protected:
 CImageObject* m_pImageObject;
```

Now open the ImageViewerView.cpp file and make the following changes to the constructor and destructor:

```
CImageViewerView::CImageViewerView()
 : CFormView(CImageViewerView::IDD)
{
 m_pImageObject = NULL;
}

CImageViewerView::~CImageViewerView()
{
 delete m_pImageObject;
 m_pImageObject = NULL;
}
```

Next, modify the view's `OnInitialUpdate()` function so that it looks like the following code. The first thing the code does is to retrieve the name of the image file from the document object. Then, the size of the image is retrieved via the `CImageObject::GetWidth()` and `CImageObject::GetHeight()` functions. The values returned from these functions are then passed to the `SetScrollSizes()` function so that the view will automatically adjust the vertical and horizontal scrollbars according to the view's size and how much of the image is within the view's viewing area.

```
void CImageViewerView::OnDraw(CDC* pDC)
{
void CImageViewerView::OnInitialUpdate()
{
 CScrollView::OnInitialUpdate();

 CDocument* pDoc = GetDocument();
 ASSERT_VALID(pDoc);
 if (pDoc)
 {
  CString strPathName = pDoc->GetPathName();
  ASSERT(0 < strPathName.GetLength());
  if (0 < strPathName.GetLength())
  {
   m_pImageObject = new CImageObject(strPathName);

   CSize sizeTotal;
   sizeTotal.cx = m_pImageObject->GetWidth();
   sizeTotal.cy = m_pImageObject->GetHeight();
   SetScrollSizes(MM_TEXT, sizeTotal);
   ResizeParentToFit();
  }
 }
}
```

After modifying the OnInitialUpdate() function, modify the `OnDraw()` function so that it looks as follows:

```
 if (m_pImageObject)
 {
  m_pImageObject->SetPalette(pDC);
  m_pImageObject->Draw(pDC);
 }
}
```

After finishing with the view, use ClassWizard to create a `Cdocument`-derived class called CImageViewerDoc. Once the files have been created for this new class, all you need to do to finish with the document class is to open the ImageViewerDoc.cpp file and remove the following line.

```
#include "  \ add additional includes here"
```

Encapsulating the image document and view in a class

Now that you have coded the view and the document class, it's time to concentrate on the important part of this demo: encapsulating the document and view in a DLL. First, create a file called ImageViewer.h. It will be a very simple file used to expose a `CImageViewer` class with a single function, `CImageViewer::Init()`. This `Init()` function is what an application will call in order to use the document and view that are coded in this DLL.

The ImageViewer.h file should look like the following.

```
#pragma once

class AFX_EXT_CLASS CImageViewer
{
public:
 BOOL Init();
};
```

Once you have created and saved the ImageViewer.h file, add the following `#include` directives to the "ImageViewer.cpp" file.

```
#include "ImageViewer.h"
#include "resource.h"
#include "ImageViewerDoc.h"
#include "ImageViewerView.h"
```

Add the `Init()` function, as follows. This function simply takes as its only argument a pointer to the application object. It's needed for the `AddDocTemplate` function call. After that, this function creates a `CMultiDocTemplate` and adds it to the application object's list of document templates via the `AddDocTemplate` function.

```
BOOL CImageViewer::Init(CWinApp* pApp)
{
```

```
 BOOL bSuccess = FALSE;

  CWinApp* pApp = AfxGetApp();
  ASSERT(pApp);
  if (pApp)
  {
   CMultiDocTemplate* pDocTemplate;

   pDocTemplate = new CMultiDocTemplate(
    IDR_IMAGEDOCTYPE,
    RUNTIME_CLASS(CImageViewerDoc),
    RUNTIME_CLASS(CMDIChildWnd),
    RUNTIME_CLASS(CImageViewerView));

   ASSERT(pDocTemplate);
   if (pDocTemplate)
   {
    pApp->AddDocTemplate(pDocTemplate);
    bSuccess = TRUE;
   }
  }

  return bSuccess;
}
```

For the document template to be created, you need to create a string table in the DLL's resource file and add a document entry. It should have an ID of `IDR_IMAGEDOCTYPE` and have a value of `\nImageV\nImageV\nImage Files (*.jpg, *.gif, *.bmp)\n.jpg;.gif;.bmp;\nImage Viewer.Document \nImageV Document`.

The last step before building the DLL is to link to the ImageObject and ImageLoad import libraries. (There is a debug and release library for both.) Don't forget that in order to run the test application, you not only need to copy the DLL you are coding now to the appropriate folder, but you also need to install the ImageObject library from the CD.

Building a test for the image document and view DLL

Now that you have written the MFC Extension DLL to house the document and view for the types of files you will allow users to open, it's time to do the easy part: create the application.

Using AppWizard, create a MDI application named ImageViewerClient. Make sure that the Document/View checkbox is checked. Once the project's files have been created, open the ImageViewerClient.h file and add the following `#include` directive before the declaration of the `CImageViewerClientApp` class:

```
#include "ImageViewer.h"
```

Open the ImageViewerClient.cpp file and add the following line to the application object's constructor:

```
m_pImageViewer = new CImageViewer();
```

Locate the `InitInstance()` function. Replace the entire function body with the following code:

```
BOOL CImageViewerClientApp::InitInstance()
{
 Enable3dControls();
 LoadStdProfileSettings();

 CMainFrame* pMainFrame = new CMainFrame;
 if (!pMainFrame->LoadFrame(IDR_MAINFRAME))
  return FALSE;

 pMainFrame->ShowWindow(m_nCmdShow);
 pMainFrame->UpdateWindow();
 m_pMainWnd = pMainFrame;

 ASSERT(m_pImageViewer != NULL);
 m_pImageViewer->Init();

 return TRUE;
}
```

Finally, create a destructor for `CImageViewerClient` to delete the `m_pImageViewer` object as follows:

```
CImageViewerClientApp::~CImageViewerClientApp()
{
 delete m_pImageViewer;
 m_pImageViewer = NULL;
}
```

Now that the code is written for the test application, simply add the import library for your MFC Extension DLL to this application's project.

Figure 22-5 shows an example of having run this application and opened a couple of .GIF files.

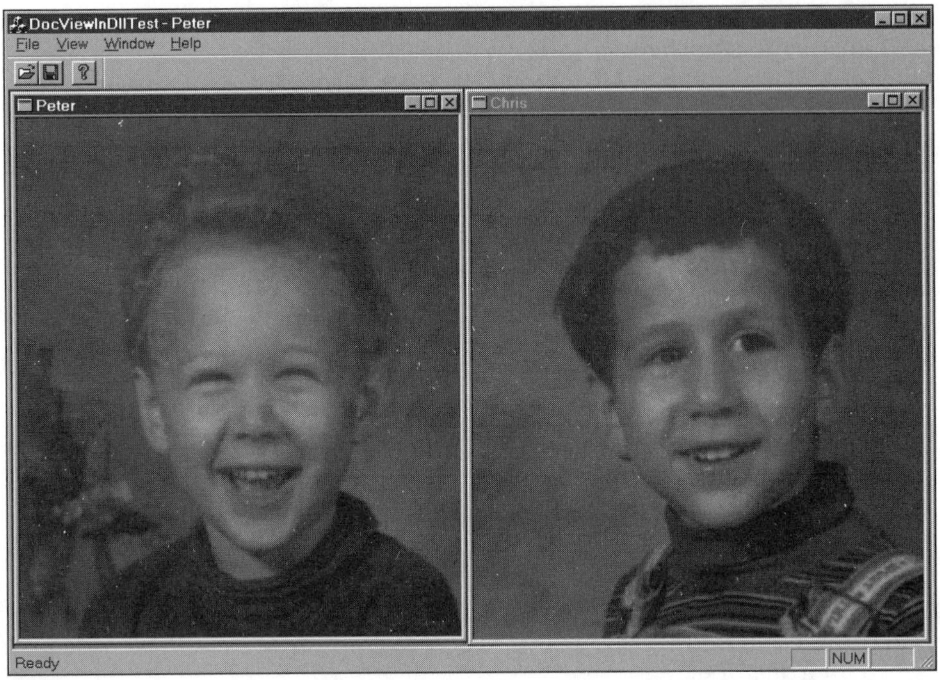

Figure 22-5: Example of encapsulating an MFC document and view in a DLL. Now any application can easily have this viewing capability simply by linking with this DLL and calling a single function.

Summary

Throughout this chapter you've seen just how easy it is to implement both regular DLLs and MFC extension DLLs to solve different programmatic problems. With regards to regular DLLs, you learned how to manage the current "module state" so that the DLL can make calls to the shared version of the MFC DLLs, and you worked through two demos: a system-level keyboard hook and an application that dynamically loads and uses DLLs with the `LoadLibrary()` and `GetProcAddress()` functions. You also learned about MFC Extension DLLs that will enable you to export whole classes or specific member functions of a class and worked through two demos that illustrated how to use nested MFC Extension DLLs and how to place documents and views in a separate DLL from the main application.

✦ ✦ ✦

CHAPTER 23

Extending Applications with Third-Party Libraries

✦ ✦ ✦ ✦

In This Chapter

Learning the advantages of third-party add-on libraries

See an overview of the ImageObject library

Understanding different image file formats

Loading, saving, and drawing images with ImageObject

Altering images with processing functions

Viewing sample programs that use ImageObject

✦ ✦ ✦ ✦

Visual C++ isn't limited to the functionality that you get with MFC or that you can add by writing your own classes. With Visual C++, you can easily link in third-party, add-on libraries that give you extra functionality such as image loading, additional database functions, and telecommunications. Linking in libraries with additional functionality extends Visual C++ because it allows you to easily perform tasks that aren't built into the language or its foundation class libraries.

Buying third-party libraries usually costs money. These extensions are rarely free, and often very costly. For instance, an imaging library that loads, saves, displays, and manipulates images will run between $250 and $2,000. But the cost might be inexpensive in comparison with how much it would cost to develop similar functionality on your own. Writing imaging functions to load, save, display, and manipulate images takes six months to a year. So, any time you consider buying an add-on library, you should calculate the cost of writing the code yourself and compare that with the cost of the library you're considering buying.

You can find third-party libraries advertised in practically every programming magazine. Catalogs such as *Programmer's Shop* and *Programmer's Warehouse* specialize in C++ libraries. In fact, add-on libraries for C++ are common place because they're cost effective ways to add functionality to Visual C++ programs.

Using a Third-Party Library

Libraries come in a variety of types. The most common form is a compiled .LIB file. To use the library, all you must do is add the library filename to the project's link section, include the .H file that will also come with the library, and make function calls to the library's API.

Suppose you bought a library with the filename *NewLib.LIB*. To add the library to your project, follow these steps:

1. Select Settings from the Project menu; the Project Settings dialog box appears.
2. Select the Link tab.
3. Set the Category combo box to General.
4. In the "Object/library modules" text box, enter the library filename.

Figure 23-1 illustrates the Project Settings dialog box with *NewLib.LIB* added. Note that "All Configurations" is selected in the "Settings For" combo box. When *NewLib.LIB* is added to the "Object/library modules" text box, it will take effect for both the release and debug versions of your application.

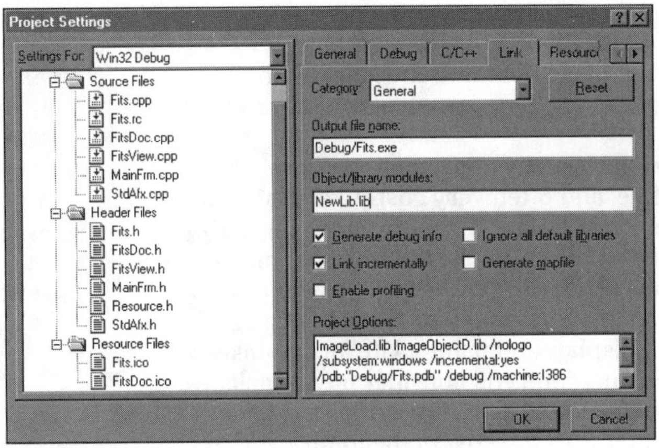

Figure 23-1: The Project Settings dialog box with Object/library modules set for NewLib.LIB

The next time you compile and link, the .LIB file will be linked to your project.

Sometimes you'll get both a release and a debug .LIB file version. If this is the case, you'll have to add the release and debug versions of the library separately. To do so, follow these steps:

1. For the release version, select Win32 Release in the Settings For combo box of the Project Settings dialog box.
2. Add the release version of the library to the "Object/library modules" text box.
3. For the debug version, select Win32 Debug in the Settings For combo box of the Project Settings dialog box.
4. Add the debug version of the library to the "Object/library modules" text box.

Debug .LIB files usually have the same name as release .LIB files except that there's a *D* appended to the name. For instance, the `NewLib.LIB` file would probably be the release version of our hypothetical example; the debug version would probably be named `NewLibD.LIB`.

Many linked libraries also come with dynamic-link library (DLL) files. These must be placed in the application's directory, the Windows directory, or the Windows\System directory. It's better if you can leave the library in the application's directory. The Windows and Windows\System directories tend to collect DLLs rapidly as software is installed. Keeping a DLL in the application's directory will help keep these important directories cleaner.

It's not always desirable, however, to put a DLL in the application's directory. If more than one application is to share a DLL, install it to the Windows\System directory. That way, you'll only need a single copy of the DLL for multiple programs. This will save the space on the user's hard drive. Multiplied over many installed applications, placing shared DLLs in the Windows\System directory can save users many megabytes of disk space.

When you get a third-party library, you'll need to tell the linker where it is so that it can find the file at link time. You'll also want to tell the compiler where the `#include` files are by following these steps:

1. Select Options from the Tools menu.
2. Select the Directories tab and choose the "Include files" option in the "Show directories for" combo box.
3. Add the directory in which the `#include` files for the compiler reside.
4. Choose "Library files" in the "Show directories for" combo box.
5. Add the directory in which the library files for the compiler reside.

Figure 23-2 shows the Options dialog box, with the library paths shown.

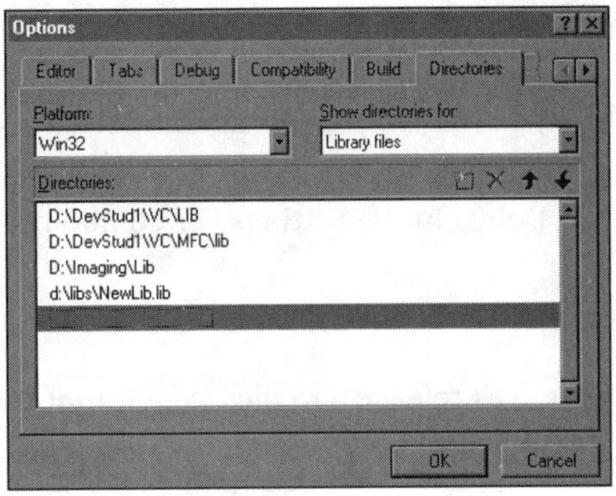

Figure 23-2: The Options dialog box showing the path for the new library

An alternative to adding the path of the library .LIB and .H files is to copy the .LIB and .H files into the directories that hold the compiler's include and library files. You might want to do this if you have already added to the paths to the include and library file and want to avoid making them any longer. Adding too many paths (especially long paths) will slow things down during compile and link time.

Some libraries come as source code modules that you must link into your project. This is rare, though, as most libraries come compiled into a .LIB file or a .LIB and .DLL combination.

The ImageObject Library in Brief

On the CD-ROM

Included on the distribution CD-ROM is a library that you can use in your programs. From the root of the CD-ROM, find a directory named `Chap23`. Inside the `Chap23` directory is a file named `IOSetup.exe`. This is a self-extracting installation file for the ImageObject library. It copies all the files to your hard drive and then sets up your compiler's include and library directories. Make sure Visual C++ isn't running when you install the installation file, otherwise the include and library directories won't be properly updated.

✦ ✦ ✦ ✦ ✦

The `ImageObject` library lets you easily load, save, display, manipulate, and image process pictures. It handles .BMP, .GIF, .JPG, .PCX, .TGA, and .TIF files. The version that comes with this book is fully functional. You can freely use it for programs that aren't commercial in any way. If you want to sell or charge for programs that use the `ImageObject` library, though, you'll have to purchase a registered version. Registration and ordering information can be found in the `Ordering.TXT` file in the Chap23 directory on the CD-ROM.

The library combines a .LIB and a .DLL file. The `ImageLoad.dll` file will be copied to your Windows\System directory. That way the DLL will always be available for applications since the Windows\System directory is always searched when the system tries to load a DLL.

There's a class library that wraps the lower-level imaging function calls. The class library makes it a snap to perform the imaging functions. For instance, you can load an image with a single line of code. You can save an image with a single line of code too. You can display an image with two lines of code from within your `OnDraw()` function.

Image manipulation functions such as cropping, stretching, and rotating are simple as well. Single lines of code perform all these functions. Many image processing functions are available to enhance your images, filter your images, or create special imaging effects. And as with all the other functionality of the `ImageObject` library, they're extremely easy to use.

An ActiveX control is also included. It automatically registers when the library files are installed. Details about using this control can be seen in Chapter 32, entitled "Using C++ and Visual Basic Together."

A demonstration program called ImageView can be found in the Chap23\ImageView directory of the CD-ROM. It demonstrates the features that are available to you when you use this add-on library. Figure 23-3 shows the ImageView application with several image windows open. Two of the images have been partially enhanced with image processing operations.

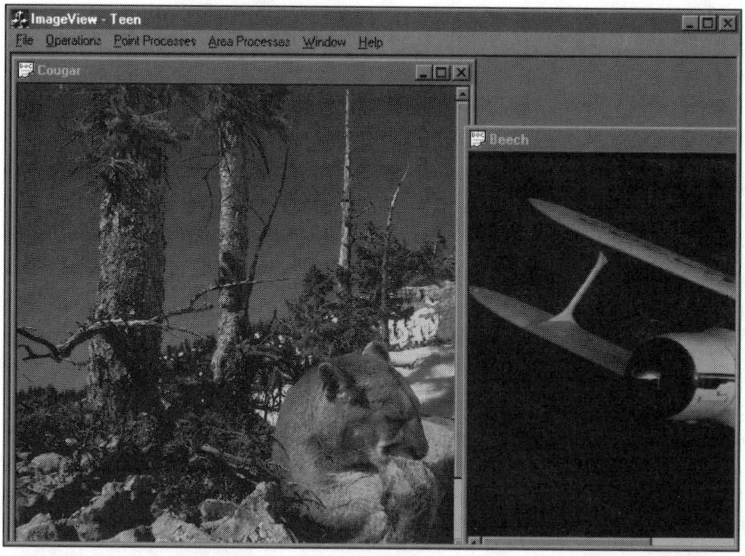

Figure 23-3: The ImageView demonstration program, showing two images that have been enhanced with the ImageObject library

Supported Image File Formats

The `ImageObject` library supports six image file formats. The supported file formats are .BMP, .GIF, .JPG, .PCX, .TGA, and .TIF. This section explains the basics of each of these file formats. Since no one file format is perfect for all situations, you'll have to decide based on the attributes of the image file format and what your needs are.

To better compare file formats, three sample images are shown below. These three images have been saved in six different file formats. The file sizes of the three images saved in each format are shown in Table 23-1. This information will enable you to decide which file format best suits a particular situation.

In the JPEG section, three versions of the sailboat image are shown at different levels of compression. Each level of compression in the JPEG format trades a quality level for file size. The lower the quality, the smaller the file size. Creators of computer art must strike a balance between huge file sizes for perfect images and smaller file sizes for somewhat degraded images.

Here's a general rule of thumb for appropriate uses of the three most common formats:

✦ A photographic image, as shown in Figure 23-4, is usually saved using the JPEG format since that format compresses them so well.

Figure 23-4: Image 1 – A photographic image using the JPEG file format

✦ Images that contain drawings are common in many applications. The next image shown in Figure 23-5 is a drawing. Frequently images such as this one are saved in the GIF format since it compresses them so well.

Figure 23-5: Image 2 – An image with a drawing can be used to demonstrate the effectiveness of some formats such as GIF.

✦ The last type of image to consider is the simple drawing, such as the one in Figure 23-6. Images of this type compress fairly well in run-length encoded (RLE) formats such as the PCX format. The PCX format loads images faster than GIF format; it can be a good choice when loading and compression are both important.

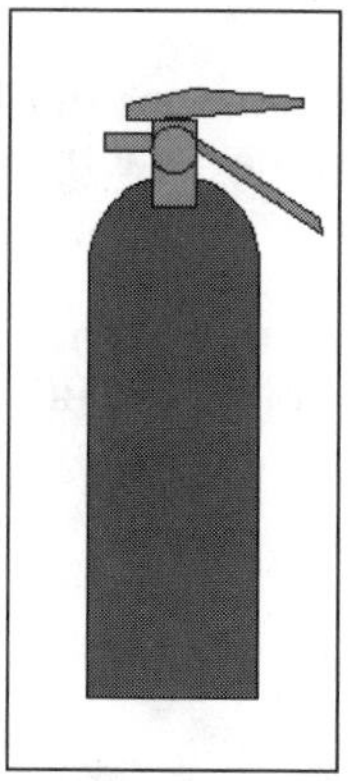

Figure 23-6: Image 3 – A very simple image might compress well in a PCX file format and load quickly too.

Table 23-1
Saved Image Sizes Using Six File Formats

Format	*Image 1 Bytes*	*Image 2 Bytes*	*Image 3 Bytes*
BMP	111,670	944,886	212,742
GIF	46,419	19,719	2,775
JPEG	141,656 (least compression)	234,124	128,547
JPEG	16,301 (moderate compression)	64,642	11,611
JPEG	8,414 (greatest compression)	30,193	7,322
PCX	88,988	92,474	13,144
TGA	331,794	944,850	212,706
TIF	112,626	945,324	213,180

The BMP file format

The Microsoft Windows Bitmap (BMP) file format is one of several graphics-file formats supported by the Microsoft Windows operating environment. As the native bitmap format of Windows, BMP is used to store virtually any type of bitmap data. Most graphics and imaging applications running under Microsoft Windows support the creation and display of BMP files.

BMP files support all the screen resolutions and color combinations that Windows supports. For this reason, a BMP file can always be created that exactly matches a screen format.

BMP files are almost always completely uncompressed. This makes them very large. A screen capture of a screen that's 800 by 600 and a color resolution of 24 bits will create a file that takes up 2,743,545 bytes. As you can see, if disk space is a consideration, this file format isn't a good choice.

The GIF file format

GIF stands for Graphics Interchange Format. Its major feature is its great compression ratios, achieved by using LZW compression. The same BMP image that's 800 by 600 with a color resolution of 24 bits, after being converted to a color resolution of 8 bits, can be as small as 20 kilobytes.

In today's age of high color resolution, one disadvantage to GIF is its limitation to 8 bits of color resolution. For most applications this is enough. For applications requiring photographic-quality images, it's not adequate.

The JPEG file format

JPEG is one of the newest file formats to become popular. Its major feature is its great compression, achieving smaller file size than even GIF's compression — but at the expense of image integrity.

Often, losing a small amount of image quality won't be noticed. In cases such as this, JPEG is a good choice because of the fantastic image compression. The same BMP image that's 800 by 600 with a color resolution of 24 bits can be as small as 5 kilobytes.

JPEGs are normally used for photographic images. That's because the small amount of image degradation can rarely be detected in a photographic image. The tradeoff between file size and an unperceived loss in quality weighs in on the side of smaller file sizes.

Figure 23-7 shows the sailboat image (Image 1) with a minimal amount of compression and almost no image degradation.

Figure 23-7: Image 1 with almost no compression suffers almost no image degradation.

Figure 23-8 shows the sailboat image (Image 1) with a moderate amount of compression and little image degradation.

Figure 23-8: Image 1 with moderate compression suffers little image degradation.

Figure 23-9 shows the sailboat image (Image 1) with the highest amount of compression and some perceivable image degradation.

Figure 23-9: Image 1 with high compression suffers some perceivable image degradation.

The PCX file format

PCX was developed by Zsoft many years ago to provide its own paint program, PC Paint, with an image-file format that offers some data compression. The compression produces a file size somewhat better than an uncompressed file, but the run-length-encoding scheme it uses can still produce large image files.

The fact that its compression doesn't save much space has PCX files fading fast from the PC scene.

The TGA file format

Targa (TGA) files were developed to support hardware devices that capture video images. The Targa file format makes it easy to store many of the video captures to disk since very little data manipulation is required.

Targa offers some compression schemes, but normally the images are stored in an uncompressed format. One big advantage that Targa files have had for some time is their support for images ranging from monochrome to those of 32-bit color resolution.

The TIFF file format

TIFF, or *tagged image file format*, was designed to be the file format that would be everything to everybody. As a result, the file format became difficult to maintain. Many vendors and third parties added their own tags, or modifications, making it hard to keep up with the changes in the file format.

It's still used in many desktop publishing applications because it handles many photometric values that are necessary when manipulating the images. It offers several compression schemes, but TIFF files are found uncompressed more often than not.

Working with the ImageObject Library

This section will show you how to use the `ImageObject` library to perform the basic image tasks such as loading, saving, and displaying. Explanations and example code fragments are presented to teach you how to use the function calls of the class library. None of the examples are full applications. Later on there's a demo program named Display that shows you how to load and display an image.

Loading images with the ImageObject library

Now you learn how to load images from disk with the ImageObject library. It's actually very simple; a single line of code will do for many situations. There are, however, some coding nuances — as well as some ways to maximize the library's built-in features — of which you should be aware; this section explains them.

The very first thing you must do is include `ImageObject.h` in any source code module that refers to the ImageObject's functions. I usually put the include directive inside another `#include` file. For instance, if my view class makes use of the ImageObject library's functions, I add `#include ImageObject.h` at the top of the view class's `#include` file.

The next thing you must do is to create a `CImageObject` class. There are two versions of the `CImageObject` constructor. The first takes no arguments and simply constructs the class. The second accepts the filename that is to be loaded into the class as an argument. The second version, which takes a filename, also has three additional optional arguments that are explained shortly.

If you create the class without a filename, you must make a call to the `Load()` function before the image is loaded. If you create the class with a filename, the image is loaded from disk at the time of the class creation. The prototypes for the `CImageObject` constructors and the `Load()` function are shown in the text that follows. Two other functions, `GetLastError()` and `GetImageInfo()` are shown as well.

Class Library

CImageObject Constuctors and Basic Functions (Load, Error, and Information)

This section shows the display functions for the `ImageObject` library. It's a summary that'll make it easy for you to do initial experiments. For more comprehensive documentation, check the `ImageObject.doc` file.

CImageObject(void);

This constructor takes no arguments. It simply creates a `CImageObject` class and initializes its internal variables.

CImageObject(const char *szFilename, CDC *pDC, int nX, int nY);

This example constructs a `CImageObject` class. The only argument required is the filename. If the `CDC` argument is given, the image will be drawn immediately after it's loaded. If `nX` or `nY` are given, their values will be stored and the image will be drawn to that location. Otherwise, the image will always be drawn to coordinates 0, 0.

BOOL Load(const char *szFilename, CDC *pDC, int nX, int nY);

This function loads a file into the `CImageObject` class. The only argument required is the filename. If the `CDC` argument is given, the image will be drawn immediately after it's loaded. If `nX` or `nY` are given, their values will be stored and the image will be drawn to that location. Otherwise, the image will always be drawn to coordinates 0, 0.

int GetLastError(void);

This function returns the last `CImageObject` error that occurred. See the Errors.h `#include` file for details.

BOOL GetImageInfo(const char *pszFilename, int *pnWidth, int *pnHeight,int *pnPlanes, int *pnBitsPerPixel, int *pnNumColors);

This function retrieves the image width, height, number of bit planes, number of bits per pixel, and number of colors. Any arguments that are NULL will not be filled in. The only mandatory argument is the filename; all others are optional.

◆ ◆ ◆ ◆ ◆

Declaring and allocating CImageObject class: version 1

The recommended way to declare and allocate a `CImageObject` class is to load an image and then delete the `CImageObject` class. In the example that follows, the hypothetical source code and the `#include` file to which the code is added are (respectively) `View.cpp` and `View.h`.

1. Add to the top of `View.h`:

   ```
   #include "ImageObject.h"
   ```

2. In `View.h`, add a public variable to the `View` class:

   ```
   CImageObject *m_pImageObject;
   ```

3. In `View.cpp`, add the following to the `View` constructor:

   ```
   m_pImageObject = new CImageObject( "Filename.bmp" );
   ```

4. In `View.cpp`, add the following to the `View` destructor:

```
if( m_pImageObject != NULL )
  delete m_pImageObject;
```

Declaring and allocating CImageObject class: version 2

Another way to create a `CImageObject` class and load the image— also easy— may suit your purposes better:

1. Add the following at the top of `View.h`:

```
#include "ImageObject.h"
```

2. In `View.h`, add a public variable to the `View` class:

```
CImageObject m_ImageObject;
```

3. In `View.cpp`, add the following to the `View` constructor:

```
m_pImageObject.Load( "Filename.bmp" );
```

Either creation method is simple to implement. After you've created the `CImageObject` class, the image is in memory, ready to use later when you want to display it in a device context. There are a few details that you should consider, one of which is error trapping.

The `Load()` function returns a boolean flag indicating success or failure. If the image loads successfully, the return value will be `TRUE`. If the image load doesn't work correctly for some reason, the return value will be `FALSE`. You can use the `GetLastError()` function of the `CImageObject` class to retrieve the value for the last error that occurred. Using this value, you can alert users to the specific problem that prevented an image from being loaded.

Expert Tip

Deleting Classes Created with the New Operator

If you create a `CImageObject` object with the new operator, make sure that you delete it before leaving your application (or when you're done with the object). If you don't delete it, the memory that was allocated for the class won't be freed, and the internal memory that the class creates will also not be freed.

◆ ◆ ◆ ◆ ◆

Following is a simple example of alerting users to errors that occur during image loading:

CImageObject pImageObject;

```
pImageObject = new CImageObject();
if( m_pImageObject == NULL )
 AfxMessageBox("Allocation error creating CImageObject");
else if( !pImageObject->Load( "File name.bmp" ) ){
```

```
switch( pImageObject->GetLastError() ){
 case IMAGELIB_FILE_OPEN_ERROR:
  AfxMessageBox("The image file could not be opened.");
  break;
 case IMAGELIB_FILE_READ_ERROR:
  AfxMessageBox("There was a read error.");
  break;
 case IMAGELIB_MEMORY_ALLOCATION_ERROR:
  AfxMessageBox("There was a memory allocation error.");
  break;
 case IMAGELIB_MEMORY_LOCK_ERROR:
  AfxMessageBox("There was a memory lock error.");
  break;
 case IMAGELIB_UNSUPPORTED_FILETYPE:
  AfxMessageBox("The file is unsupported.");
  break;
 default:
  AfxMessageBox("An image loading error occurred.");
 }
}
```

One more thing that you might need before you actually load an image is to retrieve information about an image. The `GetImageInfo()` function returns important information that will allow you to prepare for loading an image. Such preparations include creating a window of the correct size and creating a new view class. The following code shows you how to retrieve and display information about an image.

```
CImageObject ImageObject;
int nWidth, nHeight, nPlanes, nBitsPerPixel, nNumColors;
char szDisplayInfo[200];
ImageObject.GetImageInfo( "Filename.bmp", &nWidth,
 &nHeight, &nPlanes, &nBitsPerPixel, &nNumColors );
CString strInfo;
StrInfo.Format(
  "Width:%d Height:%d Planes:%d Bits:%d Colors:%d",
  nWidth, nHeight, nPlanes, nBitsPerPixel, nNumColors );
AfxMessageBox( strInfo );
```

Nutshell

Simple Loading of Images

The steps necessary to load images using the ImageObject class library are summarized here.

1. Include `ImageObject.h` in your source code or one of your source code's `#include` files.
2. Link in `ImageLoad.lib` and `ImageObject.lib` (`ImageObjectD.lib`) for the debug version.

3. Declare a `CImageObject` object as one of the following:

```
CImageObject ImageObject;
```
or
```
CImageObject *pImageObject;
```

4. Load in the image from disk by using the `Load()` function or allowing the `CImageObject` constructor to load the image. Three different methods follow:

- `CImageObject` **objects not declared as pointers:**

```
ImageObject.Load( "Filename.bmp" );
```

- `CImageObject` **objects declared as pointers:**

```
pImageObject = new CImageObject( "Filename.bmp" );
```

- `CImageObject` **objects declared as pointers and loaded with the** `Load()` **function:**

```
pImageObject = new CImageObject;
pImageObject->Load( "Filename.bmp" );
```

◆ ◆ ◆ ◆ ◆

Saving images with the ImageObject library

To save an image, a valid `CImageObject` class must already be created. The class must also contain a valid image. When you save, you have two options. One `Save()` function takes no arguments, the other takes two arguments. The two arguments of the second version of the `Save()` function are the filename and an integer value with the file type that is to be saved.

The prototypes for the `Save()` functions, as well as the functions used to retrieve image information, appear in the sidebar that discusses "CImageObject Save() and Additional Information Functions."

Class Library

CImageObject Save() and Additional Information Functions

This class library shows you the `ImageObject` functions that allow you to perform other important operations such as saving the image to disk. Check the `ImageObject.doc` file for in-depth documentation.

BOOL Save(void);

This function saves the currently loaded image. It's saved with the same filename and file type that are stored as properties in the class. This function returns `TRUE` if it succeeds, `FALSE` if it fails. For specific error codes, use the `GetLastError()` function to retrieve the error value and consult the Errors.h `#include` file to see the defines for each error.

BOOL Save(const char *pszFilename, int nFileType);

This function saves the currently loaded image. It's saved as a file with the name that's passed in. The `nFileType` parameter is optional. If it's not given, the image is saved as the same image type. As with the previous version of `Save()`, this function returns `TRUE` if it succeeds, `FALSE` if it fails. For specific error codes, use the `GetLastError()` function to retrieve the error value and consult the Errors.h `#include` file to see the defines for each error. After an image is saved with a new filename and type, those are retained in the class's properties until further changes are made.

int GetWidth(void);

This function returns the pixel width of the image.

int GetHeight(void);

This function returns the pixel height of the image.

int GetNumBits(void);

This function returns the pixel depth of the image. Common values are 8, 16, and 24.

int GetNumColors(void);

This function returns the number of colors that are in the image.

void GetFilename(char *pszFilename);

This function returns the filename of the image. You must pass in a char buffer that will then be populated with the image filename. Make sure the `char` buffer is at least 256 characters to accommodate long path and filename combinations.

✦ ✦ ✦ ✦ ✦

Now that you've seen the functions that will be used for saving images and getting image information, we'll create some code examples that use the functions. The first example loads an image and then displays information about the image.

```
BeginWaitCursor();
CImageObject ImageObject( "File name.bmp" );
EndWaitCursor();

char szDisplayInfo[500], szFile name[300];
ImageObject.GetFilename( szFilename );

CString strInfo;
strInfo.Format(
  "File name:%s Width:%d Height:%d Bits:%d Colors:%d",
  szFile name.GetBuffer( 0 ),
```

```
    ImageObject.GetWidth(),
    ImageObject.GetHeight(),
    ImageObject.GetNumBits(),
    ImageObject.GetNumColors() );

  AfxMessageBox( strInfo );
```

The next code example loads in a file called Filename.bmp and saves it out as Filename.gif. Notice that the `Save()` function takes a filename argument specifying `Filename.gif` and a second argument that specifies the image type to be saved as `IMAGETYPE_GIF`.

```
BeginWaitCursor();
CImageObject ImageObject( "Filename.bmp" );
ImageObject.Save( "Filename.gif", IMAGETYPE_GIF );
EndWaitCursor();
```

There are six supported image types. They are listed below in Table 23-2; next to each file type is the define to use when saving images.

Table 23-2
File-Type Defines

File Type	*Define Name*
BMP	IMAGETYPE_BMP
GIF	IMAGETYPE_GIF
JPG	IMAGETYPE_JPG
PCX	IMAGETYPE_PCX
TGA	IMAGETYPE_TGA
TIFF	IMAGETYPE_TIF

An operator that might come in handy is the = operator that enables you to create a new class easily by using a copy of the contents of another class. For instance, suppose you already have a `CImageObject` class named `Image1` and you want to create a copy of it named `Image2`. The following code shows you how to create a second copy of an existing `CImageObject` class.

```
CImageObject Image2;
Image2 = Image1;
```

The = operator might be especially useful when you want to save an image with another filename and a different file type. You can create a copy of the original CImageObject class, then save it with a new filename and file type. The following example shows a function that accepts a CImageObject pointer as an argument. It accepts a new filename and a new file type. It creates a copy of the original class and then saves the new class with the new filename and type.

```
void CMyClass::SaveAs( CImageObject *pImage,
 char *pszNewFilename, int nNewType )
{

  CImageObject NewImage;
  NewImage = *pImage;
  NewImage.Save( pszNewFilename, nNewType );

}
```

Often you'll want to reload an image if you save it as a JPEG. That's because if the quality used for saving is low, the image quality will be degraded as it's saved to disk. The next time you load it, you might be surprised at the difference in quality; for this reason, you might want to reload the image immediately. The following example saves an image as a JPEG file, reloads it, then causes a redraw of the application window. The example assumes that a CImageObject class named Image has already been loaded.

```
Image.SetQuality( 70 );
Image.Save( "Filename.jpg", IMAGETYPE_JPG );
Image.Load( "Filename.jpg" );
InvalidateRect( NULL, FALSE );
UpdateWindow();
```

Drawing images with the ImageObject library

In most cases, you'll want to display images that you load. It just takes a single line of code to draw the image with the Draw() function. Before drawing to the window, you must load an image into your CImageObject class. If there's no valid image, the Draw() function will simply return without attempting to draw.

The prototypes and explanations for CImageObject Draw() functions can be studied in their own sidebar.

Class Library

CImageObject Draw() and SetPalette() Functions

Two ImageObject functions are needed for drawing the images in the device context and for setting the palette.

BOOL Draw(CDC *pDC, int nX, int nY, int nWidth, int nHeight);

This function draws the image to the device context. Only the `CDC` pointer is required, all other parameters are optional. The *x* and *y* coordinates of the `CImageObject` class default to 0, 0. If you never specify coordinates `nX` and `nY` when you call the `Draw()` function, the coordinates will stay at 0, 0. If you do pass some values to `nX` and `nY`, the `CImageObject` class will remember those coordinates and always draw to those coordinates until you pass in other values. The `nWidth` and `nHeight` parameters specify the width and height of the destination rectangle to which the image will be drawn. The `CImageObject` class doesn't remember these; if you don't pass the `nWidth` and `nHeight` arguments, the `Draw()` function will draw the image in the destination rectangle based on the pixel width of the image itself. If you want to specify `nWidth` and `nHeight` without changing the values for the *x* and *y* coordinates to which the image will be drawn, pass values of –1 to the `nX` and `nY` parameters.

BOOL SetPalette(CDC *pDC);

This function sets the palette on the basis of the image's palette. For 16-, 24-, and 32-bit images, this function has no effect.

◆ ◆ ◆ ◆ ◆

The easiest way to draw an image is from your view window's `OnDraw()` function. The following example uses the `OnDraw()` function from a simple demo program to draw an image from a `CImageObject` class named `Image`. It lets the `CImageObject` class draw to the coordinates it has stored (0, 0 in most cases) and lets it draw to the destination rectangle in the same pixel width and height of the image.

```
void CArtisteView::OnDraw(CDC* pDC)
{
 CArtisteDoc* pDoc = GetDocument();
 ASSERT_VALID(pDoc);
 Image.Draw( pDC );
}
```

Nutshell

Simple Loading and Display of an Image

The steps to load and display an image are simple. This summary will give you a handy reference when you begin to load and display images in your own program.

1. Include `ImageObject.h` in your source code or one of your source code's `#include` files.
2. Link in `ImageLoad.lib` and `ImageObject.lib (ImageObjectD.lib)` for the debug version.
3. Declare a `CImageObject` object as one of the following:

   ```
   CImageObject ImageObject;
   ```

   or

   ```
   CImageObject *pImageObject;
   ```

4. Load in the image from disk by using the `Load()` function or allowing the `CImageObject` constructor to load the image. Three different methods follow:

   - **`CImageObject` objects not declared as pointers:**

     ```
     ImageObject.Load( "Filename.bmp" );
     ```

   - **`CImageObject` objects declared as pointers:**

     ```
     pImageObject = new CImageObject( "Filename.bmp" );
     ```

   - **`CImageObeject` objects declared as pointers and then loaded with the `Load()` function:**

     ```
     pImageObject = new CImageObject;
     pImageObject->Load( "Filename.bmp" );
     ```

5. Draw the image into the device context as follows:

   - **CImageObject objects that are not declared as pointers**

     ```
     ImageObject.Draw( pDC );
     ```

   - **CImageObject objects that are declared as pointers**

     ```
     PImageObject->Draw( pDC );
     ```

◆ ◆ ◆ ◆ ◆

You can draw the image to a different location simply by passing `nX` and `nY` coordinates to the `Draw()` function. The following example draws the `CImageObject` named Image to *x*, *y* coordinates 25, 60.

```
void CArtisteView::OnDraw(CDC* pDC)
{
 CArtisteDoc* pDoc = GetDocument();
 ASSERT_VALID(pDoc);
 Image.Draw( pDC, 25, 60 );
}
```

Try This

Create a Simple Display Program

It's time to try your hand at loading and displaying images. Follow these steps to create a simple program that loads and displays images:

1. Create a single-document, AppWizard project named **SimpleDisplay**.
2. Include **ImageObject.h** at the top of **SimpleDisplayView.h**.
3. Declare a `CImageObject` member in any of the public sections of `SimpleDisplayView.h` as follows:

   ```
   CImageObject *m_pImageObject;
   ```

4. With Paint create a 24-bit image file in your project's directory named **Filename.bmp**.
5. Add the following to your `CSimpleDisplayView` class constructor:

```
m_pImageObject = new CImageObject( "Filename.bmp" );
```

6. Add the following to your `CsimpleDisplayView` class destructor:

```
delete m_pImageObject;
```

7. Link in `ImageLoad.lib` and `ImageObject.lib (ImageObjectD.lib)` for the debug version.
8. Add the following line to your `OnDraw()` function in the `CSimpleDisplayView` class:

```
m_pImageObject->Draw( pDC );
```

✦ ✦ ✦ ✦ ✦

Moving one step further, you can draw the image at coordinates 25, 60 with a width of exactly 100 pixels and a height of exactly 75 pixels with code such as the next example.

```
void CArtisteView::OnDraw(CDC* pDC)
{
 CArtisteDoc* pDoc = GetDocument();
 ASSERT_VALID(pDoc);
 Image.Draw( pDC, 25, 60, 100, 75 );
}
```

If you want to leave the *x* and *y* coordinates alone, you must pass –1 to the second and third arguments. The following example draws the image to the coordinates stored in the `CImageObject` class, but draws the image with a width of 100 and a height of 75.

```
void CArtisteView::OnDraw(CDC* pDC)
{
 CArtisteDoc* pDoc = GetDocument();
 ASSERT_VALID(pDoc);
 Image.Draw( pDC, -1, -1, 100, 75 );
}
```

You might have a need to draw an image that's twice as wide and twice as high as the original image. You can use the `GetWidth()` and `GetHeight()` functions to help you do that. The follow example draws an image at 0, 0 with a width and height that are twice as large as the original image.

```
void CArtisteView::OnDraw(CDC* pDC)
{
```

```
  CArtisteDoc* pDoc = GetDocument();
  ASSERT_VALID(pDoc);
  Image.Draw( pDC, 0, 0,
   Image.GetWidth() * 2,
   Image.GetHeight() * 2 );
}
```

Images with pixel depths of 8 bits or less have a palette that must be set. This should be done each time the image is drawn. You can set the palette of an image with pixel depths greater than 8. If you make a call to the `SetPalette()` function for an image with a pixel depth greater than 8, the `CImageObject` class will simply return without attempting to set the palette.

The following example adds a call to the `SetPalette()` function before making a call to the `Draw()` function. This is the recommended procedure.

```
void CArtisteView::OnDraw(CDC* pDC)
{
  CArtisteDoc* pDoc = GetDocument();
  ASSERT_VALID(pDoc);
  Image.SetPalette( pDC );
  Image.Draw( pDC );
}
```

You might have the need to fit an image exactly to the background of your view window. This can easily be done by drawing with a width and height that are obtained from the view window. The following example shows you how to create such an effect from inside your `OnDraw()` function.

```
void CArtisteView::OnDraw(CDC* pDC)
{
  CArtisteDoc* pDoc = GetDocument();
  ASSERT_VALID(pDoc);
  RECT Rect;
  GetClientRect( &Rect );
  Image.SetPalette( pDC );
  Image.Draw( pDC, 0, 0, Rect.right, Rect.bottom );
}
```

The previous code was compiled into an example program. Figure 23-10 shows the view window with the image drawn with the correct aspect ratio. It's not distorted horizontally or vertically because the view window's size has been adjusted to be correct for the image.

Figure 23-10: As you can see, the image looks good if the window is sized to the same proportion as the original image.

If users resize the view window and cause the window to be out of proportion with the original image, the image that's drawn in the view window will also be out of proportion. Figure 23-11 shows a narrow version of the parrot image after a user has resized the view window.

Figure 23-11: If users resize the window so it's out of proportion with the original image, the image will be drawn out of proportion.

The Display Program

This program shows you how to load and display an image in a window. It's a bare bones application so that you can focus in on the code that loads and displays images. After studying this program, you should try to write your own program, or embellish this one.

This program links in `ImageLoad.lib` and `ImageObject.lib`. It also expects to find `ImageLoad.dll` in the path.

Demo Program

Display
CD-ROM Location: **Chap023\Display**
Program Name: **Display.EXE**
Source Code Modules in Text: **DisplayView.cpp**

◆ ◆ ◆ ◆ ◆

Listing 23-1: **The Display Program**

```
// DisplayView.cpp : implementation of
// the CDisplayView class
//

/////////////////////////////////////////////////////////
// CDisplayView construction/destruction

CDisplayView::CDisplayView()
{

  // Make sure the CImageObject pointer
  // is NULLed so that we don't try
  // to delete it in the destructor
  // if for some reason it isn't
  // allocated.
  m_pImageObject = NULL;

}

CDisplayView::~CDisplayView()
{

  // If the CImageObject pointer
  // has been allocated, delete it.
  if( m_pImageObject != NULL )
    delete m_pImageObject;

}

/////////////////////////////////////////////////////////
// CDisplayView drawing

void CDisplayView::OnDraw(CDC* pDC)
{
  CDisplayDoc* pDoc = GetDocument();
  ASSERT_VALID(pDoc);

  // If the CImageObject pointer is NULL,
  // we allocate it and load the .BMP
  // file at the same time.
  if( m_pImageObject == NULL )
    m_pImageObject = new CImageObject( "FILE.BMP" );
```

```
    // If the CImageObject pointer is not NULL
    // display the image to the window.
    if( m_pImageObject != NULL ){

      // If this window has the focus, set
      // the palette. If the image has a color
      // depth greater than 8-bits and the hardware
      // display is greater than 8-bits, this call
      // will have no effect.
      if( GetFocus() == this )
        m_pImageObject->SetPalette( pDC );

      // Call the function that draws the image.
      m_pImageObject->Draw( pDC );
      }

  }
```

Cropping and Stretching Images

There are two operations that can be important for your applications. They are cropping and stretching an image. Cropping reduces an image from the full image down to any specific portion. Stretching changes the size of an image (either larger or smaller) to a new scaled image.

Two functions do all the work when you want to crop and scale images. Their prototypes and explanations can be found in the "Cropping and Stretching Functions" sidebar.

Class Library

Cropping and Stretching Functions

ImageObject's copping and stretching functions are detailed here. These two functions make it possible to manipulate images so that they fit in specified rectangles.

BOOL Crop(int nX1, int nY1, int nX2 int nY2);

This function crops an image from its original size to the portion of the image specified with the four arguments that are passed in as `nX1`, `nY1`, `nX2`, and `nY2`. For instance, if an image that has a width of 400 and a height of 300 is cropped, the arguments passed in might be 50, 100, 149, 199. If this is the case, the new image will be the rectangular portion of the original image that's bounded by the rectangle 50, 100, 149, 199. The new image will have a width of 100 and a height of 100. The function returns `TRUE` if it's successful and `FALSE` if it fails.

BOOL Stretch(int nNewWidth, int nNewHeight);

This function stretches an image from its original size to a new size. The two arguments that are given are the width and the height of the new image. For instance, if an image that has a width of 300 an a height of 200 are stretched, the arguments passed in might be 500 and 350. If this is the case, the image will be stretched larger and the size of the new image will be 500 by 350. The function returns `TRUE` if it's successful and `FALSE` if it fails.

◆ ◆ ◆ ◆ ◆

Here's an example that loads in an image, then crops it so that it becomes the portion of the original image bounded by the rectangular region 40, 50, 200, 100.

```
CImageObject ImageObject( "Filename.bmp" );
// ImageObject.GetWidth() will show a value of 500
// ImageObject.GetHeight() will show a value of 400
ImageObject.Crop( 40, 50, 200, 100 );
```

This next cropping example crops an image to the original image minus a 10 pixel boundary around each edge. The new image will be the same as the old image except for a 10 pixel border that goes around each edge.

```
CImageObject ImageObject( "Filename.bmp" );
ImageObject.Crop( 10, 10,
  ImageObject.GetWidth() - 10,
  ImageObject.GetHeight() - 10 );
```

The next example shrinks an image down to half of its original size. It does this by using the `Stretch()` function to change to half of the width and height obtained with the `GetWidth()` and `GetHeight()` functions.

```
CImageObject ImageObject( "Filename.bmp" );
ImageObject.Stretch( ImageObject.GetWidth() / 2,
  ImageObject.GetHeight() / 2 );
```

The CropStretch Program

Often, your application will need to change the size of an image. It might also need to crop an image to a selected rectangular region. The `CImageObject` class has functions to perform both of the operations. This program shows you how to use them.

The image that's loaded into memory will be scaled to fit the view window's client area exactly every time it's redrawn. It does so by creating a temporary `CImageObject` object, copying the current image into it, scaling the temporary image, and then drawing to the view window with the temporary object.

You can crop the image too. To do this, just click the left mouse button inside of the view window. The rectangular region around the mouse will be copied and used to create a new display image.

Demo Program

CropStretch
CD-ROM Location: **Chap023\CropStretch**
Program Name: **CropStetch.EXE**
Source Code Modules in Text: **CropStretchView.cpp**

◆ ◆ ◆ ◆ ◆

Listing 23-2: **The CropStretch Program**

```
// CropStretchView.cpp : implementation of
// the CCropStretchView class
//

/////////////////////////////////////////////////////////////
// CCropStretchView construction/destruction

CCropStretchView::CCropStretchView()

{

  // Allocate the CImageObject class and
  // load the image at the same time.
  m_pImageObject = new CImageObject( "FILE.BMP" );

}

CCropStretchView::~CCropStretchView()
{

  // If the CImageObject class was allocated,
  // delete it.
  if( m_pImageObject != NULL )
    delete m_pImageObject;

}

/////////////////////////////////////////////////////////////
// CCropStretchView drawing

void CCropStretchView::OnDraw(CDC* pDC)
{
  CCropStretchDoc* pDoc = GetDocument();
  ASSERT_VALID(pDoc);
  if( m_pImageObject != NULL ){
    // If this window has the focus, set
    // the palette.
    if( GetFocus() == this )
      m_pImageObject->SetPalette( pDC );
```

(continued)

Listing 23-2 (continued)

```
    // Create a temporary object.
    CImageObject ImageObject;

    // Call the function that populates
    // our temporary object with a
    // scaled image.
    CreateTempImage( ImageObject );

    // Draw the image.
    ImageObject.Draw( pDC );
    }

}

void CCropStretchView::CreateTempImage(
  CImageObject& ImageObject )
{

  // Make sure our CImageObject class member
  // is not NULL.
  if( m_pImageObject == NULL )
    return;

  // Get the client rectangle so that we
  // can dynamically size the image to
  // fit the the client rectangle exactly.
  RECT ClientRect;
  GetClientRect( &ClientRect );

  // Copy the contents of m_pImageObject
  // to the object that was passed in.
  ImageObject = *m_pImageObject;

  // Resize the display image so that it's
  // the size of the client rectangle.
  ImageObject.Stretch( ClientRect.right,
    ClientRect.bottom );

}

///////////////////////////////////////////////////////////
// CCropStretchView message handlers

void CCropStretchView::OnLButtonDown(UINT nFlags,
  CPoint point)
{

  if( m_pImageObject != NULL ){

    // Create a temporary object.
```

```
    CImageObject ImageObject;

    // Call the function that populates
    // our temporary object with a
    // scaled image.
    CreateTempImage( ImageObject );

    // Crop the image.
    ImageObject.Crop( point.x - 100,
      point.y - 100, point.x + 100,
      point.y + 100 );

    // Copy the new image contents into
    // our CImageObject class member
    *m_pImageObject = ImageObject;

    // Cause a window redraw.
    InvalidateRect( NULL, FALSE );
    UpdateWindow();

    }

  CView::OnLButtonDown(nFlags, point);
}

void CCropStretchView::OnFileRestoreimage()
{

  // Delete the old image.
  if( m_pImageObject != NULL )
    delete m_pImageObject;

  // Allocate a new CImageObject class
  // and load in the image file.
  m_pImageObject = new CImageObject( "FILE.BMP" );

  // Cause a window redraw.
  InvalidateRect( NULL, FALSE );
  UpdateWindow();

}
```

Changing Color Depth of an Image

By *color depth*, we mean the number of bits per pixel. A 256-color image has 8 bits per pixel while an image of more than 16 million colors has 24 bits per pixel. It will be rare that you change the color depth of an image before displaying it. That's because the image library takes care of displaying images of one color depth to a display adapter of another color depth.

The value of the `ChangeFormat()` function that changes an image's color depth is usually when you want to convert an image and resave it with a new color depth. You might want to convert one or more images so that another application can make optimal use of an image by matching it to the display adapter that will be used.

The following example reduces an image with a color depth of 24 bits down to an image with a color depth of 8 bits. It goes from having over 16 million colors down to having only 256 colors.

```
CImageObject ImageObject( "Filename.bmp" );
// ImageObject.GetNumBits() will show a value of 24
ImageObject.ChangeFormat( 8 );
```

Image Processing

A host of image-processing functions are available with two classes that reside in the ImageObject library. They are the `CImagePointProcesses` and `CImageAreaProcesses` classes. As you might guess, the `CImagePointProcesses` class performs several point process operations while the `CImageAreaProcesses` class performs several area process operations.

The prototypes and descriptions of the functions follow. The "Image Processing" sidebar explains them so that you can use them in your programs.

Two class libraries for image processing

There are two image-processing classes: `CImageAreaProcesses` and `CImagePointProcesses`.

The CImageAreaProcesses Class

This class processes areas of pixels. Most of the functions that are available fall into the category of filters. They're all described below.

CImageAreaProcesses();

This example is the `CImageAreaProcesses` class constructor, which takes no arguments. If this constructor is used, when using any of the image processing functions, you must pass in the address of a value `CImageObject` class.

CImageAreaProcesses(CImageObject *);

This class constructor, `CImageAreaProcesses`, takes the address of a `CImageObject` class. Later, when you perform image processing functions, you don't need to worry about passing in the address of a `CImageObject` class since the `CImageAreaProcesses` class will already have it stored.

BOOL MedianFilter(int nX1, int nY1, int nX2, int nY2, CImageObject *pImageObject);

This function performs a median filtering operation on an image. All the parameters are optional. If no coordinates are specified, the operation is performed on the entire image. Otherwise, you can specify a portion of the image to which the operation will be performed. You only need to pass the address of a `CImageObject` if one wasn't given in the `CImageAreaProcesses` class constructor.

BOOL EqualizeContrast(int nX1, int nY1, int nX2, int nY2, int nThresholdFactor, CImageObject *pImageObject);

This function equalizes the contrast of an image. All the parameters are optional. If no coordinates are specified, the operation is performed on the entire image. Otherwise, you can specify a portion of the image to which the operation will be performed. Typical threshold values are low, in the range of about 10. You only need to pass the address of a `CImageObject` if one wasn't given in the `CImageAreaProcesses` class constructor.

BOOL HighpassFilter(int nX1, int nY1, int nX2, int nY2, CImageObject *pImageObject);

This function performs a high-pass filtering operation on an image. All the parameters are optional. If no coordinates are specified, the operation is performed on the entire image. Otherwise, you can specify a portion of the image to which the operation will be performed. You only need to pass the address of a `CImageObject` if one wasn't given in the `CImageAreaProcesses` class constructor.

BOOL LowpassFilter(int nX1, int nY1, int nX2, int nY2, DWORD *dwFact, CImageObject *pImageObject);

This function performs a low-pass filtering operation on an image. All the parameters are optional. If no coordinates are specified, the operation is performed on the entire image. Otherwise, you can specify a portion of the image to which the operation will be performed. The `dwFact` parameter should always be NULL from an application. You only need to pass the address of a `CImageObject` if one wasn't given in the `CImageAreaProcesses` class constructor.

BOOL EdgeEnhance(int nX1, int nY1, int nX2, int nY2, CImageObject *pImageObject);

This function performs an edge-enhancing operation on an image. All the parameters are optional. If no coordinates are specified, the operation is performed on the entire image. Otherwise, you can specify a portion of the image to which the operation will be performed. You only need to pass the address of a `CImageObject` if one wasn't given in the `CImageAreaProcesses` class constructor.

✦ ✦ ✦ ✦ ✦

The CImagePointProcesses Class

The CImagePointProcesses class covers functions that process single pixels. Operations include colorization and brightness adjustment.

CImagePointProcesses();

This `CImagePointProcesses` class constructor takes no arguments. If you use this constructor, then you must pass in the address of a value `CImageObject` class when you use any image-processing functions.

CImagePointProcesses(CImageObject *);

This `CImagePointProcesses` class constructor takes the address of a `CImageObject` class. Later, when you perform image-processing functions, you don't need to worry about passing in the address of a `CImageObject` class; the `CImagePointProcesses` class will already have it stored.

BOOL ChangeBrightness(int nBrightness, int nX1, int nY1, int nX2, int nY2, CImageObject *pImageObject);

This function changes the brightness of an image. The first of its parameters specifies the percentage of the original brightness that you want the resulting image to have. All the remaining parameters are optional. If no coordinates are specified, the operation is performed on the entire image. Otherwise, you can specify a portion of the image to which the operation will be performed. You only need to pass the address of a `CImageObject` if one wasn't given in the `CImagePointProcesses` class constructor.

BOOL ReverseColors(int nX1, int nY1, int nX2, int nY2, CImageObject *pImageObject);

This function reverses the colors of an image. All the parameters are optional. If no coordinates are specified, the operation is performed on the entire image. Otherwise, you can specify a portion of the image to which the operation will be performed. You only need to pass the address of a `CImageObject` if one wasn't given in the `CImagePointProcesses` class constructor.

BOOL MakeGray(BOOL bSetPalette, CImageObject *pImageObject);

This function changes an image into a gray-scale image. All the parameters are optional. The `bSetPalette` parameter defaults to `TRUE`. You only need to pass the address of a `CImageObject` if one wasn't given in the `CImagePointProcesses` class constructor.

BOOL Colorize(int, int, int, int, COLORREF, CImageObject *pImageObject);

This function colorizes an image. Only the last parameter is optional. You must specify the coordinates to which the operation will be performed. You also must pass the color to which the image will be colorized. You only need to pass the address of a `CImageObject` if one wasn't given in the `CImagePointProcesses` class constructor.

◆ ◆ ◆ ◆ ◆

Class Library

Several examples that perform image processing tasks follow. The first one colorizes the rectangular region of an image bounded by the rectangular region 20, 40, 120, 140. The region will be colorized with red:

```
CImageObject ImageObject( "File name.bmp" );
 CImagePointProcesses PointProcesses( &ImageObject );
 PointProcesses.Colorize( 20, 40, 120, 140,
  RGB( 255, 0, 0 ) );
```

The next example shows you how to perform a median filtering operation on the rectangular region of an image bounded by 100, 100, 200, 200:

```
CImageObject ImageObject( "File name.bmp" );
 CImageAreaProcesses AreaProcesses( &ImageObject );
 AreaProcesses( 100, 100, 200, 200 );
```

The last example shows you how to increase the brightness of an entire image to 150 percent of its original brightness:

```
CImageObject ImageObject( "Filename.bmp" );
 CImagePointProcesses PointProcesses( &ImageObject );
 PointProcesses.ChangeBrightness( 150 );
```

◆ ◆ ◆ ◆ ◆

The ProcessImage Program

There are lots of things that you can do with the image processing capabilities that come with the ImageObject package, and this program shows you many of them. You'll be able to perform operations such as colorization and median filtering.

You'll probably enjoy using this program since it's fun to see what the outcome of enhancement and filtering operations is. If you have children, let them try it. They'll love altering the images.

This program links in the ImageAreaProcess.lib and ImagePointProcesses.lib files.

Demo Program

ProcessImage
CD-ROM Location: **Chap023\ProcessImage**
Program Name: **ProcessImage.EXE**
Source Code Modules in Text: **ProcessImageView.cpp**

◆ ◆ ◆ ◆ ◆

Listing 23-3: The ProcessImage Program

```
// ProcessImageView.cpp : implementation of
// the CProcessImageView class
//

/////////////////////////////////////////////////////////////////////////////
// CProcessImageView message handlers

void CProcessImageView::OnAreaprocessesChangecontract()
{

  // The brightness dialog box can also be used
  // to get any other value from 0-200. All we
  // have to do is set the dialog box class members
  // to change the title and label.
  CBrightness Brightness;
  strcpy( Brightness.m_szTitle, "Set Contrast" );
  strcpy( Brightness.m_szLabel, "Contrast" );
  if( Brightness.DoModal() != IDOK ) return;

  // Create a CImageAreaProcess class and attach
  // our CImageObject class member.
  CImageAreaProcesses AreaProcesses( m_pImageObject );
  // Change to hourglass.
  BeginWaitCursor();
  // Perform the process.
  AreaProcesses.ChangeContrast(Brightness.m_nBrightness);
  // Change from the hourglass.
  EndWaitCursor();

  // Cause a window redraw.
  InvalidateRect( NULL, FALSE );
  UpdateWindow();

}

void CProcessImageView::OnAreaprocessesEdgeenhance()
{

  // Create a CImageAreaProcess class and attach
  // our CImageObject class member.
  CImageAreaProcesses AreaProcesses( m_pImageObject );
  // Change to hourglass.
  BeginWaitCursor();
  // Perform the process.
  AreaProcesses.EdgeEnhance();
  // Change from the hourglass.
  EndWaitCursor();

  // Cause a window redraw.
  InvalidateRect( NULL, FALSE );
```

```
  UpdateWindow();
}

void CProcessImageView::OnAreaprocessesEqualizecontrast()
{

  // Create a CImageAreaProcess class and attach
  // our CImageObject class member.
  CImageAreaProcesses AreaProcesses( m_pImageObject );
  // Change to hourglass.
  BeginWaitCursor();
  // Perform the process.
  AreaProcesses.EqualizeContrast();
  // Change from the hourglass.
  EndWaitCursor();

  // Cause a window redraw.
  InvalidateRect( NULL, FALSE );
  UpdateWindow();
}

void CProcessImageView::OnAreaprocessesHighpassfilter()
{

  // Create a CImageAreaProcess class and attach
  // our CImageObject class member.
  CImageAreaProcesses AreaProcesses( m_pImageObject );
  // Change to hourglass.
  BeginWaitCursor();
  // Perform the process.
  AreaProcesses.HighpassFilter();
  // Change from the hourglass.
  EndWaitCursor();

  // Cause a window redraw.
  InvalidateRect( NULL, FALSE );
  UpdateWindow();
}

void CProcessImageView::OnAreaprocessesLowpassfilter()
{

  // Create a CImageAreaProcess class and attach
  // our CImageObject class member.
  CImageAreaProcesses AreaProcesses( m_pImageObject );
  // Change to hourglass.
  BeginWaitCursor();
  // Perform the process.
  AreaProcesses.LowpassFilter();
  // Change from the hourglass.
  EndWaitCursor();
```

(continued)

Listing 23-3 *(continued)*

```
  // Cause a window redraw.
  InvalidateRect( NULL, FALSE );
  UpdateWindow();

  }

void CProcessImageView::OnAreaprocessesMedianfilter()
{

  // Create a CImageAreaProcess class and attach
  // our CImageObject class member.
  CImageAreaProcesses AreaProcesses( m_pImageObject );
  // Change to hourglass.
  BeginWaitCursor();
  // Perform the process.
  AreaProcesses.MedianFilter();
  // Change from the hourglass.
  EndWaitCursor();

  // Cause a window redraw.
  InvalidateRect( NULL, FALSE );
  UpdateWindow();

  }

void CProcessImageView::OnPointprocessesChangebrightness()
{
  CBrightness Brightness;
  if( Brightness.DoModal() != IDOK ) return;

  // Create a CImagePointProcess class and attach
  // our CImageObject class member.
  CImagePointProcesses PointProcesses( m_pImageObject );
  // Change to hourglass.
  BeginWaitCursor();
  // Perform the process.
  PointProcesses.ChangeBrightness(
    Brightness.m_nBrightness );
  // Change from the hourglass.
  EndWaitCursor();

  // Cause a window redraw.
  InvalidateRect( NULL, FALSE );
  UpdateWindow();

  }

void CProcessImageView::OnPointprocessesColorize()
{
  CColorDialog ColorDialog;
```

```
  if( ColorDialog.DoModal() != IDOK ) return;

  // Create a CImagePointProcess class and attach
  // our CImageObject class member.
  CImagePointProcesses PointProcesses( m_pImageObject );
  // Change to hourglass.
  BeginWaitCursor();
  // Perform the process.
  PointProcesses.Colorize( 0, 0,
    m_pImageObject->GetWidth() - 1,
    m_pImageObject->GetHeight() - 1,
    ColorDialog.GetColor() );
  // Change from the hourglass.
  EndWaitCursor();

  // Cause a window redraw.
  InvalidateRect( NULL, FALSE );
  UpdateWindow();
}

void CProcessImageView::OnPointprocessesMakegray()
{

  // Create a CImagePointProcess class and attach
  // our CImageObject class member.
  CImagePointProcesses PointProcesses( m_pImageObject );
  // Change to hourglass.
  BeginWaitCursor();
  // Perform the process.
  PointProcesses.MakeGray( TRUE );
  // Change from the hourglass.
  EndWaitCursor();

  // Cause a window redraw.
  InvalidateRect( NULL, FALSE );
  UpdateWindow();

  }

void CProcessImageView::OnPointprocessesReversecolors()
{

  // Create a CImagePointProcess class and attach
  // our CImageObject class member.
  CImagePointProcesses PointProcesses( m_pImageObject );
  // Change to hourglass.
  BeginWaitCursor();
  // Perform the process.
  PointProcesses.ReverseColors();
  // Change from the hourglass.
  EndWaitCursor();
```

(continued)

Listing 23-3 *(continued)*

```
    // Cause a window redraw.
    InvalidateRect( NULL, FALSE );
    UpdateWindow();

}
```

Summary

In this chapter, you've learned that using third-party add-on libraries can save you time and money, adding functionality to your programs that you might not otherwise achieve.

Now that you've worked through the chapter, you can easily load and display images in your applications. Altering the images — by cropping, scaling, and using image-processing techniques — is also in your arsenal.

Images will make your application look great. You'll have the competitive edge you need. And displaying images has never been as easy. Just link in the CImageObject library class and add a few lines of code to your program.

Send me your applications at `ivt-rcl@interpath.com`. I'd love to see what you come up with.

✦ ✦ ✦

CHAPTER 24

Data Encryption

✦ ✦ ✦ ✦

In This Chapter

Learning basic cryptographic terms

Learning about the different types of cryptography

Examining hash functions

Using Microsoft's CryptoAPI

✦ ✦ ✦ ✦

In this chapter, we will explore the basics of cryptography. Cryptography is the science of keeping data, or messages, secure. In the past, people usually associated cryptography with the military or, perhaps, spies. Many times, talk of secret codes or encrypted messages would conjure up images of cloak-and-dagger espionage. In any case, encryption was used to keep sensitive data secure.

With the advent of personal computers and the Internet, the demand for encryption has skyrocketed. Individuals and businesses are connected in ways never imagined in the past. As the world continues on its digital trend, an ever-increasing amount of data is being shuttled from one place to another. A simple data transmission such as a Web browser that requests an HTML page from a server certainly does not need to be secured. However, if that same browser is transmitting a credit card number, then definite steps should be taken to secure the data.

Basic Cryptographic Terms

Before we can begin any serious discussion of cryptography, we should first define a common vocabulary to describe some basic concepts:

- **Cryptography**—The science of securing data through the use of mathematical algorithms.
- **Plaintext**—Data that has not been encrypted.
- **Ciphertext**—Plain text that has been encrypted.
- **Hash function**—A mathematical function that takes variable-length data and converts it to a fixed-length format, generally smaller than the original data.
- **Encryption key**—A value or token used to encrypt data.
- **Decryption key**—A value or token used to decrypt data.
- **Symmetric algorithm**—An encryption algorithm whose encryption key can be derived from the decryption key.

✦ **Public-key algorithm** — An encryption algorithm whose encryption key cannot easily be derived from the decryption key.

Different Types of Cryptography

Almost all cryptography algorithms fall into one of two distinct categories: symmetric or public-key cryptography. Because these two categories encompass the vast majority of cryptography systems in use today, we should spend some time discussing the differences between the two types of algorithms.

Symmetric algorithms

The family of algorithms classified as *symmetric* algorithms are the oldest and most common of the two types. In fact, when most people think of cryptography, they think of symmetric algorithms, whether they realize it or not. Symmetric algorithms are based on an encryption operation that allows the ciphertext (data that has been encrypted) to be decrypted by simply "rolling back" the encryption operation. A simple substitution scheme best illustrates this.

For the sake of example, let's assume the following message needs to be encrypted:

HARRY — GUARDS ARE AT THE CONSULATE. MEET ME AT THE DOCKS AT 11:45 TONIGHT.

Now, let's also assume the encryption key is the number 5. The algorithm shifts each letter five letters to the right so the ciphertext looks like this:

MFWW4 — LZFWIX FWJ FY YMJ HTSXZQFYJ. RJJY RJ FY YMJ ITHPX FY 66:90 YTSNLMY.

Doesn't look very much like the original, does it?

Because this is a symmetric algorithm, all that is required to decrypt the data is to roll back the encryption operation. In this case, all we need do is shift each character of the ciphertext five letters to the left to recover the data:

HARRY — GUARDS ARE AT THE CONSULATE. MEET ME AT THE DOCKS AT 11:45 TONIGHT.

The symmetric properties of this algorithm make it very easy to understand and use. It is this simplicity that also makes substitution schemes like this very insecure. Any third party who wanted to recover the message could determine that a substitution algorithm was used by analyzing character frequency. Notice how the letter *J* is repeated several times throughout the ciphertext. The frequency of the *J*s matches the frequency of the letter *E* in the plain text. *E* happens to be the most used letter in the English language so any reasonably competent cryptanalyst could use this information to decrypt the ciphertext in a short period of time.

In reality, symmetric algorithms are typically broken using a technique called *brute force*. This technique is normally used when the number of possible solutions is relatively small. Each and every combination is tried until the plain text is revealed. For a simple algorithm such as ours, the plain text could be recovered in a matter of seconds. In contrast, some of the most secure algorithms, such as SkipJack (the algorithm used in the Clipper chip), would take thousands of years to brute force a solution.

In most cases, symmetric algorithms like this are applied in several stages, or rounds. This means the ciphertext from the first step is used as the input message for the next step. The ciphertext from our previous example would look like this after five rounds through the substitution operation:

7ZIIL — 6FZI3H ZI4 ZG G74 2BCHFEZG4. D44G D4 ZG G74 3B20H ZG TT:QP GBC867G.

Although applying a symmetric algorithm in several rounds increases the algorithm's security, we still have character frequency problems in the five-round ciphertext. The character *4* shows up just as many times as the character *E* does in the original plain text. This character frequency issue continues to weaken the algorithm.

Many times, symmetric algorithms will be applied to data that has been compressed. Compressing data, especially text, reduces the amount of redundancy contained within the data. Any mechanism that can be used to reduce repetition should be used. In our example, we could first use WinZip to compress the text file and then encrypt the binary image of the compressed file. While our algorithm is still not high-grade military stuff, the data compression step would make it more difficult to retrieve the plain text message.

The Substitution Algorithm demo program

The SubDemo program demonstrates how to implement a simple substitution algorithm. The algorithm implemented is the same one we've explored thus far. SubDemo will read a text file of up to 10,000 bytes and, using its substitution algorithm, shift each letter and/or number contained in the file five characters to the right.

All of the algorithm's functionality is located in the member function `CSubdemoDlg::DoEncrypt()`. `DoEncrypt()` iterates through each position of a `CString` buffer and performs a lookup of that character into the array `AlphaIndex`. Once the character's position in the array has been found, the algorithm adds five to the character's current position. This produces the effect of shifting the character five positions to the right. If the position is near the end of the array and can't be shifted without moving past the upper bound, then the algorithm will wrap around to the beginning of `AlphaIndex`. This substitution scheme is applied three times.

SubDemo
CD-ROM Location: **Chap24\SubDemo**
Program Name: **SubDemo**
Source Code Modules in Text: **subdemodlg.h** and **subdemodlg.cpp**

✦ ✦ ✦ ✦ ✦

Listing 24-1: The Code for SubDemo

```
// Implementation
protected:
  HICON m_hIcon;

  // Generated message map functions
  //{{AFX_MSG(CSubdemoDlg)
  virtual BOOL OnInitDialog();
  afx_msg void OnPaint();
  afx_msg HCURSOR OnQueryDragIcon();
  afx_msg void OnEncrypt();
  //}}AFX_MSG
  DECLARE_MESSAGE_MAP()
private:
  CString DoEncrypt(CString strInput);
  CString EncryptMsg(CString strMsg);

};

// subdemoDlg.cpp : implementation file
//

#include "stdafx.h"
#include "subdemo.h"
#include "subdemoDlg.h"

#ifdef _DEBUG
#define new DEBUG_NEW
#undef THIS_FILE
static char THIS_FILE[] = __FILE__;
#endif

//////////////////////////////////////////////////////////////////
//////////////
// CSubdemoDlg dialog

CSubdemoDlg::CSubdemoDlg(CWnd* pParent /*=NULL*/)
  : CDialog(CSubdemoDlg::IDD, pParent)
{
  //{{AFX_DATA_INIT(CSubdemoDlg)
  //}}AFX_DATA_INIT
  // Note that LoadIcon does not require a
      subsequent DestroyIcon in Win32
```

```
  m_hIcon = AfxGetApp()->LoadIcon(IDR_MAINFRAME);
}

void CSubdemoDlg::DoDataExchange(CDataExchange* pDX)
{
  CDialog::DoDataExchange(pDX);
  //{{AFX_DATA_MAP(CSubdemoDlg)
  DDX_Control(pDX, IDC_PTPATH, m_PTPath);
  DDX_Control(pDX, IDC_CTPATH, m_CTPath);
  //}}AFX_DATA_MAP
}

BEGIN_MESSAGE_MAP(CSubdemoDlg, CDialog)
  //{{AFX_MSG_MAP(CSubdemoDlg)
  ON_WM_PAINT()
  ON_WM_QUERYDRAGICON()
  ON_BN_CLICKED(IDC_ENCRYPT, OnEncrypt)
  //}}AFX_MSG_MAP
END_MESSAGE_MAP()

/////////////////////////////////////////////////////////////////
//////////////
// CSubdemoDlg message handlers

BOOL CSubdemoDlg::OnInitDialog()
{
  CDialog::OnInitDialog();

  // Set the icon for this dialog.  The framework
  // does this automatically when the
  // application's main window is not a dialog

  //  SetIcon(m_hIcon, TRUE);   // Set big icon
  SetIcon(m_hIcon, FALSE);      // Set small icon

  return TRUE;  // return TRUE  unless you set the
                // focus to a control
}

// If you add a minimize button to your dialog, you will need
// the code below to draw the icon.  For MFC applications using
// the document/view model, this is automatically done for you
// by the framework.

void CSubdemoDlg::OnPaint()
{
  if (IsIconic())
  {
    CPaintDC dc(this); // device context for painting

    SendMessage(WM_ICONERASEBKGND, (WPARAM)
      dc.GetSafeHdc(), 0);
```

(continued)

Listing 24-1 *(continued)*

```
    // Center icon in client rectangle
    int cxIcon = GetSystemMetrics(SM_CXICON);
    int cyIcon = GetSystemMetrics(SM_CYICON);
    CRect rect;
    GetClientRect(&rect);
    int x = (rect.Width() - cxIcon + 1) / 2;
    int y = (rect.Height() - cyIcon + 1) / 2;

    // Draw the icon
    dc.DrawIcon(x, y, m_hIcon);
  }
  else
  {
    CDialog::OnPaint();
  }
}

// The system calls this to obtain the cursor to
// display while the user drags the minimized window.

      HCURSOR CSubdemoDlg::OnQueryDragIcon()
{
  return (HCURSOR) m_hIcon;
}

void CSubdemoDlg::OnEncrypt()
{
  CString strPTPath, strCTPath;
  // Set the default ciphertext file path to be
  // the same as the plaintext path and add
  //'.enc' to the end

  m_PTPath.GetWindowText(strPTPath);
  for(int t=0;t<strPTPath.GetLength()-3;t++)
  {
    strCTPath+=strPTPath[t];
  }
  strCTPath+="enc";
  m_CTPath.SetWindowText(strCTPath);

  CFile filePlain;
  CFile fileCipher;
  CString strBuf;
  char szBuf[MAX_BUF_SIZE];

  filePlain.Open(strPTPath,CFile::modeRead);

  fileCipher.Open(strCTPath,CFile::modeCreate |
    CFile::modeWrite);

  filePlain.SeekToBegin();
```

```
  int len=filePlain.GetLength();

  filePlain.Read(szBuf,len);

  for (t=0;t<len+1;t++)
  {
    strBuf+=szBuf[t];
  }
  CString strEncrypt=EncryptMsg(strBuf);

  fileCipher.SeekToBegin();
  fileCipher.Write((LPCTSTR) strEncrypt,
   strEncrypt.GetLength());
}
CString CSubdemoDlg::EncryptMsg(CString strMsg)
{
  CString strRound1, strRound2, strRound3;

  strRound1=DoEncrypt(strMsg); // First round
  strRound2=DoEncrypt(strRound1); // Second round
  strRound3=DoEncrypt(strRound2); // Third and final
                                  // round
  return strRound3;
}
CString CSubdemoDlg::DoEncrypt(CString strInput)
{
  char AlphaIndex[37]="ABCDEFGHIJKLMNOP
                        QRSTUVWXYZ1234567890";
  CString strRound, strBuf;
  BOOL bFound;

  for (int t=0;t<strInput.GetLength();t++)
  {
    strBuf=strInput[t];
    strBuf.MakeUpper();
    bFound=FALSE;
    for (int i=0;i<38;i++)
    {
      if (AlphaIndex[i]==strBuf)
      {
        bFound=TRUE;
        if (i+5>37)
        {
          i=0+(37-i);
        }
        else
        {
          i+=5;
        }
        strRound+=AlphaIndex[i];
        break;
      }
```

(continued)

Listing 24-1 (continued)

```
      }
      if (bFound==FALSE)
        strRound+=strBuf;
    }
    return strRound;
  }
```

Try This

Extending the SubDemo

To further your understanding of a basic symmetric algorithm, you should try to extend SubDemo to decrypt files as well. All the parts you need are already contained in the source code. To decrypt a file encrypted with this algorithm, do the following:

1. Open the plain text file and read it into a buffer.
2. Iterate through the buffer, looking up the substitution index position of each character.
3. If the character is contained within the substitution table, perform the following steps:
   a. If the position is > 5, then the new character position in the substitution index = 38 – (5 – current position).
   b. If the position is < 5, then the new position = current position – 5.
   c. Append the character at the new position in the lookup table to a decrypt buffer.
4. If the character is not contained in the substitution table, append it directly to the decrypt buffer.
5. Iterate through the file buffer until you reach the end.
6. Perform steps 1 through 5 three times to recover the plain text.

✦ ✦ ✦ ✦ ✦

Public-key cryptography

In addition to symmetric algorithms, one other group of algorithms is widely used. This group is referred to as *public-key*, or *asymmetric*, algorithms. The strength of this family of algorithms relies on the fact that the encryption key and decryption key have nothing in common. In other words, if I possessed both a ciphertext message and the decryption key, I would not be able to derive the encryption key. This unique attribute of the encrypt and decrypt keys also makes public-key cryptography well suited to a number of additional applications besides data encryption. Public-key cryptography can be used to provide a digital signature of sorts.

Let's say you possess two keys. One key is kept private and is used by you to decrypt data. The other key is widely published and can be used by anyone to encrypt messages that only you can decrypt with your privately held key. These keys are commonly referred to as *private* and *public keys*. A private key can only decrypt information that has been encryped with its matching public key. No one intercepting the message can decrypt it, and you don't have to pass your private key to anyone for them to send you an encrypted message.

When you send a message, such as an e-mail or Usenet newsgroup posting, you can "sign" the end of your message by computing a combination of your private key and the message itself. People who possess a copy of your public key can use it to determine the validity of the signature. If they can properly interpret the digital signature, they can be sure the message came from you and wasn't altered in transit.

Public-key cryptography is based on some rather complex mathematics that deal with one-way hash functions. Rolling back the operation of a one-way hash function is extremely difficult. So difficult, in fact, that even on very powerful computers, such as Cray mainframes, it would take hundreds of thousands of years to discover the encryption key. The hash function operates in the "easy" direction when it is encrypting data. We will discuss hash functions in the next section. For now, just remember that a one-way hash function is a mathematical operation which is very difficult to roll back. As the function processes each chunk of plain text, it is generating hash values. In order to decrypt the data and roll the operation back, you would need to know a vital piece of information about the function. This is the private key.

Hash Functions

Let's move away from our high-level overview and consider one of the basic building blocks for most secure cryptographic algorithms: the *hash function*. Strictly speaking, a hash function takes variable length data, such as a text message, and performs one or more mathematical operations to convert the variable length data into a fixed length format.

Hash functions are used not only in cryptography, but also in many other areas of computer science such as checksums and compiler technology. Hash functions are handy things indeed. Hash functions are so useful because the function creates a "fingerprint" of the data, or plain text, it processes. The fingerprint is normally expressed as a number — which computers are very good at understanding.

As an example, let's compute a very simple hash function, using the string "apple". Our function will use the ASCII values of each character to compute the hash value, as follows:

Character	ASCII value	ASCII value mod 23
a	97	5
p	112	20
p	112	20
l	108	16
e	101	9

The hash value is computed by taking the ASCII value mod 23. The number 23 was selected because it is a prime number and would produce a relatively unique hash. The hash value for this string is simply the sum of the third column. In our example, the hash value is 70. The hash value 70 now represents the word "apple".

Our sample hash function is not a very good hash function because it would produce *hash collisions*. A hash collision is when two different strings produce the same hash value. Collisions reduce the usefulness and effectiveness of the function because collisions introduce uncertainty when interpreting the results. A good hash function is designed to produce a minimal number of collisions.

Researching hash functions is a popular field of study within the mathematics community. Many mathematicians spend much of their careers investigating the properties of new and existing hash functions. Part of the popularity of hash functions can be attributed to their wide range of applications, including cryptography.

Many of the world's most secure cryptographic algorithms rely on very strong hash functions. These functions are so strong that they are often termed *one-way* hash functions. This means there is no easy way to deduce the input value of the function from the output value. Most functions of this type operate on groups of bits rather than whole characters. Operating at such a low level allows the hash function to escape from problems like the character-frequency problems previously discussed.

The HFDemo Program

The second demo program in this chapter demonstrates a robust hash function that operates at the bit-level of a message. The hash function used in the demonstration program is used by many UNIX C/C++ compilers to write intermediate object files.

The interesting thing to note about this algorithm, which is implemented in `CHfdemoDlg::SimpleHash()`, is its use of bitwise operators. The hash function makes extensive use of AND and XOR operations to produce the hash value.

Demo Program

HFDemo
CD-ROM Location: **Chap24\HFDemo**
Program Name: **HFDemo**
Source Code Modules in Text: **HFDemoDlg.h** and **HFDemoDlg.cpp**

◆ ◆ ◆ ◆ ◆

Listing 24-2: The HFDemo Code

```
class CHfdemoDlg : public CDialog
{
// Construction
public:
  CHfdemoDlg(CWnd* pParent = NULL);  // standard
                                     //constructor

// Dialog Data
  //{{AFX_DATA(CHfdemoDlg)
  enum { IDD = IDD_HFDEMO_DIALOG };
  CEdit  m_PText;
  CEdit  m_HText;
  //}}AFX_DATA

  // ClassWizard generated virtual function overrides
  //{{AFX_VIRTUAL(CHfdemoDlg)
  protected:
  virtual void DoDataExchange(CDataExchange* pDX);
  // DDX/DDV support
  //}}AFX_VIRTUAL

// Implementation
protected:
  HICON m_hIcon;

  // Generated message map functions
  //{{AFX_MSG(CHfdemoDlg)
  virtual BOOL OnInitDialog();
  afx_msg void OnPaint();
  afx_msg HCURSOR OnQueryDragIcon();
  afx_msg void OnDohash();
  //}}AFX_MSG
  DECLARE_MESSAGE_MAP()
private:
  unsigned long SimpleHash( const char *value);
};

// hfdemoDlg.cpp : implementation file
//

#include "stdafx.h"
```

(continued)

Listing 24-2 (continued)

```
#include "hfdemo.h"
#include "hfdemoDlg.h"

#ifdef _DEBUG
#define new DEBUG_NEW
#undef THIS_FILE
static char THIS_FILE[] = __FILE__;
#endif

/////////////////////////////////////////////////////////////////
// CHfdemoDlg dialog

CHfdemoDlg::CHfdemoDlg(CWnd* pParent /*=NULL*/)
  : CDialog(CHfdemoDlg::IDD, pParent)
{
  //{{AFX_DATA_INIT(CHfdemoDlg)
  //}}AFX_DATA_INIT
  // Note that LoadIcon does not require a subsequent
 //DestroyIcon in Win32
  m_hIcon = AfxGetApp()->LoadIcon(IDR_MAINFRAME);
}

void CHfdemoDlg::DoDataExchange(CDataExchange* pDX)
{
  CDialog::DoDataExchange(pDX);
  //{{AFX_DATA_MAP(CHfdemoDlg)
  DDX_Control(pDX, IDC_PLAINTEXT, m_PText);
  DDX_Control(pDX, IDC_HASHEDTEXT, m_HText);
  //}}AFX_DATA_MAP
}

BEGIN_MESSAGE_MAP(CHfdemoDlg, CDialog)
  //{{AFX_MSG_MAP(CHfdemoDlg)
  ON_WM_PAINT()
  ON_WM_QUERYDRAGICON()
  ON_BN_CLICKED(ID_DOHASH, OnDohash)
  //}}AFX_MSG_MAP
END_MESSAGE_MAP()

/////////////////////////////////////////////////////////////////
// CHfdemoDlg message handlers

BOOL CHfdemoDlg::OnInitDialog()
{
  CDialog::OnInitDialog();

  // Set the icon for this dialog.  The framework does this
  // automatically when the application's main window is not
  // a dialog

  SetIcon(m_hIcon, TRUE);      // Set big icon
```

```
  SetIcon(m_hIcon, FALSE);    // Set small icon

  return TRUE;  // return TRUE  unless you set the focus
                // to a control
}

// If you add a minimize button to your dialog, you
// will need the code below to draw the icon.  For MFC
// applications using the document/view model, this is
// automatically done for you by the framework.

void CHfdemoDlg::OnPaint()
{
  if (IsIconic())
  {
    CPaintDC dc(this); // device context for painting

    SendMessage(WM_ICONERASEBKGND, (WPARAM)
      dc.GetSafeHdc(), 0);

    // Center icon in client rectangle
    int cxIcon = GetSystemMetrics(SM_CXICON);
    int cyIcon = GetSystemMetrics(SM_CYICON);
    CRect rect;
    GetClientRect(&rect);
    int x = (rect.Width() - cxIcon + 1) / 2;
    int y = (rect.Height() - cyIcon + 1) / 2;

    // Draw the icon
    dc.DrawIcon(x, y, m_hIcon);
  }
  else
  {
    CDialog::OnPaint();
  }
}

// The system calls this to obtain the cursor to
// display while the user drags the minimized window.

HCURSOR CHfdemoDlg::OnQueryDragIcon()
{
  return (HCURSOR) m_hIcon;
}

void CHfdemoDlg::OnDohash()
{
  char *plaintext="";
  int limit=255;
  unsigned long hashresults=0;
  CString strResults;
```

(continued)

Listing 24-2 *(continued)*

```
  m_PText.GetWindowText(plaintext,limit);
  hashresults=SimpleHash(plaintext);
  strResults.Format("%d",hashresults);
  m_HText.SetWindowText(strResults);

}

unsigned long CHfdemoDlg::SimpleHash(const char * value)
{
  unsigned long h=0, g;

  while (*value)
  {
    h=( h << 4) + *value++;
    if (g=h & 0xF000000)
      h^=g>24;
    h&=~g;
  }

  return h;
}
```

Using Microsoft's CryptoAPI

In an attempt to make cryptography more widespread and easier for us normal mortals to use in our applications, Microsoft has designed and released a cryptography API for Windows 95 and Windows NT 4.0. This API is called CryptoAPI and is available either through Internet Explorer 3.01 or greater or as part of Windows NT 4.0.

CryptoAPI is organized in a modular fashion. Encryption and decryption services are provided by modules called *C*ryptographic *S*ervice *P*roviders (CSP for short). These modules are responsible for implementing different encryption schemes as well as guaranteeing the security of the encryption/decryption process. Microsoft has also released a CSP SDK for persons interested in developing their own CSPs. This information can be accessed at `http://www.microsoft.com/security`.

For now, let's look at the structure of CryptoAPI. The API can be dissected into four discrete sections: key functions, encryption/decryption functions, hashing functions, and CSP functions. We will cover the sections of most interest to us: key functions and encryption/decryption.

Before you can write any code to use the CryptoAPI, you must establish a set of cryptographic keys for the user and configure a default CSP. If you skip this step, none of your CryptoAPI code will execute. Microsoft provides the source code to a utility that sets up the crypto environment. The utility is called inituser.exe, and the source code file is called inituser.c. Both are included on the CD that accompanies this book.

Once you have configured your crypto environment, you can start writing programs that use CryptoAPI. Because examples teach better than describing, let's walk through the steps necessary to encrypt a file.

Note

Make sure you include WINCRYPT.H in your project. This file contains all the CryptoAPI specific types, constants, and functions needed to compile your application with CryptoAPI support.

◆ ◆ ◆ ◆ ◆

First, retrieve a handle, stored in a variable of type `HCRYPTPROV`, to the default CSP using `CryptAcquireContext()`:

```
HCRYPTPROV hCryptProv;
CryptAcquireContext(&hCryptProv, NULL, NULL, PROV_RSA_FULL,
NULL);
```

Next, open the system certificate store and retrieve the user's exchange key:

```
HCERTSTORE        hStoreHandle = NULL;
hStoreHandle = CertOpenSystemStore(hCryptProv, "MY");
```

Then, retrieve the user's key and generate an exportable key:

```
HCRYPTKEY hKey, hExportKey;
CryptGetUserKey(hCryptProv, AT_KEYEXCHANGE,
  &hExportKey);
CryptGenKey(hCryptProv, CALG_RC2, CRYPT_EXPORTABLE,
  &hKey);
```

Next, create the blob (*b*inary *l*arge *ob*ject) to hold the exported key:

```
DWORD dwBytesRequired=0;
BYTE pBuf[2112];
CryptExportKey(hKey, hExportKey, SIMPLEBLOB, 0, NULL,
  dwBytesRequired);
CryptExportKey(hKey, hExportKey, SIMPLEBLOB, 0, pBuf,
  &dwBytesRequired);
```

Note that calling `CryptExportKey()` with a null fifth parameter causes it to return the number of bytes necessary to hold the blob.

The variable `pBuf` now holds the exported key in simple blob format. This format is secure for writing and reading from disk.

Next, we open the input and output files and then write the key blob to disk:

```
WriteFile (hCryptFile, &dwBytesRequired,
sizeof(dwBytesRequired), &dwBytesWritten, NULL);
WriteFile(hCryptFile, pBuf, dwBytesRequired,
  &dwBytesWritten, NULL);
```

Now comes the meat of encrypting a file. We loop through reading in data from the plain text file, encrypt the data with a call to `CryptEncrypt()`, and then write the encrypted data to disk. This loop ends when there is no more data to read.

```
do {
  ReadFile(hPlainFile, pBuf, 2048, &dwBytesRequired, NULL);
  bFinished=(dwBytesRequired<2048);
  CryptEncrypt(hKey, 0, bFinished, 0, pBuf,
    &dwBytesRequired, 2112);
  WriteFile(hCryptFile, pBuf, dwBytesRequired,
    &dwBytesWritten,NULL);
} while (!bFinished);
```

Once we have encrypted all the data in the file, we need to perform some basic clean-up:

```
CryptDestroyKey(hKey);
CryptDestroyKey(hExportKey);
CryptReleaseContext(hCryptProv, 0);
CloseHandle(hCryptFile);
CloseHandle(hPlainFile);
```

That's it! We have now securely encrypted a text file that cannot easily be decrypted. Decrypting the file is mostly the reverse of the above process. There are just a few considerations to remember:

- ✦ The input buffer size for the encrypted file must be a multiple of 4, 8, or 64.
- ✦ The key blobs must be read and used in the same order they were written.

The CryptDemo Program

This demo program demonstrates how to incorporate CryptoAPI into a dialog-based application.

Demo Program

CryptDemo
CD-ROM Location: **Chap24\CryptDemo**
Program Name: **CryptDemo**
Source Code Modules in Text: **CryptDemoDlg.h** and **CryptDemoDlg.cpp**

✦ ✦ ✦ ✦ ✦

```
class CCryptDemoDlg : public CDialog
{
// Construction
public:
  CCryptDemoDlg(CWnd* pParent = NULL);  // standard
                              // constructor

// Dialog Data
  //{{AFX_DATA(CCryptDemoDlg)
  enum { IDD = IDD_CRYPTDEMO_DIALOG };
  CEdit  m_PlainText;
  CEdit  m_CipherText;
  //}}AFX_DATA

  // ClassWizard generated virtual function overrides
  //{{AFX_VIRTUAL(CCryptDemoDlg)
  protected:
  virtual void DoDataExchange(CDataExchange* pDX);
  // DDX/DDV support
  //}}AFX_VIRTUAL

// Implementation
protected:
  HICON m_hIcon;

  // Generated message map functions
  //{{AFX_MSG(CCryptDemoDlg)
  virtual BOOL OnInitDialog();
  afx_msg void OnPaint();
  afx_msg HCURSOR OnQueryDragIcon();
  afx_msg void OnEncrypt();
  afx_msg void OnKillfocusPlaintext();
  //}}AFX_MSG
  DECLARE_MESSAGE_MAP()
};

// CryptDemoDlg.cpp : implementation file
//

#include "stdafx.h"
#include "CryptDemo.h"
#include "CryptDemoDlg.h"
#include "wincrypt.h"

#ifdef _DEBUG
#define new DEBUG_NEW
#undef THIS_FILE
static char THIS_FILE[] = __FILE__;
#endif

/////////////////////////////////////////////////////////////////
// CCryptDemoDlg dialog

CCryptDemoDlg::CCryptDemoDlg(CWnd* pParent /*=NULL*/)
```

```
  : CDialog(CCryptDemoDlg::IDD, pParent)
{
  //{{AFX_DATA_INIT(CCryptDemoDlg)
  //}}AFX_DATA_INIT
  // Note that LoadIcon does not require a subsequent
  // DestroyIcon in Win32
  m_hIcon = AfxGetApp()->LoadIcon(IDR_MAINFRAME);
}

void CCryptDemoDlg::DoDataExchange(CDataExchange* pDX)
{
  CDialog::DoDataExchange(pDX);
  //{{AFX_DATA_MAP(CCryptDemoDlg)
  DDX_Control(pDX, IDC_PLAINTEXT, m_PlainText);
  DDX_Control(pDX, IDC_CIPHERTEXT, m_CipherText);
  //}}AFX_DATA_MAP
}

BEGIN_MESSAGE_MAP(CCryptDemoDlg, CDialog)
  //{{AFX_MSG_MAP(CCryptDemoDlg)
  ON_WM_PAINT()
  ON_WM_QUERYDRAGICON()
  ON_BN_CLICKED(ID_ENCRYPT, OnEncrypt)
  ON_EN_KILLFOCUS(IDC_PLAINTEXT, OnKillfocusPlaintext)
  //}}AFX_MSG_MAP
END_MESSAGE_MAP()

/////////////////////////////////////////////////////////////////
// CCryptDemoDlg message handlers

BOOL CCryptDemoDlg::OnInitDialog()
{
  CDialog::OnInitDialog();

  // Set the icon for this dialog.  The framework does
//   this automatically when the application's main
//   window is not a dialog
  SetIcon(m_hIcon, TRUE);       // Set big icon
  SetIcon(m_hIcon, FALSE);    // Set small icon

  return TRUE;  // return TRUE  unless you set the
                // focus to a control
}

// If you add a minimize button to your dialog, you
// will need the code below to draw the icon.  For MFC
// applications using the document/view model, this is //
automatically done for you by the framework.

void CCryptDemoDlg::OnPaint()
{
  if (IsIconic())
  {
    CPaintDC dc(this); // device context for painting
```

```
    SendMessage(WM_ICONERASEBKGND, (WPARAM)
      dc.GetSafeHdc(), 0);

    // Center icon in client rectangle
    int cxIcon = GetSystemMetrics(SM_CXICON);
    int cyIcon = GetSystemMetrics(SM_CYICON);
    CRect rect;
    GetClientRect(&rect);
    int x = (rect.Width() - cxIcon + 1) / 2;
    int y = (rect.Height() - cyIcon + 1) / 2;

    // Draw the icon
    dc.DrawIcon(x, y, m_hIcon);
  }
  else
  {
    CDialog::OnPaint();
  }
}

// The system calls this to obtain the cursor to
// display while the user drags the minimized window.
//

HCURSOR CCryptDemoDlg::OnQueryDragIcon()
{
  return (HCURSOR) m_hIcon;
}

void CCryptDemoDlg::OnEncrypt()
{
  BOOL bFinished;
  HCRYPTPROV hCryptProv;
  HCRYPTKEY hKey=0, hExportKey=0;
  DWORD dwBytesRequired, dwBytesWritten;
  HANDLE hPlainFile, hCryptFile;
  CString strPlainFile, strCryptFile;
  BYTE pBuf[2112];

  m_PlainText.GetWindowText(strPlainFile);
  m_CipherText.GetWindowText(strCryptFile);

  CryptAcquireContext(&hCryptProv, NULL, NULL,
    PROV_RSA_FULL, 0);

  hPlainFile=CreateFile(strPlainFile, GENERIC_READ,
    FILE_SHARE_READ, NULL, OPEN_EXISTING,
    FILE_ATTRIBUTE_NORMAL, NULL);

  hCryptFile=CreateFile(strCryptFile, GENERIC_WRITE,
    FILE_SHARE_READ, NULL, CREATE_ALWAYS,
    FILE_ATTRIBUTE_NORMAL, NULL);

  CryptGetUserKey(hCryptProv, AT_KEYEXCHANGE,
```

```
    &hExportKey);

  CryptGenKey(hCryptProv, CALG_RC2, CRYPT_EXPORTABLE,
    &hKey);

  CryptExportKey(hKey, hExportKey, SIMPLEBLOB, 0, NULL,
    &dwBytesRequired);

  CryptExportKey(hKey, hExportKey, SIMPLEBLOB,
    0,pBuf,&dwBytesRequired);

  WriteFile(hCryptFile, &dwBytesRequired,
    sizeof(dwBytesRequired), &dwBytesWritten, NULL);

  WriteFile(hCryptFile, pBuf, dwBytesRequired,
    &dwBytesWritten, NULL);

  do {
    ReadFile(hPlainFile, pBuf, 2048, &dwBytesRequired, NULL);
    bFinished=(dwBytesRequired<2048);
    CryptEncrypt(hKey, 0, bFinished, 0, pBuf,
      &dwBytesRequired, 2112);
    WriteFile(hCryptFile, pBuf, dwBytesRequired,
      &dwBytesWritten,NULL);
  } while (!bFinished);

  CryptDestroyKey(hKey);
  CryptDestroyKey(hExportKey);

  CryptReleaseContext(hCryptProv,0);
  CloseHandle(hPlainFile);
  CloseHandle(hCryptFile);
  AfxMessageBox ("Encryption of " + strPlainFile + " is
    complete.");

  return;
}



void CCryptDemoDlg::OnKillfocusPlaintext()
{
  CString strPlainText, strTemp;

  m_PlainText.GetWindowText(strPlainText);
  for(int t=0;t<strPlainText.GetLength()-4;t++)
  {
    strTemp+=strPlainText[t];
  }
  strTemp+=".enc";
  m_CipherText.SetWindowText(strTemp);
}
```

Summary

This chapter has just barely touched the surface on the complex subject of data encryption. A comprehensive introduction and overview of data encryption methods would require a book just as large as the one you now hold in your hands. I hope you are now familiar with the basic concepts of cryptography and feel comfortable incorporating Microsoft's CryptoAPI into your applications.

For further reading, here is a list of resources that you should find helpful:

- *Applied Cryptography* by Bruce Schneier (John Wiley & Sons, 1996). This book is, without a doubt, the most thorough examination of modern crytographic methods. It is considered by many cryptography experts to be the bible on the subject. And if that wasn't enough, it also comes with source code for several secure, public domain algorithms.
- The `http//www.microsoft.com/security` Web site. This site contains the latest and greatest information regarding Microsoft's CryptoAPI product.
- The Cypherpunks mailing list. The Cypherpunks are a group of people who are interested in learning about and teaching cryptography. The mailing list archives are available at `ftp://csua.berkeley.edu/pub/cyperpunks`. Interested parties can join the mailing list by sending e-mail to `majordomo@toad.com`.
- Usenet newsgroups `sci.crypt` and `sci.crypt.research`. The `sci.crypt` newsgroup is the all-purpose Usenet newsgroup on cryptography. While there is a high noise ratio, there is an occasional interesting posting. The `sci.crypt.research` newsgroup is a moderated group with less traffic than `sci.crypt`, and it generally has more interesting posts.

✦ ✦ ✦

PART

VI

Common Object Model Programming

Microsoft says "COM is the glue that holds everything together." That might be true. Today, more and more software components are COM objects that can be reused by many applications, as long as the development language supports COM objects. With Microsoft's emphasis on COM, Visual C++, Visual Basic, Visual J++, and Visual InterDev all can all use COM objects.

This section shows you how to create and use COM objects — more commonly known as ActiveX controls. You learn the basics of the topic, and can probably use the techniques in your own development immediately.

✦ ✦ ✦ ✦

In This Part

Chapter 25
Introduction to ActiveX

Chapter 26
Containers and Servers

Chapter 27
Automation and ActiveX Controls

Chapter 28
Active Template Library

✦ ✦ ✦ ✦

CHAPTER 25

Introduction to ActiveX

✦ ✦ ✦ ✦

In This Chapter

Looking back at OLE 1.0

Seeing how OLE 2.0 improves upon OLE 1.0

Introducing ActiveX and COM

Learning about ActiveX applications and components

✦ ✦ ✦ ✦

If you fancy yourself a rocket scientist, you may have actually attempted to read one of the many reference books on ActiveX programming. But, when you started to read, you most likely had a humbling experience. ActiveX, and the COM system upon which it's built, is a complex beast — downright mind-boggling. Expert programmers take a year or more to wade through all the documentation and figure out how to put the concepts to work. Although your chances of mastering this new technology without a year of full-time work on ActiveX is slim, you shouldn't give up hope.

MFC to the rescue! As you may have guessed, MFC features classes that help tame ActiveX and make it easier to use in your own programs. Moreover, AppWizard can create skeleton applications that support ActiveX, leaving you only to fine-tune the result. This makes ActiveX manageable even for the weekend programmer. In this chapter, you get an introduction to ActiveX, which is as much an integral part of Windows 98 as it was an integral part of Windows 95.

OLE 1.0

You may have noticed in Windows 95 and Windows 98 that documents rather than applications are the focus of an operating system. In other words, the user needn't be as concerned with what application does what job. She needs to know only the type of document she wants to create, letting the operating system find and load the appropriate application. Moreover, when the user wants to create a document containing different types of data elements — for example, both text and graphics — she doesn't have to leave the editing environment to create the new data. Instead, the appropriate editing tools should merge with the current application, providing a seamless document creation and editing experience. This whole idea of a document-centric operating system started with a technology Microsoft dubbed *OLE,* which stands for Object Linking and Embedding. Figure 25-1 illustrates this concept.

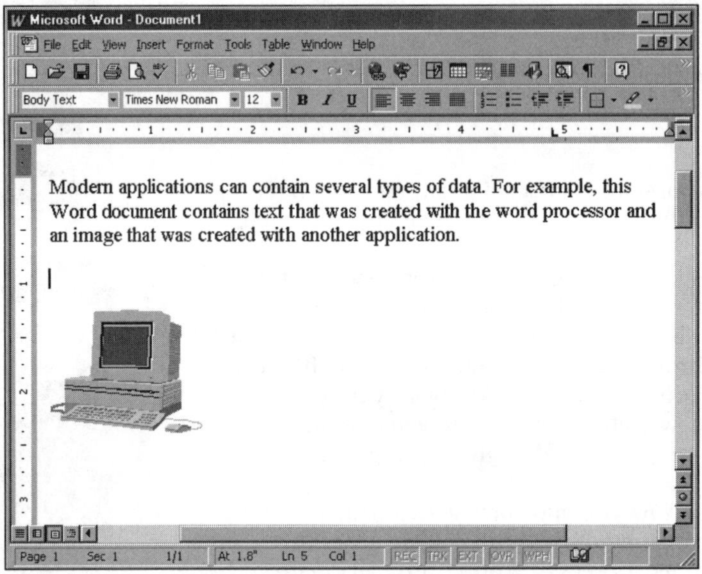

Figure 25-1: With OLE, applications can contain more than one type of data.

OLE is a system that enables applications to share data more easily through data linking and data embedding. The application that holds the linked or embedded data is called a *container application*, whereas the application that supplies editing services for the linked or embedded data is called the *server application*. (There's nothing to stop an application from being both a container *and* a server.) When a dataset is linked into a document (see Figure 25-2), the document maintains a connection to the dataset as part of the document. Even so, the linked data stays in its own file as a discrete object. Because the document maintains only a link to the dataset, the document stays up to date as the dataset changes.

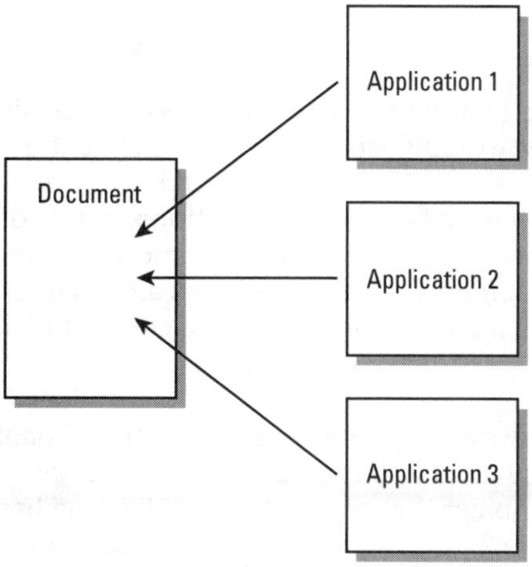

Figure 25-2: Linked data remains in its own file.

When a dataset is embedded into a document, the document no longer maintains a connection with the dataset's file. Instead, the dataset is actually copied into the document (see Figure 25-3). Because there is no longer a connection between the containing document and the original dataset, the document no longer changes when the dataset changes. To update the embedded data, the user would have to load the document and change the data manually.

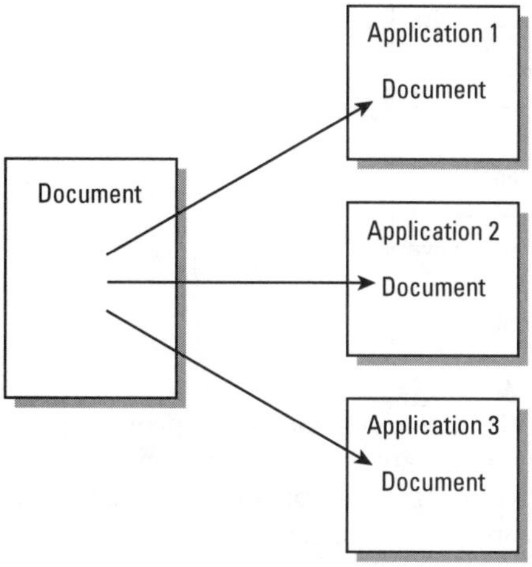

Figure 25-3: Embedded data is copied into the containing document.

Although linked and embedded data behave a little differently, in either case, OLE enables the user to edit the data easily, by automatically calling up the application that created the data. Usually, the user double-clicks the linked or embedded item, which causes the editing application to appear in its own window, or, if it supports in-place editing, the editor can actually merge its toolbars and menus with the application that contains the linked or embedded data.

OLE 2.0

OLE 1.0 was a big leap forward in making computers easier to use—but the first version of OLE was only a shell of what it would become, lacking many features that would enable applications to take a second seat to documents. OLE 2.0 extends OLE's abilities to include not only data sharing between applications, but also functionality sharing between applications. By creating an application as a set of *programmable objects* (also called *OLE components*), applications can call upon each other for the capabilities they need, further generalizing the concept of an application.

Suppose, for example, that you're writing a word processing application. Thanks to OLE, your application doesn't necessarily need to have its own spell checker. Instead, it can call upon a spell-checker object that some other application has already registered with the system. Figure 25-4 illustrates this idea. Notice how the word processor in the figure supplies three programmable objects that can be accessed by other applications. The text editor is currently calling upon the services of the spell-checking component.

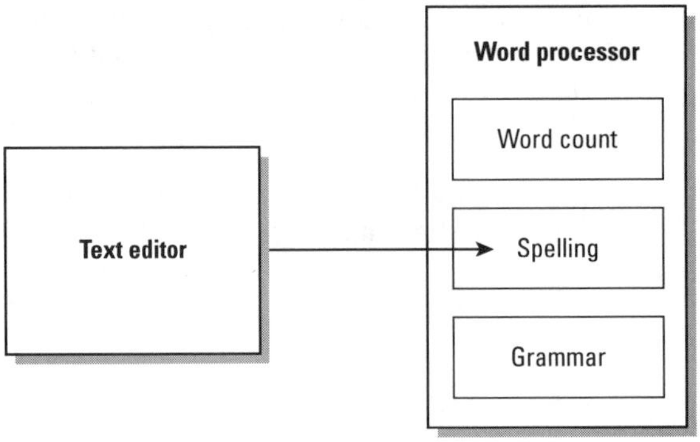

Figure 25-4: Applications can supply programmable objects that can be accessed by other applications.

In Figure 25-4, the word processor is the *OLE server* (because it's providing a service) and the text editor is an *OLE client* (because it's using a service). The process of controlling another application's programmable objects is called *OLE automation*. So, you could also call the word processor an *automation server* and the text editor an *automation client*. Whatever terminology you want to use, programmable objects blur the boundaries between one application and another, making all the applications in the system seem to work together.

Today it's widely accepted that OLE automation can make life easier for both application users and application developers. Users can take full advantage of the capabilities represented by all applications installed in the system, without having to know where those capabilities originate. The user can concentrate on the document and let the applications take care of themselves.

Unfortunately for developers, OLE's advantages come with some big disadvantages. Although developers no longer need to reinvent software that's been developed and installed on the user's system, they must now support OLE in their applications, which adds another layer of complexity to the development process — an obstacle perceived as insurmountable by many programmers. Luckily, as you'll see in the following chapters, Visual C++ developers can let MFC handle most of the intricacies of developing OLE applications.

When OLE 2.0 was introduced so too was the concept of *OLE controls*, programmable objects that can be embedded into an application and so become an integral part of the application in much the same way an embedded document becomes a part of a containing document. Originally, OLE controls were conceived as a way to create buttons, sliders, progress indicators, and other types of custom controls. (They are called OLE *controls*, after all.) The idea soon grew to include mini-applications that offer complex services to host applications. For example, Figure 25-5 shows an application containing a Microsoft calendar control. As you can see, this control goes way beyond a custom button or slider, being more akin to a complete application than a lowly button.

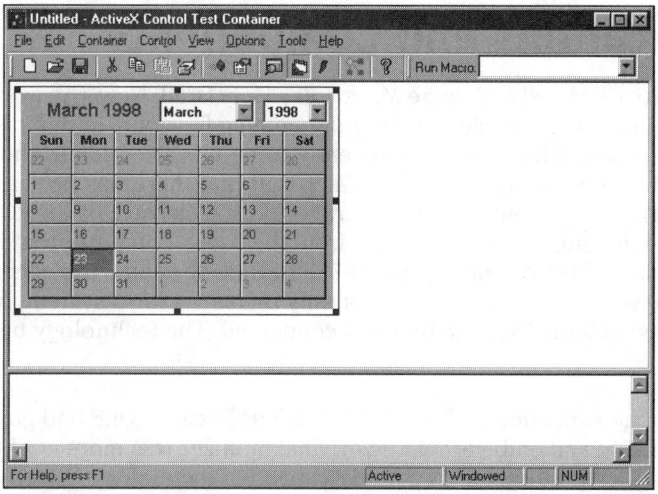

Figure 25-5: Microsoft's calendar control demonstrates how OLE controls can be complex, mini-applications.

COM

Behind all this OLE stuff hides another equally complex technology called COM. *COM* stands for Component Object Model and provides the underpinnings of OLE. Put simply, COM is a specification for creating binary objects. These binary objects can communicate with each other, controlling functions and setting properties. In a nutshell, a binary object is like a program that loads into the system, but is not necessarily visible on the screen. *DLLs*, or dynamic link libraries, are objects of a similar type; they contain functions that other modules in the system can call.

Simply, the COM specification comprises rules that specify how a developer should create and manage binary objects. These rules define a method through which applications can query a binary object to discover the types of interfaces the object supports. Some of these interfaces are standard, whereas others are proprietary. In any case, by adhering to the specifications, objects can be accessed and manipulated by any OLE-capable application.

Here's the good news: If you're programming with Visual C++ and MFC, you can pretty much forget about COM. Although it's always a good idea to have a little background on the technology you're using, as you'll soon discover, Visual C++'s amazing AppWizard can provide your application with most of the basic OLE functionality your program needs. All you have to do is refine the generated source code for your specific purposes.

ActiveX Applications and Components

A couple of years ago, COM and OLE were Microsoft's Holy Grail. Now, the word "ActiveX" pops up everywhere in Microsoft's programming literature and in the Visual C++ documentation. When Microsoft recently turned its attention to the Internet, it occurred to the decision-makers at Microsoft that there was no reason not to treat the Internet as just another peripheral — like a disk drive or CD-ROM drive. Why not make the Internet so accessible from the user's computer that it seemed to become part of the operating system? With this idea came the necessity of extending OLE 2.0 so it would encompass not only the user's local system, but also any network to which the local system was connected. The technology behind ActiveX was born.

But what should this new technology be called? OLE 3.0? Because OLE had gone so far beyond object linking and embedding, the original moniker was more confusing than descriptive. So Microsoft named this newly expanded technology ActiveX. Now, virtually everywhere the word OLE is used, the word ActiveX is substituted. For example, OLE components are now ActiveX components, OLE controls are now ActiveX controls, and OLE documents are now ActiveX documents.

ActiveX objects, however, are more powerful than their old OLE predecessors, expanding the original OLE concepts to the Web. ActiveX controls, for example, can be placed in Web pages and transmitted automatically to the browser that's viewing the Web page. ActiveX documents, too, are much more powerful than OLE documents. Not only can these objects be transmitted over the Web, ActiveX documents also tell the receiving browser how the document should be displayed. You can think of an ActiveX document as being a storage object for information that can be interpreted, displayed, and manipulated by a receiving application.

In the following chapters, you'll learn to program ActiveX applications and controls using AppWizard and MFC. As you work through these chapters, keep in mind that ActiveX is an immense technology that's worthy of a complete book (or books) of its own. In fact, Microsoft's own ActiveX manuals run to thousands of pages. Although this book provides only an introduction to ActiveX, the following chapters cover the major types of ActiveX projects: containers, servers, automation, and ActiveX controls. The following sections in this chapter introduce you to these concepts. If, however, you'd like still more information, take a look at *Discover ActiveX* by Richard Mansfield, published by IDG Books Worldwide (1997). Advanced programmers may want to check out *Inside OLE* by Kraig Brockschmidt.

ActiveX container applications

An ActiveX container is an application that can hold linked or embedded data. Such an application must not only be able to display the linked or embedded data, but also enable the user to select, move, delete, and edit the data. Figure 25-6, for example, shows Microsoft Word displaying a document that contains an embedded graphic.

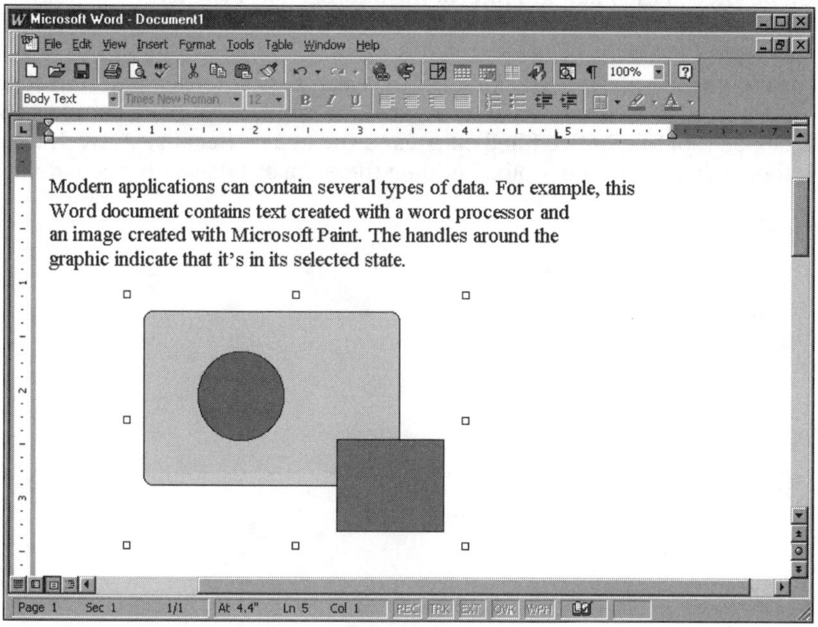

Figure 25-6: Microsoft Word can act as a container application.

In the figure, the Paint object includes sizing handles that enable the user to resize the image. The user can also move the image to any position in the document, as well as delete the image by selecting the Edit menu's Clear command, or by pressing the Delete key on the keyboard.

When Microsoft Word contains linked or embedded data, it's acting as an ActiveX container. Many Windows applications support ActiveX in this way. In Chapter 26, "Containers and Servers," you'll discover how to program your own ActiveX container applications.

ActiveX server applications

In the previous section, you saw how Microsoft Word can act as a container application, containing both text and a graphic image. The graphical object was created with Microsoft Paint, which makes Paint the server application. If the user wants to edit the embedded graphic, he can double-click it. The server then should respond in one of two ways: by opening the graphic in a separate editing window or by merging its user interface with Word's.

How the server application responds to the edit command depends on the capabilities the developer added to the application. If the application supports in-place editing (recommended), ActiveX merges the server's toolbars and menus with the container application's. This enables the user to edit the item without ever switching windows or applications. Figure 25-7 shows Microsoft Word after the user has double-clicked the Paint graphic. In the figure, Paint has merged its toolbars and menus with Word's.

With the merged menus and toolbars, the user can now edit the Paint object just as if the object were loaded into Paint. In Figure 25-8, for example, the user has used Paint's ellipse tool to add two filled ellipses to the image. Because ActiveX makes all Paint's tools available in the toolbar, adding the ellipses takes only seconds.

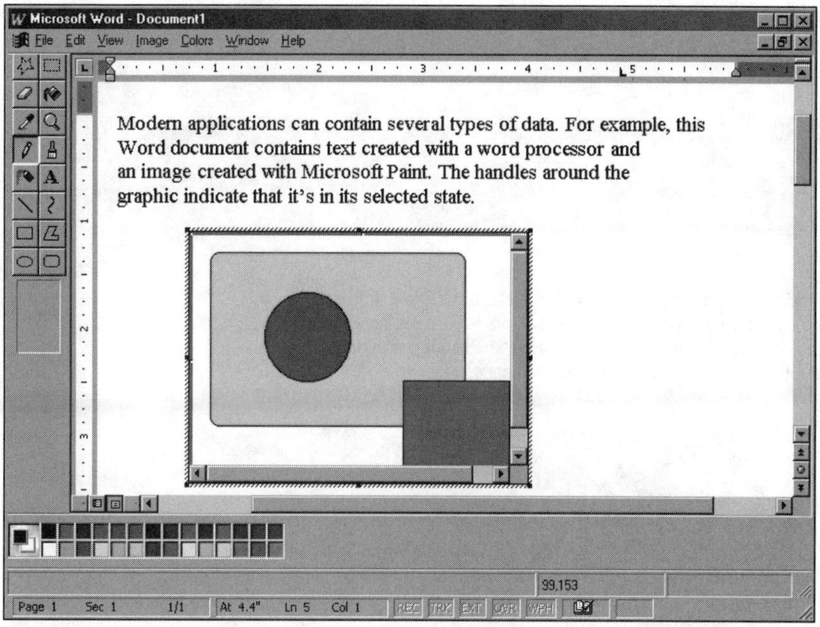

Figure 25-7: Paint's toolbars and menu bars are now merged with Word's.

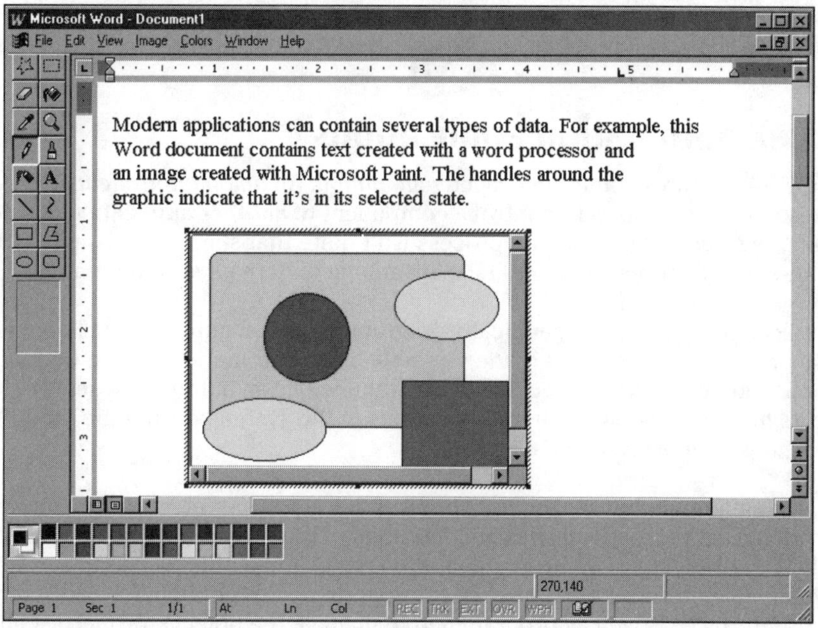

Figure 25-8: Here, the user has edited the image using Paint's tools.

When he's finished editing, a quick mouse click restores Word's own toolbars and menus. The newly edited graphic appears in the document, as shown in Figure 25-9.

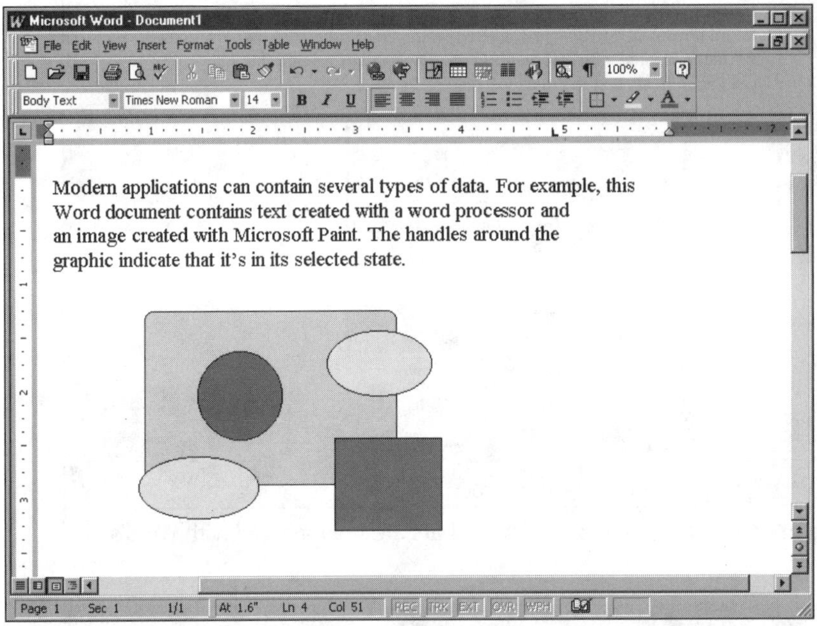

Figure 25-9: The edited image now appears in the Word document.

ActiveX automation applications

ActiveX also features something called *automation*. An *automation-client* application reaches out in the system to control a component of another application, called the *automation server*. Of course, the process isn't quite that simple. Both applications must be specially programmed to take advantage of ActiveX automation.

An application that wasn't specifically programmed as an automation client cannot access programmable objects made available by an automation server. Conversely, an application that wasn't specifically programmed as an automation server cannot share its functionality with other applications in the system, even if the other applications support ActiveX automation.

To create an automation server, the application's developer must define interfaces that provide access to properties and methods of the programmable objects supplied by the server. On the client side, when an application wants to access a programmable object, it must have been programmed to obtain a reference to the object's interface, as well as programmed to manage the object's properties and call the object's methods. For example, reusing the spell-checker example, an application that wanted to take advantage of another application's spell-checker (assuming that the spell checker is a programmable object) would acquire a reference to the spell checker's interface and call the spell checker's functions through that interface. You learn to create automation applications, both clients and servers, in Chapter 27, "Automation and ActiveX Controls."

ActiveX controls

One special type of ActiveX object is the ActiveX control. ActiveX controls are like mini-applications that you can embed into other applications. They take the idea of programmable components and separate those components from the server. That is, ActiveX components are complete entities unto themselves, and do not need to be managed by a server application.

Web developers often use ActiveX controls on the Internet as a way to provide computing power to Web pages. In this way, ActiveX controls can act much like Java applets. Virtually any type of program can be programmed as an ActiveX control and added to a Web page. When the user logs onto the Web page, the system checks whether the ActiveX control is available locally. If it isn't, the system automatically downloads the control and displays it in the Web page. You learn to program ActiveX controls in Chapter 27, "Automation and ActiveX Controls."

ActiveX documents

These days, most people who use a computer also use the Internet, especially the World Wide Web. Because of the Web's popularity, Microsoft decided it needed to expand its new document-oriented philosophy to the Internet. ActiveX documents are Microsoft's answer to enabling Web browsers and other ActiveX client applications to interpret and display documents in much the same way OLE documents enabled data sharing on a local computer system. ActiveX documents are, to put it simply, super-powered OLE documents.

One important feature of ActiveX documents is their capability to be transmitted over the Internet to a remote ActiveX client application, usually a Web browser. In much the same way your local computer system can link or embed a Microsoft Paint document into a Microsoft Word document, so too can a Web browser embed an ActiveX document in its window. Even so, this ActiveX document may or may not be located on the local computer. It may have been received from the other side of the world.

Another important feature of ActiveX documents is how they take the concept of a document and expand it to define a more complete data object, one that contains not only data but also the tools needed to display that data. Many ActiveX documents don't look like documents at all, but rather like complete applications running inside a client application's window. For example, an ActiveX document that represents a 3D scene would contain not only the data that defines the scene (the traditional idea of a document), but also all the information needed for a client application to display and manipulate the 3D scene. You could say that an ActiveX document knows how to manage itself, making it easy for a client application to display the document.

Summary

Now that you have a general idea of what ActiveX is and what it does, you're ready to get your hands dirty with some actual ActiveX programming. In the following chapter, you create your first ActiveX container application. In the remaining ActiveX chapters, you discover even more about this complex-but-exciting technology.

✦ ✦ ✦

CHAPTER 26

Containers and Servers

✦ ✦ ✦ ✦

In This Chapter

Creating a skeleton container application

Modifying an ActiveX item's class

Using the mouse to select items

Deleting embedded items

Creating a skeleton server application

Displaying server items both in the server and a container

Discovering the three ways to run a server

✦ ✦ ✦ ✦

Container and server applications have been around for years. After all, even the very first version of OLE enabled applications to share data through linking or embedding objects in an application's window. Although OLE's change to ActiveX has greatly expanded the capabilities of container and server applications, linking and embedding is still an important part of incorporating ActiveX into your applications. In this chapter, you learn to create container and server applications, as well as see how these applications interact when they're run.

Container Applications

To be considered fully compliant with Windows 98, an application must support all applicable Windows 98 features. One of those features is ActiveX. One way a program can support ActiveX is to be an ActiveX container, which is an application that can link or embed files created by other applications. We introduced container applications in the previous chapter. In this chapter, you build your own ActiveX container application using AppWizard and other Visual C++ tools. This application, called *Container,* shows you how to link objects to or embed objects in an application's document, as well as how to enable users to edit, move, and delete objects. You can find the complete Container application in the Chap26\Container folder of this book's CD-ROM.

Creating a skeleton container application

In many other programming projects in this book, you started your application with AppWizard. Your container application, too, begins as an AppWizard project, which enables Visual C++ to generate the basic source code for the program's classes. In a container application, these classes include not only the usual application, frame window, document (now derived from the `COleDocument` class instead of `CDocument`), and view window classes, but also an additional class derived from MFC's `COleClientItem` class. In this application, AppWizard will call the derived class `CContainerCntrItem`. This class represents any linked or embedded item in the application's window.

Note

You should read through all the application-building steps in this section, whether or not you actually build the Container application yourself, because the steps include explanations of the programming techniques needed to build a container application.

◆ ◆ ◆ ◆ ◆

Demo Program

Container

CD-ROM Location: **Chap26\Container**

Program Name: **Container.EXE**

Source Code Modules in Text: **None**

◆ ◆ ◆ ◆ ◆

To create the skeleton for `Container`, perform the following steps.

1. Start a new AppWizard project called *Container,* as shown in Figure 26-1.

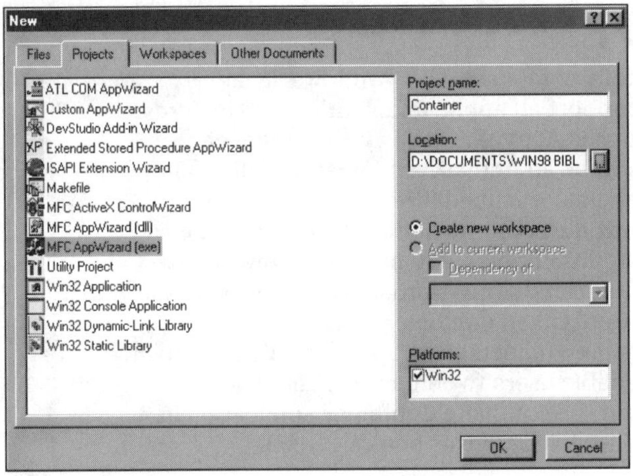

Figure 26-1: The new container application project is called *Container.*

2. In the MFC AppWizard - Step 1 of 6 dialog box, select the Single Document option.
3. Click the Next button twice, accepting the default options in the Step 2 of 6 dialog box.

4. In the Step 3 of 6 dialog box, select the Container option, as shown in Figure 26-2, and click the Next button.

   Selecting the Container feature tells AppWizard to generate the ActiveX source code needed to create a skeleton container application. The skeleton application will be able to link and embed data created by other applications.

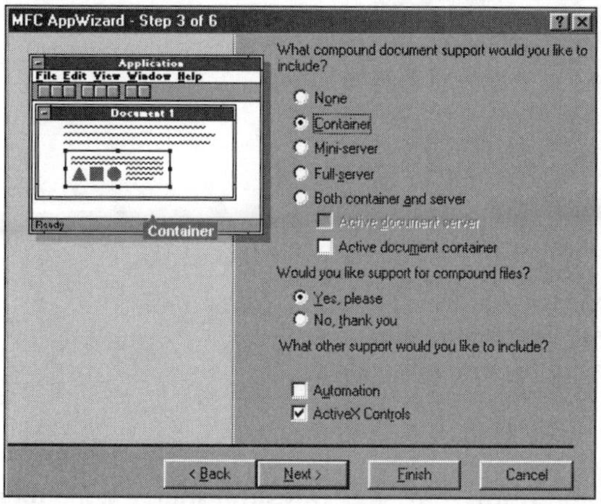

Figure 26-2: AppWizard can generate the code needed to create a container application.

5. In the Step 4 of 6 dialog box, turn off all features except 3D Controls, and then click the Next button.
6. In the Step 5 of 6 dialog box, select the option labeled "as a statically linked library". Accept the default MFC Standard project style and the option labeled "Yes, please" to generate source file comments.
7. Click the Finish button. Your New Project Information dialog box should look like the one in Figure 26-3, except your install directory may be different depending on the directory you chose when you created the project in Step 1.

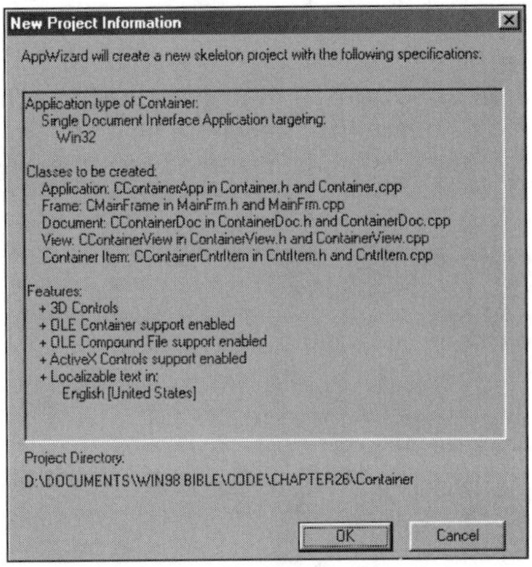

Figure 26-3: The New Project Information dialog box displays the container application's final options.

8. Click the OK button, and AppWizard generates the source code files for the skeleton application.

You've now completed the Container skeleton application. Save your work.

Compile and run the application. Next, link or embed an item into the application's open document. To do this, select the Edit menu's Insert New Object command. The Insert Object dialog box appears, as shown in Figure 26-4. You can choose to create a new item of the type selected in the Object Type box, or you can choose a file to link to or embed into the document.

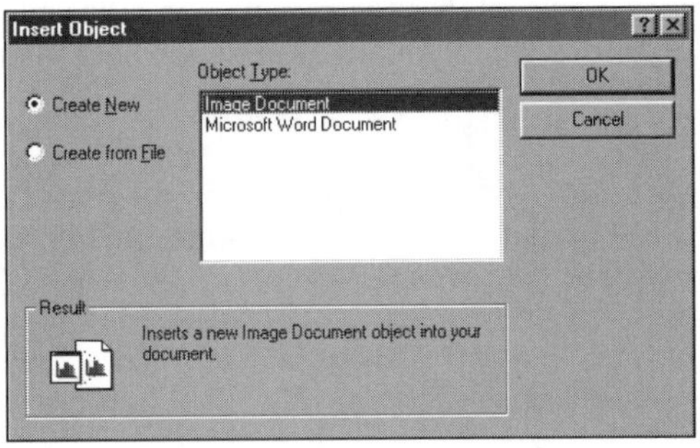

Figure 26-4: The skeleton application already supports linking and embedding.

For now, click the Create from File option. Click the Browse button, and when the Browse dialog box appears, navigate to the test.bmp file included with the Container application on this book's CD-ROM (in the Chap26\Container folder). Double-click the test.bmp file, and then click OK in the Insert Object dialog box. The application inserts the bitmap file into the current document, as shown in Figure 26-5. You haven't added even one line of code on your own, yet the application already has ActiveX functionality, thanks to AppWizard's Container option.

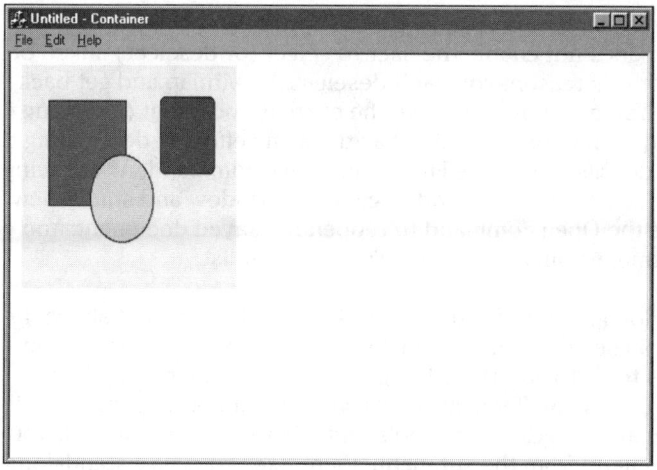

Figure 26-5: Here, a bitmap object is embedded into the application's document.

Now, display the Edit command's Bitmap Image Object submenu. Select the Edit command from this submenu. When you do, Microsoft Paint's menus and toolbars merge with the Container application's window so that you can edit the image. Figure 26-6 shows what the application looks like with the merged Paint tools.

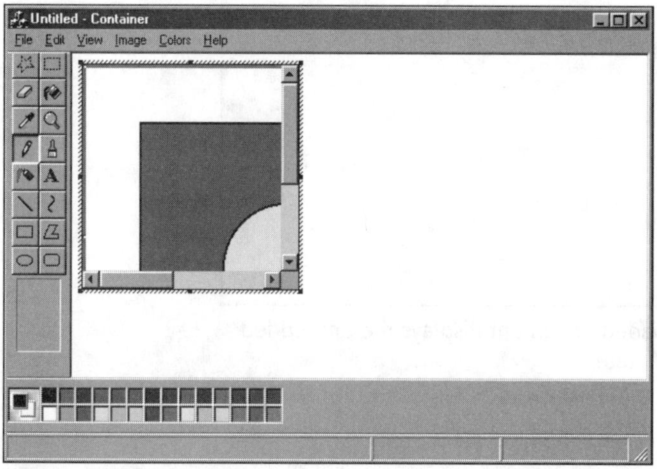

Figure 26-6: You can draw on the bitmap just as if you had started Paint as a standalone application.

Notice that the bitmap object now has a set of sizing handles. Use the handles to enlarge the image so you can see it all, and then use Paint's tools to draw a few new shapes on the bitmap. Because the container application now sports all of Paint's tools and menus, you can do almost anything with the bitmap that you could do if you were actually running Paint.

Unfortunately, there's a bit of a problem with the application. Specifically, the skeleton application does not enable the user to select (or deselect) linked or embedded items. For this reason, you can't deselect the bitmap and get back to the regular application. You can, however, save the current document (including its embedded item) and then reload it, which has the same effect of deselecting the embedded item. To do this, select the File menu's Save command. After saving the file, select the File menu's New command to clear the window and start a new document. Now, use the Open command to reopen the saved document. You can also select the document from the File menu's document list.

After reloading the document, the window looks something like that shown in Figure 26-7. (What you see depends on the figure you drew, of course.) If you want to bring back Paint's tools to edit the bitmap, you can find the bitmap item represented on the Edit menu. If you again select Edit from Bitmap Image Object's submenu, ActiveX again merges Paint's tools and menus into Container. If you select the Open command from the submenu, Paint itself runs as a standalone application. When you're finished experimenting with the Container application, close it.

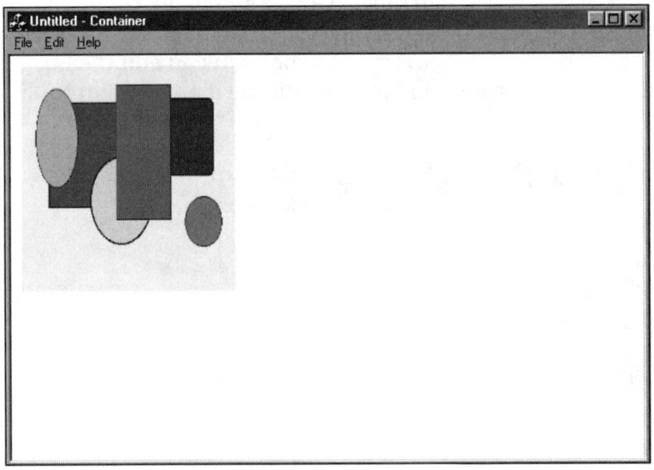

Figure 26-7: The reloaded document displays the embedded item in its deselected state.

Managing an embedded object's size and position

The first thing you must do to complete the Container application is to modify the CContainerCntrItem class so linked and embedded items can manage their own sizes and positions. When AppWizard generated the CContainerCntrItem class, it created hard-coded coordinates for objects of the class. You don't want to use hard-coded sizes and coordinates because the user will want to size and position embedded items as is appropriate for his current document. Perform the following steps to complete the CContainerCntrItem class:

1. Display the Add Member Variable dialog box. Select CContainerCntrItem. In the dialog box, type **CRect** in the Variable Type box, type **m_objectRect** in the Variable Declaration box, and select Public access.

   Here, you're adding the m_objectRect member variable to the class that represents items embedded in the application's document. This member variable will hold the object's size and position.

2. Add the following lines to the CContainerCntrItem class's OnChangeItemPosition() function, right after the TODO comment:

   ```
   m_objectRect = rectPos;
   CContainerDoc* pDoc = GetDocument();
   pDoc->SetModifiedFlag();
   pDoc->UpdateAllViews(NULL);
   ```

   MFC calls the OnChangeItemPosition() function when the user changes the position of a linked or embedded item. The lines you added to the function save the item's new position and update all views of the document to reflect the new position.

3. Add the following line to the OnGetItemPosition() function, after deleting the call to SetRect() that's already there:

   ```
   rPosition = m_objectRect;
   ```

   The framework calls OnGetItemPosition() when it needs the location of an embedded item. The line you added sets the position to the coordinates saved in the m_objectRect object.

4. Add the following line to the CContainerCntrItem class's constructor:

   ```
   m_objectRect.SetRect(20, 20, 150, 150);
   ```

   This line initializes the item's starting position. That is, when the user creates a new item, the item will first appear in the size and position contained in m_objectRect.

5. Add the following line to the CContainerCntrItem class's Serialize() function, right after the TODO: add storing code here comment:

```
ar << m_objectRect;
```

   This line saves the item's size and position when the rest of the document gets saved.

6. Add the following line to the CContainerCntrItem class's Serialize() function, right after the TODO: add loading code here comment:

```
ar > m_objectRect;
```

   This line loads the item's size and position when the rest of the document gets loaded.

Because you now have completed the CContainerCntrItem class, you should save your work before continuing. If you like, you can compile and run the application, but, at this point, the application looks and acts the same as the previous version, except that new objects (not objects loaded from a file) start off smaller when first added to the document.

Using the mouse to select items

Another thing you must do to complete the Container application is enable selection and deselection of linked and embedded items. This includes not only clicking the object for selection, but also starting the editing process by double-clicking the object. The following steps show how to add item selection to Container:

1. In the CContainerView class's OnDraw() function, remove or comment out all the lines following the TODO: remove this code when final draw code is complete comment.

   The lines you removed in this step used AppWizard's default location to display an embedded object in the container application's window. By removing these lines, you can add your own code for displaying multiple items at the locations contained in their m_objectRect member variables.

2. Add the lines shown in Listing 26-1 to the OnDraw() function, in place of the lines you removed in Step 1.

   These lines draw all linked and embedded items in their proper positions. The CRectTracker object draws the appropriate outline around the object, depending on the item's state. (CRectTracker objects also display the appropriate mouse cursor for an object.) InitRectTracker(), which initializes a tracker object, is a function you add to the program yourself later in these steps.

Listing 26-1: Lines for the OnDraw() Function

```
POSITION pos = pDoc->GetStartPosition();

while(pos != NULL)
{
    CContainerCntrItem* pObject =
        (CContainerCntrItem*) pDoc->GetNextItem(pos);
    pObject->Draw(pDC, pObject->m_objectRect);
    CRectTracker tracker;
    InitRectTracker(&tracker, pObject);
    tracker.Draw(pDC);
}
```

3. Use the ClassWizard to add the `OnSetCursor()` function (which MFC calls in response to a `WM_SETCURSOR` Windows message) to the `CContainerView` class. Make sure you have `CContainerView` selected in ClassWizard's Class Name box.
4. Add the lines shown in Listing 26-2 to the `OnSetCursor()` function, right after the `TODO` comment.

   The lines in Listing 26-2 check whether the cursor is over a selected embedded item. If it is, the program creates a `CRectTracker` object to set the cursor to the appropriate shape for the selected item. The `pWnd` variable is a pointer to the window that received the `WM_SETCURSOR` message, and `m_pSelection`, which is a member variable of the view class, is a pointer to any selected item.

Class Wizard

Handling a WM_SETCURSOR message
Message: **WM_SETCURSOR**
Function Created: **OnSetCursor()**
Source Code Module: **ContainerView.cpp**

◆ ◆ ◆ ◆ ◆

Listing 26-2: Lines for the OnSetCursor() Function

```
if ((m_pSelection != NULL) && (pWnd == this))
{
    CRectTracker tracker;
    InitRectTracker(&tracker, m_pSelection);
    BOOL cursorSetByTracker =
        tracker.SetCursor(this, nHitTest);
    if (cursorSetByTracker)
        return TRUE;
}
```

5. Use ClassWizard to add the `OnLButtonDown()` function to the `CContainerView` class.

6. Add the lines shown in Listing 26-3 to the `OnLButtonDown()` function, right after the `TODO` comment.

   These new lines first determine whether the user's mouse-button click should select or deselect an item. If the user is selecting the item, a `CRectTracker` object draws the appropriate border around the item. Calling the tracker's `Track()` member function enables the user to manipulate the item, after which the window is updated and the document marked as dirty (that is, needing to be saved). The `FindItemHit()` function determines whether the mouse was clicked over an embedded item. You add `FindItemHit()` to the program later in these steps.

Class Wizard

Handling a WM_LBUTTONDOWN message

Message: **WM_LBUTTONDOWN**
Function Created: **OnLButtonDown()**
Source Code Module: **ContainerView.cpp**

◆ ◆ ◆ ◆ ◆

Listing 26-3: Lines for the OnLButtonDown() Function

```
CContainerCntrItem* pHitItem = FindItemHit(point);
SetObjectAsSelected(pHitItem);

if (pHitItem == NULL)
    return;

CRectTracker tracker;
InitRectTracker(&tracker, pHitItem);
UpdateWindow();

if (!tracker.Track(this, point))
    return;

Invalidate();

pHitItem->m_objectRect = tracker.m_rect;
CContainerDoc* pDoc = GetDocument();
pDoc->SetModifiedFlag();
```

7. Use ClassWizard to add the `OnLButtonDblClk()` function to the `CContainerView` class.

8. Add the lines shown in Listing 26-4 to the `OnLButtonDblClk()` function, right after the `TODO` comment.

These new lines first call `OnLButtonDown()`, which handles item selection. Then, if the user has selected an item (rather than deselected an item), the program gets the state of the keyboard's Ctrl key. Holding down the Ctrl key when double-clicking an item signals that the item should be opened. If the Ctrl key isn't pressed, the double-click should trigger the item's primary verb, which is often Edit. As you can see, Visual C++ defines constants for these standard OLE verbs. (An OLE verb is an action that can be performed on an ActiveX object.)

Class Wizard

Handling a WM_LBUTTONDBLCLK message

Message: **WM_LBUTTONDBLCLK**
Function Created: **OnLButtonDblClk()**
Source Code Module: **ContainerView.cpp**

◆ ◆ ◆ ◆ ◆

Listing 26-4: **Lines for the OnLButtonDblClk() Function**

```
OnLButtonDown(nFlags, point);

if (m_pSelection == NULL)
    return;

SHORT keyState = GetKeyState(VK_CONTROL);
LONG oleVerb;

if (keyState < 0)
    oleVerb = OLEIVERB_OPEN;

else
    oleVerb = OLEIVERB_PRIMARY;

m_pSelection->DoVerb(oleVerb, this);
```

9. Add the `InitRectTracker()` member function to the `CContainerView` class. To do this, the Function Type should be `void`, the Function Declaration should be `InitRectTracker(CRectTracker* pTracker, CContainerCntrItem* pObject)`, and the Access should be Protected.

10. Add the lines shown in Listing 26-5 to the `InitRectTracker()` function.

To see a tracker object doing what it does best, just look at the `InitRectTracker()` function. There, the program gets the size of the selected item and then, through the tracker object, draws resize handles on the item. The program then determines whether the item is linked or embedded and draws the appropriate outline for the item's OLE state. Finally, if the item is being edited, the program draws a crosshatch pattern on the item in the document, indicating that it's not currently available.

Listing 26-5: Lines for the InitRectTracker() Function

```
pTracker->m_rect = pObject->m_objectRect;

if (pObject == m_pSelection)
    pTracker->m_nStyle |= CRectTracker::resizeInside;

OLE_OBJTYPE objType = pObject->GetType();

if (objType == OT_EMBEDDED)
    pTracker->m_nStyle |= CRectTracker::solidLine;
else if (objType == OT_LINK)
    pTracker->m_nStyle |= CRectTracker::dottedLine;

UINT objectState = pObject->GetItemState();

if ((objectState == COleClientItem::activeUIState) ||
    (objectState == COleClientItem::openState))
    pTracker->m_nStyle |= CRectTracker::hatchInside;
```

11. Add the `FindItemHit()` member function to the `CContainerView` class. To do this, the Function Type should be `CContainerCntrItem*`, the Function Declaration should be `FindItemHit(CPoint point)`, and the Access should be Protected.
12. Add the lines shown in Listing 26-6 to the `FindItemHit()` function.

    In the `FindItemHit()` function, the program compares each linked or embedded item's position with the point passed into the function as its single parameter. If the given point falls inside an item, that item is considered "hit" and is passed back from the function.

Listing 26-6: Lines for the FindItemHit() Function

```
CContainerCntrItem* pObjectHit = NULL;
CContainerDoc* pDoc = GetDocument();
BOOL objectHit;

POSITION pos = pDoc->GetStartPosition();

while (pos != NULL)
{
    CContainerCntrItem* pObject =
        (CContainerCntrItem*)pDoc->GetNextItem(pos);
    objectHit = pObject->m_objectRect.PtInRect(point);

    if (objectHit)
        pObjectHit = pObject;
```

```
    }

    return pObjectHit;
```

13. Add the `SetObjectAsSelected()` member function to the `CContainerView` class. To do this, the Function Type should be `void`, the Function Declaration should be `SetObjectAsSelected(CContainerCntrItem* pObject)`, and the Access should be Protected.

14. Add the lines shown in Listing 26-7 to the `SetObjectAsSelected()` function.

    `SetObjectAsSelected()` determines whether the user clicked an item or just an empty portion of the window. If an item is being selected, and there's already another item selected, the function closes the previously selected item. The `m_pSelection` member variable gets the pointer to the selected item, and the call to `Invalidate()` updates the window.

Listing 26-7: Lines for the SetObjectAsSelected() Function

```
CContainerDoc* pDoc = GetDocument();

if ((m_pSelection != pObject) || (pObject == NULL))
{
    COleClientItem* pActiveObject =
        pDoc->GetInPlaceActiveItem(this);

    if ((pActiveObject != pObject) &&
            (pActiveObject != NULL))
        pActiveObject->Close();
}

m_pSelection = pObject;
Invalidate();
```

Now that you have completed this version of the `Container` application, save your work and then compile and run the application. When the main window appears, you can embed and edit an object in the current document just as you did with earlier versions of the program. Now, however, when you click in the window outside of the embedded object, the program reverts to its own menus, as shown in Figure 26-8.

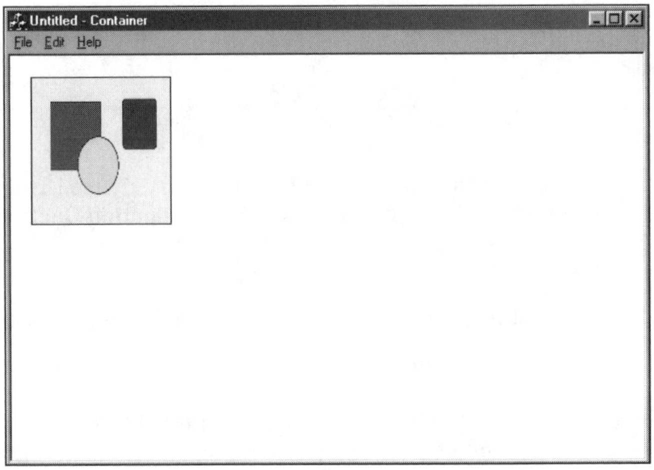

Figure 26-8: The application now can discard a server application's toolbars and menus.

When you click an object to select it, the object's sizing handles appear and the mouse pointer changes into a cross cursor, which indicates that the object can be dragged to a new location. By dragging the object's sizing handles with the mouse pointer, you can make the object any size you like. The image in the object automatically resizes as well.

This new version of Container can hold multiple embedded and linked items, rather than just a single object. Figure 26-9, for example, shows the application with two bitmaps and a Word object embedded in the window. Notice how Word's menus and toolbars have merged with the Container application's window.

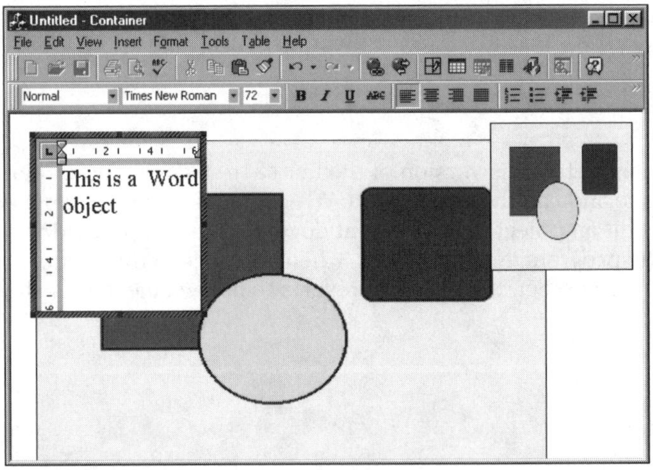

Figure 26-9: Container can manage multiple embedded objects.

Deleting embedded items

Although the Container application enables you to move around and resize linked or embedded items, you can't delete objects from the window. You need some way to delete objects. Enabling the user to delete an embedded item isn't difficult: You just have to call the selected item's `Delete()` member function. However, you do need to add the delete command to the application's user interface. The common solution is to add some sort of delete command to the application's Edit menu, as well as respond to the keyboard's Delete key. You should already be familiar with creating and responding to menu commands. Here, you see how to respond to the Delete key to delete an embedded item.

To add a delete command to the Container application, load the project, and then use ClassWizard to add the `OnKeyDown()` function to the `CContainerView` class. In `OnKeyDown()`, you need to check whether the user pressed the Delete key and whether an item is selected. If both of these conditions are true, you call the selected items' `Delete()` function and then call `UpdateAllViews()` to redraw all the view windows that may be displaying the document. Listing 26-8 shows the final `OnKeyDown()` function.

Class Wizard

Handling a WM_KEYDOWN message

Message: **WM_KEYDOWN**

Function Created: **OnKeyDown()**

Source Code Module: **ContainerView.cpp**

◆ ◆ ◆ ◆ ◆

Listing 26-8: Lines for the OnKeyDown() Function

```
void CContainerView::OnKeyDown
    (UINT nChar, UINT nRepCnt, UINT nFlags)
{
    // TODO: Add your message handler code here
    //   and/or call default

    if ((m_pSelection == NULL) || (nChar != VK_DELETE))
        return;

    m_pSelection->Delete();
    m_pSelection = NULL;
    CContainerDoc* pDoc = GetDocument();
    pDoc->UpdateAllViews(NULL);

    CView::OnKeyDown(nChar, nRepCnt, nFlags);
}
```

Nutshell

Creating a Simple ActiveX Container

These steps sum up the process of creating a container application.

1. Use AppWizard to create the skeleton application, being sure to select the Container option in the AppWizard Step 3 of 6 dialog box.
2. Write code for the item class's `OnChangeItemPosition()` function so the item stores its new position whenever it's moved.
3. Implement the item class's `OnGetItemPosition()` function so the function sets the `rPosition` variable to the item's current position.
4. Add to the item class's `Serialize()` function the code needed to save and load the item's position.
5. In the view class's `OnDraw()` function, write the code needed to draw each embedded or linked object.
6. In the view class, implement message-response functions for the `WM_SETCURSOR`, `WM_LBUTTONDOWN`, and `WM_LBUTTONDBLCLK` messages. In these functions, handle the selection of an object with the mouse.
7. Provide a command that enables the user to delete embedded or linked items from the document. Usually, this is done with a Delete command on the edit menu or by responding to the keyboard's Delete key.

✦ ✦ ✦ ✦ ✦

Server Applications

In this section, you put together the Server application, which supports ActiveX server features such as OLE menus, ActiveX document classes, ActiveX frame-window classes, and server item classes. You also see how to program a server to draw its items when those items are embedded in another application's window. You can find the complete application in the Chap26\Server folder of this book's CD-ROM.

Creating a skeleton server application

Just as with the container application, you use AppWizard to start your server application. Visual C++ then generates the basic source code for the program's classes. In a server application, these classes include not only the usual application, frame window, document (now derived from the `COleServerDoc` class instead of `CDocument`), and view window classes, but also an additional class derived from MFC's `COleServerItem` class. In the Server application, AppWizard names the derived class `CServerSrvrItem`. This class represents the server side of any of the application's items, linked or embedded, in a container application's window.

Note

You should read through all the application-building steps in this section, whether or not you actually build the Server application yourself, because the steps include explanations of the programming techniques needed to build a server application.

◆ ◆ ◆ ◆ ◆

Demo Program

Server
CD-ROM Location: **Chap26\Server**
Program Name: **Server.EXE**
Source Code Modules in Text: **None**

◆ ◆ ◆ ◆ ◆

To create the skeleton server application, perform the following steps:

1. Start a new AppWizard project called *Server*, as shown in Figure 26-10.

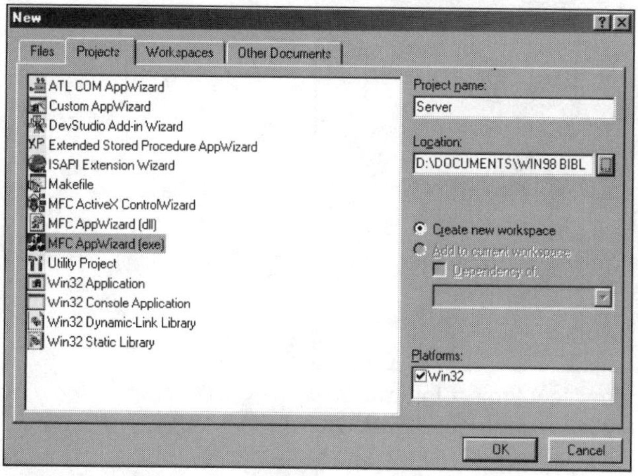

Figure 26-10: The new server application project is called *Server*.

2. In the MFC AppWizard - Step 1 of 6 dialog box, select the Single Document option.
3. Click the Next button twice, accepting the default options in the Step 2 of 6 dialog box.
4. In the Step 3 of 6 dialog box, select the Full-server option and click the Next button.

   When you select the Full-server feature, you're telling AppWizard to generate the source code needed to create a skeleton ActiveX server application. The skeleton application will be able to link its documents to and embed its documents in applications that act as ActiveX containers. (A mini-server application, another option you can select, cannot run as a standalone application and supports only embedded objects.)

5. In the Step 4 of 6 dialog box, turn off all features except 3D Controls, and then click the Next button.

6. In the Step 5 of 6 dialog box, select the option labelled "as a statically linked library." Accept the default MFC Standard project style, as well as the default option labelled "Yes, please" to generate source file comments.

7. Click the Finish button. Your New Project Information dialog box should look like the one in Figure 26-11, except your install directory may be different depending on the directory you chose when you created the project in Step 1.

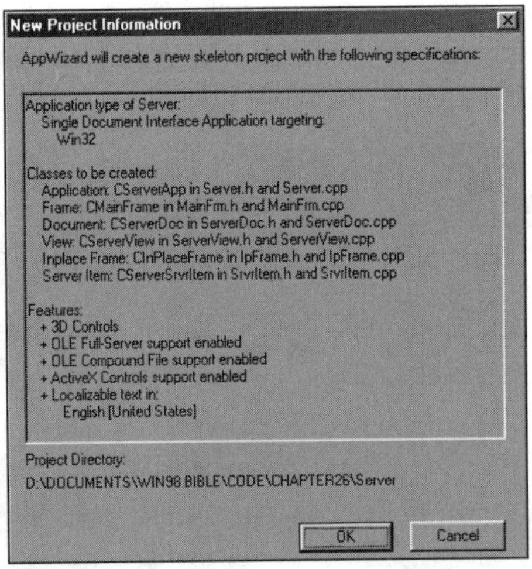

Figure 26-11: The New Project Information dialog box displays the server application's final options.

8. Click the OK button, and AppWizard generates the source code files for the skeleton application.

Now that you've completed the Server skeleton application, save your work by selecting the File menu's Save All command.

Compile and run the application so you can link its document to or embed its document in the Container application you created earlier in this chapter. To do this, start Container and select the Edit menu's Insert New Object command. The Insert Object dialog box appears. In the Object Type box, find Server Document, as shown in Figure 26-12.

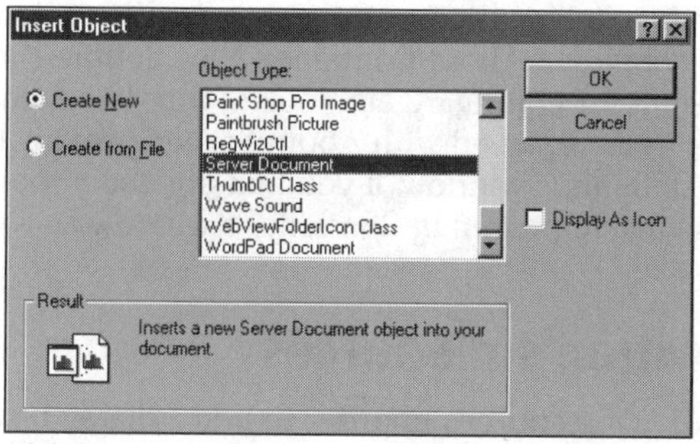

Figure 26-12: The Server application has already registered its document type with the Windows system Registry.

Note

Make sure you have compiled and run Server before running Container. If you fail to run Server, Visual C++ won't register the application's document type in your system Registry, and you won't find the Server Document document type in the Insert Object dialog box.

◆ ◆ ◆ ◆ ◆

Visual C++ names Server's default document type Server Document. If you select this document type from the Insert New Object dialog box, Windows embeds a document from Server into the currently open Container document, as shown in Figure 26-13. Something interesting happens as well. As long as the Server Document object is selected for editing, Server's menus take the place of Container's.

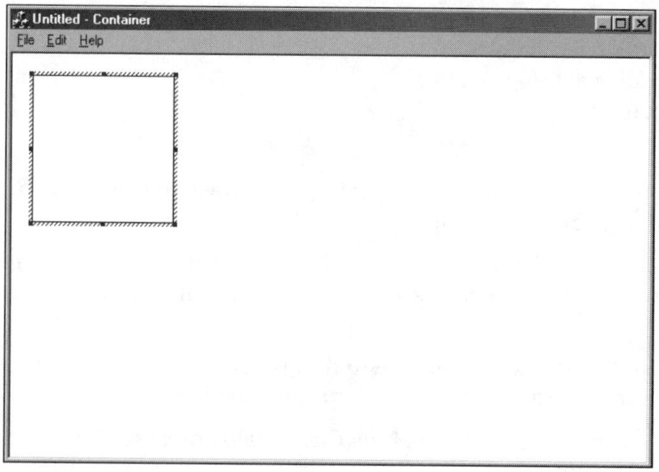

Figure 26-13: Container showing off its new Server Document object along with Server's menu bar

Deselect the Server Document item by clicking the Container window. Next, look at the Help menu. You should see the command About Container. Now double-click the Server Document object to select it for editing. Again, look at the Help menu. The About Container command has been replaced with About Server, proving that Server's menus have appeared in Container's window. If you had created a toolbar for the Server application, it would have appeared in Container's window as well.

Customizing the application's resources

Now it's time to modify the application's resources in order to add a dialog box and complete the application's menus. Perform the following steps to complete the Server application's resources:

1. Select the Resource command from Visual C++'s Insert menu. When the Insert Resource box appears, select the Dialog resource (see Figure 26-14), and click the New button.

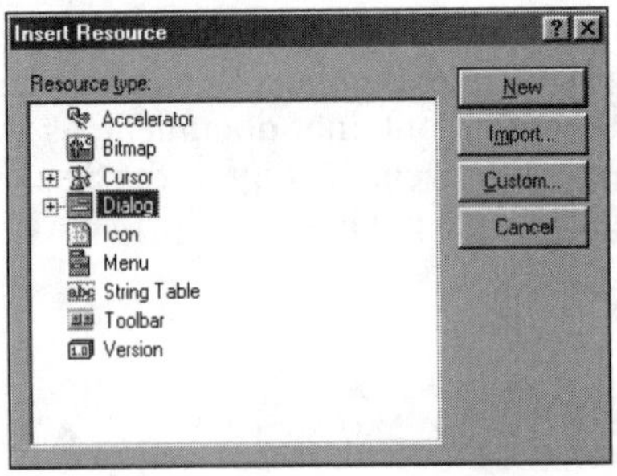

Figure 26-14: Adding a dialog box to the Server application

2. Use the dialog-box editor to create the dialog box shown in Figure 26-15, going with the default IDs for all controls.

   The server application displays a set of lines as the contents of its document. The dialog box enables the user to specify the number of lines in the document.

3. Double-click the dialog box you just created to bring up the Adding a Class dialog box. Select the Create a New Class option and click OK.

4. Name the new class `CLineDlg` in the New Class dialog box (see Figure 26-16), and click the OK button.

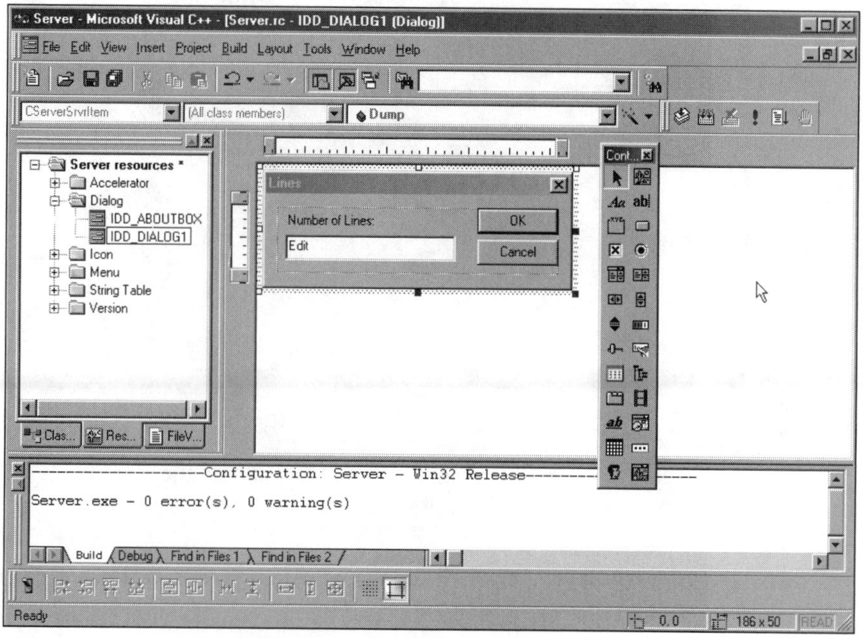

Figure 26-15: The finished dialog box looks like this.

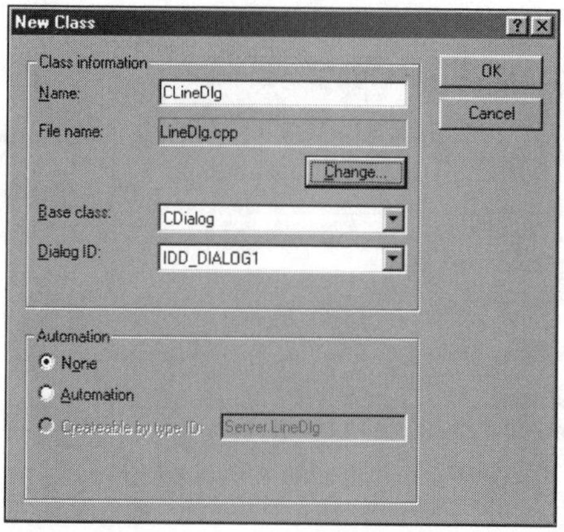

Figure 26-16: The new dialog class will be called CLineDlg.

5. In the MFC Class Wizard property sheet, display the Member Variables page, and then double-click `IDC_EDIT1` and create a variable named `m_lines` for the control, as shown in Figure 26-17.

6. Back in ClassWizard, enter 1 and 10 as `m_lines`'s minimum and maximum allowable values. Click OK to close the ClassWizard property sheet.

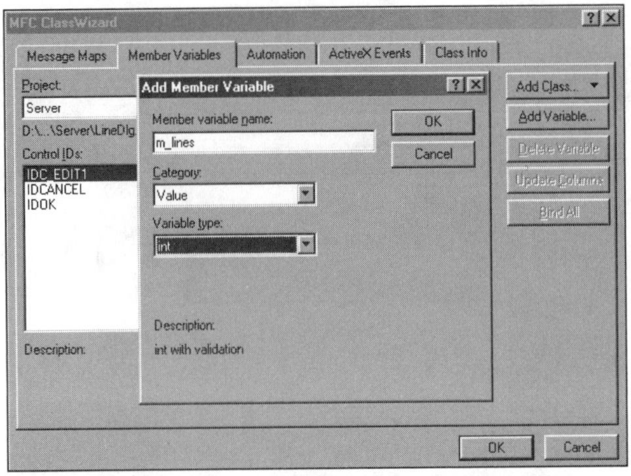

Figure 26-17: The m_lines member variable will hold the value the user enters in the edit box.

7. In the ResourceView page of the Project Workspace window, double-click the `IDR_MAINFRAME` menu ID to display the menu in the menu editor.
8. Add the Number of Lines menu item to the Lines menu, as shown in Figure 26-18, giving the Number of Lines item the ID `ID_LINES_NUMBEROFLINES`.

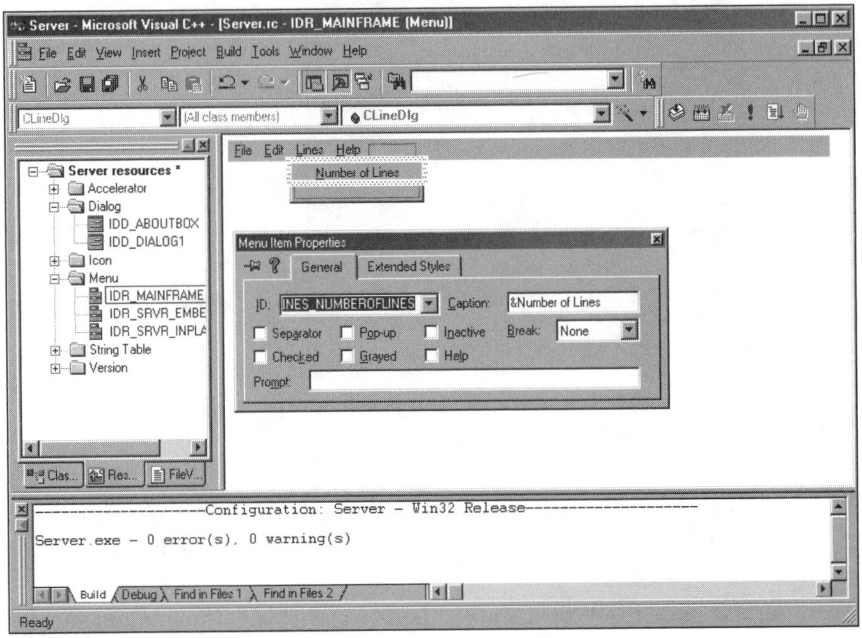

Figure 26-18: The user will be able to call up the Lines dialog box using the Lines menu's Number of Lines command.

9. Add the Lines menu to the IDR_SRVR_EMBEDDED (see Figure 26-19) and IDR_SRVR_INPLACE (see Figure 26-20) menus. Use the ID_LINES_NUMBEROFLINES ID for the Number of Lines command on each menu. (If you like, you can use Visual C++'s copy and paste commands to duplicate the Lines menu in the server menus.)

As you can tell from the menu IDs, Windows will use these additional menus to display menu bars in a container application that's editing a Server document. The double bars in the IDR_SRVR_INPLACE menu specify where additional menus can be merged into the menu bar.

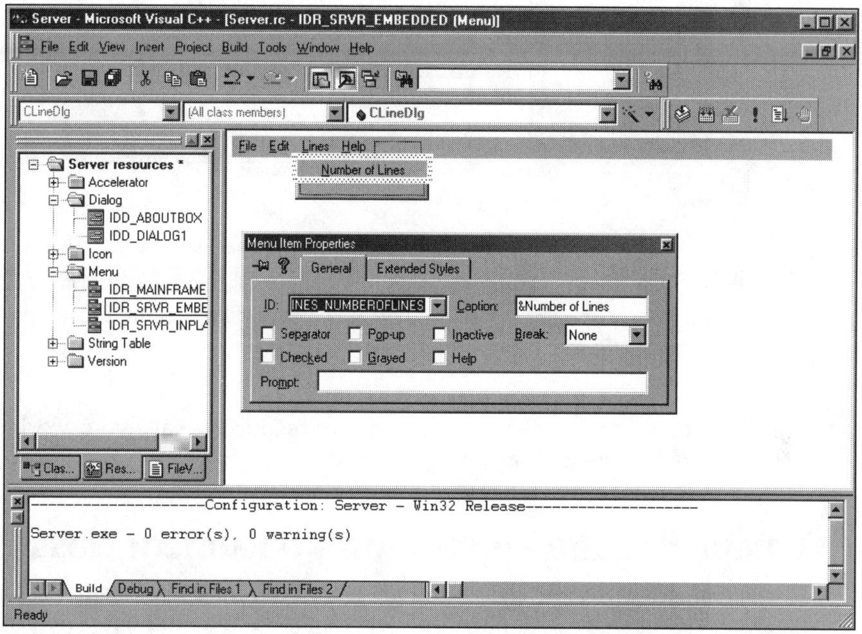

Figure 26-19: You should duplicate server editing commands in the IDR_SRVR_EMBEDDED menu.

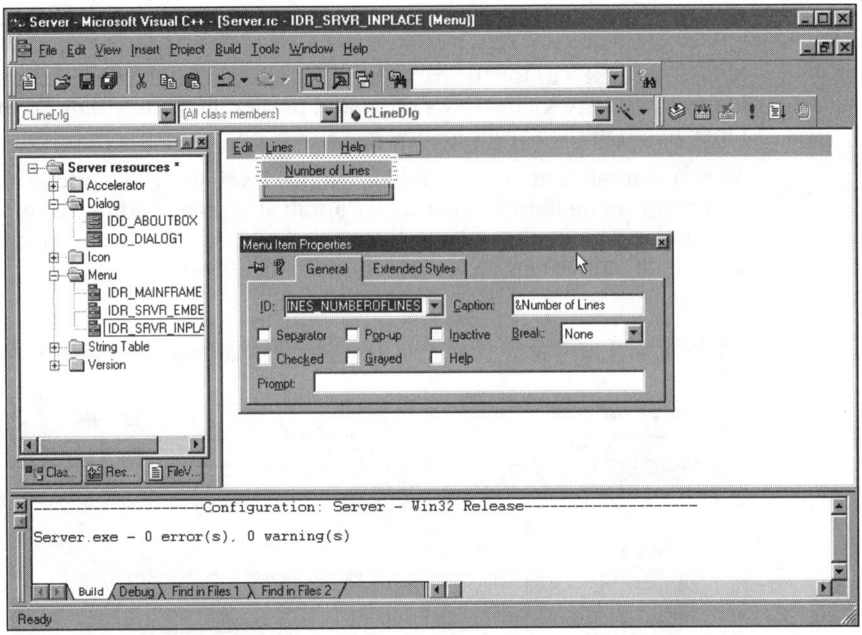

Figure 26-20: You should also duplicate server editing commands in the IDR_SRVR_INPLACE menu.

Now that you've completed the application's resources, save your work by selecting the File menu's Save All command.

Completing the application's document class

Just like most AppWizard-generated programs, Server's document class holds the data that represents the application's currently open document. An ActiveX server application's document class is much like any other application's document class, providing not only member variables to hold the document's data, but also the code needed to initialize a new document as well as to save and load a document. Perform the following steps to complete Server's document class, `CServerDoc`:

1. Right-click `CServerDoc` in the ClassView page of the Project Workspace window, and select Add Member Variable from the menu that appears.
2. When the Add Member Variable dialog appears, type **int** in the Variable Type box, type **m_lines** in the Variable Declaration box, and select the Public access option, as shown in Figure 26-21.

   The `m_lines` variable will hold the number of lines that appear in the Server document. This variable is the only value that determines how a Server document looks on the screen.

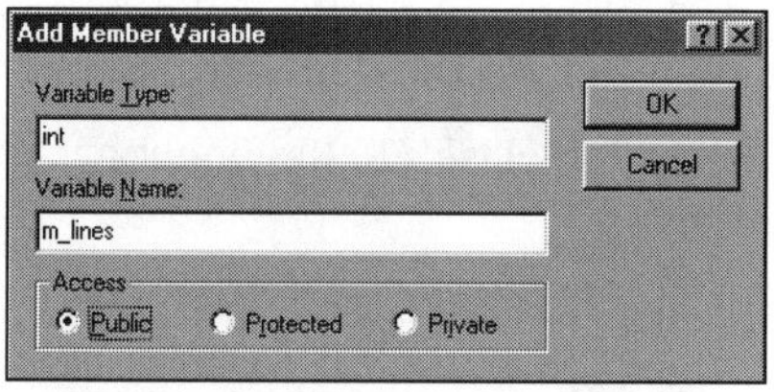

Figure 26-21: The appearance of a Server document is controlled by the value of a single variable.

3. Add the following line to the document class's `Serialize()` function. Place the line after the `add storing code here` comment.

```
ar << m_lines;
```

4. Add the following line to the document class's `Serialize()` function. Place the line after the `add loading code here` comment.

```
ar > m_lines;
```

5. Add the `OnEditCopy()` function to the document class, as shown in Figure 26-22.

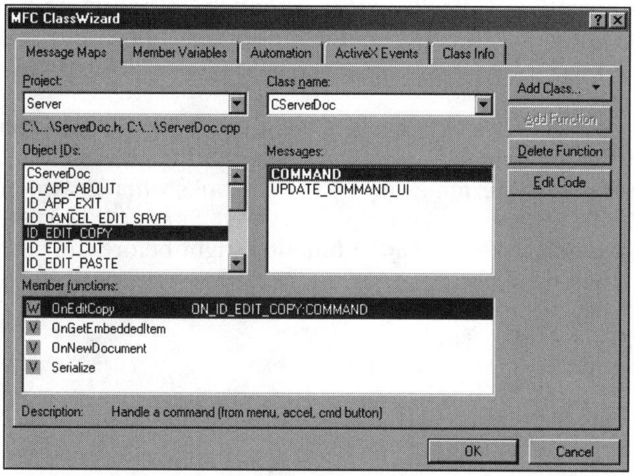

Figure 26-22: You use ClassWizard to add the OnEditCopy() function to the document class.

6. Click the Edit Code button and then add the following lines to the new `OnEditCopy()` function:

```
CServerSrvrItem* pItem = GetEmbeddedItem();
pItem->CopyToClipboard(TRUE);
```

Now, when the user selects a Paste Link command, the `OnEditCopy()` function copies the Server Document item to the Clipboard.

7. Add the following line to the `CServerDoc` class's `OnNewDocument()` member function, right after the `TODO` comment:

```
m_lines = 5;
```

This line initializes the rectangle size to its default value.

Now that you've completed the Server application's document class, select the File menu's Save All command to save your work.

Completing the server item's class

Earlier in this chapter, in the section on container applications, you discovered that AppWizard creates a class derived from `COleClientItem` that represents the ActiveX object currently embedded in the container's document. The server, too, has a similar class, but the server version of the class represents an ActiveX item for which the server is supplying editing functions. You could say that this server item class, derived from `COleServerItem`, is the other side of the ActiveX item coin.

On the container side, the ActiveX object (represented by an object of the `COleClientItem` class) has to know its own size and where it's positioned. On the server side of things, the same object (now represented by the `COleServerItem` class) has to know how to draw itself. That is, although the container application positions the ActiveX item in the window, it is the server application that displays the item.

To complete Server's server item class, you need to provide the code that draws the item. Similar to an application's view class, a server item class contains an `OnDraw()` function, which determines how the item looks when drawn in a container application's window. To complete Server's `CServerSrvrItem` class, add the following lines to the class's `OnDraw()` function, right before the `return` statement:

```
pDC->SetMapMode(MM_TEXT);
for (int x=0; x<pDoc->m_lines; ++x)
{
    pDC->MoveTo(10, x*5+10);
    pDC->LineTo(100, x*5+10);
}
```

The `OnDraw()` function displays the inactive embedded object in a container application's window. The mapping mode should be set to the same mode used in the view class's `OnDraw()` function, which draws the document in the server's window when the server is being run as a standalone application.

Completing the view class

In an ActiveX server application running as a standalone application, the view class displays a document. The view class also supplies editing functions for the application. These editing functions are usually callable from a container application through the server menus that Windows merges with the container's menus (when the user selects an embedded item for editing). In the following steps, you complete the view class's `OnDraw()` function, as well as enable the user to display the Lines dialog box. Using the Lines dialog box, the user can edit a Server document by changing the number of lines that represent the document.

1. Add the following lines to the `CServerView` class's `OnDraw()` function, right after the `TODO` comment:

   ```
   pDC->SetMapMode(MM_TEXT);
   for (int x=0; x<pDoc->m_lines; ++x)
   {
       pDC->MoveTo(10, x*5+10);
       pDC->LineTo(100, x*5+10);
   }
   ```

   These lines draw the document when it's being displayed in the server application's own window. Notice that these lines are identical to the lines you added to the item's `OnDraw()` function.

2. Press Ctrl+W to display ClassWizard, and then add the `OnLinesNumberoflines()` message-response function for the `ID_LINES_NUMBEROFLINES` command ID.

3. Add the lines in Listing 26-9 to the `OnLinesNumberoflines()` function.

Listing 26-9: Lines for the `OnLinesNumberoflines()` Function

```
CLineDlg dlg;

CServerDoc* pDoc = GetDocument();
dlg.m_lines = pDoc->m_lines;

int result = dlg.DoModal();
if (result == IDOK)
{
    pDoc->m_lines = dlg.m_lines;
    pDoc->SetModifiedFlag();
    pDoc->NotifyChanged();
    Invalidate();
}
```

The `OnLinesNumberoflines()` function sets up the Lines dialog box and displays it to the user. If the user dismisses the dialog with the OK button, `OnLinesNumberoflines()` sets the document's `m_lines` member variable to the new value entered by the user and then updates both the locally displayed document and the embedded item (if any). Calling the document class's `NotifyChanged()` function is all it takes to notify any items embedded in containers that their displays need to be repainted.

4. Add the following line to the top of the view class's implementation file (ServerView.cpp), after the line that's already there, `#include "ServerView.h"`:

```
#include "LineDlg.h"
```

Now that you've completed the Server sample ActiveX server application, select the Build Server.exe command from Visual C++'s Build menu to compile and link your changes.

Nutshell

Creating a Simple ActiveX Server

These steps sum up the process of creating a basic server application.

1. Use AppWizard to create the skeleton application, being sure to select the Full-server option in the AppWizard Step 3 of 6 dialog box.
2. When constructing the server's menu bar, duplicate server-item commands in the `IDR_SRVR_EMBEDDED` and `IDR_SRVR_INPLACE` menus.
3. Complete the application's document class just as you would for any standalone application.
4. Complete the server item's `OnDraw()` function, which displays the item in a container application's window.
5. Complete the view class's `OnDraw()` function, which displays the item when the program is run as a standalone application.

◆ ◆ ◆ ◆ ◆

Running the server application

You can run a server application several ways. The most obvious way is to run the server just like any other application, as a standalone program. Second, a server application can run as an in-place editing tool in a container application. To run the server this way, you select for editing a linked or embedded server item in a container application's window. Finally, you can run the server application by selecting for editing a linked item in a container application. In this case, the server runs in its own window, editing the file to which the linked item is associated.

Running Server as a standalone application

To run Server on its own, double-click the program's executable file, or select the execute command from Visual C++'s toolbar or Build menu. You then see the window shown in Figure 26-23. The lines in the window's upper-left corner represent the application's default document, which consists of five lines.

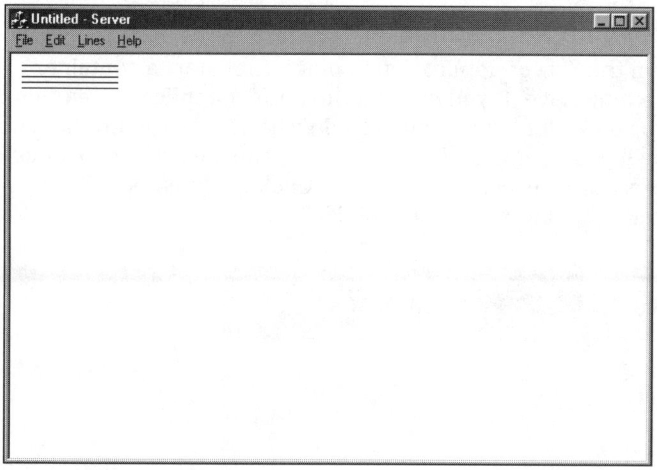

Figure 26-23: This is Server running as a standalone application.

The only way you can edit the document in this simple example is to change the number of the lines. You do this by selecting the Lines menu's Number of Lines command, which displays the Lines dialog box. In this dialog box, you can specify a number from 1 to 10 for the lines. Figure 26-24 shows the application after the user has given the document 10 lines.

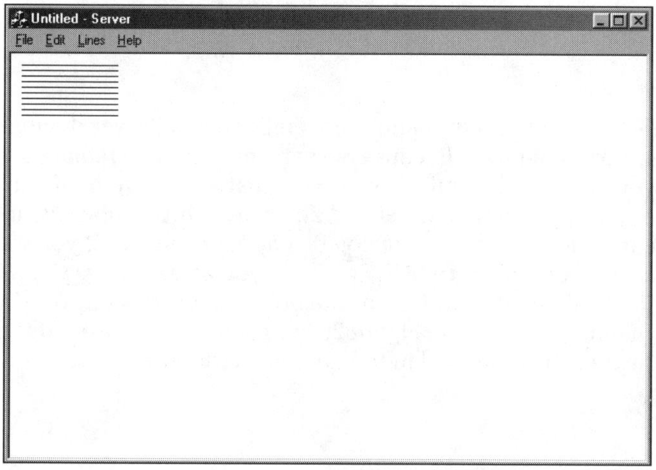

Figure 26-24: Here, the number of lines has been reset to 10.

Before closing the Server application, save the document under the name test.srv. Later in this chapter, you use this file to link an item into a container application's window.

Running Server as an in-place editor

When you want to run the Server application in place, first start a container application. As luck would have it, you created the perfect application earlier in this chapter. (Okay, maybe luck didn't have much to do with it.) So, run Container, and select its Insert New Object command from the Edit menu. Select Server Document in the Object Type box of the Insert Object dialog. Click OK to embed the item in the container application's window (see Figure 26-25).

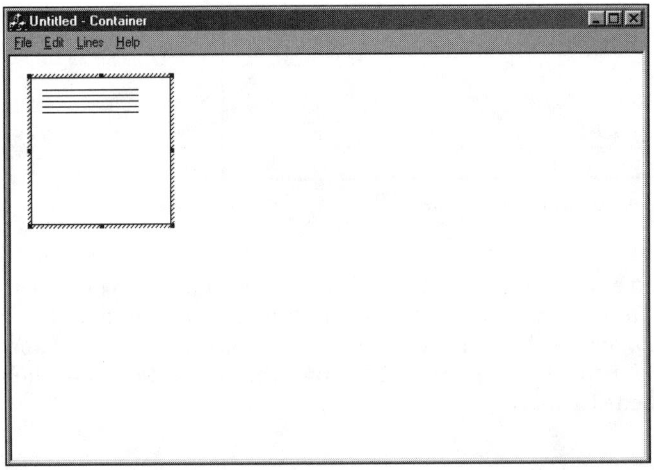

Figure 26-25: Here's Container with its embedded Server Document item.

Notice in Figure 26-25 that the application not only embedded a Server document object, but it also ran Server in-place. Because Server's menus have replaced Container's menus, you can edit the embedded object just as you would if you had run Server as a standalone application. Go ahead and select the Number of Lines command from the Lines menu. The Lines dialog box appears, just as if you were running Server rather than Container (which, in a way, you are). Change the number of lines to 10, and then click outside of the object to deselect it. Windows restores Container's menus, as shown in Figure 26-26. The solid line around the Server item means the item is embedded in the container window.

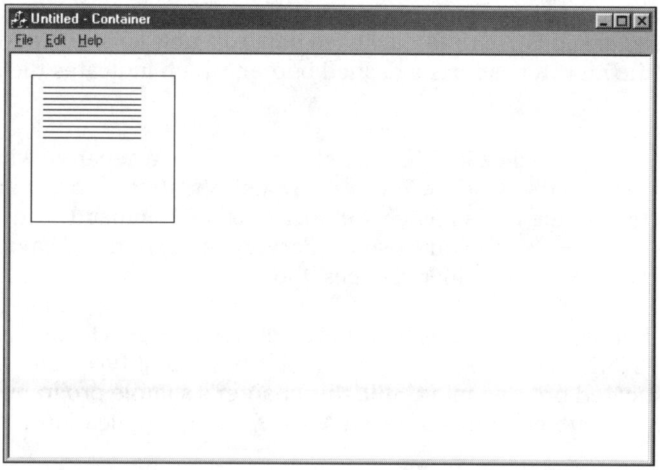

Figure 26-26: Windows has reset the Container's menu.

Running Server as an editor for a linked item

In the previous section, you used the Container application as a container for an embedded Server item. Because the item is embedded, the item's data exists only as a part of the container application's document; that is, the item used in Container doesn't have a file of its own. When you link a Server item, on the other hand, you select a Server file. In this case, when the file is edited, the linked item in the container window changes automatically to the new version of the document.

To see this in action, again select the Insert New Object command from Container's Edit menu. When the Insert Object dialog box appears, select the Create from File option. The Object Type box changes to a File box with a Browser button, as shown in Figure 26-27. Use the Browse button to locate and select the test.srv file you saved when running Server as a standalone application. Select the Link option in the Insert Object dialog box. Click OK to link the file to Container's window.

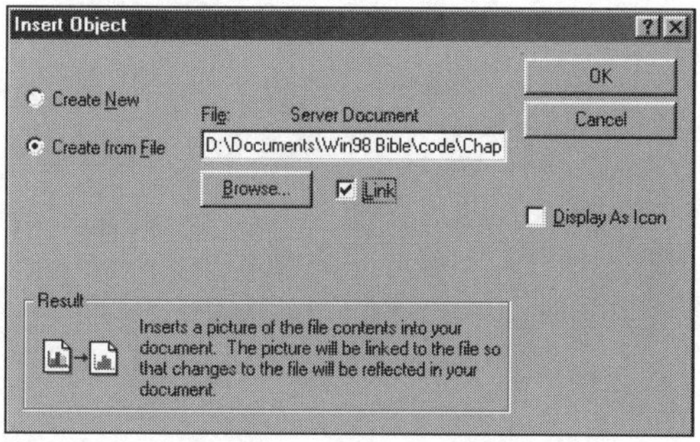

Figure 26-27: You can use the Insert Object dialog to link, as well as embed, items.

When the newly linked Server item first appears, it covers the previously embedded item. Use your mouse to drag the linked item to a new location in the window. Notice that the new item sports a dashed border, which indicates the item is linked.

To edit the linked item, double-click it. Windows starts Server in a separate window and loads the linked file into the window. You can now edit the item by bringing up the Lines dialog box (select the Lines menu's Number of Lines command) and changing the number of lines. When you close the Server application and save the changed file, the linked item in Container changes, too.

That's all there is to building and running a basic server application. Of course, your own server applications will feature more complex document types and will require more sophisticated programming. Still, this chapter's sample program ought to get you started with creating your own ActiveX server applications.

Summary

AppWizard does an amazing job of generating the code an application needs to be an ActiveX container. Still, the basic functionality supplied by AppWizard is rarely adequate for a complete application. AppWizard leaves many details of implementing a container to the programmer. In this chapter, you learned how to give the skeleton container application extra capabilities, such as enabling the user to select, move, and delete embedded items.

A basic server application is easier to build than a container application. Still, there's a lot to learn to master the programming of ActiveX server applications. This chapter presented an introduction to server programming. If you want to know more, you should pick up an ActiveX programming book that covers writing container and server applications with Visual C++ and MFC.

✦ ✦ ✦

CHAPTER 27

Automation and ActiveX Controls

✦ ✦ ✦ ✦

In This Chapter

Building an automation server application

Building an automation client application

Controlling an automation server from the client application

Building an ActiveX control

Responding to the control's user interface

Testing an ActiveX control

✦ ✦ ✦ ✦

As you learned in Chapter 25, ActiveX Automation gives applications the capability to control each other. Using automation, for example, you can program features in one program and then use those features in any other program you write—reusability at its best. You might, for example, have an application that can, among other things, count the number of words in a document. If you make this application into an automation server, other applications can call the function that counts words and not need to implement that function themselves. In this chapter, you'll learn how to create both automation server and automation client applications.

You'll also learn how to create ActiveX controls, which, although they are used differently than automation servers, have a lot in common with servers. For example, both automation servers and ActiveX controls define properties and methods that can be controlled from another application. In this chapter, you create a sample ActiveX control and discover how to use these controls in Web pages and other applications.

Automation Servers

In this section, you put together the *AutoServer* application, which supports automation features such as properties and methods that can be accessed by a client application. Along the way, you learn to define an interface through which client applications can control an automation server. Because a server application is only half the picture, you also create a client application called *AutoClient*. You can find these applications in the Chap27\AutoServer and Chap27\AutoClient folders of this book's CD-ROM.

The Automation Server Application

In the first part of this chapter, you learn to program a simple automation server. As you already know, an automation server provides some sort of service that can be accessed and controlled by a client application. For example, an automation server might provide a spell-checker that other applications can use to spell-check their documents. In this chapter, you won't create a server that sophisticated, but you'll get a look at how this handy technology works. You can find this section's sample application, AutoServer, in the Chap27\AutoServer folder of this book's CD-ROM.

Creating a skeleton automation server

You can use AppWizard to generate the basic source code your automation server started, leaving you to fill in the details appropriate for your specific application. You create an automation server with AppWizard in much the same way you create any other type of application. You just specify slightly different AppWizard options. Perform the following steps to create the AutoServer skeleton application:

Note

You should read through all the application-building steps in this chapter, whether or not you actually build the automation server application yourself, because the steps include explanations of the programming techniques needed to build an automation server application.

◆ ◆ ◆ ◆ ◆

Caution

AutoServer

CD-ROM Location: **Chap27\AutoServer**
Program Name: **AutoServer.exe**
Source Code Modules in Text: **None**

◆ ◆ ◆ ◆ ◆

1. Start a new AppWizard project called *AutoServer*, as shown in Figure 27-1.
2. In the MFC AppWizard – Step 1 dialog box, select the Single Document option.
3. Click the Next button twice, accepting the default options in the Step 2 dialog box.
4. In the Step 3 of 6 dialog box, select the Automation option. Click the Next button.

   When you select the Automation feature, you're telling AppWizard to generate the source code needed to create a skeleton automation server application. The skeleton application will be able to define properties and methods that can be accessed by other applications.
5. In the Step 4 of 6 dialog box, turn off all features except 3D Controls, and then click the Next button.

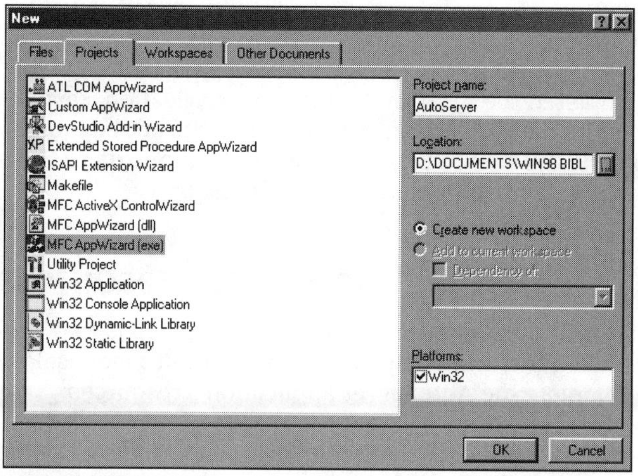

Figure 27-1: The new automation server application is called *AutoServer*.

6. In the Step 5 of 6 dialog box, select the "as a statically linked library" option.
7. Click the Finish button. Your New Project Information dialog box should look like the one in Figure 27-2, except your install directory may be different depending on the directory you chose when you created the project in Step 1.

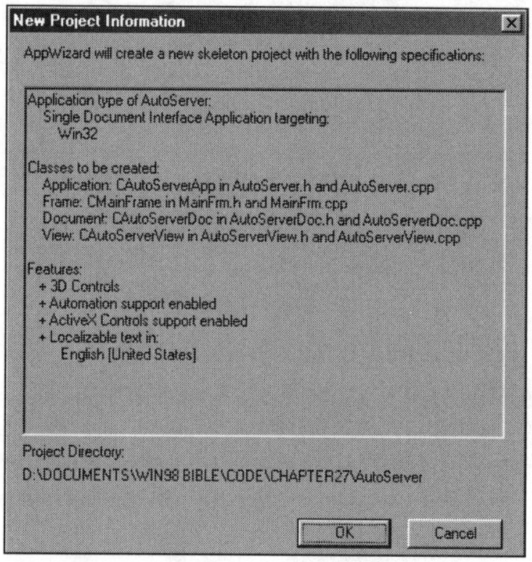

Figure 27-2: The New Project Information dialog box displays the automation server's final options.

8. Click the OK button and AppWizard generates the source code files for the skeleton application.

Now that you've completed the AutoServer skeleton application, save your work by selecting the File menu's Save All command. Currently, the application does nothing useful, so don't compile the source files yet. Instead, continue on to the next set of steps, where you complete the automation server's resources.

Customizing the automation server's resources

At this point, you've built the basic application. The next step is to customize the resources to add a dialog box and complete the application's menus. Perform the following steps to complete the AutoServer application's resources:

1. In the ResourceView page of the Project Workspace window, double-click the `IDR_MAINFRAME` menu ID to display the menu in the menu editor.
2. Click the resource's Edit menu and delete the menu from the menu bar.
3. Remove all commands from the File menu except Exit.
4. Add the Color menu shown in Figure 27-3, giving the submenu's Set Color command the ID `ID_COLOR_SETCOLOR`.

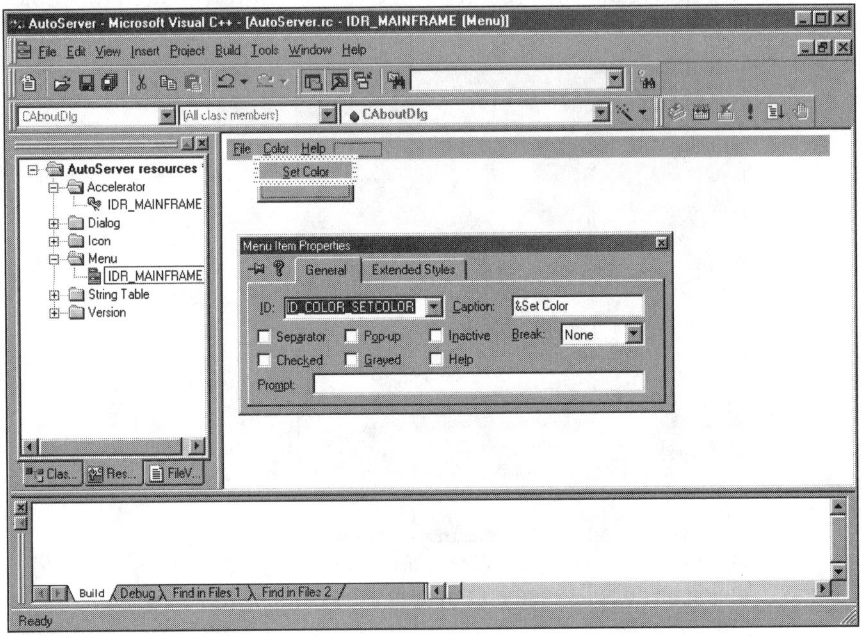

Figure 27-3: The user will be able to select the Set Color command from the Color menu.

5. In the ResourceView window, click the IDR_MAINFRAME accelerator resource and delete all accelerators from the project.

Now that you've completed the application's resources, save your work by selecting the Edit menu's Save All command.

Completing the automation server's document class

In Chapter 12, you learned about MFC's document/view architecture. So, it should be no surprise to you that, as in many MFC programs, AutoServer's document class holds the data that represents the application's currently open document. An automation server application's document class is much like any other application's document class, providing member variables that hold the document's data as well as providing the functions that initialize that data. The document class can, of course, also serialize (save and load) the application's document. The AutoServer application doesn't save and load files. Even so, it does have a single variable that controls how the document (a text string) looks. Perform the following steps to complete AutoServer's document class, CAutoServerDoc:

1. First, add a member variable to CAutoServerDoc. In the Add Member Variable dialog box, type `UINT` in the Variable Type box, type `m_color` in the Variable Declaration box, and select the Public access option.

   The m_color variable will hold the color of the document's text string.

2. Add the following line to the CAutoServerDoc class's OnNewDocument() member function, right after the TODO comment:

   ```
   m_color = 0;
   ```

   This line initializes the text color to the default value.

Now that you've completed the AutoServer application's document class, select the File menu's Save All command to save your work.

Completing the automation server's view class

In the following steps, you complete the view class's OnDraw() function, as well as enable the program to respond to the Set Color command. Using the Set Color command, the user can change the color of the application's text display.

1. Add the lines shown in Listing 27.1 to the CAutoServerView class's OnDraw() function, right after the TODO comment:

Listing 27-1: **Lines for the OnDraw() Function**

```
LOGFONT logFont;
logFont.lfHeight = 48;
logFont.lfWidth = 0;
logFont.lfEscapement = 0;
logFont.lfOrientation = 0;
logFont.lfWeight = FW_BOLD;
logFont.lfItalic = 0;
logFont.lfUnderline = 0;
logFont.lfStrikeOut = 0;
logFont.lfCharSet = ANSI_CHARSET;
logFont.lfOutPrecision = OUT_DEFAULT_PRECIS;
logFont.lfClipPrecision = CLIP_DEFAULT_PRECIS;
logFont.lfQuality = PROOF_QUALITY;
logFont.lfPitchIn addition,Family = VARIABLE_PITCH | FF_ROMAN;
strcpy(logFont.lfFaceName, "Times New Roman");

CFont font;
font.CreateFontIndirect(&logFont);

CFont* pOldFont = pDC->SelectObject(&font);

COLORREF color;
if (pDoc->m_color == 0)
  color = RGB(0,0,0);
else if (pDoc->m_color == 1)
  color = RGB(255,0,0);
else if (pDoc->m_color == 2)
  color = RGB(0,255,0);
else
  color = RGB(0,0,255);

pDC->SetTextColor(color);
pDC->TextOut(20, 20, "AutoServer's Display String");

pDC->SelectObject(pOldFont);
```

These lines create a large font for the display string, set the text color on the basis of the current color setting, and display the display string.

2. Use the ClassWizard to add the `OnColorSetcolor()` message-response function, as shown in Figure 27-4.

Note

Handling a menu message

Message: **ID_COLOR_SETCOLOR**
Function Created: **OnColorSetcolor()**
Source Code Module: **AutoServerView.cpp**

✦ ✦ ✦ ✦ ✦

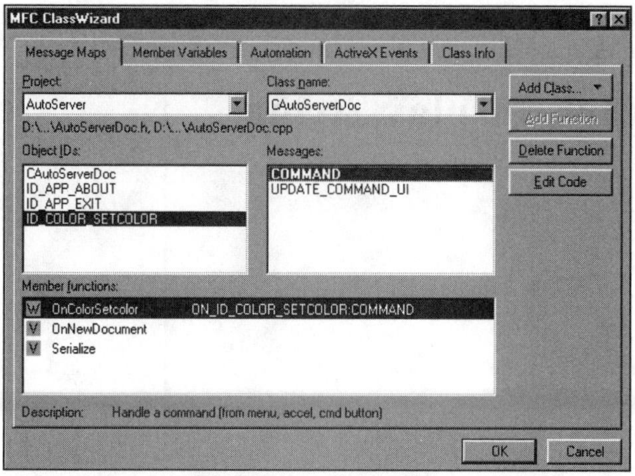

Figure 27-4: Use ClassWizard to add the `OnColorSetcolor()` function to the view class.

3. Add the following lines to the `OnColorSetcolor()` function:

```
CAutoServerDoc* pDoc = GetDocument();

++pDoc->m_color;
if (pDoc->m_color > 3)
  pDoc->m_color = 0;

Invalidate();
```

4. The `OnColorSetcolor()` function increments the color value stored in the application's document object. The value of `m_color` controls the color of the application's display string. The call to `Invalidate()` forces the application to redraw its display.

Now that you've completed AutoServer's view class, select the File menu's Save All command to save your work. Compile and run the application and you discover that it runs just like any other AppWizard application, with no obvious automation features. You can select the Color menu's Set Color command to change the color of the display text (see Figure 27-5), but that's about it. To create the automation server, you must define properties and methods, which you do in the next section.

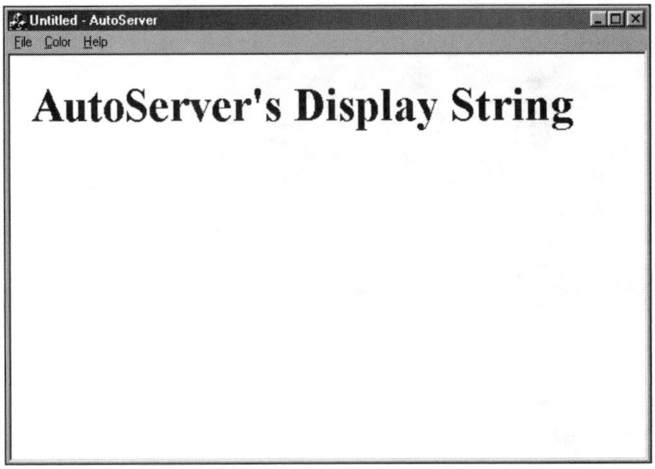

Figure 27-5: At this point, AutoServer runs with no obvious automation features.

Defining the server's properties and methods

To enable an automation client application to control the automation server, the server must define an interface consisting of properties and methods. To add properties and methods to AutoServer, perform the following steps:

1. Open the ClassWizard and select the Automation tab.
2. Select `CAutoServerDoc` in the Class Name box and click the Add Property button.
3. In the Add Property dialog, enter **Color** in the External Name box, select short in the Type box, and select the Get/Set methods option (see Figure 27-6).

   `Color` will be the name of the property that client applications will use to control the color of the display text. To retrieve this value from the automation server, a client application calls the `GetColor()` method. Similarly, to change the Color property, a client application calls the `SetColor()` method.
4. In ClassWizard, click the Add Method button. In the Add Method dialog box, type **DisplayServerWindow** in the External Name box (the Internal Name box mirrors your typing), and select void in the Return Type box, as shown in Figure 27-7. Click OK to dismiss the Add Method dialog.

   The `DisplayServerWindow()` method enables client applications to display the server application's window.

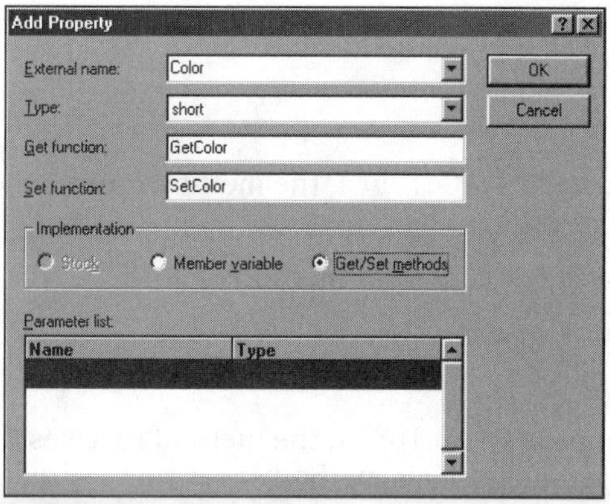

Figure 27-6: The Color property controls the text color.

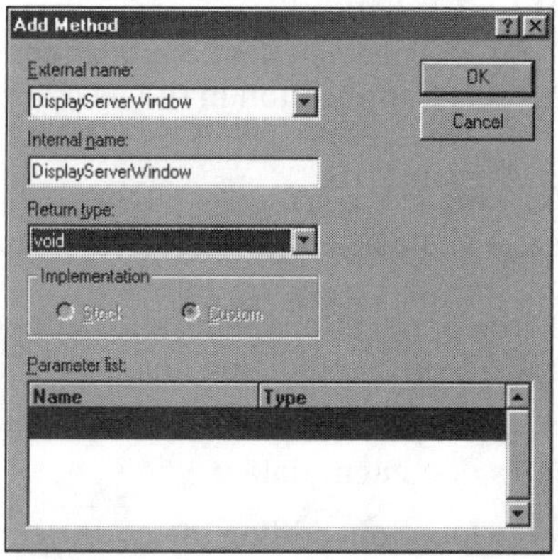

Figure 27-7: ClassWizard can also define methods for the automation interface.

5. With `DisplayServerWindow` highlighted in ClassWizard's External Name box, click the Edit Code button. Add the following lines to the `DisplayServerWindow()` method:

```
CFrameWnd* pWnd = (CFrameWnd*)AfxGetMainWnd();
pWnd->ActivateFrame(SW_SHOW);
```

Now, when a client application calls `DisplayServerWindow()`, the server gets a pointer to the main window and displays the window by calling its `ActivateFrame()` function.

6. In the `GetColor()` method, replace the `return` statement with the following line:

```
return (short)m_color;
```

When a client application calls `GetColor()`, the method returns the value of `m_color`, the text's current color.

7. Add the following lines to the `SetColor()` method:

```
m_color = nNewValue;
UpdateAllViews(NULL);
```

When a client application calls `SetColor()`, the method receives the new value in the `nNewValue` parameter. This method saves the new value in `m_color` and then redraws all views so the new color has an immediate effect on the display.

You've now completed the AutoServer sample application. Compile and link your changes, then save your application. Although AutoServer now supports ActiveX automation through its new interface, you still need a client application that knows how to control the server. You build the client application in the next section.

Nutshell

Creating a Simple Automation Server

These steps sum up the process of creating a basic automation server application.

1. Use AppWizard to create the skeleton application, being sure to select the Automation option in the AppWizard Step 3 of 6 dialog box.
2. Complete the server's document class by defining member variables for the data that makes up the application's document data.
3. Complete the view class's `OnDraw()` function, adding the code needed to display the application's document data.
4. Use ClassWizard to define the server's properties and methods. You do this on ClassWizard's Automation page. You also need to write the code for the body of each method you add.

✦ ✦ ✦ ✦ ✦

The Automation Client Application

As you may have guessed, automation is a two-sided process. Now that you have a server application that supplies automation services, you need a client application that knows how to use those services. In this section, you construct a client application that knows how to access AutoServer's automation interface. After completing the client application, you discover how the server and client work together. You can find this section's sample application, AutoClient, in the Chap27\AutoClient folder of the accompanying CD-ROM.

Creating the automation client skeleton

AppWizard can get your client server started just as easily as it got your server application started. Then you can fill in the details that are appropriate for your specific client application. As you'll soon see, creating an automation client application using AppWizard is not unlike creating any other type of application. Perform the following steps to create the AutoClient skeleton application.

Caution

AutoClient
CD-ROM Location: **Chap27\AutoClient**
Program Name: **AutoClient.exe**
Source Code Modules in Text: **None**

◆ ◆ ◆ ◆ ◆

1. Start a new AppWizard project called *AutoClient*.
2. In the MFC AppWizard – Step 1 dialog box, select the Single Document option.
3. Click the Next button three times, accepting the default options in the Step 2 and Step 3 dialog boxes.
4. In the Step 4 of 6 dialog box, turn off all features except 3D Controls, and then click the Next button.
5. In the Step 5 of 6 dialog box, select the As a Statically Linked Library option.
6. Click the Finish button. Your New Project Information dialog box should look like the one in Figure 27-8, except your install directory may be different depending on the directory you chose when you created the project in Step 1.

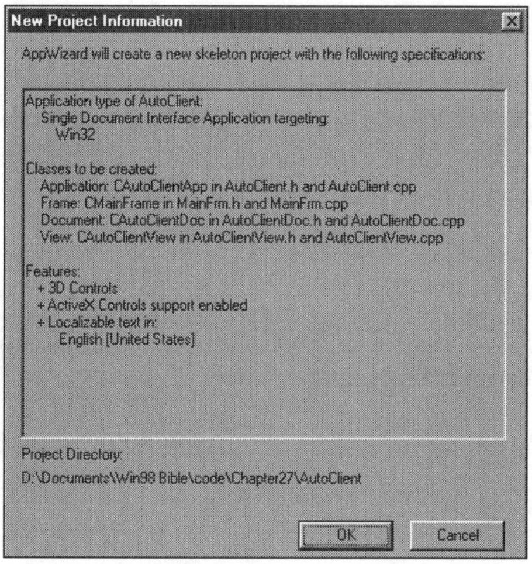

Figure 27-8: The New Project Information dialog box displays the automation client's final options.

7. Click the OK button and AppWizard generates the source code files for the skeleton application.

Customizing the client application's resources

Now that you've built the basic client application, you can customize the resources to complete the application's menus. Follow the steps following to complete this task:

1. In the ResourceView page of the Project Workspace window, double-click the `IDR_MAINFRAME` menu ID to display the menu in the menu editor.
2. Add the Automation menu shown in Figure 27-9, giving the Set Color and Show Window commands the IDs `ID_AUTOMATION_SETCOLOR` and `ID_AUTOMATION_SHOWWINDOW`, respectively.

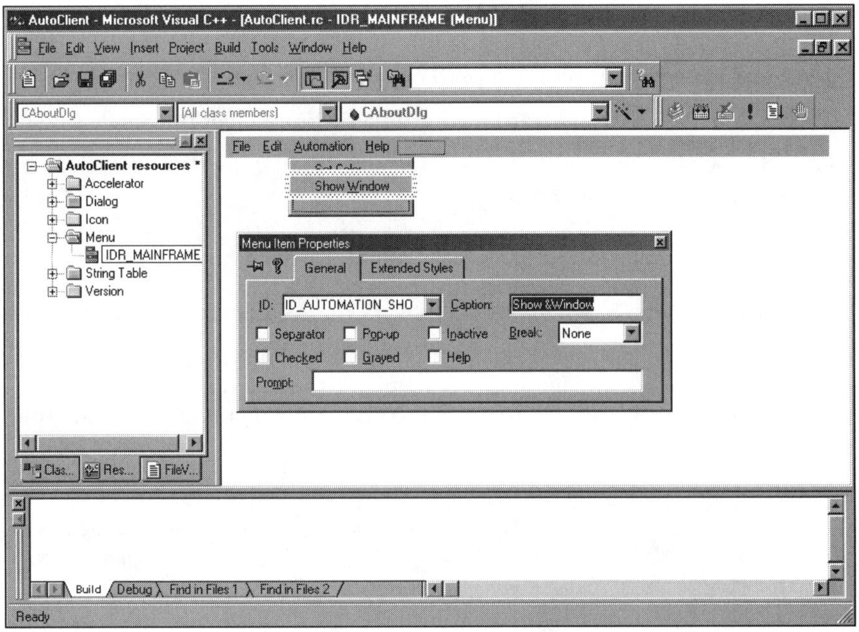

Figure 27-9: The final Automation menu should look like this.

3. Select the Edit menu and delete it.
4. In the ResourceView window, select the `IDR_MAINFRAME` accelerator resource and delete all accelerators from the project.

Now that you've completed the application's resources, save your work by selecting Save All in the File menu.

Completing the client application's view class

In the previous section, you created new menu commands for the automation client application. Somewhere in the application's classes, the program must respond to those commands. In the case of AutoClient, the view class is charged with responding to menu messages. Because some of those menu messages must manipulate the server application, the view class must have access to the server application's properties and methods. This access is provided by an interface you can create from the server application's type library. To create that interface and the menu commands' message-response functions, follow these steps:

1. Open ClassWizard, and then select the Message Maps tab. Click the Add Class button and select the From a Type Library option, as shown in Figure 27-10. The Import From Type Library dialog box appears.

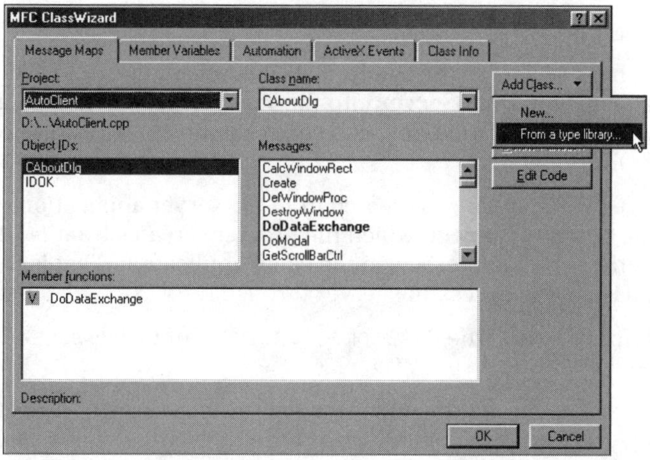

Figure 27-10: ClassWizard can create classes from type libraries.

2. In the Import from Type Library dialog, navigate to the AutoServer.tlb file in your server application's Release or Debug directory and select it.
3. In the Confirm Classes dialog (see Figure 27-11), click OK to accept the suggested names for the new class and the class's source code files; then close ClassWizard.

   The type library contains information about the server's properties and methods. ClassWizard can read the type library and create a class for the interface represented by the class library. This new class makes it easy for your application to access the server's properties and call the server's methods.

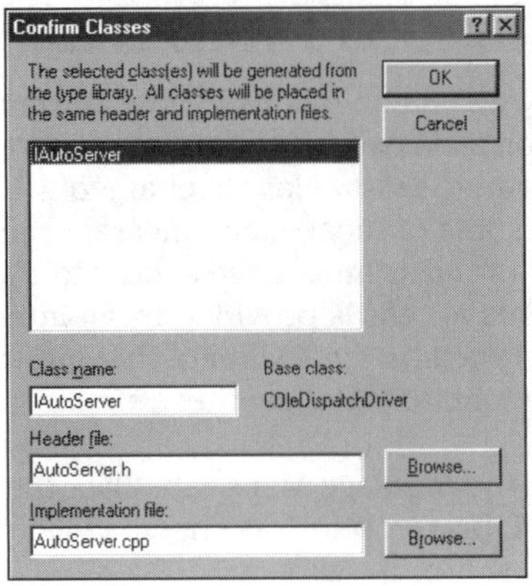

Figure 27-11: ClassWizard converts the server's interface into a class.

4. Add a member variable to the CAutoClientView class. In the Add Member Variable dialog, type **IAutoServer** into the Variable Type box, type **m_server** into the Variable Declaration box, and select the Protected access option; then click OK.
5. `IAutoServer` is the class you created from the server application's type library. The `m_server` object, which the program creates from `IAutoServer`, represents the server's interface in the client application. That is, the client application is able to access the server through the `m_server` object.
6. Use ClassWizard to add the `OnAutomationSetcolor()` message-response function to the `CAutoClientView` class.
7. Add the following lines to the new `OnAutomationSetcolor()` function:

Note

Handling a menu message
Message: **ID_AUTOMATION_SETCOLOR**
Function Created: **OnAutomationSetcolor()**
Source Code Module: **ClientServerView.cpp**

```
int color = m_server.GetColor();
++color;
if (color > 3)
    color = 0;
m_server.SetColor(color);
```

◆ ◆ ◆ ◆ ◆

These lines get the current text color number from the server, calculate a new color number, and call the server to set the new color.

8. Use ClassWizard to add the `OnAutomationShowwindow()` message-response function.

9. Add the following line to the new `OnAutomationShowwindow()` function:

Note

Handling a menu message

Message: **ID_AUTOMATION_SHOWWINDOW**
Function Created: **OnAutomationShowwindow()**
Source Code Module: **AutoClientView.cpp**

✦ ✦ ✦ ✦ ✦

```
m_server.DisplayServerWindow();
```

This line calls the server's `DisplayServerWindow()` method to display the server's main window, which remains hidden unless the client calls this method.

10. Use ClassWizard to add the `OnCreate()` message-response function.
11. Add the following lines to the new `OnCreate()` function, right after the `TODO: Add your specialized creation code here` comment:

```
BOOL loaded =
   m_server.CreateDispatch("AutoServerApp.Document");

if (!loaded)
    return -1;
```

These lines load the automation server. If the server fails to load, the return value of –1 tells MFC that the window cannot be created properly and the application should terminate.

Now that you've completed the client application's view class, you'll add the code needed to initialize ActiveX. Then, you'll run both the server and client applications to see how they work together.

Initializing ActiveX in the client application

At this point, the AutoClient application is nearly finished. The last thing to do is to enable ActiveX by calling the MFC `AfxOleInit()` function. If you fail to do this, your client application will be unable to access the server. The best place to call `AfxOleInit()` is in the application class's `InitInstance()` function. Load the `CAutoClientApp` class's implementation file, and add the following lines to the very beginning of the `InitInstance()` function, right after the function's opening brace:

```
BOOL OleEnabled = AfxOleInit();
if (!OleEnabled)
    return FALSE;
```

You've now completed the automation client application. In the following section, you'll finally get to run both the server and the client and see the power of automation.

Creating a Simple Automation Client

These steps sum up the process of creating a basic automation client application.

1. Use AppWizard to create the skeleton application. You don't need to select any ActiveX options.
2. Modify the application's resources to provide commands for controlling the server. You might, for example, provide a menu that contains server commands.
3. Create a class that represents the server's interface. To do this, use ClassWizard's Add Class button and create the class from the server's type library.
4. In the view class, create a member variable that's an object of the server interface class.
5. In the view class's `OnCreate()` function, call the server object's `CreateDispatch()` function to load the server.
6. Implement message-response functions for the server commands supported by the client application.
7. In the application class's `InitInstance()` function, call `AfxOleInit()` to initialize ActiveX.

◆ ◆ ◆ ◆ ◆

Controlling the Server from the Client

Now you've created both an automation server application and a client application, the two sides of the automation process. You're ready to see ActiveX automation in action. First, though, be sure that you've run the server application at least once. When you run the server the first time, it registers itself with Windows as an automation server. Until the server has been registered with Windows, the client application cannot control it.

Now, if the server application is still running, close it. You don't need to have the server running to control it from the client; the client application loads the server automatically. Run the AutoClient application, and you'll see the window shown in Figure 27-12.

When you start AutoClient, although you can't see the server application, it's already loaded into memory. To prove this, select the Set Color command from the AutoClient's Automation menu. What happened? Nothing? Actually, a lot is going on behind the scenes. Every time you select the Set Color command, AutoClient calls the automation server and changes the text color. The problem is that the server's window isn't visible, so you can't see the changes.

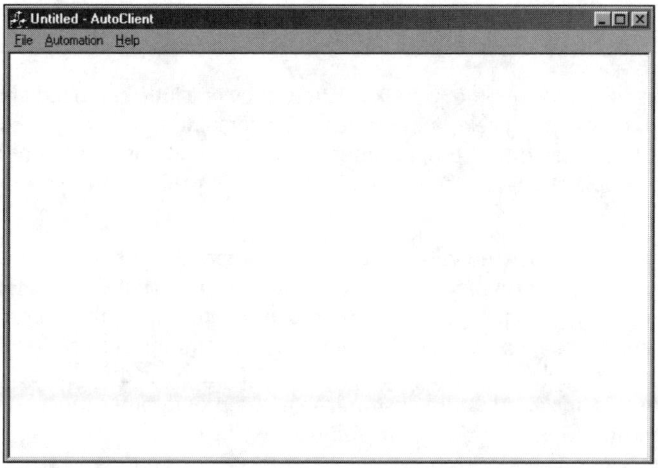

Figure 27-12: This is AutoClient when you first run it.

To remedy this problem, select the Show Window command from AutoClient's Automation menu. Up pops the server's window, and there you can see that your Set Color selection really did have an effect, because the text is a different color. Arrange both windows so you can see them both. (You can make the client application window smaller to save on room.) Now, select the Set Color command again, watching as the text color changes in AutoServer's window.

ActiveX Controls

ActiveX controls are like mini-applications that you can embed in other application's windows. ActiveX controls are popping up all over the Word Wide Web, in much the same way that some people use Java applets. Because ActiveX controls can do just about anything a small application can do, they enable Web developers to create Web pages that actually do something inside the user's browser, rather than just present information. On Web sites, you can find ActiveX controls that do everything from play Tic-Tac-Toe to calculate the payment schedule on a loan. In this section, you get an introduction to creating ActiveX controls. Along the way, you'll create a working ActiveX control called SquareRoot that'll find the square root of a number given by the user. You can find the sample control in the Chapter27\SquareRoot folder of this book's CD-ROM.

A Control's Programmer, Developer, and User

Often, when programmers first start creating ActiveX controls, they're a little confused about the way controls are used during the development process. Understanding a control's complete development cycle, from the control programmer to the eventual appearance of the control in a Web page or application, is essential to understanding the control-programming process.

There are three types of people associated with a control: a programmer, a developer, and a user. The *programmer* is the person who creates the control using Visual C++ or some other development environment. This programmer isn't much different from the programmer of any other type of application, except that the control's programmer must remember to make the control as customizable as possible for the developer, who is the next person associated with the control. To make a control customizable, the programmer must create control properties that the developer can change to suit his specific needs.

The developer in this case isn't the same thing as a programmer. Rather, the *developer* is a person who's going to use the control in one of his own Web pages or in the development of another application. The developer will often customize the control's properties to fit the requirements of his project. This is why it's so important for the control's programmer to provide customizable properties.

Finally, the last person associated with the control is the user. In this case, the *user* is the person who logs onto the developer's Web page or runs the developer's application, either of which contains the control. The user sees the control in its customized form. That is, the control appears in the Web page or application as the developer designed it to appear when he or she customized the control's properties. The user cannot change the control's properties or access the control in any way except through its user interface, just as with any other type of application.

Creating a skeleton ActiveX control

When you use AppWizard to create a skeleton control, the resultant control is fully functional without your having to enter a single line of source code. Of course, if you want to create a useful control, you have to do a little programming. In this section, you use ActiveX ControlWizard to create the basic control. In later sections, you change this skeleton control into a simple square-root generator. Perform the following steps to create the skeleton control.

Note

You should read through all the application-building steps in this chapter, whether or not you actually build the ActiveX control yourself, because the steps include explanations of the programming techniques needed to build an ActiveX control.

◆ ◆ ◆ ◆ ◆

Caution

SquareRoot
CD-ROM Location: **Chap27\SquareRoot**
Program Name: **SquareRoot.ocx**
Source Code Modules in Text: **None**

◆ ◆ ◆ ◆ ◆

1. Start a new MFC ActiveX ControlWizard project called SquareRoot, as shown in Figure 27-13.

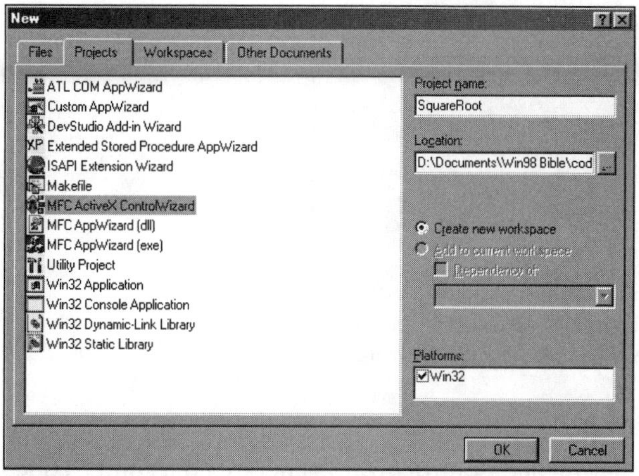

Figure 27-13: The new control project is called SquareRoot.

2. In the MFC ActiveX ControlWizard – Step 1 of 2 dialog box, accept all default options and click the Finish button (see Figure 27-14).

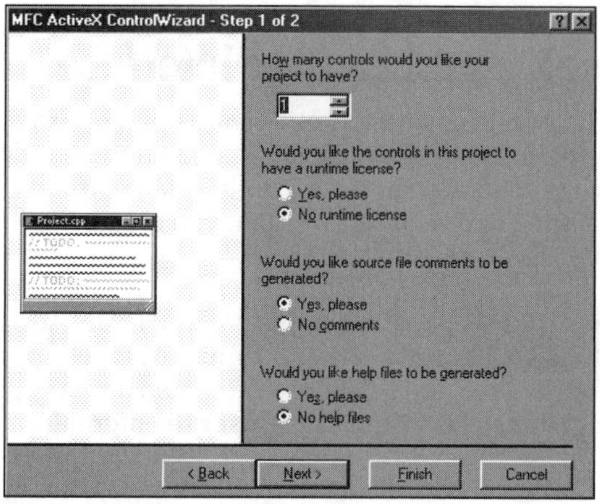

Figure 27-14: The default options will work fine for the sample ActiveX control.

3. Your New Project Information dialog box should look like Figure 27-15, except your install directory may be different depending on the directory you chose when you created the project in Step 1.

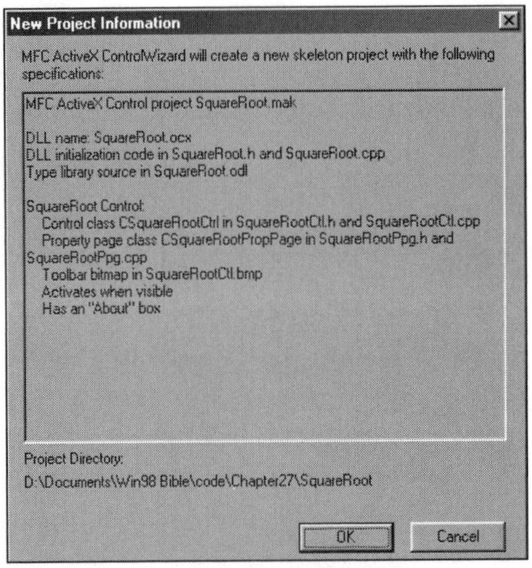

Figure 27-15: The New Project Information dialog box displays the ActiveX control's final options.

4. Click the OK button and ControlWizard generates the source code files for the skeleton application.

Now that you've completed the SquareRoot skeleton ActiveX control, save your work by selecting the File menu's Save All. Currently, the application does nothing useful, so you don't need to compile the source files. Instead, continue on to the next set of steps, where you complete the control's user interface.

Creating the ActiveX control's user interface

Some ActiveX controls are interactive, whereas others are not. For example, an ActiveX control might do nothing more than display an animated image. Even so, SquareRoot, being a simple calculator, requires a user interface through which the user can communicate with the control. In this section, you create that interface by completing the following steps:

1. Add a member variable to the `CSquareRootCtrl` class. In the Add Member Variable dialog box, type **CEdit** in the Variable Type box, type **m_numberEdit** in the Variable Declaration box, and select the Protected access option. The edit box you're adding to the class enables the user to enter information into the control.

2. Bring up the Add Member Variable dialog box again, and type **CEdit** in the Variable Type box, type **m_resultEdit** in the Variable Declaration box, and select the Protected access option. This edit box will display the square root that the user requested.

3. Bring up the Add Member Variable dialog box again, and type **CButton** in the Variable Type box, type **m_button** in the Variable Declaration box, and select the Protected access option. This button will be another interactive element of the ActiveX control, enabling the user to tell the control to process text entered into the edit box.

4. Use ClassWizard to add the `OnCreate()` function.

5. Add the following lines to the `OnCreate()` function, right after the `TODO` comment:

Class Wizard

Handling a WM_CREATE message

Message: **WM_CREATE**
Function Created: **OnCreate()**
Source Code Module: **SquareRootCtl.cpp**

◆ ◆ ◆ ◆ ◆

```
m_numberEdit.Create(WS_CHILD | WS_BORDER |
  WS_VISIBLE | ES_AUTOHSCROLL,
  CRect(20, 70, 120, 100), this, IDC_NUMBEREDIT);
m_resultEdit.Create(WS_CHILD | WS_BORDER |
  WS_VISIBLE | ES_AUTOHSCROLL,
  CRect(20, 110, 120, 140), this, IDC_RESULTEDIT);
m_button.Create("Calc", WS_CHILD | WS_BORDER |
  WS_VISIBLE | BS_PUSHBUTTON,
  CRect(130, 70, 230, 100), this, IDC_BUTTON);
```

6. Add the lines shown in Listing 27-2 to the `CSquareRootCtrl` class's `OnDraw()` function, right after the `TODO` comment, replacing the two lines already there:

Listing 27-2: Lines for the OnDraw() Function

```
pdc->TextOut(20, 50, "Enter Number:");

LOGFONT logFont;
logFont.lfHeight = 32;
logFont.lfWidth = 0;
logFont.lfEscapement = 0;
logFont.lfOrientation = 0;
logFont.lfWeight = FW_BOLD;
logFont.lfItalic = 0;
logFont.lfUnderline = 0;
logFont.lfStrikeOut = 0;
logFont.lfCharSet = ANSI_CHARSET;
```

(continued)

Listing 27-2 *(continued)*

```
logFont.lfOutPrecision = OUT_DEFAULT_PRECIS;
logFont.lfClipPrecision = CLIP_DEFAULT_PRECIS;
logFont.lfQuality = PROOF_QUALITY;
logFont.lfPitchIn addition,Family = VARIABLE_PITCH | FF_ROMAN;
strcpy(logFont.lfFaceName, "Times New Roman");

CFont font;
font.CreateFontIndirect(&logFont);
CFont* pOldFont = pdc->SelectObject(&font);
pdc->TextOut(20, 10, "SquareRoot");
pdc->SelectObject(pOldFont);
```

7. Select the Resource Symbols command from Visual C++'s View menu. The Resource Symbols dialog box appears, displaying the resource IDs defined in the program (see Figure 27-16).

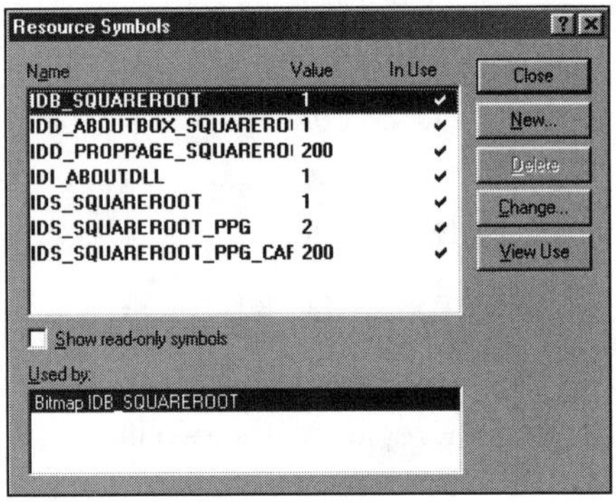

Figure 27-16: The Resource Symbols dialog box enables you to see defined IDs, as well as see how the IDs are used.

8. Create a new resource symbol named **IDC_NUMBEREDIT**. (Visual C++ automatically provides a value.) You use this ID to identify the ActiveX control's first edit box.

9. Create two more resource symbols: **IDC_RESULTEDIT**, which you use to identify the ActiveX control's second edit box; and **IDC_BUTTON**, which you use to identify the ActiveX control's button.

Now that you've completed the control's basic user interface, you can see what the control looks like when its embedded in a program. First, use the Build command to compile and link the control. Visual C++ registers the new control with the system so that you can include it in other applications or in Web pages.

To get a look at the new control, select the ActiveX Control Test Container command from Visual C++'s Tools menu. The test container application appears. In the text container's Edit menu, select the Insert New Control command. In the Insert OLE Control dialog, find the SquareRoot Control in the Object Type box (see Figure 27–17), and double-click it. The control appears in the test container's window.

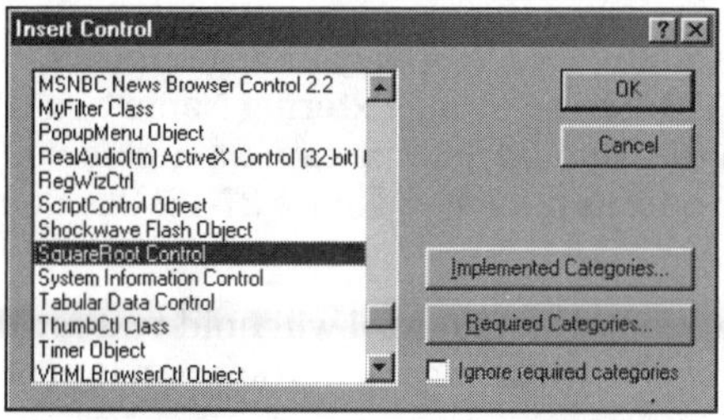

Figure 27-17: The Insert Control dialog box lists the controls that are registered on your machine.

When the control first appears, resize it with the mouse. Although the control has its full user interface, the controls won't do anything yet. You still have to add the code that makes the control do what it's designed to do. You accomplish that task in the following sections.

Creating properties and methods

You've learned that an ActiveX control is like a mini-application that can be placed in windows of other applications or in Web pages. When you create properties and methods for the control, developers (a developer in this case meaning the person adding the control to a window) can customize the way the control looks and acts. For example, the developer might want to change the control's title string "SquareRoot" to something else. You can do this by making the title string a property of the control.

Like properties, methods also determine how the control looks and acts. Methods are functions in a control that can be called from the control's container. The SquareRoot control already has one method generated by AppWizard: the function that displays its About dialog box. This method is called `AboutBox()` and looks like this:

```
void CSquareRootCtrl::AboutBox()
{
  CDialog dlgAbout(IDD_ABOUTBOX_SQUAREROOT);
  dlgAbout.DoModal();
}
```

You can add other methods to your controls as well. The SquareRoot control, for example, will have methods for setting and getting properties. You create control properties in much the same way you create properties for automation applications. Perform the following steps to add properties and methods to the SquareRoot control.

1. Open ClassWizard, and then click the Automation tab.
2. Click the Add Property button. When the Add Property dialog appears, select the Get/Set Methods option, type **TitleString** in the External Name box (ClassWizard automatically fills in the Get and Set function names as you type), and select `BSTR` in the Type box, as shown in Figure 27-18. Click OK to create the property.

   The `TitleString` property of the SquareRoot control will hold text for the control's title. `BSTR` is a data type used with strings in automation functions.

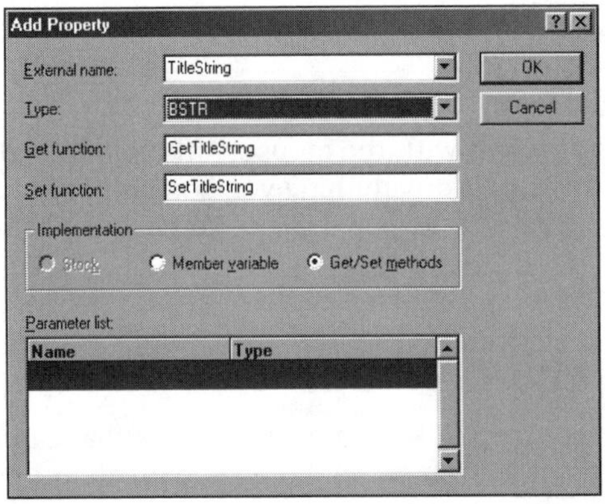

Figure 27-18: You use the Add Property dialog box to create your control's properties.

3. Click the Add Property button again. When the Add Property dialog appears, select the Get/Set Methods option, type **ButtonCaption** in the External Name box, and select `BSTR` in the Type box. Click OK to create the property.

   The `ButtonCaption` property of the SquareRoot control will hold the caption for the control's single button.
4. Add a member variable to the `CSquareRootCtrl` class. In the Add Member Variable dialog, type **CString** in the Variable Type box, type **m_titleString** in the Variable Declaration box, and select the Protected access option.

   The `m_titleString` member variable will hold the string assigned to the `TitleString` property.

5. Display the Add Member Variable dialog again, type **CString** in the Variable Type box, type **m_buttonCaption** in the Variable Declaration box, and select the Protected access option.

   The m_buttonCaption member variable will hold the string assigned to the ButtonCaption property.

6. Add the following line to the GetTitleString() method, after the TODO comment:

   ```
   strResult = m_titleString;
   ```

   This line sets the string to be returned by the function to the string stored in the m_titleString member variable.

7. Add the following lines to the SetTitleString() method, after the TODO comment:

   ```
   m_titleString = lpszNewValue;
   InvalidateControl();
   ```

   These lines set the m_titleString member variable to the new string value and then redraw the control.

8. Add the following line to the GetButtonCaption() method, after the TODO comment:

   ```
   strResult = m_buttonCaption;
   ```

   This line sets the string to be returned by the function to the string stored in the m_buttonCaption member variable.

9. Add the following lines to the SetButtonCaption() method, after the TODO comment:

   ```
   m_buttonCaption = lpszNewValue;
   m_button.SetWindowText(m_buttonCaption);
   ```

   These lines set the m_buttonCaption member variable and the button caption to the new string value.

10. In the OnDraw() function, change the "SquareRoot" in the second call to TextOut() to m_titleString.

    The OnDraw() function will now display the current value of the TitleString property instead of a hard-coded value.

11. In the OnCreate() function, change the "Calc" in the m_button.Create() call to m_buttonCaption.

    The control's button will now display the caption string stored in the ButtonCaption property instead of a hard-coded value.

12. Add the following lines to the end of the `CSquareRootCtrl()` constructor:

```
m_titleString = "SquareRoot";
m_buttonCaption = "Calc";
```

These lines give the `TitleString` and `ButtonCaption` properties their default values.

13. Add the following lines to the end of the `CSquareRootCtrl` class's `DoPropExchange()` function:

```
PX_String(pPX, "TitleString", m_titleString,
  "SquareRoot");
PX_String(pPX, "ButtonCaption", m_buttonCaption,
  "Calc");
```

These lines implement the same sort of data transfer mechanism that MFC dialog boxes employ. In the case of a control, the `DoPropExchange()` function takes care of transferring values to the control's properties when the control first loads and saves the control's properties when the control closes. This mechanism is the heart of *persistent properties*, a topic you learn more about later in this chapter.

Now that you've created your ActiveX control's properties and methods, you write the code that makes the control's button act as it should.

Responding to the control's button

To complete the SquareRoot control, all you've to do now is make the control's button respond to the user's clicks. You can do this using Windows messages, as you'll see when you complete the following steps:

1. Add a member function to the `CSquareRootCtrl` class. In the Add Member Function dialog, type **afx_msg void** in the Function Type box, type **OnButtonClicked()** in the Variable Declaration box, and select the Protected access option.

2. Add the following line to the `CSquareRootCtrl` class's message map (found near the top of the SquareRootCtl.cpp file), right after the `ON_OLEVERB()` macro that's already there:

```
ON_BN_CLICKED(IDC_BUTTON, OnButtonClicked)
```

3. Add the lines in Listing 27-3 to the `OnButtonClicked()` function:

Listing 27-3: Lines for the OnButtonClicked() Function

```
CString str;
m_numberEdit.GetWindowText(str);
float number = (float)atof(str);
```

```
float result = (float)sqrt(number);
char resultString[11];
sprintf(resultString, "%f", result);
resultString[10] = 0;
m_resultEdit.SetWindowText(resultString);
```

Now, when the user clicks the Calc button, the control's `OnButtonClicked()` function gets called, which extracts the user's number from the first edit box and calculates the number's square root. The function displays the result by converting it to a string and using the string to set the second edit control's contents.

4. Add the following line near the top of the SquareRootCtl.cpp file, after the line `#include "SquareRootPpg.h"` that's already there:

```
#include "math.h"
```

You've now completed the SquareRoot control. Compile, link, and register the control.

Nutshell

Creating an ActiveX Control

These steps sum up the process of creating a basic ActiveX control.

1. Use ControlWizard to create the skeleton control.
2. Create the ActiveX control's user interface by creating controls (such as buttons and edit boxes) as member variables of the ActiveX control's class.
3. Add an `OnCreate()` function to the ActiveX control's main class, and add to the function the code needed to create the elements of the control's user's interface.
4. Complete the control's `OnDraw()` function to draw user interface elements (such as text) that aren't created in the `OnCreate()` function.
5. Use ClassWizard's Automation page to add properties and methods to the control.
6. In the control's main class, define member variables to hold data for the control's properties and complete the properties' get and set methods.
7. Complete the code for the control's methods, and create message-response functions for the elements of the control's user interface. (For example, if the user interface contains a button, write a function that responds to button presses.)
8. Complete the control's `DoPropExchange()` function for all persistent properties.

◆ ◆ ◆ ◆ ◆

Testing the ActiveX control

Now that you're done building the control, you can see SquareRoot do its stuff. Run ActiveX Control Test Container from Visual C++'s Tools menu. When the application appears, select the Insert New Control command from the container's Edit menu. Double-click SquareRoot Control in the Insert New Control dialog box, and then resize and position the control so that you can see it properly. Type the number 5 into the first edit box and click the Calc button. The number 2.236068 should appear in the second edit box, as shown in Figure 27–19.

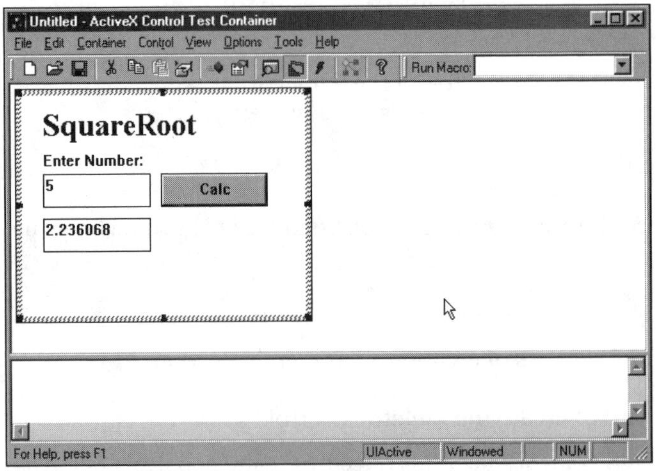

Figure 27-19: Here's the SquareRoot control after the user calculates the square root of 5.

A control is more flexible if the developer can customize the way it looks and acts. SquareRoot enables you to change its properties, setting the control's title and button caption. To try this, select the Properties command from the container application's View menu. The Properties dialog box appears. Select `TitleString` in the Property list box, type **My Title** into the Value box, and click the Apply button.

Now, using the same procedure you used to set the `TitleString` property, set the `ButtonCaption` property to Show SQRT. When you click the Apply button, the control's button caption changes to the new one.

Persistent properties

Persistent properties are control properties saved when the control closes and reloaded when the control next runs. Using persistent properties, a Web page or application developer can not only include the control in his project, but also customize the control's properties to better suit her needs. For example, if you were designing a Web page that used the SquareRoot ActiveX control, and you changed the button's caption property to "Get SQRT," you'd want the new caption to appear in the button every time the Web page or application loaded the control. Persistent properties make this sort of customization possible.

To implement persistent properties, you must include in the control's DoPropExchange() function a PX_ program line for each persistent property. MFC defines 16 of these functions, each for a particular type of data. The PX_ functions are PX_Blob(), PX_Bool(), PX_Color(), PX_Currency(), PX_DataPath(), PX_Double(), PX_Float(), PX_Font(), PX_IUnknown(), PX_Long(), PX_Picture(), PX_Short(), PX_ULong(), PX_UShort(), and PX_VBXFontConvert(). Each PX_ function requires four arguments, which are a pointer to a CPropExchange object, a string holding the property name, the variable in which the property is stored, and the property's default value.

The SquareRoot control's DoPropExchange() function defines two persistent properties, one for the control's title string and one for the control's button caption. To see persistent properties in action, start your old friend ActiveX Control Test Container and load the SquareRoot control into the application. Next, change the ButtonCaption property to "Get SQRT," and then select the application's Save To Stream command (found on the Control menu). This command saves an instance of the control, including your property changes, to disk. Finally, select the Insert Control From Stream command from the Edit menu to load another instance of the control.

Notice that the button in the new control instance still contains your new caption. This is thanks to the DoPropExchange() function. If you didn't have a PX_ program line for the button caption in DoPropExchange(), the new instance of the control would have the original "Calc" button caption. To prove this, you can comment out the button caption's PX_ line in DoPropExchange(), recompile the control, and then try the previous experiment again. The button will not remember any caption changes you make.

Placing an ActiveX control on a Web page

Including an ActiveX control in your Web page isn't much harder than including a Java applet. The biggest difference is that ActiveX controls are identified by a GUID (globally unique ID), and before you can add a control to a Web page, you've to know what that GUID is. An easy way to find the GUID is to look up the control in your registry.

First, click your Windows 98 Start menu and select the Run command. When the Run dialog appears, type **regedit** into the Open box and click the OK button. The Registry editor appears on your screen and displays the main folders in your systems registry (see Figure 27-20).

Select the Edit menu's Find command. In the Find dialog box, type SquareRoot Control, and click the Find Next button. The registry editor searches for the SquareRoot control in the registry. Press F3 to search again, until you find the SQUAREROOT.SquareRootCtrl.1 entry in the left hand pane. You see that this entry has a subfolder called CLSID (see Figure 27-21). Click CLSID to display the control's GUID (also known as a class ID, or CLSID).

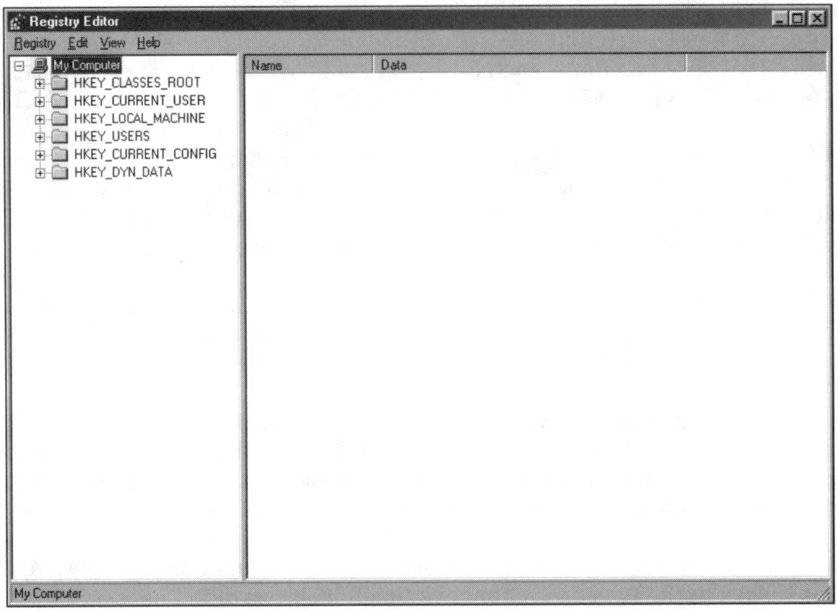

Figure 27-20: Windows 98's registry editor is a handy application for exploring your system's Registry.

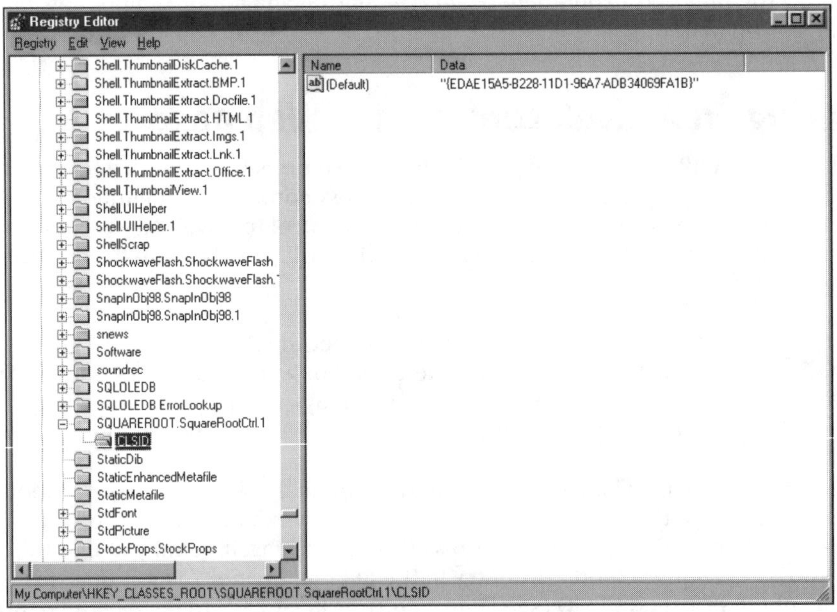

Figure 27-21: This is the Registry entry you're looking for.

Double-click the word "default" in the right hand pane to bring up the ID in Value Data box of the Edit String dialog box (see Figure 27-22). Then, press Ctrl+C to copy the ID to the Clipboard. You'll need the ID to add the control to your HTML document, and it's a heck of a lot easier to copy it this way than to try to type it manually. Close the Registry editor.

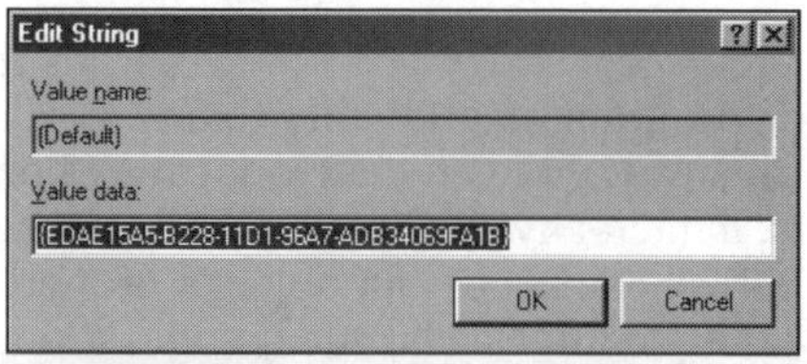

Figure 27-22: It's easy to copy the GUID from the Edit String dialog box.

The next step is to add the control to your HTML file, which you do with the `<OBJECT>` tag. Listing 27-4 is an example HTML document for the SquareRoot control:

Listing 27-4: **Loading SquareRoot in an HTML Document**

```
<HTML>

<HEAD>
  <TITLE>ActiveX Control Example</TITLE>
</HEAD>

<BODY>
<CENTER>

<OBJECT
  classid="clsid:EDAE15A5-B228-11D1-96A7-ADB34069FA1B"
  id=SquareRoot height=150 width=300>
</OBJECT>

</CENTER>
</BODY>
</HTML>
```

Note

If you created the SquareRoot control using the steps presented throughout this chapter, your version of the control will have a different GUID (or CLSID) than the one shown in Listing 27-4. Every control has its own GUID so that the computer can tell one control from another.

✦ ✦ ✦ ✦ ✦

The `<OBJECT>` tag is similar to many other HTML tags, containing attributes that enable you to control the element's ID and size. The most important thing to notice about the `<OBJECT>` tag is the way it specifies the control's `classid` attribute. The value for this attribute is the GUID you found with the Registry editor.

Summary

Using automation servers, you can provide program functionality to any application that can access the server. In this way, you can develop features once and reuse those features in future projects. In fact, any application that can create an interface class from the server's type library can access an object's properties and methods. A server can even provide multiple interfaces, and so offer a set of features to other programs.

ActiveX controls take the idea of automation one step further, by enabling you to embed a programmable object into an application's window or a Web page. Creating an ActiveX control with Visual C++ and MFC is much easier than programming one from scratch, thanks to the MFC ActiveX Control Wizard. Using this handy wizard, you can concentrate on writing the code that makes your control do what it needs to do, rather than having to write the general code common to all ActiveX controls.

✦ ✦ ✦

CHAPTER 28

Active Template Library

In This Chapter

Learning the background of the Active Template Library

Creating an Active Template Library control

Using an Active Template Library control from C++

Converting between string types

The Active Template Library (ATL) was designed from the ground up to make developing COM objects in C++ easy and flexible. ATL is fairly minimal, which is its greatest strength. (The original version of the ATL shipped as four C++ header files, one of which was empty!) Using ATL, you can build fairly small, self-contained binaries without requiring any additional runtime DLLs.

ATL is representative of the movement away from monolithic, single-tier applications and serves as a good foundation from which to develop the lightweight COM components required for modern distributed applications. ATL is less of a massive, MFC-like infrastructure than it is a modular, time-saving library that keeps thousands of programmers from implementing IUnknown and IClassFactory over and over again.

ATL does not try to be all things to all people. Version 1 provides very reasonable support for implementing IUnknown, IClassFactory, IDispatch, IConnectionPointContainer, and COM enumeration. Version 2 offers enhanced versions of the original ATL classes in addition to support for writing ActiveX™controls. ATL does not provide collections and strings (ATL assumes you will use the Standard C++ Library classes for these); ODBC support (the world is moving to COM-based data access that doesn't need wrapping); WinSock wrappers (sockets are already dated); or a complete wrapper for the Win32 API (ATL 2.0's control implementation provides support for implementing dialogs and WndProcs). Also missing from ATL is MFC's document/view model. Instead, ATL assumes you will use the more scalable and flexible COM approach of connectable outbound COM interfaces (ActiveX controls, for instance) to notify the UI-based objects.

The key idea is to use the right tool for the job. If you are building nonvisual COM components, ATL is likely to be a much better choice than MFC in terms of development effort, scalability, runtime performance, and executable size. For modern user interfaces based on ActiveX controls, ATL also produces faster code, and less of it, than MFC does. On the other hand, ATL requires more COM knowledge than is needed to operate MFC's Class Wizard. For building double-clickable single-tier applications, ATL is currently no more helpful than the Standard Template Library (STL). For this, MFC remains the superior choice.

The design of ATL is inspired by STL, which has become part of the Standard C++ Library included with all ANSI/ISO-compliant C++ compilers. Like STL, ATL uses C++ templates aggressively. Templates are one of the more controversial features in C++. When abused, templates can lead to bloated executables, poor performance, and unintelligible code. Used judiciously, templates provide a degree of generality combined with type safety that is impossible to achieve otherwise. Like STL, ATL falls between these two extremes. Fortunately, compiler and linker technology is advancing at about the same pace as aggressive template usage, making STL and ATL reasonable choices for current and future development.

Despite its extensive use of templates internally, you can use ATL without ever having to type an angle bracket. This is because ATL ships with the ATL Object Wizard, which generates a variety of default object implementations based on ATL's template classes. The ATL Object Wizard enables anyone to get a COM object up and running in a matter of minutes without thinking about COM or ATL. Of course, to take full advantage of ATL, you do need to understand C++, templates, and COM programming techniques. For a large class of objects, however, the ATL Object Wizard's default implementations require only the addition of method implementations for any custom interfaces being exported, which for most developers is the whole point of implementing a COM object in the first place.

At first glance, the ATL architecture may seem quite bizarre and arcane. For mainstream component developers just getting up to speed on COM, the actual ATL architecture is irrelevant because the wizards generate reasonable skeletons that only require method definitions. For serious COM developers and systems programmers, ATL provides an elegant, extensible architecture for building COM components in C++. Once you understand the architecture and move beyond the wizards, ATL can be as expressive and powerful as raw COM programming.

Creating an ATL Control

This section demonstrates how to create a simple ATL control that draws a spirograph in the view window. Two functions will be added that enable the radius and color of the design that's drawn to be altered.

Start by selecting New from the File menu. When the New dialog box appears, click the Projects tab. Choose ATL COM AppWizard, and enter **SpiroGrph** as the project name. The dialog box should look like the one shown in Figure 28-1.

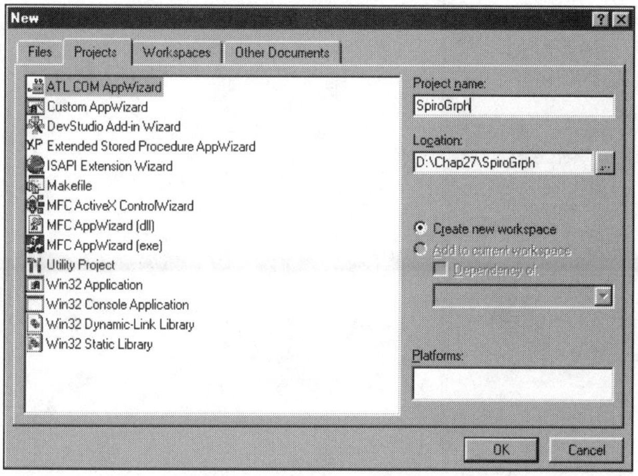

Figure 28-1: The New dialog box with ATL COM AppWizard selected and the project named SpiroGrph

The ATL COM AppWizard gives you choices for the project's options. The first dialog box that appears enables you to set how you want the ATL file saved. The dialog actually asks you to specify a server type, but this translates into how the control will save. Most of the time, you'll want it saved as a DLL. This example uses the default choice of a DLL, as shown in Figure 28-2.

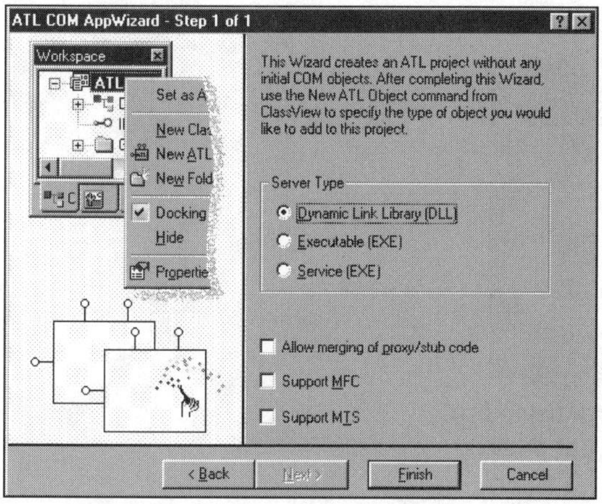

Figure 28-2: The Step 1 of 1 dialog box shows that your control will be saved as a DLL.

The last step in the AppWizard creation process is a review of your choices. The New Project Information dialog box, as shown in Figure 28-3, lets you see the choices you've made.

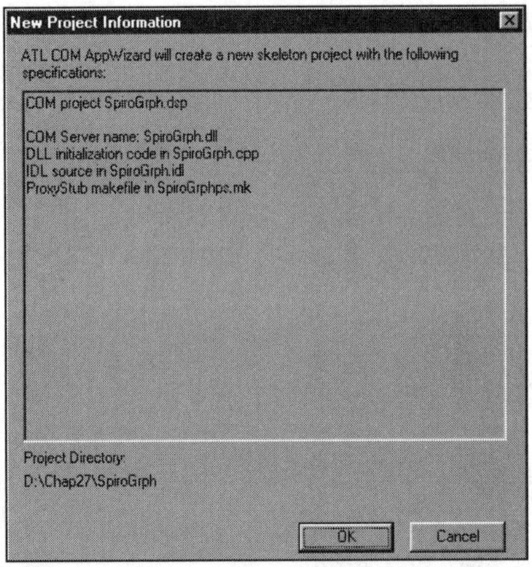

Figure 28-3: You can review all your choices in the New Project Information dialog box.

Adding a COM Object to the Project

To add a COM object to the project, you select New ATL Object from the Insert menu. A dialog box is then displayed that gives you a selection of COM objects you can add to your project, as shown in Figure 28-4.

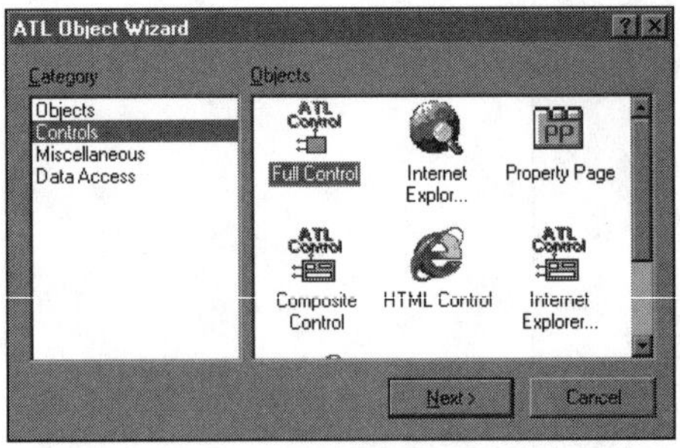

Figure 28-4: The ATL Object Wizard dialog box lists COM objects you can add to your project.

The dialog box offers four sets of COM components to choose from: Objects, Controls, Miscellaneous, and Data Access. You'll be creating a control, so make sure Controls is selected in the Category list and choose the Full Control item from the Objects list.

You need to enter the name for the COM component in the dialog box that appears. For this project, enter Spiro in Short Name field, as shown in Figure 28-5. This is used as the basis for the C++ class name that implements the component and for the names of the files containing the C++ code. It is also the basis for the name of the CoClass, which is the component class; the name of the interface, ISpiro, that the component will support; the type name; and the Prog ID that will appear in the registry. Note that the component class is not a C++ class — it's a COM class that identifies the interfaces the component supports.

All the other project attributes are the default settings. For almost all of your ATL projects, these will work best.

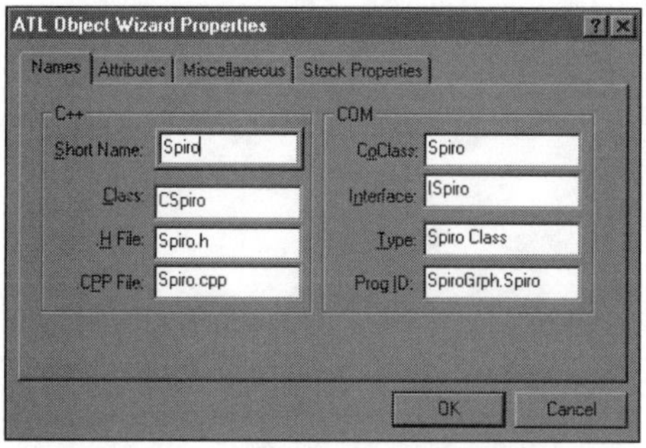

Figure 28-5: You can specify the names for the classes, files, and objects in the ATL Object Wizard Properties dialog box.

The Attributes tab in the dialog box provides options for implementing the component, as shown in Figure 28-6.

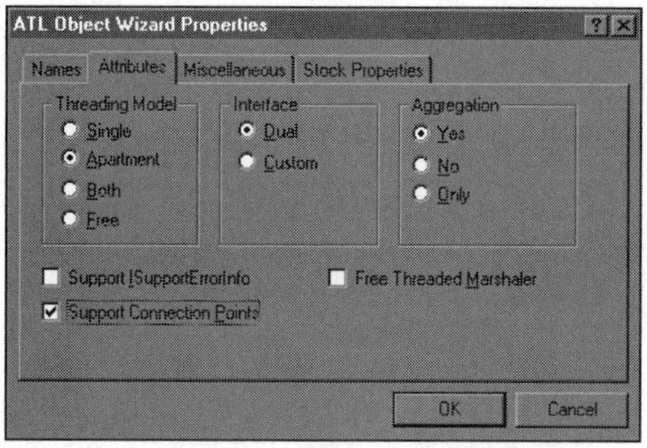

Figure 28-6: You can set the attributes for the object in the Attributes tab pane.

Adding the Draw Code

The first thing to do is add some variables to the CSpiro class, which appears in the Spiro.h file as follows:

```
unsigned char m_Red, m_Green, m_Blue;
int m_nIterations;
int R, r, O;
```

Make sure you include math.h at the top of the Spiro.h file. Now you must initialize these variables so that the OnDraw() code will produce something that looks like a spirograph. You do this in the CSpiro constructor, which is found in the Spiro.h file. Edit the constructor as follows:

```
CSpiro()
 {

  m_Red = 0xff;
  m_Green = 0x00;
  m_Blue = 0x80;

  m_nIterations = 400;

  R = 50;
  r = 10;
  O = 5;

 }
```

The last thing you must do is add the draw code to the OnDraw() function. The OnDraw() function can be found in the Spiro.cpp file. First make sure math.h is included at the top of Spiro.cpp, and then edit the OnDraw() function as follows:

```
HRESULT CSpiro::OnDraw(ATL_DRAWINFO& di)
{
 int x = 0;
 int y = 0;
 int prevx;
 int prevy;
 int t;
 int nCenterX, nCenterY;

 HPEN hOldPen, hPen;
 hPen = CreatePen( PS_SOLID, 1,
  RGB( m_Red, m_Green, m_Blue ) );
 hOldPen = (HPEN) SelectObject( di.hdcDraw, hPen );

 nCenterX =
  ( di.prcBounds->right - di.prcBounds->left ) / 2;
 nCenterY =
  ( di.prcBounds->bottom - di.prcBounds->top ) / 2;
```

```
for( t=0; t<=m_nIterations; t++ ){
 prevx = x;
 prevy = y;

 x = (int) ( (double) ( R + r ) *
  cos( (double) t ) -
  (double) ( r + 0 ) *
   cos( (double) ( ( ( R + r ) / r ) * t ) ) );
 y = (int) ( (double) ( R + r ) *
  sin( (double) t ) -
  (double) ( r + 0 ) *
   sin( (double) ( ( ( R + r ) / r ) * t ) ) );

 if( t > 0 ){
  MoveToEx( di.hdcDraw,
   prevx + nCenterX,
   prevy + nCenterY, NULL );
  LineTo( di.hdcDraw,
   x + nCenterX, y + nCenterY );
  }
 }

SelectObject( di.hdcDraw, hOldPen );
DeleteObject( hPen );

return S_OK;

}
```

Compile the control, and then choose the ActiveX Control Test Container from the Tools menu. Select the `Spiro` class, and you'll see the control draw a shape as shown in Figure 28-7.

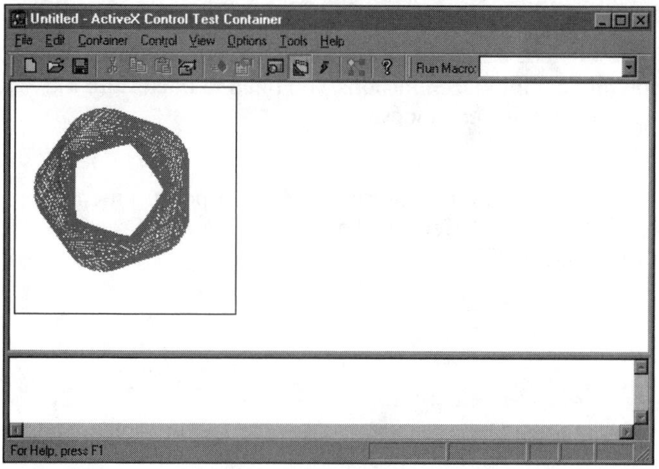

Figure 28-7: The spirograph in the ActiveX Control Test Container window

Implementing the Interface Functions

We need two functions to change the appearance of the control's drawn pattern. One, named `SetRadius()`, alters the radius of the spirograph. The other, named `SetColor()`, changes the color in which the pattern will be drawn.

You must add these functions so that calling applications can find them. To do this, you must implement interface functions. Start by clicking the Classes tab in the InfoViewer window, as shown in Figure 28-8.

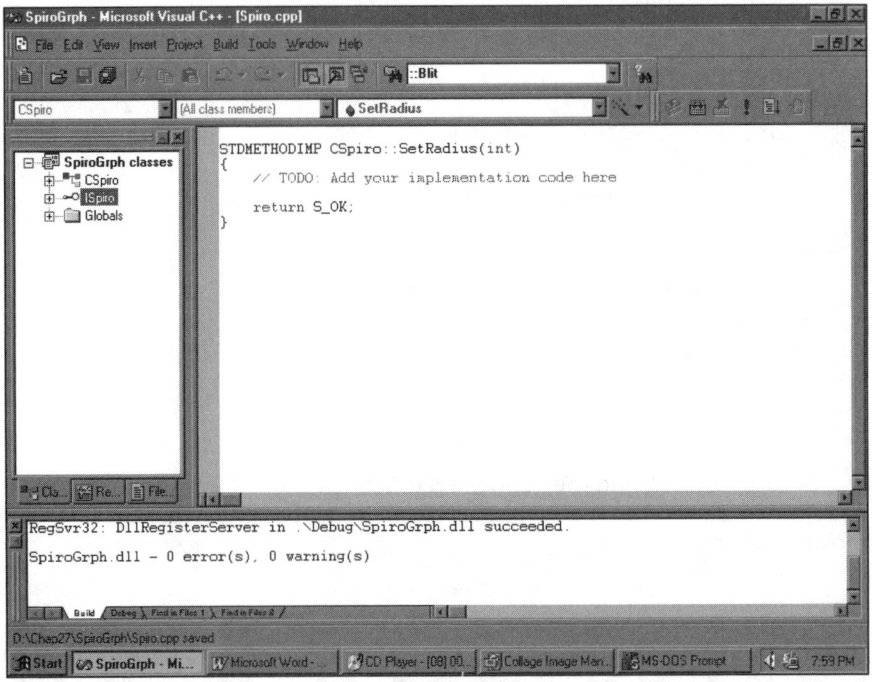

Figure 28-8: Before you add the interface functions, you need to make sure the Classes tab is selected in the InfoViewer window.

Now, click the right mouse button on the ISpiro interface. A pop-up menu appears with several selections. Choose Add Method. The Add Method to Interface dialog box appears, as shown in Figure 28-9.

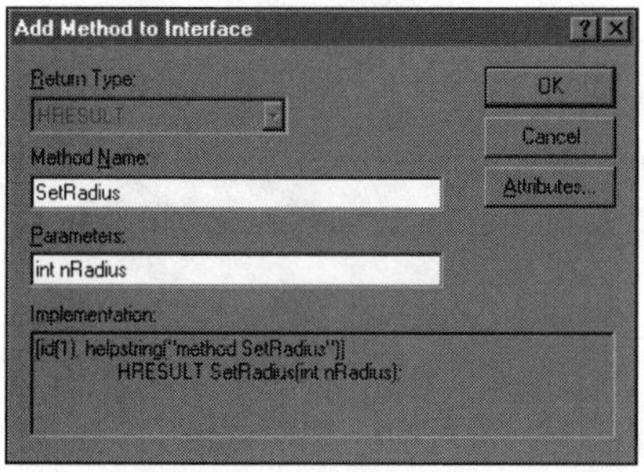

Figure 28-9: The Add Method to Interface dialog box enables you to specify the method name and parameters.

Now all you have to do is open the Spiro.cpp file and add code to the three methods that you just added. The code for the methods is as follows:

```
STDMETHODIMP CSpiro::SetRadius(int)
{

  r = nRadius;
  InvalidateRect( NULL, FALSE );
  UpdateWindow();

  return S_OK;
}

STDMETHODIMP CSpiro::SetColor(long)
{

  m_Red = (unsigned char) ( color > 16 );
  m_Green = (unsigned char) ( ( color & 0x00ff00 ) > 8 );
  m_Blue = (unsigned char) ( color & 0x0000ff );
  InvalidateRect( NULL, FALSE );
  UpdateWindow();

  return S_OK;
}

STDMETHODIMP CSpiro::Draw(int nHdc)
{
  int x = 0;
  int y = 0;
  int prevx;
  int prevy;
  int t;
  int nCenterX, nCenterY;
  HWND hWnd;

  HPEN hOldPen, hPen;
  hPen = CreatePen( PS_SOLID, 1,
    RGB( m_Red, m_Green, m_Blue ) );
  hOldPen = (HPEN) SelectObject( (HDC) nHdc, hPen );
```

```
    hWNd = ::GetWindowDC( (HDC) nHdc );
    RECT Rect;
    ::GetClientRect( hWnd, &Rect );

    nCenterX = Rect.right / 2;
    nCenterY = Rect.bottom / 2;
    for( t=0; t<=m_nIterations; t++ ){
      prevx = x;
      prevy = y;

      x = (int) ( (double) ( R + r ) *
        cos( (double) t ) -
        (double) ( r + 0 ) *
          cos( (double) ( ( ( R + r ) / r ) * t ) ) );
      y = (int) ( (double) ( R + r ) *
        sin( (double) t ) -
        (double) ( r + 0 ) *
          sin( (double) ( ( ( R + r ) / r ) * t ) ) );

      if( t > 0 ){
        MoveToEx( (HDC) nHdc,
          prevx + nCenterX,
          prevy + nCenterY, NULL );
        LineTo( (HDC) nHdc,
          x + nCenterX, y + nCenterY );
        }
      }

    SelectObject( (HDC) nHdc, hOldPen );
    DeleteObject( hPen );

    return S_OK;

  }
```

Using the Control from C++

The last thing you do is create a separate application that will use the control. Create an MFC application with an SDI interface and all other options as defaults.

Invoke the ClassWizard, click the New Class button, and then select From Type Library. A file selector appears from which you must locate and select the type library file of the control. Type libraries normally have .tlb extensions; look for SpiroGrph.tlb from the previously created project, as shown in Figure 28-10.

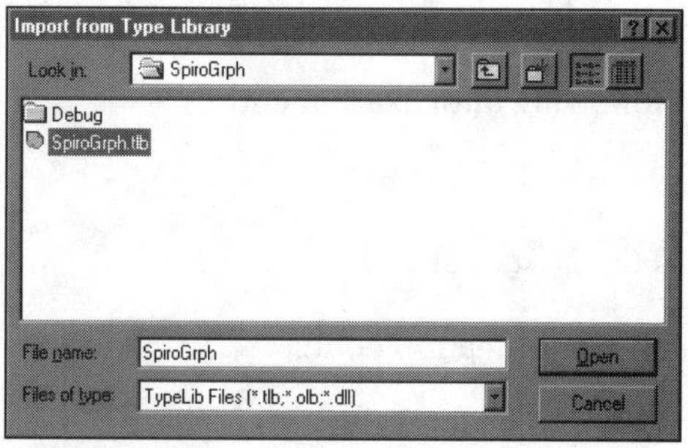

Figure 28-10: The Import from Type Library dialog box showing the SpiroGrph control selected

Once you've selected the type library file, you have the chance to change file and interface names from the defaults assigned by the ClassWizard. Keep the defaults as shown in Figure 28-11 and click the OK button. Next, click the OK button on the ClassWizard's main dialog box.

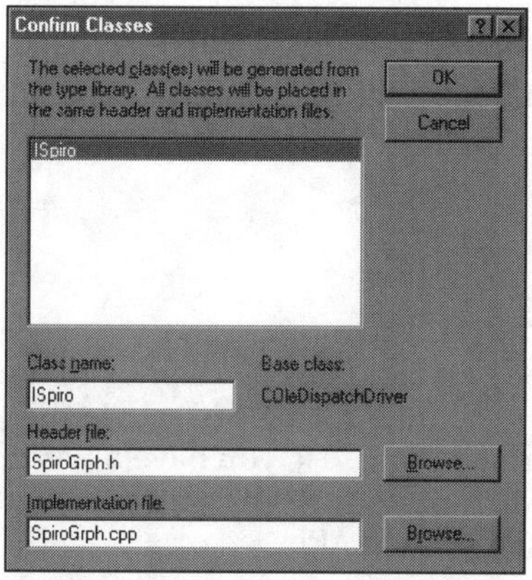

Figure 28-11: The Confirm Classes dialog box enables you to change the default names.

The last thing you must do is declare a class in your program source code and initialize it. First include spirogrph.h (this file was created by the ClassWizard) at the top of your application's view class .h file, and then add the following public declaration in the view class .h file:

```
ISpiro *m_pSpiro;
```

In the view class constructor, add the following initialization code:

```
CoInitialize( NULL );
m_pSpiro = new ISpiro;
m_pSpiro->CreateDispatch( _T( "Spiro.Spiro.1" ) );
```

In the view class destructor, add the following cleanup code:

```
delete m_pSpiro;
CoUninitialize();
```

The spirograph functions are there to be used by your control via the ISpiro class. Add the following line to your view class's OnDraw() function, and the Spirograph will draw:

```
m_pSpiro->Draw( (int) pDC->m_hDC );
```

Data Types

If your control is written in C++ and only C++ programs use it, you'll be OK if you pass character strings back and forth. But other languages such as Basic need to pass character strings as BSTRs. This section shows you how to perform the necessary conversions to and from BSTRs.

Converting to and from BSTRs

A BSTR is an OLECHAR* or a pointer to a Unicode string. The DWORD prior to the OLECHAR* indicates the actual length of the BSTR, and this value is set via the SysAllocString API. In other words, by referencing a BSTR, you have a basic Unicode string and can use the Unicode-to-ANSI macros that follow. If you want to free a BSTR, however, you have to use the SysFreeString API.

The syntax of the ATL string-conversion macro is:

```
MACRONAME( StringAddress )
```

For example:

```
A2W( lpa )
```

In the macro names, the source string type is on the left (for example, A) and the destination string type is on the right (for example, W). A stands for LPSTR, OLE stands for LPOLESTR, T stands for LPTSTR, and W stands for LPWSTR.

Thus, A2W converts an LPSTR to an LPWSTR, OLE2T converts an LPOLESTR to an LPTSTR, and so on. The destination string is created using _alloca, except when the destination type is BSTR. Using _alloca allocates memory off the stack so that when your function returns, it is automatically cleaned up.

If a C occurs in the macro name, the macro converts to a const string. For example, W2CA converts an LPWSTR to an LPCSTR. When using an ATL string conversion macro, specify the USES_CONVERSION macro at the beginning of your function in order to avoid compiler errors. For example:

```
void func( LPSTR lpsz )
{
   USES_CONVERSION;
   ...
   LPWSTR x = A2W(lpsz)
   // Do something with x
   ...
}
```

It is better to use the macros that have *T* and *OLE* in them, as they will resolve to the correct format when compiling for UNICODE or ANSI.

In addition, Don Box has developed some classes that help with conversions of this type. You can get them at http://www.develop.com/dbox/yacl.htm. Don also wrote an article for the August 1995 MSJ that explains various conversion techniques.

Comparing BSTRs

ATL's CComBSTR class doesn't support comparison. So, you have to find other ways to do this. Below are some of your options.

You can convert the BSTRs to either ANSI or Unicode strings and do the comparison from there. For example:

```
if( strcmp( OLE2A( bstr1 ), OLE2A( bstr2 ) ) == 0 )
or
if( _tcscmp( OLE2T( bstr1 ), OLE2T( bstr2 ) ) == 0 )
```

The Unicode version is better because BSTRs can contain embedded nulls, and the ANSI conversion functions will terminate when they encounter the first null. This approach also does a bitwise comparison. If you want to maintain any locale-specific information, you should use the Win32 CompareString API.

Looking through ATL's implementation of CComVariant, you'll find an implementation of BSTR comparison that does this:

```
return
  ( ::SysStringByteLen(bstrVal) ==
::SysStringByteLen(varSrc.bstrVal)) &&
  ( ::memcmp(bstrVal, varSrc.bstrVal,
::SysStringByteLen(bstrVal)) == 0 );
```

Viewing the contents of a BSTR in the debugger

First, be sure to enable the display of Unicode strings via Tools ➪ Options ➪ Debug ➪ Display Unicode strings. This should enable viewing of BSTR types. Wrappers for BSTR, though, still cause problems.

To display _bstr_t types, add this to your \DevStudio\SharedIDE\bin\autoexp.dat file:

```
_variant_t =vt=<vt,x> str=<bstrVal,su> short=<iVal>
long=<lVal>dbl=<dblVal,g>
_bstr_t =<m_Data->m_wstr,su>
tagVARIANT =vt=<vt,x> str=<bstrVal,su> short=<iVal>
long=<lVal>dbl=<dblVal,g>
```

Embedding an ActiveX Control in a Web Page

To get this section to work, you need to have an ActiveX-aware browser installed on your PC. Internet Explorer 3.0 or later from Microsoft will do, as will any other browser that supports ActiveX. If you can access the Internet but don't have an ActiveX-capable browser, you can download Internet Explorer free of charge. You'll find it at `http://www.microsoft.com`.

Web pages are defined using something called Hypertext Markup Language, commonly known as HTML. The elements of a Web page are specified by HTML tags, which usually occur in pairs and are delimited by angle brackets.

Here's an example of how to add the SpiroGrph control to a Web page:

```
<HTML>
<HEAD>
<TITLE> A Page with a SpiroGraph</TITLE>
</HEAD>
<BODY>
<OBJECT ID="SpiroGrph1" WIDTH=400 HEIGHT=300
  CLASSID="CLSID: B0819F01-B460-11D1-B719-0080AD17AF01">
</OBJECT>
</BODY>
</HTML>
```

In this example, the specification of the name of the object to be inserted and the `CLASSID` for the object that identifies what kind of object it is both appear in the opening `<OBJECT>` tag along with the width and height of the control. We've specified the `CLASSID` between quotes as the characters `CLSID` followed by the hexadecimal digits for the `CLSID` that appeared in the arguments to the `IMPLEMENT_OLECREATE_EX` macro.

Summary

In this chapter, you've learned some background on Active Template Controls. You've also learned how to create text controls from Developer Studio. Instructions for using controls in Web pages were given so that you could dive right in and bring your Web page into the leading edge of technology. Now you can begin your own experimentation and really take advantage of what you know.

Creating and using ActiveX controls can be daunting at first because you need to learn so many new things. But the power you get from them is worth the effort. Not only will your applications be able to share code written for and by other languages, but your Web applications will become much more powerful.

✦ ✦ ✦

PART

VII

Distributed Computing

Do you need to load files from half a world away? Do you need to connect to a computer in a remote part of the hemisphere? Or do you just need to send files to your company's office on the other side of town? In any case, this section teaches you how to use the Internet to connect with other computers and share data.

You'll learn the ins and outs of FTP, HTTP, and sockets. You'll also learn how to create simple Web browsers.

✦ ✦ ✦ ✦

In This Part

Chapter 29
Internet Programming

Chapter 30
CHtmlView

✦ ✦ ✦ ✦

CHAPTER 29

Internet Programming

✦ ✦ ✦ ✦

In This Chapter

Creating Internet sessions

Learning about Internet sessions

Retrieving URL data from remote servers

Understanding how to use MFC FTP classes to access FTP servers

Seeing a demo program that accesses an FTP server

Learning about Web crawlers

Seeing a demo program that crawls the Web

✦ ✦ ✦ ✦

The Internet is part of just about everyone's vocabulary, and programming applications that use the Internet for data transfer should be part of every programmer's bag of tricks. Many salespeople who travel around the country transfer information back to headquarters daily via the Internet. Some educational institutions use the Internet to share instructional materials with other institutions and students; electronic commerce (in the form of shopping and financial transactions over the Internet) is commonplace.

We're at the very beginning of our venture into worldwide communications and data sharing. The possibilities are almost endless. Application developers must be ready to meet the current challenge, and prepare for future challenges that will appear. Learning to use the MFC classes to access Internet data is just the first step, and this chapter provides the foundations for doing that. The next step is to be creative and formulate additional and inventive uses for your newly found data-sharing techniques.

We'll delve into three main areas: the Internet protocols specific to HTTP, FTP, and Gopher. These are at the heart of data transfer methods for the Internet.

Getting Started with CInternetSession

Before you can connect to an FTP server or retrieve an HTTP file, you must establish an Internet session. MFC provides a class, called `CInternetSession`, that encapsulates the details of the Internet session. This all-important class creates and initializes a single session or several simultaneous Internet sessions. If necessary, you can describe your proxy server when you create the CInternetSession class. The following code shows how to create a CInternetSession class:

```
// Simple CInternetSession creation.
CInternetSession *pInternetSession;
pInetSession = new CInternetSession;
```

Six optional parameters can be used when creating a CInternetSession class. The prototype for the CInternetSession constructor follows, along with the descriptions of the optional parameters:

```
CInternetSession( LPCTSTR pstrAgent = NULL,
  DWORD dwContext = 1,
  DWORD dwAccessType = INTERNET_OPEN_TYPE_PRECONFIG,
  LPCTSTR pstrProxyName = NULL,
  LPCTSTR pstrProxyBypass = NULL, DWORD dwFlags = 0 );
```

The first parameter, pstrAgent, is a pointer to a string that identifies the name of the application or entity calling the Internet functions. If pstrAgent is NULL (the default), the framework calls the global function AfxGetAppName(), which returns a null-terminated string that contains an application's name. Some protocols use this string to identify your application to the server.

The second parameter, dwContext, is the context identifier for the operation. This parameter identifies the operation's status information returned by CInternetSession::OnStatusCallback(). The default is set to 1; however, you can explicitly assign a specific context ID for the operation. The object and any work it does will be associated with that context ID. If dwFlags includes INTERNET_FLAG_ASYNC, objects created by this object have asynchronous behavior as long as a status callback routine is registered.

The third parameter, dwAccessType, is the type of access required. You can't combine these flags as you can others with OR operators; only one value may be used. Table 29-1 gives the valid values, exactly one of which may be supplied.

Table 29-1
Valid Access-Type Values

Type	*Description*
INTERNET_OPEN_TYPE_PRECONFIG	Preconfigured (in the registry). This access type is set as the default.
INTERNET_OPEN_TYPE_DIRECT	Direct to Internet.
INTERNET_OPEN_TYPE_PROXY	Through CERN proxy.

The fourth parameter, pstrProxyName, is the name of the preferred CERN proxy if dwAccessType is set as INTERNET_OPEN_TYPE_PROXY. The default is NULL.

The fifth parameter, pstrProxyBypass, is a pointer to a string that contains an optional list of server addresses. These addresses may be bypassed when using proxy access. If a NULL value is supplied, the bypass list will be read from the registry. This parameter is meaningful only if dwAccessType is set to INTERNET_OPEN_TYPE_PROXY.

The sixth and last parameter, dwFlags, indicates various options such as caching and asynchronous behavior. The default is set to 0. The possible values are listed in Table 29-2.

Table 29-2
Possible Options Flags

Type	***Description***
INTERNET_FLAG_DONT_CACHE	Do not cache the data, either locally or in any gateway servers
INTERNET_FLAG_ASYNC	Future operations on this object may fail with ERROR_IO_PENDING. A status callback will be made with INTERNET_STATUS_REQUEST_COMPLETE when the operation finishes. This callback is on a thread other than the one for the original request. You must call the EnableStatusCallback() function to establish a status callback routine, or the functions will be completed synchronously.
INTERNET_FLAG_OFFLINE	Download operations are satisfied through the persistent cache only. If the item does not exist in the cache, an appropriate error code is returned. This flag may be combined with the bitwise OR (|) operator.

After you've established an Internet session, you can retrieve files using the OpenURL() function; you can also create FTP, HTTP, and Gopher connections.

During an Internet session, a transaction such as a search or data download can take appreciable time. The user might want to continue working, or might want to have status information about the progress of the transaction. To handle this problem, CInternetSession provides for searches and data transfer to occur asynchronously, allowing the user to perform other tasks while waiting for the transfer to complete. Another alternative is to perform Internet transactions in threads.

Creating a Simple Web Browser

The following code example reads a URL; what you do with the URL data is up to you. This simple code snippet doesn't display the latest JPG files in a window; it just saves the data to a disk file.

```
#include <afxinet.h>

CInternetSession InternetSession;
CStdioFile *pFile;
CFile OutFile;

int nBytes;
char cbBuffer[1024];

// Open a local disk file to which the
// file will be saved.
OutFile.Open( "demo.html",
  CFile::modeCreate | CFile::modeWrite );

// Open a file that references the URL.
pFile =
  pInternetSession.OpenURL("www.site.com/demo.html");

// Read all bytes of the file and write them
// to a local disk file.
while( ( nBytes = pFile->Read( cbBuffer,
  sizeof( cbBuffer ) ) ) > 0 )
  OutFile.Write( cbBuffer, nBytes );

// CStdioFile destructor calls Close().
delete pFile;

// Will close when InternetSession goes out of scope.
InternetSession.Close();
```

When you look at the example just given, note that some important processes are occurring or set up to occur:

- ✦ The `OpenURL()` function returns a pointer to a `CStdioFile` object. `CStdioFile` is derived from `CFile`, so `CFile` functions such as `GetLength()` are available to you.
- ✦ The `CStdioFile::Read()` function returns the number of bytes read. You can use this to check whether you've reached the end of the file. If you have, the value returned for the bytes read `that's` will be zero.
- ✦ The destructor for `CStdioFile` will close the file. When you delete the `CStdioFile` object, the file closes automatically. If you don't delete the object, be sure to close the file; otherwise you might have problems later with open resources that aren't freed.

✦ The `CInternetSession` object's destructor will call the `Close()` function. In the example, the `Close()` function was called because in this case it was unclear when the `CInternetSession` object would go out of scope and be destroyed.

Expert Tip

Parsing URL Strings

If you're accepting a URL address from users, they may not type it in so that the MFC Internet functions such as `OpenURL()` can understand it. If your application relies on users to specify the URL, try the following code as a safety feature. It parses user-given URLs into a format that the Internet functions understand. For the code to work, you must pass in the URL and the service type. Service types include `ftp://`, `http://`, and `gopher://`:

```
BOOL CClass::ConnectionFunction( CString& strURL,
  CString& strService )
{
  DWORD dwServiceType;
  CString strServer, strObject;
  int nPort;

  // Parse the URL initially. If we get a FALSE
  // return value, the parsing didn't succeed.
  if( !AfxParseURL( strURL, dwServiceType,
    strServer, strObject, nPort ) ){

    // Create a new URL string with the service
    // as a prefix. Services include ftp://
    // http:// and gopher://
    CString strNewURL = strService;
    strNewURL += strURL;

    // Make another attempt to parse the URL.
    if( !AfxParseURL( strNewURL, dwServiceType,
      strServer, strObject, nPort ) )
      return( FALSE );

    strURL = strNewURL;

    }

  return( TRUE );

}
```

◆ ◆ ◆ ◆ ◆

Nutshell

Simple Retrieval of an HTTP File

This set of steps is intended as a summary of how to read an HTTP file from a remote server. The bare bones steps are listed, with no handling of the actual data that was retrieved.

1. Create a `CInternetSession` class.
2. Use the `CInternetSession`'s `OpenURL()` function to create a `CStdioFile` object. Make sure to obtain a pointer to the `CStdioFile` object.
3. Read the data, preferably in small chunks such as 1,024 bytes. (Small chunks provide an opportunity to keep in synch with the data that's coming in over a slow line such as a dial-up connection.
4. Close the `CStdioFile` object and delete it later, or just delete it and let its destructor close the file.
5. Close the `CInternetSession` object and delete it later, or just delete it and let its destructor close the session. If the `CInternetSession` object is not a pointer, you can just let it go out of scope — this closes the session and Deletes the object.

✦ ✦ ✦ ✦ ✦

Connecting to an FTP Server

You must connect to an FTP server before retrieving files from it. There are two simple steps you must perform to make the connection. The first thing you have to do is create a `CInternetSession` object. The second thing you do is to obtain an Ftp connection with `CInternetSession`'s `GetFtpConnection()` function.

The MFC class `CFtpConnection` both manages your FTP connection to an Internet server and allows direct manipulation of directories and files on that server. FTP is one of the three Internet services recognized by the MFC WinInet classes. You can only communicate with an FTP Internet server after you first create an instance of `CInternetSession`, and then create a `CFtpConnection` object. You never create a `CFtpConnection` object directly; instead, you call `CInternetSession::GetFtpConnection()`, which creates the `CFtpConnection` object and returns a pointer to it.

Now for a simple example. The following code connects to `ftp.microsoft.com`:

```
// The internet session is created
// when the CInternetSession object
// is declared.
CInternetSession InternetSession;
CFtpConnection *m_pFtpConnection;

  try{
    // Get an FTP connection to ftp.microsoft.com.
    m_pFtpConnection =
      InternetSession.GetFtpConnection("ftp.microsoft.com");
```

```
    }

  // Catch any exceptions that are thrown as a result of
  // of attempting the FTP connection.
  catch( CInternetException *pEx ){
    TCHAR szError[1024];
    if( pEx->GetErrorMessage( szError, 1024 ) )
      AfxMessageBox( szError );
    else
      AfxMessageBox( "There was an exception." );
    pEx->Delete();
    m_pFtpConnection = NULL;
    }

  // Perform FTP operations here...

  // Close the FTP connection and delete
  // the object.
  if( m_pFtpConnection != NULL ){
    m_pFtpConnection->Close();
    delete m_pFtpConnection;
}

  // The CInternetSession destructor will close the
  // internet session.
```

Try This

Connect to an FTP Server

Take some time now and use what we've just talked about before moving on. Let's create a simple program that connects to an FTP server:

1. Create a single-document application named FTPConnect.
2. Include <afxinet.h> in `FTPConnectView.h`.
3. Declare the following in `FTPConnectView.h`:

```
CInternetSession *m_pInternetSession;
CFtpConnection *m_pFtpConnection;
```

4. Add the following code to the constructor in `FTPConnectView.cpp`:

```
m_pInternetSession = new CInternetSession;
```

5. Add the following code to the destructor in `FTPConnectView.cpp`:

```
if( m_pInternetSession != NULL )
  delete m_pInternetSession;
```

6. Add `WM_CREATE` and `WM_TIMER` handlers for the CFTPConnectView class.

7. Edit the `OnCreate()` function as follows:

```
SetTimer( 1, 1000, NULL );
```

8. Edit the `OnTimer()` function as follows:

```
KillTimer( nIDEvent );

try{
  // Get an FTP connection to ftp.microsoft.com.
  m_pFtpConnection =
    m_pInternetSession.GetFtpConnection(
      "ftp.microsoft.com");
  }

// Catch any exceptions that are thrown as a result of
// of attempting the FTP connection.
catch( CInternetException *pEx ){
  pEx->Delete();
  m_pFtpConnection = NULL;
  }
```

9. Set a breakpoint in the `OnTimer()` function where the `KillTimer()` function is called.

10. Run the program in debug mode and watch each line execute. You should connect to `ftp.microsoft.com`. Make sure you set a breakpoint inside the catch block so that if an exception is thrown, you'll be able to see it.

✦ ✦ ✦ ✦ ✦

Retrieving a File from an FTP Server

After an FTP connection has been established, it's a simple matter to retrieve a file from an FTP server. The `CFtpConnection` class has a high-level function called `GetFile()` that handles everything for you. A single line of code is all you need to pull a file down from a remote FTP server. The following code gets the file named `disclaimer.txt` from `ftp.microsoft.com` with an existing `CFtpConnection` class, and saves it to the current directory as a file named copy.txt:

```
// m_pFtpConnection was established before
// getting to this section of code.
m_pFtpConnection->GetFile("disclaimer.txt", "copy.txt" );
```

The sidebar titled "The GetFile() Function" gives full details about the `GetFile()` function.

The GetFile() Function

Prototype

You call the GetFile() function member function to get a file from an FTP server and store it on the local machine. GetFile() is a high-level routine that handles all the overhead associated with reading a file from an FTP server and storing it locally. If dwFlags is FILE_TRANSFER_TYPE_ASCII, translation of file data also converts control and formatting characters to Windows equivalents. The default transfer is binary mode, in which the file is downloaded in the same format as it is stored on the server. Consider this code:

```
BOOL GetFile( LPCTSTR pstrRemoteFile, LPCTSTR pstrLocalFile, BOOL
bFailIfExists, DWORD dwAttributes, DWORD dwFlags,DWORD dwContext);
```

Both pstrRemoteFile and pstrLocalFile can be either partially qualified filenames relative to the current directory or fully qualified. A backslash (\) or forward slash (/) can be used as the directory separator for either name. GetFile() translates the directory name separators to the appropriate characters before they are used.

Override the dwContext default to set the context identifier to a value of your choosing. The context identifier is associated with the specific operation of the CFtpConnection object created by its CInternetSession object. The value is returned to CInternetSession::OnStatusCallback() to provide status on the operation with which it is identified.

The function returns nonzero if successful; otherwise, it returns zero. If the call fails, the Win32 function GetLastError may be called to determine the cause of the error.

Parameters

The first parameter, pstrRemoteFile, is a pointer to a null-terminated string containing the name of a file to retrieve from the FTP server.

The next parameter, pstrLocalFile, is a pointer to a null-terminated string containing the name of the file to create on the local system.

The third parameter, bFailIfExists, indicates whether the filename may already be used by an existing file. If the local filename already exists, and this parameter is TRUE, GetFile() fails. Otherwise, GetFile() erases the existing copy of the file.

The next parameter, dwAttributes, indicates the attributes of the file. This can be any combination of the following flags:

- FILE_ATTRIBUTE_ARCHIVE — Indicates that the file is an archive file. Applications use this attribute to mark files for backup or removal.
- FILE_ATTRIBUTE_COMPRESSED — Indicates that the file or directory is compressed. For a file, compression means that all the data in the file is compressed. For a directory, compression is the default for newly created files and subdirectories.
- FILE_ATTRIBUTE_DIRECTORY — Indicates that the file is a directory.

(continued)

(continued)

- FILE_ATTRIBUTE_NORMAL — Indicates that the file has no other attributes set. This attribute is valid only if used alone. All other file attributes override FILE_ATTRIBUTE_NORMAL.
- FILE_ATTRIBUTE_HIDDEN — Indicates that the file is hidden. It is not to be included in an ordinary directory listing.
- FILE_ATTRIBUTE_READONLY — Indicates that the file is read only. Applications can read the file but cannot write to it or delete it.
- FILE_ATTRIBUTE_SYSTEM — Indicates that the file is part of or is used exclusively by the operating system.
- FILE_ATTRIBUTE_TEMPORARY — Indicates that the file is being used for temporary storage. Applications should only write to the file if absolutely necessary. Most of the file's data remains in memory without being flushed to the media because the file will soon be deleted.

The fifth parameter, dwFlags, specifies the conditions under which the transfer occurs. This can be any of the following transfer type flags:

- FTP_TRANSFER_TYPE_ASCII — Transfers the file using FTP's ASCII (Type A) transfer method. Converts control and formatting information to local equivalents.
- FTP_TRANSFER_TYPE_BINARY — Transfers data using the FTP Image (Type I) transfer method. The file transfers data exactly as it exists, with no changes. This is the default transfer method.

The last parameter, dwContext, is the context identifier for the file retrieval.

The FtpDemo Program

One of the most powerful tools at your command is the FtpDemo program, which gives you the ability to use FTP to retrieve and update files on a remote server.

FtpDemo shows you how to log on to an FTP server, and how to retrieve a file from the server. It performs its FTP operations from inside of threads — if it didn't, the application would hang up before the FTP operations were completed.

Caution

FtpDemo

CD-ROM Location: **Chap29\FtpDemo**
Program Name: **FtpDemo.EXE**
Source Code Modules in Text: **FtpDemoView.cpp**

✦ ✦ ✦ ✦ ✦

Listing 29-1: FtpDemo Program

```
// FtpDemoView.cpp : implementation of
// the CFTPDemoView class
//

/////////////////////////////////////////////////////////////
// CFTPDemoView message handlers

// The data structure in which
// information the threads need
// is stored.
typedef struct{
  BOOL bInProgress;
  int nErrorCode;
  char szHostname[300];
  char szSrcFile[300];
  char szDestFile[300];
  char szAppName[300];
  HWND hWnd;
} FTPINFO;

FTPINFO FtpInfo;

UINT GetFile( LPVOID Info )
{
  FTPINFO *pFtpInfo = (FTPINFO *) Info;
  CInternetSession *pInetSession;
  CFtpConnection *pFtpConnection;

  // Set the flag so that we know
  // a threaded operation is in progress.
  pFtpInfo->bInProgress = TRUE;

  // Allocate a CInternetSession object.
  pInetSession = new CInternetSession(
    pFtpInfo->szAppName, 1,
    PRE_CONFIG_INTERNET_ACCESS );

  // If the CInternetSession object didn't
  // allocate, send a message to the window
  // that's contained in the FtpInfo structure.
  if( pInetSession == NULL ){
    ::PostMessage( pFtpInfo->hWnd, WM_COMMAND,
      WM_USER + 10, FTP_INET_SESSION_NULL );
    pFtpInfo->bInProgress = FALSE;
    return( 0 );
    }
  // Attempt to make the Ftp connection.
  try{
```

(continued)

Listing 29-1 *(continued)*

```
    pFtpConnection =
      pInetSession->GetFtpConnection(
        pFtpInfo->szHostname );
    }

  // If GetFtpConnection() throws an exception,
  // catch it, clean up, and return.
  catch( CInternetException *pEx ){
    pEx->Delete();
    delete pInetSession;
    ::PostMessage( pFtpInfo->hWnd, WM_COMMAND,
      WM_USER + 10, FTP_CONNECTION_ERROR );
    pFtpInfo->bInProgress = FALSE;
    return( 0 );
    }

  // Attempt to get retrieve the file from
  // the remote server to the local machine.
  if( !pFtpConnection->GetFile( pFtpInfo->szSrcFile,
    pFtpInfo->szDestFile ) )
    // If an error occurred, post a message
    // to the window found in the FtpInfo
    // structure.
    ::PostMessage( pFtpInfo->hWnd, WM_COMMAND,
    WM_USER + 10, FTP_GET_FILE_ERROR );

  else
    // If no error occurred, post a message
    // to the window found in the FtpInfo
    // structure.
    ::PostMessage( pFtpInfo->hWnd, WM_COMMAND,
    WM_USER + 10, FTP_GET_FILE_SUCCESS );

  // Close the Ftp connection and delete
  // the CFtpConnection and CInternetSession
  // objects.
  pFtpConnection->Close();
  delete pFtpConnection;
  delete pInetSession;

  // Let the main app know that we're
  // done in the thread.
  pFtpInfo->bInProgress = FALSE;

  return( 0 );

}

UINT GetDir( LPVOID Info )
{
  FTPINFO *pFtpInfo = (FTPINFO *) Info;
```

```
CInternetSession *pInetSession;
CFtpConnection *pFtpConnection;
CFtpFileFind *pFtpFind = NULL;
HGLOBAL hGlobal = NULL;
BOOL bContinue;

// Set the flag so that we know
// a threaded operation is in progress.
pFtpInfo->bInProgress = TRUE;

// Allocate a CInternetSession object.
pInetSession = new CInternetSession(
  pFtpInfo->szAppName, 1,
  PRE_CONFIG_INTERNET_ACCESS );

// If the CInternetSession object didn't
// allocate, send a message to the window
// that's contained in the FtpInfo structure.
if( pInetSession == NULL ){
  ::PostMessage( pFtpInfo->hWnd, WM_COMMAND,
    WM_USER + 10, FTP_INET_SESSION_NULL );
  pFtpInfo->bInProgress = FALSE;
  return( 0 );
  }
// Attempt to make the Ftp connection.
try{
  pFtpConnection =
    pInetSession->GetFtpConnection(
      pFtpInfo->szHostname );
  }

// If GetFtpConnection() throws an exception,
// catch it, clean up, and return.
catch( CInternetException *pEx ){
  pEx->Delete();
  delete pInetSession;
  ::PostMessage( pFtpInfo->hWnd, WM_COMMAND,
    WM_USER + 10, FTP_CONNECTION_ERROR );
  pFtpInfo->bInProgress = FALSE;
  return( 0 );
  }

// Create a new CFtpFileFind object.
pFtpFind = new CFtpFileFind( pFtpConnection );
if( pFtpFind == NULL )
  goto GetDirBailout;

// Allocate the memory into which
// we'll place the directory entries.
hGlobal =
  GlobalAlloc( GMEM_MOVEABLE | GMEM_ZEROINIT,
```

(continued)

Listing 29-1 *(continued)*

```
      20000 );

  // If the memory wasn't allocated,
  // bail out.
  if( hGlobal == NULL )
    goto GetDirBailout;

  // Look for the first file.
  bContinue = pFtpFind->FindFile( "*" );

  // If there aren't any files,
  // bail out.
  if( !bContinue )
    goto GetDirBailout;

  // While files are found, stay in this
  // loop.
  while( bContinue ){

    // Get the next file.
    bContinue = pFtpFind->FindNextFile();

    // Get the file name.
    CString strFilename = pFtpFind->GetFileName();

    // Bracket the file name if it's
    // a directory and add CR/LF.
    if( pFtpFind->IsDirectory() )
      strFilename = "[" + strFilename + "]";
    strFilename += "\15\12";

    // Lock the memory and concatenate
    // this file name to the list.
    char *pDest = (char *) GlobalLock( hGlobal );
    if( pDest != NULL ){
      strcat( pDest, strFilename );
      GlobalUnlock( hGlobal );
      }
    }

  // Post a message to the calling window and
  // send the memory handle.
  ::PostMessage( pFtpInfo->hWnd, WM_COMMAND,
    WM_USER + 10, (long) hGlobal );

  // Make sure we don't try to free
  // the memory. That will be the calling
  // window's responsibility.
  hGlobal = NULL;

GetDirBailout:
```

```
  // If we allocated a CFtpFileFind object,
  // close and then delete.
  if( pFtpFind != NULL ){
    pFtpFind->Close();
    delete pFtpFind;
    }

  // If the memory is not NULL, free it.
  if( hGlobal != NULL )
    GlobalFree( hGlobal );

  // Close the Ftp connection and delete
  // the CFtpConnection and CInternetSession
  // objects.
  pFtpConnection->Close();
  delete pFtpConnection;
  delete pInetSession;

  // Let the main app know that we're
  // done in the thread.
  pFtpInfo->bInProgress = FALSE;

  return( 0 );

}

void CFTPDemoView::OnFileGetfileviaftp()
{
  CGetFtpFile GetFtpFile;

  if( GetFtpFile.DoModal() == IDOK ){
    // Clear the FtpInfo structure.
    memset( &FtpInfo, 0, sizeof( FTPINFO ) );
    // Copy the host name into the
    // FtpInfo structure.
    strcpy( FtpInfo.szHostname,
      GetFtpFile.m_strHostname );
    // Copy the source filename into the
    // FtpInfo structure.
    strcpy( FtpInfo.szSrcFile,
      GetFtpFile.m_strSrcFile );
    // Copy the destination filename into the
    // FtpInfo structure.
    strcpy( FtpInfo.szDestFile,
      GetFtpFile.m_strDestFile );
    // Copy the application name into the
    // FtpInfo structure.
    strcpy( FtpInfo.szAppName, AfxGetAppName() );
    // Remember the window handle.
    FtpInfo.hWnd = m_hWnd;
    // Kick off the thread.
    AfxBeginThread( (AFX_THREADPROC) GetFile,
```

(continued)

Listing 29-1 *(continued)*

```
      (LPVOID) &FtpInfo );
    }

}

void CFTPDemoView::OnUpdateFileGetfileviaftp(
  CCmdUI* pCmdUI)
{

  // Disable if a threaded
  // operation is in progress.
  pCmdUI->Enable( !FtpInfo.bInProgress );

}

void CFTPDemoView::OnFileGetftpdirectory()
{
  CGetFtpFir GetFtpDir;

  if( GetFtpDir.DoModal() == IDOK ){
    // Clear the FtpInfo structure.
    memset( &FtpInfo, 0, sizeof( FTPINFO ) );
    // Copy the host name into the
    // FtpInfo structure.
    strcpy( FtpInfo.szHostname,
      GetFtpDir.m_strHostname );
    // Copy the application name into the
    // FtpInfo structure.
    strcpy( FtpInfo.szAppName, AfxGetAppName() );
    // Remember the window handle.
    FtpInfo.hWnd = m_hWnd;
    // Kick off the thread.
    AfxBeginThread( (AFX_THREADPROC) GetDir,
      (LPVOID) &FtpInfo );
    }

}

void CFTPDemoView::OnUpdateFileGetftpdirectory(
  CCmdUI* pCmdUI)
{

  // Disable if a threaded
  // operation is in progress.
  pCmdUI->Enable( !FtpInfo.bInProgress );

}

BOOL CFTPDemoView::OnCommand(WPARAM wParam,
  LPARAM lParam)
{
```

```
    // This is a message sent from one of
    // our threads.
    if( wParam == WM_USER + 10 ){
      if( lParam > FTP_DIR_SUCCESS ){
        // Handle complete directory.
        GlobalFree( (HGLOBAL) lParam );
        }
      else{
        // Handle other events.
        }
      return( TRUE );
      }

    return CView::OnCommand(wParam, lParam);
  }
```

Web Robots

A Web robot is a program that automatically traverses the Web's hypertext structure by retrieving a document, and recursively retrieving all documents that are referenced. Note that the definition of recursive in this case isn't limited to any specific traversal algorithm — even if a robot applies some heuristic to the selection and order of documents to visit, and spaces out requests over a long space of time, it is still a robot.

A normal Web browser is not a robot because it is operated by a human being and doesn't automatically retrieve referenced documents (other than inline images).

Web robots are sometimes referred to as *Web wanderers*, *Web crawlers*, or *spiders*. These names are a bit misleading; they give the impression that the software itself moves between sites like a virus, which is not the case — a robot simply visits sites by requesting documents from them.

Agents

Some robots are known as *agents*. There are several types of agents, as described in the following list:

- ✦ *Autonomous agents* are programs that travel between sites, deciding themselves when to move and what to do. These agents can only travel between special servers and are currently not widespread on the Internet.
- ✦ *Intelligent agents* are programs that help users with such chores as choosing a product, guiding a user through form-filling steps, or even helping users find specific information. These operations generally have little to do with networking.

- *User-agent* is a technical name for programs that perform networking tasks for a user, such as Web user-agents like Netscape Navigator and Microsoft Internet Explorer, and e-mail user-agents like Qualcomm Eudora.

- A *search engine* is a program that searches through some dataset. In the context of the Web, the term search engine is most often used for search forms that search through databases of HTML documents gathered by a robot.

The trouble with robots

Some people believe robots are bad for the Web, for these reasons:

- Certain robot implementations can (and have in the past) overloaded networks and servers. This happens especially when people are just starting to write a robot. Even so, most modern robots contain sufficient information to prevent some of these mistakes.
- Robots are operated by human beings, who make mistakes in configuration or simply don't consider the implications of their actions. This means people need to be careful, and robot authors need to make it difficult for people to make mistakes with bad effects.
- Web-wide indexing robots build a central database of documents, which doesn't scale too well to millions of documents on millions of sites.

Most robots are well designed, professionally operated, cause no problems, and provide a valuable service in the absence of widely deployed better solutions. So, robots are neither inherently bad nor inherently brilliant — they just need careful attention.

Where a robot decides to visit depends on the robot — each one uses a different strategy. In general, they start from a historical list of URLs, especially of document files such as .doc and .txt files with many links elsewhere, such as server lists, "What's New" pages, and the most popular sites on the Web.

Most indexing services also allow you to submit URLs manually, which will then be queued and visited by the robot. Sometimes other sources for URLs are used, such as scanners through USENET postings and published mailing list archives. Given those starting points, a robot can select URLs to visit and index, and to parse and use as a source for new URLs.

If an indexing robot knows about a document, it may decide to parse it and insert it into its database. How this is done depends on the robot: Some robots index the HTML Titles or the first few paragraphs. Other robots parse the entire HTML and index all words, with weightings that depend on HTML constructs. Still others parse the META tag or other special hidden tags.

The Crawler Program

You may have a good understanding of how Web robots work. Even so, creating a Web crawler is a tough assignment. We accepted the challenge, though, and created a simple, yet powerful Web crawler program.

This program operates by taking a single starting URL address. From that point, it loads in Web pages, parses through and removes additional URL references, and then adds them to a list of pending URLs. The list of pending URLs grows faster than the list of processed URLs because most Web pages have multiple links.

This crawler application could be expanded to perform useful tasks such as evaluating and rating Web sites. The list of pending and processed URLs are kept in a `CStringArray` class. If you want to expand this application so that it stores hundreds of thousands of URLs in the lists, you'll have to store the pending and processed lists in a database rather than in memory.

Crawler
CD-ROM Location: **Chap29\ Crawler**
Program Name: **Crawler.EXE**
Source Code Modules in Text: **WebCrawler.cpp**

◆ ◆ ◆ ◆ ◆

Listing 29-2: Crawler

```
// WebCrawler.cpp

#include "stdafx.h"
#include "WebCrawler.h"

CWebCrawler::CWebCrawler( HWND hWnd,
  const char *lpszStartURL )
{

  // Get the application name so
  // that we can open the internet
  // session with it.
  strcpy( m_CrawlerInfo.szAppName,
    AfxGetAppName() );

  // Remember the window handle so that
  // we'll know where to send messages
  // while inside of the thread.
  m_CrawlerInfo.hWnd = hWnd;

  // Store the starting URL.
```

(continued)

Listing 29-2 *(continued)*

```
  strcpy( m_CrawlerInfo.szStartURL, lpszStartURL );

}

CWebCrawler::~CWebCrawler()
{

}

void CWebCrawler::BeginCrawl( void )
{

  // Kick off the thread.
  AfxBeginThread(
    (AFX_THREADPROC) CWebCrawler::CrawlThread,
    (LPVOID) &m_CrawlerInfo );

}

UINT CWebCrawler::CrawlThread( LPVOID Info )
{
  CRAWLER_INFO CrawlInfo;
  CInternetSession *lpInetSession;
  CString strHttpData;
  CString strServerLoc;
  CString strCurrentURL;
  CStringArray PendingList, ProcessedList, LocalList;
  BOOL bRead;
  HGLOBAL hAbort, hData;
  int nCount, i, nSuccessCount = 0;
  static char szFormat[] =
       "Pending:%d Processed:%d\
 Total:%d Success:%d        \15\12";

  // Create a memory handle so that we can
  // safely communicate with the application's
  // window.
  hAbort = GlobalAlloc( GMEM_MOVEABLE | GMEM_ZEROINIT,
    sizeof( BOOL ) );

  // Make a copy of the crawler startup information
  // structure.
  memcpy( &CrawlInfo, Info, sizeof( CRAWLER_INFO ) );

  // Create and initialize the CInternetSession
  // object.
  lpInetSession =
    new CInternetSession( CrawlInfo.szAppName,
      PRE_CONFIG_INTERNET_ACCESS );

  // If the CInternetSession object didn't
```

```
// allocate, bail out.
if( lpInetSession == NULL )
  goto CrawlThreadBailout;

// Create a CString object with the
// starting URL.
strCurrentURL = CrawlInfo.szStartURL;

// Continue crawling until we get a signal
// to abort.
while( !Aborted( hAbort, CrawlInfo.hWnd ) ){

  // Read the Http data for
  // the current URL.
  bRead = ReadHttpFileData( strHttpData,
    strCurrentURL, lpInetSession );

  // Move this URL from the Pending
  // to the Processed list.
  PendingToProcessed( strCurrentURL,
    PendingList, ProcessedList );

  // If the read was successful...
  if( bRead ){

    // Increment our success counter.
    nSuccessCount++;

    // Create the server location from
    // the current URL.
    ServerLocFromURL( strCurrentURL, strServerLoc );

    // Get a list of URLs from the HttpFileData
    // and add it to the pending list.
    ListURLs( strHttpData, strServerLoc,
      &nCount, PendingList, ProcessedList, LocalList );

    // If we found some URL reference in the
    // HTTP data, perform the following code.
    if( nCount > 0 ){

      // Allocate memory for the data
      // transfer.
      hData = GlobalAlloc(
        GMEM_MOVEABLE | GMEM_ZEROINIT, 20000 );

      // If the memory allocation succeeded...
      if( hData != NULL ){

        // Lock the memory handle.
        char *pData = (char *) GlobalLock( hData );
```

(continued)

Listing 29-2 (continued)

```
        if( pData != NULL ){

          // Format statistics about current
          // crawler status.
          wsprintf( pData,
            szFormat,
            PendingList.GetSize(),
            ProcessedList.GetSize(),
            PendingList.GetSize() +
              ProcessedList.GetSize(),
            nSuccessCount );

          // Concatenate the current URL.
          strcat( pData, strCurrentURL );
          strcat( pData, "\15\12" );

          // Loop through and concatenate
          // all the URLs in the list.
          for( i=0; i<nCount; i++ ){
            strcat( pData, "   " );
            strcat( pData, LocalList.GetAt( i ) );
            strcat( pData, "\15\12" );
            }

          // Unlock the memory.
          GlobalUnlock( hData );
          }

        // Post a message to the application
        // window with the memory containing
        // the list of URLs.
        ::PostMessage( CrawlInfo.hWnd,
          WM_COMMAND, WM_USER + 12, (long) hData );
        }
      }
    }
  else{

    // For some reason, buried inside of the OpenURL()
    // code is a problem. It might be within MFC, or
    // somewhere deeper. If OpenURL() throws an
    // exception, it's highly likely that the internet
    // session handle will become invalid. For this
    // reason, we delete the CInternetSession object
    // and recreate it.

    // Delete the CInternetSession object
    delete lpInetSession;


    // Create and initialize the CInternetSession
```

```
        // object.
        lpInetSession =
          new CInternetSession( CrawlInfo.szAppName,
            PRE_CONFIG_INTERNET_ACCESS );

        // If the CInternetSession object didn't
        // allocate, bail out.
        if( lpInetSession == NULL )
          goto CrawlThreadBailout;

        }

      // If there are no more items in the pending
      // list, we need to bail out since the
      // crawler will no longer function.
      if( PendingList.GetSize() == 0 )
        goto CrawlThreadBailout;

      // Get the current url from the first
      // entry in the pending list.
      strCurrentURL = PendingList.GetAt( 0 );

      }

CrawlThreadBailout:

  // Delete the CInternetSession object
  if( lpInetSession != NULL )
    delete lpInetSession;

  // Delete the memory handle.
  if( hAbort != NULL )
    GlobalFree( hAbort );

  return( 0 );

}


BOOL CWebCrawler::ReadHttpFileData(
  CString& strHttpFileData, const char *lpszURL,
  CInternetSession *lpInetSession )
{

  // Start off by emtying the CString object. If this
  // function fails, we don't want calling functions to
  // mistakenly thing there's valid data in the CString
  // object.
  strHttpFileData.Empty();

  // If the CInternetSession object is NULL, nothing will
```

(continued)

Listing 29-2 *(continued)*

```
// work so we return indicating failure.
if( lpInetSession == NULL )
  return( FALSE );

// Try to open the URL.
CHttpFile *lpHttpFile;
try{

  lpHttpFile =
    (CHttpFile *) lpInetSession->OpenURL( lpszURL );

  // If lpHttpFile is NULL then something went wrong.
  // This probably never happens. If something goes
  // wrong, it should throw an exception.
  if( lpHttpFile == NULL )
    return( FALSE );

  // Get the the handle type.
  DWORD dwResult = AfxGetInternetHandleType(
    lpHttpFile->m_hFile );

  // Make sure the handle type is the one
  // we're looking for. If it isn't we'll
  // bail out.
  if( dwResult != INTERNET_HANDLE_TYPE_HTTP_REQUEST ){
    lpHttpFile->Close();
    delete lpHttpFile;
    return( FALSE );
    }

  }
catch( CInternetException *e ){
  // Delete the exception and return indicating
  // failure.
  e->Delete();
  return( FALSE );
  }

// CHttpFile is derived from CFile. So to get the
// size of the file, we use the CFile.GetLength()
// function.
long nFileLength = lpHttpFile->GetLength();

// Allocate a buffer large enough for the HTTP file.
char *lpBuffer = new char [nFileLength+1000];

// Check to make sure the allocation didn't fail.
if( lpBuffer == NULL ){

  // Close the CHttpFile object.
  lpHttpFile->Close();
```

```
  // Delete the CHttpFile object.
  delete lpHttpFile;

  // Return indicating failure.
  return( FALSE );

  }

// Clear out the buffer in which the HTTP file
// will be read. We're going to use strlen()
// functions later, and need to make sure the
// string is NULL terminated.
memset( lpBuffer, 0, nFileLength + 1000 );

// Try to read the HTTP file into the buffer.
// We must make sure to catch any exceptions.
try{
  int nBytesRead, nTotalBytes = 0, nTries = 0;

  // Since each read may not bring in all the
  // data, we must make several retries. This
  // insures that we get all of the data in the
  // incoming stream.
  while( nTotalBytes < nFileLength && nTries < 4 ){
    nBytesRead =
      lpHttpFile->Read( &lpBuffer[nTotalBytes],
        nFileLength );
    nTotalBytes += nBytesRead;
    if( nTotalBytes < nFileLength )
      Sleep( 500 );
    nTries++;
    }

  }
catch( CInternetException *e ){
  e->Delete();
  }

// Close the CHttpFile object.
lpHttpFile->Close();

// Delete the CHttpFile object;
delete lpHttpFile;

// Set our CString object to contain the
// HTTP file data that was read into lpBuffer.
strHttpFileData = lpBuffer;

// Delete lpBuffer since we no longer need it.
delete [] lpBuffer;
```

(continued)

Listing 29-2 *(continued)*

```
  // Return indicating success.
  return( TRUE );

}


BOOL CWebCrawler::Aborted( HGLOBAL hGlobal, HWND hWnd )
{
  BOOL bRet, *pData;

  // If the memory handle is NULL,
  // return and indicate no abort.
  if( hGlobal == NULL )
    return( FALSE );

  // Post a message to the hWnd and expext hGlobal
  // to receive the value of an Abort BOOL.
  ::PostMessage( hWnd, WM_COMMAND,
    WM_USER + 11, (long) hGlobal );

  // Lock the memory handle and get the
  // BOOL value from the hWnd.
  pData = (BOOL *) ::GlobalLock( hGlobal );
  if( pData != NULL ){
    bRet = *pData;
    ::GlobalUnlock( hGlobal );
    }

  // Return the result.
  return( bRet );

}

void CWebCrawler::PendingToProcessed(
  CString& strURL, CStringArray& PendingList,
  CStringArray& ProcessedList )
{
  int nCount, i;

  // Get the count of URLs in the ProcessedList
  // CStringArray object.
  nCount = PendingList.GetSize();

  // Loop through the processed strings and see
  // if this string (strURL) is there.
  for( i=0; i<nCount; i++ ){

    // If we find the string, remove it from the list.
    if( PendingList.GetAt( i ) == strURL ){
      PendingList.RemoveAt( i );
```

```
        break;
        }

      }

    // Get the count of URLs in the PendingList
    // CStringArray object.
    nCount = ProcessedList.GetSize();

    // Loop through the pending strings and see
    // if this string (strURL) is there.
    for( i=0; i<nCount; i++ ){

      // If we find the string, return FALSE so
      // that the calling function knows this string
      // has been found. We don't add it again.
      if( ProcessedList.GetAt( i ) == strURL )
        return;

      }

    // Add the string.
    ProcessedList.Add( strURL );

}

BOOL CWebCrawler::AlreadyFound(
  CString& strURL, CStringArray& PendingList,
  CStringArray& ProcessedList )
{
  int nCount, i;

  // Get the count of URLs in the ProcessedList
  // CStringArray object.
  nCount = ProcessedList.GetSize();

  // Loop through the processed strings and see
  // if this string (strURL) is there.
  for( i=0; i<nCount; i++ ){

    // If we find the string, return TRUE so
    // that the calling function knows this string
    // has been found.
    if( ProcessedList.GetAt( i ) == strURL )
      return( TRUE );

    }

  // Get the count of URLs in the PendingList
  // CStringArray object.
  nCount = PendingList.GetSize();
```

(continued)

Listing 29-2 *(continued)*

```
  // Loop through the pending strings and see
  // if this string (strURL) is there.
  for( i=0; i<nCount; i++ ){

    // If we find the string, return TRUE so
    // that the calling function knows this string
    // has been found.
    if( PendingList.GetAt( i ) == strURL )
      return( TRUE );

    }

  // Return indicating we didn't
  // find this string.
  return( FALSE );

}

BOOL CWebCrawler::LegalExtension( CString& strURL )
{
  static char *szLegalExtensions[] = { ".cgi",
    ".map", ".zip", ".z", ".gif", ".jpg", ".class", "" };

  // Make sure we have a valid URL string.
  if( strURL.GetLength() == 0 )
    return( FALSE );

  // Find the '.' character
  int nIndex = strURL.ReverseFind( '.' );
  if( nIndex == -1 )
    return( TRUE );

  // Get a pointer to the URL data.
  char *lpURLData = strURL.GetBuffer( 0 );

  // Loop through the extensions list and look for
  // legal extensions.
  int i = 0;
  while( szLegalExtensions[i][0] != 0 ){
    if( !stricmp( &lpURLData[nIndex],
      szLegalExtensions[i] ) )
      return( FALSE );
      i++;
    }

  // Return indicating this extension is OK.
  return( TRUE );

}

BOOL CWebCrawler::ListURLs(
```

```
  CString& strHttpFileData,
  CString& strServerLoc, int *lpnCount,
  CStringArray& PendingList,
  CStringArray& ProcessedList,
  CStringArray& LocalList )
{

  // Set caller's count to zero;
  *lpnCount = 0;

  LocalList.RemoveAll();

  // Check to make sure we have some valid HTTP file
  // data.
  if( strHttpFileData.GetLength() < 4 )
    return( FALSE );

  // nIndex keeps track of where we are in the HTTP file
  // data as we step through it. nLength keeps track of
  // the length of the HTTP file data.
  int nIndex = 1;
  int nLength = strHttpFileData.GetLength();

  // Get a pointer to the CString data.
  char *lpStringData =
    strHttpFileData.GetBuffer( nLength );

  // First, make sure we're not at the end of the buffer.
  // Second, look for an occurance of "HREF".
  while( nIndex < nLength - 4 ){

    // Check to see if the character before and after the
    // "HREF" are both non-alphanumeric characters. If
    // they aren't, the "HREF" string that was found was
    // part of another string and we don't want to treat
    // like a URL reference. If they are both non-
    // alphanumeric then we can be sure we've found a
    // reference to a URL.
    if( !strnicmp( &lpStringData[nIndex], "HREF", 4 )&&
      !isalnum( (int) lpStringData[nIndex-1] ) &&
      !isalnum( (int) lpStringData[nIndex+4] ) ){

      // Now skip past any non-alphanumeric
      // characters that might precede the URL.
      nIndex += 4;
      while( lpStringData[nIndex] != 0 &&
        !isalnum( (int) lpStringData[nIndex] ) )
        nIndex++;

      // Now we must get the actual URL name
      // and store it in strURL.
```

(continued)

Listing 29-2 *(continued)*

```
        CString strURL;
        while( lpStringData[nIndex] != 0 &&
          lpStringData[nIndex] != '>' &&
          lpStringData[nIndex] != '=' &&
          lpStringData[nIndex] != '%' &&
          lpStringData[nIndex] != '?' &&
          lpStringData[nIndex] != ',' &&
          lpStringData[nIndex] != ' ' &&
          lpStringData[nIndex] != '\42' ){
          strURL += lpStringData[nIndex++];
          }

        // First, see if we have a "MAILTO:" reference. If
        // we do, it's not a URL and we don't want to mess
        // with it. We then look to see if this URL isn't
        // one with an extension that we're going to
        // ignore. We skip files with extensions such as
        // .jpg and .gif.
        if( strnicmp( strURL.GetBuffer( 0 ), "MAILTO:", 7 )
          && LegalExtension( strURL ) ){

          // In case the URL name is something such as
          // NAME.HTM or IMAGES/TEST.HTM we need to
          // put the server name in front of it. This
          // function does that.
          FormURLName( strServerLoc, strURL );

          // Call a function that looks to see
          // if we've already found this URL.
          if( !AlreadyFound( strURL,
            PendingList, ProcessedList ) ){
            PendingList.Add( strURL );
            LocalList.Add( strURL );
            (*lpnCount)++;
            }

          }

      }

      // Because the character before and after the "HREF"
      // weren't both non-alphanumeric characters and
      // therefore the "HREF" string that was found was
      // part of another string, we increment nIndex
      // and continue searching.
      else nIndex++;

      }

    return( TRUE );
```

```
}

BOOL CWebCrawler::FormURLName( CString& strServerLoc,
  CString& strURL )
{

  // We need a pointer the the strURL data.
  // We'll use the pointer along with strnicmp
  // functions. We won't have to call ReleaseBuffer()
  // since we're not going to alter the contents
  // of strURL.
  char *lpURLData = strURL.GetBuffer( 0 );

  // Set our flag initially to indicate that the server
  // name is not part of the URL.
  BOOL bServerInURL = FALSE;

  // Check for URLs that start with http:// ftp://
  // and gopher://
  if( !strnicmp( lpURLData, "http://", 7 ) )
    return( TRUE );
  else if( !strnicmp( lpURLData, "ftp://", 6 ) )
    return( TRUE );
  else if( !strnicmp( lpURLData, "gopher://", 9 ) )
    return( TRUE );
  else if( !strnicmp( lpURLData, "www.", 4 ) ||
    !strnicmp( lpURLData, "www2.", 5 ) ){
    strURL = "http://" + strURL;
    return( TRUE );
    }
  else if( lpURLData[0] == '/' ||
    isalnum( lpURLData[0] ) ){
    strURL = strServerLoc + strURL;
    return( TRUE );
    }
  else{

    // Find the '.' and the '/' at the end of the string.
    int nDot = strURL.ReverseFind( '.' );
    int nSlash = strURL.ReverseFind( '/' );

    // If there's a '.' to the right of the '/'
    // then a server name was given as part of the URL
    if( nDot > nSlash )
      bServerInURL = TRUE;

    // If there was not '/' charater, then there
    // was no server name given.
    if( nSlash == -1 && nDot != -1 )
      bServerInURL = FALSE;
    }
```

(continued)

Listing 29-2 *(continued)*

```
  // If there was not server in the URL, we form
  // a new string in strURL with the server name
  // at the beginning.
  if( !bServerInURL ){

    // Store the URL in a temp CString object.
    CString strTemp = strURL;

    // Store the server location in strURL.
    strURL = strServerLoc;

    // If the server name doesn't end with '/'
    // add one on.
    if( strURL.GetAt( strURL.GetLength() - 1 ) != '/' )
      strURL += '/';

    // Concatenate the URL to the server name.
    strURL += strTemp;

    }

  return( TRUE );

}

BOOL CWebCrawler::ServerLocFromURL(
  CString& strURL,
  CString& strServerLoc )
{

  // Empty the server location CString object.
  strServerLoc.Empty();

  // See if the URL is NULL or contains no data.
  if( strURL.GetLength() == 0 )
    return( FALSE );

  // If the URL ends with '/', it's the server location
  // with no actual file.
  if( strURL.GetAt( strURL.GetLength() - 1 ) == '/' )
    strServerLoc = strURL;

  else{

    // Look for a '.' and '/' character.
    int nSlash = strURL.ReverseFind( '/' );
    int nDot = strURL.ReverseFind( '.' );

    // No dot, assume the entire thing is the
    // server location.
    if( nDot == -1 )
```

```
      strServerLoc = strURL;

    // A dot and a slash, assume the server location
    // ends with the slash.
    else if( nSlash != -1 )
      strServerLoc = strURL.Left( nSlash + 1 );
    }

  // Return indicating success.
  return( TRUE );

}
```

Guidelines for Robot Writers

Are you sure you really need a robot? Robots put a strain on network and processing resources all over the world, so consider if your robot is really worth it. Also, the purpose for which you want to run your robot is probably not as novel as you think—there are already many other spiders out there. Perhaps you can make use of the data collected by one of the other spiders. Finally, are you sure you can cope with the results? Retrieving the entire Web is not a scaleable solution because it's just too big. If you do decide to do it, only go a few levels deep—don't aim to traverse the entire Web.

Be accountable

If you do decide you want to write and/or run a robot, make sure that if your actions do cause problems, people can easily contact you and start a dialog. Specifically:

✦ Identify your Web wanderer. HTTP supports a User-agent field to identify a WWW browser. As your robot is a kind of WWW browser, use this field to name your robot (for example, **NottinghamRobot/1.0**). This allows server maintainers to set your robot apart from human users who are using Interactive browsers. In addition, you should run the robot from a machine registered in the DNS, which makes it easier to recognize, and lets people know where you are.

✦ Identify yourself. HTTP supports a From field to identify the user who runs the WWW browser. Use this to advertise your e-mail address (for example, `j.smith@somewhere.edu`). This allows server maintainers to contact you in case of problems, so you can start a dialog on better terms than if you were hard to track down.

✦ Announce your robot. Post a message to `comp.infosystems.www.providers` before running your robot. If people know in advance that your robot's on its way, they can keep an eye out for it.

- Announce your robot to the target. If you're only targeting a single site, or a few, contact the site administrator and inform him or her.
- Be informative. Server maintainers often wonder why their server is hit. If you use the HTTP Referer field, you can tell them. This requires little effort on your part, but can be very informative to others.
- Be there close to the spider machine to watch the operations. Don't set your Web wanderer going and then take off for a couple of days. If in your absence the robot does things that upset people, you're the only one who can fix it. It is best that you remain logged in to the machine that is running your robot, so people can use "finger" and "talk" to contact you.
- If you do have to be away, suspend the robot when you're not there in a place from which you can monitor the spider for a number of days (for example, over the weekend)—only run it in your presence. Yes, it may be better for the performance of the machine if you run it over night, but that implies that you don't think about the performance overhead of other machines. Yes, it takes longer for the robot to run, but this is more an indication that robots are not always the best way to do things. Why run it continually—after all, what's the rush?
- Notify your authorities. It is advisable to tell your system administrator and/or network provider what you're planning to do. You'll be asking a lot of the services they offer— if something goes wrong, they like to hear it from you first, not from external people.

Test locally

Don't run repeated tests on remote servers. Instead, run a number of servers locally and use them to test your robot first. When going offsite for the first time, stay close to home initially, as with a page with local servers. After doing a small run, analyze your performance and your results, and estimate how they'll measure up to thousands of documents. It may soon become obvious you can't cope.

Don't hog resources

Robots consume a lot of resources. To minimize the impact, keep the following in mind:

- Make sure your robot runs slowly. Although robots can handle hundreds of documents per minute, this puts a large strain on a server and is guaranteed to infuriate the server maintainer. Instead, put a sleep in, or if you're clever, rotate queries between different servers in a round-robin fashion. Retrieving one document per minute is a lot better than one per second. One per five minutes is better still.
- Use `If-modified-since` or `HEAD` where possible. If your application can use the HTTP `If-modified-since` header or the `HEAD` method for its purposes, there will be less overhead than with full `GET`s.

✦ Ask for what you want. HTTP has an Accept field in which a browser (or your robot) can specify the kinds of data it can handle. Use it. For example, if you only analyze text, say so. This allows clever servers to not bother sending you data that you can't handle (and will have to throw away anyway). Also, make use of URL suffixes if they're there.

✦ Build in some logic yourself. For example, if a link refers to a `.ps`, `.zip`, `.Z`, `".gif`, or the like — but you only handle text — then don't ask for that link.

✦ Look out for gateways (URLs starting with `finger`) — news gateways, WAIS gateways, and so on; think about other protocols (such as `news:` or `wais:`) because if it encounters them, your program has to use different ports and protocols.

✦ Don't forget the subpage references (`<A HREF="#abstract">`) — don't retrieve the same page more than once. It's imperative that you make a list of places *not* to visit — *before* you start.

✦ Check URLs. Don't assume that the HTML documents you're going to get back will be sensible. When scanning for a URL, be wary of things like `<A HREF="http://somehost.somedom/doc"`. A lot of sites don't put the trailing / on URLs for directories — a naive strategy of concatenating the names of sub-URLs that can result in bad names.

✦ Check the results. If a server refuses a number of documents in a row, verify what it is saying. It may be that the server refuses to let you retrieve these things because you're a robot.

✦ Don't loop or repeat. Remember all the places you have visited, so you can ensure that you're not looping. It is imperative that you check to see whether the different machine addresses you have are not in fact the same box (for example, `web.nexor.co.uk` might be the same machine as `hercules.nexor.co.uk` and `128.243.219.1`) so you don't have to go to this site again.

✦ Run at opportune times. Some systems have preferred times of access, when the machine is only lightly loaded. If you plan to do many automatic requests from one particular site, find out from its administrator when the preferred time of access is.

✦ Don't run your robot often. How often people find acceptable differs, but I'd say once every two months is probably too often. Also, when you rerun your robot, make use of your previous data, such as the URLs to avoid.

✦ Make a list of volatile links (like the What's New page, and the meta-index). Use this list to get pointers to other documents and concentrate on new links — this way you'll get a high initial yield, and if you stop your robot for some reason, at least it has spent its time well.

✦ Don't try queries. Some WWW documents are searchable (ISINDEX) or contain forms. Don't follow these. For example, the Fish Search may result in a search for "cars" being sent to databases with computer science Ph.D.s, people in the X.500 directory, or botanical data. Not sensible.

Stay with it

It is vital that you know what your robot is doing, and that it remains under control. Remember the following guidelines:

✦ Make sure your robot provides ample logging. It wouldn't hurt to keep track of certain statistics, such as the number of successes and failures, the hosts accessed recently, and the average size of recent files. This ties in with the "Don't loop or repeat" point made earlier— *To prevent looping, log where you have been*. Again, estimate the required disk space to make sure you can cope.

✦ Be interactive. Make sure you're able to guide your robot. Commands that suspend or cancel the robot, or make it skip the current host, can be very useful. In addition, checkpoint your robot frequently. This way you won't lose everything if it falls over.

✦ Be prepared. Your robot will visit hundreds of sites. It will probably upset a number of people. Be ready to respond quickly to inquirers and tell them what you're doing.

✦ Be understanding. If your robot upsets someone, instruct it to not visit his or her site, or to visit only the home page. Don't lecture him or her about why your cause is worth it, because he or she probably isn't in the least interested.

Summary

In this chapter, you learned how to communicate with other computers via the Internet. With relatively little code, you now can save and load files from an FTP site. You also know how to retrieve files from an HTML server.

Storing files to and retrieving files from the Internet is an important capability for many of today's programs. In addition, with the MFC classes that come with Visual C++, Internet transfers aren't all that difficult. If you spend some time studying the example demo programs introduced in this chapter, you'll get a grasp of how to use the MFC classes for your purposes. You can then experiment on your own and become a real expert.

✦ ✦ ✦

CHAPTER 30

CHtmlView

The Microsoft Web Browser control can be used by application developers to add the capability to browse sites on the World Wide Web, or folders and files on a local or networked file system. It's easy to create a Web application because there are relatively few steps to creating these programs compared with what it takes to develop your own browser control. The Web Browser control supports Web browsing through point-and-click hyperlinking, and through direct navigation to URLs. The control even maintains a history list that enables you to browse forward and backward through previous browsed sites, folders, and documents.

Applications can also use the Web Browser control as an Active Document container to host other active documents. This means richly formatted documents, such as a Microsoft Excel spreadsheet or Microsoft Word document, can be opened and edited in-place from within the Web Browser control. Web Browser is also an ActiveX Control container that can host any ActiveX Control.

As if the Web Browser weren't enough, Microsoft has also provided an MFC class that encapsulates it so it's even easier to use. The `CHtmlView` class provides the functionality of the WebBrowser control within the context of MFC's document view architecture.

The WebBrowser ActiveX control (and, therefore, `CHtmlView`) is available only to programs running under Windows 95 and Windows NT Versions 3.51 and later, in which Internet Explorer 4.0 (or later) has been installed.

Some `CHtmlView` member functions apply to the Internet Explorer application only. These functions will succeed on the WebBrowser control, but they will have no visible effect. These functions are `GetAddressBar()`, `GetFullName()`, `GetStatusBar()`, `SetAddressBar()`, `SetFullScreen()`, `SetMenuBar()`, `SetStatusBar()`, and `SetToolBar()`.

✦ ✦ ✦ ✦

In This Chapter

Exploring Microsoft's Web browser

Creating a CHtmlView project

Converting projects to CHtmlView projects

Navigating URLs

Creating a Demo Program Using CHtmlView

Creating a URL Control Using CHtmlView

✦ ✦ ✦ ✦

Creating a CHtmlView Project

Creating an application based on the `CHtmlView` class is a no-brainer. You start with the AppWizard. The application should be some form of a document/view program, whether it's a single-document or multiple-document program.

Most of the options, such as those that determine whether you have a toolbar or allow print and print preview, don't make any difference in the program's capability to use the `CHtmlView` class. You can set these as you wish and the application will support the Web Browser control with no problem.

The only thing you must remember during the AppWizard creation process comes toward the end. When the sixth dialog box (labeled appropriately "6 of 6") comes up, you have the chance to change the base class of the view class to something besides the vanilla `CView` class. At this point, you need to select the `CHtmlView` class, as shown in Figure 30–1.

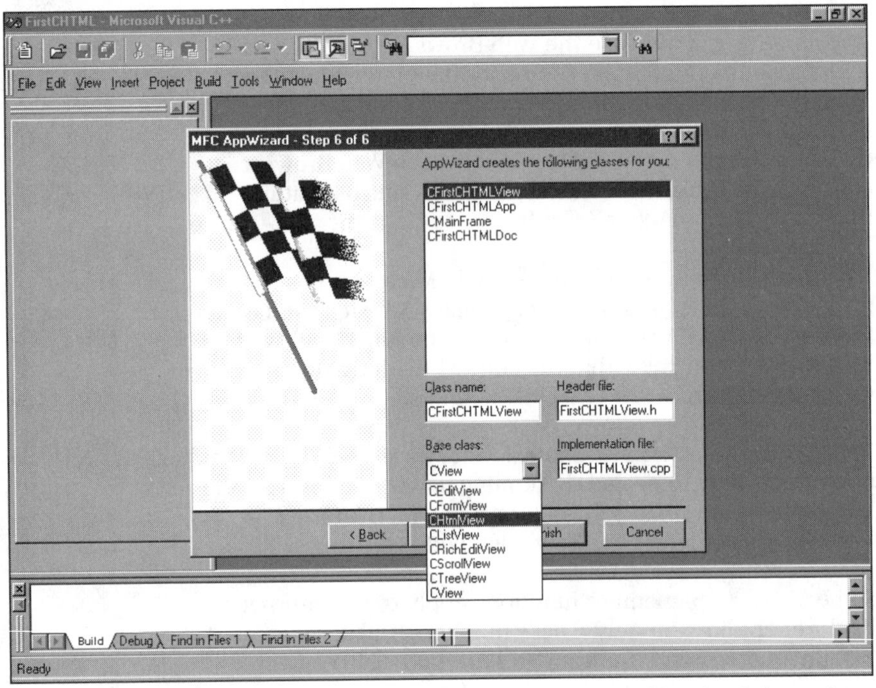

Figure 30-1: You have to select the CHtmlView class as your view class's base class.

After you create the `CHtmlView`-based product, compile it and run it. The default URL points to Microsoft's Visual C++ Web page at `www.microsoft.com/visualc`, as shown in Figure 30-2.

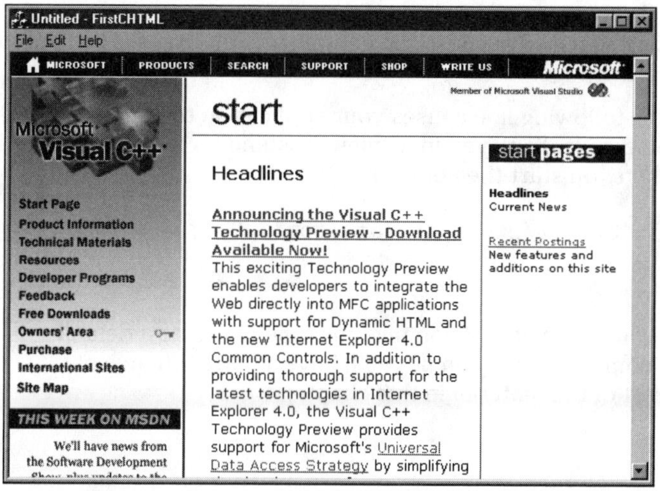

Figure 30-2: A Web page automatically comes up when the project first runs.

You can easily change the starting URL by editing the `OnInitialUpdate()` function. For instance, if you want the application to start at `www.yahoo.com`, you'd change the `OnInitialUpdate()` function as follows:

```
void CFirstCHTMLView::OnInitialUpdate()
{
  CHtmlView::OnInitialUpdate();

  Navigate2(_T("http://www.yahoo.com"),NULL,NULL);
}
```

Converting Projects to Use CHtmlView

You may have existing projects you want to convert from a `CView`-based application to a `CHtmlView`-based application. Following is the procedure to convert an application's view class to `CHtmlView`:

1. Use the Find/Replace feature to replace all instances of your current view class (usually `CView`) in your view's .CPP file with `CHtmlView`.
2. Repeat the same substitution in your view's .H file, replacing your current view class with `CHtmlView`.
3. In your application's STDAFX.H file, append the following line:

```
#include <afxhtml.h>
```

4. Override the `OnInitialUpdate()` member function of your application's view class.

5. In the function body of `OnInitialUpdate()`, add a call to `CHtmlView::Navigate()` to cause the contained WebBrowser control to load the specified HTML page.

   For example, the following line causes your application to start with Microsoft's home page displayed in its view (assuming you're connected to the Internet when you start the application):

   ```
   Navigate( _T("http://www.microsoft.com"),0,0,0);
   ```

Try This

Create a Browser

Now it's time to try your hand at it. If you take the time to create a default `CHtmlView` project, compile it, and run it, you'll have a better chance of understanding the rest of the material in this chapter.

Follows these steps:

1. Run AppWizard.
2. Select an MFC exe project and name it FirstCHTML.
3. Select a single-document interface that supports document/view.
4. Choose all default options until dialog box 4. In that dialog box, deselect the docking toolbar, status bar, and printing options.
5. Keep the default settings for dialog box 5.
6. When dialog box 6 appears, change the `FirstCHTMLView` class so its base class is `CHtmlView`.
7. Compile the application.
8. Run the application.

◆ ◆ ◆ ◆ ◆

Navigating CHtmlViews

When a program that's based on the `CHtmlView` class runs, users can navigate for themselves by clicking the HTML hyperlinks. This requires absolutely no code for the application developer—the underlying Web Browser control takes care of everything. But, somewhere along the way, you may have a reason for navigating to different URLs and this section shows you how to do it.

The first obvious thing you want to provide users with is the ability to go backward and forward through the history list. For instance, if they're at a Web page and they want to back up to the Web page where they were previously, you must give them a way to do this. Internet Explorer has the right and left arrow icons on the toolbar that enable users to back up and go forward. But these aren't built into the Web Browser control.

The easiest user interface that will enable users to go forward and backward is made up of a few menu selections. Later, you can add buttons to your toolbar. The following function moves to the previous Web page:

```
void CMyHtmlView::Back()
{

        GoBack();

}
```

The following function moves to the next page:

```
void CMyHtmlView::Forward()
{

        GoForward();

}
```

Three other important functions that users will want are `Stop()`, `Refresh()`, `GoHome()`, and `GoSearch()`. The `Stop()` function terminates retrieval of the current Web page contents. The `Refresh()` function refreshes the current Web page by re-retrieving the data from the Web server. If users want to go to their home pages, the `GoHome()` function can be used (the home page is retrieved from the registry preferences, which are set by Internet Explorer). In addition, the `GoSearch()` function takes the user to his default search page (once again, this is set with Internet Explorer).

Two functions enable you to take users directly to a new URL. The `Navigate()` and `Navigate2()` functions are the ones we're interested in here. The only difference between them is the way in which each interprets the URL. The `Navigate()` function expects URLs to be relative, and the `Navigate2()` function expects URLs to contain a full path.

For example, a user may be viewing a Web page that's located at `www.myserver.com/first/second/test.html` and want to move to `www.myserver.com/first/second/third/othertest.html`. The new URL is simply one level deeper in the subdirectory hierarchy. The following code will work perfectly to go to the new URL:

```
Navigate( "third/othertest.html" );
```

The following code, though, would not work because the `Navigate2()` function expects an absolute address:

```
Navigate2( "third/othertest.html" );
```

Instead, if you wanted to use the `Navigate2()` function, you'd have to do the following:

```
Navigate2(
  "www.myserver.com/first.second/third/othertest.html");
```

CHtmlDemo1

Our first demo program is a simple browser contained within a `CHtmlView` window. It uses a total of six functions from the `CHtmlView` class. They are `Stop()`, `GoBack()`, `GoForward()`, `GoHome()`, `GoSearch()`, and `Navigate2()`.

Users can navigate by clicking the HTML hyperlinks. They can also use the menus or toolbar buttons that navigate back, forward, and to a specific URL, among other things. With the exception of a simple dialog box that enables users to enter a new URL, all the code added to the project can be found in the CHtmlDemo1View.cpp source code module (see also Listing 30-1).

CHtmlDemo1
CD-ROM Location: **Chap30\CHtmlDemo1**
Program Name: **CHtmlDemo1.EXE**
Source Code Modules in Text: **CHtmlDemo1View.cpp**

✦ ✦ ✦ ✦ ✦

Listing 30-1: **CHtmlDemo1View**

```
// CHtmlDemo1View.cpp : implementation of the
// CCHtmlDemo1View class
//

#include "stdafx.h"
#include "CHtmlDemo1.h"

#include "CHtmlDemo1Doc.h"
#include "CHtmlDemo1View.h"

#include "NewURL.h"

/////////////////////////////////////////////////////////////
// CCHtmlDemo1View construction/destruction

CCHtmlDemo1View::CCHtmlDemo1View()
{
}

CCHtmlDemo1View::~CCHtmlDemo1View()
{
```

```
}

BOOL CCHtmlDemo1View::PreCreateWindow(CREATESTRUCT& cs)
{
  return CHtmlView::PreCreateWindow(cs);
}

/////////////////////////////////////////////////////////////////
// CCHtmlDemo1View drawing

void CCHtmlDemo1View::OnDraw(CDC* pDC)
{
  CCHtmlDemo1Doc* pDoc = GetDocument();
  ASSERT_VALID(pDoc);
}

void CCHtmlDemo1View::OnInitialUpdate()
{
  CHtmlView::OnInitialUpdate();

  Navigate2(_T("http://www.microsoft.com/visualc/"),
    NULL,NULL);
}

/////////////////////////////////////////////////////////////////
// CCHtmlDemo1View message handlers

void CCHtmlDemo1View::OnNavigateBack()
{

  GoBack();

}

void CCHtmlDemo1View::OnNavigateForward()
{

  GoForward();

}

void CCHtmlDemo1View::OnNavigateGoto()
{
  CNewURL NewURL;

  if( NewURL.DoModal() == IDOK )
    Navigate2( NewURL.m_strNewURL, 0, 0, 0 );

}

void CCHtmlDemo1View::OnNavigateHome()
```

(continued)

Listing 30-1 *(continued)*

```
{

  GoHome();

}

void CCHtmlDemo1View::OnNavigateSearch()
{

  GoSearch();

}

void CCHtmlDemo1View::OnNavigateStop()
{

  Stop();

}
```

When the program first runs, it will display the Web page at Microsoft's Visual C++ site. You can use the navigation buttons to get to other sites, such as `www.excite.com`, as shown in Figure 30-3.

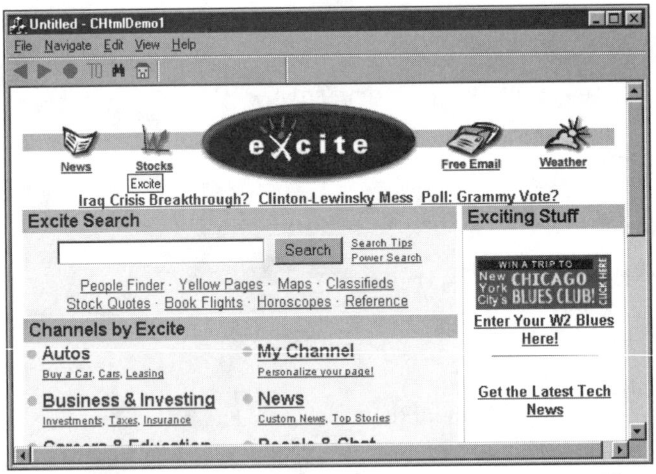

Figure 30-3: This simple browser will take you about anywhere, such as http://www.excite.com.

HTML Document Information Retrieval

Despite the fact that the Web Browser control does most everything for you, a lot of interactions are still possible between the application and the control. For example, obtaining the current URL so you can update your program and display the URL for users will probably be important to you. The following code gets the location name and sets the frame windows text so users can see the location they're currently viewing:

```
CMainFrame *pFrame = (CMainFrame *) AfxGetMainWnd();
pFrame->SetWindowText( GetLocationName() );
```

It may be important for you to know the state of the Web Browser control. You may decide to wait on some activities if the control is in the middle of a transfer or update. The `GetReadyState()` function can be used to retrieve the control's current state, as follows:

```
int State = GetReadyState();
```

The values you get back are described in Table 30–1.

Table 30-1
Return values from GetReadyState()

Value	*Description*
READYSTATE_UNINITIALIZED	The default initialization state.
READYSTATE_LOADING	The object is currently loading its properties.
READYSTATE_LOADED	The object has been initialized.
READYSTATE_INTERACTIVE	The object is interactive, but not all its data is available.
READYSTATE_COMPLETE	The object has received all its data.

If all you must know is whether the Web Browser control is busy, there's a simpler function than `GetReadyState()`. It's `GetBusy()`, and it returns `TRUE` or `FALSE`. If the control is busy retrieving data or downloading a file, the return value will be `TRUE`; otherwise, the return value will be `FALSE`.

Two functions, `GetOffline()` and `SetOffline()`, may be useful if you want to know if the Web Browser control is offline or if you want to set it to offline. The following code illustrates how you can find out whether the control is online or offline:

```
BOOL bOffline = GetOffline();
if( bOffline )
  AfxMessageBox("The Web Browser control is offline.");
```

```
else
  AfxMessageBox("The Web Browser control is online.");
```

The next two functions set the control to an offline state and an online state, respectively:

```
void SetControlToOffline( void )
{
  SetOffline( TRUE );
}

void SetControlToOnline( void )
{
  SetOffline( FALSE );
}
```

Some `CHtmlView` member functions apply only to the Internet Explorer application. These functions will succeed on the Web Browser control, but they will have no visible effect. These functions are `GetAddressBar()`, `GetFullName()`, `GetStatusBar()`, `SetAddressBar()`, `SetFullScreen()`, `SetMenuBar()`, `SetStatusBar()`, and `SetToolBar()`.

Blocking and Logging URLs for a CHtmlView Application

One of today's hot topics is blocking Internet sites (to keep children from pornographic sites, to keep employees from goofing off at entertainment sites, or to prevent access to certain sites from public terminals, for example). You can write your own browser program and use the functions in the `CHtmlView` class to carry this out easily.

The function we use to perform the blocking operations is `OnBeforeNavigate2()`. This function can be declared in your `CHtmlView`-derived class as a virtual function. It will then be called every time the Web Browser control is ready to navigate to a new URL. The prototype for this function is as follows:

```
virtual void OnBeforeNavigate2( LPCTSTR lpszURL, DWORD nFlags,
LPCTSTR lpszTargetFrameName, CByteArray& baPostedData,
LPCTSTR lpszHeaders, BOOL* pbCancel );
```

The parameters of this function are described in Table 30-2.

Table 30-2
The OnBeforeNavigate2() Parameters

Parameter	*Description*
lpszURL	A pointer to a string containing the URL to which to navigate.
nFlags	Reserved for future use.
lpszTargetFrameName	A string that contains the name of the frame in which to display the resource or NULL if no named frame is targeted for the resource.
baPostedData	A reference to a CByteArray object that contains the data to send to the server if the HTTP POST transaction is being used.
lpszHeaders	A pointer to a string containing additional HTTP headers to send to the server (HTTP URLs only). The headers can specify such things as the action required of the server, the type of data being passed to the server, or a status code.
pbCancel	A pointer to a cancel flag. An application can set this parameter to nonzero to cancel the navigation operation, or to zero to allow it to proceed.

It's easy to deny access to a URL. Simply check your own code to see if you want to deny a URL and if you do, set `pbCancel` to `TRUE`. The following code performs just such an operation:

```
void CCHtmlDemo2View::OnBeforeNavigate2( LPCTSTR lpszURL,
  DWORD nFlags, LPCTSTR lpszTargetFrameName,
  CByteArray& baPostedData, LPCTSTR lpszHeaders,
  BOOL* pbCancel )
{
  // Call a function elsewhere in the class
  // to see if we should block this site.
  BOOL bFound = ShouldThisURLBeBlocked( lpszURL );

  // If the URL was found in the list, we'll block.
  // First, alert users to the block, then set
  // *pbCancel to TRUE so the Web Browser control
  // will not navigate to the URL.
  if( bFound ){
    AfxMessageBox( "The site is blocked." );
    *pbCancel = TRUE;
    }

}
```

Another important function you may want to perform is to log all URLs to a file (to look through a log file and see if undesirable sites have been navigated, for example). The function we'll use to log URLs to which we've navigated is `OnNavigateComplete2()`. This function can be declared in your `CHtmlView`-derived class as a virtual function. It will then be called every time the Web Browser control completes navigation to a new URL. The prototype for this function is as follows:

```
virtual void OnNavigateComplete2( LPCTSTR strURL );
```

The `strURL` parameter is a string expression that evaluates to the URL, UNC filename, or PIDL (a pointer to an item identifier list) that was navigated to.

The URL parameter can be a PIDL in the case of a shell name space entity for which there is no URL representation. The URL contained in `strURL` can be different from the URL the browser was told to navigate to, because this URL is the canonicalized and qualified URL. For example, if an application specifies a URL of `www.microsoft.com` in a call to `Navigate()` or `Navigate2()`, the URL passed by `OnNavigateComplete2` will be `"http://www.microsoft.com/"`. Also, if the server has redirected the browser to a different URL, the redirected URL will be reflected here.

To log URLs that have been navigated to, simply open a file for writing (in append mode) and write the URL. You may consider writing other information, such as the time and date, as shown in the following code:

```
void CCHtmlDemo2View::OnNavigateComplete2(LPCTSTR strURL)
{
  CFile cf;

  // Attempt to open an existing file.
  if( !cf.Open( "URLHist.dat",
    CFile::modeRead | CFile::modeWrite ) ){

    // If the file didn't exist, attempt to create it.
    if( !cf.Open( "URLHist.dat",
      CFile::modeCreate | CFile::modeWrite ) )
      return;
    }

  // Seek to the end of the file so we'll append.
  cf.SeekToEnd();
  // Write the URL.
  cf.Write( strURL, strlen( strURL ) );
  // Write a carriage return/line feed pair.
  cf.Write( "\15\12", 2 );

}
```

CHtmlViewDemo2

The second demo program in this chapter, `CHtmlViewDemo2`, does two important things: it keeps a list of URLs to block in a Block.dat file, and it logs into a URLHist.dat log file all URLs that were navigated to. Users can add to the block list at any time when the program is running. Additional URLs can also be added to the Block.dat file with a text editor — these additions will be loaded the next time the `CHtmlViewDemo2` program runs.

After each URL is successfully navigated to, the URL is logged to the URLHist.dat file. Later you can look at the log file to see where a user has gone. The sites that are blocked aren't added to the log file; this may be a useful addition to the logging capability.

Demo Program

CHtmlDemo2

CD-ROM Location: **Chap30\CHtmlDemo2**

Program Name: **CHtmlDemo2.EXE**

Source Code Modules in Text: **CHtmlDemo2View.cpp**

◆ ◆ ◆ ◆ ◆

Listing 30-2: CHtmlDemo2View

```
// CHtmlDemo2View.cpp : implementation of the
// CCHtmlDemo2View class
//

#include "stdafx.h"
#include "CHtmlDemo2.h"

#include "CHtmlDemo2Doc.h"
#include "CHtmlDemo2View.h"

#include "NewURL.h"
#include "NewBlock.h"

#include "MainFrm.h"

/////////////////////////////////////////////////////////////
// CCHtmlDemo2View construction/destruction

CCHtmlDemo2View::CCHtmlDemo2View()
{

  LoadBlockList();

}
```

(continued)

Listing 30-2 *(continued)*

```
CCHtmlDemo2View::~CCHtmlDemo2View()
{
}

BOOL CCHtmlDemo2View::PreCreateWindow(CREATESTRUCT& cs)
{
  return CHtmlView::PreCreateWindow(cs);
}

/////////////////////////////////////////////////////////////////////////////
// CCHtmlDemo2View drawing

void CCHtmlDemo2View::OnDraw(CDC* pDC)
{
  CCHtmlDemo2Doc* pDoc = GetDocument();
  ASSERT_VALID(pDoc);
}

void CCHtmlDemo2View::OnInitialUpdate()
{
  CHtmlView::OnInitialUpdate();

  Navigate2(_T("http://www.microsoft.com/visualc/"),
    NULL,NULL);
}

/////////////////////////////////////////////////////////////////////////////
// CCHtmlDemo2View message handlers

void CCHtmlDemo2View::OnNavigateBack()
{

  GoBack();

}

void CCHtmlDemo2View::OnNavigateForward()
{

  GoForward();

}

void CCHtmlDemo2View::OnNavigateGoto()
{
  CNewURL NewURL;

  if( NewURL.DoModal() == IDOK )
    Navigate2( NewURL.m_strNewURL, 0, 0, 0 );
```

```
}

void CCHtmlDemo2View::OnNavigateHome()
{

  GoHome();

}

void CCHtmlDemo2View::OnNavigateSearch()
{

  GoSearch();

}

void CCHtmlDemo2View::OnNavigateStop()
{

  Stop();

}

void CCHtmlDemo2View::LoadBlockList( void )
{
  CStdioFile cf;

  // Attempt to open the data file that contains the list
  // of URLs to block. If it's not there, there are no
  // URLs to block so we just return.
  if( !cf.Open( "Block.dat",
    CFile::modeRead | CFile::typeText ) )
    return;

  // Read through each line of the file and store the
  // result in the CStringArray.
  CString strTemp;
  while( cf.ReadString( strTemp ) )
    m_strBlockList.Add( strTemp );

}

void CCHtmlDemo2View::OnNavigateAdditemtoblocklist()
{
  CNewBlock NewBlock;

  // Instantiate the dialog box in which users will
  // enter a URL which the want blocked. Remember, if
  // users who are navigating to a specific site enter
  // www.excite.com, the OnBeforeNavigate2() function
  // will actually receive http://www.excite.com/
```

(continued)

Listing 30-2 *(continued)*

```
  if( NewBlock.DoModal() == IDOK ){
    CFile cf;

    // Add the string to the list.
    m_strBlockList.Add( NewBlock.m_strNewBlock );

    // Attempt to open the file which
    // contains the URLs to block.
    if( !cf.Open( "Block.dat",
      CFile::modeRead | CFile::modeWrite ) ){

      // If the file doesn't open, attempt to create
      // a file.
      if( !cf.Open( "Block.dat",
        CFile::modeCreate | CFile::modeWrite ) ){

        // If the file creation fails, alert the user
        // to the problem and return.
        AfxMessageBox( "Error while opening data file" );
        return;
        }
      }

    // Seek to the end of the file so
    // that we'll be appending.
    cf.SeekToEnd();

    // Write the URL to the file.
    cf.Write( NewBlock.m_strNewBlock + "\15\12",
      NewBlock.m_strNewBlock.GetLength() + 2 );

    }

}

void CCHtmlDemo2View::OnBeforeNavigate2( LPCTSTR lpszURL,
  DWORD nFlags, LPCTSTR lpszTargetFrameName,
  CByteArray& baPostedData, LPCTSTR lpszHeaders,
  BOOL* pbCancel )
{

  // Look through the list.
  for( int i=0; i<m_strBlockList.GetSize(); i++ ){

    // Pull out the string at this index. It's
    // easier to work with a single CString than
    // messing with the CStringArray.
    CString strTemp;
```

```
      strTemp = m_strBlockList.GetAt( i );

      // Use strnicmp to compare the string in the list
      // with the string that's passed in.
      if( !strnicmp( lpszURL, strTemp,
        strTemp.GetLength() ) ){

        // If we find a match, we'll block.
        *pbCancel = TRUE;

        // Alert user to the block.
        AfxMessageBox( "The site is blocked." );
        break;
        }
      }

}

void CCHtmlDemo2View::OnNavigateComplete2(LPCTSTR strURL)
{
  CFile cf;

  // Attempt to open an existing file.
  if( !cf.Open( "URLHist.dat",
    CFile::modeRead | CFile::modeWrite ) ){

    // If the file didn't exist, attempt to create it.
    if( !cf.Open( "URLHist.dat",
      CFile::modeCreate | CFile::modeWrite ) )
        return;
    }

  // Seek to the end of the file so we'll append.
  cf.SeekToEnd();
  // Write the URL.
  cf.Write( strURL, strlen( strURL ) );
  // Write a carriage return/line feed pair.
  cf.Write( "\15\12", 2 );

  // Get a pointer to the frame window.
  CMainFrame *pFrame = (CMainFrame *) AfxGetMainWnd();
  // Set the frame window's caption text to contain
  // the URL.
  pFrame->SetWindowText( strURL );

}
```

When the program runs, it will look just like the `CHtmlDemo1` program, but if you add any items to your block list, you'll get the message shown in Figure 30-4.

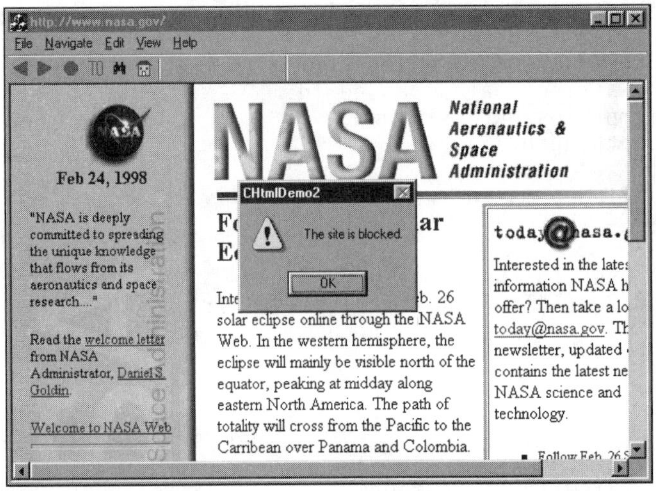

Figure 30-4: After a URL is in the block list, users won't be able to go there.

Summary

MFC's `CHtmlView` class is a powerful tool in the realm of Internet programming. It makes using the Microsoft Web Browser control easy. You can have a Web browser application working in a matter of minutes. Before Microsoft's Web Browser control was made available as a control, software developers either spent months parsing HTML files and displaying them, or spent hundreds of dollars for third-party libraries. The Web Browser control cut development times down to minutes instead of months. In addition, the CHtmlView class goes even further to make the Web Browser control easy to use. After reading this chapter, you should have no trouble creating a browser for your specific needs.

✦ ✦ ✦

PART

VIII

Using Visual Studio Tools

I've often thought there are many development tools for programmers that are just dying to be developed. The only problem is that such tools should be integrated with the integrated development environment (IDE). Good news: This section shows you how to write your own Wizards — so now you can create that add-on tool for Visual C++ that you've always wanted to add.

You learn how to use different programming languages in conjunction — Visual Basic with Visual C++, and Visual J++ with Visual C++. Reading this section can enhance your opportunities to use *all* the tools in Visual Studio.

✦ ✦ ✦ ✦

In This Part

Chapter 31
Using J++ with C++

Chapter 32
Using C++ and Visual Basic Together

Chapter 33
Writing a Custom AppWizard

✦ ✦ ✦ ✦

CHAPTER 31

Using J++ with C++

In This Chapter

Why use J++?

Creating a J++ project

Working with Java images

Making Java live on the Web

Working with a banner applet

Understanding the MakeBanner program

You bought Visual Studio because it has all the tools, such as Visual C++, Visual J++, Visual InterDev, and Visual Basic. The challenge is to find a use for all these tools, not just your favorite development tool. It's even better if you can get the tools to work in tandem. This chapter gives you a way to use J++ and C++ together. There are many more methods you can use, and after you work through this chapter, you'll easily come up with some of them.

In this chapter, you create a Java banner applet embedded in a Web page. The applet uses two alternating images to present information to users. Such banners usually contain advertisements. A C++ program creates banner images and uploads them to the Web. This C++ program could even edit the HTML file on the Web to accommodate changes made necessary by varying image sizes. This automatic HTML formatting feature isn't implemented in our demo program, but you could make the modification fairly easily; doing so might be a good exercise after you have completed the demo project. After reading and working through this chapter, you'll be equipped to use J++ and C++ together to automate Web updates.

Creating a J++ Project

The Banner applet project is included on the CD-ROM, so we won't be creating it as part of the chapter's tutorial. The applet, however, can be found on the CD-ROM for you to use in your web pages. It will, however, be helpful to go through the basic procedure for creating an applet in case you're not familiar with it. Then we'll show you how to edit the applet source code to incorporate the elements necessary for applets such as the banner applet, and delete elements that aren't necessary.

Start by running J++. Select New Project from the File menu. A New Project dialog box will appear. Make sure the New tab is selected. In the Visual J++ Projects folder, open the Web Pages folder. With the Web Pages folder open, you'll see an object in the right side of the dialog box labeled "Applet on HTML." First, enter your project name in the Name field (the name we used is `Demo1`; for this exercise, name yours **Demo1** as well). Then add something suitable in the Location field (our location is d:\work\Demo1). Select the "Applet on HTML" object and click the Open button. Figure 31-1 shows the New Project dialog box for our Demo1 Web applet project.

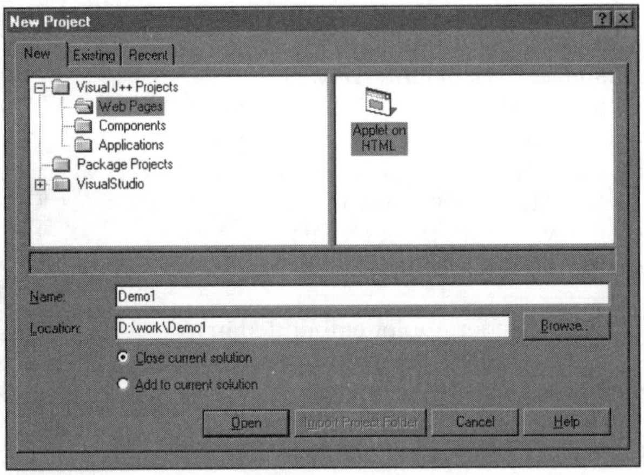

Figure 31-1: The New Project dialog box set to create a Web applet project named Demo1.

After the project has been created, find the Project Explorer window. If you can't find it, use the View menu and select Project Explorer to bring it into view. Open the Demo1 item in the Project Explorer window, and you'll see two files: `Applet1.jav` and `Page1.htm`. Open the `Applet1.java` file by double-clicking it. Figure 31-2 shows our project with the Project Explorer window in view and the Applet1.java source code displayed.

Before going any further, we'll compile and run the applet. From the Build menu, select Build Demo1. Then select Start Without Debugging from the Debug menu. The applet will appear with the text `Applet1 (param)`.

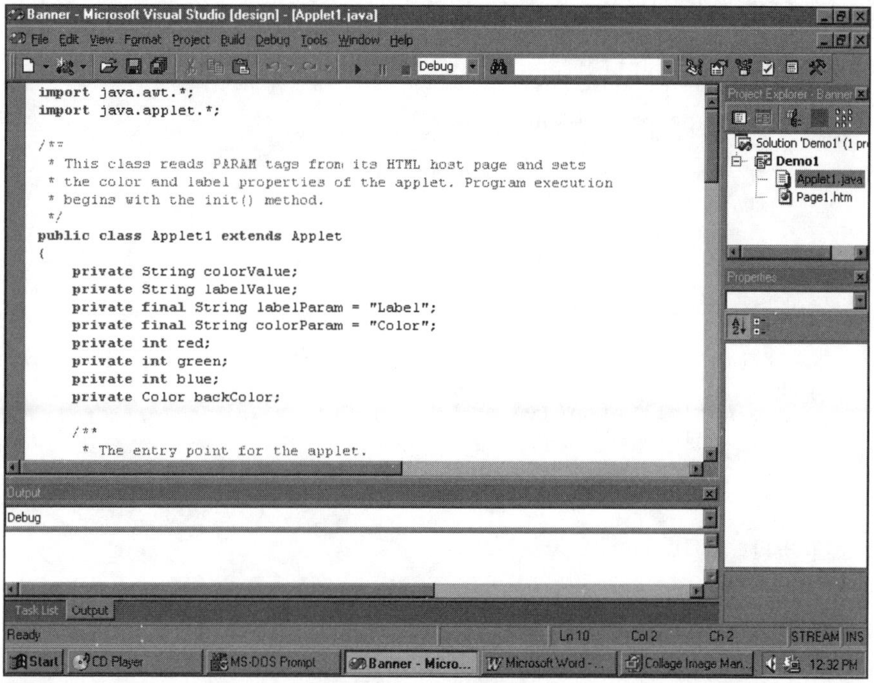

Figure 31-2: Here's how our Demo1 project looks with the Project Explorer window in view and the Applet1.java source code opened.

Making a threaded applet

The first thing we need to do is add code to the applet so it's running as a threaded applet. The difference between threaded applets and non-threaded applets is that non-threaded applets just respond to events; threaded applets maintain an execution loop inside of a `run()` method that allows them to perform actions at various intervals. Adding support for threading is easy—you just add a global Thread class named Applet1 and three methods.

First, add the following class declaration at the top of the Applet1 class above the `private String colorValue` line:

```
private Thread m_Applet1 = null;
```

Next, add the following three methods to your applet:

```
public void start()
  {
    if (m_Applet1 == null)
    {
      m_Applet1 = new Thread(this);
      m_Applet1.start();
    }
  }

  public void stop()
  {
    if (m_Applet1 != null)
    {
      m_Applet1.stop();
      m_Applet1 = null;
    }
  }

  public void run()
  {
    while (true)
    {
      try
      {
        repaint();
        Thread.sleep(500);
      }
      catch (InterruptedException e)
      {
        stop();
      }
    }
  }
```

Next, you add the text **implements Runnable** to the `Applet1` class specification, as follows:

```
public class Applet1 extends Applet implements Runnable
```

After you've made these changes, compile the applet to make sure you haven't made any typos. The output window displays the message `Solution Build SUCCEEDED` if everything goes okay.

Removing unnecessary code

Some code in this applet is placed there for your convenience: `getParameterInfo()`, `initError()`, and `initForm()`. Now that they've served their purpose, we can remove these items so the applet is simpler and easier to understand. One last thing is to remove any reference to `label1`.

Adding code that draws to the applet window

The first thing we need to do to be able to draw to the applet window is to add our own `paint()` method to override the native `paint()` method. The following code can be added anywhere in the class:

```
public void paint(Graphics g)
{
  g.drawString( "m_value=" + m_value, 30, 30 );
}
```

You may have noticed a variable in the `paint()` method named `m_value`. We need to declare that variable and another named `m_addition`. Add the following two declarations right below where the Demo1 Thread is declared:

```
private int m_value = 0;
private int m_addition = 10;
```

There's one last thing to do before you see anything happen. We're going to add the `m_addition` value to the `m_value` variable each time through the execution loop. Our modified `run()` method follows:

```
public void run()
  {
    while (true)
    {
      try
      {
        repaint();
        Thread.sleep(500);
        m_value += m_addtion;
      }
      catch (InterruptedException e)
      {
        stop();
      }
    }
  }
```

Compile the applet and then run it. You'll see `m_value` increase by 10 every 500 milliseconds. Figure 31-3 shows our applet running.

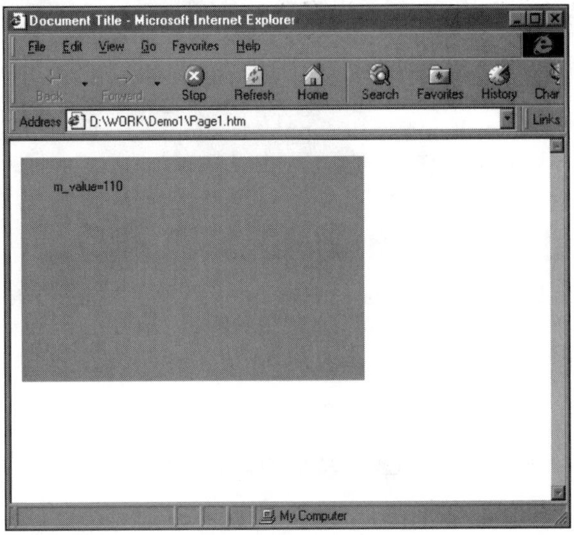

Figure 31-3: After adding the thread and draw support for our Demo1 applet, we can see the m_value increase in value every half second.

Applet parameters

Sometimes you may want to give an applet a parameter so values can change easily without compiling the applet. Continuing with our `Demo1` applet, we'll add the ability to change the value of `m_addition`. That way, we can change how much the `m_value` variable changes each time through the execution loop. We can even make the parameter a negative value and have `m_value` decrease.

There are two things we must do to add the parameter support for the `m_addition` variable. First, we have to add the value to the HTML file. (Note that the applet was created with two default HTML parameters, named Label and Color.) Let's set the value of `m_addition` to 25. Here's how we'll add an HTML parameter that does this:

```
<applet
  code=Applet1.class
  name=Applet1
  width=320
  height=200 >
  <param name=Label value="Applet1 (param)">
  <param name=Color value="8888FF">
  <param name=Addition value="25">
</applet>
```

The next thing we must do is load the parameter value from our applet code. If you look at the `init()` method, you'll see `getParameter()`used twice—once for the Label parameter and once for the Color parameter. The thing I don't like about this code is that if either parameter is missing from the HTML file, the applet causes an exception. The exception is dutifully caught in the default code, but the applet is still prevented from running. The best solution is to have a default value for any parameter variables, and check to see if the appropriate parameter is contained in the HTML file. If it is, go ahead and assign the varaible with its value. If it's not there, skip over the assignment and use the default value. The following code shows you how to safely get an HTML parameter without generating an exception if the parameter isn't in the HTML file:

```
String param;
param = getParameter("Addition");
if (param != null)
  m_addition = Integer.parseInt( param );
```

Java Images

Basic image handling in Java is easy. The Image class in `java.awt` provides abstract methods to represent common image behavior, and special methods defined in Applet and Graphics give you everything needed to load and display images in your applet as easily as drawing a rectangle. In this section, you'll learn about how to get and draw images in your applets.

Loading images

To display an image in your applet, you must first load that image over the net into your applet. Images are stored as separate files from your Java class files, so you have to tell the applet where to find them.

The Applet class provides a method called `getImage()`, which loads an image and automatically creates an instance of the Image class for you. To use it, all you have to do is import the `java.awt.Image` class, and then give `getImage()` the URL of the image you want to load. There are two ways of performing the latter step:

- ✦ The `getImage()` method with a single argument (an object of type URL) retrieves the image at that URL.
- ✦ The `getImage()` method with two arguments — the base URL (also a URL object) and a string representing the path or filename of the actual image (relative to the base) — retrieves the image.

Although the first method may seem easier (just plug in the URL as a URL object), the second is more flexible. Remember, because you're compiling Java files, if you include a hard-coded URL of an image and then move your files around to a different location, you have to recompile all your files.

The latter method, therefore, is usually the one to use. In fact, the Applet class provides two additional methods that help with the base URL argument to this `getImage()`:

✦ The `getDocumentBase()` method returns a URL object representing the directory of the HTML file that contains the applet. So, for example, if the HTML file is located at `http://www.myserver.com/htmlfiles/javahtml`, `getDocumentBase()` returns a URL pointing to that path.

✦ The `getCodeBase()` method returns a string representing the directory where this applet is contained — which may or may not be the same directory as the HTML file, depending on if the `CODEBASE` attribute in `<APPLET>` is set.

The decision about whether to use `getDocumentBase()` or `getCodeBase()` depends on if your images are relative to your HTML files or relative to your Java class files. Use the one that applies to your situation. Not that either of these methods is more flexible than hard-coding a URL or pathname into the `getImage()` method — using either `getDocumentBase()` or `getCodeBase()` enables you to move your HTML files and applets around, and Java can still find your images.

The following examples can give you an idea of how to use `getImage()`.

The first call to `getImage()` retrieves the file at that specific URL (`http://www.server.com/files/image.gif`). If any part of that URL changes, you have to recompile your applet to take the new path into account.

```
Image img =
  getImage( ""http://www.server.com/files/image.gif"" );
```

In the next form of `getImage()`, the image.gif file is in the same directory as the HTML files that refer to this applet:

```
Image img =
  getImage( getDocumentBase(), ""image.gif"" );
```

The following example is in the form in which the file image.gif is in the same directory as the applet itself:

```
Image img =
  getImage( getCodeBase(), "image.gif" );
```

If you have lots of image files, it's common to put them into their own subdirectory. The next example looks for the file image.gif in the images directory, which is in the same directory as the Java applet:

```
Image img =
  getImage( getCodeBase(), "images/image.gif" );
```

If the image file you specify can't be found, `getImage()` returns null. Your applet continues to run — you just don't see that image appear when you try to draw it.

Expert Tip

Image Formats

Currently, Java supports images in GIF and JPEG formats. Other formats may be available later; however, for now, your images should be in either GIF or JPEG format.

◆ ◆ ◆ ◆ ◆

Drawing images

All that `getImage()` does is retrieve an image and place it into an instance of the Image class. Now that the image has been loaded, you have to do something with it.

The most likely thing you're going to want to do is display it somewhere in the applet window. The `Graphics` class provides two methods to do just that, and both are named `drawImage()`.

The first version of `drawImage()` takes four arguments: the image to display, the *x* and *y* coordinates of the top-left corner to which the image is drawn, and `this`. The following example draws an `Image` class named `img` inside the `paint()` method at position (10, 10):

```
public void paint(Graphics g)
{
  g.drawImage( img, 10, 10, this );
}
```

This `drawImage()` method does what you'd expect it to: It draws an image in its original dimensions with the top-left corner of the image positioned at the given x and y position. Listing 31-1 shows an extremely simple applet that loads an image and displays it in the `paint()` method. The `paint()` method is an overridable Java method that handles all Java window redraws. (This applet project isn't on the CD-ROM, but is presented here as an example.)

List 31-1: Simple Applet That Loads and Displays an Image

```
import java.awt.Graphics;
import java.awt.Image;
public class Simple extends Applet
{
  Image img;

  public void init()
  {
    img = getImage( getCodeBase(), "image.gif" );
  }

  public void paint(Graphics g)
  {
```

```
      g.drawImage( img, 0, 0, this );
    }
  }
```

The second `drawImage()` method takes six arguments: the image to draw, the *x* and *y* coordinates, destination width and height values, and `this`. If the width and height arguments for the destination are smaller or larger than the actual image, the image is automatically scaled to fit. Using those extra arguments enables you to squeeze and expand images into whatever space you need them to fit. Keep in mind, however, that you may get some image degradation from scaling it differently from its original size.

One helpful hint for scaling images is to find out the size of the actual image that you've loaded, so you can scale it to a specific percentage and retain the width-to-height aspect ratio. Two member methods for the `Image` class enable you to get the image dimensions—they are the `getWidth()` and `getHeight()` methods. Both take a single argument, an instance of `ImageObserver`, which tracks the loading of the image. Most of the time you can use `this` as the argument to either `getWidth()` or `getHeight()`.

Revisiting the example in Listing 31-1, we're going to change it so it draws the image with a width and height of 25 percent of the original image. The modified applet can be seen in Listing 31-2.

Listing 31-2: Applet That Loads an Image and Draws It at 25 Percent Original Size

```
import java.awt.Graphics;
import java.awt.Image;
public class Simple extends Applet
{
  Image img;

  public void init()
  {
    img = getImage( getCodeBase(), "image.gif" );
  }

  public void paint(Graphics g)
  {
    int width = img.getWidth( this );
    int height = img.getHeight( this );
    g.drawImage( img, 0, 0, width / 4, height / 4, this );
  }
}
```

Making Java Live on the Web

After you've created an applet, the chances are pretty good that you'll want to make it available to the entire Web population. To do this, you must upload the various files that make up the applet to a Web site, and test them to make sure nothing breaks in the process.

Uploading applets

Uploading applets to a Web site assumes that you have the authority, and the tools (such as an FTP tool), to do so. If the site you want to add the applet to is maintained by someone other than yourself, you'll have to obtain permission, and perhaps even get the access passwords, if you plan to upload the materials yourself. If you don't already have such authority, you can give the applet and the various files it uses to someone who has the authority to perform the upload.

Creating the Web server directory layout

If this is the first time that Java is being used at a site, it might be a good idea to create a directory structure to contain the Java classes and other associated files, such as audio and graphics files. This is pretty straightforward and similar to how the directory structure is set up on your local drive.

Make sure you know the name of the directory in which the initial HTML file will be located. Many services require an index HTML file in a directory; Web browsers that hit the site load this particular file automatically. If your service has this requirement, then you probably want to place your Java files within this directory.

Connecting to the server

If you have permission to upload files to a site on the Web, then you're ready to get started. A great program to use to upload files is WS_FTP32. If you don't have a copy of this program, you can download a trial version from `http://www.ipswitch.com/junodj/ws_ftp32.htm`. To connect to a server with WS_FTP32, follow these steps:

1. After WS_FTP32 is installed, run it. The Session Properties dialog box (shown in Figure 31-4) appears on top of the main program window.

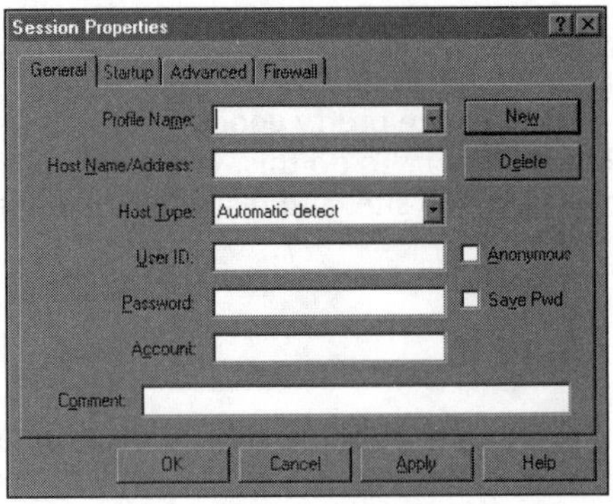

Figure 31-4: The Session Properties dialog box appears when WS_FTP32 first runs.

2. In the Session Properties dialog box, enter information about the destination server, including its name (or IP address), your login name, and your password. If you have the Save Pwd check box selected, all the information is saved, including the password, and you can log in by simply selecting the server from the list.
3. Fill in the Profile Name with something you'll easily recognize from the list of FTP sites.
4. When the information is correctly entered, click the OK button; the program tries to log on to the server.

   After the Profile Session dialog box is gone, you'll see that the application has two sides. The left list box contains a listing of the current directory, even when you're not logged on to a server. Once logged in, you'll see a directory listing in the list box on the right half of the screen (as shown in Figure 31-5). This only shows the names of the files and directories, not file and directory details. To get full file and directory information, click the DirInfo button.

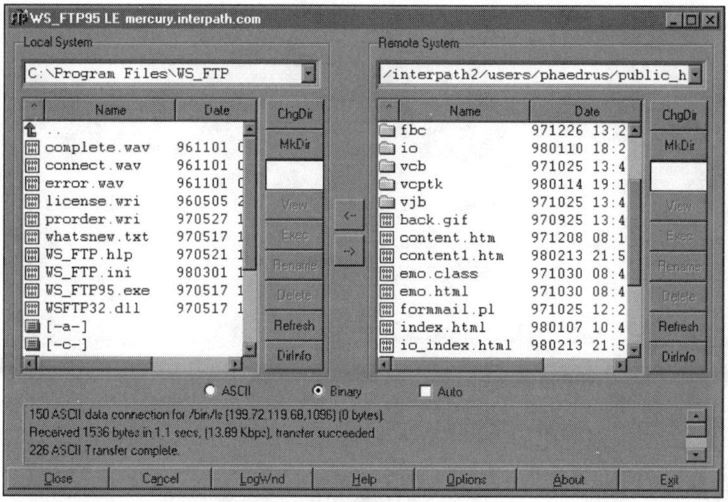

Figure 31-5: The left list box contains the current local directory and the right list box contains the current server directory.

Uploading the applet

After you're connected, you can upload the files. I'll use the Banner applet as an example. You must upload the `Banner.class`, `Banner.html`, `Banner1.gif`, and `Banner2.gif` files. Here are the steps for uploading files:

1. Navigate the left list box so it shows all the Banner files, and highlight them (as shown in Figure 31-6).
2. Click the → button.

   The files are uploaded to the server. Because the files are short and most modem connections are relatively fast, you won't see much more than a flash as the upload-progress box appears during the upload. For longer files, the upload progress box stays visible long enough for you to see it.

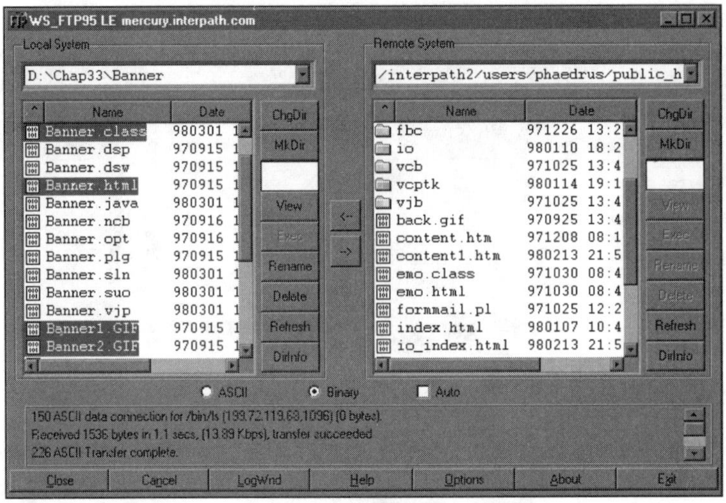

Figure 31-6: Highlight the files you want to upload, and then click the → button.

Editing the HTML file

Editing the HTML file is an easy way to change the way your applet looks. You can center the applet, justify it on the left side of the browser window, or justify it on the right side of the browser window. Many of the applets you'll create have parameters that reside in the HTML file. Changing them alters the behavior of the applet.

After the five Banner files are on the server in the correct directory, the main HTML file (index.html in my case) must be edited so users have the chance to see your applet. For now, we'll just have the main HTML file bring up the Banner.html file in response to a user selection. Add the following text to your main HTML file:

```
<h3><p>Run <a href=Banner.html><I>Banner</a></h3></i><p>
```

The Banner link appears when your browser opens the main HTML file on your site. When you click the HTML line, you'll see the Banner applet run in your browser.

The Banner Applet

After talking about the Banner applet, it's about time we showed it to you. The source code for the applet follows. You can study it so you have a better understanding of all the techniques for threading and images we've been discussing.

Demo Program

Banner
CD-ROM Location: **Chap31\Banner**
Program Name: **Banner.class**
Source Code Modules in Text: **Banner.java**

◆ ◆ ◆ ◆ ◆

Listing 31-3: **The Java Source Code for the Banner Applet**

```
import java.applet.*;
import java.awt.*;

public class Banner extends Applet implements Runnable
{
  private Thread   m_Banner = null;

  // There are two images that alternate.
  // The image data is contained in the
  // classes m_image1 and m_image2.
  // The image filenames are contained in
  // the classes m_image1Name and m_image2Name.
  private Image m_image1;
  private Image m_image2;
  private String m_image1Name;
  private String m_image2Name;

  // The delay contains the delay value
  // for the movement of the image.
  private int m_delay;

  // This is a flag so that the paint()
  // method knows when the images have
  // been loaded.
  private boolean m_loadedImages;

  // We use this to draw to an offscreen image.
  private Image m_offscreenImage;

  // Use these variables to keep track of the
  // image that's currently being drawn and
  // the applet window dimension.
  private int m_currentImage;
  private Dimension m_dimension;

  // Use these variables to keep track of the
  // x and y points at which the image is being
  // drawn, the current effect, and whether we're
  // currently drawing an effect (as opposed to
  // simply allowing refresh drawing).
  private int m_x, m_y;
```

(continued)

Listing 31-3 *(continued)*

```
private int m_effect;
private boolean m_doEffect;

public void init()
{

  // Set initial values in our
  // variables. The following assignments
  // indicate that the images haven't been
  // loaded, the delay is 100 milliseconds,
  // the current image is 1, we're drawing
  // to coordinate ( 0, 0 ), we're not
  // currently drawing an effect, and the
  // current effect is 0.
  m_loadedImages = false;
  m_delay = 1000;
  m_currentImage = 0;
  m_x = m_y = 0;
  m_doEffect = false;
  m_effect = 0;

  // The following code retrieves the
  // applet paremeters from the HTML file.
  // We get both image names and the
  // delay value.
  String param;

  param = getParameter("Image1");
  if (param != null)
    m_image1Name = param;

  param = getParameter("Image2");
  if (param != null)
    m_image2Name = param;

  param = getParameter("Delay");
  if (param != null)
    m_delay = Integer.parseInt(param);

  // Here we get the applet window size.
  m_dimension = getSize();

  // Create an offscreen image that's
  // the same size as the applet window.
  m_offscreenImage =
    createImage(m_dimension.width, m_dimension.height);

}

// This method loads an image. After the
// image load has been initiated, it waits
```

```
// for completion before returning.
public Image waitForImage( String imageName )
{
  Image image;
  MediaTracker tracker = new MediaTracker( this );

  // Initiate the image load.
  image = getImage( getCodeBase(), imageName );

  // Add the image to the MediaTracker and wait
  // for completion.
  tracker.addImage( image, 0 );
  try{ tracker.waitForID( 0 ); }
  catch( InterruptedException e ){}

  return( image );
}

public void paint(Graphics g)
{

  // We don't want to draw if the
  // images haven't been loaded yet.
  if( !m_loadedImages )
    return;

  // Get a Graphics class for the offscreen image
  // with which we'll do our offscreen drawing.
  Graphics offscreen =
    m_offscreenImage.getGraphics();

  // There are two cases. The first case is
  // when m_image1 is the applet background
  // and m_image2 is being drawn on top of it.
  if( m_currentImage == 0 )
  {
    offscreen.drawImage( m_image1, 0, 0, this );
    if( m_doEffect )
      offscreen.drawImage( m_image2, m_x, m_y, this );
  }
  // The second case is when m_image2 is the
  // applet background and m_image1 is being
  // drawn on top of it.
  else
  {
    offscreen.drawImage( m_image2, 0, 0, this );
    if( m_doEffect )
      offscreen.drawImage( m_image1, m_x, m_y, this );
  }

  // Draw the offscreen image to the visible
  // applet Graphics context.
```

(continued)

Listing 31-3 *(continued)*

```
    g.drawImage( m_offscreenImage, 0, 0, this );

  }

  public void start()
  {
    if (m_Banner == null)
    {
      m_Banner = new Thread(this);
      m_Banner.start();
    }
  }

  public void stop()
  {
    if (m_Banner != null)
    {
      m_Banner.stop();
      m_Banner = null;
    }
  }

  // We overrode update() so that we could
  // call paint() without drawing a solid
  // rectangle to the applet window as
  // the default update() method does. This
  // would cause window flicker each time
  // repaint() was called from the run()
  // method.
  public void update(Graphics g)
  {
    paint(g);
  }

  public void run()
  {

    // Load the images then indicate
    // that we're done so that the
    // paint() method will perform its
    // job.
    m_image1 = waitForImage( m_image1Name );
    m_image2 = waitForImage( m_image2Name );
    m_loadedImages = true;

    while (true)
    {
      try
      {
        // Repaint the applet window,
        // then sleep for 'delay' milliseconds.
```

```
repaint();
Thread.sleep(m_delay);

switch( m_effect )
{
  case 0:
    // Indicate we're doing
    // an effect, and make
    // the first coordinate
    // adjustment.
    m_doEffect = true;
    m_x = m_dimension.width - 10;
    do{
      // Repaint and sleep.
      repaint();
      Thread.sleep( 50 );
      // Adjust the coordinate
      // and check to see
      // if we're done.
      m_x -= 10;
      if( m_x < 0 )
        m_x = 0;
    }while( m_x > 0 );
    // Set so we know we're
    // not doing an effect,
    // toggle to the alternate
    // image, and set to the
    // next effect.
    m_doEffect = false;
    m_currentImage ^= 1;
    m_effect = 1;
    break;
  case 1:
    // Indicate we're doing
    // an effect, and make
    // the first coordinate
    // adjustment.
    m_doEffect = true;
    m_x = 10 - m_dimension.width;
    do{
      // Repaint and sleep.
      repaint();
      Thread.sleep( 50 );
      // Adjust the coordinate
      // and check to see
      // if we're done.
      m_x += 10;
      if( m_x > 0 )
        m_x = 0;
    }while( m_x < 0 );
    // Set so we know we're
    // not doing an effect,
```

(continued)

Listing 31-3 (continued)

```
      // toggle to the alternate
      // image, and set to the
      // next effect.
      m_doEffect = false;
      m_currentImage ^= 1;
      m_effect = 2;
      break;
    case 2:
      // Indicate we're doing
      // an effect, and make
      // the first coordinate
      // adjustment.
      m_doEffect = true;
      m_y = m_dimension.height - 10;
      do{
        // Repaint and sleep.
        repaint();
        Thread.sleep( 50 );
        // Adjust the coordinate
        // and check to see
        // if we're done.
        m_y -= 10;
        if( m_y < 0  )
          m_y = 0;
      }while( m_y > 0 );
      // Set so we know we're
      // not doing an effect,
      // toggle to the alternate
      // image, and set to the
      // next effect.
      m_doEffect = false;
      m_currentImage ^= 1;
      m_effect = 3;
      break;
    case 3:
      // Indicate we're doing
      // an effect, and make
      // the first coordinate
      // adjustment.
      m_doEffect = true;
      m_y = 10 - m_dimension.height;
      do{
        // Repaint and sleep.
        repaint();
        Thread.sleep( 50 );
        // Adjust the coordinate
        // and check to see
        // if we're done.
        m_y += 10;
        if( m_y > 0  )
          m_y = 0;
```

```
                }while( m_y < 0 );
                // Set so we know we're
                // not doing an effect,
                // toggle to the alternate
                // image, and set to the
                // next effect.
                m_doEffect = false;
                m_currentImage ^= 1;
                m_effect = 0;
                break;
            }

        }
        catch (InterruptedException e)
        {
          stop();
        }
      }
    }

  }
```

The MakeBanner Program

We've written a program that creates two banners for the Banner applet. It does this by loading tiles from a collection of 18 tiles, placing the tiles into a larger banner image, and overlaying a logo image. There's a tile selector dialog box that lets you pick the tile you want for each of the two banner images.

There are many places to change the program to make it more flexible. For example, the banner size is hard coded to a width of 500 and a height of 90. These dimensions could easily be altered via a dialog box that gives users a choice.

After the banner images are created, they can be uploaded to a Web server via FTP. If you select Upload Images, you'll be prompted for a server name, user name, password, and directory. The program uses this information to upload Banner1.gif and Banner2.gif to the server. Here again, allowing users to choose different filenames would be another example of enhancing the program's extensibility.

Demo Program

MakeBanner

CD-ROM Location: **Chap31\MakeBanner**

Program Name: **MakeBanner.EXE**

Source Code Modules in Text: **MakeBannerView.cpp**

✦ ✦ ✦ ✦ ✦

Listing 31-4: **The MakeBannerView.cpp File**

```
// MakeBannerView.cpp : implementation of the
// CMakeBannerView class
//

#include "stdafx.h"
#include "MakeBanner.h"

#include "MakeBannerDoc.h"
#include "MakeBannerView.h"

#include "SelectTile.h"
#include "FTPParams.h"
#include <afxinet.h>

/////////////////////////////////////////////////////////
// CMakeBannerView construction/destruction

CMakeBannerView::CMakeBannerView()
{
  // Set our current tiles to 0 and 9.
  m_nTileOne = 0;
  m_nTileTwo = 9;
  // Set the correct file names.
  m_strTileOne = "Tiles\\Tile1.gif";
  m_strTileTwo = "Tiles\\Tile1.jpg";
  // Create the banner images.
  m_pBannerOne =
    new CImageObject( 500, 90,
      1, 24, RGB( 0, 255, 0 ) );
  m_pBannerTwo =
    new CImageObject( 500, 90,
      1, 24, RGB( 0, 0, 255 ) );
  // Load the logo images.
  m_LogoOne.Load( "Logo1.gif" );
  m_LogoTwo.Load( "Logo2.gif" );
  // Create the banners based on the tile and the logo.
  CreateBanner( m_pBannerTwo,
    &m_LogoTwo, &m_strTileTwo );
  CreateBanner( m_pBannerOne,
    &m_LogoOne, &m_strTileOne );
}

CMakeBannerView::~CMakeBannerView()
{
  // Delete the two dynamically
  // allocated CImageObject pointers.
  delete m_pBannerOne;
  delete m_pBannerTwo;
}

BOOL CMakeBannerView::PreCreateWindow(CREATESTRUCT& cs)
```

```
{
  return CScrollView::PreCreateWindow(cs);
}

///////////////////////////////////////////////////////////
// CMakeBannerView drawing

void CMakeBannerView::OnDraw(CDC* pDC)
{
  CMakeBannerDoc* pDoc = GetDocument();
  ASSERT_VALID(pDoc);

  // Draw both banner images. It's
  // not necessary to set the palette
  // since they're 24-bit.
  m_pBannerOne->Draw( pDC, 10, 10 );
  m_pBannerTwo->Draw( pDC, 10,
    20 + m_pBannerOne->GetHeight() );
}

void CMakeBannerView::OnInitialUpdate()
{
  CScrollView::OnInitialUpdate();

  CSize sizeTotal;
  sizeTotal.cx = sizeTotal.cy = 100;
  SetScrollSizes(MM_TEXT, sizeTotal);
}

///////////////////////////////////////////////////////////
// CMakeBannerView message handlers

void CMakeBannerView::OnTilesSelecttileforimage1()
{
  CSelectTile SelectTile;

  // Set the dialog's tile variable to
  // the one that's currently selected.
  SelectTile.m_nCurrentImage = m_nTileOne;
  // Invoke the dialog box and remember
  // the results if we get IDOK.
  if( SelectTile.DoModal() == IDOK ){
    m_nTileOne = SelectTile.m_nCurrentImage;
    m_strTileOne = SelectTile.m_strFilename;
    }

}

void CMakeBannerView::OnTilesSelecttimeforimage2()
{
  CSelectTile SelectTile;
```

(continued)

Listing 31-4 *(continued)*

```
  // Set the dialog's tile variable to
  // the one that's currently selected.
  SelectTile.m_nCurrentImage = m_nTileTwo;
  // Invoke the dialog box and remember
  // the results if we get IDOK.
  if( SelectTile.DoModal() == IDOK ){
    m_nTileTwo = SelectTile.m_nCurrentImage;
    m_strTileTwo = SelectTile.m_strFilename;
    }

}

void CMakeBannerView::OnTilesCreatefirstbanner()
{

  // Create the banner image.
  CreateBanner( m_pBannerOne,
    &m_LogoOne, &m_strTileOne );
  // Update the window.
  InvalidateRect( NULL, FALSE );
  UpdateWindow();

}

void CMakeBannerView::OnTilesCreatesecondbanner()
{

  // Create the banner image.
  CreateBanner( m_pBannerTwo, &m_LogoTwo,
    &m_strTileTwo );
  // Update the window.
  InvalidateRect( NULL, FALSE );
  UpdateWindow();

}

void CMakeBannerView::CreateBanner(
  CImageObject *pImage, CImageObject *pLogo,
  CString *pFilename )
{
  // Create and load the file.
  CImageObject Tile( *pFilename );

  // Draw the tiles into the banner
  // image.
  int y = 0;
  while( y < pImage->GetHeight() ){
    int x = 0;
    while( x < pImage->GetWidth() ){
      pImage->Blit( &Tile, x, y );
      x += Tile.GetWidth();
```

```
      }
    y += Tile.GetHeight();
    }

  // Now blit the logo to the banner
  // image in transparent mode.
  pImage->Blit( pLogo,
    ( pImage->GetWidth() - pLogo->GetWidth() ) / 2,
    ( pImage->GetHeight() - pLogo->GetHeight() ) / 2,
    BLIT_MASK );

}

void CMakeBannerView::OnTilesUploadimages()
{

  // Set the dialog box to the
  // values that the view class
  // has stored.
  CFTPParams FtpParams;
  FtpParams.m_strFTPServer = m_strFTPServer;
  FtpParams.m_strUser = m_strUser;
  FtpParams.m_strPassword = m_strPassword;
  FtpParams.m_strDirectory = m_strDirectory;

  // Invoke the dialog and bail out if
  // we get IDCANCEL.
  if( FtpParams.DoModal() == IDCANCEL )
    return;

  // Store user data so we can remember it
  // later when the dialog is invoked again.
  m_strFTPServer = FtpParams.m_strFTPServer;
  m_strUser = FtpParams.m_strUser;
  m_strPassword = FtpParams.m_strPassword;
  m_strDirectory = FtpParams.m_strDirectory;

  // Save both images as 8-bit gif images.
  // Do this by converting with a temp
  // image and then save as Banner1.gif
  // and Banner2.gif.
  CImageObject m_TempImage;

  m_TempImage = *m_pBannerOne;
  m_TempImage.ChangeFormat( 8 );
  m_TempImage.Save( "Banner1.gif" );

  m_TempImage = *m_pBannerTwo;
  m_TempImage.ChangeFormat( 8 );
  m_TempImage.Save( "Banner2.gif" );

  // Create an Internet Session object.
```

(continued)

Listing 31-4 (continued)

```
    CInternetSession *pInetSession;
    pInetSession = new CInternetSession(
      AfxGetAppName(), 1,
      PRE_CONFIG_INTERNET_ACCESS );

    if( pInetSession == NULL )
      return;

    // Get an Ftp connection to the server.
    CFtpConnection *pFtpConnection;
    try{
      pFtpConnection =
        pInetSession->GetFtpConnection(
          m_strFTPServer, m_strUser, m_strPassword );
      }
    // Catch any exceptions and bail out.
    catch( CInternetException *pEx ){
      pEx->Delete();
      delete pInetSession;
      return;
      }

    // Change directories if necessary.
    if( m_strDirectory.GetLength() > 0 )
      pFtpConnection->SetCurrentDirectory(m_strDirectory);

    // Copy both files to the server.
    pFtpConnection->PutFile( "Banner1.gif",
      "Banner1.gif" );
    pFtpConnection->PutFile( "Banner2.gif",
      "Banner2.gif" );

    // Close the connection and delete the
    // objects we created.
    pFtpConnection->Close();
    delete pFtpConnection;
    delete pInetSession;

  }
```

Summary

Yes, you can use J++ and C++ together. If you're really creative, you'll think of scads of other ideas. I'll be interested in hearing from you; drop me a line with your ideas. Please e-mail me at `ivt-rcl@interpath.com`. I hope I can include your idea in my next book!

✦ ✦ ✦

CHAPTER 32

Using C++ and Visual Basic Together

✦ ✦ ✦ ✦

In This Chapter

Development language biases

Creating RegistryControl with Visual C++

Using RegistryControl from Visual Basic

Creating OhmsCalculator with Visual Basic

Using OhmsCalculator from Visual C++

Visual Basic graphics coordinates

An Imaging Control

✦ ✦ ✦ ✦

I have to admit it, I have a C++ bias. I love the language and prefer it to all other development tools. At the Visual 6 summit, hosted by Microsoft in January 1998, I listened politely to the Visual Basic developers. They spoke of short development times, robustness without the debugging cycle of typical C++ projects, and short learning curves for those new to Visual Basic.

All that made sense to me — I couldn't disagree. But I kept thinking of the 2MB project that a HelloWorld program would create (my exaggeration — upward) as opposed to the 20K equivalent C++ program (once again, my exaggeration — downward). In my mind I added the speed factor. A Visual C++ program is about 100 times faster than a Visual Basic program. As the Visual Basic programmers spoke, I kept thinking of why I didn't want to use Visual Basic — for anything.

Paul Gross, one of Microsoft's vice presidents, made a presentation in which he talked about "world-class applications." It seems that Microsoft spent some time identifying the best applications on the market. They arrived at 42 applications that were good enough to be classified as world-class. (Of course, he was diplomatic enough not to mention the names of these applications.) Of these 42, 38 were written in Microsoft Visual C++. Aha! — this was further ammunition for my argument against Visual Basic, and I smugly knew the conference would validate my feelings.

As the conference progressed, I couldn't help wonder why Microsoft had so little coverage of Visual C++. The Visual C++ product manager spoke for about half an hour, and Mike Blaszczak and Christian Beaumont spoke for about an hour. Most of the rest of the time was spent with the dreaded Visual Basic. The Active Data Object (ADO) team used Visual Basic exclusively to talk about ADO development — that is, except for the ten obligatory minutes in which they showed us how to do simple ADO access from C++. The guy who talked about dynamic HTML used Visual Basic for everything he demonstrated. It went on like this for two days.

At lunch on the second day, I sat with the ADO development team. The team leader looked at me and asked, "What is it you C++ guys have against RAD tools?" (RAD stands for rapid application development, one of Visual Basic's big selling points.) I was somewhat taken aback. The rest of the table then proceeded to pile it on with comments like, "Yeah, I think C++ programmers like a lot of code so they can be macho." Now this was a battle I was bound to lose, so I politely migrated the subject to ADO.

When I arrived back at my office, my boss told me I needed to have a demo application running in two days for a big client. After I informed him that this would be impossible, he explained that the success of the entire account rode on the demonstration program. While I was casting about for answers, a colleague suggested Visual Basic. The one thing this unsavory choice did for me was provide the possibility of some sleep over the next two-day period—I knew if I used Visual C++, the demo program would take me two days of nonstop programming.

To make a long story short, I wrote an ActiveX control in Visual C++ that displayed and processed images, and I created the rest of the program in Visual Basic. Everything worked great, and our company reaped the rewards (not to mention my future salary reviews).

Since then, I've talked to many developers who have the philosophy that different development tools all have a place in a software developer's arsenal. In spite of my Visual C++ snobbery, I now agree with that. This chapter is dedicated to the marriage of Visual C++ and Visual Basic. In the first section, I show you how to write a C++ control that's used from a Visual Basic program; in the second section, you learn how to write a Visual Basic control that's used from a C++ program.

The functionality of the controls were selected based on the strengths of Visual C++ and Visual Basic. The control written in C++ accesses the Registry. It's a task that's fairly easy from C++, but not that easy from Visual Basic. The control written in Visual Basic is a simple form-based program that calculates voltage, resistance, and amperage with Ohm's law. Programs like this are extremely easy in Visual Basic—I think it took me about ten minutes to implement.

The RegistryControl ATL Control

This first project is an ATL control written in C++. Its purpose is to make it easy for developers to read and write to the system Registry. It uses the `CRegistry` class from Chapter 9 for the actual Registry functionality. The `CUseRegistry` class is the layer between the control and the `CRegistry` functions.

Notice that all the strings passed in from Basic are BSTRs. Because this control was written in C++, and the `CRegistry` class expects `char` pointers, the BSTRs all need to be converted to `char` arrays. Throughout the source code in Listing 32-1, you can see the conversion macros at work taking care of this detail.

Demo Program

RegistryControl

CD-ROM Location: **Chap32\RegistryControl**
Program Name: **RegistryControl.dll**
Source Code Modules in Text: **UseRegistry.cpp**

◆ ◆ ◆ ◆ ◆

Listing 32-1: The Salient Source Code for the RegistryControl Project

```
// UseRegistry.cpp : Implementation of CUseRegistry
#include "stdafx.h"
#include "RegistryControl.h"
#include "UseRegistry.h"

/////////////////////////////////////////////////////////////////////////////
// CUseRegistry

STDMETHODIMP CUseRegistry::Open(long hKey, BSTR lSubKey)
{
  USES_CONVERSION;

  // Open the registry for the subkey. The W2CA
  // macro is used to convert the BSTR to a char
  // pointer.
  m_Registry.Open( (HKEY) hKey, W2CA( lSubKey ) );

  return S_OK;
}

STDMETHODIMP CUseRegistry::Close()
{

  // Close the registry.
  m_Registry.Close();

  return S_OK;
}

STDMETHODIMP CUseRegistry::IsOpen(long *pnIsOpen)
{

  // See if the registry is open.
  *pnIsOpen = (long) m_Registry.IsOpen();
```

(continued)

Listing 32-1 *(continued)*

```
  return S_OK;
}

STDMETHODIMP CUseRegistry::ReadDWORD(BSTR lValueName,
  long * lValue)
{
  USES_CONVERSION;

  // Read a binary DWORD from the registry. The W2CA
  // macro is used to convert the BSTR to a char pointer.
  m_Registry.ReadDWORD( W2CA( lValueName ),
    (unsigned long *) lValue );

  return S_OK;
}

STDMETHODIMP CUseRegistry::ReadString(BSTR lValueName,
  BSTR lValue)
{
  USES_CONVERSION;

  // Declare, allocate, and clear a char
  // array into which the registry string
  // will be read.
  char *lpReturnValue;
  lpReturnValue = new char [5000];
  memset( lpReturnValue, 0, 5000 );

  // Read the string from the registry. The W2CA
  // macro is used to convert the BSTR to a char
  // pointer.
  m_Registry.ReadString( W2CA( lValueName ),
    lpReturnValue );

  // Copy the string into the BSTR using the A2CW
  // conversion macro.
  memcpy( lValue, A2CW( lpReturnValue ),
    sizeof( WORD ) * ( strlen( lpReturnValue ) + 1 ) );

  // Delete the allocated memory.
  delete [] lpReturnValue;

  return S_OK;
}

STDMETHODIMP CUseRegistry::WriteDWORD(BSTR lValueName,
  long lValue)
{
  USES_CONVERSION;
```

```
  // Write a binary DWORD to the registry. The W2CA macro
  // is used to convert the BSTR to a char pointer.
  m_Registry.WriteDWORD( W2CA( lValueName ), lValue );

  return S_OK;
}

STDMETHODIMP CUseRegistry::WriteString(BSTR lValueName,
  BSTR lValue)
{
  USES_CONVERSION;

  // Write a string to the registry. The W2CA macro
  // is used twice in the function call to convert
  // the BSTRs to char pointers.
  m_Registry.WriteString( W2CA( lValueName ),
    (void *) W2CA( lValue ) );

  return S_OK;
}

STDMETHODIMP CUseRegistry::CreateKey(long hKey,
  BSTR lSubKey, BSTR lClass)
{
  USES_CONVERSION;

  // Call the CRegistry static function named
  // CreateKey() that creates a key in the registry.
  // The W2CA macro is used to convert the BSTR to
  // a char pointer.
  CRegistry::CreateKey( (HKEY) hKey, W2CA( lSubKey ),
    W2CA( lClass ) );

  return S_OK;
}

STDMETHODIMP CUseRegistry::DeleteKey(long hKey,
  BSTR lSubKey)
{
  USES_CONVERSION;

  // Call the CRegistry static function named
  // DeleteKey() that deletes a key from the registry.
  // The W2CA macro is used to convert the BSTR to
  // a char pointer.
  CRegistry::DeleteKey( (HKEY) hKey, W2CA( lSubKey ) );

  return S_OK;
}
```

After the RegistryControl project is successfully compiled, it's registered as a control and can be instantiated from any application on your computer. If you distribute this or any other control to clients, it has to be registered as a control on their system. To do this, use the Regsvr32.exe program that's found in the Windows\System directory. You can use the Run selection from the Start menu. Figure 32-1 shows how you can register the RegistryControl control.

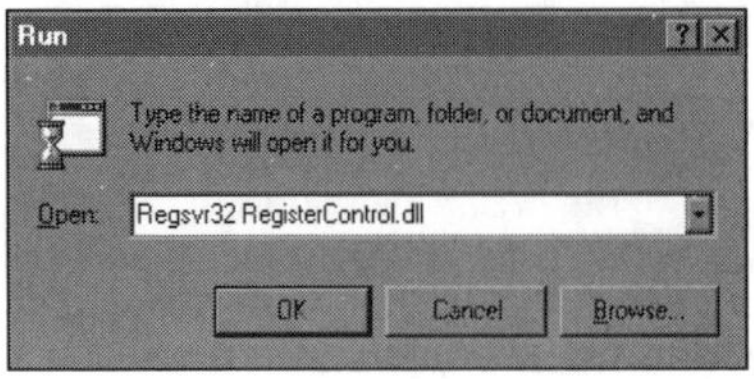

Figure 32-1: You can register a control from the Run selection of the Start menu.

If your application is being installed with an InstallShield or Wise Install, the controls can be automatically registered when the installation takes place. There's an option in both of these systems that allows you to have all controls registered at installation time.

One other option is to call `WinExec()` from your own installation program. The following code registers the RegistryControl control in this way:

```
WinExec( "Regsvr32 RegistryControl.dll" );
```

Now that the C++ control has been compiled and registered, we just need to write a Visual Basic program and pull the control in. To use a control from Visual Basic, select it from the list of references. Begin by selecting References from the Visual Basic Project menu. A dialog box appears that lists all the controls found on the system. Each item has a check box to the left, and if the check box is selected, you can use the control in your Visual Basic program. Figure 32-2 shows the list of controls and a check mark by the RegistryControl control that I wrote in Visual C++.

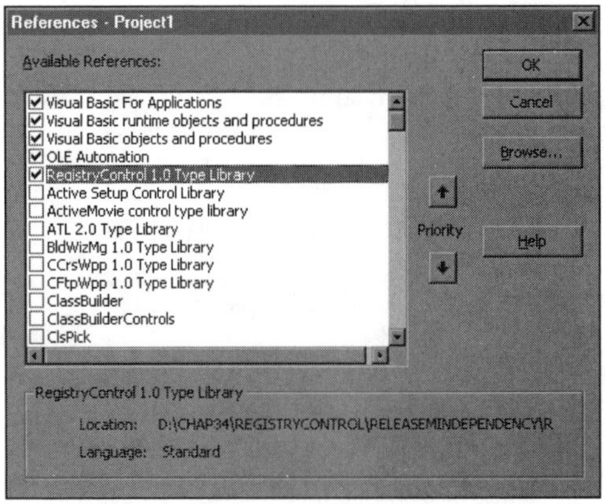

Figure 32-2: Visual Basic gives you a list of registered controls from which you can select and use for your programs.

The last thing to do is write code for the Visual Basic program that uses the control. The next section talks about a program I wrote and shows the source code.

The Register Visual Basic Program

This section shows you the Register program, which is a Visual Basic program I built to load in and use the RegistryControl ATL control. There's a lot more functionality to the control than this program uses, but I wanted to keep this program simple so you could easily see how to instantiate and use the control.

Four of the control's methods are used. The first is `CreateKey()`. This method creates a key in the Registry into which your program's configuration data can be stored. The first argument in the `CreateKey()` method determines where the newly created key will be placed. Our example puts it into `HKEY_LOCAL_MACHINE`. This is determined by specifying the value `&H80000002`. Table 32-1 shows the values for the various Registry sections.

Table 32-1
Values for Registry Sections

Section	*Value*
HKEY_CLASSES_ROOT	80000000
HKEY_CURRENT_USER	80000001
HKEY_LOCAL_MACHINE	80000002
HKEY_USERS	80000003
HKEY_PERFORMANCE_DATA	80000004
HKEY_CURRENT_CONFIG	80000005
HKEY_DYN_DATA	80000006

The second RegistryControl method used is `Open()`, which opens the Registry key so data can be written to it and enables data to be read from the Registry. The `IsOpen() method` is used to determine if the Registry was successfully opened—this is important so that your users can be notified in case of Registry errors. Data is written to the Registry key with the `WriteString()` method. Finally, the Registry key is closed with the `Close()` method.

Demo Program

Register
CD-ROM Location: **Chap32\Register**
Program Name: **Register.exe**
Source Code Modules in Text: **Register.frm**

✦ ✦ ✦ ✦ ✦

Listing 32-2: The Source Code for the Register Project

```
Private Sub Form_Load()

Dim obj As New UseRegistry

' Create the registry subkey
obj.CreateKey &H80000002, "SOFTWARE\UseRegistry", "Test"

' Open the registry subkey
obj.Open &H80000002, "SOFTWARE\UseRegistry"

' Check to make sure the open was successful
Dim IsOpen As Long
obj.IsOpen IsOpen

If IsOpen <> 0 Then
    ' Write data to the entry
    obj.WriteString "TestValue", "My Name"
    ' Close the registry key
    obj.Close
End If

End Sub
```

When you run the Register program, you won't see anything except a blank form. That's because the RegistryControl control doesn't display a user interface. Instead, it performs the tasks it's told to do, and when it's done, it comes back to the Visual Basic program.

You can, however, see the results of the actions that the control took. Begin by running Regedit. Open the `HKEY_LOCAL_MACHINE` section and open the `SOFTWARE` key. You should see a key named `UseRegistry`. Open the `UseRegistry` key and look inside to see the data that was saved to it. The data is named "TestValue," and the data string that's stored is "My Name." Figure 32-3 shows what our Registry looked like after running the program and opening the `UseRegistry` subkey.

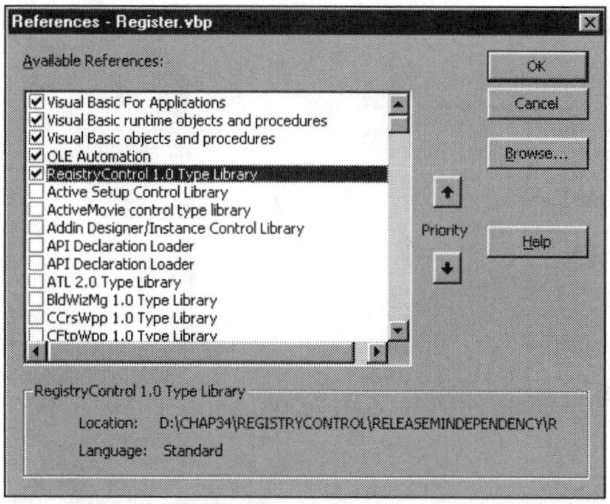

Figure 32-3: Although the Register program doesn't show you what's going on, you can use Regedit to find out what it did.

The next thing you're going to do in this chapter is take advantage of Visual Basic's ability to easily create a form-based user interface. I show you how to write a control that you can load into a Visual C++ program. That way you get the best of both worlds — a quickly built user interface, with the ability to perform on the level of a C++ program.

The OhmsCalculator Basic ActiveX Control

The control you've built with Visual Basic is called OhmsCalculator. It enables users to enter three values into a form: voltage, resistance, and amperage. Three buttons appear at the bottom of the form. One causes the control to calculate the voltage from the resistance and amperage values; another causes the control to calculate the resistance from the voltage and amperage values; and the third causes the control to calculate the amperage from the voltage and resistance values.

The program was written in about ten minutes, including the time it took to look up Ohm's Law in a physics book. The procedure consisted of putting three labels on the form, three text fields, and three buttons. Code was then added to each button so that an appropriate value is calculated and placed in a field. For example, if the user presses the Calculate Voltage button, the voltage text field is populated based on a calculation from values obtained from the resistance and amperage fields. Figure 32-4 shows the control interface as it appears in the Visual Basic editor.

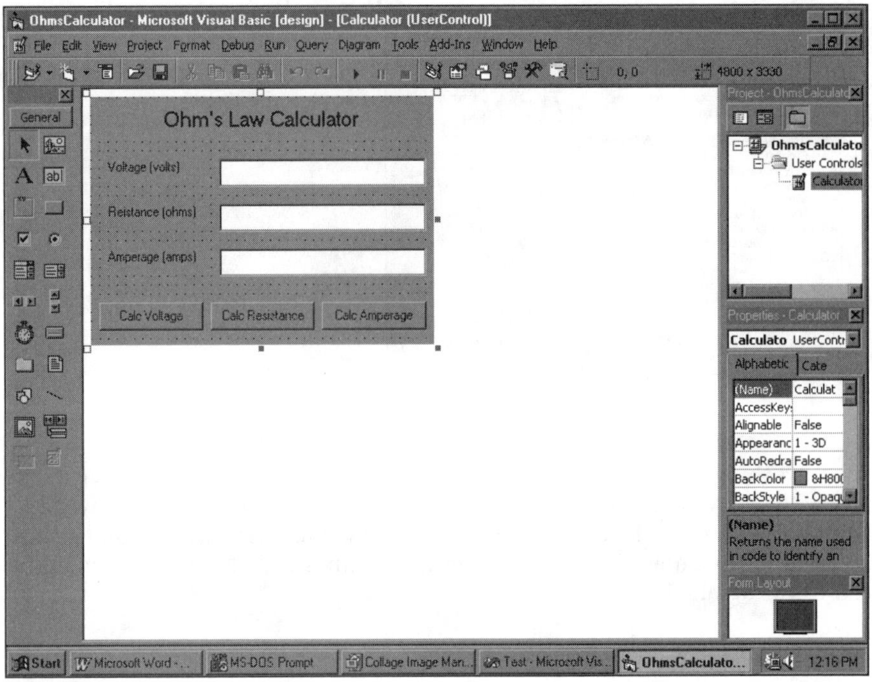

Figure 32-4: The Visual Basic editor makes it a snap to create form-based controls.

Demo Program

OhmsCalculator
CD-ROM Location: **Chap32\OhmsCalculator**
Program Name: **OhmsCalculator.ocx**
Source Code Modules in Text: **OhmsCalculator.frm**

✦ ✦ ✦ ✦ ✦

Listing 32-3: The OhmsCalculator Visual Basic ActiveX Control Source Code

```
Private Sub Command1_Click()

' Get the values from the fields
Dim Amps As Double
Amps = Val(Text3(1).Text)
Dim Ohms As Double
Ohms = Val(Text2(1).Text)

' Calculate the voltage
Dim Volts As Double
Volts = Amps * Ohms
```

```
' Set the voltage field to the value
Text1(0).Text = Volts

End Sub

Private Sub Command2_Click()

' Get the values from the fields
Dim Amps As Double
Amps = Val(Text3(1).Text)
Dim Volts As Double
Volts = Val(Text1(0).Text)

Dim Ohms As Double
If Amps = 0 Then
    ' Here we're checking for divide by zero. Alert
    ' them to the error.
    Text2(1).Text = "Can't calculate when Amps=0"
Else
    ' Calculate the resistance
    Ohms = Volts / Amps
    ' Set the voltage field to the value
    Text2(1).Text = Ohms
End If

End Sub

Private Sub Command3_Click()

' Get the values from the fields
Dim Ohms As Double
Ohms = Val(Text2(1).Text)
Dim Volts As Double
Volts = Val(Text1(0).Text)

Dim Amps As Double
If Ohms = 0 Then
    ' Here we're checking for divide by zero. Alert
    ' them to the error.
    Text3(1).Text = "Can't calculate when Ohms=0"
Else
    ' Calculate the amperage
    Amps = Volts / Ohms
    ' Set the voltage field to the value
    Text3(1).Text = Amps
End If

End Sub

Private Sub UserControl_Initialize()

End Sub
```

When you create a control such as OhmsCalculator, you can't run it from Visual Basic to test it. If you want to test it before you try using it from Visual C++ (a highly recommended procedure), you need to create a separate Visual Basic project that pulls the control in and uses it.

Another alternative for loading a control that you can use before creating a C++ wrapper for the control is to employ the Visual C++ ActiveX Control Test Container tool from the Visual C++ Tools menu, as described in the next section.

The UseOhmsCalculator C++ Program

Using a control from Visual C++ isn't quite as easy as using a control from Visual Basic. (All the Visual Basic fans are out there saying, "No surprise!") First, you identify the control you want to use. To do this, select Add to Project from the Project menu, and then select Components and Controls from the Add to Project submenu. In the Components and Controls Gallery dialog box, open the Registered ActiveX Controls folder, and find the control you want. In this case, the control is named OhmsCalculator.Calculator. One important note: *This control must have been registered either by building the .ocx file or by running Regsvr32 on it.* Figure 32-5 shows OhmsCalculator.Calculator in the control list.

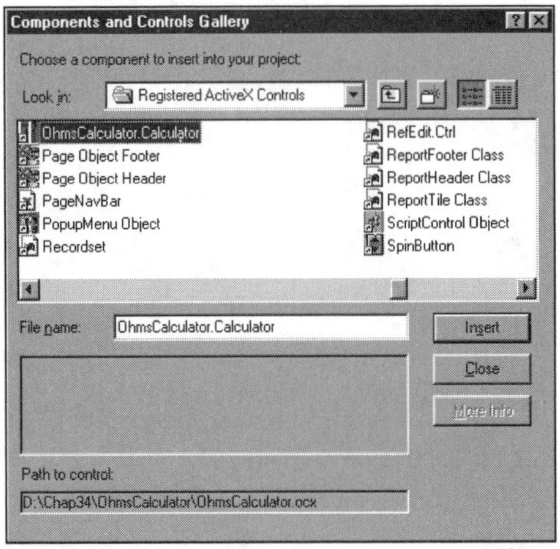

Figure 32-5: Find the control you want in the list – in this case it's OhmsCalculator.Calculator.

Next, click the Insert button. Another dialog box appears in which you can name the C++ control wrapper class and the filenames into which the source code will be saved. Figure 32-6 shows what our Confirm Classes dialog box looks like.

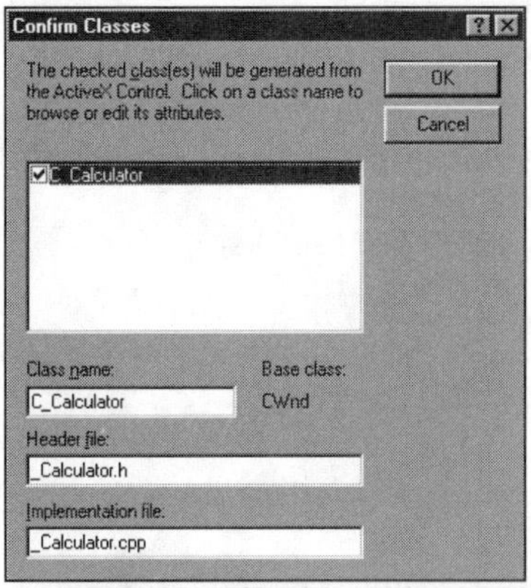

Figure 32-6: You get the opportunity to name the C++ class that wraps the control and the source code files for the class.

Demo Program

UseOhmsCalculator

CD-ROM Location: **Chap32\UseOhmsCalculator**
Program Name: **UseOhmsCalculator.exe**
Source Code Modules in Text: **UseOhmsCalculatorView.cpp**

◆ ◆ ◆ ◆ ◆

Listing 32-4: Highlights of the C++ Source Code for the UseOhmsCalculator Program

```
// UseOhmsCalculatorView.cpp : implementation of the
// CUseOhmsCalculatorView class
//

#include "stdafx.h"
#include "UseOhmsCalculator.h"

#include "UseOhmsCalculatorDoc.h"
#include "UseOhmsCalculatorView.h"

/////////////////////////////////////////////////////////////
// CUseOhmsCalculatorView

IMPLEMENT_DYNCREATE(CUseOhmsCalculatorView, CView)

BEGIN_MESSAGE_MAP(CUseOhmsCalculatorView, CView)
  //{{AFX_MSG_MAP(CUseOhmsCalculatorView)
  ON_WM_TIMER()
  ON_WM_CREATE()
  //}}AFX_MSG_MAP
END_MESSAGE_MAP()
```

(continued)

Listing 32-4 *(continued)*

```
///////////////////////////////////////////////////////////
// CUseOhmsCalculatorView construction/destruction

CUseOhmsCalculatorView::CUseOhmsCalculatorView()
{
}

CUseOhmsCalculatorView::~CUseOhmsCalculatorView()
{
}

BOOL
CUseOhmsCalculatorView::PreCreateWindow(CREATESTRUCT& cs)
{
  return CView::PreCreateWindow(cs);
}

///////////////////////////////////////////////////////////
// CUseOhmsCalculatorView drawing

void CUseOhmsCalculatorView::OnDraw(CDC* pDC)
{
  CUseOhmsCalculatorDoc* pDoc = GetDocument();
  ASSERT_VALID(pDoc);
}

///////////////////////////////////////////////////////////
// CUseOhmsCalculatorView message handlers

void CUseOhmsCalculatorView::OnTimer(UINT nIDEvent)
{

  // Kill the time since we only want to
  // do this once.
  KillTimer( nIDEvent );

  // Get a dc to the main screen so we can get the
  // logical pixel values.
  CWindowDC WindowDC( NULL );

  // Set the rectangle coordinates so they're the
  // correct size. We do this by adjusting to TWIPS.
  // (The window sizes were obtained from the
  // OhmsCalculator project.)
  RECT Rect;
  Rect.left = 0;
  Rect.top = 0;
  Rect.right =
    ( WindowDC.GetDeviceCaps( LOGPIXELSX ) *
```

```
      4800 ) / 1440;
  Rect.bottom =
    ( WindowDC.GetDeviceCaps( LOGPIXELSY ) *
      3300 ) / 1440;

  // Create the control.
  m_Calculator.Create( NULL, "OhmsCalculator",
    WS_VISIBLE, Rect, this, 2000 );

  CView::OnTimer(nIDEvent);
}

int CUseOhmsCalculatorView::OnCreate(
  LPCREATESTRUCT lpCreateStruct)
{
  if (CView::OnCreate(lpCreateStruct) == -1)
    return -1;

  // Kick off the timer.
  SetTimer( 1, 200, NULL );

  return 0;
}
```

When the Visual C++ program runs, you should see the control that was written in Visual Basic appear in the View window, as shown in Figure 32-7. Go ahead and try it out. It works like a charm. This is a great way to easily add user interface components to your Visual C++ programs.

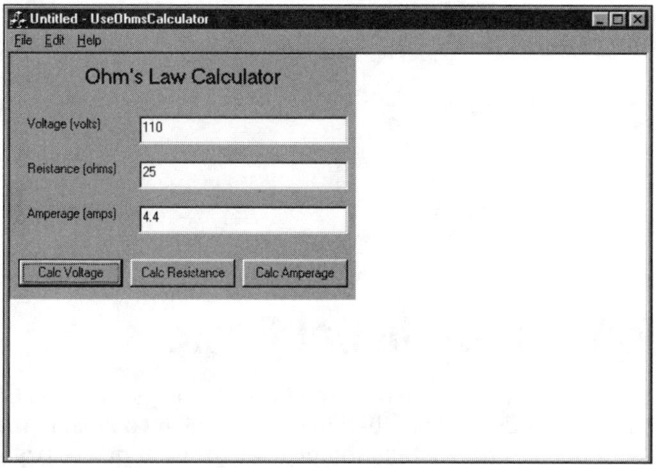

Figure 32-7: Here you can see the Visual Basic control in the Visual C++ View window.

Visual Basic Graphics Coordinates

There's one warning for anyone who writes a Visual C++ control that interacts graphically with a Visual Basic device context: Visual Basic graphics coordinates are all in twips. *Twips* is a mapping mode in which there are 1,440 logical units per inch. These logical units aren't the same as device units or pixels.

The problem is Visual Basic doesn't set its mapping mode to twips. It uses twips internally for graphics, but other programs won't know by obtaining the mapping mode of a Visual Basic window that Visual Basic is using twips. For this reason, you have to perform conversions from a control written in Visual C++ if you want to draw to the Visual Basic window.

Two conversion functions, `VbTwipsToVcMMTextX()` and `VbTwipsToVcMMTextY()`, follow. Each one converts from the Visual Basic twips to the Visual C++ `MM_TEXT` mapping mode.

```
int VbTwipsToVcMMTextX( int  x )
{
  CWindowDC WindowDC( NULL );
  int nMMTextX;

  nMMTextX  = ( WindowDC.GetDeviceCaps( LOGPIXELSX ) *
    x ) / 1440;

  return( nMMTextX );

}

int VbTwipsToVcMMTextY( int  y )
{
  CWindowDC WindowDC( NULL );
  int nMMTextY;

  nMMTextY  = ( WindowDC.GetDeviceCaps( LOGPIXELSY ) * \
    y ) / 1440;

  return( nMMTextY );

}
```

An Imaging Control for Visual Basic

There's a very nice imaging control included on the CD that comes with this book. It's part of the imaging add-on library described in Chapter 23. If you install the ImageObject library with the IOSetup installation program, the IOCntl control is registered, and you can use it from Visual Basic.

I've written a Visual Basic program called Pictures to show you how easy this control makes it to load and display images. With the control, you can write a program in about five minutes that loads and displays an image.

The first thing you have to do to use this control is select References from the Project menu. Find the IOCntl control and turn the check box on. All you have to do then is simply instantiate the control and use it. Figure 32-8 shows the Visual Basic program running with an image drawn to the Form1 window.

Figure 32-8: It's easy to display an image in your Form window, as this screen shot shows.

Demo Program

Pictures
CD-ROM Location: **Chap32\Pictures**
Program Name: **Pictures.exe**
Source Code Modules in Text: **Pictures.frm**

✦ ✦ ✦ ✦ ✦

Listing 32-5: **Source Code for the Pictures Visual Basic Program**

```
Private obj As New ImageControl

Private Sub Form_Load()
obj.Load "d:\chap32\pictures\Cougar.bmp"
End Sub
```

(continued)

Listing 32-5 *(continued)*

```
Private Sub Form_Paint()
obj.Draw Me.hDC
End Sub
```

Summary

OK, I was wrong about Visual Basic. It's a powerful tool that shortens development time and costs in many cases. Don't hesitate to use it whenever you see that it makes more sense than Visual C++. At the same time, make sure you fully utilize Visual C++ for components that are awkward in Visual Basic. Do as I've done—drop the Visual C++ snobbery (or Visual Basic snobbery, if that's your bias). You'll go far if you integrate these two powerful tools.

✦ ✦ ✦

CHAPTER 33

Writing a Custom AppWizard

✦ ✦ ✦ ✦

In This Chapter

Discovering how the AppWizard works internally

Learning about AppWizard templates and macros

Creating a custom AppWizard

Changing a project's default settings with a custom AppWizard

Creating a custom AppWizard to include personal information on every About box

Adding custom dialog boxes to AppWizard

Modifying templates to customize the skeleton code created by AppWizard

Changing the AppWizard's confirmation dialog

Using the Registry to store persistent custom AppWizard information

✦ ✦ ✦ ✦

The AppWizard is definitely one aspect of the Microsoft development environment that all programmers, regardless of ability, are infinitely aware of. As you have seen countless times throughout this book, AppWizard is used to quickly build the skeleton framework for an MFC application or DLL. This is because the AppWizard application provides an incredibly easy way to create a Visual C++ project and source code files for a Windows application or DLL. All you have to do is follow a series of dialogs, select the different options that characterize your application (such as database support, file support, MAPI support, and so on), and voilà, AppWizard creates a complete set of source files necessary to build your project on the basis of the options you selected. You are then free to modify the resulting source code files to your heart's content, knowing that AppWizard has freed you from the tedious and time-consuming task of creating the framework for your project. Thus the biggest benefit of AppWizard is that it saves you considerable time in your development cycle.

As great a tool as AppWizard is, it is not without its limitations. Let's not forget that several hundred thousand programmers use AppWizard worldwide. Therefore, AppWizard has to provide a very generic set of functions and defaults. Even so, you, the individual developer, are not bound by the same constraints. You may, for example, know that every application you're going to build for your current company is going to be an SDI application with Automation support. Microsoft doesn't make Automation support the default simply because the majority of programmers using MFC are not using Automation. If they were, inclusion of Automation in an AppWizard-generated application would be the default. The same thing can be said about any default setting in the AppWizard, but that doesn't make your job any easier; every time you use AppWizard to create a project, you must remember to set all the appropriate options.

Wouldn't it be great if you could define your own AppWizards with dialogs, options, and default settings that are specific to your current needs? In addition, it would really help if this user-defined AppWizard allowed you to add files and libraries that you always include in every project, but sometimes forget until you get the compiler and linker errors. In addition, while we're at it, a user AppWizard that interfaces to the regular AppWizard would really be useful. After all, there are times when you simply want to keep all the standard AppWizard defaults and add one more option or one more dialog of options.

For several versions of Visual C++, programmers could only sit around and wonder what if. Even so, that changed in Version 4 of Visual C++ with the introduction of custom AppWizards. With custom AppWizards, you can do everything described previously and a lot more. This chapter is based on that technology — and how to exploit it to make the AppWizard an even more productive tool for you.

The Internal Workings of the AppWizard

Before jumping into how to create a custom AppWizard, let's take a moment and look at exactly how the AppWizard goes about creating a project from the options you choose.

The first thing you see when you run the AppWizard is a series of dialog boxes. As you enter your project options into these dialog boxes, AppWizard is storing these values in a string map. In some cases, AppWizard uses these values to aid it in the process of presenting the dialog boxes. To see an example of this, press Ctrl+N to create a new file. Select the Projects tab and select the "MFC AppWizard (exe)" entry in the Projects list. After you're presented with the first dialog, take a look at the different types of project options available: single-document (SDI), multiple-document (MDI), and dialog-based. These different project types are referred to as *tracks*. For now, select a project type of "Multiple document" and click the Next button. The second dialog displays options dealing with a document-based application. These options include things such as file support, database view support, and the like. If you click the Back button and select the "Dialog-based" project type, the next dialog displays options for dialog-based applications (such as whether you want an "About box" on the system menu). This is an example of where the AppWizard uses a value you entered (the project type) to control which dialog boxes will appear and in what order.

Recall that the different project types are referred to as tracks. Well, each track is defined as having a specific sequence of dialogs that will be displayed when that track is being used. AppWizard simply changed the track type according to the option you selected on the first dialog.

Whereas the example just described shows where AppWizard uses an option you specified to direct the operation of the AppWizard, the majority of the time the options you specify are used as *substitution macros* in the code that is produced for your project. Ever wonder how when you create an application that contains an About box, the About box's title bar contains the name of your project? This works because the AppWizard has a generic set of source files for each track. Because these files are used as the base for the source files that will eventually be created in your project's folder, they are called *templates*. For example, the template for the English-language version of a dialog-based application's resource file ("`Dlgloc_enu.rcLoc_enu.rc`") has the following lines to define the About box:

```
...
IDD_ABOUTBOX DIALOGEX 0, 0, 160, 129
STYLE DS_MODALFRAME | WS_POPUP | WS_CAPTION | WS_SYSMENU
CAPTION "About $$ROOT$$"
...
```

In this code sample, `$$ROOT$$` represents a variable, or macro, that you set when you completed the AppWizard's dialog boxes. Actually, the `$$ROOT$$` macro represents the name of the project. This is how the title bar of your dialog's About box always states the correct project name. Upon completion of the dialog boxes, AppWizard simply substitutes the values you specified on the different dialog boxes in the appropriate places in the templates.

So what do we know at this point? Well, up to now we know that AppWizard displays a series of dialog boxes where you specify the different options for your project. AppWizard then takes these different options, or macros, and uses them to substitute everywhere in the template files that contains a `$$placeholder$$` sequence, where "placeholder" is a valid macro known to AppWizard. Figure 33-1 shows how this works.

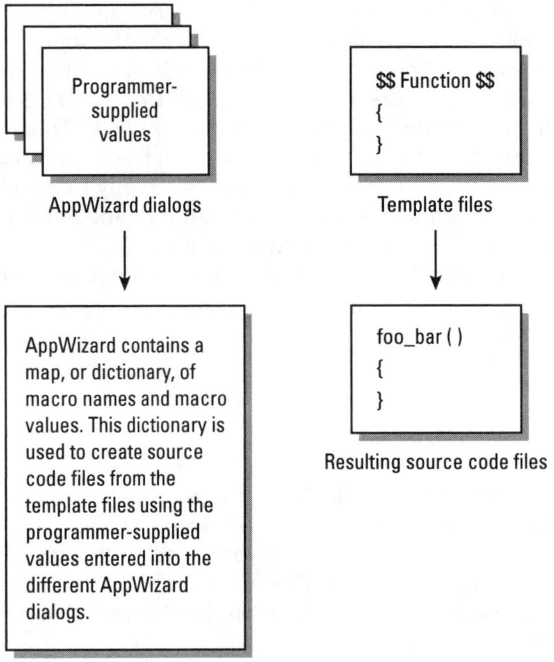

Figure 33-1: Overview of how AppWizard does that thing it does so well

Okay. I've done enough talking about AppWizards and custom AppWizards. It's time to see how this works firsthand.

Creating a Custom AppWizard

As you might have guessed, you create the framework for a custom AppWizard with the AppWizard. Press Ctrl+N to display the New dialog. From the Projects tab, select the Custom AppWizard. You should now see the first of two dialog boxes used to create the base source files for your custom AppWizard.

There are only three fields on the first dialog box. The first field is the starting point for the new custom AppWizard. There are three options available in this field:

- ✦ **Existing project** — Select this option when you have a fully implemented project that you want to use as the framework for new projects. There are two caveats to this option: choose a project that was generated by the MFC AppWizard, and the files and classes that were generated need to have the same generic names that were created by AppWizard. Remember the code snippet earlier with the `$$ROOT$$` macro? When you create a project with the MFC AppWizard, the template files for the document class declare the document class name as being C+`$$ROOT$$`+Doc. Therefore, if your base project name was called MyAwesomeToolkit, AppWizard would have named the document class `CMyAwesomeToolkitDoc`. If, however, you modified this class name after AppWizard created it, the custom AppWizard will not be able to understand that fact because it has no way of locating your document class without using the same rules that the original MFC AppWizard used when the base project was created.

✦ **Standard MFC AppWizard steps**—When creating a custom AppWizard, this is the most commonly used option. By selecting this option, you're basically telling AppWizard, "Create for me every single template that could be used for every project type supported." At this point, you have the most flexibility in terms of being able to modify any header file, implementation file, resource file, and so on that is used to create an MFC project. Because this is the most common custom AppWizard type, and the most difficult to implement, the examples and demos in this chapter will use this starting point.

✦ **Your own customized steps**—This option is used when you want to display an entirely new set of dialogs and options for the programmer. For example, let's say that you're creating a custom AppWizard to automate the creation of a non-MFC application. You would still have some options the programmer would need to select; however, none of the MFC dialogs make any sense to your non-MFC application. You would, therefore, select this option and create all your own customized dialog boxes. Although this type of custom AppWizard won't be covered explicitly, most of what you would do to create it will be covered in the examples and demos in this chapter.

The next field allows you to name the new custom AppWizard. This name will be used in the New dialog's Project list.

The last field on this dialog box is where you specify how many custom steps, or dialogs, to add to the new custom AppWizard. There are some cases when you'll not want to add any steps. Let's say you simply want to change some default MFC AppWizard settings such as project type or Automation support. In this case, you would specify a value of 0 for this option. (This example is actually covered in the next section.)

When you have finished this dialog and begun the second dialog, only two fields remain. The first field defines whether the new custom AppWizard will be used to create an MFC application or an MFC DLL. The second field stipulates which languages will be supported.

In the next section you'll see how easy it is to create a custom AppWizard that has different default project settings than the generic AppWizard.

Changing a Project's Default Settings

As mentioned earlier, there are a number of instances when you might want to change the default settings of a project. In this section, you'll create a custom AppWizard demo project called `SDIAutomationWiz`. After the custom AppWizard has been created, you'll modify it so that any project created with this custom AppWizard has a default project type of SDI as well as Automation support.

Creating the SDIAutomationWiz demo project

The instructions in this section will allow you to code a custom AppWizard. Even so, if you just want to read along and look at the code later, the source code can be found on the companion CD in the \Demos\SDIAutomationWiz folder.

To begin, create a new custom AppWizard project called **SDIAutomationWiz**. On the first dialog, specify the "Standard MFC AppWizard steps" as the starting point. Set the Project list name to anything you would want to see in your Project list. I typically like to name my custom AppWizards so those Wizards with common functionality are grouped together in the Project list. In other words, since this custom AppWizard will basically be an MFC AppWizard with some minor default settings changed, I named the demo "MFC AppWizard (exe) – SDI/Automation." Finally, since we will not be adding dialogs in the particular custom AppWizard, set the number of custom steps to 0 and press the Enter key. On the next dialog, select "MFC AppWizard Executable" and press the Enter key to dismiss this dialog. When the confirmation dialog box is displayed, click the OK button to create the project for your new custom AppWizard.

Changing AppWizard macros

As you've already learned, the term *macro*, as it applies to custom AppWizards, simply refers to the settings for a given project. Regardless of the macro you're setting, there are only two things to know to be able to read a macro's value or set its value. The first thing is that the class that represents the custom AppWizard is called `CCustomAppWiz`. The second thing is that the macro values are stored in a member variable of the `CCustomAppWiz` class. This member variable, actually a `CMapStringToString`, is referred to as the Dictionary.

Defining the CCustomAppWiz class

Even though custom AppWizards have a special suffix (.awx), they are still the same run-of-the-mill DLLs you're accustomed to using. If you open the SDIAutomationWiz.cpp file that you created in this project, you'll see the following `DLLMain` function defined:

```
extern "C" int APIENTRY
DllMain(HINSTANCE hInstance, DWORD dwReason, LPVOID lpReserved)
{
```

```
    if (dwReason == DLL_PROCESS_ATTACH)
    {
     TRACE0("SDIAUTOMATIONWIZ.AWX Initializing!\n");

     // Extension DLL one-time initialization
     AfxInitExtensionModule(SDIAutomationWizDLL, hInstance);

     // Insert this DLL into the resource chain
     new CDynLinkLibrary(SDIAutomationWizDLL);

     // Register this custom AppWizard with MFCAPWZ.DLL
     SetCustomAppWizClass(&SDIAutomationWizaw);
    }
    else if (dwReason == DLL_PROCESS_DETACH)
    {
     TRACE0("SDIAUTOMATIONWIZ.AWX Terminating!\n");

     // Terminate the library before destructors are called
     AfxTermExtensionModule(SDIAutomationWizDLL);
    }
    return 1;   // ok
   }
```

In addition to the usual tasks like the creation of a `CDynLinkLibrary`, which is always created for an MFC extension DLL, there is also a call to the `SetCustomAppWizClass()` function. This is a function that is exported by the AppWizard DLL (MFCAPWZ.DLL). It simply connects the AppWizard DLL to this custom AppWizard DLL so that they can communicate when they need to. Always remember that even though you have created a custom AppWizard, the base AppWizard is still in control. In other words, your custom AppWizard is simply used to do things such as displaying a new dialog, changing the order of the dialog boxes, and setting defaults. It is still the base AppWizard that does the parsing of the templates, the merging of the templates and macros, and the creation of the project's files.

Having said that, it is probably apparent what the `CCustomAppWiz` class does. It serves as a means of communicating with the AppWizard. Actually, AppWizard tells your `CCustomAppWiz` object when it needs something by calling the appropriate functions.

Although there are about ten functions in the `CCustomAppWiz` class, only about five are routinely seen and used. The purpose of most of these functions can be deduced by their names. For example, the `InitCustomAppWiz()` function is called after the custom AppWizard is loaded to give it an opportunity do any initialization it needs to do. This is where you would want to do things such as initializing AppWizard macros. Besides the `InitCustomAppWiz()` function, there is also an `ExitCustomAppWiz()` function that is called when the custom AppWizard is about to be unloaded.

Two functions that are used to control the ordering of the dialogs are the `Next()` and `Back()` functions. As you probably guessed, these functions directly correlate to the Next and Back buttons on the AppWizard's dialog boxes.

The last function of importance here is the `CustomizeProject()` function. After the programmer has finished setting the project's options, AppWizard creates the project's "make" file and defines the default Debug and Release configurations for the project. The AppWizard then calls `CustomizeProject()` function so that the custom AppWizard has an opportunity to change any "make" files settings before the project is saved.

Working with macro dictionaries

Now that you know about the `CCustomAppWiz` class and the fact that you normally set a macro's initial value in the `InitCustomAppWiz()` function of this class, it's time to actually work with the different macros. As mentioned earlier, the `CCustomAppWiz` class contains a member variable, `m_Dictionary`, that stores the macro names and their values. Because this member variable is a `CMapStringToString`, you can simply use the standard MFC map functions to get and set the different macros, as the following code snippet indicates:

```
// retrieve value for Automation
CString strValue;
m_Dictionary.Lookup(_T("AUTOMATION"), strValue);

// Include support for context sensitive help
m_Dictionary.SetAt(_T("HELP"), strValue.Compare("1"));
```

At this point, open the SDIAutomationWizappAW.cpp file and type the following code at the end of the `InitCustomAppWiz()` function:

```
m_Dictionary.RemoveKey(_T("PROJTYPE_MDI"));
m_Dictionary.SetAt(_T("PROJTYPE_SDI"), _T("1"));
m_Dictionary.SetAt(_T("AUTOMATION"), _T("1"));
```

Now you can build the custom AppWizard project. If you watch the Output window, you'll see that the custom AppWizard has been copied to a specially designated folder (\Program Files\Microsoft Visual Studio\Common\msdev98\Template). After you have built the custom AppWizard, it should appear as an option in the Project list of the New dialog box when you're creating new projects. If you select this custom AppWizard, you'll see that the defaults are now SDI and Automation support.

It is important to realize that if you create custom AppWizards for distribution, you'll only need to distribute the .awx file. The .awx file will then need to be copied into the same folder on the destination PC. If, for some reason, your custom AppWizard is not located in the correct folder, it will not appear on the New dialog's Project list when the programmer attempts to create a new project.

Including Personal Information on Every About Box

You may have noticed that throughout this book, all the dialog-based demos have an About box button. You may have also noticed that all the demos (SDI, MDI, and dialog-based) have an About box that displays a description of the program, the programmer's name (either Rick or me), and a button that when clicked takes you to one of our Web pages. When I originally wrote the code for this nifty, albeit simple About box, I didn't want to have to remember to put the code for it into every demo application. This was to become my very first custom AppWizard. It is also the subject of the second demo for this chapter: AboutWiz.

Creating the AboutWiz demo project

The source code for this demo can be found on the companion CD in the Demos\AboutWiz folder. If you're actually performing the procedures in this chapter as you go along (as opposed to just reading them), create a new custom AppWizard project and call it **AboutWiz**. On the first dialog, specify the "Standard MFC AppWizard steps" as the starting point. Set the Project list name to anything you would want to see in your Project list. In keeping with my naming convention discussed in the first demo, I named mine "MFC AppWizard (exe) – About Box". Because an extra dialog is going to be used in this custom AppWizard, set the number of custom steps to 1 and press the Enter key. On the next dialog, select "MFC AppWizard Executable" and press Enter to dismiss this dialog; then press OK to dismiss the confirmation dialog.

Adding a custom dialog

First, create the custom dialog box that will be used to gather the information that will later appear on every project's About box created with the `AboutWiz` custom AppWizard.

Select the Resource tab on the AboutWiz's workspace dialog bar. Under the entry for Dialog resources, you should find a dialog with a resource ID of `IDD_CUSTOM1`. As you can see, it looks almost like the base dialog box AppWizard supplies for you when you create a dialog-based MFC application. At this point, let's add the necessary controls to the dialog. Here are the different style settings for the three input controls (all three are Edit controls):

- **Programmer**: `ID= IDC_EDT_PROGRAMMER`
- **Web Page**: `ID= IDC_EDT_WEB_PAGE`
- **General Information:** `ID= IDC_EDT_GENERAL_INFO, Multiline=YES, AutoHScroll=NO, AutoVScroll=YES`

Figure 33-2 shows how this dialog box should appear when you're finished adding the controls.

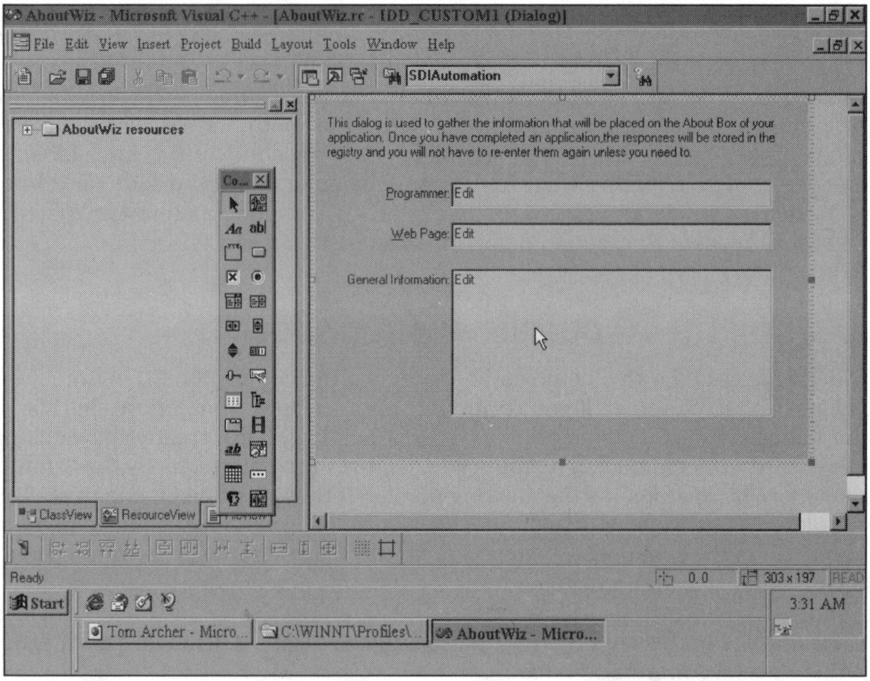

Figure 33-2: The dialog box for the AboutWiz demo after the new controls have been added

After you have added the new controls to the dialog resource, use ClassWizard to create a `CString` member variable for the Programmer, Web Page, and General Information Edit controls called `m_strProgrammer`, `m_strWebPage`, and `m_strGeneralInfo`, respectively. Open the cstm1dlg.cpp file and add the following lines to the end of the `CCustom1Dlg::OnInitDialog()` function (before the `return` statement):

```
AboutWizAW.m_Dictionary.Lookup("PROGRAMMER",
 m_strProgrammer);
AboutWizAW.m_Dictionary.Lookup("GENERAL_INFO",
 m_strGeneralInfo);
AboutWizAW.m_Dictionary.Lookup("WEB_PAGE",
 m_strWebPage);

UpdateData(FALSE);
```

Because a macro Dictionary is nothing more than a `CStringToString` object, the way to retrieve a Dictionary value is simply by calling the Dictionary's Lookup function.

Note

In case you're curious about the `AboutWizAW` object and where it came from, it is a global object of type `CCustomAppWiz`. You can see its definition in the AboutWizAW.h file. The reason that this object was made a global object is that, unlike a regular MFC application, there is no application object that every module in the application has access to.

◆ ◆ ◆ ◆ ◆

After you've changed the `CCustom1Dlg::OnInitDialog()` function, delete the three initialization lines from the `CCustom1Dlg`'s constructor. Their values will be initialized in the `CAboutWizAppWiz::InitCustomAppWiz()` function.

Finally, save the data by changing the `CCustom1Dlg::OnDismiss()` function to look like the following:

```
BOOL CCustom1Dlg::OnDismiss()
{
 if (!UpdateData(TRUE)) return FALSE;

 AboutWizAW.m_Dictionary.SetAt("PROGRAMMER",
  m_strProgrammer);
 AboutWizAW.m_Dictionary.SetAt("GENERAL_INFO",
  m_strGeneralInfo);
 AboutWizAW.m_Dictionary.SetAt("WEB_PAGE",
  m_strWebPage);

 return TRUE;
}
```

If you were to build the custom AppWizard and use it to create a new project, you would see your new dialog. Consider the values that were entered into the custom dialog and then saved as macros in the AppWizard's Dictionary—now the question is, *How do they get used in the new project?* The answer: They are referenced in template files that the AppWizard uses to build the new project. In the next section, you'll see how to create a new file template that will be copied to every project created with your new custom AppWizard.

Creating your own templates

Because our About box is very simple, we will put the code to declare and implement the `CAboutDlg` class in one header file: about.h. Create a file named `about.h` in the project's Template folder. Make sure that it looks like the following:

```
#pragma once

////////////////////////////////////////////////////////////////
CAboutDlg dialog used for App $$Root$$
```

```
class CAboutDlg : public CDialog
{
 public:
 CAboutDlg();

 // Dialog Data
 //{{AFX_DATA(CAboutDlg)
 enum { IDD = IDD_ABOUTBOX };
 //}}AFX_DATA

 // ClassWizard generated virtual function overrides
 //{{AFX_VIRTUAL(CAboutDlg)
 protected:
 virtual void DoDataExchange(CDataExchange* pDX);
 //}}AFX_VIRTUAL

 // Implementation
 protected:
 //{{AFX_MSG(CAboutDlg)
  afx_msg void OnOk();
 //}}AFX_MSG
 DECLARE_MESSAGE_MAP()
 };

CAboutDlg::CAboutDlg() : CDialog(CAboutDlg::IDD)
{
//{{AFX_DATA_INIT(CAboutDlg)
//}}AFX_DATA_INIT
}

void CAboutDlg::DoDataExchange(CDataExchange* pDX)
{
 CDialog::DoDataExchange(pDX);
 //{{AFX_DATA_MAP(CAboutDlg)
 //}}AFX_DATA_MAP
}

BEGIN_MESSAGE_MAP(CAboutDlg, CDialog)
 //{{AFX_MSG_MAP(CAboutDlg)
 ON_BN_CLICKED(IDOK, OnOk)
 //}}AFX_MSG_MAP
END_MESSAGE_MAP()

void CAboutDlg::OnOk()
{
 CString strURL;
 GetDlgItem(IDOK)->GetWindowText(strURL);
 if (!strURL.IsEmpty())
 {
  if (32 >= (int)ShellExecute(NULL, "open", strURL,
   NULL, NULL, SW_SHOWNORMAL))
  {
   AfxMessageBox("::ShellExecute failed to open "
    "this link!");
```

```
    }
  }
  else
  {
    AfxMessageBox("No URL defined on button!");
  }
}
```

As you can see, the only major thing added is the `OnOk()` handler. The function will take the About button's text and use it in a call to the Win32 SDK ShellExecute function. Where did the button get its text value? This will be answered in the "Changing the AppWizard templates" section later in this chapter. But before we get to that, there is still one more thing you must do to add a template to a project.

As I mentioned earlier, when a project is created using your custom AppWizard, it is AppWizard that creates the project's files using your templates. So, how do you tell AppWizard that you have a new template that needs to be created when the other files of the new project are created? A file named `newproj.inf` exists for this very purpose.

Changing the newproj.inf file

This file is sort of like a "bill of materials" for the custom AppWizard. AppWizard uses this file to know how to build a new project that is created with your custom AppWizard. When you open this file, your first impression is likely to be something along the lines of what mine was: "I thought I was programming in C++. What the heck is this stuff?" You'll see quite a few lines of "directives" that help AppWizard carry out its job of combining the templates and macros to create source code files for new projects. Instead of simply rehashing what you can read at the top of this file and what you can easily find in online help, let's look at a few lines of the `newproj.inf` file. After you understand the different directives, you'll be able to read the rest of the file without any difficulty.

The first thing to notice is that all directives begin with two dollar signs ("$$"). Because you can probably guess that the string below "Canned parts, with canned names" isn't code, it's easy to decipher `$$//` at the beginning of a line — it's used to insert a comment.

```
$$// Canned parts, with canned names
```

Normally when you see a template that is to be copied as one of the new project's files, a macro is used to help name the destination file. Even so, there are some standard files that will always have the same name regardless of the type of build. The standard `include` file, `stdafx.h`, is an example of this.

The lines following simply instruct the AppWizard to copy the `stdafx.h` and `stdafx.cpp` files to the new project folder, keeping the same filenames.

```
stdafx.h    StdAfx.h
stdafx.cpp  StdAfx.cpp
```

Note

The AppWizard uses the Tab character to delimit the two files' names (source template file and destination file). Therefore, if you insert a line of code similar to that given here, be sure to type a Tab character between the two files — *not* a space or series of spaces.

◆ ◆ ◆ ◆ ◆

The next directive to take note of in the `newproj.inf` file is `$$IF`. This directive simply tests the Boolean state of the macro enclosed in parenthesis. Note here that it is the `$$IF` directive that requires the parenthesis, not the use of the macro itself. In other words, if you want to refer to the macro in other places in your code, that is done by encasing the macro name with `$$` (for example, `$$PROGRAMMER$$`). As you can see in this next code snippet, the first two lines simply instruct that if the project type is not a DLL and it is not a dialog-based application, copy the `frame.h` and `frame.cpp` templates to files whose filenames are dictated by the `frame_hfile` and `frame_ifile` macros. You may recall, from using AppWizard to create an MDI application, that the last dialog box allows you to name the files that house the different classes. That's why a macro has to be used here. That particular dialog box, just like the custom dialog you saw in the previous section, used the filenames entered into it and updated the macros in the dictionary. Here they are being used to actually name the destination files:

```
$$IF(!PROJTYPE_DLL)
$$IF(!PROJTYPE_DLG)
frame.h     $$frame_hfile$$.h
frame.cpp   $$frame_ifile$$.cpp
```

This `$$IF` line works just like the two previous `$$IF` lines. The only differences are the macro being tested and the resulting template-to-file copy.

```
$$IF(MDICHILD)
childfrm.h      $$child_frame_hfile$$.h
childfrm.cpp    $$child_frame_ifile$$.cpp
```

Finally, as you might expect, each `$$IF` directive must have a matching `$$ENDIF` directive. Also notice that like C++, you can add a comment to the end of a line with the `//` character sequence.

```
$$ENDIF //MDICHILD
$$ENDIF //!PROJTYPE_DLG
```

Now that you see how easy it is to read the `newproj.inf` file, insert the following lines at the top of the file (after the comments explaining how to read and use the directives):

```
$$IF(PROJTYPE_DLG)
$$IF(ABOUT)
about.h  about.h
$$ENDIF //ABOUT
$$ELIF(PROJTYPE_MDI)
```

```
about.h  about.h
$$ELIF(PROJTYPE_SDI)
about.h  about.h
$$ENDIF //PROJTYPE_DLG
```

What we're basically doing with this code is making sure that the `about.h` file is copied in each of three scenarios: when the project type is dialog-based and the programmer did not uncheck the About box, when the project type is SDI, or when the project type is MDI.

Changing the AppWizard templates

In the previous section, you learned how to create a new template and have it added to the new project (via the `newproj.inf` file). Now you'll learn how to alter some of the generic templates created for you by the AppWizard when you created your custom AppWizard.

Changing the template resource files

Because we are going to add a new dialog, the first thing we will do is to insert a dialog template resource to the resource template file. When you created the custom AppWizard, you specified that you wanted your starting point to be "Standard MFC AppWizard steps." If you're following along by typing the demo in, take a look in your project's Template folder. All the template files necessary for creating every type of MFC executable have been copied there. This means that you can change anything you want. The first problem, however, is figuring out what to change! We know that we want to change a resource file, but which one? My beta version of AppWizard has just created 17 different resource files! With a little investigation, it is easy to see which resource files will need to change.

The majority of these resource files end in a three-letter suffix that indicates the language support (English=`enu`, German=`deu`, and so on). There are also localized Macintosh versions of each resource file. Therefore, for an English demo that is targeting an Intel PC running Windows 95, Windows 98, or Windows NT, we can already pare the number of resource files to contend with down to four: `all.rc`, `dlgall.rc`, `dlgloc_enu.rc`, and `loc_enu.rc`.

If you open the `all.rc` and `dlgall.rc` files and look at the directives and macros, you notice that these are base-resource files for all languages and platforms. These files, in turn, include the necessary language-specific and platform-specific resource files for things such as string tables and dialog resources. By process of elimination, we have discovered that the two files that need to be updated with the new dialog resource are the `loc_enu.rc` and `dlgloc_enu.rc` files. The reason that two resource files exist for each language is because one file (`loc_enu.rc`) is used for document-based applications (SDI or MDI) and the other file (`dlgloc_enu.rc`) is used for dialog-based applications.

Now that we finally know which resource files to alter, we can add our dialog. Unfortunately, you can not use the resource editor to create your dialog as you're probably accustomed to doing. This is because when you attempt to open the template resource file, the resource editor compiles the file's resources. Because the files contain the special directives you've learned about, the file won't compile and, hence, DevStudio won't allow you to edit it. You can, however, open a template resource file by setting the Open As option to Text in the File Open dialog. Even so, since you certainly don't want to manually type in the code required to define the dialog template resource, there has to be a better way. The method I used was to create the dialog in a separate resource file. In fact, to speed things up, I simply created a dummy project solely for this purpose. That way, I could open the resource editor on the dummy project's resource file and create my About box. When I finished, I opened the dummy project's resource file in text mode and copied the lines of resource code that defined the dialog to the clipboard. I then returned to the custom AppWizard, and upon opening the two different template resource files (`loc_enu.rc` and `dlgloc_enu.rc`), I manually replaced the existing `IDD_ABOUT` dialog resource definition as follows. Elegant? Definitely not. But it got the job done.

```
$$IF(ABOUT)
 IDD_ABOUTBOX DIALOGEX 0, 0, 160, 129
 STYLE DS_MODALFRAME | WS_POPUP | WS_CAPTION | WS_SYSMENU
 CAPTION "About $$ROOT$$"
 FONT 8, "MS Sans Serif"
 BEGIN
  CTEXT           "Written by"
   " $$PROGRAMMER$$",99998,7,64,143,12,NOT WS_GROUP,
   WS_EX_CLIENTEDGE | WS_EX_STATICEDGE
  LTEXT           "$$GENERAL_INFO$$",99999,7,7,144,40
  DEFPUSHBUTTON   "$$WEB_PAGE$$",
   IDOK,7,89,143,14,WS_GROUP
  PUSHBUTTON      "Cl&ose",IDCANCEL,7,107,143,14
 END
$$ENDIF //ABOUT
```

The only difference between the two files was that, in the case of the `dlgloc_enu.rc` file, I "wrapped" the dialog's definition with a `$$IF(ABOUT)` / `$$ENDIF` directive pair.

Notice how the macros are being used in the dialog's definition. This is how the information the user entered in your custom AppWizard's dialog finally ends up in a resource file.

Now we have our About box defined. Let's say we continue with these changes being the only changes we make to the template resource files. Now, the user of our custom AppWizard chooses a dialog-based application, fills out the programmer and Web-page information, and builds the system. Even so, what if the end user of his application never looks at the system menu? This About box is meant to be seen! After all, you're creating this About box to get the end user to your Web site. Therefore, the last change that needs to be made to the template resource file is to add an About button to the main dialog defined in the `dlgloc_enu.rc` file. To do this, simply open the dlgloc_enu.rc file and replace the main dialog with the following code:

```
IDD_$$SAFE_ROOT$$_DIALOG DIALOGEX  0, 0, 185, 92
STYLE DS_MODALFRAME | WS_POPUP | WS_VISIBLE | WS_CAPTION |
WS_SYSMENU
EXSTYLE WS_EX_APPWINDOW
CAPTION "$$TITLE$$"
FONT 8, "MS Sans Serif"
BEGIN
 DEFPUSHBUTTON   "OK",IDOK,128,7,50,14
 PUSHBUTTON      "Cancel",IDCANCEL,128,23,50,14

 $$IF(ABOUT)
  PUSHBUTTON
  "&About",ID_APP_ABOUT,128,45,50,14
  $$IF(HELP)
   PUSHBUTTON      "&Help",IDHELP,128,62,50,14
  $$ENDIF // HELP
 $$ELIF(HELP)
  PUSHBUTTON      "&Help",IDHELP,128,45,50,14
 $$ENDIF

 LTEXT           "TODO: Place dialog controls
here.",IDC_STATIC,5,34,113,8
END
```

Notice that I not only added an About button, but also positioned the Help button on the basis of whether an About button would be created. Due to the changes that we've made to the template resource files, every About box for every SDI, MDI, or dialog-based application will have the same About box, and the dialog-based applications will have a button on the main dialog that displays the About box. (By the way, the reason that we didn't have to make any more changes to the loc_enu.rc file is because every SDI or MDI application has an About option on the Help menu, and this option can not be turned off through the AppWizard.)

Changing the view and dialog template files

The very last code change that we now need to make involves changes to the view and dialog class implementation and header files. The reason that we have to change these is because the default view and dialog implementation files declare the CAboutDlg class. We don't want this, however, because we've done this ourselves in the about.h file that is to be copied by AppWizard along with the other templates. (By the way, the reason the About box code was moved to another file is so two different templates don't contain duplicate code.)

If you use the AppWizard to create an SDI application called "MyApp," the main application object will be declared in a filenamed "MyApp.h," and it will be implemented in a filenamed "MyApp.cpp." This is because a macro named $$ROOT$$ exists that contains the string value of your project name. The newproj.inf file contains the following lines that pertain to copying the template files that relate to document-based applications (SDI and MDI):

```
root.h    $$root$$.h
root.cpp  $$root$$.cpp
```

As you can see, the template header and implementation files for a document-based application are named `root.h` and `root.cpp`, respectively. Open the `root.h` file and insert the following function declaration in the `//{{AFX_MSG ($$APP_CLASS$$)`:

```
afx_msg void OnAppAbout();
```

After you have saved the `root.h` file, open the `root.cpp` file and make the following changes:

1. Remove the `CAboutDlg` class declaration at the top of the file.
2. Remove any `CAboutDlg` functions from the file.
3. Include the about .h file at the top of the file.
4. Add `ON_COMMAND (ID_APP_ABOUT, OnAppAbout)` to the `MESSAGE_MAP` section.
5. Add the following function definition at the end of the file:

```
// App command to run the About dialog
void $$APP_CLASS$$::OnAppAbout()
{
 CAboutDlg().DoModal();
}
```

Now that the document-based template files are done, it's time to modify the dialog-based template files. Much like root.h and root.cpp are the template files used to define the application class for all document-based applications, dlgroot.h and dlgroot.cpp are used for the same purpose for any dialog-based applications. Even so, unlike a document-based application, the `CAboutDlg` dialog for a dialog-based application is not defined in the same files as the application class. Instead, it is defined in the main dialog's implementation file, which is named dialog.cpp.

Open the dialog.cpp file and make the following changes:

1. Remove the `CAboutDlg` class declaration at the top of the file.
2. Remove any `CAboutDlg` functions from the file.
3. Include the about .h file at the top of the file, as follows:

```
$$IF(ABOUT)
#include "about.h"
$$ENDIF //ABOUT
```

4. Locate the `$$IF(ABOUT)` entry line in the `MESSAGE_MAP` section, and add the following line:

```
ON_BN_CLICKED(ID_APP_ABOUT, OnAbout)
```

5. Add the following function definition to the end of the file:

```
$$IF(ABOUT)
void $$DLG_CLASS$$::OnAbout()
{
 CAboutDlg().DoModal();
}
$$ENDIF //ABOUT
```

We are finished with the main code necessary to make our custom AppWizard work. Even so, let's add a couple of niceties to the application before building and testing it. Every time you use AppWizard to generate a project, the last dialog is a confirmation dialog that displays the options you have selected throughout the sequence of dialog boxes that were displayed to you. In the next section, you'll learn how incredibly easy it is to modify this file to also display the options that were selected from your custom dialog(s).

Changing the CONFIRM.INF file

If you open the confirm.inf file, you'll see that it looks a great deal like the newproj.inf file in terms of making heavy use of the AppWizard directives and macros. All you have to do to add your text to this file is simply type it using the macros that you defined. Here is an example of how you might want to display the information entered for the About box:

```
$$IF(PROJTYPE_DLG)
$$IF(ABOUT)
About Box Information
     Programmer: $$PROGRAMMER$$
     Web Page:   $$WEB_PAGE$$
     App Desc:   $$GENERAL_INFO$$
$$ENDIF //ABOUT
$$ELIF(PROJTYPE_MDI)
About Box Information
     Programmer: $$PROGRAMMER$$
     Web Page:   $$WEB_PAGE$$
     App Desc:   $$GENERAL_INFO$$
$$ELIF(PROJTYPE_SDI)
About Box Information
     Programmer: $$PROGRAMMER$$
     Web Page:   $$WEB_PAGE$$
     App Desc:   $$GENERAL_INFO$$
$$ENDIF //PROJTYPE_DLG
```

As you may recall, the `$$IF/$$ELIF/$$ENDIF` structure mimics exactly what's in the newproj.inf to determine whether the about.h file is to be copied for the new project. The lines between these directives are simply lines of text displayed, verbatim, on the AppWizard's Confirmation dialog.

Using the Registry for persistent macros

Let's think about the application we've done in terms of usability. We have this application (a custom AppWizard) that allows a programmer to create an MFC application that always contains an About box which displays the programmer's contact information. Even so, this information needs to be entered every time the programmer creates a new project. Even if the programmer is going to place an application description in the General Information macro, two out of the three macros he has to enter are the same every time he runs the custom AppWizard. Adding to that is the possibility that someone may use the custom AppWizard and want the same description for every application. For example, he or she may want the General Information macro to have a value like "Please check out my Web page by clicking the button following to other really cool applications I've done."

Modifying the CAboutWizAppWiz class to use the Registry

Using the `CRegistry` class introduced earlier in the book makes this part quite simple. As a matter of fact, there is only one class to modify (`CAboutWizAppWiz`). When you have completed the steps outlined in this section, you'll be ready to build and test your new custom AppWizard.

Open the AboutWizAppAW.cpp file and do the following:

1. Add the following Registry key value:

```
#define ABOUTWIZ_KEY \
 "Software\\Programming Windows 98 Bible\\AboutWiz"
```

2. Define the following static structure to contain the macro names, default macro values, Registry value names, and macro default values. The Registry value names are used to search the Registry in the key specified by `ABOUTWIZ_KEY`. If a value can not be found (for example, the first time the application is run), the value contained in the macro default value is used to populate the custom dialog.

```
static struct
{
  char szMacroName[50];
  char szRegistryValueName[50];
  char szMacroDefaultValue[50];
} macroPairs[] = {
 "PROGRAMMER", "Programmer", "Programmer Name",
 "GENERAL_INFO", "General Info", "App Desc",
 "WEB_PAGE", "Web Page", "Web Page"
};
```

3. Place the following code at the end of the `CAboutWizAppWiz::InitCustomAppWiz()` function. As you can see, this code simply creates a `CRegistry` object on the stack and then iterates through the static macros structure defined in step 2. For each entry in the macros structure, the code reads the Registry to try to locate the value for it. If a value can not be located, a default value is used. In either case, once a macro value has been established, the Dictionary is updated to reflect the macro's value.

```
CRegistry reg(HKEY_LOCAL_MACHINE, ABOUTWIZ_KEY);
CString strValue;
for (int i = 0; i < sizeof macros / sizeof macros[0];
 i++)
{
 if (reg.ReadString(macros[i].szRegValName,
  strValue.GetBuffer(strValue.GetLength())))
 {
  m_Dictionary.SetAt(macros[i].szMacroName, strValue);
 }
 else
 {
  m_Dictionary.SetAt(macros[i].szMacroName,
   macros[i].szMacroDefaultValue);
  if (m_Dictionary.Lookup(macros[i].szMacroName,
   strValue))
  {
   reg.WriteString(macros[i].szRegValName,
    strValue.GetBuffer(strValue.GetLength()));
  }
 }
}
```

4. Place the following code at the end of the `CAboutWizAppWiz::ExitCustomAppWiz()` function. The AppWizard DLL calls this function when the custom AppWizard DLL is being unloaded. We will use this function to save the values entered by the user.

```
CRegistry reg(HKEY_LOCAL_MACHINE, ABOUTWIZ_KEY);
CString strValue;
for (int i = 0; i < sizeof macros / sizeof macros[0];
 i++)
{
 if (reg.ReadString(macros[i].szRegValName,
  strValue.GetBuffer(strValue.GetLength())))
 {
  m_Dictionary.SetAt(macros[i].szMacroName, strValue);
 }
 else
 {
  m_Dictionary.SetAt(macros[i].szMacroName,
   macros[i].szMacroDefaultValue);
  if (m_Dictionary.Lookup(macros[i].szMacroName,
   strValue))
```

```
        {
         reg.WriteString(macros[i].szRegValName,
          strValue.GetBuffer(strValue.GetLength()));
        }
      }
    }
```

Now it's time to build and test the custom AppWizard. First, specify the active configuration as a Release build. Then, build the project.

As mentioned earlier, the DLL will be copied into the \Program Files\Microsoft Visual Studio\Common\msdev98\Template folder. The custom AppWizard DLL file will have the name of the project used to create it with an extension of "awx." This extension is how AppWizard knows which files in this folder are custom AppWizards.

After you have built the project, you can test it by simply creating a new project and selecting the Wizard that you just created. For example, create a dialog-based application called TestAboutWiz. The custom dialog will be the last dialog box displayed. Figure 33-3 shows the custom dialog box at work. After you have entered the information for this dialog and clicked the Finish button, the Confirmation dialog will appear. Verify that the information entered on the custom dialog also appears on this dialog. Click the OK button to create the TestAboutWiz project.

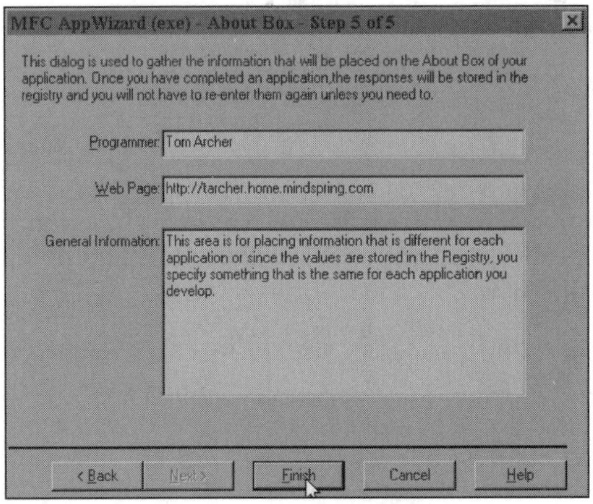

Figure 33-3: An example of entering information into the AboutWiz custom dialog box

After the TestAboutWiz project has been created, build it and run it. It should appear with an OK button, a Cancel button, and an About button. Clicking the "About" button should produce results similar to those shown in Figure 33-4.

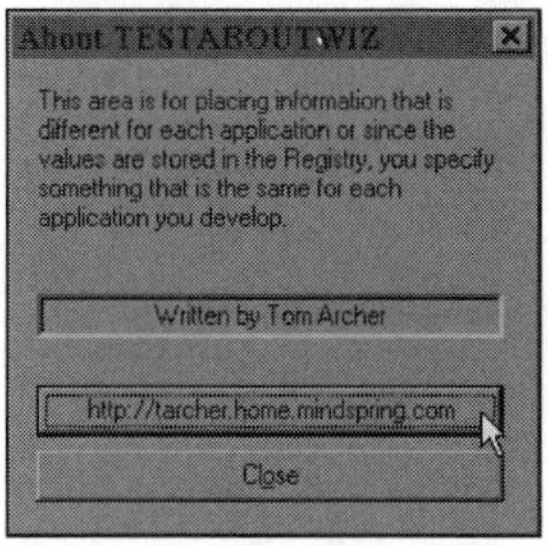

Figure 33-4: This About box is created for every new project you create with the AboutWiz custom AppWizard, enabling you to place important contact information on every application you develop.

That's it! You now have a custom AppWizard that will place an About box displaying your name, general information, and Web page in every application you create.

Summary

As you've seen throughout this chapter, the capability to create custom AppWizards is a great tool for increasing productivity because it allows you to define generic functionality in a given class of projects. Although the steps involved are not difficult, they are time-consuming until you get used to them.

The first custom AppWizard I programmed was the AboutWiz DLL that was used as the main demo in this chapter. Due to learning curves, lack of documentation, and the fact that I was doing this with a Beta compiler, it took me approximately 10 hours to finish. Even so, after I knew what I was doing, my second custom AppWizard took me 45 minutes. By showing you what I've learned, I hope this chapter enables you to traverse that learning curve a little quicker and create your first custom AppWizard in much less time than it took me.

✦ ✦ ✦

APPENDIX

What's on the CD-ROM

The CD-ROM accompanying this text is organized into two sections. The first section contains the chapter-related content: all of the demonstration programs and supporting files can be found here. Each chapter except Chapter 25 has a folder. For instance, the folder for Chapter 3 is named Chap3, the folder for Chapter 29 is named Chap29, and so on. Within each of the chapter folders are subfolders for each of the demonstration programs noted in the chapter. For a guide to this section of the CD-ROM, see the following "Chapter Content."

Note that throughout the text of the book, when a demonstration program is mentioned, the folder in which it resides is listed. For instance, in Chapter 5, the first demo program has a line above it as follows:

CD-ROM Location: **Chap5\BlitDemo**

Note also, if you use Explorer to copy the demonstration program folders to your hard drive, all the files will have the read-only attribute set. You can fix this from DOS. While you are in any of the folders on your hard drive, type **ATTRIB *.* /s -r**. This removes the read-only attribute for all files in the folder and its child folders.

You can also copy the files with the DOS XCOPY command. When you do this, the attribute bits won't be set.

There's one additional alternative. All the chapter content folders have been collected into a self-extracting file named InstallContents.EXE. If you run this program, the chapter content folders will be installed to your hard drive with none of the read-only attribute bits set.

The second organizational section on the CD-ROM is for programming tools. For descriptions of these tools, see the following "Programming Tools." The files can all be found on the CD-ROM in the Programming Tools folder.

Chapter Content

This section describes all the CD-ROM contents that directly relate to the chapter content.

Chapter 1

This chapter is an introduction to Windows 98 and the Visual Studio set of tools. Included are C++ programs, an ATL-created ActiveX control, a J++ applet, a J++ application, and a Visual Basic Program.

HelloWorld1

The first program created for this chapter is a variation of the traditional "Hello World" program with which all C and C++ programmers start. The program was created with the MFC AppWizard. The only one of the default settings throughout the AppWizard process that was changed was to make the application a single-document interface program.

Important to note is you can now create programs with AppWizard that don't have document/view architecture support. This is a tremendously valuable option. Many times I created document/view programs that simply displayed graphics or images and totally ignored all the document features. Every time this happened, I'd look at the files in the project and long to delete the document source code files. (Good thing I never did; the project wouldn't compile if I had.)

HelloWorld2

I never thought there was a place for Win32 console applications until two things happened. First, I began teaching C++ at Rockingham Community College. The first thing I started with was creating AppWizard-based Windows applications. It only took about 15 minutes before I realized how lost everyone was. I then quickly learned about Win32 console applications. With these gems, I was able to teach C++ concepts without students getting lost in the myriad project and MFC classes.

Once I made this startling revelation, I began to realize the Win32 console applications are handy for utilities that don't need a user interface. With almost no effort, I can create programs that do useful things, such as move and rename files, convert binary files to source code, and other things software developers need. I don't yearn for the old days when I could whip up a DOS application in five minutes to automate some programming tasks. And I don't even have to worry about segmented pointers or running out of memory (usually!).

This second program is a Win32 console application "Hello Visual C++ Console World!" When you create a Win32 console application, one of the choices, believe it or not, is a "Hello World" application.

HelloWorld3

It won't be long into your programming career, especially with the direction in which Microsoft is pushing, that you need to create ActiveX controls. For most situations, the best way to do this is with the Active Template Library (ATL) Wizard. This creates the startup code for an ATL project and saves you the time and drudgery of doing it yourself.

Despite the ease with which you can create an ATL control, the footprint turns out to be relatively small. A full control with minimal code that's added (such as the HelloWorld3 control) ends up at about 37K. ATL controls have many options; one is the capability to use MFC. If you want to use MFC, be prepared for another 80–100KB that'll be added to the footprint.

HelloWorld4

Somewhere along the way, everyone creates several Java applets and/or applications. Some go on to master the language and extensively use J++ as a development tool. I initially got into Java because it's so easy to use images and I like spicing up my Web site. Eventually, I learned all the other aspects of Java and, low and behold, I inherited several E-Commerce applets I maintain at work. This was an unwanted side benefit of my Java development.

All kidding aside, you need to know some Java to keep up with today's development requirements. And Visual Studio gives you J++, a powerful, easy-to-use tool for Java development.

The HelloWorld4 applet was written in about two minutes. Java is fairly easy to learn and J++ creates enough startup code so you needn't fool with it yourself.

HelloWorld5

Someone out there is now saying "Java is a real language, what about applications?" Serious Java devotees may even be mixing it up with some expletives. Yeah, Java is a real language that can be used to write good applications. As a matter of fact, Id Software, developers of Doom and Quake, are now using Java to develop some of their utility programs. If it's good enough for them, it's good enough for us.

Truthfully, Java is a great language. It's object-oriented, not like the hybrid variety of OOP that C++ implements. You can write a serious application with Java, no question about it. My only concern is the Virtual Machine is not all that fast. I haven't written any large applications with Java yet; I think I'll wait until the VM gets faster. But for small applications, it's a good choice.

The HelloWorld5 program is a Java application that displays a text string in the application's window caption bar.

HelloWorld6

Visual Basic is another power tool in the Visual Studio 6 aresenal. With Visual Basic you can easily create useful applications. When I say easily, this means in several short minutes. And it's not just form-based applications that are easy. Writing NT services is a snap. Creating ActiveX components is a piece of cake. If you don't use Visual Basic, you need to take a look. It's a sophisticated tool, which, in many cases, can save you time and money.

The HelloWorld6 application took about a minute and a half to write. It took more time to run the program, capture the screen, and save the image than it took to write. And there's absolutely no source code for the program. What you see is all automatically based on some form properties and a single object placed on the form.

Chapter 2

This chapters covers the topic of menus and handling menu input. Two demonstration programs show you how to create and respond to simple menus, create and respond to context menus, and deal with advanced topics such as pop-up menus.

MenuDemo1

To illustrate the basic techniques of handling menu input, we created a demo program named MenuDemo1. It performs simple menu command and update functions in response to menu input.

MenuDemo2

The MenuDemo2 program shows you how to create context menus and use them to effect changes in a window. The program divides the view window into four quadrants. One is red, one green, one blue, and one white. If you click the right mouse button in the view window, the program calculates which quadrant you're in. It then displays a context menu and enables you to set the brightness of the quadrant's color.

Chapter 3

This chapter shows you how to respond to mouse and keyboard events. Three demo programs teach you how to create ClassWizard handlers and then use the command functions to respond.

MouseDemo1

We created a simple demo program that shows you how to respond to the main mouse events. It handles mouse movement events, mouse-button-down events, and mouse-button-up events. It does not handle middle mouse-button events.

MouseDemo2

To demonstrate how to change mouse cursors within an application, we wrote a special program named MouseDemo2. The program loads in 16 cursors and sets the cursor depending on the mouse position.

The application looks at where inside of the view window the mouse currently is. Dividing the view window into 16 rectangular regions allows the program to decide which of 16 mouse cursors to use. When you run the program and move the mouse around inside the view window, you see the mouse cursor change. The name of the mouse cursor is also displayed.

Keyboard Demo Program start here

Now that you've learned about keyboard input, it's time to show you a program that demonstrates the principles. We built and included a simple program named KeyboardDemo. It displays `WM_KEYDOWN`, `WM_KEYUP`, and `WM_CHAR` messages that are sent to the View window.

Chapter 4

Chapter 4 covers the topic of graphics. The three demo programs that accompany this chapter show readers how to perform basic draw operations.

PenBrushDemo

The first demo program in this chapter shows you how to use `CPen` and `CBrush` objects. Because these MFC classes encapsulate GDI pens and brushes, they make it easier for programmers to draw with pens and brushes.

With a menu selection, you can alternate between drawing lines and rectangles to the window. Another menu selection enables you to set the line width with which the lines and rectangle border will be drawn.

When lines are drawn to the window, you'll see the defined line patterns such as `PS_DASH` and `PS_DOT`. When rectangles are drawn to the window, you'll see the defined fill patterns such as `HS_BDIAGONAL` and `HS_CROSS`.

GraphicsDemo1

The GraphicsDemo1 program illustrates the basic techniques of drawing to a window. When the program runs, you can draw lines, rectangles, and ellipses. You can select the color with which the program will draw with the color selector common dialog. Additionally, you can set the ROP code so draw operations are performed with different results.

To draw in the window, click the left mouse in the window. To change the draw operation, draw color, and ROP code, use the menu selections.

GraphicsDemo2

This program shows you how to create a clipping rectangle and use it to limit the window area in which draw operations occur. The program enables you to move the clipping rectangle around on the screen so you can experiment. To change the clipping rectangle to a different location, click the left mouse button in the window.

To draw the star-shaped figure, move the mouse around in the window. It'll draw in the window, centered around the mouse coordinates. You will, however, only see part of the figure because there's a rectangular clipping region selected.

Chapter 5

Chapter 5 covers bitmaps and palettes. The subfolders in the Chap05 folder all contain programs and files related to the material in Chapter 5.

BlitDemo

This demo program shows you how to load and display bitmaps. The bitmaps are stored as resource objects and the program loads them with the `LoadBitmap()` function. Four different `BitBlt()` rasters operations are shown: `SRCCOPY`, `SRCINVERT`, `SRCAND`, and `SRCPAINT`.

ShowDIB

This program contains a specially-written class named `CDib`. The `CDib` class makes it easy to load, display, and save DIBs. You can use the `CDib` class in any of your programs by using the DIB.cpp and DIB.h files from this program.

Miscellaneous

In the Chap5 folder are two files. The HSV.c file contains a single function that converts RGB values to HSV values. The Transparent.c file contains a single function that draws a `CBitmap` object to the screen, but masks it with a transparent color.

Chapter 6: FileExceptionTest

This dialog-based application illustrates how to throw and catch exceptions (of type `CFileException`) in your C++/MFC code. The different `CFileException` causes are loaded into a combo box in `OnInitDialog()`. When an entry in the combo box is selected, an exception of that type is thrown and caught. The resulting exception description is then displayed on the dialog. The purpose of this demo is to illustrate how to throw and catch exceptions across function boundaries.

Chapter 7: CodeFinder

This dialog-based application is "built up" throughout the dialog/controls chapter and demonstrates many techniques useful in designing and programming dialogs. Almost all the "basic" controls (static, edit, listbox, combobox, radio buttons, and so forth) have been used in an attempt to show the reader how each of these controls needs to be programmed. In addition, the demo teaches the concepts of how to use DDX and DDV to make moving the data from the dialog's controls to the application's variables easier. While the main dialog is modal, there is also a modeless dialog that illustrates how to program that functionality into your application. This modeless dialog implements a "find" feature so the reader can see a realistic example of having a modal dialog and a modeless dialog present at the same time and communicating information back and forth. In addition, the demo also illustrates how to program a "folded" dialog. Folded dialogs are dialogs that resize to show less information or additional information as the result of the user clicking a button.

Chapter 8: ModalPropertySheetDemo

This demo shows how to create and control programmatically a modal property sheet and its property pages. In addition, techniques for doing things not inherently supported with property sheets and property pages such as disabling tabs, enabling mnemonics, changing a tab's font, and so forth, are illustrated.

Chapter 9

This chapter covers the topic of Data I/O. Subjects such as string manipulation, file I/O, and registry access are covered.

StringDemo

To show you how to use the basic `CString` functions, we created a demo program named `StringDemo`. The application loads a file named AESOP.txt when it first runs. This text file contains many fables from *Aesop's Fables.*

You can search the text for any string. You can choose to do a case-sensitive search or a noncase-sensitive search. You can also perform a search and replace operation on the file. Once the search and replace operation is done, you can see the altered text inside of WordPad. (When you see it in WordPad, though, make sure WordPad is set for text wrapping.)

FileDemo

You'll use the `CFile` class to load and save buffers of data often. For this reason, a program named FileDemo was written that does this. It enables you to create a list of files and then saves all the files to one large file.

You can also copy a single file from one source to a destination. To do this, just select Copy First File. The program will then copy the first file in the list to a destination file you select.

One handy function you may want to remove and place in your own program is the `CopyFile()` function. It's useful for a wide variety of applications that need to copy files from one place to another.

Chapter 10

This chapter covers the topics of sound and music. Playing wave files, MIDI files, and CD audio tracks is taught.

WaveDemo

The first demo program in this chapter plays six different prerecorded sounds. Three of the sounds are saved to disk as .wav files. The other three are part of the program's resource file. Users can select any of the six sounds and have them play. The sounds can either be played directly from disk or the resource file, or they can be loaded and then played at a later time. You can see what the program looks like in Figure 10-1.

MIDIDemo

The MIDIDemo program shows you how to play and manage MIDI files. Four MIDI files are in the MIDIDemo folder and any one of them can be loaded and played. The program uses the `CMidi` class for performing MIDI operations. It will make playing MIDI files easy. The MIDIDemo program can be seen in Figure 10-2.

CDPlayer

Few programs play CD audio music. Most programs load and play MIDI files. This program plays the high-quality sound data found on audio CDs. It does so with the `CCDAudio` class.

Because the CD that comes with the book doesn't have any CD audio tracks, you'll have to put one of your own in the CD drive. After you do this, you can play any of the tracks on the CD. This program also enables you to pause playback and move around inside of each track. You can see the CDPlayer application pictured in Figure 10-3.

Library

For convenience, use the Sound.lib and Sound.h files found in the Chap10\Library folder of the CD-ROM. This makes adding sounds to any of your applications easier because you won't have to link in any source code.

Chapter 11

This chapter covers the topic of Timers and Idle Processing. Both these techniques can make your program work smoother by letting things happen on a periodic basis.

Clock

The first demo program shows you how to create a clock application using a timer. The `SetTimer()` function passes a `NULL` as its third parameter and, therefore, causes a `WM_TIMER` message to be posted to the window.

This program enables you to view either an analog clock or a digital clock. To change the display, simply change the setting in the Type menu.

OnIdleDemo

The OnIdleDemo program shows you how to override and use the `OnIdle()` function. It shows numeric values for the `OnIdle lCount` value and the elapsed time since `lCount` was reset.

The OnIdleDemo program shows you a bar graph with the relative amount of time given to the program's `OnIdle()` function.

The program also draws a bargraph to give a graphical indication of the relative amount of idle processing the application has made available to the `OnIdle()` function. If you move the mouse around or perform window operations, such as resizing, the graph decreases. That's because all the messages Windows services reduce the amount of processing time available to the `OnIdle()` function.

Chapter 12

Chapter 12 covers documents and views as they apply to a single-document interface (SDI) application. The subfolders in the Chap12 folder all contain programs and files related to the material in Chapter 12.

RectApp

This sample application demonstrates all the basic programming techniques needed to create a complete SDI application. The program covers modifying document and view classes, including how to serialize (save and load) document data and how to display document data.

RectApp2

This sample application is similar to this chapter's RectApp, except it uses a persistent object to store data for the document class. The program shows how to create a persistent class (a class that can serialize its own state and contents) and how to use that class in the context of an SDI application.

Chapter 13

Chapter 13 covers dynamic and static splitter windows. The subfolders in the Chap13 folder all contain programs and files related to the material in Chapter 13.

DynSplitter

This sample application demonstrates how to program an application with a dynamic splitter window. The application displays 100 lines of text the user can split horizontally and/or vertically to create up to four views of the text.

MDISplitter

This sample application demonstrates how to use splitter windows in an MDI application. The user can create child document windows, each of which contains 100 lines of text that can be split horizontally and vertically, just as was done in the DynSplitter application.

MultViewSplitter

This sample application demonstrates how to create a custom splitter-window class that can display data in different formats in each of its splitter panes. In this case, when users split the pane horizontally, they see two different lines of text, one in each pane.

StatSplitter

This sample application demonstrates how to program static splitter windows. Specifically, the application displays 12 static splitter panes, each of which contains 100 lines of text and has its own horizontal and vertical scroll bars.

Chapter 14: MDIDemo

Chapter 14 covers multiple-document interface (MDI) applications. The subfolders in the Chap14 folder all contain programs and files related to the material in Chapter 14.

The MDIDemo sample application demonstrates how to program an MDI application. The application is similar to Chapter 12's RectApp2, except each new document appears in its own child document window. The program covers completing document and view classes, including how to serialize (save and load) document data and how to display document data.

Chapter 15

Chapter 15 covers printing documents from an MFC application. The subfolders in the Chap15 folder all contain programs and files related to the material in Chapter 15.

RectPrint

This sample application demonstrates how to handle printing and print preview for an application that displays a graphical document. The application is yet another version of Chapter 12's RectApp2, except the window displays a ruler across the top and fully implements printing and print preview.

TextPrint

This sample application demonstrates how to handle printing and print preview for an application that displays a text document. The application enables the user to open and print a text file, demonstrating such advanced features as pagination and controlling the Print dialog box.

Chapter 16: MFC Extensions

This application contains several small C++ classes that extend the functionality of MFC in different ways. The UI controls include a "gray edit" control like the one seen in Quicken where the edit control's text is in an italicized gray font until the control has focus or until the control loses focus and the user has typed in data. Another control is an "underline edit" control where, as the name implies, instead of a rectangle, the edit control's border consists of a single underline. These controls are useful for applications like invoicing and purchasing where end users are accustomed to seeing dialogs that more closely approximate a printed document. In addition to these UI controls, there is an "auto complete" combo box that functions like the "URL" combo box seen in most browsers where the combo box is continually searching its list and "auto completing" the entry as the user types. The last two classes presented include a class for making a form view more closely represent a 3D piece of paper and a `CCtrlView`-derived class (`CListBoxView`) that has a listbox that occupies the entire client area and works exactly like the other MFC provided `CCtrlView`-derived classes.

Chapter 17: SBDemo

This chapter covers available MFC support for two user-interface objects: toolbars and status bars. *Toolbars* are windows with buttons that enable users to issue commands with a single mouse click. This makes toolbar commands somewhat more accessible to users, because menus require at least two mouse clicks (or a mouse click and drag). Because they occupy screen space, however, toolbars should be used for only the most commonly requested commands. For the same reason, most users want to be able to hide unwanted toolbars. AppWizard automatically provides this capability in the toolbars it creates for you. We'll show you how to create additional toolbars, as well as how to show them and hide them as desired.

The SBDemo demo program illustrates how to customize the appearance of a status bar at runtime. Many of the techniques we discussed in this chapter are used in this application. These techniques include custom status bar indicators, controlling the status bar, and dynamically changing the status bar panes.

The status bar creation process is located in MainFrm.cpp and specifically in the member function `CMainFrame::OnCreate()`. In here, you can find the modifications made to the indicatos array, as well as the initial call to `CStatusBar::Create()`.

Most of the actual modifications to the status bar are located in Sbdemoview.cpp. The dynamic modification of the status bar occurs in the mouse command message handlers `OnLButtonDown()`, `OnRButtonDown()`, and `OnMouseMove()`. In the button handler functions, each of the status bar panes are toggled between a "popped" out and recessed appearance. The code contained in the `OnMouseMove()` handler updates two of the status bar panes with the current *x* and *y* coordinates of the mouse cursor.

Chapter 18: ThreadDemo

This chapter covers the difficult topic of threads. How to use them and how to avoid the pitfalls are taught.

The ThreadDemo program implements a multiple-document framework. Each separate window is drawn by a separately instantiated thread. So if you create four child windows, four threads are at work drawing each window.

The thread functions draw a spirograph pattern in the windows. Three values determine the shape and pattern of the spirograph pattern: the integers `nFixedRadius`, `nMovingRadius`, and `nMovingOffset`. Each time the window is drawn, these values are incremented. This makes the pattern change over time for a continuous variety of effects.

Chapter 19

ODBCDemo

This is the first demo of the ODBC chapter and shows the basics of using the ODBC SDK. Boiler plate code is presented to allocate the different environment handles, connect to a data source, disconnect from a data source, and free the environment handles. In addition, this demo dynamically prepares SQL statements, executes the prepared SQL statements, binds program variables to result set columns, and fetches data from a result set using numerous ODBC SDK functions. This folder contains a Microsoft Access database (Chapter19.mdb) used for all the demos in this chapter. Another important thing to note is you must create a DSN for the sample database for these demos to work. The steps for creating the DSN are outlined in Chapter 19.

ODBCInfoDll

This application presents a powerful class (CODBCInfo) that shows off some of the more powerful capabilities of ODBC. While this class specifically was written to retrieve data attributes for any given data type supported by the data source, the internals of the class are what's interesting here. As the chapter explains, this class shows how to code to the ODBC SDK in such a way that data can be retrieved from a data source without knowing the database schema until runtime. The class accomplishes this using the SQLNumResultCols() and SQLDescribeCol() functions to query the data type dynamically that was returned for each column in a specified result set. Then, each column's SQL type is converted into its corresponding C data type so the correct amount of memory can be allocate for each column of data. Once the memory has been allocated, the SQLGetData90 function is actually used to retrieve the data. Based on the type of data being read in, this memory is mapped into the appropriate CDbVariant member variable.

ODBCInfoClient

This application provides the reader with a boiler-plate example of how to use the CODBCInfo class. A dialog-based application, ODBCInfoClient, displays a button, which, when clicked, creates an instance of the CODBCInfo class. The CODBCInfo object is then used to query a sample database (provided with the sample) as to several of the data attributes of the SQL type SQL_CHAR. These values are then displayed in a message box.

Chapter 20

UserMaintenance

This demo uses the MFC database classes to present a fully functional "User" maintenance application. The MFC database classes used are CDatabase and CRecordset and are used to provide all the basic database operations (add/delete/update) for a sample Microsoft Access database (provided on the CD). Both sequential and random access I/O are used in this application to illustrate to the reader how each type of I/O is accomplished with the MFC database classes. When the application initializes, all the Users in the UserMaster table are read and loaded into a listbox, illustrating for the reader the manner in which a CRecordset object can be used to navigate a set of records sequentially. When a User is selected from the listbox, its data (User Name, User Status, and so forth) is displayed on the dialog. Once the User's data is displayed on the dialog, it can be changed and updated via a command button. Updates and deletes are performed via the CDatabase class' ExecuteSQL() function. Please note, the demos in this chapter use the same database used with Chapter 19. Therefore, you need to create a DSN as outlined in Chapter 19 for these demos to work properly.

Parameterized

This application displays a dialog that allows the search and retrieval of Users from a sample database (provided with the application). This search is done via a parameterized CRecordset. The different steps necessary to create and use parameterized CRecordset are outlined in Chapter 20. In addition, once a record is retrieved, another CRecordset-derived class is used to retrieve other data concerning the User. This second record set is based on a multitable Microsoft Access query that returns data.

Chapter 21: DaoUserMaintenance

This application uses the MFC DAO classes to present a fully functional "User" maintenance application. The MFC DAO classes used are CDaoDatabase and CDaoRecordset and are used to provide all the basic database operations (add/delete/update) for a sample Microsoft Access database (DaoDemo.mdb) provided with the application. All the Users in the UserMaster table are read and loaded into a listbox when the application is started, illustrating for the reader the manner in which a CDaoRecordset object can be used to sequentially navigate a set of records. When a User is selected from the listbox, its data (User Name, User Status, and so forth) is then displayed on the dialog. Once the User's data is displayed on the dialog, it can be changed and updated via a command button. Updates and deletes are performed via the CDaoDatabase class' Execute() function.

Chapter 22

Chapter 22, all about writing your own DLLs, contains several demo programs to illustrate DLL concepts.

CommClientApp

If you ever wondered how the Control Panel works or if you ever needed the same functionality in your application, this demo may be just what you need. The idea behind the Control Panel is a simple one. Microsoft needed a way to have the Control Panel provide an interface to certain applications without having the Control Panel itself know anything about the applications. This way, Control Panel applets could be added and removed without the Control Panel application changing. How does this work? When the Control Panel starts up, it performs a LoadLibrary() on all files it finds in the Windows folder matching a specified file mask (extension of .cpl). Files that are Control Panel applets must export a predefined set of functions. Control Panel then uses the GetProcAddr() function to get the addresses of these functions from the loaded module and dynamically makes the necessary calls to do such things as display the applet's icon, run the applet, and communicate with the applet. This sample application shows how to implement this functionality from within your application. The demo consists of a main application that loads all DLLs (via LoadLibrary()) found in its folder. The GetProcAddr() function is then used to query each DLL to make sure it is one understood by the demo. Each supported DLL exports a function that returns a string describing the DLL. The application fills a listbox with each of these descriptions. When one of the listbox's entries is selected, another of the associated DLLs exported functions is called and the DLL displays a dialog.

ImageViewer

This DLL demonstrates how to implement MFC document/view support for a given file type in a DLL. Basically it works by defining the document, view, frame, and resources needed for the document template and exporting an initialization function for any application that needs support for the file type. Now any time an application needs to implement support for this file type, the programmer only needs to link the application with the DLL and calls the DLL's initialization function. The DLL automatically takes care of creating the document template and adds it to the application object's document template list.

ImageViewerClient

This is the client application for the ImageViewer DLL. Using this application, you can open any graphics files supported by `ImageObject`. The document template used for opening and displaying the files is actually contained in the ImageViewer DLL. This application simply calls a single exported function and, viola!, the application automatically has support for any files the document template supports.

KeybdHook

The DLL exports several functions to illustrate how to install, control, and de-install a Windows hook function for monitoring keyboard activity. While the demo application was written specifically for the purpose of a keyboard hook function, the chapter and the majority of the source code can be used for almost any type of Windows hook function.

Chapter 23

This chapter covers the topic of using third-party libraries to enhance applications. It does so with the `ImageObject` imaging library.

Display

This program shows you how to load and display an image in a window. It's a bare-bones application, so you can focus on the code that loads and displays images. After studying this program, you should try to write your own program or embellish this one.

This program links in ImageLoad.lib and ImageObject.lib. It also expects to find ImageLoad.dll in the path.

CropStretch

Many times, your application needs to change the size of an image. It may also need to crop an image to a selected rectangular region. The `CImageObject` class has functions to perform both of the operations. This program shows you how to use them.

The image loaded into memory will be scaled to fit the view window's client area exactly every time it's redrawn. It does so by creating a temporary `CImageObject` object, copying the current image into it, scaling the temporary image, and then drawing to the view window with the temporary object.

You can crop the image, too. To do this, click the left mouse button inside of the view window. The rectangular region around the mouse will be copied and used to create a new display image.

ProcessImage

You can do lots of things with the image-processing capabilities that come with the `ImageObject` package, and this program shows you many of them. You can perform operations such as colorization and median filtering.

You'll probably enjoy using this program because it's fun to see what the outcome of enhancement and filtering operations is. If you have children, let them try it. They'll love altering the images.

This program links in the ImageAreaProcess.lib and ImagePointProcesses.lib files.

Chapter 24

In this chapter, we explore the basics of cryptography. The topics include: learning basic cryptographic terms, learning about the different types of cryptography, examining hash functions, and using Microsoft's CryptoAPI.

Substitution Algorithm Demo Program

The SubDemo program demonstrates how to implement a simple substitution algorithm. The algorithm implemented is the same one we've explored thus far. SubDemo reads a text file of up to 10,000 bytes and, using its substitution algorithm, shifts each letter and/or number contained in the file five characters to the right.

All the algorithm's functionality is located in the member function `CSubdemoDlg::DoEncrypt()`. `DoEncrypt()` iterates through each position of a `Cstring()` buffer and performs a lookup of that character into the array `AlphaIndex()`. Once the character's position in the array has been found, the algorithm adds five to the character's current position. This produces the effect of shifting the character five positions to the right. If the position is near the end of the array and can't be shifted without moving past the upper bound, then the algorithm wraps around to the beginning of `AlphaIndex()`. This substitution scheme is applied three times.

The HFDemo Program

The second demo program in this chapter demonstrates a robust hash function that operates at the bit-level of a message. The hash function used in the demonstration program is used by many UNIX C/C++ compilers to write intermediate object files.

The interesting thing to note about this algorithm, which is implemented in `CHfdemoDlg::SimpleHash()`, is its use of bitwise operators. The hash function makes extensive use of AND and XOR operations to produce the hash value.

Chapter 26

Chapter 26 covers ActiveX container and server applications. The subfolders in the Chap26 folder all contain programs and files related to the material in Chapter 26.

Container

This sample program demonstrates how to program an ActiveX container application. The application enables the user to embed into its document ActiveX objects created by other applications. These embedded objects can be anything from text documents to ActiveX controls. The application shows how a server application's menus and toolbars can merge with the container's to support in-place editing.

Server

This sample program demonstrates how to program an ActiveX server application. The application can display its document in a container application, merging its menus with the container application's menus. The application can be run invisibly as a server or run as a full, stand-alone application with its own window and controls.

Chapter 27

Chapter 27 covers ActiveX automation clients and servers, as well as ActiveX controls. The subfolders in the Chap27 folder all contain programs and files related to the material in Chapter 27.

AutoClient

This sample program demonstrates how to program an ActiveX automation client application. The application can control the AutoServer application, another sample application included in this chapter.

AutoServer

This sample program demonstrates how to program an ActiveX automation server application. The application can be controlled by any application that can access the AutoServer's automation interface. Specially, the AutoServer displays a text string whose color can be changed by the automation client application. The AutoClient sample application, described previously, can access AutoServer's automation interface and so can manipulate AutoServer's display string.

SquareRoot

This sample program demonstrates how to program an ActiveX control. The control enables the user to calculate the square roots.

Chapter 28

This chapter covers the topic of the Active Template Library (ATL). In this chapter, you learn how to create ATL controls and use them in C++ programs.

SpiroGrph

This directory contains a project aht, a simple ATL control that draws a spirograph in the view window. Two functions will be added that allow the radius and color of the design drawn to be altered. Code is added to the control's `OnDraw()` function to draw the spirograph.

TestSpiroGrph

Once the ATL SpiroGrph control has been created, you need a separate application that will use the control. This program is a simple, single-document program. Visual C++ has the capability to load and create a wrapper class for ActiveX components easily and that's how this program was created.

Chapter 29

This chapter covers Internet programming. How to send and receive files using FTP, and how to retrieve http files are emphasized.

FtpDemo

One of the most powerful tools at your command is the ability to use FTP to retrieve and update files on a remote server. This program shows you how to log on to an FTP server and how to retrieve a file from the server.

The program performs its FTP operations from inside of threads. If it didn't, the application would hang up while the FTP operations completed.

Crawler

You may have a good understanding of how Web robots work. Even so, creating a Web crawler is a tough assignment. We accepted the challenge, though, and created a simple, yet powerful, Web crawler program.

This program operate by taking a single starting URL address. From this point, it loads in Web pages, parses through and removes additional URL references, and then adds them to a list of pending URLs. The list of pending URLs grows faster than the list of processed URLs because most Web pages have multiple links.

This crawler application could be expanded to perform useful tasks, such as to evaluate and rate Web sites. The list of pending and processed URLs are kept in a `CStringArray` class. If you want to expand this application so it stores hundreds of thousands of URLs in the lists, you must store the pending and processed lists in a database, rather than in memory.

Chapter 30

This chapter covers the topic of the `CHtmlView` class. The class is taught and demo programs built to teach you how to use this powerful class.

CHtmlDemo1

Our first demo program is a simple browser contained within a `CHtmlView` window. It uses a total of six functions from the `CHtmlView` class. They are `Stop()`, `GoBack()`, `GoForward()`, `GoHome()`, `GoSearch()`, and `Navigate2()`.

Users can navigate by clicking the HTML hyperlinks. They can also use the menus or toolbar buttons that navigate back, forward, and to a specific URL, among other things. With the exception of a simple dialog that enables users to enter in a new URL, all the code added to the project can be found in the CHtmlDemo1View.cpp source code module.

CHtmlViewDemo2

The second demo program in this chapter does two important things. It keeps a list of URLs to block and logs all URLs navigated to into a log file. Users can add to the block list at any time when the program is running. Additional URLs can also be added to the Block.dat with a text editor — these additions will be loaded the next time the CHtmlViewDemo2 program runs.

After each URL is successfully navigated to, the URL is logged to the URLHist.dat file. Later, you can look at the log file to see where a user has gone. The sites that are blocked are not added to the log file; this may be a useful addition to the logging capability.

Chapter 31

This chapter covers using J++ and C++ together.

Banner

After talking about the Banner applet, it's time we showed it to you. The source code for the applet is included here. You can study it so you have a better understanding of all the techniques for threading and images we've been discussing.

MakeBanner

We've written a program that creates two banners for the Banner applet. It does this by loading tiles from a collection of 18 tiles, placing the tiles into a larger banner image, and overlaying a logo image. There's a tile selector dialog box that enables you to pick the tile you want for each of the two banner images.

There are many places to change the program so it's more flexible. For example, the banner size is hard coded to a width of 500 and a height of 90. These dimensions could easily be altered via a dialog box that gives users a choice.

Once the banner images are created, they can be uploaded to a Web server via FTP protocol. If you select Upload Images, you'll be prompted for a server name, user name, password, and folder. The program uses this information to upload Banner1.gif and Banner2.gif to the server. Here again, enabling users to choose different file names would be another example of how the program's extensibility can be enhanced.

Chapter 32

This chapter covers using Visual Basic and C++ together. Mostly, it's about using ActiveX controls written in one, but loaded into the other.

RegistryControl

This first project is an ATL control written in C++. The purpose of RegistryControl is to make reading and writing to the system registry easy for developers. It uses the `CRegistry` class from the Data I/O chapter for the actual registry functionality. The `CUseRegistry` class is the layer between the control and the `CRegistry` functions.

You'll notice all the strings passed in from Basic are BSTRs. Because this control was written in C++ and the `CRegistry` class expects char pointers, the BSTRs all need to be converted to char arrays. Throughout the source code in listing 34-1, you'll see the conversion macros at work taking care of this detail.

Register

This section shows you the Basic program we built to load in and use the RegistryControl ATL control. There's a lot more functionality to the control than this program uses. But we want to keep this program simple so you can easily see how to instantiate and use the control.

Four of the control's methods are used. The first is `CreateKey()`. This method creates a key in the registry into which your program's configuration data can be stored. The first argument in the `CreateKey()` method determines in which of the registry sections the newly created key will be placed. Our example puts it into `HKEY_LOCAL_MACHINE`. This is determined by specifying the value &H80000002.

The second RegistryControl method used is `Open()`. This opens the registry key so data can be written to it. This also allows data to be read from the registry.

The `IsOpen()` method is used to determine if the registry was successfully opened. This is important so your users can be notified in case of registry errors. Data is written to the registry key with the `WriteString()` method. Finally, the registry key is closed with the `Close()` method.

OhmsCalculator

The control we built with Visual Basic is called *OhmsCalculator*. It enables users to enter three values: voltage, resistance, and amperage. There are three buttons at the bottom of the form. One causes the control to calculate the voltage from the resistance and amperage values; another causes the control to calculate the resistance from the voltage and amperage values; and the third causes the control to calculate the amperage from the voltage and resistance values.

The program was written in about ten minutes, including the time it took to look up Ohm's Law in a physics book. The procedure consisted of putting three labels on the form, three text fields, and three buttons. Then, code was added to each button so an appropriate value was calculated and placed in a field. For example, if the 'Calculate Voltage' button was pressed, the voltage text field is populated based on a calculation from values obtained from the resistance and amperage fields.

UseOhmsCalculator

Using a control from Visual C++ isn't quite as easy as using a control from Visual Basic. (All the Visual Basic fans are out there saying "No surprise!") The first thing you must do is identify the control you want to use. To do this, select Add to Project from the Project menu and then select Components and Controls from the Add to Project submenu. Open the Registered ActiveX Controls folder and find the control you want. In this case, the control will be named OhmsCalculator.Calculator. One important note: *This control must have been registered either by building the .ocx file or by running Regsvr32 on it.*

The next thing you must do is click the Insert button. Another dialog will appear in which you can name the C++ control wrapper class and the file names into which the source code will be saved.

Chapter 33

This chapter covers writing your own custom Wizards. The demo programs show two possible Wizards you can write.

SDIAutomationWiz

This is a custom AppWizard that shows how to set default options for new projects. This particular application sets the project type to SDI and turns Automation on for every new project created with this custom AppWizard. Custom AppWizards are great for situations where you need to have the same default settings for multiple projects. Using this application's source code as a template, you can easily personalize it to preset almost any setting for your own custom AppWizard. To use the custom AppWizard without building it, you need to copy the SDIAutomationWiz.awx file into the Visual Studio template folder. By default, this folder is located on C:\Program Files\Microsoft Visual Studio\Common\MSDev98\Template.

AboutWiz

A much more advanced custom AppWizard, this application illustrates how to create and display customized dialogs, how to retrieve and set user-defined variables, and how to control which dialogs appear — and in what order — based on user-interaction with the AppWizard. The end result is a custom AppWizard that automatically adds an "About box" into every new project created with this custom AppWizard. The About box provided contains contact information and a command button that brings up your Web page in a browser for the end users of the application that was built with this custom AppWizard. The custom AppWizard even saves this information in the system registry so the reader needn't type it in every time a new project is created. To use the custom AppWizard without building it, you need to copy the AboutWiz.awx file into the Visual Studio template folder. By default, this folder is located on C:\Program Files\Microsoft Visual Studio\Common\MSDev98\Template.

Programming Tools

The ProgrammingTools folder on the CD-ROM contains programs that'll help you when you need extensions to MFC. A few of the programs are full-blown applications based on a programming library. Some of the programs are demonstrations of programming tools. The libraries will make your job easier by adding functionality you need.

Three companies are represented in the collection of programming tools. Stingray software, Dundas software, and LeadTools software. This section organizes these tools by company.

Most of the programs on the CD-ROM are self-extracting programs that automatically install when you run them. If the files have .exe extensions, run the program and it will install. If a file has a .zip extension, you need to use a program similar to WinZip or PKUNZIP to uncompress the file. Instructions for installing files that are compressed into a .zip file can be found after the archive has been uncompressed.

Stingray Software

Stingray software specializes in MFC extensions. These tools will give your programs what they need to compete with the best software on the market.

Objective Grid Samples

File name: **OG60DB.exe**

This file illustrates the various features of the Objective Grid. This tool gives your MFC applications a great grid control. With this grid control, you can create spreadsheet-type applications or many other things requiring a grid.

Objective Grid Demobrowser

File name: **og60dbx.exe**

This demo shows off a DAO bound grid, with a dynamic splitter and a Status Bar Record Counter. It does data access using the MFC DAO classes.

Objective Grid Designer

File name: **OGDesign.exe**

This is the Objective Grid designer that ships with Objective Grid 6.0. This tool enables you to specify the layout of the grid with no programming. You can load up the sample .OGL files provided.

Objective Grid CCE Evaluation Version

File name: **ogcceeval.exe**

This is the evaluation version of Objective Grid CCE. This advanced version of the Objective Grid control enables you to experiment with creating your own grid-based programs.

Objective Toolkit

File name: **OT_Demo.exe**

Now, for the first time, see all the Objective Toolkit features in one easy-to-use Explorer-style demobrowser. You'll be amazed at how many features exist when they are all put in an easily navigable tree. This toolkit sports MFC extension features such as extended tree controls and enhanced toolbars.

Objective Toolkit/X

File name: **OTX_Eval.exe**

Objective Toolkit/X, or OT/X, makes the power of Objective Toolkit Pro available as an ActiveX control. With the strength of OT Pro and the flexibility of ActiveX, OT/X creates a unique, untapped market for a modern, Win32 GUI, with the ease of VB.

Objective Toolkit Demos

File name: **otpdemos.exe**

This file contains the additional features you can use in the Objective Toolkit. By running these demos, you'll see how flexible and full-featured Objective Toolkit is.

Objective Chart Demobrowser

File name: **OC_Demo.exe**

This is the new Objective Chart demo. It shows you how to use the Objective Chart library. With it, you can add charts and graphs to your MFC programs.

Diagram Demobrowser

File name: **od10demo.zip**

This file includes Circuit, Logger, and white paper all in one package. These programs show you how to use the Diagram controls. All demos include full source.

Objective Edit Demobrowser

File name: **oe10demo.exe**

This file contains the Objective Edit Demobrowser. It's a tool that enables you to perform editing functions far more versatile and useful than the edit controls that come with MFC.

Dundas Software

Dundas Software specialize in grid controls and wizard-creation tools. Their libraries and tools are intended for use in MFC-based programs.

Ultimate Grid 97 for MFC Demo

File name: **ug97demo.exe**

This demonstration program shows most of the grid's main features. Over 30 subdemonstrations are included, with each one covering a separate function group. Features such as text style, cell types, scrolling, highlighting, column swapping, graphics, ballistics, finding, sorting, column and row locking, Excel style, Access style, charting, real-time data, calendar, hints, and more are included.

Ultimate Wizard Factory

File name: **uwfdemo.exe**

This program demonstrates the use of the wizards you can create with the Ultimate Wizard Factory. Because most of our customers are C++ developers, we feel a program that executes a wizard to create class skeleton files would be a nice utility to have around. Until, of course, you can make your own using the Ultimate Wizard Factory.

Index

SYMBOLS

- &, ampersand, 27, 230
- /, forward slash, 839
- <>, angle brackets, 826
- ==, equality operator, 292
- \, backslash, 839
- [ ], array operator, 291
- << operator, 377
- = operator, 692
- > operator, 377

A

- About dialog box, 803, 939–953
- Accel Properties dialog box, 42
- accelerator. *See* keyboard accelerators
- access keys, 40–41
- access-type values, Internet, 832
- Active Data Object (ADO), 913
- Active Template Library (ATL), 813–827
  - adding COM object, 816
  - BSTRs
    - comparing, 825
    - converting, 824–825
    - viewing, 826
  - COM AppWizard, 815–816
  - control
    - RegistryControl, 914–919
    - Visual Basic, 914–919, 921–924
  - creating control, 814–816
  - default settings, 817
  - embedding controls in Web page, 826
  - HelloWorld program, 11–14
  - interface functions, 820–822
  - Object Wizard, 814, 816–817
  - OnDraw function, 818–819
  - overview, 813–814
  - using from C++, 822–824
  - Wizard, 11
- ActiveX, 742–748
  - automation, 781–797
    - applications, 746–747
    - client application, 790–795
      - creating skeleton, 791, 796
      - customizing resources, 792
      - demo program, 791
      - initializing, 795
      - view class, 793–795
    - servers, 781–790
      - controlling from client, 796–797
      - creating skeleton, 782–784, 790
      - customizing resources, 784
      - demo program, 782
      - document class, 785
      - properties and methods, 788
      - view class, 785–788
  - COM (Component Object Model), 742
  - container applications, 743–744, 749–764
    - creating skeleton, 749–754, 764
    - deleting embedded items, 763
    - demo programs, 750
    - embedded object size and position, 755–756
    - selecting items with mouse, 756–762
      - FindItemHit function, 758, 760
      - InitRectTracter function, 759–760
      - OnDraw function, 756–757
      - OnLButtonDblClk function, 7587
      - OnLButtonDown function, 758
      - OnSetCursor function, 757
      - SetObjectAsSelected, 761
    - Web Browser, 867
  - controls, 747
    - ControlWizard, 798–799
    - creating skeleton, 798–800, 807
    - demo program, 799

(continued)

ActiveX (*continued*)
persistent properties, 808–809
properties and methods, 803–806
response to button, 806–807
Test Container, 14, 924
testing, 808
user interface, 800–803
Web Browser, 867
Web page placement, 809–812
documents, 747–748
information resources, 743
OLE
1.0, 737–739
2.0, 740–741
automation, 740–741
controls, 741
overview, 742–743
server applications, 744–746, 764–780
COleServerItem class, 774–775
creating skeleton, 764–767
CServerDoc class, 772–774
customizing resources, 768–772
demo program, 765–768
running
as editor for linked item, 779–780
as in place editor, 778–779
as standalone, 776–778
view class, 775–776
ActiveX Control Test Container, 14, 924
Add Member Variable dialog box, 237, 374, 595
Add Method to Interface dialog box, 821
Add Property dialog box, ActiveX controls, 804
AfxBeginThread(), 503–506, 513
AfxEndThread(), 508
AFX_EXT_CLASS, 667–668
AfxGetAppName, 832
AfxGetResourceHandle() function, 48
AFX_IDW_STATUS_BAR, 487, 489
AfxOleInit() function, 795
agents, 847–848
algorithms
public-key, 714, 720–722
symmetric, 713, 714–720
alignment
dialog controls, 233
text, 116–117
Alt key. *See also* mnemonics
accelerators, 44–45
virtual key codes, 84
ampersand, 27, 230
angle brackets (<>), 826
animations
raster operations, 165
worker threads, 502
ANSI
double-byte character sets, 295
literal strings, 290
applets, Java
creating, 887–893
paint method, 891
parameters, 892–893
threaded, 889–890
demo programs
Banner applet, 900–907
MakeBanner, 907–912
images
drawing, 895–896
formats supported, 895
loading, 893–895
scaling, 896
uploading to Web sites, 897–900
Applications key, 41, 55, 82
AppWizard
accelerator table, 40
ActiveX control, 798
automation server, 782–784
CHtmlView class, 868
container application, 749–753
custom, 934–953
About box, 939

CCustomAppWiz class, 936–938, 950–953
confirm.inf file, 949–950
default settings, changing, 936–938
demo projects
AboutWiz, 939
SDIAutomationWiz, 936
dialog, 939–941
macros, 936, 938
persistent, 950–953
newproj.inf file, 943–945
options, creation, 934–935
templates
creating new, 941–945
resource files, changing, 945–947
view and dialog files, 947–949
default dialog box, 229
default menu, 25
dialog-based application, 228–229
DLLs, regular, 646
document/view applications, 6, 370, 372–375
Explorer-style applications, 7
limitations, 931–932
MDI, 411–412, 420–422
OnDraw() function, 107–108
overview, 932–934
printing and, 428–429, 432, 435
server applications, 765–767
splitter windows
dynamic, 395–397
MDI, 404–405
multiple view, 407–408
static, 401–402
status bars, 480, 486, 489
toolbars, 481
arithmetics, 146
array operator [ ], 291
arrow
keys, 89
two-headed pointer, 231
ASCII
accelerator, 42–43, 84
scan code conversion, 83
asymmetric algorithms, 714, 720–722
ATL. *See* Active Template Library (ATL)
ATL Object Wizard dialog box, 816–817
Attach() function, 53–54
audio. *See* sound
auto complete, 456–458
AutoDelete threads, 508, 511
automation, 781–797
ActiveX applications, 746–747
client application, 790–795
creating skeleton, 791, 796
customizing resources, 792
demo program, 791
initializing ActiveX in, 795
view class, 793–795
DAO, 607–608, 614–616
OLE, 740–741
servers, 781–790
controlling from client, 796–797
creating skeleton, 782–784, 790
customizing resources, 784
demo program, 782
document class, 785
properties and methods, 788
view class, 785–788
autosave, 349
awx suffix, 936, 938. *See also* AppWizard, custom

B

background attributes, 104, 113
background tasks, 501, 502
backslash (\), 839
Banner applet demo, 900–912
binary objects
blob (binary large object), 727–728
COM and, 742
binary resources, viewing, 650

bit depth, 157
bit planes, 157, 158
bit-blitting, 470
BitBlt() function, 161–164, 193
Bitmap Image Object submenu, 753–754
BITMAPFILEHEADER data structure, 181–182
BITMAPINFOHEADER data structure, 181–182
bitmaps, 155–194
  caching, 100
  CBitmap object, 157–173
    CD-ROM demo program, 167–173
    content, loading and setting, 159–161
    creating, 157–159
    drawing to screen, 161–164
  color depth, 157, 181–182
  device-independent (DIBs), 180–192
    CDib class, 183–189
    CD-ROM demo program, 189–192
    file structure, 181–182
  double buffering, 192–194
  overview, 155–156
  palettes, 173–180, 182, 189
  as pseudodevices, 102–103
  raster graphics, 99–100
  space requirements, 100, 103
  toolbar buttons, 479, 481
blitting, 470
blob (binary large object), 727–728
blocking Internet sites, 876–884
BMP file format, 682
BOOL ChangeBrightness, 706
BOOL Colorize, 706
BOOL Crop, 699
BOOL Draw, 693
BOOL EdgeEnhance, 705
BOOL EqualizeContrast, 705
BOOL GetImageInfo, 686
BOOL HighpassFilter, 705
BOOL Load, 686
BOOL LowpassFilter, 705
BOOL MakeGray, 706
BOOL MedianFilter, 705
BOOL ReverseColors, 706
BOOL Save, 689–690
BOOL SetPalette, 693
BOOL Stretch, 700
borders, 471–472
Box, Don, 825
brightness, image, 706, 707
browsers, Web. *See also* Internet Explorer
  ActiveX and, 747
  creating simple, 834
  Microsoft Web Browser, 867–884
  Netscape Navigator, 848
brushes
  demo program, 129–133
  hatch, 128–129
  solid, 127
BSTR
  comparing, 825
  converting, 824–825, 915
  viewing, 826
buffer, character, 292–293, 690
buttons. *See also* toolbars
  caption, changing, 278–279
  removing, 276–277
  repositioning, 277–278

C

C++
  ActiveX Control Test Container, 924
  ATL control, 914–918
  dbDAO, 614–615
  debugger, 119–120
  DLLs, 645–674
  exception handling, 195–196
  HelloWorld1 program, 6–9
  IDE, 5
  J++, 887–912
  libraries, third-party, 675–712
  MIDI, 332
  pointer, 52
  project types, 6

- registering ATL controls, 14
- RegistryControl demo, 914–918
- runtime library, 517–518
- sound, 324
- UseOhmsCalculator program, 924–927
- View Window, 927
- Visual Basic and, 913–930
- Win32 console application, 10–11

C runtime library, 517–518
CAccessDb class, 199–203
caching bitmap images, 100
CallNextHook, 660, 662
CapsLock key, 484–485
Caption property dialog, 229–230
captions
- button, changing, 278
- menu field, 27
- tab, 269, 283–285

capturing the mouse, 79–80
CArchive class serialization, 377, 381
CArchive() object, 252
catch block, 197–198
- code content, 218–219
- DAO errors, 617–618, 633
- database classes, 583, 598–599, 602, 604
- database code, 565
- multiple exceptions, 206–207
- superfluous, 217

CAutoCompleteComboBox, 456–458
CBitmap class. *See* bitmaps
CBN_prefix, 240
CBrush class, 127–129
CCDAudio class, 339–347
CChildFrame class, 413, 417–420, 421
- header file, 418
- implementation file, 419–420

CClientDC object, 112
CComboBox class, 236–238, 246, 456–458
CContainerCntrlItem, 750
CControlBar, 480
CCtrlView class, 474–476
CCustomAppWiz class. *See also* AppWizard, custom
- defining, 936–937
- macros, 938
- Registry use, 950–953

CD audio 338–347
- CCD audio class, 339
  - functions, 341–342
  - MCI (Media Control Interface), 339–341
- CDPlayer program, 342–347

CDaoDatabase, 616–619, 625, 638
CDaoException, 617–618
CDaoRecordset, 620–630
CDaoWorkspace, 619–620
CDatabase, 564–567, 591
CDBException class, 565, 584, 604
CDialog class, 235, 269. *See also* dialogs
CDialogBar class, 480
CDib class
- Draw function, 187–188
- Load function, 183–186
- Save function, 186–187
- Set Palette function, 189

CDocument, 370
CDPlayer program, 342–347
CD-ROM demos
- ActiveX controls, 799
  - OhmsCalculator, 922–924
  - RegistryControl, 914–919
- applet, Banner, 901–912
- ATL controls, 914–917
- automation client, 791
- automation server, 782
- bitmap objects, 167–173
- CFileException, 210–212
- CHtmlView class, 872–874, 879–884
- clipping graphics, 151–153
- clock program, 354–360
- CodeFinder application, 228
- container applications, 750

(continued)

CD-ROM demos (*continued*)
  DAO, 620
  DIBs (device-independent bitmaps), 189–192
  document/view architecture, 371–380, 382–388
  encryption
    CryptoAPI, 728–732
    hash functions, 722–726
    substitution algorithm, 715–720
  exception handling, 210–212
  FTP, 840–847
  graphics, 137–142, 151–153
    Crop/Stretch, 700–703
    Display, 697–699
    ProcessImage, 707–712
  HelloWorld program, 8, 10, 11, 15, 19, 23
  idle processing, 363–366
  keyboard input demo, 96
  MakeBanner program, 907–912
  MDIDemo, 417–420
  menu demo, 34, 51
  MFC extensions, 455
  mouse cursor demo, 76
  mouse events, 68
  ODBC
    fetching data, 537–545
    functionality, encapsulating, 545–561
  OhmsCalculator
    ActiveX control, 922–924
    C++ use of, 924–927
  OnIdle program, 363–366
  PenBrush demo, 130–133
  printing
    graphics application, 446–447
    text application, 430–432
  RectApp, 371–380, 382–388
  Register program, 919–921
  RegistryControl, 914–917
  RGB to HSV conversion, 177
  saving files, 305–312
  screen flicker file, 192
  server applications, 765
  sound
    CDPlayer program, 342–347
    MidiDemo, 334–338
    WaveDemo, 329–332
  splitter windows
    dynamic, 395–397
    MDI, 399–402
    multiple view, 407–408
    static, 399–402
  status bar, 492–498
  strings, 296–302
  threads, 518–522
  timers, 354–360
  URLs, blocking and logging, 879–884
  Visual Basic
    image control, 929–930
    OhmsCalculator, 922–924
    Register, 919–921
  WebCrawler, 849–863
  window drawing, 137–142
CDynLinkLibrary, 937
centering text, 148–149
CERN proxy, 833
CException class, 196, 203–215
  creating and deleting objects, 204
  derived classes, defining
    CFileException, 208–212
    custom, 212–215
  error information retrieval, 205–206
  multiple exception types, catching, 206–207
CfieldExchange, 575
CFile class, 302–312, 834
  CD-ROM demo program, 305–312
  CMemFile, 313
  CStdioFile, 313–314
  exception handling, 195
  I/O operations, 305
  Open() member function, 302–305

saving files, 305–312
CFileException class, 208–212
CFont object, 118–121
CFormBackground, 469–474
CFormView class, 669
CFrameWnd, 413
docking toolbars, 483
CFtpConnection, 836–840
CGA video, 157
CGreyEdit, 458–464
ChangeFormat() function, 704
char arrays, BSTR conversion of, 915
characters
buffer, 292–293, 690
frequency and encryption, 714–715
map program, 118
sets, multibyte (MBCs), 289, 295
sizes, 435–440
CHARMAP, 119
child controls, 235
child windows, 411–423, 482
CHtmlView class, 5, 867–884
blocking and logging URLs, 876–884
converting projects to, 869–870
creating projects, 868–869, 870
demo programs, 872–874, 879–884
HTML document information retrieval, 875
navigating, 870–872
CImageAreaProcesses class, 704–705
CImagePointProcesses class, 706–707
CInternetSession class, 831
CFTPConnection, 836–838
parameters, optional, 832–833
Ciphertext. *See* encryption
CLASSID, 826
ClassWizard
automation interface and, 788–789
CODBCDemoDlg, 543–544
command ranges, 33, 51
default names, 29
DeleteContents() function, 375–376
menu items, 29–31
MFC Database classes, 585–586, 588–589, 597
mouse capture, 80
mouse messages, 65–66, 74
OnNotify() function, 281
property pages, 269, 274–275, 281, 283
radio button, 242
recordsets, 568–572, 620–622, 626, 635
status bars and, 491
timers, 351–352
type library and, 793
ClientToScreen() function, 67
clipboard
commands, 45
screen shots, 100
Clipper chip, 715
clipping
drawing attributes, 104
fonts, 123
regions, 149–153
windows boundaries, 101–102
clipping precision, font, 123
clipping the pointer, 81
CListBoxView, 474–477
CListView class, 474–475
clock program, 354–360
CLSID (class ID), 809
CMapStringToString, 936, 938
CMDIChildWnd class, 413, 421
CMDIFrameWnd class, 413
CMemFile class, 313
CMenu
class functions, 49–50
menu flags, 51–52
getting object, 48–49
MFC creation of, 54
CMidi class, 333–334
CMY color space, 176
CN_UPDATE_COMMAND_UI message, 30
CodeFinder application, 226–265

COleResizeBar, 480
COleServerItem, 774
collisions, hash, 722
color
  additive vs subtractive, 173
  brush, 127
  CMY color space, 176
  default values, 115
  depth, 157, 181–182, 703–704
  GetSysColor function, 465
  HSV color system, 176–177
  logical, 114
  masking, 164, 166–167
  pallettes, logical, 174–179
  pen, 126–127
  raster operations, 135–136
  reversing, 706
  RGB, 114–115, 173–174
  Set Color command, 784, 787
  static, 174
  text, 115–116
  transparent, 164, 166–167
  video memory and, 157, 159
colorizing image, 706–707
COLORREF, 113–116
COM (Component Object Model), 742. *See also* ActiveX
  Active Template Library (ATL), 813–827
  class identifiers, 319
COM ports, 314
combo box
  auto complete, 456–458
  CComboBox class, 236–238, 246
  message handling, 239–240
  notification, 240, 247
  resizing, 233
  strings, 246
  URL address, 236
Common User Access (CUA), 665
Components and Controls Gallery dialog box, 924
compression, image, 680–685
Confirm Classes dialog box, 823, 925
confirm.inf file, 949–950
conformance levels, ODBC, 529–530
console application, 10–11
container applications, 749–764
  ActiveX, 743-744
  creating skeleton, 749–754, 764
  defined, 738
  deleting embedded items, 763
  demo programs, 750
  embedded object size and position, 755–756
  selecting items with mouse, 756–762
    FindItemHit function, 758, 760
    InitRectTracter function, 759–760
    OnDraw function, 756–757
    OnLButtonDblClk function, 7587
    OnLButtonDown function, 758
    OnSetCursor function, 757
    SetObjectAsSelected, 761
context identifier, 839
context menus and Applications key, 82
contrast, image, 705
controls. *See also* ActiveX, controls
  adding, 231–233
  child, 235
  dialog
    changing properties, 230
    defined, 226
  dominant, 233–234
  enabling and disabling, 243–244
  registering, 918
  removing, 230
  resizng, 231
  tab order, 234
  toolbar, 231
coordinates
  converting screen and window, 67–68
  drawing, 109
  embedded objects, 755

font clipping precision, 123
images, 693–695
mapping modes, 133–135
scaling, 448–451
text, calculating, 144–149
text alignment, 116–117
Visual Basic graphics, 928
CopyFile() function, 306, 310
Core level, ODBC, 529
CorelDRAW, 118
CPalette class, 178
cpp file, 339
CPrintDialog object, 434
CPrintInfo, 433–436
CProject class, creating, 241
CPropertyPage class. *See* property pages
CPropertySheet class. *See* property sheets
CPtrArray class, 373, 377, 382–383
CPtrArray member function, 385–387
crawlers, Web. *See* robots, Web
Create() function, CDialog class, 260–261
CreateBitmapIndirect() function, 158–159
CreateCompatibleBitmap() function, 159, 193
CreateCompatibleDC(), 193
CreateDC(), printer, 426–427
CreateFont() function parameters, 121–123
CreateKey () method, 919
CreateStatic() function, 401
CreateStockObject()
fonts, 119
pens, 126
CreateView() function, 406–407
CreateWorkspace() method, 612
CRecordset, 568–578, 592–604
CRecordView class, 564
CRegistry class, 914, 950–951
cropping images, 699–703
Cryptographic Service Providers (CSP), 726–272
cryptography. *See* encryption
CScrollView class, 396–397, 401
CSerial class, 315–317
CServerDoc, 772–774
CServerSrvrItem, 764
CSimpleException class, 213–214
CSplitterWnd
custom splitter class, 407–409
member function table, 392–393
CStatusBar class, 480, 484, 487–488
style flags, 487–488
CStdioFile class, 313–314, 834
CString class, 289–302
allocating objects, 290
character buffer, 292–293
demo program, 296–302
object combo boxes, 237
reference counts, 290
TCHAR data type, 295
Unicode support, 295
CToolBar, 480–483
CTreeView class, 474–475
Ctrl key
accelerators, 44–45
virtual key codes, 84
CUA (Common User Access), 665
CUnderlineEdit, 464–468
cursors. *See also specific cursors*
dynamic DLL loading and, 650
keyboard, creating and managing, 87–89
raster graphics, 99
CUseRegistry class, 914–917
CUserException class, 213
CustomizeProject () function, AppWizard, 938
CView class, 370
printing functions, 432–446
CWave class
CD-ROM demo program, 329–332
functions, 326–328
overview, 324
CWinApp classes, DLLs, 646–647
CWinThreads. *See* threads
CWnd class, 235

CControlBar, 480
CPropertySheet, 269
CSplitterWnd class, 391
CView class, 370
EnableWindow function, 243–244
keyboard cursors, 87
threads, 514
toolbars, 480, 483

D

DAC (Digital Adapter Color), 174
DAO, 617–618, 633
DAO (data access objects), 607–641
hierarchy, 610–614
Databases collection, 612
Databases object, 612–613
DBEngine object, 610
Recordsets collection, 613
Recordsets object, 613–614
Workspace object, 611–612
Workspaces collection object, 610
interfaces, 614–615
DAO Automation interfaces, 614
db DAO C++ classes, 614–615
MFC DAO classes, 615
MFC DAO classes, 615–641
CDaoDatabase, 616–619, 625, 638
CDaoRecordset, 620–630, 632
CDaoWorkspace, 619–620
demo programs, 630–641
MFC Database classes compared, 615–616
overview, 608–610
Data Definition Language (DDL), 526, 608, 616
data encryption. *See* encryption
data input/output, 289–321
CFile class, 302–312
CMemFile class, 313
CSerial class, 314–317
CStdioFile class, 313–314
CString class, 289–302
Registry, 317–321
serial communications, 314–317
strings, 289–302
data manipulation language (DML), 526
data source. *See also* ODBC
CDatabase class, 564–567
connecting to, 532–533
CRecordset class, 568–578
defined, 526, 527, 531–532
disconnecting from, 536
ODBC Direct Workspace, 612
querying, 534
database classes, 583–584, 598–599
database management system. *See* DBMS (database management system)
database member functions, 565
Database object, 612–613
Database Options dialog box, 569, 621
databases
DAO, 607–641
MFC Database classes, 563–605
ODBC, 525–562
replication, 609–610
Databases collection, 612
DBCS (double-byte character sets), 295
dbDAO C++ classes, 614–615
DBEngine object, 610, 614
DBMS (database management system). *See also* ODBC
defined, 525, 526
standard, ODBC, 526–529
DDL (data definition language), 526, 608, 616
DDX (dynamic data exchange), 581, 585, 595, 635
combo box project, 237
modal property sheets, 274
debug version, library, 676–677
debugging
CFont objects, 119–120
multithread applications, 501
DECLAR_SERIAL macro, 382
Delete() function

CException class, 204
container applications, 763
DeleteContents() function, 370, 375–377
deleting exceptions, 204
Department of Justice, 4
depth
bitmap, 180
color, 157, 181–182, 703–704
destruction
CString object, 290
dialog, 247, 252, 257
Detach() function, 53–54
device context
coordinates, 109
drawing attributes, 103–107
drawing images, 693
fonts and, 119–124
OnDraw() function, 107–108, 120–121
printer, 425–429, 433–437
SelectObject function, 119–123
text attributes, 112–118
DevStudio, 546
Control menu, 231
dialog tab order, setting, 234
MFC Database classes demo, 593
resource editor, 228
viewing DLL and EXE resources, 210
DFX (DAO field exchange), 626
dialog bars, 480
Dialog Data Exchange (DDX), 236–238
dialog template resource, 228, 229, 269, 945
Dialog toolbar, 233
dialogs, 225–266
applications, dialog-based, 227–228
bars, 480
CDialog class, 235
CFormBackground, 469
communication between modeless and modal, 261–265
controls, enabling and disabling, 243–244
CProject class
creation, 241
serialization, 249–253
DDX (dialog data exchange), 236–238
destructor, 247, 252, 257
initialization, 242–243, 248
message handling, 239–240
MFC control classes, 235–236
MFC DAO classes demo, 631–640
MFC Database classes demo, 570–581
modal, 253–258
modeless, 258–265
new button, 242–243
ODBCDemo, 538–539
overview, 226
Parameterized CRecordset and Query demo, 594–595
resource editor
changing box properties, 229–230
controls
adding, 231–233
changing properties, 230
removing, 230
resizing, 231
tool bar, 231
tab order, 234
saving data, 244–249
serialization, 249–253, 257
server applications, 768–769
tabbed, 267–288
templates, 228, 229, 253, 255, 269, 945
title bar, 933
toolbar, 233
underline edit control, 464–468
DIBs (device-independent bitmaps), 180–192
CDib class, 183–189
draw function, 187–188
load function, 183–186
save function, 186–187
Set Palette function, 189
CD-ROM demo program, 189–192
file structure, 181–182

Dictionary, AppWizard, 936, 938, 941
Digital Adapter Color (DAC), 174
directory separators, 839
DirectSound technology, 324
disabling tabs, 279–281
DLLMain() function, 646–647, 936–937
DLLs (Dynamic Link Libraries), 645–674. *See also* libraries
  AppWizard, 936–937
  ATL controls, 815
  demo programs
    document and view support, 669–673
    dynamic loading of DLLs, 650–658
    keyboard hook, 661–666
  Internet Explorer, 5
  MFC Extension, 666–673
    AFX_EXT_CLASS, 667–668
    encapsulating documents and views, 669–673
    exporting class, 667
    nested, 668
    regular DLLs compared, 666–667
    resources, locating, 669
  ODBC Driver Manager, 528, 529
  regular, 645–666
    advantages, 646
    dynamic loading, 648–658
    hooks, 658–666
    linking MFC support, 646
  shared, 677
  third-party libraries, 677
  viewing resources, 210
DML (data manipulation language), 526
docking toolbars, 480, 483
document class, 369–388
  automation server, 785
  DeleteContents() function, 370, 375–377
  editing functions, 379–381
  header files, 382–383
  implementing document/view architecture, 369–370
  member variable declaration, 373–374
  mouse, response to, 379–380, 387
  OnNewDocument() function, 370, 374–375
  public member functions, 383
  sample programs, 371–380, 382–388
  Serialize() function, 370, 377–378
    non-persistent objects, 387–388
    persistent objects, 381–388
  server applications, 772–774
DoEncrypt(), 715
DoFieldExchange() function, 573, 575, 601–602, 626, 627
DoModal() function, 269–270, 275
DoPropExchange() function, 806, 809
double buffering, 192–194
Draw() function
  CDib, 187–188
  ImageObject library, 692–696
DrawBitmap() function, 162–163
DrawFocusRect() function, 90–91
DrawFormBackground() function, 470–472
drawImage() method, 895–896
drawing. *See also* graphics
  attributes, 103–107
  functions, GDI text, 142–144
DrawShadow() function, 473
DrawTransparent() function, 166–167
drivers, native 32-bit code, 3
DSN (data source name), 537
  ODBC and, 531–532
DWORD
  BSTR and, 824
  CRegistry class, 320–321
  variable, 161
dynamic data exchange. *See* DDX (dynamic data exchange)
Dynamic Link Libraries. *See* DLLs (Dynamic Link Libraries)
dynamic recordset, 613
dynamic splitter window. *See* splitter windows

dynasets, 568, 613, 620. *See also* recordsets
DynSplitter application, 393–399

E

echoing keyboard focus, 86–93
edge enhancement, image, 705
Edit String dialog box, 811
EGA video, 157
embedding data. *See* ActiveX; container applications; OLE
EnableTab function, 282–283
EnableWindow(), 243–244
encryption, 713–733
  CryptoAPI, 726–732
  demo programs
    CryptoAPI, 728–732
    hash function, 722–726
    substitution algorithm, 715–720
  hash functions, 721–726
  information resources, 733
  public-key algorithms, 714, 720–722
  symmetric algorithms, 713, 714–720
  terms defined, 713–714
enum structure, 208, 210, 214–215
EnumFontFamilies() function, 123
EnumPrinters() function, 426
equality operator (==), 292
erasing focus rectangles, 91
errors. *See also* exception handling
  CException functions, 205–206
  exception handling, 195–223
  GetLastError function, 839
  return codes, 198–203
Esc key, 44
escapement, font, 121
Eudora, 848
exception handling, 195–223
  advanced techniques, 215–223
    catch block code content, 218–219
    try block code content, 217–218
    virtual function exceptions, 219–223
  applets, 893
  CD-ROM demo program, 210–212
  CException class, 203–215
    creating and deleting objects, 204
    derived classes, defining, 207
      CFileException, 208–212
      custom, 212–215
    error information retrieval, 205–206
    multiple exception types, catching, 206–207
  Cfile I/O operations, 305
  DAO, 617–618, 633
  database classes, 583–584, 598–599
  database member functions, 565
  return codes compared, 198–203
  SEH vs C++, 195–196
  syntax, 196–198
    catch, 197–198
    throw, 196–197
    try, 197
Excite Web page, 874
ExecuteSQL() function, 564, 566, 591
ExitCustomAppWiz() function, 937, 951

F

F10 key, 665
FAT file system, 3
field exchange
  DAO, 626
  record, 573–574, 575
file commands, 45
File Transfer Protocol. *See* FTP (File Transfer Protocol)
files
  filename size, 3
  graphics formats, 680–685
  memory, 313
  metafile, 102–103
  retrieving
    FTP, 838–840
    HTTP, 835–836
  saving demo program, 305–312
filtering records, 574–576

filters, 658–662
Find dialog
  demo application, 272–288
  modeless dialog box, 258–265
FindItemHit() function, 758, 760
flags
  CCDAudio, MCI, 340–341
  CFile Open, 303–304
  CStatusBar, 487
  Internet options, 833
  menu, 50–52
  palette entry, 175–176
  PlaySound() function, 325
  printer, 426
  SetPaneStyle, 489
  style, 482
  text alignment, 117
  timers, 352–353
flicker, screen, 110–111, 192–193
floating-point arithmetic, 146
focus rectangles, 89–92
fonts, 118–124
  GetTextMetrics function, 437
  as graphics, 98
  point size, 144–146
  selecting
    nonstock font, 120–124
    stock font, 119–120
  tab, changing, 286
forward slash (/), 839
forward-only recordset, 613
frame window
  accelerator table connection, 40
  initializing, 40
  menu connection, 29
FTP (File Transfer Protocol)
  connecting to server, 836–838
  retrieving files, 840–847
  uploading applets, 897
function keys, 41
function seam, 527, 649

G

gateways, 865
GDI (graphics device interface), 101–103
  color support, 113–114
  device context, 103–108
  overview, 97–98
  palette manger, 174–175
  physical devices, 101–102
  pseudodevices, 102–103
raster operations, 135–136
GenerateDb() function, 199–202
GetBuffer() function, 197, 217, 290, 293
GetBusy() function, 875
getCodeBase() method, 894
GetDefaultConnect() function, 573
GetDeviceCaps() function, 157, 448–449
getDocumentBase() method, 894
GetErrorMessage() function, 205–206, 209
GetException() function, 211
GetFile() function, CFTPConnection, 838–840
getImage, Applet class, 893–894
GetImageInfo() function, 688
GetLastError function, 839
GetObject() function, 158
GetOffline() function, 875
GetParent(), 514–516
GetProcAddress() function, 648, 650, 654–656
GetReadyState() function, 875
GetStatus(), CFile class, 305
GetSysColor() function, 92, 465
GetTextMetrics() function, 436–438
GIF (Graphics Interchange Format) file
    format, 681, 682, 895
GoSearch() function, 871
graphics, 97–153. *See also* bitmaps; images
  clipping regions, 149–153
  coordinates, 109
  cropping, 699–703
  file formats, 680–685
  fonts, 118–124
  GDI (Graphics Device Interface)

devices, 101–103
context, 103–108
physical, 101–102
pseudodevices, 102–103
overview, 97–98
Image Object library, 678, 685–712, 928
drawing images, 692–693, 694
loading images, 685–689, 693–694
sample load/display programs, 694–699
saving images, 689–692
image processing, 704–712
mapping modes, 133–135
messages, drawing
other, 111–112
WM_PAINT, 108–111
pens and brushes, 124–133
CBrush class, 127
CPen class, 124–127
demo program, 127
raster operations, 135–136
rubber sheet, 109
sample programs
Crop/Stretch, 700–703
Display, 697–699
ProcessImage, 707–712
stretching, 699–703
text, 112–118
coordinate calculations, 144–149
drawing functions, 142–144
third-party libraries, 675–712
twips, 134, 928
types, 98–100
raster, 99–100
text, 99
vector, 100
Graphics class, Java, 895–896
grey edit control, 458–464
GUID (globally unique ID), 809–812

H

handle maps, 52–54
handlers
creating menu, 29–31
mouse messages, creating, 65–66
hash functions, 713, 721–726
hatch styles table, 128
HBITMAP, 155–156
headers
CChildFrame class, 418
CCustomSplitterWnd class, 408–409
dialogs, 582, 632–633
ODBC, 538, 546–549
template, AppWizard, 947–948
unavailable to DLL, 650
height
applet images, 896
bitmap, 158, 161, 181
character, 435, 438–440
font, 121
images, 693, 695–696, 699–700
HelloWorld program, 6–9
AppWizard, 6–9
ATL control, 11–14
CD-ROM demos, 8, 10, 11, 15, 19, 23
Java applet, 14–18
Java application, 18–23
view class, 8–9
Visual Basic application, 23–24
Win32 console application, 10–11
HKEY_CLASSES_ROOT key, 318–319
HKEY_CLASSES_USER key, 318
HKEY_CURRENT_CONFIG key, 318
HKEY_CURRENT_USER key, 319
HKEY_DYN_DATA key, 318
HKEY_LOCAL_MACHINE, 920
HKEY_LOCAL_MACHINE key, 317–318
HKEY_USERS key, 318–319
hooks, 658–666
CallNextHook, 660, 662
defined, 658
demo program, 661–666
SetWindowsHookEx(), 659–660, 663

(continued)

hooks (*continued*)
  table of functions, 659
  UnhookWindowsHookEx(), 660, 663
hourglass cursor, 75
HSV color system, 176–177
HTML (Hypertext Markup Language)
  editing applets, 900
  tags, 826
HTTP file retrieval, 835–836
hue, 176

I

icons
  minimized windows, 416
  raster graphics, 99
  video memory and, 155
Id Software, 18
ID_AUTOMATION_SETCOLOR, 794
ID_AUTOMATION_SHOWWINDOW, 795
ID_COLOR_SETCOLOR, 784, 786
ID_DATABASE_CONNECT, 485–486
IDE (integrated development environment), 5
IDispatch interface, 614
idle processing, 361–366
  CD-ROM demo program, 363–366
  OnIdle() function, 361–366
  uses, 349
IDs
  button, 276
  CLASSID, 826
  dialog resource, 229–230
  GUIDs (globally unique IDs), 809–812
  menu resource, 26–29
  range of command, 33, 51
ID_SEPARATOR, 484
If-modified-since, 864
ImageObject library, 678, 685–712, 928
  CImage Object class creation, 685–687
  drawing images, 692–693, 694
  loading images, 685–689, 693–694
  sample programs
    CropStretch, 700–703
    Display, 697–699
    ProcessImage, 707–712
  saving images, 689–692
images. *See also* graphics
  color depth, 703–704
  colorizing, 706–707
  cropping, 699–703
  file formats, 680–685
    BMP, 682file-type defines table, 691
    GIF (Graphics Interchange Format), 681, 682, 895
    JPEG, 680, 683–684
    PCX, 681, 684
    saved image sizes, 682
    TGA (Targa), 684
    TIFF (tagged image file format), 684–685
  Java
    banners, 900–912
    drawing, 895–896
    formats supported, 895
    loading, 893–895
    scaling, 896
  photographs, 680, 682–684
  processing, 704–712
  resizing windows, 696–697
  sample programs
    CropStretch, 700–703
    Display, 697–699
    ProcessImage, 707–712
  stretching, 699–703
  video capture, 684
  Visual Basic control of, 928–930
ImageViewer demo application, 669–673
  imaging library, 675
IMPLEMENT_SERIAL macro, 383
mport from Type Library dialog box, 823
indicators, status bar, 490
inheritance, priority, 512–513
InitCustomAppWiz() function, 937–938, 951
initialization, dialog, 242–243

InitRectTracker() function, 759–760
inline functions, 514
input, 289–321. *See also* keyboard; mouse
Insert Control dialog box, 803
Insert New Object command, 752
Insert New Object dialog box, 767
Insert Object dialog box, 752–753, 767
Insert Resource dialog, 269–273
insertion points, 89
InstallShield, 918
integrated development environment (IDE), 5
IntelliSense, 6–7
interfaces. *See also* user interface (UI)
  DAO, 614–615
  GDI (Graphics Device Interface), 97–98
  MDI (Multiple-Document Interface), 45, 372, 402–405, 411–423, 932
  Media Control, 325–326, 339–341
  MIDI (Musical Instrument Digital Interface), 333–338, 351
  SDI (Single-Document Interface), 372, 402, 412–413, 422, 932
Internet. *See also* Internet Explorer; World Wide Web (WWW)
  ActiveX and, 747
  blocking sites, 876–884
  HTML, 826, 900
  programming, 831–866
    CInternetSession, 831
      parameters, optional, 832–833
    creating simple browser, 834
    FTP
      connecting to server, 836–838
      demo program, 840–847
      retrieving files, 838–840
    HTTP file retrieval, 835–836
    robots, Web
      agents, 847–848
      demo program, 849–863
      problems with, 848
Internet Explorer
  ActiveX and, 826
  CryptoAPI, 726
  DLLs, 5
  integration with Windows 98, 4–5
  Navigation, 870–872
  search page, 871
  as user-agent, 848
  Web Browser ActiveX control, 867
interoperability, DBMS, 526
Intuit, 458
Invalidate() function, 110
IsOpen() method, 919
item data, 246

J

J++, 887–912
  creating applets, 887–893
    paint method, 891
    parameters, 892–893
    threaded, 889–890
  demo programs
    Banner, 900–907
    MakeBanner, 907–912
  HelloWorld applet, 14–18
  IDE, 5
  Java images
    drawing, 895–893
    loading, 893–895
  uploading applets to Web sites, 897–900
Java. *See also* J++
  applets
    ActiveX controls compared, 747
    demo programs, 900–912
    uploading to Web sites, 897–900
  HelloWorld program, 18–23
  Id Software, 18
  images, 893–895
Jet. *See* DAO

JPEG
file format, 680, 683–684
Java, 895
viewing, 669
justification, text, 106, 113, 118

K

keyboard accelerators, 40–48
editor, 41
keyboard, input, 40–41
menu hints, 43
selecting appropriate, 43–46
standard commands, 44–45
table resource, creating, 41–43
tables
multiple, 46–48
window class, 47–48
virtual key codes, 84–86
Windows 98 native functions, 46–47
keyboard hook DLL demo, 661–666
keyboard input, 81–93
CD-ROM demo, 93
echoing keyboard focus, 86–93
cursors, creating and maintaining, 87–89
focus rectangles, 89–92
selection state, 92–93
languages, foreign, 83
mnemonics, 27
translation of, 82–86
physical keyboard, 82–83
printable character messages, 84–86
Windows logical keyboard, 84
keys. *See also* keyboard accelerators
Alt, 44–45, 84
Applications key, 41, 55, 82
arrow, 89
CapsLock key, 484–485
Ctrl key, 44–45, 84
encryption, 713–714, 720–722, 727–727
Esc key, 44
F10 key, 665
mode, 41
modifier, 41
NumLock, 484–485
Registry, 317–319
Shift key, 43, 45, 84
SysReq key, 82
Tab key, 89
toggle keys, 41
virtual, 42, 84–86
Windows key, 41, 82
KillTimer() function, 353

L

leading, 147
libraries. *See also* DLLs (Dynamic Link Libraries)
C runtime, 517–518
ImageObject library, 678, 685–712
CImage Object class creation, 685–687
drawing images, 692–693, 694
loading images, 685–689, 693–694
sample programs
CropStretch, 700–703
Display, 697–699
ProcessImage, 707–712
saving images, 689–692
STL (Standard Template Library), 814
third-party, 675–712
cost, 675
using, 676–678
Unicode, 295
Wave class, 324
Windows multimedia, 324, 332–333
line styles table, 125
listbox, 474–477
Load() function, CDib, 183–186
LoadAccelerators() function, 46
LoadBitmap() function, 160, 162
LoadLibrary() function, 648, 650, 654–656
LoadMappedBitmap() function, 161
logical colors, 114
logical font, 120

logical keyboard, 83–84
logical palettes, 174–179
LOGPALETTE, 175, 178, 292–295

M

macros
  DECLAR_SERIAL, 382
  dictionaries, 938
  IMPLEMENT_SERIAL, 383
  persistent, 950–953
  RGB(), 113–115
  substitution, 933
MakeBanner demo program, 907–912
mapping modes, 133–135
  MM_TEXT, 105, 109, 134
  twips, 928
Marlett font, 99
masking, bitmap color, 164, 166–167
MCGA video, 157
MDI (Multiple-Document Interface), 372, 411–413
  AppWizard, 411–412, 420–422, 932
  commands, 45
  creating applications, 420–421
  demo application, 414–420
  menus, 413, 415, 421–422, 423
  SDI compared, 412–413, 422
  splitter windows, 402–405
MDIDemo application, 414–420
MDISplitter application, 403–405
Media Control Interface
  CD audio, 339–341
    commands table, 340
    flags table, 340–341
  waveform audio, 325–326
    commands table, 326
memory file, 313
menu bar, MDI frame window, 413, 415, 421–422, 423
Menu Item Properties dialog box, editing, 26
menus, 25–61
  C menu
    class functions, 49–50
    menu flags, 51–52
  CD-ROM demos, 34, 57
  changing default, 25–31
    creating menu handlers, 29–31
    creating menus, 29
    editing menu resources, 26–28
      adding prompts, 28
      Caption field, 27
      ID field, 26–27
      keyboard mnemonics, 27
      naming conventions, 27
      Prompt field, 28
  changing dynamically, 48–54
    MFC handle maps, 52–54
    pop-up, existing, 49–52
  command ranges, 33–34
  context, 49–52, 54–61
    changing dynamically, 48–54
    parameters, 55–56
    windows, changing with, 56–61
  editor, 26–28
  flags, 50–52
  hints, accelerator, 43
  input handling, 34–39
  keyboard accelerators, 40–48
  menu bar, MDI frame window, 413, 415, 421–422, 423
  messages in MFC, 31–32
  server applications, 770–772
message handling
  CDialog class, 239–240
  mouse, 65–66, 68–74
  statusbars, 491
message map, 33
metafile, 102–103
MFC Database Classes, 563–605
  CDatabase, 564–567, 591
  CRecordset, 568–578, 592–604

(continued)

MFC Database Classes (*continued*)
demo applications
Create/Read/Update/Delete (CRUD), 578–592
parameterized recordsets, 592–604
overview, 563–564
parameterized recordsets, 568–578, 592–604
MFC Extension classes, 666–673
AFX_EXT_CLASS, 667–668
encapsulating documents and views, 669–673
exporting class, 667
nested, 668
regular DLLs compared, 666–667
resources, locating, 669
MFC (Microsoft Foundation Classes). *See also specific classes*
accelerator tables, 47
ATL controls, 11
command message routing, 32
command ranges, 33–34, 51
control classes, 235–236
database classes, 563–605
exception handling, 195–223
extending classes, 455–477
Extension DLLs, 666–673
frame window class, 29
handle maps, 52–54
Internet Explorer, 5
menu messages, 31–32
message handling, 30
mouse event program, 68–74
persistent objects, 381–388
printing graphics, 446
OnCreate function, 450
OnDraw function, 450–452
OnPreparePrinting function, 452
sample application, 446–447
scaling, 447–452
printing text, 428–446
member functions, 433–446428–446
OnBeginPinting, 435–441433–435
OnEndPrinting, 445, 446
OnPrepareDC, 441–443, 444
OnPreparePinting, 433–435
OnPrint, 443–445
Unicode support, 295
Microsoft
Access, 525, 568
DAO, 607–641
Developer Studio, 546
Control menu, 231
dialog tab order, setting, 234
MFC Database classes demo, 593
resource editor, 228
viewing DLL and EXE resources, 210
Explorer Address combo box, 456
Foundation Classes (MFC) (*See* MFC (Microsoft Foundation Classes))
Internet Explorer
ActiveX and, 826
CryptoAPI, 726
DLLs, 5
integration with Windows 98, 4–5
Navigation, 870–872
search page, 871
as user-agent, 848
Web Browser ActiveX control, 867
Paint as ActiveX server application, 744–746
SQL server, 525
Web Browser
CHtmlView class, 867–884
HTML information retrieval, 867–884
Word as ActiveX container application, 743–746
MIDI (Musical Instrument Digital Interface)
CD-ROM demo program, 334–338
CMidi class, 333–334
defined, 333
timers, multimedia, 351

Minimum Grammar, SQL, 530
MM_TEXT mapping mode, 109, 134
mnemonics
  keyboard, 27, 230
  property page tabs, 286–288
modal dialogs, 253–258
modal property sheets
  creating, 269–270
  demo application, 272–288
mode keys, 41
modems, 314–315
modifier keys, 41
monitors, 99, 157
mouse, 63–81
  capturing, 79–80
  CD-ROM demos, 68, 76
  coordinates, screen/window conversion of, 67–68
  cursor, changing, 75–79
  linked and embedded item selection, 756–757
  message handlers, creating, 65–66
    MFC programs, 68–74
  MFC event handler, 68–74
  non-client events, 74–75
  OnLButtonDown() function, 379–380
  pointer
    clipping, 81
    two-headed arrow, 231
  windows input messages, 64–65
MulDiv() helper function, 145
multibyte character sets (MBCs), CString class, 289, 295
multilingual applications, 649
Multiple-Document Interface (MDI). *See* MDI (Multiple-Document Interface)
multitasking, 3–4. *See also* threads
MultViewSplitter application, 405–409
music
  CD audio, 338–347
  MIDI, 332–338
Musical Instrument Digital Interface (MIDI). *See* MIDI (Musical Instrument Digital Interface)

N

Navigate() function, 871
Navigate2() function, 871–872
nesting MFC Extension DLLs, 668
Netscape Navigator, 848
New button, 242–243
New Class dialog box, 569, 621
New dialog box, ATL COM AppWizard, 815
New Project dialog box, 888
New Project Information dialog box
  container application, 752
  RectApp demo, 373
  server application, 766, 783, 791
    ActiveX control, 800
    ATL COM AppWizard, 816
newproj.inf file, 943–945
nIndex parameter, 488
nonclient mouse events, 74–75
NumLock keys, 484–485

O

OBJECT tag, 812
ODBC Data Source Administrator, 529
ODBC (Open Database Connectivity), 525–562
  conformance levels, 529–530
  definitions, 525–526
  demo applications
    encapsulating functionality, 545–561
    fetching data, 537–545
  DirectWorkspace, 612
  drivers, 527–534, 531
  encapsulating functionality, 545–561
  function seams, 649
  header files, 538, 546–549
  implementation, 530–536
    configuring, 530–532
    data source

(continued)

ODBC (*continued*)
connecting to, 532–533
disconnecting from, 536
querying, 534
retrieving data, 535–536
SQL requests, 534–535
Microsoft Access and, 607
standard, 526–529
version, setting, 533
OhmsCalculator ActiveX control, 921–924
OLE (Object Linking and Embedding). *See also* ActiveX
automation, 607, 608, 614–616, 740–741
controls, 741
OLE 1.0, 737–739
OLE 2.0, 740–741
Registry and, 317, 319
verbs, 759
OnAutomationSetColor() function, 794
OnAutomationShowwindow() function, 795
OnBeforeNavigate2 () function, 876–877
OnBeginPrinting() function, 435–441
OnButtonClicked() function, 806–807
OnCancel() function, 664
OnChangeItemPosition() function, 755
OncolorSetColor(), 786–787
OnCreate() function
ActiveX controls, 801
automation client, 795
character height, 440
printing graphics, 450
status bars, 484, 487, 490
OnCreateClient() function, splitter windows
dynamic, 395–398
MDI, 404
static, 400–402
OnCtlColor() function, 465–466
OnDestroy() virtual function, 657
OnDismiss() function, 941
OnDraw() function, 107–108, 387
ActiveX controls, 801–802
ATL, 818
automation server, 785
bitmaps, 159, 162, 163
CFormBackground, 470
CPalette objects, 178
document/view architecture, 370
font creation example, 120–121
linked and embedded items, 756–757
printing, 429, 438–442, 441
graphics, 451–452
screen flicker, 192–193
server applications, 774–775
view class, 378–379
OnEditCopy() function, 773
OnEndPrinting() function, 445–446
OnGetItemPosition() function, 755
OnIdle() function, 349, 361–366
OnInitDialog () function, 240, 250–252, 272, 941
OnInitialUpdate() function, 398
OnKeyDown() function, 763
OnLButtonDblClk() function, 758–759
OnLButtonDown() function, 379, 387, 758
OnLinesNumberoflines() function, 775–776
OnMouseMove() function, 67
OnNavigateComplete2() function, 878
OnNewDocument() function, 370, 374–375
OnNotify() function, 281
OnPrepareDC() function, 441–443, 444
OnPreparePrinting() function, 433–435, 452
OnPrint() function, 443–445
OnSetCursor() function, 757
OnTimer(), 350
OOP programming, 381
Open() member function, CFile, 303–305
operators
array, 291
equality, 292
logical "or," 567
relational, 291
scope, 46

Options dialog box, 678
Oracle Server, 525
orientation, font, 121–122

P

Paint() function
  applets, 891
  Java, 895
  underlining, 467
palettes
  default, 114–115
  DIBs, 182, 189
  entry flags, 175–176
  events, 179–180
  logical, 174–179
panes. *See* windows
PANOSE font IDs, 120
parsing URL strings, 835
PatBlt() function, 100
Pause() function, CCDAudio, 342
PC Paint, 684
PCX file format, 681, 684
Peachtree Accounting, 458
PenBrushDemo program, 129–133
pens
  CPen class, 124–127
    color, 126
    style, 125–126
    width, 126
  demo program, 129–133
permissions, database, 600–604
persistent objects, 381–388, 613
persistent properties, 808–809
photographs, 680, 682–684. *See also* images
PIDL, 878
pitch, font, 123
pixels. *See* graphics
Plaintext. *See* encryption
PlaySound() function, 325
point size, font, 144–146
pointer clipping, 81
pop-up menus, 49–52, 54–61
  changing existing, 49–52
precision, font output, 122
PreCreateWindow() function, 47, 417–420
preemptive multitasking, 3–4
PreTranslateMessage() function, 46–47, 457–458
Print dialog box, 432
Print Preview, AppWizard, 429
Print Setup dialog box, 432
printable character messages, 84–86
printing, 425–452
  CPrintInfo, 433–436
  device context and, 103
  logical colors, 114
  MFC, 428–446
    graphics
      OnCreate function, 451
      OnDraw function, 451–452
      OnPreparePrinting function, 452
      sample application, 446–447
      scaling, 447–452
    member functions
      OnBeginPrinting, 435–441
      OnEndPrinting, 445–446
      OnPrepareDC, 441–443, 444
      OnPreparePrinting, 433–435
      OnPrint, 443–445
  overview, 425–428
  sample applications, 430–432, 446–447
  spooling, 102
  StartDoc function, 427–428
priority
  classes, 513–514
  inheritance, 512–513
  threads, 504, 512–513
private key, 721
process priority classes, 513–514
programmable objects, 740–741. *See also* OLE
Project Explorer window, 888
Project Settings dialog box, 676

Prompt field, menu, 28
property pages, 267–288
property sheets, 267–288
  buttons
    caption, changing, 278–279
    removing, 276–277
    repositioning, 277–278
  embedded, 271
  modal, 269–270
    example, 275
  modeless, 270–271
  tabs
    captions, 283–285
    disabling, 279–281
    font, 286
    mnemonics, 286–288
    re-enabling, 281–283
protected data members, 381
PrtScr key, 100
pseudodevices, 102–103
public member
  functions, 383
  variables, 381
public-key cryptography, 714, 720–722

Q

Qualcomm Eudora, 848
queries, parameterized, 592–604, 600–604
Quicken, 458

R

RAD tools, 914
radio buttons, 242
raster operations, 91, 135–136, 164–167
  fonts, 122
  GDI drawing, 135–136
  graphics, 99–100
  table of, 165
readability, code, 201–203
record field exchange (RXF), 573–574
Record() function, CWave class, 328
Recordset object, 613–614
recordsets
  constructing, 573
  CRecordset, 568–578, 592–604
  DAO, 613–614
    CDaoRecordset, 620–630, 632
      constructing, 625
      deleting, 630
      DFX (DAO field exchange), 626
      filtering, 626–628
      navigation, 629
      opening, 625
      parameterized, 627–628
      saving, 629–630
      sorting, 628–629
    demo application, 630–641
    types, 613, 620
  deleting, 578
  filtering, 574–576, 593, 597
  navigating, 577, 584
  opening, 573, 583
  parameterized, 574–576
    demo, 592–604
    queries, 600–604
  Recordsets collection, 613
  Recordsets object, 613–614
  RFX (record field exchange), 573–574
  saving, 577–578
  sorting returned records, 576–577
Recordsets collection, 613
RectPrint sample application, 446–447
redrawing, 110–111
Refresh() function, 871
Register demo program, 919–921
registering controls, 918
Registry, 317–321
  CRegistry class, 319–321
  editor, 810
  keys, 317–319
  persistent macros, 950–953
  section values, 919
  SetOption override, 610

subtrees, 319
values, 317
RegistryControl, 914–918
Regsvr32, ATL controls, 14
relational operators, 291
ReleaseBuffer() member function, 293
ReleaseLibrary() function, 656
RemoveAll() function, 376
ReportError() function, 205
resizing
COleResizeBar, 480
combo box, 233
dialog box, 231
images, 697
linked or embedded items, 762
resource
editor, 946
dialogs, 226–235
property pages, 269–273
file templates, 945–947
IDs, 276, 485
summary list, 26
resource script (.RC) file, 26
Resource symbols dialog box, 802
ResumeThread(), 507
return codes, exception handling compared, 198–203
return codes compared, 198–203
RFX (record field exchange), 573–574
RGB
additive color system, 173
CMY value calculation, 176
default windows palette, 174
HSV conversion of, 177
video memory, 157, 159
RGB() macro, 113–115
robots, Web
agents, 847–848
demo program, 849–863
problems with, 848
writing guidelines, 863–866
accountability, 863–864
control, 866
resource use, 864–865
testing, local, 864
routing command messages, 32
RTTI (runtime type information), 198
rubber sheet graphics, 109

S

sample applications. *See* CD-ROM demos
saturation, color, 176
Save() function
CDib, 186–187
CWave class, 328
dialogs, 244
saving
files, CD-ROM demo, 305–312
persistent and nonpersistent objects, 387–388
with Serialize() function, 370, 377–378
scaling, 447–452
DBMS, 526
images, 699–703
Java applet images, 896
scan code, 82–83
scheduling, thread, 512–513
scope operators, 46
screen flicker, 110–111, 192–193
screen shots, 100
scroll bars
CScrollView class, 396–397, 401
OnInitialUpdate function, 398
shared, 400
splitter windows, 389, 393–394, 396–400
SDI (single-document interface), 372
AppWizard option, 932
MDI compared, 412–413, 422
splitter windows, 402
search engines, 848. *See also* robots, Web
security
encryption, data, 713–733
threads, 503

SEH (structured exception handling), 195–196
Select Database Tables dialog box, 570, 622
SelectClipRgn() function, 149–153
selection state, 92–93
  color and, 92
  window focus and, 92
SelectObject() function, fonts, 119, 123
serial communication, 314–317
serialization
  dialog data, 249–253, 257
  persistent objects, 381–388
  Serialize() function, 377–378, 756
    document/view architecture, 370
    persistent objects, 381–388
server applications, 764–780
  COleServerItem class, 774–775
  creating skeleton, 764–767
  CServerDoc class, 772–774
  customizing resources, 768–772
  defined, 738
  demo program, 765–768
  running
    as editor for linked item, 779–780
    as in-place editor, 778–779
    as standalone, 776–778
  view class, 775–776
Session Properties dialog box, 898
SetBitmapBits() function, 160
SetEnabledText() function, 282
SetItem function, tab caption, 283–285
SetObjectAsSelected() function, 761
SetOffline() function, 875–876
SetPalette() function, 189, 696
SetPaneStyle(), 488–489
SetResults() function, tab caption, 284
SetSystemPaletteUse() function, 180
SetTextAlign(), 117
SetTimer(), 350–354
SetViewportOrg() function, 441–442
SetWindowsHookEx, 659–660, 663
shade, 177
shadows, 473–474
Shift key
  keyboard accelerators, 43, 45
  virtual key codes, 84
shortcuts, keyboard. *See* keyboard accelerators
single-document interface (SDI). *See* SDI (single-document interface)
sizing handles, 762
SkipJack, 715
Sleep() function, 507
sleeping thread, 507
SMP (symmetric multiprocessing), 512
snapshots, 568, 613, 620. *See also* recordsets
SOFTWARE key, 920
sorting, recordset, 576–577
sound, 323–348
  CD audio, 338–347
    CCDAudio class, 339
      functions, 341–342
      MCI (Media Control Interface), 339–341
    CDPlayer program, 342–347
  MIDI
    CD-ROM demo program, 334–338
    CMidi class, 333–334
    defined, 333
  waveform audio, 324–332
    CD-ROM demo program, 329–332
    CWave class, 324, 326–328
    MCI (Media Control Interface), 325–326
spacing, text, 113
spell checker
  automation applications, 746–747
  OLE and, 740
  threads, 501
spiders. *See* robots, Web
splitter windows, 389–410
  CSplitterWnd class, 391
    custom splitter class, 407–409
    member functions table, 392–393

dynamic, 389–391, 393–399, 404–405
MDI, 402–405
multiple view, 405–409
overview, 389–391
sample applications
dynamic splitter, 393–399
MDI splitter, 403–405
multiple view splitter, 405–409
static splitter, 399–402
static, 391, 399–402
spooling, 102, 427
SQL (Structured Query Language). *See also* ODBC
conformance levels, 530
data source connection, 532–533
defined, 526
Minimum Grammar, 530
preparing and executing requests, 534–535
querying data, 534
syntax, 608
SQL UPDATE, 591
SQLAllocHandle(), 532–534, 540–541
SQLBindCol(), 535–536, 541
SQLConnect(), 541
SQLDescribeCol(), 535, 557
SQLDisconnect(), 536
SQLFetch(), 535–536, 541, 557
SQLGetData(), 535
SQLGetFunctions(), 534
SQLGetTypeInfo(), 534, 545, 548, 556–559
SQLNumResultCols(), 535
Standard Template Library (STL), 814
StartDoc() function, 427–428
statement completion, 6–7
StatSplitter application, 399–402
status bars, 484–499
AppWizard, 480, 486, 489
constants, 485
controlling, 489–492
creating, 484–485
custom, 487–489
CStatusBar, 480
demo program, 492–498
displaying, 485–486
message handlers, 491
StCustomAppWizClass() function, 937
stretching images, 699–703
strings, 289–302
BSTR, 824–827
CD-ROM demo program, 296–302
combo box, 237, 246
CRegistry class, 321
CString class, 289–302
parsing URL, 835
searching, 296
Unicode, 295
Structured Query Language. *See* SQL (Structured Query Language)
style flags, 482
substitution algorithms, 714–720
substitution macros, 933
subtractive color system, 173, 176
SuspendThread(), 507
Sybase SQL Server, 525
symmetric algorithms, 713, 714–720
symmetric multiprocessing (SMP), 512
syntax, 196–198
catch, 197–198
throw, 196–197
try, 197
syntax, exception-handling, 196–198
SysReq key, 82
system commands, 44

T

Tab character, 944
Tab key, 89
TableDefs collection, 613
tabs
captions, 283–285
dialogs, 267–288
disabling, 279–281

(continued)

Tabs (*continued*)
  font, 286
  mnemonics, 286–288
  order, setting, 234
  re-enabling, 281–283
Targa (TGA) file format, 684
Task Manager, 82, 89
TCHAR data type, 295
Teletype machines, 314–315
templates, AppWizard
  creating new, 941–945
  resource files, changing, 945–947
  view and dialog files, 947–949
TerminateThread, 511
test container, ATL controls, 13–14, 924
text
  coordinate calculations, 144–149
    centering text, 148–149
    next string, next line, 147–148
    next string, same line, 146–147
  device context attributes, 112–118
    alignment, 116–117
    color, 113–116
    justification, 118
    table of, 113
  drawing attributes, 106
  drawing functions, 142–144
  editing windows, 80
  fonts, 118–124
  as graphics, 98
  grey edit control, 458–464
  justification, 106, 113, 118
  keys, 40
  mouse capture, 80
  printing, 425–452
TEXTMETRIC structure, 437–438
TGA (Targa) file format, 684
threaded applet, 889–890
ThreadFunc, 503–504
threads, 501–522
  C runtime functions, 517–522
  CD-ROM demo program, 518–522
  FTP file retrieval, 840
  Internet transactions, 833
  overview, 501–502
  priority classes, 513–514
  scheduling, 512–513
  sharing MFC objects, 514–517
  sleeping, 507
  suspending and resuming, 507
  terminating, 508
    from another thread, 508–511
  user interface, 502
    creating, 505–506
  worker, 502–505
    creating, 503–504
    thread function, 504–505
throw statement, 196–197. *See also* exception handling
Thumbtack icon, 26
timers, 349–360
  clock program demo, 354–360
  multimedia, 351
  notification, 350
  setting
    by callback procedure, 352–354
    by WM_TIMER, 350–352
  uses, 349
tint, 177
title bar, dialog, 933
toggle keys, 41
tone, 177
toolbars, 479–483
  AppWizard, 481
  controls, 229
  creating, 481–483
  Dialog, 233
  dialog bars, 480
  docking, 480, 483
  MFC control bars, 480–481
  showing and hiding, 483
  ToolTips, 480–481

ToolTips, 480–481
tracks, AppWizard, 932
transactions
  boundaries, 620
  CDaoWorkspace class, 619
  CDatabase class, 567
TranslateAccelerator(), 46
TranslateMessage(), 82, 84
transparent color, 164, 166–167
try block, 197, 199
  code content, 217–218
  constructors, 203
  DAO errors, 617–618, 633
  database classes, 583
  database code, 565
  multiple exceptions, 206–207
  re-throwing exceptions, 216–217
twips, 134, 928
type library, 793, 822–823
typeface, font, 123

U

UINTs, 490
underline edit control, 464–468
UnhookWindowsHookEx, 660, 663
Unicode
  BSTR and, 824
  CString class, 289, 290, 295
update functions, naming, 29
UpdateAllViews(), 377, 386
UPDATE_COMMAND_UI, 29
UpdateWindow() call, 111
URL
  blocking, 876–884
  image retrieval, 893
  logging, 876–884
  navigating, 870–872
  parsing strings, 835
  Web robots and, 848–863
UseOhmsCalculator program, 924–927
user interface (UI)
  ActiveX controls, 800–803
  form-based, 921
  threads, 502, 505–506
User Maintenance demo application, 578–592
User Master table, 568, 581, 592, 595–600, 620–624
UseRegistry key, 920

V

vector graphics, 100
verbs, OLE, 759
VGA monitors, 157
video captures, 684
video memory, 155–156
  CGA, 157
  DAC (Digital Adapter Color), 174
  MCGA, 157
  palletized, 174
view class, 369–388
  automation client, 793–795
  automation server, 785–788
  CCtrlView, 474–476
  CFormView, 669
  CFTPConnect, 837
  CHtmlView, 5, 867–884
  CListBoxView, 474–477
  CListView, 474–475
  CRecordView, 564
  CScrollView, 396–397, 401
  CTreeView, 474–475
  CView, 370, 432–446
  implementing document/view architecture, 387
  include file, 685
  OnDraw() function, 370, 378–379
  OnInitialUpdate function, 398
  public member variables, 381
  server applications, 775–776
  splitter windows, 391
Viewing DLL and EXE resources, 210
viewport origin, 441–443

virtual functions
  exceptions, 219–223
  OnNotify(), 281
virtual key codes, 42
  scan code conversion, 83–84
  table of, 85–86
Virtual Machine (VM), 18
Visual Basic, 609
  ATL controls
    Basic, 921–924
    C++, 914–919
  C++ and, 913–930
  editor, 921–922
  graphics coordinates, 928
  HelloWorld program, 23–24
  IDE, 5
  mapping mode, 928
  OhmsCalculator ActiveX control, 921–924
  Pictures demo program, 929
  Register demo program, 919–921
  twips, 928
Visual C++. *See* C++
Visual InterDev, 5
Visual J++. *See* J++
Visual Studio, 5–24. *See also* C++; J++; Visual Basic
  accelerator-table editor, 41
  context menus, 54
  new features, 5
  resource editor, 29

W

WaitForSingleObject(), 510–511
wanderers, Web. *See* robots, Web
Wave class library, 324
waveform audio, 324–332
  CD-ROM demo program, 329–332
  CWave class, 324, 326–328
  MCI (Media Control Interface), 325–326
  PlaySound() function, 325
Web Browser, Microsoft
  CHtmlView class, 867–884
  HTML information retrieval, 867–884
weight, font, 122
width
  applet images, 896
  bitmap, 158, 161, 181
  DIBs, 182
  font, 121
  images, 693, 695–696, 699–700
  pen, 126
Win32 console application, 10–11
window extra bytes, 53
windows. *See also* dialogs
  boundaries, 101–102
  changing with context menus, 56–61
  drawing demo program, 136–142
  keyboard focus, 86–93
  minimized as icons, 416
  mouse capture, 79–80
  raster graphics and movement, 99
  redrawing, 110–111
  resizing, 697
  splitter (*See* splitter windows)
  UI threads, 502
Windows key, 41, 82
Windows multimedia library, 324, 332–333
WinExec() function, registration, 918
Wise Install, 918
WM_CHAR, 81–82, 84–85
WM_COMMAND message, 30
WM_CREATE message, 440, 801
WM_DESTROY message, 640, 657
WM_KEYDOWN message, 81–82, 84–85, 763
WM_LBUTTONDBLCLK message, 759
WM_LBUTTONDOWN message, 64, 79–80, 758
WM_MOUSEMOVE, 64, 80
WM_PAINT message, 91–92, 108–111
  priority, 110
  requesting, 110–111

WM_PALETTECHANGED message, 180
WM_QUERYNEWPALETTE message, 179
WM_QUIT message, 505, 508
WM_SETCURSOR, 75
WM_SETCURSOR message, 757
WM_SETFOCUS message, 90–91
WM_TIMER, 350–360
worker threads, 502–505
Workspace object, 611–612
Workspaces collection object, 610
World Wide Web (WWW)
    ActiveX, 747, 809–812, 826
    blocking access to sites, 876–884
    embedding controls, 826
    Java applets, 897–912
WriteString () method, 919
WS_FTP32 program, 897
WS_VISIBLE windowing style, 483

X

XOR
    animations, 165
    hash functions, 722
    raster operations, 135, 165–167

Z

Zsoft, 684

Notes

Notes

Notes

Notes

Notes

Notes

Notes

Notes

Notes

Notes

IDG BOOKS WORLDWIDE, INC. END-USER LICENSE AGREEMENT

READ THIS. You should carefully read these terms and conditions before opening the software packet(s) included with this book ("Book"). This is a license agreement ("Agreement") between you and IDG Books Worldwide, Inc. ("IDGB"). By opening the accompanying software packet(s), you acknowledge that you have read and accept the following terms and conditions. If you do not agree and do not want to be bound by such terms and conditions, promptly return the Book and the unopened software packet(s) to the place you obtained them for a full refund.

1. **License Grant.** IDGB grants to you (either an individual or entity) a nonexclusive license to use one copy of the enclosed software program(s) (collectively, the "Software") solely for your own personal or business purposes on a single computer (whether a standard computer or a workstation component of a multiuser network). The Software is in use on a computer when it is loaded into temporary memory (RAM) or installed into permanent memory (hard disk, CD-ROM, or other storage device). IDGB reserves all rights not expressly granted herein.

2. **Ownership.** IDGB is the owner of all right, title, and interest, including copyright, in and to the compilation of the Software recorded on the disk(s) or CD-ROM ("Software Media"). Copyright to the individual programs recorded on the Software Media is owned by the author or other authorized copyright owner of each program. Ownership of the Software and all proprietary rights relating thereto remain with IDGB and its licensers.

3. **Restrictions on Use and Transfer.**

   (a) You may only (i) make one copy of the Software for backup or archival purposes, or (ii) transfer the Software to a single hard disk, provided that you keep the original for backup or archival purposes. You may not (i) rent or lease the Software, (ii) copy or reproduce the Software through a LAN or other network system or through any computer subscriber system or bulletin-board system, or (iii) modify, adapt, or create derivative works based on the Software.

   (b) You may not reverse engineer, decompile, or disassemble the Software. You may transfer the Software and user documentation on a permanent basis, provided that the transferee agrees to accept the terms and conditions of this Agreement and you retain no copies. If the Software is an update or has been updated, any transfer must include the most recent update and all prior versions.

4. **Restrictions on Use of Individual Programs.** You must follow the individual requirements and restrictions detailed for each individual program in the appendix, "What's on the CD-ROM" of this Book. These limitations are also contained in the individual license agreements recorded on the Software Media. These limitations may include a requirement that after using the program for a specified period of time, the user must pay a registration fee or

discontinue use. By opening the Software packet(s), you will be agreeing to abide by the licenses and restrictions for these individual programs that are detailed in the appendix, "What's on the CD-ROM" and on the Software Media. None of the material on this Software Media or listed in this Book may ever be redistributed, in original or modified form, for commercial purposes.

5. Limited Warranty.

(a) IDGB warrants that the Software and Software Media are free from defects in materials and workmanship under normal use for a period of sixty (60) days from the date of purchase of this Book. If IDGB receives notification within the warranty period of defects in materials or workmanship, IDGB will replace the defective Software Media.

(b) IDGB AND THE AUTHORs OF THE BOOK DISCLAIM ALL OTHER WARRANTIES, EXPRESS OR IMPLIED, INCLUDING WITHOUT LIMITATION IMPLIED WARRANTIES OF MERCHANTABILITY AND FITNESS FOR A PARTICULAR PURPOSE, WITH RESPECT TO THE SOFTWARE, THE PROGRAMS, THE SOURCE CODE CONTAINED THEREIN, AND/OR THE TECHNIQUES DESCRIBED IN THIS BOOK. IDGB DOES NOT WARRANT THAT THE FUNCTIONS CONTAINED IN THE SOFTWARE WILL MEET YOUR REQUIREMENTS OR THAT THE OPERATION OF THE SOFTWARE WILL BE ERROR FREE.

(c) This limited warranty gives you specific legal rights, and you may have other rights that vary from jurisdiction to jurisdiction.

6. Remedies.

(a) IDGB's entire liability and your exclusive remedy for defects in materials and workmanship shall be limited to replacement of the Software Media, which may be returned to IDGB with a copy of your receipt at the following address: Software Media Fulfillment Department, Attn.: *Windows 98 Programming Bible*, IDG Books Worldwide, Inc., 7260 Shadeland Station, Ste. 100, Indianapolis, IN 46256, or call 1-800-762-2974. Please allow three to four weeks for delivery. This Limited Warranty is void if failure of the Software Media has resulted from accident, abuse, or misapplication. Any replacement Software Media will be warranted for the remainder of the original warranty period or thirty (30) days, whichever is longer.

(b) In no event shall IDGB or the authors be liable for any damages whatsoever (including without limitation damages for loss of business profits, business interruption, loss of business information, or any other pecuniary loss) arising from the use of or inability to use the Book or the Software, even if IDGB has been advised of the possibility of such damages.

(c) Because some jurisdictions do not allow the exclusion or limitation of liability for consequential or incidental damages, the above limitation or exclusion may not apply to you.

7. **U.S. Government Restricted Rights.** Use, duplication, or disclosure of the Software by the U.S. Government is subject to restrictions stated in paragraph (c)(1)(ii) of the Rights in Technical Data and Computer Software clause of DFARS 252.227-7013, and in subparagraphs (a) through (d) of the Commercial Computer—Restricted Rights clause at FAR 52.227-19, and in similar clauses in the NASA FAR supplement, when applicable.

8. **General.** This Agreement constitutes the entire understanding of the parties and revokes and supersedes all prior agreements, oral or written, between them and may not be modified or amended except in a writing signed by both parties hereto that specifically refers to this Agreement. This Agreement shall take precedence over any other documents that may be in conflict herewith. If any one or more provisions contained in this Agreement are held by any court or tribunal to be invalid, illegal, or otherwise unenforceable, each and every other provision shall remain in full force and effect.

CD-ROM Installation Instructions

The CD-ROM that accompanies this book contains a complete set of demonstration programs developed in the text, plus a selection of programming tools from several vendors.

- ✦ To install the demo programs described in the text, simply copy the files into a new folder on your hard disk (see the appendix for notes on dealing with read-only attributes to files copied from the CD) or run the `InstallContents.EXE` file to install all the demo programs at once.
- ✦ To install the programming tools, simply double-click each self-extracting installer to install the files.
- ✦ For more details on the content of the CD-ROM and how to use it, see the appendix.